Human
Sexuality

Human Sexuality

a contemporary introduction

edited by Caroline F. Pukall

OXFORD
UNIVERSITY PRESS

OXFORD

UNIVERSITY PRESS

Oxford University Press is a department of the University of Oxford.
It furthers the University's objective of excellence in research, scholarship,
and education by publishing worldwide. Oxford is a registered trade mark
of Oxford University Press in the UK and in certain other countries.

Published in Canada by
Oxford University Press
8 Sampson Mews, Suite 204,
Don Mills, Ontario M3C 0H5 Canada

www.oupcanada.com

Library and Archives Canada Cataloguing in Publication
Human sexuality (2014)
Human sexuality : a contemporary introduction / edited
by Caroline F. Pukall.

Includes bibliographical references and index.
ISBN 978-0-19-544135-2 (pbk.)

1. Sex—Textbooks. 2. Sex (Biology) —Textbooks. 3. Sex customs—
Textbooks. 4. Sexual ethics—Textbooks. 5. Sexual health—Textbooks.
I. Pukall, Caroline F., author, editor of compilation II. Title.

HQ21.H82 2014   306.7   C2013-904434-5

Cover image: igor kisselev/Shutterstock.com

Printed and bound in the United States of America

1 2 3 4 — 17 16 15 14

Contents in Brief

Contents

4 Sexual Anatomy: The Parts, the Pieces, and How They Respond 77

Caroline F. Pukall and Richard J. Wassersug

5 Sex Hormones and Human Sexuality 107

Gillian Einstein and Jennifer Blake

6 Pregnancy and Childbirth 131

Samantha Waxman and Beverley Chalmers

7 Contraception and Pregnancy Options 157

Katherine S. Sutton and Beverley Chalmers

8 Sexually Transmitted Infections: At the Junction of Biology and Behaviour 183

William A. Fisher and Marc Steben

9 Sexuality over the Lifespan 214

Elke D. Reissing and Heather L. Armstrong

10 Gender 236

Meredith L. Chivers

11 Sexual/Affectional Orientations and Diversity 263

Kevin Alderson

15 Variations in Sexual Behaviour 365

Katherine S. Sutton and Caroline F. Pukall

16 Sexual Dysfunctions 391

Peggy J. Kleinplatz

17 The Dark Side of Sex: Assault and Harassment 417

Scott T. Ronis

18 Selling and Buying Sex 446

Kevin Alderson

19 Sex Education in Canada 466

Stéphanie C. Boyer and Shannon M. Coyle

About the Editor

Caroline F. Pukall obtained her Ph.D. in clinical psychology from McGill University and is currently an associate professor in the Department of Psychology at Queen's University. She is also the director of the Sex Therapy Service at Queen's University, through which she trains and supervises clinical psychology graduate students in sex and couple therapy. In addition, she supervises several graduate and undergraduate students in the Sexual Health Research Laboratory on projects spanning many aspects of sexual function and dysfunction, including vulvodynia and sexual arousal. In her research, Caroline uses multiple methodologies, including self-report measures, online surveys, sensory testing, genital blood flow measurement, and brain imaging.

Over the years, Caroline has contributed her expertise to a number of works and organizations. She has published over thirty articles in peer-reviewed journals, and she has written numerous book chapters. She is also a co-editor of a professional book entitled *Female Sexual Pain Disorders: Evaluation and Management* (Wiley-Blackwell, 2009), a co-author of *When Sex Hurts: A Woman's Guide to Banishing Sexual Pain* (Da Capo Press, 2011), and an associate editor for *The Journal of Sexual Medicine*. She was an advisor to the task force and work group of the *DSM-5* definition of the sexual pain disorders, and she is a reviewer for several scientific journals in the areas of sexuality and pain. In addition, she is an active member of several university-based committees and professional organizations.

Contributor Biographies

Kevin Alderson, Ph.D., is an associate professor at the University of Calgary. Dr Alderson's research interests are in the areas of LGBTTIQQ studies and human sexuality. His recent books include *Counseling LGBTI Clients* and *Breaking Out II: The Complete Guide to Building a Positive LGBTI Identity*. He has authored several book chapters and journal articles and is the editor-in-chief of the *Canadian Journal of Counselling and Psychotherapy*.

Heather L. Armstrong, Ph.D., is a postdoctoral fellow with the Centres for Disease Control and Prevention's Division of Adolescent and School Health. Her research focuses on the experiences of sexual minority individuals, specifically sexual attitudes, motivations, and protective factors and interventions to improve health outcomes among LGBT youth.

Karen L. Blair, Ph.D., obtained her degree from the Department of Psychology at Queen's University. Her work focusses on relationships and health in same- and mixed-sex couples, and she is currently researching public displays of affection and physiological health outcomes in same-sex couples as a CIHR-funded postdoctoral fellow at the University of Utah.

Jennifer Blake, M.D., is Chief Executive Officer of the Society of Obstetricians and Gynaecologists of Canada (SOGC), which is a leading authority on women's sexual and reproductive health representing thousands of specialists across the country. She is an experienced physician and respected leader who has facilitated major organizational change in both hospital and academic sectors.

Stéphanie C. Boyer, M.Sc., is a doctoral student in the Department of Psychology at Queen's University. Her research interests include women's health and sexual dysfunctions, particularly in the area of female genital pain. She has published her work in sexuality and women's health journals and has co-authored book chapters on the topic of female sexual pain disorders.

Beverley Chalmers, D.Sc. (Med.) & Ph.D., is an adjunct full professor in the Department of Obstetrics and Gynecology, and an affiliate investigator in the Ottawa Health Research Institute, at the University of Ottawa. She has served as an international perinatal health consultant to numerous agencies including WHO/PAHO, UNICEF, Médecins Sans Frontières, Save the Children, the Academy for Educational Development (USA), the Open Society Foundation, the Norwegian Board of Health, and the Ministry of Health of Moldova. She has undertaken 141 missions in 26 countries. She has over 260 publications including 50 books or book chapters. She promotes a multidisciplinary, multicultural, and psycho-socially sensitive approach to perinatal care.

Meredith L. Chivers, Ph.D., is an associate professor and a Queen's national scholar in the Department of Psychology at Queen's University. Her research examines gender differences in sexual psychophysiology, sexual attraction, and sexual functioning, with a focus on women's sexuality.

Shannon M. Coyle, M.A., is a research associate in the Sexual Health Research Lab in the Department of Psychology at Queen's University and is an adjunct professor at St Lawrence College. Her research and teaching interests include human sexuality, sex education in Canada, and health promotion and fitness.

Gillian Einstein, Ph.D., is an associate professor of psychology at the University of Toronto. Her research focusses on the effects of estrogens and culture on women's biologies. She has edited and annotated a book for MIT Press on foundational papers in hormones and behaviour, *Sex and the Brain*. She has consulted on female genital circumcision/mutilation/cutting (FGC) for the World Health Organization and is on the advisory board of the Institute of Gender and Health of the Canadian Institutes of Health Research.

Erin E. Fallis, M.A., is a doctoral student in the Clinical Psychology Program at the University of Waterloo. Her research focusses on how characteristics of couples' romantic relationships (e.g., relationship satisfaction, communication) influence sexual satisfaction and sexual functioning. Erin's research is supported by the Social Sciences and Humanities Research Council of Canada.

Melissa A. Farmer, Ph.D., is a postdoctoral fellow in the Department of Physiology at Northwestern University. She has conducted human and animal sexuality research, with a focus on vulvodynia and pelvic pain conditions, as well as received training in sex and pain management therapy as a clinical psychologist at McGill University. She has published several articles, reviews, and book chapters bridging animal and human sex research.

William A. Fisher, Ph.D., is a distinguished professor in the Department of Psychology and the Department of Obstetrics and Gynaecology at University of Western

Ontario. Dr Fisher has conducted research on the prediction and prevention of sexual and reproductive health risk for the past three decades, and he is co-originator of the Information–Motivation–Behavioural skills model of sexual and reproductive health behaviour. His work has been funded by the US National Institutes of Health and Health Canada.

Peggy J. Kleinplatz, Ph.D., is a professor of medicine and a clinical professor of psychology at the University of Ottawa where she is also Director of Sex and Couples Therapy Training. She has edited three books, most recently *New Directions in Sex Therapy: Innovations and Alternatives*, winner of the AASECT 2013 Book Award. Her current research focusses on optimal sexual experience, with a particular interest in sexual health in the elderly and other marginalized populations.

Sheila MacNeil, Ph.D., is a clinical psychologist with Dalhousie University's Counselling and Psychological Services and has a part-time private practice in sex therapy. Her research interests are in the areas of sexual satisfaction, sexual dysfunction, and communication.

Caroline F. Pukall, Ph.D., is an associate professor and the director of the Sex Therapy Service in the Department of Psychology at Queen's University. She works in the area of human sexuality, with a focus on vulvodynia and sexual arousal, and she has published numerous articles, books, and book chapters.

Uzma S. Rehman, Ph.D., is an associate professor in the Department of Psychology at the University of Waterloo. Her research focusses on intimate relationships and couples' sexuality. Her research is funded by the Canadian Institutes of Health Research, the Ontario Mental Health Foundation, and the Social Sciences and Humanities Research Council of Canada.

Elke D. Reissing, Ph.D., is an associate professor at the School of Psychology and the director of the Human Sexuality Research Laboratory at the University of Ottawa. She teaches sexuality and clinical psychology courses, and her research focusses on female sexual dysfunction and older adults' sexuality.

Scott T. Ronis, Ph.D., is an assistant professor of psychology at the University of New Brunswick. His research focusses on the development of emotional and behavioural problems among youth, dynamic family processes, juvenile sexual offending, and childhood sexual experiences. He has published various articles and book chapters, and his research is funded by the Canadian Institutes of Health Research and the Social Sciences and Humanities Research Council of Canada.

Natalie O. Rosen, Ph.D., is an assistant professor in the Department of Psychology and Neuroscience and the Department of Obstetrics and Gynaecology at Dalhousie University. Her research and clinical interests are in the area of human sexuality and intimate relationships, with a focus on vulvodynia. She has published a growing number of articles and book chapters on this topic.

Kelly B. Smith, Ph.D., is a postdoctoral fellow in the Department of Obstetrics and Gynaecology at the University of British Columbia. She works in the area of sexuality, with a particular research and clinical focus on vulvodynia. She has received several research awards, including a Post-Doctoral Fellowship from the Michael Smith Foundation for Health Research, and has published several articles and book chapters.

Marc Steben, M.D., is a family practitioner who works at Quebec's National Institute of Public Health, focussing on sexually transmitted infections. He is a member of both the Department of Social and Preventive Medicine and the Department of Obstetrics and Gynecology in the Faculty of Medicine at l'Université de Montréal. He is the medical director of Clinique A McGill Street, a clinic devoted to multidisciplinary approaches to sexual health. He is a member of the Canadian STI guidelines expert group and lead author on HPV, genital herpes, and genital ulceration chapters.

Katherine S. Sutton, Ph.D., is a postdoctoral fellow at the Centre for Addiction and Mental Health in Toronto, Ontario. Her research focusses on various aspects of health and human sexuality, including vulvodynia, hypersexuality, and paraphilias. She has published numerous articles and book chapters on these topics. Her clinical areas of practice include sex therapy, gender identity disorders, and the assessment and treatment of adult sexual offenders.

Richard J. Wassersug, Ph.D., is an adjunct professor in the Department of Urologic Sciences at the University of British Columbia and scientist in residence for the Men's Health Initiative of BC. He is also an adjunct professor at the Australian Research Centre in Sex, Health, and Society. His research focusses on the psychology of androgen deprivation in various populations ranging from male-to-female transsexual to advanced prostate cancer patients.

Samantha Waxman, Ph.D., is a clinical psychologist working in private practice. Her areas of practice include clinical and health psychology with individuals and couples. Her Ph.D. research focussed on women's sexual arousal.

Editor's Preface

My goals in launching *Human Sexuality: A Contemporary Introduction* are numerous: to create the first-ever "from-the-ground-up" Canadian human sexuality textbook, to construct a textbook that conveys expertise in each and every chapter, to focus on Canadian research and policy while including international and diverse perspectives, and to make the book as accessible as possible to students in order to stimulate interest and critical thinking. Having taught human sexuality courses for a decade, I have always been impressed with the range of available sexuality textbooks. However, I have found some of them too biological, some too clinical, and some not "Canadian" enough. *Human Sexuality: A Contemporary Introduction* offers a balance of the biological and clinical and of Canadian and international content, and each chapter is written by one or more experts in the field at a level that is engaging and thought-provoking for all.

Information about the Book

A course on human sexuality, for me, is a win–win situation for the students and the instructor. The topic is interesting for all who are in the class: the students *want* to learn, and the instructor can't help but be passionate about the field—especially with so many engaged and interested students in the class and wonderful research findings in the literature. This textbook is designed to capitalize on and enhance this inherent interest for the students.

The authors, the editorial team at Oxford University Press, and I have done our best to ensure that each chapter is interesting, relevant, current, and well-written in order to engage and inform the reader. Although the chapters are comprehensive, there is not too much detail to get lost in. Studies of high quality are cited, and when relevant, stories and information from the news and online sources are used to illustrate points and themes in relation to research findings. This way, the reader is encouraged to be an informed consumer of information from media sources. Canadian content is emphasized, but not to the exclusion of information from other parts of the world.

Human Sexuality is intended for use in a survey course. Although many readers may have taken prior courses and/or had prior formal training in sexuality, this book assumes no prior background. The biological and psychological aspects of sexuality presented in this book also require no prior exposure to these areas of study. Taken together, the chapters offer a broad and comprehensive introduction to the study of human sexuality, but not all chapters need to be covered in every course. All chapters are written to be relatively independent of one another, and where applicable, helpful cross-references guide students to relevant material in other chapters.

Outstanding Contributors

The authors of each chapter come from a variety of backgrounds, including psychology, urological sciences, gynecology, kinesiology and health, physiology, and public health. Overwhelmingly, the discipline most represented is psychology, but the backgrounds of all authors represent the interdisciplinary nature of the study of human sexuality. All authors, at the time of their initial agreement, held positions in Canada, emphasizing the Canadian focus of this textbook. Authors are well published and respected in the field. Examples of authorities in cutting-edge research areas include Elke Reissing (chapters 2 and 9), a female sexual dysfunction expert who also focusses on sexuality in older adults; Richard Wassersug (Chapter 4), an expert in the area of men who undergo voluntary castration, and in anatomy; Gillian Einstein and Jennifer Blake (Chapter 5), leading researchers in women's health and endocrinology/hormones; Beverley Chalmers (chapters 6 and 7), a leading expert in women's reproductive health issues and policy; Bill Fisher and Marc Steben (Chapter 8), authorities in the areas of sexually transmitted infections; Meredith Chivers (Chapter 10), a pioneer in the field of sexual psychophysiology; Uzma Rehman (Chapter 13), a leading researcher in communication and healthy relationships, and Peggy Kleinplatz (Chapter 16), a forerunner in the area of sexual dysfunction.

Given the expertise and diverse backgrounds of the authors who contributed to this book, it is not surprising that several of the chapters are unique: the stand-alone chapter on communication (Chapter 13) offers original reflections on the importance of this behaviour in intimate (and other) relationships; the innovative approach to sexual/affectional orientation in the sexual/affectional orientations and diversity chapter (Chapter 11) showcases the evolution of myriad identities in society; the chapter on variations in sexual behaviour (Chapter 15) contains exclusive information not found in other texts; and the sexual dysfunction chapter (Chapter 16) is thoroughly distinct in its approach. This flavour of uniqueness has resulted from the strengths of each and every author, and it provides the backbone for the exceptional information provided in this book.

Acknowledgements

I would like to thank Jacqueline Mason (formerly at Oxford University Press), who first approached me about this textbook and who worked with me on the early stages of making this marvellous volume a reality. A tremendous thank you goes to Sarah Carmichael (developmental editor, Oxford University Press), who responded to every single email I sent her about all aspects of this multistage process; without her expertise, attention to detail, wonderful sense of humour, and confidence in my abilities, this book would not be the trailblazing tome that it is. I also would like to extend heartfelt gratitude and thanks to Janice Evans, senior editor *extraordinaire* at Oxford, who worked tirelessly to make this volume utterly magnificent. Without her magical touch, this book would not be the perfect specimen that it is. An enormous thank you goes to Steven Hall, Production Manager in Creative Services, who shaped this book to the highest degree of excellence in terms of all visual aspects. Thanks also to all of you at Oxford University Press who worked tirelessly on various parts of this textbook behind the scenes. I also extend infinite appreciation and heartfelt gratitude to each and every contributor for their wonderful expertise. It has been a pleasure working alongside you all.

I would like to dedicate this book to my family: my parents, who supported me in every undertaking without question; my sister, who always believed in me and pushed me to be (and do) my very best in all endeavours; my husband, who is the best partner in all areas of life that I could ever wish for (I am so lucky!); and my twins and stepson, who keep me balanced and fulfilled in many more ways than words can describe.

Finally, I would like to acknowledge the contributions of the following reviewers, whose thoughtful comments and suggestions have helped to shape this book:

Irving M. Binik, McGill University
Lori Brotto, University of British Columbia
Cindy Clarke, Lakehead University and University of Guelph
Michelle Everest, Western University
Lindsay Harris, Algonquin College
Terry Humphreys, Trent University
Scott Mattson, University of Windsor
Dawn More, Algonquin College
Jennifer M. Ostovich, McMaster University
B.J. Rye, St Jerome's University
Stacey Sasaki, University of Manitoba
Monika Stelzl, St Thomas University
Paul Vasey, University of Lethbridge

Caroline F. Pukall,
Queen's University

From the Publisher

Human sexuality is a subject that affects us all, in some way or another, throughout our entire lives. While some topics are fairly straightforward and receive at least some attention in primary and secondary schools—anatomy, pregnancy, safer sex—others are more complex and unfamiliar to many young adults. Interpretations of gender, attraction, love, and communication are but a few aspects of human sexuality that require higher-level thought and analysis to be understood in a meaningful way. Also deserving of thoughtful consideration are the many emotionally charged issues, such as the legal status of sex-trade work and the content of sex education programs for children and teens, embedded within considerations of human sexuality.

Recognizing the vital importance of providing today's students with comprehensive, balanced coverage of these and other topics, Oxford University Press is proud to present *Human Sexuality: A Contemporary Introduction*. This exciting new work offers students an informative, practical, thought-provoking introduction to all areas of human sexuality. This book has been carefully designed to ensure students get the most from their learning experience.

1. *A student-friendly tone.* Each contributor has written in a style that is clear and inviting to students new to the study of human sexuality.

2. *A broad approach.* Perspectives from psychology, biology, sociology, cultural studies, public policy, legal studies, and medicine are incorporated throughout the text, offering students well-rounded coverage of key topics.

3. *Expert editor and contributors.* Chapters have been written by leading Canadian scholars, researchers, and sexual health clinicians working in the field today. Together, the chapters bring to life editor Caroline F. Pukall's vision of a highly accessible, thoroughly Canadian, research-based introduction to human sexuality.

4. *Cutting-edge material.* Each chapter draws on the latest research findings and theories to ensure that all material reflects the current state of the discipline. *Human Sexuality* also features up-to-date explorations of such evolving topics as what constitutes "atypical" sexual behaviour and how to label and interpret sexual dysfunctions, with detailed coverage of how sexual dysfunctions are treated in the *DSM-5*.

5. *A wide array of practical examples.* Examples drawn from people's lived experiences demonstrate how concepts, approaches, and theories manifest in the real world.

6. *A visually stimulating design.* A contemporary, fresh design reflects the vibrancy and excitement of the discipline and helps students navigate through the key features of the text.

Key Features

Human Sexuality includes a wide variety of features guaranteed to engage readers' interest and promote student learning.

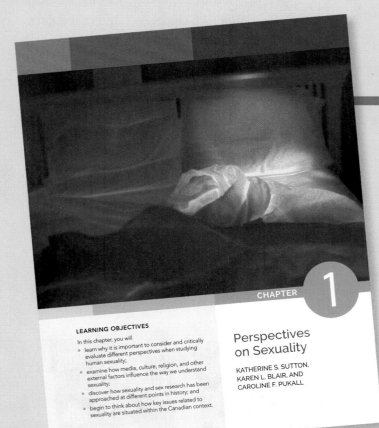

LEARNING OBJECTIVES

In this chapter, you will

- learn why it is important to consider and critically evaluate different perspectives when studying human sexuality;
- examine how media, culture, religion, and other external factors influence the way we understand sexuality;
- discover how sexuality and sex research has been approached at different points in history; and
- begin to think about how key issues related to sexuality are situated within the Canadian context.

CHAPTER 1

Perspectives on Sexuality

KATHERINE S. SUTTON,
KAREN L. BLAIR, AND
CAROLINE F. PUKALL

- **Lists of learning objectives** prepare students for what is to come by providing a concise overview of each chapter.

- **Chapter-opening case studies** engage students' imagination through detailed descriptions of real-world situations. **Questions for critical thought and reflection** follow each case study, encouraging readers to actively think about the subject matter as they progress through each chapter.

What Is the Reproductive Advantage of Same-Sex Sexual Orientation?

According to evolutionary theory and natural selection, if something is encoded in our genes, then there must be some reproductive advantage associated with it. But what is the reproductive advantage of same-sex sexual orientation, given that gay and lesbian couples are, strictly speaking, unable to conceive children without assistance? Sociobiologists have proposed an explanation.

Canadian researchers Paul Vasey and Doug VanderLaan (2010) studied a group of culturally accepted transgendered men, known locally as *fa'afafine*, in Samoa. In Samoan culture, the biologically male fa'afafine are seen as occupying a gender category other than that of "male" or "female," and they predominantly engage sexually with men. Even though fa'afafine individuals do not typically father their own children, they do share genes with other members of their families, such as their nieces and nephews. Therefore, the researchers suggest, from an evolutionary perspective, it is in the fa'afafine's best interest to look after these family members in order to ensure that some of their genetic traits are passed on to future generations (see Figure 2.1).

In this study, the researchers compared avuncular tendencies (such as investing resources in family members) of the fa'afafine to those of male-gendered men with children and male-gendered men without children. As would be predicted by evolutionary theory, the fa'afafine showed stronger avuncular tendencies and were more likely to do things for the children, like take care of them for a week while their parents were away. This notion of "inclusive fitness" has been used

FIGURE 2.1 Can evolutionary theory explain sexual orientation? The *fa'afafine* of Samoa assist in caring for their nieces and nephews, thus helping to ensure that some of the genes they share with their relatives will be passed on to future generations.

to explain altruism, and it has been observed in the animal world, as some animals will risk their lives with alarm calls to protect their family group. Inclusive fitness could explain the adaptive advantage of having gay and lesbian family members.

QUESTIONS FOR CRITICAL THOUGHT AND REFLECTION

As you read through the chapter, keep the following questions in mind:

1. Do you think that evolutionary theory can fully explain sexual orientation? What other factors might be involved?
2. What other aspects of human sexuality might evolutionary theory help to explain?
3. What is the value of using scientific theories to explain human behaviour?

- **Visually engaging photos, cartoons, figures, and tables** bring the discussion to life and help students approach complex concepts and data in new ways.

---

114   Human Sexuality

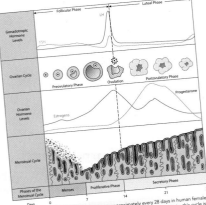

FIGURE 5.4 The reproductive cycle repeats approximately every 28 days in human females. When it is described according to the development and release of the oocyte, this cycle is called the ovarian cycle. When it is described according to the development and clearing of the uterine lining, it is called the menstrual cycle.

aromatase An enzyme that converts androgens to estrogens.

receptor A molecule, most often found on the surface of a cell, that receives chemical signals directing a cell to do something (e.g., make proteins).

FSH is the first hormone to increase in level; as noted above, it initiates the growth and maturation of ovarian follicles and stimulates enzymes that are essential for the production of estrogens, notably **aromatase**. The rising levels of estrogen have a positive feedback effect on LH secretion. LH in turn stimulates increased steroid synthesis in the theca cells of the ovary; as LH increases, so do androgen levels. The androgens pass to the granulosa cells of the follicles, where the aromatase enzyme acts to convert androgens to estrogens. Estrogen, however, has a negative impact on the production of FSH: the level of FSH drops as estrogen levels increase. Fortunately FSH induces its own **receptor** on the follicles, which means that as it becomes scarcer, only those follicles with the most receptors will still be able to bind FSH and continue to develop. This enables the selection and success of the dominant follicle and dramatically increases the likelihood of a single oocyte (egg) being released. As women age and their pool of remaining follicles diminishes in size, inhibin levels are reduced, allowing FSH levels in the early part of the cycle to rise. The elevated level of FSH can result in more than one follicle maturing, thus contributing to an increased risk of multiple pregnancy.

---

8 • Sexually Transmitted Infections: At the Junction of Biology and Behaviour   187

(Sexually Transmitted Disease, 2013). Syphilis remains a problem around the world, including in Canada, today (see Figure 8.4).

If we fast forward five centuries, from the syphilis epidemic in Europe in the 1500s to North America in the 1980s, we arrive at the age of herpes, what your parents probably thought of as "The New Scarlet Letter"—an indelible mark (and incurable infection) that broadcast one's sexual activity to the world. Herpes causes cold sores that inconveniently locate themselves on one's genitals and are readily transmitted to a sexual partner's genitals. Herpes can be transmitted in genital-genital sex and in oral-genital contact. It represented the leading edge of what came to be recognized as the era of sexually transmitted viruses, which include the herpes simplex virus (HSV), the human papillomavirus (HPV), and the human immunodeficiency virus (HIV). While STIs that are caused by bacteria (such as syphilis, gonorrhea, and chlamydia) can all be cured with antibiotics, most STIs caused by viruses cannot be cured (hepatitis B and C can be cured). Before swearing off sex for the rest of your life, however, consider that viral STIs can be avoided (e.g., screening tests for HIV infection), prevented (in the case of HPV, by preventive vaccination, and in the case of HIV, by consistent condom use), and treated to reduce the damage done to one's health and to limit transmission to partners or from mother to baby during childbirth.

FIGURE 8.3 A poster announcing a cure for syphilis (c. 1930s).

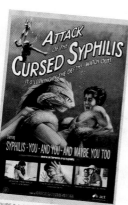

FIGURE 8.4 A 2010 AIDS Committee of Toronto poster promoting awareness of a syphilis outbreak among men who have sex with men.

---

422   Human Sexuality

remain. Clearly, these laws symbolize the reach of traditional social values and seem to be biased against people who have anal sex.

Prevalence and Incidence of Sexual Assault

Researchers have used multiple methods to estimate the scope of sexual assault (Gannon & Ward, 2008). For example, some researchers have used surveys to obtain **prevalence estimates**, by identifying the percentage of surveyed individuals who report having been sexually assaulted or having sexually assaulted someone else at least once. Others have used official reports to obtain **incidence estimates**, by examining the number of sexual assaults that are officially reported. Both types of estimates are biased and are assumed to undercount incidents of sexual assault.

Prevalence estimates of sexual assault vary substantially, depending on the definitions, measures, and samples used. In 1993, Statistics Canada conducted the first nationally representative survey dedicated to studying violence against women, which was called the Violence Against Women Survey (VAWS). The VAWS was a special one-time survey funded by the federal government that established a baseline and an understanding of physical and sexual violence among Canadian women; its methodology has since been replicated in other countries. The survey found that 51 per cent of all Canadian women had been sexually or physically abused by a man at least once, and that approximately 60 per cent of these women had survived more than one incident of violence. However, researchers have since pointed out that design flaws in the study may have led to an elevated perception of the problem of violence against women.

Since 1993, a number of smaller surveys investigating sexual assault have been conducted in Canada, both in the general population and on university campuses, and the findings are sobering. For instance, according to Statistics Canada's 2004 General Social

prevalence estimates Estimates based on the percentage of surveyed individuals who report having participated in or experienced a certain condition in a given period of time.

incidence estimates Estimates based on the documented instances of a certain condition in a given period of time.

TABLE 17.1 This table illustrates whether a sexual relationship between two people of different ages is legally consensual in Canada. Red indicates that consent cannot be given, orange indicates that consent can be given in some cases, and yellow indicates that consent can be given in all cases.											
The youth is . . .	Under 12	12	13	14	15	16	17	18	19	20	
And the other person is . . .	No*	No	No	No	No	No	No	Yes	Yes	Yes	
Under 12	No*	Yes	Yes	Yes	Yes	Yes	Yes	Yes	Yes	Yes	
Same age	No	Yes	Yes	Yes	Yes	Yes	Yes	Yes	Yes	Yes	
Less than one year older	No	Yes	Yes	Yes	Yes	Yes	Yes	Yes	Yes	Yes	
Less than two years older	No	No	No	Yes	Yes	Yes	Yes	Yes	Yes	Yes	
Less than three years older	No	No	No	No	Yes	Yes	Yes	Yes	Yes	Yes	
Less than four years older	No	No	No	No	No	Yes	Yes	Yes	Yes	Yes	
Less than five years older	No	No	No	No	No	No	Yes	Yes	Yes	Yes	
More than five years older	No	No	No	No	No	No	Yes	Yes	Yes	Yes	

*Children under the age of 12 cannot legally consent to any sexual activity. However, it is not an offence if two children under the age of 12 engage in sexual activities with each other.

Note: Even close-in-age exceptions are not considered consensual when one of the individuals is in a position of trust or authority with the other, one is in a relationship of dependency with the other, or if the relationship between them is found to be exploitative. Furthermore, there are protections for people mental or physical disabilities, regardless of age.

- **Marginal definitions of key terms** ensure students understand the meaning of discipline-specific terminology used in the discussion. These definitions also appear in the **glossary** for quick-reference and review.

- **"Culture and Diversity" boxes** offer insight into perspectives and issues that are common in other parts of the world, encouraging students to think outside the box of ethnocentricity.

52   Human Sexuality

random samples Study participants who have been selected at random to accurately represent the population of interest in terms of gender, racial, socioeconomic, behavioural, and/or other characteristics.

questionnaire A set of multiple-choice or short-answer questions that is designed to obtain specific information.

use **random samples**. A related challenge is representing the types of people who are disinclined to volunteer to participate in sexuality research, as there is evidence that individuals who are willing to participate in sexuality research differ in important ways from individuals who are unwilling to participate (Strassberg & Lowe, 1995).

Another challenge is finding a research method that participants will not find intimidating. Many people are comfortable with filling out a **questionnaire** about sexuality, but some might find such a task daunting, especially if the questions ask them to think about negative sexual experiences. Perhaps even more daunting, for some people, is research that involves the use of invasive devices that monitor physiological responses to visual or tactile sexual stimulation. Regardless of the methods involved, it is the responsibility of the researchers to ensure that the participants feel safe in the laboratory setting.

In addition, it may be difficult for the research to remain free of bias. Recall, from Chapter 1, that personal, cultural, religious, and even political ideas about sexuality often influence how sexuality is defined, which questions are asked, and how information is interpreted. Although responsible researchers try to design studies that will not be coloured by personal bias, this is not always possible. Indeed, many forms of bias have, to some extent, coloured all sex research, and biases will undoubtedly continue to shape this research in the future. After all, sex always occurs within a context that is influenced by a complex mixture of forces—interpersonal relationship dynamics, psychological pressures that reflect a person's unique experiences, cultural definitions of what is and is not normal, religious ideas that link sex with moral responsibility, biological

Culture & Diversity

Using Research to Explore Sexuality in Asian Canadians

Given the strong role that culture plays in the expression of sexuality, surprisingly little research has been done to investigate how first- and second-generation immigrants' sexual beliefs are influenced by the sexual mores of both their traditional cultures and the culture of their new home. Lori Brotto, a clinical psychologist at the University of British Columbia, has delved into how this cross-cultural interaction influences sexual attitudes, knowledge of sexuality and sexual health, and sexual function. Based on previous observations of heightened sexual conservatism in Asian Canadians, Brotto queried Asian- and Euro-Canadian men and women in universities and in the Vancouver community about their sexual lives and the extent to which they had adjusted to the Western values held by Canadians—in other words, the extent to which they had acculturated. She discovered that Asian-Canadian women reported less sexual knowledge, more conservative sexual attitudes, more sexual guilt, and poorer sexual function (e.g., lower

desire, arousal, pleasure) than did their European-Canadian peers. Using statistical regression modelling, she determined that more highly acculturated Asian-Canadian females reported less sexual guilt, and that lower levels of sexual guilt in turn had a positive impact on sexual desire (Woo, Brotto, & Gorzalka, 2011). Interestingly, despite the previous reports of poorer sexual function in Asian-Canadian women, vaginal blood flow patterns in these women were comparable to those found in European-Canadian women (Yule, Woo, & Brotto, 2010). Researchers often observe vaginal blood flow patterns as a physiological indicator of sexual arousal; thus, these findings suggest that the psychological attitudes about sexuality do not necessarily inhibit a woman's ability to achieve sexual arousal. This research raises awareness about the complex interaction of culture, sexual beliefs, and sexual functioning in influencing how women experience their sexuality, which has yet to be explored in other ethnic minorities in Canada.

---

9 • Sexuality over the Lifespan   225

Ethical Debate

Sexuality and Disability

Sexuality is universal among all people, from the very young to the very old. Unfortunately, some people hold very negative views about sex and disability. Some are prejudiced against those with physical or cognitive disabilities and would never consider forming a sexual relationship with them. Others mistakenly believe that people with disabilities are less sexual than people without disabilities. Such views may lead to discrimination, intentional or not; for example, parents of an adult with a disability who lives in their home might not allow their adult child to have private time for sexual activities with a partner or even by him or herself. Additionally, some people with disabilities may have internalized negativity about their bodies and may feel as though they are "unsexy" or not allowed to be sexual. In all of these cases, some education about sexuality could go a long way to overcoming prejudice and discrimination.

For most people with disabilities and their partners, sex is much like sex between two people without disabilities; it may simply require some additional communication and creativity, things that most sexual couples—regardless of their abilities—could benefit from (Figure 9.9)! Yet in some cases that involve people who live with severe disabilities, the matter may be much more complex and may even pose some ethical dilemmas, not only for the person with the disability but also for her or his partner(s) and/or the people who love and care for that person. For example, what is the role of the caretakers when a couple with severe disabilities wishes to conceive a child, and at what point, if any, can one decide that the couple is "too disabled" to take care of a child? If the couple does not wish to conceive but are not able to effectively and/or consistently use contraceptives on their own, does the caretaker have a duty to assist with birth control? If so, how far does this duty extend? Similarly, how

FIGURE 9.9 Good sex is creative sex! People with physical disabilities may have to be more creative when having sex, but this can actually lead to more sexual enjoyment and satisfaction.

far does the caretaker's role extend in ensuring that the couple uses condoms or dental dams to protect against STIs? Does the caretaker have a right to deny assistance if he or she feels uncomfortable doing so? Further, in cases involving an individual or individuals with cognitive disabilities, who decides when the disabilities are too severe to assume consent to participate in sexual relationships?

would have seemed impossible even 20 years ago. In addition, email and social networking sites have changed the way people meet and maintain relationships. Social networking sites such as Facebook offer many benefits—they allow for increased social connection, and they can help couples in long-distance relationships stay in close contact (see the "Research vs Real Life" box). Yet they also present potential dangers. Canadian researcher Amy Muise and colleagues (2009) have found, for example, that

- **"Ethical Debate" boxes** inspire students to contemplate and discuss the role of ethics in studies and considerations of human sexuality. These boxes ask such provocative questions as "Should sexual orientation be considered a human right?" "How do we define 'normal' sexuality?" "Should parents help their children to become gender conforming?" and "How far must researchers go to protect the confidentiality of study participants?"

- **"Research vs Real Life" boxes** address disparities between research findings and real-life experiences. Students will discover how and to what purpose research findings are translated or misconstrued by the media and the general population.

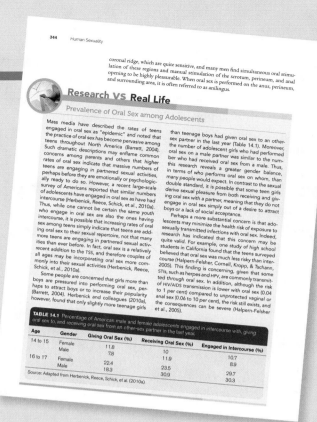

- **Chapter summaries** highlight key concepts to help students synthesize what has been covered in the chapter and review for tests and exams.
- **End-of-chapter debate and review questions** promote classroom discussion and critical thought.
- **Extensive lists of recommended websites, books, articles, and video resources** encourage students to continue their learning journey beyond the page and classroom.

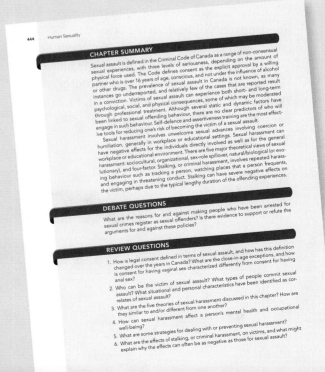

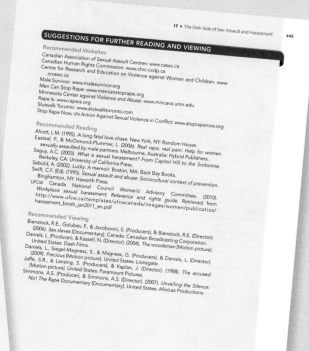

Online Supplements

Human Sexuality is supported by an outstanding array of ancillary materials for both students and instructors, all available on the companion website: www.oupcanada.com/Pukall.

FOR INSTRUCTORS

The following instructor's resources are available to qualifying adopters. Please contact your OUP Canada sales representative for more information.

- **An instructor's manual** includes comprehensive chapter overviews, topics for classroom discussion and debate, recommended readings, links to relevant video clips, and sample syllabi.
- **A test generator** offers a comprehensive set of multiple-choice, true/false, short-answer, and essay questions.
- **PowerPoint slides** for use in classroom lectures summarize key points from each chapter.
- **An image bank** includes a wide selection of stunning images that will enhance the vibrancy of slides and handouts.

FOR STUDENTS

A comprehensive study guide offers students additional activities and content to help them understand key concepts presented in each chapter and review for tests and exams.

OXFORD NEXT FOR *HUMAN SEXUALITY*

Human Sexuality is accompanied by *Oxford Next*, an interactive site that offers a wide variety of exercises, activities, self-quizzes, experiments, and videos designed to help students understand important concepts and principles. Access to *Oxford Next* is available for free with purchase of a new copy of *Human Sexuality* and also includes an e-book and additional study resources for students.

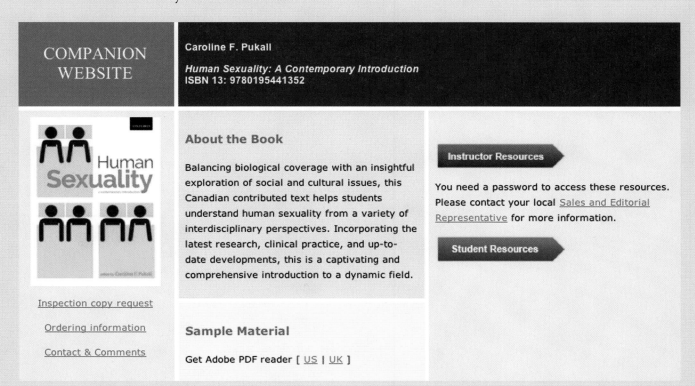

www.oupcanada.com/Pukall

Perspectives on Sexuality

KATHERINE S. SUTTON,
KAREN L. BLAIR, AND
CAROLINE F. PUKALL

LEARNING OBJECTIVES

In this chapter, you will

- learn why it is important to consider and critically evaluate different perspectives when studying human sexuality;

- examine how media, culture, religion, and other external factors influence the way we understand sexuality;

- discover how sexuality and sex research has been approached at different points in history; and

- begin to think about how key issues related to sexuality are situated within the Canadian context.

What to Expect from a Sexuality Class?

Chris was excited but nervous. She was on her way to the first session of the human sexuality class that she had heard so much about. Her friends had told her that she was in for a treat, and although outwardly she seemed open and excited about the course, inwardly she felt a little uncomfortable and awkward about sitting in class with others learning about such a private topic. So many questions raced through her head. Would she see pictures of genitals? Would the students have to talk about their own sexual experiences, or lack thereof? Would they watch pornographic films? Would people think that she was a pervert for taking the class, or maybe even super sexually open? Neither was the case. She had heard that interesting research was covered in this course.

What kind of research was done in the area of sexuality anyway? Sexuality didn't seem to be a topic of scientific study like personality or depression. What did she get herself into?! She walked to the lecture hall and sat down, waiting to learn about something that was never really discussed openly in her family.

QUESTIONS FOR CRITICAL THOUGHT AND REFLECTION

1. What do you expect to learn from a class on human sexuality?
2. What thoughts (positive and negative) were going through your head as you registered for this course?

Introduction

masturbation Manual stimulation of one's own genitals for sexual pleasure, commonly resulting in orgasm.

As you may already know, the topic of sexuality is never a neutral one. People have different ideas about sexuality, and many can get quite defensive of their own beliefs about things like sexuality education, **masturbation**, sex outside a committed relationship, abortion, and same-sex relationships—if they are able to talk about these topics at all! Even if sexuality is not openly discussed in one's family or relationships, it is hard to ignore the many sexual messages "out there" that can range from being explicit to being very subtle. The purpose of this chapter is to discuss the many ways in which we are all exposed to messages (good and bad) about sexuality and to get you thinking about these messages in different ways.

Sex and Media

Media play a large role in the formation of our identities and norms. Media help to shape how we think of ourselves, and others, in terms of gender, class, and race. Media also help to create and dictate societal norms, including norms about sexuality (Kellner, 2003). From media, we learn what is "normal" (Chapter 15), what we "should" desire, and what to buy—or buy into—in order to achieve the most satisfaction and normalcy. The idea of what is "good" and what is "bad" is a social construction, and much of this social construction is created through media. Sometimes media are blatantly obvious in their intentions, but many times messages are conveyed through subtle advertising (Figure 1.1). What is portrayed in media does not necessarily reflect the reality of society; however, the ways in which characters are developed, plots played out, and topics focused on (or not) certainly provide insight into underlying attitudes about sexuality and **LGBTTIQQ** individuals.

LGBTTIQQ Lesbian, gay, bisexual, transgender, two-spirited, intersex, queer, questioning.

A History of Sex and Advertising in Western Culture

Because of the influence of religious doctrines, reference to sexuality was censored in Western culture for many centuries, forcing media to find subtle ways of injecting it into the mainstream. This was particularly true in the Victorian era, at which time many politicians and social moralists were concerned that high levels of sexual activity would lead to a population increase that would overtax diminishing natural resources, as predicted by the scholar Thomas Robert Malthus (1766–1834) (Marsh, 2011). Despite concerns about population growth, contraceptives were illegal to sell or advertise, although they were available to those who knew whom to approach and what to say to get them.

Items that were explicitly sexual were disguised in advertising, while non-sexual items were often sold with sexy campaigns. For example, vibrators were first used as a medical device to relieve **hysteria** by inducing orgasm in women (Maines, 1999). Marketing for handheld vibrators first appeared in magazine advertisements in the early 1900s; in these ads, the vibrators were disguised as massaging devices for health promotion rather than for sexual stimulation. Over time, however, it became more common for advertisers to use aspects of sexuality to sell non-sexual products—for example, Lux soap was once touted as a product that could "keep romance aflame" (Woman's Home Companion, July 1935), and "pin-up girls" were widely used in the 1940s and '50s to sell products such as Royal Crown Cola (Figure 1.2).

In the 1950s, advertisers increasingly used sex in their campaigns as topics of sexuality came to be presented somewhat more openly in other venues of popular media. This openness was brought about, to a great extent, by the publication of Alfred Kinsey's controversial "Kinsey Reports": *Sexual Behaviour in the Human Male (1948)* and *Sexual Behaviour in the Human Female* (1953). In fact, at least three major 1950s ad campaigns—Maidenform's "I dream," Revlon's "fire and ice," and Clairol's "Does she or doesn't she?" (colour her hair, that is!)—were inspired by Kinsey's findings.

In the following years, many advertisers continued to focus on female sexuality in their campaigns, although ads showing scantily clad men, such as those for Calvin Klein underwear in the 1980s, also began to appear. Women's magazines, such as *Cosmopolitan*, came to be a major venue for such sexualized ads, particularly those featuring women. Although many of these magazines may, on the surface, seem to be pro-woman, they often contain content that creates and then exploits women's insecurities, especially those related to sexuality and appearance. They convince women to buy into patriarchal views of the ideal woman, and all of the products that come with these views. Advertisers work to convince readers that they can close the gap between themselves and the ideal by buying the advertiser's product (Dines & Humez, 2003).

Although it is commonly believed that "sex sells," studies that explore the validity of this belief have produced conflicting results. A study conducted by Severn, Belch, and Belch (1990), for example, concluded that unless an ad is for something sexual, people are more likely to remember that the scene was sexy than to recall the product that was being advertised. On the other hand, a study by Gallup and Robinson Research (2012) found that, when used effectively, sex increases recall for products an

FIGURE 1.1 Media can affect our attitudes toward sexuality, particularly when we are young; however, this is a difficult area to research because ethical concerns prevent researchers from randomizing groups and exposing some youths to sexuality or pornography while withholding this exposure from others. This area of research is also difficult for logistical reasons: we cannot raise children in an isolated environment where we can ensure that they are not exposed to media. In doing an experiment that compares a group of youths who report having viewed a lot of sexuality in media to a group of youths who report having viewed little sexuality in media, what might be some of the confounding (third variable) problems?

hysteria A controversial mental illness/disease that was seen as being specific to women and characterized by the conversion of psychological stresses (specifically, sexual frustration) into physical symptoms (e.g., gastrointestinal and nervous system problems), as well as volatile emotions and attention-seeking behaviours.

average of 77 per cent over the average recall for products advertised with ads that are not sexual.

Sex in Film and on Television

The concern about the amount of sexuality in media is related to advances in technology (Lane, 2000); however, sexual themes and innuendos have been present in literature and theatre throughout the history of the Western tradition. For example, the play *Lysistrata*, written by the ancient Greek playwright Aristophanes (c. 450–c. 385 BCE), is a comedy rampant with sexual jokes; in one scene, a woman is described as having arrived from "A very lovely land, well cropped, and trimmed, and spruced with pennyroyal," a known contraceptive (Riddle, 1992). Yet the film industry came to appeal to wider audiences than the theatre had, and this broad appeal was a particular worry for those wanting to censure sexuality. In 1896, a film called *The Kiss* depicted a quick kiss between a heterosexual couple; this scene garnered much negative feedback, including the comment that "such things call for police action." It was not long before mainstream films became more sexually explicit, with the first non-pornographic film to depict nudity, *Inspiration*, released in 1915. Sexually explicit films, made specifically to sexually arouse viewers, were produced very soon after the invention of the motion picture camera in 1895.

Having nudity in a Hollywood film affects the film's rating code, as determined by the Motion Picture Association of America. Genital nudity, particularly male frontal nudity, is still rare in mainstream North American films; however, female nudity, especially toplessness, has become much more acceptable and often does not result in an **R rating**. The European film industry, reflecting European societies' more open attitudes toward sexuality, uses nude scenes much more liberally. Filmed full frontal nudity of both men and women is much more common and far less stigmatized in Europe than it is in Hollywood, where the decision to do a nude scene can dramatically impact an actor's reputation.

Television has also been an area of concern when it comes to sexual messages. Over the years, many questions have arisen: Who is allowed to have sex on television? How explicit can the sexual content be? Should sexual violence be shown? How does sexual content affect the sexual behaviour of viewers? The first televised scene of a married couple sharing a bed appeared on the *Mary Kay and Johnny* show in 1947; however, it would be another few decades before scenes of a shared marital bed would become commonplace on television, and even longer before it would become acceptable to depict married (and unmarried) couples having sex in their shared bed.

When television shows and films push the boundaries of what viewers expect to see in terms of sexual content, they are often made to suffer the consequences of their actions. This is particularly true in North America, where censorship boards have the power to impose fines when they deem content to be sexually inappropriate. For example, the broadcasting corporation CBS was fined $3.6 million in 2006 by the Federal Communications Commission (FCC) for showing a teenage orgy on the crime show *Without a Trace*. Even reportedly unintentional sexual content can come under fire, as was the case in the United States in 2004, when immense controversy emerged over the "wardrobe malfunction" in which Janet Jackson's nipple was exposed at the

FIGURE 1.2 Pin-up girls were argued by some to be a healthy portrayal of female beauty and empowerment. Others argued that these images were associated with corrupting societal morals and objectifying women for their sexuality. Either way, images of pin-up girls quickly became a part of mass media, both as images in and of themselves, and through their use in advertisements.

R rating Restricted rating from the Motion Picture Association of America, requiring individuals under the age of 17 to be accompanied by a parent or adult guardian.

Super Bowl XXXVIII halftime show. In Canada, this same incident resulted in fewer than two hundred complaints to the Canadian Broadcast Standards Council (CBSC, 2004).

Sex and the Internet

The Internet has greatly increased the ease with which individuals are able to access sexual content and activity. This development has led to the need for a variety of parental control features to help parents monitor the content that their children access online. The proliferation of online chat sites, message boards, role-playing systems (e.g., Second Life), and social networking sites (e.g., Facebook, MySpace) has inadvertently provided sexual predators with a ripe new hunting ground for young victims. As a result, entirely new divisions of law enforcement have emerged to focus specifically on sex crimes facilitated by the Internet.

Although it is often associated with increased risks in relation to sexuality, the Internet has also played a positive role in promoting healthy, safe, and diverse human sexuality and behaviour. For example, the Internet has become a source of accessible sex education, has contributed to the normalizing of sexuality and diverse sexual identities, and has provided a new means of meeting potential partners. Online dating sites are one of the fastest-growing online industries and gross over $1 billion annually. Stories abound of individuals meeting online, as the process has become more commonplace and less taboo. According to one poll, 25 per cent of Canadians reported having used online dating services, and this number increases to 36 per cent among individuals 18 to 34 years of age (Goodyear, 2011). Online dating has been particularly useful for individuals seeking marginalized types of relationships, such as same-sex relationships. In fact, same-sex couples are three times more likely than mixed-sex couples to have met online (Rosenbloom, 2011), partly due to the fact that those seeking same-sex relationships hold fewer notions of taboos associated with online dating than does society in general (Custer, Holmberg, Blair, & Orbuch, 2008).

Safer Sex Messages

The popular message expressed in the last few decades is that media sources are not often helpful in promoting safer sex behaviours, including the use of contraceptives, in sexual situations, particularly those involving oral sex. The "fantasy model" of sex portrayed in today's media—including films, television shows, song lyrics, and music videos—seems immune to pregnancy and **sexually transmitted infections** (STIs). While fantasizing about sex can be a good thing, idealizing **sexual scripts** that do not include safer sex behaviours can be dangerous. Many people still use the excuse of getting caught in the heat of the moment for not using contraceptives, and even when **contraception** has been considered, contraceptives are not always used effectively. In the movie *Grease* (1978), for example, Rizzo and Kenickie mention contraception but continue to have sex in the back seat of his car even after the condom breaks.

Although some form of sexual content is present in 70 per cent of television programs (Roberts, Henriksen, & Foehr, 2009), most programs do not address the issue of safer sex. According to the "Sex on TV 4" study by the Kaiser Family Foundation (2005), only 11 per cent of primetime television shows that bring up sex also include information about safer sex or the risks associated with sex (Kunkel, Eyal, Finnerty, Biely, & Donnerstein, 2005). In addition, research examining sexual scenes rather than entire shows reveals that only 2 per cent of sex scenes address sexual precautions (Kunkel et al., 2003). There is an average of 5.9 sexual scenes per hour in primetime television shows (Kunkel et al., 2003). Given this high prevalence of sex without apparent consequences, many studies have been conducted to assess whether there is an

sexually transmitted infection (STI) An illness, disease, or infection transmitted from one person to another by means of sexual behaviour, including sexual intercourse (both vaginal and anal), oral sex, and the use of shared sex toys.

sexual script A series of learned and predictable actions that lead up to sexual encounters.

contraception The deliberate use of natural techniques, an artificially created barrier, or hormonal methods to prevent pregnancy as a result of sexual intercourse.

FIGURE 1.3 Although some of the popular media have sensationalized teen pregnancy by adding a flair of romance or excitement, *Juno* addresses many of the troubles that can arise from teen pregnancy.

impact on adolescent sexual risk taking. These studies have found high correlations between exposure to sex in media and risky sexual behaviour (e.g., Roberts et al., 2009).

On the other hand, there are some positive media messages about the real consequences of sex. Sex in media has been a useful tool for disseminating important information about safer sex and about LGBTTIQQ individuals. For example, in the movie *Juno* (2007), a 16-year-old girl deals with the consequences of becoming pregnant and decides to put her child up for adoption (Figure 1.3).

Portrayals of the consequences of unsafe sex also appear on television. There is the example of Rachel becoming pregnant when a condom breaks during a one-night stand on the sitcom *Friends*. Many episodes of *Degrassi*, a Canadian television show aimed at teens, also take a realistic look at sex and contraception. Although the information is not always accurate, safer sex among LGBTQ individuals is at least addressed as a topic on the drama *Queer as Folk*. *Sex and the City*, at times, addresses issues such as unplanned pregnancy and STIs, most prominently in an episode in which Miranda is diagnosed with chlamydia and must inform all of her recent sexual partners and encourage them to be tested, even if they are asymptomatic. More recently, the *Glee* episode "Sexy" was entirely dedicated to sex education and safer sex.

Television, with its wide reach, has the power to educate viewers on important issues related to sexual health. For example, an online survey found that men who have sex with men (MSM) who had seen an episode of *ER* that addressed syphilis transmission among MSM were more likely than men who had not seen the episode to say they intended to be screened for syphilis (Knapp-Whittier, Kennedy, St Lawrence, Seeley, & Beck, 2005). In addition, individuals at risk for HIV infection often learn about health issues through television programming (Beck, Pollard, & Greenberg, 2000). Soap operas have also been shown to effect positive behavioural changes on audiences (e.g., Kennedy, O'Leary, Beck, Pollard, & Simpson, 2004). Since 1995, annual "Soap Summits" have been held in order to encourage positive social and health messages in American television soap operas.

Outside of North America, telenovelas and other soap opera–like shows are a popular and effective means of spreading important messages on themes of sexuality such as family planning and safe sex. The South African series *Soul City* (1992), for example, promotes the use of condoms to its 12 million viewers. Studies have found that regular viewers of the show are almost four times more likely than non-viewers to use condoms. Telenovelas about family planning have proved effective in countries such as Saint Lucia, Brazil, and Mexico. Mexico's National Council on Population found that after nine months of episodes of *Acompáñame* (*Accompany Me*), sales of birth control pills rose 23 per cent in one year (compared with a 7 per cent rise the previous year), and there was a 33 per cent increase in the number of women who signed up to participate in family planning programs (Andaló, 2003). Similar findings emerged in India, where the show *Humraachi* (*Come Along with Me*) effected attitude changes about increasing the ideal age of marriage, and in Kenya, where several shows including *Tushauriane* (*Let's Talk about It*) were thought to have been responsible for a 58 per cent increase in contraceptive use, as well as attitude changes toward smaller ideal family sizes.

Safer and healthy sex has also been promoted on television and radio talk shows by people such as Sue Johanson (Figure 1.4), a Canadian sex educator and therapist who hosted the *Sunday Night Sex Show*. She answered questions about everything from contraception and STIs to masturbation, **BDSM**, and sex toys.

LGBTTIQQ Issues

Some prime media figures have also made attempts to address prejudice against the LGBTTIQQ communities. For example, ThinkB4youspeak.com has put out public service announcements with the theme "It's not okay to say 'that's so gay.'" A study examining queer women's thoughts and feelings about LGBT content on television found that, although they believed that representation of the queer community was done in a stereotypical manner, half of the participants identified a show that had an impact on the development of their queer identity (Houseman, 2011). The first female–female kiss on television occurred in 1991 on the drama series *L.A. Law*, while the first televised male–male kiss was in a 1960 BBC production of the play *Colombe*. Transgender issues have come to the forefront in media with the 2012 Miss Universe Canada contestant Jenna Talackova, who was initially disqualified from the competition because she is transgender. After much controversy, she was reinstated into the competition. She made it into the top 12 contestants and received one of four "Miss Congeniality" titles.

FIGURE 1.4 Sue Johanson, host of the *Sunday Night Sex Show*—on the radio from 1984 to 1998, and on television from 1996 to 2005—earned an appointment to the Order of Canada in 2001 for her work on sexuality.

Cultural Diversity

The first interracial kiss depicted in film occurred in 1903 in the film *What Happened in the Tunnel*, when a white woman and her black maid switch places in the dark to play a joke on a man who is persistently flirting with the white woman. The first interracial kiss on American television was not until years later, in 1968, on *Star Trek* between Captain Kirk and Lieutenant Uhura. However, the film *The Barbarian* (1933) featured an interracial romance between an American girl and her Egyptian guide; the film went so far as to include a "topless" bathtub scene (the girl was wearing a flesh-tinted bodysuit). The first mainstream contemplation of interracial marriage was presented in *Guess Who's Coming to Dinner* in 1967. Films and literature also use the stereotype of the black male and the white female to portray the black race in a negative light (Courtney, 2005). For example, the mistaken notion of an assault taking place rather than a simple argument between a black man and a white woman results in the man being beaten by police in the 1991 film *Jungle Fever*.

Hollywood tends to focus on white characters. Indeed, white actors received 80 per cent of all the roles in Hollywood in 1996 (Robinson, 1999). Traditionally, individuals of other races have been marginalized or portrayed in a negative light. Hollywood films also tend to dehumanize black males by objectifying their bodies during sex scenes far more often than occurs with white males. In addition, black males are often given roles in which sex without intimacy is the norm and sexual partners are acknowledged through domination and/or violence (Jones, 1993). Black music videos are also more sexualized than are white music videos, and a study by Turner (2011) concluded that this sexualization poses the greatest danger to black women, who are most likely to model what they see in these videos. Media may contribute to the relatively high rates

BDSM A type of role play or lifestyle choice between two or more individuals that involves a wide range of activities involving safe and consensual manipulations of erotic power. The term stands for "bondage and discipline, dominance and submission, sadism and masochism."

of STIs in the black population in the United States (Turner, 2011); hopefully, media will be used to address this issue in the future. For more information about the role of culture in media portrayals of sexuality, see the "Culture and Diversity" box.

Culture & Diversity

Sex and Media in Arabic and Japanese Cultures

Arabic Films

The term *Arabic films* generally refers to Egyptian films, as the majority of Arab films are created in Egypt. It is clear from changes in this industry in the last ten years that filmmakers are pushing traditional sexual boundaries. For example, the controversial 2003 film *Sleepless Nights* counters the popular belief in the Middle East that a man never marries a woman he slept with out of wedlock. One of the plotlines in the film sympathetically examines a couple who live together without being married; however, tradition wins out in the end when they do eventually marry. The Egyptian novel *The Yacoubian Building*, written by Alaa Al-Aswany and published in 2002, addresses—among other topics—the life of gay males in Cairo. In 2006, the film adaptation of this novel became the first Egyptian film to depict gay men and was the biggest-budget Arab film made until that point (Diab, 2006). *Her Man*, by female filmmaker Ayten Amin, was another controversial film; released in 2007, it examined the relationship between a man's first wife and his younger second bride. His first wife sleeps with the young bride and leaves a mark on her breast in the hopes that her husband will think that she is cheating. Released in 2010, the Lebanese film *Out Loud* (2010), by Samer Daboul, addresses topics such as premarital heterosexual sex and gay male relationships. Sexual content is also becoming widespread in many contemporary music videos in Egypt and Lebanon. Sex has also made headlines in the social media that helped drive the 2011 Egyptian revolution. For example, an Egyptian university student, Alia Al-Mahdi posted a nude picture of herself on a blog as a means of speaking out against oppression. Her post resulted in a mixture of reactions around the world and amongst revolutionaries, from extreme anger to sympathy, to strong support.

Anime

Anime is an animated form of movie or television show, usually based on Japanese comics or graphic

FIGURE 1.5 What impact do you think viewing gender-fluid characters has on children? Do such characters convey a positive, negative, or neutral message about gender and sexuality? Make note of your answer now, and think about this question again after reading Chapter 10, on gender.

novels (see Figure 1.5). This is an area of media in which the fluidity of gender roles and sexuality are explored to a greater degree than they are in North American film and television. Characters display greater sexual and gender fluidity and do not always conform to Western dichotomous understandings of gender (i.e., male and female), thereby raising themes related to intersex and transgender issues. Some critics argue that these transgender themes and characters still display a conservative view of gender because their purpose is for comic relief, although this is not always the case.

Nonetheless, these themes are still raised in anime, while broadcast companies in North America remain more reluctant to do so, especially when the shows are directed at children. As an example, when the popular anime series *Sailor Moon* was introduced to a North American audience, Optimum Productions significantly censored storylines through visual cropping and inaccurate translations to present same-sex couples as cousins and to erase gender-fluid and transgender characters. Ultimately, when the gender and sexual fluidity of characters became too difficult to hide through editing, only episodes that depicted traditional gender norms and heterosexual characters were aired on television in North America (Hoskin, 2012).

Hentai

The term *hentai*, in the English usage, refers to sexually explicit pictures, movies, comics, and games, particularly those of Japanese origin. There are many types of hentai. Some forms depict "run of the mill" sexual activity between adult males and females, males and males, and females and females. Other forms, however, depict characters of younger ages.

A common practice in hentai is to stretch sex acts beyond the limits of what one might expect: such acts can include sex with animals, sexual slavery, aural sex (penetration of the ear by a penis or tongue, for example), and nasal sex (penetration of the nostrils, or using the nose to penetrate a vagina, for example). Rape scenes are also common and can involve anything from robots raping young females to tentacles raping adult women to lesbians who transform into penises and then rape robots! It may come as no surprise that in Japanese, the term *hentai* means "pervert" or "strange desires."

Despite the explicit and boundary-pushing sexual themes in hentai and anime in general, Japanese society is not overly accepting of sexual and gender diversity. Outside of media, sexuality is considered a private matter (Gauntlett, 1999).

A Brief History of Sex Research

Ancient Texts

Ancient sexual texts date back almost 5,000 years to Asia, where Chinese handbooks of sex were written by (or for) Emperor Huang-ti, the "Yellow Emperor." These texts described various sexual positions and were used as prescriptions for a long and healthy life. In the latter half of the Zhou dynasty (1122–221 BCE), at which time Taoist thought was present though Taoism was not yet a formal religion, people believed that women had an endless supply of yin and men had a limited amount of yang. Men could acquire yin by bringing a woman to orgasm, and they were instructed to prolong ejaculation until they had taken in enough yin. The consequences of not doing so were said to be illness and even death. Male masturbation and male–male relations were frowned upon because they resulted in a man using up his yang without getting any yin. When Taoist doctrines were popular, additional sexual texts, including *Secrets of the Jade Chamber* (c. 200 BCE), emerged. The Kama Sutra (second century BCE), by Vātsyāyana (Figure 1.6), is one of the remaining texts of the 64 arts, a series of sexual literary pieces created in ancient India. Although the Kama Sutra contains information on sexual pleasure, most notably in the popular section on sexual positions, the book in its entirety is also a guide to virtuous living and love (see Chapter 3).

FIGURE 1.6 A painted scene from the Kama Sutra. This text has been popularized in our culture, with many different versions available on the shelves of mainstream bookstores. What do you think makes this book acceptable to sell in mainstream stores when "pornography" is made more discreet or available only in adult stores?

The Middle Ages

In medieval times, interest in sex and culturally appropriate social norms dictating how to conduct oneself sexually spanned many realms, including literature, medicine, and religion. Although many literary works and other texts about sex had been written and distributed in earlier times, Judeo-Christian religious authorities, beginning with St Augustine in the fourth century CE, condemned those who wrote about or participated in the pleasures of sex. The Church held that sex was intended for the purposes of procreation only, and its insistence on this principle helped it to maintain a great deal of control over the population at large. In his book *Speculum Doctrinale*, a morale guide published in the Middle Ages, Vincent of Beauvais (c. 1190–1264) upheld the view that moral citizens should engage in sex for **reproduction** rather than for pleasure. He also advised that a man should love his wife with his judgment rather than with his affections. In contrast with the religious authorities of the time, medieval physicians promoted a regular, but not excessive, amount of sexual intercourse as a part of good health, stating that abstaining from sex could lead to a dangerous buildup of **body humours** (Heckel, n.d.).

Modern History

Censorship of erotic literature became commonplace with the rise of the printing press in the mid- to late fifteenth century. Censors were particularly concerned about the influence of **libertinism**, which was a popular philosophy from the seventeenth to the nineteenth century, particularly in Britain and France. Possibly the most heavily censored—and most widely known—libertine author was the Marquis de Sade (1740–1814), who wrote a number of erotic works that pushed the boundaries of "normal" sexuality (see Chapter 15).

Yet the early modern era was also a time of great scientific breakthroughs related to sex and sexuality, and research conducted at this time began to offer a better grasp on sexuality from biological and evolutionary perspectives. In 1677, scientists discovered that seminal fluid contained millions of individual sperm. Centuries later, in 1827, the female egg was discovered, and in 1843 the mechanism of conception was first officially recognized. Charles Darwin (1809–1882) also has a place in the history of sex research. His works on sexual selection eventually led to the field of evolutionary psychology (see Chapter 2), which examines various aspects of sexual relationships, including mate preference and gender differences in jealousy.

In 1886, Richard von Krafft-Ebing (1840–1902) published his book *Psychopathia Sexualis*, which was the first text to bring sexuality into the realm of scientific study. In this text, he introduced the terms **sadism** and **masochism** to psychiatry, and he discussed sexual function and sexual crimes. Unfortunately, as is often the case, this "scientific" study was greatly coloured by the cultural norms of the time, as exemplified in Krafft-Ebing's classification of "perversions" as sexual acts that could not result in pregnancy. Krafft-Ebing also concluded that masturbation was the cause of all sexual deviation, a finding that was not so much scientific as it was reflective of the repressive sexual morals of the period. Despite Krafft-Ebing's initial beliefs about perversions, however, he later concluded that "homosexuals" did not suffer from perversion. He also suggested that gender identity disorder could be "fixed" through sex reassignment surgery.

Other eighteenth-century researchers—including Iwan Bloch (1872–1922), known as "the father of sexology" (see Chapter 3), and Henry Havelock Ellis (1859–1939)—were more consistently positive about sexuality. Ellis wrote seven volumes, collectively entitled *Studies in the Psychology of Sex*, in which he discussed his sexual research. He

reproduction The process by which new organisms (offspring) are produced from progenitor organisms (parents).

body humours The four humours of Hippocratic medicine believed to directly influence an individual's temperament and health: black bile, yellow bile, phlegm, and blood.

libertinism A philosophy, lifestyle, or pattern of behaviour characterized by self-indulgence and lack of restraint, especially one involving sexual promiscuity.

sadism The practice of deriving pleasure or sexual gratification from inflicting pain, humiliation, or suffering on other people.

masochism The practice of deriving pleasure or sexual gratification from the experience of suffering physical pain or humiliation.

concluded that sexual behaviour is determined by social and cultural context, and that if humans were left to their own desires, they would display a range of sexual behaviours, many of which should be considered "normal." He acknowledged that masturbation was widespread and recognized a continuum of sexual orientations. He also recognized women as sexual beings with their own desires and orgasms, and he stated that sexual difficulties for both men and women resulted from psychological problems.

On the topic of psychosexual problems and dysfunctions, Sigmund Freud (1856–1939) is probably the best-known and possibly the most influential figure in the modern history of sexuality. Although his dissemination of his ideas about sex—gleaned from his **psychoanalytic** therapy practice—led to sex being a more mainstream topic (particularly within the field of medicine), his theories on sexuality pathologized adults, especially females. He theorized that psychological dysfunction in adults was a consequence of problems in psychosexual development. He identified five stages of sexual development in children and believed that psychological problems arose if an individual did not successfully make it through each of the stages (Chapter 2).

The first institute for sex research and the first sexuality journal were founded by Magnus Hirschfeld (1868–1935), a German physician. Hirschfeld was in charge of the first large-scale survey about sex, which he administered to over 10,000 participants. Sadly, the Nazis destroyed much of his work, and Hirschfeld died in exile. The oldest survey research that we have access to today was conducted by Alfred Kinsey (1894–1956), founder of the Institute for Sex Research at Indiana University (now commonly referred to as the "Kinsey Institute"). Until recently, his statistics on sexuality were the most accurate that were available. Summaries of Kinsey's findings were also published in magazines such as *Time* and *Life*. Kinsey became quite famous in his lifetime, and references to him and his work appeared in various forms of popular culture, such as the song "Too Darn Hot," from the Broadway Musical *Kiss me, Kate* (1948), which contains the lyrics "According to the Kinsey Report, every average man you know much prefers to play his favourite sport when the temperature is low."

There was no great attempt to replicate Kinsey's findings or do further survey-based research on sexuality until the Hunt Report, conducted by *Playboy* in the early 1970s. Following the publication of this report, *Redbook* magazine conducted a large-scale survey of women's sexual attitudes and behaviours. Though neither survey was representative of the general population, both generated some interesting discussions about human sexuality. Shere Hite's *Hite Report of Female Sexuality* (1976) explored female sexuality and was followed in 1981 by her book on male sexuality. Much of Hite's work also contained non-representative samples (Chapter 3), so it is difficult to make generalizations based on her work. The 1992 National Health and Social Life Survey (NHSLS) was done with random sampling methodology, allowing results to be more generalizable to the public at large. The research was done through face-to-face interviews throughout the United States. Findings suggested that although Americans engage in a variety of sexual activities, they are less sexually active than suggested by earlier surveys. Despite this, respondents were, for the most part, content with their sex lives (Laumann, Gagnon, Michael, & Michaels, 1994).

Survey research is one way to discover what is going on behind closed doors, but self-report measures such as these have their drawbacks. One way to overcome the limitations of self-report measures is to study sex through observational techniques. Kinsey had observed people engaging in sexual acts as a part of his research, but it was William Masters (1915–2001) and Virginia Johnson (1925–2013) who pioneered the use of instruments that measure **physiological** responses that occur during masturbation and intercourse (see the "Research vs Real Life" box, and Chapters 3 and 4).

psychoanalytic Relating to or incorporating the methods and theories of psychiatric treatment originated by Sigmund Freud.

physiological Relating to the physical functioning of living organisms.

Research VS Real Life

Observing Sexual Response as It Happens in the Lab

As one might imagine, many areas of sexuality research can be extremely personal, delving into some of the most private details of human experience. To further compound this issue, many aspects of human sexual behaviour do not lend themselves to survey research. One such area is the physiology of sexual arousal and response. Most individuals are unaware of the inner workings of their organs during sexual activity, and even if they were aware, very few would be interested in stopping part way through to answer a survey about their experiences! This makes studying the actual physiological processes that occur during sexual activity difficult. These challenges have not, however, prevented researchers from attempting to study sex "up close and personal."

William Masters and Virginia Johnson were pioneer researchers in this field and have provided the basis of most of what we now know about sexual physiology and the **sexual response cycle**. In the early 1950s, Masters was a researcher in the Department of Obstetrics and Gynaecology at Washington University in St Louis, Missouri, and he wanted to begin a study investigating the physiological responses of individuals engaged in sexual activity. In the process of getting his study up and running, he placed an advertisement for a research assistant and came across Virginia Johnson, who would become his research partner and later his wife. Together, Masters and Johnson were the first to systematically observe, monitor, and film individuals having sex or masturbating for the purposes of examining their physiological responses. But how did they find people who were willing to participate in their research?

Originally, Masters had determined that he could use sex trade workers (STWs) as his research subjects, based on the assumption that such individuals were accustomed to performing on demand and would not feel uncomfortable engaging in sexual activity within a laboratory environment. Through the process of interviewing 188 female STWs and 27 male STWs, Masters determined that there would likely be problems in using these individuals because they tended to have transient lifestyles, which would make them difficult to follow over time, and health issues that affected their sexual responses. Masters was somewhat stumped as to how to find other

participants and began discussing his research with colleagues. Much to his surprise, he found that many were willing to participate in his research themselves! Eventually, Masters and Johnson were able to recruit almost 700 participants (312 men and 382 women) who were willing to have their physiological responses recorded while they either masturbated or engaged in partnered coitus within the laboratory setting (Masters & Johnson, 1966). It has been conservatively estimated that they collected data on more than 10,000 orgasms.

Despite the wealth of information collected, Masters and Johnson originally had difficulty disseminating their research findings. Between 1959 and 1965, many of the top medical journals refused to publish their results, and a large number of doctors and scientists with whom they shared their findings disapproved of the study and accused the research team of immorality and voyeurism. (It should be noted that this research was being conducted at a time when even talking about sex openly was frowned upon; thus, the thought of studying sex occurring in a public place such as a research lab was very off-putting to many individuals.) Even more controversial was the "coition machine" that the team invented, which consisted of a clear artificial penis that was equipped with a camera in order to provide visual images of the interior of the vagina during sexual penetration.

> **sexual response cycle**
> The four-stage model of physiological responses during sexual stimulation proposed/discovered by Masters and Johnson's research. The phases are excitement, plateau, orgasmic, and resolution.

The results of Masters and Johnson's research have been used extensively in the treatment of sexual dysfunction, infertility, and contraceptive failure. Researchers today still make frequent reference to the sexual response cycle, as detailed by Masters and Johnson (Chapter 4), and their methods served to bring the study of sexual activity into the laboratory. Contemporary sex researchers have found a number of other ways to study various aspects of sexual physiology (Chapter 3), but it can often remain difficult to receive ethical approval from university research ethics boards for research that involves physically invasive investigation into sexual activity.

How Have Societal Influences Shaped Views of Sexuality?

Historical Views on Masturbation

Modern researchers have found that masturbation is, compared to other sexual activities, a more efficient and successful method of reaching orgasm for many people, especially women. Kinsey found that 45 per cent of self-reported masturbators were able to reach orgasm in less than three minutes and that the majority of women—many of whom reported being unable to reach orgasm through partnered sexual activity, especially vaginal intercourse—could reach orgasm through masturbation within four minutes. This and other research has shown masturbation to be a common practice, with the majority of individuals (up to 97 per cent of males and 78 per cent of females) engaging in some form of sexual self-pleasuring, yet Western society has historically considered masturbation to be at best taboo and at worst dangerous, perverse, sinful, and even illegal (Maines, 1999).

Depictions of masturbation date back to prehistoric times and can be found in rock paintings around the world. Many ancient civilizations, such as the ancient Greeks and the ancient Egyptians, viewed masturbation as a normal and healthy alternative to other sexual pleasures, and at times they incorporated it into religious or spiritual practices, or depicted it in art (Figure 1.7).

The relaxed views of these civilizations later gave way to more rigid and conservative views on sexuality, which saw masturbation as a sin that carried serious medical consequences. In the 1656 criminal code of the Puritan colony of New Haven, Connecticut, masturbation was identified as a crime that was punishable by death. In the early 1700s, an extensive pamphlet entitled "Onania: The Heinous Sin of Self-Pollution" was published in both England and the United States detailing the dangers of chronic masturbation, arguing that, in excess, it could even lead to death. In 1760, Swiss physician Samuel-Auguste Tissot produced perhaps one of the most damning publications against masturbation. Entitled *L'Onanisme*, the work was a medical treatise on the negative consequences associated with masturbation, including weakness, memory loss, blurred vision, gout, and headaches. Tissot's work was very influential and, as a result, masturbation was predominantly viewed as a debilitating illness for the following two centuries, both in Europe and in the New World.

Concerns about the negative consequences of masturbation and consideration of the activity as a debilitating illness inspired some doctors to investigate potential cures for chronic masturbators. The American doctor John Harvey Kellogg (1852–1943), a zealous opponent of masturbation, went so far as to recommend burning off the clitoris on girls and sewing shut the foreskin on boys in attempts to prevent masturbation. Less severe recommendations included eating a bland diet, to which end Kellogg invented the breakfast cereal Corn Flakes in 1894. Kellogg was not alone in his views; Sylvester Graham (1974–1851), an American minister, had previously invented Graham crackers for the same purpose.

FIGURE 1.7 This depiction of a mythological satyr masturbating, which appears on a Greek vase dating from the sixth century BCE, is representative of the ancient Greek's relatively open view of masturbation.

It was not until the turn of the twentieth century that some physicians began to challenge the idea that masturbation could cause such dire medical consequences. Havelock Ellis attempted to challenge Tissot's claims on a case-by-case basis. His approach entailed finding individuals who were chronic masturbators but did not suffer from any of the ailments presented in Tissot's treatise. Roughly half a century later, Alfred Kinsey's survey results suggested that masturbation was in fact a normative and healthy behaviour. Medical and social views changed more slowly. In the 1980s, philosopher Michel Foucault argued that it was an inappropriate exercise of power for parents to deny their children the knowledge of self-pleasure. Today, the topic continues to carry with it a heavy sense of taboo, especially when the question of educating children and teens about masturbation arises. In 1994, for example, the surgeon general of the United States, Dr Joycelyn Elders, was forced to resign after suggesting that educators should inform high school students that masturbation is a healthy and safe activity, and a good way to prevent pregnancy and STI transmission (Jelq, 2009). More recently, in 2010, the attempt to introduce information about masturbation into the Ontario sexual education curriculum generated a great deal of controversy among parents and members of the Catholic School Board in the province, as well as among the general public (see Chapter 19).

History of the Vibrator

The invention of the vibrator may not come from the source that you would expect. It was not the sex industry but rather the medical profession that spearheaded the invention of the vibrator, although with somewhat different motives than those held by today's sex-toy manufacturers. The medical profession's interest in generating female orgasms dates back to the writings of Hippocrates (c. 460–c. 377 BCE), which included discussion of how to properly treat a woman suffering from hysteria, a medical condition that was seen as resulting from the intrinsic pathology of the feminine state. Literally, *hysteria* comes from the Greek word for "that which proceeds from the uterus" and was considered a "disease of the womb" treatable with exercise and massage (i.e., genital massage leading to orgasm, called "paroxysm" in earlier times). In today's terms, such a "condition" might amount to sexual frustration or dissatisfaction, but instead of turning toward self-pleasuring or a partner for relief, women were frequently treated by their physicians. It was quite commonplace for physicians to provide treatment through the massage of the genitals until the woman reached orgasm. Treatment of this nature continued well into the twentieth century, at which point doctors became interested in increasing the efficiency of their "treatment."

In an effort to increase the number of patients that could be treated in a day as well as the speed at which each individual could be treated, the medical profession invented the first electric vibrators, the history of which was recently popularized by the Hollywood film *Hysteria* (2011). Originally, vibrators were used only within doctor's offices, but they quickly became commercialized for home use. In the early decades of the twentieth century, it was not uncommon to see advertisements for vibrators in such widely available publications as needlework magazines or the Sears catalogue, some even with suggestive headlines such as "Aids that every woman appreciates" (Figure 1.8). The devices were advertised as essential relaxation tools, and they were said to aid in maintaining youth and happiness. Beginning in the 1930s, however, it became clearer what these devices were truly being used for, and they were seen as a rival to the "natural sexual acts between a man and his wife." Thus vibrators became taboo and they were no longer publicly advertised. It was not until the 1960s that vibrators returned to catalogues and advertisements, this time promoted by the adult novelty industry.

Even today, however, the vibrator remains somewhat of a taboo subject, despite the fact that more than half of American women between the ages of 18 and 60 report having used a vibrator at some point (Herbenick et al., 2009). In the 1980s and 1990s, many American states began passing legislation that prohibited the distribution and acquisition of sexual devices. Many of these laws have since been challenged and repealed, but in three states—Alabama, Mississippi, and Virginia—the marketing and sale of sexual devices are still prohibited by criminal law. The law against vibrators in the state of Texas was removed only in 2008.

History of Sex Education in Canada

The teaching of sex education in Canadian schools, discussed in more detail in Chapter 19, has encountered varying levels of acceptance and controversy based on the shifting social climates throughout Canadian history. In the 1940s, there was a strong push for sex education to become part of the public school curriculum as a result of rising concerns related to the spread of "venereal diseases" (i.e., STIs) throughout the Canadian military's enlisted men, which was seen as a threat to victory in World War II. Because mothers at the time were participating in the workforce as part of the war movement, it was believed that young girls were not receiving the moral instruction and practical information necessary to prevent the spread of STIs. As a result, a curriculum was in place by 1944 that included both moral and biological content aimed at preventing premarital sexual behaviour and educating youth about reproductive biology. This curriculum proved to be somewhat ahead of its time, however, as the focus on biological information did not sit well with most people in the conservative postwar era. Opponents of the curriculum argued that providing youth with information on how to avoid the negative consequences of sexual behaviour would lead to an increase in the number and frequency of young people engaging in premarital sex. As a result, by 1949 the curriculum had been stripped of all physiological information and the remaining content focussed on transmitting Anglo-Saxon heterosexual values related to marriage and childrearing.

In the late 1960s, the topic of sexual education once again became controversial after an Ontario legislative committee recommended that a new curriculum be introduced that consisted of "family living; planned parenthood; morals and sex in our culture; the sex act and the reproductive process; contraception; venereal diseases; the psychological and emotional implications of sex" (CBC News Archives, 2012). Although the curriculum was approved, it was not until 1994 that the Public Health Agency of Canada produced the first edition of *The Canadian Guidelines for Sexual Health Education*.

Sex education continues to be a controversial subject across the country, particularly when governments introduce new curricula that include enhanced coverage of sex and sexuality. Such was the case in Ontario, in 2010, when the provincial government

FIGURE 1.8 Vibrator advertisements—such as this one from the 1930s—appeared in commonplace publications throughout the early decades of the twentieth century. The commercialization of the hand-held home vibrator followed from the immense popularity of this device in physicians' offices.

attempted to implement curriculum changes that require sex education to be taught in all schools, including religious schools, and that remove parents' ability to excuse their children from certain aspects of the curriculum. One of the most controversial issues has been the inclusion of information about sexual orientation and gender identity, especially within the context of introducing these subjects to elementary school students. Opponents of the curriculum argue that these topics should not be "forced" on children, and that they may lead to "confusion." Organized opponents even placed paid advertisements, in newspapers and at bus stops, that displayed pictures of sad-looking children with captions such as "Please! Don't confuse me. I'm a girl. Don't teach me to question if I'm a boy, transsexual, transgendered, intersexed, or two-spirited." The ads were misleading and did not accurately represent the nature of the information being provided to students, but they were effective in creating a great deal of concern among Ontario parents. Despite the opposition, the legislation mandating that the curriculum be taught in all schools has remained.

Research suggests that exposure to sex education can have a positive impact on teens. A recent study found that the higher quality of sex education that has emerged over the last couple of decades in Canada has contributed to a 36.9 per cent decline in the country's teen birth and abortion rate (McKay & Barrett, 2010). Indeed, a 2006 report found that compared to other industrialized countries, Canada had the lowest teen birth and abortion rate among girls aged 15 to 19 (McKay & Barrett, 2010). Conversely, other studies have shown that abstinence-only programs, which are common in the United States, are associated with higher percentages of teens becoming pregnant (Kohler, Manhart, & Lafferty, 2008).

The Internet has also become a source of sex education in Canada. A creative group of Canadian gynecologists—the Society of Obstetricians and Gynaecologists of Canada—introduced a Facebook game called "Sex Quest," which allows young people to participate in a trivia game concerning sexual health topics. As players progress through the questions, they can obtain different levels of mastery, similar to those found in other online games. Other games and apps are also available on the Society's website, SexualityandU.ca, including an interactive quiz that allows users to test their "sexual IQ."

Religious and Cultural Views of Sexuality

ethnocentrism The tendency to believe that one's ethnic or cultural group is the norm, and to view other ethnicities or cultures as abnormal or different.

Ethnocentrism affects our understanding of human sexuality, leading to the belief that it is our version of sex that is "normal"; as a result of such thinking, we often forget or refuse to acknowledge the spectrum of normality that exists around the world. One thing that we all have in common is that societies around the world regulate sexuality in some way (DeLamater, 1987). Universal regulations include incest taboos and, with a few exceptions, prohibitions against rape. However, many cultural perceptions of what constitutes acceptable sexual activities are not universal. For example, in the Mehinaku culture, kissing on the lips does not occur (Gregor, 1985).

RELIGION AND FEMALE SEXUALITY

Traditional narratives about the origin of humankind are telling of how a particular culture views women and gender (Witcombe, 2000). In Western culture, the origin of humankind is rooted in the narrative of Adam and Eve, which is present in Judaism, Christianity, and Islam. However, the notion of placing the blame for original sin on a woman goes back much further than the story of Eve, to the ancient Greek myth of Pandora. Like Eve, Pandora is the mother of all women, and it is because of her that women must be punished. She gave in to temptation by opening a vessel that held all the world's evils, a vessel that has been compared to a woman's womb (Reeder, 1995). Before Pandora, there was no sickness, evil, or death. Eve has a similar story of giving in to temptation by picking an apple from the forbidden tree of knowledge. But without the apple, the world would not have knowledge; so, although women are blamed for original sin, they also represent a frightening amount of power to men, and some scholars believe that this is why they have been subjugated throughout history (Tyree, 1998). The story of Eve also reveals two persistent stereotypes: that women give in too easily to temptation, and that they are sources of temptation for males.

In societies influenced by the Christian tradition, a dichotomy arose between "Eve" and "Mary," the biblical mother of Jesus; as a result, women came to be perceived as either "Madonnas" (like Mary) or "whores" (as was the perception of Eve). This gender dualism has worked to maintain a heterosexual norm in which women are "naturally" made to be vessels for male consumption (Galloway, 1997). In this dualistic view, Mary represents the pure woman, a role earlier filled by the goddess Isis in ancient Egyptian culture. These figures represent feminine purity and obedience, the ideal for womanhood in a male-dominated society. Eve, on the other hand, represents the corrupt woman, the opposite of the ideal (Figure 1.9). In many societies, prostitution was permitted because it saved the virtuous women from becoming the objects of uncontrollable male lust. Note that mistresses in many cultures and throughout history have been seen as less than the ideal woman and, as such, were often allowed to possess intellect, wit, and other "male" qualities that have not traditionally been permitted to "pure" woman. Yet, while they are allowed some sense of agency, their ultimate purpose is still to be consumed and controlled by males.

" Eve is a nice addition, except you inadvertently created a lot of sexual tension. "

FIGURE 1.9 Eve's sexuality has been regarded as dangerous because it was she who tempted Adam to bite into the apple, which resulted in the banishment from the Garden of Eden and punishment for humankind.

Sexuality and the Monotheistic Religions

Sexuality, or the control of sexuality, is a major theme in all of the major **monotheistic religions**, although each has a slightly different view of the matter. Even among followers of one of these religious traditions, views often differ, based on varying interpretations of religious texts. The following sections provide a general overview of the sexual norms and taboos of these religions, touching on such topics as marriage, sexual orientation, abortion, and masturbation.

monotheistic religions Religions that believe in only one deity, as opposed to those that believe in multiple deities.

Judaism

Sexual relations are viewed as basically good in the Torah, the religious writings of Judaism, because they are a part of God's creation; the Hebrew word *yada* means both "entering another sexually" and "knowing God" (Galloway, 1997). However, as is true of all three major monotheistic religions, sexuality is often dealt with in a contradictory manner. While on the one hand sex is good, on the other, sex is viewed as a source of impurity. In traditional practice, **nocturnal emissions**, menstruation, and childbearing require a ritual cleansing. The period of abstinence brought about during menstruation is said to increase sexual desire in the couple (Bishop, 1996).

nocturnal emission An involuntary ejaculation of semen during sleep (commonly known as "wet dream").

adultery Sexual intercourse between a married individual and someone who is not his or her spouse.

polygamy The practice or custom of having more than one wife or husband at the same time.

monogamy The practice or state of being married to or in an intimate relationship with one person at a time.

menopause The stage of life at which a woman ceases to menstruate, usually between the ages of 45 and 55.

According to various books of the Torah, taboos punishable by death in early Judaism included incest, bestiality, male–male sexual behaviour, and **adultery**; however, the definition of adultery was not always applied equally to men and women. If a married man had sexual relations with an unmarried woman, this was not considered to be adultery. Sex between spouses was expected and encouraged, and having children was viewed as a way of propagating the religion. In early Judaism, **polygamy** was permitted, though by the end of the first century BCE most Jewish couples were **monogamous**. Sex between unmarried people or between a married man and an unmarried woman was permitted, but having a child out of wedlock resulted in slander and ostracism (Wiesner-Hanks, 2000). Additionally, if a man accused his wife of not being a virgin at the time of their marriage and the accusation was "proved" true, the woman was to be stoned to death.

In the modern practice of Judaism, the primary purpose of sex is to reinforce the marital bond. Sex is permitted even without the possibility of conception, such as when a woman is pregnant or after she has entered **menopause**. Certain forms of contraception that do not block the passage of sperm are also permitted, as long as the couple plans to have, or already has, children. For example, the birth control pill is permitted, but a condom is not. Sex is taught to be an act of pleasure that should never be used to manipulate, and that should never involve force. In addition, sex is the woman's right, not the man's, and it is his duty to provide her pleasure. Foreplay is encouraged. If the husband consistently abstains from having sex with his wife, she even has grounds for divorce. In favour of the husband, the wife also is not allowed to withhold sex for reasons of punishing her husband. Divorce is permitted for many reasons in Judaism, with the idea that it is better for two people to separate than to live in discord. Abortion is permitted when the fetus is endangering the life of the mother. Male–male sexual acts are forbidden, but there is no comment on sexual orientation or sexual acts between females. The Torah implicitly prohibits male masturbation, but it does not comment on female masturbation; nevertheless, female masturbation is generally frowned upon (Rich, 1999).

Christianity

Early Christianity espoused a wide variety of beliefs about sexuality, as there was no central authority over the church in the first century CE. Some authorities permitted marriage, but others felt that virginity was ideal and represented the ultimate devotion to God. There was no great push for Christians to have sex in order to "be fruitful and multiply," as many followers interpreted the purpose of this biblical instruction as creating enough people of faith so that the Messiah would arrive, and for them the Messiah had arisen. And, although they were still constrained by societal norms and generally seen to be inferior to men, women had much more freedom in the early days of the church than they were to have in the subsequent centuries.

Many of the church's later, more repressive views on sexuality were based on the teachings of the Church Fathers, a small group of early theologians whose writings came to be viewed as highly authoritative within the Christian tradition. These men, and the church leaders who followed them, used theology to justify condemnation of all forms of sexuality, turning to asceticism and celibacy as the ultimate attainment of closeness to God. Despite their professed views, however, many of the Church Fathers and other leaders within the church were men with active sexual lives who had difficulty controlling their sexual desires (Bishop, 1996); indeed, it was not until the eleventh century that men in the clergy were required to remain unmarried and celibate. One of the most prominent Church Fathers, St Augustine (354–430), believed that sexual desire overcame reason and will, resulting in disobedience of God. He also believed that the original sin of Adam and Eve was transmitted to every human through ejaculation, because children are born of sexual activity. This and similar views led to the Catholic Church's view of sex as shameful and unclean. Augustine also suggested that the **missionary position** was the only appropriate way to engage in intercourse while acknowledging women's position as inferior to men.

Feminist scholars argue that while the text of the Bible itself is not inherently anti-feminist, the way in which the Church has interpreted this text through centuries of male domination makes the work seem strongly opposed to women's equality. They believe that women and men were created equal, as partners (Galloway, 1997), but that Christians use Eve to justify the subordinate position of women in the post–Garden-of-Eden world (Parsons, 1996). It is evident that women were prominent missionaries, leaders, and even apostles in early Christianity (Kung, 2005). A few women retained some sense of power and fame in the Church even later through monasteries and nunneries. For example, Hildegard of Bingen (1098–1179), a Benedictine nun, wrote about medicine and natural sciences; her writings even include her thoughts on miscarriage being more common among very young and older women (French, 2002). Women who chose to remain virgins represented an equal sexual threat to those who chose to be sexually active because they were also claiming control over their own bodies, rather than submitting to men. The act of sex for women was controlled through marriage or relegated to STWs, and even those females who chose virginity were referred to as "brides of Christ," suggesting that they too were subjugated within the constraints of a (symbolic) marriage (Tyree, 1998).

Early Christianity developed in a society that practised contraception, abortion, and **infanticide**. Although many early figures in the church believed that a fetus does not have a soul until it begins to kick and move in the womb, the present belief among most Christians is that ensoulment occurs at the time of fertilization. Thus, the official stance of most Christian denominations is a strong opposition to abortion, but many offer exceptions if a woman's health is at risk. This official stance is not necessarily shared by all of the followers of these religions; indeed, two-thirds of women who have had abortions in the United States identify as Christian (Guttmacher Institute, 2011).

Today, the Catholic Church prohibits not only abortion, but also artificial forms of contraception and sexual acts that do not have the potential for procreation. Such acts include those between members of the same sex and masturbation, which is viewed as sinful because it wastes seed (in men) and indulges in lust (in both sexes). The sole purpose of sex in Catholicism was, and for many remains, to procreate. However, it was not until the fourth century that sexual activity that did not involve penile-vaginal penetration was forbidden and criminally punished. Presently, the Catholic Church accepts the use of natural methods of birth control (see Chapter 7), but it is still opposed to hormonal and barrier methods. At the same time, several contemporary groups such as Catholics for a Free Choice argue that many Catholics believe a person can still be a "good Catholic" without following the Church's beliefs about contraception (Catholics for a Free Choice, 1998). Many other Christian denominations are more accepting of a wider variety of contraceptive methods, but this leniency exists to varying degrees and even differs within a particular church. While sexual relations outside of marriage are generally frowned upon across the various Christian denominations, views on masturbation and same-sex relationships vary by group, with some (e.g., the United Church) being more liberal than others.

missionary position A position for sexual intercourse in which the heterosexual couple lies face to face with the woman underneath the man.

infanticide The act of killing a child within a year of its birth.

Islam

The Prophet Muhammad was born in 570, at a time when nomadic tribes of the Middle East were fading as people started settling in fixed communities, a trend that lessened women's power status in these societies. This change promoted the rise of patriarchy and the fall of any matrilineal traditions that had been present in tribal life, where men and women were treated mostly as equals for many years. Judaism and Christianity were known in the Arab world at the time, and Muhammad respected them above any of the existing polytheistic religions. According to tradition, the religion of Islam was born when the angel Gabriel visited Muhammad. His first wife, Khadija, encouraged him to trust this vision (French, 2002). Muhammad's second and most influential wife, Aisha, became important following the Prophet's death and challenged the misogynistic views that began to prevail in Islam, stating in protest to separating prayer spaces by gender that "The Prophet would pray while I lay before him on the bed!" (French, 2002, p. 256).

Treatment of women in Islam has varied greatly throughout the religion's history, depending upon Qur'anic interpretation and political motivations. Under the Prophet's rule, Islam was still subject to the gender roles of the time, but there was far more equal treatment and less division of gender roles between the sexes than would follow after his death. For example, in early Islam women fought in all battles, and they were welcome in the mosques with men until the tenth century (French, 2002). Also, Islam initially held Adam and Eve equally responsible for sin; however, as time passed, the familiar interpretation of Eve as the source of sin emerged.

Unlike the Christian leaders of the time, the Prophet did not promote celibacy, provided that sex occurred within a marriage. He promoted sexual pleasures between husband and wife or wives, except during the time of menstruation, a period of forty days after a woman had given birth, pilgrimage, and the daylight hours of Ramadan, the ritual month of fasting in Islam (Bishop, 1996). Foreplay is noted to be important, and the sage Al-Ghazali wrote that a husband should not concentrate only on his own satisfaction, but rather focus on providing pleasure and orgasm to his wife or wives (Ali, 2006).

Because sex within marriage for the sake of enjoyment was promoted, birth control was acceptable, but only with permission of the wife, in order that her sexual pleasure would not be reduced. The most common form of birth control at the time of the Prophet was **withdrawal** (see Chapter 7). Female-controlled forms of contraception were also permitted; because of this, Arab knowledge of contraception was far ahead of that of most Europeans until the nineteenth century. Presently, many Islamic leaders tout the use of contraceptive measures as a way of controlling the size of one's family for economic and other practical purposes, but acceptance of birth control is not universal in the Islamic world (Shaikh, 2003).

The Qur'an states, "Marry such of the women as seems good to you; two, or three, or four . . . if you fear that you may not be fair [to several wives], then take only one" (quoted in Bishop, 1996, p. 76). This statement can be interpreted as permitting polygamy, but some say that it is actually promoting monogamy, since no man but the Prophet could be fair to more than one wife. Today, most Muslims have only one wife, although Shia Muslims are permitted *Nikah Mut'ah*, which is a temporary "marriage" that can last anywhere from a few minutes to many years and is often used as a loophole that permits individuals to engage in casual sex. Divorce is allowed, though not encouraged or common (French, 2002). If the man initiates a divorce, there is a waiting period of three months before the divorce is official, likely to prevent potential confusion over paternity. A woman does not have to wait three months to divorce her

withdrawal A method of controlling fertility in which the man withdraws his penis from the woman's vagina before ejaculating, with the plan of preventing sperm from entering the cervix.

husband, but she must take her request to court, and her request might be denied, depending upon circumstances. Rape of one's wife is forbidden, but with the caveat that a woman who rejects her husband is cursed (French, 2002).

According to Islam, a fetus is ensouled at 120 days (Shaikh, 2003), but abortion is accepted after this time if the mother's life is in danger or the fetus is deformed in some way. Masturbation is generally forbidden, but in some interpretations of Islam it is allowed in "extenuating" circumstances, such as when an individual fears that she or he will commit an even graver sin (e.g., engage in extramarital sex).

Same-sex acts are treated similarly in Islam as they are in the other major mono-theistic religions, and the basis for not accepting same-sex sexuality is in the story of Lot, which appears in the sacred texts of all three religions. According to the version that appears in the Qur'an, Lot, who is a prophet in Islam, is sent to preach about monotheism in the cities of Sodom and Gomorrah. It has commonly been interpreted that he was sent to preach against the same-sex male relations that were occurring. Male–male sexual behaviour is a crime in most Muslim countries, and it may even be punishable by death. Yet the condemnation of same-sex sexual behaviour in Islam has not always been as damning or clear-cut as many believe. It has largely been tolerated throughout Islam's history, and one Islamic scholar has written that the Qur'an con-demns only those same-sex acts that are violent or exploitative (Kugle, 2010). Despite this historical tolerance, there are still many Muslims who do condemn same-sex acts. In contrast, there are a number of groups that have formed in support of LGBTTIQQ Muslims, one of which is the Salaam Queer Muslim Community, a Canadian advocacy and support group.

Sexual Diversity in Canada

POLYAMORY

Polyamory can be found in a variety of cultures worldwide and can take many differ-ent forms (see Chapter 14). Some polyamorous partners live together, while others live separately. If the individuals involved in a polyamorous relationship are married, the practice is known as polygamy; globally, **polygyny** is more common than **polyandry**.

The legality of polyamory and polygamy varies around the world. While most coun-tries do not specifically outlaw *polyamory*, many Western nations, including Canada, do criminalize *polygamy*. Anti-polygamy laws were added to the Criminal Code of Canada in the 1880s, when an influx of Mormons, members of the Church of Jesus Christ of Latter-Day Saints (LDS), brought the issue to the attention of authorities. Section 293 of the Criminal Code allows for up to five years in prison for individuals found guilty of polygamy. Until the 1950s, the law specifically referenced Mormons. Today, only members of the Fundamentalist Church of Jesus Christ of Latter-Day Saints (FLDS) practise polygamy (CBC News, 2011).

Section 293 of the Criminal Code has recently been at the centre of several high-profile debates in British Columbia. In 2009, British Columbia's provincial govern-ment attempted to charge two prominent members of the FLDS in Bountiful, British Columbia, with polygamy (Figure 1.10). The charges were dropped before the case went to trial, but, as a result of these events, the province launched a constitutional exam-ination of Section 293 to determine whether the law was in violation of the **Charter of Rights and Freedoms**, with respect to the protection of religious freedom. In the end, the law against polygamy was not found to be unconstitutional, but the case brought the issue to the forefront, leading to the question of whether Canada's anti-polygamy law could be applied to polyamorists. The federal government claimed that

polyamory The practice of having multiple sexual and/or conjugal partners; being romantically and sexually involved with more than one person at the same time.

polygyny Polygamy in which a man has more than one wife.

polyandry Polygamy in which a woman has more than one husband.

Charter of Rights and Freedoms The Canadian bill of rights entrenched in the Constitution of Canada, which sets out the rights of all Canadians.

FIGURE 1.10 Winston Blackmore, shown here with several of his daughters and grandchildren, was one of the prominent leaders of the FLDS community in Bountiful, British Columbia, charged with polygamy in 2009.

polyamorists would be breaking the law only if they had formal marriage ceremonies, but many people have observed that the actual text of the law *could* be interpreted to include polyamorists and even those who engage in adultery. A number of political review committees have unsuccessfully recommended the removal of the section from the Criminal Code (CBC News, 2011).

Although no case of polygamy has been successfully prosecuted in over sixty years in Canada, the law has been used to deny family-sponsored visas to immigrants attempting to sponsor multiple spouses from a country where polygamist marriage is legal. Unlike some other countries, such as the United Kingdom and Australia, Canada does not recognize polygamist marriages performed abroad as legal.

FEMALE TOPLESSNESS

When a woman goes topless, is it a sexual act? This was the question that faced an Ontario Court of Appeals in 1996, when Gwen Jacobs challenged her conviction for committing an indecent act after having taken off her shirt on a hot summer day in Guelph, Ontario, in 1991. In many European nations, it is quite common for women to go topless, especially on beaches, but in North America, it is still seen as taboo. In the United States, it is illegal for a woman to go topless, and it is considered an indecent act. In Canada, it was illegal across much of the country until 1996, when Jacobs won her appeal. Since then, there have been successful challenges to the law in other provinces as well, and it is thus assumed that women have the right to go topless across the country (Yelaja, 2011).

The argument in favour of women going topless points out that a woman's chest is made up of the same anatomical parts as a man's chest, but that the additional mammary glands and fatty tissue change the appearance of breasts on women, as compared to men. The original judge in the Jacobs case, who ruled against Jacobs, argued that female breasts were sexualized by men and therefore, unlike male breasts, considered a private body part. The Court of Appeals overruled this decision, recognizing the inherent sexism and double standard that it embodied. Despite the successful challenge to the law, you are not likely to see a great number of women walking the streets of Canada without their tops, as the act itself is still quite taboo and garners a significant amount of, likely unwanted, attention. A 1998 Compas survey of Canadian adults found that men were more likely than women to view female topless sunbathing as appropriate; in addition, individuals living in Quebec and British Columbia were most likely to have favourable views of women going topless at the beach, while those living in Saskatchewan were least supportive of the practice (Fischtein, Herold, & Desmarais, 2005).

SAME-SEX MARRIAGE

Canada became the fourth country to legalize same-sex marriage at the federal level in 2005; however, Canadian same-sex couples have had access to the benefits and obligations of marriage since 1999. In 1999, the outcome of a Supreme Court case between two lesbian women resulted in changes to the definition of *spouse* to include mixed- *and* same-sex common-law partners. The court ruled that it was against **Section 15 of the Canadian Charter of Rights and Freedoms** to deny same-sex couples the protections afforded to heterosexuals in **common-law relationships**; these protections include division of assets, alimony, access to pensions, shared income taxes, and inheritance statutes. This ruling was the catalyst for the public debate on same-sex marriage in Canada, and it led to a number of provincial challenges seeking to legalize same-sex marriage.

In 2003, Liberal Prime Minister Jean Chrétien announced legislation that would make same-sex marriage legal and requested that the Supreme Court review whether the federal government had the right to define marriage. In December 2004, the Supreme Court of Canada ruled that the federal government was within its rights to redefine marriage to include same-sex couples, but it was not until 2005 that the government debated and passed Bill C-38, which gave same-sex couples the legal right to marry on a federal level. This officially made Canada the fourth country in the world to legalize same-sex marriage after the Netherlands, Belgium, and Spain. At the time, Conservative leader Stephen Harper vowed that if his party were to form the next government they would repeal the law. Harper followed through with this vow by tabling a motion on 7 December 2006 to re-open the debate on same-sex marriage. The motion was defeated in the House of Commons by a vote of 175 to 123, with a number of Conservative members of Parliament breaking party lines to vote against the motion. In 2012, the federal government began working on legislation that would allow foreign same-sex couples that got married in Canada to legally divorce, as the previous legislation required that couples reside in Canada for at least one year prior to being able to file for divorce in Canada. In early 2013, Bill C-32 passed, allowing non-residents married in Canada to file for divorce. This legislation was primarily required due to same-sex marriage not being recognized by other nations, therefore not allowing couples that came to Canada to get married any means for getting divorced.

Statistics Canada has included questions that are inclusive of same-sex couples since 2001, and according to the data available from the 2006 census, the number of same-sex couples in Canada (common-law or married) was 45,300 in 2006. Of these, 16.5 per cent were legally married and 83.5 per cent were in common-law relationships. Of those who were legally married, 53.7 per cent were male and 46.3 per cent were female (Statistics Canada, 2011).

The path to legalized same-sex marriage has been much longer in the United States than it was in Canada. As of September 2013, 14 (out of 50) states have legalized same-sex marriage, with the majority of states still prohibiting same-sex marriages. Until recently, federal benefits were not available to any same-sex couples, and the majority of states that prohibit same-sex marriage also fail to recognize same-sex marriages from other jurisdictions. Additionally, not all states that have legalized same-sex marriage will perform marriages for out-of-state residents, causing many same-sex couples from the US to get married in Canada. Given the close proximity of Canada to the US, many might wonder why there are such differences between the two countries when it comes to the legalization of same-sex marriage. The difference is not that shocking, however, when one examines the historical progression of LGBTQ rights in each country (Table 1.1). For example, Canada decriminalized same-sex sexual acts in 1969, but it was not until 2003 that such acts became legal in the US. As a point of contrast, while Canada was legalizing same-sex sexuality, the US was legalizing interracial marriage, something that was never officially criminalized in Canada at any point. The Canadian government removed the ban on allowing gay men and lesbians to serve openly in the Canadian Armed Forces in 1992; in the US, the "Don't Ask Don't Tell" policy, which

Section 15 of the Canadian Charter of Rights and Freedoms The section of the Charter that deals with equality rights, such as the right to equal treatment before and under the law as well as equal protection and benefit of the law.

common-law relationship A legally recognized relationship in which two people involved in a romantic relationship and who are not married have lived together for at least 12 months.

TABLE 1.1 Landmark developments in lesbian and gay rights in Canada and the United States.

	Canada	United States
1967	Everett Klippert, a NWT man who had admitted to police in 1965 that he was gay and would not change, is sent to prison indefinitely as a dangerous sexual offender, leading to a public debate over whether or not gay men should be incarcerated for their private, consensual sexual activities	
1969	"Homosexuality" is decriminalized through an amendment to the Criminal Code	Occurrence of the "Stonewall Riots," which are considered to be the start of the modern gay rights movement. LGBTTIQQ individuals rioted after the police raided a gay bar in Greenwich Village, New York City.
1970		First Pride march in New York City takes place
1971	Everett Klippert is released and is officially the last individual to have been incarcerated for "homosexuality" in Canada	
1976		In New Jersey, transgender people are able to marry based on their gender identity, regardless of assigned gender (*MT v. JT*). (This decision was rejected in a Texas court in 1999.)
1988	BC MP Svend Robinson announces he is gay, making him the first "out" member of parliament	
1992	Gay men and lesbians are allowed to serve openly in the Canadian Armed Forces	
1993		Minnesota becomes the first state to ban employment discrimination based on perceived gender identity.
1995	Sexual orientation is added to Section 15 of the Charter of Rights and Freedoms (*Egan v. Canada*)[a]	
1996		The federal Defense of Marriage Act (DOMA) is enacted; it defines marriage as a legal union between one man and one woman, preventing the federal government from recognizing the validity of same-sex marriages
1999	The definition of *spouse* is changed by the Supreme Court of Canada, recognizing conjugal common-law relationships between same-sex partners (*M. v. H.*)	
2000	Bill C-23 is passed in the House of Commons, extending all marriage rights to same-sex common-law couples (but retaining the definition of *marriage* as a union between one man and one woman)	
2003	Prime Minister Jean Chrétien announces that the federal government will not stand in opposition to efforts to legalize same-sex marriage across the country. Ontario and British Columbia become the first provinces to recognize same-sex marriage.	Same-sex sexual activity becomes legal following the Supreme Court's striking down of the sodomy law in *Lawrence v. Texas*

TABLE 1.1 Continued

	Canada	United States
2004		Massachusetts becomes the first state to grant marriage licences to same-sex couples; several other states have since followed this lead.
2005	Bill C-38 gains royal assent on 20 July, legalizing same-sex marriage across the country	
2006	A motion that would have reopened the same-sex marriage debate in the House of Commons fails on 7 December	
2008	Sex reassignment surgery (SRS) is re-listed as an OHIP-covered surgery in Ontario, after having been unlisted in 1998.	
2009		In response to the murders of Matthew Shepard and James Byrd Jr, the Matthew Shepard and James Byrd Jr Hate Crimes Prevention Act is passed. This act adds gender, sexual orientation, and gender identity to the hate crimes legislation and is the first federal law to protect transgender people.
2011		The controversial "Don't Ask Don't Tell" policy is repealed, thus allowing gay men and lesbians to serve openly in the US military
2012	Ontario becomes the first province in Canada to allow transgender people to change the gender on their birth certificate without having sex reassignment surgery.	Barack Obama becomes the first sitting US president to publicly declare support for the legalization of same-sex marriage; in July, President Obama's administration asks the Supreme Court to review DOMA
2013	The Honourable Glen Murray, member of provincial parliament in Ontario, calls on the Canadian federal government to respond to the anti-gay legislation passed in Russia and to ensure the safety of Canada's LGBTQ athletes at the 2014 Olympic Winter Games in Sochi, Russia. In 2013, Russia passed its "anti-propaganda" law that criminalized providing positive information about sexual diversity and same-sex relationships to minors (or in public). Simple acts such as displaying a rainbow flag are deemed criminal under the new law, as are public displays of affection by same-sex couples.	On 26 June 2013, the Supreme Court of the United States of America ruled that the Defense of Marriage Act was unconstitutional in the case of *United States v. Windsor*. The ruling led the federal government to move forward in recognizing same-sex marriages across the US and within the US military. Under President Obama, the federal government announced that all same-sex marriages would be recognized as legal for the purposes of federal income taxes processed by the IRS and that married same-sex couples in the military would receive veterans benefits and be treated equally with mixed-sex married couples.

[a] At the same time in the US, it is still legal, in 29 states, to discriminate against individuals in the workplace based on sexual orientation.

saw thousands of gay men and lesbians discharged from the military, was not removed until 2011. The situation in the United States has been constantly improving, especially during President Obama's administration. In 2012, Obama became the first sitting US president to announce support for same-sex marriage; however, on the same day that Obama made his announcement, North Carolina residents voted to ban same-sex marriage and all forms of same-sex civil unions and domestic partnerships, essentially denying same-sex couples the rights and protections—including those against domestic violence—that are granted to mixed-sex couples. In June 2013, the Supreme Court of the United States (SCOTUS) ruled in favour of Edie Windsor in *United States v. Windsor*, declaring that the Defense of Marriage Act (DOMA), which prevented the federal government from recognizing same-sex marriages, was unconstitutional. In 2007, Edie Windsor and her partner Thea Spyer were married in Canada by the first openly gay Canadian Judge, Harvey Brownstone. Two years later, in 2009, Thea died from multiple sclerosis and left her estate to her wife, Edie. As a result of DOMA and the federal government's inability to recognize same-sex marriages, Edie was taxed $363,053 on the inheritance of her wife's estate, a tax that would not have been levied against the surviving spouse of a mixed-sex couple. As a result of the SCOTUS ruling, the federal government was ordered to pay back the tax bill with interest. Consequently, the federal government now recognizes same-sex marriages, regardless of the jurisdiction in which the marriage took place (i.e., Canada, a US state, or internationally). This recognition brings with it a number of rights, obligations, and privileges, including survivor benefits and the ability to file joint federal tax returns. The US military also announced that it would grant all service members 10 days leave if they wished to travel to a state in which same-sex marriage is legal for the purposes of getting married and consequently becoming eligible to receive military couples' benefits.

Are same-sex couples significantly different from mixed-sex couples? The majority of the research comparing both types of couples fails to find very many differences. Both are likely to have disputes about finances and who does the dishes, and individuals in each type of relationship are equally devastated by the disintegration of a relationship or the loss of a partner. Some research has found that the division of labour is more equal and less gendered in same-sex relationships, and other studies have pointed to higher levels of sexual satisfaction and desire in same-sex relationships, but research in this area has produced conflicting results. What has been shown, however, is that the approval one receives of one's relationship from friends and family is equally important to both same-sex and mixed-sex couples (Blair & Holmberg, 2008). Not only is social approval of one's relationship associated with increased relationship satisfaction, it is also associated with positive mental and physical health for the individuals within the relationship. As such, this may be an indication that institutionalized forms of social support for relationships (e.g., legalized marriage) can play an important role in the health and wellness of same-sex couples.

SEX TRADE WORK

Although the actual act of exchanging money for sex has never been illegal in Canada, the government has put in place a number of laws that prohibit related behaviours, thereby making sex trade work (STW), commonly referred to as prostitution (Chapter 18), difficult to practise legally within the country. Practising in private, however, and communicating using private media such as the telephone or the Internet, is legal, and thus the law does allow for the legal practice of STW under very specific circumstances.

In recent years, controversial debates have taken place between those who would like to see STW of all forms eliminated and those who would like to see it decriminalized. Opponents of legalized STW argue that it is an exploitative and immoral practice, while proponents argue that decriminalizing STW would allow it to be practised more openly and also subject to regulations and protections (for both service providers and customers). Those in favour of legalized STW argue that the status quo serves the interests of customers (most often men) over the interests of workers (most often women),

Ethical Debate

Should Sexual Orientation Be Considered a Human Right?

The question of whether sexual orientation should be considered a human right has been debated recently by various world organizations, including the United Nations (UN) and the Commonwealth of Nations. Canada includes sexual orientation in Section 15 of its Charter of Rights and Freedoms, prohibiting discrimination based on sexual orientation, but many countries around the world still criminally prosecute men who engage in same-sex sexual behaviours, and some even enforce the death penalty in such cases. Should organizations such as the UN interfere in the laws of nations by levying sanctions against those who do not view sexual orientation as a human right? Should the more industrialized and wealthy Commonwealth nations withhold foreign aid from other Commonwealth countries that still have criminal laws against same-sex sexuality?

A report issued at the 2011 biannual Summit of the Commonwealth called for the creation of a human rights commissioner who would, among other things, monitor the legal and social treatment of LGBTQ individuals in Commonwealth countries. The suggestion was not carried through, however, possibly because 41 of the 52 Commonwealth countries still have laws against same-sex sexual activity. Many of these laws are a legacy of the British Empire laws, which have been modified in Western Commonwealth nations but held onto in other countries, especially those in Africa. For example, Nigeria's House of Representatives recently passed a bill that outlaws the recognition of same-sex marriages and allows for up to 14 years in prison for anyone who enters into a same-sex marriage or civil union. The law goes so far as to criminalize public displays of affection between same-sex couples and participation in LGBTQ organizations. Britain's prime minister announced at the summit that funding to some countries would be restricted or reduced based on their treatment of sexual diversity. One of the countries that would see their aid significantly reduced by this policy is Uganda, and a representative from that country argued that it was not fair to reduce aid when the country is facing very important issues of poverty, corruption, education, and hunger, which he considered to be more critical than the rights of same-sex oriented individuals in Uganda. Is it ethically right to make a developing nation's foreign aid dependent upon its treatment of human rights issues? The consensus on this question appears to be that, yes, human rights violations are a legitimate cause for withholding or restricting foreign aid, but the question that has been less clearly answered is whether sexual diversity should be considered a human rights issue? This question has recently drawn a great deal of global attention as a result of Russia's new anti-propaganda laws, which, passed under the guise of protecting children, effectively criminalize the display of rainbow flags, same-sex public displays of affection, or any verbal acknowledgement of same-sex sexualities in a positive light. Protestors have called upon the International Olympic Committee (IOC) to remove the upcoming 2014 Olympic Games from Sochi, Russia, arguing that the anti-propaganda laws are a violation of the Olympic Committee's charter, which prohibits discrimination based on sexual orientation. On a larger scale, the United Nations passed a resolution in 2011, which recognized the rights of LGBT individuals as being human rights, but to date there has been little consensus concerning how or when the global community should intervene to protect the rights of LGBT citizens around the world.

such that the illegality of the practice both stigmatizes and marginalizes STWs, who feel unable to seek the assistance of the authorities and who are placed at the mercy of their clientele with respect to potential violence and health risks. Legalization of STW and related activities would allow regulations to be put in place to safeguard the health of both workers and clients, as well as make legal protection more widely available to STWs.

When prostitution is not regulated or legally protected by the authorities, STWs are subject to exploitation and violence, often at the hands of their pimps and their clientele. In Canada, the majority of STWs in large urban cities report working for themselves, with the presence and influence of pimps being strongest in the Prairie provinces and the Maritimes (Shaver, 2011). With respect to clientele, a 1998 Gallup poll found that 7 per cent of Canadian men have paid for sex at least once during their lifetime (Weitzer, 1999).

CHAPTER SUMMARY

Sexuality is a topic of great interest to researchers and laypeople alike. Though many people do not like to talk about their own sex lives, what goes on behind closed doors is being influenced immensely in both positive and negative ways by media, politics, religion, and culture. Such external influences are not new; they have existed throughout our long history. However, with advances in technology, information about sexuality is at our fingertips in a way that it never was before. The challenge with the immense amount of information available, not all of which is accurate, is to develop the ability to think critically about the information one reads, question the norms that media is presenting, and explore one's own sexuality while respecting that of others.

DEBATE QUESTIONS

In what ways have media (e.g., films and advertising) promoted positive and safer sexuality? In what ways have they promoted a fantasy model of sex in which there are few, if any, consequences?

REVIEW QUESTIONS

1. Who were some of the most influential figures in the history of the study of sexuality? What is their lasting influence in today's society?

2. Do you think that conducting observational studies such as those of Masters and Johnson is an appropriate way to study sexual activity? Would you be comfortable participating in such a study?

3. How have views of masturbation changed throughout history? Which cultures accepted this practice, which condemned it, and why?

4. How did interpretations of the narrative of Adam and Eve help shape the roles of men and women in Western society?

5. How is the vibrator related to hysteria?

6. What are the arguments of the two sides in the debate on same-sex marriage in Canada?

7. How does ethnocentrism affect our society's view of sexuality? How does it affect your own views?

SUGGESTIONS FOR FURTHER READING AND VIEWING

Recommended Websites

The International Encyclopedia of Sexuality: www2.hu-berlin.de/sexology/IES/canada.html

It Gets Better Project (LGBTTIQQ website): www.itgetsbetter.org

Journal of Sex Research: http://sexscience.org/journal_of_sex_research

Media Smarts (see "Digital and Media Literacy"): www.media-awareness.ca/english/index.cfm

Queereka: http://queereka.com/2012/01/03/perspectives-introduction

Science of Relationships: www.scienceofrelationships.com

Sex Education Opposition Advertisements in Ontario:

> http://ca.news.yahoo.com/blogs/dailybrew/national-post-gets-heat-running -apparent-anti-gay-165525989.html

> www.2bmag.com/2011/09/ dont-confuse-whom-exactly-national-post-publishes-transphobic-ad-5773

> www.xtra.ca/public/national/toronto_sun_will_not_apologize_for_transphobic_ ad-10850.aspx

> www.adweek.com/adfreak/canadian-group-accused-transphobia-newspaper-ad -135343

Sex in Advertising: www.gallup-robinson.com/tableofcontents.html

The Sex Information and Education Council of Canada: www.sieccan.org

Sex Scrolls: www.sexscrolls.net

SexualityandU.ca: www.sexualityandu.ca

Spread the Word (documentaries on sexuality): www.sprword.com/sex.html

Top Documentary Films (films on sexuality): http://topdocumentaryfilms.com/category/sex

Transgender Issues (map of surgeries covered in different Canadian provinces): http://www.xtra.ca/public/National/Sex_reassignment_surgery_in_Canada_whats_ covered_and_where-7706.aspx

Recommended Reading

Hawkes, G., & Scott, J. (2005). *Perspectives in human sexuality.* New York, NY: Oxford University Press.

Heasley, R., & Crane, B. (2002). *Sexual lives: A reader on the theories and realities of human sexualities.* New York, NY: McGraw Hill.

Horrocks, R. (1997). *An introduction to the study of sexuality.* London, UK: MacMillan Press.

Maines, R. (1999). *The technology of orgasm: Hysteria, the vibrator and women's sexual satisfaction.* Baltimore, MD: Johns Hopkins University Press.

Ryan, C., & Jethá, C. (2010). *Sex at dawn.* New York, NY: HarperCollins Press.

Tiefer, L. (2004). *Sex is not a natural act and other essays.* Boulder, CO: Westview Press.

Trees, A. (2009). *Decoding love: Why it takes 12 frogs to find a prince and other revelations from the science of attraction.* New York, NY: Penguin.

Weeks, J. (2010). *Sexuality* (3rd Ed.). New York, NY: Routledge Press.

Recommended Viewing

B., M. (Director). (2004). *Silence: In search of black female sexuality in America* [Documentary]. United States: Shoot Films, Not People Productions.

Condon, B. (Director & Writer). (2004). *Kinsey* [Motion picture]. United States: American Zoetrope.

Cronenberg, C. (Director). (2011). *A dangerous method* [Motion picture]. United States: Recorded Picture Company.

Wexler, T. (Director). (2011). *Hysteria* [Motion picture]. United Kingdom: Informant Media.

Theoretical Approaches to Studying Human Sexuality

ELKE D. REISSING AND
HEATHER L. ARMSTRONG

LEARNING OBJECTIVES

In this chapter, you will

- discover how theories can help us understand real-world phenomena;

- become familiar with a variety of theories that attempt to describe and explain aspects of human sexuality; and

- discover how researchers employ, test, refine, and/or refute theories to build our understanding of sexuality.

What Is the Reproductive Advantage of Same-Sex Sexual Orientation?

According to evolutionary theory and natural selection, if something is encoded in our genes, then there must be some reproductive advantage associated with it. But what is the reproductive advantage of same-sex sexual orientation, given that gay and lesbian couples are, strictly speaking, unable to conceive children without assistance? Sociobiologists have proposed an explanation.

Canadian researchers Paul Vasey and Doug VanderLaan (2010) studied a group of culturally accepted transgendered men, known locally as *fa'afafine*, in Samoa. In Samoan culture, the biologically male fa'afafine are seen as occupying a gender category other than that of "male" or "female," and they pre-dominantly engage sexually with men. Even though fa'afafine individuals do not typically father their own children, they do share genes with other members of their families, such as their nieces and nephews. Therefore, the researchers suggest, from an evolutionary perspective, it is in the fa'afafine's best interest to look after these family members in order to ensure that some of their genetic traits are passed on to future generations (see Figure 2.1).

In this study, the researchers compared avuncular tendencies (such as investing resources in family members) of the fa'afafine to those of male-gendered men with children and male-gendered men without children. As would be predicted by evolutionary theory, the fa'afafine showed stronger avuncular tendencies and were more likely to do things for the children, like take care of them for a week while their parents were away. This notion of "inclusive fitness" has been used

FIGURE 2.1 Can evolutionary theory explain sexual orientation? The *fa'afafine* of Samoa assist in caring for their nieces and nephews, thus helping to ensure that some of the genes they share with their relatives will be passed on to future generations.

to explain altruism, and it has been observed in the animal world, as some animals will risk their lives with alarm calls to protect their family group. Inclusive fitness could explain the adaptive advantage of having gay and lesbian family members.

QUESTIONS FOR CRITICAL THOUGHT AND REFLECTION

As you read through the chapter, keep the following questions in mind:
1. Do you think that evolutionary theory can fully explain sexual orientation? What other factors might be involved?
2. What other aspects of human sexuality might evolutionary theory help to explain?
3. What is the value of using scientific theories to explain human behaviour?

Introduction

While sexuality is generally considered to be an exciting topic, the theory of sexuality does not have the same reputation. Yet theoretical reasoning is the basis for all knowledge, and it provides the foundation for further exploration and deeper understanding. Theory, in everyday language, stands for a hunch, an idea about something that has not been proven. **Scientific theory**, on the other hand, represents a set of conclusions or explanations that have been thoroughly tested and are generally agreed upon as the current state of understanding. Theories, however, can be refuted if new information emerges—and this organized quest for explanations and the ultimate truth is what science is all about.

scientific theory A set of thoroughly tested, generally agreed upon conclusions about, or explanations of, certain phenomena.

Scientific theory in sexuality helps us to

➡ Organize, self-correct, and generate knowledge

➡ Communicate about sexuality

➡ Develop research ideas and methods

➡ Interpret research results

FIGURE 2.2 What's so important about theory? Theories are like compasses—they help guide the study of sexuality.

hypothesis A prediction, based on theory, about the expected outcomes of a research study.

psychodynamic theory A theory that attempts to explain the conscious and unconscious psychological forces that underlie human personality, motivation, and behaviour.

id The portion of an individual's personality that represents unconscious and/or instinctual urges and desires.

ego The portion of an individual's personality that mediates between the realities of the outside world, the individual's urges and desires, and the individual's conscience.

superego The portion of an individual's personality that represents that person's internalized standards, which are based on social and parental learning.

Theory makes it possible for us to formally talk about sexuality and explain otherwise intensely personal or even secret physical and emotional events. Thanks to theory, things that are often considered taboo and that may elicit uncomfortable laughter can actually be researched and discussed in an academic manner. Take, for example, erectile function. While it may make some people uncomfortable to discuss this issue on a personal level, researchers and clinicians have pointed out that some erectile problems are physical problems that can be treated with medications. This understanding has helped normalize the problem and legitimize the personal distress many men experience. Furthermore, we are able to talk about the normal changes in erectile function associated with aging and prevent unnecessary anxiety and distress that can further exacerbate difficulties in having and maintaining erections.

Theory also guides how researchers examine a topic, facilitates researchers' interpretation of results, and helps researchers come up with predictions, or **hypotheses**, that can then be tested through experimentation (Figure 2.2). Sexuality research is carried out by a diverse group of professionals such as psychologists, sociologists, anthropologists, and biologists, to name only a few. Some researchers may be more interested in the reproductive aspects of sexuality, which align well with biological and evolutionary theories. Other researchers may be interested in the role of culture in shaping sexuality, which may align better with social constructionist theories.

Take our example of erectile function. If researchers wanted to study how a man's anxiety about maintaining an erection affects his ability to do so, they would begin by formulating a hypothesis—an "if . . . then . . ." kind of statement—that reflects their theoretical stance. For example, *if* a man has fears about his erectile capacity during sexual activity, *then* he will be more likely to experience erectile problems. This hypothesis is based on the cognitive theory of sexuality, described below, which highlights the importance of our thinking patterns in how we experience and respond sexually during our sexual encounters. Researchers can choose a number of ways to test this hypothesis, as will be explained in Chapter 3. If the findings are in line with the prediction, the theory is supported. If not, the theory can be revised and further tested. In this way, the scientific study of sexuality based on theory is always developing and self-correcting in order to provide the most complete and accurate knowledge possible. Human sexual development, sexual identity, and sexual behaviours are very complex, universal human phenomena that are affected by biology, culture, thinking, learning, feeling, and an individual's particular history and circumstance. Obviously, no one theory can capture all aspects of human sexuality. In the following sections, we will discuss the major theories that have been proposed to help us understand the diverse and complex aspects of human sexuality. Each one has merit, and as a collective they are advancing organized thinking toward greater knowledge about sexuality. Broadly speaking, they normalize variation and diversity, and they assist in addressing sexual problems.

Psychological Theories of Sexuality

Psychodynamic Theory

Sigmund Freud (1856–1939) (Figure 2.3), a medical doctor, was the first to present a comprehensive theoretical framework to explain human psychosexual development. According to Freud's **psychodynamic theory**, an individual's personality is divided into three parts: the **id**, the **ego**, and the **superego**. These elements operate on conscious, preconscious, and unconscious levels. **Psychoanalysis** can help an individual to bring parts of his or her personality to conscious awareness, in order to examine, correct, and balance any disruptions that may be present.

Psychodynamic theory explains that basic personality formation is the result of the successful (or not so successful) transition through specific stages in the first six years of a person's life (Figure 2.4). In the oral stage (birth to two years), the **erogenous zone** to which all **libidinal energy** is directed is the mouth. If the infant is not satisfied in his or her need to suck, bite, and so on, the libidinal energy is blocked and the child may experience **fixation**. This fixation may result in particular adult personality traits such as dependence or aggression. The major challenge of the anal stage (two to four years) is mastering control over one's bladder and bowel movements. Fixation at this stage is thought to result in personality traits with a strong focus on cleanliness and orderliness or, on the flip side, carelessness and lack of self-control.

FIGURE 2.3 Sometimes a cigar is just a cigar . . . or is it? Sigmund Freud, the father of psychoanalysis, used dream analysis to access the unconscious level of a person's personality. He believed that dreams contain symbols that contain deeper, hidden meanings—for example, a cigar may be seen as a phallic symbol, and a dream about smoking a cigar could be interpreted as expressing a hidden desire for sexual contact involving a penis.

psychoanalysis Therapy conducted between a therapist (psychoanalyst) and a client, with the goal of examining, correcting, and balancing any disruptions in the client's personality.

erogenous zone An area of the body with heightened sensitivity.

libidinal energy Psychic energy associated with mental desires and drives.

fixation A condition that occurs when needs are not met in childhood, resulting in blocked libidinal energy and unsuccessful resolution of the psychosexual stages of development.

In the phallic stage (four to six years), libidinal energy is focussed on the genitals. During this stage, boys develop an **Oedipus complex**, which Freud characterized as a boy's falling in love with his mother and wanting to eliminate his father, in order to secure his mother's attention. These feelings, in turn, result in fears that the father will retaliate, which the boy experiences as **castration anxiety**. Successful completion of the phallic stage and resolution of the Oedipus complex sees the boy identifying with his father instead of competing against him for his mother's affection. The equivalent of the Oedipus complex in girls is the **Electra complex**, thus named by Carl Jung in 1912, and first described by Freud as "penis envy." In this stage, a girl is initially also attached to her mother but, realizing she does not have a penis, she shifts her attachment to her father. The idea of the Electra complex has never been fully accepted, even in psychoanalytic circles, and Freud has been much criticized for the sexist undertones of his notion of penis envy. Psychoanalytic theory suggests that the inability to resolve the Oedipus or Electra complex will result in problems with gender-role identification, with adult intimate relationships, and with learning to delay gratification.

Oedipus complex In boys, a desire for the mother's love coupled with fears of retaliation from the father.

castration anxiety Anxiety due to fear of loss of or injury to one's genitals.

Electra complex In girls, an attachment to the mother followed by a shift in attachment to the father as a way to resolve penis envy.

The next stage is the latency stage (age six to puberty), during which all libidinal energy is said to lie dormant; however, as you will read in Chapter 9, preadolescence is marked by an increase in interest in all things sexual, and it is a time when gender roles are learned and practised. Yet Freud argued that in the years leading up to puberty, libidinal energy is waiting to reemerge in the final psychosexual developmental stage, the genital stage. Freud described the final stage as a time when physical sexual changes reawaken repressed needs, and sexual feelings are directed toward others for sexual gratification.

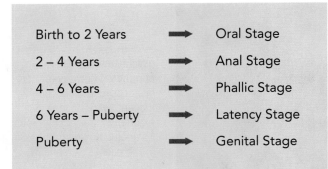

Birth to 2 Years	➡	Oral Stage
2 – 4 Years	➡	Anal Stage
4 – 6 Years	➡	Phallic Stage
6 Years – Puberty	➡	Latency Stage
Puberty	➡	Genital Stage

FIGURE 2.4 The sexual child? Freud believed that the successful resolution of each of the psychosexual stages would lead to healthy gender and sexual identity.

falsifiable Able to be proven false by research.

classical conditioning A process through which an individual is repeatedly exposed to a neutral stimulus and an unconditioned stimulus at the same time, until the neutral stimulus comes to elicit a response initially brought forth by the unconditioned stimulus.

Freud also believed that at this stage, women need to move from an immature, adolescent orgasm focussed on the clitoris to a mature, vaginal orgasm. This particular assertion has been completely refuted, as you will discover in the discussion of the variability of the orgasmic experience in Chapter 4.

Over the years, Freud's psychodynamic theory has been both criticized from every imaginable angle by its opponents and hotly defended by its proponents. Critiques have focussed on the overemphasis on sex—in particular, the overemphasis on sex from the male point of view—and the lack of supporting data. Freud's theory is based on information gleaned from therapy, not data from experiments, and some argue that the clinical data were flawed and inaccurate. Moreover, Freud's theory is impossible to examine experimentally—technically speaking, it is not **falsifiable**. As a result, some people have argued that it is not in fact a *real* theory. In addition, Freud's take on female psychosexual development has been critiqued as inadequately developed and sexist. On the other hand, some point out, Freud was one of the first to highlight the importance of childhood experiences in influencing personality development, and he provided a theoretical framework to address psychological problems via psychoanalysis. When seen in their historical context, Freud's contributions to theory and psychotherapy were considerable.

Classical Conditioning

Classical conditioning is associated with the seminal work of Russian physiologist Ivan Pavlov (1849–1936), who discovered that repeatedly pairing a neutral stimulus with an unconditioned stimulus that elicits an unconditioned response will result in a conditioned response. Pavlov noted this phenomenon when he paired a ringing bell (the neutral stimulus) with his dogs' food (the unconditioned stimulus). Initially, the dogs would salivate at the sight of the food (the unconditioned response) but not in response to the sound of the bell. However, with repeated presentation of both the bell and the food at the same time, the dogs began to salivate at the sound of the bell (the conditioned response), even when the food was not present (Figure 2.5). This theory can explain why we might have very vivid memories or experience specific feelings when, for example, we smell familiar cologne or see a particular piece of clothing.

In sexuality research and therapy, classical conditioning has been used to understand the development of some forms of compulsive sexual behaviours and fetishes, and to develop treatments for unwanted sexual behaviours. For example, a sex therapy client can be instructed to imagine becoming sexually aroused by his unwanted or problematic fetish; when he actually becomes aroused, he can then be instructed to smell ammonia salt capsules, which will make him feel extremely nauseated. He may also be instructed to imagine the worst consequence of his behaviour for

FIGURE 2.5 Ivan Pavlov's early twentieth-century experiments with dogs led to a deeper understanding of how we come to associate certain stimuli with one another, and how such associations can influence our behaviour. Later theories of sexuality, such as Daryl Bem's "exotic becomes erotic" theory, expand on Pavlov's findings to suggest that classical conditioning can explain certain sexual preferences.

his family and himself. This combination of an unpleasant physiological response and a vividly imagined aversive consequence can effect significant changes in behaviour (Kafka, 2007).

Classical conditioning has also been used to explain sexual orientation. For example, in his "exotic becomes erotic" theory, Daryl Bem (1996) proposed a method of sexual orientation development based on classical conditioning; this theory has been used to explain both heterosexual and same-sex orientations. According to this theory, children's temperaments influence their gender (non)conformity (see Chapter 10). Most children will engage in activities that are typical of their gender and go on to develop heterosexual orientations. However, some will identify more strongly with the opposite gender and engage in activities more typical of *that* gender. As a result, these individuals start to feel different from their same-sex peers; in other words, the same-sex peers become exotic. These exotic same-sex peers become a source of non-specific arousal, which is then interpreted as erotic and/or romantic attraction. This is an application of classical conditioning, as the sense of the exotic (unconditioned stimulus) elicits non-specific arousal (unconditioned response), and when this is repeatedly associated with same-sex peers (neutral stimulus), the arousal becomes erotic attraction (conditioned response). In this line of thinking, of course, the assumption is that sexual orientation is not innate but rather something that people learn through their experiences.

Operant Conditioning

Operant conditioning is associated with the pioneering work of psychologist B.F. Skinner (1904–1990), who invented the **operant conditioning chamber** to test his theories on **reinforcement**. Skinner's research suggested that an individual who encounters reinforcement when she or he engages in a certain behaviour (an **operant**) is more likely to repeat that behaviour in the future. Conversely, the individual is less likely to repeat a behaviour that results in punishment. Some rewards, such as sex or food, are particularly powerful because they are intrinsically rewarding. These are called **primary reinforcers**.

Sex is both a primary reinforcer *and* a behaviour that can be shaped by rewards and punishments. This implies that sexuality is both innate and a learned phenomenon. Consider the following example. A man who works in a high-stress office environment takes little time for anything else but work. When he feels very stressed, he likes to masturbate to pornographic images on the Internet. This gives him pleasant feelings and relief of sexual tension (a primary reinforcer) while at the same time decreasing his overall tension (offering reinforcement). This temporary, euphoric sexual high offers a nice break from his usual stressful routine, and he finds himself masturbating more and more often. He begins taking risks by looking at pornography during work time, and he starts spending a great deal of money trying to find more stimulating websites. The risk of being discovered and fear of negative consequences at work act as punishment, decreasing the frequency of his viewing pornography and masturbating (at least at work). As he continues to masturbate, the temporary feelings of relief come to be followed by feelings of guilt, shame, remorse, and even depression. Eventually, what was once an enjoyable activity becomes a source of added stress. This is an example of the sexual addiction model for this kind of hypersexual behaviour first described by Patrick Carnes in 1983 (but see the "Research vs Real Life" box for an alternative approach to the explanation of compulsive sexual behaviour).

Operant conditioning also teaches us that learning about sexuality can take place throughout one's life. As a consequence of this theory, sex therapy often has a strong educational element and uses behavioural rehearsal to increase successful outcomes.

operant conditioning A process through which an individual's behaviour is modified by its consequences or the reinforcement that he or she receives.

operant conditioning chamber Originally, a small box that contains a lever or other device that an animal can use to receive reinforcement (e.g., food) or to avoid punishment (e.g., a shock); also known as "Skinner's box."

reinforcement Something that encourages a specific behaviour.

operant A behaviour.

primary reinforcer A powerful reward that is intrinsically satisfying.

Research VS Real Life

Should Sex Offenders Avoid Sex?

The use of operant conditioning to explain problematic and/or hyperactive sexual behaviour has received a good deal of criticism, and research has been conducted to explore alternative models that better explain problematic sexual behaviours, and that have the potential to improve treatment interventions. An excellent example comes from the work of Canadian researcher and clinician Dr Paul Fedoroff, who has contributed the following:

Sex crimes, by definition, involve problematic sexual behaviours. But does this mean we can conclude that "sex" is the cause of the problem and must therefore be avoided in all forms? In the 1990s, the idea of "sex addiction" became popular. Some thought that "sex addicts" should abstain from sex in the same way that drug addicts or alcoholics abstain from substances of abuse. Our group attempted to test this hypothesis by proposing a three-way crossover design in which convicted pedophiles would be randomly assigned to one of three groups: a) no change in masturbation frequency, b) no

masturbation, and c) double baseline frequency of masturbation. After thirty days, each group would be randomly switched to one of the two remaining conditions. After an additional thirty days, they would be switched to whichever condition they had not already been assigned. When we submitted the proposal for ethical review, the review board did not approve it, commenting that it was "unethical to encourage sex offenders to masturbate." We therefore cut the "increase frequency of masturbation" arm of the study.

We found that most (13 out of 17) study participants thought not masturbating was a bad idea, and some thought their risk of reoffending actually increased. The majority reported increased sexual interests when not masturbating (Brown, Traverso, Fedoroff, 1996). After the first study was published in a peer-reviewed journal, we returned to the review board and explained that we had done the dangerous study (preventing sex offenders from masturbating) and, to its

---

When a new behaviour demonstrates encouraging results, the feeling of accomplishment will further reinforce change. For example, a man learning ejaculatory control is given instructions on how to masturbate until the point when he feels he is just about to experience orgasm. At first, he is instructed to stop stimulating himself at this point, until the "edge" of excitement has passed; later, he will be instructed to merely slow down. When he starts to experience success by having longer-lasting erections, he will feel motivated to continue practising masturbatory control.

Social Learning Theory

social learning theory
A theory based on the idea that learning occurs through modelling of observed behaviour.

Social learning theory has its origin in the work of psychologists Julian Rotter (1916–) and Albert Bandura (1925–). It is based on the principles of operant conditioning but also recognizes the importance of social context and environmental factors. Social learning theory posits that human behaviour is learned by observing other people's behaviours, attitudes, and outcomes. When it comes to choosing one learned behaviour over another, we do so based on our *individual* expectations about rewards or punishments. Social learning theories have been used to explain such things as sexual development in adolescents and young adults, contraception use, and coercive sexual behaviours. These theories are also the basis for intervention programs designed to promote healthy behaviours—for example, groups in which young people are given the

credit, the board agreed that a prospective three-way crossover study would be ethical. Remarkably, no other research group has ever undertaken the proposed study, and it is still on our lab's to-do list.

This study highlights a recurrent theme in forensic sexology. Most contemporary researchers agree that sex itself is not pathological. Sex crimes result from abnormal sexual interests (e.g., sexual interest in children) or disinhibited behaviour (e.g., intoxication). Therefore, the notion that it is dangerous to tell sex offenders to masturbate more frequently is a hypothesis that needs testing, especially since the data from the study described above suggests that forbidding masturbation in sex offenders may be more dangerous than encouraging, or at least allowing, it. In spite of this, many programs that treat sex offenders either ignore the topic of masturbation or suggest that if it occurs, it should be done in the absence of adult consensual pornography, which is designed to offer adults an outlet for their sexual impulses. Thus, it becomes the researcher's tasks to educate

policy-makers as well as the general population on the value of research findings versus popular opinion.

Recently, a major North American study of sex offenders' use of the Internet found that participants who reported more "Internet preoccupation" (and who therefore had greater access to online pornography) were significantly less likely to have committed known, in-person sexual offences than were offenders who used the Internet less often (Prentky et al., 2010). The effect was less significant but still important for offenders with higher levels of conduct-disordered behaviour. This study and a host of others like it suggest that pornography may be a diversion from in-person sexual activity. The question remains: If the aim of treatment is to direct sex interests toward "normal" sexual scenarios, why not expose sex offenders to adult pornography that features consensual activity between adults?

J. Paul Fedoroff, MD, FRCPC, is a psychiatrist and director of forensic research at the University of Ottawa's Institute of Mental Health Research, and at the Integrated Forensic Program at the Royal Ottawa Health Care Centre.

---

opportunity to discuss how they cope with contraceptive use and safe-sex strategies. The participants in such programs often respond by showing an increase in their perception of risk and greater confidence in their ability to be proactive and take responsibility over safe sex (Pedlow & Carey, 2000).

Albert Bandura (1977) suggested that a person who can successfully perform a specific behaviour will experience a sense of competence, or **self-efficacy**. In the sexual context, high levels of *sexual self-efficacy*, the belief that one can be a competent lover, have been associated with positive sexual adjustment and sexual satisfaction. For example, researchers at the University of Ottawa have shown that young women are more likely to have positive sexual adjustment if they also have higher levels of sexual self-efficacy (Reissing, Laliberté, & Davis, 2005). The researchers further showed that the first intercourse experience is very influential: most people clearly remember losing their virginity, and the emotional experience of this event can set the stage for adult sexual adjustment by either increasing or decreasing sexual self-efficacy (Reissing, Andruff, & Wentland, 2010). What this finding suggests is that some people with low levels of sexual self-efficacy can become stuck in a harmful cycle of assuming that they cannot be good lovers and therefore avoiding the very experiences that could *disconfirm* those beliefs; this avoidance in turn will further feed into their low sexual self-efficacy, ultimately resulting in impairment of sexual response.

self-efficacy A person's belief that she or he can competently perform a specific behaviour.

Social Exchange Theory

social exchange theory A theory based on the idea that interpersonal relationships operate on a system of costs (or losses) and rewards (or gains) within which individuals try to maximize rewards and minimize costs, or at least find balance between the two.

Social exchange theory describes how, in any relationship, people try to maximize rewards and minimize costs. The theory is based on four components: the balance of costs and rewards, equity/equality, comparison level, and comparison level for alternatives (Byers & Wang, 2004). Within this theory, *comparison level* refers to what a person expects to get out of the relationship in comparison to what she or he puts into it, and *comparison level for alternatives* refers to how a person feels that the current relationship compared to other available options.

Researchers E. Sandra Byers and Adrienne Wang (2004), at the University of New Brunswick, have applied the social exchange theory to sexuality in intimate relationships. They found that people are more likely to stay in an intimate relationship in which the rewards are high and the costs are low. Additionally, in order for a relationship to be stable and for both partners to be satisfied, the partners need to experience a balance of costs and rewards. If one partner feels as though she or he is contributing more to the relationship and the other partner is reaping all the benefits, the partner who feels he or she is contributing more may become unhappy and seek additional rewards outside of the relationship in an attempt to re-establish a balance. Within an intimate relationship, people are more likely to be satisfied and to stay in the relationship if their expectations, or comparison levels, of what they should contribute to and receive from a relationship are being met. Finally, people are more likely to stay in a relationship when the comparison level for alternatives is low. In other words, people are more likely to stay with their partner if there are no attractive alternatives available.

Cognitive Theories

cognitive theories Theories that attempt to understand human behaviour by focussing on thought processes.

dyspareunia Genital and/or pelvic pain during or after sexual activity.

Cognitive theories are associated with a number of researchers who describe how our thinking affects how we feel and behave (e.g., Dobson, 2002). These theories recognize that our thoughts are subject to a number of misconceptions, distortions, false assumptions, and errors in evaluating situations or information. These errors can result in frustration, distress, and even psychological disorders, as well as inappropriate or even harmful behaviours.

Cognitive theories have been very influential in explaining a host of sexual problems and patterns of behaviour—remember, from the introduction to this chapter, how feelings of anxiety and distress can exacerbate erectile problems. Take, as another example, a woman who does not experience orgasm with intercourse alone, and who assumes that all women should reach orgasm every time they have intercourse. As a result of her false assumption, this woman may think that she is an inadequate lover, and she may avoid sexual activities that do not involve intercourse, even though she might find such activities to be pleasurable and, ultimately, facilitate orgasm. During sex, she may be preoccupied with her perceived failure as a lover. As a result, her levels of sexual arousal may decrease, and she may experience **dyspareunia**. The subsequent lack of enjoyment from sexual encounters may leave her with a dwindling level of sexual desire, and it may make her feel emotionally distanced from her partner (Figure 2.6). While this scenario might sound extreme, sex therapists work on a regular basis with individuals who are caught in such vicious cycles

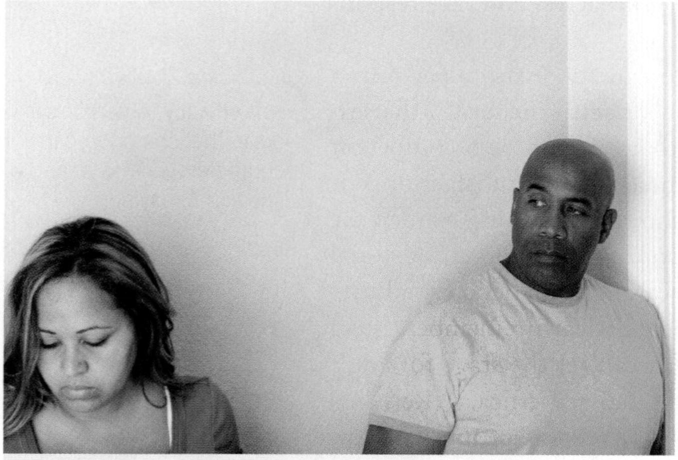

FIGURE 2.6 Faulty beliefs and negative thinking can lead to sexual problems and disorders. Cognitive therapists challenge their clients to confront this thinking in the hopes of improving sexuality.

in which inaccurate beliefs about sexuality and the behavioural consequences of these beliefs create other faulty beliefs and more sexual problems (Leiblum, 2007).

Biological Theories of Sexuality

Genetic Theory

Genetic theory, as it relates to the study of sexuality, explains how our genetics play a large part in regulating hormone production, reproductive cycles, ovulation, ejaculation, conception, and pregnancy (see Figure 2.7). According to this theory, genetics can also explain sexual orientation and gender identity. Many people who identify as gay or lesbian describe how they have always felt that they were somehow different from others and how they knew at a young age that they did not fit in with the majority of their peers. Some describe wanting to dress up as members of the other sex, while others recall joining in the activities of their other-sex peers. To find evidence of a genetic component to sexual orientation, studies with both male (Bailey & Pillard, 1991) and female (Bailey, Pillard, Neale, & Agyei, 1993) participants have been conducted using identical twins (who have identical DNA), fraternal twins (who have related DNA), and adoptive siblings (who have unrelated DNA). In these studies, the **concordance rate** of same-sex sexual attraction was significantly higher for the identical twins (48 to 52 per cent) than for the fraternal twins (16 to 22 per cent) or the adopted siblings (6 to 11 per cent). Childhood gender nonconformity has also been shown to be similarly heritable in male and female twins (Bailey, Dunne, & Martin, 2000).

Further evidence of the role that genetics plays in human sexuality can be found in genetic disorders and sexual problems that have genetic causes. One example of a genetic disorder that impacts sexuality is Klinefelter's syndrome (see Chapter 10). In this syndrome, genetic males (whose sex chromosomes are normally XY) carry an additional X chromosome (XXY); these men are essentially infertile and have a variable degree of typical physical characteristics such as sparse body hair, narrow shoulders, wide hips, and a lanky build. Sexual problems that can have genetic or biological causes include **erectile dysfunction** and dyspareunia. Such problems are often treated medically or in combination with sex therapy.

Sociobiological Theory

Sociobiological theory is the application of **evolutionary biology** to explain social behaviours—for example, aggression—in animals, including humans (Barash, 1977; Wilson, 1975). In many ways, sociobiology is similar to **evolutionary psychology**.

Evolutionary theory describes how all living things have changed over time and developed into their current form. These changes are determined by how adaptive a given characteristic is to the environment, as well as the likelihood that an organism exhibiting a certain characteristic will survive *and* reproduce. This process is referred to as **natural selection**, an important component of which is **sexual selection**. Sexual selection works through two processes: **intrasexual competition** (e.g., when male deer fight

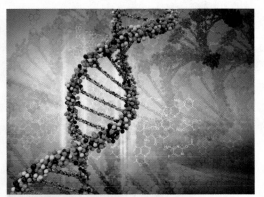

FIGURE 2.7 It's in my genes! As technology improves, scientists are discovering that much of human sexuality can be explained (at least partly) by a person's genetic makeup.

genetic theory A theory that examines the role of genes in influencing behaviour.

concordance rate The probability that two individuals will have the same trait, given that one individual has the trait.

erectile dysfunction The inability to develop or maintain an erection of sufficient rigidity to engage in intercourse.

sociobiological theory A theory based on the idea that the way we behave in social situations is influenced by our biological makeup, which has evolved over the history of our species.

evolutionary biology The application of evolutionary theories to understand how species have adapted and changed over time.

evolutionary psychology The application of evolutionary theories to understand emotional and psychological processes, mainly in human beings.

natural selection The evolutionary process in which organisms best adapted to their environment are most likely to survive and reproduce.

sexual selection The evolutionary process of mate selection, which can be either intrasexual or intersexual.

intrasexual competition Competition between members of the same sex for access to breeding with members of the other sex.

intersexual selection
Preferentially picking one mate over others.

to determine who has the most powerful antlers and therefore the right to mate with the best females) and **intersexual selection** (e.g., when a female bird chooses the mate who has the brightest plumage) (Figure 2.8).

Sociobiological theory recognizes that, generally speaking, reproduction takes a greater investment of time and effort from a female than from a male. After all, it is the female who becomes pregnant and gives birth, and in many species the female is most responsible for the care of the offspring. When choosing a mate, therefore, a female should look for a male who will contribute good genes and can provide useful resources and protection, to make sure her offspring will survive and reproduce in turn. For a male, conversely, it usually takes little investment to impregnate females. A male needs to ensure that his offspring survive, but, unlike a female who actually gives birth, he can never be completely certain that the offspring he cares for are biologically his. This dilemma is met with two possible strategies (Trivers, 1972). Males can choose to provide little or no parental care, mate as much as possible, and trust the odds that at least some of their offspring will make it to adulthood and reproduce. Alternatively, males can choose to mate with a specific female and then provide resources and protection to that female and her offspring, thereby assuring that a few offspring that are likely his will survive. Broadly speaking, in birds with few differences in plumage and size, such as the swallow, the male provides more parental care and wows the female with a good nest and abundant food. On the other hand, in birds with notable differences, such as the peacock, males provide little or no care for the females or their offspring, and they compete with other males for access to females via colorful displays of plumage and ruffles, which females take as a sign of good genes (Breedlove, Rosenzweig, & Watson, 2007).

As you might expect, evolutionary forces have been implicated in a number of human sexual behaviours. Evolutionary forces may also relate to a number of our short-term and long-term mating strategies (see the "Research vs Real Life" box on **sexual strategies theory**).

sexual strategies theory
A theory based on the idea that human mating strategies have evolved to overcome mating problems faced by our ancestors.

dual control model of sexuality A theory that suggests that an individual's sexual responses are influenced by the balance between neurobiological, environmental, and cultural processes that activate or suppress sexual response.

The Dual Control Model of Sexuality

The **dual control model of sexuality**, developed by John Bancroft and Erick Janssen (2000) at the Kinsey Institute, suggests that each person's sexual responses involve an interaction between sexual excitatory and sexual inhibitory neurobiological processes.

FIGURE 2.8 (Left) In some species, males compete with one another to impress and win the most eligible mates. (Right) In other species, members of one sex will choose the most beautiful mate (or the mate with the longest neck, or the mate with the sweetest song).

These processes have developed in human beings in response to evolutionarily adaptive pressures. Mating and having offspring is, of course, imperative to passing on one's genes, but under certain environmental conditions—for example, in times of famine or war—it is useful to be able to suppress one's sexual response. People differ in their propensity toward excitation and inhibition, and in line with evolutionary theory, gender differences have emerged such that women exhibit a greater propensity toward inhibition and men display a greater propensity toward excitation. Factors that activate inhibitory or excitatory systems vary for each person. Thus, this theory provides a possible explanation for the significant variability of sexual expression across cultures and individuals.

Cynthia Graham, Stephanie Sanders, and Canadian researcher Robin Milhausen (2006) have identified factors in the propensity for sexual inhibition and excitation in women in a sample of over five hundred randomly selected women. Inhibitory factors include a relationship context that does not meet the needs of the woman, the woman's susceptibility to having her sexual arousal disrupted by situational factors, and worries over sexual functioning. Factors for sexual excitation include the ability to become aroused in a variety of situations, partner characteristics and behaviours that enhance arousal, agreeable sexual power dynamics, olfactory factors that enhance arousal, and an agreeable setting. Although sexual inhibition can be useful in certain situations, it can lead to sexual difficulties when an individual desires to become aroused. Indeed, Graham, Sanders, and Milhausen found that inhibitory factors were the strongest predictors for current and lifetime sexual problems in women.

While the dual control model of sexuality is still a relative newcomer on the sexual theory scene, it is a promising attempt to combine biological and psychological factors in a unified theory of sexuality. Researchers and clinicians are beginning to explore the clinical usefulness of the theory in relation to a variety of sexual problems (Bancroft, 2009).

Social Constructionist Theories of Sexuality

Sociological Theory

Sociological theory highlights the importance of social institutions, such as family and religion, in regulating sexuality. Sexuality is linked to societal structures of power, kinship, and ideology, and these structures determine, to a large degree, how sexuality is defined, expressed, and regulated within a certain culture or community. For example, people from Quebec tend to view common-law marriage as a more acceptable institution for regulating sexuality than do individuals from other parts of Canada (see the "Culture and Diversity" box).

Differences in perceptions of sexuality—particularly, of what constitutes acceptable sexual behaviour—tend to be most remarkable between countries that have very different cultural histories. For example, consider how male same-sex sexual behaviour is viewed around the world. In Canada, as you know, individuals' freedom to exhibit same-sex sexual behaviour is protected under the Charter of Rights and Freedoms. However, in Saudi Arabia, male same-sex sexual behaviour is subject to the death penalty, and in Mexico, it is considered acceptable only for the man who is perceived to be "the top" or the "dominant" figure during the sexual act. In Melanesia, on the other hand, same-sex encounters among men are considered an essential developmental phase (Herdt, 1984).

Social Script Theory

Social script theory suggests that there are specific sequences of behaviours, based on societal beliefs and values, that individuals consider to be appropriate for particular

sociological theory A theory that attempts to investigate and explain social phenomena by examining patterns and influences in various social contexts.

social script theory A theory based on the idea that our social interactions tend to follow, or are at least heavily influenced by, predefined, culturally recognizable sequences of behaviours.

Research VS Real Life

It's Evolution: Casual Sex and Sexual Strategies Theory
Contributed by Jocelyn Wentland, Ph.D., University of Ottawa

Sexual strategies theory (SST), as proposed by evolutionary psychologists David Buss and David Schmitt (1993), suggests that the mating behaviours that men and women exhibit are strategic and evolved to solve specific mating problems that our ancestors faced in the evolutionary past. As discussed in the description of the evolutionary theory of sexuality, males generally invest different amounts of time and energy in reproducing than do females. In humans, as is the case with most species, men can have many children with minimal investment, or they can invest in a limited number of offspring that they assume to be theirs. Reproductive costs are higher for women, however, given the energy and time they invest in caring for young offspring; as a result, women need to ensure they have adequate resources available in case they become pregnant.

It follows from these observations that the strategies that men employ when looking for either a short-term mate (a casual sex partner) or a long-term mate (a relationship partner) are quite different from the strategies that women use in these situations. Buss and Schmitt developed SST to explain the differences between men's mating styles and women's mating styles, and to explain how the context will determine which strategy a man or a woman uses. For example, in a population where there is an uneven sex ratio (e.g., in China, where there are more males than females), members of the sex that is underrepresented may be able to engage in their preferred mating strategy.

The use of the word *strategies* is important in relation to this theory because these mating behaviours are goal-directed and aimed at problem solving, although they are not consciously planned or articulated. SST is commonly cited in the evolutionary literature because it takes into account the *context* and *situation* in which males or females may deploy any one specific mating strategy. The 11 specific tenets of SST are listed in Table 2.1.

Now, recall the importance of testing and refining—and sometimes even refuting—theory. Recent research in Canada has put Buss and Schmitt's theory to the test, and the findings challenge tenets five and eight of this theory. Wentland and Reissing

(2011) recruited university-aged male and female participants for a series of focus groups (females only, males only, females and males, and female and male sexuality experts) to discuss how various casual sexual relationships are initiated, maintained, and terminated, including whether the individuals remain in contact after the sexual relationship ends. Participants agreed on specific terms and rules of conduct for four different types of casual sexual interactions: one-night stands, booty calls, fuck buddies, and friends with benefits.

According to SST, one would expect that women view casual sex differently than men do. Yet Wentland and Reissing's study found that both male and female participants in all four groups were able to discuss the various scripts associated with each type of casual sexual relationship. For example, participants readily identified how the various sexual relationships start, how often the individuals spend time with each other, whether or not the individuals engage in sexual activity or sexual activity *and* social activity, how the individuals contact each other (e.g., by texting, through Facebook), and the level of communication that takes place between the individuals in regard to sex and/or other relational issues. The only gender difference that the researchers observed was in the terminology that (some) men used to refer to various sexual relationships. Men in the male-only group mentioned terms like *dick 'em and dump 'em*, *hit it and quit it*, and *use 'em and lose 'em*, whereas these terms were not mentioned by participants in the female-only group or the co-ed groups. In regard to the themes that were identified, there were no gender differences, and both genders identified the specific components that differentiate these casual sexual relationships—namely, frequency of contact, type of contact (sexual and/or social), personal disclosure, discussion of the relationship, and friendship.

According to SST, there are two specific constraints on women's short-term mating: (1) extracting resources immediately from a partner and (2) assessing the potential for short-term mates to become long-term mates. These constraints are interrelated because a mate's ability to provide resources in the short term may indicate that he could also provide resources in the long term and, thus, be a good long-term mate. Thus, SST suggests that women should think of short-term mates as potential long-term mates, and that they should evaluate short-term mates based on the resources these mates provide. However, the purpose of casual sexual relationships is for partners to repeatedly engage in sexual activity without the potential problems that are commonly associated with long-term, committed relationships (Bisson & Levine, 2009; Knight, n.d.). As a result, with the exception of friends with benefits, who may engage in social activities (e.g., go to a movie together) in addition to engaging in sexual activity, casual sexual relationships centre upon engaging in sexual activity. Thus, women may not be assessing their casual sexual partners based on the immediate resources they supply, such as payment for dinner or tangible gifts; rather, they are more likely to assess these partners for their ability to engage in satisfactory sexual activity.

Furthermore, both male *and* female participants in Wentland and Reissing's study stated that they were less inclined to consider dating someone with whom they had repeatedly engaged in casual sexual activity than to consider dating someone with whom they had had a one-night stand. The researchers hypothesize that participants would consider dating a previous one-night stand because they do not know this person very well and, thus, the development of a long-term relationship remains a possibility. Thus, the results of this study provide an interesting perspective on how individuals assess mates both for short-term or long-term mating.

Modern casual sexual relationships may offer both men and women the opportunity to engage in short-term sexual behaviour that has traditionally been associated with male sexual behaviour. Thus, although SST suggests that men and women should use different mating strategies in the context of short-term mating, it appears that casual sexual relationships may be used similarly by both young men and young women. Further research with more participants and non–university-aged participants is underway to determine if expected gendered patterns can be detected in other age groups, especially among slightly older individuals, for whom long-term mate selection may be more important.

TABLE 2.1 Tenets of sexual strategies theory.

1	Men and women pursue short-term mating (STM) and long-term mating (LTM) when reproductive benefits outweigh costs
2	STM must solve different adaptive problems than LTM
3	Men dedicate more time to STM than women do because of asymmetry in parental investment
4	The adaptive problems that men must solve are different from those that women must solve because of differences in reproductive opportunities and constraints
5	There are four reproductive constraints on men for STM: partner number, identifying fertile women, identifying sexually accessible women, and minimizing commitment and investment
6	There are four reproductive constraints on men for LTM: identifying reproductively valuable women, ensuring certainty in paternity (and avoiding being tricked into caring for another male's offspring), identifying women with good parenting skills, and identifying women who are willing and able to commit to LTM
7	Women are constrained by the quantity and quality of external resources they can secure for themselves and their offspring (and by the quality of the genes that their potential mates carry)
8	There are two reproductive constraints on women for STM: extracting resources immediately and assessing prospective long-term mates
9	There are four reproductive constraints on women for LTM: identifying men with the ability and willingness to invest resources in her and her offspring, identifying men with good parenting skills, identifying men willing to commit to LTM, and identifying men who are able and willing to protect her and her offspring
10	Men and women evolved specific psychological mechanisms to solve problems associated with STM and LTM
11	These mechanisms and their associated behaviour manifestations, along with the context, result in the evolved sexual strategies that men and women employ today

Culture & Diversity

I Do—Do You?

Theories can help us understand the differences in how sexuality is expressed across cultures. For example, social constructionist theories teach us that sexuality is regulated in all cultures and that social institutions such as marriage, family, and the law dictate, to a large degree, how sexuality is expressed. Some marriages are the result of romantic attachment, as they often are in Canada, but other marriages result from other factors, such as family arrangements, as is often the case in India, or financial motivations, such as having multiple wives to display wealth and power, as can be seen in numerous African tribes. Yet cultural differences do not arise only between countries on different continents.

In Canada, we observe a striking difference in perceptions of common-law marriage as an alternative to formal marriage, particularly in Quebec as compared to the rest of the country. Across Canada, the trend to live in common-law relationships has increased as social and legal recognition of common-law unions has increased. The laws in each province differ, but generally speaking you are recognized as being in a common-law relationship if you have lived with your partner for two years or more, or if you live with your partner and have dependent children with that partner. Outside of Quebec, a common-law couple has many of the same rights and privileges of a formally married couple, including the right to spousal support. Under the Civil Code of Quebec, however, common-law marriages are considered civil unions

or "de facto unions"; the partners in such a union are allowed to share social benefits such as spousal health care plans, but they are given very few of the legal rights granted to formally married couples.

Yet, according to the 2006 census, common-law unions are more common in Quebec, where 29 per cent of family units are common-law, than they are in the rest of Canada, where 16 per cent of family units are common-law (Statistics Canada, 2007). One reason for the higher tendency to live in common-law relationships in Quebec may be the historical influence of Catholicism. The Catholic Church has traditionally permeated every aspect of Quebec society, wielding significant power and influence over the social, economic, and political lives of Quebecers (Bélanger, 2000a). High marriage and birth rates were part of the traditional way of life sanctioned and promoted by the Church. With the Quiet Revolution (1960–1966) came an increasingly negative view of the Church as standing in the way of change and modernization (Bélanger, 2000b). Values and ideas from the past were questioned, and profound changes took place in Quebec society. As a result, the Church lost most of its power. Today, many Quebecers reject formal (church) marriage in favour of civil unions, and the province has one of the lowest birth rates in the country. For many Quebec couples, rejecting formal marriage is part of living in a new, secularized society and minimizing the power of the Catholic Church.

sexual situations (Gagnon & Simon, 1973). When a sexual encounter occurs between people of the same societal background, the individuals involved can use these scripts to interpret the sexual situation. For example, a typical sexual script suggests that couples will progress from kissing to touching to oral sex and then to sexual intercourse, not necessarily all in one evening, but generally in that order. When both partners follow the sexual script, they generally know what to expect and can be assured that their date and/or relationship is progressing well. However, imagine the disaster that could occur if one of the partners did not following the typical pattern and instead tried to initiate sexual intercourse without having ever tried to kiss her or his partner!

While knowing what to expect can be reassuring, adhering rigidly to limited, conventional sexual scripts can lead to low satisfaction, boredom, and difficulties with arousal and desire, especially in established relationships. Sex therapists often assess existing sexual scripts and work with clients to modify their scripts to provide greater pleasure and satisfaction. For example, Canadian researcher and clinician Sophie Bergeron, from the University of Montreal, has included script modification in her treatment of women who experience vulvodynia, a condition that results in pain with intercourse (Bergeron et al., 2001). Dr Bergeron stresses the importance of de-emphasizing the role that vaginal penetration plays in the typical heterosexual script, and she works with her clients to rewrite their scripts and expand their sexual repertoire. As a result of this treatment, clients can enjoy sexuality—sometimes for the first time in their lives—while working toward decreasing the pain they feel with vaginal penetration.

Feminist Theory

According to most **feminist theories**, sexuality is socially constructed, and what is thought of as "typical" sexual behaviour is determined by a male agenda focussed on male pleasure; vaginal intercourse is assumed to be imposed upon women. There is no uniform feminist theory; rather, there is a shared motivation to examine the inequalities of male–female relationships and their effects on women's sexuality. Focus is placed on studying the experiences of women from their point of view. Feminist researchers agree with other researchers on the importance of contextual and especially relational factors in the sexual experiences of women. This view of sexuality as less focussed on genital responses and more focussed on the entire person and her context has resulted in an alternative view of sexual difficulties in women (see Chapter 16).

> **feminist theory** A theory based on the idea that society has been shaped around the desires of heterosexual males, and that it thus fosters gender inequality.

Leonore Tiefer has proposed "the new view" of women's sexual problems, which recognizes the importance of emotional, physical, and relational factors in influencing a woman's sexual experience (Kaschak & Tiefer, 2001). Tiefer and other feminist researchers and clinicians also warn against the increasing medicalization of sexuality and, more recently, have raised attention to the issue of cosmetic vulvar surgery (see Chapter 4). Some consider this kind of surgery to be Western-styled genital mutilation because the procedure is not medically necessary and can cause numerous complications ranging from scarring to chronic pain and even death (Liao & Creighton, 2007).

How Do Theories Inform Clinical Work with Sexual Problems?

Up to this point, you have seen how various theories can help us study and understand human sexuality. Some are better suited to describing specific phenomena, while others provide more general frameworks. No one theory is better or worse than the others; rather, they all help us appreciate the complexity, richness, and diversity of human sexual expression. In addition, each theory can help researchers and clinicians identify, explain, and treat sexual problems in a clinical setting. Consider the following example: Some men experience ejaculation more quickly than they or their partner(s) desire. In some cases, this issue might result from the man's or his partner's unrealistic expectations. Some men, however, have little or no ejaculatory control and ejaculate very quickly when stimulated; in such cases, the man and/or his partner may feel very distressed about this condition, commonly known as "premature ejaculation" (PE) (see Chapter 16). Seeking help, a man experiencing PE might choose to visit a clinician specializing in men's sexual difficulties. The clinician's approach to this problem would likely depend on the theoretical framework from which she or he is working. Table 2.2 describes how different theoretical orientations might guide a clinician's explanation of the origin of the problem and his or her first-choice intervention.

In reality, clinicians are likely to draw on a variety of theories in order to perform a comprehensive assessment, and they will likely use a range of therapeutic techniques, such as behavioural exercises and psychotherapy, to increase ejaculatory control and latency, decrease performance anxiety, increase focus on pleasure and the ebb and flow of arousal, expand sexual repertoire, and work toward increasing intimacy and communication in the couple. (See the "Ethical Debate" box for another example of how theory can help us understand real-world behaviours.)

TABLE 2.2 How theoretical orientations might guide clinicians' decisions in the treatment of premature ejaculation.

Method	Description	Rationale
Psychodynamic	Passive-aggressive personality; unconscious hostile feelings toward partner	Engaging in psychoanalysis to bring to conscious knowledge source of hostility and resolve conflict
Classical Conditioning	Ejaculation via masturbation associated with fear of discovery (had to be fast to avoid discovery)	Learning techniques to control and/or delay ejaculation
Operant Conditioning	Feels good to have an orgasm even if partner is not happy	Focussing on the pleasure of pleasing partner to reinforce learning techniques to control and/or delay ejaculation
Social Learning	Low sexual self-efficacy prevents man from fully exploring/experiencing his sexuality	Increasing sexual self-efficacy by exploring sexuality in general and expectancies about erectile performance in particular
Cognitive	Attempt to delay orgasm by thinking about things unrelated to arousal, leading to lack of sensory awareness; thoughts that distract attention from controlling ejaculation; performance anxiety	Examining thoughts that interfere with attending to progression of arousal; identifying and addressing cognitive misconceptions and worries about performance
Biological	Genetic predisposition; hypo or hyper function of serotonin receptors; penile hypersensitivity/nerve conduction abnormalities	Prescribing serotonin reuptake inhibitors, tricyclic antidepressants, and/or anesthetic creams
Social Script	Sexual script focussed on vaginal penetration	Expanding sexual repertoire
Feminist	Problem in power relationship between the man and his female partner(s)	Focussing on sexuality beyond intercourse; examining and resolving power issues in the relationship(s)

Ethical Debate

To What Extent Can You Use Theory to Justify Your Own Sexual Choices?

David has been in a relationship with Maria for three years. They met at the end of their undergraduate studies and fell for each other while working on a shared study project. They moved in together one year ago and have started, in the past six months, discussing marriage. David and Maria enjoyed their sexual relationship over the past few years but noted a decrease in the frequency of their sexual encounters.

Two months ago, David was approached by a female colleague to consider a "no-strings attached"

casual sexual relationship. He accepted and has been meeting up with his colleague at lunchtime ever since. He has not told Maria about his sexual affair. He feels a bit guilty about it, but he generally believes that this is a sex-only arrangement and, as such, has nothing to do with his long-term relationship with Maria.

One day, Maria decides to surprise David with an impromptu lunch. When she arrives at his office, she sees David driving off with a woman she does not know. That evening, Maria questions David about his relationship with this woman.

David decides not to lie. Rather, he tries to explain why he entered into the relationship with his colleague and why his actions do not pose a threat to his relationship with Maria. Conveniently, he remembers his undergraduate sexuality class on theories of sexuality and has a choice of explanations. . . .

David starts by explaining that he, as a male mammal, feels the imperative to spread his genes by mating with multiple women. To manage this urge, he used to limit himself to masturbation and pornographic materials, but these outlets proved insufficient over time. He says this is the only time he has been involved with another woman, and it will not keep him from attending to his primary relationship with Maria and investing in their future offspring.

Seeing that Maria is about to attack the male mammal, David decides on another approach. He explains that he grew up in a culture in which a man's occasional sexual indiscretion was silently accepted, as long as the man did not neglect his spouse or his family. This is the way it was in his family, and he is just doing what he learned while growing up.

This second explanation diffuses Maria a little bit because she is a very empathic person and can see how David's early experiences could have influenced his later behaviour. Yet this explanation is not going to help her deal with David's disregard for the impact his infidelity has had on her, and it will not help her regain her trust in him.

Ultimately, David and Maria decide that their relationship is too important to lose over evolutionary imperatives and early-learning experiences, so they consult with a psychologist. With the help of their therapist, they re-evaluate the course of their relationship. They learn that early on in most sexual relationships, the strong physical attraction individuals feel for each other is driven by biological processes, as their brains release a variety of chemicals that facilitate sexual infatuation and arousal. After some months, sometimes years, these feelings of strong sexual drive dissipate and are replaced by increasing feelings of love and commitment. For David and Maria, this shift coincided with moving in together and developing a far more predictable lifestyle. Further, they learn from each other that they have both become bored with their sexual script over the past few years. They also discover that David had become quite anxious about the prospect of getting married, and that his sexual encounters with his colleague might have helped him diffuse some of his anxiety.

As they continue to work with their therapist, David and Maria begin to expand their sexual repertoire. They make sex a priority in their lives, and they make efforts to increase their emotional intimacy and communication. David also begins to explore ways other than using the primary reinforcement of sex to manage his anxiety. In time, he comes to recognize the impact his infidelity has had on Maria, and he shares with her his deep regret for having hurt her. Eventually, Maria's trust in David will likely begin to grow again, and they may be able to advance in their relationship with a greater awareness of their own and each other's needs.

David and Maria's situation is not unusual, and it raises a number of difficult questions. To what extent can we use explanations based in theory to justify our behaviours? What obligations do our partners have to accept such explanations? Is it inevitable that we stray in our relationships, because of our biology and because of what we sometimes see in our families and in media?

CHAPTER SUMMARY

Scientific theory represents a set of conclusions or explanations about certain phenomena; these explanations have been thoroughly tested and represent the state-of-the-art knowledge at a given time. Theories can be tested, refuted, and built upon. In the study of sexuality, they are particularly useful in helping us to communicate about topics that are often considered private, sensitive, and value-laden. Theories also help researchers come up with predictions (develop hypotheses), guide the design of research studies, and are essential in the interpretation of research findings. Some theories of sexuality focus on the biological basis of sexuality, while others focus on psychological factors that affect sexuality, while still others focus on the social construction of sexuality. All have merit, and taken together they do justice to the diversity and complexity of human sexuality.

DEBATE QUESTIONS

What are the benefits of following a typical sexual script? What are the drawbacks?

REVIEW QUESTIONS

1. Which theory explains sexuality best for you? Does it depend on the specific issue?
2. Do different theoretical views cancel one another out, or is there merit in taking all theories into account when examining a phenomenon?
3. According to Freud, what are the six stages of psychosexual development?
4. How can a fetish for leather be explained by classical conditioning?
5. How is sex both a primary reinforcer and an operant?
6. How do evolutionary theories explain gender differences in sexuality?
7. What are the two processes described by the dual control model of sexuality?

SUGGESTIONS FOR FURTHER READING AND VIEWING

Recommended Websites

American Psychological Association, on Sexuality: www.apa.org/topics/sexuality/index.aspx

American Sociological Association, Section on Sexualities: www2.asanet.org/sectionsex

Behavior Online: www.behavior.net

Center for Evolutionary Psychology: www.psych.ucsb.edu/research/cep/primer.html

Rainbow Health Ontario: www.rainbowhealthontario.ca/home.cfm

The Sex Information and Education Council of Canada: www.sieccan.org/index.html

The Society for the Scientific Study of Sexuality: www.sexscience.org

True Nature: A Theory of Human Sexual Evolution (blog): www.humansexualevolution.com

Recommended Reading

Abramson, P.R., & Pinkerton, S.D. (2002). *With pleasure: Thoughts on the nature of human sexuality.* New York, NY: Oxford University Press.

Bancroft, J. (2008). *Human sexuality and its problems* (3rd ed.). Philadelphia, PA: Churchill Livingstone.

Bancroft, J. (Ed.). (2000). *The role of theory in sex research.* Bloomington: Indiana University Press.

Baumeister, R.F. (Ed.). (2001). *Social psychology and human sexuality: Essential readings.* London, England: Psychology Press.

D'Emilio, J. (1998). *Sexual politics, sexual communities: The making of a homosexual minority in the United States, 1940–1970* (2nd ed.). Chicago, IL: University of Chicago Press.

Fisher H. (2004). *Why we love: The nature and chemistry of romantic love.* New York, NY: Henry Holt.

Fisher, H. (1992). *Anatomy of love: A natural history of mating, marriage, and why we stray.* New York, NY: Random House.

Freud, S. (1920). *Three contributions to the theory of sex* (A.A. Brill, Trans.). New York, NY: Nervous and Mental Disease Publish Co. (Original work published 1905). Available at www.gutenberg.org/files/14969/14969-h/14969-h.htm

Gagnon, J.H., & Simon, W. (2005). *Sexual conduct: The social sources of human sexuality* (2nd ed.). New Brunswick, NJ; Aldine Transaction.

Weis, D.L. (Ed.). (1998). *Journal of Sex Research*, 35(1). Available at www.tandfonline.com/toc/hjsr20/35/1

Recommended Viewing

Berg, A.D., & Stacker, A.D. (Writers). (1997). Sexual attraction [Television series episode]. In T. Golden (Producer), *The unexplained.* United States: Towers Production (A&E Network).

Daley, S. (Director). (2000). The nature of sex [Television series episode]. In R Godeanu (Producer), *Nature.* United States: Thirteen/WNET New York.

Miles, C. (Writer & Director). (1997). *Love in the ancient world* [Documentary]. United States: A&E Television Networks.

3

Sex Research Methods

MELISSA A. FARMER

LEARNING OBJECTIVES

In this chapter, you will

- learn about how researchers have studied human sexuality in the past and today;
- discover the strengths and weaknesses of certain research methods and designs;
- find out why psychophysiological approaches are so valuable in studies of human sexuality; and
- see how research into the sexual behaviours of animals can inform our understanding of human sexuality.

Participating in a Sex Research Study

Elle stepped tentatively into the laboratory and was met by a smiling young woman in a white lab coat. Elle nervously smiled back, wiping the sweat from her clammy hands on her jeans. She had seen an ad on her university's website asking for women with a history of childhood sexual abuse to volunteer for a study focussing on female sexuality, and she felt compelled to participate in research that could help other women like herself.

The researcher led Elle into a private, dimly lit room with a large flat-screen television on the wall, a large purple leather recliner facing the television, and a smaller chair set close to the recliner. Once she had settled into the plush leather chair and the researcher had taken a seat in the smaller chair, Elle admitted, "I have never done anything like this before. I have never spoken to anyone about what has happened to me."

The researcher's eyes softened, and she leaned forward to reassure Elle: "You are here of your own free will. If you feel uncomfortable or distressed at any point, you can stop participating immediately. You are calling the shots, okay?"

Elle released the breath she had been holding in and felt her muscles relax. The researcher explained the study procedures in detail, and Elle signed a document verifying that she understood and agreed to participate in the study. Then, the researcher handed Elle a collection of questionnaires that contained questions about her mood, her sexual life, and her traumatic childhood experiences. Elle was surprised by the questions, because she had never thought about her sexuality in such detail before. She had not realized, for example, that she felt only "occasional" but not "frequent" pleasure with sexual activity, and she wondered whether this was normal.

After completing the questionnaires, the researcher showed Elle a small tampon-shaped device with a long cord attached. "This device gives off infrared light and detects your vaginal blood flow based on how much of the light is reflected back from the walls of your vagina," the woman said, handing the device to Elle. "When I leave the room, I will lock the door behind me. I would like you to place the device into your vagina and relax on the recliner. You'll see two movies: the first one will be a documentary on Russian culture, and the second one will be an erotic film that was created by a woman director. I would like you to continuously rate how turned on you feel throughout the second film using the lever beside the recliner. You will always be able to talk to me via intercom if you feel the need to stop, or if you start having intrusive thoughts that make you uncomfortable. None of the information we collect will be associated with you, individually. Do you have any questions?" Elle shook her head. "Let's begin."

QUESTIONS FOR CRITICAL THOUGHT AND REFLECTION

1. How would you feel about participating in a study such as the one described above?
2. If you were Elle, what questions would you have for the researcher?

Introduction

Human sexuality studies can be challenging to conduct for a number of reasons. For one thing, given the highly sensitive nature of the subject matter, researchers may have difficulty *finding* participants who are willing to openly and honestly disclose their thoughts and feelings about their sexual experiences. This problem becomes even more pronounced when the researcher is interested in understanding a population of individuals who have difficulty with sexuality, which is often the case in clinical research. In such cases, the researcher must take many precautions to earn participants' trust. The opening case study illustrates this challenge.

Perhaps even more difficult than finding willing participants is finding interested participants who are representative of the *entire* population that the researchers are interested in studying. In order to find a group that represents a wide range of ethnicities, backgrounds, beliefs, and experiences, researchers must try as much as possible to

random samples Study participants who have been selected at random to accurately represent the population of interest in terms of gender, racial, socioeconomic, behavioural, and/or other characteristics.

questionnaire A set of multiple-choice or short-answer questions that is designed to obtain specific information.

use **random samples**. A related challenge is representing the types of people who are disinclined to volunteer to participate in sexuality research, as there is evidence that individuals who are willing to participate in sexuality research differ in important ways from individuals who are unwilling to participate (Strassberg & Lowe, 1995).

Another challenge is finding a research method that participants will not find intimidating. Many people are comfortable with filling out a **questionnaire** about sexuality, but some might find such a task daunting, especially if the questions ask them to think about negative sexual experiences. Perhaps even more daunting, for some people, is research that involves the use of invasive devices that monitor physiological responses to visual or tactile sexual stimulation. Regardless of the methods involved, it is the responsibility of the researchers to ensure that the participants feel safe in the laboratory setting.

In addition, it may be difficult for the research to remain free of bias. Recall, from Chapter 1, that personal, cultural, religious, and even political ideas about sexuality often influence how sexuality is defined, which questions are asked, and how information is interpreted. Although responsible researchers try to design studies that will not be coloured by personal bias, this is not always possible. Indeed, many forms of bias have, to some extent, coloured all sex research, and biases will undoubtedly continue to shape this research in the future. After all, sex always occurs within a context that is influenced by a complex mixture of forces—interpersonal relationship dynamics, psychological pressures that reflect a person's unique experiences, cultural definitions of what is and is not normal, religious ideas that link sex with moral responsibility, biological

Culture & Diversity

Using Research to Explore Sexuality in Asian Canadians

Given the strong role that culture plays in the expression of sexuality, surprisingly little research has been done to investigate how first- and second-generation immigrants' sexual beliefs are influenced by the sexual mores of both their traditional cultures and the culture of their new home. Lori Brotto, a clinical psychologist at the University of British Columbia, has delved into how this cross-cultural interaction influences sexual attitudes, knowledge of sexuality and sexual health, and sexual function. Based on previous observations of heightened sexual conservatism in Asian Canadians, Brotto queried Asian- and Euro-Canadian men and women in universities and in the Vancouver community about their sexual lives and the extent to which they had adjusted to the Western values held by Canadians—in other words, the extent to which they had acculturated. She discovered that Asian-Canadian women reported less sexual knowledge, more conservative sexual attitudes, more sexual guilt, and poorer sexual function (e.g., lower

desire, arousal, pleasure) than did their European-Canadian peers. Using statistical regression modelling, she determined that more highly acculturated Asian-Canadian females reported less sexual guilt, and that lower levels of sexual guilt in turn had a positive impact on sexual desire (Woo, Brotto, & Gorzalka, 2011). Interestingly, despite the previous reports of poorer sexual function in Asian-Canadian women, vaginal blood flow patterns in these women were comparable to those found in European-Canadian women (Yule, Woo, & Brotto, 2010). Researchers often observe vaginal blood flow patterns as a physiological indicator of sexual arousal; thus, these findings suggest that the psychological attitudes about sexuality do not necessarily inhibit a woman's ability to achieve sexual arousal. This research raises awareness about the complex interaction of culture, sexual beliefs, and sexual functioning in influencing how women experience their sexuality, which has yet to be explored in other ethnic minorities in Canada.

drives, and so on. These forces can have a significant impact on how individuals perceive their own sexuality as well as sex in general (see the "Culture and Diversity" box).

Given these contextual considerations, it is easy to appreciate the difficulty in approaching the study of sexuality from the strictly **positivist** perspective that characterizes modern science (Farmer & Binik, 2005). The reliance on positivist thinking in sex research reflects the desire to understand and measure the personal and social experience of sexuality. One of the earliest and longest-standing attempts of this kind is the challenge to clearly define "normal" versus "abnormal" types of sexual behaviour, an issue we still struggle with today (see the "Ethical Debate" box). The positivist approach to sex research has been criticized for its over-simplification of sexuality to include only measurable, observable physical and behavioural events. The opponents of the positivist approach emphasize the importance of personal experience within the context of sex, as this experience is based on the personal values, religious mores, and cultural influences that give sex its emotional meanings. This view is exemplified by recent controversy about whether variations in female sexual function are "dysfunctional." Scholars argue that contemporary "medicalized" models of female sexuality, which are guided by strict definitions of "normal" sexual function, base expectations of the female sexual response on patterns observed in the male sexual response, despite

positivism The philosophy underlying scientific inquiry that requires that knowledge is based on reproducible experimental verification of natural phenomena, rather than on personal experience.

Ethical Debate

"Normal" Sexuality and Clinical Definitions of Sexual Dysfunction

Sex researchers often consult the ***Diagnostic and Statistical Manual of Mental Disorders*** (*DSM*) when they need to define clinically problematic sexual dysfunctions, including problems with sexual desire and arousal, aversion, pain, erectile disorder, premature ejaculation, and other sexual difficulties that impair intimate sexual relationships and quality of life. In other words, researchers use this manual when they need to define what is *not* "normal" sexuality.

The *DSM* has been revised several times since it was first published in 1952, and over the years it has faced criticism on several points. Most notably, some critics have argued that because the *DSM*'s diagnostic criteria are based on "expert consensus," any ideological biases that the "experts" have will influence how researchers and clinicians understand and diagnose sexual problems. These diagnoses, in turn, impact the biomedical and psychotherapeutic treatments patients receive, and ultimately they affect how patients understand and experience their own sexuality.

Ethically, the impact of these diagnoses on the patient is key, and some critics have even argued that practitioners' reliance on the *DSM*'s diagnoses constitutes a form of medically driven social control. Also troubling is the fact that, despite the *DSM*'s insistence that its diagnoses are based on **empirical** evidence when it is available, results from sex research do not seem to drive many of the *DSM*'s criteria for sexual dysfunction; in the worst cases, some diagnostic criteria are completely unsupported by research findings.

As "experts" continue to revise the definitions presented in new versions of the *DSM*, they, along with every doctor and psychotherapist who uses the *DSM*, must keep in mind the significant impact their definitions and diagnoses can have on patients' lives. At its core, this task hearkens back to the core questions underlying the foundations of sexology: What is normal sexuality? Who decides which sexual attitudes and behaviours are treated as pathological?

Diagnostic and Statistical Manual of Mental Disorders A handbook published by the American Psychiatric Association (APA) that describes and offers standard criteria for diagnosing mental disorders.

empirical Methods that rely on direct observation and experiments, rather than theory alone, to confirm a phenomenon.

the many interpersonal, cultural, and political factors that influence men's experiences of sexuality in a different manner than they influence women's experiences (Moynihan, 2003; Tiefer, 2001).

This chapter highlights many of the advantages of taking a positivist approach to research. At the same time, it also acknowledges the limitations of this approach and explores alternative ways of conducting sexuality research. The following section expands on the brief history of sex research you encountered in Chapter 1. This material is meant to give you a glimpse into how sexuality has been studied in the past. Later in the chapter, you will find detailed descriptions of the various methods that researchers use today, as well as illustrative examples of how each method has been used in actual research studies. The concepts and methods covered in this chapter will provide you with a foundation of knowledge that you can use to critically assess the validity and quality of sexuality research that you encounter in later chapters and in your future studies.

A Historical Overview of Sex Research Methods

Early Texts

Early formal texts on sexuality served instructional, cultural, and religious purposes for those who had the education and wealth to access them. One of the best-known sexual manuals is the Kama Sutra of Vātsyāyana, written in Sanskrit around the second century, which consists of erotic instruction related to courtship, sexual intercourse, a man's interactions with his wife and other women, and tips on improving sexual vitality (Daniélou, 1993).

Early sex manuals, while often considered historical curiosities, in fact preserve detailed descriptions of how sexuality was viewed in past times. For example, a sixteenth-century Arabic text by Sheikh Nefzaoui, *The Perfumed Garden for the Soul's Recreation*, provides the following description of sex:

> The acme of enjoyment, which is produced by the abundance and impetuous ejaculation of the sperm, depends upon one circumstance, and this is, that the vulva is furnished with a suction-pump (orifice of the uterus), which will clasp the virile member, and suck up the sperm with an irresistible force. The member once seized by the orifice, the lover is powerless to retain the sperm, for the orifice will not relax its hold until it has extracted every drop of the sperm, and certainly if the crisis arrives before this gripping of the gland takes place, the pleasure of the ejaculation will not be complete (Burton, 1886/1964, p. 111).

This passage contains references to what was later referred to as the "upsuck theory of orgasm," which suggests that the function of female orgasm may be to "suck up" sperm in order to make fertilization possible. Centuries after this text was written, Masters and Johnson (1966) investigated this theory, but they failed to observe any "sucking up" of sperm. The "clasping" of the cervix likely refers to orgasm-induced cervix contractions, which *have* been observed in experiments (van Netten, Georgiadis, Nieuwenburg, & Kortekaas, 2008). Interestingly, Nefzaoui's account advocates for simultaneous orgasms, as the male's "pleasure" depends on the "gripping of the [female] gland" (Burton, 1886/1964, p. 111).

In Western nations, texts that discussed sexuality were often censored (see Chapter 1), although texts encouraging individuals to *suppress* their sexual desires were generally allowed to circulate. In the Victorian era, for example, there were abundant marriage and love manuals that promoted the suppression of sexual desire and behaviour, except for the purposes of procreation. Examples of such titles that appeared in the United States at this time include John Harvey Kellogg's *Plain Facts for Old and Young* (1877) and Henry Guernsey's *Plain Talks on Avoided Subjects* (1882).

Modern Texts

Texts on sexuality continued to serve primarily instructive purposes until the late nineteenth century. As you learned in Chapter 1, Richard von Krafft-Ebing's *Psychopathia Sexualis* (1886) is often credited as the first text to approach sexuality from a modern scientific perspective. Yet this work was heavily influenced by the social values of the time, and it **pathologized** a number of sexual expressions that were considered to be "abnormal," including same-sex attraction, sexual fetishes, sadism, and masochism.

In contrast, Iwan Bloch's *The Sexual Life of Our Time in Its Relations to Modern Civilization* (1906) took a more objective look at sexuality. Often referred to as "the father of **sexology**," Bloch aimed to describe natural variations in sexual phenomena, like masturbation and same-sex attraction, by describing their occurrence across cultures and in healthy, "normal" individuals. Whereas Krafft-Ebing's work seemed to argue for a clear separation between "normal" and "pathological" sexuality, Bloch's work suggested that all aspects of sexuality lie along a continuum.

The early twentieth century also saw a rise in the publication of sex manuals written by women. Many of these texts—such as Margaret Sanger's *What Every Mother Should Know* (1911)—were designed to educate women about sexuality, and to promote the use of birth control within the context of marriage (Melody & Peterson, 1999). Some of the manuals of this time, such as Marie Stopes's *Married Love* (1918), also contain early feminist critiques of the repressive Victorian models of sexuality.

pathologize The act of identifying a condition as abnormal or indicative of disease.

sexology The scientific study of human sexuality.

interviews Self-report research tools designed to collect data about an individual's experiences and/or perceptions.

Kinsey's Interview-Based Approach

The dawn of analytical, large-scale sex research began with Alfred Kinsey (Figure 3.1). Kinsey began his formal study of human sexual behaviour in 1939 by **interviewing** 62 male and female college students; within a year, he had recruited 733 participants. The questions Kinsey used in these interviews addressed a wide variety of topics, including marriage, sexual education, physical history, nocturnal sex dreams, masturbation, heterosexual experiences, same-sex sexual activity, and sexual contact with animals. Kinsey's plan was to collect data from many subjects who spanned the continuum of every possible sexual interest, and to develop a classification system based on these data. The detailed categories and subgroupings he identified allowed him to compare sexual behaviour between different groups based on sex, age, religious affiliation, marital status, social class, and education. Over the course of 18 years, he and his colleagues Wardell Pomeroy, Paul Gebhard, and Clyde Martin conducted 17,500 interviews (Brecher, 1969).

Kinsey's work gained wide recognition in academic and non-academic circles with the publication of *Sexual Behaviour in the Human Male* (1948) and

FIGURE 3.1 Alfred Kinsey's studies of human sexuality were based on thousands of personal interviews in which he gathered information about the sexual beliefs and behaviours of individuals from a variety of age groups—from teen to elderly—and backgrounds, including prison inmates and sex workers. Originally trained as a zoologist, Kinsey applied the attention to subtle variations in detail that he learned in his early studies of gall wasps to his descriptions of variations in sexuality.

Sexual Behaviour in the Human Female (1953), which were based on interviews of more than ten thousand men and women. Among other achievements, these works challenged the Victorian ideas that women were uninterested in sex. They also normalized same-sex attraction and bisexual fantasies and behaviour, thus contributing to later social movements that supported the recognition and acceptance of same-sex attraction. Perhaps most surprising was Kinsey's success in obtaining detailed and intimate information about interviewees' experiences that did not conform to what was generally perceived to be "normal" sexual behaviour—for example, same-sex sexual behaviour and sexual interactions with animals. Kinsey and his colleagues attributed their success to their interviewing techniques, which normalized a wide variety of sexual behaviours by framing questions with the assumption that every individual had engaged in the entire spectrum of sexual behaviours. The researchers also avoided using slang in their interviews, as such informal language could cast a negative light on sexual activities.

Despite its general success, Kinsey's work has been criticized by some. Major criticisms have focussed on Kinsey's oversampling of white men and women (and thus underrepresenting non-white ethnic groups); his use of **non-random samples**; possible inaccuracies in the reported prevalence of various behaviours and disorders, especially given that some of his data on this topic conflicted with that from other sources; and the emphasis on a person's sexual *behaviour* rather than how the person *experiences* his or her own sexuality. Nevertheless, Kinsey's contribution to the scientific study of sexuality has made an undeniable impact on sexology and society.

non-random samples
Study participants who have not been selected at random and therefore do not accurately represent the population of interest in terms of gender, racial, socioeconomic, behavioural, and/or other characteristics.

FIGURE 3.2 William Masters and Virginia Johnson conducted many groundbreaking studies into the nature of sexual response and the diagnosis and treatment of sexual disorders and dysfunctions from 1957 to the 1990s. Current understandings of "normal" sexual function are often still based on these early studies.

Masters and Johnson's Observational Approach

The first systematic, large-scale study of physiological sexual responses in humans was conducted by William Masters and Virginia Johnson (Figure 3.2) in the late 1950s. Inspired by Alfred Kinsey's work, Masters and Johnson sought to understand human sexuality through direct observation of individuals' sexual responses. To achieve this goal, they used various electronic instruments and filming of procedures (see the "Research vs Real Life" box in Chapter 1).

Although Masters and Johnson are often credited with being the first to use observational techniques to study physiological sexual responses in humans, a number of researchers had used similar methods to monitor such responses long before Masters and Johnson. For example, French researcher Félix Roubaud, who published a detailed description of genital responses to sexual intercourse in 1855, had observed the mechanical interaction between a vagina and a penis, changes in blood flow resulting from sexual excitement, and even behavioural changes before and during orgasm. Another example comes from the work of American doctor Joseph R. Beck, who in 1874 described his direct observations of cervical contractions and blood flow changes during orgasm in a female patient. In addition, cardiovascular activity during sexual intercourse and orgasm was documented by American researchers Ernst P. Boas and Ernst Goldschmidt in 1932. Furthermore, American gynecologist Robert L. Dickinson (1861–1950) was the first to use the technique of inserting an illuminated glass tube into the vagina to observe changes of the vagina and cervix, a technique also used by Masters and Johnson.

In contrast to their predecessors, Masters and Johnson's empirical approach was innovative because it enabled the researchers to *measure* sexual responses. In addition, their observations of 694 men and women during masturbation and sexual intercourse allowed them to speculate about patterns of sexual excitement, plateau, orgasm, and post-orgasmic resolution (see Chapter 4). They published their views on "normal" sexual behaviour in *Human Sexual Response* (1966), and they attempted to characterize abnormal sexual function as a departure from these standards in *Human Sexual Inadequacy* (1970). Although their work was instrumental in characterizing sexual physiology and in developing the first sex therapy program, it was also criticized for oversampling white individuals, focussing on orgasm as the goal and outcome of "normal" sex, pathologizing same-sex sexual behaviour, and overemphasizing the mechanical aspects of intercourse.

Qualitative vs Quantitative Approaches to Research

Recall from the introduction to this chapter, and from Chapter 1, that a person's sexual experiences are influenced by a wide variety of social, psychological, cultural, and even political factors. These psychosocial factors interact with biological systems and physical processes related to sexuality. Thus, contemporary researchers who seek a complete understanding of sex and sexuality must devise methods that can account for a broad array of factors. To meet this goal, researchers generally use a combination of qualitative and quantitative approaches. The value of using **qualitative research methods** is that they are able to account for subjective aspects of sexuality that are difficult to measure—for example, a person's attitudes, beliefs, and emotions about sexuality. The value of using **quantitative research methods**, on the other hand, is that they allow the researcher to objectively identify and measure behaviour and physical processes (erection, vaginal lubrication, etc.) that occur during sexual activity. Quantitative methods can also be very useful in identifying the cause-and-effect relationships between sexual variables, and in classifying certain types of sexual behaviour.

The importance of considering both qualitative and quantitative sexual information is evident in Alfred Kinsey's systematic evaluation of different types of sexual

qualitative research methods Research methods that explore variation in the individual, interpersonal, and/or group understanding of phenomena by using flexible, open-ended questions.

quantitative research methods Research methods that measure and organize naturally occurring variation, often with the aim of identifying causal relationships.

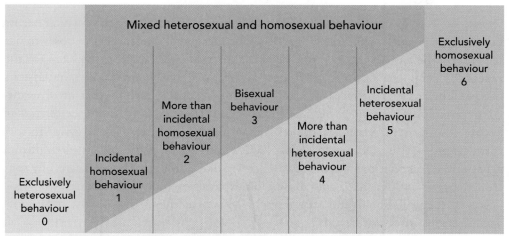

FIGURE 3.3 Kinsey's scale of sexual orientation attempts to describe a person's sexual identity at a given time. A score of 0 indicates that a person is exclusively heterosexual and a score of 6 indicates that a person is exclusively same-sex oriented. Kinsey assigned an additional grade, listed as "X," to those people (males and females) who were asexual.

behaviours based on participant interviews. His initial interviews were designed to *qualitatively* evaluate participants' entire range of sexual behaviours without making judgments about whether individuals should or should not engage in the behaviours; he then used the self-report information he had collected to create measurable categories of sexual behaviours that could be studied *quantitatively* with statistics. For example, he found that many individuals who reported that they were heterosexual also experienced erotic thoughts about or engaged in sexual behaviours with members of their own sex, whereas other individuals who reported that they were same-sex oriented also acknowledged having sexual thoughts about or experiences with members of the other sex. By using qualitative as well as quantitative methods, Kinsey was able to classify his participants along a seven-point scale of sexual orientation (Figure 3.3).

Despite his reliance on interviews in much of his work, Kinsey has been accused of downplaying important qualitative aspects of sexuality by preferring to focus on easily measurable sexual behaviours. Thus, his work also contains examples of the limitations sex researchers face when they neglect qualitative approaches. In his studies of orgasm, for example, Kinsey carefully recorded the occurrence of orgasms, but he did not investigate how the characteristics of orgasms—including the quality of orgasm-related sensations, orgasm intensity, or the subjective experience of orgasms—differed between individuals (Robinson, 1976). As a result, his research did not fully explore all aspects of orgasms. In fact, it was not until 2002 that the characteristics of orgasms were carefully studied, when Kenneth Mah and Irv Binik of McGill University used hundreds of qualitative descriptions from young men and women to develop a two-dimensional model of orgasm (Mah & Binik, 2002).

Although some researchers have viewed qualitative approaches as unnecessary to the research process—perhaps because they consider such approaches to be unempirical, or not applicable to general populations—most sex researchers today recognize that qualitative approaches have an important place in sexuality research. Qualitative approaches can be particularly useful at the beginning of a research project because they can help researchers understand the aspects of sexuality that cannot be captured by general summaries of information—for example, meaning, morality, social norms, religion, ethnicity, socioeconomic influences, sexual orientation, and context.

Sex Research Methods and Designs

Researchers use a variety of methods to study human sexuality, each of which has its own strengths and weaknesses (Table 3.1). The method(s) a researcher chooses to use depend on the type of question she or he wants to answer, which is the basis for the **research design**. For example, if the goal of the research is to *describe* certain patterns of sexual behaviour, the researcher might choose to design a study that involves direct observation, case studies, and/or interviews. If the goal is to study the *correlation* between two or more variables, the researcher might choose to use surveys or to sort through pre-existing records to collect data. Alternatively, if the goal is to confirm a cause-and-effect relationship, the researcher will likely decide to design a carefully controlled *experiment*. The following discussion explores each of these research designs—descriptive, correlational, and experimental—as well as the methods most commonly used in each type of research.

Descriptive Designs

Descriptive research designs are useful when researchers wish to summarize patterns of sexual attitudes and behaviour, and/or generate ideas for future research

research design A researcher's plan for how she or he will collect and analyze data.

descriptive research designs Research designs that allow researchers to summarize patterns of sexual phenomena through observation and self-report.

TABLE 3.1 Strengths and weaknesses of commonly used sex research methods and designs.

Design/Method	Description	Strengths	Weaknesses
Descriptive Design	summarizing patterns in attitudes toward sex and sexual behaviours; generally used in qualitative research, but can also be used in quantitative research	enables researchers to uncover detailed descriptions that reflect the richness of individuals' lived experiences	results are not usually generalizable; cannot be used to prove causation or relationships among variables
Direct Observation	monitoring and recording patterns in sexual and/or relational behaviour; generally used in qualitative research	descriptive; increased ecological validity and accuracy; can provide much contextual information	does not allow the researcher to manipulate or influence behaviours of interest
Interview	collecting detailed self-report data about an individual's experience and/or perceptions of sexuality; generally used in qualitative research	descriptive; provides a detailed account of sexuality; organized around a semi-structured framework	susceptible to memory bias and responder bias, difficult to organize all the information obtained
Case Study	examining a single individual, event, or group of interest in great detail over a period of several months or years; generally used in qualitative research	descriptive; provides a detailed longitudinal account, which can suggest causal relationships	susceptible to interpretation bias; difficult to generalize findings in one individual or group to the rest of the population
Content Analysis	identifying themes of meaning in a text or set of observations; generally used in qualitative research	descriptive; retains meaning and richness of data	difficult to quantify without reducing information from data
Correlational Design	examining two or more variables that change in relation to one another; generally used in quantitative research	enables an evaluation of the relationship between two complex variables	cannot infer causation; may be confounded by related but distinct constructs
Survey	collecting information through standardized or unstandardized questionnaires about sexual beliefs, attitudes, and behaviour; generally used in quantitative research	allows for the collection of large amounts of information; relatively inexpensive to conduct; useful in correlational and statistical analyses; participants can remain anonymous	susceptible to participants' memory bias, responder bias, and influences from demand characteristics; questionnaires may oversimplify sexual constructs
Archival Data-Mining	sorting through pre-existing data or records; generally used in quantitative research	convenient; can reveal much about past conditions in general, or a patient's medical history in specific	prone to inaccuracies when records are incomplete; variables in past records may not be ideal measures of current interests
Experiments	using standardized procedures to evaluate the causal relationship between two variables using randomization; generally used in quantitative research	can make strong inferences about cause and effect; offers control over experimental variables	can be ethically implausible to use in research involving human subjects
Quasi-experiments	using standardized procedures to evaluate correlation between two variables; does not use random assignment; generally used in quantitative research	convenient; can evaluate clinically important patient groups; offers some degree of control over experimental parameters	cannot be used to make strong statements about cause and effect; unknown influence of confounding variables

by documenting aspects of sexuality through observation and participants' self-report. Researchers can use descriptive methods in both qualitative and quantitative approaches, with qualitative descriptive methods relying on open-ended questions to draw detailed descriptions from small samples of individuals, and quantitative descriptive methods summarizing data from large samples. The descriptive methods outlined here are found in qualitative and quantitative research designs.

DIRECT OBSERVATION

The most basic and non-intrusive descriptive method is **direct observation**, which involves monitoring and recording sexual or relational behaviour. This method is most often used in qualitative approaches, as it can take into account a wide variety of contextual factors. Alternatively, it is also used in quantitative approaches to measure the frequency at which certain behavioural variables occur. Masters and Johnson's studies of sexual response were initially based on observational methods, as these methods allowed them to understand the basic principles of physiological sexual arousal and orgasm. When conducting observational studies, researchers generally try to avoid interfering with the phenomena they are observing in order to preserve the **ecological validity** of their findings.

Observational studies can capture readily observable events either in a laboratory setting that is designed to interfere as little as possible with what is being studied, or in a naturalistic, public environment (Figure 3.4). In some cases, a researcher or a trained observer may monitor events as they occur—either in person, or via a real-time digital transmission (e.g., a webcast). In other cases, the researcher may set up audio, video, or digital recording devices to capture the events for review at a later time; this approach has the benefit of reducing the observer's **memory bias**. Because human behaviours are not always predictable, observation studies must be carefully planned so that the period of observation coincides with times at which the behaviour(s) of interest will most likely occur.

The advantages of direct observation are evident from John Gottman's work on couple communication in the prediction of divorce. Using video recordings, Gottman monitored conversations between mixed-sex and same-sex couples at his laboratory. He found that participants' expressions of positive or negative emotion during a 15-minute couple conversation about marital conflict could predict marital outcome years later (Carrère & Gottman, 1999).

Of course, direct observation also has clear limitations for sex research, given that most sexual activity occurs in private settings. An additional limitation is the fact that subjects may not behave naturally if they are aware that they are being observed. Furthermore, the observer must carefully guard against his or her own **interpretation bias**; to avoid this bias, researchers must carefully **operationalize** all behaviours.

INTERVIEW

Interviews can provide detailed self-report data about individuals' experiences of sexuality, sexual histories, and attitudes that shape expectations

direct observation Observing and recording patterns in behaviour, either in a natural setting or in a laboratory.

ecological validity The extent to which the behaviours that are observed in a research setting are representative of what actually happens in the real world.

memory bias A bias that results from cognitive processes that interfere with the way in which a person remembers an event.

interpretation bias A bias that results from the fact that different people interpret behaviours and situations in different ways, based on their personal experiences, opinions, beliefs, and so on.

operationalize To clearly define a concept so that different people will understand it in the same way.

FIGURE 3.4 Observational studies conducted in public settings can allow researchers to observe how people interact with one another in a natural setting, such as a city park, yet they do not allow researchers to have any control over when they might observe the behaviour(s) they are interested in studying.

about sex and relationships. When interpreting an interview, an interviewer may consider observations and visual cues, including the individual's level of comfort in discussing his or her sexual history, current mood, and reactions that suggest additional open-ended questioning is needed. A major benefit of using interviews is that they generate a great amount of data; indeed, as you have seen, Alfred Kinsey's intricate characterization of sexual behaviour was largely based on data he collected through interviews.

Interviews also have a place in clinical settings, where researchers and clinicians can administer structured interviews to help formulate a subclinical or psychiatric diagnosis that plays a prominent role in the participant's experience of sexuality. The screening procedures for **sexual psychophysiology** research (see below), for example, typically include a clinical interview to determine the presence of sexual dysfunction; the questions in such an interview are generally based on criteria outlined in the most recent edition of the *Diagnostic and Statistical Manual of Mental Disorders*.

The main weakness of the interview technique is that, as with all self-report techniques of data collection, it is susceptible to memory bias—on the part of the researcher as well as on the part of the participant—as well as **responder bias**. Often, responder bias creeps in when participants feel that they need to respond to sexual questions in a manner they deem to be socially acceptable (Paulhus, 2002).

CASE STUDY

A **case study** is an in-depth, descriptive, **longitudinal** examination of a single individual, event, or group of interest using interviews, observations, questionnaires, and/or information from experiments (see below). In sexuality research, a case study typically refers to the analysis of an individual within a sexual context, with the researcher collecting detailed information about the individual's sexual development and history, recent or current sexual experiences, sexual relationships, sexual function, and previous treatments. A case study may illustrate a common sexual experience, or it may offer insight into a poorly understood aspect of sexuality that would be unethical to study with experiments. In either case, such studies can uncover a vast amount of qualitative and quantitative information.

A drawback to the case study approach is that the analysis of case study data is susceptible to interpretation bias. The case study of Anna O., presented in Sigmund Freud and Josef Breuer's *Studies on Hysteria* (1895), is a classic example of how a certain type of interpretation bias—**theoretical bias**—can limit the objective interpretation of an individual's behaviour. In the case of Anna O., the researchers inferred a causal relationship between childhood sexual abuse and hysteria because they were—consciously or subconsciously—*looking* for a connection to support their theoretical approach. Other factors that limit the usefulness of case studies are their poor **generalizability** and their lack of a control group or experimental design, which prevents the researcher from being able to draw any conclusions about cause-and-effect relationships.

CONTENT ANALYSIS

Content analysis, a common component of descriptive studies, allows researchers to systematically sort through the information they collect from their research in the form of observational notes, transcripts of interviews or **focus group** sessions (Figure 3.5), participants' personal narratives, audio recordings, and/or video recordings. Content analysis can be used qualitatively, to uncover patterns or themes that naturally emerge from the research, and to develop new ways of describing certain phenomena. It can also be used quantitatively, to sort data into predetermined categories, although much of the richness of the original descriptions can be lost in such an approach.

sexual psychophysiology The study of physiological sexual processes that underlie psychological sexual responses.

responder bias The tendency for a participant to answer questions in a way she or he believes the researcher expects.

case study An in-depth study of an individual or a group.

longitudinal studies Studies that examine psychological and/or behavioural information in a single individual or group over a long period of time (usually months to years).

theoretical bias A bias that can result from an individual's strict adherence to a specific theoretical approach.

generalizability The extent to which the conclusions drawn from particular findings in a sample population can be extended to principles that are present in the population at large.

content analysis A method of data analysis by which a researcher identifies patterns or themes of meaning in a transcript or across observations, and often relates these patterns or themes to predetermined theories.

focus group A small group of demographically diverse individuals who participate in a guided discussion to help the researcher better understand a certain belief, behaviour, or phenomenon.

FIGURE 3.5 A focus group can bring together individuals who exhibit a range of attitudes and opinions about sexuality, sexual experience, or sexual problems. In a focus group session, a moderator asks questions that will elicit a wide range of responses, with the aim of understanding a topic from as many perspectives as possible.

An example of qualitative content analysis comes from the work of Cindy Graham and her colleagues at the Kinsey Institute, who wanted to identify factors that can increase or decrease the level of a woman's sexual arousal. They began by holding focus groups, after which they used content analysis to draw meaning from the sessions' transcripts. Based on the transcripts, the researchers noted that the participants judged how sexually aroused they felt based on certain physical cues, including genital "tingling, warmth, fullness, swelling, and lubrication." The researchers also noted that the participants described how certain thoughts or emotions could prevent them from feeling sexually aroused. In the words of one woman, "It's not as easy to feel aroused when I'm not feeling good about myself and my body." The researchers then used the information they had gathered from the transcripts to develop new theoretical views of sexual arousal (Bancroft, Graham, Janssen, & Sanders, 2009; Graham, Sanders, Milhausen, & McBride, 2004).

Correlational Designs

correlational research designs Research designs that allow researchers to study how two or more variables co-vary, or change, in relation to one another.

Correlational research designs allow researchers to study how multiple variables change in relation to one another. The primary limitation of correlational designs is evident in the scientific mantra *correlation does not imply causation*. Correlational research can uncover strong positive or negative relationships between two or more variables, but it cannot indicate which variable causes changes in the other, or whether there is a third, unknown variable that causes both variables to vary in a seemingly related pattern. For instance, a negative correlation between genital sensitivity and number of past sexual partners may suggest that individuals who have had many sexual partners have lower genital sensation than do individuals who have had few sexual partners. Yet this correlation can easily be explained by a third variable: age. Indeed, loss of genital sensitivity is a natural consequence of aging, and older individuals, as compared to younger individuals, are also likely to report higher numbers of sexual partners because they have had more years of sexual opportunities. Given this difficulty in inferring clear causal relationships, correlational designs are often seen as exploratory efforts that generate ideas for experimental studies.

SURVEY

survey method A research method in which participants are asked to respond to questionnaires.

Researchers often use the **survey method** to collect data for correlational studies. This method requires that participants complete **standardized** or **unstandardized questionnaires** that contain questions about sexual beliefs, attitudes, and behaviour. Sexuality questionnaires are designed to tap into highly specific sexual constructs, such as sexual self-efficacy, sexual desire, or sexual guilt. When recruiting participants for a survey, researchers must be careful to avoid over-sampling from any one group, as over-sampling could bias the results. Thus, they try to select participants at random from a group that is large enough to include individuals with a wide variety of demographic characteristics, to improve the generalizability of the survey data.

standardized questionnaire A research tool consisting of a fixed set of questions and corresponding response options.

unstandardized questionnaire A research tool consisting of a fixed set of questions, with room for individualized responses.

An example of a survey that produced highly generalizable results is the National Health and Social Life Survey (NHSLS), which explored the prevalence of different types of sexual difficulties among individuals aged 18 to 59. In total, the researchers involved in the study sampled 1749 women and 1410 men at random from across the United States. The study identified a variety of sexual problems in women under the age of 30: 32 per cent reported a lack of interest in sex, 26 per cent reported an inability to achieve orgasm, and 21 per cent reported pain during sexual intercourse. It also unearthed sexual problems faced by men under the age of 30: 14 per cent reported a lack of interest in sex, 7 per cent reported orgasm difficulties, 30 per cent reported that they reach orgasm "too early," and 7 per cent reported that they had difficulty getting erections (Laumann, Paik, & Rosen, 1999). Information from this broad survey has helped to shape researchers' understanding of how common different sexual problems are.

The validity and reliability of survey data depend on how well the survey questions are worded. Ideally, questions should be stated in a clear, simple sentence, and consistent wording should be used throughout the questionnaire. Confusing terms must be explicitly defined (e.g., "*Sexual intercourse* includes any of the following activities: oral sex, penile-vaginal intercourse, and penile-anal penetration."). In addition, the questions should be followed by a set of clearly worded multiple-choice responses, rather than open-ended responses. Clear wording and ample definitions are particularly important when the concepts in question overlap, as is the case with such concepts as *sexual desire* and *arousal*, particularly in newer models of sexual response (Basson, 2000).

Survey research offers a number of advantages. One is that it allows researchers to set up the study to allow participants to retain a sense of anonymity, which often helps participants feel free to give honest answers about even the most sensitive of sexual topics. Indeed, research has shown that women are more likely to report a higher prevalence of sexual arousal problems and genital pain when responding to self-report questionnaires than when responding to in-person interviews (Hayes, Bennett, Dennerstein, Taffe, & Fairley, 2008). Another advantage is that surveys are very cost-effective to conduct, especially when they are presented online. Finally, surveys can gather a large amount of data on a great number of topics very quickly.

Yet there are also drawbacks to this method. As with all self-report methods of data collection, the survey method is susceptible to participants' memory bias as well as responder bias, although these biases can be mitigated to some degree if participants feel that they will remain anonymous. Surveys are also susceptible to participants' responses being influenced by **demand characteristics**.

ARCHIVAL DATA-MINING

Archival data-mining offers a window into the past, and this method can be a rich source of correlational information. Archival analysis can incorporate quantitative information (e.g., age of first diagnosis, presence of positive cultures from genital exams, number of previous sexual partners) as well as qualitative information (e.g., descriptions of interventions as "biomedical" or "behavioural" treatments), with the aim of uncovering trends in data across time, evaluating relationships between sexual health and demographic variables, and assessing the possible outcomes of a given treatment.

Recently, researchers have retrospectively analyzed Statistics Canada data to reveal longitudinal patterns in the sexual behaviour of Canadian teenagers. Their analysis revealed that the percentage of Canadian teens between the ages of 15 and 19 who had engaged in sexual intercourse was lower in 2005 than it had been in 1996/1997, in all provinces except Newfoundland and Labrador, Nova Scotia, and Manitoba

demand characteristics
Experimental cues that indicate the type of behaviour or responding that the researcher expects.

archival data-mining
Sorting through pre-existing data or records to uncover new insights into past phenomena.

experimental research designs Research designs that use standardized procedures and randomization to evaluate the causal relationship between two variables.

confounding variables Psychological, behavioural, and/or biological variables that change along with the manipulated experimental variable, thereby affecting a researcher's ability to discern a true cause-and-effect relationship between two variables.

random assignment The process of dividing research participants into different treatment or experimental groups, so that each participant has an equal chance of being placed in any group.

quasi-experimental research designs Research designs that use standardized experiment-like procedures but that do not use random assignment and provide researchers with only a limited ability to manipulate independent variables.

independent variables The variables that are being manipulated in an experiment.

dependent variables The variables that are being measured in an experiment.

delayed control-group design A research design that includes groups receiving the same treatment, tested at different points in time to better understand the time course of the treatment effects.

(Rotermann, 2008). This analysis of existing data provided new information about longitudinal patterns in teenage sexual behaviour.

The major benefits of archival analysis include its cost-effectiveness and its lack of interference with how the data were collected. Yet it also has notable drawbacks, as records may be incomplete or inconsistent, and these records can only reveal information about past occurrences of sexuality-related variables.

Experimental and Quasi-experimental Designs

Experimental research designs allow researchers to manipulate an experimental variable, carefully control for potential **confounding variables**, and use standardized procedures that expose each subject to the same experimental conditions. Thus, they are capable of leading to strong evidence of cause-and-effect relationships. "True" experiments are defined by the use of **random assignment** of subjects to experimental and control groups and/or treatments, which allows a researcher to make claims about causality. However, given that random assignment is impractical, unethical, and/or impossible in most sex research involving humans, the use of experimental design is rare in human sexuality research. At the same time, it *is* frequently used in research into the sexual behaviour of animals, and such research can help us understand certain aspects of our own sexuality, as will be discussed later in the chapter.

Given the difficulties associated with conducting true experiments involving humans, many sex researchers have turned to **quasi-experimental research designs** in their studies. As you might expect, there is a major drawback to using such methods—by definition, quasi-experimental studies do not use random assignment, and therefore researchers cannot be certain whether confounding variables are affecting **independent** and/or **dependent variables** in a way that distorts the results of the research.

Quasi-experiments are frequently used to study many pre-existing subject characteristics, such as sex, age, behavioural history, and the presence of clinically meaningful sexual dysfunction. In such studies, researchers identify naturally occurring groups of interest within a population and assign individuals to either an experimental group or a non-randomly selected control group. Members of control groups can be selected based on how well their characteristics (e.g., age, romantic involvement, level of depression) match those seen in the experimental group, to reduce the confounding effect of these characteristics.

The quasi-experimental control group design is a common feature of sex research on interventions and therapies. This design includes experimental and control groups, with various pre- and post-testing schedules based on the research question. A majority of clinical sexuality studies rely on this type of design because clinical researchers are interested in identifying and studying populations with pre-existing demographic and/or sexual characteristics. Cindy Meston used an interesting variation on this design, called the **delayed control-group design**, to investigate whether physical activity that increases activation of the central nervous system, such as exercise, can enhance sexual arousal in women (Meston & Gorzalka, 1995). In her study, she compared three groups of healthy women, each of whom participated in two counterbalanced testing sessions. In the first session, which did not involve physical exercise, the participants viewed erotic films while an electronic device detected their vaginal blood flow (a proxy for sexual arousal). This session was the same for all three groups. In the second session, participants began by exercising for 20 minutes, and then they viewed another erotic film. In this second session, Meston measured vaginal blood flow at 5 minutes post-exercise in one group, 10 minutes post-exercise in another group, and 15 minutes post-exercise in the third group, to determine the interaction between increased activity in the central nervous system and genital arousal. She found that exercise enhanced genital blood flow yet had no impact on how "turned on" the women felt.

One drawback of using either experimental or quasi-experimental research designs is the potential for demand characteristics to interfere with participants' behaviour. For example, in one study where subjects were asked to rate the intensity of erotic stimuli, individuals fitted with electronic monitoring devices rated the same stimuli as more erotic than did their peers who were not equipped with the devices (Amoroso, Brown, Pruesse, Ware, & Pilkey, 1970). The authors suggested that the process of applying the monitoring devices created the expectancy that the subjects would get sexually aroused.

Psychophysiological Approaches to Research

Psychophysiological approaches are very popular in contemporary sex research because they allow researchers to relate an individual's subjective experience of feeling "turned on" to a measurable physiological response. In a typical psychophysiological research project, participants are equipped with devices that monitor physiological or neurological changes associated with a sexual response; they are then presented with experimentally manipulated sexual stimuli (e.g., an erotic film or image, or sensual music). The idea behind this approach is that the stimuli will elicit a psychological response, and that the physiological and neurological responses that are unique to this psychological response can then be monitored and recorded as objective indications of the psychological response. Traditionally, psychophysiological researchers have examined genital responses as physiological measures of sexual arousal, although more recently they have turned to examining brain activity for this purpose.

Measures of Genital Response

In its current state, sexual psychophysiology and its methods are closely linked to the sexual response cycle outlined by Masters and Johnson. Recall, from Chapter 1, that this cycle describes the "typical" stages of sexual stimulation as excitement, plateau, orgasm, and resolution. Masters and Johnson observed that sexual arousal is associated with increased genital blood flow in both men and women. As a result of this observation, researchers who want to gauge sexual arousal generally use methods that directly or indirectly measure the physiological process of genital **vasocongestion** and its effects (Table 3.2). In women, vaginal blood flow and genital temperature are the primary physiological indices of sexual arousal; in men, penile tumescence (swelling) and genital temperature indicate arousal. These proxy measures of sexual arousal are reproducible in the laboratory, and they are assumed to be valid measures of sexual arousal because other types of positive and negative states of non-sexual arousal (e.g., positive mood, good humour, fear) are not associated with these genital responses.

Devices that measure female sexual arousal are designed to capture signs of the increased blood flow that makes the vagina and vulva swell as a woman becomes aroused. One of the most widely used methods is **vaginal photoplethysmography**, which involves the use of an acrylic tampon-shaped device that fits comfortably into the vagina. This device emits infrared light that hits the walls of the vagina and is then reflected back to a photosensitive detector in the device to produce a signal called the **vaginal pulse amplitude (VPA)**. In theory, the amount of light that gets reflected back to the detector provides a measure of the woman's arousal, as a greater amount of light is thought to be reflected when the vaginal capillaries are filled with more blood during sexual arousal than when they contain less blood during a non-sexually aroused state. Despite these assumptions, the causal relationship between vasocongestion and

vasocongestion The increased vascular blood flow in the genitals during sexual arousal, which results in swelling of the vagina and vulva in women and erection in men.

vaginal photoplethysmography A physiological method used to indirectly measure vaginal blood flow associated with female sexual arousal.

vaginal pulse amplitude (VPA) A measure of short-term changes in vaginal blood flow, generally with each heartbeat.

TABLE 3.2 Strengths and weaknesses of sexual psychophysiology measures commonly used to study the physiological changes associated with sexual arousal.

Method	Description	Rationale	Strengths	Weaknesses
Females				
Vaginal Photoplethysmography	A tampon-shaped plastic probe surrounding a device that emits and recognizes infrared light; the device is inserted into the vagina	The amount of light reflected back from the vaginal wall to the device provides an indirect measure of genital blood flow	Takes only seconds to show changes in blood flow; comfortable; can be inserted in private; data are uniquely associated with sexual arousal	Can be biased by body movements; there is no typical "baseline" blood flow; individuals can vary in baseline blood flow between testing sessions
Labial Thermistor	A sensor that provides a measure of surface temperature; the device is attached to the labia skin with a metal clip	The surface temperature of the labia reflects changes in blood flow associated with sexual arousal	Measures of temperature are reproducible over different testing sessions; temperature correlates with self-reports of sexual arousal; can be used during menstruation	Takes minutes to show changes in temperature; long time to return to baseline temperature after arousal; labial temperature may be affected by room temperature
Males and Females				
Thermography	A heat-sensing camera takes thermal images of genitals	The surface temperature of the genitals reflects changes in blood flow	Temperature can be compared among participants with high accuracy; equipment does not touch subject; can be used in females and males	Expensive equipment; takes minutes to show changes in temperature; cannot evaluate rapid changes in sexual arousal
Doppler Ultrasonography	A transducer emits sound waves that interact with tissue and blood, and the sound waves are "bounced back" to the transducer	The movement of blood in and around the clitoris or penis changes the frequency of the sound waves that are detected by the device	Immediate information about properties of genital blood flow; provides information about anatomy (clitoris or penis); can be used in females and males	Differences in placement or in level of experience of tester may affect data; drugs that increase blood flow may be needed to see the greatest changes; does not correlate with self-report of sexual arousal in women
Laser Doppler Imaging	A low power, infra-red laser beam images blood perfusion to a depth of about 2–3 mm over a skin surface	Moving blood in the microvasculature causes a Doppler frequency shift of the scattered laser light, which is photodetected and processed into a colour-coded map of blood flow	Non contact; direct measure of blood flow; a colour photograph is also taken to improve identification of structures in the blood flow map	Can be biased by body movements; takes minutes to show change in blood flow; measurement can be affected by presence of thick pubic hair

TABLE 3.2 Continued

Method	Description	Rationale	Strengths	Weaknesses
Males				
Penile Volume Plethysmography	The penis is inserted into a container; as penis volume increases, the amount of "free" space in the container reduces	As arousal-related blood flow increases, the penis increases in size	Reliable; accounts for arousal-related changes in penile length and girth	Containers are bulky and awkward; does not provide information about firmness of erection
Penile Strain Gauge	A ring is placed around the penis shaft; the ring expands as penis volume increases	As blood flow increases, the penis circumference increases	Reliable; many commercially available types accommodate different penis sizes and shapes	Does not provide information about firmness of an erection; movement and body position may affect measurements
Penile Photoplethysmography	A device that emits and detects light is mounted on the penis above the dorsal artery	Light reflected back from the penile dorsal artery to the device provides an indirect measure of genital blood flow	Changes are measurable seconds after penis circumference changes	Onset of erection may be associated with short periods of reduced blood flow

the amount of light that gets reflected has yet to be conclusively proven, and some researchers have suggested that other physiological factors may affect the amount of reflected light. Nonetheless, this method has been used widely to assess arousal in healthy women as well as women with various sexual problems, including difficulties with desire, arousal, orgasm, and genital pain. Interestingly, increases in VPA do not always correlate with self-reported "subjective" sexual arousal (Chivers, Seto, Lalumière, Laan, & Grimbos, 2010), suggesting that this physiological measure of arousal does not reliably reflect the emotional and psychological experience of arousal. An additional difficulty with this measure is that there is no "baseline" for vaginal blood flow against which increases can be compared, given that the "typical" rates of blood flow vary between individuals and across even short periods of time.

In efforts to improve upon the limitations of vaginal photoplethysmography, researchers have used other direct and indirect measures of vaginal vasocongestion to measure female sexual arousal. Theoretically, methods based on more direct measures of blood flow, like **Doppler ultrasonography**, should provide superior measures of female sexual arousal. Ultrasound methods have shown, for example, that penile insertion into the vagina indirectly stimulates the anatomical structures associated with the clitoris, suggesting that the physiological processes underlying vaginal and clitoral orgasm may be very similar (Buisson, Foldes, Jannini, & Mimoun, 2010). In healthy women, however, clitoral Doppler ultrasound was unable to show a correlation between increased clitoral blood flow and self-reported sexual arousal (Kukkonen et al., 2006).

Other methods for measuring female sexual arousal, including the **labial thermistor** and **thermography**, evaluate external genital temperature changes. An advantage to using temperature-based measures is that the baseline body temperature—around 37 degrees Celsius in humans—may be used to detect absolute changes in temperature.

Doppler ultrasonography A physiological method used to measure female and male sexual arousal by detecting properties of blood flow in genital tissue.

labial thermistor A physiological method used to measure female sexual arousal by recording the surface temperature of labia skin.

thermography In sex research, a physiological method used to measure female and male sexual arousal by using a heat-sensing camera to record the temperature of genital skin.

Thus, temperature-based methods are thought to be more appropriate than internal blood flow–based methods for arousal comparisons between subjects. The primary disadvantage of these methods, however, is that body temperature changes very slowly—over several minutes, rather than the seconds it takes for VPA to show change—when an individual becomes sexually aroused. In addition, similar to the problem of relying on VPA, it is unclear how closely the temperature changes in the external genitals reflect vaginal vasocongestion.

The measurement of male sexual arousal has focussed on changes in penile circumference associated with erection, which is an indirect measure of vascular blood flow in the penis. Studies have revealed that increases in penile circumference correlate with a man's subjective report that he feels sexually aroused. Thus, devices that measure changes in penile circumference have been used to understand the effect of cognitive beliefs on sexual arousal. For example, one study found that listening to stories about a man using a condom during a sexual encounter did not affect the increase in penile circumference, suggesting that the idea of condom use likely does not reduce male sexual arousal (Gaither, Rosenkranz, Amato-Henderson, Plaud, & Bigwood, 1996). The most common and reliable method for testing erection-associated increases in penile circumference is the **penile strain gauge**. In fact, other measures of male sexual arousal are often validated by comparing them with the penile strain gauge. When researchers are interested in comparing physiological responses in males *and* females, they may prefer to use a method that can be used on both sexes, such as thermography, because use of the same measure of arousal increases the researcher's confidence that the same physiological processes are being compared between the sexes.

Although the classic sexual response cycle described by Masters and Johnson has historically provided the benchmark for the validity of sexual psychophysiology studies, much controversy surrounds the validity of this model. There is general agreement that an erection indicates a sexually aroused state in a man, yet the validity and precision of similar indices in women have been seriously questioned. Can vaginal blood flow really be unique to sexual arousal, given that simple physical exercise also increases vaginal blood flow (Meston & Gorzalka, 1995)? Could such a measure be confounded by an individual's previous sexual history of arousal without orgasmic release, as shown in Masters and Johnson's (1966) study of female sex workers with persistent pelvic vasocongestion?

One of the most significant methodological criticisms of vaginal blood flow- and tumescence-based measures of physiological sexual arousal is that analyses of these measures must be restricted to within-subject comparisons, such as per cent change, because individuals vary widely in the magnitude of their responses. Anatomical differences, such as penile circumference, prevents any between-subject comparisons of tumescence; similarly, anatomical and circulation differences may yield very distinct ranges of vaginal blood flow between women. For these reasons, measures such as thermography and genital thermistors are increasingly preferred by researchers because temperature provides an absolute scale of measurement that can be compared among participants (Woodard & Diamond, 2009).

Quantitative Sensory Testing

Researchers can also use psychophysiological methods to evaluate how individuals discriminate between different types of sensory stimulation that may influence the body's ability to become aroused. **Quantitative sensory testing** requires that an individual make simple perceptual judgments on whether a stimulus is detectable, whether the stimulus is more or less intense than a previous sensation, and in some cases whether the stimulus is painful. Genital sensory testing provides information about how the body

penile strain gauge A physiological method used to assess male sexual arousal by measuring increases in penile circumference.

quantitative sensory testing A standardized assessment of how an individual perceives distinct sensations caused by the placement of various stimuli (e.g., pressure, temperature) onto the skin's surface.

processes sensations at rest and during a sexually aroused state, which can vary based on the type of stimulus (e.g., pressure, heat, vibration, or electrical shock) and the characteristics of the examined skin (e.g., genital or non-genital). In sensory testing, non-genital "control" sites are often used to determine whether sensation differences are unique to genital tissue. Notably, the perception of sensation can be influenced by psychological factors that also influence sexuality, including attention, distraction, and mood.

Quantitative sensory testing must account for natural differences in skin sensitivity, which can vary greatly based on where the skin is located. The skin on the palm of the hand, for example, is far more sensitive than the tissue inside the mouth. Similarly, genital skin differs from other types of skin in important ways. The genital organs (e.g., the penis, the vulva, the vagina) and non-genital erogenous zones (e.g., the breasts, the upper thighs) consist of skin and muscle tissue, as well as visceral (organ) tissue. Figure 3.6 shows the theoretical relationship between mechanical (pressure) force and genital touch sensitivity, which indicates the amount of force needed to first detect the presence of light pressure. Sexual arousal appears to have opposite effects on genital touch sensitivity in males and females; in males, more force is required to detect non-painful pressure on the penis after sexual arousal compared to the baseline state, whereas less force is needed to detect light pressure on the vulva after sexual arousal in women (Payne et al., 2007; Payne, Thaler, Kukkonen, Carrier, & Binik, 2007).

Perhaps the most clinically useful applications of quantitative sensory testing deal with the assessment of different types of sexual problems. For example, researchers have used quantitative sensory testing methods to study abnormal sensations associated with Genito-Pelvic Pain/Penetration Disorder, formerly called the "sexual pain disorders" (i.e., dyspareunia and **vaginismus**). The importance of genital sensory testing has been demonstrated by a Canadian group consisting of Irv Binik, Caroline Pukall, and colleagues; this group has generated the majority of data describing sensory abnormalities in men and women with genital pain. These researchers have found that women with the most common type of dyspareunia (provoked vestibulodynia, previously known as vulvar vestibulitis) have increased genital and non-genital touch and pain sensitivity (Pukall, Binik, Khalifé, Amsel, & Abbott, 2002). Similar observations have been made in men with chronic prostatitis pain (Davis, Maykut, Binik, Amsel, & Carrier, 2011). These studies have established that, in individuals with sexual pain disorders, there are measurable physiological changes in how an individual's body transmits pain signals, and these changes may interact with psychological variables such as sexual aversion, anxiety, depression, and lack of sexual desire.

vaginismus A condition in which vaginal penetration is difficult or impossible due to marked fear and/ or tightening of the pelvic floor muscles.

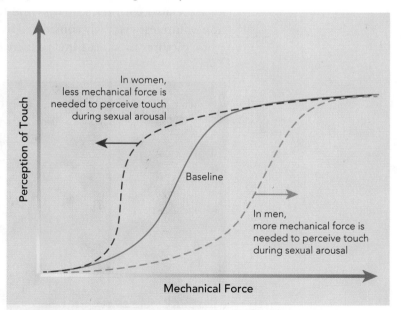

FIGURE 3.6 Sexual arousal can change how sensory stimulation is perceived in both men and women. In the baseline (pre-aroused) state, increasing mechanical force initiates an increasing perception of touch on the genitals. When women are sexually aroused, less force against the vulva is needed to evoke the perception of touch, indicating that sexual arousal enhances a woman's ability to feel genital touch. In contrast, when men are aroused, more force must be applied to the penile shaft before touch is perceived, and this indicates that sexual arousal reduces the ability for males to perceive genital touch.

Brain Imaging Methods

Until recently, the field of sexual psychophysiology had focussed on physiological changes in the pelvis, such as changes in genital blood flow and temperature. For years, researchers have been aware of the impact of psychological responses on sexual arousal in men and women, but it has been only in the past twenty years that they have had access to technologies that can help them to reliably study these responses. Brain imaging technologies have begun to unravel the brain activity related to sexual function and dysfunction, although these technologies are still limited in the type of information they can provide. Functional magnetic resonance imaging (fMRI), which indirectly detects changes in blood flow associated with brain regional neural activity, is the most common technique used to assess cognitive, emotional, and sensory processes associated with sexual arousal, orgasm, genital pain, and even romantic love (Ortigue, Bianchi-Demicheli, Patel, Frum, & Lewis, 2010; Woodard & Diamond, 2009; Figure 3.7).

As with the previously described psychophysiological measures, fMRI methods are used to correlate a stimulus with a neural response. When conducting fMRI-based studies, researchers design their studies based on their knowledge of cognitive psychology and perception. Stimulus presentation patterns in fMRI studies may reflect **block designs**, such as multiple non-successive depictions of erotic images for fixed periods of time (usually lasting for several seconds or more) separated by periods with no visual image presented. Alternatively, they may reflect **event-related designs**, which are used to measure brain activity associated with varying types of stimuli, such as a participant's perception of an event shortly after it occurs. However, the relationship among the perception of a stimulus, the resulting brain activity, and the measurable shift in the magnetic properties of cerebral blood flow can vary greatly between individuals and situations. As a result, the relationship between the brain activity related to a stimulus and the detectable changes in blood flow, as well as the influence of confounding variables, are mathematically modelled by the researcher.

Numerous cognitive and physiological processes can bias neuroimaging data. For one thing, brain activity observed during sexual arousal is likely biased by the physical effects of general autonomic arousal (Kagerer et al., 2011). Additionally, brain activity associated with the experimental task—but not with the experimental manipulation of interest—is rarely considered in such studies. For instance, studies that provide erotic pictures or short films to increase sexual arousal often do not include neutral

block designs Research designs, used in brain imaging research, that consist of the alternating presence or absence of the stimuli of interest.

event-related designs Research designs, used in brain imaging research, that incorporate different types of intermixed stimuli.

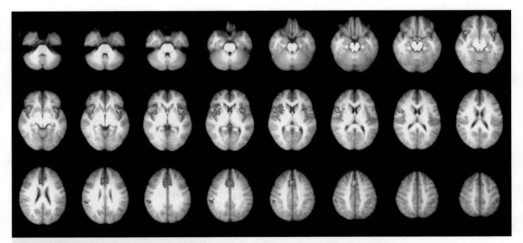

FIGURE 3.7 Brain activity related to physical sensations, sexual thoughts and feelings, and sexual arousal can be evaluated using fMRI methods. The images shown here reveal areas of brain activation associated with the perception of vulvar pain in women with chronic dyspareunia due to provoked vestibulodynia. Areas that are commonly active during pain—such as the insular cortex, anterior cingulate cortex, thalamus, prefrontal cortex, and related brain regions—are active in response to painful vulvar stimulation, as well. Note that statistical significance is represented by colour-coding when these images are produced, with red and orange regions showing moderate brain activation and yellow regions showing the greatest brain activity.

(non-erotic) stimuli and simply assume that the absence of the erotic stimulus is an adequate control. A neutral "control" task, which is commonly included in sexual psychophysiology research designs, would enhance the validity of the study by identifying and controlling for brain activity related to the testing process but unrelated to the manipulated variables. For example, Caroline Pukall's inclusion of a non-painful pressure control task in her analysis of vulvar discomfort in women with chronic vulvar pain allowed her to extract measures of brain activity that were specifically related to the perception of pain (Pukall et al., 2005). In contrast, the early studies of brain activity during orgasm (e.g., Komisaruk et al., 2004) did not include comparisons to neutral tasks that statistically accounted for orgasm-related muscle contractions, autonomic changes, and emotional responses that an individual experiences during orgasm. Each of these potential confounding variables reduces confidence that one is, in fact, observing brain activity unique to orgasm alone.

Many methodological problems affect fMRI data. First, fMRI has poor temporal precision, given that the magnetic changes in blood properties are measurable only seconds *after* an area has used the glucose and oxygen related to the initial brain activity of interest. Second, it has poor spatial precision, as the unit of measurement is a 1 millimetre by 5 millimetres cube of space (called a voxel, or a volumetric pixel), which consists of millions of neurons (Arthurs & Boniface, 2002). Third, anatomical locations are approximate rather than definite, as the brain image must be statistically "stretched" to fit a standard brain. Fourth, as suggested above, fMRI studies often fail to include a control condition, which is necessary to separate distinct pieces of a more complicated cognitive process. Fifth, fMRI data is only as good as the researcher's ability to identify when important brain activity occurs and to interpret that activity. Furthermore, different scanners produced by different manufacturers do not necessarily produce data of similar quality, and many research groups use customized data analysis strategies that are not replicable by other research groups. For these reasons, fMRI data should be interpreted with great caution; remember, a finding is valid only when it is reproducible and can be confirmed with numerous types of analyses.

Relevance of Animal Sexuality

The complexity of the cognitive, social, and biological factors that influence human sexuality can complicate our understanding of the simple principles that underlie sexual physiology and behaviour. Because of this, researchers who seek to understand the most basic biological, motivational, and behavioural processes that characterize sex in humans often turn to the study of non-human **model organisms**. The objectives of using animal models are threefold: a) to describe normal and abnormal (pathological) biological phenomena; b) to clarify cause-and-effect relationships; and c) to facilitate the assessment of medical treatments that will benefit humans (Giuliano et al., 2010).

Animal models are cost-effective, convenient tools that enable true experimental control—whereas research involving human subjects is limited by many confounding variables, animal models allow researchers to systematically manipulate experimental variables in an attempt to understand the causal relationships between biology and behaviour. In many cases, it would be unethical to conduct such experiments with humans. **Translational models** that extend research findings from animal research to human research are becoming increasingly important. Researchers are encouraged to develop animal models that closely parallel what is observed in humans, including behaviours, symptoms of disease, and physiological changes associated with disease. A close correspondence between an animal model and the condition it is intended to represent suggests that it is a valid translational model.

model organisms Animals that share important physiological and biological characteristics with humans, to the degree that they can be studied to reveal broad biological and behavioural patterns that are also present in humans.

translational model A simplified representation of a more complex human condition or situation that generalizes an experimental finding to the clinical setting (and vice versa).

Behavioural Indicators of Sexual Response in Animals

Most animals cannot communicate their internal state directly, so researchers who work with animals must rely on observable behaviours to infer what an animal experiences. For this reason, animal research has historically been interpreted through the lens of **behaviourism**. In the past few decades, new technological advances have allowed researchers to correlate sexual behaviour with changes in how cells function, and today animal sexuality is studied under the rubric of **behavioural neuroscience**. In this newer approach, sexual behaviours are studied in relation to the physiological processes that underlie these behaviours. The traditional way to explore these relationships is by altering or preventing normal responses in the peripheral and/or central nervous systems and observing how these manipulations change an animal's behaviour. To date, animal sexual behaviour has been studied in terms of sensation and perception of sexual stimuli, sexual motivation, hormonal effects on sexual behaviour (i.e., how testosterone, estrogen, progesterone, oxytocin, etc. affect behaviour), and the link between learning and sexual behaviour. The following discussion explores the techniques used to study these relationships, as well as what experiments have taught us about the value of animal models.

The most basic unit of animal behaviour is the withdrawal reflex, which consists of an observable movement in an animal in response to a stimulus—for example, the withdrawal of a paw in response to a sudden prick underneath the paw. The physical movement suggests that the animal has *perceived* the stimulus. This simple assumption has enabled researchers to measure an animal's perception of genital sensations, and to examine such things as how genital and non-genital sensitivity to pressure changes throughout the **estrus cycle** in female rodents. In addition, the withdrawal response has allowed researchers to apply the same sensory testing methods that are used to study genital sensation in women to rodents. For example, by applying hair-like plastic fibres that exerted different ranges of force to the vulva skin of mice, a group at McGill, led by Melissa Farmer and Jeffrey Mogil, discovered that repeated yeast infections can make a mouse's genital skin highly sensitive to touch (Farmer et al., 2011). Other researchers have made a similar observation in women who have longstanding vulvar pain as well as a history of repeated yeast infections. The similarity in these findings suggests that this animal model of vulvar pain is a valid model of chronic vulvar pain in women.

Over the years, other studies have found in animals sexual behaviours that are similar to sexual behaviours observed in humans. One example comes from Frank Beach's (1976) investigation of what he calls **attractivity**, which is the "attractiveness" of a female based on her appearance, her scent, and/or her vocalizations. Beach based his concept of attractivity on Charles Darwin's observations of intersexual selection in animals (see Chapter 2), and he reasoned that a female's attractivity can be inferred by the willingness of males to approach her. Beach further divided female sexual behaviour into **proceptivity** and **receptivity**; the latter is indicated by a female's arching of her spine to raise her haunches and thus facilitate copulation. Further research has revealed that a sexually receptive female rodent automatically arches her spine in this way in response to a light touch against her rump (Pfaus, Kippin, & Coria-Avila, 2003). The concepts that Beach identified are directly relevant to current models of female sexual response in humans, including sexual desire (which reflects attractivity and proceptivity) and sexual arousal (which reflects receptivity).

Animal studies have also given us insight into male sexual behaviour, which is broadly defined in animals as a combination of **appetitive**, **pre-copulatory**, and **consummatory** behaviours (Giuliano et al., 2010). Appetitive behaviours are patterns

behaviourism A theoretical approach that assumes observable behaviours are the only measurable and therefore knowable indications of psychological processes.

behavioural neuroscience The study of how parts of the peripheral nervous system (the nerves and nerve cells outside the central nervous system) and the central nervous system (the spinal cord and the brain), as well as hormones and other chemicals that affect these systems, influence animal behaviour.

estrus cycle The physical processes that occur in the female reproductive tract caused by hormones in sexually mature mammals.

attractivity A female's visual, auditory, and/or chemical cues that provoke approach behaviours in males.

proceptivity A female's approach behaviour in response to contact with a male.

receptivity A female's capacity to engage in copulation.

appetitive behaviours In male animals, behavioural patterns that orient a male toward a female.

pre-copulatory behaviours In male animals, behaviours that reflect motivation toward a specific sexual target, which is influenced by concurrent sexual arousal.

consummatory behaviours In male animals, mounting, intromissions (penile-vaginal insertions), and ejaculation.

of behaviour that orient a male toward a female before the male becomes sexually aroused; these behaviours include motor movement (e.g., grooming, active investigation) and preference for a female based on her attractivity. Appetitive behaviours drive the male to interact with the female, which initiates pre-copulatory behaviours that reflect a male's interest in a particular sexual partner (Figure 3.8). These behaviours, aimed toward a preferred and sexually receptive female partner, result in consummatory behaviour (see Figure 3.8). In humans, males follow a similar progression of behaviours as they become oriented toward, begin to desire, and finally consummate a sexual act with their desired partner.

Rodents as Model Organisms

The systematic study of sexual behaviour has primarily been conducted using rodents in laboratory settings. Many of the discoveries resulting from these model organisms have proven generalizable to other animal species, as well as humans. The earliest attempts to study rodent sexual behaviour were called "open field tests," because the testing apparatus consisted of a box (or "field") within which a male rat and a female rat could freely move. Using this "field," researchers monitored male-initiated sexual behaviour, including the frequency of mounts onto the female, intromissions, ejaculations, and physical contact between the copulating couple. They also collected a large volume of information about male sexual function and motivation, including the impact of learning, hormonal, and drug manipulations that improve or impair male sexual behaviour. For example, one study demonstrated the reliance of male sexual behaviour on gonadal hormones by showing that castration of male rats greatly reduced

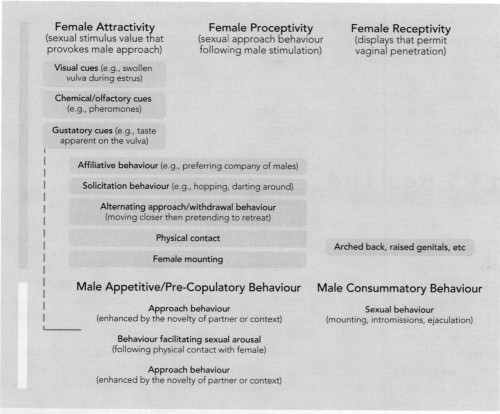

FIGURE 3.8 This visual representation depicts how the sexual behaviours of female animals (which reflect attractivity, proceptivity, and receptivity) relate to the sexual behaviours of male animals (which include appetitive/pre-copulatory and consummatory behaviours).

their sexual behaviour (Pfaus, Kippin, & Coria-Avila, 2003). Similarly, research examining the roles of estrogen and progesterone in female-paced (or female-controlled) sexual behaviour has revealed that both hormones are necessary for female-initiated sexual approach behaviours (Pfaus, Smith, & Coopersmith, 1999). Such experiments have added to our understanding of the hormonal control of human female sexuality, including changes of female sexual behaviour across the menstrual cycle, with oral contraceptive use, and following medical treatments that reduce sex hormone production and function (e.g., ovariectomy, radiotherapy for cancer).

Researchers soon developed a testing apparatus to measure female sexual motivation (Pfaus, Kippin, & Coria-Avila, 2003). This apparatus, which was called a "paced" mating chamber because it allowed a female to control the rate and timing of copulation, has become the primary method by which researchers study hormonal, neurological, and pharmacological influences on female sexual desire in the laboratory rat. The pacing chamber allows the female to approach, hide from, and interact with a sexually interested male. Importantly, the development of the paced mating design allowed researchers to investigate differences between male and female sexual motivation. Given the broad sex differences in human sexual motivation, such experiments allow researchers to unravel the factors that guide sexual desire and behaviour in men and women.

Researchers often use rodents in experiments designed to test new drug treatments before these treatments are given to humans. For example, Canadian neuroscientist James Pfaus has used rats in his research about drugs that may improve sexual arousal in human women (Pfaus, Shadiack, Van Soest, Tse, & Molinoff, 2004). In his experiments, he began by randomly assigning rats to treatment and control groups. He then controlled for differences in hormone levels by surgically removing the rats' ovaries, which produce estrogen and progesterone, and then restoring hormone levels to ensure that all of the rats had similar hormone levels. Next, he administered a drug that binds to certain types of melanocortin receptors, to see if activating the rats' melanocortin system (which modulates pain, inflammation, and skin pigmentation) would increase sexual behaviour. He discovered that the drug did indeed increase sexual behaviour in the rats, a finding that suggests that melanocortin drugs may be promising libido-enhancing tools in women (see the "Research vs Real Life" box). The use of random assignment, the use of hormone replacement to control female sexual behaviour, and the capacity to

Research VS Real Life

Translation of Animal Research to Human Sexual Functioning

One goal of research on animal sexuality is to identify and develop compounds to enhance the human sexual response. Sometimes, studies of drugs developed for medical purposes unrelated to sexuality result in findings of interest to the field of sexual research. Such was the case when researchers at the University of Arizona were testing a synthetic melanocortin drug for its sunless tanning properties, and the dermatologists leading the study realized that the drug had the side effect of enhancing erection and sexual motivation in study participants (Hadley, 2005). Subsequent studies have confirmed that melanocortins produce signs of physical arousal in male rodents (i.e., erections) and increase sexual motivation in female rodents. These animal studies have shown that the effects of melanocortin drugs on sexual interest and arousal are unlike the effects of other drugs marketed to improve sexuality, such as Viagra. Thus, these studies suggest that additional clinical trials may confirm that melanocortin drugs may help improve sexual problems with arousal and motivation in men and women.

manipulate the concentrations of drugs enabled Pfaus to draw strong causal inferences about the relationship between melanocortins and female sexual behaviour.

Limitations of Animal Models

The primary limitation of using animal models is that they are *models*, which are by definition oversimplifications. The causes and effects of sexual behaviour vary across different species of animals and can at times constitute serious limitations on how relevant and valid an animal model is to human sexual behaviour. Furthermore, animal research relies on assumptions about the internal states of animals based solely on observable behaviour, and these internal states cannot be conclusively proven with experiments. In addition, equating animal sexual behaviour and human sexual behaviour is a type of **anthropomorphizing**, which can be viewed as a type of observer bias. Finally, ethical concerns about animal experimentation may limit public support of such research. However, strict ethical guidelines set forth by the Canadian Council on Animal Care carefully regulate and enforce ethical practices in animal research.

anthropomorphizing
Perceiving human qualities or characteristics in non-human entities.

CHAPTER SUMMARY

The motivation underlying much of early sex research was to explore and define the limits of "normal" sexuality. Contemporary approaches in the study of sexuality have expanded the definition of normal sexual behaviour by considering variations due to ethnicity, acculturation, sexual orientation, sex roles, and physiological factors. Today, many researchers acknowledge the importance of using qualitative as well as quantitative approaches to arrive at a well-rounded understanding of sexuality, and they employ a variety of research methods and designs in their studies. Descriptive studies focus on describing patterns of sexual attitudes and behaviour while preserving the meanings of these patterns; correlation studies, on the other hand, depict how two or more variables change in relation to one another; and quasi-experimental studies allow researchers to evaluate sexuality in a quantitatively rigorous manner. Most quasi-experiments that investigate human sexuality rely on psychophysiological methods that measure physiological and/or neurological responses to sexual stimuli; these responses are taken as an indication of sexual arousal. Given the numerous ethical limitations associated with research involving humans, true experiments in the study of sex are possible only in animal models, which provide convenient means to investigate perceptual, hormonal, and neurobiological factors that may also influence human sexuality.

DEBATE QUESTION

The reliability and validity of human sex research depends on an individual's willingness to honestly and accurately report on her or his experiences of sexuality. If a researcher takes all appropriate precautions—ensuring anonymity, confidentiality, the individual's feelings of safety—can we fully trust self-reports about sexual thoughts, feelings, and behaviours?

REVIEW QUESTIONS

1. What steps can researchers take to ensure that their participants feel comfortable? What type of participant reporting biases must researchers overcome in obtaining accurate information?

2. Given the goals of positivism, which historical figure(s) in sex research contributed the most to the growth of the scientific study of sexuality, and why was this contribution seminal?

3. What are the strengths and weaknesses of qualitative research? What are the strengths of quantitative research? How can the two approaches complement each other?

4. How are descriptive research designs, correlational research designs, and experimental or quasi-experimental research designs used in sex research involving humans? What are the strengths and weaknesses of each type of design?

5. What are the assumptions about genital physiology that underlie many sexual psychophysiological methods? Do these assumptions accurately capture your experience of sexual arousal?

6. What are the advantages and disadvantages of using animal models to study human sexuality?

SUGGESTIONS FOR FURTHER READING AND VIEWING

Recommended Websites

Canadian Council on Animal Care in Science: http://ccac.ca
Canadian Sex Research Forum: http://csrf.ca
The Kinsey Institute: www.kinseyinstitute.org

Recommended Reading

Bancroft, M.D. (1997). *Researching sexual behavior: Methodological issues.* Bloomington, IN: Indiana University Press.

Bullough, V.L. (1994). *Science in the bedroom: A history of sex research.* New York, NY: Basic Books.

Carroll, J.L. (2010). *Sexuality now: Embracing diversity* (3rd ed.). Belmont, CA: Wadsworth Cengage Learning.

Crews, D. (1994). Animal sexuality. *Scientific American, 270,* 109–14.

Maier, T. (2009). *Masters of Sex: The life and times of William Masters and Virginia Johnson, the couple who taught America to love.* New York, NY: Basic Books.

Roach, M. (2008). *Bonk: The curious coupling of science and sex.* New York, NY: W.W. Norton & Company.

Wiederman, M.W., & Whitley, B.E. (2002). *Handbook for conducting research on human sexuality.* Mahwah, NJ: L. Erlbaum.

Recommended Viewing

Ashford, M. (Writer & Executive Producer). (2013). *Masters of sex* [Television series]. United States: Showtime.

Canner, L. (Producer & Director). (2009). *Orgasm Inc.* [Documentary]. United States: First Run Features.

4 CHAPTER

Sexual Anatomy: The Parts, the Pieces, and How They Respond

CAROLINE F. PUKALL AND
RICHARD J. WASSERSUG

LEARNING OBJECTIVES

In this chapter, you will

- learn about how external and internal genital organs function in males and in females;
- discover the role that genital organs and other sensitive areas play in sexual response; and
- find out how different researchers have described sexual response cycles.

Why Would Anyone Want to Become a Eunuch?

I can tell you, for me it was an overwhelming desire to have my testicles removed. Some would say it is a form of sexual dysphoria, which sounds a little extreme, however, an overwhelming desire is probably the one somewhat common reason I have heard from other **eunuchs** trying to explain [what motivated them]. [. . .] For me, one pro is that for the first time in my life, I feel in control of my body and am very happy—and I no longer accidentally sit on my nuts. [. . .] One of the physiological cons to castration beyond the actual procedure [. . .] is the real likelihood of osteoporosis. [. . .]

Who would want to undergo voluntary castration? Well, the eunuch community is full of people whom you might never guess are eunuchs. They are farmers, photographers, restaurant owners, postal workers, computer programmers, and more. They come from all walks of life and the only way that you would know it is if they told you or by fondling their privates. Perhaps even a co-worker, friend, or acquaintance of yours might be a eunuch.

This body modification is, by its nature, not for everyone. Then again, there is no one body modification for everyone. [. . .] Castration was the best one for me. There are some social stigmas attached, but rarely do folks walk up and pat one another just to see if they have the family jewels. My doctor chuckles. He says I'm easy to check for a hernia.

Talula, retrieved from http://news.bmezine.com/wp-content/uploads/2008/09/pubring/talula/20030606.html on 19 August 2011 and edited for grammar by chapter authors.

QUESTIONS FOR CRITICAL THOUGHT AND REFLECTION

1. What, if any, ethical implications are there for health care professionals performing this surgery on healthy males?
2. How would you react if a close male friend of yours was interested in undergoing voluntary castration?

eunuch A castrated human male.

Introduction

This chapter offers core information about genital anatomy and function, sexual response, and the biomechanics of sex. It also discusses rarely mentioned topics, such as voluntary castration, and frequently debated issues, such as female genital mutilation and male circumcision. Ultimately, the material you encounter in this chapter should help you to become more aware of, and more comfortable with, your own genitals. It should give you the vocabulary and understanding you need to knowledgeably discuss issues related to sexual anatomy and response.

Female Genitals

External Genitals

The external genitals of the female (Figure 4.1) consist of the mons pubis, the clitoris, the labia majora, the labia minora, the vulvar vestibule, and the urethral and vaginal openings. Together, these organs are called the *vulva*. Although many women commonly refer to their vulvar region as their vagina, the vagina is an internal passageway; only its opening is in the vulva. Indeed, the popular play *The Vagina Monologues* could be more accurately called *The Vulva Monologues*. The appearance of the vulva varies greatly from one woman to the next, and this variation is completely normal.

THE MONS PUBIS

The mons pubis is the rounded fatty pad of tissue that covers the pubic symphysis (the place where the left and right sides of the pelvis meet in the midline); it is sensitive to touch. At puberty, the mons becomes covered with pubic hair, which varies in colour, texture, and thickness from woman to woman.

Pubic Hair

There are three major theories to explain why pubic hair exists. First, pubic hair is believed to play a role in sexual communication through pheromonal signalling, by helping to dissipate volatile compounds (Pagel & Bodmer, 2003). Second, it is assumed to provide protective padding during the friction of intercourse (Ramsey, Sweeney, Fraser, & Oades, 2009). Third, it visually signals sexual maturity. Despite these functions, women have been removing their pubic hair since at least the times of ancient Egypt and Greece, when a lack of pubic hair was likely considered sexually attractive (Kilmer, 1982). In the Middle Ages, pubic hair removal was practised as a way to avoid pubic lice. Today, the removal of pubic hair is more common for women than for men (Ramsey et al., 2009), although some men remove their pubic hair to create the illusion of a longer penis (Trager, 2006). Both men and women also report removing their pubic hair to increase feelings of attractiveness and cleanliness (Riddell, Varto, & Hodgson, 2010), to increase sensitivity to touch in the genital area, to make it easier to locate anatomical areas (e.g., the clitoral hood), and for other sexual reasons (e.g., to avoid hair becoming caught in the teeth during oral sex) (Ramsey et al., 2009).

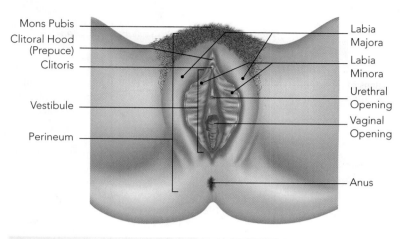

FIGURE 4.1 The vulva consists of the external female genitals. It protects the vaginal opening via a "double door" made up of the labia majora and the labia minora.

Herbenick and colleagues (2010), who conducted an online survey on body hair removal in women, have uncovered a number of trends associated with the removal of pubic hair. For one thing, they found that sexually active women engaged in a variety of practices for hair removal, ranging from shaving and waxing (most common) to electrolysis and laser hair removal (least common). They also found that women who removed all of their pubic hair were generally younger, more likely to engage in oral sex, more likely to have a more positive perception of their own genitals, and reported higher sexual function. In addition, complete hair removal was more common in women who self-identified as bisexual, rather than heterosexual or lesbian. Further, the researchers found that the frequency of hair removal varied substantially. Finally, the survey revealed that although about 20 per cent of younger women (18 to 24 years old) removed their pubic hair, the activity was less common in older women.

THE CLITORIS

The clitoris is an exceptionally sensitive organ, far more sensitive than the vagina, that has approximately the same number of nerve endings as the glans of the penis. The clitoris is important for female sexual response; in fact, clitoral stimulation is the most common way that women achieve arousal and orgasm during masturbation and partnered sexual activity. The only known function of the clitoris is sexual pleasure. The size, shape, and position of the clitoris varies from woman to woman.

The clitoris has two externally located components, the glans and the shaft, which are situated just below the pubic symphysis (Figure 4.2). It also has two substantial, internally located crura, or roots, that project inward from each side of the shaft and run backward along the medial edge of the bars of bone that define our true anatomical

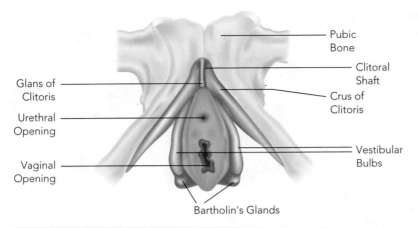

Glans of Clitoris

Urethral Opening

Vaginal Opening

Pubic Bone

Clitoral Shaft

Crus of Clitoris

Vestibular Bulbs

Bartholin's Glands

FIGURE 4.2 The clitoris and its underlying structures. The clitoris is much larger than most people think: including the inner portion, it measures, on average, about 10 centimetres long, but only about 1.5 centimetres is exposed.

perineum The area between the pubic symphysis and the coccyx (tail bone).

smegma Secretions made up of dead skin cells, oils, and moisture, which can form in the genital folds of males and females.

bottom, or **perineum**, the area between the pubic symphysis and the coccyx (tail bone) (Figure 4.1). The perineum includes the anus in both sexes and the vaginal and urethral openings in females.

The glans and shaft of the clitoris are covered by the clitoral hood (or prepuce). **Smegma** sometimes accumulates under the clitoral hood; this buildup can be prevented by pulling back on the hood when washing the genital area.

The glans of the clitoris is a small knob of tissue that appears smooth, round, and somewhat transparent. It can be seen under the clitoral hood when the hood is retracted. The relatively short shaft of the clitoris, however, cannot be seen. It consists of two areas of corpora cavernosa (i.e., erectile tissue) that extend back as the crura, which are longer than the shaft and run into the body along the sides of the vagina. The corpora cavernosa of both the shaft and the crura fill with blood during sexual arousal.

THE LABIA MAJORA

The labia majora, sometimes called "the outer lips," are pads of fatty tissue lateral to the labia minora and the urethral and vaginal openings. They extend downward from the mons pubis on each side of the vulva, and their outer surfaces are covered with pubic hair. The skin of the labia majora is typically darker than that of the thighs. The labia majora are richly supplied with nerve endings and are important for sexual stimulation and arousal. They also provide padding and protection for the sensitive labia minora, clitoris, and vaginal opening.

THE LABIA MINORA

Also referred to as "the inner lips," the labia minora are hairless folds of skin located between the labia majora. They extend upward and forward toward the clitoris to form the clitoral hood (prepuce), and they meet posterior to the vaginal opening, in an area called the fourchette. The labia minora darken in colour during pregnancy and after childbirth. They contain oil glands, sweat glands, blood vessels, and an abundance of nerve endings, and they are important in sexual stimulation and arousal.

Often the labia minora protrude from between the labia majora, and sometimes they are folded over, concealing the vaginal opening until they are spread apart. The labia may be asymmetrical, with one labium longer than the other. These variations are normal; labia minora vary substantially from woman to woman (Figure 4.3). As such, there is no universally accepted standard for what they "should" look like. However, some women choose to undergo elective surgery to alter the appearance of their labia minora in order to "look normal" or to reduce their sexual inhibitions due to fear of a partner's negative evaluation of their genitals (Bramwell, Morland, & Garden, 2007).

One of the most commonly performed voluntary genital alteration procedures is **labiaplasty**. This surgery encompasses a variety of different procedures, and it is usually done to make the labia minora plumper, more symmetrical, and/or smaller.

labiaplasty A form of cosmetic surgery to change the appearance of the labia minora.

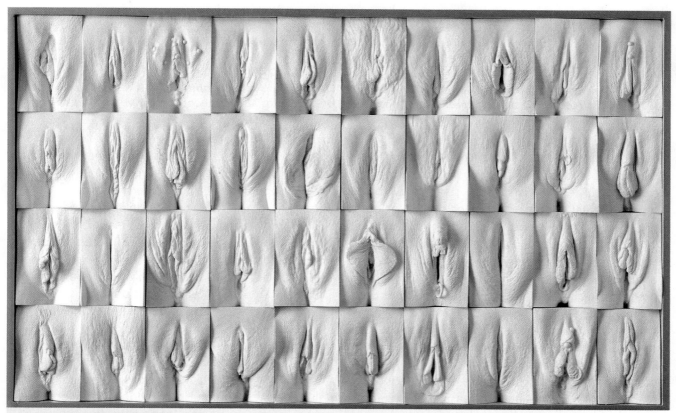

FIGURE 4.3 Variations in the appearance of labia minora, as documented in plaster casts by British artist Jamie McCartney for his project *The Great Wall of Vagina*. This image shows one of ten panels. In all, there are 400 plaster casts of vulvas, all of them unique. The age of women who underwent the vulvar casting is from 18 to 76, and casts include pairs of mothers and daughters, pairs of identical twins, and transsexuals, as well as a woman pre- and post-partum and another woman before and after labiaplasty.

Risks associated with labiaplasty include infection, decrease in pleasurable sensations, scarring, and unpleasant hypersensitivity in the area (Goodman et al., 2007; Rouzier, Louis-Sylvestre, Paniel, & Haddad, 2000). In addition, although some studies report excellent outcomes and few complications (e.g., Goodman et al., 2010), 20 per cent of patients in one study reported that the surgeon did not adequately explain the procedure and what to expect in terms of outcome; indeed, 17 per cent were unsatisfied with the results (Rouzier et al., 2000). In some parts of the world, women undergo a more invasive surgery known as female genital mutilation (FGM), which often involves full removal of the labia minora as well as most or all of the rest of the woman's external genital organs (see the "Culture and Diversity" box).

THE VULVAR VESTIBULE

The vulvar vestibule is the teardrop-shaped area of the vulva inside the labia minora. The word *vestibule* means "entranceway," and within the vestibule lie the vaginal and urethral openings. The vestibular area is well-endowed with nerve endings and blood vessels; it consists of erogenous tissue, which is sensitive to pleasurable stimulation. In some women, however, the vestibule is so sensitive that any touch to the area—whether it be sexual (e.g., attempted vaginal penetration) or non-sexual (e.g., speculum insertion during a gynecological examination)—is painful and unpleasant. This condition is called *vestibulodynia*.

Culture & Diversity

Female Genital Mutilation

This box is based on Chalmers and Omer-Hashi (2003) and was contributed by Beverley Chalmers, DSc(Med), PhD, adjunct professor, Department of Obstetrics and Gynecology, University of Ottawa.

As defined by the World Health Organization (WHO, 1997), female genital mutilation (FGM) (or female circumcision) involves the "partial or total removal of the external female genitals or other injury to the female genital organs whether for cultural or other non-therapeutic reasons" (p. 3). It is estimated that 100 million to 140 million women worldwide (about 15 per cent of all women) have been circumcised and that two million or more girls experience this procedure each year (approximately 5500 per day). Most of these women live in East and West African countries, although FGM is also common in parts of Arabia, including Yemen, Oman, and the United Arab Emirates. It is also practised, albeit less frequently, in a few Asian countries—such as Indonesia, Malaysia, and India—and increasingly in Europe, Canada, Australia, and the United States. While FGM may be prohibited and rarely practised in most Western countries, families who live in a Western country but are originally from a country where FGM is more commonly practised may send their daughters back to their country of origin to have the procedure performed. The age at which female circumcision is performed varies widely, but most commonly it is performed between the ages of four and

nine. Girls are not typically aware of the specifics of the procedure, as strict secrecy is maintained about it both prior to and after the event.

The operation is often done by "excisors," who are older female relatives, designated women in the community, or religious or tribal leaders. They use special knives, scissors, scalpels, pieces of glass, razor blades, or even, on occasion, sharp stones or hot rocks for the procedure. Anesthesia is rarely used, and the girl is usually held down by a number of women, frequently including her relatives. The wound is covered with substances such as alcohol, vinegar, lemon juice, eggs, herbal mixtures, porridge, soap, or cow dung. Bleeding may be controlled by the application of goat excreta, oils, salt, alum paste, or myrrh, in addition to applied pressure. In affluent sectors of society, the procedure may be performed in a health care facility by qualified health practitioners.

Regardless of who performs the procedure, there are a number of negative health consequences associated with FGM. The severity of these consequences depends on the type of procedure, the extent of the cutting, the skill of the operator, the cleanliness of the tools, the environment, and the physical condition of

THE URETHRAL OPENING

The urethral opening lies about halfway between the clitoris and the vaginal opening, within the vulvar vestibule. The urethra is the tube that transports urine collected in the bladder to where it is expelled from the body. In general, the urethral opening is not highly sensitive to sexual stimulation.

THE VAGINAL OPENING

The vaginal opening is a highly sensitive region located in the posterior area of the vulvar vestibule, below the urethral opening. It varies in size from woman to woman, but it is normally considerably larger than the urethral opening. After a woman has given birth vaginally, the vaginal opening generally appears more "open" and may feel looser to the woman and/or her partner.

The Hymen

The hymen is a thin membrane that partially covers the vaginal opening. It is believed to protect the vaginal tissues early in life. It is usually present at birth, and it generally remains intact until first intercourse, when it is commonly torn. Some women,

the girl who is being operated on. Immediate risks include severe pain and bleeding, infection, difficulty passing urine, injury or trauma to adjoining organs, and death. The emotional consequences—of hurt and pain induced by those the girl trusts and loves—may be indelible. The long-term effects include severe scarring, chronic kidney and urinary tract infections, painful menstruation or the accumulation of menstrual blood in the vagina, and acute or chronic **pelvic inflammatory disease** that can result in infertility, internal damage, cysts or scarring of the perineal area, miscarriage, complications during childbirth, and pain during sexual intercourse. Infection with HIV/AIDS and other diseases is also a possibility if the equipment used was not properly sterilized. For all of these reasons, FGM is considered to be a serious health hazard, and it is internationally recognized as a violation of human rights (WHO, 2001).

Many women who have undergone FGM experience various forms and degrees of sexual pain and dysfunction, as well as emotional trauma that may inhibit the sexual response. Typically, the more extensive the procedure, the more muted the sexual response. Orgasm capacity is, not surprisingly, lost in many genitally-mutilated women. Yet these women presumably experience comparable levels of sexual

desire as women with intact genitals, and in many cases, they may be able to experience some degree of sexual enjoyment. While clitoral stimulation is an integral part of women's sexual response, non-vulvar erogenous zones also contribute to sexual response, as does cognitive function.

Many reasons are given for maintaining the practice of FGM; these include psychosexual (e.g., it is thought to ensure chastity before marriage), socio-cultural (e.g., it is a rite of passage that guarantees marriage and subsequent economic security), hygienic/aesthetic (e.g., external female genitals are considered dirty and unsightly in some cultures), and/or religious (e.g., it is meant to fulfill religious requirements). Importantly, parents do not circumcise their daughters to cause harm, but rather out of love. In addition, in some cultures, not having the procedure may be psychologically more disturbing than having it, as an uncircumcised woman may feel less connected to the community than a circumcised woman feels. In fact, most women who have undergone the procedure report that they are pleased that they were circumcised.

> **pelvic inflammatory disease (PID)** A bacterial infection of the female reproductive organs that causes lower abdominal pain.

however, are born without a hymen, and some women who are born with one may unknowingly tear it during sporting or other non-sexual activities. Thus, the assumption that a woman without an intact hymen is not a virgin is not always correct. Some bleeding and pain may result when the hymen is torn; however, this tearing is not usually traumatic or highly uncomfortable. Interestingly, if the hymen is partial, thin, and/or flexible enough, it may remain intact even after intercourse. In such cases, the assumption that an intact hymen indicates virginity is also wrong!

Although there are different configurations of hymenal integrity (Figure 4.4), most of them have some degree of opening that allows for the passing of menstrual blood and for the insertion of tampons (generally, tampons are too small to tear the hymen). Sometimes, the membrane is too thick to break easily during sexual intercourse, and sometimes an imperforate hymen traps menstrual blood in the vagina. Medical intervention is needed in these cases.

The hymen and its rupture at first intercourse is a controversial topic. In some cultures that condemn coital sex before marriage, the presence of an intact hymen has been taken as sole evidence of virginity, over and above the word of the woman. As such, some future husbands insist on a pelvic examination to "prove" the woman's virginity

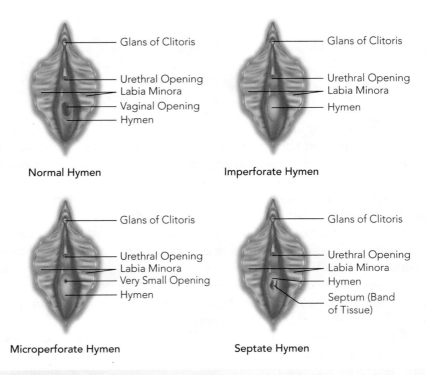

FIGURE 4.4 Different hymenal configurations. The *normal hymen* typically covers the lower part of the vaginal opening. The *imperforate hymen* covers the entire vaginal opening and may require minor surgery to allow for the passing of menstrual blood as well as vaginal penetration. The *microperforate hymen* covers most of the vaginal opening but contains small holes that allow for the passing of menstrual blood. The *septate hymen* partially obstructs the vaginal opening with a band or series of bands of tissue.

hymenoplasty A cosmetic surgery to reposition the remnants of the broken hymen or a small flap of vaginal skin to approximate the hymen.

before marriage. In some countries, some women seek **hymenoplasty**, or hymen reconstruction surgery, to hide the fact that they no longer have an intact hymen (Cook & Dickens, 2009; also see the "Ethical Debate" box in Chapter 14).

Internal Organs

The internal sex organs of the female consist of the vagina, the Bartholin glands, the vestibular bulbs, the Skene's glands, the cervix and uterus, the ovaries, and the fallopian tubes (Figure 4.5).

THE VAGINA

The vagina is a canal that starts at the vaginal opening and extends into the body. It is oriented upward and tilts slightly backward, toward the sacrum, (i.e., the base of the spine). It connects with the cervix, the lowest part of and entrance to the uterus. In an unaroused state, the vagina is about 7.5 to 12.5 centimetres long. When a woman is aroused, her vagina lengthens by about 5 to 7.5 centimetres. The vagina can stretch in order to accommodate not only a penis or sex toy, but also the passage of a baby during childbirth.

endometriosis A condition in which the type of cells that normally line the uterus grow outside of the uterus, causing pain.

The vagina consists of three layers of tissue. The outermost layer is the vaginal mucosa, which is similar in texture to the tissue inside the mouth. The rugae (ridged walls) of this layer are soft and moist. These walls release secretions to maintain a healthy, slightly acidic chemical balance. Other than regularly washing between the vulvar folds, nothing needs to be done to keep this balance. Some women use products such as douches that are meant to rinse out the vagina; however, douches can alter this balance. Vaginal douches should not be used unless they are medically prescribed, as they can increase a woman's chances of medical problems, including

ectopic pregnancy A pregnancy in which the fertilized egg implants outside of the uterus.

endometriosis, **ectopic pregnancy**, and decreased fertility.

When a woman is sexually aroused, the mucosa releases a clear, slippery lubricant—a unique feature of the vagina. This lubrication generally begins about 10 to 30 seconds after effective sexual stimulation (Masters and Johnson, 1966). Lubrication is associated with increased blood flow to the vaginal walls (i.e., vasocongestion) and serves two major functions. First, it raises the chances of conception by increasing the alkalinity of the normally acidic vaginal environment, rendering this environment more hospitable to sperm. Second, it increases sexual pleasure; without lubrication, penetration can be uncomfortable for the woman and/or her partner. Vaginal lubrication also exudes a scent that can be an erotic stimulus. If a woman feels she is not lubricating enough, she can use saliva, lubricated condoms, and/or a water-based lubricant to supplement her body's production.

The middle layer of the vagina is muscular and is most prominent in the lower third of the vagina, closest to the vaginal opening. The muscles of this layer tighten during sexual arousal and, along with other muscles of the pelvic floor, contract rapidly and rhythmically during orgasm.

The deepest layer of the vagina consists of fibrous tissue. This layer resists expansion of the vagina and helps keep the vagina in place within the pelvis.

The lower third of the vagina is particularly rich in sensory nerves, which respond precisely to touch and pressure. This region is highly sensitive to mechanical stimulation. The upper portion of the vagina, on the other hand, receives autonomic innervation and is relatively insensitive to localized touch. This insensitivity accounts in part for why women do not feel tampons or diaphragms once they are in the vaginal canal. This tissue, though, is sensitive to deep pressure and stretching.

THE BARTHOLIN GLANDS

The Bartholin glands, a pair of small glands, lie just inside the labia minora on the left and right sides of the vagina (Figure 4.6). Their function is unknown, although some assume that their relatively minute secretions just before orgasm contribute to vaginal lubrication.

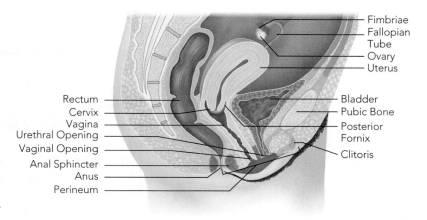

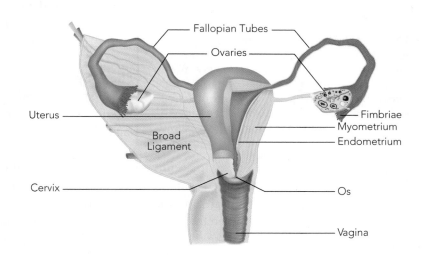

FIGURE 4.5 Internal female genital anatomy, as viewed from the side (top) and from the front (bottom). When most people think of female genitals, they think "vagina," but there is much more to women's internal genitals than this part. Parts of the uterus, ovaries, and vagina are depicted as cut away to give a sense of the internal complexity of the structures.

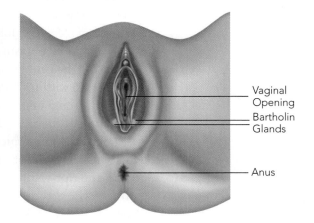

FIGURE 4.6 The Bartholin glands are approximately 0.5 centimetres in diameter and are found in the lower portion of the labia minora. These glands were first described by Caspar Bartholin, a Dutch anatomist, in 1677.

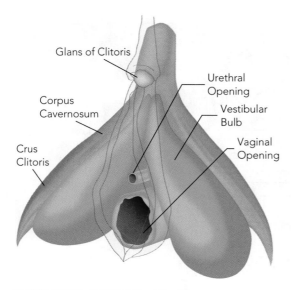

Glans of Clitoris

Corpus
Cavernosum

Crus
Clitoris

Urethral
Opening

Vestibular
Bulb

Vaginal
Opening

FIGURE 4.7 The clitoris is a complex structure. The glans clitoris, which is roughly the size and shape of a pea, is estimated to have more sensory nerve endings than any other part of the female body. When the highly sensitive glans is stimulated, the vestibular bulbs, along with the corpora cavernosa and the crura clitoris, fill with blood and expand.

THE VESTIBULAR BULBS

The vestibular bulbs are not the bulbs of the vulvar vestibule, but the bulbs of the clitoris. They lie on either side of the vagina, near the vaginal opening and along the crura of the clitoris (Figure 4.7). They are composed of erectile tissue similar to the corpus spongiosum of the penis and fill with blood during sexual arousal; this process results in the swelling of the vulvar area.

THE SKENE'S GLANDS

Women have a pair of Skene's glands (also called the lesser vestibular or paraurethral glands) that are located on the anterior (front) wall of the vagina close to the lower end of the urethra; their ducts empty into the urethra (Zaviačič, Jakubovská, Belošovič, & Breza, 2000). There is growing evidence based on both their anatomy and secretions that they are the female equivalent to the male prostate gland (Wunsch & Schober, 2007). The Skene's glands are believed to contribute to the sensitivity of the G-spot (see below).

The G-Spot

The G-spot, or Grafenberg spot, is a highly sensitive area on the anterior (front) vaginal wall, about five centimetres from the vaginal opening (Grafenberg, 1950). It is a large and diffuse area—not a single spot—that includes the Skene's glands and ducts, as well as adjacent vaginal and urethral tissues. Stimulation of the glands and the tissue around them can be highly pleasurable for some women (Figure 4.8), leading to sexual arousal, orgasm, and in some women even ejaculation (Perry & Whipple, 1981). Other women find this kind of stimulation uncomfortable, or at least not sexually arousing.

Like the semen of male ejaculation, the fluid of female ejaculation exits from the urethra. The fluid contains enzymes and other chemicals similar to those secreted by the male prostate gland (Wimpissinger, Stifter, Wolfgang, & Stackl, 2007). The amount of fluid secreted varies from woman to woman: some women produce very little, whereas others secrete abundant amounts. In addition, just as penile stimulation alone can lead to ejaculation in males, female ejaculation can occur as a result of clitoral stimulation alone.

Not every woman has G-spot orgasms or ejaculates. From a sample of over 300 women, Masters, Johnson, and Kolodny (1988) reported that only 4.7 per cent expelled fluid at orgasm. In one study examining over 1200 professional women in Canada and the United States, just over 60 per cent of the participants reported a highly sensitive area within their vagina, which was responsive to sexual stimulation. However, only about three quarters of these women experienced orgasm and ejaculation from stimulation of the area (Darling, Davidson, & Conway-Welch, 1990).

The precise anatomical site for G-spot orgasms remains controversial. The problem is that the roots of the clitoris lie just to the sides of this region, and any pressure on the anterior vaginal wall in the area of the Skene's glands is likely to indirectly stimulate the clitoral roots as well as the urethra. This complicated situation has led some researchers to prefer referring to this general region as the "clitourethraovaginal complex" and to downplay the idea of the G-spot as a precise and isolated erogenous site (Buisson, Foldes, Jannini, & Mimoun, 2010). Certainly during penile-vaginal intercourse, the pressure on the vaginal walls is great enough to stimulate all of the surfaces in the region, making it difficult to claim a specific anatomical target as the singular source of the sensory stimulation.

A disturbing service offered by some cosmetic surgeons is "G-spot amplification," which purportedly enhances sexual arousal and response. In this procedure, collagen is injected into the G-spot region to enlarge it and supposedly increase sensation. However, the American College of Obstetricians and Gynecologists (ACOG) states, "women should be informed about the lack of data supporting the effectiveness of these procedures and their potential complications" (ACOG, 2007). Women who have undergone the procedure have reported various complications, including infections, scarring, and pain during intercourse.

THE CERVIX AND THE UTERUS

The cervix is the lower third, or neck, of the uterus (Figure 4.5). It is located at the top of the vagina and contains mucous-secreting glands. Sperm travel from the vagina into the uterus through the os (the opening in the centre of the cervix). The upper two-thirds of the uterus is the fundus, or body. The major function of the uterus is to hold and nourish a developing fetus during pregnancy. The uterus is usually tilted forward (anteflexed), but in some women it is tipped back toward the spine (retroflexed) (see the "Ethical Debate" box below).

The uterus consists of three layers. The innermost layer or lining, which is continuous with the mucosa of the vagina, is the endometrium; this layer is richly supplied

FIGURE 4.8 The area known as the G-spot, a large part of which is believed to encompass the area of the Skene's glands. Many women find stimulation of this area highly arousing, yet there is much debate as to whether this area is really distinct from the surrounding areas, in terms of its potential for providing sexual pleasure in response to stimulation. The urethral opening is the exit point for the ejaculate, which has led some women to believe that they are urinating as opposed to ejaculating.

Ethical Debate

The Anatomical Problem with Backroom Abortions

Due to the anatomical position of the uterus, which usually tips forward in relation to the long axis of the vagina, an effort to disrupt a pregnancy by sticking a stiff probe—such as a straightened coat hanger—up the vagina and into the cervix can all too easily miss the target. The object will instead enter the deepest portion of the vagina, called the posterior fornix, which lies just behind the cervix (Figure 4.5). Here, the vaginal wall is very thin; if it is pierced, as is too often the case with many non-professional abortion attempts, the piercing object can enter the body cavity itself.

If the probe is not sterile, piercing the thin wall of the vagina can lead to massive and potentially lethal infection within the abdominal cavity. Many women have died from such infections. Indeed, the straightened wire from a common coat hanger has been used so many times in attempted abortions that the coat hanger has become a symbol of backroom abortions—that is, procedures that can be easily attempted but can go dreadfully wrong. Knowing the medical risks should discourage women from seeking non-medical abortions or attempting self-abortions. Yet women across the globe undergo these sorts of procedures all too frequently. What might drive women to seek a non-medical abortion? Why might unlicensed individuals agree to perform such procedures, even if they know the risk involved? What can be done to reduce the problem? (See Chapter 7 for more information on abortions.)

with hormone-secreting glands and blood vessels. Its state varies according to age and menstrual-cycle phase. The endometrium is shed during menstruation and normally regenerates with each menstrual cycle. The second layer, the myometrium, is muscular. The elasticity of the myometrium allows for the stretching needed to accommodate a fetus as it grows, and this layer contracts during labour to expel the fetus. The deepest layer, the perimetrium, is a thin, smooth membrane. It is continuous with a similar layer covering all the internal organs that move within the abdominal and pelvic cavity during normal functions.

Cervical Cancer

In Canada, roughly 1350 women will be diagnosed with cervical cancer each year, and about 390 of these women will die from this disease (Canadian Cancer Society, 2012). Although it is not the most common or lethal cancer, cervical cancer is among the most easily prevented.

The first warning sign of cervical cancer is **cervical dysplasia**, which can be identified through the detection of precancerous cells. Dysplasia of the cervix is not cancer, but it can develop into cancer if left untreated (Canadian Cancer Society, 2008). The test that detects these changes is the **Pap test** invented by and named after the prominent Greek doctor Georgios Papanikolaou. During this test, a doctor inserts a **speculum** into the vagina and uses a small brush or spatula to take a sample of cervical cells. Although having a Pap test is likely not on the top of most women's "to do" lists, it can reduce a woman's risk of cervical cancer. Since the Pap test has become a routine part of health care for women (usually done every two years), the cervical cancer rate in Canada has decreased by 50 per cent, and the death rate associated with the disease has decreased by 60 per cent (Canadian Cancer Society, 2008). Women at highest risk for cervical cancer are those who do not have regular Pap tests, who became sexually active at a young age, who have had many sexual partners (or a partner who has had many partners), and who have used birth control pills for over five years. Sexual activity can lead to cervical cancer because of the strong link between cancer and human papillomavirus (HPV) infection (see Chapter 8).

cervical dysplasia Growth of abnormal cells on the surface of the cervix.

Pap test A test in which a sample of cells is taken from a woman's cervix with a small brush or spatula to detect precancerous changes.

speculum A plastic or metal device shaped like a duck's bill, used to open a body cavity in a medical examination.

THE OVARIES

Females have two ovaries, one on each side of their uterus (Figure 4.5). The ovaries are endocrine glands that produce estrogens, most notably estradiol, and progestins, mainly progesterone. Estrogens influence the development of physical sex characteristics in females and, along with progesterone, regulate the menstrual cycle. In addition, progesterone plays an important role in preparing the uterine lining for pregnancy.

The ovaries also, as their name implies, produce ova, or eggs. When a female is born, her ovaries contain approximately 1,000,000 immature ova (Federman, 2006); when she experiences her first menstruation (menarche), they contain about 500,000. During a woman's reproductive years, typically one ovum matures with each menstrual cycle (during ovulation) and is released by one or the other ovary; the side usually alternates from cycle to cycle. Sometimes two ova mature and are released at the same time; if both are fertilized and successfully implanted, the resulting fetuses will develop into non-identical (fraternal) twins.

THE FALLOPIAN TUBES

The fallopian tubes, also called the oviducts or the uterine tubes, transport the ova from the ovaries to the uterus. They are about 10 centimetres long, with one located on each side of the pelvic cavity (Figure 4.5). The eggs move down the fallopian tubes via waves of movement in microscopic hair-like projections, called cilia, and peristaltic contractions of muscle in the walls of the tubes. The part of the fallopian tube closest to the ovary is called the infundibulum, and it is here that fertilization typically occurs. The infundibulum has finger-like projections called fimbriae, which extend toward the ovary and draw the egg (whether fertilized or not) from the ovary into the tube. If the egg is fertilized, it will then normally implant in the uterus. Sometimes, though, the fertilized egg implants in tissue outside the uterus, resulting in an ectopic pregnancy. Most ectopic implantations are in the tubes themselves, but they can also occur in the vagina or the abdominal cavity.

Male Genitals

External Genitals

The external genital organs of the male consist of the penis and the scrotum (Figure 4.9), with the testes located inside the scrotum.

THE PENIS

The penis plays an essential role in sexual pleasure, reproduction, and urination. This cylindrical organ consists of blood vessels, fibrous tissue, and three distinct tubes of spongy tissue. In humans, the penis does not contain any bone. The only muscles present are the **smooth muscles** associated with the walls of blood vessels and the muscles at the base of the penis that aid in the ejection of semen and urine through the urethra.

smooth muscles Involuntary non-striated muscles.

The penis consists of three sections: the roots, the shaft, and the glans. The roots of the penis extend internally and attach to the same bars of the pubic bone that the roots of the clitoris attach to in females. The shaft is the main external part of the penis. It is hairless and covered with loose skin when the penis is **flaccid**; this skin becomes taut when the penis is engorged with blood (erect). The shaft starts at the base of the penis and ends at the coronal ridge (the rim of the glans), which separates the shaft from the enlarged, acorn-shaped glans at the tip of the penis. The entire penis is sensitive to stimulation, but the glans is the most sensitive part.

flaccid Non-erect.

The foreskin (or prepuce) either partially or fully covers the glans in males who are not circumcised (see the "Research vs Real Life" box). It is a retractable fold of skin that protects the glans when the penis is flaccid. Usually, the foreskin is easily retracted to

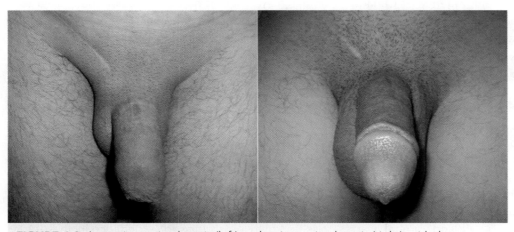

FIGURE 4.9 An uncircumcised penis (left) and a circumcised penis (right), with the scrotum visible behind the penis. These photos were taken before and after an adult man underwent a circumcision procedure. Although the procedure is occasionally performed on adults, circumcision usually occurs shortly after a male infant is born, with the child's parents choosing the procedure for a variety of religious, cultural, hygienic, and/or aesthetic reasons.

clean the glans. If the glans is not adequately cleaned, smegma can accumulate and cause an unpleasant smell; if bacteria or fungi accumulate, balanitis (inflammation of the glans and neighbouring shaft) is possible.

Inside the Penis

Running the length of the penile shaft are three cylindrical spongy bodies (Figure 4.10). The two larger ones, the corpora cavernosa, lie side by side on the upper part of the shaft and continue inward for quite some length as the crura, or roots, of the penis

Research VS Real Life

Circumcision

Circumcision is the surgical procedure of removing the foreskin of the penis. The procedure is usually done shortly after birth. Much of the time, circumcision is done for religious reasons (e.g., it is traditional for Jews and Muslims to circumcise their male children), but some parents choose it for non-religious reasons, including family tradition, hygiene/health, and esthetics/appearance. Although circumcision is not currently recommended as a standard procedure in Canada (Fetus and Newborn Committee, Canadian Pediatric Association, 1996; it is more positively viewed in the US at this time), parents-to-be are urged to make the best informed decision for their male child by discussing the procedure with their health professionals.

Globally and in North America, about 30 per cent of men are circumcised (Weiss, Polonsky, Bailey, Hankins, Halperin, & Schmid, 2007). The rate of circumcision in Canada varies greatly by province. A survey of Canadian maternity practices, conducted in 2006–7 by the Public Health Agency of Canada (2009), found that 44.3 per cent of males in Alberta were circumcised, compared to only 6.8 per cent in Nova Scotia.

Some people believe that circumcision is essential for the health of a male and his partner; others argue that it is medically unnecessary and risky, especially for a male newborn. Still others view it as genital mutilation. Proponents of routine circumcision have documented health benefits including the following: a decrease in the incidence of infant and childhood urinary tract infections, a decrease in some sexually transmitted infections (including HIV, the virus that causes AIDS, and genital wart infections), and a decrease in the incidence of adult penile cancer (Dickerman, 2007). In addition,

circumcision can prevent or correct a painful condition called *phimosis*, in which the penile foreskin is too tight to retract.

Those who oppose routine circumcision, however, indicate that the procedure entails a number of risks, including hemorrhage, infection, shock, penile mutilation, and psychological trauma; in rare cases, death can also occur. In addition, the procedure is painful. Male infants circumcised without anesthetic were found to exhibit heightened pain responses to vaccinations four to six months post-circumcision (Taddio, Katz, Hersich, & Koren, 1997). In recent years, the debate has intensified with the rise of a social-political movement of "intactivists" who want the procedure to be made illegal. In 2011, these individuals fought, but failed, to have a question about banning circumcision placed on a ballot in San Francisco.

One question often asked is whether sexual function differs between circumcised and uncircumcised (intact) men. There is no consensus on the answer to this question. Masters and Johnson (1966) found no difference in the sensitivity of the circumcised versus intact penis, and a more recent study from McGill University similarly found no differences in penile sensitivity or sexual arousal response in circumcised versus intact men (Payne, Thaler, Kukkonen, Carrier, & Binik, 2007). At the same time, Sorrells and colleagues (2007) found that the glans of the circumcised penis is less sensitive than that of the intact penis. Anecdotal reports suggest that some men who undergo circumcision in adulthood (and who have therefore had sexual experiences while uncircumcised and while circumcised) experience increases in sexual pleasure, while others experience decreases in sexual pleasure. Obviously, more research is needed.

anchored to the pubic bones. Under the pair of corpora cavernosa lies the thinner spongy body, the corpus spongiosum. The corpus spongiosum runs the length of the penis—with the urethra running through the middle of it—and expands at the end of the penis to form the glans. During erection, the corpus spongiosum can sometimes be seen as a raised column on the underside of the penis.

All three components of the shaft have a multitude of tiny irregular spaces separated by fibrous bands, and they are richly supplied with blood vessels and nerves. When the penis is flaccid, the spaces contain little blood. However, when the male is sexually excited, the spaces in all three chambers fill with blood, as the smooth muscles in the walls of the arteries that deliver blood to the penis dilate. The elevated blood pressure in the penis causes the veins that normally drain blood from the penis to be compressed, limiting blood flow out. As a result, the blood volume in the penis increases, causing the shaft to grow in length and girth. Many neurotransmitters are involved in this process, the main one being nitric oxide, which causes the smooth muscles in the walls of the arteries to dilate. Epinephrine and norepinephrine are involved in the loss of an erection after orgasm, because they stimulate muscles in the walls of the arteries to constrict. This limits blood flow into the penis and reduces the pressure on the veins to allow blood to drain from the penis.

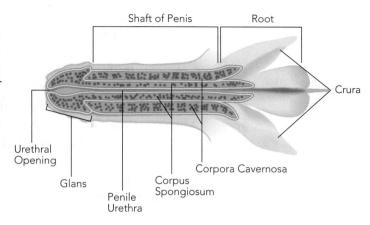

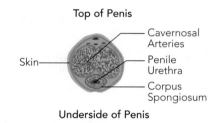

FIGURE 4.10 Interior structure of the penis, as viewed from the side (top) and the front (bottom). Note that, unlike the penises of most mammals, human penises do not contain a bone. Most researchers assume that humans lost the os (penis) bone, or baculum, at some point in the evolution of our species, although why this happened is not known. Note that, in the top image, the corporus spongiosum and urethra are depicted although they are actually completely covered by the corpora cavernosa, as indicated in the bottom image.

Corpora Cavernosa versus Corpus Spongiosum: What's the Difference?

There is an important difference between the two corpora cavernosa and the corpus spongiosum. The cavernous bodies are wrapped in a tight fibrous sleeve that becomes taut when those cylinders are filled with blood, as occurs with a full erection. This makes the erect penis stiff and firm. The spongy portion, however, lacks this tight wrapping and, as a result, it remains quite soft and spongy when it fills with blood. This arrangement is essential for sexual functioning—if the corpus spongiosum became as stiff as the corpora cavernosa during an erection, or if the corpora cavernosa wrapped completely around the urethra instead of lying above it, the pressure on the urethra would be too great for semen to escape. Ejaculation would be inhibited.

Penis Size

Penis size preference, surprisingly, varies across cultures and historical periods. In ancient Greece, for example, a small penis was considered a desirable trait in a man, as it was believed to be better for conception than was a large penis; artist's renderings of male figures with large penises were meant to convey contempt or ridicule (Friedman, 2001). Symbolically, however, erect (and thus large) penises have typically denoted attributes such as fertility, intelligence, power, and strength (Wylie & Eardley, 2007). Methods of increasing penis size have been documented throughout history, and they have included such measures as hanging weights from the penis in order to stretch it and encouraging poisonous snakes to bite the penis in order to make it swell.

More men believe that their penis is smaller, rather than larger, than average; however, most men fall in the average range and have a fully functional penis (Vardi, Harshai, Gil, & Gruenwald, 2008). It is important to distinguish between the size of a penis in the flaccid state and the size of a penis in the erect state. Masters and Johnson (1966) found that there was a poor relationship between the size of a flaccid penis and the size of an erect penis: small flaccid penises tend to increase more in size when erect than do larger flaccid penises. In a review article, Wylie & Eardley (2007) noted great consistency among studies measuring different facets of penis size: the average length of a flaccid penis was about 9.5 centimetres, while the average length of an erect penis was about 15 centimetres. In addition, the mean diameter of a flaccid penis was about 2.5 centimetres, whereas the mean diameter of an erect penis was about 4 centimetres.

Some men, even if they consider their penis to be of average size, believe that an average-sized penis is not enough to satisfy themselves or their partners. Some of these men may try various kinds of non-surgical methods—e.g., penile extenders, liquid injectable silicone—to enlarge their penises, and the outcomes of such methods range from no change to a slight change (Nugteren et al., 2010; Oderda & Gontero, 2010). Others may opt for surgical intervention, which can entail serious complications (e.g., penile deformity, penile shortening, scarring, and sexual dysfunction) and generally offers only very modest increases (about 1.3 centimetres in length and 2.5 centimetres in circumference). Overall, short- and long-term satisfaction rates from penile enhancement surgery are low (Vardi et al., 2008).

It is important to note that large penises are not essential for sexual pleasure during intercourse, and not all women and men prefer them. Studies examining how women in California, New Zealand, and Cameroon, for example, rate the attractiveness of non-erect penises found that women in all of these regions rated penises of intermediate length as most attractive (Dixson, Dixson, Morgan, & Anderson, 2007; Dixson, Dixson, Bishop, & Parish, 2010).

The Angle of the Dangle

Erections have several features that can facilitate rewarding coital sex for both partners, as well as insemination. Compared to a flaccid penis, an erect penis is longer, wider, and firmer. Its stiffness makes penetration possible, and its size means that it can fill a vagina or an anus.

How erect should a penis be? If a male is standing upright with a full erection, the average angle is only about 10 degrees above horizontal, but this angle commonly ranges from 0 degrees to 40 degrees. The roots of the penis are typically more horizontal, so that the erect penis bends upward at the junction between the roots in the perineum and the external shaft. When an erection is not full, the angle is diminished. A reduced angle is a sign of mild erectile dysfunction. If the penis is not firm enough, penetration during vaginal or anal sex may not be possible. If the angle is not great enough, maintaining penetration during sexual intercourse may become difficult.

THE SCROTUM

The scrotum, the loose pouch of skin that contains the testes (discussed below), hangs directly under the base of the penis. The scrotum consists of two thin layers: an outer layer of skin with little hair, and an inner sheet of **involuntary muscle** called the dartos. The dartos muscle responds to temperature and contracts if the testes are cold. This contraction causes the testes to rise, the scrotum to look smaller, and the skin of the scrotum to wrinkle.

involuntary muscle A muscle that contracts without conscious control, usually found in the walls of internal organs.

Internal Organs

The internal sex organs of the male consist of the testes, the seminiferous tubules, the epididymis, the vas deferens, the seminal vesicles, the prostate gland, and the Cowper's glands (Figures 4.11 and 4.12).

THE TESTES

There are two testes, or testicles, inside the scrotum (Figure 4.12). The testes are the male reproductive glands, or gonads; they are analogous to the female ovaries. They secrete male sex hormones (androgens) and produce sperm. Although the testes are roughly the same size, they are somewhat asymmetrical; the left testis usually hangs lower than the right. The spermatic cord suspends each testis in the scrotum and contains the vas deferens, blood vessels, and nerves. The cord on each side, as well as the testis itself, is surrounded by a layer of muscle called the cremaster, which lifts the testis when it contracts.

Why would the testes need muscle around them? For sperm to develop normally and remain healthy, the testes need to be at a fairly constant temperature that is slightly lower than the core body temperature. The cremaster helps to maintain this temperature by adjusting how close the testicles are to the torso. When men jump into cold water, for example, the cremaster muscle reflexively contracts to bring the testes closer to the abdomen to keep them warm. Conversely, when the testes are in a comparatively hot environment, the muscle relaxes and the testes hang farther away from the body to cool off. Some people believe that keeping the testes in a hot environment—by taking long hot baths and wearing tight athletic supporters, for example—can cause infertility. Although some sperm can certainly be damaged by this practice, this is not an effective form of contraception. Men who have jobs that involve sitting in a warm area all day (e.g., cab drivers) may have a lower-than-normal sperm count, but a low sperm count may be due to other environmental factors as well.

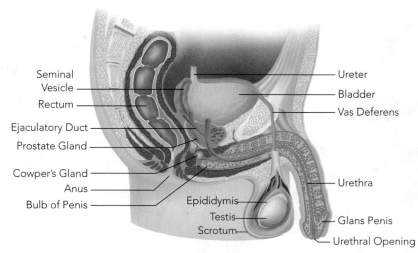

FIGURE 4.11 Internal male genital anatomy, as viewed from the side. Note that the vas deferens and seminal vesicle are not normally visible on a midline view; these structures are shown here schematically.

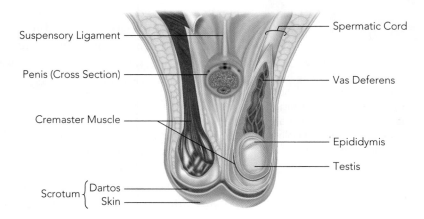

FIGURE 4.12 Inside the scrotum. In the Middle Ages, men who wanted to produce male offspring sometimes had their left testicle removed because people believed that the right testicle made "boy" sperm and the left made "girl" sperm.

The Development of the Testes

When a male fetus first starts to develop testes, these organs are not in the scrotum but up in the fetus's abdominal cavity. The testes then descend through the lower edge of the abdominal wall, just to the side of the pubic symphysis, and down into the scrotum. This normally occurs in the last month or so before birth. About 3 per cent of all boys are born with one undescended testis, but this usually corrects itself within the first year of life. If it does not, surgical intervention is necessary because undescended testicles reduce fertility and increase the risk of testicular tumors.

As the testes descend into the scrotum, they drag with them their blood supply, their nerves, and the duct that drains the testes of sperm—the vas deferens (see below). Since the testes first form in the abdomen, they are innervated as if they are abdominal viscera, and they sense stretching or compression much like other viscera. As a result, pain from compression can be intense, but it is not precisely localized. It is typically felt deep in the body cavity where the testes first developed. This is why men who are in pain after being hit in the scrotum often bend over holding their abdomen, where they feel the pain, rather than their scrotum, where the trauma actually occurred. Males can confirm this for themselves just by squeezing their testes and noting how they sense the resulting pain deep in their abdomen.

Castration

Castrating a male by removing or destroying his testicles is a practice that most people now consider barbarous, yet human castrations have been practised across much of human history, particularly in Asia and the Mediterranean region (Figure 4.13). Today, a typical Westerner may think of a eunuch as a guard in an ancient harem, protecting but *not* inseminating the wives and mistresses of a sultan or a potentate. However, "harems" were more than a collection of women confined behind walls within some Middle Eastern palace. They were the places where government business took place. In that setting, eunuchs were far more than guards; they were managers, teachers, administrators, senior diplomats, and high-ranking military officials.

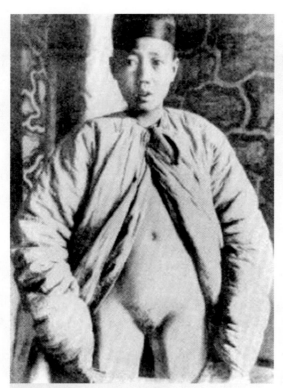

FIGURE 4.13 A eunuch from the end of the Chinese empires. The last living eunuch from China was Sun Yaoting, who was castrated in 1911, when he was eight years old, by his father. His father anticipated that he would serve in the imperial palace, but the empire collapsed a few months later.

In past times, castrations were typically performed before puberty. As a result, the males did not go through puberty and as adults looked very different from their non-castrated contemporaries. They did not develop secondary sexual characteristics, such as a deep voice or facial hair, and they grew to be taller than non-castrated males. Because of their large size and high-pitched voices, they often had dramatic stage presence and voices. For this reason, eunuchs were a part of many European choirs, including the Vatican's choir beginning around 1550. From there, the role of the singing eunuch evolved into that of the castrati, the secular operatic stars of Europe from about 1600 to 1850.

While it is generally assumed that eunuchs had no interest in or ability to be sexual, history shows that this is not uniformly true. While some eunuchs were asexual monks, others were lascivious lovers. They also varied in terms of their sexual partners, in some instances being encouraged (or at least allowed) to marry women, as was the case in some Chinese dynasties and the Ottoman Empire, and in other cases being partnered with males.

The socially condoned castration of healthy males in order to make them into eunuchs who could fill established social and cultural roles ended in the early years of the twentieth century, with the collapse of the Chinese and Ottoman empires. The last known castrato of the Vatican's choir, Alessandro Moreschi, died in 1922.

Some males are still castrated in our society, but rarely before puberty, and for very different reasons than in the past. Castrations are now done either surgically or chemically. Castration results in androgen deprivation, which can be very beneficial in the treatment of some diseases, in particular prostate cancer, but also carries with it certain negative side effects. For example, adult men who are androgen-deprived typically lose muscle mass and gain weight. They are at increased risk of developing diabetes and osteoporosis, and they can experience reduced libido and some menopausal symptoms, such as hot flashes. And, of course, they are sterile. They are not, however, likely to become sopranos or lose their facial hair, as those features become fixed with puberty. Depending on the drugs that are used, and how long they are used for, the androgen deprivation caused by chemical agents may be reversible.

Most androgen-deprived males in the modern world are prostate cancer patients, who undergo short- or long-term **chemical castration** to extend their lives. In North America today, approximately half a million prostate cancer patients are on androgen-depriving drugs. However, this treatment is rarely referred to as "castration." Most medically castrated men are said to be on "hormonal therapy," and they rarely refer to themselves "eunuchs." This shift in terminology is largely a result of current cultural perceptions, which consider castration cruel, and emasculation shameful. Indeed, to say that someone is "a eunuch" or "has no balls" is to imply a level of powerlessness that goes well beyond the inability to impregnate a female.

chemical castration Administration of medication that suppresses androgens and, as a result, reduces a male's sex drive.

THE SEMINIFEROUS TUBULES

Within the testes are the seminiferous tubules (Figure 4.14) and the interstitial cells (Leydig's cells), both of which are involved in sperm production and storage. The seminiferous tubules are long, thin, coiled tubes that are packed into the testes. **Spermatogenesis** occurs in these tubules after the onset of puberty and throughout adulthood but decreases as men get older. Sperm storage also takes place in these tubules. The interstitial cells are located between the tubules, and they produce the male hormones (androgens), most notably testosterone, which they secrete directly into the bloodstream.

spermatogenesis Sperm production.

THE EPIDIDYMIS

The epididymis is a C-shaped structure covering part of each testis (Figures 4.11 and 4.14). It consists of a narrow, tightly coiled tube and has three parts: a head, a body, and a tail. Immature sperm produced in the seminiferous tubules move through the ducts into the epididymis, where they mature and are once again stored.

THE VAS DEFERENS

Sperm stored in the epididymis drain into the vas deferens, a thin duct that is part of the spermatic cord (Figure 4.12). The vas deferens carries the sperm up through the lower abdominal wall (via the inguinal canal) and around the bladder to the prostate gland (see below). From there, the sperm enter the urethra to ultimately exit the penis upon ejaculation (Figure 4.11). This circuitous route, from the testicles to the tip of the penis, reflects the fact that the testes first developed in the abdomen.

Up until the sperm reach the prostate, they are moved by cilia and muscle contractions in the walls of the epididymis and the vas deferens. Once at the prostate, they mix with the fluids secreted by the seminal vesicles and become independently mobile, propelling themselves by the cork-screw action of their tails.

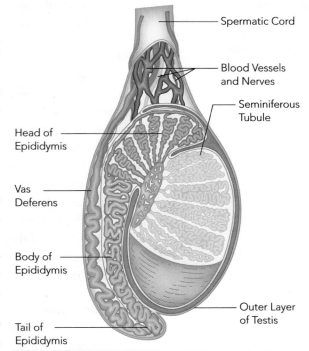

Labels: Spermatic Cord; Blood Vessels and Nerves; Seminiferous Tubule; Head of Epididymis; Vas Deferens; Body of Epididymis; Tail of Epididymis; Outer Layer of Testis

FIGURE 4.14 A schematic drawing of the inside of a testis. Each testis contains a complex arrangement of seminiferous tubules; a single testis may contain 300 to 500 metres of these tubules.

THE SEMINAL VESICLES

The seminal vesicles (Figure 4.11) are two tubular glands next to the prostate gland, near the ends of the vas deferens. They secrete a sugary, alkaline fluid that constitutes up to 70 per cent of the ejaculate; the remaining portion (about 30 per cent) is produced by the prostate gland. The fluid produced by the seminal vesicles, whose purpose has yet to be fully determined, contains a multitude of chemicals.

THE PROSTATE GLAND

The prostate gland lies directly below the bladder (Figure 4.11) and consists of glandular tissue and muscle. The prostate secretes a thin, milky, alkaline fluid, resulting in a chemically safe environment to maintain sperm. The alkalinity of semen counteracts the harmful acidity of the male urethra and the female vagina.

Prostate Cancer

Prostate cancer is the most common malignancy in males; at least 1 in 7 men in Canada can expect to be diagnosed with this disease in his lifetime, and about 1 in 27 men will die of it. Prostate cancer is rare in men under 40, although it becomes increasingly common with age. Right now, the mean age for diagnosis is the mid-60s; most men will have it by the time they are 90, although it is not always diagnosed.

Regular screening for prostate cancer is recommended for men if they have a family history of the disease. Screening involves a blood test for a protein (prostate specific antigen, PSA) secreted into the bloodstream by prostate cells, as well as a digital rectal examination, in which a physician inserts a gloved finger up the rectum and feels for lumps and irregularities in the gland through the wall of the rectum. The prostate can be easily reached in this way because it lies directly in front of the rectum.

prostatectomy The surgical removal of all or part of the prostate gland, usually performed to remove cancer.

If the cancer is caught early and is still localized within the prostate gland, it can be treated in various ways—for example, through radiation therapy or surgical **prostatectomy**. But if it has spread to other parts of the body, curative treatments are no longer an option. Instead, it is treated first with androgen deprivation therapy and then with various chemotherapeutic agents.

Androgen deprivation can be achieved by either surgical removal of the testes (an orchiectomy) or chemical castration. It was the Canadian physician Charles Huggins who first realized that one could treat prostate cancer and certain other cancers of the reproductive system by controlling hormones. The cells that make the prostate gland function are stimulated to grow by androgens. Thus, removing androgens from the body shuts down those cells.

Unfortunately, androgen deprivation for prostate cancer is rarely a long-term cure and has many side effects (see above). At the same time, prostate cancer is generally slow-growing and often asymptomatic. This has led to heated debate about when men should be treated if they have early-stage prostate cancer, and whether they should be screened at all, particularly if they are elderly, since most elderly men would not benefit from treatment.

Semen and Sperm

Semen is made up mostly of fluid from the seminal vesicles and the prostate gland. A male releases about one teaspoon of semen each time he ejaculates, but the amount can be affected by several factors, including the length of time since the last ejaculation (the greater the length of time, the more ejaculate), the length of time of arousal before ejaculation (the longer the duration of arousal, the more ejaculate), and age (younger men tend to produce more fluid than older men do).

A single ejaculation typically contains between 200 and 500 million sperm, yet surprisingly sperm account for only about 1 per cent of the volume of the ejaculatory fluid. Other substances in the fluid include fructose, ascorbic and citric acids, and water.

A single mature sperm is tiny—about 60 micrometres in length. It is composed of a head, a midpiece, and a tail (Figure 4.15). Normally, the 23 chromosomes carried in the head of a sperm combine with the 23 from an egg to produce the full complement of 46 chromosomes in humans. Sperm can live in the female reproductive tract for about four days.

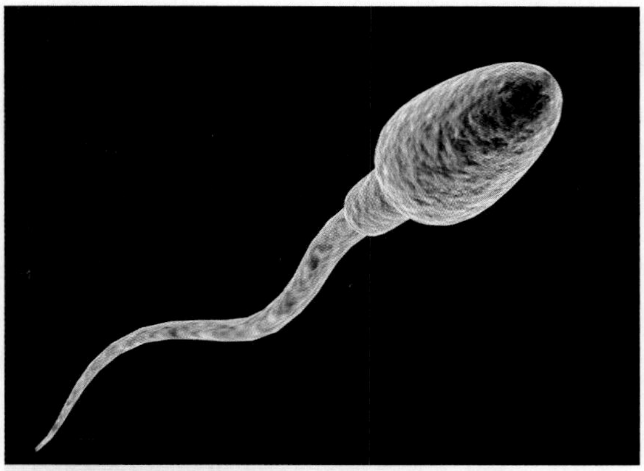

THE COWPER'S GLANDS

The Cowper's glands (bulbourethral glands) are two pea-sized structures that lie on each side of the urethra, below the prostate (Figure 4.11); their ducts empty into the urethra. During sexual arousal, they secrete a small amount of clear, slippery, alkaline fluid (**pre-ejaculate**, or pre-cum) that is believed to counteract the acidity of the urethra and prepare the urethra for the flow of seminal fluid. This pre-ejaculatory fluid may contain active and healthy sperm; for this reason, the withdrawal method is not a reliable means of birth control.

FIGURE 4.15 Human Sperm (magnified). The term *sperm* comes from the Greek *sperma*, meaning "seed." Some have hypothesized that pregnant women who are continually exposed to the fetus's father's semen are less like to suffer from morning sickness. Although likely appealing to dads-to-be, this theory has not been tested.

pre-ejaculate A clear fluid released from the tip of the penis when a man is sexually aroused.

Other Areas of Interest: Erogenous Zones

An erogenous zone is an area of the human body that can result in sexual arousal upon tactile stimulation. Aside from the obvious—the penis and the clitoris—there are many areas that can be included in this category. For example, the scrotum, the anus and surrounding perineal area, the buttocks, the wrists, the ears, the neck, the axillae (armpits), the breasts, and the nipples are often cited as pleasure zones. Interestingly, people who have spinal cord injuries and have lost sensation in various parts of their lower bodies may experience a shift of their lower erogenous regions to the border between their sensitive and insensitive skin (Lundberg, Ertekin, Ghezzi, Swash, & Vodusek, 2001).

Female Breasts

As with the vulva, there is large variation in the size and shape of breasts and nipples from woman to woman. In fact, there are often differences in breast size in the same woman, as one breast is usually slightly larger than the other. As well, the colour and size of the **areola** around the nipple differ from woman to woman. Although such variation is natural, one common issue is that many women are not satisfied with their breast size (Koff & Benavage, 1998). Some of these women undergo surgery to either increase or decrease the size. Overly large breasts can cause chronic pain in the neck, shoulder, and back areas, and they can lead to secondary health issues such as poor blood circulation and impaired breathing (Noone, 2010). However, breast reduction surgery (as with all surgeries) can have negative consequences, including decreased nipple sensitivity, infection, and hematoma (a localized swelling filled with blood that may need to be surgically drained) (Noone, 2010). At the other extreme, breasts that are perceived to be smaller than average may impact a woman's sense of her own attractiveness, and a recent review on breast augmentation surgery indicated high satisfaction with the procedure (Thorne, 2010). Nonetheless, breast augmentation surgery can result in a number of complications, including excessive bleeding, infection, implant rupture or deflation, and scarring. In some cases, complications are severe enough that the implant may need to be removed.

areola The round, coloured area around the nipple.

BREAST CANCER

Breast cancer is the most common cancer affecting women. In Canada each year, an estimated 22,700 women will be diagnosed with breast cancer, and 5100 will die from it (Canadian Cancer Society, 2012). Men can also have breast cancer, and it is estimated that in Canada, 200 men will be diagnosed with the disease and 55 men will die from it annually (Canadian Cancer Society, 2012). Although it is not clear what causes breast cancer, some modifiable risk factors—for example, body weight, physical activity, alcohol use, tobacco use/exposure—have been identified.

The Canadian Breast Cancer Foundation (CBCF) states that, because breasts change throughout life, being "breast aware" is the best way to detect changes that may indicate cancer. There are five steps to being breast aware: (1) know how your breasts normally look and feel; (2) know what changes to look for; (3) look and feel for changes; (4) report any changes to a doctor; and (5) get a mammogram if recommended by your doctor. Remember that a change in one's breasts is not necessarily a sign of breast cancer; some changes, such as those that arise when a woman is breastfeeding, are normal. If an abnormal lump is detected, breast imaging techniques, sometimes followed by a biopsy (during which a sample of the lump is taken), are usually the first steps to finding out what is happening. There are several ways to treat breast cancer; depending on the type and stage of cancer, these treatments can be directed specifically to the disease in the breast and neighboring body wall (local) or they can reach cells throughout the body by traveling through the bloodstream (systemic).

The Mechanics of Coital Sex

During the most common position for coitus in our species—the missionary position—pressure is applied by the penis to both the anterior vaginal wall and the clitoris with each hip thrust. If the penis is firm enough and the angle is appropriate, the movements of the penis in the vagina are not simply in and out; rather, the movements include some translation of the male's torso upward and downward in relation to the female's body (Figure 4.16). The clitoris lies directly below the pubic symphysis, so a slight movement upward by the male applies a pulse of pressure to the clitoris.

As the male moves upward, the female's pubic symphysis acts as a fulcrum or rotation point for his penis; thus, as he moves upward, the tip of his penis rotates downward. If the penis is not firm enough and the erection angle is not appropriate and stable, the male risks having his penis slip out of the vagina as his pelvic thrusts shift him upward. On the other hand, if he restricts his movements to reduce the chance of separation, his stimulation of the clitoris is reduced.

An under-appreciated anatomical feature of the penis is the suspensory ligament that attaches the base of the penis to the male's pubic symphysis. This tough, fibrous band acts as a spring for the penis during erection and penetration. One can check out its spring-like function by simply rotating an erect penis upward toward the front of the male's abdomen. It should rotate up easily. Next, try to rotate it downward. The penis resists downward rotation, in part because this motion stretches the

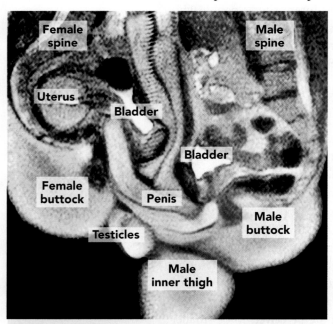

FIGURE 4.16 An inside view of male-female intercourse in the missionary position. Depictions of this position appear in the pottery and art of ancient civilizations, suggesting that humans have been using it since ancient times. It is also likely that the position was in use far before humans evolved, since it is also used by the great apes and other primates.

suspensory ligament. The springiness of this system helps provide pulsatile pressure to the clitoris during coitus. It also helps to prevent the penis from slipping out of the vagina every time the male moves his body upward.

But what if the penis is not quite fully erect? If the angle of the erection is too low, as the male thrusts forward and upward, the penis can rotate downward and slide out of the vagina. This lowering in the angle of the erect penis is a subtle but common indication of mild erectile dysfunction. When a man is experiencing mild erectile dysfunction, his erection may appear to be as long, wide, and firm as usual, but the shaft will be more flexible than normal, causing the penis to drop to a lower-than-normal angle; this extra mobility has been called "the hinge effect." This effect is not always recognized by couples trying to have sex when there is mild erectile dysfunction. They may feel that they have to adjust their posture to avoid separation, and this conscious adjustment can distract from the primal reflexive nature of the sexual act. Erectile dysfunction treatments that are not 100 per cent effective commonly fail due to the hinge effect.

Sexual Response Cycles

The sexual response cycle is defined as the sequence of events that occur when a person becomes sexually aroused and engages in sexually stimulating activities (e.g., intercourse, masturbation). Although primarily based on physiological processes, it also involves psychological, cognitive, and experiential processes that depend on a less obvious sex organ—the brain. When reading the following sections, keep in mind that people's sexual response cycles are highly variable and individualized; they evolve over time and change depending on the person's mood, sexual history, the situation, and partner factors. However, there are some basic biological processes that occur in most people, most of the time. The following discussion considers the various models that have been proposed to explain the sensations that are involved in a full sexual response, and how these sensations may vary between males and females.

Masters and Johnson's Sexual Response Cycle

William Masters and Virginia Johnson are credited with being the first researchers to objectively investigate the sexual response cycle; indeed, they studied sexual response rigorously and published their findings in their 1966 book, *Human Sexual Response.* Masters and Johnson studied the sexual response of over 350 women and over 300 men who experienced more than 10,000 cycles of arousal and orgasm in a laboratory setting (see the "Research vs Real Life" box in Chapter 1). Masters and Johnson focused on the physiological processes of sexual response—monitoring such indicators as heart rate, blood pressure, and respiration rate, directly observing changes in genital and non-genital regions of the body. They also included measurements of changes inside the vagina during arousal and orgasm during "artificial coition" by using a clear phallic-shaped dildo that contained a tiny surgical camera.

Armed with these data, Masters and Johnson described a four-phase model of sexual response (Figure 4.17) based on two fundamental processes: vasocongestion and **myotonia**. Vasocongestion refers to the pooling of blood in the blood vessels of a bodily region, and it can occur in both genital and non-genital areas during sexual arousal. Normally, when an individual is in a non-sexually aroused state, the inflow of blood to tissue and organs via arteries is balanced by an equal outflow through veins. However, during sexual arousal, the dilation of the arteries results in an inflow over and above what the veins carry away. The affected area then appears red and swollen, and it may feel warm and more sensitive. Myotonia refers to the increased muscle tension in

myotonia The increased muscle tension in genital and non-genital areas of the body during sexual arousal.

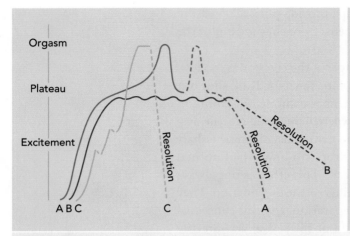
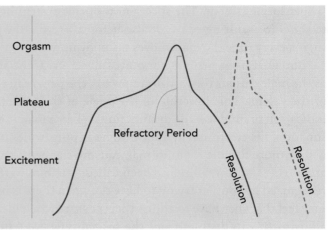

FIGURE 4.17 The sexual response cycle in females (left) and males (right), as depicted by Masters and Johnson. The graphs show the four phases identified by Masters and Johnson: excitement, plateau, orgasm, and resolution. In the graph of the cycle in females, the solid lines indicate common patterns of increasing sexual response, while the dashed lines indicate common patterns of loss of sexual response. This loss develops as a reverse response pattern, from plateau to excitement to a resolved (i.e., unstimulated) state. Note that the facility of multiple orgasm in females is highest when effective sexual stimulation is started at plateau levels of response, as depicted in Pattern A. In addition, this graph shows three variations of the cycle in women: Pattern A depicts a female with a gradual buildup of sexual tensions, culminating in an orgasm, after which another orgasm is experienced, followed by the resolution response. Pattern B illustrates a woman with a gradual buildup of sexual tension, but with no orgasm experience; as a result of the lack of physical release with orgasm, the refractory period is longer. Pattern C represents a woman with a quick and intense sexual response, and an equally quick resolution phase. The graph of the cycle in males shows a cycle similar to that represented by Pattern A on the left. The "refractory period" refers to the period of time following orgasm/ejaculation in which another orgasm cannot occur, although some men can experience multiple orgasms.

genital and non-genital areas of the body during sexual arousal. This tension can cause certain areas of the body to experience sudden, perceptible muscle spasms.

Note that the four phases of the response cycle are the same regardless of the type of sexual stimulation. Also, although separated for ease of comprehension here, the phases do not indicate discrete steps that are independent of one another.

THE FIRST PHASE: EXCITEMENT

The excitement phase refers to the processes that signal the beginning of sexual arousal. The fundamental process that occurs during this stage is vasocongestion, which results in penile erection and vaginal lubrication (Figure 4.18a). Vasocongestion can be triggered by direct genital and/or non-genital stimulation or by sexual thoughts, and it occurs rapidly—usually within a few seconds in young males, and within 10 to 30 seconds in young females (barring high alcohol levels and fatigue, which lengthen the response time).

Other genital changes also take place in the excitement phase. In males, the dartos muscle in the wall of the scrotum and the cremaster muscle around the testes contract. The former tightens (and wrinkles) the skin of the scrotum, while the latter elevates the testes. In females, the glans and the crura of the clitoris and the vestibular bulbs swell. The labia majora separate away from the vaginal opening, and the labia minora swell and darken in colour. In addition, the inner two-thirds of the vagina expands significantly, and the vaginal walls open somewhat like an inflated balloon to accommodate penile entry. As part of this accommodation response, the cervix and uterus also elevate.

Non-genital changes take place in this phase as well. Nipple erection occurs in both males and females due to myotonia. In females, breasts may swell and enlarge to a

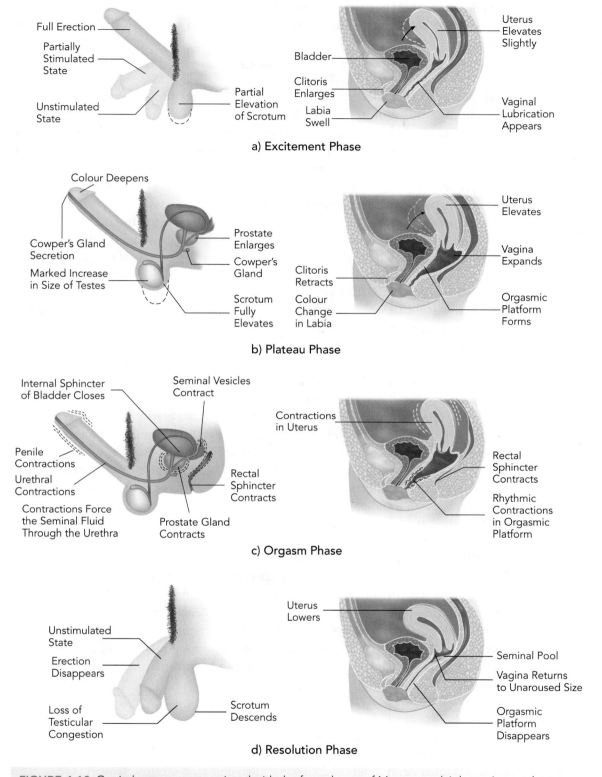

a) Excitement Phase

b) Plateau Phase

c) Orgasm Phase

d) Resolution Phase

FIGURE 4.18 Genital responses associated with the four phases of Masters and Johnson's sexual response cycle. a) In the first phase, the male's penis becomes fully erect and his testes become elevated. The female's clitoris and labia swell, her vagina lengthens and expands, and her cervix and uterus elevate. b) In the second phase, the male's testes and the female's uterus elevate further, and the female's clitoris may retract slightly. Note that many men release little to no Cowper's Gland secretion. c) In the third and briefest phase, both men and women experience orgasm and involuntary muscle spasms throughout their body; in men, this phase is characterized by ejaculation, and in women it is characterized by rhythmical contractions in the vagina, uterus, and pelvic floor. d) In the fourth and final phase, the genitals return to their unaroused states.

variable degree. Along with increases in heart rate and blood pressure, a "sex flush"—a pink or red blush on the chest that is more common in women than in men—may also occur.

THE SECOND PHASE: PLATEAU

Despite the fact that the term *plateau* implies a levelling off of responses, Masters and Johnson used this term to refer to a dramatic surge of sexual tension in males and females. During this stage, most of the processes that begin in the excitement phase increase until the individual reaches the peak that leads to orgasm (Figure 4.18b). For example, heart rate, blood pressure, and myotonia increase in both sexes, testicular engorgement and elevation become more pronounced in males, and the uterus becomes increasingly elevated in females. In addition, the external portion of the clitoris may retract under its hood (as stimulation may become too intense to be pleasurable), and the lower third of the vagina becomes significantly engorged, leading to a tightening of this region that results in increased muscle tension of the pelvic floor.

THE THIRD PHASE: ORGASM

As effective stimulation is continued, some people (more males than females) will reach the orgasmic phase (Figure 4.18c). This stage is the briefest of all the stages, usually lasting only a few seconds. During this stage, involuntary muscle spasms occur throughout the body, including the rectal sphincter and the neighbouring pelvic floor, and heart rate and blood pressure reach maximal levels. In males, ejaculation, which occurs with orgasm, occurs in two steps: the emission phase, in which the internal structures, notably the muscle in the wall of the prostate gland, contract, resulting in the pooling of seminal fluid in the urethral bulb, and the expulsion phase, in which semen is expelled via contractions of muscles at the base of the penis that surround the bulb. In females, the lower third of the vagina and the uterus contract rhythmically with orgasm; in addition, rectal pressure, an indicator of perineal muscle activity, oscillates between 8 and 13 hertz (van Netten, Georgiadis, Nieuwenburg, & Kortekaas, 2008). There are no further changes in the breasts or the clitoris.

THE FINAL PHASE: RESOLUTION

The final phase of the sexual response cycle is resolution, during which the sexual system returns to its unaroused state (Figure 4.18d). This phase starts right after orgasm if no further stimulation occurs. Some processes (e.g., heart rate, blood pressure, and sex flush) resolve quickly, whereas others (e.g., clitoral engorgement and penile erection) take longer. If orgasm has not occurred and no further stimulation is experienced, the resolution phase will take longer, especially after a lengthy period of high arousal.

Other Sexual Response Cycle Models

KAPLAN'S THREE-STAGE MODEL

Australian-American sex therapist Helen Singer Kaplan (1974) proposed a model of sexual response containing the following three phases: desire, excitement, and orgasm (Figure 4.19). The strength of this model lies in its inclusion of desire as the first stage of sexual response, acknowledging the importance of psychological—in addition to physiological—processes in sexual response.

BASSON'S MODEL OF FEMALE SEXUAL RESPONSE

Rosemary Basson, from the University of British Columbia, constructed a model of female sexual response (Figure 4.20) based on her work with women who experience low sexual desire (Basson, 2002). One key element of her model is that it accounts for the fact that while many women experience spontaneous sexual desire and seek ways to be sexual in response to their desire, others—especially those in long-term relationships—may not experience desire in this way; rather, they may engage in sexual activity for non-sexual or sexually neutral reasons (e.g., to feel emotionally closer to a partner). Once sexual sensations start to build, and if other psychological, relational, and environmental cues are satisfactory, these women's sexual desire may increase, and this desire may drive them to want to continue the activity to satisfy this desire.

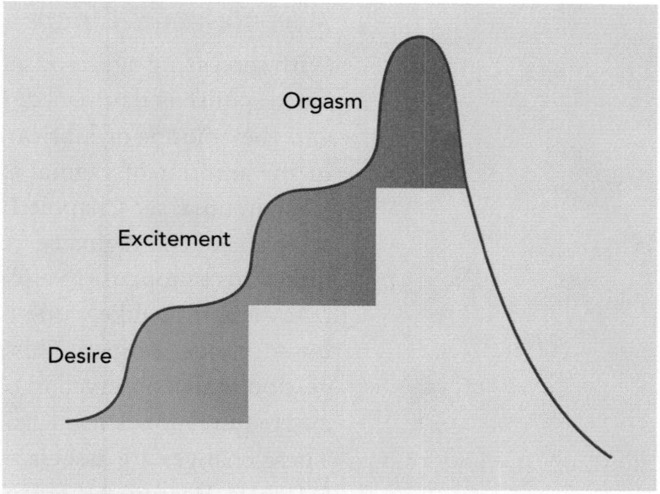

Comparing the Models: Sexual Function and Dysfunction

Sand and Fisher (2007) surveyed over one hundred female registered nurses, asking questions about sexual function and the type of sexual response cycle that best described their experience: Masters and Johnson's four-phase model, Kaplan's three-stage model, or Basson's model. Interestingly, women in this sample were equally likely to endorse each model, yet those who endorsed Basson's model were more likely to report greater sexual dysfunction and more dissatisfaction with their emotional relationship with their partner.

FIGURE 4.19 Helen Singer Kaplan's three-stage model of sexual response. This model is most notable for its inclusion of *desire* and, thus, its recognition that psychological processes play a role in sexual response.

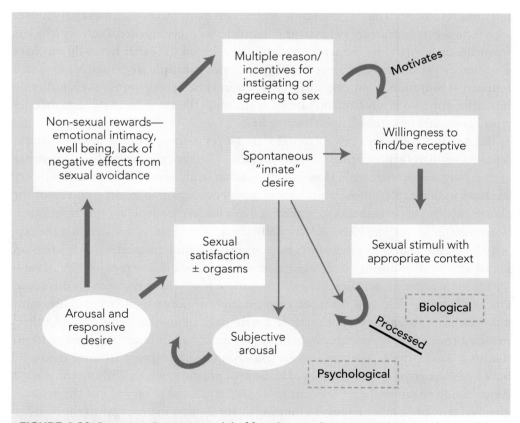

FIGURE 4.20 Rosemary Basson's model of female sexual response. This complex model is unique in that it accounts for a variety of reasons for which women choose to engage in sexual activity.

Age-Related Decreases in Sexual Response

With increasing age, arousal takes longer, and the intensity of all aspects of one's sexual response is dampened. For example, in women, vaginal lubrication takes longer, and the amount of lubrication secreted is reduced; in combination with a reduction in the amount of vaginal expansion, these changes may lead to painful intercourse (dyspareunia; see Chapter 16) (Koch, Mansfield, Thurau, & Carey, 2005). In addition, the walls of the vagina become less flexible as a woman ages. These changes are often linked to menopause (Nelson, 2008). On the other hand, the resolution phase typically takes less time, likely due to the fact that the degree of vasocongestion is generally lower in older women. This pattern of faster resolution and lower degrees of vasocongestion is also observed in older men. As men get older, erections take longer to occur and require more stimulation, and the degree of firmness is less than in younger males. These changes are associated with the normal decline of testosterone levels with age (Morales, Heaton, & Carson, 2000), among other factors such as presence and type of disease and availability of partner.

Sex Differences in Sexual Response

Although there is much similarity between the sexes in terms of the biological processes of sexual response, there are some notable differences.

THE REFRACTORY PERIOD AND MULTIPLE ORGASMS

During the resolution phase, there is an important difference between males and females in terms of their physiological readiness for further sexual stimulation. Once orgasm occurs, males usually experience a **refractory period**, which can last from a few minutes to days. The length of time depends on many factors, such as age (younger men have shorter refractory periods) and frequency of previous sexual activity (the less frequent, the shorter the refractory period). Females, on the other hand, do not have a refractory period and can more readily experience **multiple orgasms**. Masters and Johnson (1966) found that orgasms that occur in close succession to one another do not differ physiologically from one another, although the second and subsequent ones typically require less stimulation than the first.

Kinsey and colleagues (1953) found that 14 per cent of women in their sample reported regularly experiencing multiple orgasms. Theoretically, women can experience as many orgasms as they wish. However, a Canadian study of over 170 female university students indicated that most women experience post-orgasmic hypersensitivity of the clitoris, which the participants identified as a motivation for avoiding further stimulation (Humphries & Cioe, 2009). Additionally, some researchers have stated that the capacity for multiple orgasms in women may be greater during masturbation or same-sex sexual activity than during penile-vaginal intercourse alone (Masters & Johnson, 1966).

Multiple orgasms in males also exist, but there is very little research on this topic. One study found that men described their multiple orgasm experience variably: some reported having orgasms without ejaculation followed by an ejaculatory orgasm, others reported the reverse experience, and still others described different response patterns (Dunn & Trost, 1989). There is also evidence of multiple orgasms in some men who have had their prostate gland removed because of prostate cancer. Without the gland's contribution to semen, "dry" orgasms result, but the speed of recovery of the prostate gland after an orgasm is no longer a limiting factor for how many orgasms the men can have. Interestingly, in an account from one male who no longer had a prostate gland and reported being multi-orgasmic, the orgasm was described as radiating out of the deep pelvis rather than being focussed in the area of the body where the gland used to reside (Warkentin, Gray, & Wassersug, 2006).

refractory period In males, the period of time following orgasm in which another orgasm cannot occur regardless of stimulation received.

multiple orgasms More than one orgasm experienced within a short period of time.

VARIABILITY OF ORGASMIC EXPERIENCE

The occurrence of orgasm varies greatly between males and females. Based on Kinsey's data (Kinsey, Pomeroy, & Martin, 1948; Kinsey et al., 1953), the frequency of ejaculation in boys increases from 5 per cent to 100 per cent between the ages of 10 and 15, whereas a more gradual increase is seen in women across a 25-year span starting at about 15 years of age, and the frequency does not appear to exceed 90 per cent. In addition, the types of stimulation needed for orgasm vary between sexes. Although about 90 per cent of women are orgasmic from some form of sexual stimulation (e.g., direct or indirect clitoral stimulation), most women do not regularly experience orgasm "solely" from sexual intercourse. Indeed, some women *never* experience orgasm this way. Contrast this experience with that of men: almost 100 per cent of men regularly experience orgasm via sexual intercourse alone. This difference likely reflects evolutionary and/or social processes (Wallen & Lloyd, 2011).

Narjani (1924) proposed that if the distance between a woman's clitoral glans and her urethra is less than 2.5 centimetres or so (and therefore the possibility of clitoral stimulation via penile penetration is enhanced), the likelihood of orgasms solely from sexual intercourse may be increased. Indeed, it was found that women with shorter distances between these two regions were more likely to report experiencing orgasms from vaginal penetration alone (Wallen & Lloyd, 2011). As described earlier, the pubic symphysis acts as a fulcrum during intercourse; the penis essentially rolls over it during coital pelvic thrusting. If the clitoris is located right between the shaft of the penis and the pubic symphysis, it would receive maximal stimulation during intercourse. It is hard, though, to isolate which body structures and surfaces are being stimulated for females during coital sex. This argues against the notion of vaginal orgasms being a sign of sexual maturity over and above orgasms from clitoral stimulation, as posited by Freud (1905/2000). Indeed, Masters and Johnson (1966) reported that physiological processes did not differ between their classifications of vaginal versus clitoral orgasms. In addition, descriptions of the experience of male orgasms and female orgasms have been found to be indistinguishable (e.g., Mah & Binik, 2002).

CHAPTER SUMMARY

There is great variation in the appearance and functioning of the sexual organs. Although variation in appearance is normal, some people feel the need to undergo surgical procedures to alter the appearance of their external genitals or breasts; most of these surgeries carry with them a variety of risks. A number of researchers, most notably Masters and Johnson, have attempted to characterize a sexual response cycle in humans. There is great variation in the ways in which people experience sexual response, with the greatest variation occurring between the sexes during sexual response in, for example, the facility for experiencing multiple orgasms. Despite these differences, human sexual response is physiologically similar between the sexes.

DEBATE QUESTIONS

In our society over the last few decades, we have had increasing interest in, and acceptance of, body modification surgeries. But should there be limits on such surgeries? If so, where should we draw the line?

REVIEW QUESTIONS

1. What are some functions of pubic hair?
2. What are common anatomical features of the clitoris and the penis?
3. What is the function of the prostate gland in males?
4. What are believed to be the health benefits and risks of male circumcision?
5. What is the difference between the sexual response cycle described by Masters and Johnson and that described by Basson?

SUGGESTIONS FOR FURTHER READING AND VIEWING

Recommended Websites

3-D Vulva: www.3dvulva.com

Boston University School of Medicine, Sexual Medicine: www.bumc.bu.edu/sexualmedicine/physicianinformation/female-genital-anatomy

Canadian Breast Cancer Foundation: www.cbcf.org

Canadian Cancer Society: www.cancer.ca

Female Genital Anatomy for Dummies: www.dummies.com/how-to/content/the-human-vagina-and-other-female-sexual-parts.html

Male Genital Anatomy for Dummies: www.dummies.com/how-to/content/anatomy-of-the-human-penis.seriesId-225283.html

MedScape, Male Reproductive Organ Anatomy: http://emedicine.medscape.com/article/1899075-overview

Recommended Reading

Anderson, W.R., Summerton, D.J., & Holmes, S.A. (2003). The urologist's guide to genital piercing. *British Journal of Urology International*, *91*, 245–51. doi:10.1046/j.1464-4096.2003.04049.x

LeVay, S., & Baldwin, J. (2008). *Human Sexuality* (3rd ed.). Sunderland, MA: Sinauer Associates.

Livoti, C., & Topp, E. (2004). *Vaginas: An owner's manual*. New York, NY: Thunder's Mouth Press.

Moore, M., & de Costa, C. (2003). *Dick: A user's guide*. New York, NY: Marlowe.

Roach, M. (2008). *Bonk: The curious coupling of sex and science*. New York, NY: W.W. Norton.

Wassersug, R.J., & Johnson, T.W. (2007). Modern-day eunuchs: Motivations for and consequences of contemporary castration. *Perspectives in Biology and Medicine*, *50*, 544–56. doi: 10.1353/pbm.2007.0058

Recommended Viewing

Arnold, C. (Director). (2006). *The O tapes* [Documentary]. United States: Roseworks.

Dodson, B. (Producer). (n.d.) *Betty Dodson's bodysex workshop* [Web film]. Available at http://dodsonandross.com/product/betty-dodsons-bodysex-workshop-01bs

Gordon, K. (Writer). (1999). Phallacies [Television series episode]. In V. Mathur (Producer), *The nature of things*. Canada: CBC.

Land, E. (2012). *Centrefold* [Documentary]. United Kingdom: Wellcome Trust. Available at www.thecentrefoldproject.org

Leach, H. (Director). (2008). *The perfect vagina* [Documentary]. United Kingdom: Channel 4.

McNamara, M. (Director). (2005). *Penis dementia: The search for the perfect penis* [Documentary]. Canada: Markham Street Films.

5 CHAPTER

Sex Hormones and Human Sexuality

GILLIAN EINSTEIN
AND JENNIFER BLAKE

LEARNING OBJECTIVES

In this chapter, you will

- discover how important hormones are to sexual development, sexuality, and reproduction;
- come to understand how hormones connect the brain and nervous system to the reproductive system; and
- find out how hormonal changes associated with aging influence sexuality.

Photo above: Testosterone crystal; transmitted light micrograph; 4x magnification.

The Role of Hormones in Sexuality

James, a 37-year-old man, had been experiencing erectile dysfunction for two years and diminished libido for at least four years. When he had first experienced erectile difficulties, James was upset, but he was uncomfortable discussing the problem with anyone, even his wife, Eve. He began avoiding any form of intimacy, afraid it might lead to more disappointment. Eve, initially understanding, began to feel hurt and increasingly lonely. She felt her husband was avoiding, or even rejecting, her. The couple had attended relationship counselling, but without benefit. James was in otherwise good health, and he was successful in his work.

Recently, James and Eve decided that they would like to have a baby. Finally ready to seek medical help, James contacted his family doctor, who referred him to an endocrinologist. The specialist took a careful history of James's experiences over the past four years and performed a preliminary physical examination, which revealed that everything was normal, with the exception that James's testes were decreased in size. Blood tests revealed an elevated prolactin **hormone** level, and brain imaging with magnetic resonance imaging (MRI) revealed a mass in James's pituitary gland. This mass, which was identified as a prolactin-secreting tumour, proved to be the source of James's overabundance of prolactin and, hence, his decreased libido. James's doctors treated him with a medication that suppressed his prolactin synthesis, and his previous level of sexual function was restored.

Although grateful that James could be sexually active, James and Eve were both very upset that the delay in diagnosis and treatment had caused them so much distress, and they were concerned that it might be too late to reverse the psychological damage. Eventually, with the help of a counsellor, James and Eve were able to repair their relationship. Within a few months Eve was pregnant, and they were looking forward to the birth of their first child.

QUESTIONS FOR CRITICAL THOUGHT AND REFLECTION

1. How do you think that erectile dysfunction made James feel as a person?
2. What kind of psychological damage do you think might result if one partner is not capable of sexual intercourse?
3. Are there characteristic features of physiologic dysfunction that might have led to an earlier diagnosis?

hormone A chemical released by a cell or group of cells (gland) in one part of an organism that affects cells in other parts of the organism via the circulatory system.

Introduction

Recall, from the previous chapters, that the brain plays a central role in sexual function. Indeed, our thoughts and self-perceptions have an enormous influence on our sexual actions. But to understand how our thoughts are able to influence sexual action and, potentially, reproduction, we must understand the role of hormones. Hormones provide the connections within and between the nervous system (the brain, the spinal cord, and the peripheral nerves and muscles) and the reproductive system (the ovaries, the testes, and the genitals). Thus, a full understanding of human sexuality requires a careful examination of the hormones involved in sexuality and reproduction. As you will discover in this chapter, sex hormones can affect every body system involved in sexual behaviour—from the reproductive system, including the genitals, to the nervous system, which includes the brain.

What Are Hormones?

The word *hormone* was coined in 1905 by Ernest Starling, a British physiologist. It is derived from the Greek verb *ormao*, which means "to arouse" or "to excite." Starling defined hormones as "chemical messengers" that a body produces and that are carried to the organ(s) they affect via the circulatory system. Today, we know that hormones play a very complex role in a vast array of biological processes, including growth, aging, metabolism, immune response, sexual response, and reproduction. We also know that hormones can affect not only cells and tissues within the originating body, or person, but also cells and tissues in different persons (e.g., through smell).

Hormones are released into the bloodstream by **endocrine organs** such as the **gonads** and the brain. Once they are in the bloodstream, hormones have the potential to affect every organ in the body. For example, sex hormones, once released, can cause the entire body to experience sexual desire and attraction and they can prime all of the body's components for sexual relations, orgasm, **gamete** release, pregnancy, **parturition**, production and release of milk for breastfeeding, **affiliation**, and **bonding**. Thus, these hormones have a unifying effect on all aspects of sexuality and reproduction.

Hormones can be grouped into three classes, depending on their molecular composition:

1. *lipid and phospholipid hormones*, which are derived from lipids and include two major groups:
   a. *steroid hormones* (e.g., androgens, estrogens, and progestogens), which are structurally composed of carbon rings and derived from cholesterol (Figure 5.1) and
   b. *eicosanoid hormones* (e.g., prostaglandins), which are long-chain fatty acids derived from arachadonic acid;
2. *peptide hormones* (e.g., follicle stimulating hormone, luteinizing hormone, vasopressin, and oxytocin), which consist of peptides (short chains of amino acids, the building blocks of protein); and
3. *monoamine hormones*, such as adrenaline and noradrenaline, which are derived from aromatic amino acids like phenylalanine, tyrosine, and tryptophan.

The main hormones associated with sexual development, reproduction, and/or behaviour, and which will therefore be discussed in greatest detail later in this chapter, are the steroid hormones estradiol, testosterone, and progesterone; the peptide hormones vasopressin, oxytocin, and prolactin; and the glycoprotein hormones luteinizing hormone (LH) and follicle-stimulating hormone (FSH).

Hormones act in **trace** amounts, but they can produce strong effects. They can change the chemical reactions that take place within cells by causing protein synthesis, ultimately having wide-ranging effects on multiple cells and tissues. Given that minute amounts produce strong effects, hormones are finely regulated by **feedback signals** from every organ affected, especially the brain. These signals indicate the difference between the actual level of a hormone and the expected level of that hormone. If the actual level is too low, the signal indicates that more of the hormone must be produced; if the level is too high, the signal lets the producing endocrine organs know that they should decrease their output of the hormone. Hormones have reciprocal relationships with all their target organs: just as the brain affects hormone synthesis, hormones affect the brain to regulate their own synthesis.

Hormone Synthesis

Sex steroids can be synthesized and secreted by both peripheral and central nervous system tissues. Estrogens and androgens are primarily synthesized and secreted by the gonads (the ovaries and the testes). However, the **adrenal glands**, as well as **adipose tissue**, also contribute to the total quantity of androgens and estrogens that circulate within the body. The ovaries and the adrenals both produce androgens and their **precursors** in women, although they produce less of these substances after

---

endocrine organs Organs that secrete hormones into the blood to affect tissues distant from the site of the gland.

gonads Glands in which gametes are produced; in humans, the ovaries and the testes.

gamete A cell with half the number of chromosomes necessary for reproduction that fuses with another such cell during conception.

parturition Childbirth.

affiliation Attachment or connection with others of the same species, often to care for young, reduce stress, and/or confer a survival benefit on the group.

bonding Joining together for social and physical support, as through affiliation.

trace A very small amount that is detectable by extremely sensitive instrumentation but not quantifiable.

feedback signal The part of a control system that provides a measure of the level of a certain substance.

adrenal glands Endocrine glands that make and secrete sex hormones such as estrogens and androgens, stress hormones such as cortisol, and catecholamines.

adipose tissue Body fat.

precursor In biochemistry, a compound, cell, or cellular component from which another substance, cell, or cellular component is formed.

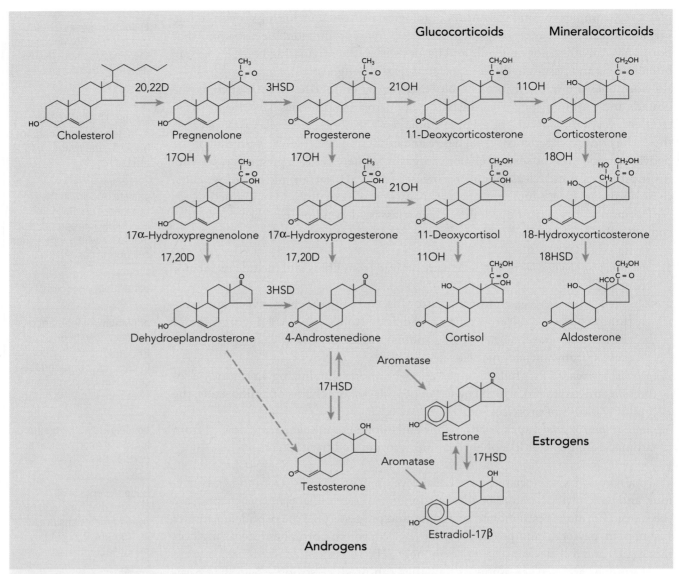

FIGURE 5.1 All of the sex steroids must be made from cholesterol. This figure shows the major pathways for the synthesis of androgens, estrogens, and progestagens. These pathways are common to the ovaries, the testes, the adrenals, and the brain; thus, men and women both produce androgens as well as estrogens. Note that androgens (androstenedione and/or testosterone) must be produced before estrogens can be synthesized. Also note the similarity in the structures of estradiol (a highly potent estrogen) and testosterone (an important androgen)—they differ from each other only by the presence of a single double bond.

menopause (Spencer, Klein, Kumar, & Azziz, 2007). The adrenals and adipose tissue are the source of most of the circulating estrogens in menopausal women as well as in men. The brain is also a source of estrogens (Toran-Allerand, Tinnikov, Singh, & Nethrapalli, 2005).

The peptide hormones LH and FSH are synthesized by the **anterior pituitary** gland (Figure 5.2). Oxytocin and vasopressin are synthesized in the paraventricular and supraoptic nuclei of the **hypothalamus**, respectively. From there, they are transported via **axons** either to target areas of the brain, where they act as **neurotransmitters**, or to the **posterior pituitary** (Figure 5.2), where they are released as hormones. The pathway from the hypothalamus to the pituitary is through the hypothalamic-pituitary-gonadal (HPG) axis (see Figure 5.3).

anterior pituitary The gland within the pituitary that synthesizes and secretes hormones such as growth hormone (GH), thyroid-stimulating hormone (TSH), prolactin (PRL), luteinizing hormone (LH), and follicle-stimulating hormone (FSH).

What Are Sex Hormones?

Hormones are considered sex hormones if they play a large role in sexual maturity and reproduction. The main sex hormones in humans are androgens, estrogens, LH, and FSH. In addition, because of their roles in behaviours that either lead to or result from sexual activity, such as breastfeeding and pair bonding, oxytocin and vasopressin can also be considered sex hormones.

Androgens and estrogens (as well as progestagens) are key players in the maturation of the gonads, the production of gametes, and the rate at which the reproductive system matures. FSH and LH play major roles in reproduction. In females, FSH stimulates the growth and maturation of the **Graafian follicle** and induces enzymes that are required to convert androstenedione to estradiol (see Figure 5.1). LH acts on the cells of the ovary to stimulate the synthesis of steroid hormones, notably androstenedione. LH is also critical for **ovulation**, as an LH surge is necessary for rupture of the follicle that contains the egg, and it stimulates the growth of the **corpus luteum**. In males, LH activates sperm-producing cells in the testes and the growth of the testes, while FSH plays an important role in driving the early stages of spermatogenesis.

Calling these hormones *sex hormones* may suggest that they are associated with sexual functioning in *either* men or women. Yet this is hardly the case. As mentioned above, both the testes and the ovaries synthesize and secrete androgens (often designated as "male" hormones) and estrogens (often designated as "female" hormones), as do the adrenals of both sexes. In fact, estrogens are critical in shaping the development of the male brain (for a review, see Einstein, 2007), and they are vital to the activation of sperm production (Smith et al., 1994). In addition, androgens must be present in both males and females because estrogens are synthesized *from* androgens (again, refer to Figure 5.1).

THE HPG AXIS AND THE REGULATION OF SEX HORMONES

We have known for millennia that many species of animal regulate their sex hormones according to the time of year; many are fertile and willing to mate during certain seasons but not others. Although humans mate year round, careful analysis of birth

hypothalamus A portion of the brain that contains numerous small groupings of neurons, all of which play a role in visceral functions such as sex, and that connects the nervous system to the endocrine system via the pituitary.

axon A thin fibre that projects from a nerve cell.

neurotransmitters Biochemicals made by the nervous system that transmit signals from one neuron to another.

posterior pituitary A collection of axons projecting from the hypothalamus that terminates behind the anterior pituitary gland.

Graafian follicle A small sac, embedded in the ovary, that contains an egg.

ovulation The second phase of the menstrual cycle, during which a mature egg is released from the ovaries; in the ovarian cycle, the stage just after the LH surge.

corpus luteum A temporary, functional cyst that develops out of a Graafian follicle after the follicle has released its egg; its major function is to produce progesterone and estradiol to support a pregnancy.

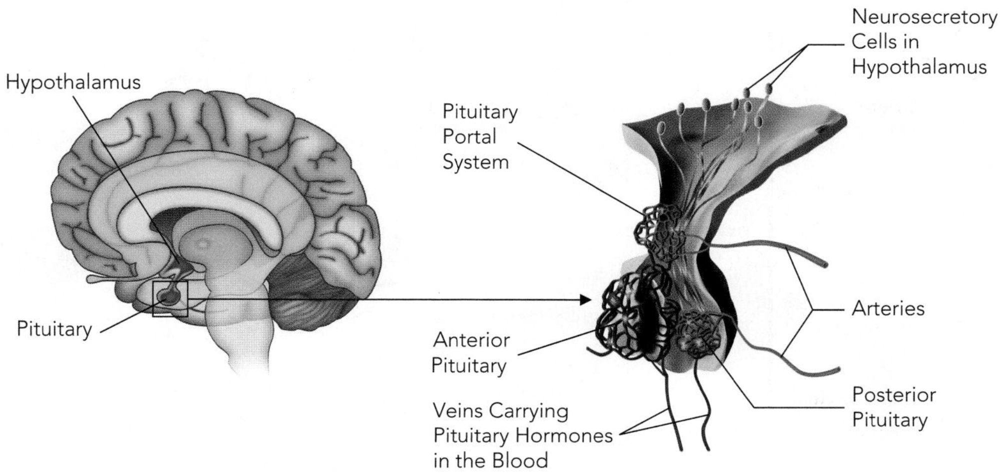

FIGURE 5.2 The "pituitary gland," which lies just below the hypothalamus in the brain, consists of two structures, one that is a gland (the anterior pituitary) and one that is part of the nervous system (the posterior pituitary). These structures are both intimately connected to the hypothalamus, but in very different ways.

records reveals that even in humans there is a seasonal pattern, with birth rates being highest in late summer and early autumn, and lowest in late winter and early spring. This finding points to peak conception rates in the darkest winter months, and lowest conception rates in the early summer months. This pattern has deviated slightly (by about 5 per cent) in modern times, suggesting that cultural and societal developments have caused this pattern to weaken (Roenneberg & Aschoff, 1990), but still it remains strikingly consistent. Of course, seasonal variation is not the only factor that drives human mating practices, but this example does provide evidence for a role of the seasons in regulating the production of sex hormones underscoring a relationship between the outside world, the brain, and the reproductive system. After all, we register changes in the seasons through our senses—through differences in light, temperature, and smell—and sensory information is processed by neurons in our brain.

The mechanism by which the brain is connected to the reproductive system is known as the HPG axis (Figure 5.3). This axis first came to be conceptualized following British physiologist Geoffrey Harris's demonstration, in 1955, that the pituitary is controlled by the hypothalamus (Raisman, 1997). Harris's experiments revealed that nerve fibres from the hypothalamus release **humoural substances** into the capillaries of the median eminence, a region between the brain and the pituitary, which the portal vessels then carry to the anterior pituitary (see Figure 5.2). This discovery led to further clarification of the roles played by the pituitary and the hypothalamus, how they communicate with each other, and how they communicate with the gonads via hormones.

humoural substances Any substance that forms part of the body fluids.

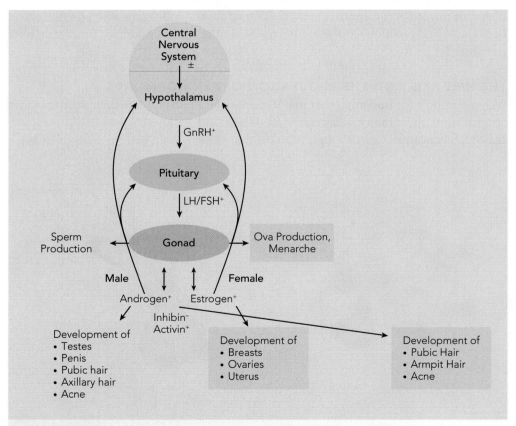

FIGURE 5.3 The hypothalamic-pituitary-gonadal (HPG) axis helps to transmit and regulate sex hormones in the human body. It is a two-way system, with feedback pathways at every component level, meaning that it can transmit information to and from the brain. In the diagram, the plus signs (+) indicate stimulatory effects, while the minus signs (−) indicate inhibitory effects.

Regulation of the Reproductive Cycle by Sex Hormones

The HPG axis is known to be of critical importance to the secretion and regulation of the gonadal hormones—estrogens, progestogens, and androgens—as well as the **gonadotropic hormones** FSH and LH. As you will discover from the following sections, these hormones play essential roles in the development and regulation of the reproductive cycles in humans. This development begins at **puberty**, and it generally follows one of two patterns, depending on whether an individual is born male or female. For an example of a condition that can result in an exception to this pattern, however, see the "Ethical Debate" box.

Female Reproduction

The interaction of the different components of the HPG axis—including the hormones—regulates the female reproductive cycle (Figure 5.4). The purpose of the ovarian cycle is reproduction. If conception does not take place in a given cycle, a new cycle will begin in the ovary before **menstruation**.

From the time of puberty, the hypothalamus produces pulsatile secretions of gonadotropin-releasing hormone (GnRH), which travel to the anterior pituitary via the portal blood supply. GnRH binds to **secretory cells** in the pituitary. These cells are then stimulated to produce LH and FSH, which travel via the blood supply to the gonads (refer back to figures 5.2 and 5.3). Upon reaching the gonads, LH and FSH stimulate the synthesis of androgens and estrogens. Estrogens produced by the ovaries travel to the brain via the blood supply; once there, they inhibit the release of FSH and stimulate the release of increasing amounts of LH, leading to a surge of LH and ovulation. Inhibin (a glycoprotein hormone) is also produced in the ovary and helps to regulate the ovarian cycle.

gonadotropic hormones Hormones that stimulate the gonads.

puberty A stage of life in which an adolescent reaches sexual maturity and becomes capable of reproduction.

menstruation The shedding of the uterine lining that has built up in anticipation of a fertilized egg.

secretory cells Cells that secrete.

Ethical Debate

Is It a Boy or a Girl?

Lila was 24-weeks pregnant when she attended a local clinic for an ultrasound. She had already had an amniocentesis, and she had been told that the sex of her child was male. The ultrasound technician was unable to identify a penis, even though the picture showed a very good view of the genital region. The technician suggested that Lila go for a repeat ultrasound at the hospital that had referred her to the clinic. The second ultrasound identified structures resembling testes, but no penis. In the medical literature, this developmental condition is called *micropenis* or *absent penis*.

Lila and her husband were referred to a children's hospital to meet with the prenatal diagnosis team for a discussion of what it means for an infant to be born with a micropenis and the care decisions that they, as parents, might want to make. They were told that they had two options: to rear their child as a

male with a small penis, or to raise their child as a female, which would require sex reassignment surgery and hormone therapy. They were also advised that the research and clinical literature is divided on the best course of action with respect to the child's psychological well-being and quality of life.

Lila and her husband were devastated by the news. They did not feel that either option was compatible with full enjoyment of life, and they wondered what right they had to make this decision for the adult their child would eventually become. They also wondered what determines sexual identity: chromosomes (XX or XY), hormones, or society?

If you were Lila and her husband, what ethical principles would guide your decision? If you chose to raise your child as a female, what concerns might you have about the effects and limitations of hormone therapy?

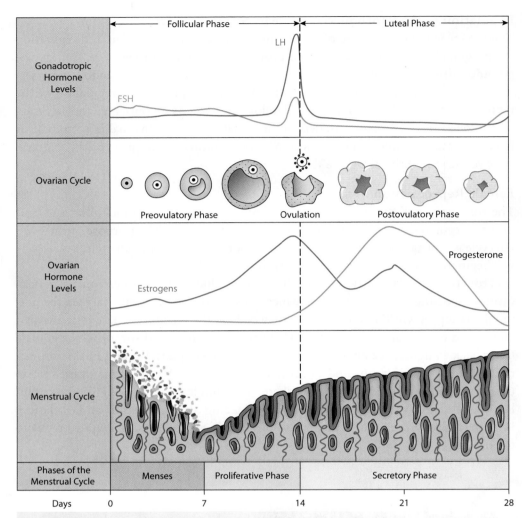

FIGURE 5.4 The reproductive cycle repeats approximately every 28 days in human females. When it is described according to the development and release of the oocyte, this cycle is called the *ovarian cycle*. When it is described according to the development and clearing of the uterine lining, it is called the *menstrual cycle*.

aromatase An enzyme that converts androgens to estrogens.

receptor A molecule, most often found on the surface of a cell, that receives chemical signals directing a cell to do something (e.g., make proteins).

FSH is the first hormone to increase in level; as noted above, it initiates the growth and maturation of ovarian follicles and stimulates enzymes that are essential for the production of estrogens, notably **aromatase**. The rising levels of estrogen have a positive feedback effect on LH secretion. LH in turn stimulates increased steroid synthesis in the theca cells of the ovary; as LH increases, so do androgen levels. The androgens pass to the granulsoa cells of the follicles, where the aromatase enzyme acts to convert androgens to estrogens. Estrogen, however, has a negative impact on the production of FSH: the level of FSH drops as estrogen levels increase. Fortunately FSH induces its own **receptor** on the follicles, which means that as it becomes scarcer, only those follicles with the most receptors will still be able to bind FSH and continue to develop. This enables the selection and success of the dominant follicle and dramatically increases the likelihood of a single oocyte (egg) being released. As women age and their pool of remaining follicles diminishes in size, inhibin levels are reduced, allowing FSH levels in the early part of the cycle to rise. The elevated level of FSH can result in more than one follicle maturing, thus contributing to an increased risk of multiple pregnancy.

Rapidly rising levels of estrogen trigger the LH surge, which leads to the rupture of the mature follicle(s) and the release of the egg, or *ovum*. The ruptured follicle continues to play an essential role in reproduction: it reorganizes as the corpus luteum and begins production of progesterone. The increased androgen production brought about by LH enables increased conversion to estrogens, but this increase in androgen production also results in increased testosterone levels, just at the time of maximum fertility. Androgens have biological and behavioural roles in the menstrual cycle: androgens contribute to the degeneration of non-dominant follicles in the late follicular phase, leading to increased sex drive at the time of maximal fertility.

The menstrual cycle is a manifestation of the ovarian cycle; it involves the buildup and shedding of the uterine lining (the endometrium) in preparation for the implantation of a fertilized egg. The menstrual cycle, like the ovarian cycle, is ultimately regulated by GnRH, but it is also directly responsive to cyclic changes in estrogen and progesterone levels. These hormones control the development and shedding of the uterine lining. In the **follicular phase** (also referred to as the proliferative phase), estrogen stimulates the growth of the lining. After ovulation, in the **luteal phase** (also called the secretory phase), progesterone action increases the complexity and the energy stores of the endometrium. If conception does not occur, the corpus luteum will regress, estrogen and progesterone production will decline, and menstruation will follow. Thus the cycle of maturing and releasing an egg for fertilization begins anew (see Figure 5.4). In the absence of impregnation, menstruation is the outwardly visible sign of human female fertility; as such, many cultures have attached much significance to it.

The menstrual cycle has also been associated with a number of psychological phenomena, such as mood disorders; these disorders are approximately twice as prevalent in women as in men (Zukov et al., 2010). Since this sex difference is observed only during the period between puberty and menopause, many have hypothesized that it is due to the cyclical fluctuation of ovarian steroids. This hypothesis, along with other factors, has led to the different phases of the menstrual cycle often being associated with mood changes in women; for instance, many women tend to report negative mood more commonly during the luteal phase than during the follicular phase or ovulation. Indeed, some mood-related disorders, such **premenstrual dysphoric disorder (PMDD)** (known as **premenstrual syndrome**, or **PMS**, to most people), has been named in relation to phases of the menstrual cycle (American Psychiatric Association, 2013). Depression and anxiety can affect desire for, performance of, and experience of sex.

Despite reports of a link between menstrual phase and self-reported mood, however, a direct relationship between ovarian hormones and mood is not well established, even in cases of PMDD. For example, studies on the effects of hormones on mood in postmenopausal women have revealed contradictory results: estrogen administration has been shown to reduce, increase, or have no significant effect on negative mood (Rubinow & Schmidt, 2006). Progesterone has also been proposed as a treatment, but it has been found to be ineffective for premenstrual mood disturbances. In other studies of randomly recruited, non-help-seeking women, no correspondence was observed between either menstrual phase or ovarian steroids and mood. Rather, it was psychosocial factors—stress and physical health—that were highly correlated with mood (Schwartz, Romans, Meiyappan, DeSouza, & Einstein, 2012). There is no doubt, however, that many women do suffer cyclic mood changes that can significantly impair their quality of life.

Male Reproduction

In males, LH binds to cells in the testes, causing them to secrete testosterone. Testosterone is required for normal spermatogenesis, but high circulating levels can

follicular phase The first phase of the menstrual cycle, during which the ovarian follicles mature and estrogen stimulates the growth of the endometrium.

luteal phase The third phase of the menstrual cycle, which begins with the formation of the corpus luteum and ends in either pregnancy or involution of the corpus luteum.

premenstrual dysphoric disorder (PMDD) A mood disorder associated primarily with the luteal phase of the menstrual cycle and characterized by feelings of anxiety, anger, and depression.

premenstrual syndrome (PMS) A wide range of physical and/or emotional symptoms typically occurring 5 to 11 days prior to menstruation.

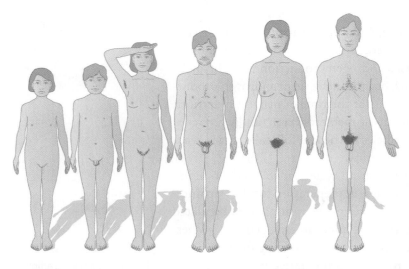

FIGURE 5.5 Human beings do not arrive in the world sexually mature. While the scaffolding for sexual differentiation is established in utero, full sexual maturation requires a sustained increase in sex hormones over a number of years; this process of pubertal development occurs mainly in adolescence, but some of the changes will continue into early adulthood.

inhibit hypothalamic production of GnRH. FSH stimulates other cells to release androgen-binding protein, which promotes testosterone binding. After puberty, the levels of LH, FSH, and testosterone remain relatively constant in males.

The Role of Hormones in the Development of Secondary Sex Characteristics

The activation of the HPG axis in both males and females during puberty also affects the acquisition of secondary sex characteristics (Figure 5.5). In women, rising estrogen levels cause the lower half of the pelvis and the hips to widen (providing space for a larger birth canal). Fat tissue increases to a greater percentage of the body composition in women than in males, and this tissue is typically distributed to the breasts, hips, buttocks, thighs, upper arms, and pubis. In men, there is a dramatic increase in the number of muscle cells during puberty, leading to the divergence in physical strength between men and women after puberty. This progressive differentiation in fat distribution and muscle mass, as well as in local skeletal growth, contributes to the formation of the typical male or female body shape by the end of puberty. At puberty, androgens result in the growth of pubic and axillary (underarm) hair in both sexes, and the growth of the testes, the lowering of the voice, and facial hair in men. Estrogens lead to the cessation of the growth of the long bones in both sexes, the viability of sperm in males, and the development of breasts in women. All of these characteristics become marks of sexual maturity and, ultimately, the basis of physical attraction.

The Sexual Brain

The brain is also shaped by the developing gonads and becomes a critical player in the HPG axis. As suggested above, the hypothalamus region of the brain is a major part of the HPG axis; it is highly responsive to steroid and peptide hormones, and it appears to be involved not only in the production of sex hormones but also in sexual acts and an individual's experience of sexuality. Even outside of the HPG axis, there is virtually no brain region that is not affected by sex hormones—either directly or, through connections with other regions, indirectly. It is because of the brain's responsiveness to sex hormones, as well as its role in processing sexual stimuli and regulating sexual behaviour, that this organ has come to be known as the main sex organ of the body.

In many cases, the responsiveness of a person's brain to sex hormones, as well as differential responses between females and males, results from prenatal exposure to androgens and estrogens. Indeed, the hypothalamus is extremely sensitive to hormones even in utero. Additionally, research has shown that sexual differentiation of the brain occurs due to hormonal influences during a critical developmental period (Figure 5.6). This differentiation plays a role in establishing the neuronal connections

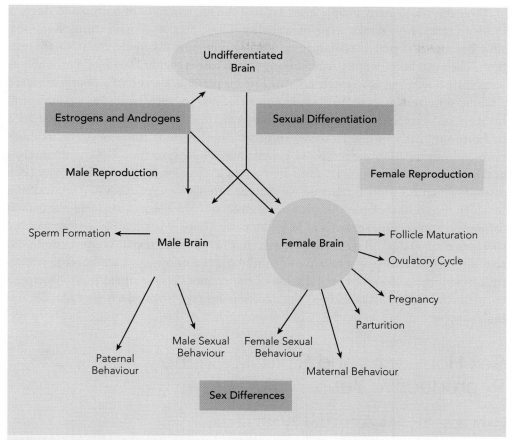

FIGURE 5.6 A fetus's brain becomes differentiated as either male or female at a critical point in its development, and the path it takes will affect the individual's reproductive cycle and sexual behaviour later in life. This process is part of the whole body's sexual differentiation, and brain regions that control the male and female HPG axis, such as the hypothalamus, are affected during this time. Other brain regions that play a role in more subtle sexual behaviours—for example, the cerebral cortex—may also be affected.

involved in the ovarian cycle. Raisman and Field (1973) used rodents to demonstrate that females have a neural circuitry that produces an LH surge and consequently ovulation, while males do not. Interestingly, it is possible to prevent this circuitry from forming in females by exposing them to estrogens during the critical developmental period, and males have the potential to develop this circuitry if they are exposed to neither androgens nor estrogens during this same critical period.

Some researchers have speculated that early hormonal influences might shape neuronal circuits to affect sexuality—gender identity and sexual attraction. For example, some have suggested that variations such as transsexuality and same-sex sexual orientation may result from different exposures to hormones during a critical developmental period of the **sexual brain**. Consequently, neuroscientists have studied the brains of heterosexual, lesbian, gay, bisexual, and transgendered individuals to explore issues such as whether structures in the brains of gay men resemble those in the brains of straight women, or whether male-to-female transsexuals have neural responses similar to those of women who were born chromosomally female. While the research on such issues has produced mixed results, what does seem certain is that prior to hormone administration in preparation for a sex change, neither male-to-female nor female-to-male transsexuals have circulating sex steroids that place them out of the normal range of that of their chromosomal sex (Einstein, 2007; 2012).

sexual brain The part of the brain that mediates sexual behaviour.

Over the years, many people have debated the relative roles of nature and nurture in forming an individual's sense of sexuality. These debates remain unresolved, possibly because it is not *either* nature *or* nurture but most assuredly a combination of both. The most famous story surrounding this debate is that of David Reimer, who was born male but raised as a female after he lost his penis as a result of a poorly executed circumcision (see Chapter 10). Reimer never adjusted to being treated as a female, and his story suggests that the brain centres that mediate sexuality are permanently shaped by hormones early in life. However, in other cases, such as those of XY individuals born without testosterone receptors, genetic males have grown up viewing themselves as female because they look like and are treated as females. Similarly, there have been cases in which XX individuals with congenital adrenal hyperplasia (CAH), a condition in which the adrenal glands overproduce androgens (which can cause male-like genital formation and eventual growth of facial hair; see Chapter 10), have grown up viewing themselves as males. All we really know is that because the sexual brain is connected to brain regions that play a role in our thinking, perceptions, and self-control, sexuality, attraction, desire, and a sexual sense of self cannot be uncoupled from life experience (Einstein & Flannagan, 2003). For additional perspectives on whether females and males are born or made, see the "Culture and Diversity" box.

Sex Hormones and Sexuality in the Reproductive Years

How Hormones Affect Sexuality

We have seen that sex hormones play an undeniable role in establishing our reproductive capacities, our secondary sex characteristics, and, potentially, our brain connections related to sex. In addition, although the specific role that sex hormones play in influencing human sexuality is still a matter of some debate, there is strong evidence that these hormones may directly affect sexual attraction, desire, and performance.

Androgens and estrogens may influence peripheral as well as brain responses, as androgen and estrogen receptors are dispersed widely throughout genital and neural tissues in both women and men. Both hormones play a direct role in genital and subjective arousal; administration of testosterone can increase genital sexual arousal in both women and men (Tuiten et al., 2000), while administration of estradiol to menopausal women increases vaginal wall thickness and elasticity, lubrication, and vasocongestion (Traish, Botchevar, & Kim, 2010). In addition, androgens may be strongly linked with **libido** and desire in men, and androgen insufficiency may cause a decrease in sexual desire in women (Bachmann et al., 2002). Thus, administration of androgens has been used to treat sexual dysfunctions—broadly speaking—in both men and women. Yet the literature is conflicting, and other studies on the effects of circulating androgens in women did not find that low levels of these hormones were associated with low sexual desire. Thus, more research is needed before we can draw firm conclusions about the role of androgens in sexual desire in women.

libido Sex drive.

SEXUAL DESIRE AND CLOSENESS

In reproductive-aged women, androgens may be more closely associated with closeness than with sexual desire. One study demonstrated that while women's testosterone levels were generally higher pre-intercourse than pre-control activity (control activities included cuddling and exercise), and higher post-intercourse than post-control activity, changes in testosterone levels from pre- to post-activity were *greatest* for cuddling, followed by intercourse, and then exercise (van Anders, Hamilton, Schmidt, & Watson,

Culture & Diversity

Are Females and Males Born or *Made*?

The Western explanation of whether we become female or male is based on observations of how the fetus develops. Initially, an embryo contains a region called *the indifferent gonad*. In XY organisms, there is a gene called *SRY* located on the Y chromosome; when this gene is switched on, it will start the metamorphosis of the indifferent gonad into the testes. Once this process begins, the Leydig cells in the testes will begin to secrete testosterone, along with the resultant androgens and estrogens, and the Sertoli cells will begin to secrete Mullerian-inhibiting factor (MIF), leading to the suppression of the female internal reproductive system. The presence of androgens, insulin-like factors, and MIF leads to the full development of the testes, the male internal piping, and the penis. In the XX organism, the indifferent gonad transforms into the ovaries, which secrete relatively little androgens or estrogens until puberty. It is possible that ovarian-activating factors are involved, but these have not been studied as of yet. The uterus and the female internal reproductive piping develop from the Müllerian ducts. The subsequent presence or absence of androgens and estrogens affects every body system including the developing brain to create the male or female body type. Thus, in the West,

infants are assumed to be male or female at birth by virtue of the early interactions of genes and hormones.

Other cultures, however, do not share this explanation. In regions of North Eastern (Sahel) Africa, for example, the common belief is that female and male babies are born sexually equivalent. This is understandable since there is enormous variation in the appearance of infants' genitals at birth, and certain genetic conditions might lead to an XX baby being thought of as XY (e.g., CAH) or an XY baby being thought of as XX (e.g., a condition called "testes-at-12"). As well, prior to puberty, few visible characteristics clearly differentiate XX children from XY children (refer back to Figure 5.5). The thought in these cultures, then, is that males and females need to be *made*, especially if they are to be reproductively successful. The male is thought to have female parts—the foreskin of the penis—that must be removed to make a full male; similarly, the female is thought to have a male part—the external portion of the clitoris—that must be removed to make a full female. It is believed that if this is not done, the individual will not be able to reproduce successfully and will occupy a territory that few cultures find acceptable: the space between male and female.

2007). These results suggest that testosterone is linked more closely with cuddling than with intercourse!

Another study revealed that among women, testosterone was not correlated with sexual desire; estrogen, on the other hand, was significantly correlated with women's overall sexual desire, but not with solitary (as opposed to partnered) sexual desire. Different patterns emerge for men: testosterone is associated with some types of sexual desire—such as desire for solitary sexual activity—but not others (van Anders & Dunn, 2009), and estrogens do not seem to play a role in overall desire for men. Thus, sexual desire is linked to sex hormones in complex and different ways for women and men.

PARTNERED AND PAIRED SEX

Although sexual assertiveness and testosterone levels do not seem to be significantly correlated in either females or males (van Anders & Dunn, 2009), testosterone may be correlated with the type of sex a person desires. A study by van Anders and Watson (2006) found that, in general, partnered women and men have lower testosterone levels than their unpartnered counterparts. However, among women, this finding was significant only in lesbian women. The study also found that the number of partners is a critical factor for testosterone levels in men: monoamorous (single-partnered) men had the lowest testosterone levels of any group studied, male or female. However, in heterosexual women, testosterone is also significantly correlated with certain aspects of partnered sex. When van Anders and Dunn (2009) evaluated heterosexual women with high and low levels of testosterone, they found that those with high testosterone levels reported relaxation, or peaceful, soothing, and relaxing sensations related to partnered sex.

MULTIPLE-PARTNERED, OR POLYAMOROUS, SEX

Singles of both sexes have higher testosterone levels than both males and females in long-term partnered relationships. Being in a casual relationship (which is more similar to being single than to being in a long-term partnered relationship) is associated with higher testosterone levels in men but not in women. However, van Anders and Watson have noted the increasing trend toward polyamory (an open, committed, multi-partnered sexuality; see Chapter 14) and suggested that individuals oriented toward polyamory might have different levels of estrogens and androgens, compared to individuals who are not oriented toward polyamory. This hypothesis was borne out; both men and women in polyamorous relationships had higher testosterone levels than their single or dyadic counterparts. Thus, higher levels of testosterone are linked to a higher likelihood of entering shorter-term relationships, with testosterone levels being associated with "frequency of sex" for women and "interest in new partners" for men (van Anders & Watson, 2006), both of which are fulfilled by polyamorous relationships.

MASTURBATION

Researchers have fairly consistently found an association between testosterone and masturbation in men (van Anders, Brotto, Farrell, & Yule, 2009). In women, however, it is estrogens that are significantly correlated with masturbation. One study that measured six contributing components of solitary sexual desire in women—building, flooding (the feeling of blood flowing), flushing, spurting, throbbing, and general spasms—found that flooding and flushing in female masturbation were significantly correlated with estradiol (van Anders & Dunn, 2009).

ORGASM

There is some evidence that among healthy women of reproductive age, orgasm occurrence and frequency are correlated with testosterone as well as estradiol. In one study of the effects of estradiol, participants were asked to indicate how often they a) engaged in partnered sexual activity; b) engaged in masturbation; and c) experienced orgasm with their partner during the past 7 days, 30 days, and six months. The results suggested that while testosterone was correlated with the psychological experience of orgasm, estradiol was strongly correlated with the physiological experience of orgasm in women. Interestingly, no correlations have been found between testosterone or estradiol and orgasm in men (van Anders & Dunn, 2009).

How Sexual Activity and Other Life Factors Affect Hormone Levels

We often think of hormones as driving sexual response, but sexual activity, as well as other life experiences, can also affect levels of estrogens and testosterone. In fact, the relationship between sex and sex steroids is reciprocal. Of course, cause-and-effect relationships involving hormones are very difficult to establish, and the associations may be different for men than for women. However, the evidence suggests a number of correlations. For example, it seems that sexual activity *increases* testosterone in women (van Anders et al., 2007) and perhaps in men as well (Dabbs & Mohammed, 1992). In addition, intimate physical interactions, whether they are of a sexual or non-sexual nature, can increase testosterone in women. Further, sexual arousal decreases levels of cortisol (a steroid hormone associated with stress) and increases levels of estradiol in women (Goldey & van Anders, 2011). Finally, it seems that anticipation of intercourse may lead to increased testosterone in both men and women (van Anders et al., 2007). So we see that the relationship between actions and hormones doesn't just flow in one direction.

LONG-DISTANCE RELATIONSHIPS

Above, you learned that testosterone levels can affect an individual's relationship preferences, but it also seems that the proximity of one's partner can affect testosterone levels. For example, the physical presence of a partner is associated with lower testosterone among those in mixed-sex and same-sex relationships (van Anders & Watson, 2007). Further, testosterone levels vary in males and females depending on whether individuals are single, in long-distance relationships, or in same-city relationships; single men tend to have higher testosterone levels than men in long-distance or same-city relationships, while women in same-city relationships have lower testosterone levels than single women or women in long-distance relationships. Additionally, because men in same-city relationships have testosterone levels similar to those of men in long-distance relationships, the association between partnering and low levels of testosterone in men does not seem to require the physical presence of a partner. In contrast, this association may require a physical presence for women, because women in same-city relationships have lower testosterone levels than do women in long-distance relationships (van Anders & Watson, 2007). What is clear from these observations is that knowing that a partner exists (cognition) can influence hormone levels just as surely as direct sexual activity can!

ABSTINENCE

Abstinence also affects testosterone levels, but in less direct ways. In one study, although baseline testosterone levels did not differ between men who had abstained from sexual activity for three weeks and those who had not, levels were higher immediately before and during presentation of erotic visual stimuli and masturbation among men who had abstained (Exton et al., 2001). Thus, in men, abstinence appears to modulate testosterone levels in response to the sexual context. In women, abstinence does not seem to modulate testosterone levels under any circumstances (van Anders et al., 2009).

SEXUAL THOUGHTS

Even imagining sexual interactions may affect testosterone levels. In one study, naturally cycling women (i.e., those not on hormonal contraceptives) were asked to imagine either a sexual condition or one of three non-sexual conditions (positive, neutral, or stressful). The results showed that thoughts related to the sexual condition increased testosterone levels to a greater degree than did thoughts related to the other conditions. In another study, viewing erotic stimuli was shown to increase testosterone levels in men but not in women; rather, estradiol levels were shown to increase when women viewed erotic stimuli (van Anders et al., 2009). Thus, we again find that the relationship between sexual thoughts and sex steroids is reciprocal.

Oxytocin and Vasopressin: Pleasure, Bonding, and Affiliation

So far you have learned about the roles of estrogens and androgens in different aspects of sexual behaviour. However, there are other hormones that play a role in sexual as well

FIGURE 5.7 Oxytocin plays a significant role in mother–infant bonding. When a mother nurses her child, simultaneous touch and eye contact may enhance the mother's already elevated levels of oxytocin and thus encourage maternal bonding; it also encourages the infant to bond with its mother and may help the infant develop an ability to affiliate later in life.

milk let-down response
A series of neural events that leads to milk ejection from the mammary glands (breasts).

as other reproductive behaviours, with perhaps the two most important ones being oxytocin and vasopressin. As mentioned previously, these peptide hormones are synthesized by the hypothalamus and act as either neurotransmitters in the brain or hormones when they are released into the body. They are very similar in structure, with only two of their nine amino acids differing from one another.

Oxytocin is strongly associated with childbirth and lactation as well as maternal behaviour and bonding. A study at McGill University found a strong relationship between high levels of oxytocin and high levels of maternal care in animals (Shahrokh, Zhang, Diorio, Gratton, & Meaney, 2010), and another at the University of Toronto has suggested that oxytocin plays a role in mother–infant bonding through touch and eye gaze in humans (Figure 5.7) (Corter & Fleming, 2002).

Vasopressin is perhaps best known for its involvement in fluid balance and cardiovascular and autonomic regulation. However, like oxytocin, it is involved in multiple aspects of human social/sexual functions.

More broadly, oxytocin and vasopressin tend to act synergistically, with increases in oxytocin leading to reductions in social stress and increases in affiliative behaviour and increases in vasopressin leading to aggression and anxiety. Both oxytocin and vasopressin are well known for their role in stimulating uterine contractions during the birthing process and initiating the **milk let-down response** and, hence, breastfeeding post-birth. It seems that the neural circuits involved with these functions integrate sensory cues such as olfaction and touch with oxytocin and vasopressin synthesis and dopamine release to reinforce social bonding with pleasurable sensations.

While oxytocin has been shown to facilitate receptive sexual display in female rodents and penile erection in male rodents, its role in human sexual response is much less direct. We know that oxytocin levels rise with sexual arousal, cervical-vaginal stimulation, and orgasm. Interestingly, when human participants were given oxytocin by nasal spray (so it can quickly enter the brain), they *perceived* that their genital arousal was greater, even though their physiological reactions did not indicate an actual increase in genital arousal. In the same vein, oxytocin levels are correlated positively with subjective reports of orgasm intensity in multi-orgasmic women (Carmichael, Warburton, Dixen, & Davidson, 1994). However, with the exception of being increased post-orgasm in both men and women, there does not seem to be a direct role for either oxytocin or vasopressin in human sexual behaviour.

While oxytocin does not *cause* genital arousal in humans, it does seem to play a role in establishing social bonds that can lead to sexual arousal. Befriending and affiliating is thought to require the synthesis and release of oxytocin to allow each of the individuals to let down her or his guard in order to be in close proximity to others. Thus, one hypothesis about oxytocin's role in sex is that by helping humans overcome a natural avoidance of proximity to others, it facilitates approach behaviour and thus smoothes the way to sexual contact (Insel & Young, 2001).

Researchers have found evidence for oxytocin's role in establishing affiliative bonds in the animal kingdom. Perhaps the most striking evidence comes from observations of sexual and maternal behaviour in two different vole species, the monogamous prairie vole and the polygamous montane vole. Prairie voles form life-long monogamous relationships, and they have much higher oxytocin levels and concentration of oxytocin receptors than do montane voles (Figure 5.8). In addition, researchers have shown that a local infusion of oxytocin can induce montane voles to become monogamous, while administration of a chemical that blocks the action of oxytocin can abolish prairie vole monogamy (Young, Gobrogge, Liu, & Wang, 2011).

In humans, oxytocin has been found to increase perception of trustworthiness, and there is evidence that it also increases the perception of another's attractiveness, seemingly key elements in partnered relationships (see Chapter 12). One study randomized university students to receive either 24 units of oxytocin or a placebo. They were then shown images of faces and asked to rate each face on attractiveness and trustworthiness. Both the men and women who had been administered oxytocin rated the faces as more attractive and more trustworthy than did those who had received the placebo (Theodoridou, Rowe, Penton-Voak, & Rogers, 2009).

FIGURE 5.8 Oxytocin and monogamy are correlated in prairie voles. Because they are monogamous, prairie vole parents watch over and raise their young together. If these were montane voles, which have lower levels of oxytocin and are polygamous, the mother would be caring for the young by herself.

But does this mean that oxytocin can make you fall in love? Well, it certainly seems to make people more susceptible to the precursors of love. As well, researchers have found that the feeling of love itself is marked by a broad variety of changes in neurohormones and neuropeptides, particularly oxytocin. When functional magnetic imaging (fMRI) is carried out on individuals who describe themselves as being in love, the resulting brain images show activation of the dopaminergic reward systems, which contain dopamine, oxytocin, and vasopressin receptors and have been shown to reinforce pleasure. As well, the participants being imaged have increased levels of neurotrophins (basic proteins that support the growth and survival of neurons), leading to increased activity in the endocrine system, which in turn recruits the neurobiological substrates that mediate arousal and desire, two key factors in sexual response (Ortigue, Bianchi-Demicheli, Patel, Frum, & Lewis, 2010). In addition, studies have shown that women viewing pictures of loved ones have high brain activity in dopaminergic pathways associated with reward, as do people who describe themselves as being "intensely in love." These same regions also contain high numbers of oxytocin and vasopressin receptors, however, no study has conclusively shown that being in a relationship, or being "in love," is associated with high levels of oxytocin (Campbell, 2010).

In sum, oxytocin and vasopressin clearly play a role in many behaviours that are critical for humans to form lasting, trusting, sexual relationships. While there is evidence in lower mammals that both hormones may play a role in sexual behaviours, the evidence is slimmer, but nevertheless enticing, in humans. Perhaps, given these hormones' roles in particularly human aspects of sexuality and their direct connection with the steroid hormone system, which is linked to sexual behaviour, this is close enough for us to consider them as being significant in relation to human sexuality (Figure 5.9).

Prolactin

Another peptide hormone potentially involved in sex is prolactin. Its link to sexual behaviour is even more distant than oxytocin's or vasopressin's, but it is worth a mention. Prolactin levels surge at the time of orgasm and have been associated with feelings

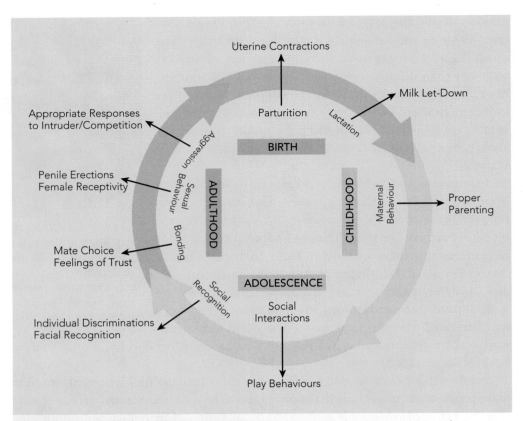

FIGURE 5.9 While not technically a sex hormone, oxytocin plays an important role in species propagation. It can affect behaviours and physiology at numerous points in the life cycle to facilitate social interactions, play behaviours, mate choice and trust, sexual behaviours, uterine contractions, milk let-down, and maternal behaviours.

of sexual satisfaction. An excess of prolactin, however, creates problems for both sexual function and fertility in men and women, as evidenced by the effects of prolactin-secreting tumours. These benign tumours, which are not uncommon in women, lead to a cessation of the ovarian cycle and diminished desire. Therefore, it is clear that, like oxytocin, prolactin is linked to major sex hormones. In men, prolactin-secreting tumours are less common but more directly linked to sexuality. Affected men report a loss of sexual desire and erectile dysfunction—recall that this was the case for James in the case study at the beginning of this chapter. Sperm count and semen volume also diminish. Men may be slow to report the symptoms to their doctor, and these issues are often misdiagnosed as being psychologically based. Treatment of these tumours can be either surgical or medical, and both are effective in restoring sexual function and fertility.

Does the Act of Smelling Sex Hormones Lead to Sexual Behaviour?

The sense that we call "smell" is, along with taste, technically referred to as "chemo-sensation," which exists in even the simplest types of microorganisms. In more sophisticated organisms, complex organs are devoted to receiving and processing these chemo-sensations, and to using this information to make decisions. Olfactory signals (smells) activate areas in our thinking cortical brain, but they can be directly appreciated by the limbic system, our emotional brain, without our even being aware of it. In fact, the olfactory nerve is the only sensory nerve that projects directly into the brain without intermediary processing. Thus, it is not surprising that olfaction, memory, and sexual responses are strongly linked.

While environmental olfactory signals are detected in the main olfactory bulb, **pheromones** are detected by receptors in another olfactory organ, the vomeronasal organ (Figure 5.10). This structure, which lies between the nose and the mouth, is responsible for the first stage of the **accessory olfactory system** in most terrestrial mammals, although its functionality in humans is unclear.

Researchers have been investigating olfactory cues to sexual behaviour using animal models since Frank Beach first demonstrated, in 1949, that odours related to estrus (the name for the ovulatory cycle in non-human mammals) stimulate mounting behaviour in male rats, and that the loss of smell in sexually inexperienced male rodents blocks these rodent's ability to copulate. Jim Pfaus and his colleagues at Concordia University have continued this tradition, demonstrating that male rats allowed to copulate to ejaculation with females bearing an almond scent will later preferentially choose females bearing that scent for mounting and copulation. Thus, the association of a neutral (non-sexual) odour with a sexual reward provides sufficient conditioned incentive to influence partner choice (e.g., Kippin & Pfaus, 2001a; 2001b). Among female rats, female–female mounting can be elicited by exposure to urine from estrus females and blocked by lesions of the olfactory bulb. However, researchers have yet to demonstrate conclusively that there are olfactory cues for human sexual behaviour.

Pheromones

Pheromones are a special kind of olfactory signal capable of acting outside the body of the secreting individual to engender particular behaviours in the receiving individual. They have long been known to play an active role in the animal kingdom, where they appear to influence mating habits and other behaviours in insects, fish, reptiles, amphibians, and mammals; accumulating research demonstrates that pheromones may also play a role in human sexuality (Bhutta, 2007). In humans, pheromones are produced by **apocrine glands**, primarily in the axilla (armpit) and pubic areas, body regions that become active with puberty. The synthesis of pheromones in both women and men is controlled by androgens.

Four categories of pheromones—territorial, menstrual/fertile, sexual, and maternal-infant—have been identified in humans. The strongest evidence that menstrual pheromones can affect human behaviour comes from the work of Martha McClintock (1971), who observed that women living together develop menstrual synchrony. She postulated that this synchronicity resulted from an olfactory effect and demonstrated that women exposed to the smell of other women's sweat sped up or slowed down their menstrual cycles depending on whether the sweat was collected before, during, or after ovulation. She postulated that at least one pheromone was involved in this synchronization effect, but the actual molecule has not yet been identified.

Other researchers have suggested that steroid hormones such as androstadienone (a non-androgenic steroid found in men's sweat) can affect the salience of emotional information in both women and men who are exposed to amounts so low they cannot be consciously detected (Hummer & McClintock, 2009), as well as alter cortisol levels in women (Wyart et al., 2007). Exposure to this hormone under negative circumstances also reportedly

pheromones Olfactory signals that trigger a social response in members of the same species.

accessory olfactory system A secondary system of smell, present in many mammals, that detects and processes pheromones.

apocrine glands Glands that open at the surface of the skin and whose cells bleb off a portion of themselves in the release of their secretions.

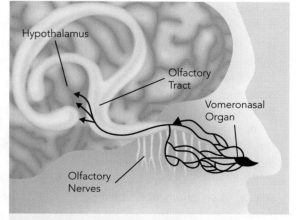

Hypothalamus

Olfactory Tract

Vomeronasal Organ

Olfactory Nerves

FIGURE 5.10 Although researchers do not all agree on the functionality of the vomeronasal organ in humans, many believe that this structure is important in conveying olfactory signals from the nose into the brain, especially to the hypothalamus. In other animals, the organ has been shown to be highly sensitive to pheromonal signals, which are detected by a complex array of receptors.

increases women's perception of pain (Villemure & Bushnell, 2007). In addition, exposure to androstadienone seems to increase blood flow to certain regions of women's brains involved in female sexual behaviours in non-human animals. Similarly, the steroid estratetraenol (found in women's urine) seems to increase blood flow to certain regions of men's brains involved in male sexual behaviours in non-human animals. Further, when same- and other-sex oriented males were exposed to both androstadienone and estratetraenol, same-sex oriented males exhibited increased cerebral blood flow in response to androstadienone, and heterosexual males exhibited increased cerebral blood flow in response to estratetraenol (Savic, Berglund, & Lindström, 2005). Whether it is sexual orientation that alters hypothalamic response or hypothalamic response to these putative human pheromones that establishes sexual orientation is still an open question.

Vaginal pheromones vary throughout the menstrual cycle, and with pregnancy. **Major histocompatibility complex (MHC)** compounds have been found in these secretions, suggesting that women have a way of communicating their genetic makeup to potential or current sexual partners. Analyses of MHC genes have revealed great diversity among individuals, and this diversity may be linked to more or less robust offspring and better or worse reproductive outcome. It has been hypothesized that being able to detect someone's MHC may provide an important survival benefit when choosing a mate (see Chapter 12). This has been well documented in mice, but less so in humans. Yet, given the potential potency of MHC compounds, it is striking to reflect on the lengths to which we will go in order to mask—or perhaps amplify—our natural body scent. See the "Research vs Real Life" box for more on MHC.

major histocompatibility complex (MHC) A group of genes that code for proteins found on the surfaces of cells that help the immune system recognize foreign substances.

Research VS Real Life

Passing the Sniff Test, or What Your T-Shirt Might Be Saying about You

As early as the mid-1970s, researchers demonstrated that humans can correctly identify sex from axillary odours, and that they can recognize their own axillary odours as well as those of others. Women can detect certain compounds found in the axillary odours of men at a concentration 1000 times lower than men can, and women's ability to detect these complexes improves during the fertile phase of the menstrual cycle. Men, in turn, find a woman's scent more pleasant when she is in the fertile phase of her cycle. There is some evidence that the perfumes we select, often pheromone based, amplify our MHC.

Women have repeatedly been found to prefer the scent of a t-shirt worn by a man who is genetically dissimilar to them, based on their MHC (Wedekind, Seebeck, Bettens, & Paepke, 1995; Jacob, McClintock, Zelano, & Ober, 2002), and this preference is most marked around the time of ovulation. Women taking oral contraceptives, by contrast, do not show any such preference; in fact, they exhibit preference for MHCs with scents similar to their own. The same pattern emerges among pregnant women, possibly because of the potential benefit of close kin to the pregnant woman. By contrast, men do not show as strong a preference for the scent of a t-shirt worn by a woman; this difference may result because reproduction comes at a much higher cost to a woman than to a man.

Of course, women's preference for certain scents is not the only factor that drives their choice in mates, but the evidence shows that it may be a strong one. For example, some evidence indicates that women who share similar MHC patterns with their husbands are more likely to engage in sex outside the relationship with a male with dissimilar MHC-patterns, and that a disproportionate number of these couplings occur during the fertile phase of the cycle. Thus, the drive to bring in new genetic material—even in women not consciously desiring to reproduce—may be stronger than we are aware of consciously.

Sex Hormones, Sexuality, and Aging

As we age, our levels of sex hormones change, as does the functioning of our HPG axis. What happens to sexuality when women and men age and their levels of sex hormones change? This is an area of growing study, but there is still much to be learned about healthy sexual aging. Below we discuss what is known about women and men's hormonal changes and how these changes may affect sexuality.

Menopause

At some point in a woman's life, typically when she is in her late 40s, she will enter a phase in which her ovaries begin to secrete less and less estradiol. This change coincides with the depletion of the reserve of oocytes and Graafian follicles, resulting in loss of fertility. During this time, women stop menstruating regularly, and their hormone levels wax and wane. This stage of life is called the **perimenopausal** period. In this period, the fluctuating levels of estrogens and progestogens can lead to hot flashes, sleeplessness, night sweats, joint pain, irritability, and frequent changes in mood. Once menstruation has stopped for 12 months or more, a woman is said to be **menopausal**.

> **perimenopause** The years prior to menopause when hormonal levels are fluctuating and declining.

> **menopause** The period of time after a woman has ceased to menstruate.

For most women, the symptoms of perimenopause will eventually subside, and they will feel healthy and energetic again. However, a decline in sexual interest and function is not uncommon in perimenopausal and menopausal women, and this decline may result in distress, even in women who otherwise feel healthy and vital. This decline in libido has been linked with declining estradiol levels, as estradiol affects brain regions associated with sexuality as well as vaginal and clitoral tissues. This link should come as no surprise, based on the previously discussed role of estradiol in female sexuality.

Sexual concerns are among the most frequent complaints among women attending menopause clinics. In a Melbourne, Australia, study of women aged 45 to 55, the frequency of self-reported sexual problems rose from 42 per cent in early perimenopause to 88 per cent after eight years in the menopausal period. These otherwise healthy women reported decreases in frequency of sexual activity, libido, sexual responsiveness, arousal, enjoyment, and orgasm. While declining sexual activity is not related only to age and hormone levels—indeed, it may be associated with state of health, fitness, psychological wellness, and relationship factors—this study suggested that these changes may in large part be due to declining estradiol levels (Dennerstein, Randolph, Taffe, Dudley, & Burger, 2002; see also Chapter 9).

Of course, along with hormonal changes come changes in a woman's perception of herself as a sexual being. In addition, individual ideas about aging, changing body shape and size, and general life circumstances can all have a huge impact on a woman's sexuality, independent of any hormonal changes. Basson and colleagues (2005) analyzed female sexual function and dysfunction during menopause, and their results have provided a highly nuanced understanding of female sexuality that emphasizes the importance of a woman's perception of her sexual function and acknowledges the importance of context and rewarding experience in sustaining sexual interest and activity.

WOMEN, AGING, AND ANDROGENS

The most prevalent sexual problem among women of all ages is low sexual desire; surveys have suggested that anywhere from 34 to 43 per cent of women in Western countries may experience this problem. Desire decreases with age in both men and women, but the decrease is more dramatic in women. As suggested above, this decrease is often linked with declining estradiol levels, but researchers also suggest that decreasing levels of androgens, particularly testosterone, may play a role. Research has shown that the role that androgen levels play differs at different stages in perimenopause, yet the exact relationship between androgens and sex drive in older women remains unclear.

Levels of circulating testosterone in women decline gradually from young adulthood through menopause, leaving women in their sixties with approximately half the circulating testosterone of women in their forties, who in turn have approximately half the testosterone of women in their twenties. Adrenal production of other androgens also declines with age, and researchers have documented an accelerated rate of reduction for adrenal androgens during menopause.

Clinical complaints of low sexual desire are most common in women between 40 and 60 years of age. Notably, these are also the busiest and most stressful times of women's lives, as they are often the times when women undertake multiple caregiving roles. In fact, age and duration of relationship appear to be more significant than hormone levels in explaining waning desire in this age group. Thus we again find evidence that factors other than hormone levels may contribute significantly to lower sexual desire in women.

In spite of the lack of evidence for a correlation between low sexual desire and declining androgen levels, several trials of androgen administration have had positive effects on women's libido. The evidence is clearest in women who have had their ovaries surgically removed, where testosterone replacement was helpful in restoring lost sexual function (Shifren et al., 2000). Likewise, a study of postmenopausal women demonstrated that combined estradiol-androgen injections increased sexual desire and arousal, and occasionally increased the frequency of sexual intercourse and orgasm, more than did either estradiol alone or a placebo (Sherwin, 2002). When testosterone was administered to women seeking treatment for low sexual desire, women who were treated scored higher on a sexual desire inventory than did untreated women. Thus, in women who have complaints of low libido, androgen administration may have a beneficial effect.

Andropause

As men age, the key change related to sex hormones seems to be a decline in the synthesis of testosterone and, thus, a decline in testosterone levels. These decreasing levels are primarily due to changes in Leydig cell production, which decreases due to changes in responsiveness to LH. The morning peak of testosterone that often leads to morning erections is blunted; the penis becomes less responsive to testosterone, while the prostate becomes more responsive. This change in testosterone levels is accompanied by increases in levels of circulating LH and FSH. It is really not known what levels of testosterone are "healthy" in aging men because the natural decrease in testosterone level with aging is most often compared with levels in young men.

In some men over 50, decreasing levels of testosterone may lead to a clinical syndrome called "andropause." Symptoms associated with this syndrome include low libido (with or without erectile dysfunction); decreased strength, energy, and/or stamina; increased irritability, and a decreased enjoyment of life. There may also be changes in cognitive function as well as loss of bone and muscle mass, increased visceral fat, testicular atrophy, and the development of breasts. Any and all of these changes may affect sexuality, and there are few clinical trials of androgen replacement to demonstrate the effectiveness of testosterone administration in reversing these changes (Practice Committee of the ASRM, 2008). In fact, the levels of testosterone necessary to have and maintain an erection are relatively low, and testosterone levels seldom actually fall below that level in healthy aging men. Thus, although the reported incidence of erectile dysfunction increases as men age, most men consulting their physician have enough testosterone to maintain erections. It is important to consider issues such as atherosclerosis and psychosocial aspects of aging, which may have a greater effect on sexual function.

Even as men age, complaints of persistent sexual problems are uncommon—only 6.2 per cent of male sexual problems persist for more than six months. The most common problem, low libido, seems to be caused principally by **hypogonadism**, symptoms of which include poor morning erection, low sexual desire, erectile dysfunction, and measurably low levels of testosterone. This condition can be treated with androgens, but only after other metabolic and psychological causes are ruled out. Once treated, men who have had sexual difficulties tend to regain their erections, ejaculation, orgasm, and penile sensation.

Overall, there is good reason to believe that androgen loss in and of itself does not directly affect sexuality or sexual function in aging men. However, as is the case in women, much more research is required to elucidate which symptoms are caused by losses in sex steroids, and which are caused by psychosocial factors.

hypogonadism A condition in which the gonads produce little or no hormones.

CHAPTER SUMMARY

The key sex hormones in humans are estradiol and testosterone. These hormones affect the development and regulation of reproductive cycles, the development of the sexual brain, the expression of sexual desire, and the experience of sexual sensations. With age, these hormones may wax and wane, creating new challenges for our sexual lives and sexualities. Oxytocin and vasopressin also play important roles in human sexuality, with oxytocin being most significant in its promotion of maternal behaviour and affiliative bonds. Hormones may also serve as pheromones, signaling social messages to potential mates. It is important to remember, however, that sex hormones' effects on sexualities are neither unidirectional nor invariant, and that hormones alone do not control our sexual desires and behaviours.

DEBATE QUESTIONS

Do hormones or psychosocial issues have a greater effect on sexual desire and attraction? In what ways might hormonal and psychosocial factors interact?

REVIEW QUESTIONS

1. What are the major sex hormones?
2. What are the components of the HPG axis? How do the effects of the HPG axis differ in females and males?
3. How do hormones regulate the menstrual cycle in women? In what ways might a woman's experience of sexuality vary with different stages of the menstrual cycle? In what ways might her attractiveness to males change along with these stages?
4. What effects does testosterone have on sexual desire and performance in males?
5. What role does testosterone play in female sexuality?

6. How do levels of sex hormones change with age, and what is the effect of those changes on sexuality?

7. In what ways do hormones affect behaviour? In what ways do sexual thoughts and behaviours affects hormone levels?

8. How do the peptide hormones oxytocin, vasopressin, and prolactin influence human sexuality?

SUGGESTIONS FOR FURTHER READING

Recommended Websites

Estrogen and Testosterone Hormones: http://health.howstuffworks.com/sexual-health/sexuality/estrogen-and-testosterone-hormones-dictionary.htm

Hormones of the Reproductive System: http://users.rcn.com/jkimball.ma.ultranet/BiologyPages/S/SexHormones.html

Urology Care Foundation: www.urologyhealth.org/pediatric/index.cfm?cat=01&topic=110

Society for Human Sexuality: www.sexuality.org/l/incoming/sexdiff.html

Recommended Reading

Arnold, C. (1982). *Sex hormones: why males and females are different*. New York, NY: HarperCollins.

Einstein, G. (2007). *Sex and the brain: A reader*. Cambridge, MA: MIT Press.

Fausto-Sterling, A. (2000). *Sexing the body: Gender politics and the construction of sexuality*. New York, NY: Basic Books.

Fisher, H. (2004). *Why we love: The nature and chemistry of romantic love*. New York, NY: Henry Holt and Company.

Komisaruk, B., Beyer-Flores, C., & Whipple, B. (2006). *The science of orgasm*. Baltimore, MD: Johns Hopkins University Press.

LeVay, S. (1994). *The sexual brain*. Cambridge, MA: MIT Press.

Oudshoorm, N. (1994). *Beyond the natural body: An archaeology of sex hormones*. New York, NY: Routledge.

Roberts, C. (2007). *Messengers of sex: hormones, biomedicine, and feminism*. New York, NY: Cambridge University Press.

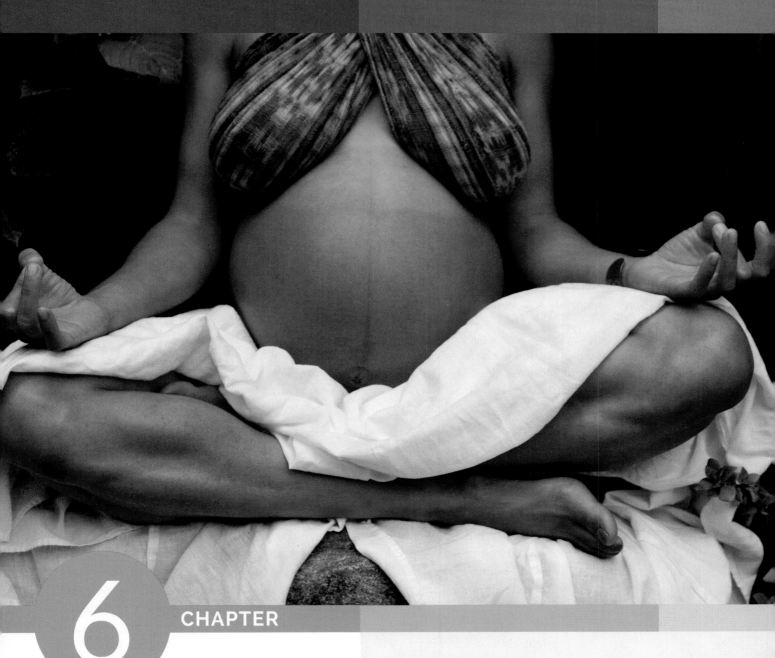

6 CHAPTER

Pregnancy and Childbirth

SAMANTHA WAXMAN
AND BEVERLEY CHALMERS

LEARNING OBJECTIVES

In this chapter, you will

- learn about conception, the stages of fetal development in an uncomplicated pregnancy, and delivery options;
- discover how pregnancy and childbirth can affect a woman's sexuality;
- become aware of the complications that can arise in a pregnancy; and
- become familiar with the various treatment options available to couples experiencing infertility.

Facebook "Unlikes" Breastfeeding

The online social networking site Facebook garnered a great deal of media attention in the past few years after it deleted pictures of women nursing their babies. The website claimed the photos to be obscene. According to an article in the *New York Times* (Wortham, 2009), the controversy started when several women noticed that their pictures had been flagged for removal. Facebook stated that it does not have any issues with breastfeeding but feels that pictures that show nipples are in violation of their policy. In response to the actions taken by Facebook, a group was formed called "Hey Facebook, Breastfeeding Is Not Obscene!" The group's main goal is to protest the policy prohibiting photos of exposed breasts on Facebook.

In Canada, the right to breastfeed in any location and at any time is protected by the Canadian Charter of Rights and Freedoms. Each province has a human rights code that protects women from discrimination based on sex. To date, only Ontario and British Columbia have specific legislations that pertain to mothers' right to breastfeed their children. The provisions specify time, access, and accommodation in the workplace and in public.

QUESTIONS FOR CRITICAL THOUGHT AND REFLECTION

1. Do you think Facebook has the right to remove pictures of women breastfeeding their babies?
2. Is the act of showing one's breast or nipple for the purposes of breastfeeding "obscene"?
3. How does the Canadian Charter of Rights and Freedoms fit with the policies set out by Facebook?

Introduction

conception Fertilization of the egg by the sperm.

This chapter provides a summary of some of the most significant psychological, physiological, cognitive, emotional, and sexual changes that occur during **conception**, pregnancy, birth, and the postpartum period (after the baby is born). Issues related to sexuality and sexual experiences are an integral part of the transition to new parenthood. Sexual response and enjoyment during pregnancy, after birth, and during breastfeeding are important issues for couples, and these issues are not always well addressed by health care providers. In addition, infertility and the consequent need for assisted reproductive technologies is becoming an increasing concern globally, particularly as women in many countries are choosing to give birth for the first time at a much older age than in previous decades. New technological developments that facilitate conception in couples dealing with infertility are emerging rapidly today, and the most commonly used are described in this chapter. Although this chapter focusses on childbirth in the Western industrialized world, some concerns regarding childbirth in other regions are also mentioned.

Conception

How does a woman get pregnant? Several systems need to work together for pregnancy to occur. Hormones need to be at the right levels, ejaculation needs to happen, sperm needs to reach the egg, and so on. This section will describe all the necessary steps for conception to occur.

The first development necessary for conception is ovulation, which occurs on approximately day 14 of a woman's menstrual cycle. After the egg (or ovum) is released into the ovary, it is picked up by the fimbriae (finger-like structures at the opening of the fallopian tube) and enters the fallopian tube. Consequently, the egg moves down the fallopian tube to the uterus. The egg must be fertilized (i.e., the sperm must penetrate the egg; Figure 6.1) within 12 to 24 hours after its release, or it will disintegrate.

During sexual activity the woman's cervix secretes mucus to prepare the passageway for the arrival of the sperm. In penile-vaginal intercourse, the man's orgasm typically results in the release of sperm into the woman's vagina. A typical ejaculate measures approximately three millilitres (or a teaspoon) in volume and contains between 200 and 400 million sperm. Although this may seem like an incredibly large number of sperm to fertilize one egg, most of the sperm are lost on the way to meet the egg. About one-half of the deposited sperm will flow out of the vagina (due mostly to gravity). Other sperm may be killed by the acidity of the woman's vagina. Of those sperm that make it to the fallopian tubes, approximately one-half will swim up the tube that does not contain the egg. Sperm typically live for 48 hours inside a woman's body; however, some sperm are capable of living for as long as eight days.

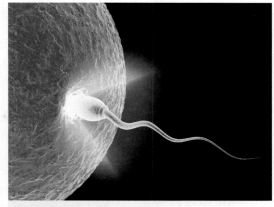

FIGURE 6.1 At the moment of conception, the sperm meets and enters the egg.

Once in the correct tube, the journey is not yet over as the sperm still have to make their way to the egg. Sperm are capable of swimming one to three centimetres every hour. Once the sperm arrive at the egg, they have travelled approximately 3000 times their own length. Although 200 to 400 million sperm originally start out on the journey to fertilize the egg, only 200 to 300 sperm get near to it. The long and difficult journey helps to ensure that only the healthiest sperm have the opportunity to reach and fertilize the egg, thereby reducing the likelihood of birth defects.

Fertilization of the egg by the sperm takes place in the fallopian tubes. Human sperm are believed to follow chemical signals released by the egg (Spehr et al., 2003). The egg contains chromosomes, proteins, fats, and nutritious fluid, and it is surrounded by a gelatinous layer called the zona pellucida. In order for fertilization to occur, sperm must penetrate this layer (Primakoff & Myles, 2002); in order to do so, they must undergo a process known as **capacitation** (Cohen-Dayag, Tur-Kaspa, Dor, Mashiach, & Eisenbach, 1995). The sperm then swarm the egg and release a substance known as hyaluronidase, which dissolves the zona pellucida and permits the penetration of the egg by one (or sometimes more) lucky sperm. This is the moment that conception occurs. The zona then thickens to lock out other sperm from entering the egg.

capacitation Removal of the plasma membrane overlying the sperm to allow for greater binding between the sperm and the egg.

The fertilized egg, or zygote, continues to travel down the fallopian tube, making its way to the uterus for implantation. This process takes approximately five days (Cunningham et al., 2010). Throughout this process, cell division takes place. Eggs carry an X sex chromosome, while sperm carry either an X or a Y sex chromosome. The ratio of male to female fetuses is about 106 to 100, respectively. This imbalance is due to a greater loss of female embryos during early pregnancy (Cunningham et al., 2010).

Pregnancy Detection

Once conception has occurred, there are a number of ways for a woman to detect that she is pregnant. Perhaps the best-known sign of pregnancy is a cessation of menstruation, yet this is not always as clear an indicator as many think. Although menstruation ceases following conception, spotting or light bleeding may occur during the implantation of the egg. In addition, some women may continue to have light spotting during the pregnancy, which may be a cause of much concern. On the other hand, the absence of blood is not an accurate indicator of pregnancy, as factors such as stress can result in a "missed" period.

basal body temperature The lowest waking temperature.

Besides observing a missed period, there are several ways for a woman to determine that she may be pregnant. One method involves examining her **basal body temperature** (Davidson, London, & Ladewig, 2008). An abrupt rise in body temperature at about the time that ovulation would normally occur that continues to stay elevated for more than two weeks indicates a high probability that a woman is pregnant. This temperature change is generally 0.2 to 0.4 degrees Celsius above the mean temperature of the preovulatory phase (Gibbs, Karlan, Haney, & Nygaard, 2008), and it is detectable only if the woman has been keeping track of her body temperature before she conceived. The increase in temperature is the result of large amounts of progesterone being made by the corpus luteum, and then later by the **placenta**. Other early indicators of pregnancy may include tenderness of the woman's breasts and nipples, nausea and vomiting, more frequent urination, and feelings of fatigue.

placenta An organ that connects the fetus to the uterine wall for gas and nutrient exchange.

human chorionic gonadotropin (HCG) A hormone produced by the chorionic villi of the placenta.

Chemical tests can also help a woman determine if she is pregnant. Most of these tests are designed to detect **human chorionic gonadotropin (HCG)** in the woman's urine. Some home pregnancy tests work by having the woman urinate on a stick, while others involve dipping a diagnostic strip into a container of collected urine. Home pregnancy tests purport to detect pregnancy at the time of a missed period, but they may not be as accurate when performed at home as when performed under laboratory conditions (Bastian, Nanda, Hasselblad, & Simel, 1998; Wilcox, Baird, & Weinberg, 1999).

Women may also visit their health care providers to have additional tests for pregnancy performed. Using a pelvic exam, a health care practitioner can detect a soft spot between the uterine body and the cervix; this spot is commonly called "Hegar's sign," and it can be detected at approximately one month following conception. By the third or fourth month of pregnancy, health care practitioners can look for other signs, including the beating of the fetus's heart, fetal movement, and ultrasound detection of the fetal skeleton.

The expected delivery date is usually calculated using Nägele's rule, which recommends taking the date of the first day of the woman's last menstrual period, subtracting three months, adding seven days, and then adding one year. Thus, normal gestation is about 280 days. However, most singleton babies are not born on the actual anticipated date but within a 10-day span on either side of the date.

Fetal Development

Pregnancy is divided into three periods, or trimesters, each spanning roughly three months. The first trimester occurs from the time of fertilization to the end of the third month of pregnancy, the second trimester is the middle three months, and the third trimester is the last three months and ends with delivery of the baby.

First Trimester

amniotic sac A sac, filled with amniotic fluid, that helps protect the embryo from outside damage and harmful temperature changes.

The embryonic stage (Figure 6.2) occurs following fertilization and lasts for the first eight weeks of pregnancy. The placenta and **amniotic sac** develop during this stage. The placenta provides the fetus with nourishment and oxygen from its mother's blood, and it helps to keep the circulatory systems of the mother and baby separate. It is also responsible for secreting hormones, primarily estrogen and progesterone. The amniotic sac acts like a cushion to help protect the embryo from outside damage and also helps to maintain a stable temperature for the embryo.

During the first month of gestation, the embryo starts to develop most of its major organs and organ systems, including the heart, the digestive system, and the central nervous system. During the second month of gestation, the umbilical cord becomes visible; once fully developed, the cord typically measures 50 to 60 centimetres in length. The umbilical cord attaches the embryo to the placenta. This stage also involves the development of facial features, hands, feet, and body tissue, as well as the major blood vessels in the body. The liver, pancreas, and kidneys are formed by the end of this stage.

The final month of the first trimester is when the embryo starts to be referred to as the fetus. During this stage, the fetus develops distinctively human physical characteristics, including more pronounced limbs and digits; in males, the testicular tissue develops. By the end of this stage, the fetus will have fingernails, toenails, hair follicles, and eyelids (Figure 6.3), and the sex of the fetus can usually be determined by an examination of the external genitalia using ultrasound.

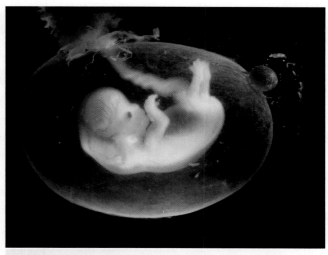

FIGURE 6.2 During gestation, the embryo (later the fetus) is suspended in the amniotic sac to help protect it from the outside world.

EFFECTS ON THE PREGNANT WOMAN

The first trimester is often accompanied by several side effects for the pregnant woman. She will likely experience tenderness, tingling sensations, or fullness in her breasts due to hormonal stimulation of the mammary glands. She may also feel nausea, fatigue, and changes in appetite (e.g., cravings for or revulsion toward certain foods). Finally, there is the likelihood of more frequent urination, irregular bowel movements, and increased vaginal secretion.

One common side effect of pregnancy in this trimester is "morning sickness." This term is actually a misnomer because the nausea, vomiting, and/or aversions to certain foods and/or odours can occur at any time of day or night. A review of 20,000 pregnancy records found that morning sickness was associated with a healthy outcome, including lower incidences of miscarriage and stillbirth (Flaxman & Sherman, 2000). In fact, women who experienced nausea and vomiting during pregnancy were significantly less likely to miscarry (i.e., lose the pregnancy) than women who did not (Flaxman & Sherman, 2000; Weigel & Weigel, 1989).

primiparous Pregnant for the first time.

Second Trimester

The mother can sometimes detect fetal movement at around 13 to 16 weeks; however, for **primiparous** women, detection of fetal movement may not occur until weeks 18 to 20. By the fifth month, the fetus' heartbeat can be heard with a stethoscope. By the sixth month, the fetus can open its eyes, and it becomes sensitive to light and sounds by the twenty-fourth week of gestation. Although the fetus goes through considerable development during this phase, it is still not capable of living on its own. For instance, it has immature lungs that are unable to supply enough oxygen for it to survive without the help of its mother's body (or technological assistance, in the case of a baby born before term).

A baby born before 24 weeks has a much lower chance of survival compared to babies born later in the pregnancy. For example, babies born earlier in the second trimester (e.g., around week 23) have about a 20 per cent chance of survival, while babies born nearer to the beginning of the eighth month (e.g., around week 28) have close to a

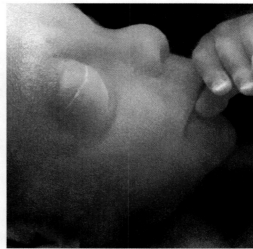

FIGURE 6.3 By the end of the twelfth week of gestation, the fetus has developed many characteristics that resemble a typical baby, including fingernails, toenails, hair follicles, and eyelids.

90 per cent chance. Although a baby born in the second trimester cannot survive on its own, the technologies offered at neonatal intensive care units (NICUs), which specialize in caring for sick or premature newborn babies, can help the baby survive this critical period.

EFFECTS ON THE PREGNANT WOMAN

The second trimester is often accompanied by indigestion and constipation as the fetus grows and puts pressure on the mother's internal organs. The placenta generates hormones that aid in the production of breast milk and, as a result, the breasts and areola enlarge, and the nipples and areola darken. The pregnant woman is also likely to develop stretch marks on the skin of her stomach as it stretches to accommodate the growing fetus; stretch marks may also appear on her breasts as they enlarge. Women, however, generally report feeling well during the second trimester, as the nausea and vomiting have generally dissipated by this point, and the discomfort of the later months of pregnancy caused by the enlarged abdomen is not yet an issue.

Third Trimester

By the end of the seventh month, fetal development of the brain and nervous system are complete. The fetus's skin is wrinkled and covered with down-like hair, which helps to regulate body temperature and is typically lost by the eighth month. By the end of the eighth month, the average fetus weighs 2500 grams, while the average full-term baby in Canada weighs approximately 3400 grams (Cunningham et al., 2010). The fetus usually prepares itself for delivery by settling into the head-down position, which is known as cephalic presentation (Figure 6.4). However, not all fetuses will turn before delivery. Sometimes, the fetus remains in a breech presentation (legs or bottom first) or a shoulder-first presentation. In such cases, a medical professional may try to coax the fetus into a head-down position by pushing on the mother's stomach (a process called external cephalic version). Braxton-Hicks (or false-labour) contractions are also common during the final months of pregnancy.

EFFECTS ON THE PREGNANT WOMAN

The third trimester is often the most uncomfortable. The increased size of the fetus can cause the pregnant woman to shift her centre of gravity, creating difficulties with her balance. She may also develop backache, leg cramps, frequent urination, shortness of breath, edema (i.e., swelling) of her hands and feet, and varicose veins in the rectum (hemorrhoids) or legs. During pregnancy, the average weight gain for normal-weight individuals is between 25 and 35 pounds (Health Canada, 2010). The amount of weight ideally gained is related to the normal weight of the woman: women who are overweight to begin with should ideally gain less weight, as obesity may add complications to birth, while those who are underweight at the start of pregnancy should gain more (Cunningham et al., 2010).

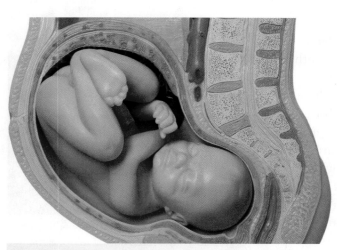

FIGURE 6.4 The fetus prepares for delivery by moving head-first toward the vaginal canal. This position is commonly called cephalic presentation.

Sexuality during Pregnancy

Generally speaking, it is safe for a woman to continue to engage in sexual activity throughout her pregnancy, until the start of labour. There is no reason to be concerned that the male's penis will hurt the fetus. The fetus is well protected by the amniotic sac, and the mucous plug that forms at the base of the cervix helps prevent bacteria and other germs from passing from the vagina into the uterus. However, if the pregnancy has not been developing as expected, if there is a history of miscarriage, or if there has been cramping or spotting, a health care provider may recommend that the pregnant woman abstains from sexual activity that could cause her to have an orgasm, as the resulting contractions of the uterus may trigger labour (Cunningham et al., 2010).

Masters and Johnson (1966) reported an initial decline in sexual interest and satisfaction among women during the first trimester. A second decline has also been found during the third trimester (De Judicibus & McCabe, 2002; von Sydow, 1999). However, women's sexual desire and physiological response have been found to increase during the second trimester. This increase may be related to the fact that the earlier symptoms of pregnancy (e.g., nausea) have subsided and the size of the woman's abdomen has yet to become intrusive.

In addition, pregnancy increases the blood volume in a woman's breasts, pelvis, and external genitals. Therefore, the vasocongestion associated with sexual arousal may be accentuated due to the already increased blood volume in these parts, creating greater sensitivity to touch and pressure. For some women, this increased sensitivity may make sexual contact uncomfortable or at least not pleasurable, but for others it may have the opposite effect, making sexual activity even more enjoyable.

Pregnant women are often encouraged to explore different sexual positions and activities to discover what works best for them. Due to physical changes in a pregnant woman's body, particularly the increasing size of her abdomen, the couple may prefer positions that involve the woman being on top, side entry, or rear entry to male-on-top positions. Partners are also encouraged to continue the use of non-penetrative sexual activities, including manual and oral stimulation. Once the woman's membranes have ruptured at the start of labour, she should abstain from intercourse and oral stimulation, as these activities carry a risk of fetal infection at this time.

A survey study by De Judicibus and McCabe (2002) found that women who were more satisfied with their partnered relationships reported greater sexual satisfaction during pregnancy. They were also more positive about their anticipated role as a mother, and they had lower rates of fatigue and depressive symptoms, both of which likely contributed to their high levels of sexual satisfaction. Other research has suggested that the experience of pregnancy and childbirth—the many physical changes, the frequent obstetric examinations, the increased familiarity with intimate bodily functions—may facilitate increased psychological comfort with thinking and talking about sexuality within the relationship (Chalmers, 1990).

Choice of Caregiver for Normal Births

One of the many decisions that need to be made by the expectant women and her partner during pregnancy is the choice of caregiver, especially for birth. Although many women elect to have a physician deliver their baby, there are other options available that are perhaps preferable, at least for uncomplicated births. In industrialized countries such as the Scandinavian countries where midwives are primary caregivers for healthy women in pregnancy and childbirth, women have more favourable maternal and neonatal outcomes, including lower perinatal mortality rates and lower Caesarean-section (C-section) rates, than in countries where most healthy women receive care from obstetricians (Enkin et al., 2001). In Canada, women also expressed far greater satisfaction with their labour and birth if they were assisted by a midwife rather than an obstetrician or a family doctor (Chalmers, Dzakpasu, Heaman, & Kaczorowski, 2008; Chalmers & Royle, 2009).

Midwives are trained to assist women during normal childbirth. They provide the pregnant woman and her partner with prenatal care and birth education, as well as postpartum care of both mother and baby for the first six weeks after birth. In Canada, midwives may perform at-home deliveries or work in a hospital, although they may serve as primary caregiver only for uncomplicated vaginal births. In addition, a doula is a trained labour coach who may provide emotional and physical support during

Culture & Diversity

The Traditional View of Pregnancy in India
Contributed by Caroline F. Pukall, Ph.D., C.Psych., Department of Psychology, Queen's University

"May you bathe in milk and bloom among sons" is a traditional blessing bestowed upon young women in India: milk indicates motherhood, and sons symbolize prosperity. Being a mother, especially of sons, is highly regarded in India; it is a socially powerful role, one that is expected of each girl once she marries. In contrast to the relatively medicalized approach to pregnancy in North America, pregnancy is viewed as a normal physiological process that does not require intervention by health professionals unless problems are experienced. The elder women of the family and/or community provide the pregnant woman with information, advice, and help (Choudhry, 1997).

In concert with an accepting view of life occurrences in general, most Indian women believe they have little control over their pregnancies or the outcomes of their pregnancies. There are some beliefs specific to pregnancy, however. With respect to food consumed during pregnancy, it is understood that "hot" foods are harmful and "cold" foods are beneficial—and the division of "hot" versus "cold" foods is not based on serving temperature or spiciness! Rather, pregnancy is viewed as a "hot" process, and the hotness needs to be balanced by consuming "cold" foods such as milk, wheat, and green leafy vegetables. "Hot" foods, such as meat, lentils, coffee, and garlic, are to be avoided because they are believed to lead to negative outcomes for the mother and the developing baby; they could cause maternal boils, diarrhea, fever, and coughing (e.g., Jesudason & Shirur, 1980), as well as fetal deformity or death (Nag, 1994).

Another common practice found predominantly in less affluent areas of India involves "eating down," or eating less during pregnancy. It is believed that excessive eating results in large newborns and difficult deliveries. However, it is also the case that in disadvantaged families adult females receive less food than do other family members, as they eat only after the elders, males, and children have eaten (Choudhry, 1997). As a result, many pregnant women in India gain an average of 11 to 13 pounds during pregnancy, and the average newborn birth weight is 5.5 pounds. As stated in the main text, there are many issues associated with low birth weight, and indeed, nutritional anemia, toxemia, prematurity, and low birth weight are serious issues in India (Raman, 1988).

Some other beliefs about pregnancy are also common in India. For example, twins and higher-order multiples are considered unlucky, although becoming pregnant with multiple children rather than a single child is seen as a work of fate. In addition, contrary to what one might expect, heavy bleeding before delivery is seen as a good sign, as the blood is believed to purify the uterus and "clean" the baby; further, bleeding in the fifth month of pregnancy is believed to be a sign that the expecting mother is carrying a male child. Finally, male children are considered more desirable than female children, as males are thought of as an "investible" resource; males will support their parents in old age, whereas females will need a dowry and move away when they marry. As a result, pregnant women in various parts of India may fast and/or ingest herbal medicines in the hopes of having a male child (Choudhry, 1997).

pregnancy, labour, and delivery, usually in addition to the physician, nurses, midwife, and the woman's partner. For information regarding the traditional view of pregnancy in India, see the "Culture and Diversity" box.

Delivery Options

A pregnant woman may deliver her baby in one of two ways: through a vaginal birth or through a C-section. Vaginal births may occur with or without pain relief, and methods of pain management may be pharmacological (e.g., administration of analgesics or anaesthetics) or non-pharmacological (e.g., water immersion, use of birthing balls, practices associated with the Lamaze method). In some cases, vaginal births may also require the use of forceps or vacuum devices to extract the baby through the vaginal canal. C-sections may be performed by physicians and require that the mother undergo either general or spinal anaesthesia. These methods are not mutually exclusive, and a delivery may require an approach that combines elements of each. For example, a woman may start labour using non-pharmacological pain management techniques but, should complications arise, she may opt for pain management drugs and delivery using **forceps** or a **vacuum extractor**, or through surgery.

Vaginal Birth

A few weeks before the onset of labour, the fetus begins the process of **engagement** (also called "dropping" or "lightening"), whereby it turns so that the widest part of its head is positioned against the woman's pelvic bones. In second or subsequent births, this process may occur later, just before labour starts. Eventually, the woman's cervix begins the process of **effacement**, during which it thins in preparation for the stretching (dilatation) required for passage of the baby. Dilatation may dislodge the mucous plug in the cervix and cause capillaries at the surface of the cervix to break. The resulting passage of a small amount of blood and mucus is sometimes referred to as a "bloody show." In about 12 per cent of women, the membranes of the amniotic sac rupture prematurely, releasing the amniotic fluid; this process is commonly referred to as the mother's "water breaking" (Davidson et al., 2008). After this event, labour typically begins within 24 hours; if it does not, labour must be induced to prevent infection.

There are three stages of vaginal childbirth.

STAGE 1

The first stage of vaginal childbirth can last a few hours to more than one day. On average, spontaneous labour lasts 8.6 hours for a first pregnancy and about half that time for a second or subsequent pregnancy. The first contractions tend to be relatively mild and widely spaced, occurring at intervals of approximately 10 to 12 minutes and lasting about 20 to 40 seconds. With time, contractions become more frequent, longer in duration, more regular, and stronger in sensation. The woman may feel an urge to push; however, her body is not yet ready. Women are encouraged to go to the hospital when the contractions are 4 to 5 minutes apart, unless, of course, they are giving birth at home.

Contractions help to efface and dilate the cervix. Dilation of the cervix is used to define the three phases of the first stage of childbirth. In the early phase, the cervix dilates up to 4 centimetres, and contractions occur every 15 to 20 minutes and last 45 to 60 seconds. In the active phase, the cervix dilates from 4 to 8 centimetres, and

forceps A tong-like instrument with cup-shaped ends that grasp the baby's head so the baby can be pulled from its mother's body through the birth canal.

vacuum extractor A cup-shaped suction device that attaches to the baby's head to extract the baby from its mother's body through the birth canal.

engagement The beginning of the descent of the fetus through the pelvic canal.

effacement The thinning and shortening of the cervix late in pregnancy or during labour.

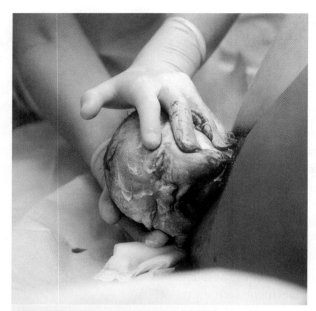

FIGURE 6.5 A baby's head emerging from its mother's vagina.

episiotomy Incision of the perineum to help with passage of the baby.

meconium The first stools passed by a newborn.

contractions become more frequent and intense. The final phase, called transition, is often the shortest and most difficult. It typically lasts 30 minutes or less, and it is at this time that the cervix fully dilates to 10 centimetres, which allows for the passage of the baby.

STAGE 2

The second stage of vaginal childbirth begins when the cervix is fully dilated and the baby's head begins to move into the vagina (birth canal); it ends with the birth of the baby (Figure 6.5). This stage is generally shorter than the first stage and can last from a few minutes to a few hours. For first pregnancies, this stage lasts, on average, 80 minutes, while for subsequent births, it typically lasts 30 minutes.

This stage of childbirth is more active than the first stage, as it is during this stage that the woman is encouraged to push or "bear down" to assist the delivery of the baby. Each contraction helps to move the baby farther along the birth canal. This stage can be quite stressful and tiring for the woman, although it is also very exciting, as it is clear that the birth is imminent. When the baby's head becomes visible at the entrance to the vagina, it is said to have "crowned." At this point, the baby will have moved along the entire length of the vagina and is ready to enter the world.

In the past, many physicians opted to perform an **episiotomy** at this point, to reduce tearing. Randomized controlled trials comparing women who underwent episiotomies to those who did not, however, have shown that routine use of episiotomy has no beneficial maternal outcomes (e.g., there is no reduction in perineal laceration, pain, or medication use) and is likely to cause harm (e.g., more pain with intercourse; Hartmann et al., 2005). As such, it is no longer endorsed in the medical literature as an appropriate routine procedure.

Once the baby's head is delivered, blood and mucus are traditionally suctioned from the baby's nose and mouth to induce breathing, although most healthy babies require no suction as they can usually clear their own airways (Enkin et al., 2001). Babies that have passed **meconium** in utero will, however, need nasal and pharyngeal suction.

STAGE 3

The final stage of vaginal childbirth may last from a few minutes to over an hour. This stage is sometimes referred to as the "placental phase," as it is at this time that the placenta detaches from the walls of the uterus and is expelled along with the fetal membranes as "afterbirth." Contractions during this stage assist the uterus to return to its smaller size. If there have been any tears, they are sewed up at this time, although minor lacerations may be left unsutured.

PAIN MANAGEMENT WITH VAGINAL BIRTHS

Childbirth preparation classes encourage the use of non-pharmacological techniques to reduce pain in labour. Using such tools as birthing balls, learning controlled breathing, soaking in a tub, walking around, using massage or distraction techniques, applying a transcutaneous electrical nerve stimulation (TENS) machine to stimulate areas of the back, and even undergoing hypnosis may all allow women to cope with labour pain and to avoid pharmacological intervention in labour and birth. Studies have found that childbirth preparation classes provide a number of benefits, including a reduction in the length of labour, lowered incidence of birth complications, a decrease in use of analgesics, a more positive attitude toward childbirth, and an increased sense of being in control (Saisto, Salmela-Aro, Nurmi, Kononen, & Halmesmaki, 2001; Slade, Escott, Spiby, Henderson, & Fraser, 2000; Zax, Sameroff, & Farum, 1975). These classes have also been associated with an increase in tolerance for pain and reduction in anxiety both before birth and in the weeks following birth (Markman & Kadushin, 1986; McClure & Brewer, 1980; Worthington, Martin, Shumate, & Carpenter, 1983).

Pharmacological analgesics and anesthetics may also be administered to manage pain in labour. Less commonly, tranquilizers and narcotics may also be used. General anaesthetics are used only for C-sections, and then only rarely, with **epidurals**, or **spinal blocks** being preferred. However, there are several problems with the use of most drugs—and in particular with epidural or spinal anesthetics—in that they may decrease the strength of a woman's uterine contractions, slow the process of cervical dilation, prolong labour, and reduce a woman's ability to push the baby through the birth canal, resulting in an increased need for an assisted delivery (vacuum extraction or forceps delivery) or a C-section (O'Brien, Young, & Chalmers, 2009; Enkin et al., 2001). Finally, the drugs are able to cross the placental membrane, meaning that the baby receives some of the anesthetic drug, which can decrease the baby's overall responsiveness and interfere with the first stages of breastfeeding and maternal–infant interactions. There is little evidence available to examine the long-term effects of pharmacological agents on either mother or baby, although short-term effects of epidural anaesthetics (e.g., backache, headache, bladder problems, tingling and numbness, and sensory confusion) have been observed. As specified above, the short-term effects of epidurals/spinal blocks are evident in both mothers (prolonged labour, etc.) and babies (decreased responsiveness resulting from the drugs).

epidural Injection of local anesthetic into the epidural space of the spinal canal to produce numbness in the lower body.

spinal block Injection of local anesthetic into the spinal fluid to produce numbness in the lower body.

C-Section

C-sections involve an incision being made through the abdomen and wall of the uterus so that the physician can retrieve the baby when delivery through the vagina is not possible (Figure 6.6). C-sections are most often necessary when the baby is too large or the mother's pelvis is too narrow to allow the baby to pass, the baby is in the breech position or is lying in a transverse position (lying across the cervical opening), or the umbilical cord is in a position such that it will pass into the cervix before the baby. Although such cases require surgical intervention, there is increasing evidence that C-sections are being performed more often than necessary. The Society of Obstetricians and Gynaecologists of Canada (SOGC), as well as the World Health Organization and most other professional bodies that deal with health issues, have taken the stance that vaginal childbirth is the safest route for the baby, and they are concerned about the rising C-section rates across the globe (see the "Research vs Real Life" box).

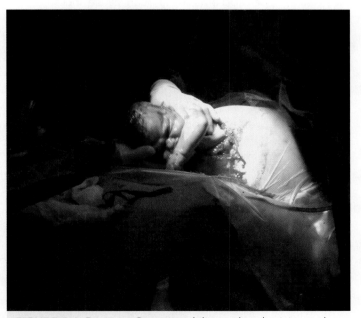

FIGURE 6.6 During a C-section delivery, the physician makes an incision in the woman's abdomen and uterine wall in order to retrieve the baby.

Research VS Real Life

C-Section—Modern-Day Miracle?

C-section rates have been on the rise in Canada since the 1970s, and the rate is currently at an all-time high (SOGC, 2004). In some areas of the country, more than 30 per cent of births occur through C-sections (Klein et al., 2009). Performing C-sections at the request of the pregnant woman is also becoming more accepted. Pop culture has likely played a role in the increasing rate of elective C-sections, given the number of celebrities touting the virtues of elective C-sections. These celebrities include Elizabeth Hurley, Britney Spears, Christina Aguilera, and Victoria Beckham; indeed, Beckham, who has been described by the media as "too posh to push," is a vocal supporter of scheduled C-sections and has used this method to deliver each of her four children.

Women in favour of elective C-sections often report that C-sections allow them to avoid the pain of vaginal delivery—although this argument discounts the pain experienced as a result of abdominal surgery. Others note that because C-sections allow them to control the timing of their deliveries, the procedure helps to create a sense of control that can be missing from "traditional" vaginal deliveries. Still others point to supposed health benefits such as a reduced rate of pelvic floor problems, which can cause incontinence, although research has shown that it is mainly pregnancy that increases the risk of urinary and fecal incontinence, and not the mode of delivery (Chaliha, Kalia, Stanton, Monga, & Sultan, 1999).

Despite the various arguments in favour of C-sections, the risks associated with the procedure seem to outweigh the potential benefits. Liu et al. (2007) report that healthy women who undergo a planned C-section are three times more likely to experience severe maternal morbidity as compared to women who have a planned vaginal birth. In general, C-sections are associated with higher risks of infection, excessive bleeding, scarring, damage to the intestines and bladder, chronic conditions related to childbirth, and even death. In addition, women who give birth by C-section have substantially longer recovery times than do women who give birth vaginally. This longer recovery time can interfere with the mother's ability to care for her baby without considerable assistance, and it can place a significant strain on the health care system.

In Canada, SOGC promotes vaginal birth as the preferred method of childbirth, as it is the safest option for most women and has fewer risks of complications than birth by C-section does (SOGC, 2004). Similarly, the UK's National Institute for Clinical Excellence (NICE) guidelines state that C-section on demand is undesirable (Kmietowicz, 2004). Yet not all national health organizations feel this strongly about the issue, and the American College of Obstetricians and Gynecologists (ACOG) has deemed it to be ethically permissible for a doctor to comply with a request for a C-section from a woman who has been informed of the risks, although it has also stated that the physician is allowed to deny the request if he or she does not feel that it is in the woman's best interest.

A recent study by Klein et al. (2009) surveyed 549 obstetricians, 897 family physicians, 545 nurses, 400 midwives, and 192 doulas from across Canada to assess their attitudes toward labour and birth. The researchers found that 42 per cent of obstetricians were in favour of a woman's right to choose a C-section without medical indication that the procedure is necessary, but only 21 per cent agreed with the statement that a C-section is as safe as a vaginal birth for women. Interestingly, only 8 per cent of the obstetricians surveyed would choose a C-section over vaginal delivery for themselves or their partners. The Canadian Maternity Experiences Survey revealed that few women (8.1 per cent) request a C-section at some time during pregnancy or before labour commences. This percentage included 5.3 per cent who had had a previous C-section (Public Health Agency of Canada, 2009).

Immediately after the Baby Is Born

Following birth, whatever the method of delivery, the umbilical cord is clamped. The cut is made about 2 to 3 centimetres from the baby's body, leaving a little stub that will dry up and fall off a few days after birth (Cunningham et al., 2010).

If both mother and baby are well, the baby should be delivered directly onto the mother's abdomen as it is born. Early skin-to-skin contact of mother and baby (and/or partner and baby) facilitates mother–infant (and partner–infant) interaction and "bonding." It is also regarded as one of the first steps in promoting breastfeeding (Chalmers, Mangiaterra, & Porter, 2001). The baby should remain in skin-to-skin contact with the mother (and/or the partner) for the first few hours after delivery, and breastfeeding should occur when the baby shows signs of readiness for a feed. The first breastfeeding usually takes place about an hour or so after a normal delivery, but it could be longer if the birth is surgically assisted or the mother is given medications for pain management.

A few hours after birth, drops of silver nitrate (or a similar drug) are placed in the baby's eyes; this delay is meant to facilitate the infant's visual contact with the mother and/or partner in the hours after birth. Vitamin K is also customarily administered to the baby through intramuscular injection to ensure that his or her blood will clot normally. Although babies may obtain high amounts of Vitamin K if they are given **colostrum** or infant formula, the injection further reduces the risk of hemorrhage, which is of great concern because it may result in death.

> **colostrum** High protein, antibody-rich fluid that flows from the breast before the full onset of lactation.

The Postpartum Period

Postpartum Emotional Issues

The expulsion of the placenta during the third stage of labour results in significant reductions in the mother's levels of estrogen and progesterone. During the weeks and months after birth, considerable physiological and psychological changes occur within the woman's body as these hormones slowly return to pre-pregnancy levels.

After giving birth, women may experience adverse emotional reactions that range in severity. Three major categories of postpartum emotional conditions have been identified: the **postpartum blues** (or baby blues), **postpartum depression (PPD)**, and **postpartum psychosis (PPP)**. The postpartum blues occurs in up to 80 per cent of women and usually resolves within a couple of weeks. PPD occurs in 10 to 20 per cent of women during the first year after birth and can last months or even years. PPP is rare, occurring in about 0.2 per cent of women, but it requires immediate medical care (Chalmers & Chalmers, 1986; Dennis, 2004; Health Canada, 2000; Samuels & Samuels, 1986; Stewart, 2006).

> **postpartum blues** Mild depression, tearfulness, anxiety, and/or irritability occurring in the first few days after delivery.

Many practitioners believe that the prevalence rates of PPD are actually much higher than 20 per cent (up to 50 per cent) but are under diagnosed or under reported (Beck and Gable, 2000; Bloch, Rotenberg, Koren, & Klein, 2005). The experience of PPD may involve extreme sadness or despair, apathy, changes in appetite and sleep, low self-esteem, and difficulty concentrating. Major predictors of PPD include a history of depression, depression or anxiety during pregnancy, recent stressful life events, and inadequate social support (Stewart, 2006). Additional factors that might contribute to PPD include hormonal changes, birth experiences, lack of experience with babies, marital stress, the number of children in the family, and demographic characteristics such as maternal age (Chalmers & Chalmers, 1986). Untreated PPD carries risks to maternal and child health (Health Canada, 2000). Supportive treatments include self-help groups, respite care, home- and child-care assistance, counselling, and psychotherapy. PPD may also require pharmacological treatment.

> **postpartum depression (PPD)** Severe depression occurring within the first year after giving birth.

> **postpartum psychosis (PPP)** Psychosis occurring within the first three months postpartum.

Perhaps the most effective way of managing PPD is early detection; however, it is often difficult to accurately identify those suffering from the condition. Many women experience their symptoms in silence (Beck & Gable, 2000), sometimes because they are unable to comprehend the reasons for their depressive feelings, or because they feel guilty that they are having negative emotions in relation to the birth of their baby. Postpartum mood changes can also be experienced by fathers. During the first year postpartum, paternal depression was found to range from 1.2 to 25.5 per cent in community samples, and from 24 to 50 per cent in men whose partners were experiencing maternal depression. In fact, maternal depression has been identified as the strongest predictor of paternal depression during the postpartum period (Goodman, 2004).

Sexuality during the Postpartum Period

Women's sexual functioning undergoes significant changes during the postpartum period. A British study of women at six months postpartum found that of the 484 respondents, 89 per cent had resumed sexual activity (Barrett et al., 2000). However, the researchers also found high levels of sexual morbidity, including dyspareunia, vaginal dryness, and decreased sexual desire. Most of the women surveyed (83 per cent) reported sexual difficulties during the first three months postpartum. This rate declined to 64 per cent at six months postpartum; however, it did not reach pre-pregnancy levels (38 per cent). De Judicibus and McCabe (2002) found similar results: at six months postpartum, most women were reporting decreased sexual desire, frequency of intercourse, and sexual satisfaction compared to pre-pregnancy conditions. Postpartum dyspareunia has been found, in some studies, to be associated with the type of delivery, with forceps delivery conferring the greatest risk, as well as perineal or other genital damage, particularly vaginal tears and episiotomies (Barrett et al., 2000). Women who experienced dyspareunia before pregnancy were four times more likely to experience it at six months postpartum compared with women who had not experienced dyspareunia before childbirth.

The resumption of sexual activity is dependent on a number of factors, including the couple's level of sexual interest, healing of genital trauma, fatigue, doctors' recommendations, and tradition. Connolly, Thorp, and Pahel (2005) found that at six, twelve, and twenty-four months postpartum, 57, 82, and 90 per cent of women had resumed intercourse, respectively. In general, couples with high sexual and relationship satisfaction prior to the arrival of the baby are less likely to report decreases in sexual desire and frequency of intercourse (De Judicibus & McCabe, 2002).

Obstetricians traditionally advised waiting a minimum of six weeks for safety (i.e., to avoid re-tearing or the risk of infection) and comfort, which corresponds to the time it takes for the uterus to return to its normal shape and size. In recent decades, however, this recommendation has been altered to support intercourse as soon after birth as the couple feels ready. Usually this corresponds with the cessation of any significant amount of postpartum bleeding or genital pain, which usually occurs within a few weeks after birth.

Breastfeeding

Breastfeeding is internationally recognized as the optimal method of infant feeding, given its beneficial effects on infant health and growth, immunity, and cognitive development (Kramer et al., 2001; Kramer & Kakuma, 2004; Kramer et al., 2008; Lucas, Morley, Cole, Lister, & Leeson-Payne, 1992). In addition, a number of benefits, such as reduced postpartum bleeding, delayed resumption of ovulation, and improved bone remineralization, have been identified in breastfeeding mothers (Rea, 2004; Public Health Agency of Canada, 2008). The Canadian Paediatric Society, Dietitians of Canada, and Health Canada (1998) recommend, for healthy full-term infants, **exclusive breastfeeding** for the first six months after birth, with the introduction of

exclusive breastfeeding
Feeding an infant only breast milk.

complementary foods at six months of age and continued breastfeeding for up to two years of age and beyond. These guidelines are consistent with recommendations from the World Health Organization and United Nations Children's Fund (WHO & UNICEF, 2003) and the World Health Assembly (WHO, 1996).

PHYSIOLOGY OF BREASTFEEDING

Milk production begins two to three days after delivery. Between birth and the time that the milk is ready, the mother's breasts produce colostrum, a substance that is high in nutrients as well as antibodies that protect the baby from infection. When the breasts are ready, the hormone prolactin is released to stimulate the production of milk. Prolactin is produced until the woman ceases breastfeeding. Once breastfeeding begins, the mother's body starts to produce oxytocin, which is needed to eject the milk from the breasts.

Exclusive breastfeeding delays the resumption of regular menstrual cycles. One study examining **lactational anovulation** and **amenorrhea** found that, on average, breastfeeding women had 322 days of anovulation and 289 days of amenorrhea (Lewis, Brown, Renfree, & Short, 1991). Therefore, exclusive breastfeeding can be an effective contraceptive (with about a 2 per cent failure rate) if rules are followed (see Chapter 7).

lactational anovulation
A lack of ovulation due to breast milk production.

amenorrhea Suppression or absence of menstruation.

Breastfeeding and Sexuality

Breastfeeding may affect a woman's sexuality in a number of ways. Masters and Johnson (1966) found that women who breastfed their babies were more likely to have higher levels of sexual interest in the months following delivery than their female counterparts who did not breastfeed; however, breastfeeding women are more likely to delay the resumption of intercourse (Adler & Bancroft, 1998; Rowland, Foxcroft, Hopman, & Patel, 2005). In contrast to Masters and Johnson's research, a review by LaMarre, Paterson, and Gorzalka (2003) found an association between breastfeeding and decreased sexual desire, which may be related to androgen levels or other factors, including fatigue and depression. Other research has suggested that women who breastfeed are four times more likely to experience dyspareunia than women who bottle feed (Signorello, Harlow, Chekos, & Repke, 2001). In addition, breastfeeding women may have positive or negative experiences with increased nipple sensitivity, leaking milk, and/or erotic feelings during breastfeeding.

As previously mentioned, oxytocin is important in the release of milk from the breasts during breastfeeding. However, as you learned in Chapter 5, that is not its only role related to sexuality. Oxytocin is also responsible for uterine contractions during orgasm and labour; therefore, contractions of the uterus may occur while a woman is breastfeeding and even up to 20 minutes after breastfeeding is complete (Riordan, 2005). These contractions assist the uterus in returning to its pre-pregnancy size. Due to the effects of oxytocin, some women may experience sexual arousal, and sometimes even orgasms, while breastfeeding. These feelings may be confusing for the woman, as the pleasurable sensations suggest a sexual context, and they may even create feelings of shame and guilt. One study found that 33 to 50 per cent of women experienced erotic feelings while breastfeeding, and of those, 25 per cent felt guilty about their experience (von Sydow, 1999). Yet there is nothing shameful about these pleasurable feelings; they are a natural response to the hormones being released and the tactile stimulation of the breasts and nipples. Oxytocin release also results in prosocial feelings, which encourage feelings of love—most important when developing a relationship between a mother and her baby.

Complicated Pregnancies

Most pregnancies and deliveries are uncomplicated and result in the birth of a healthy baby. However, problems may occur during gestation, at birth, or after the baby is born. These problems can be very distressing for both the mother and her partner and can have a significant impact on the survival of the fetus. Some of these complications are examined below.

Ectopic Pregnancy

Ectopic pregnancy occurs when a fertilized egg implants somewhere other than the inner lining of the uterus. The most common reason for an ectopic pregnancy is that the egg is unable to make its way through the fallopian tube into the uterus. In such cases, the tube may be obstructed—for example, by scar tissue that has developed as a result of chlamydia, or by an implanted intrauterine device (IUD). Most ectopic pregnancies occur in the fallopian tubes, but it is possible for the egg to implant in the abdominal cavity, the cervix, or the ovary. Once the fertilized egg implants, it begins to develop, form a placenta, and produce hormones that cause nausea and other common symptoms of pregnancy. Ectopic pregnancies may spontaneously abort, or they may grow and rupture. If a rupture occurs, it is likely to result in sharp abdominal pain, cramping, and/or vaginal bleeding. It is very important that the woman seek treatment immediately, as it is possible that she may hemorrhage, go into shock, and even die. Ectopic pregnancies have been found to occur in 2 per cent of all first-trimester pregnancies in the United States, and they account for 6 per cent of all pregnancy-related deaths (Cunningham et al., 2010).

Miscarriage (Spontaneous Abortion)

Most pregnancy losses occur within the first 20 weeks of gestation: these losses are commonly called *miscarriages*, although the appropriate medical term for unintended pregnancy loss at any time during the pregnancy is *spontaneous abortion*. These losses should be distinguished from induced abortions, which are deliberately initiated. Studies have found that approximately 25 per cent of pregnancies are miscarried by the sixth week following the woman's last menstrual period (Wilcox, Baird, & Weinberg, 1999). The most common reason for miscarriage is the presence of a defect in the embryo or fetus. Early miscarriages may appear as heavy menstrual flow, while later miscarriages may present as bad cramps, heavy bleeding, and/or the expulsion of recognizable uterine contents (e.g., placenta).

Although a woman's physical recovery from a miscarriage can be quite quick, the psychological consequences are likely to be significant and enduring. Lok and Neugebauer (2007) found that as many as 50 per cent of women who miscarried suffered some form of psychological morbidity following the loss, and that elevated levels of anxiety, depression, and grief are particularly common. The researchers also found several risk factors that may predispose a woman who miscarries to psychological distress, including a history of psychiatric illness, childlessness, lack of social support or poor relationship adjustment, prior pregnancy loss, and feelings of ambivalence toward the fetus.

Rh Incompatibility

Rh incompatibility (also referred to as D-antigen incompatibility) is a condition in which the antibodies from the pregnant woman's blood destroy red blood cells in the fetus. It occurs in cases where a woman who has Rh-negative blood (blood that does not contain Rh factor) is pregnant with a fetus that has Rh-positive blood (blood that contains Rh factor, a genetic transmission from the fetus's Rh-positive father). When the mother's Rh-negative blood mixes with Rh-positive blood, it forms antibodies; this may happen during delivery or when a miscarriage occurs. If the mother's blood mixes with Rh-positive blood for the first time during delivery, there is little risk to the baby because it will take some time for the antibodies to form. However, there will be great risk to a subsequent Rh-positive fetus, as the previously formed antibodies will attack the fetus's red blood cells when the mother's blood enters the fetus. This attack can result in fetal anemia, intellectual disability, or death. To prevent the development of these antibodies, a physician can give the woman an injection of RhoGAM shortly after she gives birth or has had a miscarriage.

Pregnancy-Induced Hypertension

There are three potential conditions related to hypertension (i.e., high blood pressure) that can be related to pregnancy: pregnancy-induced hypertension, pre-eclampsia, and **eclampsia**. Pregnancy-induced hypertension is simply high blood pressure associated with the pregnancy. Pre-eclampsia results when a woman's blood pressure is elevated and she also experiences generalized edema (fluid retention and swelling) and proteinuria (protein in the urine). Pre-eclampsia is associated with increased risk of fetal death. In severe cases, there is a risk that the woman will develop vision problems, severe headaches, and abdominal pain. In most cases, pre-eclampsia develops following the twentieth week of gestation; however, it can also occur up to six weeks post-partum. Women are most at risk for this condition if they are pregnant with their first child, obese, carrying twins or higher-order multiples, and/or of Latin-American or African-American descent (Conde-Agudelo & Belizan 2000; Sibai et al., 1997). If the condition is not well managed, the woman may develop eclampsia, which may result in convulsions, coma, and even death (Cunningham et al., 2010).

> **eclampsia** A life-threatening complication of pregnancy that is characterized by the presence of seizures.

Congenital Anomalies

Another possible complication of pregnancy is the development of major birth anomalies in the fetus. Congenital anomalies may be the result of genetics (e.g., Down's syndrome [Figure 6.7], Tay-Sachs disease), infection (e.g., from a sexually transmitted infection), maternal illness (e.g., diabetes), use of drugs and/or alcohol (e.g., fetal alcohol syndrome), or exposure to environmental chemicals. As mentioned above, the presence of a defect in the fetus may result in a miscarriage, and a recent study that investigated 544 fetuses from 486 second-trimester miscarriages found malformations or abnormalities in 13 per cent (Joó et al., 2009).

Taking folic acid supplements in the three months prior to conceiving and in the first trimester of pregnancy can significantly reduce the incidence of congenital anomalies due to neural tube defects (defects in the brain and spinal cord). All women who are considering becoming pregnant should ensure that they take folic acid (Medical Research Council Vitamin Study Research Group, 1991); this is especially true for those who are taking certain anti-convulsants (e.g., for the treatment of epilepsy), as these medications are known to increase the risk of a fetus developing a congenital anomaly.

FIGURE 6.7 Down's syndrome results when a fetus develops with an extra chromosome.

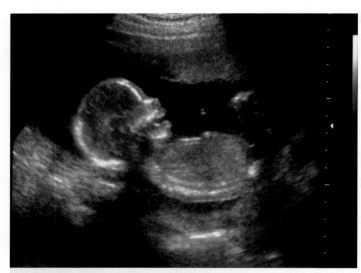

FIGURE 6.8 Sonograms are used to see the fetus in utero and ensure that it is developing normally.

sonographic examination Diagnostic imaging using ultrasound to visualize the developing fetus.

chorionic villi Finger-like projections that emerge from the sac that surrounds the developing fetus.

There are now several ways to detect congenital anomalies early in the pregnancy. One is to screen for elevated levels of the glycoprotein alpha-fetoprotein (AFP) in the mother's blood. A fetus begins to produce AFP early in the gestational period, and the fetal body wall (the outermost surface, or "skin," of the developing fetus) is supposed to protect against leakage of AFP into the amniotic fluid. However, defects in the wall (e.g., neural tube defects) will permit AFP to leak into the amniotic fluid, resulting in significantly elevated levels of AFP in the mother's blood serum (Cunningham et al., 2010). Maternal serum AFP screening is offered to women in the second trimester of pregnancy. Should an elevated value be detected, a **sonographic examination** (Figure 6.8) may be helpful in ruling out three of the common causes of AFP elevations: underestimation of gestational age, multifetal gestation, and fetal death (Cunningham et al., 2010).

Amniocentesis is a more invasive method by which congenital anomalies can be detected. It involves inserting a needle through a woman's abdomen into the uterus and withdrawing a sample of amniotic fluid. The puncture heals quickly, and the amniotic sac will replenish the lost fluid over the course of the next 24 to 48 hours. Once the sample has been obtained, the fluid is analyzed for several genetic conditions, as well as for the sex of the fetus. If an anomaly is identified, a woman can decide whether she would like to keep or abort the fetus. Although amniocentesis provides very important information, it is not without its risks. In approximately 1 per cent of cases, the procedure itself can cause a woman to miscarry. Therefore, given this risk, it is generally recommended that amniocentesis be performed only when the woman has a high risk of having a child with an anomaly (e.g., if she already has a child with a defect, if she believes she is a carrier of a genetic defect, or if she is over 35 years of age). Whether or not the women should undergo amniocentesis at all is also dependent on whether she would take any action as a result of a negative finding. If a physician determines that an amniocentesis is required and the mother gives her consent, the procedure is generally performed between the fifteenth and the twentieth week of pregnancy. Performing the procedure later in the pregnancy may increase the risk of miscarriage.

A similarly invasive method of determining congenital anomalies is chorionic villus sampling (CVS), which involves the insertion of a thin catheter through the cervix and into the uterus to obtain a small sample of **chorionic villi**. This method has been found to be as accurate as amniocentesis in detecting birth defects. The advantage of CVS over amniocentesis is that it can be performed by the eighth week of pregnancy. However, the disadvantage is that the risk of miscarriage rises to 2 per cent (Wass, Brown, Warren, & Saville, 1991). With either procedure, the period between having the test done and receiving the results can be very stressful for the woman and her partner.

Preterm Birth/Low Birth Weight

A baby is considered to be preterm if it is born before 37 completed weeks of gestation (the usual gestational period is approximately 40 weeks). Preterm birth is the primary cause of neonatal and infant mortality in industrialized countries; in fact, 60 to 80 per cent of deaths of infants without congenital anomalies are related to preterm birth (Hack & Fanaroff, 1999; Joseph et al., 1998; Joseph, Demissie, & Kramer, 2002; Kramer et al., 2000). It also accounts for a major proportion of neonatal morbidity, including acute respiratory failure, gastrointestinal complications, immunologic deficiencies, and central nervous system hemorrhage, as well as long-term motor, cognitive, visual, hearing, behavioural, and growth problems (Hack & Fanaroff, 1999; Joseph et al., 1998; Joseph et al., 2002; Kramer et al., 2000). In addition, preterm infants delivered before 32 weeks of gestation, which account for approximately 1 to 2 per cent of all babies born, account for nearly 50 per cent of all long-term neurological disorders and about 60 per cent of all perinatal deaths (Kramer et al., 2000). Compared with term babies, preterm infants incur higher costs related to early intervention, long-term hospitalization, outpatient medical procedures, and developmental and educational support (Clements, Barfield, Ayadi, & Wilber, 2007).

Preterm births have been linked to low birth weight, which is defined as a birth weight that is considerably less than that of most normal term babies, because fetuses tend to make the most weight gains during the last few weeks of gestation. However, term babies can also have low birth weight (Figure 6.9). In general, babies born at the appropriate weight for their gestational age—even if they are born before their due date—are the most likely to survive with the least adverse consequences. Those that weigh more than or less than the appropriate weight for their age are more likely to face health and developmental challenges.

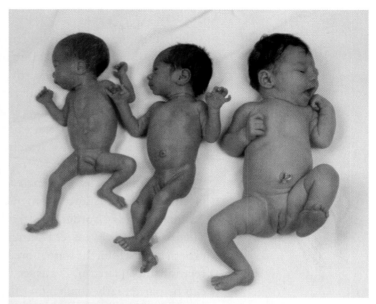

FIGURE 6.9 A baby may be born at a low birth weight if it is born premature or if it is too small for its gestational age. In this photo, the baby on the left is four weeks old and was born nine weeks premature; the baby in the centre is two weeks old and was born at full term but underweight; the baby on the right is only two days old but was born full term and of average weight.

In recent years, the preterm birth rate has been increasing in many industrialized countries. This is the case in Canada, where the preterm birth rate in 2004 was 8.2 per 100 live births (Public Health Agency of Canada, 2008). Several maternal factors have been identified as being associated with preterm births, including poor health, inadequate nutrition, heavy smoking, drug use, alcohol use, syphilis, and an interval of less than six months between pregnancies. Additionally, carrying more than one fetus at the same time is likely to increase the chance of delivering babies preterm and with low birth weight (Blickstein, Goldman, & Mazkereth, 2000). In the past two decades, increased use of assisted reproductive techniques (see below) worldwide—often associated with women's decision to delay childbearing—has resulted in an increased incidence of multiple births, which has contributed considerably to the increase in the number of preterm births in many countries (Public Health Agency of Canada, 2008).

Anoxia

The umbilical cord provides the fetus with oxygen. During delivery, the umbilical cord may be compressed as the baby passes through the birth canal. Prolonged constriction of the cord can result in anoxia (i.e., oxygen deprivation), although other conditions can also result in reduced oxygen supply to the fetus. The umbilical cord is likely to be constricted if a baby is born in the breech position, because in this position the baby's head will press the umbilical cord against the birth canal during delivery. When faced with evidence that anoxia is occurring, a physician may determine that a C-section is necessary, as prolonged anoxia can lead to cerebral palsy, brain damage, intellectual disability, and even death.

Stillbirth

Stillbirth commonly refers to babies that are born dead during the last trimester of pregnancy (Stanton, Lawn, Rahman, Wilczynska-Ketende, & Hill, 2006). A recent study found that, in 2000, the stillbirth rate in most developed countries was approximately 5 per 1000 deliveries, while the rate in most developing countries was approximately 25 per 1000 deliveries (Stanton et al., 2006). The highest stillbirth rates were in South Asia and Sub-Saharan Africa, where the average rate was 32 per 1000 deliveries. Based on the collected data, the researchers estimated that 3.2 million stillbirths occur annually worldwide.

Stillbirth often leads to increased psychological difficulties in the woman who has given birth. For instance, women commonly experience anxiety, depression, and post-traumatic stress disorder (PTSD) following a stillbirth (Hughes, Turton, & Evans, 1999; Turton, Hughes, Evans, & Fainman, 2001). A recent study also found that women who experienced stillbirths were more likely to experience the breakdown of their partnered relationships (Turton, Evans, & Hughes, 2009). Grieving the loss of a stillborn baby can be particularly challenging for several reasons (Cacciatore, 2010). First, there are often very few tangible reminders of a stillborn baby. Second, because the baby dies within its mother, the mother may blame herself or her physiological makeup for the death, even if she did everything she could to support the pregnancy. Third, even if the woman is able to acknowledge or accept the death of her baby on an emotional or intellectual level, her body still produces breast milk as though the baby were alive, potentially compounding her psychological distress (Cacciatore, 2010).

Infertility and Reproductive Technologies

Not all individuals are able to conceive naturally. In Canada, one in eight couples is affected by **infertility** (Health Canada, 2008). Infertility is defined as a biological inability to achieve pregnancy either after one year of frequent, unprotected intercourse if the woman is under 34 years of age, or after six months of such intercourse if she is over 35 years of age (Kakarla & Bradshaw, 2003). There are two types of infertility: primary, in which the couple has never been able to conceive, and secondary, in which the couple has difficulty conceiving but has been able to conceive in the past, whether or not the pregnancy ended in a miscarriage. Infertility is similar to impaired fecundity, which refers to the condition of couples who have achieved pregnancy at least twice in the past, but in which the pregnant woman has been unable to carry a fetus to a viable birth. Infertility and impaired fecundity can affect anyone trying to conceive, regardless of age, sex, sexual orientation, or background. Of all infertility cases, 40 per cent result from male infertility, 40 per cent result from female infertility, and the remaining 20 per cent result from infertility in both partners or unknown causes (Klock, 2004).

Male infertility is believed to affect 1 in 25 men. The most common problem is low sperm count, which may be due to varicoceles, or varicose veins in the testes. A typical sperm count ranges from 40 million to 150 million sperm per millilitre of sperm, and a male is determined to have low sperm count if he is producing less than 10 million sperm per millilitre (Gibbs et al., 2008). There are several factors that may account for low sperm count, including frequent ejaculations, tight underwear, frequent hot baths, use of electric blankets, and other activities that result in the scrotal temperature rising by up to approximately 1 degree Celsius (Leary, 1990). Other physical problems that lead to male infertility include irregularly shaped sperm (e.g., malformed heads and tails), low sperm motility (caused by prostate or hormonal problems, scar tissue from infections, or a genetic predisposition), chronic disease (e.g., diabetes, sexually

infertility The inability to achieve pregnancy without the assistance of reproductive technologies.

transmitted infections), injury to the testes, autoimmune responses in which antibodies produced by the man deactivate his own sperm, and a pituitary imbalance resulting from thyroid disease (Amso & O'Leary; Gibbs et al., 2008).

Female infertility affects approximately 1 in 12 women between 15 and 45 years of age. The most common fertility issue in women is irregular ovulation. A woman is considered to be at risk for ovulatory dysfunction if her cycle is less than 21 days or longer than 36 days. In addition, cycles that fall within the normal range of 21 to 36 days but vary considerably in length from month to month may also indicate ovulatory dysfunction. Another common problem that may cause infertility is the obstruction or malfunction of the reproductive tract, which can impede the passage of the sperm. Such obstructions may be caused by pelvic inflammatory disease (PID), an infection that results in the formation of bands of scar tissue (adhesions) on tissue and organs in the pelvic area. Endometriosis may also prevent proper functioning of the reproductive tract, particularly if the cells that break away from the uterine lining implant and begin to grow on the surface of the ovaries or fallopian tubes, thus blocking the passage of the eggs and/or preventing the sperm from meeting the egg. Other problems include declining hormone levels, cervical factor infertility (when the cervical mucus is too thick, too thin, or contains antibodies that attack the sperm), and advancing age (the quality and number of eggs decline with age; Amso & O'Leary, 2008).

Other factors that may result in infertility for both men and women include genetic conditions (e.g., Turner's syndrome in women, cystic fibrosis in men), environmental factors (e.g., toxins, heat, chemicals, radiation), and lifestyle factors (e.g., cigarette smoking, heavy alcohol consumption, obesity; Amso & O'Leary, 2008) Finally, couples may simply lack knowledge about intercourse and conception, and they may require education.

Psychological Impact of Infertility

The psychological and social consequences of infertility are considerable (Cousineau & Domar, 2007). The condition can lead to feelings of anger, confusion, sadness, anxiety, shame, and depression. Domar, Zuttermeister, and Friedman (1993) compared the psychological symptoms of infertile women to those of other female patients with chronic medical conditions. The researchers found that the women with infertility issues had global scores of psychological symptoms that were similar to those of women with cancer, cardiac disease, and hypertension, but lower (i.e., less severe) than those of women with chronic pain and HIV. In addition, a survey study conducted by Andrews and Halman (1992) found the stress of infertility to be associated with lower self-esteem in both partners. Although those surveyed did not report a reduction in marital satisfaction as a result of fertility issues, they did report increases in conflict and decreases in sexual satisfaction.

In general, women's experience of psychological distress resulting from infertility tends to be greater than that of their male partners. After all, women must undergo the most invasive procedures involved in identifying and attempting to treat infertility, and they are frequently forced to think about the issue, as they are responsible for daily monitoring of their menstrual cycles (Cousineau & Domar, 2007). However, infertility may also cause great distress in men; in particular, given society's expectations of men being able to reproduce, infertility may challenge a man's sense of virility and masculinity. There is even evidence that such distress can reinforce the biological causes of infertility. For example, Pook, Roehrle, and Krause (1999) found that a man's perceived stress of infertility was a risk factor for a decrease in sperm quality. Further, men may also suffer greatly because they tend to use fewer coping strategies than women do, preferring problem-solving approaches to the use of social support, which is more common in women (Jordan & Revenson, 1999).

Treatment of Infertility

Individuals and couples experiencing infertility now have several different treatment options available to them. However, many of these treatments can be highly invasive, and none are 100 per cent effective. In fact, a recent report from the US Centers for Disease Control (CDC) (Sunderam et al., 2006) suggests that the likelihood of an assisted reproductive technology (ART) procedure resulting in pregnancy and a live-birth delivery is approximately 30 per cent. In addition, there is evidence that up to 65 per cent of couples who have difficulty conceiving will eventually be able to conceive on their own, without any assistance (Rousseau, Lord, Lepage, & Van Campenhout, 1983). Therefore, couples seeking assistance with conception must consider all possible options and weigh the risks and limitations of ART treatment (discussed below) against the possibility of a naturally occurring pregnancy.

The first step in fertility treatments is often the use of "fertility drugs," which help to produce eggs at a faster rate or in larger numbers. These drugs may cause a woman's ovaries to release as many as 40 eggs in one cycle, which is why the process is often referred to as "superovulation." The drug most often used is clomiphene citrate (Clomid). It helps to stimulate the pituitary to produce luteinizing hormone and follicle-stimulating hormone, thereby inducing ovulation. Approximately 40 per cent of women treated with this drug will become pregnant (Davidson et al., 2008). If clomiphene citrate is not successful, a woman may be injected with HMG (human menopausal gonadotropin), which directly stimulates the ovaries to produce eggs. Although there is an increased chance of conceiving when using these drugs, there are also potential drawbacks. For example, the likelihood of having multiple births increases to 8 per cent with clomiphene citrate and to 20 per cent with HMG, when compared to a rate of 1.2 per cent of natural pregnancies (Davidson et al., 2008). In addition, fertility drugs also increase the risk of the ovaries becoming too large and rupturing.

Assisted Human Reproduction (AHR)

The Assisted Human Reproduction Act was introduced by the Canadian federal government in 2004 to regulate new reproductive technologies. The legislation led to the creation, in 2006, of the Assisted Human Reproduction Agency of Canada (AHRC), which helps in the maintenance of national standards and policies surrounding eggs, sperm, and embryos in the fertility clinics across Canada. As of 2006, there were approximately 25 fertility clinics across Canada. The legislation explicitly prohibits several activities, including pre-selecting or increasing the probability of having an embryo of a particular sex; transplanting a sperm, egg, embryo, or fetus of a non-human into a human being; paying a donor for sperm or eggs; buying or selling human embryos; and human cloning (see the "Ethical Debate" box). The legislation also regulates specific controlled activities, including in vitro fertilization, donor insemination, egg donation, transfer of a fertilized embryo, and research using embryos (Assisted Human Reproduction Act, 2004).

There are a number of clinical techniques used to assist reproduction, including artificial insemination (AI), in vitro fertilization (IVF), gamete intrafallopian transfer (GIFT), zygote intrafallopian transfer (ZIFT), and embryo transfer. The success rate of each of these ART techniques is typically not specified due to limited sample sizes. Rather than being reported by specific technique, information on assisted reproduction is usually grouped into four categories based on characteristics of the embryos

Ethical Debate

Cloning: How Far Is Too Far?

Cloning involves the reproduction of an individual from a single cell taken from a "donor" or "parent." The procedure requires removing the nucleus of an egg and replacing it with the nucleus from a donor, thereby producing an embryo that is genetically identical to its donor. Unaltered embryos typically contain only half of each parent's DNA; however, with cloning, the embryo is almost 100 per cent identical to its parent. The reason it is not 100 per cent the same is that the clone also receives genetic materials from the mitochondria of the original egg (Winston, 1997).

Debates over the ethical implications of cloning have intensified since 1997, when researchers successfully cloned a sheep from a single cell of an adult ewe (Wilmut, Schnieke, McWhir, Kind, & Campbell, 1997). This was the first time that a mammal had been cloned from adult DNA. The cloned sheep, who the researchers called Dolly, survived until she was six (about half the average lifespan of a regular sheep), when she was put down after having suffered from lung cancer and arthritis. Dolly had been able to produce six healthy lambs, all using "natural" reproductive strategies. Following Dolly, researchers have been able to clone several other animals, including sheep, goats, cows, mice, pigs, cats, and rabbits.

Although most people object to the idea of cloning a human, some have noted that human cloning could benefit us in a number of ways. For example, therapeutic cloning, which involves harvesting stem cells and cloning specific tissues or organs rather than entire individuals, can be used to study the treatment of disease, and it has the potential to be used to develop organs for transplantation. Reproductive cloning (the cloning of an entire organism, as described above) may also offer some benefits. For example, it could allow researchers to study various aspects of human development in new ways, and it could provide a useful alternative for those dealing with infertility (Winston, 1997). However, there remain several potential negative implications, including unpredictable genetic defects and genetic enhancement to produce specific desired traits. Indeed, it is for these and similar reasons that the Canadian government has introduced legislation that prohibits human cloning for any purpose. Yet, given the significant advances that cloning could lead to, might it be possible that popular attitudes, as well as government legislation, may one day shift to allow researchers to explore the possibilities of human cloning?

or eggs: (1) procedures that use fresh embryos from the patient's eggs, (2) procedures that use thawed eggs from the patient's eggs, (3) procedures that use fresh embryos from donor eggs, and (4) procedures that use thawed embryos from donor eggs. The 2006 CDC data (Sunderam et al., 2006) reported higher live birth rates among ART procedures that used fresh embryos from donor eggs (54 per cent) as compared to the other types.

ARTIFICIAL INSEMINATION (AI)

Artificial insemination involves the use of a thin, flexible catheter to insert sperm directly into the vagina or the uterus. The benefit of injecting the sperm directly into the uterus is that it reduces the distance that the sperm must travel in order to reach the egg. AI can occur with sperm from a partner or husband (called AIH) or from a donor (called AID). Sperm donors are often used when there is no male partner, when the male partner has a genetic condition that the couple does not want transmitted to the fetus, or when there is a problem with the quality of the sperm (e.g., after chemotherapy or radiation). If the problem is low sperm count, sperm can be collected from multiple ejaculations, frozen, and then combined to create a sample with a higher sperm count. In most cases, the sperm are collected in advance and frozen for future use, and they are inserted into the woman's body at the time of ovulation.

IN VITRO FERTILIZATION (IVF)

A woman may require in vitro fertilization when her reproductive tract is blocked, preventing the egg from reaching the fallopian tubes. This procedure involves surgically removing eggs from a woman's ovaries and fertilizing them with sperm in the laboratory. The fertilized egg is then injected into the woman's uterus (intrauterine insemination) or cervix (intracervical insemination), generally three to five days after fertilization has taken place. Intrauterine insemination in combination with medication that results in superovulation has been found to be three times more likely to result in pregnancy when compared to intracervical insemination and superovulation, or intrauterine insemination alone (Guzick et al., 1999). IVF is a very expensive and invasive procedure. Each attempt costs approximately CAD $7,000, and the procedure is not widely covered by provincial health care plans. In Ontario, for example, OHIP will pay for treatment only if a woman has bilaterally blocked fallopian tubes and has not reached her fortieth birthday at the time of treatment (see IVF Canada, 2013).

GAMETE INTRAFALLOPIAN TRANSFER (GIFT)

Gamete intrafallopian transfer is similar to IVF in that the eggs are retrieved as previously described, but the collected eggs and sperm are then deposited directly into the woman's fallopian tube, which allows for natural fertilization to occur. This procedure requires the presence of at least one healthy fallopian tube and can be very useful in cases of severe endometriosis and cervical factor infertility. Notably, some women prefer to use GIFT over either IVF or ZIFT (see below) for various cultural, ethical, or religious reasons, as it does not involve selection of the "best" fertilized eggs, fertilization occurs naturally in the fallopian tubes, and it does not result in discarded or frozen surplus eggs.

ZYGOTE INTRAFALLOPIAN TRANSFER (ZIFT)

Zygote intrafallopian transfer is essentially a combination of IVF and GIFT. This procedure involves the retrieval of the egg, which is fertilized in the laboratory. The zygote is then transferred directly into the fallopian tube to allow for natural implantation to take place.

SURROGACY

Another option available for individuals or couples who do not have a partner with a functioning uterus is surrogacy. Surrogacy involves a woman outside of the couple who desires a child bringing a child to term for that couple. The surrogate may be impregnated through any of the procedures outline above. In cases where a woman is producing healthy eggs but is unable to carry a baby to term, the egg might be retrieved from that woman, fertilized in vitro, and then implanted into the surrogate's uterus. If the couple seeking a baby cannot contribute a viable egg, one of the surrogate's own eggs may be used. In either case, the sperm may come from the couple or from a donor.

ART-Related Multiple Births

The single greatest risk of assisted human reproduction is having more than one fetus in the uterus at a time (Assisted Human Reproduction Canada, 2011). This risk is directly related to the use of assisted reproductive technologies, particularly the practice of transferring more than one embryo during an IVF cycle (Cook et al., 2011). Compared with natural ovulation fertilization, IVF is accompanied by a 20-fold increased risk of twins and a 400-fold increased risk of triplets or quadruplets (Brinsden, 2003). Overall, more than 70 per cent of all twins and 99 per cent of all higher-order multiples result from fertility treatments (Evans, Ciorica, Britt, and Fletscher, 2005).

Multiple births can cause health problems for the mother as well as the fetuses. Mothers carrying multiple fetuses are particularly susceptible to potentially life-threatening complications such as diabetes, hypertension, and pre-eclampsia. Fetuses tend to be overcrowded, as the human uterus is not designed to carry multiple fetuses, and this overcrowding can lead to preterm births as well as fetal growth restriction. Recall that the normal gestational period is about 40 weeks. However, the duration of pregnancy is inversely related to the number of fetuses such that the mean gestational age at birth for twins, triplets, and quadruplets is 35, 33, and 30 weeks, respectively (Evans et al., 2005). As a result, birth weights tend to decrease as well. These factors all contribute to greater risk of respiratory, gastrointestinal, and neurological disorders, including cerebral palsy (Little, 2010a). In addition, the risk of neonatal death in the first month of life is five times greater for twins and fifteen times greater for triplets than for singleton births (Little, 2010b).

A recent review (Cook et al., 2011) explored Canada's position within the international milieu of ART-related multiple births. The authors found that Canada and the US were tied for the highest twin rate across 21 countries. They also found that countries with the highest percentage of single-embryo transfers reported the highest rates of singleton births.

MULTIFETAL PREGNANCY REDUCTION

Multifetal pregnancy reduction (MFPR) involves removing one or more fetuses from a woman's womb, in order to increase the chance that the pregnancy will continue safely for both the mother and the remaining fetus or fetuses. The procedure is usually performed between 9 and 13 weeks of gestation, which helps to (1) ensure the fetuses are large enough to see on ultrasound, (2) allow the woman and her partner to make a decision, and (3) provide time for a possible spontaneous pregnancy loss to occur (Little, 2010b).

CHAPTER SUMMARY

This chapter has explored some of the experiences that women and their partners have and the changes that take place during normal pregnancy, birth, and the post-partum period. It has also examined some of the complications that might arise during these periods. In particular, the chapter has highlighted those aspects of the experience of becoming a parent that have particular importance with regard to sexuality and sexual experiences. Although the chapter has focussed on the experiences of couples in industrialized regions of the world, it is important to remember that pregnancy and childbirth are universal experiences: all women across the globe, whether they are rich or poor, or of any religious, social, or cultural group, experience similar physiological changes during pregnancy, childbirth, and infant feeding. While the situation in which they find themselves may differ markedly, women worldwide share a common experience when becoming mothers.

DEBATE QUESTIONS

Should parents be allowed to choose the sex of their baby through abortion or in vitro fertilization techniques? Why, or why not?

REVIEW QUESTIONS

1. How do pregnancy and childbirth affect aspects of sexuality?

2. What experiences can enhance or diminish sexual adjustment and enjoyment throughout pregnancy, birth, and the postpartum period?

3. In what ways can different medical approaches to pregnancy and childbirth impact a woman's psychological adjustment to becoming a mother? In what ways might these approaches benefit or detract from a woman's sense of fulfillment or enjoyment of her transition to parenthood?

4. If you were to advise a couple on the changes that occur to their developing fetus during each trimester of pregnancy, what information might you include? How might you prepare a couple for the birth of their child? What information do you think they would need to know about labour and delivery?

SUGGESTIONS FOR FURTHER READING AND VIEWING

Recommended Websites

CHILDBIRTH.ORG: www.childbirth.org

BabyCenter Canada: www.babycenter.ca/c3/pregnancy

The American College of Obstetricians and Gynecologists: www.yourpregnancyand childbirth.com

Parenthood.com: www.parenthood.com

PHAC's *Canadian Maternity Experiences Survey*: www.phac-aspc.gc.ca/rhs-ssg/ survey-eng.php

PHAC's *Canadian Perinatal Health Reports*: www.phac-aspc.gc.ca/publicat/2008/ cphr-rspc/index-eng.php

The Society of Obstetricians and Gynaecologists of Canada (SOGC): www.sogc.org

WHO: www.who.int

UNICEF: www.unicef.org

Recommended Reading

Boston Women's Health Book Collective. (1976). *Our bodies, ourselves: A book by and for women*. New York, NY: Simon & Schuster.

Murkoff, H. (2012). *What to expect when you're expecting* (4th ed.). New York, NY: Workman Publishing.

Recommended Viewing

Epstein, A. (Director). (2007). *The business of being born* [Documentary]. United States: Warner Bros.

Soliman, A. (Director). (2000). *Born in the USA* [Documentary]. United States: PatchWorks Films.

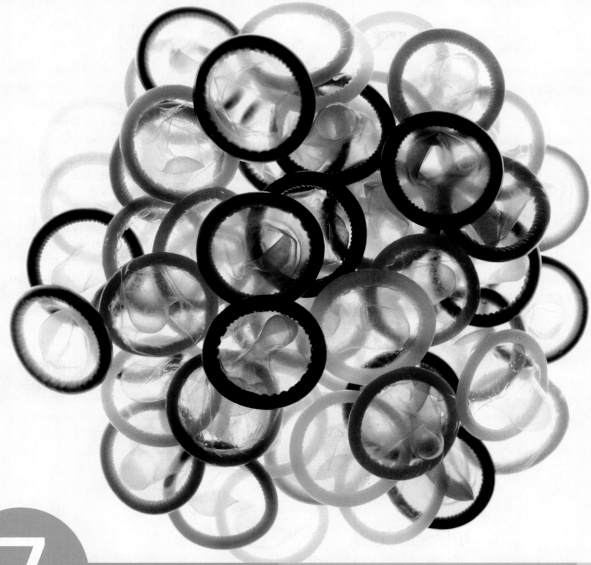

7 CHAPTER

Contraception and Pregnancy Options

KATHERINE S. SUTTON
AND BEVERLEY CHALMERS

LEARNING OBJECTIVES

In this chapter, you will

- discover the importance of taking control of one's reproductive health;
- learn about key developments in the history of birth control and the legalization of abortion;
- consider the pros and cons of various contraceptive methods available in Canada today; and
- think about the ongoing debates surrounding birth control and, especially, abortion.

Uh-oh . . .

Laura and her boyfriend, Sam, have been together for eight years and are both in their mid-twenties. They recently moved in together and subsequently became engaged. Currently, they are working their way through graduate school and working part-time jobs with modest, but stable, incomes. Both Laura and Sam are career-oriented, and they have decided to wait until their early 30s to have children.

Because waiting to have children is so important to them, the couple have always been very cautious about using contraception. They used hormonal contraceptives in the past but stopped when they discovered that the contraceptives were causing Laura to experience negative side effects, including headaches and decreased levels of sexual desire. After doing some research, they decided that condoms were the next most efficacious method, and they have been using condoms for protection for the past few years. They are usually very responsible and careful about using condoms, but one night they drank too much at a party and had unprotected sex. Although Laura was aware of the existence of the emergency contraceptive pill, she never even considered taking it after that episode of unprotected sex because she was on her period and she did not believe that she could get pregnant while menstruating. When she missed her period the next month, she took a pregnancy test. It was positive.

Laura is in a bind because she knows that Sam is against abortion, but she also knows that neither of them wants a child right now. She does not feel ready to be a mother, and if she decides to have an abortion, she wants to do it while she is still in the first 12 weeks of pregnancy. However, she has mixed feelings about having an abortion: while she is **pro-choice** when it comes to abortion, she's not sure how she feels about actually having one herself. She has heard that most women do not experience any negative psychological effects from abortion, and that she is likely to feel relieved, but what about Sam?

QUESTIONS FOR CRITICAL THOUGHT AND REFLECTION

1. How do you think Laura should deal with this situation? What are her options?
2. If you have a partner, do you know where you both stand on these issues?

pro-choice movement A movement whose followers believe that a woman has the option to choose whether or not to terminate her pregnancy.

Introduction

The study of contraception is an important one for people who wish to gain control over their reproductive health. The ability to choose when, and if, one wants to have a child has resulted in major positive changes for women in particular. The invention and subsequent widespread use of effective contraceptives is associated not only with improved maternal and fetal health, but also with an improvement in women's social status, including their ability to gain higher education and enter the workforce (Freedman & Isaacs, 1993). Having fewer children results in less financial strain on many couples, and lower birthrates in general may give us all a sense of control over the population crisis plaguing our earth. Unfortunately, despite great advances, effective contraceptives are still not universally available, and those who do have access often do not use them consistently or effectively.

Ancient Forms of Birth Control

Over the course of history, humans have developed many different concoctions for women to take in an attempt to prevent conception. Silphium, a plant used in ancient Greece for preventing pregnancy, was so popular that it eventually became extinct during the third or second century BCE. Deadly substances, including mercury and arsenic, were also ingested for contraception in many ancient cultures (Connell, 1999).

Barrier methods were also used in ancient times. In ancient Egypt, for example, women inserted tampons soaked in crocodile dung, honey, and various other substances thought to prevent conception into their vaginas before intercourse.

Other ways of controlling conception in the past involved the prevention of penile-vaginal intercourse. One example is that of menstruation taboos that required girls who had begun menstruating to seclude themselves from the general population. For the Carrier people of British Columbia, this practice involved sending newly menstruating girls into seclusion in the wilderness for three or four years (Delaney, Lupton, & Toth, 1988). Another example involved **intra-crural intercourse**, which is called *soma* in some Southern African communities that practised this alternative to penetrative intercourse (Chalmers, 1990).

Prehistorically, however, the most widely and consistently used method of population control—the larger implication of birth control—was likely infanticide (Harris, 1977). Infanticide remained fairly commonplace in Europe, India, and China until the nineteenth century, and it continues to be widely practised in some locations today (Jones, 2009). Indeed, a common criticism of China's **family planning** laws is that it drives parents to commit infanticide (see the "Ethical Debate" box).

intra-crural intercourse Rubbing the penis between the partner's thighs.

family planning Individual/partnered choice over the spacing and number of children a woman/couple will have.

A Brief History of Birth Control in Canada

Using, selling, and disseminating contraception was regarded as a crime under Canada's Criminal Code of 1892 because it was thought that contraception "corrupted morals." Under this law, a person could serve up to two years in jail if she or he was found guilty of using contraception (Bishop, 2011). Initially, the birth control movement started among the higher-educated and wealthier classes. Indeed, they were the ones who could afford the available under-the-counter forms of contraception provided covertly by birth control advocates. Although some of the more progressively minded individuals argued that everyone should have access to contraception, regardless of social class, many women were discouraged from asking their physicians about birth control, and physicians were understandably reluctant to provide this illegal information (Mitchinson, 1991).

The first formal contraception advocacy organization in Canada was formed in Vancouver, British Columbia, in 1923, and the first birth control clinic opened in Hamilton, Ontario, in 1932. Also in the 1930s, the Parents' Information Bureau for family planning and birth control was set up in Kitchener, Ontario by philanthropist A.R. Kaufman. One of the program's field workers, Dorothea Palmer, was arrested for distributing information on birth control in 1936; she won a landmark acquittal, stating that she had been working for the good of the public (Bishop, 2011).

By the 1960s, following the "baby boom" and increasing global concerns about population control, society was becoming more accepting of birth control. The International Planned Parenthood Federation was formed in 1963, and the idea of family planning as a human right was first recognized by the United Nations in 1968. Although this growing movement was opposed by several religious organizations, most notably the Catholic Church, the majority of Canadians supported the push to make contraceptives widely available. In the year following the United Nations' declaration, under Prime Minister Pierre Trudeau, the use of birth control was removed from the Canadian Criminal Code; this shift reflected Trudeau's popular position that "the state has no business in the bedrooms of the Nation." At that time it became legal for doctors to prescribe the birth control pill for contraceptive purposes; it had previously been available only as a remedy for "menstrual problems."

Ethical Debate

China's One-Child Policy

In 1978, China introduced a policy restricting the number of children per couple, in most cases to one (see Figure 7.1). The policy has been in application to varying degrees ever since, with exceptions to the one-child-per-couple rule becoming more lax over the years. Currently, ethnic minorities are excluded from the policy, and parents without siblings or those who are rich enough to pay the financial penalties imposed for a second child may have two children. In some rural areas, there are exceptions if the first child is a girl or if the child has some sort of disability. Multiple births (e.g., twins) are also allowed (Information Office of the State Council of the People's Republic of China [IOSCPRC], 1995). It has been estimated that the policy prevented 300 million to 400 million births between 1979 and 2010.

The one-child policy was created in order to alleviate the social, economic, and environmental problems of over-population that China was facing. Regarding these objectives, it has been successful, at least according to a recent systematic study of the policy (Baochang, Wang, Zhigang, & Zhang, 2007). Since the implementation of the policy, China's gross domestic product (GDP) has increased, its consumer goods market has expanded, and the per-capita net income of families has increased. Life expectancy has also risen, and the incidence of a number of diseases has decreased. Health care and education are more accessible, and women's social status has increased because women are no longer overburdened with

FIGURE 7.1 This propaganda poster from the 1980s was designed to promote China's one-child policy. The image highlights both the reality for the majority of families, in which it is the woman's responsibility to take care of family planning, and also the cultural ideal, which is to have a son.

childbearing. Without the government taking a strong approach to control the population, many more individuals in China would be starving, poverty stricken, and suffering from illnesses (IOSCPRC, 1995). So, this all sounds great, right?

However successful the policy has been in controlling the population, many have criticized the way in which it has been implemented. Some have pointed out that although the policy is officially voluntary, the rewards for following it and the punishments for

Progressive changes continued to take place over the following decades, although these changes were at first slow to come. Even by the mid-1970s, access to family planning services and contraceptives was limited, often to married couples, and there was no national policy or public education program regarding sexuality and fertility (Appleby, 1999). The situation is much improved today, although access to contraceptives is not equal in all regions of the country and for some the matter remains highly controversial. In addition, while most Canadians today have had at least some formal education about contraception, many people continue to believe certain popular myths associated with the topic (Table 7.1).

Modern Methods of Birth Control

As previously suggested, contraceptives have been used to greater or lesser degrees across human history. Primitive contraceptives were commonly used by many peoples,

violating it are such that individuals are forced to comply. Others have objected to the waiting period some couples must face in cases where the quota of children for a particular area has already been met. Still others have challenged the policy as violating the human right of a woman to control her fertility and, in some cases, the right not to be tortured. Women without birth permits for a second child have been physically forced to undergo abortions, even into the third trimester of their pregnancy (Lim, 2007). The use of physical force for abortions and sterilization was outlawed in 2002, but it is unclear whether this law is enforced (Taylor, 2005).

Statistics demonstrate that, in general, females tend to suffer more than males under the policy. For one thing, the majority of the family planning burden falls on women. Despite efforts to increase the appeal of vasectomies for Chinese men, there are many traditional and cultural barriers to promoting the equal participation of men and women in reproductive responsibilities. In addition, male children are favoured in Chinese culture and are desired for a variety of practical reasons, such as care of parents in old age. This preference for males has led many women to abort female fetuses or abandon female children in order to try for a male child. In September 1997, the World Health Organization issued a report claiming that "more than 50 million women were estimated to be 'missing' in China because of the institutionalized killing and neglect of girls due to the one-child population policy" (reported in Jones, 2009). In 2000, the ratio of males to females in China was 117 to 100, and it is estimated that by 2020 there will be 30 to 40 million unmarried men in China (Huang & Yang, 2006). The consequence of this gender imbalance is currently manifesting in increasing trafficking of women.

A recent survey by the National Population and Family Planning Commission of China (2010) found that 70.7 per cent of women in China would like to have two or more children. Feminist critique maintains that women have a right to make their own decisions about their bodies without government intervention (Dixon-Mueller, 1993); however, decisions about family planning policies in China are made exclusively by male policy makers (Thomas & Grindle, 1990). Rather than a population-control policy, therefore, it is suggested that China implement a reproductive-rights policy that would allow everyone access to contraception and abortion, as well as the freedom to choose when and how many children they want. Supporters of this idea note that it is a violation of human rights to be forced either to have (by limited access and education about contraception and abortion) or not to have (through laws and mandatory abortion, birth control, or sterilization) children. If not exclusively the right of the woman, it should be the right of the woman and her partner to make any decisions regarding their childbearing. What do you think?

and we have evidence that later civilizations developed great knowledge of birth control—for example, the tenth-century Persian text *The Canon of Medicine* documents 20 different methods of preventing conception. A major breakthrough came in the sixteenth century, with Italian anatomist Gabriello Fallopio's invention of reusable condoms, which he made from linen (Youssef, 1993), and which were later made of animal intestines (Collier, 2007). Yet religious and political influences—for example, that of the Catholic Church, and the call to repopulate Europe following the plagues—came to paint the use of contraceptives in a negative light, and it was not until well into the twentieth century, largely due to the influence of political activists such as Margaret Sanger (Figure 7.2), that Western societies in general began to once again look favourably upon birth control.

This renewed interest in birth control has led to some remarkable advances in the types of contraceptives that are widely available. Yet, despite this variety, evidence shows that most Canadians have limited familiarity with any methods beyond male condoms and oral contraceptive (OC) pills (Bishop, 2011). The following section describes the various contraceptive methods that are available today. Note that some (e.g., hormonal contraceptives) protect only against pregnancy, while others (e.g., condoms) are useful both in preventing pregnancy and also in protecting against STIs (see

menses Menstrual flow.

douche To flush out the inside of the vagina with a liquid.

TABLE 7.1 Common myths related to contraception.

Myth	Truth
A female cannot get pregnant the first time that she has sex with a male.	A female can get pregnant the first time she has sex. Females can also get pregnant before their first menstrual period because the first ovulation occurs before the first **menses**.
A female cannot get pregnant if she **douches** after sexual intercourse.	Douching is not an effective means of preventing pregnancy, as the rinse cannot reach the sperm already past the cervix; in some cases, it may even force ejaculate further into the vaginal canal. Furthermore, douching can be dangerous and is strongly discouraged for various health reasons (Chapter 4). Also, douching is not an effective way of preventing the transmission of sexually transmitted infections (STIs).
Pregnancy cannot occur if a woman has sex standing up or if the female is on top of the male during sex.	Sexual positions make little difference to whether or not conception will occur. Once the sperm is in the female's vagina, it is transported toward her cervix and into her uterus regardless of what position she is in.
A female cannot get pregnant if she does not orgasm.	It is true that during female orgasm the cervix contracts, drawing semen into the uterus. However, semen enters the uterus without this contraction, and women are fully capable of becoming pregnant without orgasm.
A female cannot get pregnant if the male does not orgasm.	Although ejaculation and orgasm often go hand-in-hand for males, it is possible for a male to experience orgasm without ejaculating and also to ejaculate without experiencing orgasm. Whether or not ejaculation occurs, when men are sexually aroused, they often release pre-ejaculate (also known as "pre-cum"), which can contain motile sperm.
A female cannot get pregnant if the male withdraws ("pulls out") before he ejaculates.	Withdrawal is not a very effective means of preventing conception, and it results in pregnancy for 1 out of 5 women who use this method (WHO, 2001). One problem is that it requires a great deal of attention and self-control from the male to withdraw in time. Another is that the male cannot control the release of pre-ejaculate. Additionally, semen released on the woman's vulva can still make their way into the female reproductive organs and fertilize the egg.
A female cannot get pregnant if she has sex during menstruation.	Menstrual cycles in women are not an exact science. Even if a woman is very aware of her cycle and knows when she is least likely to get pregnant, there is no guarantee that a pregnancy will not occur. In addition, sperm can live in the female body for several days, resulting in conception well after coitus.
Women who carry condoms are "sluts."	Carrying a condom does not mean that a woman has to have sex, but rather that she is responsible and prepared if she chooses to do so.

Chapter 8). Also note that the effectiveness of these methods depends on how they are used, with **perfect use** leading to much better results than **typical use**.

Without using of any form of contraception, the probability of getting pregnant within a year is 85 per cent if you are sexually active (Hatcher, Trussell, & Nelson, 2007). Thus, choosing a reliable method of birth control is essential if you and your partner want to avoid getting pregnant. Many people find it difficult to decide which method is best for them, and there are a number of Internet-based resources available to help you make the decision. For example, the Society of Obstetricians and Gynaecologists of Canada's website SexualityandU.ca has a great questionnaire-based tool entitled "Choosing Wisely," which was developed by Dr Mary Anne Jamieson and graduates at Queen's University. However, such guides are intended only to offer advice; they should not replace a detailed consultation with a health care provider.

FIGURE 7.2 Margaret Sanger (1879–1966) was an American nurse and activist who strongly believed in educating women about contraception. She coined the term *birth control*, in 1914, to mean the voluntary control of conception by mechanical and/or chemical means (Bishop, 2011).

perfect use Ideal situation in which the birth control method is followed 100 per cent accurately.

typical use Realistic situation in which some people will inevitably make mistakes in use, perhaps because they are misinformed, intoxicated, tired, or forgetful.

Hormonal Contraceptives

Hormonal contraceptives (Table 7.2) are reversible methods of birth control that protect against pregnancy, but not against STIs. These methods require a woman to take hormones that will drastically reduce the chances of pregnancy. Hormonal contraceptives work by inhibiting ovulation, altering the endometrium, and/or altering the consistency of the cervical mucus. In order to be effective, hormonal contraceptives must be taken regularly, whether or not the woman engages in sexual activity.

Many women choose hormonal contraceptives because, when used properly, these methods are typically more effective in preventing pregnancy than are most non-hormonal methods. They are also not methods that need to be thought about during the act of intercourse, as is the case with many barrier methods. Other benefits include increased regulation of menstrual cycles, reduced menstrual flow, and in some cases even **amenorrhea** (with progestin-only contraceptives) or a reduced risk of **chronic pelvic pain** (with Depo-Provera) or ovarian cancer. Yet hormonal contraceptives have also been linked with several side effects, including a slight increase in the risk of breast and cervical cancers, increased risk of **vaginitis** (with NuvaRing), and potential weight gain (particularly with Depo-Provera). In addition, some women experience hormonal side effects (e.g., breast tenderness, nausea, perception of mood changes), although these side effects are usually temporary, typically diminishing after the first three months of using hormonal contraceptives (Redmond, Godwin, Olson, & Lippman, 1999).

amenorrhea Absence of menstruation.

chronic pelvic pain (CPP) Chronic or recurrent pelvic pain that apparently has a gynecological origin but for which no definitive cause can be found.

Non-hormonal Intra-uterine Devices and Barrier Methods

Non-hormonal intra-uterine devices (IUDs) and barrier methods (Table 7.2) are also reversible, and they have the advantage of being safe to use while breastfeeding and

vaginitis An inflammation of the vagina, usually due to infection, that can result in discharge, irritation, and pain of the vagina and vulva.

for women with adverse reactions to hormone-based contraceptives. While IUDs must be inserted by a doctor, the barrier devices can be inserted or applied by the individual as required (although women must be fitted by a doctor for either a cervical cap or a diaphragm). Each barrier method must be applied within a specific timeframe before sex occurs. Some individuals consider this to be a drawback, arguing that the application of the contraceptives interferes with the spontaneity of sex, but others find the anticipatory period to be arousing.

TABLE 7.2 Artificial methods of birth control.

HORMONAL CONTRACEPTIVES[a]

Combination Hormonal Contraceptives

Mechanism of Action: Inhibits ovulation; thins endometrium to help prevent implantation; thickens cervical mucus to trap sperm

Pros: Menstrual cycle regulation; reduced menstrual flow; decreased acne; reduced symptoms of pre-menstrual syndrome (PMS); decreased risk of endometrial and ovarian cancer; increased bone mineral density

Cons: Possible temporary hormonal side effects, such as spotting between menses, breast tenderness, headaches, decreased levels of desire, nausea, and the perception of weight gain and mood changes; slightly increased risk of breast and cervical cancer; expensive; do not protect against STIs

Combination Oral Contraceptive Pill (estrogen and progesterone)	Transdermal Contraceptive Patch	NuvaRing
		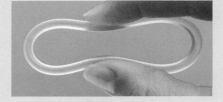
Failure Rate:[b] Perfect: 0.3%, typical: 8%[c]	**Failure Rate:** Perfect: 0.3%, typical: 8%	**Failure Rate:** Perfect: 0.3%, typical: 8%
How to Use? Pill is taken daily, with either a break for menstruation every 21 days or continuously	**How to Use?** One patch applied on the skin every week for 3 weeks, then a break for 1 week for menstruation	**How to Use?** Ring inserted into the vagina and placed at the cervix for 3 weeks, then removed for 1 week for menstruation
Pros: Easy to take	**Pros:** Need to remember only once per week	**Pros:** Need to remember only once per month
Cons: Difficult to remember to take the pill	**Cons:** Possible skin irritation from patch	**Cons:** Possible increased risk of vaginitis; interference with intercourse reported by 1 to 2.5% of women[d]

Progestin-Only Hormonal Contraceptives

Mechanism of Action: May inhibit ovulation; thins endometrium to help prevent implantation; thickens cervical mucus to trap sperm

Pros: Chance of developing amenorrhea; appropriate for women who cannot tolerate estrogen methods; appropriate for women over the age of 35 who smoke; suitable for use while breastfeeding; may reduce menstrual flow, menstrual cramps, and symptoms of PMS

Cons: Potential irregular bleeding; possible hormonal side effects (see "cons" for combination hormonal contraceptives), do not protect against STIs

TABLE 7.2 Continued

Mini-pill	Depo-Provera	Levonorgestrel-Releasing Intra-uterine System (LNG-IUS)

Failure Rate: Perfect: 0.3%, typical: 8%

How to Use? Pill taken at approximately the same time every day, without breaks for menstruation

Pros: Easy to take

Cons: Must be taken at the exact same time (within 3 hours) each day

Failure Rate: Perfect: 0.3%, typical: 8%

How to Use? Intramuscular injection by a health care provider every 3 months

Pros: Need to remember only once every 3 months; reduced risk of endometrial cancer, endometriosis, chronic pelvic pain (CPP), and PMS

Cons: Potential weight gain and mood changes; decrease in bone mineral density (which may improve after discontinuing)[e]

Failure Rate: Perfect and typical: 0.2%

How to Use? Small T-shaped device with slow-release hormone inserted into the uterus by a physician, and a plastic string passes out through the cervix so the woman can feel it is in place

Pros: Not having to think about contraception for 5 years; significantly lower dose of hormones than with OC pills, resulting in fewer side effects; significantly reduced menstrual flow

Cons: Up to 30% of women report benign ovarian cysts that usually resolve spontaneously; rare risk of uterine perforation or infection during insertion; exposure to STIs while using this method is associated with an increased risk of pelvic inflammatory disease (PID); possibility of expulsion

NON-HORMONAL CONTRACEPTIVES

Intra-uterine Device (IUD)

Mechanism of Action: Makes uterine environment inhospitable to sperm; inhibits implantation

Failure Rate: Perfect: 0.6% (most failures occur in the first 3 months of use)

How to Use? Small T-shaped device inserted into the uterus by a physician, and a plastic string passes out through cervix so the woman can feel it is in place

Pros: Lasts for 5 years; reduced risk of endometrial cancer; no hormonal side effects

Cons: Possible irregular bleeding; increase in blood loss during menstruation; exposure to STIs while using this method is associated with an increased risk of PID; possibility of expulsion or uterine perforation

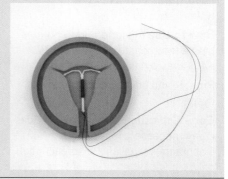

Cervical Barrier Methods

Mechanism of Action: Create barriers at the cervix so sperm cannot get through; spermicide used with these methods provides additional protection by killing some sperm

Pros: No hormonal side effects

Cons: Increased risk of toxic shock syndrome (TSS); no STI protection; unsuitable for women with recurrent vaginal or urinary tract infections (UTIs); may be difficult for some women to insert

Continued

TABLE 7.2 Continued

Contraceptive Sponge	Lea Contraceptive	Cervical Cap

Contraceptive Sponge

Failure Rate: Nulliparous: perfect: 9%, typical: 16%; Parous: perfect: 20%, typical: 32%

How to Use? Moisten with water; lasts 12 to 24 hours (depends on brand); removed 6 to 8 hours after last ejaculation

Pros: No prescription needed; one size fits all; already contains spermicide; less messy than many other spermicide methods; can be used for multiple intercourse acts within the effective period

Cons: High failure rate with typical use

Lea Contraceptive

Failure Rate: 8.7% with spermicide, 12.9% without spermicide

How to Use? Placed against the cervix, with the rounded tab that protrudes from the central ring facing the anterior vaginal wall; removed 6 to 8 hours after intercourse; can be reused for approximately 6 months

Pros: Up to 8 hours of protection; one size fits all; no prescription needed

Cons: Must be cleaned after each use

Cervical Cap

Failure Rate: Nulliparous: perfect: 9%, typical: 20%; Parous: perfect: 26%, typical: 40%[f]

How to Use? Held in place against the cervix by suction

Pros: Made of silicone (safe for women with latex allergies); can be left in for 72 hours

Cons: Can be dislodged during intercourse; may cause vaginal odour

Diaphragm	Spermicides

Diaphragm

Failure Rate: Perfect: 6%, typical: 16%

How to Use? Inserted up to 6 hours before intercourse and removed within 24 hours; replace every 2 years

Pros: Reduced incidence of cervical dysplasia

Cons: Difficult to find the spermicidal cream necessary for use with diaphragms;[g] available by prescription only; significant body weight changes require resizing of the diaphragm by a physician

Spermicides

Failure Rate: Perfect: 18%; typical: 29%

How to Use? Spermicide should be paired with barrier methods in order to be more effective; regardless of how long the spermicide is effective for, it is only effective for one act of intercourse
- Vaginal contraceptive film (VCF): inserted into the vagina at least 15 minutes, but not more than an hour, prior to intercourse
- Bioadhesive jelly: inserted with an applicator; effective immediately, for up to 24 hours
- Foam: inserted with an applicator; effective immediately, for up to 1 hour
- Suppositories: inserted 10 to 15 minutes prior to intercourse; effective for 1 hour
- Jellies or creams: primarily for use with a diaphragm or cervical cap; effective for 6 to 8 hours if used with these devices, or 1 hour if used alone

Pros: All but the VCF can also function as a lubricant; no prescription needed; can reduce the risk of PID

Cons: Many spermicides contain nonoxynol-9, which may be irritating to the skin and can increase the risk of infections, including STI transmission; they can be messy; the taste is not appealing; many take 10 to 15 minutes to take effect and are effective only for about an hour

TABLE 7.2 Continued

Female Condom

Mechanism of Action: Creates a physical barrier to trap sperm

Failure Rate: Perfect: 5%, typical: 21%

How to Use? Inserted into vagina up to 8 hours before intercourse, with flexible ring end at cervix; outer portion covers the vulva

Pros: Protects against STIs (it provides more protection than the male condom does against STIs that are transmitted by skin-to-skin contact); made from polyurethane (and therefore safe to be used by individuals with latex allergies); no prescription needed; can be used for anal intercourse (by removing the inner ring)

Cons: Bulky appearance; crinkly or suction noises during intercourse; expensive

Male Condom

Mechanism of Action: Creates a physical barrier to trap sperm

Failure Rate: Latex: perfect: 2% (0.1% when combined with hormonal contraceptives); typical: 15%; polyurethane and silicone have a higher frequency of breakage and slippage; nonoxynol-9 spermicidal condoms were once thought to be more effective but are no longer recommended because they can irritate vaginal/anal lining, increasing the risk of infection

How to Use? Rolled onto the penis (see Figure 7.3 for details); must be used with a water-based lubricant (oil-based lubricants weaken the condom structure and can result in breakage)

Pros: No prescription needed; help protect against STIs; many universities and community health centres offer free condoms; putting the condom on can be incorporated into sex play

Cons: Effectiveness decreases if not stored correctly or if expired; non-latex condoms are fairly expensive; complaints of reduced sensitivity (a small amount of a water-soluble lubricant inside the condom, as well as a thin condom, may reduce such complaints)

SURGICAL METHODS

Female Sterilization—Tubal Ligation

Mechanism of Action: Prevents the egg and sperm from ever meeting because fallopian tubes are severed

Failure Rate: 0.5%

How to Use? Surgery done either laparoscopically (most common) or transcervically; the surgeon seals the fallopian tubes through burning, clipping, cutting, or tying; a backup form of birth control should be used for 3 months following the procedure

Pros: Not having to think about contraception again

Cons: Does not protect against STIs; requires general anaesthesia and may entail post-operative side effects; possible increased risk of ectopic pregnancy[h]

Male Sterilization—Vasectomy

Mechanism of Action: Prevents sperm from entering ejaculate because vas deferens is severed

Failure Rate: 0.05% after physician clearance has been given;[i] sperm will still be in the ejaculate for 10 to 30 ejaculations following the surgery

How to Use? Surgery done either through a small puncture in the scrotal skin or through one or two incisions in the scrotal skin; the surgeon removes a 1.5 cm segment from each end of the vas deferens, and the ends are sealed with a suture, cauterization, or clips; a backup form of birth control should be used until two consecutive negative semen samples are produced

Continued

TABLE 7.2 Continued

Male Sterilization—Vasectomy (*continued*)

Pros: Relatively simple procedure with very few complications and no general anaesthesia; most studies do not find evidence of increased risk of testicular cancer; reversal surgery is available

Cons: Does not protect against STIs; potential side effects and short-term complications associated with surgery, such as infection and local pain; following surgery, semen analysis needs to be done to ensure effectiveness

[a] Unless otherwise referenced, the information in this table was adapted from Black, Francoeur, and Rowe (2004a; 2004b; 2004c). Typical and perfect use statistics were taken from Trussell (2007a).
[b] The "failure rate" reflects the probability of a woman using the method of becoming pregnant within a year.
[c] The failure rate of this pill increases in women who are obese (more than 70.5 kg overweight; Holt, Cushing-Haugen, & Daling, 2002).
[d] Roumen, Apter, Mulders, & Dieben, 2001.
[e] Supplemental estrogen may attenuate these negative effects.
[f] World Health Organization (2001).
[g] Only one is available: Contragel (Canadian Federation for Sexual Health, 2009).
[h] National Institutes of Health (2011).
[i] Royal College of Obstetricians and Gynaecologists (2004).

spermicide A contraceptive substance that kills sperm to prevent impregnation.

toxic shock syndrome (TSS) A serious but uncommon bacterial infection, originally associated with tampon use but now known to have an association with some contraceptive barrier methods.

parous Having given birth at least once.

nulliparous Never having given birth.

A variety of barrier methods are available, and each has its own advantages and disadvantages. Cervical barriers tend to be most effective when they are used with **spermicide** and/or condoms. One of the main drawbacks of these methods is that they do not protect against STIs; in addition, some women find the devices difficult to insert, and use of these devices can increase the risk of **toxic shock syndrome (TSS)**. Contraceptive sponges and cervical caps also tend to be much less effective in **parous** women than in **nulliparous** women. Condoms, on the other hand, when used correctly, have a major advantage in that they do offer protection against many STIs. Indeed, in terms of preventing HIV infection, condoms are the most effective means available (although the failure rate for HIV prevention in penile-vaginal intercourse is still 20 per cent; Weller & Davis-Beaty, 2002). Female condoms have the added benefit of providing some protection against external genital contact, which can further reduce the transmission of STIs. As is the case with all contraceptives, condoms are most effective when they are used properly and consistently (see Figure 7.3).

Surgical Methods

Surgical methods of birth control (Table 7.2) are generally non-reversible; therefore, when considering surgical options, one needs to be vigilant about making an informed decision that takes into account unanticipated situations in which one may wish to conceive in the future, such as the loss of a partner or a child.

Natural Methods

Natural methods of birth control are ones in which there are no human-made barriers or hormones. One advantage of natural methods is that they can be used in conjunction with barrier methods. In addition, they are reversible, they do not involve introducing chemicals into the body, and many are supported by religious groups, making them accessible to people who might not believe in other birth control options. A major disadvantage of all natural methods is that they do not protect against STIs.

FERTILITY AWARENESS METHODS

Fertility awareness methods rely on a woman's detailed understanding of her physiology and menstrual cycle. Thus, a major advantage to using these methods is that the woman

Ten Steps to Correct Condom Use

1. Check the expiry date on the back of the condom, and check for air bubble (ensure condom wrapper is sealed).

2. Open the condom package carefully. Do not use your teeth.

3. Blow air into the tip of the condom to figure out which way to roll the condom onto the penis.

4. Place a few drops of water-based lubricant inside the condom.

5. Place the condom on the glans of the erect penis.

6. Squeeze the tip of the condom so that there is space left to collect semen.

7. Unroll the condom down the base of the erect penis and smooth out any air bubbles.

8. Apply water-based lubricant and enjoy!

9. Withdraw the penis immediately after ejaculation, and remove the condom from the penis at a safe distance from partner's genitals.

10. Tie off the end of the condom. Dispose of the condom in the garbage. Do not flush it down the toilet.

FIGURE 7.3 These steps outline proper use of a condom. When used correctly, condoms offer protection against both pregnancy and STIs.

will acquire a greater awareness of her gynecological health and be able to recognize any abnormalities that may be cause for concern. Yet women using these methods to avoid pregnancy are limited as to when they can have intercourse. Other disadvantages include the lengthy periods of time and amount of vigilance required to learn about one's fertility signs. In addition, these methods are not as feasible if a woman has an irregular menstrual cycle, as there will be fewer days when she can have sex without risking pregnancy. These methods are also not appropriate for women experiencing a vaginal infection—when sex is not advisable in any case—as vaginal infections can alter fertility signs.

The Sympto-thermal Approach

The sympto-thermal approach (see Figure 7.4) is used to chart basal body temperature (BBT), cervical position, and cervical mucus to gain insight into when a woman is fertile and therefore likely to get pregnant. Women can track changes in their BBT by using a specific thermometer to take their temperature after first waking from at least six hours of sleep. Most women experience a rise of approximately 0.2 degrees Celsius following ovulation, and the fertile time lasts three days following this temperature rise. Cervical position and mucus consistency change throughout the menstrual cycle, with the cervix being farthest away from the vaginal opening and the mucus being clearer and more elastic approaching ovulation. Each of these signs can be charted on its own, without the others; however, a combined record of all three changes will provide the most accurate indication of fertility. These methods must be used consistently and correctly in order to be effective, and it will be a number of months before a woman new to this approach has observed enough of a pattern to make reasonably accurate predictions about her fertile time. Perfect use is 91 to 99 per cent effective, and typical use is 80 per cent effective (WHO, 2001).

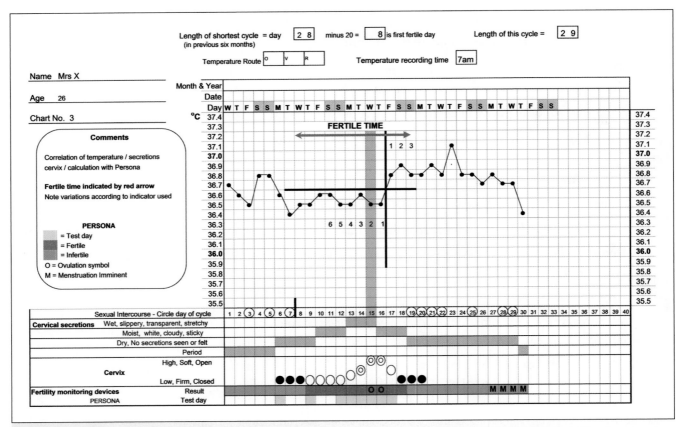

FIGURE 7.4 Sympto-thermal charts, such as the one shown here, help a woman track changes in her basal body temperature, cervical position, and cervical secretions, in order to identify when she is fertile.

CALENDAR-BASED METHODS

rhythm method A calendar-based method of family planning that estimates the start and end of the fertile time based on past cycle lengths and involves abstaining from intercourse during the fertile time.

The best-known example is the **rhythm method** in which the fertile time is calculated based on the length of the last 12 cycles. The following calculation can be used to give the start and end of the fertile time: shortest cycle minus 20 and longest cycle minus 10. This takes into account the lifespan of the sperm and the earliest possible ovulation before the start of the next period. So if the last 12 cycles were 28, 26, 31, 27, 28, 30, 29, 27, 30, 29, 28, and 27 days, the shortest cycle in the last year was 26 days and the longest cycle was 31 days. The fertile time would therefore last from day 6 to day 21. This means that a woman can have unprotected sex without worrying about becoming pregnant only on days 1 through 5 (most or all of which will be days of menstrual bleeding) and days 22 through to the start of the next cycle (as early as day 26, in this example).

The standard-days method is another (often more accurate) variation of the rhythm method that works for women whose menstrual cycles are between 26 and 32 days in length. It involves tracking a woman's cycle on a calendar or with a string of beads, and it assumes that days 8 through 19 are unsafe to have unprotected sex if pregnancy prevention is the goal. Perfect use for the standard-days method is approximately 95 per cent effective (Arévalo, Jennings, & Sinai, 2002; Hatcher et al., 2007). Despite such evidence indicating a low failure rate, calendar-based methods are not recommended as primary methods of contraception because the timing of a woman's fertile window can be unpredictable, especially at times of stress or hormonal change. In addition, because they are left with relatively few days on which they can have sex without risking pregnancy, many women and couples find these methods overly restrictive and difficult to follow in practice.

LACTATIONAL AMENORRHEA

Lactational amenorrhea, first recognized by the ancient Egyptians, occurs when breastfeeding causes hormonal suppression of ovulation. It is 98 per cent effective as a temporary postpartum method of birth control, as long as the woman's menses have not returned, the woman is exclusively breastfeeding, and the baby is less than six months of age. Intervals between breast-feeding, day and night, should not exceed six hours.

WITHDRAWAL

Withdrawal ("pulling out") has been used throughout history as a means of preventing pregnancy. It requires the man to withdraw his penis from the woman's vagina before he ejaculates, in order to prevent the ejaculated sperm from entering her cervix. For this method to work, the man must have the ability to recognize when he is going to ejaculate and the self-control to withdraw. There is not a great deal of data on the effectiveness of this method, but the WHO (2001)

FIGURE 7.5 Calendar-based methods such as the rhythm method and the standard-days method require a woman to keep track of the days of her menstrual cycle and avoid having sex on certain days.

estimates perfect use to be 96 per cent effective and typical use to be 81 per cent effective. The advantage of using this method is that neither chemicals nor barrier methods are needed. The main disadvantage is that intercourse is interrupted part way through, and some couples may dislike having to end intercourse as soon as the man is about to ejaculate. Another disadvantage is that a woman can still get pregnant from pre-ejaculate, which occurs well before a man ejaculates.

Abstinence

Some couples, particularly those who are unmarried, choose **abstinence** as a method of preventing pregnancy; this choice is often tied to religious and/or moral prohibitions against engaging in premarital sexual activity. The definition of abstinence varies from one individual to the next. For some, it means refraining from any activity that could be considered sexual, including masturbation; for others, it means refraining only from penile-vaginal intercourse; for many, it falls somewhere between these two extremes. This method can be 100 per cent effective in preventing pregnancy, but it is not a means of preventing STI transmission if the individuals are engaging in oral and/or anal sex.

abstinence Refraining from some or all aspects of sexual activity.

　　While abstinence is a healthy and positive choice for some people, it may be frustrating or too restrictive for others. Most major problems related to abstinence occur when it is taught to youth as the only option for premarital contraception: in these cases, young people may end up engaging in risky sexual practices due to a lack of knowledge about what is safe. Couples choosing this method should have a backup method available in case they change their minds—especially in the heat of the moment!

Birth Control Use around the World

The most common contraceptive methods worldwide are female sterilization and the IUD (Townsend, Sitruk-Ware, Williams, Askew, & Brill, 2011). The IUD is used by 14.5 per cent of women in the developing world and 7.6 per cent of women in the developed world (UN, 2006). Sterilization is currently used worldwide by 21 per cent of married females seeking birth control and 4 per cent of males (Clifton, Kaneda, & Ashford, 2008). The condom is more popular for use in developed countries than it is in many of the world's developing areas. For example, in 2002 in Canada, 35 per cent

Research VS Real Life

Male Contraceptive Pill/Injection

The exploration of hormonal contraceptives for men first began in 1979, when Cunningham and colleagues (1979) conducted a study to find an androgen-based male contraceptive; however, the results were unsuccessful. Thirty years later, a trial examining the use of testosterone-based contraceptives for males found that monthly injections of 500 milligrams of testosterone undecanoate provides an effective and reversible means of birth control, with no serious short-term adverse effects, for most healthy Chinese males (Gu et al., 2009). Interestingly, while 95.2 per cent of Chinese men have sperm-suppression levels necessary for this method to be effective, only about two-thirds of Caucasian men experience the necessary levels of suppression. Other research has suggested that the addition of synthetic progestogens such as levonorgestrel (commonly found in female OCs), norethisterone, and etonogestrel to the testosterone may achieve effective rates of sperm suppression in Caucasian males as well.

Interest in male hormonal contraceptives seems to be mixed. Some researchers and health professionals have argued that there is a real need for the development of these contraceptives. Indeed, a recent international survey found that between 50 and 70 per cent of men (depending on the country) would be willing to use a male hormonal contraceptive (Heinemann, Saad, Wiesemes, White, & Heinemann, 2005). Further, population conferences and women's groups have called for new male contraceptive methods (Nieschlag, 2010), and only 2 per cent of women in a culturally varied survey

reported that they would not trust their partner to use such methods properly (Glasier et al., 2004). Yet media reports continue to focus on a lack of female trust for male hormonal contraceptives (Oudshoorn, 2003), and pharmaceutical companies have been hesitant to make the necessary investments to bring these contraceptives to the market.

Why has the male hormonal contraceptive not been greeted with as much enthusiasm as the female hormonal contraceptive, especially given their similar levels of efficacy (Oudshoorn, 1999)? Perhaps it is due to the pervasiveness of the notion that a man's masculinity is reduced if he does not have the capability of impregnating a woman. Or, perhaps it is because pregnancy and contraception continue to be viewed as essentially a woman's responsibility. It may even be due to the fact that many women are reluctant to give up control over their fertility—especially given the long, hard fight many feminists have faced over the years in an effort to enable women to have this control.

Yet now it seems there may be a feminist argument for sharing the burdens of contraception with men. Leaving the responsibility of contraception solely up to the woman promotes and legitimizes a stereotypical view of gender roles, relegating women to family and reproductive issues and excluding men from this responsibility (and right). Thus, while it may be easiest to keep the status quo and continue to rely on female hormonal contraceptives, the introduction of hormonal contraceptives for men would be a definitive step toward equal partnership in contraception and family planning.

of unmarried, non-virgin, 18- to 34-year-old women were currently using condoms (Fisher, Boroditsky, & Morris, 2004), and 20.3 per cent of married women reported using condoms (UN, 2010). However, condoms are used by less than 6 per cent of married women aged 15 to 49 in many areas of Asia, the Caribbean, Latin America, and Sub-Saharan Africa (Trussell, 2007b). A new trend to look for in the coming years may be the male contraceptive pill, an invention that appears to vary in effectiveness based on culture. (See the "Research vs Real Life" box.)

Birth Control Use in Canada Today

The 2002 Canadian Contraception Study (Fisher et al., 2004) examined contraceptive behaviours of 1582 women aged 15 to 44. It found that most of the women surveyed were familiar with OCs and male condoms, and over half knew about emergency

TABLE 7.3 Birth Control use, by method, among Canadian women aged 18–44 who have ever had intercourse.

Method	Married (%)		Unmarried (%)	
	18–34	35–44	18–34	35–44
OCs	29	13	56	17
Male condom	18	12	35	11
Male sterilization	10	32	2	10
Female sterilization	7	14	1	14
Withdrawal	8	4	8	6
No method[a]	9	14	3	7

[a]But not trying to get pregnant.
Source: Adapted from Fisher, Boroditsky, and Morris (2004).

contraception. It also revealed that condoms and OCs were most popular among unmarried women aged 18 to 34, while both male and female sterilization were more common in the older age groups (Table 7.3). Notably, the study found that the use of female sterilization had dropped from 16 per cent of all women who had ever had sex in 1993 to 8 per cent in 2002, while the use of male sterilization in this demographic remained constant around 15 per cent.

Those using OCs reported choosing this method because it was effective, easy to use, and recommended by their health care provider; however, 5 per cent reported worrying "a great deal" about missing pills. Interestingly, 62 per cent of the respondents using OCs had missed at least one pill in the previous six months, and 11 per cent had missed six or more pills in the previous six months. The median age of first use was 17 years, and 34 per cent of the women started using the pill prior to having intercourse for the first time. The mean duration of use in current users was 7 years.

Those who used male condoms reported doing so because of the method's lack of side effects, ease of use, and effectiveness, as well as the fact that their use of condoms was restricted to intercourse activities. Only 7 per cent of current users indicated that they chose condoms primarily to protect against STI transmission. Unfortunately, condoms were not used consistently: 30 per cent of the women indicated that they had not always used condoms with each intercourse act in the past six months. Unmarried women under the age of 24 had significantly more favourable opinions and belief of higher efficacy of male condom use than did married women. The most common reasons for decreasing or stopping condom use were "I have only one sexual partner" and "I know and trust my husband/partner" (Fisher et al., 2004). According to another study, the most common reason for females not to use a condom is a low perception of sexual risks, and for males it is inconvenience or unavailability (Carter, McNair, Corbin, & Williams, 1999).

The Psychology of Birth Control

Why Use Birth Control? The Bigger Picture

Canada began collecting information on the teenage (ages 15 to 19) pregnancy rate in 1974, when the rate (including live births and abortions) per 1000 teenagers was 53.9.

With the exception of a slight increase from the mid-1980s to the mid-1990s, the rate has been substantially declining since 1974; in 2005, it was 29.2 per 1000 teenagers. In the United States, two-thirds of families started by a young, unmarried mother live in poverty (Carter et al., 1999). One-quarter of teen mothers receive welfare within the first three years of their child's birth, and only 38 per cent of mothers who have a child before the age of 18 finish high school. Fathers of children born to unmarried teenage mothers typically pay less than $800 in child support *per year*, as many of them are not financially stable themselves. In addition, nearly a quarter of teenage mothers have a second child within two years (Kalmuss & Namerow, 1994).

According to the World Bank, the world's population is projected to reach 9.1 billion by 2050, with the majority likely to live in the world's poorest countries. The number of children a couple has affects the overall education level, health, and income of the family. There is a clear link between fertility regulation and the achievement of broader development goals throughout the world (Singh, Darroch, Vlassoff, & Nadeau, 2004). Clearly, there are many reasons both in Canada and around the world to use birth control! However, survey results from the 2002 Canadian Contraception Study show that adherence to contraceptive methods is a challenge for many females and their partners.

Choosing Not to Use Birth Control: Sexual Risk-Taking in Canada

In Canada, 28 per cent of women have not asked their health care provider about birth control (Black, Francoeur, & Rowe, 2004c). Even those who have asked may not be taking all necessary precautions all of the time. A Canadian Community Health Survey indicated that only 41 per cent of those who list condoms as their main method of contraception used them all of the time (Statistics Canada, 1999). Another study found that the greater the number of sexual partners reported by young Canadian women, the more likely they were to be using OCs, the less likely they were to be using condoms, and the more likely they were to have had an STI (MacDonald et al., 1990).

So why do people take sexual risks? It appears that a variety of personality, situational, and relationship factors may influence an individual's decision to engage in sexual risk-taking (Cooper, 2010). For example, a study examining twin sets found that personality factors such as impulsivity, extraversion, and neuroticism are all correlated with risky sexual behaviour and that these correlations occur mainly due to overlapping genetic influences (Zietsch, Verweij, Bailey, Wright, & Martin, 2010). Situational factors including poverty, limited access to contraceptives, and substance use/abuse can all reduce one's ability to use birth control effectively. Relationship factors also play a role in birth control compliance. Factors that increase the likelihood of sexual risk-taking include abusive relationships, as well as power dynamics, particularly as they pertain to who controls the sexual situations and contraception use (Billy, Grady, & Sill, 2009). As such, researchers are now asking couples about their safe-sex practices, in order to examine how each member of the couple influences the other.

One way of identifying ways to reduce sexual risk-taking is through the **information–motivation–behavioural skills (IMB) model** (Fisher & Fisher, 2003; Chapter 8). According to this model, contraceptive information needs to be easy to understand and accessible in a timely manner. An individual needs motivation to avoid engaging in risky sexual behaviours; this motivation may come from personal attitudes and/or social norms that discourage sexual risk-taking, as well as an individual's perceived vulnerability to unwanted pregnancy or STIs. Further, a person's behavioural skills need to be developed so that she or he is self-efficacious and

information–motivation–behavioural skills (IMB) model A social psychology model that identifies three major components (information, motivation, and behavioural skills) that may directly or indirectly impact sexual health behaviours.

confident when it comes to implementing a birth control strategy; to achieve this goal, an individual must have access to her or his chosen method of birth control, and she or he must be able to discuss contraception with her or his partner(s). One way of achieving these goals is through sexual education that is focussed on providing information tailored to individual needs, developing positive attitudes toward and social norms of contraceptive use, and helping individuals build the behavioural skills they need to make good choices about contraception. After all, women or couples who are active collaborators in their choice of birth control are most likely to adhere to it (Delbanco & Daley, 1996).

Finally, emotional responses and openness about sex influence contraceptive use (Byrne & Fisher, 1983). In general, the more open one is to discussing sex and the more comfortable, rather than guilty or inhibited, one feels about sex, the more likely one is to use birth control effectively and consistently (Fisher et al., 1988). However, not all guilt is bad. For example, an individual who anticipates that he or she will feel guilt and shame if condoms are not used is more likely to use condoms (Hynie, MacDonald, & Marques, 2006).

Talking to Your Partner about Contraception

Talking to a partner about contraception is not easy for most people, but in order to have a healthy and safer sex life, it is absolutely essential. Talking about contraception is equally important whether you are with a monogamous long-term partner, a "friend with benefits," or a one-night stand. It is not a discussion to be had in the passion of the moment, but one that needs to occur before the sexual situation arises, to ensure that proper protection is available. For the single woman or man, this conversation does not need to be lengthy. A simple disclosure of the woman's being on the pill (or using some other contraceptive method) and a request for a condom (or grabbing the one you brought and making sure it is used) is perfectly fine. If you find that you are not comfortable doing this, it may be a sign that you are not ready to engage in intercourse; after all, sex is a much more intimate act than a quick discussion of safer sex practices. Talking about contraception may seem "unsexy," but it is sexier than the alternatives—ending up unintentionally pregnant or with an STI.

For couples, this discussion may need to be longer and reoccur over time as the relationship evolves and needs change. Both partners need to decide as a couple what method(s) will work for their present circumstances (Figure 7.6). They should take equal responsibility for contraception, and they both need to be honest and respectful about what choices they are willing and not willing to make when it comes to safer sex. Going to a health care professional or local contraception clinic together can be an excellent starting point for this important decision.

Emergency Contraception

Emergency contraception (EC) is any contraceptive method used after intercourse and before the time that the egg could implant in the uterine lining. EC is not the same as an abortion, and it does not have an effect on established pregnancies. It is not recommended as a regular method of birth control, but rather as a backup

FIGURE 7.6 It is important to talk to your partner about sex and contraception. Talking about sex increases both safety and satisfaction!

FIGURE 7.7 Plan B is a form of emergency contraception that involves taking two pills within 72 hours of having unprotected sex. Despite over a quarter of Canadian woman believing this pill is a form of abortion (Black, Francoeur, & Rowe, 2004a), it differs from abortion because it will not stop a pregnancy after implantation has occurred.

method when the usual one has failed (e.g., a condom broke or a pill was forgotten). There are no statistics to indicate that women in Canada are using EC as their primary means of birth control. There is also no available evidence to suggest that the introduction of EC reduces abortion rates (Glasier et al., 2004). There are two main methods of EC available in Canada: hormonal (the ECP) and the IUD.

The Emergency Contraceptive Pill

The emergency contraceptive pill, also known as "the morning-after pill," is the hormonal form of EC available as Plan B (pills that contain levonorgestrel, a progestogen; Figure 7.7) or the Yuzpe method (pills that contain levonorgestrel as well as ethinyl estradiol, and estrogen). Of the two options, Plan B is more effective and causes fewer unpleasant side effects, such as nausea. Plan B has been available in Canada since 2000, and the Yuzpe method has been in use since the 1970s. ECPs became available without a prescription in Canada in 2005. ECPs should be taken within the 72-hour period post-coitus, as their effectiveness decreases over time. Within the first 24 hours, efficacy is 95 per cent for Plan B and 77 per cent for the Yuzpe method. These rates decrease to 58 per cent for Plan B and 41 per cent for the Yuzpe method when the pills are taken between 49 and 72 hours post-intercourse (Task Force on Postovulatory Methods of Fertility Regulation, 1998).

Post-coital IUD Insertion

The other option for EC is the post-coital insertion of an IUD. The effectiveness of this method approaches 100 per cent. The IUD must be inserted within seven days of the unprotected act of intercourse. Unlike the ECP, this method requires a doctor's appointment and a prescription. Side effects of this method are similar to those associated with the use an IUD as a primary method of birth control (see Table 7.2).

Unwanted Pregnancies

The average woman will spend about thirty years of her life trying not to get pregnant, a time period far longer than the five years that most women spend attempting to conceive and being pregnant (Barot, 2008). So what happens when there is an unwanted pregnancy? Options vary based on how far along the pregnancy is, as well as the beliefs and life circumstances of the woman (and her partner). Options include keeping the baby, abortion, and adoption.

Who Gets Abortions?

therapeutic abortion An abortion performed when the mother's life is at risk, the pregnancy is likely to cause severe physical or mental health consequences in the mother, or the fetus has a congenital disorder associated with a significant risk of morbidity.

elective abortion An abortion performed for reasons other than maternal or fetal health.

In 2009, 93,775 abortions were performed across Canada. Of the women who underwent these procedures, 16 per cent were under 19, 47 per cent were between 20 and 29, and 27 per cent were 30 or older (with approximately 10 per cent of unknown age; Canadian Institute for Health Information, 2009). Although there is no evidence to suggest that women are using abortion as a means of birth control, the use of abortion services suggests that the contraceptive needs of Canadians are not being met, in one way or another: information may not be properly disseminated, or individuals may not be using methods consistently or correctly.

An abortion can be considered **therapeutic** or **elective**. Reasons for getting a therapeutic abortion include maternal health problems and fetal anomalies that threaten the health or survival of either the mother or the fetus. Reasons that women frequently cite for obtaining an elective abortion include not feeling ready to care for a(nother) child, financial concerns, concerns that a(nother) child will interfere with current responsibilities to others, avoidance of single motherhood, relationship problems, and feeling too young or immature to raise a child (Finer, Frohwirth, Dauphinee, Singh, & Moore, 2005). Other reasons for terminating a pregnancy include rape and sexual coercion. While therapeutic abortion is generally more widely accepted and legalized, elective abortion is also legal throughout Canada (*R. v. Morgentaler*, 1988). Abortion is also legal to varying degrees in the United States (*Wade v. Roe*, 1973).

A Brief History of Abortion in Canada

In 1869, abortion was made illegal in Canada, and women breaking this law could be sentenced to life in prison. It was also, like contraception, regarded as a crime under Canada's Criminal Code of 1892, and it remained illegal for over a century. When the 1967 amendments to the Criminal Code failed to legalize abortion, many activists called for reform. Foremost among them was Dr Henry Morgentaler (Figure 7.8), who defied the law by opening an abortion clinic in Montreal in 1969. In that same year, due in large part to Morgentaler's influence, abortion became legal under the very strict condition that a committee of doctors determined the pregnancy to be a danger to the woman's health.

FIGURE 7.8 Dr Henry Morgentaler was a pro-choice activist who fought for decades to provide legal and safe abortion care for Canadian women.

Viewing the change as inadequate, Morgentaler continued to perform abortions even when the woman's health was not at risk, and in 1970 he was arrested and charged with conspiracy to perform abortion. That same year, the first feminist protest in support of legalizing abortion occurred, and 30 women chained themselves to the parliamentary gallery in the House of Commons. This act resulted in the first closure of Parliament in Canadian history! Four years later, the first national abortion-rights group was formed: the Canadian Abortion Rights Action League. Abortion finally became legal in 1988, when the Supreme Court of Canada struck down the abortion law as being unconstitutional, in its decision in *R. v. Morgentaler*.

Although abortion is no longer illegal in Canada, access to abortion care varies across the country. Attacks on abortion clinics and doctors who performed abortions were prevalent in the 1990s, and although protests are more peaceful now than they have been in the past, 64 per cent of clinics still experience protests (Wu & Arthur, 2010). Today, much debate continues to surround the legal status of abortion, both in Canada and around the world (see the "Culture and Diversity" box).

Types of Abortions

There are several methods of abortion available to women in Canada. While some methods require surgical intervention, others do not. Options vary based on how far along the pregnancy is.

MEDICAL (NON-SURGICAL) ABORTIONS

Medical abortions are usually performed up to seven weeks following the last menstrual period, but they can be done up to the ninth week of **gestation**; they are not effective in later stages of pregnancy. Administration of the drugs methotrexate and

gestation In mammals, the period of time in which a fetus/embryo develops in the uterus, beginning with fertilization and ending at birth.

Culture & Diversity

Abortion around the World

The legal status of abortion varies around the world (Figure 7.9). While it is legal in North America, most European countries, China, India, and South Africa, it remains illegal in most African, South American, and Central American nations, unless there is a threat to maternal life, health, or mental health (and in some cases exceptions are made for rape or fetal defects). Abortion is illegal with no exception in El Salvador, Malta, and Vatican City (Johnston, 2005).

Generally, the incidence of abortion worldwide has declined with improvements in available family planning education and access to birth control (Sedgh, Henshaw, Singh, Bankole, & Drescher, 2007). In 1995, the worldwide abortion rate was 35 per 1000 women; by 2003, the rate had dropped to 29, and it continued to drop to 28 in 2008 (Guttmacher Institute, 2012). Approximately 83 per cent of abortions occur in developing countries, but the country with the highest rate of abortions is Russia: in 2003, Russia's abortion rate was 45 per 1000 women, much higher than the global average (Singh, Wulf, Hussain, Bankole, & Sedgh, 2009). Reasons for this high rate include a lack of religious influence under Soviet rule (when religion was largely suppressed), limited access to effective means of contraception both before and after the collapse of the Soviet Union, and decades of cultural acceptance of abortion as a primary means of birth control (Chalmers et al., 1998).

Unfortunately, the number of unsafe abortions globally has not declined, sitting just below 22 million per year in 2008, and accounting for 48 per cent of all abortions. Each year, unsafe abortion results in the hospitalization of approximately 5 million women and the death of approximately 70,000 women (Singh, 2006; see also the "Ethical Debate" box in Chapter 4). Complications from unsafe abortions result in 13 per cent of worldwide maternal deaths. Nearly all abortions in Africa, Latin America, and the Caribbean are unsafe (Vlassoff, Walker, Shearer, Newlands, & Singh, 2009).

Even where abortion is legal, it is often highly stigmatized and regarded as contrary to religious beliefs. In addition, it is not always accessible to everyone, either due to a lack of trained professionals and equipment or a lack of money and resources. For example, abortion is not affordable for most people in Pakistan, where 66 per cent of people live on less than $2 per day, and an abortion costs between $50 and $104 (Cohen, 2009). While increasing access to safe abortion is certainly a global priority, worldwide access to preventative contraceptives and family planning services—which would lead to a reduction in the need for abortions—is what is essential for women's reproductive health and autonomy.

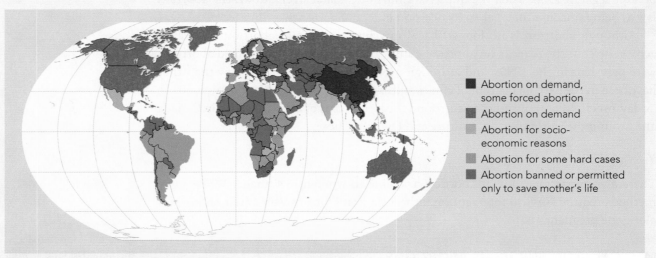

Abortion on demand, some forced abortion

Abortion on demand

Abortion for socio-economic reasons

Abortion for some hard cases

Abortion banned or permitted only to save mother's life

FIGURE 7.9 As this map shows, elective abortion is illegal in many countries. Most abortions occur in developing countries, where many women die due to complications from unsafe and illegal abortions.

misoprostol is currently the only medical option available in Canada. The procedure involves the injection of methotrexate into the hip muscle, which stops the growth of the fetus. Five to seven days later, while at home, the woman takes misoprostol, either in the form of a vaginal suppository or orally. This substance causes the uterus to contract, and the contents of the uterus are usually expelled within 24 hours; however, this process can take several days or weeks.

The main advantage of medical abortions is that they are less invasive than surgical abortions, and they therefore avoid any risk of damage from surgical instruments. However, the drugs can have unpleasant side effects, including nausea, headache, and fever, and the procedure may require several visits to a health care facility to ensure that the fetus has been expelled. In general, 90 to 98 per cent of medical abortions are effective in ending a pregnancy (Ashok, Penney, Flett, & Templeton, 1998).

SURGICAL ABORTIONS

Several surgical methods of abortion are available, depending upon fetal gestation.

Manual Vacuum Aspiration

Manual vacuum aspiration is the only surgical option available in the first seven weeks of pregnancy. In the procedure, a flexible plastic tube is inserted through the woman's cervix, and a syringe attached to the tube removes the contents of the uterus by creating suction. The procedure takes approximately 10 minutes, is generally considered to be safe and effective, and may involve the use of local anaesthetics.

Vacuum Suction Curettage

Vacuum suction curettage can be performed from the sixth to the fourteenth week of gestation in a hospital, and some private clinics will perform it up to the twentieth week. It is a 10-minute outpatient procedure performed while the patient is under general or local anaesthetic, at a hospital, a clinic, or a doctor's office. In preparation for the procedure, the woman's cervix must be dilated, either with laminaria tents (thin tubes made of sterile, dry seaweed that slowly expand as they absorb fluid) or progressively larger rod-like dilator instruments. Once the cervix has been dilated, a tube is inserted through the opening and into the uterus. The contents of the uterus, including the fetal tissue, are then suctioned out, and a curette is used to gently scrape the uterine lining to ensure that all of the tissue has been removed. The procedure is associated with little risk and generally has a failure rate of less than 1 per cent.

Dilation and Evacuation

Dilation and evacuation is usually used for abortions in the thirteenth through sixteenth weeks of gestation, though it can be performed up to the twenty-fourth week. The procedure is similar to vacuum suction curettage, but it is more complicated because of the increased size of the fetus, and it must be done in a hospital under general anaesthetic. Beyond the sixteenth week of gestation, the fetus is often removed with forceps.

Second- and Third-Trimester Abortions

Abortions that occur after the twentieth week of gestation typically require **feticide**, to ensure that the fetus is not born alive. This can be done with an injection of a substance to stop the fetal heart. The fetus is then typically removed through the cervix, with the assistance of medical devices such as forceps. In some cases, labour is induced and the dead fetus is delivered as it would be during regular labour, but such cases are rare because inducing labour carries a significant risk to the woman. A C-section may also be performed as a last resort to remove a dead fetus.

feticide A deliberate act that causes the death of a fetus.

The Psychological Effects of Abortion

Studies of the psychological consequences of abortion are often controversial, and they have produced mixed findings over the years. For example, in the mid- to late 1980s, a number of researchers reported finding evidence for a condition called "post-abortion syndrome" (PAS), which they described as a variation of post-traumatic stress disorder (PTSD); this condition was subsequently presented by many as being a common negative consequence of abortion. In 1989, however, a panel from the American Psychological Association (APA) determined that there was no evidence for the existence of PAS. The panel further concluded that severe negative psychological reactions after abortion are rare, and that most negative reactions tend to be mild, taking the form of slight regret, sadness, and/or guilt. Other research has found that the overwhelming responses are relief and happiness (Adler et al., 1992).

Why are these results so varied? In many cases, it may be that some form of bias has interfered with the results. After all, abortion is a controversial topic, and many studies are funded by private agencies whose position on the matter may influence how the research is conducted and which findings are reported. Yet not all research is influenced by such biases, and many of the most methodologically sound studies seem to indicate that the majority of women who get abortions do not experience any significant long-term mental health problems as a result of the procedure (Vignetta, Polis, Sridhara, & Blum, 2008). In addition, it seems that women who were well informed in their decision and who received support tend to have positive psychosocial outcomes (Lei, Robson, & May, 2008). At the same time, no reliable study suggests that *no* women experience negative effects after having an abortion, and some individuals may even require extensive counselling, a service that is provided by many clinics and hospitals throughout Canada. In general, women's responses vary based on such factors as age, culture, ethnicity, religious views, access to family planning, and gestational age of the fetus (Major et al., 2009).

The Pro-choice–Pro-life Debate

There are two main stances on abortion in the modern world: pro-choice and **pro-life** (sometimes called "anti-choice"). Pro-choice supporters generally believe that all women should be allowed to choose whether or not to terminate a pregnancy, while pro-life supporters generally believe that abortion should never (or almost never) be an option. The topic is subject to incredibly heated debates, and both sides receive support. A 2010 poll found that 52 per cent of Canadians who were sampled described themselves as "pro-choice," and 27 per cent described themselves as "pro-life"; 10 per cent did not affiliate themselves with either side of the debate, and 11 per cent had no response to the question (EKOS, 2010).

There are a variety of pro-life groups across Canada. They are often associated with religious groups, and their views are generally based on the political and moral stance that a fetus is a person and has a right to life. Supporters of this movement tend to advocate for either prohibition of abortion or restriction of abortion to particular therapeutic circumstances, as determined by the physician rather than the woman herself. Many even go so far as to equate abortion with murder.

Canada's pro-choice movement is often associated with Dr Henry Morgentaler as well as a feminist perspective. The pro-choice movement argues for women's reproductive rights and freedoms. Many pro-choice supporters have differing beliefs about how far along a pregnancy can be terminated, and to some extent regarding potential restrictions on abortion. These beliefs often relate to the question of exactly when life

pro-life movement A movement whose followers believe that abortion is murder and should not be conducted under any circumstances (or under limited circumstances involving the physical health of the mother).

starts: Is it at conception? At implantation? Not until birth? Perhaps when the fetus could potentially survive outside the womb, but with or without medical assistance?

Adoption

We do not have valid statistics on how many women put their babies up for adoption each year, but the number has been estimated as being in the hundreds (Canada Adopts, 2001). What is clear, however, is that the vast majority of unplanned pregnancies end either in abortion or in the woman raising the child herself. The decision to bring a baby to term only to hand it over to be raised by others—usually strangers—is a difficult one for most women to make. In addition, some mothers who initially plan to put their baby up for adoption change their mind, either at some point during the pregnancy or after the baby is born, and decide to keep the baby.

Adoption in Canada can be done through either a public (government) organization or a private, provincially approved agency. In a public adoption, the birth mother is generally not involved in the process after she has given her consent for her baby to be turned over to the adoption organization. Private adoptions, on the other hand, can offer the birth mother greater control over the process, if she chooses to be involved. In the case of both public and private adoptions, a qualified agency must conduct a formal home study of the prospective adoptive parents before the adoption is finalized, to ensure their suitability to take care of a child. Presently in Canada, private adoptions, especially of children from overseas, greatly outnumber public adoptions (Canada Adopts, 2001).

CHAPTER SUMMARY

Human desire and ability to control fertility has existed since prehistoric times. Although the use of contraceptives has not always been legal in Canada, many forms of birth control are now available. Currently, the OC pill the most commonly used form of birth control in Canada. Individuals' choice and use of contraceptives is influenced by a variety of factors, including personal attitudes toward sex and sexuality, type and frequency of sexual activity, social norms, perceived vulnerability to unwanted pregnancy and STIs, and access to contraceptives and family planning services. When contraceptives fail, some women choose to end an unwanted pregnancy through abortion, while others decide to keep the baby or give it up for adoption. Although abortion has been legal in Canada since 1988, access to safe abortions is still variable across Canada, with the greatest access being in large cities. Worldwide, the incidence of abortion has declined in recent decades, in large part due to improved access to birth control and information about family planning. At the same time, elective abortion is not currently legal in all countries, and many women around the world risk their lives undergoing unsafe abortions.

DEBATE QUESTION

What are the pros and cons of government policies aimed at population control? (Consider China as an example.)

REVIEW QUESTIONS

1. What positive changes resulted from efforts to give women and/or couples the right to control their reproductive health (e.g., access to family planning services, including abortion) in Canada?

2. What are some personal reasons an individual might have for using contraceptives? What are some population-based reasons for encouraging the use of contraceptives? Is there any overlap between the two?

3. What are the most commonly used methods of birth control in Canada? Why do you think these methods are so popular?

4. What is the impact of illegal and unsafe abortions on women around the world?

5. If a friend asked for advice on contraception, what reliable resource(s) would you recommend?

SUGGESTIONS FOR FURTHER READING AND VIEWING

Recommended Websites

SexualityandU.ca, on Birth Control: www.sexualityandu.ca/birth-control

Society of Obstetricians and Gynaecologists of Canada, Clinical Practice Guidelines: www.sogc.org/guidelines/index_e.asp

Guttmacher Institute: www.guttmacher.org

Canadian Federation for Sexual Health: www.cfsh.ca

Adoption Council of Canada: www.adoption.ca

National Abortion Federation: www.prochoice.org

United Nations, Department of Economic and Social Affairs, Population Division: www.unpopulation.org

Facts and Details, the One-Child Policy in China: http://factsanddetails.com/china.php?itemid=128&catid=4&subcatid=15

Recommended Reading

Bullough, V.L. (Ed.). (2001). *Encyclopedia of birth control*. Santa Barbara, CA: ABC-CLIO.

Dixon-Mueller, R. (1993). *Population policy & women's rights: Transforming reproductive choice*. Santa Barbara, CA: ABC-CLIO.

Hatcher, R.A., Trussell, J., & Nelson, A.L. (Eds). (2007). *Contraceptive technology* (19th ed.). New York, NY: Ardent Media.

Riddle, J.M. (1994). *Contraception and abortion from the ancient world to the renaissance*. Cambridge, MA: Harvard University Press.

Riddle, J.M. (1997). *Eve's herbs: A history of contraception and abortion in the west*. Cambridge, MA: Harvard University Press.

Society of Obstetricians and Gynecologist of Canada. (2005). *Sex Sense: Canadian Contraception Guide* (2nd ed.). Ottawa, ON: Author.

Tentler, L.W. (2004). *Catholics and contraception: An American history*. Ithaca, NY: Cornell University Press.

Recommended Viewing

Discovery Education (Producer). (2003). *Birth control: Myths & methods* (4th ed.) [DVD]. United States: Clearvue & SVE.

8 CHAPTER

Sexually Transmitted Infections: At the Junction of Biology and Behaviour

WILLIAM A. FISHER
AND MARC STEBEN

LEARNING OBJECTIVES

In this chapter, you will

- encounter brief histories of syphilis, herpes, and HIV/AIDS;
- learn about the prevalence, routes of transmission, symptoms, consequences, diagnosis, treatment, and prevention of major STIs; and
- find ways to protect yourself and your partner from becoming infected with an STI.

Judy and Chris

Getting ready for her spring-break trip to the Caribbean, Judy packs her swimsuit, plenty of sunscreen, several new outfits, and, after thinking about it for a while, a couple of condoms that were given out at the student health fair. After arriving, Judy checks out her all-inclusive resort's welcome party, and, with the help of a certain amount of rum, makes a new friend. As the evening develops, the tropical sun sets, the mood kicks in, a certain amount of additional rum is consumed, and Judy and her friend find themselves in her room. Things proceed along the lines of the sexual response cycle (see Chapter 4), and the condoms come in handy.

Two months later, Judy is talking to her classmate Chris, as the two sit in terror, trying, but failing, to make sense of an introductory calculus lecture. They agree to study together. Chris thinks that Judy is his only hope of passing the course; Judy tells her roommate that Chris is "easy on the eyes," and a relationship develops. After the final exam and several beers, Judy and Chris find their way back to Chris's dorm, and Chris's roommate develops a sudden need to go to the library. Clothing falls to the floor, and Judy tells Chris, "There is a lot of scary stuff out there . . . maybe, if we're headed where I think we're headed,

it would be a good idea to, you know, get tested." Chris agrees, and they decide to make love to each other with their hands instead of having intercourse, for the sake of safer sex. Tentative groping, accelerated murmuring, and a few sexual response cycles ensue. The next day, Judy and Chris meet at the clinic, get screened for sexually transmitted infections (STIs), and return a week later to receive the good news that each of them has tested negative for HIV, chlamydia, and gonorrhoea. They go home to celebrate, confident that their lovemaking is safe.

Judy and Chris remain a couple, faithful to each other. Some time later, however, Chris notices that he has a cluster of white bumps all over his penis; around the same time, Judy's Pap test results come back labelled "abnormal." When their doctors inform them that they have an STI, each is in shock, each wonders what the other has been up to, and each wonders how on earth this could have happened.

QUESTIONS FOR CRITICAL THOUGHT AND REFLECTION

1. What STI do you think Judy and Chris have?
2. Who gave it to whom? Does it matter?

Introduction

pathogens Bacteria, parasites, or viruses that cause infection or disease.

asymptomatic Showing no symptoms or signs of a disease.

prevalence The current extent of an infection or disease (or another condition) in a defined population.

This chapter concerns sexually transmitted infections (STIs) and ways to avoid them. We use the term *sexually transmitted infections* rather than *sexually transmitted diseases* because it is the infection of an individual with a sexually transmitted **pathogen** that concerns us, not whether he or she has evident signs of a sexually transmitted disease. Many STIs are **asymptomatic**, but they can nonetheless damage individuals' health and be transmitted to others without the affected person showing any visible symptoms.

As the title of this chapter suggests, STIs occur precisely where pathogen biology and sexual behaviour intersect. An individual's risk of contracting an STI, at a basic level, is a joint function of the **prevalence** of the sexually transmitted pathogen in question, the infectiousness of the pathogen, the individual's sexual behaviour, and the sexual behaviour of his or her partner(s) (Figure 8.1). And the news on this score isn't all that good: among young (and not so young) people in Canada today, there are lots of risky sexual behaviours, pathogen prevalence is high, and there are lots of STIs (see Figure 8.2).

The much better news, however, is that there *is* a path to being reasonably sexual in the millennium's second decade—a path to exploring and enjoying sexuality and relationships while minimizing the risk and consequences of contracting STIs. This path to safer sex is the focus of this chapter.

Rate Yourself

Selected Factors That Elevate Risk for Sexually Transmitted Infection

- I am sexually active and under 25.
- I use a non-barrier method of contraception.
- I have had a new sexual partner in the past year.
- I have been under the influence of alcohol or drugs when having sexual contact.
- I am in a polyamorous or "open" sexual relationship.
- I am in a monogamous sexual relationship and I have had (or my partner has had) sexual relationships in the past.
- I have had a one-time sexual partner.
- I have been a victim of forced sexual contact.

FIGURE 8.1 Being sexually active—even if you are in a monogamous sexual relationship—increases your risk of becoming infected with an STI.

Back to the Future: STIs Past and Present

A Brief History of Syphilis and Herpes

Theories abound about the origins of syphilis, one of the oldest STIs on record. Some speculate that Columbus and his fellow explorers brought the infection from the New World to Europe, and evidence of syphilis has been found in the skeletal remains of pre-Columbian indigenous peoples in the Americas. Others dispute this origin, instead suggesting that what was referred to as leprosy in Europe, before Columbus's voyage, was associated with sexual contact and may have in fact been syphilis (Sexually Transmitted Disease, 2013). The disease was named after Syphilis, a figure in Greek mythology who was cursed with a terrible disease, and it has been referred to as both the "French pox" (by the English) and the "English pox" (by the French).

Treatments for syphilis have varied over the centuries. From the 1500s onward, those with syphilis were treated with mercury compounds, leading to what one STI specialist has described as "a few minutes with Venus, a lifetime with Mercury" (Darrow, 1997). It was also in the 1500s that Gabriello Fallopio (1564) published the first evidence that condoms could be used to prevent the disease. From the 1900s on, syphilis was treated with arsenic, and with the advent of antibiotics in the 1940s, with penicillin (Figure 8.3).

A particularly unethical attempt to study the disease occurred between 1932 and 1972 in Tuskegee, Alabama. Beginning in 1932, the US Public Health Service recruited 600 impoverished African American men, 399 of whom were infected with syphilis and 201 of whom were not, to study the natural course of the disease. Initially, the men were treated with available compounds such as arsenic and mercury, but eventually all treatment was withheld, even after it was determined that penicillin would cure the disease. Some 100 of the infected men died of untreated syphilis, and the "research" was publicly disclosed only in the early 1970s, by an American investigative reporter

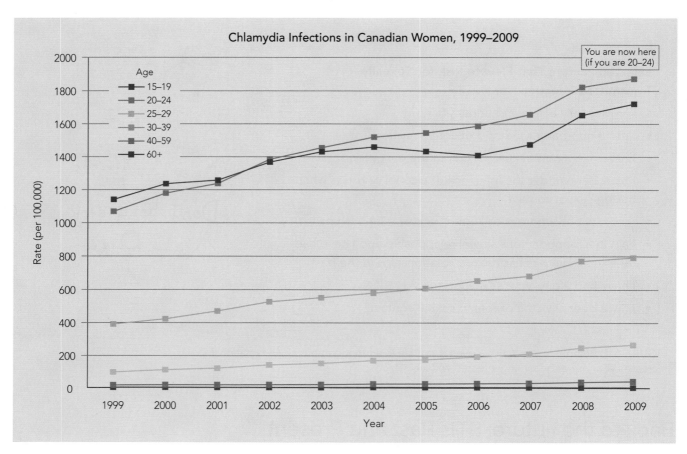

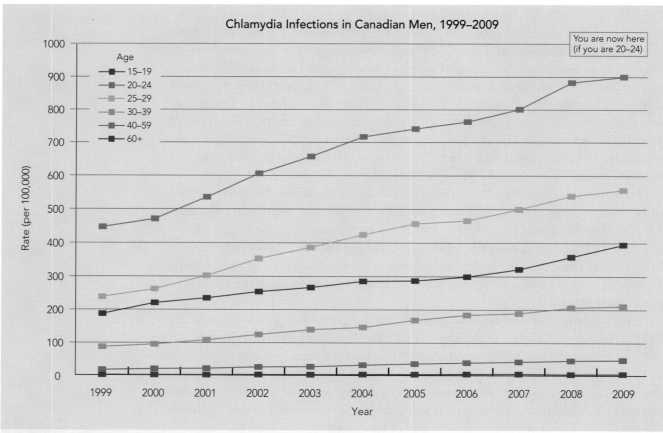

FIGURE 8.2 The market is up: chlamydia infections in Canadian women and men, 1999–2009.

(Sexually Transmitted Disease, 2013). Syphilis remains a problem around the world, including in Canada, today (see Figure 8.4).

If we fast forward five centuries, from the syphilis epidemic in Europe in the 1500s to North America in the 1980s, we arrive at the age of herpes, what your parents probably thought of as "The New Scarlet Letter"—an indelible mark (and incurable infection) that broadcast one's sexual activity to the world. Herpes causes cold sores that inconveniently locate themselves on one's genitals and are readily transmitted to a sexual partner's genitals. Herpes can be transmitted in genital-genital sex and in oral-genital contact. It represented the leading edge of what came to be recognized as the era of sexually transmitted viruses, which include the herpes simplex virus (HSV), the human papillomavirus (HPV), and the human immunodeficiency virus (HIV). While STIs that are caused by bacteria (such as syphilis, gonorrhea, and chlamydia) can all be cured with antibiotics, most STIs caused by viruses cannot be cured (hepatitis B and C can be cured). Before swearing off sex for the rest of your life, however, consider that viral STIs can be avoided (e.g., screening tests for HIV infection), prevented (in the case of HPV, by preventive vaccination, and in the case of HIV, by consistent condom use), and treated to reduce the damage done to one's health and to limit transmission to partners or from mother to baby during childbirth.

FIGURE 8.3 A poster announcing a cure for syphilis (c. 1930s).

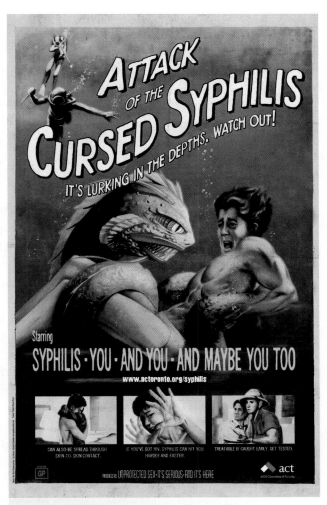

FIGURE 8.4 A 2010 AIDS Committee of Toronto poster promoting awareness of a syphilis outbreak among men who have sex with men.

A Brief History of HIV/AIDS

Perhaps the only thing that put into perspective the threat of getting herpes and the chill it put on sexual relationships was the emergence of acquired immunodeficiency syndrome (AIDS) shortly after herpes became a widespread concern. The AIDS epidemic began, in a sense, on 15 June 1981, with the publication of a brief article in the US Centers for Disease Control's *Morbidity and Mortality Weekly Report* concerning unusual infections seen in five same-sex oriented men in Los Angeles. In reality, however, AIDS, which is caused by infection with HIV, had been spreading for some time (Darrow et al., 2004). According to Hahn and colleagues (Hahn, Shaw, De Cock, & Sharp, 2000), the simian immunodeficiency virus, seen in primates, is the probable source of HIV; this virus appears to have crossed from primates to humans in Africa on a number of occasions between 1910 and 1950 (Korber et al., 2000), possibly when humans butchered primates for "bush meat" and cut themselves while doing so. Evidence has been found of HIV-like infections in human beings in Africa as early as 1959 (Nahmias et al., 1986), and the virus appears to have spread, possibly via Haiti, to North America at a later time (Chin, 2007). Widespread behaviour-driven infection among men who have sex with men and injection drug users in developed nations is thought to have begun in the 1970s (Chin, 2007).

During the 1980s and 1990s, AIDS-related deaths occurred at a terrifying rate in the US and Canada, where AIDS became the number one cause of death in men younger than 50 (Bayer & Oppenheimer, 2000; Centers for Disease Control and Prevention [CDC], 2001; Karon, Fleming, Steketee & De Cock, 2001; Public Health Agency of Canada [PHAC], 2011b). No effective treatment for AIDS was available at the time (Sepkowitz, 2001), and affected communities, notably those of gay men in New York, San Francisco, Toronto, and Vancouver, were decimated (Shilts, 1987). Characteristics of many individuals affected by AIDS—including same-sex sexual orientation, intravenous drug use, poverty, and race—and fear of contagion, led to stigma and rejection of people with AIDS, of the health care providers who were struggling to treat them, and of public health personnel who sought to prevent the spread of the disease (Bayer & Oppenheimer, 2000).

AIDS self-help groups (such as "God's Love We Deliver," founded in 1985) emerged as important sources of support for people with AIDS during an era of enormous prejudice and rejection. AIDS activists—sometimes employing "direct action" tactics such as demonstrations and disruptions of conferences, and occasionally resorting to violence and blood splattering attacks—tried desperately to influence the US and Canadian governments and the pharmaceutical industry to provide care, end discrimination, and facilitate drug availability for people with AIDS (Gay Men's Health Crisis, 2011; ACT UP, 2011). At least one AIDS activist of the 1980s was quoted as saying "Nobody's listened to us. What we need is [sic] a few assassinations" (Bayer & Oppenheimer, 2000, p. 139).

A unique chapter in the history of the fight against AIDS in Canada, and some would say a uniquely shameful one, unfolded at the University of Western Ontario in the spring of 1991. Professor James Miller, of the Department of Languages and Literature, and 22 of his students had gathered a collection of AIDS-prevention posters from around the world. After an international tour during which the posters were exhibited in museums and other settings in city after city, the exhibition returned to Western, and the posters were displayed in the university's library. The exhibition, however, was brought to the attention of the London police, who deemed it obscene, and the university was threatened with legal action unless the exhibit was removed from public display (see Figure 8.5). In what many have regarded as a shameful violation of academic freedom—indeed, as a violation of the most basic freedom of expression—the university's administration hastened to place the exhibition under lock and key in an out-of-the way university location, for limited viewing. Only a single professorial voice—that of William A. Fisher, one of the authors of this chapter—was raised in public protest.

The face of AIDS began to change fundamentally in 1996, with the announcement—in Vancouver, at the sixteenth International AIDS Conference—of the successful test of antiretroviral (ARV) drug combinations that could halt replication of HIV and stop progression from HIV infection to full-blown AIDS. Until the development of ARV therapy, the time between diagnosis of HIV and death due to AIDS was three to five years for most of those infected with the virus, and AIDS was almost always fatal. ARVs, however, if taken regularly, have the capacity to change HIV infection to a manageable condition with which the individual can live over a relatively healthy and long lifetime (Chen, Hoy, & Lewis, 2007). Since this development, ARVs have contributed to exceptionally rapid declines in AIDS-related illnesses and deaths. What is more, recent research indicates that ARVs may provide some degree of prevention of HIV infection if taken regularly by persons at risk, although

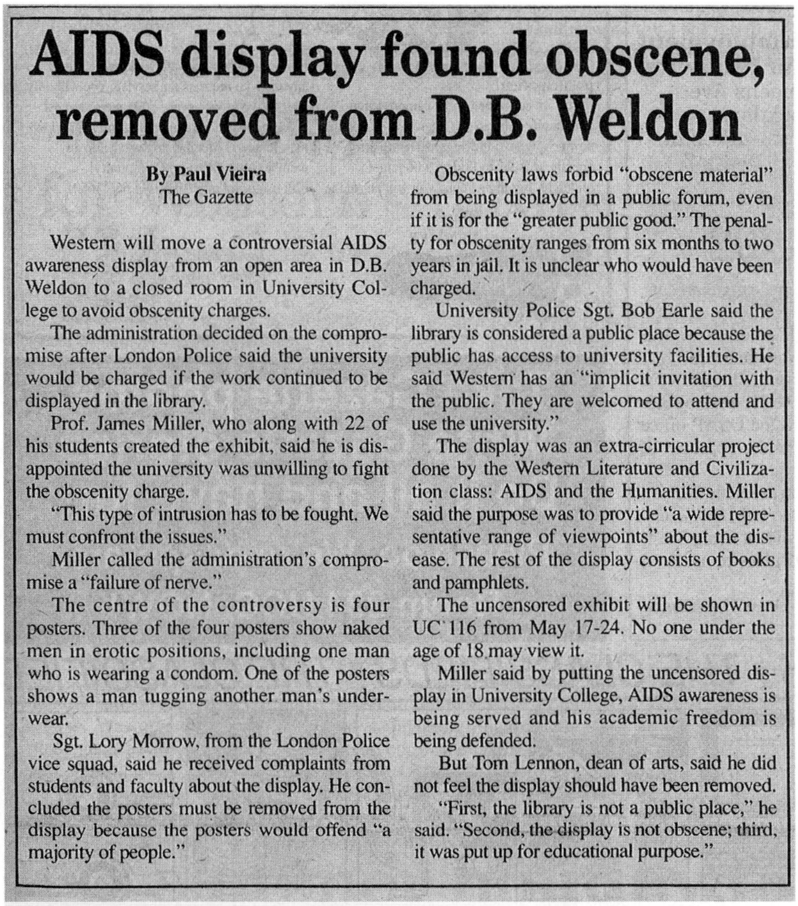

AIDS display found obscene, removed from D.B. Weldon

By Paul Vieira
The Gazette

Western will move a controversial AIDS awareness display from an open area in D.B. Weldon to a closed room in University College to avoid obscenity charges.

The administration decided on the compromise after London Police said the university would be charged if the work continued to be displayed in the library.

Prof. James Miller, who along with 22 of his students created the exhibit, said he is disappointed the university was unwilling to fight the obscenity charge.

"This type of intrusion has to be fought. We must confront the issues."

Miller called the administration's compromise a "failure of nerve."

The centre of the controversy is four posters. Three of the four posters show naked men in erotic positions, including one man who is wearing a condom. One of the posters shows a man tugging another man's underwear.

Sgt. Lory Morrow, from the London Police vice squad, said he received complaints from students and faculty about the display. He concluded the posters must be removed from the display because the posters would offend "a majority of people."

Obscenity laws forbid "obscene material" from being displayed in a public forum, even if it is for the "greater public good." The penalty for obscenity ranges from six months to two years in jail. It is unclear who would have been charged.

University Police Sgt. Bob Earle said the library is considered a public place because the public has access to university facilities. He said Western has an "implicit invitation with the public. They are welcomed to attend and use the university."

The display was an extra-cirricular project done by the Western Literature and Civilization class: AIDS and the Humanities. Miller said the purpose was to provide "a wide representative range of viewpoints" about the disease. The rest of the display consists of books and pamphlets.

The uncensored exhibit will be shown in UC 116 from May 17-24. No one under the age of 18 may view it.

Miller said by putting the uncensored display in University College, AIDS awareness is being served and his academic freedom is being defended.

But Tom Lennon, dean of arts, said he did not feel the display should have been removed.

"First, the library is not a public place," he said. "Second, the display is not obscene; third, it was put up for educational purpose."

FIGURE 8.5 This article, which appeared in the University of Western Ontario's newspaper *The Gazette* on 15 May 1991, describes reactions to the AIDS-prevention poster collection that was deemed obscene.

who should be taking such medications and the fact that ARVs provide only partial protection remain topics of considerable interest (CDC, 2010). (See the "Research vs Real Life" box for more on how societal values shape research priorities.)

Of course, this shift did not happen overnight. One problem was that ARVs were initially terribly expensive, and it took time for arrangements to be made to make them accessible to North Americans living with HIV infection. What is more, access to affordable ARV medications came much later in African and other developing nations, and access remains a serious problem in developing nations today. Another problem was—and, to some extent, continues to be—**adherence**. In order to be effective, ARVs must be taken *as prescribed*. Yet ARV therapy initially involved taking a large number of pills each day, and the pills often caused serious side effects that deterred individuals from adhering to their medication. Even today, although ARVs have become much simpler to take and have fewer side effects, many persons living with HIV infection struggle with adherence to ARVs (Conway, 2007; Lazo et al., 2007). In addition, as length of time on ARV medication increases, rates of adherence may decrease (Fumaz et al., 2008; Kleeberger et al., 2004). The challenges of providing access to affordable ARV medications worldwide and lifelong adherence to ARVs remain at the forefront of HIV/AIDS care today.

Currently, there are approximately 34 million persons living with HIV infection, and about 2.5 million incident (i.e., new) HIV infections occur worldwide each year (UNAIDS, 2012; Figure 8.6). More than 71,000 Canadians are living with HIV infection today, and between 2000 and 4000 new HIV infections occur in Canada each year (PHAC, 2011c).

adherence The degree to which an individual takes medication or complies with other instructions of a health care provider.

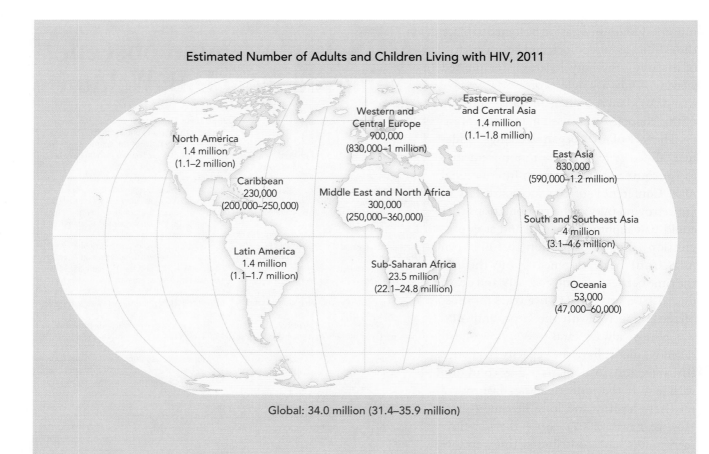

Estimated Number of Adults and Children Living with HIV, 2011

Eastern Europe
and Central Asia
1.4 million
(1.1–1.8 million)

Western and
Central Europe
900,000
(830,000–1 million)

North America
1.4 million
(1.1–2 million)

East Asia
830,000
(590,000–1.2 million)

Caribbean
230,000
(200,000–250,000)

Middle East and North Africa
300,000
(250,000–360,000)

South and Southeast Asia
4 million
(3.1–4.6 million)

Latin America
1.4 million
(1.1–1.7 million)

Sub-Saharan Africa
23.5 million
(22.1–24.8 million)

Oceania
53,000
(47,000–60,000)

Global: 34.0 million (31.4–35.9 million)

Estimated Number of Adults and Children Newly Infected with HIV, 2011

Eastern Europe
and Central Asia
140,000
(91,000–210,000)

Western and
Central Europe
30,000
(21,000–40,000)

North America
51,000
(19,000–120,000)

East Asia
89,000
(44,000–170,000)

Caribbean
13,000
(9600–16,000)

Middle East and North Africa
37,000
(29,000–46,000)

South and Southeast Asia
280,000
(170,000–370,000)

Latin America
83,000
(51,000–140,000)

Sub-Saharan Africa
1.8 million
(1.6–2 million)

Oceania
2900
(2200–3800)

Global: 2.5 million (2.2–2.8 million)

FIGURE 8.6 Worldwide, over 34 million people are living with HIV infection, and 2.5 million people become newly infected with HIV each year.

Research VS Real Life

Do Good Values Make Bad Science?

At the first quarter century of the AIDS epidemic, it is important to weigh our accomplishments against our failures in the fight against AIDS. . . . Future historians will conclude that we cannot escape responsibility for our failure to use effective, scientifically proven strategies to control the AIDS epidemic. (Stall & Mills, 2006, p. 961)

Sometimes sex research clashes with societal values, and sometimes sex research is actually shaped by societal values—in particular, the values of sex researchers themselves. In a paper titled "AIDS Exceptionalism: On the Social Psychology of HIV Prevention Research," W.A. Fisher, Kohut, and Fisher (2009) discuss the history of HIV-prevention research and the role of societal—and researchers'—values in shaping the HIV-prevention research agenda:

> As we reflect on the record of HIV prevention research in the social sciences, we are struck by an interesting and important fact. For the first two decades of the HIV epidemic, social scientists conducting HIV prevention research focussed on the promotion of preventive behaviour among members of the general public and members of so-called "high risk groups" without reference to the HIV– or HIV+ status of target populations. . . . Correspondingly, for the first two decades of the HIV epidemic, social scientists directed exceedingly little attention to creating and evaluating HIV prevention interventions specifically designed to address the prevention needs of HIV+ individuals who were capable of communicating infection to others. (p. 46)

Standard public-health practice would place the very highest priority on the development and implementation of interventions to support safer sexual behaviour among HIV-infected persons, who are capable of transmitting the infection to others. In fact, however, a reversal of standard priorities was in place, with almost all HIV-prevention intervention research focussed on helping HIV-negative persons remain uninfected. A review of all 898 HIV-prevention intervention studies published from 1986 to 2006 shows that only 58 (7 per cent!) of the studies were focussed on the development of HIV-prevention interventions to support safer sexual behaviour among HIV-infected individuals, and most such studies appeared in or after the year 2000, some two decades into the HIV epidemic (W.A. Fisher et al., 2009; Figure 8.7).

Given the very obvious fact that all new cases of HIV infection begin with existing cases of HIV infection, what can possibly explain researchers' reluctance to study HIV-transmission risk behaviour among HIV-infected individuals, and their neglect of research on HIV-prevention interventions for HIV-positive persons? According to W.A. Fisher and colleagues (2009), strongly held and indeed very good values were at play, but as the old saying goes, "the road to bad science is paved with good intentions." In particular, Fisher and colleagues pointed out that HIV caregivers and HIV-prevention researchers who chose to work in this field early in the epidemic were largely self-selected for being liberal, tolerant, and progressive, and they were often members of a marginalized minority group themselves. In an oral history of physicians and scientists who were prominent in fighting AIDS during the early years of the epidemic, Bayer and Oppenheimer (2000) reported that 50 per cent were Jewish, 40 per cent were gay or lesbian, and 30 per cent were women. Professionals with progressive values who chose to take part in the fight against AIDS early on were acutely aware that persons with this disease were demonized as carriers of a lethal illness, doubly stigmatized as being gay or injection drug users, and carrying the personal burden of a death sentence. Accordingly, researchers in the HIV-prevention field were exquisitely cautious—in retrospect perhaps a bit overly cautious—about seeming to "blame the victim" by creating interventions to support prevention among HIV-infected persons. The mere existence of such research, it was feared, would suggest that HIV-infected individuals were to be suspected of transmitting the disease.

With the development of effective ARV medications in the late 1990s, the social and biomedical

Continued

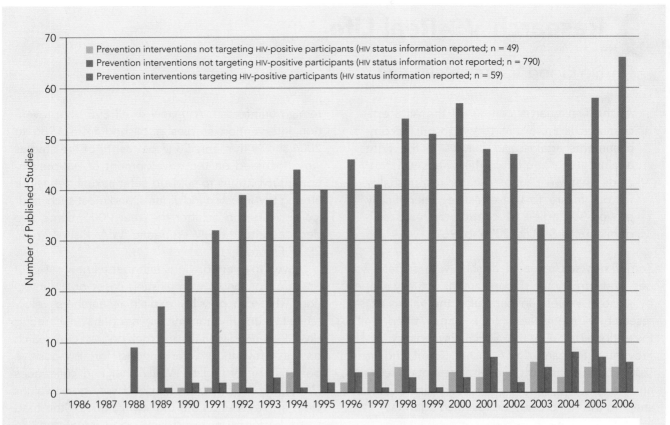

FIGURE 8.7 Studies of interventions to promote prevention of HIV infection published between 1986 and 2006.

context of HIV prevention changed. Empathic, tolerant, and altruistic professionals could now craft prevention agendas in which widespread and proactive HIV testing and research on "prevention with positives" made a great deal of sense. HIV became more "normalized" as a treatable chronic illness, and the epidemic was of long enough standing that prejudice, victim blame, and fear of contagion were somewhat lessened. Further, bringing HIV-infected individuals into effective health care and linking HIV care and HIV prevention came to be seen as an empathic and rational priority. As a result of these developments, HIV-prevention initiatives focussed on HIV-infected individuals have started to become a reality.

The STI Hit Parade

The following sections provide an overview of the Canadian prevalence, routes of transmission, symptoms, consequences, diagnosis, treatment, and prevention of major STIs, as well as the characteristics of several other strange bedfellows. Note that the STIs are divided into bacterial infections and viral infections. An important distinction between the two, as mentioned above, is that STIs caused by bacteria can be cured with antibiotics, while most STIs caused by viruses cannot be cured. Yet viral STIs can be prevented (for example, through consistent and correct use of condoms and dental dams), and they can often be treated, to reduce the severity of the consequences.

One thing that all STIs have in common is that they can cause not only adverse health consequences but also significant personal and relationship consequences. Once an STI has been diagnosed, the infected person must in most cases ensure that all of his or her partners are notified, so that they can seek treatment. Health care providers can offer advice about the appropriateness of partner notification and assistance with this task in specific situations.

Bacterial STIs

CHLAMYDIA

Canadian Prevalence

Chlamydia has the highest prevalence of any reportable STI in Canada. Young heterosexual females and males aged 20 to 24 years have the highest **incidence** of chlamydia in this country (PHAC, 2010, 2011d).

Routes of Transmission

Penile-vaginal and penile-anal intercourse are the most common ways chlamydia is transmitted, although oral sexual contact can also transmit it. Chlamydia may also be transmitted from an infected mother to her infant during childbirth (PHAC, 2011e, 2011f).

Symptoms

Chlamydia infections are most often asymptomatic or present minimal symptoms such as a mild discharge from the vagina, penis, or anus. Urinary symptoms such as burning or itching are also possible, and some women may experience vaginal bleeding (PHAC, 2010, 2011f).

Consequences

In woman, chlamydia infection may spread to the uterus and fallopian tubes and cause pelvic inflammatory disease (PID), which can cause pain with or without intercourse. PID may lead to infertility due to scarring of the fallopian tubes, increased likelihood of ectopic pregnancy, and chronic pelvic pain (CPP). Because women who are infected with chlamydia are likely to be asymptomatic, too often they find out that they have fertility issues due to PID only when they try to start a family. Consequences to the male reproductive tract are generally less severe, although chlamydia can cause **epididymitis**, which may result in infertility, and **urethritis** (figures 8.8 and 8.9).

Diagnosis

Doctors can diagnose chlamydia by taking a sample with a swab from the cervix, vagina, urethra, anus, or pharynx (throat), or by collecting and analyzing a urine sample (PHAC, 2010). Women can also test themselves for chlamydia by using a self-sampling kit and sending the swab to a lab for analysis (see http://www.iwantthekit.org/).

Treatment

Chlamydia is treated with oral antibiotics prescribed by a physician or other health care provider. Across Canada, many public health programs offer free medication to infected persons and their partners.

Prevention

Chlamydia is prevented by correct use of male or female condoms (PHAC, 2010; CDC, 2011a).

incidence The frequency of occurrence of new cases of an infection or a disease (or other condition) in a defined population.

epididymitis Inflammation of the epididymis.

urethritis Inflammation of the urethra.

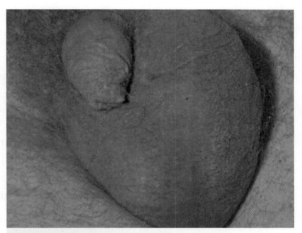

FIGURE 8.8 Epididymitis, visible as mostly unilateral swelling and redness in the scrotal area. This condition is sometimes accompanied by urethral discharge.

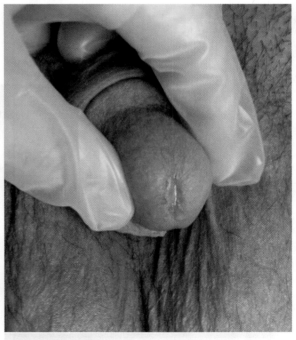

FIGURE 8.9 Chlamydia urethritis, which is often characterized by a clear discharge from the urethra.

GONORRHEA

Canadian Prevalence

Gonorrhea prevalence is highest among Canadian men who have sex with men and travellers who have had sex with locals while travelling abroad. Among heterosexual men and women, gonorrhea is becoming more prevalent but remains less common than chlamydia (PHAC, 2010, 2011d).

Routes of Transmission

Penile-vaginal and penile-anal intercourse are the most common ways gonorrhea is transmitted, although oral sexual contact can also transmit it. Gonorrhea can also be transmitted from an infected mother to her infant during childbirth (PHAC, 2011g).

Symptoms

Gonorrhea is more frequently symptomatic than chlamydia. When symptoms appear, they often include a noticeable pus-like yellowish to greenish discharge from the vagina, urethra, or anus (PHAC, 2011g; Figure 8.10). Throat pain is also common in cases of oral gonorrhea.

Consequences

In women, gonorrhea can spread to the uterus and fallopian tubes and cause PID, thereby affecting fertility; in men, consequences to the reproductive tract are generally less severe. In rare cases, untreated gonorrhea may enter the bloodstream and affect the joints, the skin, and the tissues that surround the liver, the heart, and the brain (PHAC, 2010).

Diagnosis

Doctors can diagnose gonorrhea by taking a sample with a swab from the cervix, vagina, urethra, anus, or pharynx, or by taking a blood or urine sample (PHAC, 2010, 2011g). Women can also test themselves for gonorrhea by using a self-sampling kit and sending the swab to a lab for analysis (see http://www.iwantthekit.org/).

coinfection Infection with two or more STIs at one time.

Treatment

Oral or injectable antibiotics are prescribed for treatment of gonorrhea infection of the genitals or anus. The medication has to be given in the form of a single injection if, for example, gonorrhea is present in the pharynx, or if consequences such as PID or epididymitis occur. It is recommended that persons diagnosed with gonorrhoea be treated for chlamydia as well because there are substantial rates of **coinfection** (PHAC, 2010, 2011g). Unfortunately, the development of antibiotic-resistant strains of gonorrhea is a growing concern.

Prevention

Gonorrhea is prevented by correct use of male or female condoms (PHAC, 2010; CDC, 2011a).

SYPHILIS

Canadian Prevalence

Syphilis is not common in the general population, although the risk of contracting syphilis is considerably higher among men who have sex with men, travellers who have had sexual

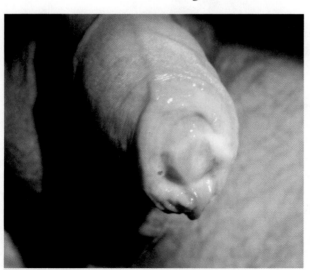

FIGURE 8.10 Gonococcal urethritis, which is often characterized by a pus-like discharge from the urethra.

contact with locals while travelling abroad in areas with high syphilis prevalence, and individuals living in or visiting certain geographic areas of Canada where outbreaks occur periodically (PHAC, 2010, 2011d).

Routes of Transmission

Penile-vaginal and penile-anal intercourse are the most common ways syphilis is transmitted, although oral sexual contact and injection drug use (through contamination of drug preparation and injection material and of the drug itself) are also possible routes of infection. Transmission of syphilis from an infected mother to her infant during pregnancy or childbirth is also possible (PHAC, 2010, 2011h).

Symptoms

Syphilis may appear with different symptoms at different stages of progression. When initially infected, an individual may show symptoms of *primary syphilis*, which include swelling of lymph nodes near the site of contact and single or multiple painless **ulcers** (Figure 8.11). The ulcers can go unnoticed if they are in the vagina, the anus, or the mouth. If untreated, the symptoms of primary syphilis may subside, but the infection will most likely progress to *secondary syphilis*, with symptoms that include a rash on the palms of the hands, the soles of the feet, and the trunk (Figure 8.12). Symptoms of secondary syphilis may also include flat, warty **lesions** in the **anogenital** area, patches of erosions and/or whitish skin in the mouth or anogenital area, fever, jaundice, muscle and/or joint aches, and patchy loss of hair (PHAC, 2010, 2011h).

Consequences

If untreated, syphilis can progress to the *tertiary stage*, in which it affects the blood vessels, heart, and eyes, and sensory or brain damage may occur. Tertiary syphilis may also cause growths called gummas on the bones or in internal organs, and it can eventually lead to death (PHAC, 2010, 2011h). Syphilis infection may also heighten the risk of HIV acquisition or transmission, particularly when ulcers or lesions are present.

Diagnosis

A blood test is used to detect specific (treponemal) or non-specific (non-treponemal) antibodies present in syphilis (PHAC, 2010). If the blood test is done early in primary-stage syphilis and it comes back negative, it may have to be repeated to be accurate.

Treatment

Injected penicillin is the drug of choice for treatment of syphilis, as oral medication is less reliable due to adherence issues.

Prevention

Proper use of male and female condoms is effective for the prevention of syphilis (PHAC, 2010).

ulcers Open sores.

lesions Abnormal changes to a body tissue.

anogenital Relating to the region of the anus and/or the genitals.

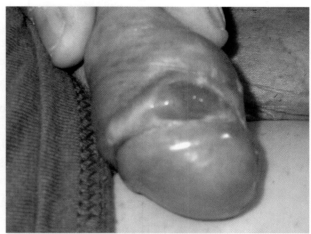

FIGURE 8.11 Single-sore, primary syphilis.

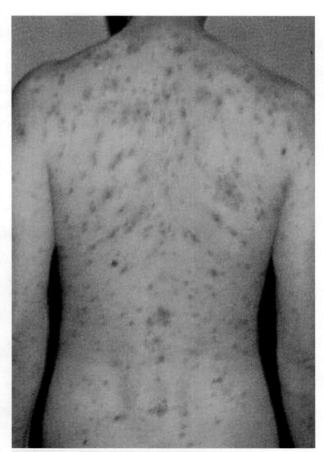

FIGURE 8.12 The rash of secondary syphilis.

Viral STIs

HERPES

Herpes can be caused by two different but closely related types of the herpes simplex virus (HSV): HSV type 1 and HSV type 2. While infections of HSV type 1 are generally found in both the orolabial (lip) and anogenital areas, infections of HSV type 2 are rarely found outside the anogenital area.

Canadian Prevalence

Herpes is not a reportable disease in Canada; consequently, precise information about its prevalence is limited. Estimates suggest that approximately half of the Canadian population may be affected by HSV type 1 in the orolabial area, and a total of one-third of Canadians may be affected by either HSV type 1 or HSV type 2 in the anogenital area (PHAC, 2010).

Routes of Transmission

Herpes is transmitted by way of genital-genital, penile-anal, oral-genital, and oral-oral contact. Infants can be infected with herpes from the mother during childbirth and from caretakers. The absence of herpes blisters in a previously infected individual is not a guarantee that transmission will not take place, as a person infected with herpes can transmit the virus to others even if she or he is asymptomatic (PHAC, 2010, 2011i).

Symptoms

Orolabial herpes generally presents as lesions on or around the lips—the classic cold sore. In the case of an anogenital infection, the lesions typically present on both sides of the genitals when an individual is first infected (Figure 8.13). When herpes recurs, the blistery lesions generally appear on one side only. The first sign of a recurrence is often a feeling of numbness or pins and needles in the affected area; 12 to 36 hours later, a red patch of skin covered in tiny, watery or pus-filled bubbles will develop. The bubbles will eventually open, crust over, and disappear. Each outbreak can last for several days. Note that the herpes virus remains within the body's nervous system for life, and herpes lesions and/or asymptomatic excretions often recur after the initial outbreak.

Consequences

Herpes blisters may become infected and cause temporary scarring, and herpes infection may cause urinary tract symptoms. Herpes infection may also heighten the risk of HIV acquisition or transmission. In addition, herpes may cause personal and relationship distress. Infants infected with herpes during childbirth or afterward can experience major neurological and other impairments, or even death (PHAC, 2010; PHAC, 2011i).

Diagnosis

Herpes is diagnosed by swabbing the lesions, preferably before they crust, and performing a viral identification test. Because herpes cannot be excluded by a negative viral identification test, a blood test can help establish the diagnosis (PHAC, 2010, 2011i).

Treatment

Oral antiviral drugs such as acyclovir, valacyclovir, and famciclovir can limit the length of an initial herpes outbreak. For patients with infrequent outbreaks, oral

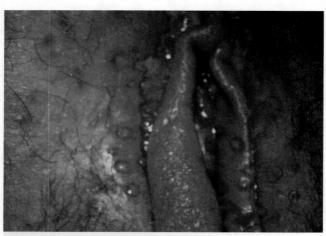

FIGURE 8.13 First-time genital infection of HSV type 1.

antiviral medication taken at the **prodromal stage** of a recurrence can prevent or shorten the outbreak. For patients with frequent outbreaks; severe recurrences; significant psychological, social, and/or sexual consequences; or the need to lower the risk of transmission to a newborn or a sexual partner, daily oral antiviral medication can be prescribed (PHAC, 2010). Local antiviral treatment is expensive and of limited value. Keeping herpes lesions clean and dry and using an over-the-counter antibiotic preparation can lessen local symptoms (see also Thomas & Maddin, 2011).

> **prodromal stage** When premonitory symptoms (symptoms forecasting that there will be an outbreak in a few hours or days) are present.

Prevention

Condoms are helpful, but herpes can be transmitted to or from areas that condoms do not cover. A blood test for herpes detection exists, yet it is usually only performed in those who are already expressing symptoms or who have a sexual partner with a history of genital herpes. Routine testing is not typically performed, as false positive results can occur in some people with a *low* likelihood of infection, leading to distress and adverse psychological effects.

HUMAN PAPILLOMAVIRUS (HPV)

Over 120 types of human papillomavirus (HPV) have been identified, more than 40 of which infect the anogenital area (Steben & Duarte-Franco, 2007). There is evidence that at least some types of HPV are associated with cervical and other cancers; those that are most closely associated with cancers are considered to be "high risk," while those least associated with cancers are considered to be "low risk."

Canadian Prevalence

While HPV is not a reportable STI in Canada, it is by all estimates the most prevalent STI in this country (PHAC, 2011j; Steben & Duarte-Franco, 2007). Up to 80 per cent of Canadians will be infected by one of the anogenital types of HPV in their lifetime (Steben & Duarte-Franco, 2007). HPV has been shown to have high rates of incident infection among university-aged women in Canada (Richardson et al., 2003; Figure 8.14), and rates are likely similar among university-aged men (Burchell et al., 2010). Because HPV is so common, it is readily acquired from first-time sexual partners, although certain factors such as a high number of sexual partners and the use of non-barrier contraceptives increase the risk of infection (Figure 8.15).

Route of Transmission

HPV infection occurs by way of skin-to-skin contact between an infected and an uninfected individual. Transmission of HPV and other viruses that infect the anogenital areas generally occurs through genital-genital, genital-anal, or oral-genital sexual contact (PHAC, 2011j).

Symptoms

Most people who have HPV do not know they are infected. Some HPV-infected persons will develop warts in genital and/or non-genital areas (see figures 8.16 and 8.17), some will have abnormal Pap tests, and some will develop cervical, penile, or other precancerous conditions or cancers long after infection occurs.

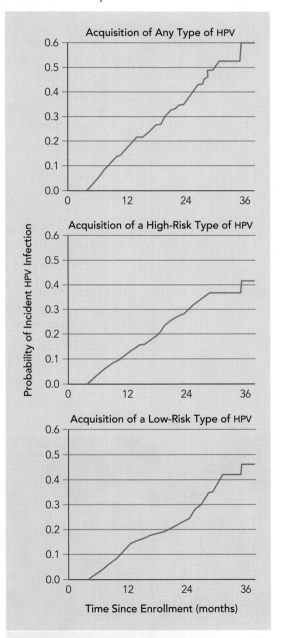

FIGURE 8.14 A university-aged woman's probability of becoming infected with HPV rises dramatically within a relatively short time span.

Factors that Increase the Risk of HPV Infection

➡ Early age of first partnered sexual activity

➡ Engaging in sexual activity with new partners

➡ Having a series of monogamous sexual partners

➡ Having multiple concurrent sexual partners

➡ Having a high number of sexual partners

➡ Engaging in sexual activity with high-risk partners

➡ Use of non-barrier methods of contraception

FIGURE 8.15 The primary risk factor for becoming infected with HPV is engaging in partnered sexual activity, although certain additional factors may increase this risk.

Consequences

Many HPV-infected individuals will spontaneously clear this viral infection with no symptoms and no physical consequences. Infection with low-risk HPV types can lead to the development of genital warts and low-grade diseases of the cervix, vagina, vulva, anus, and penis; HPV lesions will frequently be accompanied by personal or relationship distress (Pirotta et al., 2009; Drolet et al., 2011). Infection with high-risk HPV types can lead to precancerous lesions or cancers of the cervix, penis, anus, vulva, vagina, mouth, and respiratory tract (D'Souza et al., 2010; Gillison et al., 2010; Nasman et al., 2009; PHAC, 2011j). Recent research has suggested that the number of HPV-related oral and pharyngeal cancers is increasing around the world (Table 8.1), and the data indicates that the odds of acquiring head and neck cancers increase by 25 per cent if one has had more than six intercourse partners and by 336 per cent if one has had more than four oral-genital partners (Nasman et al., 2009).

Diagnosis

HPV infection resulting in genital warts is diagnosed by way of a visual exam by a health care professional. Precancerous changes to the cervix caused by a HPV infection are detected by a Pap smear, followed by a close examination of the cervix under magnification and additional tests if the results are abnormal. For precancerous or cancerous lesions, a biopsy is needed to confirm the diagnosis (PHAC, 2010, 2011j).

Treatment

Genital warts can be treated at home by an immune-stimulating drug (imiquimod) or a drug that kills cells on the surface of the skin (podophyllotoxin), both of which are applied locally and are available by prescription. They can also be treated in a health care provider's office by the application of more toxic drugs (podophyllin or trichloro-acetic acid), surgery, or cryotherapy, which involves freezing the lesions with liquid nitrogen. Precancerous lesions of the cervix can be surgically removed; HPV-related

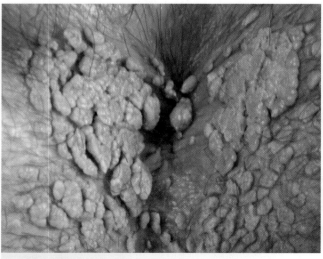

FIGURE 8.16 Anal warts.

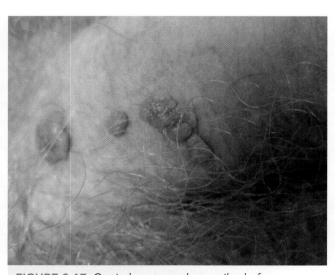

FIGURE 8.17 Genital warts on the penile shaft.

TABLE 8.1 Presence of HPV in oral and pharyngeal cancer biopsies (Sweden): an emerging STI concern.

Years	HPV-Positive Biopsies (% of total biopsies)
1970–9	23
1980–9	29
1990–9	57
2003–5	77

Source: Data based on Nasman et al. (2009).

cancers can be treated with chemotherapy, surgery, or radiation therapy (PHAC, 2010; Canadian Cancer Society, 2011).

Prevention

Two vaccines are approved for the prevention of HPV infection in Canada. The first is Gardasil, which protects against infection with the four most common types of HPV, including the two most common low-risk types that cause genital warts—HPV 6 and HPV 11—and the two most common high-risk types that cause precancerous lesions or cancers of the anogenital region—HPV 16 and HPV 18. Gardasil has been approved for use in Canada for females aged 9 to 45 years and for males aged 9 to 26 years. The second approved vaccine is Cervarix, which prevents infection with HPV 16 and HPV 18. Cervarix has been approved for use in Canada for females aged 10 to 25 years.

HPV vaccines are given in three separate injections and cost between $400 and $600 overall for the three doses. School- and community-based, cost-free HPV immunization programs exist in all jurisdictions in Canada, but most offer vaccinations only to girls between the ages of 9 and 13, and uptake of the vaccine has been somewhat uneven (see the "Research vs Real Life" box, below). For those not covered under the free programs, provincial or personal medical insurance may cover the cost of the vaccine. Pap tests remain necessary in vaccinated women, as they can help prevent cervical cancer caused by the HPV types that are not prevented by the vaccines, and some women may have been infected before they received the vaccines (PHAC, 2011j, 2011k).

HUMAN IMMUNODEFICIENCY VIRUS (HIV)

Canadian Prevalence

As mentioned earlier in this chapter, over 71,000 Canadians are living with HIV infection today, and approximately 2000 to 4000 new HIV infections are reported in Canada each year (PHAC, 2011c). HIV infections appear more commonly among men who have sex with men, injection drug users who share drug-injection materials (e.g., needles and syringes) and/or contaminated drugs, and persons from countries in which HIV is **endemic**. More than 35 per cent of new HIV infections in Canada today, however, occur among heterosexual individuals, and about 25 per cent occur among women (PHAC, 2011l). The presence of HIV infection in infants has declined dramatically in Canada since the mid-1990s due to prenatal testing of mothers and antiretroviral medication given before and during childbirth to prevent mother-to-child transmission.

endemic Common or of chronic prevalence in a certain area.

Routes of Transmission

HIV is transmitted when the blood or other bodily fluids of an infected individual come into contact with the oral, genital, or anal **mucosa** and bloodstream of an uninfected

mucosa The lining of the mouth, vagina, anus, and several other bodily orifices.

Research VS Real Life

HPV Prevention: A Revolution in Women's Health?

As noted above, HPV is an exceedingly common STI, and it is also exceedingly easy to acquire. According to an American study of a large sample of young women, having had a new sexual partner in the past year raises one's risk of HPV infection 2.6 times. Having a sexual partner who is more than two years older also raises the risk of HPV infection some 2.6 times (Dempsey, Gebremariam, Koutsky, & Manhart, 2008). Studies of Canadian university students emphasize that the probability of acquiring HPV infection in this country is also considerable. In a 2010 study of newly formed university student couples who had been sexually active for six months or less, 169 out of the 263 couples studied—64 per cent—had HPV (Burchell et al., 2010). The researchers also found that there was a significant probability that couple members were infected with the same HPV strains, strongly suggesting that couple members had infected each other. In follow-up analyses of the couples, it emerged that HPV high-risk type 16 was the most common form of the virus.

The first vaccine developed to prevent HPV, Gardasil, was approved for use in Canada in 2006, and the federal government rapidly established a $300 million fund to support school-based programs to vaccinate young girls against HPV infection prior to the onset of sexual activity. Gardasil vaccination for boys and men ages 9 to 26 has been recommended for the prevention of genital warts, precancerous conditions, and cancer of the anus, but the vaccine has not been funded in school-based or other programs for males because of the high coverage in women (PHAC, 2012). Despite the lack of action involving boys, it seemed that Canada was off to a good start in preventing HPV infection and its many serious consequences.

While there appear to be obvious reasons to welcome the development of HPV vaccines as a revolutionary advance in women's—and potentially men's—health, there has actually been considerable resistance in the Canadian popular press and professional literature, resulting in calls for caution or rejection of the school-based vaccination programs (Gulli, 2007; Lippman, Melnychuk, Shimmin, & Boscoe, 2007). Shortly after approval of the first HPV vaccine and the announcement of federal funding for the school-based vaccination programs, a cover story appeared in *Maclean's* magazine entitled "Our Girls Are Not Guinea Pigs: Is an Upcoming Mass Inoculation of a Generation Unnecessary and Potentially Dangerous?" (Gulli, 2007). The article begins with stories of serious illnesses that occurred shortly after young women were vaccinated against HPV, but that in fact were judged to have *no* connection to the vaccine. For example:

> The morning after Emily Cunningham got a shot of Gardasil, the new vaccine that protects against four strains of the human papilloma virus (HPV) that can cause cervical cancer and genital warts, she woke up with a headache, and neck and back pain. By 9 p.m. that evening in April, she had a fever so high "you could feel the heat rising from her a foot away." . . . One could discount what happened to Emily because she had a flu shot that same day, but other *really bad* reactions have been reported. (Gulli, 2007)

In fact, many safety reports indicate that this vaccine is very safe, and the long-term follow-up studies show persistent protection.

individual (Canadian AIDS Society, 2011a, 2011b). Penile-vaginal and penile-anal intercourse are high-risk behaviours for HIV transmission, as these acts can cause small tears in the mucosal linings, and these tears permit HIV to enter the bloodstream directly. Oral sexual contact entails a much lower risk than anal or vaginal penetration, but it is *not* a no-risk sexual behaviour for HIV transmission. Sharing sex toys can also transmit the infection. In addition, the presence of genital skin lesions (such as those caused by syphilis or herpes) or inflammation (which can be caused by a number of things, including STIs) increases the risk of HIV transmission. (In fact, there is a synergistic

Beyond such emotional examples, very reasonable medical questions were posed by the *Maclean's* article and by a paper by Dr Abby Lippman and colleagues (2007) appearing at about the same time in the *Canadian Medical Association Journal*. Among other questions, both articles ask how long the vaccination will confer protection against HPV. This important question arose because the vaccine's protection had been tested for only five years in only about 1200 females aged 16 to 26 years; further, the vaccine was being recommended for nine-year-old girls, in whom safety and immunogenicity studies had been done but no efficacy evaluations had been conducted, for ethical reasons. Both articles also question the need for a widespread vaccination program given that, as they point out, cervical cancer is "only" the thirteenth-leading cause of cancer-related deaths in Canada. Both papers further question the usefulness of the vaccine by emphasizing that Pap tests can detect cervical cancer at a very early stage when it can be effectively treated.

Proponents of the vaccine responded vigorously (see, for example, the Society of Obstetricians and Gynaecologists of Canada, 2007). Some have pointed out that the protection provided by the HPV vaccine is now known to last far longer than five years, that nine-year-olds' immune response to the vaccine is in fact stronger than the immune response of someone given the vaccine at a later age, and that protection would continue through the time of many Canadians' first involvement in sexual intercourse, a time of considerable risk of HPV infection. Moreover, they argue, averting cervical cancer *is* important: in Canada, more than 1350 women are diagnosed with cervical cancer and approximately 390 die from it every year, and cervical cancer is the second most common form of cancer diagnosed in 25- to 45-year-old women. In addition, it is not only cervical cancer and cervical cancer-related deaths that the vaccine can avert—it is also the stress of getting an abnormal Pap test result (which happens about 400,000 times a year in Canada), the cost (to individual women and to the medical system) of extensive follow-up examinations and/or treatments (in the event of an abnormal Pap test, findings of cancer, or the appearance of genital warts), and the potential distress of discovering HPV symptoms in oneself or one's partner. Thus, while the vaccine may appear very expensive on a per-dose basis, it seems to be the smarter, more cost-effective choice when compared to the alternatives.

Proponents of the vaccine also argue that while Pap tests *can* detect cervical cancer at its early stages, not everyone gets routine Pap tests—vulnerable women (e.g., recent immigrants, Aboriginal women, and those living in remote locations) are least likely to be screened, and overall adherence rates are only about 75 per cent. Further, Pap tests are not 100 per cent accurate (in fact, 29 per cent of women with cervical cancer never received an abnormal Pap test result), and many women who develop cervical cancer have never had a Pap test. Pap tests also do not screen for other HPV-related cancers, such as anal or vulvar cancer. At the end of the day, it has been asserted that it is obviously much smarter to prevent HPV infection rather than to attempt to detect and treat it after the fact. Proponents argue as well that, given the prevalence of sexually transmitted HPV infection, our real choice is to enter sexual activity—and HPV risk—with vaccine protection or without it. Some proponents have also wondered why resistance has emerged specifically to a vaccine that prevents an STI—is there an anti-sex subtext to this discussion? What is your opinion?

relationship between HIV and lesion-causing STIs: HIV is more contagious when genital lesions are present, and those with HIV who have a lesion-causing STI have a longer period of infectiousness, due to impaired immune responses.)

HIV can also be transmitted through various non-sexual means. The most common non-sexual route of transmission is through the sharing of equipment used to prepare and inject drugs. HIV can also be transmitted from an HIV-infected mother to her infant during childbirth or breastfeeding. Occupational exposure to HIV, such as that which might occur in a nurse, paramedic, physician, or police officer who has been exposed to the blood of an HIV-infected individual through a cut or other opening, is very rare, but it can occur. Transmission through blood transfusions and surgical transplants are very rare in Canada and in other countries in which blood products are screened.

Symptoms

At the time of initial HIV infection, the individual may experience flu-like symptoms with enlarged lymph nodes, but these symptoms do not always appear. Much later in the course of infection, an untreated HIV-infected individual will experience moderate to severe immune system damage (PHAC, 2010).

Consequences

If untreated, HIV progresses to AIDS (acquired immune deficiency syndrome), which involves severe damage of the immune system, opportunistic infections, cancers, neurologic and cardiac diseases, physical wasting, and death (PHAC, 2010).

Diagnosis

Blood tests that detect antibodies to HIV are used to diagnose this infection. Because it may take up to three months to produce antibodies and antigens in sufficient quantity for the blood test to identify, an individual must wait three months following a suspected exposure to HIV before the blood test can diagnose infection with complete accuracy. The diagnosis of infants born to HIV-infected mothers is more difficult, as these infants often possess their mother's HIV antibodies at birth, even if they are not in fact infected with HIV. Therefore, either less commonly used tests that directly detect the virus must be used, or the testing must wait until the maternal antibodies have cleared the infant's system (CGSTI, 2011; National Institutes of Health, 2011).

Treatment

As noted earlier, ARV therapy, involving a combination of drugs, can be effective in stopping the replication of HIV and preserving an HIV-infected individual's health and lifespan (for a discussion of sexuality in HIV-positive individuals, see the "Ethical Debate" box). In order to be effective, ARVs must be taken with a very high level of adherence; an individual infected with HIV must take at least 90 per cent of the pills prescribed to suppress production of HIV, halt progression to AIDS, and prevent the development of treatment-resistant viruses (Bangsberg & Deeks, 2002; Paterson et al., 2000). ARV therapy may have serious side effects (e.g., nausea, diarrhea, and abnormal fat deposits in areas of the body), and it must be maintained throughout the infected individual's lifespan. Note that while high adherence to ARV therapy will stop replication of the virus, it cannot provide a cure; HIV always remains in "reservoir" areas of an infected individual's body (e.g., the brain), and it will reappear if ARV therapy is stopped (National Institutes of Health, 2011).

ARV therapy also appears to have preventive value. Specifically, if an ARV-treated HIV-infected individual's **viral load** drops to a very low level (called "an undetectable viral load"), he or she may be at that moment less or even non-infectious. However, viral loads can rise at any time without notice, so simply being on ARVs should never be taken as a sign that an HIV-infected individual cannot pass the infection on to others (Eurosurveillance Editorial Team, 2008).

viral load A measure of the amount of a virus that an infected person has per millimetre of blood.

Prevention

Male and female condoms are effective in preventing HIV infection (Canadian AIDS Society, 2011a, 2011b; World Health Organization, 2007). Treatment of HIV-infected mothers is very effective in reducing mother-to-infant transmission. Post-exposure prophylaxis is available for professionals who suspect they have had an occupational

Ethical Debate

Which Side Are You On? Stimulating Sexual Interest and Sexual Activity among HIV-Positive Persons

In 1994, at a time when AIDS represented a nearly always fatal, untreatable STI, William A. Fisher, in his capacity as an editorial board member of the *Journal of Sex Research*, received a manuscript titled "Effects of Testosterone Replacement Therapy on Sexual Interest, Function, and Behavior in HIV+ Men," submitted for consideration for publication. Reading a manuscript concerning the intentional stimulation of sexual interest, function, and activity for persons infected with HIV, and who were capable of transmitting the virus to uninfected others, certainly attracted Fisher's interest. The manuscript raised important—actually, at the time, life-and-death—questions about research and practice ethics.

According to the research report, 80 HIV-infected men were treated with testosterone (Wagner, Rabkin, & Rabkin, 1997a), and some 90 per cent of the men who remained in treatment were reported to be clear treatment successes, with nearly uniform increases in sexual interest among the participants who lacked sexual interest at baseline, and significant increases in strength of erection during oral and anal sex. Mean frequency of oral and anal sex and mean number of sex partners in the month after testosterone treatment increased as well. The authors deemed the study to be a success: "Progressive HIV illness entails many kinds of losses; restoration of one's sexuality associated with testosterone replacement can greatly enhance quality of life and sense of vitality" (Wagner et al., 1997a, p. 27). The possibility that testosterone administration had resulted in or would result in increases in risky sex, resulting in the transmission of HIV from men infected with the virus and treated with testosterone to uninfected others, however, could not be ruled out.

During the manuscript-review process, questions arose concerning the ethics of the research that was reported, and concerning the possible wider practice of testosterone supplementation to improve the sexual quality of life of HIV-infected individuals. After considerable thought, Fisher's recommendation was to publish the study alongside an ethical critique. Issues raised in the critique, "Do No Harm: On the Ethics of Testosterone Replacement Therapy for HIV+ Persons" (W.A. Fisher, 1997), included "(a) the dubious ethics of stimulating sexual desire and sexual function in persons who carry a fatal, sexually transmitted pathogen; (b) our very limited ability to ensure that testosterone replacement therapy for HIV+ persons will not pose significant danger to uninfected persons, and (c) the relative importance of quality of life versus protection of life considerations in research and therapy in the HIV/AIDS area" (W.A. Fisher, 1997, p. 35). The critique argued that we live in a complex ethical universe in which important ethical values may collide, and we may be required to prioritize some values over others; in this case, it continued, preservation of life should trump the very important, but in this instance less important, value of quality of life.

In recommending publication of the original article and the ethical critique, Fisher's intent was to stimulate much-needed debate about ethics and practice in this area. In the spirit of stimulating such debate, responses to the critique were also invited. One of the most provocative responses included the assertion that "the logical extension of Fisher's argument is that *any* treatment for people with HIV increases societal risk because the longer they are alive the longer they pose a potential threat to the community as disease vectors" (Wagner et al., 1997b, p. 37). How would *you* have reacted, in 1994, to a study on the administration of testosterone to promote sexual activity among HIV-positive persons?

exposure to HIV, and to victims of sexual assault (CDC, 2005). Such measures involve taking ARVs starting within 72 hours of exposure (Canadian AIDS Society, 2011a, 2011b). *Pre*-exposure prophylaxis, involving the administration of ARV medications to persons at risk of HIV infection, has been found to be a relatively but not completely effective form of prevention (Grant et al., 2010). Studies conducted in African nations also demonstrate that circumcision may be more than 50 per cent effective in preventing acquisition of HIV infection in men (Bailey et al., 2007). The use of an ARV-containing vaginal gel may help prevent infection in women (Abdool Karim et al., 2010). Among injection drug users, avoidance of sharing drug-injection or drug-preparation equipment (or using only very carefully cleaned drug injection paraphernalia) is essential for HIV prevention (CDC, 2004).

HIV antibody screening tests, taken after the last at-risk sexual contact, occurrence of injection-drug paraphernalia sharing, or other suspected exposure to HIV, can confirm an individual's HIV status. Many couples engage in mutual HIV antibody testing, agreed-upon monogamy, and/or agreed-upon precautions if monogamy is not maintained (e.g., condom use and/or informing the partner) as means of HIV prevention.

VIRAL HEPATITIS

There are many types of viral hepatitis, all of which involve inflammation of the liver. The three that are of most concern to Canadians are hepatitis A, hepatitis B, and hepatitis C.

Canadian Prevalence

Hepatitis A is prevalent at epidemic levels in certain "closed" communities, such as prisons and some residential settings, in which food that is contaminated with the virus is served to a number of people. It is also common among men who have sex with men. Hepatitis B is prevalent among men who have sex with men and injection drug users. It is also common in individuals from countries in which the disease is prevalent, in countries where blood products are not screened before medical use, and in locations in which medical equipment is reused without proper disinfection. Hepatitis C is prevalent among injection drug users, in individuals from countries in which poor infection control in health care settings is practised, and in countries where blood products are not screened. Hepatitis C is also prevalent in HIV-positive men who have sex with men (CDC, 2011b; PHAC, 2011m).

Routes of Transmission

Hepatitis A is mainly transmitted by fecal-oral routes, including oral-anal sex and ingestion of food or water contaminated with feces. Hepatitis B can be transmitted through sexual contact, the sharing of contaminated drug-injection or drug-preparation equipment, or the sharing of sex toys. Hepatitis C can be transmitted through blood contact, the sharing of contaminated drug-injection or drug-preparation equipment, and sexual activities that cause trauma to the sites of sexual contact. Hepatitis C is not readily transmissible through most sexual activities (CDC, 2011b; PHAC, 2011m).

Symptoms

Jaundice (yellowing of the skin and eyes) is seen in some cases, and flu-like symptoms with abdominal pain are possible as well.

Consequences

Most people with hepatitis A survive and clear the virus from their bodies after appropriate treatment. For hepatitis B and C, the virus may remain in the individual's body, resulting in the possible development of cirrhosis of the liver and/or liver cancer.

Diagnosis

All types of hepatitis are diagnosed via a blood test.

Treatment

Hepatitis A requires symptom-specific treatment. Hepatitis B and C can be cured via interferon injections and courses of antiviral drugs (University of California San Francisco, 2011).

Prevention

For hepatitis A and B, vaccine prevention is available without cost in most jurisdictions in Canada, and most school children receive hepatitis B vaccine. With respect to hepatitis B and C, safe recreational drug-injection practices can help prevent infection (CDC, 2004).

Strange Bedfellows: Other Genital Concerns

TRICHOMONIASIS

Canadian Prevalence

Trichomoniasis ("trich") is an uncommon STI in most regions of Canada. It is prevalent in parts of Africa and other areas of the world and more common among women with multiple sexual partners (PHAC, 2011n).

Transmission

Trichomonas vaginalis, the protozoa that causes this infection, is most commonly spread through sexual contact (PHAC, 2011n).

Symptoms

Symptoms consist of a profuse yellowish vaginal discharge in women, although the infection may be asymptomatic. Trichomoniasis in men is often asymptomatic. Other symptoms include pain upon urination and itching in the genital area.

Consequences

If untreated, trichomoniasis can lead to infertility, increased risk of cervical cancer, inflammation of the uterus, endometritis (inflammation of the endometrium), and premature delivery (PHAC, 2011n).

Diagnosis

A swab of the vagina or urethra is sent to the lab to identify the trichomoniasis parasite.

Treatment

The infection is usually treated via an oral drug (metronidazole).

Prevention

Male and female condoms can help prevent trichomoniasis.

PUBIC LICE AND SCABIES

Public lice and scabies are infestations of small parasites.

Canadian Prevalence

Infestations of both pubic lice and scabies are common in Canada.

Transmission

Pubic lice and scabies can be transmitted through direct sexual or non-sexual contact with infected persons, or through contact with contaminated surfaces such as bed sheets and towels (PHAC, 2011o).

Symptoms

Pubic lice and scabies cause itchiness, especially at night. Adult pubic lice, which are about the size of a pinhead, are generally visible on the surface of the skin (Figure 8.18). The white eggs of the lice may also be visible near the skin, at the base of the individual's hair. For scabies, a rash might appear where the parasite has burrowed into the skin, often at the wrists, at the webbing of the fingers, or on the body.

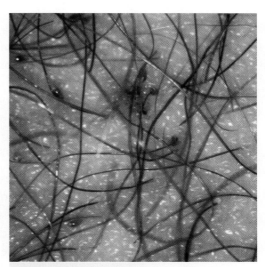

FIGURE 8.18 Pubic lice.

Consequences

Severe itchiness may be lead to bacterial infection because of the breakdown of the skin from scratching.

Diagnosis

Public lice and scabies are diagnosed by visual inspection by the patient or a health care provider. They can also be found via skin biopsy.

Treatment

Permethrin, pyrethrin-piperonyl and lindane cream or shampoo can be used to effectively treat these parasites.

Prevention

No definitive prevention or screening test for these parasites is available.

MONILIASIS

Moniliasis, also commonly referred to as *candidiasis* or *thrush*, is a vaginal yeast infection caused by the overgrowth of naturally occurring vaginal organisms. Moniliasis is part of the normal flora of the vagina and not sexually transmitted *per se*, but it can be activated by sexual activities involving the vagina (especially oral sex) or a new sexual partner; it can also be activated by antibiotics, diabetes, or immunodeficiency (PHAC, 2010).

Symptoms

Moniliasis symptoms include pain during intercourse, and vaginal itchiness and discharge that may be white and clumpy in acute cases.

Consequences

If untreated, moniliasis can cause an eczema-like reaction in the genital area and pain during sex or urination.

Diagnosis

Infrequent cases are generally diagnosed by visual inspection by a health care provider. Recurrent cases (four or more episodes in a year) are confirmed by laboratory tests.

Treatment

Oral or topical drugs are used to treat moniliasis. In the case of recurrent moniliasis, boric acid vaginal suppositories or capsules or oral fluconazole (an antifungal drug) may be used on a weekly basis over extended periods of time.

Prevention

Avoidance of wide-spectrum antibiotics can reduce the risk of developing moniliasis, since these substances destroy the bacteria and thus the equilibrium in the microbioma of the vagina and promote the overgrowth of yeast. As all people carry yeast organisms in their body from time to time, no screening for monilia is available. The use of lactobacilli preparations has not been found to prevent recurrences.

BACTERIAL VAGINOSIS

Canadian Prevalence

Bacterial vaginosis (BV) is caused by an overgrowth of bacteria that normally live in the vagina, and it is fairly common in pregnant women (PHAC, 2010; CDC, 2011c). BV is not generally considered to be an STI, and it is not entirely clear how it is caused. However, having a new sexual partner or having multiple partners appears to increase the risk, as does douching.

Symptoms

Symptoms of BV include a fishy odour, vaginal discharge, and itching around the vagina. Pain during intercourse (dyspareunia) can also result.

Consequences

If untreated, BV may cause pregnancy complications, including preterm delivery; it can also increase a woman's susceptibility to acquiring or transmitting HIV, and her susceptibility to acquiring chlamydia, gonorrhea, and herpes.

Diagnosis

Diagnosis is based upon vaginal pH, odour, the presence of clue cells under the microscope, and chemical tests done in the lab.

Treatment

BV is treated by oral medication (metronidazole), clindamycin vaginal cream, metronidazole vaginal gel, or long-acting vitamin C tablets (inserted into the vagina).

Prevention

Definitive prevention is not possible, but abstinence, avoidance of multiple sexual partners, and avoidance of douching can help. In addition, adherent use of the medication prescribed for the treatment of this condition, even if all the symptoms have disappeared, can help prevent recurrences.

STI Screening and STI Testing: How to Approach the Topic with a (Potential) Sexual Partner

Screening for STIs involves testing in the absence of evident symptoms, as a couple might decide to do before they become sexually active together or even after sexual activity has started. *Testing* for STIs is undertaken when an individual has reason to believe that he or she might have been exposed to a sexually transmitted infection—for example, through unprotected intercourse. It is always a good idea to talk to your partner about STI screening or testing *before* unprotected sexual contact. *Think positive*—"Let's get tested so we can relax and enjoy . . ."—to *stay negative* (i.e., free of STIs). Be assertive, but not aggressive, about your wishes: "I think we should get screened, and until then, let's use condoms. I won't be comfortable being sexual otherwise." It is important to remember, however, that while screening can detect several common STIs (e.g., chlamydia, gonorrhea, HIV), the two most common STIs—HPV and HSV—cannot be detected by screening.

What happens if a test reveals that you have an STI? Communicating your results to your current and/or past sexual partner(s) is often essential. Because most STIs can be asymptomatic, your partner(s) may not know they are infected (and indeed *they* may have infected *you*). They may develop serious complications if their infection goes untreated, and they can transmit the STI to others. Your health care provider can help you determine whether you need to contact past partners and, if so, how far back in time to go. If you have difficulty communicating with a partner about having an STI, your health care provider can also be of help (see PHAC, 2010).

Your health care provider can inform you about the kinds of STI testing that are available and advisable. Screening may be as simple as taking a blood test to detect HIV antibodies or giving a urine sample to detect chlamydia or gonorrhoea. It can also be more specific, depending upon your and your partner's risk factors (e.g., sexual behaviours, prevalence of specific STIs in the places you live and travel).

Is There a Reasonable Way to Be Sexual in the New Millennium?

The information about STIs presented in this chapter may seem quite daunting, but it is not intended to convince you to live the life of a sexual hermit. While abstinence from partnered sexual contact *is* an effective method of avoiding STIs, it is not a realistic solution for most Canadians. On average, the age of first sexual intercourse in Canada is somewhere in the later teens, and the average age of first marriage is around 30; between these two points, a very typical pattern is to engage in a series of affectionate, sexual, **serially monogamous** relationships (W.A. Fisher & Boroditsky, 2000). Unfortunately, this pattern carries with it an extended period of risk of contracting an STI. There is, however, a way forward, and the following discussion covers strategies for minimizing risk and consequences of STIs in the new millennium.

> **serial monogamy** A pattern of consecutive, single-partnered intimate relationships.

Think about Sex

Being sexually active involves thinking about sex *a lot*—something that comes naturally to many people! Think in advance about whether you want to be sexually active with a partner, and to what degree. Think about what's on your sexual-health wish list, including *consent* ("Have I clarified whether I, and my partner, actually want to do this?"), *contraception* ("Have I and my partner discussed, or have I personally put into place, acceptable contraceptive precautions?"), and *safer sex* ("The heck with taking a sexual history—if my partner or I *have* a sexual history, then we need to use condoms, and discuss STI screening, the limits to screening, and mutual monogamy"). And add to your sexual wish list *sexual pleasure* ("I know my partner believes that he or she is a superior lover, but I've got to figure out how to convey what I like best about what we do sexually together") and *interpersonal relationships* ("Is this relationship good for me, and good for my partner?"). Also think about what you need to know—about contraception, safer sex, sexual function, sexual communication, and relationships;—and where you can go to get the information you need, and then do your homework! (Good places to start are this textbook and the sexual and reproductive health website of the Society of Obstetricians and Gynaecologists of Canada, sexualityandU.ca). Also keep in mind that your thoughts on sex may differ from others' thoughts on sex. Conceptions of sex in general—and of such related topics as consent, safer sex, and the promotion of sexual health in particular—tend to differ across cultures and among individuals; it is important to be aware of such differences when you are at home and when you are travelling within North America or overseas (see the "Culture and Diversity" box).

Use Condoms

When used correctly and consistently, male and female condoms effectively prevent several STIs, including chlamydia, syphilis, gonorrhea, and HIV. Although they may not be as highly effective in the prevention of genital herpes and HPV infection (because those infections can be transmitted via areas that condoms do not completely cover), they still provide some protection (Winer et al., 2006; Manhart & Koutsky, 2002). Remember that condom protection works both ways: they protect the individual using the condom and the individual having sexual contact with that person. Note also that male condoms can be placed on the penis and used as a barrier to STIs in oral-penile contact, and both male and female condoms can be cut down the middle, placed over the vulva, and used as a barrier to infection in oral-vulvar or oral-anal contact. Dental dams are also effective barriers for use in any instance of oral-vulvar or oral-anal contact.

Culture & Diversity

HIV/AIDS-Prevention Interventions in the United States and South Africa

It is a long way from New Haven, Connecticut, to the province of KwaZulu-Natal, South Africa, but STIs are a health threat in both locales. Of particular concern in both locations is the threat of HIV infection. Yet HIV/AIDS-prevention interventions have been implemented successfully in both America and Africa. Although these interventions follow the same theoretical approaches, they also reflect and respond to vastly different cultural concerns.

Working to stem forward-transmission of HIV/AIDS, Jeffrey Fisher, William Fisher, and colleagues (J.D. Fisher, Cornman, Norton, & Fisher, 2006) have been at the forefront of "Prevention with Positives" HIV/AIDS-prevention interventions, which support the efforts of HIV-infected individuals to practise safer sex and safer injection drug use, in efforts to avoid transmitting the virus to uninfected others. Based on the information–motivation–behavioural skills (IMB) model (J.D. Fisher, Fisher, & Shuper, 2009; also see Chapter 7), the researchers conducted formative research to identify HIV-prevention information gaps, HIV-prevention motivational obstacles, and HIV-prevention behavioural-skills limitations among HIV-infected patients receiving care in New Haven, Connecticut (J.D. Fisher, Cornman, et al.,

2006), and in KwaZulu-Natal, South Africa (Cornman et al., 2008). They found that specific HIV-prevention information gaps, motivational obstacles, and behavioural-skills limitations differed drastically in the two cultural settings.

Equipped with a deeper understanding of individuals' requirements in each locale, the researchers were able to apply the IMB model to develop culturally appropriate HIV-prevention interventions. In New Haven, for example, efforts focussed on using the model to address culture-specific needs of HIV-infected injection drug users and gay men. In KwaZulu-Natal, HIV-prevention information efforts involved addressing the belief that traditional healers can cure HIV, motivation-focussed efforts dealt with the cultural imperative of having children (which can entail engaging in risky sexual behaviour), and efforts to identify HIV-prevention behavioural skills focussed, for women, on negotiation of condom use in what were often extremely unequal male–female relationships. In the end, the researchers' efforts paid off, and the interventions they had developed were effective in reducing HIV transmission in both cultural settings (J.D. Fisher, Fisher, et al., 2006; J.D. Fisher et al., 2012).

Carry a condom with you in a safe place. Do not store condoms in your wallet or car, where pressure and heat will make them deteriorate; rather, carry them in purses, backpacks, jacket pockets, or empty dental-floss containers. See to it that the condom is in place before any sexual contact occurs, and that it is removed only after sexual contact is finished. In addition, do not be misled by common misperceptions (e.g., that "some" genital-genital rubbing or oral-genital contact before the condom is put on is safe) or objections (e.g., condoms are cumbersome, or "unsexy"; see Table 8.2).

A common pattern among Canadian couples is to use condoms until the couple transitions from condoms to oral contraceptives, once both partners feel that they have "gotten to know" the other suitably well (MacDonald et al., 1990). Unfortunately, this practice can actually serve to facilitate their contracting an STI. Even if oral or other non-barrier contraceptives are used to avoid a pregnancy (see Chapter 7), STI risk must still be addressed (by mutual discussion and mutual screening, and perhaps continued condom use, among other precautions).

Get Vaccinated

Highly effective vaccines are available to prevent infection with HPV and hepatitis A and B. While HPV vaccination was first introduced for women, it is now recommended

TABLE 8.2 Perceived barriers to using male condoms—and how to overcome them.

Perceived Barrier	Resolution
Condoms decrease sexual pleasure or sensation.	• Put a drop of water-based lubricant or saliva in the tip of the condom or on the glans of the penis prior to putting on the condom. • Try a thinner latex condom. • Try different brands. • Try more lubrication.
Condoms decrease the spontaneity of sexual activity.	• Incorporate condom use during foreplay. • Remember that peace of mind may enhance sexual arousal and response.
Using condoms is embarrassing, juvenile, and/or "unmanly."	• Remember that being responsible is neither embarrassing nor juvenile, and that it is "manly" to protect oneself and others.
Condoms don't fit well.	• Try a smaller or larger condom. (Different sizes are readily available in many stores and health centres.)
Using condoms requires prompt withdrawal after ejaculation.	• Remember that a sexual encounter doesn't have to end with withdrawal of the penis, and suggest low-risk post-coital activities such as caressing erogenous areas.
Condoms can break, and fear of breakage may lead to loss of enjoyment.	• Keep in mind that condoms generally do not break if used properly. The use of pre-lubricated condoms can help, as can the addition of a water-based lubricant if necessary.
Condoms are difficult or unpleasant to use during oral or other non-penetrative sexual activity.	• Use a non-lubricated condom for oral-penile sexual contact. • Try flavoured condoms (but not edible condoms, which do not protect against STIs). • Cut a non-lubricated condom down the middle to form a protective sheet for oral-vulvar and oral-anal sexual contact.

for men as well (PHAC, 2012). Why? To prevent men from developing genital warts and cancers, and to protect men's partners from HPV infection.

Take Secondary Prevention Measures

While primary prevention measures, such as those outlined above, help you avoid becoming infected with an STI, secondary prevention measures help limit the health impact and spread of an STI that has occurred. Secondary prevention measures include *sign and symptom awareness, STI screening and testing, Pap tests, adherence to STI treatment*, and *partner notification and treatment. Sign and symptom awareness* involves being cognizant of changes in your or your partner's body that could signify infection. If you observe any signs of infection, you should stop engaging in sex and seek treatment from a health care provider (e.g., your family physician, or a doctor or nurse at your local student health centre or sexual health clinic). *STI screening and testing* can help you identify an asymptomatic infection of chlamydia, gonorrhea, syphilis, or HIV; screening and testing should be considered for both partners before and after they begin having sex with each other, and it can provide considerable peace of mind. *Pap tests* and regular gynecological examinations can also help women identify an infection or any abnormal changes in their reproductive tract.

If an STI is detected in any of these ways, it is critical to *adhere to the recommended treatment*, including taking all prescribed medication and attending follow-up appointments. In terms of medications, for example, antibiotics may be prescribed for chlamydia, gonorrhea, or syphilis; antiviral therapy may be recommended to suppress recurrent herpes outbreaks; and strict adherence to ARVs is necessary for the management and decreased transmissibility of HIV. Finally, *partner notification and treatment* may be essential; if one partner detects an STI infection, the other partner needs to be tested or treated. If you discover that you have an STI, ask your health care provider about the appropriateness of partner notification. And, if you develop a chronic STI, such as herpes or HIV, it becomes critical to knowledgably and sensitively discuss the issues of infection and prevention with a partner *before* sexual contact takes place, so that well-informed consent to sexual contact can be given and preventive action can be taken.

Check Out—but Don't Rely On—Your Partner's Sexual and Injection Drug Use History

Do *not* rely on the common, but largely erroneous, advice that you can reduce your risk of becoming infected with an STI by finding out about your partner's sexual and injection drug use history. If either you or your partner has been sexually intimate with another individual—including hand-genital, mouth-genital, or genital-genital contact—or has used injection drugs, you need to practise the *real* prevention strategies discussed above. An individual will likely have no idea whether a previous partner has given him or her "the gift that keeps on giving" (an asymptomatic STI), and many of the factors and activities that pose a risk of STI transmission (e.g., past sexual partners, past sexual coercion, injection drug use) are so stigmatized that individuals are reluctant to candidly discuss them with others.

Research (Williams et al., 1992) suggests that many young people use condoms and practise STI prevention "until they get to know their partner," as if after acquaintance with a partner's roommates, friends, pet hamster, and taste in music and beer, all known STIs spontaneously drop dead. As they say, "It just ain't so." Another common strategy involves invoking "theories of risk" that we may develop in the belief that we can scope out and avoid partners who might have an STI (Williams et al., 1992). While it might feel safe to avoid partners whose characteristics correspond to one's "theory of risk" (e.g., they ride a motorcycle, you met them in a bar, they drink a lot) in favour of those characteristics that do not correspond to one's theory of risk (e.g., they take the bus, you met them in class, they don't drink too much), again, "It just ain't so."

CHAPTER SUMMARY

STIs occur at the intersection of biology and behaviour. One's probability of acquiring an STI is primarily a function of sexual behaviour—one's own and that of one's partner(s)—and pathogen prevalence. In Canada, there is considerable risky sexual behaviour and considerable pathogen prevalence, and the chance that a sexually active person who is not in a permanent, exclusive sexual relationship will acquire an STI is high. The risk can be reduced, however, through primary and secondary means of prevention, including abstinence from sexual contact, consistent condom use, STI screening, vaccination against HPV and hepatitis A and B, regular Pap tests, adherence to treatment, and partner notification of STIs that occur.

DEBATE QUESTION

Some people strongly assert that individuals with an STI are responsible for telling potential sexual partners of their infectious status, and that if they fail to do so, they are committing sexual assault. Others just as strongly assert that it is every individual's responsibility to protect himself or herself from STIs. What is your opinion?

REVIEW QUESTIONS

1. What is a sexually transmitted pathogen?
2. How is STI screening different from STI testing?
3. What is the difference between the prevalence of an infection and the incidence of an infection?
4. What are effective means for preventing HIV and HPV in sexually active individuals?
5. What are the signs that a woman may be infected with chlamydia? What are the signs that a man may be infected with chlamydia?
6. What are some of the health consequences of HPV infection?

SUGGESTIONS FOR FURTHER READING AND VIEWING

Recommended Websites

American Sexual Health Association (ASHA): ashastd.org

Canadian AIDS Society: www.cdnaids.ca

Canadian Guidelines on Sexually Transmitted Infections (from PHAC): www.phac-aspc
.gc.ca/std-mts/sti-its/index-eng.php

General Information on STIs (from PHAC): www.phac-aspc.gc.ca/publicat/std-mts/
index-eng.php

General Information on STIs (from the CDC): www.cdc.gov/std

Go Ask Alice—How to Tell Partner about Herpes: www.goaskalice.columbia.edu/
1143.html

Herpes Guide: www.herpesguide.ca

UNAIDS: www.unaids.org

Recommended Reading

Albarracin, D., Gillette, J.C., Earl, A.N., Glasman, L.R., Durantini, M.R., & Ho, M. (2005). A test of major assumptions about behaviour change: A comprehensive look at the effects of passive and active HIV-prevention interventions since the beginning of the epidemic. *Psychological Bulletin, 131*, 856–97.

Bayer, R., & Oppenheim, G.M. (2000). *AIDS doctors: Voices from the epidemic.* Oxford, England: Oxford University Press.

Darrow W.W. (1998 [1977]). A few minutes with Venus, a lifetime with Mercury. In G.G. Brannigan, E.R. Allgeier, & A.R. Allgeier (Eds), *The sex scientists* (pp. 156–70). New York, NY: Addison, Wesley, Longman.

Fisher, W.A., Kohut, T., & Fisher, J.D. (2009). AIDS exceptionalism: On the social psychology of HIV prevention research. *Social Issues and Policy Review, 3*(1), 45–77.

Lippman, A., Melnychuk, R., Shimmin, C., & Boscoe, M. (2007). Human papillomavirus, vaccines and women's health: Questions and cautions. *Canadian Medical Association Journal, 177*(5) 484–7.

National Advisory Committee on Immunizations. (2007). *Canada communicable disease report.* Retrieved from www.phac-aspc.gc.ca/publicat/ccdr-rmtc/07vol33/index-eng.php

Shilts, R. (1987). *And the band played on: People, politics, and the AIDS epidemic.* New York, NY: St Martin's Press.

Society of Obstetricians and Gynaecologists of Canada. (2007, 14 August). *SOGC statement on CMAJ commentary, "Human papillomavirus, vaccines and women's health: questions and cautions."* Retrieved from www.sogc.org/media/guidelines-hpv-commentary_e.asp

Stall, R., & Mills, T.C. (2006). A quarter century of AIDS [Editorial]. *American Journal of Public Health, 96,* 959–61.

Recommended Viewing

France, D. (Director). (2012). *How to survive a plague* [Documentary]. United States: Public Square Films.

9 CHAPTER

Sexuality over the Lifespan

ELKE D. REISSING AND
HEATHER L. ARMSTRONG

LEARNING OBJECTIVES

In this chapter, you will

- gain insight into the various stages of sexual development an individual experiences over the lifespan;
- learn about the challenges and rewards associated with these stages; and
- discover the importance of maintaining a life-long positive attitude toward sexuality.

Life Stages

Two-year-old Melanie rubs her vulvar area against her mother's hip when her mother is carrying her. . . . Little Ari firmly believes that he will never marry, and he absolutely does not want to play with girls. . . . Jade is very excited about her new feelings about her body and emerging feelings for boys while trying to manage her parents' messages about sin and duty. . . . Yasmine feels confused between the way her body looks and the way she feels inside, which is more like a boy than a girl. . . . Pierre is experiencing difficulties with his erection and feels that he is alone because he believes that other young men don't have these issues. . . . Olivia would like to pursue a sexual relationship with no commitment but feels that others would judge her. . . . Daniel feels that he is moving from being in love to a deeply committed feeling that his partner is "the one," and he is considering marrying him. . . . Morris and Denise are finding it difficult to make time for their relationship because they have young children, tight work schedules, and other obligations. . . . Diane is amazed at how exciting her sex life has become at the age of 68 after falling in love with Martin, with whom she is planning a weekend away to learn about tantric sex. . . .

Every stage in a person's life brings new challenges and rewards with respect to sexuality. At times, these changes can be confusing. Knowing what to expect can help people overcome this confusion and successfully navigate new territories in their life-long journey of sexual development.

QUESTIONS FOR CRITICAL THOUGHT AND REFLECTION

1. How do you think your ideas about your body and sexuality will evolve over the next five years? What about over the next ten years?
2. Does it surprise you to know that individuals are sexual from the time they are born to the time they die?

Introduction

Just as our bodies, emotions, and perceptions continuously change throughout our lives, so does our sexuality develop as we grow and age. Certainly, there are times, such as puberty, when changes in our sexuality are very prominent, but sexuality influences our lives in many other, more subtle ways.

On a purely biological level, sex and sexuality are vital to the survival of our species, so almost all people are equipped at birth with the biological tools they will need to reproduce later in life. Other aspects of sexuality are associated with developmental and experiential learning and are influenced by one's culture and society. Differences in how human beings express their sexuality can be noted, but many similarities can also be observed. For the most part, this chapter focusses on sexual development and milestones that are similar for all people.

Understanding that sexuality is present at all stages of life and how it changes over time can help people prepare for and respond to sexual situations. Adolescence, for example, is a critical and often confusing time in a person's sexual life, but some of the confusion or even distress can be minimized if a young person knows what to expect. Likewise, some parents may be shocked when their infant displays "sexual" behaviours such as touching her or his genitals, but they may be comforted if they understand that such behaviours are a normal part of child development. Further, we can overcome the misconception that sexuality diminishes and sexual desire disappears as we age if we are aware that many people continue to be sexually active and satisfied well into their later years.

How people choose to behave sexually can have consequences on sexual function and reproductive health. With sexual development across the lifespan comes sexual responsibility to oneself and one's partner. It is important to recognize one's personal likes and dislikes, and it is also important to learn how to communicate those needs to one's partner. This facilitates moving through different life stages successfully, and meeting the changes, challenges, and rewards associated with sexuality.

Sexuality in Infancy and Early Childhood

Sexual development starts while the fetus is growing in the womb (Figure 9.1; see Chapter 6). Erections have been noted in male fetuses (Shirozu et al., 1995), and male infants may experience reflexive erections beginning shortly after birth (Meijer & Bakker, 2003). Signs of physiological arousal in female infants, such as vaginal lubrication, are harder to detect but have also been reported (De Lamater & Friedrich, 2002). Infants are able to derive physical pleasure from tactile contact with their caregivers and from sucking (e.g., breastfeeding, or sucking on pacifiers, hands, and toys), which is pleasurable because of the heightened sensitivity of the mouth. They are also able to derive physical pleasure from self-stimulation, and it is common for infants to rub their genitals against something such as a blanket or a toy; this may occur in infants as young as two months old (Kinsey, Pomeroy, & Martin, 1948; Narchi, 2003).

Young children often begin to masturbate as their manual dexterity improves, typically around the age of two or three. Around this time, naturally curious toddlers and preschoolers quickly learn that they are able to reduce tension and derive physical pleasure from manual self-stimulation (Martinson, 1994). While Kinsey and his colleagues (1948, 1953) reported that self-stimulation to orgasm is possible in children as young as four to five months, it is rare until the child becomes older. Such "sexual" behaviours as self-stimulation in young children are motivated by curiosity and exploration, rather than sexual desire, as young children do not yet have the cognitive perception of sexuality that they will develop as they grow up. Thus, early experiences that an adult might understand to be sexual, such as self-stimulating in public, may be strange or confusing but sexually neutral to a child.

All infants seek love and physical contact from their caregivers, and fulfilment or neglect of this need can shape future development and expectations (Figure 9.2). For example, if an infant cries and is promptly cradled and soothed by her mother, that child will likely learn to expect this reaction whenever she is distressed (Ainsworth, 1973). This expectation can shape her sexual development, as she may grow up expecting that her sexual and romantic partners will also respond in a loving and supportive way when she is distressed. There is even some evidence to suggest that an infant's survival depends on receiving this close physical contact. In the 1940s, it was noticed that infants in orphanages who were not receiving physical contact from their caregivers had higher than usual mortality rates, even though they were given adequate physical and medical care (Spitz, 1945, 1946). Children who receive some physical contact but are not given the opportunity to feel safely attached to an adult may develop difficulties relating to others, a problem often diagnosed in children as an attachment disorder.

Between the ages of one and two, a child begins to notice that there are physical differences between males and females (Schuhrke, 2001). As this curiosity develops, and as the child becomes older, he or she may begin to compare his or her genitals to those of siblings or parents. Children may also begin to engage in genital play, kissing, and other physical displays of affection with their friends and playmates. Games like "playing doctor" in which

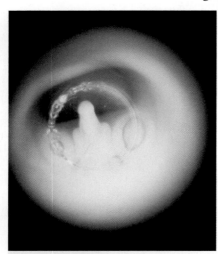

FIGURE 9.1 It's too soon to tell. In the ninth week of gestation, all human fetuses have the same genital organ, known as the indifferent phallus (as seen in this endoscopic image). It's not until around 12 weeks that this organ develops into either a penis or a clitoris.

children explore their bodies are common between the ages of two and five (Figure 9.3; Sandnabba, Santtila, Wannäs, & Krook, 2003), with almost half of children engaging in these types of games by age six (Okami, Olmstead, & Abramson, 1997). This type of playing is generally done in an attempt to understand and explore physical similarities and differences as well as gender roles, and it is not sexually motivated. Sex play may occur with same-sex or opposite-sex friends and is not indicative of sexual orientation.

Parents' reactions to their child's sexual behaviour can have significant consequences. In particular, parents' negative reactions to behaviours such as masturbation and group sex play may be detrimental to the child's developing sexuality. Such reactions can lead children to feel shameful and guilty about their sexuality, and they may affect children's future emotional and sexual adjustment (Leung & Robson, 1993). Therefore, rather than punishing a child for her or his behaviour and thus conveying the message that all sexuality deserves to be punished, it may be preferable for parents to try to teach their children appropriate ways to express their sexuality.

Sexuality Education during Childhood

When we think about "sex education," we usually think of teaching adolescents and young adults about contraception and safer sex. However, sex education is something that can and does happen at any point in our lives, beginning in early childhood. Sex education happens when a 3-year-old rubs her vulva on the sofa, or a 6-year-old asks how a baby got into the belly of a woman, or a 12-year-old experiences his first nocturnal emission. When thinking about how to discuss sexuality with children, many adults are very nervous. Do children need to be informed about their sexuality at a young age? How much should they be told? When is it appropriate to talk about what?

Thankfully, some excellent books have been published to help parents raise their children to be sexually healthy. One outstanding resource is Debra Haffner's *From Diapers to Dating: A Parent's Guide to Raising Sexually Healthy Children from Infancy to Middle School* (2008). Haffner, a sex educator and reverend, believes that sexually healthy children feel good about their bodies, are respectful of others, understand the concept of privacy, make age-appropriate decisions, feel comfortable asking their parents questions about sexuality, and are prepared for the changes of puberty. In order to help their children get to this point, parents need to make sexuality education as important as education about family responsibilities, family values, and self-esteem, and they need to be seen by their children as "askable." "Askable parents" welcome opportunities to talk to their children about sexuality, rather than waiting for questions. The key to this is taking advantage of what Haffner calls "teachable moments" or "golden opportunities." An example of such a moment may be when a parent notices that

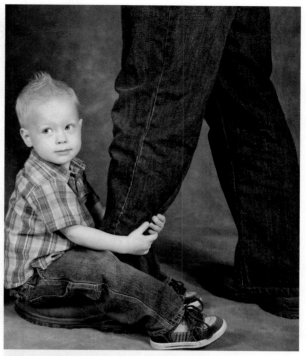

FIGURE 9.2 Where are you going?! Children who are overly clingy to their parents may be showing signs of insecure attachment, which can affect their sexual relationships as adults.

FIGURE 9.3 Children's curiosity about their own and other children's bodies is normal, and games like "playing doctor" are common between the ages of two and five. Parents need to be prepared for this type of behaviour and avoid reacting negatively, as a parent's reaction can shape a child's developing sexuality.

FIGURE 9.4 Whose turn is it? Adolescents, like children, find various socially acceptable ways to express their developing sexual interests.

his or her child has observed a same-sex couple kissing. The child might not comment or question what she or he saw, but the parent can seize the opportunity to introduce to the child that there are different kinds of couples and families, and that some people fall in love with people of the same sex. Similarly, catching their preschooler engaged in "playing doctor" with a friend can be an opportunity for parents to discuss with their child the differences between male and female bodies.

Honest, ongoing communication is key when teaching young children about sexuality. Encouraging curiosity and offering knowledgeable answers and advice in response to questions can help a child develop positive feelings about his or her own sexuality. In addition, research has demonstrated that children who know a lot about sexuality are more likely to make informed and responsible sexual choices as they get older.

Sexuality in Preadolescence

Preadolescence, which generally occurs between the ages of 8 and 12, is the developmental stage that Freud referred to as the "latency period" (see Chapter 2), suggesting that children's interest in sex and sexuality decreases during this stage. While this may be true for some preadolescents, more recent research and observations suggest that children's interest in sex typically increases during this stage, particularly around the age of 10 (Herdt & McClintock, 2000). Masturbation is the primary form of sexual expression among preadolescents, with males being more likely than females to masturbate frequently and to experience orgasm (Schwartz, 1999). In those children who show a decreased interest in their bodies and sex differences, it may be that parents' negative reactions to earlier open displays of body exploration taught them to hide when exploring their bodies. Socialization and an effort on the part of the child to adopt appropriate social norms may also result in less overt exploration activities (Friedrich, Grambsch, Broughton, Kuiper, & Beilke, 1991). Toward the end of the preadolescent period, as their interest in dating increases, many children begin to explore their emerging sexuality by playing socially acceptable sexualized games like "spin the bottle" (Figure 9.4).

In their friendships and everyday activities, preadolescent children tend to be mostly segregated by sex, and many face peer pressure to conform to social norms (De Gaston & Weed, 1996). For example, girls who previously enjoyed playing sports and other physically aggressive games may face pressure to act more feminine. Boys, on the other hand, may be teased and ridiculed by peers if they prefer quieter, more stereotypically "girl activities" like reading or playing a musical instrument. This peer pressure can help children learn social norms and how to act in a socially acceptable way toward same-sex (or same-gender) as well as other-sex (or other-gender) peers; however, it can also be isolating and damaging to a child's self-esteem if his or her sense of self is not

primary sex characteristics The main sex organs that are necessary for reproduction.

secondary sex characteristics Features not directly related to reproduction that develop at puberty.

menarche The first incidence of menstruation.

semenarche The first incidence of ejaculation.

congruent with the ideals of the peer group (Figure 9.5). For example, a boy who knows he is attracted to other boys may feel confused, ashamed, and even depressed or suicidal when he realizes that he does not fit in with the "heterosexual norms" presented by his peer group (see D'Augelli & Hershberger, 1993).

sexualization Making someone or something sexual.

Increasingly, preadolescents, especially young girls, also face problems associated with **sexualization** (Figure 9.6). Sexualization occurs when people are made to feel as though their value or worth is inextricably linked to their sexual appeal, when they equate their physical attractiveness to being sexy, when they are sexually objectified, and when sexuality is inappropriately imposed upon them (Zurbriggen et al., 2007). Evidence for the sexualization of preadolescent girls can be found in the media (television, movies, music, magazines, the Internet, etc.) as well as in consumer products marketed toward girls under 10 (e.g., Bratz dolls, thong underwear; Zurbriggen et al., 2007). Parents, teachers, and peers can also convey the message that physical attractiveness and sexuality are highly valued in young girls, and the results of this sexualization can be harmful. Self-objectification has been association with anxiety about appearance and feelings of shame in 12- and 13-year-old girls (Slater & Tiggemann, 2002). Sexualization of girls has also been linked to eating disorders, low self-esteem, and depression (Zurbriggen et al., 2007). Additionally, girls who are exposed to sexualized media are more likely to endorse sexual stereotypes of women as sexual objects, and they are more likely to place high value on appearance and physical attractiveness (Zurbriggen et al., 2007).

FIGURE 9.5 A preadolescent child who does not conform to the gender norms of his or her peers may be ostracized by the group, an experience that can be very painful and may affect how the child feels about his or her own sexuality.

Sexuality in Adolescence

Adolescence is marked by many considerable physical, cognitive, and emotional changes that contribute to an individual's sexual development. During puberty, the **primary sex characteristics** change, and **secondary sex characteristics** develop as a result of hormonal changes (see chapters 4 and 5). In females, the most salient biological change is **menarche**, although girls also begin to develop secondary sex characteristics—including pubic and axillary hair, breasts, and wider hips—several years before they begin to menstruate. In males, the testes, scrotum, and penis all increase in size; facial, body, and pubic hair begins to appear; and the larynx enlarges, causing the voice to deepen. Males also experience their first ejaculation (sometimes referred to as **semenarche**), an increase in the frequency of their erections (both related and unrelated to sexual thoughts), increased masturbation, increased sexual dreaming, and nocturnal emissions.

FIGURE 9.6 Young girls are often sexualized in Western cultures, giving them little time to be carefree children. What do girls learn about themselves by imitating adult women?

Puberty tends to begin earlier for girls than it does for boys—usually around the age of 10 or 11 for girls and 12 or 13 for boys. There is some evidence to suggest that puberty may actually be starting earlier now compared to 10 or 20 years ago because of increases in childhood obesity; it is not uncommon for girls as young as 7 to begin to develop breasts (Biro et al., 2010). Typically, puberty lasts about three to four years, with male puberty lasting a bit longer on average. During this period, teenagers may start to develop close intimate relationships with romantic partners and may even fall in love for the first time (Figure 9.7). Not surprisingly, the events that occur during this time, and the feedback that adolescents received from peers, parents, and partners, can have significant and life-long effects.

Sexual Activity during Adolescence

During adolescence, the primary sexual expression is masturbation for both males and females. However, as adolescence progresses, more and more partnered sexual activities begin to occur. Dating often begins during this time, and dating may in turn lead to exploration of sexual behaviours. Typically, sexual exploration between boys and girls follows the heterosexual sexual script, which involves kissing, followed by genital touching, oral sex, and finally sexual intercourse. Given that this script is based on heterosexual norms, LGBTTIQQ teens may find that they do not have a common script to follow, and they may be left struggling to figure out how to even find a date, and then what to do when on a date (see below).

The first experience of sexual intercourse is arguably one of the most significant events that may occur during adolescence. A Canadian study confirmed the importance of this event by showing that the emotional reaction to first intercourse is related to later adult sexual adjustment (Reissing, Andruff, & Wentland, 2010). Generally speaking, in Canada, the average age at first intercourse is 17 for both males and females. The experience is more likely to be positive if the person is in a relationship with his or her partner and is not under the influence of drugs or alcohol. It can also affect males and females differently, as there is a widely held **sexual double standard** between the sexes. For males, first intercourse is often seen as a rite of passage toward becoming a "real man"; for females, it is often seen as "losing" one's virginity or somehow becoming less pure (e.g., Carpenter, 2002). The Canadian Youth, Sexual Health, and HIV/AIDS Study found that Canadian youth have a variety of reasons for having or not having sex for the first time (Table 9.1; Boyce et al., 2006).

Once adolescents begin engaging in sexual intercourse, they run the risk of experiencing an unplanned pregnancy (Figure 9.8). Research examining teen pregnancy in five countries, including Canada, determined that ineffective and inconsistent use of contraception was the greatest predictor of teen pregnancy (Darroch, Singh, Frost, & Study Team, 2001). Teens who become pregnant and choose to have and raise their babies often face numerous health and social outcomes. Babies born to teenage

sexual double standard A set of culturally maintained standards for sexual behaviour reflecting more permissive and less restricted sexual expression by men than by women.

FIGURE 9.7 They're playing our song! High school is often the time when people have their first romantic (and often sexual) relationships. This period of growth and development will inform future adult relationships.

TABLE 9.1 Teens' reasons for having first sexual intercourse or not having had sex.

| | REASONS FOR HAVING FIRST SEXUAL INTERCOURSE (%) | | | |
| | Grade 9 | | Grade 11 | |
	Males	Females	Males	Females
Love for the Person	32	49	39	60
Curiosity/Experimentation	23	12	21	14
Influence of Alcohol/Drugs	10	9	9	6
Got Carried Away	8	14	11	7
To Lose Virginity	12	4	9	3
To Have a Relationship	5	5	5	1.7
Loneliness	0.9	0	0.4	0.5
Other	9	6	5	8

| | REASONS FOR NOT HAVING HAD INTERCOURSE (%) | | | |
| | Grade 9 | | Grade 11 | |
	Males	Females	Males	Females
Not Ready	29	40	12	30
Not Had Opportunity	32	11	42	11
Haven't Met Right Person	23	20	27	29
Want to Be a Virgin at Marriage	5	11	3	13
Fear of Pregnancy	2.7	6	2.7	6
Religious Beliefs	2.9	4	6	6
Parent's Disapproval	1	1.7	0.6	1.3
Friend's Disapproval	0.1	0.5	0.7	—
Fear of HIV/AIDS	1.7	1.0	1.0	1.9
Fear of Other STIs	0.2	0.3	0.2	—
Other	2.9	4	4.0	2.5

Source: Adapted from Boyce et al. (2006).

mothers are more likely to be underweight, which can lead to mental and physical problems as well as death in the infant (Chen et al., 2007). Additionally, Canadian research has found that being a teen mother is correlated with low socioeconomic status (Bissell, 2000; see also Chapter 7). Fortunately, teen pregnancy rates are decreasing in Canada, likely because of more effective contraceptive use, greater access to reproductive health care, better sex education, and shifting social norms that provide more support for young women (McKay & Barrett, 2010). Yet many Canadian teens continue to experience unplanned pregnancies, suggesting that there is a continuing need for improvements to sex education and access to reproductive health care, including contraception.

With the beginning of partnered sexual activity, the risk of acquiring a sexually transmitted infection (STI) also increases (see Chapter 8). In Canada, STI rates in teenagers, specifically chlamydia rates, have increased in recent years (SIECCAN, 2004). This increase may be due in part to the fact that teens are becoming increasingly likely to have a series of monogamous sexual relationships; it may also result from the fact that consistent condom use tends to *decrease* among sexually active young people from

FIGURE 9.8 Teens who engage in sexual intercourse risk becoming pregnant, especially if they are not fully aware of their contraceptive options.

rainbow parties Oral sex parties at which girls wear different colours of lipstick and leave rings of colour around the penises of the boys on whom they perform oral sex.

Grade 9 to Grade 12 (SIECCAN, 2004). When asked why they had not used a condom during their last sexual intercourse, teens in Grade 11 often said that they had used a non-barrier contraceptive method (such as the pill) or that they had a "faithful partner" (SIECCAN, 2004). This finding suggests that teens are more likely to be worried about preventing pregnancy than they are about protecting themselves against STIs.

Many teens engage in oral sex as an alternative to penile-vaginal intercourse. Indeed, data from an American study confirm that oral sex is more prevalent than vaginal sex in teenagers aged 15 to 19, with just over half of the participants reporting that they had engaged in oral sex (Lindberg, Jones, & Santelli, 2008). Research has shown that many teens believe that oral sex is less risky, more prevalent, and more acceptable than penile-vaginal intercourse; what most do not realize, however, is that many STIs can be transmitted through oral-genital contact (Halpern-Felsher, Cornell, Kropp, & Tschann, 2005; see also Chapter 8). Because of this, many teens participate in oral sex without the use of condoms or dental dams. Girls in particular may choose to engage in oral sex as a way to relieve pressure to be sexually active before they are ready to have penile-vaginal sex, as they may view oral sex as a less intimate behaviour that is still sexually satisfying. Research by Canadian journalist Sharlene Azam confirms the prevalence of this attitude in her book and documentary film *Oral Sex Is the New Goodnight Kiss* (2009). Azam even describes oral-sex parties, often referred to among teens as **rainbow parties**, where teens get together in groups to engage in unprotected oral sex with one another. It is clear that misperceptions and false beliefs about oral sex are common among adolescents, and there is a definite need for sex education that provides reliable information and emphasizes the physical and emotional health outcomes associated with oral sex.

Sexuality among LGBTTIQQ Adolescents

Adolescence is a time when many LGBTTIQQ youths start to organize and process the implications of their same-sex attractions. Even teens who have been aware of their same-sex attraction since childhood may experience confusion about how their sexual orientation fits (or does not fit) into the social norms of their peer group. Dating can be very difficult for LGBTTIQQ teenagers because of lack of opportunity and presence of social disapproval. In addition to having same-sex partners, many gay and lesbian teens also have sexual relationships with opposite-sex partners (Table 9.2; Saewyc et al., 2007). For some, sexual experimentation with opposite-sex partners is a way of exploring their sexuality; for others, it is an attempt to mask their sexual orientation in order to fit in with their peers.

Unfortunately, bullying of LGBTTIQQ youth is extremely pervasive across Canada (Mishna, Newman, Daley, & Solomon, 2009; Saewyc et al., 2007). This bullying can take place just about anywhere, from schools to malls to cyberspace, and it can be perpetrated by just about anyone—peers, teachers, even parents (Mishna et al., 2009). Victims of bullying often suffer from low self-esteem, anxiety, depression, low academic performance, and ostracism (Mishna et al., 2009; Saewyc et al., 2007); in some

TABLE 9.2 Gender of teens' sexual partners in the past year.

	MALES		
	Opposite Gender (%)	**Both Genders (%)**	**Same Gender (%)**
Heterosexual	99	1	<1
Mostly Heterosexual	94	5	1
Bisexual	55	32	14
Gay	26	19	55
	FEMALES		
	Opposite Gender (%)	**Both Genders (%)**	**Same Gender (%)**
Heterosexual	99	1	<1
Mostly Heterosexual	91	9	0
Bisexual	62	33	5
Lesbian	15	56	29

Source: Adapted from Saewyc et al., 2007.

cases, bullying can also lead to substance abuse and suicide. While bullying may involve physical acts of violence, it more commonly takes the form of verbal abuse. Many teens and even adults also unthinkingly participate in bullying by using anti-LGBTTIQQ language—for example, by saying "that's so gay" when they mean "that's so stupid." Such language may seem harmless to some, but it can have a significant impact on LGBTTIQQ youth. In recent years, anti-bullying campaigns such as "Think before You Speak" (www.thinkb4youspeak.com) have been launched in Canada and many other Western nations to help raise awareness of and eliminate all forms of bullying, and there is hope that these sorts of educative efforts will have a positive impact on the social experiences of LGBTTIQQ youth.

Sexuality in Adulthood

As people go through their adult lives, they will likely experience a variety of different lifestyles that will influence how they experience sexuality. Most people will be single at some point; many will experience **cohabitation** with a partner. Most adults go on to marry at least once in their lives, and of these some will experience infidelity and divorce. These life stages provide different experiences and opportunities for further sexual growth and development.

cohabitation People involved in a romantic and/or sexual relationship living together without being married.

Different people will also experience different levels of interest in sex, whatever their relationship status. Further, despite common stereotypes, not all men are more interested than women in having sex or in having sex with many different partners. While some men desire a lot of sex, others prefer less frequent sexual encounters. Some prefer to have sex only within a monogamous relationship, others want to experience sex with a variety of partners. Women's interests in sex and preferences for certain types of sexual partnerships are similarly varied. Some women do tend to be less interested than most men in having sex and/or in having sex with multiple partners, and various theories have suggested that there may be physiological, behavioural, social, evolutionary, and other reasons for such differences between men and women (see Chapter 2). Yet other women defy the social expectation that women will be less sexual than men;

these women tend to be highly sexually assertive and confident, and they appear to have rejected the traditional sexual script often followed by less sexually assertive woman (Wentland, Herold, Desmarais, & Milhausen, 2009).

As adults gain experience with different types of relationships, most will come to understand that sex can be more than just a physical sensation; it is often a sensual and emotional experience that creates intimacy between partners. Most will also come to understand that sexual attraction can be very complex, and that an intelligent mind and a good sense of humour can be just as attractive—if not more so—than a "sexy" body. Experience also gives individuals the opportunity to identify what they most enjoy about sex and practise communicating their sexual needs and desires to their partner(s). This sort of communication is essential in all sexual relationships, and it can help to correct common misconceptions related to sex and sexuality, such as those about sexuality and disability (see the "Ethical Debate" box).

Being Single

Many adults are single at various times in their lives. Some people choose to remain single for their whole lives, while others choose to be single for only a portion, perhaps while they focus on other aspects of their lives, such as their careers. Still others would rather be in a relationship but are single because they have not yet found the right partner. While single, a person may express his or her sexuality in a variety of different ways at different times. Some people choose to engage in casual sex; others practise celibacy. One of the most common and accepted strategies is serial monogamy, which involves having a series of exclusive, intimate relationships, one following immediately or closely after the termination of another.

Casual sexual encounters appear to be increasingly common among single men and women, especially among younger adults (Wentland & Reissing, 2011). Canadian researchers Jocelyn Wentland and Elke Reissing (2011) examined different types of casual sexual relationships and identified four distinct categories: one-night stands, booty calls, fuck buddies, and friends with benefits. Both male and female participants in Wentland and Reissing's study agreed that these types of relationships are distinctly different from one another in terms of such factors as frequency of contact, type of contact (sexual and/or social), personal disclosure, discussion of the relationship, and friendship; they also agreed that these differences are governed by specific, tacitly agreed-upon rules of engagement (see the "Research vs Real Life" box in Chapter 2 for more details about this study). Casual sex increasingly appears to be an accepted rather than secret form of sexual interaction and can provide sexual release for those not in a more committed relationship; it may also serve as a "test drive" for compatibility with a potential partner.

Dating

Single people who wish to be to be in a more long-term committed relationship will often go through a period of dating in which they meet and spend time with a variety of people to determine if any might be suitable partners. While sex is often an important component of dating relationships, some couples wait for a while after they start dating before having sex, and others choose to wait until marriage. Further, while it is fairly common and acceptable in Canada for couples who are dating to have sex, sex before marriage is less common in many other countries (see the "Culture and Diversity" box).

Dating has changed significantly since the introduction of online communication technologies. Online dating sites allow people access to numerous potential mates that

Ethical Debate

Sexuality and Disability

Sexuality is universal among all people, from the very young to the very old. Unfortunately, some people hold very negative views about sex and disability. Some are prejudiced against those with physical or cognitive disabilities and would never consider forming a sexual relationship with them. Others mistakenly believe that people with disabilities are less sexual than people without disabilities. Such views may lead to discrimination, intentional or not; for example, parents of an adult with a disability who lives in their home might not allow their adult child to have private time for sexual activities with a partner or even by him or herself. Additionally, some people with disabilities may have internalized negativity about their bodies and may feel as though they are "unsexy" or not allowed to be sexual. In all of these cases, some education about sexuality could go a long way to overcoming prejudice and discrimination.

For most people with disabilities and their partners, sex is much like sex between two people without disabilities; it may simply require some additional communication and creativity, things that most sexual couples—regardless of their abilities—could benefit from (Figure 9.9)! Yet in some cases that involve people who live with severe disabilities, the matter may be much more complex and may even pose some ethical dilemmas, not only for the person with the disability but also for her or his partner(s) and/or the people who love and care for that person. For example, what is the role of the caretakers when a couple with severe disabilities wishes to conceive a child, and at what point, if any, can one decide that the couple is "too disabled" to take care of a child? If the couple does not wish to conceive but are not able to effectively and/or consistently use contraceptives on their own, does the caretaker have a duty to assist with birth control? If so, how far does this duty extend? Similarly, how

FIGURE 9.9 Good sex is creative sex! People with physical disabilities may have to be more creative when having sex, but this can actually lead to more sexual enjoyment and satisfaction.

far does the caretaker's role extend in ensuring that the couple uses condoms or dental dams to protect against STIs? Does the caretaker have a right to deny assistance if he or she feels uncomfortable doing so? Further, in cases involving an individual or individuals with cognitive disabilities, who decides when the disabilities are too severe to assume consent to participate in sexual relationships?

would have seemed impossible even 20 years ago. In addition, email and social networking sites have changed the way people meet and maintain relationships. Social networking sites such as Facebook offer many benefits—they allow for increased social connection, and they can help couples in long-distance relationships stay in close contact (see the "Research vs Real Life" box). Yet they also present potential dangers. Canadian researcher Amy Muise and colleagues (2009) have found, for example, that

Culture & Diversity

Attitudes toward Premarital Sex across Different Cultures

Attitudes toward virginity and premarital sex vary across cultures (Figure 9.10). In India, for example, sex before marriage is widely disapproved of, and the vast majority of people do not have premarital intercourse (Santhya, Acharya, Jejeebhoy, & Ram, 2011). In a large study with over 45,000 participants aged 15 to 29, only 5 per cent of women and 11 per cent of men reported having had premarital intercourse before the age of 20. By age 25, the percentages had increased to 10 per cent of women and 30 per cent of men. Those who had less education, who lived in rural areas, and who had started working before age 15 were more likely to have had sex before marriage. Use of drugs and alcohol was also associated with premarital sex, as was watching television and movies, having peers as confidantes, and having peers who engaged in premarital sex. Parental influences such as lack of support, disapproval of the relationship, and the presence of violence in the family home were also contributing factors.

In Ethiopia as well, most people place a high value on maintaining virginity until marriage, especially for women (Molla, Berhane, & Lindtjorn, 2008). In a large study of over 3700 Ethiopian youth aged 15 to 24, only 3 per cent reported having participated in premarital sex. Additionally, almost all participants

(97 per cent of males and 95 per cent of females) reported that they intended to marry someone who was a virgin. Those who had participated in premarital sex were more likely to have less traditional values, be older, use alcohol, and be more educated.

In comparison to the cultures of India and Ethiopia, Canadian culture is more permissive of premarital sex, especially when it occurs within a loving and committed relationship. Researchers at the University of British Columbia surveyed 299 European-Canadian university students and found that 57 per cent had had premarital sex (Woo & Brotto, 2008). They also surveyed 329 Asian-Canadian students (primarily of Chinese descent) and found that far fewer—only 40 per cent—had experienced premarital sex. Further, the researchers found that Asian-Canadian students who were more acculturated to Western culture and reported less affiliation with their traditional culture fared better sexually; they reported less sexual dysfunction, more sexual communication, less avoidance, and more sensuality. The researchers suggested that young people who identify more strongly with Western culture may seek more sexual experiences and, as a result, have more opportunity to increase their sexual knowledge and comfort.

FIGURE 9.10 Different cultures have different ideas about dating, marriage, and the roles of husband and wife. In India and Ethiopia, for example, most young couples do not participate in premarital sex.

people who spend more time on Facebook also report more jealousy-related feelings and behaviours (see Chapter 12). It seems as though the open and ambiguous nature of Facebook leads to increased levels of jealousy among romantic partners, since comments posted on profile pages may be taken out of context, and people may continue to be "Facebook friends" with past romantic partners. Therefore, while online communication technologies can benefit the creation and maintenance of personal relationships, they must be used with care.

Living Together

In Canada today, compared to in the past, more people are living together without being married (Le Bourdais & Lapierre-Adamcyk, 2004). In some cases, cohabitation may be a step toward getting married, and many couples who live together eventually marry. In other cases, couples may choose to live together with no plans to ever marry, and some of these couples may eventually decide to define their arrangement as a common-law relationship. People living in common-law relationships are entitled to many, but not all, of the same legal rights as married individuals, such as access to shared health care benefits and pension earnings. One potential problem with common-law marriage is that property acquired during the course of the relationship is not automatically shared, and in the circumstance of separation, financial protection for the lower income earner is not guaranteed by law.

There are advantages and disadvantages to living together before marriage. Cohabiting can give a couple a chance to get to know each other better without making a legal or financial commitment to each other, which may allow them to make a more informed decision about whether or not they want to marry. Another advantage is that cohabiting people between the ages of 25 and 29 have a higher frequency of sex than either dating or married people have (Herbenick et al., 2010). On the other hand, couples who live together may experience conflict if their visions of the future divert, particularly if one would like to marry but the other would not. Canadians who do get married after cohabiting are 50 per cent more likely to get divorced than those who marry without having first cohabited (Clark & Crompton, 2006). There may be many reasons for this higher divorce rate among couples who cohabited before marriage—for example, such couples may hold less traditional views of marriage, or they may simply view all relationships, even those formally recognized under the law, as temporary (see Smock, 2000; Milan, 2003).

Getting Married

Among Canadians who decide to marry, there is a general trend to enter into a first marriage later than was the case in previous generations. For example, the average age at first marriage was 29.1 years for women and 31.1 years for men in 2008; by comparison, the average age at first marriage in 1972 was 22.5 years for women and 24.9 years for men (Statistics Canada, 2013). This trend can be explained by several things. For one, more people are attending post-secondary education and incurring great debt in the process; as a result, more people are choosing to live at home longer and delay getting married until they are financially stable. In addition, as suggested above, more people are living together first before getting married. Further, women are less financially dependent on men than they were in the past and, as such, are able to be more selective when choosing a mate. Finally, it is much more acceptable today than in the past for women to delay childbearing until their thirties or to have children without being married, so women today likely feel less pressure to get married and start a family at a young age.

Research VS Real Life

Long-Distance Relationships Are Doomed . . . Right?
Contributed by Emma Dargie, M.Sc., Department of Psychology, Queen's University

Everyone knows that being in a long-distance dating relationship (LDDR) is difficult. Jealousy and loneliness are common, and people in LDDRs are known to grow apart from and fight with their partners. Friends of a person starting an LDDR typically respond with sympathy, support, and sometimes even pity. If these relationships are so tough, is it better to just break up rather than spend the foreseeable future in misery? Public opinion suggests that this may be the case, but research indicates that there is more to this story to consider.

Many studies show that individuals in LDDRs report comparable or greater relationship quality than individuals in geographically close relationships (GCRs). In addition, researchers have found that couples in LDDRs are less likely to break up than couples in GCRs (Stephen, 1986). Individuals in LDDRs also report being more in love and are just as satisfied, or more so, with their relationship and their

ability to communicate (Stafford & Reske, 1990). Finally, being in an LDDR is not related to a decrease in feelings of intimacy (Dellmann-Jenkins, Bernard-Paolucci, & Rushing, 1994; Guldner & Swensen, 1995). However, other researchers have found that those in LDDRs report lower relationship quality, even if they are not more likely to break up with their partner (van Horn et al., 1997). Further, those in LDDRs may not have realistic opinions about their partner, focussing more on the positive aspects and ignoring the negative, which may lead to future instability (Stafford & Reske, 1990). While reports are conflicting, they seem to indicate that there may be certain characteristics of LDDRs not found in GCRs, which are more associated with relationship problems.

Two explanations for the problems faced by couples in LDDRs that have been investigated are the physical distance between partners and how much time partners get to spend with each other

---

Sexual frequency during marriage varies, although most married people report being sexually satisfied, particularly if they tend to want sex at the same rate as their partner (Smith et al., 2011). Studies have suggested that more than half of all married adults aged 18 to 24 have intercourse at least two to three times per week; among older adults, roughly half have intercourse at least a few times per month (Herbenick et al., 2010; Reece et al., 2010). Sexual frequency tends to be the highest at the beginning of the marriage, decrease when children are born, and then increase again once children are grown and have left the house. Pressures from a variety of sources such as work, family, and financial stress may also lead to a decrease in the frequency of sex within a marriage. In addition, sexual frequency may decrease due to habituation, when one or both partners become used to the other and the relationship, or even become bored with the routine of the relationship (Call, Sprecher, & Schwartz, 1995).

Sexual satisfaction is associated with marital satisfaction in that couples who report being happy with their sex lives are also more likely to report being happy in their marriages (Young, Denny, Luquis, & Young, 1998). However, it is difficult to determine which causes which. Sexual satisfaction may enhance a couple's desire to spend time with each other doing non-sexual activities; conversely, enjoyment of shared non-sexual activities may enhance a couple's sense of sexual satisfaction. In marriages in which no sex is occurring, couples are more likely to be dissatisfied and eventually separate (Donnelly, 1993). However, it is impossible to know if the marital dissatisfaction leads to a decrease in sexual activity, or if a lack of sex in the marriage causes the partners to become unsatisfied.

Marital satisfaction follows a trend similar to that of sexual frequency: it peaks during the first few years of marriage, then declines until mid-life, and then starts to rise

in person, face-to-face. Dainton and Aylor (2001) found that individuals in LDDRs with little-to-no face-to-face contact with their partners reported significantly lower levels of trust than individuals in GCRs or individuals in LDDRs with some face-to-face contact. Similarly, Holt and Stone (1988) found that couples who were farther apart for longer periods of time reported lower levels of relationship satisfaction than those who were closer and had more face-to-face contact. However, van Horn et al. (1997) found that satisfaction did not vary based on the frequency of visits. These conflicting findings suggest that distance and frequency of visits alone do not predict relationship success.

Attitudes, perceptions, and individual factors may all play a key role in the success of LDDRs. One study has shown that when people perceive the future of their LDDR as positive, they are likely to report more satisfaction with and less distress about their relationship (Maguire, 2007). In another study (Sprecher, 1999), couples in GCRs completed subjective and objective measures of love over time. The researcher found that at each time point assessed, individuals subjectively reported being more in love than the last time they completed the questionnaires. The objective measures, however, showed that their level of love actually remained the same (Sprecher, 1999). Although this concept has not been explicitly explored with those in LDDRs, this study demonstrates the powerful role of perception in relationships. Finally, individual factors such as anxiety, attachment, and relationship style impact how a person acts in his or her relationship, whether in an LDDR or a GCR, thus impacting the success of the relationship (Pistole, Roberts, & Chapman, 2010).

At the end of the day, being in an LDDR does not doom a person's relationship. Even though a couple may be geographically far apart and get to see each other only infrequently, it is still possible for their relationship to succeed, especially when they maintain a positive attitude. Thus, the perception that LDDRs are not worth the effort it takes to make them work may be widely held, but it is not supported by the research.

again. For both men and women, the quality of the friendship between spouses is the most important factor for marital satisfaction (Gottman & Silver, 1999). According to the interpersonal exchange model of sexual satisfaction (Lawrance & Byers, 1995; see Figure 14.8), marriages are also happy when the rewards outweigh the costs of the relationship, when the expectations of the rewards and costs in the relationships are being met, and when there is perceived equality between the rewards and costs for each partner. Rewards can be things like spending quality time together, having a satisfying sexual relationship, and having shared interests. Costs can be things like arguments, feeling emotionally distant, or having financial difficulties. When the costs start to outweigh the rewards, people may end the relationship or start looking outside of the marriage for other rewards. Fortunately, most people who are married also report being happy and satisfied in their marriages (Spanier, 1976).

As discussed in Chapter 1, it has been legal for same-sex couples to marry in Canada since 2005 (Figure 9.11). A few years after this significant development, Canadian researchers Heather MacIntosh, Elke Reissing, and Heather Andruff (2010) interviewed 26 married same-sex couples to explore the impact that legal marriage had on their relationship. Participants reported higher-than-average levels of

FIGURE 9.11 The legalization of same-sex marriage in Canada has had a positive impact on the social and political landscape of the country.

relationship satisfaction and attachment security, as well as mainly positive social and political outcomes (e.g., greater understanding of their relationship by others, more legal rights). Given that this study was conducted with couples who had very recently been given the legal right to marry, it is perhaps not surprising that they reported overwhelmingly positive experiences. In the future, it will be interesting to see how same-sex and opposite-sex married couples who have grown up knowing that marriage could be an option for them compare in terms of sexual and relationship satisfaction.

Extradyadic Sex

Almost all couples, whether dating, cohabiting, or married, expect sexual exclusivity, and societal norms strongly dictate that cheating on one's partner is wrong. Yet approximately 22 to 25 per cent of men and 11 to 15 per cent of women report that they have had extramarital sex, and actual numbers are likely higher than reported given people's tendency to underreport this type of behaviour (Allen et al., 2005). People have **extramarital sex**, or **extradyadic sex**, for many reasons. Research has shown that individuals who engage in extradyadic sex tend to be male, more educated, and less religious than those who do not, and they tend to have more sexual interests, more permissive sexual values, more opportunity for sex outside of the relationship, and less satisfaction in their primary relationship (Allen et al., 2005). Relationship factors also play a role. For example, boredom, sexual dissatisfaction, a lack of support in the marriage, and conflict have all been associated with extramarital sex (Allen et al., 2005).

The effects of an extramarital affair vary. Some couples are able to discuss the issue and work through it together, while others decide to terminate the relationship. Women are more likely to be upset about emotional infidelity, whereas men are more likely to be upset about sexual infidelity (Buss, Larsen, Westen, & Semmelroth, 1992). There may be a sociobiological explanation for this difference. Remember, from Chapter 2, that sociobiologists believe that human behaviour and responses have evolved over time to promote the reproductive fitness of offspring and the survival of our species. Therefore, for a woman, an emotional affair may suggest that her partner is becoming attached to another woman and may, as a result, be dividing his resources among two women (and any potential offspring). For a man, a sexual affair may be more threatening because if a pregnancy were to result from the woman's extramarital affair, paternal certainty cannot be guaranteed (at least, this would have been the case traditionally, before the development of modern paternity tests). Thus, a man in this situation could spend his resources taking care of another man's child. For couples who decide to continue their relationship after an affair has occurred, the road may be difficult.

Extramarital or extradyadic sex may sometimes be permitted or even encouraged within a relationship. Some couples engage in consensual extradyadic sex together with other partners; this is often referred to as "swinging." Other couples have discussed and agreed to make their relationship non-monogamous, meaning that one or both partners can engage in sexual activity with other people; this is often referred to as having an "open relationship." Finally, some people practise polygamy, often for religious reasons, with polygyny being more common than polyandry (see Chapter 1). In order for any of these non-monogamous relationships to work successfully, all partners need to develop good communication and likely guidelines or rules to follow, so as to minimize any feelings of jealousy or stress that may result.

Divorce

Rates of divorce have stayed relatively stable in the last 10 to 15 years (Statistics Canada, 2009). Currently, more than one-third of Canadian marriages end in divorce (Clark &

---

extramarital sex Sex that occurs outside the context of a marriage.

extradyadic sex Sex that occurs outside the context of the primary relationship.

Crompton, 2006). There are several factors that make divorce more likely. Age may be a contributing factor, as Canadian couples who marry young may be more likely to divorce than couples who were older at the time of marriage (Clark & Crompton, 2006). In addition, religion can have a protective effect on a marriage, as Canadians who attend religious services during the year—even if only just a few—have been shown to be less likely to divorce than those who do not attend such services (Clark & Crampton, 2006). Finally, people who have been divorced before are more likely to divorce in subsequent marriages (Clark & Crompton, 2006).

After divorce, many people start to date again. However, this dating process can be frustrating given that the average age of divorce for Canadians is 43 for men and 40 for women (Statistics Canada, 2009), and dating norms may have changed since the divorced individual was last on the dating scene. In addition to figuring out a new or different dating scene, divorced Canadians will also need to consider birth control and protection from STIs, and many may not be fully aware of the increased risk of STIs associated with unprotected sexual activity (see Chapter 8).

Sexuality and Older Adults

People are living longer today than ever before. Many enter the second third of their lives healthy and vibrant, with a wide variety of interests and often more time to enjoy life. For the majority of older adults, an active sex life is an integral part of their lives (Figure 9.12). Much is made of the physical changes of aging affecting sexuality, but in fact relatively little is known about how older adults negotiate and perceive these changes. In addition, we often talk about older adults as a homogenous group; anyone over a certain age is "old." But in each age group—50s, 60s, 70s, 80s, and beyond—different challenges and opportunities present themselves. Consider that we would not talk about a 13-year-old in the same way we would talk about a 19-year-old; yet they are both teenagers and much closer in age than many people who are considered to be "older adults."

Overall, there is not a lot of research on sexuality in older adults. With the advent of Viagra and other vasoactive medications for erectile dysfunction, sexuality in later adulthood has received more attention; however, research attention tends to focus on the functional aspects of genital sexual responses. From the little existing research, we can gather that sexuality in older adults is a complex and multifactorial process. There are significant individual differences, and many factors other than the biological aspects of aging come into play to determine how older adults experience changes in their sexuality. One study that has investigated sexuality in older adults from a variety of perspectives is the Global Study of Sexual Attitudes and Behaviors (GSSAB), an international collaboration that surveyed over 27,000 adults between the ages of 40 and 80 from 29 different countries (Laumann et al., 2005). Researchers found that if they statistically controlled for factors such as physical and mental health, income, and education, aging in men was clearly associated with problems of erection, reaching orgasm, and sexual interest. In women, only a decrease in vaginal lubrication was clearly associated with aging. The researchers concluded that men experience more sexual problems associated

FIGURE 9.12 "My parents have sex??!!" Oh yes . . . and most will have sex until the end of their lives.

with the biological effects of aging. In Chapter 2, we learned that women's excitatory and inhibitory systems for sexuality depend on numerous aspects such as relationship quality and contextual factors (Graham, Sanders, & Milhausen, 2006). Hence for women, the impact of physical changes associated with aging may be attenuated by the availability of a loving partner and pleasant environmental circumstances (for example, no more kids in the home).

Physical Effects of Aging and Their Association with Changes in Sexuality

Generally speaking, quite a number of areas of functioning are affected by the biological aging process—for example, vision, hearing, muscle mass, bone density, immune system, and even brain size. However, decline is variable and depends on lifestyle factors such as nutrition, exercise, smoking, and alcohol or drug use (Skelton & Dinan-Young, 2008). How the overall physical effects of aging impact sexuality is largely unknown. More attention has been paid to hormonal changes in men and women and how these may relate to changes in sexual desire and response.

PHYSICAL AND HORMONE-RELATED CHANGES IN WOMEN

As you learned in Chapter 5, a woman typically enters perimenopause, the life stage in which the ovaries begin to produce less estrogen and progesterone, sometime in her late 40s. Initially, she might not feel any of the effects of perimenopause, but some women start to feel what are usually referred to as menopausal symptoms such as mood swings, depressive feelings, sleep disturbances, fatigue, irritability, hot flashes, and night sweats. Menstrual periods may become heavier, lighter, and/or less regular, and vaginal dryness and decreased lubrication may be noticed. Around the age of 51, women in the Western world tend to experience menopause, the life stage in which they have their last menstrual period (Kato et al., 1998); the time after the last menses is referred to as postmenopause (American Congress of Obstetricians and Gynecologists, 2010). Women today spend a significant amount of their lives in the postmenopausal stage. Hormone levels continue to fluctuate until about five years postmenopause, at which point levels stabilize and most women no longer experience menopausal symptoms.

How menopause affects sexuality and how women experience their sexuality postmenopause is still a topic under investigation. Some women appear to have few problems with this transition and adjust to decreases in lubrication by using lubricants. Others experience significant menopausal symptoms, and it is not clear whether they enjoy sexuality less because of physical changes or because they are exhausted, depressed, and/or irritable. There appears to be growing consensus that women in postmenopause experience less sexual desire and report self-stimulating less often with increasing age (e.g., Dennerstein, Alexander, & Kotz, 2003). The frequency of intercourse also decreases; however, as is the case in adulthood, the frequency of intercourse depends very much on many contextual factors (e.g., Bancroft, 2009). If women have a partner whom they perceive in positive terms, the couple is able to communicate honestly and intimately, and the couple is able to adjust to the inevitable changes of aging, little stands in the way of a fulfilling and active sex life for older women.

PHYSICAL AND HORMONE-RELATED CHANGES IN MEN

In older men, the relationship between the physical effects of aging and sexual impairment appears to be more linear than it does in women, but as with women, there is significant variation in how aging affects an individual's sexuality. Many men find that it takes them longer to have an erection, as the penis tends to become less sensitive to stimulation with age, and that their erections are less firm and less reliable. The testicles also decrease in size and ejaculations become less forceful, which can sometimes lead to decreased subjective pleasure with orgasm. Further, the refractory period after an orgasm, during which most men are unable to have another erection, increases (Masters & Johnson, 1970). With regard to sexual dysfunction, older age is associated with increasing degrees of erectile dysfunction, a decrease in sexual desire, and more difficulty having orgasm (e.g., Bacon et al., 2003). A steady decrease in testosterone in the brain and body of older men has also been associated with the decline in sexual function and, in particular, sexual desire. Lifestyle factors (e.g., smoking) can also affect erectile responsiveness, but in general, vascular and nerve damage become more pronounced as men get older.

Pharmaceutical companies have placed a premium on enhancing erectile function via medications such as Viagra that relax the penile blood vessels to allow blood to flow into the penis, thereby facilitating erection. But although physical changes play a large part in sexual function in older men, circumstances matter just as much as they do for younger men and for women (e.g., Bancroft, 2009). Men who place a lot of value on the ability to have quick and firm erections are more likely to suffer psychologically from the effects of aging because they may find it more difficult to adjust to normal changes in their sexual response, and they may experience additional interference with erections due to self-imposed performance pressures. The quality of the relationship, personality factors, physical and mental health, an active sexual history, and sexual self-esteem can all play a role in how aging affects sexuality in men (Lindau et al., 2007).

Sexual Activity in Older Adults

Despite the challenges of aging, many men and women continue to enjoy partnered sexual activity well into their later years; for example, one study found that more than 50 per cent of adults over 75 still engage in sexual activity three or more times per month (Waite, Laumann, Das, & Schumm, 2009). Another survey found that half of men and women aged 50 and older with partners were having sex at least once a week (Jacoby, 2005). Sexual expression in older adults has been described as "more quality than quantity" and may focus on kissing, caressing, and sexual touching (Figure 9.13). Older couples may take more time to enjoy each other, which can increase the overall intimacy of the encounters. In many cases, "foreplay" becomes the "mainplay," which women, in particular, may appreciate.

As suggested above, the frequency of sexual activity in older adults may be reduced by contextual factors similar to those faced by younger adults—relationship dissatisfaction, lack of communication between partners, negative attitudes toward sex, and so on. However, many older adults who reside in nursing homes or depend on help from others may face an additional contextual barrier to being sexually active: a lack of privacy. Sexuality is sometimes seen as a problem behaviour by nurses and care staff, and older adults living in care homes who are interested in having sex may be met with negative or patronizing attitudes (Rheaume & Mitty, 2008; Walker & Harrington, 2002).

FIGURE 9.13 Nothing is better than an enthusiastic demonstration of love and attraction, no matter the age!

Safer Sex among Sexually Active Older Adults

Single older adults must be just as vigilant about practising safer sex as single younger adults and adolescents. This may be particularly difficult for older adults who find themselves single—either because they have divorced or otherwise ended a long-term relationship, or because their spouse or long-term partner has died—for the first time in decades. Having sexually matured before the HIV/AIDS epidemic of the 1980s and early 1990s, not all older adults are prepared to negotiate safer sex practices. Many unmarried people over the age of 40 in Canada admit to not using condoms with a new sexual partner (Vogel, 2010). Additionally, STI rates are on the rise among Canadian baby boomers, most notably the rate of gonorrhea in men over 60 (Vogel, 2010). Older adults also face additional vulnerabilities as a result of the physiological changes of aging. For example, the lining of a woman's vagina becomes thinner as a woman ages, and it is therefore more likely to experience small tears that can increase the risk of contracting an STI. Lower immune system function associated with increased age also increases the likelihood of infection for both men and women. Finally, **ageism** on the part of health care professionals and embarrassment may stand in the way of routine STI testing.

ageism Discrimination against people because of their age.

CHAPTER SUMMARY

A person's sexuality begins to develop before birth and continues to evolve and change throughout his or her entire life. Children seek love and affection from their caregivers and tend to be curious about the world around them, including about their bodies and the bodies of others. Parents' reactions to their children's explorations can shape the way their children view sex. As children age, they begin to experience more sexual interest in others, usually around the age of 10. This interest continues through puberty and into adulthood. In the later teenage years, many people experience sexual intercourse for the first time. With the beginning of partnered sexual experience, individuals need to be conscious of practising safer sex, to reduce the risk of STIs and unintentional pregnancy. As adults, people experience a variety of living situations that influence their sexuality: being single, dating, cohabiting, marrying, and possibly going through a divorce. Older adults continue to experience changes in their sexuality, and many have active and satisfying sex lives.

DEBATE QUESTIONS

Should people live together before getting married? What are the drawbacks? What are the benefits?

REVIEW QUESTIONS

1. Is it normal for small children to masturbate? What would you do if you were a parent and you saw your young child touching his or her genitals?

2. How are young girls sexualized in our society? What are the negative consequences of this sexualization?

3. Do you consider oral–genital contact to be sex? Why or why not?

4. What is the significance of an individual's first sexual intercourse? Do you agree that it can have lasting effects on a person's life?

5. How have email, online dating sites, and social networking sites changed the face of dating?

6. When you're older and retired, do you think you will still want to have an active sex life? If so, what things can you do to help make this possible?

SUGGESTIONS FOR FURTHER READING AND VIEWING

Recommended Websites

Aging and Human Sexuality Resource Guide (American Psychological Association): www.apa.org/pi/aging/resources/guides/sexuality.aspx

Human Sexuality: Conflicts and Consensus on Youth Sexuality: www.religioustolerance .org/condom.htm

Sexuality and Aging: www.sexualityandaging.com

Sexuality and Your Child—For Children Ages 0 to 3: www.classbrain.com/artread/ publish/article_34.shtml

SexualityandU.ca, on Sexuality and Child Development: www.sexualityandu.ca/ health-care-professionals/sexuality-and-child-development

Sexuality Changes throughout the Lifespan: www.mentalhelp.net/poc/view_doc .php?type=doc&id=29724&cn=10

Think before You Speak: www.thinkb4youspeak.com

Understanding Early Sexual Development: http://kidshealth.org/parent/growth/ sexual_health/development.html

Recommended Reading

Azam, S. (2009). *Oral sex is the new goodnight kiss*. Vancouver, BC: Reluctant Hero Inc.

Carpenter, L.M., & DeLamater, J. (2012). *Sex for life: From virginity to Viagra, how sexuality changes throughout our lives*. New York, NY: New York University Press.

D'Augelli, A.R., & Patterson, C.J. (Eds). (1995). *Lesbian, gay, and bisexual identities over the lifespan: Psychological perspectives*. New York, NY: Oxford University Press.

Diamond, L.M. (2008). *Sexual fluidity: Understanding women's love and desire*. Cambridge, MA: Harvard University Press.

Haffner, D.W. (2000). *From diapers to dating: A parent's guide to raising sexually health children*. New York, NY: Newmarket Press.

Hillman, J. (2012). *Sexuality and aging: Clinical perspectives*. New York, NY: Springer.

Ontario Federation of Cerebral Palsy. (2009). *Sexuality and cerebral palsy*. Toronto, ON: Author. Available at www.ofcp.ca/pdf/book/sexuality_book.pdf

Sigelman, C.K., & Rider, E.A. (2011). *Life-span human development* (7th ed.). Belmont, CA: Wadsworth Publishing.

Zurbriggen, E.L., Collins, R.L., Lamb, S., Roberts, T.A., Tolman, D.L., Ward, L.M., & Blake, J. (2007). *Report of the APA task force on the sexualization of girls*. Washington, DC: American Psychological Association. Available at www.apa.org/pi/women/ programs/girls/report-summary.pdf

Recommended Viewing

Azam, S. (Director). (2009). *Oral sex is the new goodnight kiss* [Documentary]. Vancouver, BC: Reluctant Hero Inc.

10

CHAPTER

Gender

MEREDITH L. CHIVERS

LEARNING OBJECTIVES

In this chapter, you will

- discover that gender is a complex psychological phenomenon that arises out of the intersections between biological and socio-cultural factors;
- become familiar with disorders of sexual development that can influence how gender is experienced;
- learn about how a child's sense of gender develops; and
- find out how a person's gender identity influences that person's social interactions and experience of sexuality.

In What Gender Do We Raise Our Child?

In 1966, the Canadian parents of a young boy faced a decision that few parents ever have to make: what gender do we raise our child? At the age of 8 months, their son Bruce lost his penis to a poorly executed circumcision. After seeing Dr John Money (Figure 10.1), who was known for his work with children with disorders of sexual development, speak about child gender identity on the CBC television show *This Hour Has Seven Days*, the Reimers sought consultation with him. They brought their son to see Dr Money at Johns Hopkins University in Baltimore, Maryland.

Because Bruce's penis could not be reconstructed and it was believed that he needed to have a penis in order to have a well-formed masculine identity, Money counselled the Reimers to raise Bruce as a girl. According to Money's theory of gender identity development—termed the "theory of gender neutrality"—an individual's sense of being a girl or a boy, female or male, feminine or masculine is malleable, determined by the individual's social and cultural environment. In essence, the theory posits that a child will adopt whatever gender is assigned to her or him, regardless of the child's genetic complement or prenatal hormonal influences, provided that the child's environment is consistent. Money believed that Bruce's gender identity was still malleable at Bruce's young age, and that with female hormone treatments and surgical construction of a vagina Bruce would stand a better chance of living happily as a woman than as a man without a penis. At the age of 22 months, Bruce's testes were removed, and he was renamed "Brenda"; from this point forward, his parents raised him as a girl. What ensued was among the greatest failures in gender reassignment, a tragedy for David (the name that he later chose for himself) and his loved ones, and evidence that gender is not only learned or socially determined.

Brenda, despite receiving female hormones, dressing as a girl, and being encouraged to behave in a feminine manner, never felt like a girl. After becoming suicidal and threatening to harm herself if forced to see Dr Money again (the Reimers continued to bring Brenda for follow-up visits once a year), Brenda was told the truth about her biological sex, her male past, and her gender reassignment. At age 14, Brenda adopted the male gender role, this time as David (Figure 10.2).

Money never reported his treatment of David to be a failure; in fact, he claimed in several publications that the case provided gold-standard evidence for the success of gender reassignment at a

FIGURE 10.1 Dr John Money, who was widely recognized as the world authority on childhood gender development in the 1960s and beyond, promoted the "theory of gender neutrality," which posits that gender is primarily a learned and socio-cultural phenomenon.

FIGURE 10.2 After adopting the male gender role at age 14, David Reimer continued to live as a male for the rest of his life. He is shown here in early 2000, with his wife, Jane, whom he married in 1990, and his stepson.

young age. It wasn't until David disclosed his story to gender and sexuality researcher Milton Diamond (Figure 10.3) that the true impact of Money's work was revealed to the scientific community. Diamond urged Reimer to tell his story publicly, to dissuade physicians treating children with disorders of sexual development or genital malformations or traumas from the notion that gender identity is infinitely malleable. Sadly, David Reimer took his life in 2004, after a series of difficult personal events. His remarkable and tragic story underscores the multidimensional and complex nature of gender, and it highlights that nurture alone is not sufficient for understanding this fundamental component of our psychology. (See John Colapinto's *As Nature Made Him*, referenced in the "Recommended Reading" section, for more on David's story.)

FIGURE 10.3 Dr Milton Diamond, of the University of Hawaii, revealed that Reimer's transition to the female gender role was not as successful as Dr Money had portrayed it to be.

QUESTION FOR CRITICAL THOUGHT AND REFLECTION

1. If you had been one of David's parents, what would you have done? Imagine you are living in the 1960s, and assume you have the same information provided to the Reimers.

Introduction

gender The psychological experience of femaleness and/or maleness.

The idea of **gender** as a psychological construct was first coined in the 1960s by John Money; he used the term *gender* to describe the psychological experience of femaleness and maleness. Money's treatment of gender-variant individuals led him to co-opt the term *gender* from linguistics, creating language that describes the experiences of those whose biological sex and psychological sense of femaleness or maleness do not coincide, and giving rise to the concept of gender as a psychological phenomenon. This chapter will explore the intersections among the psychological, biological, and socio-cultural facets of gender in the arena of sexuality. It will also examine the theoretical frameworks commonly employed to understand gender and sexuality, gender differences in sexuality, the development of gender, and the experiences of those with gender variations.

biological sex The biological condition of being male and/or female, as determined by genes, chromosomes, hormones, and physical traits.

gender identity The way in which one identifies with a gender category (e.g., man, woman, neither).

Gender or Sex?

gender role The set of social and behavioural norms that are considered to be socially appropriate for individuals of a specific sex in the context of a specific culture.

On the surface, distinguishing between **biological sex** and gender seems simple; *sex* refers to biological femaleness or maleness—as indicated by genes, hormones, and physiology—whereas *gender* refers to the psychological experience of femaleness or maleness—an emergent property of the biological and socio-cultural factors that influence **gender identity** and **gender role**. As we begin to examine the underpinnings of gender and sex in more detail, however, this tidy dichotomy becomes increasingly complex.

Gender development begins much the same way as sex development begins—before birth, based on an individual's genetic makeup. After all, an individual's **phenotype** is strongly influenced by that person's **genotype**. **Chromosomal sex** plays a definite role, as the X and Y chromosomes contribute to determining whether a fetus develops as genetically female (XX) or genetically male (XY). Genes present on the X and Y chromosomes are also key players in influencing sex and gender, particularly those that instruct the indifferent gonads to develop into either ovaries (*FOXL2, WNT4, RSPO1, DAX1*) or testes (*SOX9*). The gene that determines which gonad-differentiating genes are expressed is the *SRY* gene, found on the Y chromosome. In a typically developing XY male, the presence of *SRY* overrides the ovary-promoting genes present on the X chromosome, resulting in male gonads (testes) that secrete androgens at puberty, resulting in a male-looking body (Figure 10.4). If there are ovary-determining genes present and no *SRY* gene, as in the case of a typically developing XX female, ovaries develop and will secrete estrogens at puberty and result in a female-looking body. If *SRY* is expressed on an X chromosome in an XX female (called *SRY* translocation), testes will develop, and the individual will develop to be phenotypically male. Similarly, if *SRY* is silent on a Y chromosome in an XY male, ovaries will develop, and the individual will very likely be phenotypically female. As this discussion suggests, an individual's **gonadal sex** is an important component of that person's resulting sex and gender, largely because the gonads play a role in regulating hormones and, thus, influencing the individual's **hormonal sex**.

Hormones secreted by the gonads not only influence the appearance of external sex characteristics and reproductive organs, but also affect many other sites in the body, including the brain (see Chapter 5). Throughout prenatal and postnatal development, the hormonal milieu has both organizational and activational effects on the brain, influencing subsequent behaviour and experience, sexual and otherwise. Gender could therefore be described as *brain sex*, the distal result of genetics, proximally shaped by interactions with hormonal secretions during development. Biological development does, of course, unfold within a socio-cultural and political context. The individual's experience of gender therefore becomes formulated in these contexts and is labelled as *gender identity*, corresponding to the individual's sense of femaleness and/or maleness. These core beliefs about the self are then expressed within a *gender role*, or "shared expectations that apply to individuals on the basis of their socially identified sex" (Eagly, Wood, & Diekman, 2000, p. 127), as behaviours the individual engages in, characteristics the individual possesses, and positions the individual holds in society (Blakemore, Berenbaum, & Liben,

phenotype The outward appearance or expression of a set of physical and behavioural traits, determined by genotype and environment.

genotype The genetic constitution of an organism, determined by genetic components inherited from the organism's parents.

chromosomal sex Sex determined by the combination of sex chromosomes.

gonadal sex Sex determined by the presence of female gonads (ovaries) and/or male gonads (testicles).

hormonal sex Sex determined by levels of estrogens and androgens.

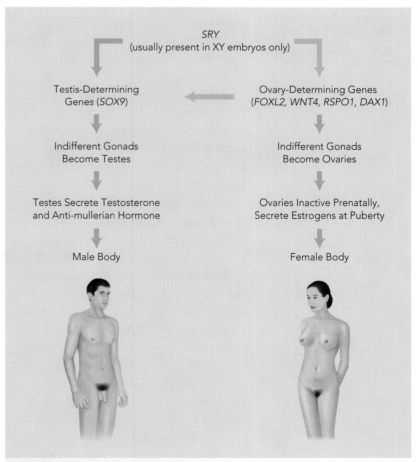

FIGURE 10.4 Genes present on the sex chromosomes are key players in determining female or male phenotypes.

gender schemas Mental frameworks based on understandings of how men and women typically behave.

gender stereotypes Widely held beliefs about the typical characteristics and behaviours of men and women.

2008). Gender role is, in turn, informed by **gender schemas** and **stereotypes**, or attitudes about what are acceptable behaviours, attributes, and positions in society for women and men. Gender role and gender identity are therefore products of the intersections among psychological, biological, and socio-cultural facets of gender.

Nature and Nurture: Theoretical Perspectives on Gender and Sexuality

Few contemporary sexuality researchers would endorse a model of gendered sexuality that suggests gender to be either purely biologically determined (i.e., determined by "nature") or purely socially constructed (i.e., determined by "nurture"); however, gender-difference research is often portrayed in media as strictly following one of these two paths. In reality, the major theoretical models of gender development typically ascribe different weights to the role of biological, psychological, and socio-cultural factors in determining gender. The following sections review the most common theoretical frameworks used to understand gender and sexuality: evolutionary psychology, social learning theory, and social structural theory.

EVOLUTIONARY PSYCHOLOGY

reproductive fitness The ability to successfully pass on genes to the next generation.

parental investment theory A theory proposed by Robert Trivers (1972) that predicts that the sex making the larger investment in offspring will be more discriminating in mating.

Evolutionary psychologists understand gender differences in sexuality as arising from evolutionary processes aimed at maximizing **reproductive fitness**. According to **parental investment theory** (Trivers, 1972), women and men are faced with different reproductive problems, owing to the biological parameters of their potential reproductive output (see Chapter 2). Thus, evolutionary psychologists propose, differences in biologically and physiologically determined reproductive roles give rise to differences in gendered psychological processes and behaviour aimed at maximizing the likelihood that children will survive and reproduce. Because a woman can produce only a limited number of children, the psychological mechanisms that regulate a woman's sexual behaviour are thought to be, on average, more conservative than those of men; thus, evolutionary forces are thought to result in women having a lower sex drive, preferring fewer sexual partners, desiring sex within the context of committed relationships with clear paternal investment in child-rearing, and preferring males with traits associated with ability to provide resources. On the other hand, because men have a greater physiological capacity to produce more offspring, the psychological mechanisms that regulate men's sexuality are thought to be less conservative, with heterosexual men expressing greater interest in casual sex, showing evidence of a higher sex drive, and preferring female partners who exhibit characteristics associated with fertility (e.g., youthfulness) (Gangestad & Simpson, 2000).

Evolutionary psychology also posits that psychological and behavioural traits associated with higher rates of reproduction (e.g., those described above) are retained through natural selection. This is because individuals who possess traits that are advantageous to successful reproduction tend to mate and transmit these traits to the next generation at a higher rate than others who do not possess these traits. Transmission of psychological traits is thought to occur mainly through genetic pathways, although cultural transmission, through memes (representations of ideas that can be learned and transmitted through a cultural group, such as how to hunt or prepare food), is another route by which information can be passed on to subsequent generations.

Another key feature of evolutionary approaches to understanding gender is its emphasis on the exceptionally important role that the *environment* plays in shaping human behaviour over successive generations. A trait's adaptiveness, or its potential to maximize reproductive fitness, can be judged only in relation to the environment within which it manifests. For example, researchers in Sub-Saharan Africa studying the adaptiveness of infant temperaments found that difficult, cranky babies do worse in times of plenty; these children create a lot of stress for their parents and are more likely to be neglected or abused than babies with calm, more even temperaments. In times of drought, however, babies with cranky temperaments are the ones most likely to survive because they demand more attention from their caregivers (de Vries, 1984). This example shows that we can judge the adaptiveness of a baby's temperament only in relation to the environment within which that temperament is expressed. Similarly, we can judge the adaptiveness of gendered sexual psychologies, such as sex drive, only in the environments in which they manifest.

SOCIAL LEARNING THEORY

According to the social learning perspective, gender differences in sexuality are the result of observational learning (Bandura, 1986). Few of us directly observe others' sexual behaviour, but our environment is awash in information about sexuality delivered via media such as the Internet, television, film, and magazines, and this information may influence how we understand and display our sexuality. For example, exposure to reality dating programs depicting gender-stereotyped romantic and sexual behaviours, such as *Who Wants to Marry a Multi-Millionaire*, is correlated with more permissive sexual attitudes and behaviours (Zurbriggen & Morgan, 2006). However, inferring causation requires an experimental design with control conditions; this correlation may reveal that individuals with more permissive attitudes are more likely to seek out media that portray sexuality in a fashion consistent with their attitudes.

A handful of researchers have conducted experimental studies that indirectly address the effects of observational learning. For example, Ward (2002) examined women's and men's endorsement of sexual stereotypes after viewing sexualized or nonsexual scenes from TV shows such as *Friends*. The sexualized scenes portrayed the following gendered sexual stereotypes: men are sex-driven, women are sexual objects, and dating is a game. Women who viewed the sexualized clips reported stronger endorsement of sexual stereotypes than did women who viewed the nonsexual clips, and the more TV they watched, the greater their endorsement of the stereotypes. Interestingly, viewing the clips did not seem to affect men in the same way; stereotype endorsement was equally high in groups exposed to the sexual clips and groups exposed to the nonsexual clips. This exhibited gender difference may provide evidence for what some researchers have termed the *female sexual fluidity hypothesis*, which proposes that female sexuality is more malleable than male sexuality in response to cultural influences (see Baumeister, 2000).

SOCIAL STRUCTURAL THEORY

Social structural theory proposes that gender differences in sexuality, particularly in relation to mate preferences, arise because of a gendered division of power that emerges from a gender-stratified workforce where men control resources (Eagly & Wood, 1999): men tend to work outside of the home and be primary breadwinners, while women are more often primary caregivers to children and secondary breadwinners. These different expectations, or gender norms, dictate the appropriate conduct for men and women, resulting in further gender-differentiated behaviours (Eagly, Wood, & Diekman, 2000). Men are expected to take on agentic roles, behaving in an assertive, independent, and dominant manner, whereas women are expected to take on communal roles, by being relationship-oriented, submissive, and dependent (Cejka & Eagly, 1999).

Gendered power inequality often manifests as the privileging of male sexuality, sexual objectification and dehumanization of women, and women prioritizing the acquisition of long-term mates with resources, as they have limited means to provide resources for themselves. Supporting this theory, women and men from more gender-egalitarian societies, as indexed by a gender-empowerment measure developed by the United Nations Development Programme (UNDP, 1995), report more similar incidence and frequency of sexual behaviours such as masturbation, vaginal intercourse, anal intercourse, and casual sex (Petersen & Hyde, 2010); yet even in these societies certain gender differences remain, in particular, masturbation and erotica use. Although power differentials do seem to influence expression of certain sexual behaviours, sexual attitudes do not seem to vary with gender empowerment.

Gender Differences or Similarities in Sexuality?

In 2005, Janet Hyde, an American psychologist at the University of Wisconsin-Madison, contended that the predominant model of differences between women and men was fundamentally flawed (Hyde, 2005). She argued that popular media representations, such as that in John Gray's bestselling *Men Are from Mars, Women Are from Venus* (1992), bias our interpretations of women's and men's behaviours, attitudes, and aptitudes in the direction of finding differences. In her detailed analysis, she demonstrated that the magnitude of the differences, measured using **Cohen's d effect size** (Cohen, 1988), was actually quite small; this observation led her to develop the *gender similarities hypothesis*, which proposes that women and men are more similar than different for most, but not all, psychological variables (Hyde, 2005). The notable exceptions include psychological factors related to physical capacities like throwing velocity and distance (Thomas & French, 1985), spatial ability (Halpern, 2000), aggressive behaviours (Archer, 2004), and certain aspects of sexuality; men show greater masturbation incidence, greater erotic materials use, more frequent casual sex behaviour, and more permissive attitudes toward casual sex (Petersen & Hyde, 2010).

Masturbation, Numbers of Sexual Partners, Attitudes toward Casual Sex, and Erotica Use

One interpretation of the consistent gender differences in masturbation frequency, reported number of sexual partners, attitudes toward casual sex, and erotica use is that they reflect a stronger and more persistent male sex drive (Baumeister, Catanese, & Vohs, 2001). Attitudes about casual sex and actual sexual behaviour in non-committed contexts have consistently shown gender differences, with men reporting greater **sociosexuality** (Lippa, 2009). According to parental investment theory, gender differences in sociosexuality reflect men's greater reproductive effort and lower cost of reproduction. This is not to say that women do not engage in casual sexual relationships; indeed they do. There is some evidence to suggest that women do so strategically at times of high fertility, by selecting male casual partners who have characteristics associated with high genetic fitness, such as facial symmetry and low vocal pitch (Gangestad & Simpson, 2000). Further, research has shown that women's interest in sex may fluctuate as a function of their menstrual cycles, with women reporting greater sexual interest and sexual receptivity when they are ovulating (Wallen, 2001). Thus, differences in men's and women's sexual behaviours may be less prominent when women are ovulating.

A study by Bailey and colleagues (1994) found that among LGBTTIQQ individuals, differences in sexuality are both gender typical—that is, congruent with what is expected for women and men based on gender norms—and gender atypical. The researchers found that gay men have similar interest in visual sexual stimuli, exhibit

---

Cohen's d effect size A measure of the strength of the relationship between two variables in a population.

sociosexuality Individual difference in the willingness to engage in casual sexual activity.

similar attitudes toward uncommitted sex, place similar importance on the physical attractiveness of their sexual partner, and reveal a similar lack of concern about their partner's social status as heterosexual men do, but they report significantly greater sociosexual behaviour, likely because they are having sex with men who also have less conservative attitudes about casual sex. Heterosexual men, however, show significantly greater preference for youthful partners and significantly greater sexual jealousy, or emotional upset at the idea of their partner having other sexual partners, than gay men do. According to evolutionary accounts of gender differences, these aspects of hetero-sexual men's mating psychology are attributable to a bias toward women of reproduct-ive age, and to a fear of their female partner giving birth to a child that is not theirs, a very costly enterprise from the perspective of reproductive fitness.

In the same study (Bailey et al., 1994), lesbian women did not differ from heterosex-ual women in their preference for youthful partners, interest in uncommitted sex, sense of the importance of their partner's physical attractiveness, or sociosexuality. Lesbian women did, however, report significantly greater interest in visual sexual stimuli than heterosexual women did, reflecting either the greater availability of erotica for lesbian women at the time, or an inherent difference in the reward value of visual sexual stim-uli for lesbian women. Heterosexual women reported significantly greater importance of a partner's social status than lesbian women did, consistent with parental invest-ment theory; heterosexual women are prioritizing mate characteristics associated with the ability to provide resources.

Social role theorists interpret reported gender differences in sexuality, such as those discussed above, as reflecting men's and women's desire to conform to gender norms, rather than differences in actual behaviour. The consequences of deviating from any social norm are high, but the costs of deviating from gender norm expectations with respect to sexuality are particularly high: men's sexual orientation or prowess may be questioned, and women's sexual integrity may be questioned (Meston & Buss, 2009). Indeed, the largest gender differences in sexual behaviours appear to be associated with agentic activities: men masturbate and use erotic materials more frequently than women do (Petersen & Hyde, 2010). Self-reports of partnered sexual activities are also influenced by gender-stereotyped expectations: men are allowed (and expected) to be more sexually permissive than women (Cohen & Shotland, 1996). Thus, men and women may report—both in formal research settings and in informal personal encoun-ters—that their sexual attitudes and behaviours are consistent with gender norms in order to avoid negative social consequences.

Sexual Orientation

Sexual orientation is one aspect of sexuality that shows a large gender difference. The majority of men report sexual attraction to women, and the majority of women report sexual attraction to men. The effect size of this gender difference is estimated to be between $d = 3.8$ (Lippa, 2005) and $d = 6.0$ (Hines, 2004) (which is massive, considering that 0.8 is considered to be a "large" effect size; Cohen, 1988). Women are, however, less likely than men to report exclusive opposite-sex attraction: 83 per cent of women, compared with 94 per cent of men (based on data from a nationally representative US survey; Chandra, Mosher, & Copen, 2010).

Are women more likely to be bisexual than men are? Chandra et al.'s (2010) study data suggest that yes, women are more likely to identify as bisexual, to report sexual behaviour with both women and men, and to report feeling sexually attracted to both women and men. Women are also more likely than men to have had same-sex sexual contact (13 per cent of women compared to 5.2 per cent of men). Among women who have had opposite-sex partners, same-sex behaviour appears to be related to their total number of opposite-sex partners; women reporting four or more opposite-sex partners in their lifetime were more likely to report same-sex behaviour (20 per cent) than were those reporting fewer numbers of opposite-sex partners (3.5 to 8.5 per cent). Among men who have had opposite-sex partners, no association between total number of opposite-sex partners and sexual behaviour with same-sex partners was shown. These data coincide with results from research by Richard Lippa (2006), which has demonstrated that as women's sex drive increases (as would be indicated by a higher number of sexual partners) so does their sexual attraction to both women and men, whereas for men no such association exists.

Another notable gender difference in sexual orientation relates to the exclusivity of same-sex attractions: cisgender women (women whose gender matches their biological sex) are far more likely than cisgender men (men whose gender matches their biological sex) to report some degree of both same- and other-sex attraction. Some interpret this gender difference to reflect a broader pattern of greater flexibility in women's sexuality, compared to that of men, when it comes to gender preferences. Bisexual- and lesbian-identified women are also more likely to change sexual identities over a 10-year period than are gay or heterosexual men; bisexual men, however, also show flexibility in their identity over time (Mock & Eibach, 2011). The reason for the seemingly greater fluidity of women's sexuality is not known, although research suggests that women's capacity to experience sexual arousal in response to a broad range of sexual stimuli may be related to higher levels of same-sex attractions among women (Chivers, 2010).

Socio-cultural factors, such as cultural prohibitions against same-sex sexuality, likely play a significant role in women's reporting of same-sex attractions. Chandra et al. (2010) found that non-Hispanic White women were less likely than Hispanic women or Black women to say they are attracted "only to the opposite sex" (81 per cent, 89 per cent, and 86 per cent, respectively). Further, women who completed the survey in Spanish were more likely than other women to say they are attracted "only to the opposite sex" (95 per cent compared to 82 per cent).

Patterns of Sexual Response

Research suggests that women and men differ in two aspects of their sexual response to sexual stimuli: **specificity of sexual arousal** and **sexual concordance**. Whereas men's patterns of sexual arousal and genital response closely correspond to their stated sexual attractions to women and/or men, heterosexual women's do not (Chivers, Seto, & Blanchard, 2007). Although women who are exclusively heterosexual report greater sexual arousal to stimuli (both visual and auditory) depicting men than that depicting women, they show genital responses to sexual stimuli depicting women as well to as that depicting men (Chivers, Haberl, & Timmers, 2011; Chivers & Timmers, 2012). Women who report same-sex attractions, however, show greater arousal to female stimuli than do women who report no same-sex attractions, and this response varies with the reported degree of their same-sex attractions (Chivers et al., 2011).

Reasons for gender differences in specificity and concordance may relate to how women and men incorporate feedback from sexual response into their emotional experience of sexual arousal and subsequent sexual desire. For women, awareness of genital arousal may not be a significant factor in determining their desire for a partner. Given that most women experience automatic genital response to sexual stimuli, the lower concordance in women may often be produced by low reports of feeling sexually aroused. Reporting biases and sexual double standards may explain why studies repeatedly find that women's minds and bodies are not as in sync as men's are.

specificity of sexual arousal Agreement between self-reported sexual attractions and sexual arousal patterns.

sexual concordance Agreement between self-reported sexual arousal and genital arousal.

Reporting Biases

As mentioned above, women's and men's self-reports about their sexuality may be biased by desires to conform to gender norms. In a research setting, biased reports can lead to inaccurate representations of women's and men's sexuality. Consider, for example, the fact that men who have sex with women report significantly higher numbers of sexual partners than do women who have sex with men. Such reports are somewhat puzzling, as we must wonder, with whom are these men having sex (Smith, 1992)?

One possible reason for this discrepancy is that men over-report their partner numbers and women under-report, consistent with the sexual double standard, whereby more liberal sexual attitudes and behaviours are tolerated in men but discouraged in women. An ingenious study conducted by Alexander and Fisher (2003) used the "bogus pipeline" methodology to help control for false accommodation of gender roles (i.e., self-reporting that falsely presents behaviours and/or attitudes as consistent with widespread gender norms). They asked young women and men to report their sexual attitudes and behaviours under three conditions: one in which participants believed they had complete anonymity, one in which participants felt a threat of exposure (the experimenter might see their responses), and one involving a "bogus pipeline," in which participants felt pressure to tell the truth because they were attached to a polygraph machine (the device was not active, but participants did not know this). The results generally showed that gender differences in sexual attitudes, autonomous sexual behaviours (e.g., masturbation, use of erotic materials), and numbers of sexual partners were smaller in the bogus pipeline group than in the exposure condition group, suggesting that women's and men's self-reports are influenced by reporting biases. It is notable, however, that gender differences did remain, but the magnitude of these differences was smaller when the threat of discovery was increased.

Because gender norms are shared expectations of men's and women's behaviours, people are usually aware of them. It is possible, however, to manipulate social and even personal norms, thereby altering self-reports. Both men and women are more likely to report being unfaithful to a previous or current dating partner when they are under the impression that promiscuity is acceptable, compared to men and women who are under the impression that promiscuity is unacceptable (Fisher, 2009). Women's self-reports of sexual arousal also vary as a function of the feedback they are given about their own sexual arousal: women who are told their genital arousal is high subsequently report more arousal than do women who are told their genital arousal is low (McCall & Meston, 2007). When evaluating gender differences research, therefore, we are well-served by carefully considering the conditions under which the data were collected.

Disorders of Sexual Development

Disorders of sexual development (DSDs) are congenital conditions in which the development of anatomical, gonadal, and/or chromosomal sex is atypical. In the past, individuals whose physical sexual characteristics, or *phenotype*, did not correspond to a typical female or male pattern, or who differed from their genetic or hormonal sex, were erroneously referred to as hermaphrodites, which properly refers only to individuals with both female and male reproductive organs. True hermaphroditism, however, is exceptionally rare among humans, although it is far more common among certain invertebrate animals, like snails. The somewhat more accurate term *pseudohermaphrodite* has also been used to describe individuals with DSDs, to suggest the presence of both female and male characteristics. In the past decade, however, activists have rejected this

disorders of sexual development (DSDs) A group of conditions in which the reproductive organs and/or genitals develop differently than expected.

intersex individuals
Individuals whose reproductive and/or sexual anatomy develops differently from what is considered to be typical in either a female or a male.

cloacal exstrophy A rare developmental variation in which the abdominal organs are exposed and the genitals develop abnormally.

penile agenesis A rare developmental variation in which a male child is born without a penis.

term as inaccurate and pejorative. Currently, in medical contexts, the more descriptive term *disorders of sexual development* (*DSDs*) is favoured to describe the congenital conditions that lead to intermediate expression of female and male phenotypes. To avoid the pejorative and stigmatizing identification of individuals as their medical conditions, individuals with DSDs often identify as **intersex**. Although many individuals who identify as intersex have DSDs that involve chromosomal and/or hormonal irregularities, not all do. For some individuals, their intersexuality relates to problems with physiological development, such as **cloacal exstrophy** or **penile agenesis**, or physical traumas such as penile ablation. The following sections discuss some of the more common and well-understood DSDs.

Sex Chromosome Variations

Recall that the typical sex chromosomal complement is either two XX chromosomes (in females) or one X and one Y chromosome (in males). In some cases, however, individuals are born with extra or fewer X or Y chromosomes. Such chromosomal anomalies can have profound effects on physical and psychological aspects of sex, sexuality, and gender. Below, two of the most frequent chromosomal abnormalities, Klinefelter's syndrome and Turner's syndrome, are discussed.

KLINEFELTER'S SYNDROME (XXY)

Klinefelter's syndrome is the most common sex chromosome trisomy disorder, affecting 1 in 500 to 1000 males of all ethnic backgrounds (Zeger et al., 2008). Males with Klinefelter's syndrome have an abnormal chromosomal complement, with the presence of one Y chromosome and two or more X chromosomes (typically XXY). The developmental differences associated with Klinefelter's syndrome are thought to result from genetic abnormalities relating to having two copies of the androgen-receptor gene present on the X chromosome. Through a complex genetic and hormonal feedback loop, the result is lower testosterone production because of cell abnormalities and impaired feedback signalling to the hypothalamic pituitary axis, resulting in high levels of follicular stimulating hormone (Bastida et al., 2007).

In the majority of cases, Klinefelter's syndrome is not diagnosed until puberty, at which time physical feminization becomes apparent. Boys with Klinefelter's syndrome often present with gynecomastia (breast development), small testes, shorter-than-average penises, low testosterone levels, tall stature, verbal cognition problems (Vawter, Harvey, & DeLisi, 2007), and compromised fertility. Many individuals with Klinefelter's syndrome report low sexual desire, later onset of masturbation in childhood, and reduced interest in partnered sexual activity. In addition, most are sexually attracted to women. Typical treatment for Klinefelter's syndrome includes testosterone supplementation (Bojesen & Gravholt, 2007).

Gender identity varies among people with Klinefelter's syndrome, and most tend to score lower than other males in masculinity on gender role inventories (e.g., the Bem Sex-Role Inventory). Many people with Klinefelter's syndrome do not identify as male, and some seek gender transition (Diamond & Watson, 2004), reflecting androgynous or female identification that can develop from an early age.

TURNER'S SYNDROME (XO)

Turner's syndrome affects approximately 1 in 2500 females. It involves abnormalities of the X chromosome that result in a missing second X chromosome, a chromosomal "monosomy." Women with Turner's syndrome tend to have a short stature, a broad chest and widely spaced nipples, under-developed female physical characteristics (e.g., breasts), and problems with ovarian development and sex hormone levels, leading to infertility (Hjerrild, Mortensen, & Gravholt, 2008). Women with Turner's syndrome are often treated with growth hormones during childhood, hormones to induce pubertal development, and hormone-replacement therapy throughout adulthood. Sexual milestones, such as first masturbation and first partnered sex, are typically reached at later ages than in unaffected women. Most women with Turner's syndrome identify as female and intersex.

Sex Hormone Variations

In some DSDs, the developmental variation relates to genetic abnormalities in some aspect of hormone synthesis or hormone receptors. Three of the most common DSDs of this sort—congenital adrenal hyperplasia (CAH), androgen insensitivity syndrome (AIS), and 5-alpha-reductase deficiency—are discussed below.

CONGENITAL ADRENAL HYPERPLASIA

Congenital adrenal hyperplasia (CAH) is an autosomal recessive genetic disorder affecting cortisol synthesis in the adrenal gland. There are at least five variations in this genetic disorder, but the most common, 21-hydroxylase deficiency and 11-beta-hydroxylase deficiency, result in increased androgen production and account for the majority of clinically diagnosed cases. It is estimated that the incidence of the 21-hydroxylase variation is between 1 in 5000 and 1 in 15,000, with some variability by ethnicity (Witchel & Azziz, 2011).

Individuals with CAH are typically exposed to elevated levels of androgens produced by their adrenal gland before they are born. Such prenatal exposure during the sixth week of gestation affects the development of female fetuses' genitals, causing varying degrees of **virilization**; larger clitorises, partially fused labia majora (Figure 10.5), shorter vaginal length, and an incomplete differentiation of the urethra and vagina are common, with observable variations ranging from slightly enlarged clitorises to typically male-appearing external genitals (e.g., a penis with a urethral opening). The development of the internal reproductive organs, the uterus and ovaries, is typically unaffected in girls. Genetic males' genital appearance is mostly unaffected by the condition. In cases in which genital anomalies are noticeable, CAH is most often diagnosed at birth. In other cases, the condition is usually diagnosed at puberty, when it may present as early onset of puberty (prior to eight years for girls, nine years for boys), accompanied by penile or clitoral enlargement. Other signs of androgen excess, such as excessive body hair, acne, hair loss (alopecia), and lack of ovulation and menstrual irregularities (in females), are typical in adolescence. In addition, about half of women with CAH may present with symptoms of polycystic ovarian syndrome, which can lead to infertility.

Children with CAH may exhibit behaviours and interests that differ from those of their non-CAH same-sex peers. Girl with CAH may show less nurturance and "tender-mindedness" (empathy), greater aggression, and less interest in infants, while boys with CAH may show less aggression and more "tender-mindedness" (Matthews, Fane, Conway, Brook, & Hines, 2009). Women with CAH are also more likely to report

virilization The biological development of sex differences, specifically changes that make a male body different from a female body.

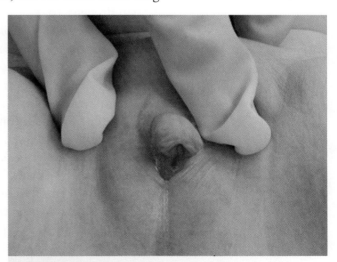

FIGURE 10.5 Congenital adrenal hyperplasia can cause varying degrees of virilization of the female genitals, including enlarged clitorises and fused labia, as shown in this image.

male-typical occupations, interest in rough sports, and interest in motor vehicles than are non-CAH women (Frisén et al., 2009).

Many women with CAH have compromised sexual functioning (Gastaud et al., 2007), and they may avoid sexual intercourse because of pain associated with a shallow vagina or consequences of genital surgeries (Minto, Liao, Woodhouse, Ransley, & Creighton, 2003). Compared with non-CAH women, women with CAH report lower sexual arousability in response to both physical and mental sexual stimuli, both with and without a partner (Zucker et al., 2004). Kenneth Zucker and his colleagues at the Centre for Addiction and Mental Health in Toronto also demonstrated that among women with CAH, sexual arousability is most strongly related to degree of heterosexual experience, suggesting that low heterosexual sexual interest may be related to lower sexual arousal among women with CAH.

The sexual orientation of women with CAH is often of particular interest to sex researchers because of the strong evidence that prenatal exposure to androgens is associated with same-sex attractions and behaviours. It is not the case that all women with CAH are same-sex attracted; in fact, the majority are heterosexual. Women with CAH do, however, show increased rates of same-sex and bisexual attractions, with positive correlations between the degree of prenatal exposure the degree of same-sex attraction (Meyer-Bahlburg, Dolezal, Baker, & New, 2008). To be clear, in these studies, women reporting "some degree of same-sex attraction" include women who report predominant attraction to men, but some occasional attraction to women. Compared to recent population-based surveys, this rate, 21%, is slightly elevated (Chandra et al., 2010).

Treatment of CAH primarily centres on addressing symptoms. Hormone therapy is commonly used to adjust the timing of puberty, manage the "salt-wasting" form of CAH (a dangerous metabolic condition), and increase fertility. Surgery may also be performed to create more female-typical appearing genitals. In some girls, genitoplasty is performed to open the vagina, with the goals of enabling vaginal penetration and creating an opening for menstrual flow. Genital surgery can also be performed to reduce the size of a woman's clitoris, although such procedures are unnecessary and may be harmful to a woman's sexual functioning.

Women who want to become pregnant and are carriers of the genes associated with CAH may be prescribed the steroid dexamethasone to interrupt the production of prenatal androgens, to reduce the chance that their child will develop CAH, although the safety and efficacy of this practice are largely unknown, and the ethics of this practice are questionable (see Dresser & Frader, 2009; Fernandez-Balsells et al., 2010). There is increasing evidence that use of this drug causes harm to fetuses, including developmental defects and cognitive deficits (Lajic, Nordenström, & Hirvikoski, 2011). In addition, dexamethasone is often administered to all pregnant women carrying the genes for CAH when only one in eight fetuses that are treated with the drug may benefit from it (one quarter of a CAH woman's pregnancies will result in a CAH infant, and half of these will be female). The remaining seven out of eight fetuses therefore receive an unnecessary treatment. Thus, pregnant women who carry the genes associated with CAH must ask themselves, is having a more stereotypical vulva worth the risk of cognitive deficits, unknown maternal effects, unknown other harms to the fetus, and the risk of impaired sexual functioning, when we know that women without DSDs show broad variation in the size and shape of all parts of their vulva (see Chapter 4)?

ANDROGEN INSENSITIVITY SYNDROME

Androgen insensitivity syndrome (AIS) is an X-linked recessive disorder in which individuals born with XY chromosomes develop typically female physical characteristics, often including external female genitalia and female breasts. During fetal development of an individual with AIS, testes develop under the influence of *SRY*, but the testes generally do not descend as they typically would. As the individual develops, the testes secrete typical levels of androgens, but mutations in the individual's androgen-receptor genes prevent the body tissues from responding to these hormones. The tissues do respond to estrogens, however, which results in the development of a female-typical phenotype.

Cases of AIS are usually categorized as either partial or complete. Individuals with partial AIS (PAIS) generally have intermediate male- and female-typical characteristics, with differing degrees of genital masculinization. In cases of complete AIS (CAIS), the genitals usually appear typically female, although the vagina may be shallower than in genetic females. Most individuals with CAIS appear female at birth, are raised as girls, and identify as heterosexual, and the majority are content with a female gender identity (Diamond & Watson, 2004; Figure 10.6). Women with CAIS highlight how female-typical psychological development is not dependent upon having two X chromosomes but rather on hormonal sex—in the absence of effective exposure to androgens, a female-typical phenotype, sexuality (attraction to males), and gender identity may develop, although many women with CAIS, just as many hormonally typical women, will not identify as heterosexual and/or female.

5-ALPHA-REDUCTASE DEFICIENCY

Another DSD affecting chromosomal males is 5-alpha-reductase deficiency (5-ARD); it results from mutations of the gene that encodes the steroid 5-alpha-reductase 2, an enzyme that converts testosterone to dihydrotestosterone (DHT). Cases are rare, although familial clusters appear in certain regions, such as in the Dominican Republic. Individuals with 5-ARD have testes (usually undescended) that secrete typical levels of testosterone, so their internal reproductive organs are male. Because of the enzyme deficiency, however, their external genitals develop as female-typical (these tissues require DHT to masculinize). As adults, most individuals with 5-ARD have typical testes, a male ejaculatory system, and a shallow vagina, with mostly female external genitals (Mendonca et al., 1996).

FIGURE 10.6 Katie Baratz is a woman with complete androgen insensitivity syndrome. Although she was born with XY chromosomes, which are typically associated with a male phenotype, she developed as phenotypically female because of a greater estrogen to androgen ratio, similar to typically developing genetic females.

Individuals with 5-ARD are typically raised as girls until puberty. As testosterone levels increase at puberty, however, masculinization of the external genitals occurs; the testes descend, the scrotum becomes pigmented, the clitoris enlarges to resemble a small penis, and the rest of the individual's body masculinizes. At this time, the majority of individuals with 5-ARD transition to a male gender identity and role, and the majority are sexually attracted to women. However, for some, such as the individual described in the following passage, the path to becoming a man may not be so direct.

Subject 8 is the youngest of 8 children of a poor farm family and was thought to be a normal female at the time of birth. His mother died when he was age 4 years, and he was raised by an older sister. He says that he felt different from other girls and began to exhibit male behaviour by age 6. By age 11, virilization of the external genitalia was apparent, male secondary sex characteristics began to appear, and he began to have erections; despite the inward feeling that he was a man he kept a female social sex and worked as a maid. At age 28 he commenced a long-term sexual relationship with a woman, and he sought medical help at age 30. Psychological evaluation revealed that he had a strong male libido and masturbated an average of 3 times a day. After surgery to correct the hypospadias, he married, adopted a child, and describes a satisfactory sexual life. (Mendonca et al., 1996, p. 66)

As this example suggests, individuals with 5-ARD may choose to undergo surgery to correct penile anomalies such as hypospadias (a developmental variation of the urethra); many may also choose hormone therapy.

Physical Traumas and Congenital Variations

Some individuals are raised in a gender role discordant with their chromosomal sex for reasons other than a genetic disorder, such as in the case of David Reimer, who lost his penis during infancy (see the chapter-opening case study). In other cases, physical developmental anomalies unrelated to sex chromosomes or sex hormones, such as penile agenesis or cloacal exstrophy, result in a genetic male not developing a penis. In the past, these males were reassigned to the female role in infancy because they lacked a penis. One review has suggested that such males who are assigned a female gender role at birth are significantly more likely to transition to the male role than those assigned to the male role at birth (Meyer-Bahlburg, 2005). Other studies following the gender identity development of genetic males with cloacal exstrophy raised as girls suggest that their gender role, and, for some, their gender identity, is more strongly associated with genetic and hormonal sex than the assigned gender. In one study examining genetic males with cloacal exstrophy, for example, 8 of 14 individuals raised as girls had transitioned to the male gender role between the ages of 5 and 12 years, and all had markedly male-typical interests (Reiner & Gearhart, 2004). These cases suggest that both nature and nurture play crucial roles in shaping gender identity.

Gender Development in Childhood

At what point in a child's development does gender identity coalesce and become expressed as gender role? Gender development involves three related processes: *detecting* gender, or being able to identify the similarities and differences between females and males; *having* gender, or recognizing in oneself characteristics shared by either boys or girls or both; and *doing* gender, or matching one's gendered behaviour with female or male gender stereotypes.

By age one, the majority of babies can detect gender, typically using gender-stereotyped physical characteristics, like hair length and clothing type, to differentiate between men and women (Leinbach & Fagot, 1993). Between two and three years of age, most children can identify what gender they *have*, whether they are a boy or a girl (Fagot & Leinbach, 1989), and most have a sense of their gender identity (Kohlberg, 1966). Yet at this age, children tend to understand gender as a superficial characteristic, believing that they can change their gender by changing their hairstyle or dress, and perhaps describing a woman with a deep voice as a man, or a man in a long wig as a woman (Kohlberg, 1966). Toward the end of this period, around the age of three or four, children come to understand gender as an inherent characteristic; in other words, they recognize *gender constancy* (Bem, 1989). *Doing* gender, behaving in stereotypic female or male ways (Messner, 2000), emerges later in childhood, typically between ages five and seven. This behaviour develops as children come to associate cultural symbols of femaleness and maleness (e.g., dolls and cars) with gender schemas (Bem, 1981), and as they are rewarded for showing preferences for gender-stereotypical activities and objects. (See the "Ethical Debate" box for a discussion of one couple's decision to raise their child genderless.)

What Factors Shape a Child's Sense of Gender Identity and Gender Roles?

From the moment babies are born, gender roles are imposed on them, and babies' behaviour is interpreted through a gendered lens. Any parent can tell you how, in Western culture, baby clothes are undeniably gendered, designed to disambiguate the

Ethical Debate

Is It Possible to Raise a Child Genderless?

Many parents attempt to minimize gender stereo-typing and strong gender schemas in their households but, to their dismay, their children end up doing gender just as other children do. I recall parents recounting how their four-year-old son, deeply engrossed in a game of cops and robbers with the neighbourhood children, had no guns to play with (these were not allowed in the house). Not wanting to be left out of the game, he improvised and brandished a doll instead, shouting "Bang! Bang!" and shooting at the fleeing suspect with the doll's mane of blonde hair.

In May 2011, Kathy Witterick and David Stocker publicly announced, in a Toronto Star article (Poisson, 2011), that they intended on raising their four-month-old baby, Storm, "genderless" (Figure 10.7). The parents, who have two older sons, Jazz and Kio, elected to not share information about their child's biological sex with the world, including the child's grandparents. Said Stocker, "If you really want to get to know someone, you don't ask what's between their legs." The parents stated that they were giving Storm the freedom to choose whom the child wants to be rather than having a gender role consistent with the child's biological sex imposed upon the child, noting that gender role socialization begins from an early age. The article generated a firestorm of public commentary, with many voicing concerns about Storm being bullied when the child entered school. Given that the family practises "unschooling," a form of home schooling where a child's curiosity drives learning in an unstructured fashion, their children are unlikely to experience bullying in a traditional elementary school. At some point in their lives, however, these children will have interactions with others in mainstream society.

This bold social experiment raises several interesting questions about the nature of the development of gender identity in children. Is it possible to be genderless in Western society? Is it ethical for Storm's parents to choose no gender identity for the child? Will Storm be marginalized for not conforming? How will Storm's gender identity be affected by Storm's parent's decision? Does this experiment have the potential to cause harm? If so, what kinds of harm?

FIGURE 10.7 Toronto couple Kathy Witterick and David Stocker have chosen to raise their youngest child, Storm (in Witterick's arms) genderless and have decided to keep Storm's sex a secret. Their other two children, Jazz (shown here on the left) and Kio, both boys, are often mistaken for girls because of their colour preferences and long hair.

gender of the tiny infant wearing them. The pink-for-girls and blue-for-boys gender stereotype is, however, a fairly recent phenomenon. In 1918, for example, the Earnshaw Knitting Company offered the following advice to new parents:

> Pink or blue? Which is intended for boys and which for girls? … There has been a great diversity of opinion on this subject, but the generally accepted rule is pink for the boy and blue for the girl. The reason is that pink being a more decided and stronger colour, is more suitable for the boy; while blue, which is more delicate and dainty, is prettier for the girl. (Krauch, 1918, cited in Maglaty, 2011)

These days, parents are hard-pressed to find clothes for girls that aren't pink (Figure 10.8).

In their classic study, John and Sandra Condry (1974) had women and men rate the presence and intensity of fear, anger, and pleasure responses of a nine-month-old baby to a teddy bear, a jack-in-the-box, a doll, and a buzzer. Half of the raters were told the infant was a boy, and half were told the infant was a girl. Those who believed the baby was a boy labelled the emotional responses as showing greater pleasure; those who believed the baby was a girl labelled the responses as showing greater intensity over all situations. Ratings of responses to the jack-in-the-box, which caused the baby to become agitated and eventually cry and scream, were most illustrative of gender stereotypes in emotional responses. Those who believed the baby was a boy rated the infant's response as "anger," whereas those who believed the baby was a girl rated the infant's response as "fear," reflecting gender stereotypes about acceptable emotional expressions.

gender socialization The learning of behaviour and attitudes considered appropriate for a given gender role.

Most parents marvel at how temperamentally different female and male children are; boys are notoriously more active, engaging in rough-and-tumble play and preferring active toys, whereas girls are typically less active, preferring to play with dolls and emulate nurturing. But are such preferences innate or adopted? Some believe that toy preferences, one expression of gender role and identity, are solely the result of **gender socialization**, a process thought to be mediated by two forms of learning. The first is observational learning, where children watch and emulate the behaviours and choices of other children and adults; the second is operational learning or shaping, whereby gender conforming behaviours are reinforced and gender nonconforming behaviours are punished. The result of such learning is that children adhere to playing with toys that are prescribed for the male or female gender role in childhood. Evidence from research on women with CAH, however, suggests that the influence of androgen during prenatal development is associated with preferring boys' toys and behaving in a gender nonconforming manner (Nordenström, Servin, Bohlin, Larsson, & Wedell, 2002).

Evidence for the biological contributions to gendered behaviour has also been found in research on non-human primates. For example, one study has shown that female and male vervet monkeys make toy choices similar to those of their human counterparts (Alexander & Hines, 2002).

FIGURE 10.8 Pink or blue? Today, most Westerners recognize pink as a "girl colour" and blue as a "boy colour," but these colours have not always been gender stereotyped in this way. The associations we make between certain colours and gender are entirely culturally constructed.

In this study, the male vervet monkeys spent more time in contact with a toy car than did the females, and the female vervet monkeys spent more time in contact with a doll, playing with the doll as if it were an infant, than did the males (Figure 10.9). Further, non-gendered toys (a stuffed dog and a picture book) attracted similar levels of attention from both males and females. This research suggests that the features of gendered toys, such as their colour, shape, and movement, interact with the characteristics of boys and girls and contribute to toy preferences. Boys may prefer cars over dolls because cars are more amenable to active play, and girls may prefer dolls because these objects facilitate the expression of nurturance. The monkeys, however, had observed other monkeys behaving in gender-specific ways (for example, female monkeys nurturing infants), so their behaviour may also reflect observational learning.

FIGURE 10.9 Research on non-human primates has shown that female monkeys prefer stereotypically female toys, and male monkeys prefer stereotypically male toys. Such findings suggest that toy preference in human children is somewhat innate.

Gender Variation in Childhood and Adolescence

Not all children adopt the gender identity or role strongly associated with their biological sex. Among gay men and lesbian women, a significant percentage of individuals recall a gender nonconforming childhood (Bailey & Zucker, 1995). In children who insist that they *are* the other sex, not simply that they *wish to be* the other sex, their transgender identity is more likely to persist into adolescence and adulthood (Steensma, Biemond, Boer, & Cohen-Kettenis, 2011; see below).

Considerable controversy surrounds the diagnosis of gender nonconforming children with gender dysphoria, and whether treatment, and what kind, should be started at a young age. Because sex hormones begin to significantly transform girls' and boys' bodies at puberty, some treatment centres are providing drugs that block the hormones associated with puberty. The aim of this treatment is to stop the feminizing or masculinizing effects of estrogens and androgens until the child is old enough to make the decision to pursue or not pursue gender transition.

Kenneth Zucker, researcher and head of the Gender Identity Service at the Centre for Addiction and Mental Health in Toronto, works with gender dysphoric children to encourage them to accept their birth sex, and with their families to address negative attitudes toward gender variance that may negatively affect their child. This approach has received considerable criticism, as it has often been misperceived as discrimination or silencing of gender minorities. Research data suggest, however, that the vast majority of gender nonconforming children lose their **gender dysphoria** (Wallien & Cohen-Kettenis, 2008), and many grow up to be happy and well-adjusted adults (Green, 1987; Bailey & Zucker, 1995). Therefore, Zucker's approach may be preferable to invasive, often irreversible medical interventions such as **transition related surgeries (TRSs)**, which can be risky and may carry long-term health consequences (Coleman et al., 2012), including infertility for the majority; circumventing this process is thought, by some, to be a more positive outcome.

gender dysphoria Distress resulting from the discrepancy between one's felt gender identity and one's biological sex and/or the gender one was assigned at birth.

transition related surgeries (TRSs) Surgical procedures to alter physical characteristics to resemble those typically associated with one's felt gender.

Trans Identities

As mentioned above, some individuals feel, often from a young age, that their gender doesn't match the gender typically associated with their biological sex. These individuals may feel as though they are trapped in the wrong body and forced to live in a gender role that doesn't match their inner self. People whose gender is opposite to their biological sex may refer to themselves as *trans* or *transgender*; following a similar nomenclature, borrowed from biochemistry, people whose gender matches their biological sex are referred to as *cis* or *cisgender*. The terms *transgender* and *transsexual* are often used interchangeably. In this chapter, however, the term *transgender* will refer to an individual whose gender identity and gender role are opposite to that person's biological sex but who has not (or has not yet) elected to have transition related surgeries (TRSs), and *transsexual* will refer to an individual who is transgender and has elected to undergo TRSs.

Biological males who identify as women are referred to as **transwomen**, and biological females who identify as men are referred to as **transmen**. The terms *male-to-female (MTF) transgender* (or *MTF transsexual*) and *female-to-male (FTM) transgender* (or *FTM transsexual*) are also used to describe transgender (or transsexual) individuals, with the initial gender term denoting biological sex at birth, and the second gender term denoting the felt gender identity (and, in the case of transsexual people, the gender associated with their acquired physical characteristics). Some individuals eschew gender categories altogether, preferring the concept of a continuum of fluid gender, or choosing to identify as **genderqueer**, similar to LGBTTIQQ individuals who choose to identify as *queer* or *unlabelled* instead of more standard labels of sexual identity (see Chapter 11).

Life Experiences and Sexual Orientations of Transmen and Transwomen

The majority of transmen recall a gender nonconforming childhood—being tomboys, preferring stereotypically male toys and physically active games, having more male than female playmates, rejecting female clothing and hairstyles, and insisting that they were boys and would eventually grow a penis. Many transmen also recall feeling distress as their bodies became more feminine during puberty. In adolescence and into adulthood, many seek to hide physical characteristics of their biological sex, binding their breasts and dressing androgynously. Research suggests that the majority of transmen report sexual attraction to women and so are, relative to their biological sex, same-sex oriented; after transitioning to the male role, these men identify as heterosexual. A minority of transmen do, however, report predominant sexual attractions to men and, after transitioning, identify as gay men. On average, transmen who are primarily attracted to women recall a somewhat more gender atypical childhood and report greater interest in sexual stimuli than do transmen who are primarily attracted to men, but both groups report similar levels of male gender identification in adulthood, and both report a desire for a masculine body (Chivers & Bailey, 2000).

The childhood experiences of transwomen are more divergent and, according to clinical research by Ray Blanchard, professor emeritus of psychology at the University of Toronto, generally fall in to two groups corresponding with the individual's sexual orientation (Blanchard, 1989). The first group is that of biological males who were very gender atypical as children—they dressed as girls, believed they were girls, preferred girls' toys and activities, had predominantly female playmates, and experienced gender dysphoria. Physically, these individuals may appear very feminine in their mannerisms, gait, voice, and physical presence, prior to any hormonal or surgical interventions or cross-living in the female role, and they may be indistinguishable from cisgender women when presenting in the female role. These transwomen typically are sexually attracted to men (are same-sex oriented relative to their biological sex) and, after transitioning to the female role, typically early in adulthood, identify as heterosexual women.

transwoman A biological male who identifies and presents as a woman.

transman A biological female who identifies and presents as a man.

genderqueer A person whose gender identification and self-presentation does not conform to gender categories.

The second group is that of transwomen who report a childhood that tended not to be gender atypical, and who report feeling predominantly sexually attracted to women. These individuals often recall feeling different from other male children, but they were not overtly gender nonconforming and generally did not experience gender dysphoria in their childhoods. Many recall dressing in women's clothing for the first time around puberty, becoming sexually aroused, and masturbating to orgasm; such behaviour is similar to that associated with transvestic fetishism (or transvestic disorder), which occurs when a non-gender dysphoric cisgender man experiences sexual pleasure from dressing in women's clothing (see Chapter 15). For many who seek transition to the female role, their eroticized cross-dressing progresses to sexual arousal at the idea of possessing female physical characteristics such a breasts and a vulva. Blanchard refers to this phenomenon as **autogynephilia** (Blanchard, 1989; see the "Research vs Real Life" box). Transwomen who are predominantly attracted to women tend to be less physically feminine in their gait, physical presence, and mannerisms, despite their strong identification as being female. Many of these transwomen seek gender transition later in life, after living as a male in a heterosexual relationship, often after an extensive history of cross-living in private. Many transwomen with a history of autogynephilia report that sexual arousal at wearing women's clothing or presenting as a woman lessens or disappears altogether after gender transition (Lawrence, 2005).

autogynephilia A sexual variation in which a man is sexually attracted to the thought of himself as a woman.

Transitioning to the Felt Gender and Sex

For most transwomen and transmen, "treatment" means processes and procedures aimed at aligning their social role and physical self with their felt gender. Health care providers committed to evidence-based and ethical practices typically follow the criteria for hormone-replacement therapy (HRT) and TRSs outlined in the World Professional Association for Transgender Health's (WPATH's) *Standards of Care for the Health of Transsexual, Transgender, and Gender-Nonconforming People* (Coleman et al., 2012). The information on the stages in gender transition described in the following sections are based on the standards set out in this publication.

PSYCHOLOGICAL AND PHYSICAL EVALUATION

The first stage is a psychological and physical evaluation by professionals with experience assisting gender transitions. Some individuals opt to start individual or group psychotherapy at this stage to recruit social and psychological support throughout gender transition, to connect with others undergoing gender transition, and to identify and negotiate potential barriers to a smooth gender transition. Because transition typically involves extensive and irreversible surgeries, the individual seeking treatment should be seen by a mental health professional to ensure that the decision is not motivated by factors other than a strong desire to match physical attributes to the felt gender role. The purpose of the physical evaluation is to determine whether the individual is intersex, and to identify any other factors that may play a role during hormonal and surgical transition, such as general health.

THE REAL-LIFE EXPERIENCE

The second stage is called the real-life experience, in which trans individuals fully transition to the social role matching their felt gender. It is recommended that the real-life experience continues for at least one year, to give individuals time to cope with adjustments in their personal and work life, and to ensure they are able to function in their felt gender role. Depending on where individuals undergo this transition, they may face significant discrimination; gender support groups can therefore provide a

Research VS Real Life

Autogynephilia

Some individuals in the transgender community reject the idea that autogynephilia is developmentally associated with a trans identity in some transwomen. These individuals argue that applying the concept of autogynephilia to transwomen equates a trans identity with psychosexual pathology or paraphilia (James, 2004), and that this equation is harmful to the trans community because it contradicts the subjective experience of transwomen as women trapped in men's bodies. No clearer example of the bitter dispute between some in the trans community and some in the scientific community on this issue exists than the backlash J. Michael Bailey received for his book, *The Man Who Would Be Queen* (2003). In this book, Bailey discusses femininity in biological males, with a chapter devoted to transgender/transsexual typologies in which he provides a detailed discussion of Blanchard's research on autogynephilia. The publication of this book sparked an onslaught of attacks on the scientific community, the majority aimed at Bailey. The conflict regarding discussions of autogynephilia in relation to transwomen in general—and in reaction to Blanchard's and Bailey's

work in particular—is surprising for many reasons, three of which are discussed below.

First, prior to Blanchard's work, there was little consensus on how to understand the variability in sexual and gender histories among transwomen, or how this variability related to the desire to transition to the felt gender role. Many typologies existed, but that of "primary" and "secondary" transwomen persisted, describing "homosexual" transwomen (those attracted to men) and "nonhomosexual"/"transvestitic" transwomen (those attracted to women), respectively (see Stoller, 1980). Along with this typology persisted the belief that "secondary" transwomen were inappropriate candidates for SRS. Because of a lack of understanding and knowledge, transwomen with a history of erotic cross-dressing were at risk of being misdiagnosed as "transvestites" and the legitimacy of their transgender identity as women being called in to question. As a result, transwomen frequently concealed their erotic cross-dressing and autogynephilia for fear they would be labelled "secondary" and denied treatment (Lawrence, 2010). Blanchard's

---

place to share stories, information, and support. In Canada, human rights laws generally prohibit discrimination against pre-operative, transitioning, and post-operative transgender and transsexual persons, although Section 15 of the Canadian Charter of Rights and Freedoms does not explicitly refer to gender minorities.

HORMONE-REPLACEMENT THERAPY (HRT)

The third stage, HRT, is usually initiated after at least one year of real-life experience, ideally under the care of an endocrinologist. Transmen begin taking injections of testosterone at this stage. The male hormone causes male-pattern hair growth on the face, chest, and body; thickening of the cartilage in the larynx, causing deepening of the voice; and changes in body fat distribution consistent with a male-typical pattern (Figure 10.10). As testosterone accumulates in the individual's system, menstrual periods cease, and the clitoris becomes larger. Many transmen undergoing hormone therapy also report increased sexual desire, more frequent sexual thoughts, stronger feelings of aggression, and greater salience of sexual stimuli; some also report a change in their preferences for visual sexual materials. Max Wolf Valerio, a transman and poet, has written about his experience of his changing sexuality after being on testosterone for almost a year:

The eye, my eyes, held and stoked by sexual imagery. I notice that I am aroused by even a benign television commercial featuring a sleek woman climbing into

research showed that transwomen reporting a history of autogynephilia also experienced significant transgender feelings and gender dysphoria, and that they should therefore receive support for gender transition. More recently, Anne Lawrence's research has demonstrated that factors associated with the autogynephilic transwoman typology are not associated with post-SRS regrets (Lawrence, 2003).

Second, rejection of the legitimacy of autogynephilic pathways to a trans identity means that transwomen with this history are silenced and marginalized within the trans community. Moreover, some within the trans community have described autogynephilia using the pejorative and judgmental term "perversion" (Conway, 2006), thus stigmatizing individuals with both atypical sexual interests and gender variation. With research clearly demonstrating the benefits of social supports to sexual and gender minorities, this fracture in the trans community may serve to further alienate autogynephilic transwomen trying to understand their gender and sexual variations, and it may increase the risk of psychological harm.

Third, although autogynephilia and its association with a trans identity has been described in the clinical and research literatures for decades, there is still only an incomplete understanding of how this sexual interest develops or how it relates to the emergence of a transgender identity. Because first cross-gender wishes typically emerge simultaneously with the onset of erotic cross-dressing in autogynephilic transwomen (Blanchard, Clemmensen, & Steiner, 1987) and well-developed transgender identities emerge only years later (Docter, 1988), both advocates and opponents (e.g., Roughgarden, 2004) of autogynephilia theory have assumed it is the autoerotic impulse that motivates gender transition in autogynephilic transwomen. In reality, however, it is not clear that there is a causal relationship between autogynephilia and gender identity in transwomen.

Fortunately, the rejection of discussions of autogynephilia in relation to trans identities was not universal. Many transwomen are relieved that autogynephilic interests, previously a taboo topic, are now being openly discussed in the trans community.

This section was written with the help of Alice Domurat Dreger, Ph.D., professor of clinical medical humanities and bioethics at Northwestern University.

a sports car with its top down. I pay more attention to women on the street. I catch myself watching, like so many other guys. . . . I get a more palpable sense of pleasure from looking. (Valerio, 2006, p. 180)

Transwomen begin taking androgen-blocking drugs and estrogens at this stage. The estrogens change body fat distribution to a more female-typical pattern and cause the skin to feel smoother. Transwomen undergoing hormone therapy will also experience breast growth, and for some this growth will be satisfactory and obviate breast augmentation. The treatment does not, however, stop male-pattern balding or beard growth; most transwomen must undergo extensive electrolysis or laser treatments to remove their male-typical facial hair permanently. The androgen-blocking treatment typically reduces sex drive, along with the frequency of erections and ejaculations. Many transwomen report relief at the subsiding of their sex drive, although some experience complete lack of sexual interest as a side effect and may take small quantities of testosterone to restore their sex drive after they have undergone SRS.

TRANSITION RELATED SURGERIES (TRSs)

The fourth stage is transition related surgeries (TRSs), which WPATH recommends to start at least one year after hormone therapy begins. This stage generally involves multiple surgeries to create genitals (bottom surgery) and a chest contour (top surgery) associated with the felt gender. For transwomen, key surgeries include bilateral orchidectomy (removal of the testicles) and reconstruction of the penile and scrotal tissues to form a vulva (labiaplasty, clitoral construction) and a vaginal canal (vaginoplasty). Depending on the extent of breast development from estrogen therapy, a transwoman might also elect to have breast augmentation surgery. Other surgeries may be

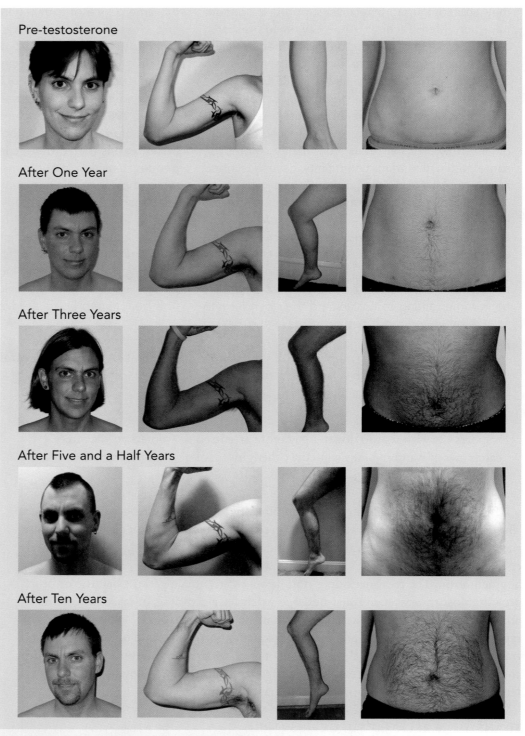

FIGURE 10.10 Ethan Daniel, an American transman, has been documenting his physical gender transition in a remarkable series of photographs (see www.ftmtransition.com/transition/testosterone/tphotos.html for the full set).The first row of photos shows him before he started testosterone therapy in 2003; the final panel shows him ten years later, in 2013.

performed to raise vocal pitch, reduce the size of the laryngeal prominence (Adam's apple), and create a more feminine facial and/or body appearance.

For transmen, top surgery involves having a bilateral mastectomy (removal of both breasts) and cosmetic surgery to create a male-typical chest appearance. Bottom surgery includes a complete hysterectomy (removal of the uterus), an oophorectomy (removal of the ovaries), and often scrotoplasty and phalloplasty (construction of a scrotum and a penis, respectively). Many transmen forego phalloplasty because creating a penis with a functioning urethra and capacity for erections (using a mechanical erection device) involves many expensive surgeries. The constructed penis, depending on the procedure, can be erotically sensitive when constructed from skin grafts from areas such as the forearm or thigh. Nerves from the graft can be connected with those on the clitoris, facilitating erotic sensation in the new penis. Many transmen opt to obtain a metoidioplasty, a surgical procedure in which the enlarged clitoris is freed from the clitoral hood and a penile shaft is created; some opt for no bottom surgery at all beyond a full hysterectomy. The result is a small, erotically sensitive penis capable of an erection and orgasm, although penetration may not be possible depending on how firm the erection is.

Post-surgery Outcomes

The majority of transsexual people report satisfaction with their surgery and improvement to their quality of life after transitioning. In a study of 232 post-operative transwomen treated by the same surgeon, the vast majority reported being satisfied with the outcome and experiencing improvement in the quality of their lives (Lawrence, 2003). Transmen who obtain hormone treatment report better quality of life than those not taking hormone therapy (Newfield, Hart, Dibble, & Kohler, 2006). Ray Blanchard and his colleagues at the Centre for Addiction and Mental Health in Toronto conducted a follow-up study of transsexual women and men; they reported that all 61 transmen and 46 out of 50 transwomen had satisfactory outcomes (Blanchard, Steiner, Clemmensen, & Dickie, 1989). All of the transwomen who reported regrets were sexually attracted to both women and men, and on average, they were older when they transitioned. Age at the time of TRSs, physical health, mental health, strong social support, a body build compatible with the chosen sex, and success of the surgery are all components that contribute to satisfaction with the transition process.

OTHER AREAS OF TRANSITION

Undergoing physical and physiological changes is only one component of a gender transition; post-operative transsexual women and men must also negotiate changes in their personal relationships. Coming out as trans can be as or more challenging than coming out as not heterosexual, particularly since many individuals may have little experience with trans people and may have negative attitudes and actively discriminate against gender minorities. Hate crime and abuse rates are higher for gender minorities than for LGBTTIQQ individuals. Some trans people face discrimination from LGBTTIQQ individuals as well, particularly if they have transitioned to become a lesbian transwoman or a gay transman.

Transsexual individuals must decide when and how to discuss their transsexuality with new romantic and sexual partners. Because transwomen are able to obtain genital surgery that creates a very natural-looking vulva and functional vagina, some transwomen are able to have sexual relationships with women and men without revealing their identity as trans; for transmen, this discussion typically happens much earlier in a sexual relationship. Fortunately, many people have positive attitudes toward gender minorities, accepting trans people as their new sex.

The Choice Not to Transition

Some transgender people opt not to transition to the opposite sex, rejecting the medical model of transsexuality, which suggests that transgender individuals have a medical disorder that requires a medical intervention to correct. These individuals may have practical reasons for not fully transitioning, such as medical conditions that preclude physical procedures, or they may reject the notion that they must choose one gender, or must possess all physical and psychological traits of one gender. In many cases, these individuals identify as genderqueer, and they may view modern Western culture's binary division of male–female, man–woman as incompatible with their personal experiences of their physical and psychological selves. This view is more consistent with that held by various societies around the world in which gender minorities are more commonly accepted (see the "Culture and Diversity" box).

Culture & Diversity

A Third (or More) Gender(s)?

Contributed by Caroline F. Pukall, Ph.D., C.Psych., Department of Psychology, Queen's University

Not all cultures have a choice of only two gender boxes to tick when you are completing forms. Australia, for example, offers a third option for gender on passport applications: in 2011, an "other" category was added to the male and female options to accommodate intersex individuals. Unfortunately, Canada lags behind in this respect: those seeking a change in gender identification on their passport are required to submit medical documentation showing that they have undergone SRS. Applicants who have not yet undergone SRS can get a passport that states their preferred gender, but these passports are valid for two years only and are issued only to applicants who can provide documentation that they will undergo SRS in the next year. These requirements have been dropped in the US and in Britain, where individuals can choose the "other" category without having had the surgery or without plans to have the surgery. Other countries have long recognized diversity in gender expression. The example of the *fa'afafine* of Samoa was discussed in Chapter 2, and in this section the focus will be on the *hijras* of India.

The *hijras* are a religious community of biological males (and a small group of intersex individuals) who dress and act like women. Their culture centres on the worship of Bahuchara Mata, a version of the Mother Goddess worshipped throughout India (Nanda, 1999). Most *hijras* undergo an operation (called *nirwaan*) in which their genitals are removed. Although

the penis, testicles, and scrotum are removed, unlike transwomen undergoing SRS, no vagina is constructed. The *hijras* are therefore defined as eunuchs (see Chapter 4), and they are seen as a third sex. *Hijras* are accorded a special status in India through their connection with the Mother Goddess and the female creative power embodied by her. They often play music, sing, and dance at ceremonies celebrating the birth of a child (usually a male), at weddings, and at temple festivals (Nanda, 1999), and their performances are believed to bring good luck.

Although many *hijras* view themselves as neither male nor female, some see themselves as females, feminine males, or androgynes. A minority of them—those who have been influenced by international discourses around LGBTTIQQ identities—may identify as transgender or as transwomen. However, unlike Western transwomen, *hijras* do not attempt to "pass" as women. Typically, *hijras* will have masculine men as sexual partners and will be (anally) penetrated by them. Although some *hijras* have "married" men in the past, the marriage is not usually recognized by law or religion.

Most *hijras* live marginalized lives and have a low socio-economic status. There are few employment opportunities for them outside of performing at ceremonies, and there is typically little money to be made from this livelihood. Many can be seen begging on the streets for money, and some turn to prostitution.

CHAPTER SUMMARY

Gender is the psychological phenomenon of femaleness and maleness arising from the intersection between biological factors (e.g., hormones, genes) and socio-cultural factors (e.g., social roles, cultural beliefs). Evolutionary psychology, social learning theory, and social structural theory are three theoretical perspectives that seek to understand gender differences and similarities in sexuality, such as those related to masturbation, numbers of sexual partners, attitudes toward casual sex, erotica use, and patterns of sexual response. Research on gender development suggests that both biological and social factors contribute to gender role behaviours in children. Individuals with disorders of sexual development have medical conditions (e.g., sex chromosome variations, hormone variations, genital development variations) that lead to intermediate expressions of female and male phenotypes, which in turn may lead to gender identity concerns in some individuals. Transmen and transwomen are people whose felt gender identity does not correspond with their biological sex; some choose to undergo a gender transition to align their physical self with their felt gender. This process involves psychological evaluation and support, living in the felt gender role, hormone therapy, and transition related surgeries.

DEBATE QUESTIONS

What are the pros and cons of performing genital surgery on infants or young children for the purpose of achieving gender-stereotypical genitals? How does the issue of consent from that infant or child bear on this decision?

REVIEW QUESTIONS

1. How do gonadal sex, hormonal sex, and genetic sex relate to gender?

2. What are three main theoretical perspectives from which social scientists seek to understand sexuality and gender, and what are the general principles of each perspective?

3. What are four gender differences in sexuality? How could each theoretical perspective account for these differences?

4. How do the variations in sex chromosomes, sex hormones, and genital development described in this chapter influence aspects of gender and sexuality?

5. What are the four major stages of a gender transition, according to the World Professional Association for Transgender Health? What is involved in each stage?

SUGGESTIONS FOR FURTHER READING AND VIEWING

Recommended Websites

Autogynephilia.org: http://autogynephilia.org

Bem Sex Role Inventory: www.neiu.edu/~tschuepf/bsri.html

Ethan Daniel's website: www.ftmtransition.com/transition/testosterone/tphotos.html

Gender Outlaw (Joshua Riverdale's FTM transition blog): http://genderoutlaw .wordpress.com

Information about Autogynephilia: www.annelawrence.com/autogynephiliaindex .html

Intersex Society of North America: www.isna.org

Recommended Reading

Bailey, J.M. (2003). *The man who would be queen: The science of gender-bending and transsexualism*. Washington, DC: Joseph Henry Press.

Colapinto, J. (2000). *As nature made him: The boy who was raised as a girl*. New York, NY: HarperCollins.

Fausto-Sterling, A. (2000). *Sexing the body: Gender politics and the construction of sexuality*. New York, NY: Basic Books.

Hines, M. (2004). *Brain gender*. New York, NY: Oxford University Press.

Lippa, R.A. (2005). *Gender, nature, and nurture* (2nd ed.). Mahwah, NJ: Erlbaum.

Mealey, L. (2000). *Sex differences: Developmental and evolutionary strategies*. San Diego, CA: Academic Press.

Pfaff, D. (2010). *Man and woman: An inside story*. New York, NY: Oxford University Press.

Poisson, J. (2011). Parents keep child's gender secret. *Toronto Star*. Retrieved from www.thestar.com/life/parent/2011/05/21/parents_keep_childs_gender_secret.html

Valerio, M.F. (2006). *The testosterone files: My hormonal and social transformation from female to male*. Emeryville, CA: Seal Press.

Recommended Viewing

Berliner, A. (Director). (1997). *Ma vie en rose* [Motion picture]. France: Sony Pictures Classics.

Elisco, D. (Director). (2009). Sex, lies, and gender [Television series episode]. In National Geographic Society (Producer), *National geographic explorer*. United States: National Geographic Television.

Gill, K. (Director & Producer). (2009). *Kiss the moon* [Documentary]. Pakistan: Little Dots Productions

MSNBC. (Producer). (2007). *Born in the wrong body* [Documentary series]. United States: MSNBC. Available at www.msnbc.msn.com/id/26392358/ns/msnbc-documentaries

11 CHAPTER

Sexual/Affectional Orientations and Diversity

KEVIN ALDERSON

LEARNING OBJECTIVES

In this chapter, you will

- learn about how sexual/affectional orientations and identities are understood and defined;
- consider the negative impacts of persistent prejudices against same-sex oriented individuals;
- become familiar with perspectives on how affectional orientation and sexual identity develop; and
- find out about the importance of self-identification and the benefits and potential risks of identity disclosure for LGBTTIQQ individuals.

Charlie's Struggle with Same-Sex Attraction

Charlie is a 65-year-old man whose wife of 40 years, Gladys, passed away a year ago. He wears his grieving on his sleeve, never quite feeling able to move on from the woman he admired and cared for throughout most of his adult life. But Charlie is also aware that he has always been sexually aroused by men. If it weren't for the fact that he grew up in a time when to be sexually involved with other men was both illegal and considered a mental disorder, he laments, he might have explored his sexuality. He recalls the harsh messages and tone of voice when people used *queer*, *faggot*, *fairy*, *homo*, and other choice words in a derogatory manner to refer to gay people.

As Charlie's mental health practitioner, you are concerned about his continual grieving and his expression of same-sex attraction. Charlie has told you he doesn't want to spend the rest of his life alone. You begin asking him some questions, and you get the following responses:

You: If you were to be left on a deserted island with only one other person, and you knew you would never be found or discovered, would you rather that person be a man or a woman?
Charlie: I would prefer to be with a woman—Gladys was always there for me, very nurturant. I don't find that most men have that characteristic.

You: Tell me about the crushes you've had throughout your life.
Charlie: I've had several. There was Tracy in Grade 11, and my homeroom teacher, Miss Fenton, in Grade 12. I also worshipped Marilyn Monroe and thought she would have made a fine wife.

You: When you are at the beach and notice a really attractive couple, who do you spend the most time focussed on: the man or the woman?

Charlie: I would have to say both, actually—I have always been impressed by muscular men, and I enjoy looking at men's crotches. I never felt that I was well-enough equipped to satisfy Gladys, although she never complained. I always felt insecure about my penis size. I also love a woman's breasts and curves.

You: When you masturbated or had sex with your wife, to what extent did you focus on sexual fantasies involving men as opposed to women?
Charlie: Well, I never focussed much on men at all. I usually fantasized about having sex with women.

You: Did you ever fall in love with anyone romantically before or after you met Gladys?
Charlie: Well, yes, I did—I fell very hard in love with Sandra Jensen, a woman I dated for six months. It took me several months to get over her.

QUESTIONS FOR CRITICAL THOUGHT AND REFLECTION

1. What impressions do you get regarding Charlie's sexual/affectional orientation? What is the likelihood that Charlie will fall in love romantically with a man?
2. What issues need to be dealt with before Charlie would be ready for another relationship with either a man or a woman?
3. If Charlie decides he wants to have sex with a man (or with a woman, for that matter), what safety concerns would you have? What psychological concerns would you have? What information would Charlie need to know before he embarks on this quest?
4. Besides engaging in same-sex behaviour, what other actions might Charlie take to help himself come to a greater acceptance of his sexuality?

Introduction

Occasionally, you read about historical figures who were purportedly gay or lesbian. For example, were Alexander the Great and Michelangelo gay? Were Joan of Arc and Florence Nightingale lesbian? Such questions are intriguing, but they are ultimately unanswerable, as there were no such constructs as "gay" or "lesbian" in the periods in which these individuals lived. Underlying the consideration that these constructs did not exist is the question of definition. Attributions, both personal and those offered by others, are based on characteristics, whether internal or external. Stereotypes, for example, are often expressed externally, while cognitions and emotions are internal—at least until they are shared in some way. What does it mean to be gay or lesbian or bisexual or heterosexual? This question will be answered in the following sections.

Sexual/Affectional Orientations and Identities

Sexual vs Affectional Orientations

When discussing peoples' intimate, sexual, and romantic attractions to others, most researchers and laypersons alike focus on the sexual aspects of such attractions, using the term *sexual orientation* to refer to an individual's tendency to be attracted to men and/or women. Yet many have noted that this term is too limited, as it overemphasizes the sexual aspects of an orientation and thus oversimplifies what an orientation is. As a result, there is growing support for rejecting the term *sexual orientation* in favour of the more inclusive term ***affectional orientation***. Indeed, most current researchers recognize that an orientation has a significant emotional attachment component (Pedersen, Crethar, & Carlson, 2008).

There are also political reasons for moving away from the trend to classify an individual's orientation based solely on his or her sexual behaviours. In modern times, sexual behaviour has often been used to classify people. In the past, divisions between "heterosexual" and "homosexual" did not exist. If a man had sex with another man, it didn't challenge his identity. In fact, the word *homosexual* did not even enter the English language until 1869 (see Bullough & Bullough, 1997). Before then, everyone was assumed to be heterosexual and to have a **heterosexual orientation**; **same-sex orientations** and **bisexual orientations** were simply not recognized. As the word *homosexual* became popular in general usage, those who engaged in same-sex sexual activity were no longer viewed as *doing* a behaviour—they instead *became* a certain creature. The *homosexual* was born.

These *homosexuals* were believed to be treacherous, immoral, corrupt creatures, and they were blamed for a lot of what was wrong in society. They were viewed as neurotic, lonely, depressed, promiscuous, unhappy, fixated, unfulfilled, undependable, defective, mentally ill, incapable of intimacy, shallow, narcissistic, effeminate, predatory, prudish, and overly chatty (Beard & Glickauf-Hughes, 1994). Other less-commonly held beliefs included that they could not whistle, they lacked body hair, they caused the American defeat in Vietnam, and they were to blame for World War II (Hetrick & Martin, 1984). Even members of the scientific community put forth negative views of homosexuality. For example, reputed physician David Reuben, in his highly influential book *Everything You Always Wanted to Know about Sex but Were Afraid to Ask* (1969), explained that "the primary interest [in homosexuality] is the penis, not the person" (p. 163). Reuben also expressed a debasing attitude toward lesbian women.

It should not sound surprising, given this history, that those men and women who were developing real relationships with others of the same sex became insulted by this now pejorative term, *homosexual*. It overemphasized sex, and it had developed an incredibly negative connotation. As a result, the term *homosexual* fell out of use, and individuals who were attracted to members of their own sex began to refer to themselves as *gay* or *lesbian*. Along with this change in terminology came new perspectives on same-sex attraction as well as the acknowledgement that some people actually *do* fall in love romantically with members of their own sex—a recognition that is better reflected by the concept of *affectional orientation* than *sexual orientation*.

affectional orientation The interaction between affect and cognition such that it produces attraction, erotic desire, and ultimately feelings of love for members of the other sex, the same sex, or both.

heterosexual orientation An affectional orientation where affect and cognition are exclusively directed at members of the other sex.

same-sex orientation An affectional orientation where affect and cognition are exclusively directed at members of the same sex.

bisexual orientation An affectional orientation where affect and cognition are directed at members of both sexes, to one extent or another.

Attempts to Measure Sexual/Affectional Orientation

Several researchers have attempted to measure sexual/affectional orientation through the use of scales, thereby creating operational definitions of these constructs. (An operational definition defines something by how it is measured.) For example, the Kinsey Scale (see Figure 3.3, on p. 57) offers operational definitions of sexual orientation that range from exclusively heterosexual (a score of 0) to exclusively homosexual (a score of 6). Placement on the scale is determined primarily by self-reported sexual behaviour and secondarily by self-reported sexual desires and attractions.

Another notable scale is the one developed by Klein, Sepekoff, and Wolf (1985). It is commonly referred to as the Klein Sexual Orientation Grid (Figure 11.1) and includes measures of seven components: sexual attraction, sexual behaviour, sexual fantasies, emotional preference, social preference, self-identification, and heterosexual/homosexual lifestyle. Each component is assigned a number from 1 (other sex only) to 7 (same sex only) in terms of past, present (over the past 12 months), and self-defined "ideal" circumstances. As a whole, this scale is more detailed and inclusive than is the Kinsey Scale.

An even more detailed scale is the relatively recent one created by Alderson, Orzeck, Davis, and Boyes (2013). This scale, which is based on the Sexuality Questionnaire (Figure 11.2), incorporates suggestions made by several researchers to measure affectional orientation on two separate scales: one that measures interest in males, and

Klein Sexual Orientation Grid

Variable	Past	Present	Ideal
Sexual Attraction			
Sexual Behaviour			
Sexual Fantasies			
Emotional Preference			
Social Preference			
Self-Identification			
Heterosexual/Homosexual Lifestyle			

Please rate the first five variables in the above table according to the following scale:

1	2	3	4	5	6	7
Other sex only	Other sex mostly	Other sex somewhat more	Both sexes equally	Same sex somewhat more	Same sex mostly	Same sex only

Please rate the last two variables in the above table according to the following scale:

1	2	3	4	5	6	7
Heterosexual only	Heterosexual mostly	Heterosexual somewhat more	Heterosexual/ Homosexual equally	Homosexual somewhat more	Homosexual mostly	Homosexual only

FIGURE 11.1 The Klein Sexual Orientation Grid measures seven components related to sexual/affectional orientation over time (past and present) and in a self-defined "ideal" state.

The Sexuality Questionnaire

The following questions pertain to the magnitude of your opposite-gender and same-gender interests. To what extent have you experienced the following during the two time periods indicated?

SEXUAL ATTRACTION: This refers to feeling sexually aroused by someone you find attractive.

Magnitude [Use the following ratings]:
0 = zero or none   1 = unsure   2 = low   3 = moderate   4 = high

#	Item	Interest in Males/Men					Interest in Females/Women				
		zero	unsure	low	mod	high	zero	unsure	low	mod	high
1	During the past 12 months	0	1	2	3	4	0	1	2	3	4
2	*During ages 12 to 19 (Note: if you are currently 19 years of age or younger, complete this question from ages 12 to a year ago. Follow this same procedure in all subsequent sections.)										

SEXUAL FANTASIES: This refers to your sexual fantasies experienced during either masturbation or during sex with a partner.

Magnitude [Use the following ratings]:
0 = zero or none   1 = unsure   2 = low   3 = moderate   4 = high

#	Item	Interest in Males/Men					Interest in Females/Women				
		zero	unsure	low	mod	high	zero	unsure	low	mod	high
1	During the past 12 months	0	1	2	3	4	0	1	2	3	4
2	*During ages 12 to 19										

SEXUAL PREFERENCE: This refers to your preference for having male and/or female **sexual** partners.

Magnitude [Use the following ratings]:
0 = zero or none   1 = unsure   2 = low   3 = moderate   4 = high

#	Item	Interest in Males/Men					Interest in Females/Women				
		zero	unsure	low	mod	high	zero	unsure	low	mod	high
1	During the past 12 months	0	1	2	3	4	0	1	2	3	4
2	*During ages 12 to 19										

PROPENSITY TO FALL IN LOVE ROMANTICALLY: This refers to your natural **inclination** to have crushes and fall in love romantically with males and/or females.

Magnitude [Use the following ratings]:
0 = zero or none   1 = unsure   2 = low   3 = moderate   4 = high

#	Item	Interest in Males/Men					Interest in Females/Women				
		zero	unsure	low	mod	high	zero	unsure	low	mod	high
1	During the past 12 months	0	1	2	3	4	0	1	2	3	4
2	*During ages 12 to 19										

BEING IN LOVE ROMANTICALLY: This refers to how often you have **actually** felt romantic love (liking the person, having chemistry or feelings of lust toward this person, and feeling some degree of commitment toward this individual).

Magnitude [Use the following ratings]:
0 = zero or none   1 = unsure   2 = low   3 = moderate   4 = high

#	Item	Interest in Males/Men					Interest in Females/Women				
		zero	unsure	low	mod	high	zero	unsure	low	mod	high
1	During the past 12 months	0	1	2	3	4	0	1	2	3	4
2	*During ages 12 to 19										

SEXUAL PARTNERS: This refers to how often you have had sexual partners who are male and/or female. [Note: "sexual partner" refers to anyone you have engaged in penetrative sexual acts with, including oral, vaginal, and anal sex.]

Magnitude [Use the following ratings]:
0 = zero or none   1 = unsure   2 = low   3 = moderate   4 = high

#	Item	Interest in Males/Men					Interest in Females/Women				
		zero	unsure	low	mod	high	zero	unsure	low	mod	high
1	During the past 12 months	0	1	2	3	4	0	1	2	3	4
2	*During ages 12 to 19										

FIGURE 11.2 The Sexuality Questionnaire captures various aspects of affectional orientation.

one that measures interest in females. Factor analytic work has shown that affectional orientation can operationally be defined and measured as a combination of six components: sexual attraction, sexual fantasies, sexual preference, propensity to fall in love romantically, being in love romantically, and the extent to which one has male and/or female sexual partners (Alderson et al., 2013).

Identity Labels

Regardless of the debates between essentialists (who believe that there is something innate about sexual desire and affectional orientation) and social constructionists (who believe that all aspects of our sexuality are constructed as a result of interactions among historical, social, and psychological variables and contexts), there is little question that **sexual identity labels** are socially constructed. Such labels as **gay identity**, **lesbian identity**, and **bisexual identity** indicate more than just preference for engaging in sexual and romantic relationships with members of a certain sex; they also entail certain self-perceptions and worldviews. For example, while both males and females may label themselves as *gay*, most gay females prefer to refer to themselves as *lesbian* because a lesbian identity generally carries with it certain political allegiances to female solidarity and feminist ideology; women who identify as *lesbian* find that these political and ideological views have personal significance to them. In fact, an important factor in adopting a certain sexual identity label is that the identity it signifies has *a personal significance* to the individual.

The sexual identity labels people give themselves may change over the course of their lives. Most gay, lesbian, and bisexual individuals, for example, at some point defined themselves as heterosexual, which is the default label in most societies. Many bisexual individuals may also have identified as gay or lesbian before coming to a bisexual label. In some cases, people assume a label that does not accurately reflect their sexual/affectional orientation because they are unaware of their romantic proclivities; this is often the case when gay, lesbian, or bisexual individuals assume the default label of *heterosexual* early in their lives. Others assume a label that they deem to be most socially acceptable, which is often the case for individuals who assume a heterosexual identity despite their involvement in same-sex sexual relationships.

A nationally representative American study by Laumann, Gagnon, Michael, and Michaels (1994) found that there were often discrepancies among sexual identity, sexual behaviour, and sexual desire. Most men reported a same-sex sexual experience at some point in their lives but did not self-identify as gay. For reasons such as this, HIV-prevention efforts are targeted at men who have sex with men (Figure 11.3), not at gay or bisexual men. Unsafe sexual behaviour can lead to HIV infection (see Chapter 8), regardless of one's sexual identity label. Furthermore, Laumann et al. found that 22 per cent of men and 13 per cent of women reported engaging in same-sex behaviour despite reporting no sexual desire for members of the same sex.

Some individuals today prefer not to use identity labels to describe themselves. This preference has its roots in the relatively new field of queer studies, which generally accepts the social constructionist view that our sexuality in its entirety is socially constructed. Individuals who are trying to avoid sexual identity labels often identify as *queer* or *unlabelled*. However, a **queer identity** is, in a sense, an oxymoron—to say one has a queer identity *is* to label one's identity.

Finally, note that such words as *lesbian, gay, bisexual, queer,* and *heterosexual* are better used as adjectives than as nouns. Recognizing that identity labels are socially constructed, we must remember that they refer to an identity and not to a person's "essence," meaning they are not intrinsically predetermined (e.g., genetically, biologically). The

---

sexual identity label The general label one chooses to use to describe one's sexual attractions (typically gay, lesbian, bisexual, questioning, or queer).

gay identity An identity status denoting those individuals who have come to identify themselves as having primarily same-sex oriented cognition, affect, and/or behaviour, and who have adopted the construct of "gay" as having personal significance to them.

lesbian identity An identity status denoting those female-gendered individuals who have adopted the construct of "lesbian" as having personal significance to them.

bisexual identity An identity status denoting individuals who have come to identify themselves as having both other-sex and same-sex oriented cognition, affect, and/or behaviour, and who have adopted the construct of "bisexual" as having personal significance to them.

queer identity An identity status that is intended to not label one's sexuality.

cause of affectional orientation is still debated, and some believe the debate between essentialism and social constructionism can never be resolved. Identities, however, are ascribed; hence, the words that signify them are descriptive rather than concrete—adjectives, not nouns.

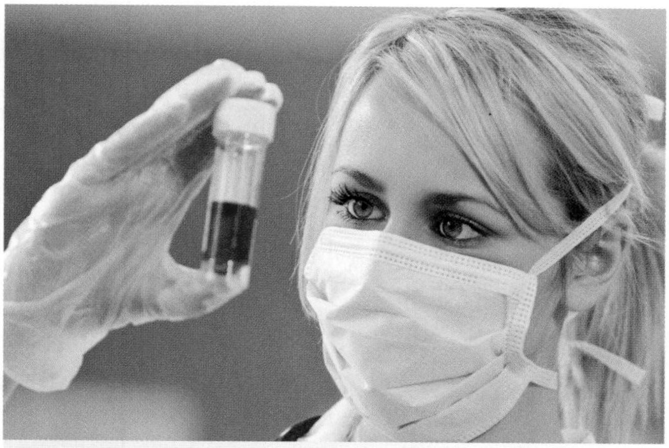

Asexuality

There is also the special case of asexuality. A recent national probability sample from Britain found that approximately 1 per cent of individuals in the sample ($N > 18,000$) indicated that they were asexual (Bogaert, 2004). Bogaert (2006) provided arguments both for and against classifying asexuality as a separate "sexual orientation" (his definition of *sexual orientation* was "one's subjective sexual attraction to the sex of others," p. 244).

FIGURE 11.3 HIV-prevention efforts are aimed at all men who have sex with men because unprotected anal sex carries a high risk of HIV transmission.

There are various definitions of asexuality that focus on low levels of sexual attraction, lack of interest in sexual behaviour, lack of sexual orientation, and/or lack of sexual excitation. Lori Brotto, from the University of British Columbia, and her colleagues conducted two studies in order to understand asexuality. In their first study, they surveyed 54 self-identified asexual men and 133 self-identified asexual women; in their second study, they telephone interviewed 15 from their original sample. They found that although men in the asexual group reported lower sexual response than is indicated by available normative data for men, these men masturbated with the same frequency as normative men. The combined data from both studies suggested that asexuality "is best conceptualized as a lack of sexual attraction; however, asexuals varied greatly in their experience of sexual response and behaviour" (Brotto, Knudson, Inskip, Rhodes, & Erskine, 2010, p. 599).

Prause and Graham (2007) concluded from their content analysis of 41 questionnaires completed by self-identified asexual individuals that low sexual desire was the primary feature contributing to the construction of an **asexual identity**. They also found that masturbation frequency among these individuals was in the normative range. Neither Brotto et al. (2010) nor Prause and Graham (2007) found that participants were distressed because of their reported asexuality. Prause and Graham found, however, that the majority emphasized romantic as opposed to sexual aspects of their relationships.

asexual identity An identity label acknowledging that a person perceives little or no interest in engaging sexually with others.

Given our understanding of asexuality to date, we can surmise that asexual individuals have an affectional orientation—they have the capacity to fall in love romantically with another person, even if they do not feel sexual desire for that person. Further, they may or may not construct an asexual identity. Finally, compared with non-asexual individuals, they report lower interest in engaging sexually with others.

Prejudice against Same-Sex Oriented Individuals

Although the constructs of "gay" and "lesbian" developed fairly recently, relative to human history, the vast majority of past civilizations disapproved of, or at least marginalized, same-sex sexual behaviour. The Ancient Greeks may have held more positive views of male–male sexual behaviour than did other cultures, but available evidence suggests that even they held mixed views; such behaviours were acceptable only for members of the upper classes, caused much moral debate among the philosophers, and were never viewed positively by the majority of citizens (Percy, 1996).

Today, negative views of same-sex sexual behaviours persist, to varying degrees, in most societies around the world. Such views also often lead to prejudices against individuals who engage in same-sex behaviour, or anyone who is deemed to not fit neatly into the category of "heterosexual." **Heterosexism**, whether it occurs consciously or unconsciously, minimizes LGBTTIQQ people, either by assuming that they do not exist or by projecting a belief that they are somehow inferior to their heterosexual counterparts. It is a continual process that manifests itself in nearly every setting (e.g., at home, at work, and at school).

Heterosexist attitudes often manifest most strongly as **homophobia**, **biphobia**, and **queerphobia**, which can lead to acts of hate and violence against members of the LGBTTIQQ community (see the "Research vs Real Life" box). In some cases, these attitudes also lead to **internalized homophobia**, which may cause gay and lesbian individuals to fear and even hate themselves, other gay and lesbian people, and those whom they perceive as having a gay or lesbian identity and/or a same-sex sexual/affectional orientation. Further, widespread **homonegativity** may make some individuals with same-sex orientations feel that they must hide or ignore their same-sex attractions, sometimes even convincing themselves that they are not actually attracted to members of their own sex.

Conversion Therapy

Fear and disapproval of same-sex oriented individuals has led to efforts to change individuals' same-sex or bisexual orientations into heterosexual orientations. Such efforts are often referred to as **conversion therapy** or, when they are driven by religiously motivated people, attempts to "pray away the gay." A substantial literature has developed in this area over the past few decades, particularly following a controversial 2003 report from a highly influential psychiatrist and professor, Robert Spitzer (Figure 11.4).

Spitzer (2003) provided data showing that some gay men who were highly motivated, usually by anti-gay religious beliefs, reported that they had changed their sexual orientations (*not* affectional orientations, although some also claimed this occurred) from same-sex oriented to heterosexual. His results were highly contested by researchers who believe that sexual orientation cannot be changed, with criticisms focussed on sampling bias and the retrospective nature of the participants' reports (see *Archives of Sexual Behavior, 2003, 32*(5), pp. 419–68, for these critiques). Nearly ten years after he published his original report, Spitzer apologized to the gay community for "making unproven claims of the efficacy of reparative therapy" (Becker, 2012, para. 5).

Earlier, Nicolosi, Byrd, and Potts (2000) had provided similar reports of

heterosexism Prejudice and discrimination against individuals of other sexual orientations and genders, based on the implicit assumption that heterosexuality is the norm.

homophobia The fear, dislike, and/or intolerance of gay and/or lesbian individuals.

biphobia The fear, dislike, and/or intolerance of bisexual individuals.

queerphobia The fear, dislike, and/or intolerance of members of the LGBTTIQQ community.

internalized homophobia The fear, dislike, and/or intolerance that gay and lesbian individuals feel toward themselves and/or others with a same-sex orientation.

homonegativity Explicitly negative attitudes toward gay and lesbian people.

conversion therapy Therapy directed at changing a same-sex or bisexual orientation into a heterosexual orientation.

FIGURE 11.4 Dr Spitzer is a retired professor of psychiatry. He is considered to be one of the most influential psychiatrists of the twentieth century, and he was influential in having "homosexuality" removed as a mental disorder from the second edition of the *Diagnostic and Statistical Manual of Mental Disorders* in 1973.

some gay men who felt they had become heterosexual after undergoing conversion therapy and/or engaging in "self-help" practices. Although these and other researchers have interpreted such self-reports of changes in sexual orientation as evidence that conversion therapy can be successful in its goals, the meaning of these self-reports is not entirely clear. After all, it is easy to change one's sexual identity label: straight

Research VS Real Life

The Negative Effects of Hate Speech

Despite the fact that research has shown variations in affectional orientation, sexual identity, and gender identity (see Chapter 10) to be normal, LGBTTIQQ individuals continue to suffer from varying degrees of prejudice, discrimination, and oppression worldwide. Same-sex sexual relationships remain illegal in over 70 countries, and in some places offenders are flogged or even put to death. Even in countries in which such relationships are legal, gay, lesbian, and bisexual individuals frequently face the effects of homophobia in their daily lives. All too often, the prejudices they face take the form of hate speech. Indeed, research consistently finds that the vast majority of gay and lesbian individuals have been verbally abused at some point in their lives.

Research also reveals that hate speech targeted at LGBTTIQQ individuals has very negative effects on these individuals. Perhaps the most visible impact of hate speech is its capacity to incite physical violence against members of a targeted population. A recent, nationally representative American study found that negative beliefs surrounding the *morality* of same-sex sexual behaviours are the strongest predictors of hate-crime victimization of LGBTTIQQ individuals (Alden & Parker, 2005). Negative epithets targeting the morality of same-sex oriented individuals lead to the development of homonegative beliefs, which in turn increase the probability of antigay violence. Statistical evidence reveals just how real the threat of violence is for same-sex oriented individuals— approximately 10 per cent of lesbian women and 20 per cent of gay men have been physically assaulted in their lives.

Hate speech can also impact its targets in more subtle ways. For example, hate speech can lead to internalized homophobia and concomitant compromised mental health: "Internalized homophobia . . . develops from the negative messages society puts forth about gays, lesbians, and bisexuals" (Dworkin, 2000, p. 169). Such internalized views can lead to self-harm. A study conducted in Calgary found that gays, lesbians, and bisexuals were 13.9 times at greater risk of making a serious suicide attempt compared to heterosexuals (Bagley & Tremblay, 1997). In addition, hate speech can nullify freedom of speech for gays and lesbians by convincing people that these individuals are so different from the majority that they are outsiders whose opinions do not matter.

Hate speech can be particularly harmful when it is directed against young people. Unfortunately, LGBTTIQQ youth are commonly targeted by their peers, and investigations reveal that Canadian schools remain havens for the verbal and physical abuse of LGBTTIQQ youth. A relatively recent and painful example of the adverse consequences that can result from bullying of LGBTTIQQ youth is the suicide of Jamie Hubley, on 14 October 2011, at the age of 15. Jamie was the only openly gay teenager in his Ottawa high school, and he was teased and taunted so mercilessly by his peers that he decided his only way out was to take his own life.

In Canada, hate speech against same-sex oriented individuals does a grave disservice to the promotion of respect for diversity within the Canadian mosaic. It is particularly dangerous in its ability to perpetuate and intensify feelings of hate directed toward the targeted population. Homophobia— along with the hateful acts it engenders—is the antithesis of love. We would do well to remember that people with same-sex sexual orientations are found in every society and every culture, and that they are members of every religion worldwide. Like everyone else, they need the love and support of their families and friends to grow into loving people themselves.

to gay to bisexual to back again, and in any direction. Each of us owns our label, and we decide whether to share it with others or to put forth another label that we feel might be more socially acceptable in a given context. Furthermore, such reports say little about affectional orientation. Many people are capable of enjoying sexual relations with either males or females—bodies respond to sexual stimulation, and sexual stimulation is enjoyable in most consensual circumstances—and such enjoyment may be interpreted as indicating a certain sexual orientation. But affectional orientations are much more complex, involving a variety of interpersonal factors; to further complicate the matter, some people may not be fully aware of their propensities when it comes to falling in love romantically. Further, there is little evidence that the goals of conversion therapy are maintained in the long run, as many individuals, including leaders within the ex-gay movement, eventually return to their previous lives as gay men and lesbian women.

Regardless of whether conversion therapy works, there are serious ethical concerns associated with such efforts of conversion. Conversion therapy should be immediately suspect from an ethical perspective because it targets only individuals with same-sex orientations, and its goal is essentially to "fix" a minority population that is deemed to have undesirable traits. Further, conversion efforts seem out of line with guideline to "avoid bringing harm to the client" that every reputable mental health professional is obliged to follow (Cramer, Golom, LoPresto, & Kirkley, 2008, p. 110). It is difficult to believe that conversion therapists are following this ethic, given ample research evidence demonstrating the negative consequences associated with conversion therapy: increased suicidality; increased anxiety and depression; decreased self-esteem and increased feelings of shame and self-loathing; increased levels of internalized homophobia and distorted perceptions of same-sex sexuality; intrusive imagery; sexual dysfunction; preoccupation with speech, mannerisms, and gender-role expression; loss of family connections, religiosity, and spirituality; phobic anxiety toward attractive members of one's own sex; increased aggression and hostility; feelings of inauthenticity; slowing of the self-identification process; social isolation and loss of same-sex partners; irrational fear of being a child abuser (as a consequence of the once-prevalent stereotype that "homosexuals" are pedophiles); and difficulty in establishing intimate relationships (Cramer et al., 2008). Indeed, it is no wonder that most professional organizations for mental health practitioners stipulate that offering conversion therapy in its various forms constitutes unethical practice.

For individuals who struggle with their same-sex sexual/affectional orientations, a more positive and helpful form of guidance may come from **LGBTTIQQ affirmative therapy**. Standing in stark contrast to conversion therapy, this form of therapy is offered by people who view LGBTTIQQ individuals as being equal and as deserving of equal rights to those sharing the dominant discourse (usually heterosexuality). LGBTTIQQ affirmative therapists may hold and practise from any theoretical orientation (e.g., psychodynamic, behavioural): the important aspect is that their attitudes and behaviours are affirming of LGBTTIQQ individuals.

LGBTTIQQ affirmative therapy Therapy directed at helping LGBTTIQQ individuals view their sexual/affectional orientation, sexual identity, and/or gender identity in a positive light.

Theories of Affectional Orientation and Sexual Identity Development

Questions about what causes us to develop the way we do are fraught with difficulty. It is especially in these lines of inquiry that we see full enactment of the nature-vs-nurture controversy: is our development caused by biological, physical, and genetic factors or by environmental, social, and psychological factors? As Kitzinger and Wilkinson

(1995) state, the question is moot: it cannot be answered through the quantitative and qualitative methodologies available to researchers. When researchers do attempt to provide an answer—at least, in relation to conditions that have a psychosocial component to them—they invariably find that the way we develop is a combination of nature and nurture. The following sections provide an overview of various research studies and theories that have contributed to our understanding of how nature and nurture influence the development of our affectional orientations and our sexual identities.

Affectional Orientation Development

Compared to the study of other conditions that have both biological and psychosocial aspects—for example, schizophrenia, chronic recurring depression, addiction, anxiety disorders—the study of affectional orientation is qualitatively different. After all, affectional orientation has many components—sexual attraction, sexual fantasies, sexual preference, propensity to fall in love romantically, being in love romantically, and the extent to which one has male and/or female sexual partners (Alderson et al., 2013). Each of these components is undoubtedly complex enough to warrant investigations into how it develops in different people.

Further, given that variations of affectional orientation are considered normal, we must wonder why it is that most research related to affectional orientation development is directed at understanding the development only of those who end up with a same-sex or bisexual orientation. Indeed, few studies are constructed to find a "heterosexual gene" or to discover how childhood social interactions might lead an individual to develop a heterosexual orientation. Unfortunately, the widespread bias that assumes heterosexuality to be the "default" orientation seems to have affected how researchers frame their questions about the development of affectional orientations.

Another issue that confounds studies regarding the etiology of affectional orientations is the fact that most researchers simply rely on a person's sexual identity label (e.g., gay, lesbian, bisexual, heterosexual, asexual) to separate participants into groups. As you have seen, however, sexual identity and affectional orientations are different constructs. Further, an individual who identifies as gay or lesbian at the time in which they are participating in a study may identify as heterosexual or bisexual at a different point in time. Despite these issues, however, researchers have managed to uncover some interesting insights into how and why individuals' affectional orientations develop the way they do.

BIOLOGICAL EXPLANATIONS

In a recent investigation involving expert analysis and critical review of the available literature, Jannini, Blanchard, Camperio-Ciani, and Bancroft (2010) investigated the role of biological as well as cultural factors in determining affectional orientation. They restricted their focus to male–male sexuality for three reasons: (a) same-sex sexual behaviour is more common among males than among females, (b) there is more scientific research regarding male–male sexual behaviour, and (c) religious and moral concerns are more focussed on male–male sexuality as compared to female–female sexuality. Jannini et al. concluded that the issues are "complicated and multifactorial" (p. 3245), and neither biological nor environmental factors can explain all cases of same-sex orientation in males. In relation to biological factors, they noted that certain "genetic and immunological factors, birth order, and fertility of relatives" seem to play a role in the development of affectional orientation (p. 3245; see Table 11.1 for a summary of the findings Jannini et al. reviewed.)

Most research looking at biological explanations of sexual/affectional orientation focusses on either the structures or the functioning of the brain. Studies that focus

TABLE 11.1 Findings that suggest a biological component to male same-sex sexual/affectional orientation.

Site or Mechanism	Finding
Anatomy (autopsies)	In the postmortem examination of the brains of same-sex oriented males, the suprachiasmatic nucleus of the hypothalamus was found to be twice the size of its counterpart in heterosexual males.
	The third interstitial notch of the anterior hypothalamus is two to three times smaller in same-sex oriented men than it is in heterosexual men.
	The anterior commissure of the hypothalamus is significantly larger in same-sex oriented men than it is in heterosexual men.
	The brain's functional response patterns to sexual stimuli contain sufficient information to predict individual sexual orientation with high accuracy.
Genetics (twin studies)	Where at least one twin was homosexual, 52% of monozygotic twins and 22% of dizygotic twins were both homosexual. (By comparison, in cases in which at least one adoptive brother was homosexual, 11% of these brothers were both homosexual.)
Genetics (Xq28)[a]	The estimated level of Xq28 allele sharing between gay brothers is 64% instead of the expected 50%.
	The Xq28 linkage is not completely confirmed. There is evidence for linkage at three other sites—on chromosomes 7, 8, and 10.
	Linkage between the Xq28 markers and sexual orientation was detected within the families of gay males but not within the families of lesbian females.
Immunology	Following maternal immunization against male-specific molecules, maternal anti-male antibodies may divert the sexual differentiation of the fetal brain from the male-typical pathway.
Hormones/Neural Processes	There are higher levels of circulating androgens in adult same-sex oriented men than in adult heterosexual men.
	Gay men and heterosexual women respond similarly to male pheromones. Both gay men and heterosexual women display a brain activation pattern distinct from that of heterosexual men.

[a]Xq28 is a band of genes located on the X axis.
Source: Adapted from Jannini et al's (2010) review of various studies.

on the brain's structures usually involve measuring the size of certain brain regions in same-sex oriented and other-sex oriented individuals. An example of such a study is Simon Levay's (1991) investigation that found that a part of the hypothalamus was two to three times smaller in gay men than it was in heterosexual men. Other studies focussing on brain structures have found that gay men have a larger corpus callosum (this structure connects the two hemispheres of the brain) than do straight men (e.g., Witelson et al., 2008). Studies that focus on the functioning of the brain generally investigate how neural processes occur. These sorts of studies have led to the finding that the brain is activated differently (faster or slower) in some gay men than it is in some straight men, and that it is activated differently in some lesbian women than it is in some straight women (Alexander, 2000).

The two most consistent findings that support a biological causality of same-sex sexual/affectional orientation concern hand preference and fraternal birth order (Blanchard, Cantor, Bogaert, Breedlove, & Ellis, 2006). Blanchard et al. (2006) note that many studies have found that gay men are more frequently left-handed compared to heterosexual men, and that one study (Lalumière, Blanchard, & Zucker, 2000) has suggested that gay men have a 34 per cent greater chance of being left-handed. They also note that Blanchard (2004) found, in a meta-analysis representing 10,143 males, that the greater number of older brothers a male has, the more likely he will identify as gay. Blanchard et al.'s own research qualified this finding, suggesting it is true only for gay males who are right-handed. It also suggested that gay males without older brothers are more likely to be left-handed than are heterosexual males without older brothers (Blanchard et al., 2006).

Well-known researcher John Money, whose work with children with disorders of sexual development was discussed in Chapter 10, provided evidence that sexual orientation is determined largely by prenatal hormones. His research suggested that males who are prenatally exposed to too little testosterone have an increased chance of identifying as gay later in life, and that females who are prenatally exposed to too much testosterone have an increased chance of identifying as either bisexual or lesbian later in life (Money, 1987). More recent research, however, suggests that Money's conclusions regarding the link between prenatal hormones and sexual orientation in females were too broad. For example, Brown, Finn, Cooke, and Breedlove (2002) suggest that prenatal exposure to high levels of androgens in females plays a role only in some cases of masculine lesbian women but not in feminine lesbian women.

Studies with twins have shown that there may be a genetic component to same-sex sexual/affectional orientation. For example, in an Australian study comparing 25,000 pairs of male identical and fraternal twins aged 18 to 52, Kirk, Bailey, and Martin (2000) found evidence that components of sexuality related to sexual/affectional orientation are inherited. They found that genetic influences could explain approximately 42 to 60 per cent of the observed variance in such components as sexual feelings and fantasies, sexual attraction toward men, attitudes toward same-sex sexual behaviour, and the number of actual male and female sexual partners.

PSYCHOSOCIAL EXPLANATIONS

Many researchers have proposed that affectional orientation development is heavily influenced by psychosocial factors. For example, Stein (1997) supported the social constructionist view that this development occurs as we process our experiences of ourselves interacting with others (a helpful overview of the differences between social constructionism and essentialism can be found in DeLameter & Hyde, 1998). Similarly, Michael D. Storms has proposed that sexual/affectional orientation (which he referred to as "erotic orientation") "emerges from an interaction between sex drive development and social development during early adolescence" (Storms, 1981, p. 340).

Due to the complex, often unmeasurable ways in which social interactions shape psychological development, it is difficult for researchers to provide conclusive evidence to support psychosocial explanations of how an individual's affectional orientation develops. Thus, such explanations remain largely theoretical. In addition, it seems that theories about how psychosocial factors influence affectional orientation development become less supportable as they become more specific. Consider, for example, that few people would object to the broad suggestion that childhood and adolescent experiences may affect how our affectional orientations develop. Now, consider the more specific proposition that men who were raised with overly close mothers and distant fathers are more likely to develop same-sex affectional orientations later in life. This idea seems almost immediately suspect because the family dynamic it relies on is that of the traditional heterosexual union in which the father is the breadwinner who spends much of his time away from his family unit and the mother stays at home to care for the children. This model of the nuclear family was the norm in North America and elsewhere for much of our modern history, yet most children who grew up in these families did not develop a same-sex affectional orientation.

Nonetheless, investigations into the psychosocial aspects of affectional orientation development have given us some significant insights. First, it seems that an individual's affectional orientation is not dependent on the affectional orientation of her or his parents—most gay and lesbian people were raised by heterosexual parents, and most children raised by same-sex parents turn out heterosexual. Second, although childhood sexual abuse can cause psychological damage and lead to confusion regarding one's sexual identity (Relf, 2001), there is no evidence that such trauma can alter one's affectional orientation. Third, although same-sex oriented individuals may question their sexual identity to a greater extent at some point in their lives than do their heterosexual counterparts, most gay men believe they always had a strong sexual/affectional orientation to men (Savin-Williams, 2005). Fourth, although it is clear that social and cultural influences can significantly shape how we understand and express our gender and sexual identity (Herdt, 1997), it is less clear that such influences have a great impact on our ability to fall in love romantically with males, females, or both. Finally, most research does not find etiological differences between gay men and heterosexual men, or between lesbian women and heterosexual women, in terms of how affectional orientation develops. Available research does suggest, however, that affectional orientation may develop differently in women than it does in men. For example, it seems that affectional orientation is substantially more fluid for women than for men (Diamond, 2008).

Sexual Identity Development

Numerous models of sexual identity development have been advanced since the 1970s, but the only such model that has received any popularity is the one developed by Vivienne Cass (1979, 1996). Cass's model proposes that gay and lesbian individuals go through six stages of development (see Table 11.2). Like any model, Cass's has been criticized, mainly by those who note that not all women pass through all the stages or in the prescribed order. Further, certain aspects of the model have become less relevant than they were when Cass first proposed the model in 1979. For example, the fifth

TABLE 11.2 Cass's six stages of gay/lesbian development.

Stage	Name	Milestones
1	Identity Confusion	The individual labels some of his or her thoughts, emotions, and/or behaviours as homosexual, which creates a deeper question of whether the person should identify as gay or lesbian.
2	Identity Comparison	The feelings of being different result in some degree of social alienation, and further questioning occurs.
3	Identity Tolerance	The individual moves closer to identifying as a gay or lesbian person, expressed in the statement, "I probably am a gay or lesbian person." The individual begins to seek out the company of other gay or lesbian individuals and their subculture.
4	Identity Acceptance	The individual accepts a gay or lesbian identity instead of merely tolerating and exploring it.
5	Identity Pride	The individual is absorbed into the gay and lesbian community, spending most of his or her time with people in this community, and develops a certain distrust of heterosexual people.
6	Identity Synthesis	The individual's homosexual identity becomes integrated with his or her other identities. It no longer rules the person's interactions with others.

Source: Adapted from Cass (1979, 1996).

stage ("Identity Pride") has been viewed as being less important as the gay liberation movement progressed (Sophie, 1985–6). Today, this stage might not occur for the majority of those who develop a gay or lesbian identity within a reasonably tolerant social environment.

More recently, Kevin Alderson (2013) has proposed a theory of development called the ecological model of LGBTI identity (Figure 11.5). This model, originally constructed to refer to gay male identity development only (Alderson, 2003), is based in human ecology theory, which is concerned with looking at people in interaction with their environments. By looking at these interacting influences, the theory suggests, the quality of daily life can be improved by creating healthy human environments.

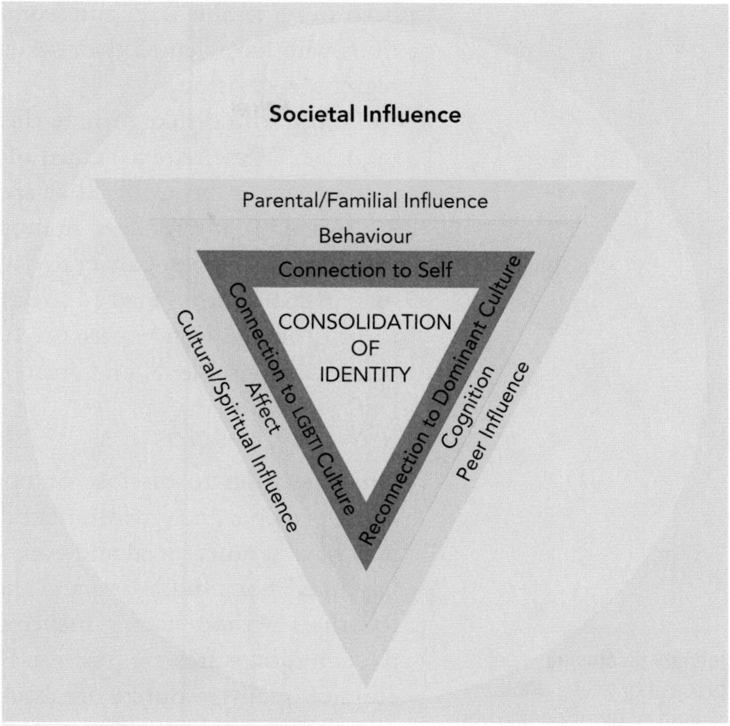

The model recognizes that a person's sexual identity (and transgender/transsexual identity) occurs within a complex environmental context. This context is shaped by the society in which the individual lives (represented in Figure 11.5 by the yellow circle) as well as cultural/spiritual, parental/familial, and peer influences (represented by the green triangle). Thus, the model recognizes that identity formation and disclosure of that identity will be substantially different, for example, for a person born and raised in Lebanon who is Muslim compared to someone born in Canada who is atheist.

If LGBTTIQQ individuals are able to question their identity (partly or wholly dependent on the four contextual influences), they will begin to reflect upon their behaviour, their cognition, and their affect (represented by the blue triangle). If their analysis of these personal dynamics suggests an LGBTTIQQ identity, and if catalysts (positive influences) outweigh hindrances (negative influences), they may begin to assume an LGBTTIQQ identity. This effort will also involve doing inner psychological work, connecting in some way to LGBTTIQQ culture, and reconnecting with this new identity to the dominant culture (represented by the red triangle). From this stage, individuals will move to the final stage (represented by the pink triangle), in which they develop a consolidated sense of their unique LGBTTIQQ identity.

FIGURE 11.5 The ecological model of LGBTI identity acknowledges that a person's sexual identity occurs within a complex environmental context.

Self-Identification and Identity Disclosure

Self-Identification as Lesbian, Gay, or Bisexual

In Canada and the US, **self-identification** as lesbian, gay, or bisexual has been considered a necessary prerequisite for optimal emotional health among LGB individuals. Every theory of sexual identity formation requires the self-identification process to occur before a positive identity can develop. For some LGB individuals, however, internalized homophobia or biphobia can be so great that the self-identification process becomes effectively blocked, either through denial, a destructive defense mechanism, or self-loathing. Erik Erikson (1968) believed that people need to have a secure identity before they can become capable of true intimacy and love. Those who block their sexuality by attempting to make it invisible are likely to make bad decisions. There have

self-identification The process of coming to accept for oneself a particular sexual identity label.

been innumerable men and women with strong same-sex sexual/affectional orientations who have denied their sexual identity and married heterosexually, only to later regret this decision.

Those who dislike or hate their affectional orientation can develop very negative sequelae. "If men are ashamed of themselves because of their same-sex feelings, they may engage in behaviors that are harmful [i.e., unprotected sex]" (Suarez & Kauth, 2001, p. 659). Internalized homophobia usually underlies this self-loathing, and it is viewed as the biggest barrier to developing a positive LGB identity. A recent study based on 156 LGB youths (aged 14 to 21) in New York City found that those who had greater identity integration experienced fewer symptoms of depression and anxiety, fewer behavioural problems, and greater self-esteem (Rosario, Schrimshaw, & Hunter, 2011).

Identity Disclosure

One's decision to disclose or not disclose an LGBTTIQQ identity is dependent on many personal and environmental factors. In some countries, disclosing a gay identity may have serious social and even life-threatening consequences (see the "Culture and Diversity" box). In Canada and the US, many people are able to disclose their identity to others without facing insurmountable consequences, although not all reactions to such disclosures are positive. For those who have reservations about **identity disclosure**, many resources are available from organizations such as Parents, Families, and Friends of Lesbians and Gays (PFLAG), which has a Canadian contingent (see www.pflagcanada.ca/en/index-e.asp). The general trend over the past few years is that LGBTTIQQ individuals are both self-identifying and disclosing their identities at younger ages than in the past (Savin-Williams, 2005).

For LGB individuals, self-identifying as gay, lesbian, or bisexual and disclosing this identity to others is associated with having better physical and mental health. Cole, Kemeny, Taylor, and Visscher (1996) tracked the incidence of cancer, pneumonia, bronchitis, sinusitis, and tuberculosis in a sample of 222 gay and bisexual men over a period of five years. Overall, the incidence of these diseases was higher among the men who hid their gay identity from others. Several studies have also found that gay men and lesbian women who disclose their sexual identity to others experience greater mental health outcomes (e.g., Chow & Cheng, 2010). At the same time, it is not entirely clear whether disclosure leads to good mental health or if good mental health makes it easier to disclose.

Some LGB individuals may also have very good reasons for *not* disclosing their sexual identity to others. For example, dependent children who feel that their parents might react very negatively to such a disclosure might choose not to confront the issue until they are older and able to support themselves. Indeed, many homeless LGBT-TIQQ youth have ended up on the streets because they were rejected by their families (Hunter, 2008). Some adults may also choose not to disclose their sexual identity to their coworkers for fear that they may be denied advancement opportunities. Despite legislation meant to prevent discrimination based on sexual identity, some employers continue to favour those who fit the dominant cultural discourse (most often, able-bodied, heterosexual males). Identity disclosure may also be particularly difficult for LGB individuals who are deeply connected to communities in which homophobia is highly prevalent. This is often the case for Black and Latino men in Canada and the United States, who may feel that disclosing an other-than-heterosexual identity will lead to their being ostracized from their community.

In some cases, parents may be aware of their child's same-sex sexual/affectional orientation before the child discloses to them (see the "Ethical Debate" box). This awareness may result from their child displaying atypical gender interests (e.g., a boy

identity disclosure The process of telling another person or other people your sexual identity label.

Culture & Diversity

Global and Cross-Cultural Findings Regarding Sexual Diversity

Across the globe, attitudes toward individuals who openly identify as being attracted to members of their own sex differ greatly. In Canada and the United States, most people are accepting or at least tolerant of these individuals, and most LGB people feel comfortable disclosing their identity to others. In Japan, attitudes toward LGB individuals are less positive, and many Japanese LGB people avoid publicly disclosing their identity; some lesbian and gay people even deny their sexual identity and end up marrying members of the other sex. Similarly, in Russia, many LGB individuals avoid disclosing their identity for fear that such a disclosure will lead to ostracism. In many Middle Eastern countries in which Islam is the dominant religion, such as Iran, disclosing a gay identity may prove fatal, as those caught engaging in same-sex sexual activity may be sentenced to death. In Egypt and many other countries, men are simply expected to marry, and a visible gay identity does not exist.

Other countries are accepting of only some expressions of an LGB identity. In Brazil, for example, masculine gay men are generally accepted, while feminine gay men experience extremely negative stereotyping; consequently, most Brazilian gay men attempt to come across as masculine. In Turkey,

feminine gay men are generally despised in everyday interactions, yet the population is fascinated with popular transsexual singers. Transsexual entertainers are also popular in Thailand (Figure 11.6), although individuals who cross-dress in their daily lives are often targets of sexual harassment and various forms of violence.

In many Western regions, public events aimed at promoting LGBTTIQQ rights and celebrating LGBT-TIQQ culture are encouraged. In Canada, the United States, most European countries, and elsewhere, millions of people gather every year as major cities host a variety of Pride parades and events. Yet Pride marches have also been banned in recent years in such major cities as Budapest, Hungary; Bucharest, Romania; Chisinau, Moldova; Moscow, Russia; and Riga, Latvia. In Belgrade, Serbia, the country's first Pride march in 2001 erupted into violence after marchers were attacked by over 1000 anti-gay protesters (Gruszczynska, 2009; Figure 11.7). Similar violence occurred during the 2005 Pride march in Warsaw, Poland, yet the march occurred there the following year without any major disturbances (Gruszczynska, 2009).

FIGURE 11.6 A transgender singer performs in Pattaya, Thailand.

FIGURE 11.7 After paraders clashed with protesters in 2001, the next Pride parade through the city centre of Belgrade did not occur until October 2010. Police again had to deal with anti-gay protesters.

preferring traditionally girl activities), from an earlier disclosure of same-sex attractions, or because the parents are non-homophobic and more sensitive to early signs of a possible same-sex orientation. However, even if parents suspect that their child has

Ethical Debate

Should You Help a Child Become Gender Conforming?

Parents are often concerned that their child will develop a same-sex orientation if he or she displays behaviours more typical of the other gender. Research supports that many males who display highly effeminate behaviour in childhood later experience same-sex attraction and behaviour (Drummond, Bradley, Peterson-Badali, & Zucker, 2008). Similarly, some females who display highly masculine behaviour in childhood later experience same-sex attraction and behaviour.

Imagine you are a mental health practitioner and a distraught mother and father come to see you about their son, Peter. Peter is 10 years old and spends most of his time playing house with two neighbourhood girls. He also avoids rough-and-tumble play and does not like getting dirty. His parents have caught him on one occasion dressing in his sister's clothing and immediately chastised him. Both parents have negative views of same-sex sexual/affectional orientation,

partly based on their religion, which views same-sex sexual behaviour as sinful.

The parents do not ask you to attempt to change Peter's affectional orientation, as they are not aware of what it is at his young age. Instead, they ask that you intervene to help Peter develop more masculine-typed behaviours and reduce his displays of feminine-typed behaviours. Given that they have not asked you to alter Peter's affectional orientation, any work you would do would not be included under the rubric of conversion therapy.

What are the ethical implications of attempting to change gender-typed behaviours? To what extent should Peter's wishes be considered in making an ethical decision? Would you honour the parents' request by attempting to make Peter more gender typical in his behaviours? Why or why not? What might be the advantages and disadvantages for Peter if he were to display more gender-typical behaviours?

a same-sex sexual/affectional orientation, they should not impose a gay, lesbian, or bisexual identity on that child; rather, they should let their child self-disclose on his or her own terms.

Relationships and Sex

An individual's affectional orientation and sexual identity both impact his or her tendency to form sexual relationships with men, women, or both. For many people, the relationships they form are often the most visible display of their affectional orientation and sexual identity. For this reason, this chapter includes a discussion, below, of a number of research findings related to same-sex and mixed-sex relationships, as well as some findings related to same-sex sexual behaviour. (The topics of relationships and sexual behaviours will be discussed in more detail in Chapter 14.)

Before we begin, however, you should note that a limitation of all research with members of the LGBTTIQQ community is sample bias. Many members of this community are secretive or closeted, and the people who take part in research are those who choose to participate. Furthermore, not all aspects of same-sex relationships have been studied to the same extent as aspects of mixed-sex relationships have been studied. Thus, what follows does not constitute a comprehensive overview of all aspects of same-sex relationships, but rather a summary of what researchers have found so far.

Intimate Relationships

In general, the more committed people are in their relationships, the better their sense of well-being. A recent American study compared a large group of heterosexual couples with gay and lesbian couples (Wienke & Hill, 2009). Results indicated that the happiest group was the married mixed-sex couples (there were no married same-sex couples in the study), followed next by cohabiting mixed- and same-sex couples (no differences were found between these two groups), and least happy were the single people, regardless of their sexual identity.

In terms of relationship satisfaction, research has found that lesbian couples report greater relationship satisfaction than do either gay or heterosexual couples (Spitalnick & McNair, 2005). Reasons include (a) their desire for and achievement of equality in their relationships, (b) the high value placed on emotional intimacy, (c) their attachment styles, (d) their ability to resolve conflict, (e) their high levels of self-esteem, and (f) the social support they garner for their lives together. For gay men, relationship satisfaction does not seem to depend on monogamy: non-monogamous gay male couples are as satisfied in their relationships as monogamous gay male couples. Furthermore, the most satisfied men in open relationships are those who have explicit rules about outside sexual activity (Ramirez & Brown, 2010).

Regardless of affectional orientation, men are more inclined to look for an attractive partner whereas women place greater value on their partner's personality (Townsend, 1998). Women also tend to be more expressive in their relationships compared to men (Gottman & Levenson, 2010). One difference between mixed- and same-sex relationships is that same-sex partners are more likely than mixed-sex partners to remain friends after relationship dissolution (Rothblum, 2009). Same-sex oriented individuals are also less likely to seek partners whose demographic characteristics—including age, race, and socioeconomic status—are similar to their own (Rothblum, 2009). Further, both gay and lesbian couples tend to be less controlling and to use fewer hostile tactics during times of conflict compared to mixed-sex couples (Gottman & Levenson, 2010).

Current research finds few differences between same- and mixed-sex relationships regarding relationship quality (Balsam, Beauchaine, Rothblum, & Solomon, 2008; Kurdek, 2006). Research does suggest, however, that same-sex relationships have a higher likelihood of ending compared to mixed-sex relationships. This finding is based on comparisons between cohabiting same-sex couples and cohabiting mixed-sex couples (Rothblum, 2009). Researchers from Norway and Sweden, where registered domestic partnerships (not marriages) have been recognized since the 1990s, have found similar results (Andersson, Noack, Seierstad, & Weedon-Fekjaer, 2006).

The majority of gay and lesbian individuals (74 per cent) express the desire to get married at some point (Kaiser Family Foundation, 2001; Figure 11.8). Indeed, many same-sex couples have elected to get married in Canada since the country legalized same-sex marriage in 2005. We do not currently know, however, whether same-sex marriages in Canada will persist as long as mixed-sex marriages. Given that most same-sex couples are not raising children (Hinds, 2011), and that many unhappy heterosexual couples remain together only so that they can raise their children together, it seems logical that there may be a greater percentage of same-sex divorces compared to mixed-sex divorces.

FIGURE 11.8 The legalization of same-sex marriage in Canada and elsewhere helps gay and lesbian individuals see their relationships as real, and this perception enhances their search for finding an ideal partner.

Research from Denmark, Sweden, and Norway has found that lesbian couples have a higher divorce rate (divorce from registered domestic partnerships, that is) compared to gay men (Andersson et al., 2006; Noack, Seierstad, & Weedon-Fekjaer, 2005). Andersson et al. (2006) postulate that this difference may be because women are generally more sensitive to the quality of their relationships than men are, regardless of affectional orientation, or that men and women enter into registered partnerships for different reasons that have not been explored. By comparison, Kurdek's (1998) American study of 66 gay and 51 lesbian cohabiting couples living together for five years found no significant difference in dissolution rates between the two groups.

Internalized homophobia is one of the worst obstacles to establishing and maintaining same-sex relationships (Alderson, 2013). It prevents gay men and lesbian women from having the ability to fully give of themselves and commit wholeheartedly to their partner. Another factor that makes it difficult for gay men to create sustainable relationships is, as research has shown, that they are particularly sensitive to interpersonal rejection, a factor that can play havoc during times of conflict.

Bisexuality and Relationships

Sigmund Freud (1925/1959) believed that we are all constitutionally bisexual. Are we? Is it just because of socialization that most of us lose our bisexuality and end up preferring to form relationships with members of one sex only? If we lived in a society in which it made no difference whatsoever if we were sexually involved with men or women, would we find ourselves forming sexual relationships with both men and women throughout our lives?

Of course, we cannot answer such a question empirically because no such society exists. We can, however, consider this question by examining the components of affectional orientation (sexual attraction, sexual fantasies, sexual preference, the extent to which one has male and/or female sexual partners, propensity to fall in love romantically, and being in love romantically), as in most cases an individual's affectional orientation directly influences whether that person will build intimate relationships with men, women, or both.

The first four of these components do not seem to rule out the likelihood of our forming relationships with men as well as women. For one thing, we know that some changes to our sexual attraction mechanism occur over time. Many adolescents have some degree of sexual interest in members of their own sex, and some enjoy sexual activity with members of their own sex. Thus, the fact that the majority of the population focusses exclusively on heterosexual relations in adulthood may simply indicate that bisexuality is eventually lost through socialization. In addition, many people have sexual fantasies that involve both men and women; if people are asked to spend more time sexually fantasizing about one sex or the other than is typical, they can generally do it while maintaining sexual arousability. Regarding sexual preference, most people prefer having sex with members of the other sex, likely a necessary requirement for sustaining the human race, but not all do; further, *preference* for having sex with members of one sex does not rule out interest in having sex with members of the other sex. Who we actually have sex with depends on several factors (e.g., personal values, the availability of members of the preferred sex/gender, our ability to attract these individuals). When it comes to consensual sex, there are many choices available to us.

That brings us to the two components that have to do with romantic love, which for most people is central to the desire to build a long-term relationship with another person. Most people believe that who we do or do not fall in love with romantically is not something that we consciously choose or that we can control. Anecdotally, there are innumerable examples of people who fell in love with and formed an intimate relationship with someone they did not believe was "right for them," just as examples abound of those who could not fall in love with someone who met their conscious criteria. Ultimately, observation evidence does not seem to suggest that the majority of people fall in love romantically with members of both sexes. If this were the case, we would likely see increased reports of individuals who were confused by their feelings of love for members of a sex that is not consistent with what they would expect, based on their sexual identity. We would also, at some point in history, likely have seen at least one example of a society where the proportion of same-sex relationships was nearly equal to that of mixed-sex relationships. This has never been the case, past or present.

BISEXUAL INDIVIDUALS IN RELATIONSHIPS

Most bisexual individuals enter heterosexual relationships long before they begin exploring their same-sex interests. In a large-scale study of bisexual individuals from eight countries, Rust (2001) concluded that both bisexual men and bisexual women are more emotionally attracted to women but more sexually attracted to men. Less than 20 per cent of bisexual people in one study were involved with men and women simultaneously (Matteson, 1996). A more recent study found that 33 per cent of those surveyed were living a polyamorous lifestyle, with 54 per cent of the sample reporting that polyamory was their preferred lifestyle (Page, 2004).

While many bisexual men and women maintain monogamous relationships, others regularly engage in sexual activities outside of their primary relationship. Bisexual individuals who choose to establish open relationships must deal with the same issues that others face when creating non-monogamous arrangements, such as handling jealousy, setting boundaries, and maintaining open communication. When handled well, open relationships can be highly satisfying to all involved. In one study of 26 married couples where the husband engaged in outside same-sex sexual behaviour, most couples reported that they were happy in their marriage (Wolf, 1985). There were caveats, however. While all of the wives were aware of their husbands' same-sex sexual behaviour, the couples did report "intense conflict dealing with their open marriage styles" (Wolf, 1985, p. 135). Furthermore, participants in this study were highly educated and earned high incomes, meaning that their reactions may not reflect those of the general population.

Due to the small percentage of individuals who define themselves as bisexual (0.9 per cent of women and 0.6 per cent of men; Reasons, Conley, & Debro, 2002), a substantial bisexual community does not exist. Many bisexual men and women report feeling isolated, at least in part because they are often viewed by non-bisexual individuals as "fence-sitters" who hedonistically pursue pleasure without taking on the stigma that too often comes with a gay or lesbian identity.

Same-Sex Sexual Behaviour

Not surprisingly, couples vary in the amount of sex they have. Research has established that, generally speaking, gay men in relationships have the most sex, lesbian couples have the least, and mixed-sex couples fall somewhere in between (Rothblum, 2009). Over time, the amount of sex diminishes for all relationship types, and gay male couples (in contrast to lesbian and straight couples) tend to become less monogamous (Rothblum, 2009).

On average, gay males have 42.8 sexual partners in their lifetime, heterosexual males have 16.5, lesbian women have 9.4, and heterosexual women have 4.6 (Laumann et al., 1994). Large-scale representative research from the US (N = 9487 males and 12,336

anilingus Oral stimulation of the anus, perineum, and surrounding area.

top A gay man who assumes the penetrator role in anal sex.

bottom A gay man who assumes the penetratee role in anal sex.

versatile A gay man who is willing to assume either the top or bottom role in anal sex.

scissoring The sexual practice where two women wrap their legs around each other and rub their vulvas together.

tribadism The sexual practice where a woman rubs her vulva against any part of her partner's body.

females) reveals that the prevalence of women having sex with other women increased during the twentieth century, while findings for men are more ambiguous. However, there is evidence that the proportion of men having sex with men increased through the 1990s (Turner, Villarroel, Chromy, Eggleston, & Rogers, 2005).

Gay boys report having sex with other boys (on average, around 13 or 14 years of age) earlier than lesbian girls report having sex with other girls (on average, around 14 or 15 years of age) (Savin-Williams, 2005). Almost 9 out of 10 gay adolescent boys have had manual and oral sex with another male, and about half have tried oral-anal contact (Savin-Williams, 2005). For boys who further explore having sex with other boys, there is a typical order in which sexual activities occur, if they occur: oral sex, anal sex, **anilingus** (sometimes called "rimming"), and anal-dildo penetration. For girls who have sex with girls, the typical order in which sexual activities occur, if they occur, is oral sex, vaginal-digital penetration, anilingus, vaginal-dildo penetration, and anal-dildo penetration (Savin-Williams, 2005).

The most common sexual practices among men who have sex with men are, in order of prevalence, mutual masturbation, oral sex, and anal intercourse (Ross & Schonnesson, 2000). A gay man who engages in anal sex may refer to himself as a **top**, as a **bottom**, or as **versatile**. Blumstein and Schwartz (1983) found that approximately 30 per cent of the gay male couples they studied rarely or never engaged in anal sex.

The most commonly reported sexual activities among women who have sex with women include oral sex, vaginal-digital penetration, and mutual masturbation (Bailey, Farquhar, Owen, & Whittaker, 2003). Genital-genital contact, especially in the **scissoring** position, and other forms of **tribadism** are also common. There is some difficulty noted in the literature regarding varying definitions of what constitutes having sex, and several aspects of lesbian sex would be viewed by many heterosexual individuals as "foreplay," as they do not involve penile penetration (Peplau & Fingerhut, 2007).

Comparing 407 18- to 62-year-old lesbian women with 370 17- to 59-year-old heterosexual women, Coleman, Hoon, and Hoon (1983) found that the lesbian sample reported having sex more frequently, experiencing more orgasms, and experiencing greater sexual satisfaction. Women in this sample were also more likely to have a greater number of sexual partners. In Loulan's (1988) study of 1566 lesbian women, 89 per cent reported masturbating and 88 per cent reported having partnered sex. Just over 50 per cent of the sample reported they enjoyed sex either fairly well or completely.

FIGURE 11.9 This lesbian couple is raising a young boy. Research suggests that most lesbian couples do an exemplary job of raising both girls and boys.

LGB Parenting and Adoption

Research regarding LGB parenting has increased in recent years, especially since the legalization of same-sex marriage throughout Canada and in some US states. The available psychological research suggests that same-sex relationships are not appreciably different from mixed-sex ones, and parents' sexual orientation has no bearing on parents' capacity to provide a safe, healthy, and nurturant environment for children (Patterson, 2009). Some research has actually shown that children raised by lesbian-mother families from birth demonstrate more competencies and express fewer behavioural problems compared to children raised by mixed-sex parents (Gartrell & Bos, 2010; Figure 11.9).

Overall, the available research indicates that parental sexual orientation is unrelated to outcomes regarding the socialization of children (Patterson & Hastings, 2007). While research does suggest that psychological outcomes are generally better when children are raised by two parents instead of only one (Biblarz & Stacey, 2010), variables such as parental gender, marital status, and sexual identity appear to have no measurable effect (Biblarz & Stacey, 2010).

In Canada, same-sex couples are legally entitled to adopt children. However, research has shown that they are less likely to actually be matched to children compared to mixed-sex couples (Sullivan & Harrington, 2009).

CHAPTER SUMMARY

Historically, the constructs of "gay" and "lesbian" did not exist, but most societies have held negative opinions about individuals, especially men, who engage in same-sex sexual activity. Even today, some people promote the unethical practice of conversion therapy in an attempt to "fix" same-sex oriented individuals. When discussing an individual's tendency to be sexually attracted to and develop romantic feelings toward members of a certain sex, the term *affectional orientation* is preferred over the term *sexual orientation*. An individual's affectional orientation can be heterosexual, same-sex oriented, or bisexual. Asexuality is best construed as having low sexual desire for others; for some, it also becomes their sexual identity label. Various theories attempt to explain affectional orientation development and sexual identity development, although much about these developments is still not well understood. Self-identification and identity disclosure are important stages in an individual's sexual identity development, especially for LGBTTIQQ individuals; at the same time, LGBTTIQQ individuals need to remain discerning in this regard, as some may face consequences to disclosing their sexual identity to others.

DEBATE QUESTION

From a child's perspective, what are the pros and cons of being raised by a gay male couple or a lesbian couple?

REVIEW QUESTIONS

1. What is the difference between sexual orientation and affectional orientation?
2. What enhancements did Klein et al.'s (1985) Sexual Orientation Grid provide over the original Kinsey Scale?
3. How do sexual identity, sexual behaviour, and sexual desire relate to one another?
4. Why is offering conversion therapy considered unethical practice by most mental health organizations?
5. What difficulties might an individual face in self-identifying as a gay, lesbian, or bisexual? What are the potential benefits of disclosing one's sexual identity to others? In what situations might an LGB individual decide not to disclose her or his sexual identity?

SUGGESTIONS FOR FURTHER READING AND VIEWING

Recommended Websites

Bisexual Resource Center: www.biresource.org

Egale Canada Human Rights Trust: www.egale.ca

GLBT Historical Society: www.glbthistory.org

Lesbian, Gay, Bisexual, and Transgender Health (from the CDC): www.cdc.gov/lgbthealth/youth-resources.htm

MyGSA.ca: www.mygsa.ca

NOH8 Campaign: www.noh8campaign.com

PFLAG Canada: www.pflagcanada.ca

Religious Tolerance: www.religioustolerance.org

Resources for Those Who Are Lesbian, Gay, Bisexual, or Unsure (from Avert): www.avert.org/gaylesbianhelp.htm

Recommended Reading

Abelove, H., Barale, M.A., & Halperin, D.M. (1993). *The lesbian and gay studies reader.* New York, NY: Routledge.

Alderson, K.G. (2013). *Counseling LGBTI clients.* Thousand Oaks, CA: Sage.

American Psychological Association. (2008). *Answers to your questions: For a better understanding of sexual orientation and homosexuality.* Washington, DC: Author. Retrieved from www.apa.org/topics/sexuality/sorientation.pdf

Bronski, M. (2011). *A queer history of the United States.* Boston, MA: Beacon Press.

Clark, D. (1997). *Loving someone gay* (Rev. ed.). Berkeley, CA: Celestial Arts.

Jannini, E.A., Blanchard, R., Camperio-Ciani, A., & Bancroft, J. (2010). Male homosexuality: Nature or culture? *Journal of Sexual Medicine, 7*(10), 3245–53. doi:10.1111/j.1743-6109.2010.02024.x

Parker, R., & Aggleton, P. (2007). *Culture, society and sexuality: A reader.* New York, NY: Routledge.

Rayside, D., & Wilson, C. (2011). *Faith, politics, and sexual diversity in Canada and the United States.* Vancouver, BC: UBC Press.

Warner, T. (2002). *Never going back: A history of queer activism in Canada.* Toronto, ON: University of Toronto Press.

Recommended Viewing

Anderson, K., & Gold, T. (Producers & Directors). (2009). *Out at work* [DVD]. United States: AndersonGold Films. Available from www.newday.com/films/outatwork.html

Epstein, R., & Friedman, J. (Producers & Directors). (1995). *The celluloid closet* [Motion picture]. United States: Sony Pictures.

Hunt, D., White, D.J., & Klainberg, L. (Producers), & Scagliotti, J. (Director). (1999). *After Stonewall* [Motion picture]. United States: Knightscove-Ellis International.

12 CHAPTER

Attraction, Intimacy, and Love

KELLY B. SMITH

LEARNING OBJECTIVES

In this chapter, you will

- explore the connections among attraction, intimacy, love, and sexuality;
- consider the factors that draw us toward (or away from) another person;
- reflect upon the definition and different types of intimacy and the applicability of attachment theory for understanding why we seek or avoid intimacy;
- encounter several theories that attempt to explain love; and
- examine the topics of optimal sexuality, jealousy, and online technologies with regard to intimate relationships.

Keeping the Magic Alive

Kerry and Sam presented for couples therapy after six years of marriage. Although they reported being generally happy with each other and their marriage, they also felt they had "lost the spark" that was present in the early stages of their relationship. A detailed assessment indicated that both Kerry and Sam felt deeply committed to their relationship and reported being "best friends" who loved and regularly confided in each other, often about the stresses they each experienced in their demanding careers. Kerry travelled regularly for business, yet she and Sam shared social and recreational activities (e.g., hosting dinner parties, playing tennis) when both were in town. They reported engaging in sexual activity with each other a few times per month, and they described this frequency as much lower than what they experienced in the initial years of their relationship. Both of them reported that they were still attracted to each other but stated that their sexual activity had become more routine and predictable over the years.

QUESTIONS FOR CRITICAL THOUGHT AND REFLECTION

1. How may attraction, intimacy, and love change over time in a relationship?
2. What does this case study reveal about different types (and components) of love that may exist in a relationship over time?
3. How may sexual behaviour be affected by one's attraction to, intimacy with, and love for another person?

Introduction

intimacy Feelings of closeness and connection that one feels with another.

Sexual relationships often involve physical attraction, feelings of **intimacy**, and love. These factors may be present to varying degrees in different sexual relationships. For example, some such relationships involve strong attraction to a sexual partner without feelings of love, others are rooted in feelings of love but involve little attraction between partners, and still other relationships include partners who are in love and share both an emotional and a sexual connection. Certainly, there are often close links among sexuality, attraction, intimacy, and love—for instance, feelings of attraction and love often influence people's decisions to engage in sexual activity with another person. It is thus important to consider the topics of attraction, intimacy, and love in a textbook devoted to understanding human sexuality.

Attraction

Attraction is often a key reason for engaging in sexual activity; in fact, in one study, both male and female undergraduates reported that being attracted to a person was the number one reason for engaging in sexual intercourse (Meston & Buss, 2007). In addition, attraction often provides motivation to enter into a romantic relationship (Figure 12.1). This section will provide an overview of what is known about attraction based on research findings that provide insight into the behavioural components of attraction as well as some of the biological underpinnings of sexual attraction.

FIGURE 12.1 Attraction is an important factor in the decision to engage in sexual activity, and it is a strong motivator for entering into a romantic relationship with another person.

Proximity

In order for attraction to develop, we first need to meet the people we become attracted to, and there is indeed a strong relationship between proximity and attraction. Students in one study who were randomly assigned to seats were rated as more likeable by those sitting near them compared to those seated farther away (Back, Schmukle, & Egloff, 2008), and living near someone increases the chance of partnering with that person. At least part of the association between proximity and attraction may be explained by the **mere-repeated-exposure effect**. This effect was demonstrated in a study in which four women posing as students in a large psychology course attended a different number of classes (zero, five, ten, or fifteen) during the term but did not interact with others in the class (Moreland & Beach, 1992). At end of the term, the students in the class were shown pictures of the women and asked to rate the women on several measures. The women who had attended a greater number of classes were rated as more attractive, and students reported they would be more likely to befriend these women. Thus, this study demonstrated that repeated exposure can influence attraction. Overall, proximity makes it more likely that people will be repeatedly exposed to one another, and it provides an opportunity for people to meet and develop attraction to one another.

> **mere-repeated-exposure effect** The tendency for repeated exposure to a stimulus (e.g., another person) to increase our preference for that stimulus.

Physical Attractiveness

Physical characteristics play a major role in attraction. While both men and women may select non-physical characteristics such as intelligence and honesty as most important in a long-term partner, physical attraction may just be what propels us toward another in the first place. Students are more likely to emphasize physical attraction and sex appeal when considering a short-term sexual partner, and research has found that physical attractiveness was the strongest predictor of undergraduate students' attraction during a speed-dating experiment (Luo & Zhang, 2009). Although physical attractiveness is important to both men and women, gender differences have been noted among heterosexual participants: specifically, men seem to place more emphasis on opposite-sex physical attractiveness than do women.

FACES

In general, people seem to be most attracted to faces that are "average" and symmetrical. Studies in which photographs of faces are combined to create an "average" composite (Figure 12.2) have shown that the composite faces tend to be rated as more attractive by both men and women compared to the individual faces used to create the composite. Note that the term *average* refers here to the statistical sense of the word; the composite faces are not plain or undistinguished or average in terms of attractiveness. Instead, the averaged faces tend to be "quite good looking" (Langlois, Roggman, & Musselman, 1994, p. 214)! There is also a relationship between level of femininity and attractiveness for female faces, with more feminine faces (e.g., those with large eyes) generally reported to be more attractive. The findings are more mixed for male faces, as both feminine and masculine faces have been rated as attractive in men. (See the discussion of menstrual-cycle effects below.)

FIGURE 12.2 These "average" male and female faces represent the types of images used in studies to measure facial attractiveness (e.g., Rhodes, Sumich, and Byatt, 1999). Such faces tend to be rated as more attractive compared to the individual faces that were combined to create the averaged composites.

BODIES

In the Western world, women with body-mass indexes (BMIs) and waist-to-hip ratios (WHRs) that are on the lower end of the typical range for females tend to be considered more attractive than women with higher BMIs and WHRs. In contrast, men with higher WHRs, higher rates of muscle, and lower levels of body fat are generally considered more attractive. With regard to cross-cultural differences, men in some foraging societies in South America and Africa seem to disregard WHRs and tend to prefer women who are relatively heavy; across many cultures, however, it seems that men prefer women with WHRs that are lower than average (as reviewed in Gangestad & Scheyd, 2005).

Reciprocity and Uncertainty

In general, we tend to like and be attracted to people who show signs of liking and being attracted to us (reciprocity). Put another way, reciprocity of attraction is the idea that "attraction breeds attraction." Recent research has examined reciprocity and attraction using an experiment involving Facebook (Whitchurch, Wilson, & Gilbert, 2011). Female undergraduate participants were told that their Facebook profiles had been viewed by male students and that they would be viewing the Facebook profiles of four of these men. Participants subsequently proceeded to view four profiles of men that were, unbeknownst to them, fictitious. Participants who were told they were going to view the profiles of men who liked them best reported more attraction to the men than did the participants who were told they would view profiles of men who had rated them as average.

Interestingly, this study also suggested that uncertainty increases attraction: women who were told that it was not known how the men had rated them reported the highest level of attraction to the profiled men. These women also reported thinking about the men more than those in the "liked-best" condition did, suggesting that uncertainty may enhance attraction because it increases the frequency with which one thinks about another. Thus, the authors of this study suggest that there may be an exception to the principle of reciprocity—namely that, as long as there is initial attraction, people may be more attracted to someone when they are uncertain about how much the other person likes them.

Similarity

We also tend to like and be attracted to others who are similar to us. This preference is captured by the saying "birds of a feather flock together." With regard to similarity and attraction, *homophily* ("love of the same") is the term used to refer to our tendency to associate and connect with others who are similar to us. Indeed, people tend to be attracted to others whose age, level of education, religious views, political views, socioeconomic status, and other such characteristics are similar to their own. As well, people tend to choose and often marry partners who are similar to themselves, a tendency known as **assortative mating**. Research has suggested that attitude similarity can also be a basis for attraction. When students were asked to read an attitude scale that they were told was completed by a stranger (but that in actuality was manipulated to display attitudes similar or dissimilar to those of the students), there was a strong association between attraction and proportion of attitudes shared with the "stranger": those whose attitudes were more similar to those of the stranger reported that they would like and enjoying working with the stranger more (Byrne & Nelson, 1965).

Menstrual-Cycle Effects

Research has suggested that what women perceive as attractive varies at different stages in their menstrual cycles. As an example, women seem to prefer men with more masculine facial features (e.g., a large jaw, a prominent brow ridge; Figure 12.3) when

homophily The principle that we are more likely to have contact and affiliate with people who are similar to us.

assortative mating The tendency to choose a partner who is similar to oneself on one or more characteristics.

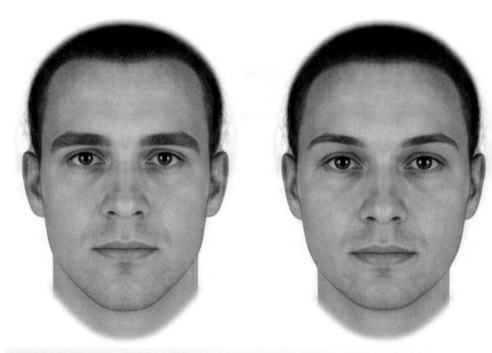

FIGURE 12.3 Are masculine faces more attractive? If you are a woman at your most fertile time of the month, chances are you will consider the more masculine face (left) to be more attractive! The above images come from an article by Jones and colleagues (2008); they show a composite male face, which was altered to increase (left) and decrease (right) masculinity.

they are most fertile (i.e., during the follicular phase of the menstrual cycle). Given that masculine traits are thought to indicate increased immunity, one theory is that females prefer masculine traits when most fertile in order to increase the chance that their offspring will be healthy and inherit good genes. Women also tend to prefer more feminine male and female faces at times of low fertility. Shifts in women's preferences for symmetrical faces have also been found, with symmetrical faces judged to be more attractive during times of increased fertility. Furthermore, research from Queen's University found that a more masculine gait was most attractive to women during the follicular phase versus the less fertile luteal phase of the menstrual cycle (Provost, Troje, & Quinsey, 2008). Men have also been found to rate women's faces as more attractive when the women are most fertile (Roberts et al., 2004).

Attraction to the scent of the opposite sex has also been found to vary during women's menstrual cycles. Studies have been conducted in which people were asked to sleep in the same t-shirt for consecutive nights; these shirts were then smelled by participants who rated the intensity, pleasantness, and sexiness of the body odour left on the t-shirt. In one such study, men rated women's body odour as more sexy and pleasant during the women's follicular phase compared to the less fertile luteal phase of the menstrual cycle, suggesting that ovulation-related odours may be linked to mate selection in males (Singh & Bronstad, 2001).

Do Opposites Attract?

As discussed previously, people tend to be attracted to similar others. One area in which humans may prefer *dissimilarity* in potential partners, however, involves the immune system. More specifically, it involves the major histocompatibility complex (MHC), which is a set of genes in vertebrates that are used by the immune system to distinguish self from non-self factors (e.g., infectious agents). Individuals who are not related are likely to have different MHC genes, and there is evidence to suggest that people prefer partners who have MHC genes that are dissimilar to their own.

Why may MHC dissimilarity between partners be important? It is hypothesized that it may function to (1) produce offspring with better immunocompetence (as distinct MHC alleles may allow the immune system to recognize and resist more pathogens), and (2) avoid in-breeding and the associated negative genetic consequences (Penn & Potts, 1999). Some t-shirt–smelling studies have highlighted a connection between MHC dissimilarity and attraction between partners (see the "Research vs Real Life" box in Chapter 5). Generally, participants in these studies have shown a preference for the odours of individuals who are dissimilar to them with regard to MHC. As an example, women who were not using oral contraceptives rated the odours of t-shirts worn by men with dissimilar MHC as more pleasant than did women whose MHC was similar to that of the men (Wedekind, Seebeck, Bettens, & Paepke, 1995). In this same study, the odours of men who were dissimilar to women in MHC were twice as likely to remind the women of their own current or ex-partners compared to the odours of MHC-similar men. This study suggests that human mating choices are influenced by body-scent preferences that indicate MHC similarity/dissimilarity. Furthermore, there is initial evidence to suggest that MHC similarity/dissimilarity may affect women's sexual behaviour and attraction to individuals who are not their primary partners (Garver-Apgar, Gangestad, Thornhill, Miller, & Olp, 2006). Among 48 heterosexual couples, increased MHC similarity between partners was associated with women's decreased sexual responsiveness to their partner and increased attraction to other men; as well, these women reported having more sexual partners outside of their primary relationship. The same pattern of results was not found for the men in this study. The MHC findings are intriguing: they highlight the complexity of human sexual attraction and suggest that some influences on attraction may be based in genetics.

Pick-Up Strategies: What Works for Men, and What Works for Women?

pick-up line A verbal statement made by someone in order to initiate a romantic encounter.

Imagine this scenario: You are in a bar or other type of social setting, notice someone you think is attractive, and decide to approach (Figure 12.4). What type of opening or **pick-up line** would you use? Research has identified different types to choose from: cute-flippant (e.g., "your place or mine?"), innocuous (e.g., "what do you think of the music?"), and direct (e.g., "can I buy you lunch?") (Kleinke, Meeker, & Staneski, 1986; Figure 12.5). The use of pick-up lines has been tested empirically, both in lab-based settings and in the field. Such research has revealed that, in general, both men and women seem to prefer innocuous and direct lines over cute-flippant ones; women, however, tend to dislike cute-flippant remarks and prefer innocuous remarks more so than men do (e.g., Kleinke et al., 1986). One study set in the "spontaneous, beer-saturated ecology" of a bar (Cunningham, 1989, p. 29) found that males who were approached by a female experimenter tended to respond positively regardless of the type of line used. The same study found that female patrons were more

FIGURE 12.4 Picking up? Although the bar can be a popular place to meet a potential sexual and/or romantic partner, research with Canadian undergraduate women indicates that 95 per cent of young women do not anticipate meeting someone to have sex with when going to a bar (Huber & Herold, 2006).

discerning when a male experimenter approached them; women tended to vary their response according to the type of pick-up line used, with cute-flippant lines receiving the least-positive responses (Cunningham, 1989).

Attempts at humour and using a third-party such as a friend to make the introduction are also popular pick-up strategies (Weber, Goodboy, & Cayanus, 2010). In fact, a recent study found that, for a male initiating conversation with a female in a bar setting, third-party introductions were perceived to be more effective than cute-flippant lines, humorous statements, direct compliments, and direct introductions (Weber et al., 2010). Based on such findings, the authors assert that single men who are looking to approach a woman "would be well-advised to consider using sponsorship from third parties to initiate flirtatious conversation with women. If third-party sponsorship is unavailable, men should consider using direct-introduction opening lines and should avoid using direct compliments, humour attempts, and cute-flippant lines" (p. 190). In any case, verbal approaches seem to be much more effective than sexually overt approach behaviours (e.g., grinding); research conducted with female participants at the University of Guelph found that verbal approaches were the most preferred method of approaching and being approached by someone in a bar, and only 1 of the over 140 women surveyed preferred a sexually overt approach (Huber & Herold, 2006).

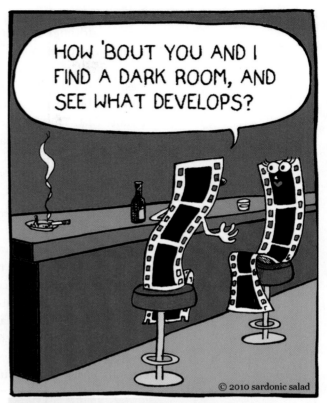

FIGURE 12.5 Are different types of pick-up lines equally effective? Not necessarily! Cute-flippant lines tend to be the least preferred type of pick-up line, especially by women.

Intimacy

Intimacy in relationships is highly valued in Western culture, and satisfying intimate relationships are associated with numerous benefits, including psychological well-being and happiness, social support, and increased physical health. Many people seek intimacy in their close sexual and non-sexual relationships, and in this section we will (1) seek to answer the question "what is intimacy?"; (2) examine a prominent theory regarding people's approaches to intimacy with others; and (3) review research regarding the role of intimacy and lack of intimacy in sexual relationships.

What Is Intimacy?

In general, intimacy is often characterized by affection, caring, trust, understanding, sharing, and togetherness, and it is associated with feelings of closeness in a relationship. Moss and Schwebel (1993) define intimacy as the "level of commitment and positive affective, cognitive, and physical closeness one experiences with a partner in a reciprocal (although not necessarily symmetrical) relationship" (p. 33). This definition defines intimacy in terms of both commitment and closeness, with the latter involving emotional (e.g., deep caring), cognitive (e.g., sharing personal information), and physical (e.g., close proximity) components. Research with couples indicates that romantic and married partners do indeed experience and express intimacy and closeness in various ways, including providing care, sharing thoughts and feelings, spending time together, and showing physical affection (e.g., Ben-Ari & Lavee, 2007). The above definition also proposes that intimacy does not need to be equivalent between partners, although it does need to be mutual.

Different types of intimacy have been described—for example, emotional, social, sexual, intellectual, and recreational. These five types of intimacy are commonly assessed with the Personal Assessment of Intimacy in Relationships (PAIR) measure developed by Schaefer and Olson (1981). Examples of items from the PAIR are shown in Table 12.1. These authors also describe intimacy as a "process" that likely requires effort to maintain in a relationship.

Attachment Theory

People differ in the degree to which they seek out or avoid intimacy with others, and attachment theory has been widely used to understand and explain these differences. Attachment theory states that our formation of relationships in adulthood is shaped by our early experiences and attachment to caregivers in childhood. An early article on adult attachment and romantic relationships documented that patterns of attachment found in infancy occur at a similar rate in adulthood (Hazan & Shaver, 1987). This article also highlighted that different attachment styles are associated with different experiences in romantic relationships; for example, adults with a secure attachment style (i.e., those with a positive view of themselves who are able to easily form close relationships with others) reported experiencing happiness and trust in their relationships, whereas adults with less secure styles reported negative experiences such as romantic jealousy (Hazan & Shaver, 1987).

Over the last few decades, a large body of literature has continued to examine adult attachment. In particular, Kim Bartholomew, a researcher at Simon Fraser University in British Columbia, has developed a two-dimensional model of adult attachment (Figure 12.6). This model demonstrates how some adult relationships are characterized by an avoidance of intimacy (Bartholomew, 1990). With this model, Bartholomew identifies four styles of adult attachment that can be understood in terms of two underlying dimensions: the model of the self (i.e., how one views herself or himself) and the model of the other (i.e., how one views other people). Individuals who have a positive view of themselves have an internalized sense of self-worth and expect others to react positively to them; individuals who have a positive view of other people expect others to be supportive and available. A positive model of self is associated with being confident (as opposed to anxious and dependent) in relationships, whereas a positive model of other is associated with seeking out (rather than avoiding) intimacy.

As outlined by Bartholomew (1990), a *secure* style of attachment is associated with positive views of both the self and others: people with a secure style have high

TABLE 12.1 Examples of items from the Personal Assessment of Intimacy in Relationships (PAIR) questionnaire.

Type of Intimacy Assessed	Item Example
Emotional	My partner listens to me when I need someone to talk to.
Social	Having time together with friends is an important part of our shared activities.
Sexual	Sexual expression is an essential part of our relationship.
Intellectual	My partner helps me clarify my thoughts.
Recreational	We enjoy the same recreational activities.

Source: Adapted from Schaefer & Olson (1981).

self-esteem and are able to form and maintain close intimate relationships without difficulty. A *preoccupied* style is characterized by a negative view of the self and a positive view of others: preoccupied individuals often feel unworthy, are markedly dependent on other people for approval, and may be demanding in their relationships. A *fearful* style of attachment involves a negative view of both the self and others: persons with a fearful style experience low self-worth and, although they may desire intimacy, actively avoid intimacy with others for fear of being rejected. Finally, the fourth style of attachment, the *dismissing* style, is characterized by a positive view of the self and a negative view of others: individuals who are dismissing feel self-reliant and perceive intimacy with others as unimportant. In the young adults they sampled, Bartholomew and Horowitz (1991) reported that 47 to 57 per cent had a secure style of attachment, 10 to 14 per cent had a preoccupied style, 15 to 21 per cent had a fearful style, and 18 per cent had a dismissing style. Examples of descriptions of the four styles are shown in Table 12.2.

There are also other ways of thinking about the dimensions that underlie adult romantic attachments. Indeed, a common view is that avoidance (of intimacy) and anxiety (about rejection or abandonment), rather than people's perceptions of self and other, are the underlying dimensions that explain differences in adult attachment patterns. Examining the four styles of attachment using this framework, we can see that secure individuals would be low in avoidance and anxiety, preoccupied individuals would be low in avoidance and high in anxiety, fearful individuals would be high on both dimensions, and dismissing individuals would be high in avoidance but low in anxiety (Fraley & Shaver, 2000).

Attachment theory and related research have important implications for understanding intimate relationships. For example, although attachment styles can change, attachment theory reminds us that history and past experiences help shape our

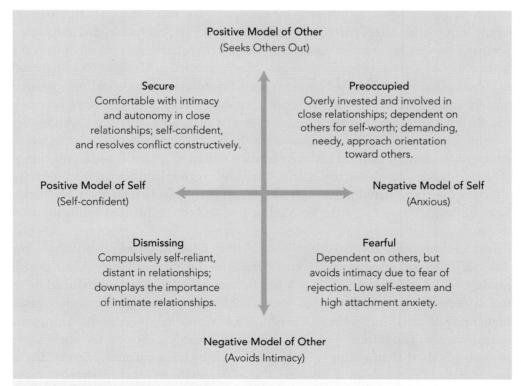

FIGURE 12.6 Bartholomew's (1990) two-dimensional model of adult attachment outlines four styles of attachment: secure, preoccupied, fearful, and dismissing.

Source: Adapted from Henderson et al. (2005).

TABLE 12.2 Examples of the four attachment styles described in the two-dimensional model of adult attachment.

Type of Attachment Style	Description
Secure	It is easy for me to become emotionally close to others. I am comfortable depending on others and having others depend on me. I don't worry about being alone or having others not accept me.
Preoccupied	I want to be completely emotionally intimate with others, but I often find that others are reluctant to get as close as I would like. I am uncomfortable being without close relationships, but I sometimes worry that others don't value me as much as I value them.
Fearful	I am uncomfortable getting close to others. I want emotionally close relationships, but I find it difficult to trust others completely, or to depend on them. I worry that I will be hurt if I allow myself to become too close to others.
Dismissing	I am comfortable without close emotional relationships. It is very important to me to feel independent and self-sufficient, and I prefer not to depend on others or have others depend on me.

Source: Based on Bartholomew and Horowitz (1991).

current relationships. Research has found that attachment styles are associated with satisfaction in romantic relationships for both individuals and their partners, with a secure attachment style associated with having a romantic partner who is highly satisfied (e.g., Guerrero, Farinelli, & McEwan, 2009). Recent research also suggests that attachment styles may influence relationship satisfaction through specific expression of emotion; preoccupied attachment, for example, was associated with destructive use of anger (e.g., criticism of partner) in one study, which in turn was related to having a partner who was less satisfied (Guerrero et al., 2009). Interestingly, research with the first cohort of same-sex couples who were legally married in Canada (20 lesbian and 6 gay couples) found that the couples reported significantly less attachment-related anxiety and avoidance, as well as higher relationship satisfaction, in comparison to norms for heterosexual married couples. In addition, all of the same-sex couples were in the secure range of attachment on the questionnaire used in this study; in comparison, only 70 per cent of heterosexual married couples fall within this range (MacIntosh, Reissing, & Andruff, 2010). The same-sex couples reported many positive effects of marriage, including feeling more emotionally close to each other, and it may be that the couples' attachment both influenced and was influenced by the decision to marry.

Attachment styles are also related to one's sexuality and sexual relationships. For example, based on responses from participants in the Niagara Young Adult Health Study, Bogaert and Sadava (2002) of Brock University found that anxious attachment was associated with an earlier age of first sexual intercourse, more lifetime partners, a higher rate of infidelity within relationships, and recent use of condoms during sexual intercourse. The authors suggested that persons with less secure attachment styles may adopt a short-term mating strategy, such as having many partners, because "to the extent that adult attachment processes reflect early childhood experience with primary caretakers . . . an unstable relationship with parents suggests their adult environments are likely to be unstable and not conducive to a stable long-term mating life history" (p. 200). The authors also suggested that increased condom use may reflect a higher number of sexual partners among those with less secure attachment. In contrast, using daily sampling methods, researchers in a different study found that individuals with high attachment anxiety were *less* likely to use condoms in their sexual interactions with their dating partner, perhaps because using condoms may be viewed as reducing intimacy and threatening their relationships (Strachman & Impett, 2009). Such studies highlight how attachment styles may influence individuals' sexuality and also suggest that the way individuals approach their sexual interactions is a reflection of their general tendency to either seek out or avoid intimacy with others.

Hooking Up and Casual Sex

While many people engage in sexual activity for emotional reasons, such as a desire for emotional closeness and intimacy, people also have sex for reasons *not* related to emotional factors—for example, the desire for physical pleasure. Sexual encounters that do not occur between partners in an established romantic relationship are often referred to as "**hooking up**" or "casual sex." Hooking up is generally defined as "casual sex practices, includ[ing] anything from kissing to intercourse" in which "the interactions have no strings attached" (Stinson, 2010, p. 99). Hooking up is different from dating in that (1) people who hook up often do so after they have been drinking alcohol, for example, at a bar or a party; (2) hooking up is not indicative of emotional intimacy or commitment between the sex partners; and (3) although a small percentage of hook-up experiences may transition into a romantic relationship (e.g., Paul, McManus, & Hayes, 2000), the encounter between the hook-up partners is typically short term, often lasting just one night.

> **hooking up** Casual sex interactions with no strings attached.

Research has documented that hooking up is a common experience among college and university students; hooking up is even referred to as "the norm" in some college environments. Research with American college students indicates that hooking up may occur in over half to three-quarters of the student population (as reviewed by Stinson, 2010); in fact, one study found that more than 75 per cent of a randomly selected sample of students living on campus reported having hooked up (Paul et al., 2000). Research examining Canadian students' casual sex experiences during spring vacation in Daytona Beach found lower numbers: 15 per cent of men and 13 per cent of women reported that they had engaged in casual sex (Maticka-Tyndale, Herold, & Mewhinney, 1998).

One explanation for the prominent hook-up culture among undergraduates is that historical and social changes have helped make it more convenient and acceptable for young people to participate in such partnered sexual activities. For example, the development of advanced contraceptive methods such as oral contraceptive pills allowed people to engage in sexual activity without facing a high likelihood that the sexual act would result in a pregnancy. In addition, the latter half of the twentieth century witnessed the development of more permissive attitudes toward sexuality and an increase in sexual activity before marriage. Young adults, as well as adolescents, are also faced with the developmental task of establishing a sexual identity (Stinson, 2010), and experimenting with sexuality through hooking up may be one way in which they try to accomplish this task.

Research has shown that hooking up has both pros and cons for the individual. Students who have participated in hooking up report a range of both positive and negative emotions associated with their experiences. Examples of reported positive emotions include happiness or excitement, whereas examples of negative emotions include confusion or disappointment. Young adults, particularly women, may also feel pressure to participate in the hook-up culture and, as a result, may engage in unwanted sexual experiences (e.g., Paul & Hayes, 2002). As well, women may struggle with the sexual double standard that exists, whereby women who hook up are often viewed more negatively compared to their male counterparts (Stinson, 2010).

Love

It is important to consider the role that love plays in human sexual experiences and relationships. Although romantic love and sexual desire may be distinct experiences with different neurobiological substrates (Diamond, 2004), many people experience love together with sexual activity and feelings of sexual desire. Research that has asked undergraduate students to provide accounts of how love and sex are linked in their romantic relationships has demonstrated that people often consider love and sex to be intertwined (Hendrick & Hendrick, 2002). Love is also one of the top reasons reported for engaging in sexual intercourse; Meston and Buss (2007), for example, found that "I wanted to express my love for the person" was the fifth most common reason women reported and the eighth most common reason men reported for having sex (participants chose from a list of 237 reasons). In this section, we will focus on love and consider (1) the question "what is love?"; (2) different types of love, namely passionate and companionate love; (3) cutting-edge research that has used brain imaging to examine love; and 4) three major theories of love. This section will conclude with a brief overview of love for non-human objects.

What Is Love?

The word *love*, in a sense, surrounds us. Turn on the radio and you are likely to hear the word sung through the speakers, turn on the television or pick up a magazine and you are likely to see images designed to convey love. As Helen Fisher notes: "everywhere people sing for love, pray for love, work for love, live for love, kill for love, and die for love" (Fisher, 2006, p. 107). Nevertheless, researchers acknowledge that the word *love* is often used broadly and in several different ways. For example, the word is often used to refer to such diverse matters as food preferences; feelings toward another person, activity, or object; and affections for a pet. Pause for a moment and think about your use of the word *love*; have you used the word to refer to a favourite song, ice cream flavour, or person, for example?

Indeed, the word *love* has different meanings, and there is no singular definition of *love*, even among members of the same cultural group (see the "Culture and Diversity" box to learn about cross-cultural views on love). In order to understand how the concept of love is generally understood, Fehr (1988) conducted a series of studies with undergraduate students at the University of British Columbia (UBC). When students were asked to list features of love, caring, happiness, acceptance, and trust were listed frequently; sexual passion and physical attraction were also listed, albeit less frequently. Fehr (1988) also asked a different group of UBC students to rate how central certain identified features were to their concept of love. The students gave trust, caring, honesty, friendship, and respect the highest ratings. This research, as well as other studies, suggests that people do not have formal definitions of love but instead consider certain features to be characteristic of love. Interestingly, research specifically examining romantic love has found that undergraduate students rate sexual attraction/desire as a central feature of romantic love, and that they list sexual attraction/desire as a feature of romantic love more frequently than any other feature except trust (Regan, Kocan, & Whitlock, 1998).

Culture & Diversity

Cross-cultural Views on Love

Researchers have identified both differences and similarities in the ways in which various cultures view love and relationships. One dimension along which cultures differ is individualism–collectivism. In cultures in which individualism predominates, such as those of Canada and the US, personal autonomy is emphasized, and people are concerned mainly with their individual goals and those of their immediate family. Cultures that are characterized by collectivism, such as those of China and India, emphasize communal goals, group membership, duty, and personal sacrifice for the larger social group. With regard to love, individualist societies generally emphasize passionate love as a basis for marriage more so than do collectivist societies; **arranged marriages** are more common in collectivist cultures, with arranged marriages being the norm for about half of the world's population (Penn, 2011).

When college students from Australia, Brazil, England, Hong Kong, India, Japan, Mexico, Pakistan, the Philippines, Thailand, and the US were asked, "If a man (woman) had all the other qualities you desired, would you marry this person if you were not in love with him (her)?" (Levine, Sato, Hashimoto, & Verma, 1995), participants from individualist countries were significantly more likely to perceive love as necessary for marriage. Eighty per cent or more of the students from the US, Brazil, England, Mexico, and Australia answered "no" to this question, as compared to 24 per cent of students from India, 39.1 per cent from Pakistan, and 33.8 per cent from Thailand. The percentage of students from Hong Kong, Japan, or the Philippines who answered "no" to this question ranged from 62 per cent (Japan) to 77.6 per cent (Hong Kong).

Research conducted with undergraduates at the University of Toronto examined the love styles of students with different ethnocultural backgrounds (Dion & Dion, 1993; see also the discussion of love styles on pp. 303–305). This research found that students from various Asian backgrounds (Chinese, Japanese, Korean, Indian, Pakistani) were more likely to endorse a view of love based on friendship (i.e., a storge love style) compared to students from Anglo-Celtic and European backgrounds. As well, it found that female students from Asian backgrounds other than Chinese had a more altruistic (i.e., agapic) view of love in comparison to women from Anglo-Celtic backgrounds. Such findings support a distinction between collectivist and individualist cultures with regard to how love is viewed, as many Asian cultures tend to be more collectivist compared to Anglo-Celtic and European cultures.

Similarities with regard to love and relationships, however, have also been documented cross-culturally. Passionate love has been observed in the majority of societies around the world, and it has consequently been deemed a near-universal experience. There also seems to be a trend toward more individualism in cultures that have traditionally been collectivist in their approaches to marriage. Furthermore, upon surveying more than 9000 individuals from 33 countries about the characteristics they find desirable in a potential mate, strong similarities were found across cultures (Buss et al., 1990). Almost all samples in this survey viewed dependability, emotional stability, intelligence, kindness and understanding, and mutual attraction/love as highly desirable characteristics. The authors suggest that such findings support the presence of a species-typical mate preference for humans; that is, they suggest that humans, regardless of their unique backgrounds, may prefer certain similar characteristics in a mate.

> **arranged marriage** A marriage in which family members, typically parents, choose a partner for a person to marry.

Different Types of Love: Passionate and Companionate

The two most common types of love are **passionate love** and **companionate love**. Passionate love is a state of intense longing for union with another; it is sometimes referred to as "being in love" and has been described as a "hot" and "fiery" state (Hatfield

> **passionate love** A state of intense longing for union with another.

companionate love
Affection and tenderness felt for someone with whom one's life is deeply connected.

& Rapson, 1993). The intense longing of passionate love consists of behavioural components (e.g., doing something to make the loved one happy), cognitive components (e.g., preoccupation with and idealization of the loved one), and emotional components (e.g., longing for reciprocal love). Other experiences associated with passionate love may include feelings of euphoria, increased energy, and obsessive thinking about the beloved; unrequited passionate love is associated with despair and anxiety (Hatfield & Rapson, 1993). Research suggests that most people have likely experienced unrequited love. For example, one study involving undergraduate students found that almost 93 per cent had had a moderate or powerful experience of loving someone who did not love them in return (Baumeister, Wotman, & Stillwell, 1993).

In comparison, companionate love has been deemed a "warm" state: it is "cooler" than passionate love. Companionate love is the affection and tenderness we feel for someone with whom our lives are deeply connected (Hatfield & Rapson, 1993). This type of love is based on deep friendship and is comfortable and trusting (Sternberg, 1986).

LOVE AND THE BRAIN

Over the last decade, studies have been conducted to investigate the role of certain brain areas associated with passionate and companionate love. In these studies, participants who are deeply or intensely in love (in the early stages of love) are typically shown pictures of their beloved and their friends or acquaintances; they are asked to think about the person whose picture they are viewing while functional magnetic resonance imaging (fMRI) is used to scan their brains. Such studies have found that viewing pictures of one's romantic partner is associated with increased activity in dopamine-rich reward and motivation systems of the brain (e.g., the caudate nucleus) and decreased activity in brain areas involved in social judgment and emotions such as fear and grief (e.g., the amygdala). Interestingly, passionate love seems to share brain patterns with other euphoric states such as cocaine-induced euphoria! Bartels and Zeki (2004) have argued that passionate love deactivates brain areas involved in critical assessment of others and negative emotions—perhaps also offering a neurological explanation for the common observation that "love is blind" (Figure 12.7)—and works to bond people by activating brain areas associated with reward. These brain patterns are similar in both males and females, as well as in same-sex and opposite-sex oriented individuals (Zeki & Romaya, 2010). Furthermore, the first study to examine brain activation patterns of individuals involved in long-term romantic relationships found results similar to those of the research involving participants in the intense, early stages of love. However, researchers found that brain areas associated with attachment (e.g., the anterior cingulate) were also activated in the long-term partnered individuals (Acevedo, Aron, Fisher, & Brown, 2011).

"I don't care if he's a basketball! We're in love!"

FIGURE 12.7 Is love blind? Research shows that partners tend to idealize, and have positive illusions about, their significant others (Swami & Furnham, 2008).

REJECTION AND THE BRAIN

What happens in the brain when one is rejected in love? A recent New York–based study has found that dopamine-rich areas of the brain associated with motivation and reward were activated in individuals who viewed a photo of their ex-partner (Fisher, Brown, Aron, Strong, & Mashek, 2010). This study also found that areas of the brain associated with craving for cocaine were activated when participants viewed their ex-partner. As suggested by the authors, the fact that romantic rejection and cocaine craving share common brain correlates may help explain some of the obsessive behaviours that can occur with rejection (e.g., thinking obsessively about the ex-partner).

Theories of Love

The following discussion will explore three major theories of love: (1) the duplex theory of love; (2) the theory of love styles; and (3) the two-factor theory.

THE DUPLEX THEORY OF LOVE

Robert Sternberg's duplex theory of love focusses on both the structure and the development of love. It consists of two parts or subtheories, the triangular theory of love and the theory of love as a story.

The Triangular Theory of Love

The triangular theory of love, a leading theory in the field, focusses on the structure of love. Specifically, Sternberg posits that there are three components of love that, in different combinations, form different types of love. These three components are intimacy, passion, and **commitment** (decision). In this theory, intimacy involves feelings of closeness and connection to a loved one and includes feelings that lead to warmth in a relationship (Sternberg, 2006). Passion involves physical arousal and attraction and often is characterized by a drive to be sexual with one's partner; at the same time, other strong needs, such as a need to be nurtured by one's partner, may also add to the experience of passion in a relationship. Passion is often the earliest of the components to emerge in a romantic relationship, and, given that it is the component that is least under conscious control, it is the most difficult to sustain (Sternberg, 1986). Commitment, in the short term, is the decision that one person loves another; in the long term, it is the decision to maintain that love. The short- and long-term aspects of commitment do not always go together, as one can love someone in the short term yet not be committed to the relationship over a long period of time, or vice versa. According to Sternberg, each component of love is associated with a set of actions. For example, intimacy may be expressed by spending time with one's partner, passion by sexual activity, and commitment by marrying (Sternberg, 2006).

These three components are each viewed as forming one side of a triangle (Figure 12.8), with the triangle representing the love that one feels for another. Each of the three components can differ in amount; accordingly, triangles will vary in shape and size. For example, an equilateral triangle would represent a love that contains fairly equal amounts of intimacy, passion, and commitment. The specific amounts of the components may shift over time in a relationship and may differ from

commitment In the short term, the decision that one person loves another. In the long term, the decision to maintain the love that one has for another person.

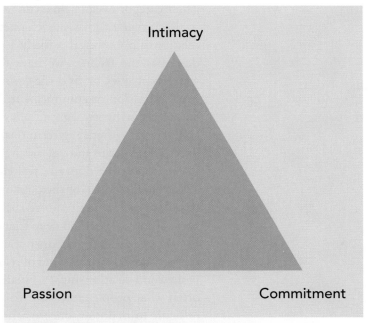

FIGURE 12.8 The triangular theory of love proposes that there are three components of love: intimacy, passion, and commitment.

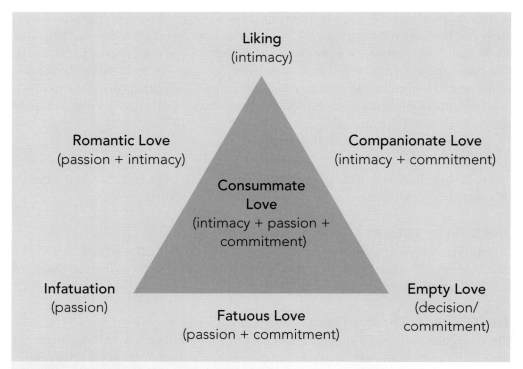

FIGURE 12.9 The triangular theory of love proposes that there are eight different types of love. Seven are shown here. The eighth, *nonlove*, is characterized by an absence of intimacy, passion, and commitment.

one relationship to another. Triangles may also differ between partners in a couple: partners whose triangles are more closely matched are predicted to be more satisfied in their relationship compared to couples in which partners' triangles are less matched (Sternberg, 1986). Using this theory, Sternberg has proposed that intimacy, passion, and commitment come together in various combinations to form different types of love, and that these components ultimately generate eight types of love (Figure 12.9). These categories can help us understand the different forms of love we may experience.

Each type of love may characterize a certain kind or phase of a relationship: no relationship, however, is likely a pure example of any one type. *Liking*, or friendship, describes the feelings we have for those with whom we experience closeness and warmth; it goes beyond the feelings we have for casual acquaintances but does not involve passion or commitment. *Infatuated love* can be likened to "love at first sight" and tends to involve signs of physical arousal such as a rapid heartbeat. *Empty love* may characterize either long-term relationships in which intimacy and physical attraction have faded or the start of arranged marriages in which one may commit to love his or her spouse yet does not feel close or physically attracted to that person. *Romantic love* is characteristic of the passionate, intimate relationships commonly presented in popular media and literature such as *Romeo and Juliet*. *Companionate love*, as described above, is often based on deep friendship and involves both intimacy and commitment. *Fatuous love* generally occurs in relationships in which people meet and marry or commit very quickly; these types of relationships are at high risk for divorce (think of many Hollywood relationships!). Finally, *consummate love*, also known as complete love, is often what people endeavour for in romantic relationships; this type of love may be difficult to maintain once reached. Sternberg's theory also includes the category of *nonlove* (not shown in Figure 12.9), which represents most of our casual interactions with others (Sternberg, 1986).

Sternberg also proposes that passion, intimacy, and commitment change over time in a relationship in a specified direction. Specifically, he posits that passion and intimacy will decrease over time as one's partner becomes less arousing and more predictable. Commitment is expected to increase over time and eventually level off. Research examining these predictions has found mixed support. For example, some research has found declines in intimacy as predicted, while other research has found that more serious relationships are associated with some aspects of increased intimacy. In support of Sternberg's predictions, lower levels of passion and higher levels of commitment have been found with longer or more serious relationships (Acker & Davis, 1992; Lemieux & Hale, 2002). (See the "Research vs Real Life" box for more information on how certain relationship factors may change over time.)

The Theory of Love as a Story

The theory of love as a story tries to explain how different types of triangles and love develop. It states that we are exposed to various stories about what love is—by watching other people or movies or reading fairy tales, for example—and eventually develop our own **love stories** based on our own personalities and experiences. The theory also suggests that we strive to fulfill these stories, and that relationships are most satisfying when partners' stories are closely matched—indeed, research has found that the greater the similarity between love stories, the more likely partners are to be satisfied in their relationship (Sternberg, Hojjat, & Barnes, 2001).

> **love stories** Stories that express different beliefs and ideas about what love is like.

Upon examining stories from American research participants and stories contained in literature and other forms of art, Sternberg and colleagues identified 26 specific love stories (although Sternberg also acknowledges that an infinite number of stories is probable). The most popular stories are the travel story (i.e., love is a journey), the gardening story (i.e., relationships require tending and nurture), the democratic government story (i.e., partners share equal power in the relationship), and the history story (i.e., relationship events form a record to keep); in contrast, the horror story (i.e., a relationship is interesting when a partner is terrorized or terrorizes), the collector story (i.e., partner is viewed in a detached manner and as fitting into an overall scheme), the autocratic government story (i.e., one partner is controlled/dominated by the other), and the game story (i.e., love is a sport) are the least popular love stories. People can have multiple love stories, and each story contains roles for two people in a relationship. Some stories may lead to more durable relationships than others, and the stories we hold influence our actions and beliefs (Sternberg, 2006). Interestingly, maladaptive stories such as the horror story are related to less satisfaction in a relationship, yet more positive stories such as the gardening story have not shown a significant association with relationship satisfaction.

THE THEORY OF LOVE STYLES

Based on historical analysis of literature regarding love and also on interviews, Canadian sociologist John Lee (1973) proposed that there are six major ways of loving called love styles: eros, storge, ludus, pragma, mania, and agape. *Eros* refers to romantic, erotic, and passionate love. An eros lover is passionate and intense and wishes to know a partner on all levels; at the same time, such lovers have appropriate boundaries in their relationships and are open and trusting. *Storge* is love based on friendship and compatibility. A person with a storge love style is someone who likely values commitment in the long term over excitement in the short term, and thus values similarity in a partner over sexual gratification or physical appearance. *Ludus* is game-playing love that does not involve commitment. A ludic lover may have intimate and/or sexual

Research VS Real Life

Attraction, Intimacy, and Love over Time

Western society tends to promote passionate love as the basis for serious relationships and marriage. What we don't often hear, however, is the ways in which passion and relationships can change; as such, some people may experience distress when their relationship undergoes common changes that they may not expect. Relationships evolve and so too do our attraction to, intimacy with, and love for another person. Perhaps in contrast to romantic societal notions, it is generally assumed in the research literature that the heat of passionate love fades over time and transitions into companionate love.

There is research to support the assertion that passionate love evolves into a companionate form of love in longer-term relationships. For example, studies have found that couples tend to have sexual intercourse (which may be an indicator of attraction to and passion for a partner) less frequently with time, and reduced levels of passion have been reported with longer relationships. Age-related declines in sexual frequency do occur; however, **habituation** also likely occurs within longer-term relationships as partners become accustomed to each other and sexual interactions within the relationship lose their novelty. In support of this notion, qualitative research conducted with married women with low sexual desire found that while these women valued commitment, closeness, and intimacy in their marriage, they also viewed these relationship factors as contributing to their reduced sexual passion; over-familiarity with one's partner brought loss of romance and decreased desire (Sims & Meana, 2010). Research conducted at Simon Fraser University has also found that relationship quality generally decreases over time among newly married couples (Poyner-Del Vento & Cobb, 2011). As well, brain imaging data suggests that brain activity patterns associated with love change over time; particularly, brain areas associated with attachment become activated in individuals in longer-term relationships (Fisher, Aron, & Brown, 2005).

Recently, however, some researchers have challenged the notion that attraction and love diminish with time (Acevedo & Aron, 2009). In particular, these researchers argue that intense romantic love, including sexual interest for one's partner, can indeed endure in long-term relationships. When long-term romantic love is considered apart from the obsessional features of early stage passionate love (e.g., obsessive thinking about one's partner), some couples do report the presence of intense love in long-term relationships; that is, these couples report high levels of romantic love but without the obsession that characterizes new (passionate) love (Acevedo & Aron, 2009). Indeed, the first study to assess the prevalence of intense romantic love in long-term relationships was recently published (O'Leary, Acevedo, Aron, Huddy, & Mashek, 2012). Using two random samples of married individuals in the US, O'Leary and colleagues found that 29 to 40 per cent of individuals who were married for more than 10 years reported being "very intensely in love" with their partner (O'Leary et al., 2012). Acevedo and Aron (2009) recognize that findings in support of long-term romantic love contrast the predictions of some major theories of love and may be distressing to some long-term couples who do not experience intense feelings of romantic love. At the same time, they suggest that such findings may serve as inspiration for some couples.

> **habituation** A decrease in behavioural response to a repeated stimulus. Sexual habituation occurs when increased accessibility to a partner and predictability in sexual interactions leads to reduced sexual interest.

relationships with numerous others; a person with this style views love as a game to be enjoyed mutually and aims "to enjoy relationships with a variety of people, with everyone having fun and no one getting hurt" (Hendrick, 2004, p. 16). *Pragma* is practical love that involves rational decision-making. Someone with this style is pragmatic and may have a list of qualities she or he is looking for in a partner; computer dating services may suit a pragmatic lover well, as they allow for the screening of potential partners. *Mania* is dependent, possessive, and obsessional love. People with a manic love style experience emotional ups and downs in a relationship; while they may long for love, they are generally mistrustful, jealous, and insecure. *Agape* is altruistic love that is characterized by giving rather than receiving. An agapic lover is compassionate and places more importance on a partner's well-being than on her or his own; this type of love style is rare, and pure agapic love may be unlikely. Although individuals may have fairly consistent love styles throughout their lives, people can also express the different love styles to varying degrees within a romantic relationship, and different styles may predominate with different partners (Hendrick & Hendrick, 1997; Hendrick, 2004).

Researchers have often conceptualized the love styles as attitudes or beliefs, and Hendrick and Hendrick (1986) developed the Love Attitudes Scale to assess these styles. Examples of items from the Love Attitudes Scale are shown in Table 12.3. Upon administering the scale to undergraduate students, the researchers found that students who were in love at the time subscribed more to the eros and agape and less to the ludus and pragma styles as compared to students who were not in love. Males were also found to subscribe more to a ludus style of love compared to females. As well, some research has found that young, never-married persons report more ludus, more mania, and less agape styles compared to married people (see Hendrick, 2004, for a review). Love styles have also been linked to relationship and sexual satisfaction, with eros associated with higher levels of both types of satisfaction. Ludus has been found to be negatively related to satisfaction in romantic relationships, in that the more one subscribes to a ludus style of loving the less likely that person is to be satisfied in his or her relationship (e.g., Fricker & Moore, 2002). Love styles have also been linked to sexual-moral attitudes; for example, participants with liberal attitudes toward sexuality (e.g., those opposed to anti-pornography laws) were more likely to endorse a more ludus style of love compared to conservative participants (Lacey, Reifman, Scott, Harris, & Fitzpatrick, 2004).

THE TWO-FACTOR THEORY OF LOVE

The two-factor theory of love is an application of the two-factor theory of emotion, which posits that emotions result from the interaction of physiological arousal and cognition. This theory has been used to explain passionate love. Berscheid and Walster (1974) proposed that passionate love arises when two conditions are met: (1) intense physiological arousal is experienced by an individual, and (2) situational cues (e.g., the

TABLE 12.3 Examples of items from the Love Attitudes Scale.

Type of Love Style Measured	Item Example
Eros	My lover and I have the right physical "chemistry" between us.
Storge	The best kind of love grows out of a long friendship.
Ludus	I believe that what my lover doesn't know about me won't hurt him/her.
Pragma	A main consideration in choosing a lover is how he/she reflects on my family.
Mania	When my lover doesn't pay attention to me, I feel sick all over.
Agape	I would rather suffer myself than let my lover suffer.

Source: Based on Hendrick and Hendrick (1986).

presence of another person) prompt the individual to apply a cognitive label, "love," to the arousal. According to this theory, love occurs when feelings of physiological arousal are attributed to the presence of another person, for example, and interpreted as love. However, the same physiological responses can result from different situations, and for different reasons; as an example, rapid heartbeat, flushing in the face, and butterflies in the stomach may occur when we are near a person for whom we have romantic feelings, but we also can experience such sensations in an anxiety-provoking situation such as giving a presentation in front of our peers. It is thus possible for **misattribution of arousal** to occur when arousal produced from one experience (e.g., fear) is misinterpreted as love.

> **misattribution of arousal**
> When physiological arousal stemming from one state (e.g., fear) is misinterpreted as stemming from another state (e.g., love).

Some support has been found for the misattribution explanation of passionate love. Dutton and Aron (1974) examined the link between fear and attraction in a study utilizing the Capilano Suspension Bridge in North Vancouver (Figure 12.10). In one portion of the study, men were approached by an attractive female interviewer while standing on the swaying, "fear-arousing" Capilano Suspension Bridge; this bridge has low handrails and is situated 70 metres above rocks and rapids. In another portion of the study, other men were approached by the same interviewer while standing on a control bridge that was sturdy, non-swaying, and approximately 3 metres above shallow water. The interviewer asked the men to complete a questionnaire and write a story while they were on the bridge, and the stories were later scored for sexual content. Upon completion of the questionnaire and story, the interviewer provided each participant with her name and phone number.

More sexual content was found in the stories created by the men on the fear-arousing bridge. Additionally, more men who had been on the fear-arousing bridge subsequently called the female interviewer; this finding suggests that the men on the

FIGURE 12.10 The Capilano Suspension Bridge spans 137 metres across and 70 metres above Capilano River in Vancouver, British Columbia. The slogan for this attraction—"Can you say you've made it?"—highlights the fear that many people experience while crossing (or while even thinking about crossing!) this bridge.

suspension bridge were more attracted to the interviewer than were the men on the control bridge. These results were not found when the interviewer was male. While other explanations for such findings are possible—reduced anxiety may have occurred, for example, with the presence of the interviewer and led to increased attraction—Dutton and Aron's (1974) findings have been used as evidence for the two-factor theory of love. According to this theory, the men on the fear-arousing bridge should have been more physiologically aroused compared to the men on the control bridge; in the presence of the attractive female, this arousal may have been interpreted as attraction.

Love for Objects

While almost all research on romantic love focusses on love directed toward other people, it is also important to consider that some people may experience such love for non-human objects. This romantic love for objects is referred to as **objectùm sexuality** (OS). People with OS feel emotionally and physically attracted to and fall in love with an object or objects; OS is often described as a sexual orientation. People with OS may have a love relationship with and feel deeply connected to an object, with some even marrying the object and taking on the object's name (e.g., Erika Eiffel, who changed her last name after marrying the Eiffel Tower; Terry, 2010). In recent years, increased media attention has been directed toward OS, and online communities have developed for people with OS to connect with one another. Very little research, however, has been conducted in this area, and the prevalence rate of OS is not known. Nevertheless, OS highlights the diversity that exists among people with regard to sexual attraction and love, and it reminds us that different forms of love exist.

objectùm sexuality Emotional and physical attraction to and love for an object or objects.

Optimal Sexuality

In recent years, Peggy Kleinplatz of the University of Ottawa and her colleagues have been conducting research to answer questions such as "what lessons can be gleaned from those who seek and attain extraordinary sexual relations?" and "what does it take to make sex more than merely functional or even satisfying but truly memorable and extraordinary?" (Kleinplatz and Ménard, 2007, p. 72). Kleinplatz and colleagues argue that the study of **optimal sexuality** has been largely absent from the academic literature, and that information about "great sex" has typically been conveyed in popular magazines and self-help manuals. An analysis of the ways in which "great sex" is depicted in five popular magazines (e.g., *Cosmopolitan*, *Men's Health*) found that these magazines often focus on sexual techniques and variety as means to achieve great sex (Ménard & Kleinplatz, 2008). Moreover, magazine advice on how to experience great sex is typically presented in a manner that promotes sexual stereotypes, gender-role stereotypes, and narrow sexual and relationship scripts; for example, it does not address the possibility of great sex with casual partners.

optimal sexuality Having sexual experiences that are (subjectively) extraordinary.

In order to study great sex, Kleinplatz and colleagues (2009) went straight to the source: they conducted interviews with 44 persons reporting great sex and 20 sex therapists. Participants described their best sexual experiences—or, for the therapists, offered their professional insights—during the interviews, and the researchers subsequently identified themes from the interviews to capture the components of great sex. What emerged were the following eight major components of optimal sexuality: authenticity; being present; connection with a partner; exploration/interpersonal risk-taking; extraordinary communication/heightened empathy; transcendence; vulnerability; and deep sexual and erotic intimacy. Two minor, less frequently emphasized components were also identified: intense physical sensation/orgasm and attraction/chemistry/desire/lust. Kleinplatz et al. (2009) noted that although participants were from diverse backgrounds, the major components were described in a strikingly similar manner across the sample.

Now, given that this chapter focusses on attraction, intimacy, and love, let's explore the findings with regard to the major component of *deep sexual and erotic intimacy* and the minor component involving *attraction*. The sexual and erotic intimacy associated with great sex appears to be characterized by deep mutual respect, caring, acceptance, admiration, and trust of one's partner. Kleinplatz et al. (2009) observed that the majority of their participants described many features of love (without using the word *love*) to highlight the deep emotional bond they felt with their partners during great sex. In fact, intimacy seems to be a pivotal component of optimal sexuality; when reporting the initial findings of their research, Kleinplatz and Ménard (2007) wrote that "regardless of what else sexual partners bring to an encounter, it was intimacy that made an exponential difference" (p. 75). Kleinplatz (2010) also notes that continued attention to emotional intimacy, including trust and communication about sexual desires, is key to experiencing great sex. As reported by older research participants, optimal sexuality may flourish over time as partners experience a deepening of their relationship (Kleinplatz, 2010). Notably, however, the optimal sexuality research also highlights that great sex and deep erotic intimacy can occur both inside and outside of a long-term relationship.

With regard to attraction, desire, and mutual lust or chemistry between partners, these factors were present in some of the participants' best sexual experiences, yet they were considered a minor component of optimal sexuality. Similarly, although orgasm was reported to be a common experience in great sex, the majority of participants did not consider it a necessary or sufficient component. In fact, sexual functioning and sexual techniques played little role in participants' descriptions of optimal sexuality; rather, it was psychological and interpersonal factors that made for great sex. This research challenges the view of "great sex" put forth in the popular media in many ways. The researchers warn, however, that their findings should not be used to impose higher standards for sexual performance.

Jealousy

jealousy A negative emotional response to potential or actual rejection from a partner or to loss of a relationship due to a rival.

Jealousy, or the "green-eyed monster," is often experienced in romantic relationships and can be defined as an emotional response to (potential or actual) rejection by a partner for a rival (Desteno, Valdesolo, & Bartlett, 2006). While jealousy can invoke various reactions and emotions, anger and fear appear to be central features. The emotional response of jealousy can be extreme, in some cases leading to violence and even homicide.

Different theories have been proposed to explain jealousy. Some models emphasize the link among thoughts, feelings, and behaviours in the experience of jealousy. White and Mullen (1989), for example, suggest that jealousy ensues when a situation is perceived as threatening to one's relationship or self-esteem; this perception, whether accurate or not, can then lead to physiological arousal, emotions (e.g., fear), and behaviours (e.g., aggression) in response to the threat. Evolutionary theory has also been applied to the study of jealousy and posits that jealousy is a response that evolved to protect valued relationships and helps to ensure reproductive success and certainty. From this perspective, humans who were attentive to the potential loss of their mate and who defended their relationship against such a threat were more likely to produce offspring and pass on their genes; in addition, male partners could be more certain that their partner's off-spring were indeed theirs.

Different Types of Jealousy: Sexual and Emotional

The evolutionary perspective has been used to explain sex differences in response to different types of jeal-ousy and jealousy-provoking scenarios (Figure 12.11). While thinking about a partner's sexual and/or emo-tional infidelity may be upsetting to both men and women, the evolutionary perspective posits that men should be more jealous and upset about sexual infidel-ity in their relationship, and women should be more jealous and upset about emotional infidelity. Why would such a difference exist? Well, according to this theory, men whose female partners are sexual with another male risk paternal uncertainty and the possi-bility of raising another man's children; they also have less chance of successfully passing on their genes. This perspective also suggests that women, on the other hand, are more upset by emotional infidelity because they risk losing their partner's investment, commitment, resources, and co-parenting efforts if the partner becomes attached to a rival.

FIGURE 12.11 Are there sex differences in jealousy? Evolutionary theory posits that men should be more jealous in response to sexual infidelity, and women should be more jealous in response to emotional infidelity.

And what does the research find? Upon asking undergraduates what would upset or distress them more—their partner "enjoying passionate sexual intercourse" with some-one else or their partner "forming a deep emotional attachment" to that person—60 per cent of males versus 17 per cent of females reported greater distress about the imagined sexual infidelity (Buss, Larsen, Westen, & Semmelroth, 1992). Some research has sug-gested that this jealousy-related sex difference is context-dependent; no difference was found between men and women with regard to sexual versus emotional jealousy when participants were asked to imagine their partner with someone of the same sex (i.e., when conceiving a child would have been impossible in the imagined scenario; Sagarin, Becker, Guadagno, Nicastle, & Millevoi, 2003).

Social Networking Sites and Jealousy

While evolutionary theory looks to our history to account for jealousy, a more mod-ern-day concern is the role social networking sites (SNSs) may play in provoking jeal-ousy. Recent years have seen the development of SNSs such as Facebook and MySpace, with these sites becoming a popular way to maintain relationships that begin offline. Facebook, for example, has exploded with popularity since it was founded in 2004, and there are currently more than a billion active Facebook users (Facebook, 2013); indeed, terms such as *tag me* and *Facebook me* have become commonplace vernacular for many people today. With the advent and increasing popularity of SNSs, anecdotal information and media reports point to these sites as a potential trigger for romantic jealousy. Researchers have also started to examine these sites with regard to jealousy in romantic relationships.

Canadian researchers at the University of Guelph were the first to link Facebook use with jealousy (Muise, Christofides, & Desmarais, 2009). As part of a larger study,

308 undergraduate students, approximately two-thirds of whom were in a relationship, completed an online survey regarding their use of Facebook. The survey included the Facebook Jealousy Scale (FJS), created specifically for the study, and an open-ended question about jealousy associated with Facebook. Women scored significantly higher on the FJS and reported spending more time on Facebook in comparison to men. In addition, upon controlling for other variables such as gender, time spent on Facebook was a significant predictor of Facebook-associated jealousy. Results from the open-ended question also suggested that the accessibility of information and lack of context on Facebook may trigger jealousy, and 16 per cent of the participants who answered the open-ended question explicitly linked the use of Facebook with the experience of jealousy (either their own jealousy or their partner's). As this study highlights, Facebook may be ripe for creating jealousy for several reasons, including that (1) Facebook provides people with information about their partner that may otherwise be inaccessible, and (2) Facebook contains information such as wall postings and photos that may be ambiguous and perceived as threatening. Further, jealousy may arise when one has past romantic partners and people who are unknown to one's current partner as "friends" on Facebook.

Moreover, a recent study of undergraduates in Australia examined Facebook intrusion in relation to romantic jealousy and dissatisfaction with one's relationship (Elphinston & Noller, 2011). The researchers describe Facebook intrusion as "an excessive attachment to Facebook, which interferes with day-to-day activities and with relationship functioning" (p. 631), and they measured jealousy by assessing cognitive jealousy and surveillance behaviours (e.g., calling just to see if one's partner is home). The authors found a significant association between Facebook intrusion and relationship dissatisfaction that was fully mediated by cognitive jealousy and surveillance behaviours. In other words, if an individual experienced jealousy, Facebook intrusion seemed to lead to relationship dissatisfaction. Thus, while Facebook and other SNSs may be beneficial for maintaining relationships, as they provide a relatively easy way to keep in touch and feel connected to others, the above two studies indicate that such sites may also have potentially negative relationship consequences (some food for thought for the next time you log in!) And stay tuned: we are likely to witness much more research regarding SNSs and intimate relationships in upcoming years.

The Role of Online Technologies in Love, Attraction, and Intimacy

As highlighted from the Facebook studies reviewed above, there is no doubt that online technologies have the power to greatly influence our social relationships. Internet use has become a part of daily life for many people: the 2009 Canadian Internet Use Survey reported that 80 per cent of Canadians who are 16 years of age or older use the Internet for personal reasons (Statistics Canada, 2009). In addition, research from the University of Victoria found that almost 42 per cent of the undergraduates sampled had sought connections with new people using the Internet, over 12 per cent had utilized online dating services, and over 6 per cent used the Internet as their primary means of communicating with their partner (Boies, 2002).

How has the rise of online technologies changed relationships? First, let's start with the potential positive effects. The Internet can be an effective tool for maintaining relationships by allowing for increased communication and contact. The Internet also offers a way for people to meet potential partners, with many of these relationships progressing to close partnerships offline. Further, the Internet offers access to people and communities that one may otherwise not have in person such as access to people with similar sexual interests. Undergraduates who are lonely are also more likely to report that it is easier to make friends online and that they are more themselves when online (Morahan-Martin & Schumacher, 2003). Recent research surveying people who have had sexual experiences via their avatars in Second Life, a 3-D virtual world, found that participants reported similar levels of sexual satisfaction in real life and in Second Life (Gilbert, Gonzalez, & Murphy, 2011).

There can be a darker side to online technologies and relationships as well. For example, the Internet can facilitate **infidelity** (see the "Ethical Debate" box for a more general discussion of sexual infidelity). One online dating service, Ashley Madison, promotes itself with the catch phrase "Life is short. Have an affair." Currently, this site reports having over 18 million members. While many of the affairs arranged online may result in real-life sexual encounters, others may be limited to online sexual contact. In one study, partners (mostly women) of persons who were greatly involved in **cybersex** reported painful consequences associated with the cybersex behaviour (Schneider, 2000). For example, these partners reported strong negative emotions, including betrayal, rage, and devastation; feelings of sexual inadequacy; and sexual problems such as loss of desire in the couple relationship. As well, approximately 22 per cent reported that cybersex was a major contributor to divorce or separation from their partner. Research focussing on **netiquette** found that one in three married couples had at least one partner who had monitored the other's online activities without the other knowing (Helsper & Whitty, 2010).

In addition to having potentially negative effects on intimate relationships, online technologies can also expose people to much criticism from others with whom they may or may not be acquainted. A concerning trend has emerged in which girls (often pre-adolescent) post a video of themselves on YouTube and pose the question "Am I pretty?" People can respond online to these postings; a quick read of the responses to such videos shows many negative, sexualized, and potentially damaging comments. While research is needed to understand the personal and relational repercussions of such trends, we can be sure that the Internet has dramatically altered our social world by allowing us access (for better or worse) to other people in a rapid, often anonymous, and unprecedented manner.

As well, a study with people who have Second Life avatars in an intimate relationship examined the impact of these Second Life relationships on participants' real-life romantic relationships (Gilbert, Murphy, & Ávalos, 2011). The majority of participants reported that Second Life intimate relationships were just as real as those formed in actual life, although equal numbers of participants agreed and disagreed as to whether Second Life and real-life love are different forms of love. A subset of the sample (36 per cent) had both a Second Life and a real-life romantic relationship. More than one-third of this subset reported that their real-life partner was uncomfortable with their Second Life relationship. In addition, approximately one-quarter of participants reported problems in their real-life relationship or had thought about leaving their real-life partner because of their virtual relationship. Although less than 10 per cent of participants had ended a real-life relationship as a result of their Second Life relationship, almost half reported that they could be more open with their virtual partner about their feelings, and almost a quarter reported loving their real-life and virtual partners equally. Such results suggest that, for some people, involvement in a virtual relationship may lead to problems with real-life partnerships.

infidelity Engaging in sexual and/or emotional relations with someone who is not one's primary partner when in a monogamous relationship.

cybersex Sexual activity that takes place via the Internet.

netiquette Rules outlining acceptable and unacceptable Internet activities.

Ethical Debate

Infidelity

One topic that people tend to have very strong opinions about, and that is often associated with intense feelings of jealousy, is infidelity. Indeed, research indicates that most people strongly disapprove of extramarital sex and believe that it is almost always or always wrong for married individuals to have sex with someone other than their spouse (e.g., Widmer, Treas, & Newcomb, 1998). (Note that much of the infidelity research has focussed on marriage; thus, the term *extramarital* is often used.) Even individuals who are rated liberal in terms of attitudes toward sexuality tend to believe that extramarital sexual activity is wrong (e.g., Lacey et al., 2004). For persons who experience infidelity in their relationships, the consequences can be extreme: for example, longitudinal data show that infidelity increases the risk for relationship dissolution and divorce (Previti & Amato, 2004). As well, a partner's infidelity may increase one's risk of suffering from major depression and distressing emotions. Despite disapproving views and negative consequences associated with infidelity, studies have indicated that more than 20 per cent of men and 10 per cent of women have engaged in extramarital sex (e.g., Wiederman, 1997). Research suggests that some same-sex couples may be more accepting of sex outside the primary relationship, yet that such encounters may still be associated with negative emotions when a partner has been sexual with someone else (e.g., Worth, Reid, & McMillan, 2002).

One question that arises is why do so many people engage in behaviours that are generally considered wrong by most people? A recent online study conducted with over 900 North American participants examined predictors of sexual infidelity, including relationship factors such as happiness and sexual satisfaction (Mark, Janssen, & Milhausen, 2011). Participants were individuals who reported being in a heterosexual, monogamous relationship. When asked whether they had ever cheated on their partner—cheating was defined as having sexual interactions with someone other than their primary partner that could jeopardize their relationship with that partner—over 20 per cent of the sample said yes. While infidelity in men was predicted by personality variables related to sexual behaviours and response (e.g., engaging in regrettable sexual behaviour during negative mood states), infidelity in women was predicted by both personality and relationship factors; for example, women were 2.6 times more likely to have cheated if they also reported low levels of happiness in their relationship. These results suggest that sexual factors (for both men and women) and relationship factors (particularly for women) are relevant to understanding infidelity. Another study that followed married individuals in the US for over 17 years concluded that sexual infidelity is both a cause and a consequence of deterioration in a relationship (Previti & Amato, 2004).

In addition to providing insight into factors that may lead to infidelity, research investigating sexual infidelity highlights some of the effects that this behaviour may have on a relationship. With regard to recovery from infidelity, some couples do stay together and heal, and therapists who work with couples often encounter the issue of infidelity in their practice. A comprehensive review noted that infidelity "can be a confusing and heart-wrenching experience for all involved, including the therapist who may have his or her own personal fears and values related to infidelity" (Blow & Hartnett, 2005, p. 217). Certainly, infidelity is a topic that can give rise to strong feelings and perspectives among many people. More studies are needed to fully understand the complexities of infidelity, including research to answer questions such as "how does the undesirable behaviour become desirable?" and "how do people weigh the decision against the extreme cost?" (Blow & Hartnett, 2005, p. 230).

CHAPTER SUMMARY

For many people, sexual relationships involve attraction, intimacy, and love. Physical proximity and repeated exposure influence attraction, and individuals tend to be attracted to others who like them in return and with whom they share similar characteristics. Other, perhaps more subtle influences on attraction include menstrual-cycle variations and immune-related odour cues. Intimacy is often highly valued in relationships, although individuals differ in the degree to which they seek or avoid intimacy with others. The most common types of love are passionate love and companionate love; research suggests that passionate love involves dopamine-rich reward and motivation systems of the brain. Several theories of love exist and have helped us to understand different types of love and the development of love. Researchers have investigated topics such as optimal sexuality, jealousy, and online technologies with regard to sexual relationships. Going forward, new and fascinating research is likely to teach us even more about attraction, intimacy, and love; some research, for example, has started to challenge the traditional notion that love and attraction to a partner decreases over time, and love for non-human objects has received increased public attention. Given that most research investigating attraction, intimacy, and love to date has focussed on heterosexual individuals, it will be important for future studies to examine these factors in same-sex oriented individuals.

DEBATE QUESTIONS

Do online technologies enhance or jeopardize intimate relationships? Why? What may be the relationship benefits of using these technologies? What may be the drawbacks?

REVIEW QUESTIONS

1. In what ways may attraction vary with changes in the menstrual cycle?
2. What are the four styles of attachment described in the two-dimensional model of adult attachment? How may each style affect intimacy with another person?
3. What are some ways in which hooking up is different from dating?
4. How does passionate love differ from companionate love?
5. What are the major theories of love that are presented in this chapter? How does research evidence support or refute each of these theories?
6. What are some of the major components of optimal sexuality?
7. From an evolutionary standpoint, why may there be sex differences with regard to jealousy?

SUGGESTIONS FOR FURTHER READING AND VIEWING

Recommended Websites

Elaine Hatfield's site: www.elainehatfield.com
International Association for Relationship Research: www.iarr.org
Helen Fisher's site: www.helenfisher.com
Objectùm-Sexuality Internationale: www.objectum-sexuality.org
Dr Kim Bartholomew's Research Lab: www.sfu.ca/psyc/faculty/bartholomew

Recommended Reading

Blow, A.J., & Hartnett, K. (2005). Infidelity in committed relationships II: A substantive review. *Journal of Marital and Family Therapy, 31*(2), 217–33. doi:10.1111/j.1752-0606.2005.tb01556.x

Grenier, G. (2007). *The 10 conversations you must have before you get married (and how to have them).* Toronto, ON: Key Porter.

Jones, B.C., DeBruine, L.M., Perrett, D.I., Little, A.C., Feinberg, D.R., & Smith, M.J.L. (2008). Effects of menstrual cycle phase on face preferences. *Archives of Sexual Behavior, 37*(1), 78–84. doi:10.1007/s10508-007-9268-y

Ortigue, S., Bianchi-Demicheli, F., Patel, N., Frum, C., & Lewis, J.W. (2010). Neuroimaging of love: fMRI meta-analysis evidence toward new perspectives in sexual medicine. *Journal of Sexual Medicine, 7*(11), 3541–52. doi:10.1111/j.1743-6109.2010.01999.x

Penn, D.J., & Potts, W.K. (1999). The evolution of mating preferences and major histocompatibility complex genes. *The American Naturalist, 153*(2), 145–64. doi:10.1086/303166

Ryan, C., & Jethá, C. (2010). *Sex at dawn: The prehistoric origins of modern sexuality.* New York, NY: HarperCollins.

Sternberg, R.J., & Weis, K. (Eds). (2006). *The new psychology of love.* New Haven, CT: Yale.

Stinson, R.D. (2010). Hooking up in young adulthood: A review of factors influencing the sexual behavior of college students. *Journal of College Student Psychotherapy, 24*(2), 98–115. doi:10.1080/87568220903558596

Whitty, M.T. (2008). Liberating or debilitating? An examination of romantic relationships, sexual relationships, and friendships on the Net. *Computers in Human Behavior, 24*(5), 1837–50. doi:10.1016/j.chb.2008.02.009

Recommended Viewing

Discovery Channel (Producer). (n.d.). *The science of sex appeal* [Video file]. United States: Discovery Channel. Retrieved from http://dsc.discovery.com/videos/science-of-sex-appeal

Fisher, H. (Speaker). (2006). *Helen Fisher: Why we love, why we cheat* [Video file]. United States: TED. Retrieved from www.ted.com/talks/helen_fisher_tells_us_why_we_love_cheat.html

13 CHAPTER

Sexual Communication

UZMA S. REHMAN
AND ERIN E. FALLIS

LEARNING OBJECTIVES

In this chapter, you will

- learn about different ways in which intimate partners communicate with each other, particularly about sex and sexuality;
- consider differences in the ways women and men communicate;
- discover common approaches to the study of sexual communication; and
- encounter valuable advice on what to do—and what not to do—in order to communicate effectively with a sexual partner.

Let's Talk about Sex

Lana and Scott are both in their mid-twenties and have been together since their third year of university. At the beginning of their relationship, Scott was very attracted to Lana but was hesitant to initiate any physical contact; he had grown up in a strict religious home where sexuality was rarely discussed, except as a vice. After moving away from home, Scott had begun to develop his own beliefs and started to drift away from the strict religious code of his family. He wanted to date, but his attempts at connecting with women usually resulted in friendship rather than romantic connections. When his male friends talked about their respective girlfriends, he felt embarrassed about his lack of experience.

Lana had a very different background. Her parents were very open to discussing sexuality with her and her siblings, and by the time she started university she had been in a two-year committed relationship. When Lana and Scott began to date, she wondered why he never tried to kiss her. She took the lead and, although Scott was surprised by her boldness, they awkwardly moved forward with their sexual relationship. Both wished that they could talk more openly about their sex life, but neither of them took the first step.

A few months into their relationship, as they were making out, Lana asked Scott to share one of his sexual fantasies with her. Scott became embarrassed and mumbled that he couldn't think of anything. Lana felt rejected and reacted angrily, telling Scott she had never met anyone as uptight as he was about sex. Scott left the room and they didn't speak for several days. Lana had hoped that a conversation about fantasies would increase their

intimacy, and she was hurt and surprised by Scott's reaction. Meanwhile, Scott wondered why Lana was so "brazen" and wished that she was less pushy in her communication style. Scott and Lana moved on from this incident and continued to date, eventually deciding to live together. However, they never again discussed the event and, as their relationship progressed, they developed a tacit agreement not to discuss any aspect of their sexual life openly.

A year or so after the couple began living together, Lana's concerns about the monotony of their sex life peaked, but she wasn't sure how to talk to Scott about the issue. After having sex one evening, she told Scott that she was feeling bored by their sexual relationship and asked if he would be open to trying sex toys. Scott responded by insulting Lana, irate that she had raised this issue immediately after they had had sex. Lana felt both upset and scared by his reaction and responded by rolling over and trying to sleep. As Lana replayed the fight in her mind, she thought about how the two of them were able to discuss pretty much anything; she didn't understand why their sex life had to be their Achilles' heel.

QUESTIONS FOR CRITICAL THOUGHT AND REFLECTION

1. In what way did Scott's background contribute to his reactions when he and Lana discussed their sexual relationship?
2. Given their different communication styles, is it possible for Lana and Scott to have a positive, long-lasting sexual relationship?

Introduction

Take a moment and recall a time in your life when you felt truly heard or understood by another person. You may refer to it as being "of one mind" or "on the same wavelength," but you are likely also remembering a time of great intimacy and closeness, of sharing and belonging. When we are fortunate, such moments of connection are frequent. However, in some relationships, or at different times in the same relationship, they can be fleeting and elusive. As the case of Lana and Scott suggests, communication is a complex process that can prove very challenging, especially when we are discussing such intimate issues as sexuality. Hurdles are frequently encountered, even for individuals who are skilled communicators. In this chapter, we will examine communication between romantic partners and will focus specifically on **sexual communication**.

sexual communication
The processes by which intimate partners share their sexual likes and dislikes with each other and negotiate sexuality in their relationship.

In particular, we will address the issues that often make sexual communication challenging for couples.

Communication in Intimate Relationships

Let's begin by considering what we mean when we use the term *communication*, and by broadly examining the role of communication in romantic relationships. *Communication* is a term commonly used in everyday encounters, and this can be both a blessing and a curse. Our frequent use of this term points to the relevance and importance that we attach to communication, but people often mean very different things when they use the word. Researchers are not immune to this problem and, as a result, the word *communication* has been used differently across research studies; this, of course, leads to confusion and makes it difficult to compare the results of different research studies. In this chapter, we use the term **couples' communication** to refer to ongoing verbal, behavioural, and affective (i.e., emotional) exchanges between partners. Thus, this definition recognizes that a raised eyebrow, a scowl, and a silent reproach are just as much components of communication as are the actual words a person uses. This definition also considers couples' communication to be an ongoing exchange between two partners and a process that unfolds over time. Thus, to truly understand a communicative exchange, we need to examine the roles of both partners.

Couples' Communication Behaviours

Researchers investigating how couples communicate initially began with the question: In what ways are the communication behaviours of distressed couples different from the communication behaviours of non-distressed couples? Not surprisingly, they discovered that distressed couples tend to engage in more negative behaviours and fewer positive behaviours than non-distressed couples do. For example, couples in distressed relationships tend to demonstrate lower levels of validation and empathy toward each other. Researchers investigating negative behaviours have found that some types of negative behaviours are particularly bad for relationships.

John Gottman, a well-known relationship researcher and therapist, has identified four negative behaviours that are particularly strong predictors of declines in relationship satisfaction: **criticism**, **contempt**, **defensiveness**, and **stonewalling**. He has labelled these behaviours with the provocative title, "the four horsemen of the apocalypse" (Gottman, 1999). Criticism can be hurtful because it involves attacking a person's character or personality rather than addressing a particular issue at hand. Thus, Lana calling Scott "uptight" would be considered criticism. Contempt goes one step further than criticism and involves putting down and being disrespectful toward one's partner. Examples of contempt include eye-rolls, name-calling, and mean humour. Defensive behaviour generally occurs when one partner feels that he or she is being attacked and must protect himself or herself by denying responsibility (e.g., "no, I didn't"), making excuses (e.g., "you did it first"), or counter-complaining (e.g., "but you do it too"). Stonewalling occurs when someone simply refuses to engage in the discussion at hand (Figure 13.1). When Scott left the room in anger in the middle of an argument, he was stonewalling. It is important to note here that disengaging from a conflict is not

couples' communication An ongoing exchange between two partners that unfolds over time and consists of verbal, behavioural, and affective exchanges.

criticism A negative communication behaviour that entails attacking a partner's character or personality rather than focussing specifically on the behaviour that is upsetting.

contempt A negative communication behaviour that entails putting down and/ or expressing disrespect toward one's partner.

defensiveness A negative communication behaviour in which someone protects himself or herself from a perceived verbal assault by denying responsibility, making excuses, or counter-complaining.

stonewalling A negative communication behaviour that entails refusing to respond and resisting influence by not engaging in the discussion at hand.

FIGURE 13.1 This young woman's distant stare, crossed arms, and refusal to speak are good indications that she is stonewalling.

FIGURE 13.2 Do actions speak louder than words? No matter what this couple is saying, it would be difficult for their words to overshadow the anger and exasperation being communicated by their facial expressions and gestures.

always a bad thing, especially when both partners agree on ending the conflict for the time being. Certainly, in some situations disengaging can be a helpful way to prevent the conflict from getting too intense and out of control. In contrast to this practice of collaborative disengagement, however, stonewalling is an action taken by one person that is experienced negatively by his or her partner.

NON-VERBAL COMMUNICATION

The examples of communication behaviours described above often have both verbal and non-verbal components. For example, a verbal comment signalling contempt could be, "I couldn't care less about what you think," and this verbal behaviour is almost always accompanied by **non-verbal communication** elements such as a curling of the lip, a dismissive tone of voice, or a shrug of the shoulder (Figure 13.2).

In their book on non-verbal communication, Guerrero and Floyd (2006) argue that the study of non-verbal communication can help us better understand the dynamics of intimate relationships. First, research shows us that the predominant way in which people communicate with one another is non-verbal. Even by conservative estimates, non-verbal communication accounts for 60 to 65 per cent of the information exchanged in an interpersonal interaction. Also, when information being received by non-verbal channels contradicts verbal messages, people are more likely to believe the message they are receiving non-verbally. Thus, if an individual turns to his or her spouse and says, "I do love you" in a defensive tone of voice, the spouse is likely to read frustration or annoyance, rather than affection, in the message. Research evidence shows that the quality of non-verbal communication between partners is a stronger predictor of relationship satisfaction, as compared to the quality of their verbal communication (Guerrero & Floyd, 2006).

> **non-verbal communication** All communication behaviours that are not words, including but not limited to body posture, voice qualities, facial expressions, and gestures.

Patterns of Couples' Communication

Although examinations of different types of communication behaviours can help us understand why specific attempts at communication may be successful or unsuccessful, we must also consider the patterns or sequences of communication that develop within a relationship. After all, communication is a process that unfolds over time. Indeed, research has identified certain interaction patterns that distinguish distressed couples from non-distressed couples. For example, distressed couples are more likely than non-distressed couples to fall into patterns of **negative reciprocity** and **demand-withdraw**.

Negative reciprocity is the tendency of partners to maintain or escalate negative communication once it has started (Gottman, 1979). Researchers have shown that distressed couples are significantly more likely than non-distressed couples to escalate their negative behaviours (e.g., Margolin & Wampold, 1981). Thus, once distressed couples find themselves in a negative exchange, it is very difficult for them to end the exchange. Consequently, these couples are less flexible in how their interactions unfold.

In the demand-withdraw pattern, "one partner pressures the other through emotional demands, criticisms, and complaints, while the other retreats through withdrawal, defensiveness, and passive inaction" (Christensen & Heavey, 1990, p. 73). This pattern has been described by couples as "the endless chase." Indeed, the more one

> **negative reciprocity** A communication pattern in which each partner tends to respond to the other with negative comments or behaviours, thereby escalating the conflict.

> **demand-withdraw** A communication pattern in which one partner puts pressure on the other (e.g., by nagging or criticizing), and the other partner does not engage or is defensive.

partner tries to push the other to engage, the more the other is likely to withdraw. In this way, couples get trapped in a vicious no-win cycle that becomes more entrenched over time. There is also evidence showing that spouses who engage in this type of interaction grow more distant from each other over time, leading to greater chances of separation and divorce (e.g., Levenson & Gottman, 1983).

How Do Researchers Study Couples' Communication?

As you read about these different communication behaviours and patterns, you might wonder how researchers study couples' communication. Typically, relationship researchers use either self-report methods or observational methods to study communication processes in couples. When using self-report methods, researchers administer a standardized questionnaire and ask respondents to rate the quality of communication in their relationship. In contrast, when researchers use observational methods, they typically invite a couple to come to a research laboratory and ask the couple to engage in a conversation while being videotaped. The length of the communication task varies by different research groups and studies, but it is typically between seven and fifteen minutes (Heyman, 2001). The topic of conversation is sometimes picked by the researcher beforehand, but more often a topic is selected by following research protocols that involve asking the couple to identify problems they are currently facing in their relationship. The researchers later watch the recorded interaction and code for certain behaviours, so the information becomes quantitative.

The focus of the coding system can vary greatly. Let's say a researcher wants to examine how spouses try to get each other to change their habits. In this instance, the researcher will use a coding system that focusses specifically on identifying different types of influence techniques. In contrast, a researcher interested in the emotions displayed during couples' discussions will use a system like Coan and Gottman's (2007) Specific Affect Coding System. The coding is usually done by **blind coders**, often student research volunteers, rather than the primary researchers who know the study hypotheses and may therefore unwittingly be biased to support these hypotheses. Observational researchers train coders to agree on the extent to which participants are displaying certain behaviours of interest, and they demonstrate that the coding is consistent through measures of **interrater reliability**.

At this point, you might be asking yourself whether couples in an artificial setting such as a laboratory act as they normally would in their everyday lives. You might wonder whether couples who tend to behave quite negatively in their home environment would do so in front of a video camera. These are very valid questions that relate to the issue of ecological validity (see Chapter 3). After all, laboratory conditions are clearly different from real-world conditions. For example, as noted above, researchers generally specify how long the participating couple will engage in a discussion, after which time a research assistant may knock on the door and ask the participants to end their discussion. In real life, however, such time limits generally do not exist (Figure 13.3). In one of the earliest studies seeking to establish the ecological validity of laboratory observations of couples, Gottman (1979)

blind coders Coders who are not familiar with the specific hypotheses of the study.

interrater reliability The extent to which two independent observers obtain the same results when using the same coding system.

"Time's up. I'm through listening."

FIGURE 13.3 Although some partners might wish they could impose time limits on their discussions, the fact that they cannot marks an important distinction between natural discussions and those that occur during research studies.

compared home and laboratory discussions of couples. The results indicated that, for the most part, couples communicated similarly across the two settings, although lab discussions were less negative.

Other studies have found that, when asked to rate how similar lab discussions are to discussions they have at home, couples report that the in-lab interactions are representative of their typical interactions (e.g., Margolin, John, & Gleberman, 1988). Interestingly, a study conducted by Vincent, Friedman, Nugnet, and Messerly (1979) found that even when couples were instructed to "fake good" or "fake bad," observers were able to reliably differentiate between couples who were truly satisfied with their relationship and those who were not. Thus, the consensus seems to be that laboratory procedures do elicit reasonably naturalistic interactions.

Of the two methods described above (self-report and observational), is one method superior to the other? It depends on the research questions that are being asked in a particular study. For example, let's say that a researcher wants to know whether depressed individuals are more likely than non-depressed individuals to repeatedly seek reassurance about their partner's commitment to their relationship. The researcher could attempt to answer this question by using self-report methods and ask depressed and non-depressed individuals in relationships to rate the degree to which they engage in this type of behaviour. However, this approach could create problems in interpreting the findings from the study. For example, if the depressed individuals reported seeking reassurance more often than did the non-depressed individuals, it could be that this finding accurately reflects differences in behaviours, or it could be that the depressed individuals are more likely to *report* engaging in negative interaction patterns because they view themselves more negatively. Thus, in this case, observational methods would be preferable because they do not rely on participants' self-perceptions. In contrast, if the researcher wanted to examine whether depressed individuals *perceive* themselves as engaging in reassurance-seeking behaviour more often than non-depressed individuals do, self-report methods would be more appropriate.

Gender Differences in Heterosexual Couples' Communication

Before we begin our discussion of gender differences in couples' communication, you should consider a cautionary note. Popular books like *Men Are from Mars, Women Are from Venus* (Gray, 1992) tend to exaggerate both the degree and importance of gender differences. For example, in the introduction, Gray (1992) claims that his book "reveals how men and women differ in all areas of their lives. Not only do men and women communicate differently but they think, perceive, react, respond, love, need, and appreciate differently. They almost seem to be from different planets, speaking different languages and needing different nourishment" (p. 5). Indeed, jokes and quips that play up the "typical" qualities of males and females abound in Western culture (Figure 13.4). Jokes aside, though, emphasizing the "otherness" of each gender in relation to the other while ignoring the many similarities is problematic for many reasons. For example, this approach perpetuates myths about how the other gender is unknowable; minimizes the many similarities between men and women in terms of their basic needs, motivations, and desires; and reinforces gender stereotypes. When considering the insights provided by scientific inquiry into gender differences, we must not forget that there are many similarities between men and women and that gender differences, when they exist, are actually rather small.

With this cautionary note in mind, let's turn to research on gender differences in couples' communication. A number of studies have examined whether men and women differ in their communication styles in romantic relationships, and if so, how.

Contrary to the gender stereotype hypothesis, which predicts that women will be passive, positive, and conciliatory in conflict situations while men will be combative and aggressive, research findings show that men and women are much more similar than different in their conflict behaviours (Cupach & Canary, 1995). When gender differences do exist, they vary by context. For example, whereas women may be more likely than men to defer when interacting with strangers, they are more likely to directly confront and demand when interacting with their romantic partners (Gottman & Carrère, 1994).

Building on the idea that women are more likely to adopt the role of the "demander" in the relationship, researchers investigating the demand-withdraw interaction pattern have consistently found that women are more like to make demands and men are more likely to withdraw (e.g., Christensen & Heavey, 1990; Rubin, 1983). A number of different theories have been advanced to explain this finding (see Christensen & Heavey, 1990, and Heavey, Layne, & Christensen, 1993, for a detailed discussion of the different theories).

"I'm not afraid of intimacy, as long as it's shallow, meaningless intimacy that doesn't reveal too much about me."

FIGURE 13.4 This cartoon offers a humorous representation of the stereotypical view that men fear intimacy.

One perspective holds that this gender difference is a result of the different personality characteristics of men and women; these characteristics, in turn, result from a combination of socialization and biology. In terms of socialization, for example, women are encouraged to be expressive and to promote unity in interpersonal relationships, while men are encouraged to be independent and to avoid being emotionally stifled by partners. In a similar vein, Gilligan (1982) and Rubin (1983) have suggested that women's identities are developed in the context of relationships, while men's identities are developed in the context of separation. Further, Christensen (1987) found that heterosexual couples in which the female partner had a greater need for intimacy (also referred to as "closeness") and the male partner had a greater need for autonomy (also referred to as "independence") displayed a higher frequency of demand-withdraw behaviour, with the woman making demands and the man withdrawing. In terms of biology, evidence suggests that men react with stronger physiological responses (e.g., increased heart rate and skin temperature) to extreme emotions than do women. Based on this information, Gottman and Levenson (1988) proposed that men would find conflict more aversive and would consequently withdraw in an attempt to prevent the conflict—and their negative physiological responses—from increasing.

Another theoretical perspective that has been advanced to explain the noted gender difference in the demand-withdraw pattern reflects the relative positions of men and women in Western society. For instance, Jacobson (1983) states that men stand to benefit more from the traditional marital relationship, in that they are typically responsible for less housework and child care than their wives are, and thus seek to maintain the status quo. Women, on the other hand, are typically responsible for a greater portion of the household and child-care tasks and are thus more likely to desire change in their relationships. According to this notion, the main method by which women can bring about change in their relationships is to engage their partners in discussions about change. Men, in turn, avoid such discussions because the status quo is more beneficial to them. Support for this view comes from research showing that in Western cultures, it is women who initiate conversations about potential conflicts in the relationship 80 per cent of the time (Ball, Cowan, & Cowan, 1995).

In 1993, Christensen and colleagues concluded that the well-replicated finding that women are demanding and men are withdrawing results from "additive effects of gender differences in conflict style plus the extant social structure" (Heavey, Layne, & Christensen, 1993, p. 25). Subsequently, Holtzworth-Munroe, Smutzler, and Stuart (1998) also found that whether the husband or wife adopted the role of the demander depended upon the topic under investigation. That is, when husbands were the ones who wanted change, they were more likely to make demands, and when wives were the ones who wanted change, they were more likely to make demands. The researchers concluded that their "findings lend strong support to the notion that the typical gender patterns observed (i.e., wife demands and husband withdraws) are not due to inherent differences between men and women but rather are context specific—that is, the partner who wants change, demands it" (p. 741). See the "Culture and Diversity" box for an examination of how couples' communication styles may differ across cultures.

Sexual Communication

Sexual communication is the process by which intimate partners share their sexual likes and dislikes with each other and negotiate sexual behaviour in their relationship. Lana and Scott's story illustrates many of the challenges and difficulties associated with this sort of communication. Given his background, his lack of experience with communicating about sexual matters, and his anxieties about his lack of sexual experience, it's not surprising that Scott became upset when he perceived Lana's communication style to be too pushy and that he viewed her expressions of her sexuality as "brazen." Although Lana was more experienced in discussing sexuality, her concerns about Scott being "uptight" and her worries that her sexual relationship with Scott would be boring made her initiate and respond to sexual discussions in a way that did not serve their relationship well. As a result of their inability to communicate effectively about their sexual likes and dislikes, discussing sexual issues became such a high-stakes endeavour that it was easier for Lana and Scott to avoid talking about their sex life altogether than to threaten their relationship with such conversations. Unfortunately, as a long-term strategy, avoidance is likely to increase resentment between intimate partners, as was the case with Lana and Scott.

Importance of Sexual Communication

Effective communication with one's partner about sexuality is important because it is associated with positive outcomes for couples. One reason for this association is that effective sexual communication can help couples overcome the incompatibilities they will inevitably experience in their sexual relationships (Lloyd, 1987). Lana and Scott's differing interest in exploring their sexual fantasies is one example of a sexual incompatibility. Others include disagreements about the timing of sex, what type of sexual activities to engage in, and how long sexual activity should last, as well as mismatches in sexual desire. If couples are not able to discuss their incompatibilities, anger and frustration can result. However, open discussions about sexual interests and differences can lead to greater closeness and intimacy. Indeed, several studies have found that effectively communicating one's sexual preferences and desires to one's partner can result in increased sexual and general relationship satisfaction (e.g., MacNeil & Byers, 1997, 2005, 2009; Cupach & Metts, 1991).

Culture & Diversity

Differences in Couples' Communication Styles across Cultures

Researchers have found similarities and differences in the ways in which couples from different cultural backgrounds communicate. For example, a study by Halford, Hahlweg, and Dunne (1990) found some evidence for cross-cultural similarities as well as cross-cultural differences in communication styles among couples from Germany and Australia. In this study, the researchers compared the communication patterns of four samples of couples: maritally distressed couples from Germany, maritally non-distressed couples from Germany, maritally distressed couples from Australia, and maritally non-distressed couples from Australia. In terms of similarities in communication behaviours, the researchers found that compared to the distressed German and Australian couples, the non-distressed couples from both cultures displayed more verbal agreement (e.g., making statements such as "I agree" and "absolutely"), more positive non-verbal responses (e.g., nodding in agreement), and significantly fewer verbal critiques, verbal refusals, and non-verbal negative responses. Another important similarity was that, across both cultures, distressed couples demonstrated an inability to end negative interactions; their behaviour also seemed to be more predictable, in that a negative comment made by one partner almost inevitably led to a process of negative escalation. In terms of differences, the researchers found that the distressed and non-distressed German couples used significantly more negative verbal responses than their Australian counterparts did, and the German couples were significantly more likely to engage in patterns of negative reciprocity compared to the Australian couples.

In one of the few observational studies investigating the communication styles of couples in Western as well as non-Western nations, Rehman and Holtzworth-Munroe (2006, 2007) compared the communication behaviours of Pakistani couples in Pakistan to those of white American couples in the US. In particular, Rehman and Holtzworth-Munroe examined whether the demand-withdraw pattern

of couples' communication identified in previous studies of Western couples would also be present in Pakistani couples, a group expected to exhibit greater power imbalances between the genders than exhibited by the white American couples. The researchers found that Pakistani wives were significantly more likely to use indirect demands (e.g., attempting to influence their partners through behaviours such as flirtation and coyness) than direct demands (e.g., attempting to influence their partners by insisting on or demanding a change). They also found that Pakistani husbands were significantly less likely to withdraw from a conflict discussion, and significantly more likely to make direct demands, than their wives were. The authors reasoned that the findings supported the hypothesis that demanding and withdrawing behaviours are not intrinsically male or female, but rather context dependent.

Not surprisingly, then, it seems that cultural influences affect how couples communicate. Thus, what researchers have found about North American couples' communication behaviours and patterns may not be true across the globe. For example, studies in North America have consistently demonstrated that effective communication between partners is strongly linked to marital satisfaction. However, in a culture where good couples' communication is not considered to be as important (perhaps because the family structure facilitates seeking companionship and emotional closeness from other family members rather than one's spouse), couples' communication may not be as strongly related to relationship satisfaction. Further, the communication behaviours that are found to contribute to marital satisfaction or dissatisfaction may differ across cultures. Indeed, while a high level of verbal conflict is generally considered to be associated with relationship dissatisfaction in North America, Winkler and Doherty (1983) found that the relatively high levels of verbal conflict reported by Israeli couples in the US was not associated with marital dissatisfaction.

In a recent observational study, Rehman and colleagues (2011) found additional evidence to support the importance of effective sexual communication for relationship satisfaction. In this study, 15 couples were asked to discuss sexual and non-sexual problems in their relationships. The findings suggested that negative communication behaviours displayed during a sexual conflict discussion (e.g., a disagreement about frequency of sexual activity) better predicted relationship distress than did negative behaviours displayed during a non-sexual conflict discussion (e.g., a disagreement about finances). The authors reasoned that this might be because sexual conflict discussions are more likely to touch on issues that are sensitive and personal; thus, the ability to discuss these issues in a positive, productive manner may be particularly important for one's relationship satisfaction. Given that couples report they are less likely to talk about sexual, as opposed to non-sexual, problems in their relationships (Dawson, Fallis, & Rehman, 2010), and because such discussions are considered more difficult (Sanford, 2003), it is possible that sexual conflict discussions become "high-stakes" conversations. It is likely that when such a high-stakes conversation does not go well, the impact on relationship and sexual satisfaction is greater than when a more routine conflict discussion goes poorly.

Why Do Couples Find It Challenging to Talk about Their Sexual Relationship?

Although, as you have seen, good sexual communication can lead to positive relationship outcomes, many people find it difficult to talk to their partner about their sexual relationship. Sanford (2003) asked psychologists who frequently work with couples to rate 24 areas of relationship disagreement in terms of how difficult they are for couples to discuss. The psychologists identified sexual interaction as the fifth most difficult (Sanford, 2003; Figure 13.5).

Based on their clinical experience, Metts and Cupach (1989) identified a number of barriers to couples discussing sexual issues. These barriers include a) concerns that discussing sexual issues might identify discrepant sexual desires or preferences between

---

Most Difficult Topics for Couples to Discuss

1. Doubts about the future of the relationship (e.g., divorce; separation)
2. Disrespectful behaviour (e.g., intentional rudeness; lying)
3. Extramarital intimacy or boundary issues (e.g., jealousy; use of pornography)
4. Excessive or inappropriate displays of anger (e.g., unfair accusations; yelling or attacking)
5. **Sexual interaction (e.g., initiation; arousal; frequency; interest)**
6. Lack of communication (e.g., refusal to talk; not sharing feelings)
7. In-laws and extended family (e.g., conflict with in-laws; time spent with relatives)
8. Confusing, erratic, or emotional behaviour (e.g., suddenly becoming upset; sudden change of mind)
9. Criticism (e.g., correcting; challenging partner's viewpoint)
10. Poor communication skills (e.g., being unclear or hard to understand)

FIGURE 13.5 This list shows the 10 most difficult topics for couples to discuss, in order from most to least difficult, according to Sanford's 2003 study. Note that sexual interaction is the fifth most difficult topic for couples to discuss.

partners, which could, in turn, threaten the relationship; b) beliefs that talking about sex is immoral; c) related feelings of embarrassment, shame, or guilt; d) worries about partner response (e.g., "will my partner be angry or upset if I bring up a sexual issue?"); e) assumptions that it should not be necessary to discuss sex within the context of an intimate relationship; f) beliefs that emotional intimacy, not sexual intimacy, leads to closeness with one's partner; and g) lack of experience or perceived skill discussing sexual issues and resulting feelings of inadequacy. Think back to Lana and Scott's story. Which of these barriers to sexual communication did they face in their relationship?

Should We Ask Couples to Discuss Sexual Topics for Research Purposes?

Just as couples may find it difficult to discuss their sexual relationship with each other, they may also find it difficult to discuss the sexual aspects of their relationship in a research setting. Perhaps because of this difficulty, only a few studies have used observational methods that require couples to discuss topics of a sexual nature in a laboratory setting. Yet, as previously mentioned, certain research questions are best investigated through observational methods; thus, some researchers have conducted studies in which they have asked couples to discuss sexual topics for research purposes, despite the reservations couples might have about discussing aspects of their sexual relationship in front of others.

In one of the few such studies, the researchers were interested in three qualities of couples' communication: blame (i.e., assignment of responsibility), clarity (i.e., how clear the message is), and receptivity (i.e., openness to receiving messages from one's partner) (Kelly, Strassberg, & Turner, 2006). They wondered how the communication behaviours of heterosexual couples in which the female partner had **orgasmic disorder** (target couples) might differ from those of heterosexual couples in which the female partner did not have orgasmic disorder (control couples). The researchers hypothesized that the communication of the target couples would be more problematic (i.e., women would be more blaming and less clear, and men would be more blaming and less receptive) than the communication of the control couples, at least when the couples discussed sexual topics. Consistent with their hypothesis, the researchers found that both males and females in the target couples were more blaming than males and females in the control couples when they talked about sex. Contrary to their hypothesis, however, the researchers found that men in the target couples and men in the control couples did not differ in terms of how receptive they were to their partner's comments, but women with orgasmic disorder were less receptive than women without orgasmic disorder during discussions of intercourse. They did not find any differences in clarity between groups. These results highlight some communication patterns characteristic of couples in which the female partner has orgasmic disorder, and they suggest that one component of treatment for the disorder could involve addressing problematic communication (Kelly et al., 2006). As this study illustrates, observational methods are a useful and exciting tool for researchers interested in sexual communication, but we must ask ourselves: What are the potential benefits and costs of using these methods to explore how couples communicate about sexuality?

> **orgasmic disorder**
> Significant difficulty or inability to experience orgasm.

BENEFITS

From a researcher's perspective, observational methods offer a number of advantages over self-report methods when it comes to studying sexual communication. For one thing, as suggested in the section on how researchers study couples' communication, observational methods allow for more objective data collection, as they do not depend on participants' self-perceptions. Thus, observational methods allow researchers to examine more objectively such things as how certain couple characteristics relate to specific communication behaviours. In addition, these methods allow researchers to compare, in detail, how the same couple behaves under slightly different conditions. For example, a researcher could ask a couple to spend five minutes discussing a sexual topic and then five minutes discussing a non-sexual topic, after which time their two conversations would be compared for similarities and differences.

Another benefit to using observational methods for studying sexual communication is that they address a major limitation of self-report methods: **socially desirable responding** (see Paulhus & Reid, 1991). This sort of responding may be intentional, in which case it is known as **impression management**, or it may be unintentional, in which case it is known as **self-deceptive enhancement** (Paulhus & Reid, 1991). Socially desirable responding can be a problem with any type of self-report data, and there is research suggesting that both forms of socially desirable responding likely arise in self-report studies of sexuality, even when researchers take steps to ensure participants' anonymity (Meston, Heiman, Trapnell, & Paulhus, 1998). Although observational methods are not immune to participants' attempts to make themselves appear in a favourable light—for example, by trying to hide feelings of anger during discussions in research labs—they are less susceptible to them than are self-report methods.

Observational methods also allow researchers to develop a more nuanced understanding of the behaviours in which couples engage during discussions of sexual topics than would be possible with self-report measures. For example, using observational methods, researchers could examine how much time each partner spends engaged in the "four horsemen of the apocalypse" behaviours, what proportion of the time the couple spends productively discussing a given topic (versus avoiding it), and how individuals' non-verbal behaviours enhance or undermine effective sexual communication. It is unlikely that even the most self-aware participants could provide accurate reports of their behaviours in this level of detail.

Ultimately, because they allow researchers to take into account many subtle details, and because they involve relatively objective methods of data collection, observational methods can be particularly helpful when researchers are attempting to address very complex issues. For example, these sorts of methods could help a researcher understand the connections between certain communication behaviours and feelings of sexual satisfaction, or between communication patterns and the development of a sexual dysfunction; they could also help researchers identify appropriate targets for treatment of sexual problems.

COSTS

One potential cost of using observational methods in studies that examine sexual communication is that these methods may have negative effects on the couples who agree to participate in these studies. While we don't know exactly how participating in sexuality studies affects couples, research has shown that couples participating in studies of marriage may experience negative emotions as a result of their participation. One study, for example, found that 44 per cent of participants either felt anxious before, or expected to feel anxious during, their engagement in a videotaped discussion about a non-sexual marital problem (Bradbury, 1994). In addition, 4 per cent of participants reported being worried that their discussion might result in a negative interaction with their partner after leaving the lab. Given the sensitive nature of sexual discussions, it is possible that an even greater proportion of couples participating in observational

---

socially desirable responding The tendency to modify one's responses to a questionnaire or interview in order to make oneself appear in a favourable light.

impression management A form of socially desirable responding in which someone deliberately responds in a way that makes him or her look good to others.

self-deceptive enhancement A form of socially desirable responding in which someone inadvertently responds in a way that makes him or her look good to others, because he or she truly perceives himself or herself more positively than is accurate.

studies may experience negative emotions (e.g., anxiety, frustration) while anticipating or during their participation in these studies. At the same time, however, an observational study of marriage similar to the one noted above found that the vast majority of participants reported that their participation either had no effect or impacted them positively, while only 5 per cent reported having a negative reaction to their participation (Bradbury, 1994).

Canadian researcher Dr Uzma Rehman and her students at the University of Waterloo, who are currently using observational methods to investigate how couples discuss sexual problems in their relationships, have suggested another potential cost to participants. Anecdotally, they have noted that couples participating in observational studies of sexual communication more frequently report, compared to couples participating in comparable studies not involving discussions of sexual topics, feeling worried that someone might see the recording of their discussions (e.g., on YouTube). Interestingly, this difference occurred despite the fact that the information provided to participants about confidentiality and data storage procedures was comparable across studies. (For a discussion of confidentiality issues faced by psychologists and other health professionals in their work, see the "Ethical Debate" box).

Although we do not yet know the extent to which participating in observational studies of sexual communication may affect participants, researchers who conduct such studies generally take steps to try and ensure couples' experiences are positive. For example, Dr Rehman and her students take the precaution of having a research assistant meet with each partner individually and ask whether he or she is willing to discuss a proposed topic before the couple is asked to discuss that topic. If one partner is not comfortable discussing the given topic, an alternative topic is selected. However, this occurs less than 1 per cent of the time.

Do Same-Sex Couples Have Different Patterns of Sexual Communication than Mixed-Sex Couples Have?

Like other areas of sexuality research, research on sexual communication is limited in that researchers have traditionally focussed almost exclusively on communication behaviours and patterns in heterosexual couples. One of the first studies to compare the subjective sexual communication experiences of individuals in mixed-sex couples to that of individuals in same-sex couples was conducted by Canadian researchers Diane Holmberg and Karen Blair (2009). The results of Holmberg and Blair's study showed that there were no significant differences between mixed-sex couples and same-sex couples in terms of their sexual communication (Figure 13.6).

As the authors of this study note, a better understanding of how sexual communication is similar or different across same-sex and mixed-sex couples is useful for a number of reasons. Without understanding the normative experiences in both types of couples, for example, there is a danger that mixed-sex couples become the standard and any deviations from the "standard" are pathologized. Also, research findings that show similarities across different couple types might help to reduce some of the stereotypes and

FIGURE 13.6 Do same-sex and mixed-sex couples communicate differently about sex? Canadian researchers Diane Holmberg and Karen Blair (2009) have found that individuals in both types of couples have very similar experiences when it comes to sexual communication.

misconceptions that persist about same-sex relationships (e.g., the myth that gay men prefer physical pleasure to the exclusion of emotional intimacy).

How to Communicate Effectively with One's Partner about Sexuality

Research findings from the general communication literature, as well as findings from research that focusses specifically on sexual communication, offer us important insights into how an individual can communicate effectively with his or her romantic partner about sexual issues. As you can imagine, a person's attitude and beliefs about sexuality play a significant role in how well he or she communicates about sex with a partner. Returning to the story of Lana and Scott, we can see that Scott had difficulty with sexual communication because he was ashamed about his own sexuality and also embarrassed about his lack of sexual experience. Although Lana did not share these concerns, she thought about sexual chemistry in fairly rigid and absolute terms, and

Ethical Debate

What Responsibility Do Psychologists Have to Break or Protect Confidentiality If an Individual Discloses Information about Risky Sexual Behaviours?

When sexual partners don't communicate, it can sometimes lead to ethical dilemmas for psychologists and other health professionals. Health professions are regulated at the provincial level in Canada. In Ontario, as an example, the legislation that governs the practice of psychology and other health professions is called the Regulated Health Professions Act (RHPA). One of the themes of the RHPA is "an emphasis on preventing harm to the public" (Yarrow & Osborne, 2004, p. 58). Additionally under the RHPA, health professionals have a legal responsibility to keep confidential all of the information they learn in the course of completing their duties (RHPA, Section 36.1, subsection i).

There are a number of reasons that it is important and beneficial for psychologists to be able to assure clients that the information they provide is confidential. First, if such assurances were not provided, many individuals who truly need psychological services might not seek these services out of concern that their private information could be shared. Second, knowing that the information they provide will be kept confidential allows clients to be more open. For example, it allows clients to share information that may be relevant to their treatment, but that is quite personal or might get them into trouble if shared in other contexts (e.g., current use

of illegal drugs). Third, confidentiality fosters the relationship between client and therapist, promoting a sense of trust.

It is hard to dispute the fact that confidentiality is important to the therapeutic relationship. However, a major ethical dilemma for health professionals occurs when protecting a client's confidentiality puts other individuals at risk. As a society, we have decided that there are certain situations where the need to protect others' welfare trumps an individual's right to confidentiality. In this spirit, there are a few specific limitations to confidentiality that health professionals have a legal responsibility to follow. Psychologists are required to review these limitations with their clients during their first session together.

One limitation to confidentiality is that the psychologist must disclose relevant information "if there are reasonable grounds to believe that the disclosure is necessary for the purpose of eliminating or reducing a significant risk of serious bodily harm to a person or group of persons" (RHPA Section 36.1, subsection i). In some scenarios it is quite clear that the psychologist has a responsibility to break confidentiality. Examples of such scenarios include a client who is planning to commit homicide, and a client who discloses that a child is being physically

this approach prevented her from effectively communicating her own concerns about their sexual relationship. In contrast, imagine the interactions of a couple in which both partners desire open and frank dialogue about sexuality and find such communication to be a vital and enjoyable part of their sexual relationship. Such a couple would likely have little difficulty communicating with each other about sex.

In addition to the beliefs and attitudes that form the backdrop of sexual communication, the expectations that an individual has about how his or her partner is likely to behave during an upcoming discussion, as well as that individual's predictions about his or her own actions, play an important role in determining how the discussion will unfold. Returning once again to Lana and Scott's example, let's say that Lana had wanted to talk to Scott about the argument that ensued after she had asked him about his fantasies. When she brought up their fight, Scott may have thought, "Oh, I don't want to talk about this, we will never resolve this issue" or "She is never going to understand how I feel about this." Regardless of how Lana behaves, Scott's belief

or sexually abused. In such cases, the psychologist is mandated to report this information to the appropriate authorities. However, there are other scenarios where the ethical course of action is less clear. When gathering information about a client's sexual behaviour and/or history, psychologists may encounter such scenarios.

Imagine you are a licensed psychologist in the following situations:

1. You begin seeing a new couple for therapy. As part of your assessment, you first meet with the couple together and then with each member of the couple separately. When you meet with the husband alone, he discloses that he is currently having extramarital sex with several partners. He has no intention of either ending his affairs or of telling his wife about them. You inquire as to whether he uses condoms to protect against sexually transmitted infections, and he indicates that he sometimes does and sometimes doesn't. He also notes that he is currently having sex with his wife without the use of condoms.
2. You have seen a young female client for three sessions. During your last session she told you that she was recently diagnosed with genital herpes. She has not told her boyfriend, with whom she has a sexual relationship, about the diagnosis because she is afraid he will break up with her.

For each situation, consider the following questions: Ethically, what should you do? What factors would you consider in making your decision? How would you go about making the decision?

There are no clear answers to these questions, but we can clarify the main issues. In the first scenario, it is clear that the husband is engaging in risky behaviour, but we don't know whether the husband has, for example, been exposed to or contracted HIV, which would pose a significant risk of bodily harm to the wife. If we did know that the husband was HIV positive, most people would likely agree that the psychologist has a duty to break confidentiality. In contrast, if we knew with certainty that the husband had not been exposed to HIV or was using condoms during every sexual encounter, his wife would be at low risk of bodily harm, and most people would likely agree that the psychologist should not breach confidentiality. The missing information creates uncertainty in this scenario. In the second scenario, the key question is whether genital herpes should be considered a form of serious bodily harm.

A psychologist or other health professional trying to answer these questions would likely benefit from consulting with his or her professional college, as one function of professional colleges is to provide guidance around ethical dilemmas. Of course, even with professional guidance, a psychologist might wrestle with his or her personal beliefs about what constitutes the right course of action.

that Lana cannot understand his perspective will influence how he behaves and will, in turn, influence how Lana responds to him. Let's imagine that Lana thinks to herself, "I can't believe he's waiting for me to start this conversation." This thought will influence how she begins the conversation in terms of the words, gestures, tone, and body language that she chooses. In this way, their negative expectations could sabotage their attempt to communicate, making a difficult conversation even more challenging.

Note that one's expectations about how a discussion will unfold can affect how the discussion actually unfolds whether these expectations are right or wrong. Thus, even when negative expectations are not accurate, they can play a detrimental role in a conversation by making individuals less receptive and more rigid. This impact occurs because individuals are motivated to behave in ways that are consistent with their expectations (Rosenthal & Jacobson, 1968). In other words, they engage in **behavioural confirmation**. For example, research has shown that women who expected to be rejected by their partners during a discussion were likely to set up the conversation pattern to end with rejection based on their assumption that they would be rejected (Downey, Freitas, Michaelis & Khouri, 1998).

Expectancies can also be confirmed through the process of **perceptual confirmation** (Miller & Turnbull, 1986). Research has supported the idea that perceptual confirmation occurs in intimate relationships. For example, one study demonstrated that spouses' expectations for an upcoming conflict discussion were positively associated with their evaluations of those discussions afterwards, even when the actual behaviours that occurred during the discussions did not fit their expectations (McNulty & Karney, 2002).

Once the actual conversation has started, there are a number of factors that influence its course and determine whether it will create greater intimacy and enhance partners' understanding of each other, or whether it will increase the distance between them. One such factor is the effectiveness of both partners' listening skills. After all, research and clinical observations demonstrate that good listening is just as important to effective communication as good speaking is. The skilled listener listens to the message that underlies the words, is tuned in to subtleties in the speaker's emotions, and is able to put aside her or his own beliefs and judgments to try to understand the other person's perspective. When people think back to conversations that have been positive defining moments in their lives, the manner in which another person listened, with full presence, is often the quality they recall most vividly. In discussions where the communication partners' goals are at crossroads or when one partner brings up a sensitive topic, it can be particularly challenging for the listener to set aside her or his own agenda to really hear what her or his partner is saying. Yet without a receptive listener, the speaker's message will be lost, and communication will break down. We recall, for example, a couple in therapy in which the female partner, after agonizing and worrying a great deal about how to bring up the topic, said cautiously, "I'd feel more attracted to you if you were more confident in social settings," only to have her partner flash back, "I'd like you to be less shrill." She retreated immediately.

Of course, there are also certain speaking skills that partners can use to improve their communication about sensitive and difficult topics, such as sexuality. With topics that feel like emotional minefields, how the speaker starts the conversation plays a critical role in how the conversation unfolds. A softer start-up, possibly noting the difficulty in talking about a particular topic, can help to put conversational partners at ease. Another key component of skillful speaking, particularly during difficult conversations, is accessing "softer," more vulnerable emotions (e.g., embarrassment, fear, anxiety), rather than "harder" emotions (e.g., anger, frustration, disgust). It is easier for us to admit that we are angry, for example, than that we are embarrassed or scared. Look

behavioural confirmation
A process whereby someone's expectations about an upcoming event influence his or her behaviour and thus cause the event to unfold in a way that is consistent with his or her expectations.

perceptual confirmation A process whereby someone interprets an event in a way that is consistent with his or her expectations.

again to Lana and Scott's story and see if you can identify some of the more vulnerable emotions that underlie their exchanges.

Interestingly, relationship researchers have found inconsistent evidence for the role of anger in relationships, and it is not yet clear how expressions of anger relate to relationship satisfaction and stability (Heyman, 2001). One plausible reason for this lack of clarity is that anger is defined differently across different studies. When it is operationalized such that it includes behaviours like hostility and escalating negative responses, anger has a negative impact on relationships. In contrast, frustration and anger expressed in a manner that does not alienate the other person are vital components of healthy relationships, as there must be room in relationships to experience and witness both positive and negative emotions (Greenberg & Goldman, 2008).

For most people, effective communication skills do not come naturally; these skills must be developed and improved upon throughout one's life. Many of the speaking and listening skills we bring to our relationships as adults are based on the skills we develop as children and adolescents. Thus, the ways in which adults communicate with young people about sexual issues may affect not only how those youths come to view sex and sexuality, but also how they will communicate with future partners about sexuality. However, although most people would agree that such communication with young people is important, many parents and others have differing ideas of how and when sexual issues should be communicated to children. This topic is covered in the "Research vs Real Life" box, and in Chapter 19.

Research VS Real Life

Who Should Give Children "the Talk," and When Should It Happen?

One of the most controversial forms of sexual communication is providing information to children and adolescents about sexual health. People have strong opinions about what information should be given, who should be sharing this information, and how old children need to be before it is introduced. Researchers in Canada have conducted studies to find out what people think about all of these questions, and the answers may surprise you.

Research

Who Should Provide Sex Education?
Large surveys of parents in Ontario and New Brunswick have shown that the vast majority of parents (95 per cent and 94 per cent, respectively) think sexual health education should be provided in schools (McKay, Pietrusiak, & Holowaty, 1998; Weaver, Byers, Sears, Cohen, & Randall, 2002). Almost all parents also believe that providing sexual health education is a responsibility shared between parents and schools (Weaver et al., 2002). Similarly, the vast majority of teachers agree that sexual health education should

be provided in schools, and that the responsibility for teaching this information to children is shared between parents and schools (Cohen, Byers, Sears, & Weaver, 2004). Parents also feel it is important for teachers who provide sexual health education to be comfortable with and knowledgeable about the subject matter (Weaver et al., 2002).

What Information Should Be Taught in Schools, and When?

McKay and colleagues (1998) asked parents of Ontario children in kindergarten through Grade Eight which of 15 topics (e.g., avoiding sexual abuse, prevention of STIs, attraction/love/intimacy, puberty) should be covered in different grades. The majority of parents felt that every topic identified should be covered at some point in school. Weaver and colleagues (2002) conducted a study with similar goals and also found that the majority of parents felt that all of the sexual health topics identified should be covered in school (see Figure 13.7 for a list of the topics included in the study). However, some topics

Continued

Important Sexual Health Topics

- Personal safety
- Abstinence
- Puberty
- Sexual decision-making in dating relationships
- Reproduction
- Sexually transmitted infections
- Sexual coercion and sexual assault
- Birth control methods and safer sex practices
- Correct names for genitals
- Sexual pleasure and enjoyment

FIGURE 13.7 Topics included in the Weaver et al. (2002) survey asking parents which sexual health education topics should be taught in school.

were identified as more controversial, with more than 10 per cent of parents suggesting they should be excluded from the sexual health education curriculum. For example, at least 10 per cent of parents said that wet dreams, masturbation, same-sex attraction, sex as part of a loving relationship, and sexual pleasure and orgasm should not be taught at all within a school curriculum (Weaver et al., 2002).

The majority of parents believe that sexual health education should begin in elementary school and continue through high school (McKay, Pietrusiak, & Holowaty, 1998; Weaver et al., 2002), as do the majority of teachers (Cohen et al., 2004). Weaver and colleagues (2002) found that parents typically thought that most topics should be introduced between grades six and eight, but there were some topics they thought should be introduced earlier or later. Most parents thought that issues around personal safety should be introduced between kindergarten and Grade Three, and that the correct names for genitals, as well as issues around body image, sexual coercion, and sexual assault, should be introduced in Grade Five or earlier. In contrast, the majority of parents thought that sexual pleasure and orgasm should not be covered until high school.

Overall, the research findings tell us that Canadian parents and teachers think it is important to provide sexual health education at school and at home, and that the majority support the idea of beginning sexual health education in elementary school.

Real Life

Evaluations of Sexual Health Education in Canada

There is little research evaluating to what extent and how well sexual health education is delivered in Canadian schools. One study did examine how satisfied recent graduates from Ontario high schools were with their sexual health education experiences. In this study, the researchers found that students were reasonably satisfied with their sexual health education experiences (Meaney, Rye, Wood, & Solovieva, 2009). Additionally, they found that students thought that about three-quarters of the topics examined had been introduced at the appropriate grade level, but about one-quarter of the topics (e.g., birth control methods and safer sex practices, sexual coercion and sexual assault, sexual decision-making) should have been introduced earlier (i.e., between grades six and eight, as opposed to during high school; Meaney et al., 2009).

Training Teachers to Provide Sex Education

As mentioned previously, parents feel (and most people would likely agree) that it is important for teachers who are delivering sexual health education to be knowledgeable about and comfortable with the relevant content (Weaver et al., 2002). Unfortunately, Cohen and colleagues (2004) found this isn't always the case. On average, teachers felt only "somewhat knowledgeable" about sexual topics, and they felt only "somewhat comfortable" teaching about sexual topics, although comfort varied depending on the topic. Most teachers reported feeling "very comfortable" with topics such as body image, reproduction and birth, and abstinence, but the majority were less than "somewhat comfortable" teaching about masturbation, sexual pleasure, and orgasm (Cohen et al., 2004). One possible reason for teachers' lack of comfort providing sex education is that many are not trained in this area. Cohen and colleagues found that 65 per cent of the New Brunswick teachers they surveyed had received no formal training in teaching sex education, while McKay and Barrett (1999) found that only 16 per cent of Canadian faculties of education offered training in teaching sex education.

The Ontario Curriculum Controversy

Perhaps the most clear example, in recent Canadian history, of how what research tells us most people want to happen differs from what actually happens in real life is that of the failed 2010 proposal for sex education reform in Ontario. The controversy began in early 2010, when Ontario's Ministry of Education proposed a new health and physical education curriculum, to be implemented in the 2010–2011 school year (CBC News, 2010; Figure 13.8). Some of the curriculum changes highlighted in the media included that Grade One students would learn anatomically correct terms for genitals, Grade Five students would learn about reproductive systems and puberty, and Grade Seven students would learn about methods of preventing pregnancy and the transmission of sexually transmitted infections (CBC News, 2010). Representatives from several religious groups, including the Canada Christian College, protested the nature of the content. Initially, Ontario's premier, Dalton McGuinty, defended the curriculum, noting he preferred that students learn sexual health information in school versus from less reliable sources (Artuso, 2010). However, he quickly conceded to protests from the religious groups, stating that the new curriculum required a "rethink" and that it would not be introduced in schools in the fall of 2010, as planned (CBC News, 2010). Teachers were to continue to rely on the previous version of the curriculum, which had been released in 1998 (CBC News, 2010).

As McKay, Pietrusiak, and Holowaty (1998) point out, "those who oppose the provision of sexual health education in the schools or who argue that

FIGURE 13.8 How do you feel about sex education in schools? In 2010, Premier Dalton McGuinty decided not to introduce a new version of the health and physical education curriculum in Ontario schools, after religious groups protested the content related to sex education.

sexual health education should only embody a particular ideological vision of sexual health may be highly vocal and persistent in promoting their point of view, thereby giving the impression that they represent a large proportion of community opinion" (p. 140). Given what the research literature tells us about the majority of parents' preferences with regard to sex education in school, one must wonder whether Premier McGuinty was overly influenced by the values of a "vocal and persistent" minority.

CHAPTER SUMMARY

This chapter examined the centrality of communication to healthy relationship functioning. When it comes to discussing sexuality, particularly sexual conflicts, couples may find it difficult to navigate these conversations skillfully, possibly due to the sensitive and personal nature of these topics. However, findings from couples' communication research provide us with important guidance in how to have these conversations. Research on sexual communication also shows that good sexual communication contributes to a couple's sexual satisfaction by improving their intimacy and increasing each partner's understanding of the other's sexual preferences. It is important to note that when researchers use observational techniques to arrive at such findings, they must be aware of benefits and costs associated with this sort of research. On one hand, observational methods provide rich information that is helpful for developing theories and interventions for sexual problems. On the other hand, some couples may experience negative emotions before, during, or after their participation in such studies.

DEBATE QUESTION

Some people believe that telling their partner every little detail about themselves is the best thing to do to increase intimacy. Others believe that telling their partner only those things about themselves they deem to be most significant is ideal. What do you believe, and why?

REVIEW QUESTIONS

1. What are some of the key ways communication differs between distressed and non-distressed couples?

2. What are two common methods that researchers use to study couples' communication, and what are the advantages and disadvantages of each?

3. What are some of the similarities and differences between men's and women's communication patterns?

4. What are some of the barriers to effective sexual communication?

5. How does good sexual communication improve sexual satisfaction?

6. Given what you have learned about the costs and benefits of using observations methods, what would you decide to do if you were designing a study of couples' communication about sexual issues?

SUGGESTIONS FOR FURTHER READING AND VIEWING

Recommended Website
Society for Human Sexuality: www.sexuality.org

Recommended Reading
Gottman, J.M. (1979). *Marital interaction: Experimental investigations.* New York, NY: Academic Press.

Halford, K., & Markman, H. (1997). *Clinical handbook of marriage and couples interventions.* Hoboken, NJ: John Wiley & Sons.

Harvey, H.J., Wenzel, A., & Sprecher, S. (1994). *The handbook of sexuality in close relationships.* Mahwah, NJ: Lawrence Erlbaum Associates.

Jacobson, N.S, & Christensen, A. (1998). *Acceptance and change in couple therapy: A therapist's guide to transforming relationships.* New York, NY: W.W. Norton & Company.

Recommended Viewing
Johnson, S. (Creator). 2008. *Creating relationships that last: A conversation with Dr Sue Johnson* [DVD]. Canada: Rheem Media. Available from www.holdmetight.net/video.php

Johnson, S. (Creator). 2009. *Hold me tight: Conversations for connections with Dr Sue Johnson* [DVD]. Canada: Rheem Media. Available from www.holdmetight.net/video.php

14 CHAPTER

Sexual Behaviours and Relationships

NATALIE O. ROSEN
AND SHEILA MACNEIL

LEARNING OBJECTIVES

In this chapter, you will

- consider the personal and social significance of sexual behaviours, including first sexual intercourse;
- learn about a diverse array of common sexual behaviours;
- discover how people in different types of relationships engage sexually with their partner(s); and
- find out how mass media have influenced how we think about sexual behaviours and relationships.

A "Friends with Benefits" Relationship

Karen and Daryl were casual acquaintances in high school, and they became friends while living in the same university residence. One night, after walking home with Karen from a party, Daryl started to kiss Karen and she reciprocated. From that point on, they usually had sex whenever they found themselves alone together in one of their dorm rooms.

They did not explicitly talk about their relationship, and they were careful not to reveal the sexual nature of their relationship to others. It seemed implied that both were free to date other people. Karen enjoyed the affection and physical contact with Daryl when she felt lonely, and she felt more comfortable being sexual with him than she had with her last boyfriend. Daryl enjoyed the casual and undemanding interactions he had with Karen; he felt that the sex was good, too, and believed casual sex was to be a common part of the university experience.

Karen had wondered what would happen if she and Daryl were to start "dating officially," but Daryl was not the partner she had imagined for herself. At the same time, her ideal dating partner had not yet appeared. For now, this seemed to Karen to be the next best thing to a committed relationship. Daryl wasn't interested in an exclusive dating relationship at the moment, although he expected that he would have a more committed sexual relationship at some point in the future. Overall, both Karen and Daryl were satisfied with their relationship, but they tried not to think about what would happen to their friendship if the "benefits" ever came to an end.

QUESTIONS FOR CRITICAL THOUGHT AND REFLECTION

1. How does a "friends with benefits" relationship differ from a dating relationship?
2. What are the risks and benefits to Karen and Daryl's relationship? How do Karen's motives for this type of relationship differ from Daryl's?

Introduction: What Does It Mean to "Have Sex"?

People can have very different ideas about what it means to "have sex." Canadian sex researcher Sandra Byers and her colleagues surveyed 298 heterosexual first-year undergraduate students to examine their definitions of having sex (Figure 14.1; Byers, Henderson, & Hobson, 2009). Less than 5 per cent of these students thought engaging in behaviours that did not include genital touching was "having sex." Approximately 12 to 15 per cent included manual genital touching in their definition of sex, and 24 to 25 per cent included oral-genital stimulation in their definition. While 90 per cent of these students reported that engaging in penile-vaginal intercourse was having sex, this number dropped to 83 per cent for having penile-anal intercourse. On the whole, the researchers determined that students were far more likely to define a sexual activity as "having sex" if it involved mutual genital contact and orgasm.

A person's definition of sex can have a number of important implications to her or his sexual health and behaviours. For example, if a person does not include a particular sexual behaviour (e.g., oral sex) in her or his definition, then that person may be less likely to use protection for that behaviour, resulting in a higher risk of contracting a sexually transmitted infection (STI). Different definitions of having sex can also be an obstacle to sex education and STI prevention. Some adolescents, for example, may respond "no" to a doctor's question about whether they are having sex even though they are having oral sex. In this case, the doctor may miss the opportunity to provide education about STIs that can be transmitted orally, such as herpes and the human papillomavirus (HPV).

As the Byers and colleagues' study underscores, many people continue to believe that intercourse involving a penis and a vagina is the "norm" for having sex (Byers et al.,

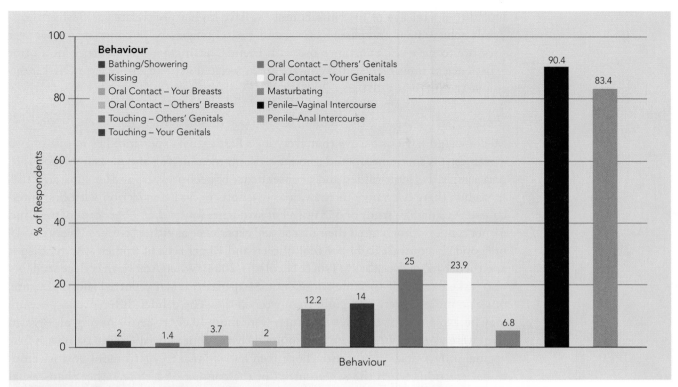

FIGURE 14.1 Percentage of students reporting that a particular behaviour constitutes "having sex."

2009). Does this mean that the partnered sexual activities engaged in by individuals who are gay or lesbian are not sex? Of course not! The "norm" of penile-vaginal intercourse is based on what has traditionally been considered to be standard sexual behaviour among heterosexual individuals; indeed, it would be interesting to find out how LGBTTIQQ individuals' definitions of "having sex" differ from those of the heterosexual students in Byers and colleagues' survey. Certainly, both heterosexual and gay couples can engage in anal intercourse, as do some lesbian couples, with the use of a dildo. It is important to recognize that couples of all sexual orientations and gender combinations engage in a diverse range of sexual activities. In this chapter, we define sex as any solo or partnered activity involving behaviours that are an expression of sexual arousal and/or desire that also results in subjective and physical feelings of arousal and desire.

First Sexual Experiences

As mentioned in Chapter 9, experiencing sexual intercourse for the first time is a significant rite of passage for many people. Many young people consider this experience to be the first time they have "had sex" with a partner. It is usually highly anticipated and can be fraught with uncertainty. Because first intercourse is thought to play such an important role in sexual development, educators and policy-makers often use age at first intercourse to identify target populations for health policies and interventions that address STI awareness and prevention, contraception and unintended pregnancies, and sexual coercion. Estimates suggest that, for both males and females, 10 to 13 per cent of 14-year-olds, 20 to 25 per cent of 15-year-olds, 40 per cent of 16-year-olds, and 50 per cent of 17-year-olds have had penile-vaginal intercourse (Maticka-Tyndale, 2001).

A number of factors play a role in determining at what age a person will first have sexual intercourse. Positive emotional connections with family members, parental disapproval of early sex and contraceptive use, and greater parental control have all been linked to a later age of first intercourse, as have higher peer-related self-esteem, academic achievement and participation, and greater religiosity. In contrast, greater peer pressure to have sex, substance use with friends, having an older partner, or a prior experience of unwanted sexual contact are associated with an earlier age of first intercourse (Laflin, Wang, & Barry, 2008).

Expectations of and Reactions to First Sexual Experiences

Media would have us believe that everyone's first sexual experience lies in one of two extremes: it is spontaneous and romantic, deeply meaningful, and pleasurable for both partners; or it is guilt-ridden and a consequence of peer-pressure and/or substance use. In reality, there is a range in emotional reactions to and satisfaction with first intercourse. A Canadian study of 358 university students found that 72 per cent of men and 61 per cent of women rated their first sexual experience as either "perfect," "very good," or "good" in contrast to 11 per cent of men and 13 per cent of women who recalled it as either "bad" or "very bad" (Tsui & Nicoladis, 2004). When American college students were asked to recall their first intercourse experience, men reported more pleasure, but also more anxiety and guilt, than women did. The gender difference in pleasure may be explained by the fact that men were more likely to recall having an orgasm than were women. Women are also more likely than men to experience pain with first vaginal intercourse. Importantly, both men and women reported more positive emotional reactions when the sex occurred in the context of a close rather than casual relationship (Sprecher, Barbee, & Schwartz, 1995). Perhaps because many people feel particularly vulnerable, both emotionally and physically, during first intercourse, the chances of having a positive experience increase when first intercourse occurs within a close relationship.

Virginity

Very few studies have examined virginity, especially beyond young adulthood, and those that have tend to focus on factors that predict losing one's virginity at an early age. This lack of research is probably due to the small number of people who remain virgins past their 20s. One American study of over 11,000 individuals 18 to 27 years old found that 98 per cent reported that they had engaged in sexual intercourse, with 8 per cent of these individuals reporting that they had waited until marriage before having had intercourse for the first time; the remaining 2 per cent were unmarried virgins (Halpern, Waller, Spriggs, & Hallfors, 2006). Reasons for abstaining from sex included religious beliefs, concerns about contracting STIs or becoming pregnant, feelings of insecurity or inadequacy concerning sexual behaviour, and not feeling loved by a potential partner. There may be some benefits associated with remaining a virgin through young adulthood, including avoiding pregnancy and STIs. In countries and cultures that forbid premarital sex, especially for women, additional benefits to remaining a virgin may include acceptance within the community and opportunities to marry; indeed, as you learned in Chapter 4, some women from such communities who have had intercourse seek hymenoplasty (hymen reconstruction surgery) to regain physical evidence of their virginity (see the "Ethical Debate" box).

There is clearly a difference between individuals who choose virginity and are happy with that choice and those who are unsatisfied with their virgin status. Individuals in this latter category are considered to be "reluctant virgins." Reluctant virgins often attribute their virginity to shyness, poor body image, lack of dating experience, poor social skills, and logistical problems related to work or living arrangements. Although the majority of reluctant virgins report feeling dissatisfied and unhappy with their

Ethical Debate

Should Doctors Perform "Revirgination" Surgery for Cultural and Social Reasons?

There is ongoing ethical debate among gynecologists and others about whether hymen reconstruction is warranted and justifiable. Some people believe that the hymen breaks only at first intercourse, when bleeding is commonly taken as a sign that the hymen has ruptured, but it may also be stretched or broken during non-sexual activities such as vaginal insertion of tampons, rigorous sports, and surgical procedures (Cook & Dickens, 2009). Hymen reconstruction, or "revirgination," is a gynecological cosmetic surgery to reposition the remnants of the broken hymen or a small flap of vaginal skin to approximate the hymen after it has broken. In some cases, women who have had this surgery may insert a small gelatin capsule containing a blood-like substance into their vagina pre-intercourse to simulate post-coital bleeding.

Some Middle Eastern and African cultures hold the tradition that young women must be virgins when they marry. Lack of evidence of a woman's virginity on the wedding night (e.g., blood on the marital bed sheets) may be a source of disgrace to a woman and her family, and it may even be cause for divorce or result in violence against the woman. Even today, there are cases of "honour killings" in which unmarried women who are suspected of having lost their virginity are killed by their family members. This practice occurs in countries including Bangladesh, the UK, Brazil, Egypt, India, Israel, Italy, Pakistan, Morocco, Sweden, Turkey, Uganda, Iran, Iraq, the US, and even Canada. Moreover, punishments are often enacted against women who have unintentionally lost their virginity through rape or coercion.

Gynecologists who support hymen reconstruction view it as promoting and protecting women's physical as well as psychological and social well-being. They also argue that women have a right to make decisions about their own bodies. Some gynecologists who oppose the procedure believe that hymen reconstruction is deceptive toward future marriage partners and their families, and that it is not medically necessary. Further, some people object to the surgery because they believe that it perpetuates the discriminatory practice of requiring women to prove their virginity (Cook & Dickens, 2009).

In the only hymen reconstruction outcome study to date, which included 20 young women in the Netherlands, all women who had undergone the surgery reported feeling satisfied with the outcome and had no regrets (Logmans, Verhoeff, Raap, Creighton, & van Lent, 1998). One study has also claimed that hymen reconstruction has reduced the rate of honour killings in Egypt by 80 per cent (Kandela, 1996). Given that the medical risks associated with this surgery are minimal when it is performed by a skilled professional who uses sterile equipment, hymen reconstruction appears to be a relatively benign procedure that may offer more benefits than drawbacks for women.

lack of sexual experience, others are primarily distressed by the lack of intimacy and love that often comes with having a romantic relationship and sex (Donnelly, Burgess, Anderson, Davis, & Dillard, 2001). Because of the social stigma that increases the longer one remains a virgin, it is often difficult for these individuals to seek help to address their barriers to becoming sexually active. Engaging in non-judgmental, open conversations with peers and finding others who share their concerns may help reluctant virgins discuss their wants and needs, and greater acceptance and awareness within media sources may help destigmatize the virgin status.

Sexual Consent

Before engaging in sexual behaviour with another person, whether or not it is for the first time, an individual must be sure that both she or he and her or his partner have given their **sexual consent**. There are two key components to giving sexual consent. The

sexual consent An individual's agreement to engage in sexual behaviour.

first is a clear understanding of what it is that the person is consenting to; the second is that the consent is given freely, without coercion or undue influence. These components are important in differentiating between consensual sexual encounters and cases of sexual assault, rape, and abuse. A controversy regarding sexual consent is whether a person's non-verbal behaviours are enough to communicate sexual consent, or whether this consent should include explicit verbal communication (Lim & Roloff, 1999).

Most sexual encounters do not follow from explicit statements of consent; rather, consent usually occurs as an unspoken but clear agreement to engage in sexual activity. One study of over 300 heterosexual university students used real and hypothetical sexual consent scenarios to examine the type of signals people use to indicate sexual consent. In this study, both men and women reported that they were more likely to give their sexual consent non-verbally than verbally (Hickman & Muehlenhard, 1999). A Canadian study of men who have sex with men and women who have sex with women found similar results: non-verbal behaviours were more commonly used to signal sexual consent than were verbal communications (Beres, Herold, & Maitland, 2004). Women have expressed a greater need for explicit verbal sexual consent as compared to men, and this finding could be explained in the context of sexual scripts (discussed in more detail in the next section). According to traditional sexual scripts, it is the man's role to initiate sexual activity, whereas the woman can accept or reject this initiation. At the same time, there is evidence that both men and women agree that sexual consent should be negotiated openly. Unfortunately, the reality is that explicit verbal consent rarely occurs.

In some cases, a person may freely consent to engaging in sexual activity even when she or he does not truly want to participate in the given activity. This sort of sexual consent is commonly referred to as **sexual compliance**. Reflecting on your own experiences, it may or may not surprise you to learn that sexual compliance appears to be quite common among sexually active university-aged individuals. Although women are more likely than men to be sexually compliant, the majority of both men and women report being sexual compliant on at least one occasion (Vannier & O'Sullivan, 2010).

What motivates people to consent to sexual activity that they do not desire? University of Toronto researcher Emily Impett and University of New Brunswick researcher Lucia O'Sullivan, along with their colleagues, have suggested that motives for sexual compliance are commonly based on relationship factors such as wanting to make one's partner happy, promoting intimacy, and avoiding relationship conflict. For some couples, sexual compliance resulting from these motives may have positive consequences, leading to more sexual satisfaction, greater feelings of closeness, and a greater sense of fun in the relationship (Impett, Peplau, & Gable, 2005). This finding could explain why there are higher rates of sexual compliance in committed relationships compared to casual sexual interactions (Vannier & O'Sullivan, 2010). Some additional reasons for engaging in sexual compliance are wanting to gain sexual experience, wanting to impress one's peers, and believing that one does not have a good reason for withholding consent.

sexual compliance An individual's willing consent to engage in sexual behaviour when she or he does not desire sexual activity.

Varieties of Sexual Behaviours

Before even becoming sexually active, North Americans are generally aware of a sequence of sexual behaviours that constitute "having sex." This sequence is what sex researchers describe as the traditional sexual script (TSS). If your class were asked to stop and write down the order of sexual activities for a couple having sex, most of you would probably list them according to the TSS: kissing, sexual touching, and intercourse, likely followed by orgasm. The TSS is an example of a cultural-level social script, and it is reflected in popular films and novels, as well as in our actual sexual practices.

In fact, many students would now include oral sex in this sequence of sexual activities, usually just prior to intercourse or orgasm. At the same time, actual sexual behaviours are much more variable than the TSS would suggest.

According to social script theory, there are two additional levels at which sexual scripts exist: the interpersonal, and the intrapsychic or individual (Gagnon, 1998). Scripts that develop at these levels show great variability, as they reflect the cultural-level TSS but also incorporate variations due to the diversity of the individuals and situational factors involved. Scripts that develop at the individual level may also reflect widespread changes in attitudes toward sex—for example, the general trend toward greater acceptance of casual sex, and the trend away from complacent acceptance of extramarital sex (see Petersen & Hyde, 2010).

Recent research does indeed suggest that North Americans are engaging in sexual practices and developing sexual scripts that are increasingly varied and flexible. For example, one study found that American adults reported 40 different combinations of sexual activities, such as tandem oral sex to mutual masturbation to anal intercourse, when describing their most recent sexual experience with a partner (Herbenick, Reece, Schick, et al., 2010b). This kind of variety is probably beneficial for the couple in terms of maintaining sexual desire and developing a mutually satisfying sexual script. Flexible sexual scripts also have the benefit of being able to overcome some of the commonly criticized limitations of the TSS, such as its focus on intercourse and orgasm as the only road to optimal sexual satisfaction and functioning. The following sections describe sexual behaviours commonly found in sexual scripts and how they vary across individuals and relationships.

Solitary Sexual Behaviours

Engaging in solitary sexual behaviours is one way in which individuals experiment with and alter the dominant sexual script of their culture, by discovering personal preferences. Sharing and negotiating these preferences with a sexual partner is another way to alter such scripts.

FANTASY

Fantasizing about sex is a sexual activity one can engage in alone or during activity with a partner. It is a normal part of a healthy sex life. Canadian research has found that people who reported more frequent positive fantasies about sex also reported more masturbation, a greater number of sexual partners, and greater sexual satisfaction (Renaud & Byers, 2001).

Sexual fantasies can originate from external sources such as media or stories, from past experiences, or from hopes and dreams. It is not abnormal for people to fantasize about sex with someone other than their primary partner, or sex with both male and female partners. These thoughts do not necessarily mean that the people having them want to cheat on their partner or are uncertain about their sexual orientation. Rather than being indicative of activities individuals intend to pursue in real life, fantasies may be one way that people explore sexual desires and adapt sexual scripts with the greatest privacy, freedom, and imagination (Gagnon, 1998).

A study of sexual fantasies among heterosexual Canadian university students found that men and women tended to fantasize about similar things, despite men engaging in sexual fantasy more often (Renaud & Byers, 1999). For at least 90 per cent of the participants, the most common topics included having intercourse with a loved partner, kissing passionately, making love outside of the bedroom, and giving or receiving oral sex. More men than women fantasized about anonymous or impersonal sex, and more

sexual fantasies Sexual thoughts or images that stimulate a person physiologically and/or emotionally.

women than men fantasized about affectionate or foreplay activities, such as "kissing passionately and being undressed" (Renaud & Byers, 1999, p. 27). Sexual fantasies of gay men and lesbian women have been found to be similar to those of heterosexual men and women, with the exception of the sex of the sexual partner (Price, Allensworth, & Hillman, 1985).

Incorporating fantasy into one's sexual activities is a strategy often introduced in sex therapy to help people struggling with low sexual desire and arousal. Fantasy can help people focus their attention on pleasurable, sexual thoughts and images rather than distracting, non-sexual thoughts (like studying!), increasing the likelihood of a satisfying sexual experience.

MASTURBATION

Although it is usually a solitary activity, masturbation, like fantasizing, is a sexual behaviour that people can engage in alone or with a partner (when with a partner, it is commonly referred to as *mutual masturbation*.) Sex therapists suggest that masturbation is a good way to learn about one's own sexual response and that it is a safe, healthy way to prepare for future satisfying sexual relationships.

Masturbation is a common behaviour in people of all ages. Children as young as 2 or 3 often begin to masturbate to explore their bodies and/or self-soothe, and later with psychosexual development masturbation becomes a sexually motivated behaviour. Teenagers engage in solitary masturbation more than any other sexual behaviour. In the United States, over 43 per cent of girls and 67 per cent of boys 14 to 15 years of age report having masturbated at some time in their life (Herbenick, Reece, Schick, et al., 2010a). The percentage of young people who masturbate rises with age, and this increase is generally more rapid for boys and more gradual for girls. By adulthood, almost all men and the majority of women are able to masturbate to orgasm (Herbenick, Reece, Schick, et al., 2010a). In addition, many women experience orgasm more often with masturbation than with vaginal intercourse (Zietsch, Miller, Bailey, & Martin, 2011).

Traditionally, masturbation has been viewed as an activity more common among men than among women, and research has found evidence in support of this view (see Petersen & Hyde, 2010). At the same time, it is not clear why this gender difference exists. Some have argued that men may have higher sex drives and therefore desire sexual satisfaction more often than do women. Others have suggested that this gender difference is a consequence of the sexual double standard that criticizes women but not men for engaging in non-reproductive sexual activity, and for finding such activity pleasurable. In support of this view, research has found that the size of the gender difference in frequency and incidence of masturbation is smaller in countries with greater gender equality than it is in those with less equality (Petersen & Hyde, 2010). Ultimately, the view that masturbation is more common and/or acceptable among men than among women may negatively impact some women, as it may discourage them from learning about and becoming more comfortable with their genitals and sexual preferences.

Partnered Sexual Behaviours

KISSING

Kissing often involves a person putting her or his lips on the lips of another person. One or both people can use their tongue to touch the inside of the mouth or tongue of the other person ("French kissing"). Kissing may also involve using the lips and mouth to stimulate other erogenous zones such as the neck, earlobes, nipples, and inner thighs. While kisses can convey platonic affection alone, kissing can also be an extremely intimate sexual behaviour because it stimulates a number of senses—touch, smell, and taste—simultaneously.

TOUCHING

Sexual touching can include stimulating genital and non-genital areas of a partner's body with the hand or other body part, or with objects (e.g., feathers, flavoured massage oils). Sexual touching, along with kissing, is commonly considered to be an element of foreplay, as it is included in the TSS as a prelude to intercourse. Some research suggests that heterosexual women, and many of their partners, *want* to spend more time in fore-play activities, such as touching, yet *do not do so* (Miller & Byers, 2004). Studies suggest that same-sex couples spend more time engaging in sensual, "non-orgasmic" activities, consider these activities to be more important, and derive more satisfaction from them than do their heterosexual counterparts, particularly heterosexual men (Holmberg & Blair, 2009). Indeed, Canadian researchers Cohen, Byers, and Walsh (2008) found that a number of the lesbian women they surveyed challenged the description of activities such as sexual touching as "foreplay." These women considered sexual touching as a continuous, partner-responsive activity rather than an isolated step in a goal-directed sequence of sexual activities. Reframing the way we think about foreplay activities—to recognize them as important sexual activities in their own right—allows us to define love-making or "having sex" more flexibly. This flexibility can be especially helpful for individuals who desire sexual intimacy and satisfaction but are unable to have or do not feel ready for intercourse.

ORAL SEX

Oral sex, stimulating a partner's genitals orally, is a practice that is increasingly common in men and women of all ages. However, the increase in frequency of oral sex in adolescents, in particular, has caught the attention of media, parents, sex researchers, and adolescents themselves (Barrett, 2004; see the "Research vs Real Life" box).

Oral sex can involve stimulating the vulva, penis, or anus with a person's lips, mouth, and tongue. When oral sex is performed on a woman's genitals, it is commonly referred to as **cunnilingus** (Figure 14.2). Many women find oral stimulation of the inner thighs, outer and inner labia, clitoris, and vaginal opening highly arousing and very satisfying. Oral sex performed on a man's genitals is referred to as **fellatio** (Figure 14.3). Fellatio usually involves oral stimulation of the penile shaft, glans, and

cunnilingus Oral stimulation of a woman's genitals by a partner.

fellatio Oral stimulation of a man's genitals by a partner.

FIGURE 14.2 A woman engaged in cunnilingus with a female partner.

FIGURE 14.3 A man engaged in fellatio with a male partner.

coronal ridge, which are quite sensitive, and many men find simultaneous oral stimulation of these regions and manual stimulation of the scrotum, perineum, and anal opening to be highly pleasurable. When oral sex is performed on the anus, perineum, and surrounding area, it is often referred to as anilingus.

Research VS Real Life

Prevalence of Oral Sex among Adolescents

Mass media have described the rates of teens engaged in oral sex as "epidemic" and noted that the practice of oral sex has become pervasive among teens throughout North America (Barrett, 2004). Such dramatic descriptions may enflame common concerns among parents and others that higher rates of oral sex indicate that massive numbers of teens are engaging in partnered sexual activities, perhaps before they are emotionally or psychologically ready to do so. However, a recent large-scale survey of Americans reported that similar numbers of adolescents have engaged in oral sex as have had intercourse (Herbenick, Reece, Schick, et al., 2010a). Thus, while one cannot be certain the same youth who engage in oral sex are also the ones having intercourse, it is possible that increasing rates of oral sex among teens simply indicate that teens are adding oral sex to their sexual repertoire, not that many more teens are engaging in partnered sexual activities than ever before. In fact, oral sex is a relatively recent addition to the TSS, and therefore couples of all ages may be incorporating oral sex more commonly into their sexual activities (Herbenick, Reece, Schick, et al., 2010a).

Some people are concerned that girls more than boys are pressured into performing oral sex, perhaps to attract boys or to increase their popularity (Barrett, 2004). Herbenick and colleagues (2010a), however, found that only slightly more teenage girls than teenage boys had given oral sex to an other-sex partner in the last year (Table 14.1). Moreover, the number of adolescent girls who had performed oral sex on a male partner was similar to the number who had received oral sex from a male. Thus, this research reveals a greater gender balance, in terms of who performs oral sex on whom, than many people would expect. In contrast to the sexual double standard, it is possible that some teen girls derive sexual pleasure from both receiving and giving oral sex with a partner, meaning that they do not engage in oral sex simply out of a desire to attract boys or a lack of social acceptance.

Perhaps a more substantial concern is that adolescents may minimize the health risk of exposure to sexually transmitted infections with oral sex. Indeed, research has indicated that this concern may be quite valid. For example, one study of high school students in California found that the teens surveyed believed that oral sex was much less risky than intercourse (Halpern-Felsher, Cornell, Kropp, & Tschann, 2005). This finding is concerning, given that some STIs, such as herpes and HPV, are commonly transmitted through oral sex. In addition, although the risk of HIV/AIDS transmission is lower with oral sex (0.04 to 1 per cent) compared to unprotected vaginal or anal sex (0.06 to 10 per cent), the risk still exists, and the consequences can be severe (Halpern-Felsher et al., 2005).

TABLE 14.1 Percentage of American male and female adolescents engaged in intercourse with, giving oral sex to, and receiving oral sex from an other-sex partner in the last year.

Age	Gender	Giving Oral Sex (%)	Receiving Oral Sex (%)	Engaged in Intercourse (%)
14 to 15	Female	11.8	10	10.7
	Male	7.8	11.9	8.9
16 to 17	Female	22.4	23.5	29.7
	Male	18.3	30.9	30.3

Source: Adapted from Herbenick, Reece, Schick, et al. (2010a).

FIGURE 14.4 A mixed-sex couple engaged in oral sex in the "69" position.

"Sixty-nine" refers to the sexual position in which partners engage in simultaneous oral stimulation of each other's genitals (Figure 14.4). Although this position may seem appealing in theory, in practice it can be quite challenging! Why? Because focussing on your partner's pleasure while simultaneously attending to your own can be quite difficult.

INTERCOURSE AND OTHER FORMS OF PARTNERED SEXUAL STIMULATION
Partnered sexual stimulation occurs in various combinations and positions. Common non-penetrative behaviours include **frottage** ("dry humping"), tribadism (in which a woman rubs her vulva against her partner's body), and **interfemoral intercourse**. Intercourse involves intromission, or the insertion of a penis, dildo, or sex toy, into either the vaginal or anal opening, usually followed by thrusting or back and forth pelvic movements. Positions for intercourse often involve standing, kneeling, lying down, or sitting, and they can vary according to comfort, preference, flexibility, and of course, creativity. Among heterosexual adults, penile-vaginal intercourse, or **coitus**, is the most common partnered sexual activity. Common coital positions include woman on top (Figure 14.5), man on top (the "missionary position"; Figure 14.6), rear entry

frottage The sexual practice in which partners (clothed or not) rub or thrust their genitals against any part of the other person's body.

interfemoral intercourse The sexual practice in which a man moves his penis between his partner's thighs without intromission.

coitus Intercourse in which a man inserts his penis into a woman's vagina.

FIGURE 14.5 A couple engaged in intercourse in the woman-on-top position.

FIGURE 14.6 A couple engaged in intercourse in the man-on-top, or "missionary," position.

FIGURE 14.7 A couple engaged in intercourse in the rear-entry position.

(Figure 14.7), and side by side (with partners either facing each other or spooning, with the man facing his partner's back).

Orgasm

Orgasm is one element of the TSS that is not, strictly speaking, a sexual behaviour. It is a sexual response (see Chapter 4). Orgasm can be evoked by solitary sexual activities, such as masturbation, or partnered activities, such as oral sex. Orgasm appears to be an important element of our cultural sexual script. For example, university students are more likely to include a sexual behaviour (e.g., oral or manual genital stimulation) in their definitions of "having sex" if that behaviour has led to orgasm than if it has not (Randall & Byers, 2003). Indeed, orgasm is often viewed as a goal of love-making, as the end of a love-making session, and as an indicator of sexual satisfaction.

As sex therapists have suggested, however, there are several problems with these common assumptions. One problem is that the pressure to achieve the "goal" of orgasm may increase performance anxiety and interfere with sexual arousal and orgasm, particularly for those who have never experienced orgasm or have orgasmic difficulties. Another problem is that the TSS suggests orgasm should follow intercourse, and that it signals a finale to love-making. This approach can be problematic for individuals, particularly women, for whom intercourse does not often lead to orgasm; indeed, a vast majority of women report having orgasms more consistently with sexual activities other than intercourse (Zietsch et al., 2011). Further, this approach may lead some women to believe they have a sexual dysfunction simply because they do not orgasm following intercourse.

Sex researchers have long described orgasm as primarily a physiological response, although more recent definitions recognize its biopsychosocial aspects (Mah & Binik, 2002). From a physiological perspective, orgasm has been described as intense sexual arousal that briefly peaks and is followed by rhythmic contractions of the pelvic muscles. In addition, orgasm is almost always associated with ejaculation in men; the same physical "evidence" of orgasm is not usually found in women, although some women do experience female version of ejaculation (see Chapter 4). From a psychological perspective, Canadian researchers Mah and Binik (2002) found that both men and women endorsed similar sets of descriptors for their experience of orgasm. These descriptors constituted a two-dimensional model that included a sensory dimension, with descriptors such as "building" and "throbbing" sensations, and a cognitive-affective dimension, with descriptors reflecting "intimacy" and "ecstasy." Another study found that a panel of health professionals could not distinguish between men's and women's written descriptions of what their orgasms felt like once descriptors of ejaculation were removed (Vance & Wagner, 1974). Therefore, while anatomy may differ, the psychological experience of orgasm appears to be more similar than different for men and women.

Sexual Satisfaction and Sexual Preferences

Sexual Satisfaction

The majority of people surveyed in committed, long-term relationships report they are satisfied with their sexual relationship (Barrett et al., 2004). Nonetheless, a browse through your local bookstore's self-help section will demonstrate the fascination we currently have as a society with enhancing our sexual satisfaction.

Through the 1990s, research identified several factors that correlate with greater sexual satisfaction. These factors include *individual factors*, such as younger age, fewer sexual problems, and greater frequency of orgasm; *relational factors*, such as relationship satisfaction and effective communication; and *lifestyle factors*, such as working the same shifts (Christopher & Sprecher, 2000). However, high levels of sexual satisfaction are also found among couples with low levels or even the absence of many of these factors. For example, many highly satisfied couples report experiencing one or more sexual problems, and the frequency of sex appears to decline more rapidly than does sexual satisfaction as couples age (Christopher & Sprecher, 2000). You might wonder, how can people experience high sexual satisfaction alongside a sexual problem and/or fewer sexual interactions?

Questions such as this have led researchers in the new millennium to improve their definition of sexual satisfaction and to test models of how the identified factors of sexual satisfaction relate to one another. One possible answer rests in distinguishing sexual satisfaction from sexual functioning. For example, Canadian researchers Lawrance and Byers (1995) have operationally defined sexual satisfaction as "an affective response arising from one's subjective evaluation of the positive and negative dimensions associated with one's sexual relationship" (p. 268). Although positively correlated with sexual functioning, sexual satisfaction may be distinguished from sexual functioning because it reflects the interpersonal and affective qualities of sex, whereas sexual functioning focusses on sexual responses, such as arousal, orgasm, and lubrication (Rosen et al., 2000). It may be the quality of sex and intimacy rather than discrete sexual functions that ultimately determine sexual satisfaction.

One such relationally focussed approach to the study of sexual satisfaction is the interpersonal exchange model of sexual satisfaction (IEMSS; Figure 14.8) developed and validated by researchers at the University of New Brunswick (Lawrance & Byers, 1995). This model is based on social exchange theory, which describes discrete interpersonal behaviours or interactions as "exchanges." According to the IEMSS, individuals can experience a sexual exchange as either a reward (pleasing), a cost (displeasing), both a reward and a cost (pleasing in some ways and displeasing in others), or neither a reward nor a cost in their relationship. Consistent with this model, after controlling for relationship satisfaction, studies found that sexual satisfaction was greater, particularly over time, when individuals experienced more sexual rewards than costs, greater sexual rewards than costs relative to their expectations, and greater equality of sexual rewards and costs (Byers & MacNeil, 2006). Further, this combination of relationship satisfaction and exchange variables accounted for more than 80 per cent of the variance in sexual satisfaction over 18 months. This suggests that we are more sexually satisfied when we are relationally satisfied *and* when our sexual interactions with a partner include more of what we find pleasing and less of what we find displeasing, both currently and as time passes. Sex researchers have yet to distinguish whether it is sexual or relationship satisfaction that plays a primary role—maybe they both play an equally important role, or perhaps it varies depending on the individual

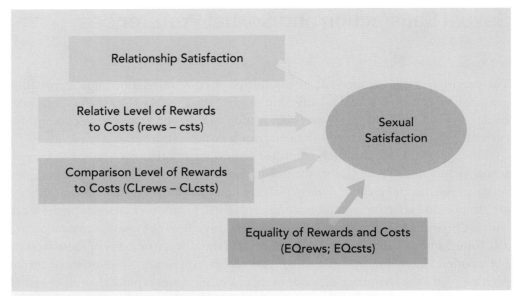

FIGURE 14.8 The Interpersonal Exchange Model of Sexual Satisfaction (IEMSS) shows the importance of relationship satisfaction, the relative level of rewards to costs, the comparison level of rewards to costs (based on what the person *expects* out of a relationship), and the perceived equality of rewards and costs to sexual satisfaction.

or couple. In the meantime, early or late in your relationship, it cannot hurt to attend to both the quality of your sexual relationship and the quality of your relationship in general.

Sex researchers are also increasingly surveying both partners within a couple to develop a more complete understanding of the relationship factors that contribute to sexual satisfaction. Byers and MacNeil (2006) found that men and women in long-term relationships were significantly more sexually satisfied the more their partner's sexual rewards exceeded costs, independent of their own level of rewards relative to costs or relationship satisfaction. In other words, a person is more sexually satisfied when both partners' sexual preferences are incorporated into love-making in a manner that maximizes rewards and minimizes costs for both.

Sexual Preferences

We have discussed how what we find sexually pleasing and displeasing is important to sexual satisfaction for both ourselves and our sexual partners. Sexual preferences, how-ever, vary somewhat between men and women and across sexual orientations. Studies have shown, for example, that heterosexual and lesbian women, and gay and bisexual men, report a greater affinity for the use of sex toys and for less orgasm-focussed sexual activities, such as sensual touching, when compared to heterosexual men (Herbenick, Reece, Schick, et al., 2010a; Holmberg & Blair, 2009). In terms of gender differences, men report engaging in masturbation more often, using **sexually explicit materials** more frequently, and having casual sex more often than women do, although some of these differences may be shrinking or explained by a reporting bias due to the sex-ual double standard (Petersen & Hyde, 2010). There also seem to be larger differen-ces within genders than between them on most sexual variables, especially when the comparison is between men and women from cultures demonstrating greater gender equality (see the "Culture and Diversity" box for more on the influence of culture, and see Chapter 10 for a more in-depth discussion of gender similarities and differences related to sexuality).

sexually explicit material
Textual, visual, and/or aud-ial material that promotes or creates sexual arousal.

Culture & Diversity

Acculturation and Sexuality in East Asian Canadians

Studies conducted in North America and Britain surveying diverse ethnic minority groups have consistently established that individuals of East Asian backgrounds have lower sexual knowledge, more conservative attitudes about sex, later first sexual experiences, less sexual experience, and fewer sexual responses compared with other minority groups (Brotto, Woo, & Ryder, 2007). In Canada, sex researcher Lori Brotto and her colleagues have studied the effects of acculturation on sexuality in East Asian Canadians living in Vancouver. (See the "Culture and Diversity" boxes in chapters 3 and 9 for more on the work of Brotto and her colleagues.) An interesting finding was that among East Asian–Canadian women who maintained strong ties with their heritage culture, greater mainstream acculturation did not reduce their sexually conservative attitudes. In contrast, among East Asian–Canadian women who relinquished their heritage culture to a greater degree, higher mainstream acculturation was associated with more liberal sexual attitudes. Further, despite the fact that sexual liberalism was lower and some sexual problems were higher for Asian-Canadian men and women, sexual satisfaction did not differ between cultural groups, nor was it affected by acculturation. What might explain this result? It is possible that Asians may have a higher tolerance for sexual problems and are therefore simply not as distressed by them, or that Asians may be less willing to report dissatisfaction because it is not culturally appropriate or because of embarrassment, anxiety, or guilt (Brotto et al., 2007). This valuable Canadian research underscores the importance of being attentive to cultural and ethnic differences in sexuality so that we can best meet the educational and treatment needs of the Canadian population.

People often believe they must find sexual partners with sexual preferences similar to their own to avoid problems or conflict. Fortunately, this does not appear to be the case, regardless of sexual orientation. Both other- and same-sex partners differ in at least a few sexual preferences, such as how frequently they desire sex (Cohen et al., 2008), and same-sex couples are no more or less sexually satisfied than their heterosexual counterparts (Holmberg & Blair, 2009). Moreover, agreement in sexual preferences explains only a small percentage of the variance in couple sexual satisfaction (Purnine & Carey, 1997). In general, it seems that partners sharing the same sexual preferences is only one of the factors contributing to greater sexual satisfaction among couples, meaning that it is unlikely that people develop sexually satisfying relationships simply by finding partners with sexual preferences that are exactly the same as their own.

How do partners successfully navigate differences in their sexual preferences, maximizing sexual rewards and minimizing sexual costs? One possibility is that couples use sexual self-disclosure and communication to negotiate a mutually pleasurable sexual script. Canadian research suggests that disclosing one's sexual preferences to one's partner contributes to greater partner awareness of one's sexual rewards, experiencing more sexual rewards relative to costs, and greater sexual satisfaction for both partners (MacNeil & Byers, 2005, 2009). Once partners have developed an interpersonal sexual script that realizes the preferences of both parties, they may reinforce this script through reciprocity and practice. Communication seems to be key, especially since many people may hold preconceived notions about their partner's sexual preferences. Indeed, research has shown that men and women often perceive their partner's sexual preferences as more stereotyped, and less flexible and compatible, than they actually are. For example, Miller and Byers (2004) found that both men's and women's perceptions of their partner's ideal duration of intercourse and foreplay were more closely related to their own stereotypes than to the actual self-reported preferences of their partners.

Use of Sex Toys to Increase Sexual Pleasure

In recent years, the use of sex toys to increase sexual stimulation and pleasure during masturbation and partnered sexual activity has grown substantially (Curtis, 2004). People may introduce sex toys into their sexual repertoire for therapeutic reasons (e.g., to treat a sexual problem), out of a desire to "spice up" their sex life, or to enhance sexual pleasure. Sex toys are widely available for purchase on the Internet, through mail-order catalogues, at sex shops, and recently via in-home sex-toy parties.

Perhaps the most widely known and used sex toys are the **dildo** and the **vibrator** (Figure 14.9). Dildos come in a variety of shapes and sizes, though many are shaped like a penis; they can be inserted into the vagina or the anus or used to stimulate other parts of the body. Some dildos are fitted with a strap so they can be worn by one partner during sexual activity ("strap-on dildos"), which frees up the wearer's hands for other activities. Vibrators also come in a variety of shapes and sizes. Small vibrators that can be placed on the finger are especially useful for clitoral stimulation. More elaborate vibrators have been developed in recent years, including the Rabbit, which consists of a dildo-like device and a vibrating clitoral stimulator, and the We-Vibe 3, a Canadian-made, hands-free vibrator that can be worn during penile-vaginal sex to stimulate both the G-spot and the clitoris. Other popular sex toys include **penis rings**, **beads** (or **balls**), **penis pumps**, and **penis extenders**.

According to one study, just under half of respondents had used sexual devices such as those listed above on at least one occasion. Women (33.1 per cent) were more likely than men (20.3 per cent) to report using a sex toy at least once during a typical four-week period (Foxman, Aral, & Holmes, 2006). A large majority of gay and bisexual men and women report using sex toys during both solo and partnered sexual activities, and they report doing so more often than do heterosexual men (Reece, Rosenberger, et al., 2010; Schick, Herbenick, Rosenberger, & Reece, 2011). Vibrator use is associated with better sexual functioning, particularly in women. Some women may be embarrassed or worried that their partner will be upset by their vibrator use. However, the majority of women's partners (male or female) expressed positive feelings toward their partner's vibrator use, and this support was in turn related to greater sexual satisfaction. It is likely that discussing and using sex toys openly contributes to feelings of sexual acceptance by one's partner and thus improves sexual functioning and satisfaction (Herbenick, Reece, Sanders, et al., 2010).

dildo A penetrative device, often shaped like a penis, that can be used to stimulate various parts of the body.

vibrator A vibrating device used to stimulate various parts of the body.

penis ring A ring placed at the base of the penis to prolong erection by keeping the blood inside the penis.

beads (or **balls**) A sex toy that consists of a series of balls connected by a string, and that can be inserted into the rectum or vagina and removed at varying speeds.

penis pump A device that draws blood into the penis, designed to assist men with erection difficulties.

penis extender A device that attaches to the penis to make the penis seem longer and/or wider.

FIGURE 14.9 Dildos and vibrators are among the most popular sex toys used in Canada.

Diversity in Sexual Relationships

Monogamous Relationships

Most people will, at some point in their lives, form a monogamous sexual relationship with another person. In Western cultures, most people's first experiences with monogamous relationships come from dating, and many people expect that they will one day "settle down" with a long-term monogamous partner. Monogamous relationships have long been a standard focus among researchers interested in studying couples' sexual behaviour and relationships, and the following sections will cover some common research findings about these sorts of relationships.

DATING

Traditionally, dating has been viewed as part of the courtship stage of a relationship. In dating relationships, partners acknowledge some uncertainty about how long they will be committed to each other. In North America, many young people start to date in preadolescence, around the age of 10 or 11. At this age, dating usually means attending parties or going on dates in large groups of both boys and girls. Dating in couples, or "going out" with someone, begins a few years later. National data suggest that adult Canadians recall starting to date at age 16 on average, but that they would ideally have started slightly later in retrospect (Bibby, 2004). Of course, dating can occur at any age and may not be exclusive to single individuals (see the discussions of non-monogamous relationships, below).

Dating Couples and Sex

In North America, dating emerges at approximately the same time, developmentally, as sexual attraction. Activities such as "spin the bottle" and other kissing games start to occur in late preadolescence; oral sex and intercourse typically occur later, often after individuals have entered into a dating relationship. Certainly, being in a committed dating relationship may contribute to partners' decisions to have intercourse, particularly for women (Sprecher, 2002). But there are several other reasons that dating couples may have sex, including to demonstrate their love to each other, to please each other, or to maintain their relationship.

As noted in Chapter 9, dating can be difficult for LGBTTIQQ adolescents, as they may face a lack of potential partners and social disapproval. Lesbian, gay, and bisexual youth, and those questioning their sexual/affectional orientation, may choose not to openly date same-sex partners in early adolescence for a number of reasons. Dating a same-sex partner can expose young people to harassment and homophobia in our society (see Chapter 11). Perhaps due to homophobia in society, coming out publicly at an earlier age has also been associated with a greater risk of negative outcomes (e.g., suicide) and discrimination (Hershberger, Pilkington, & D'Augelli, 1997). Adolescents may therefore defer same-sex dating until they feel safer. Nonetheless, LGBTTIQQ youth are often aware from an early age of a difference in their sexuality compared with society's heterosexist norms (e.g., the expectation that everyone is heterosexual, and that everyone's felt gender matches their biological sex). For example, one retrospective study of lesbian, gay, and bisexual youth aged 14 to 21 indicated that respondents were on average 10 or 11 years old when they experienced their first same-sex attraction (Rosario et al., 1996). Changes in Canadian laws to include same-sex marriages, gay–straight alliances in schools, and increasingly positive portrayals of same-sex relationships on television (e.g., on the TV show *Glee*) will hopefully improve the comfort level and outcomes for young people coming out in adolescence.

Internet Dating

Online relationships have been found to follow a similar developmental pattern to that of offline dating relationships (Sprecher, 2009). In the first stage, an individual becomes aware of a person she or he might be interested in dating, perhaps by reading that person's blog, web page, or online posts. In the second stage, the two people communicate or share some information about themselves with each other. Unlike in traditional in-person dating, in online dating at least one if not both parties have substantial information about the other gleaned from online sources. These days, one can look to Facebook, Twitter, blogs, and personal web pages to view pictures and learn about the interests, occupation, and even political and religious affiliations of a potential dating partner. This may be one reason that many Internet users perceive intimacy as developing so quickly in their online relationships. While a sense of connectedness might develop online, it is generally not until the two parties meet in person that the third stage of "couple identity" and interdependence truly emerges (Sprecher, 2009).

You may be wondering at this point whether relationships that begin and develop online stand the test of time. One study found that the majority of these relationships remained relatively stable two years later (McKenna, Green, & Gleason, 2002). In addition, recent findings suggest that between 3 and 6 per cent of current marriages or long-term relationships began online (Sprecher, 2009). Further, surveys conducted by a private research firm for Match.com found that 17 per cent of those married in the last three years met through an online dating service (Chadwick Martin Bailey, 2010). Some Internet dating sites match potential partners based on personality traits or interests, implying that this sort of matching results in longer-term relationships for their users. Marital experts, however, suggest that healthy communication and effective conflict resolution are better predictors of long-lasting relationships than are partners' similarities in interests or personality (Markman, Stanley, & Blumberg, 2010).

Overall, it appears the Internet is becoming a more common and acceptable medium by which to meet a potential partner and develop a dating relationship. Stereotypes about lonely, socially inept, or unattractive individuals seeking dates online are being challenged. Choosing to engage in online dating may depend on a range of social and psychological factors including one's peer group, cultural norms, prior dating experiences, and motivations for meeting a partner. To date, researchers have only begun to explore the growing phenomenon of online dating, and there remains a host of empirical questions for eager researchers to investigate to improve our understanding of the benefits and drawbacks of online dating.

COHABITATION AND MARRIAGE

The rate of people entering into marriages is declining in Canada among those in heterosexual relationships. This may be due to people getting married at an increasingly older age, or it may be due to an increasing number of couples cohabitating (Ambert, 2009). For example, in 2001, the number of Canadians between the ages of 18 and 34 who were married is less than half what it was 30 years earlier, while the number of cohabitating couples more than doubled in the same period of time (see Figure 14.10; Clark, 2007). It should be noted that the number of Canadians who remain single for longer has also increased considerably. This may be due to increasing numbers of young adults staying in school and completing post-secondary education before committing to longer-term relationships (Clark, 2007). In contrast to the declining marriage rate among heterosexual couples, however, the rate of same-sex marriages in Canada has increased now that the law recognizes these marriages (Ambert, 2005).

It is unclear why cohabitation has become an increasingly popular choice for heterosexual couples. One explanation is that young people may consider cohabitation helpful preparation for married life. Yet cohabitating relationships tend to be less stable than marriages, and marriages are more likely to dissolve when preceded by cohabitation. Some marital experts suggest this may be the case because couples may "slide" into a cohabitating relationship for pragmatic reasons (e.g. "it was time,"

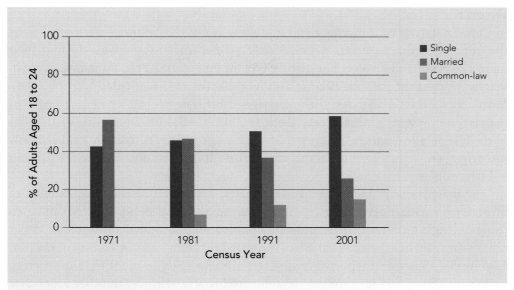

FIGURE 14.10 Percentages of Canadians aged 18 to 34 estimated to be single, married, or in common-law relationships in 1971, 1981, 1991, and 2001. Note that the 1971 Census did not enumerate common-law relationships.

Source: Adapted from Clark, 2007.

or to save on rent) rather than making a well-considered, long-term commitment to each other when moving in together, as is more often the case for those who decide to marry (Markman et al., 2010). This premise seems to be supported by the fact that cohabiting relationships tend to be slightly more stable when the couple have children (Ambert, 2009). It may be that couples are making a well-considered, long-term commitment to be together when they decide to have children, or it may be that the presence of children reinforces a couple's commitment to each other even when there is distress in the relationship. Some couples cite "the sake of the children" as a reason to stay together.

Satisfaction and Sexual Activity in Committed Relationships

A common stereotype about marriage and long-term committed relationships is that relationship satisfaction, sexual satisfaction, and frequency of sex deteriorate over time. Recent research challenges such assumptions. Sexual satisfaction can certainly fluctuate with life circumstances (e.g., childbirth, fatigue, financial stress, hormonal changes), but longitudinal studies suggest that couples who are relationally satisfied tend to stay sexually satisfied over decades, and vice versa (Christopher & Sprecher, 2000). Although the frequency of sex may decline over time, this decline is more closely associated with changes that result from the process of aging than with the duration of the relationship; in addition, as previously noted, a decrease in the frequency of sex does not necessarily indicate a decrease in sexual satisfaction. Sexual activity also appears to be most frequent, on average, for those in committed relationships (cohabiting or married) compared to those who are single or in less committed relationships. In Canada, 87 per cent of married couples and 92 per cent of cohabiting couples are having sex either monthly or weekly (Bibby, 1995). The remaining couples who report seldom or never having sex are not necessarily those who have been together the longest; rather, it is likely that other life circumstances are contributing to a decrease in the frequency of their sexual activity. Indeed, marital research suggests that most committed sexual relationships tend to ebb and flow alongside life circumstances.

Divorce

In Canada, having your marriage end in divorce is not the coin toss often implied by the popular media; however, a considerable proportion of Canadians do find their marriages ending in divorce. The divorce rate for first marriages in Canada is approximately 33 per cent and has been relatively stable for over a decade (Ambert, 2009). Most couples do not abandon their marriages quickly or easily. The average length of marriage before a couple divorces is about 14.5 years, reflecting an increase of 1.7 years in the last decade (Ambert, 2009). Because same-sex marriage has been legalized only recently, there is insufficient data to determine a long-term divorce rate for gay and lesbian couples.

The majority of people who divorce remarry, despite an increased probability of divorce with remarriage. Divorced individuals enjoy sexual opportunities similar to those of single or never-married individuals. According to Bibby (1995), while 19 per cent of divorced or separated Canadians reported that they had not had sex in the past 12 months, 38 per cent reported having sex at least weekly or monthly. Nonetheless, many individuals find it is not easy to adjust to life after divorce, and they experience new impediments to a satisfying sex life such as being older than they were the last time they were single or having children in the home. It does not appear to be an easy choice, as some might suggest, to re-enter a single life and begin dating again after having been married.

Non-monogamous Relationships

Non-monogamous sexual relationships are increasingly common and have become more socially acceptable than in the past. At the same time, while attitudes toward premarital sex are increasingly permissive, fewer people approve of extramarital sex (Petersen & Hyde, 2010). The individual variations in non-monogamous relationships often challenge common definitions of intimate relationships, making attempts to study such relationships particularly challenging for researchers. Nevertheless, researchers have conducted a variety of studies of non-monogamous relationships, and some of their findings are described below.

"FRIENDS WITH BENEFITS" RELATIONSHIPS

A covert, casual sexual relationship within a close friendship is probably not new or unique to the twenty-first century. What is emerging is greater acceptance of these relationships and a common term or idiom used to describe them—a "friends with benefits" relationship (FWBR). An example of an FWBR is described in the case study at the beginning of this chapter. An FWBR is characterized by four components: it is ongoing, it is sexual, no sexual or emotional exclusivity is required, and the relationship is rarely discussed directly or revealed to others (Bisson & Levine, 2009).

Consistent with the sexual double standard, it is possible that women are more stigmatized than men for engaging in these relationships. However, it is also possible that some women in FWBRs may enjoy more frequent sex than they would if they stuck to traditional dating relationships and expectations for their gender. Keeping the relationship secret may allow these women greater sexual expression without the risk of violating the sexual double standard publicly.

Traditional gender roles do, however, seem to influence many individuals' motivations for and expectations of these casual sexual relationships. One Internet-based study of individuals in FWBRs found that men were more often motivated by a desire for sex and hoped that the relationship would remain the same over time (Lehmiller, Vanderdrift, & Kelly, 2010). In contrast, the women surveyed were more often motivated by an emotional connection and hoped that the relationship would evolve into either a romantic relationship or a friendship without sexual involvement. Nonetheless, both men and women in this study were found to value the friendship over the sexual activity. Recent Canadian research suggests there may be some additional motivating factors for both men and women, such as considering the FWBR suitable to their stage of life and providing a sense of comfort and trust (Weaver, MacKeigan, & MacDonald, 2011).

Another study found that young people were more likely to engage in sexual activity with a romantic partner or with a casual acquaintance than with a friend. Conversely, they were more likely to engage in non-sexual activities with purely platonic friends than with friends with benefits (Furman & Shaffer, 2010). Thus, it seems that when people do opt for an FWBR, shared sexual activity is a major component of the relationship, but FWBRs are not necessarily a preferred type of sexual relationship.

Although most FWBRs are more commonly reported among younger adults, it is likely that they also occur among older adults. Recall that many individuals are staying single longer and marrying later (Ambert, 2009). In the absence of a viable potential life-partner, adults may develop more casual sexual relationships such as FWBRs.

POLYAMORY

Polyamory involves being in a romantic and sexual relationship with more than one person at the same time. In some cases, only one partner in a polyamorous relationship will be intimately involved with more than one person. In general, polyamorists describe their relationships as based more on love than on sex, relatively stable (some spanning decades), and relatively egalitarian (e.g., in terms of how time and resources will be shared among multiple partners; Barker & Langdridge, 2010). Some polyamorists are also co-parents. Limited, interview-based research suggests children may benefit from the shared resources and diverse role models provided by multidyadic parents (Barker & Langdridge, 2010). However, children being raised by polyamorous parents in societies in which polyamory is not the norm also reportedly suffer from social stigma, and they may face the loss of parental attachments if a relationship ends.

Polyamorous relationships can be very diverse in structure. In some cases, for example, two partners have a "primary" relationship, and all other relationships of the two primary partners are considered secondary or ancillary; in other cases, three or four partners form one unit, referred to as a "triad" or a "quad." While many of these emotionally bonded relationships are considered "exclusive" and partners agree to engage in sexual activity only with one another, some are "open" and partners may choose to have sexual encounters outside of the identified partnership or group. Polyamorists often have agreed-on rules to help manage jealousy, safety, and other complications of these multidyadic sexual relations. Refraining from vaginal and/or anal penetration, for example, is a common restriction on the non-primary sexual relationships (Barker & Langdridge, 2010). Note the contrast here to FWBRs, wherein polyamorists are public about at least their primary relationship, and they advocate open, direct, and honest communication about their relationships and sexual relations with others.

A diverse array of people are drawn to polyamorous relationships, for a variety of reasons. For example, self-structured polyamorous relationships often appeal to individuals who identify as bisexual, as well as individuals from the transgender, asexual, and BDSM (kink) communities (see Barker & Langdridge, 2010). As the norms of traditional sexual relationships often pose obstacles for members of these groups, it seems reasonable that polyamory may appeal to some because it offers a more flexible framework on which they can build the type of relationships they desire. Polygamous marriages, on the other hand, which can be seen as an institutionalized form of polyamorous relationships, generally appeal to heterosexual individuals who are members of groups that view polygamy as the norm, often for religious reasons.

POLYGAMY

Polygamy is a type of polyamory in which one person is married to more than one spouse simultaneously. As you learned in Chapter 1, polygyny (in which one man is married to multiple women) is far more common, globally, than is polyandry (in which one woman is married to multiple men). In North America, polygynists are predominantly heterosexual, and they tend to be conservative in their religious views and lifestyle; they also usually publicly recognize all of their marital relationships, legal or not (Bala, 2009). Wives in polygynous marriages have an emotionally and sexually exclusive relationship with their husband. Traditionally, a hierarchy of wives emerges, with older or non-childbearing (e.g., menopausal) wives and their children often holding lower statuses (Elbedour, Onwuegbuzie, Caridine, & Abu-Saad, 2002).

Historically, polygyny emerged in largely agrarian societies where having larger family units was an advantage. Today, polygynous marriages are generally associated in media with traditional Islamic beliefs that accept but do not require polygyny, and with fundamentalist Mormon communities that espouse polygyny as part of a faithful lifestyle. Modern polygyny has drawn dichotomous views of its risks and benefits, particularly for women and children. Advocates point out that in polygynous families, economic and parental responsibilities are shared, and a greater number of children (facilitated by having multiple wives) provides stability, social status, and security in parents' old age (Bala, 2009; Elbedour et al., 2002).

Research from across cultures and religious communities, however, suggests that a polygynous marital structure is often harmful to the welfare of a large number of women and children. Lack of social power, lower levels of education, significantly younger age at marriage and childbirth, parenting large numbers of children, and isolation from mainstream society are associated with the lives of women in polygynous communities (Elbedour et al., 2002). More women in polygynous marriages report psychological distress, financial stress, domestic violence, and marital problems than women in non-polygynous marriages. In addition, children from polygynous families tend to experience more behavioural, emotional, and academic difficulties than their peers from non-polygynous families (Eldebour et al., 2002).

In Canada, many had never heard of polygamy before it made front-page news in 2009, when charges of polygamy were brought against two prominent leaders of a fundamentalist Mormon group living in Bountiful, British Columbia (Bala, 2009). It is estimated that approximately 1000 individuals were living in polygynous families in Bountiful at that time. When news of the charges spread, the community referred media to a few female members who reported positive experiences in their marriages to polygynous husbands (Bala, 2009). In contrast, some women who left Bountiful, legal experts, and women and child advocates suggest that many women in the community and their children are economically and socially disadvantaged and isolated from mainstream society. (See Chapter 1 for more on this case, and on the legal status of polygamy in Canada.)

SWINGING

Swinging is the practice of both partners in an emotionally committed or married couple agreeing to and participating in sex with other individuals, usually at the same time. Swinging is notably different from polyamory because swingers do not typically emphasize feelings of love for partners other than their primary partner.

You may have heard the term *swinging* associated with the "sexual revolution" of the 1970s. However, swingers continue to place personal ads and create Internet sites to find partners, and many organize vacations together. There is nonetheless a lack of current research on swinging. Early studies indicate that most swingers are heterosexual, Caucasian, in married relationships, conservative in their political views, and similar to the average couple in the rest of their lifestyle choices (Barker & Langdridge, 2010). More recent studies suggest that many swinging women may be bisexual or "bi-curious" (Barker & Langdridge, 2010).

Couples engage in swinging for a variety of reasons, ranging from wanting to live communally with other swingers, to forming an emotional attachment with another couple, to pleasure-seeking or fun (Bruce & Severance, 2003). The couples in the former categories are obviously more likely to form closer ties with their extradyadic partners, whereas those in the pleasure-seeking category are more likely to swing with new partners more often. The two main reasons for "dropping out" of swinging are also the most common risks associated with swinging: jealousy and the risk of contracting STIs, particularly HIV/AIDS (Bruce & Severance, 2003). However, in contrast to typical participants in FWBRs, swinging couples describe practising safe sex, recognize their primary relationship publicly, and openly discuss the pros and cons of their swinging lifestyle, all of which may minimize these risks.

OPEN RELATIONSHIPS

Open relationships are more similar to swinging than to polyamorous relationships, in that most take the form of one primary and "emotionally exclusive" relationship where both partners freely consent to one or both partners having sexual relations, but not emotional bonds, with others (Barker & Langdridge, 2010, p. 759). It is dissimilar to swinging in that couples are not engaging in "partner swapping" or having sex with others at the exact same time. Similar to polyamorists and swingers, and distinct from individuals in FWBRs, couples in an open relationship tend to be public about their primary relationship and advocate open communication and safe sex to manage risks such as jealousy and STIs (Barker & Langdridge, 2010).

While some heterosexual couples, particularly during the so-called "sexual revolution," have entered into open marriages or relationships, open or non-monogamous relationships have been accepted for some time within the gay male community. And yet the majority of gay men do not engage in open relationships. Rather, many gay men seek monogamous relationships (Ambert, 2005).

INFIDELITY

Infidelity typically takes place *covertly* in the context of a relationship that is agreed by both partners to be monogamous. Infidelity is one of the most common reasons cited for separation and divorce, and one of the strongest predictors of divorce (Demaris, 2009). Infidelity can take the form of separate acts of extramarital sex or an ongoing affair, in which a married individual develops an emotional as well as sexual relationship with someone other than his or her spouse. A Canadian media poll found that almost 14 per cent of married men and 7 per cent of married women reported having had an extramarital affair (as cited in Barrett et al., 2004).

In one of the few prospective studies of risk factors for married individuals engaging in extramarital sex, Demaris (2009) surveyed a large sample of married Americans at six points over 20 years. Higher risk of extramarital sex was associated with *individual background factors*, such as being male or having divorced parents, as well as current *relational factors*, such as having considered divorcing, the presence of spousal violence, and decreased time spent with one's spouse. In contrast to retrospective research, this study found that the risk of extramarital sex was not associated with marital or sexual dissatisfaction, having had children, or opportunity to meet other potential lovers at work. It should be clearly stated, however, that researchers are not yet able to predict with a high degree of accuracy who will and who will not be unfaithful to a partner even when these individual or relational factors are present. These findings do suggest that cheating on one's spouse may have less to do with overall dissatisfaction in a relationship or opportunistic sex, and more to do with the current complaints in the relationship. Healthy communication often helps to resolve such complaints and further cements relationships (see Chapter 13).

Media

Many of the ideas people have about sex and relationships—what it means to "have sex," what behaviours are sexually exciting, what to look for in a partner, and so on—are heavily influenced by **mass media**. This should not be surprising, given that most Canadians are exposed to media content on a daily basis, and that much of this content is either obviously or subtly sexual in nature. For example, Canadians watch an average of 14 hours of television per week (Statistics Canada, 2011), and about two-thirds of the programming that appears on television in a typical week shows some kind of sexual activity (Kunkel et al., 2003). In addition, many Canadians use media, particularly the Internet, to actively seek out information on everything from safer sex to sexual techniques to how to build and maintain a sexual relationship with another person.

Theoretical Perspectives on How Media Influences Sexuality

Three theoretical perspectives have been suggested to explain how media influence individuals' sexual behaviour (Brown, 2002). These perspectives describe the impact of both overt and latent messages in media. In other words, they suggest that media influence us in ways that we are directly aware of, but also in more subtle ways that we do not consciously recognize. The first perspective is that of **agenda-setting theory**, which proposes that media affect what we think is important by highlighting what we should pay attention to; in other words, media set the agenda. From this perspective, sexual topics and issues that frequently appear in media, such as the scandalous sexual affairs of politicians or the AIDS epidemic in the 1980s, become more salient to media consumers, thereby influencing consumers' attitudes about these issues. The second perspective is that of **cultivation theory**, which suggests that we develop a shared set of values and expectations about reality based on depictions of reality in media. According to this perspective, media "cultivate" certain ideas about sex in media consumers by continually depicting sex in similar ways, according to societal values and stereotypes. The third perspective is that of **social learning theory**, which suggests that individuals will model their attitudes and behaviours after the fictional (and sometimes non-fictional) characters they see in media, especially when the models are rewarded for particular behaviours. Thus, media consumers are likely to model their sexual behaviours after sexual behaviours that are portrayed positively in media. Further, media depictions of sexual scenarios provide scripts for enacting certain sexual behaviours that people may not be exposed to elsewhere.

Positive and Negative Influences of Media on Sexuality

There are many ways in which media may negatively or positively affect our sexuality. On the one hand, being exposed to more sexual content on television is related

mass media All media technologies—including the Internet, television, newspapers, film, and radio—that are used for communicating with the public, and the organizations that distribute these technologies.

agenda-setting theory A theory that proposes that media influence our thoughts and behaviour by highlighting what we should pay attention to.

cultivation theory A theory that proposes that media portrayals create a shared set of values and expectations about reality among media consumers.

social learning theory A theory that proposes that individuals model characters seen in media, especially those who receive positive rewards.

to earlier age of first intercourse (Brown et al., 2006). What we see and hear through media may also reinforce unrealistic sexual expectations, sexually irresponsible behaviours (e.g., unsafe sex), and sex-related stereotypes. For example, the television sitcom *Will and Grace* portrayed many of the stereotypes associated with same-sex oriented men, such as being effeminate. Still, this show was one of the first to include openly gay characters in lead roles, and any media exposure to LGBTTIQQ content can be positive because it increases awareness of diversity.

On the other hand, media depictions of sexual behaviour may educate individuals about sexual-health issues, the meanings of sex-relevant terms and behaviours, and sexual and relationship norms. Brazil, for example, aims to promote awareness of sexual health and safer sex are forwarded by including messages in soap operas. It is also possible that portrayals of unsafe sex and its consequences may actually encourage adolescents to practise safer sex. Think of the popular *Friends* episode in which Rachel and Ross become pregnant when the condom they used broke. One study found that teen viewers of this episode reported more accurate information about condom effectiveness compared to non-viewers. Further, almost two-thirds of the teens surveyed reported learning to say "no" in a sexual situation by watching television, and 43 per cent said television content taught them how to talk to a partner about safe sex (Collins, Elliott, Berry, Kanouse, & Hunter, 2003).

Media may have a positive influence on sexuality in a number of other ways. First, media can provide quick access to reliable information on sexual health. A number of websites such as SexualityandU.ca, for example, provide excellent, easy-to-understand information about sexual health. Second, media offer diverse sexual models that may serve as personal role models and offer guidance for relationship interactions. Third, it is possible that media characters allow individuals to vicariously practise sexual and relationship norms and ideals. Imagine you were planning to ask a person out on a date for the first time, which for many is an intimidating task. Watching people do this on television can decrease the intimidation factor by giving ideas on how, when, and where to do it. Finally, newer media outlets such as **girl-zines** (or "grrrl-zines") may allow young women in particular an outlet for sexual expression (Ward, Day, & Epstein, 2006; Figure 14.11). Of course, it is important to actively question the credibility of the information published in these sources, as they are often based on one person's opinions and attitudes, rather than research. Still, they can encourage new perspectives for thinking about sexuality, and they provide an opportunity for young women to safely go against the sexual double standard—for example, by openly expressing their sexual desires. Clearly, access to the Internet has opened a world of possibilities for self-expression and information about sexuality.

girl-zines Self-published print or online magazines written by young women to express their thoughts and feelings about sexuality in a non-judgmental outlet.

FIGURE 14.11 Girl-zines, such as *Riot Grrrl*, are magazines written by youth to express their thoughts and feelings about sexuality.

The Internet

The Internet is perhaps the most comprehensive, easily accessible, and continuously evolving medium for sexual information, expression, and encounters. The popularity of the Internet has been described as being driven by the "triple-A engine" of accessibility, affordability, and anonymity (Cooper, Shapiro, & Powers, 1998). Indeed, the Internet allows us to access seemingly unlimited content with very little investment of financial or other resources. Anonymity, however, is a bit of a double-edged sword. While it allows individuals to explore their sexual desires in a relatively risk-free manner, people can never be certain of the identity of others with whom they communicate. This concern is especially salient for children and adolescents who may be more vulnerable to exploitation.

People use the Internet for a variety of sexual activities, including finding sexual partners, watching sexually explicit films, buying sexual toys or aids, seeking help for sexual problems, and engaging in erotic chatting. These sorts of activities are referred to as **online sexual activity (OSA)**, and they are generally grouped into three categories: (1) establishing and maintaining relationships, (2) obtaining sexuality information, and (3) obtaining sexual gratification (Goodson, McCormick, & Evans, 2000). Sexual gratification can be sought either by oneself or with a partner, and the Internet even allows partners who are in different geographic locations to connect sexually with one another by engaging in cybersex.

Research suggests that participation in OSA is quite common, particularly among young adults. According to a study of 760 Canadian undergraduate students, about half of respondents had engaged in OSA in the preceding 12 months (Boies, 2002). Forty-two per cent of these activities were relationship focussed, 53 per cent were information focussed, and 40 per cent were gratification focussed. Another study of Canadian undergraduate students found higher numbers of men (89.9 per cent) than women (54.6 per cent) participating in both solitary and partnered OSA in the previous month (Shaughnessy, Byers, & Walsh, 2010). Among men, there seem to be some notable differences in OSA. Men who have sex with men and bisexual men seem to make greater use of the Internet for sexual purposes than heterosexual men do, possibly because it serves as a safe environment for coming out or for seeking sexual encounters without publicly disclosing their sexual orientation (Daneback, Mansson, & Ross, 2007).

EFFECTS OF OSA ON RELATIONSHIPS AND INTIMACY

As you might expect, online sexual activity can have both positive and negative effects on relationships and intimacy. On the negative side, online text-based interactions may lead to communication problems between partners, especially because it is difficult to communicate emotional tone and humour without facial expressions, vocal tones, and gestures. In addition, over-involvement in solitary OSA may result in one partner neglecting his or her responsibilities toward the other, such as the responsibility to spend time engaging with the partner. A small number of cybersex users (approximately 1 per cent) develop a sexual addiction or compulsion that interferes with their relationships and ability to function in everyday activities (Griffith, 2001). Further, participating in a high level of cybersex has been associated with separation or divorce. Some partners may view cybersex as infidelity; in other cases, online affairs may lead to offline affairs. Perhaps as a consequence, the number of people seeking sex and relationship therapy for Internet-related problems has increased substantially in recent years.

In contrast and on the positive side, a survey of 8376 heterosexual adults in committed relationships found that mild or moderate amounts of OSA benefitted relationships for both men and women (Grov, Gillespie, Royce, & Lever, 2010). Specifically, OSA participants reported an increased quality and frequency of sexual activity,

online sexual activity (OSA) Activity that takes place via the Internet for any range of sexual purposes.

and increased intimacy with their partners. Further, men and women reported that engaging in OSA with their partner improved sexual communication between them. Perhaps this shared experience opens the door for couples to talk about their sexual fantasies and likes and dislikes, which otherwise may not have been discussed. Thus, while there is a tendency to focus on the detrimental impacts of OSA on relationships and intimacy, it is important to bear in mind the possible advantages and opportunities to improve one's sexual interactions when both partners are willing and when OSA is used in moderation and in the right context.

Sexually Explicit Material

Many people use sexually explicit material found on the Internet or in other media sources in their solitary and partnered sexual activities to enhance their sexual excitement and pleasure. One study found that 82 per cent of respondents aged 18 to 49 had read a sexually explicit magazine, 84 per cent had seen a sexually explicit film, and 34 per cent had watched sexually explicit films on the Internet (Traeen, Nilsen, & Stigum, 2006). Another study investigated the types of sexually explicit materials used by Canadian male undergraduate students and found that the percentage of students who viewed sexually explicit material in the preceding six months was highest for viewing nude images on the Internet and lowest for reading sexually explicit writing on the Internet (see Table 14.2; Morrison, Ellis, Morrison, Bearden, & Harriman, 2006).

Research has also found evidence that there may be differences between how men and women use sexually explicit material. For example, in a **meta-analytic review** examining gender differences in sexual behaviours and attitudes, Petersen and Hyde (2010) found that men reported more use of sexually explicit material than women did. However, this gender difference might be smaller in reality because women might underreport the frequency of their use of sexually explicit materials because they fear being negatively perceived by others.

TYPES OF SEXUALLY EXPLICIT MATERIALS

A variety of sexually explicit materials are readily available. From sexually explicit photos and videos available for free on the Internet to **soft-core** and **hard-core** magazines available for purchase at convenience stores to ads for **phone sex** services in your local paper, these materials are often difficult to avoid. Sexually explicit materials,

meta-analytic review A report that combines the effects found across multiple research studies.

soft-core Erotically suggestive without showing genitals or sexual penetration.

hard-core Explicitly depicting genitals and/or sexual penetration.

phone sex Sexual activity that takes place via telephones, either through live conversations or by listening to sexually explicit pre-recorded messages.

TABLE 14.2 Types of sexually explicit materials used by Canadian males in the preceding six months.

Sexually Explicit Material	% of Males Using Material
Video/DVD	74
Television	74
Books	41
Internet (nudity only)	77
Internet (sexual activity)	62
Internet (written materials)	32

Source: Adapted from Morrison et al. (2006).

particularly sexually explicit films, have traditionally been geared toward heterosexual men. More recently, a number of feminist directors such as Candida Royalle, Tristan Taormino, and Madison Young, some of whom began their careers as actors in sexually explicit films, have created materials that are geared more toward women and couples. Films that fall into this category tend to place a greater focus on plot and the development of relationships and intimacy before sexual activity begins. There is also a range of materials designed specifically for lesbian women and gay men, as well as people with particular sexual interests or fetishes. (See Chapter 18 for more on sexually explicit materials.)

Magazines

Probably the best-known sexually explicit magazines in North America are *Playboy* (soft-core) and *Hustler* (hard-core). Sexually explicit magazines became popular in the 1970s; however, magazine sales have declined steadily in recent decades, most likely due to the availability of sexual materials on the Internet.

Films and Videos

The 1972 film *Deep Throat* is often credited as being the first sexually explicit film to include a plot, character development, and relatively high production value. This movie paved the way for many more feature-length films of similar quality. In Canada, the television series *Bleu Nuit*, which aired in the 1980s and 1990s on weekends at midnight and typically showed European soft-core films, was popular with adults for many years, and it offered many adolescents staying up late with friends their first exposure to sexually explicit films.

Some amateur filmmakers enjoy creating their own sexually explicit movies, either for their own enjoyment, or for the enjoyment of others. These amateur movies have become increasingly easy to produce, especially with the advent of digital recording devices, and the Internet allows for fast, easy distribution and access. However, digital technologies can also pose problems for people who do not want their sexual videos to be widely shared. Once a digital video has been created, anyone with access to the video and an Internet connection can easily forward it to an entire contact list or post it to a public or semi-public Facebook page without the approval or knowledge of the video's creator.

A relatively new genre of film that bridges the gap between professional and amateur movies is that of the sexually explicit "reality" film. These movies are filmed and produced by professionals and marketed as depicting "real people having sex." A popular example is the *Girls Gone Wild* series of videos. To film this series, camera crews encourage attractive young women to expose themselves and engage in sexual activities. These women are often recruited while on spring break and staying at "all inclusive" resorts. This context makes them more vulnerable to exploitation because of frequent and heavy alcohol consumption, which may impair their judgment and increase the likelihood of their engaging in high-risk sexual behaviours (e.g., unprotected sex).

CHAPTER SUMMARY

People have different ideas about what it means to have sex. Traditionally, general conceptions of sex have reflected the TSS, which describes sex as a series of interactions between heterosexual partners and focusses on intercourse and orgasm as end goals. Today, research suggests that sexual practices and preferences are more varied and flexible than the TSS would suggest. In general, attitudes toward a wide variety of sexual behaviours and types of relationships have become more permissive and open in recent decades, although more people disapprove of infidelity today than in the past. Infidelity is one of the most common reasons cited for separation and divorce, and the deception involved marks it as different from other consensually non-monogamous relationships. The majority of Canadians express a desire to be in a committed, emotionally and sexually intimate relationship, and individuals in such relationships often develop sexual scripts, experiment with different types of sexual behaviour, and use sex toys and sexually explicit materials to enhance their sexual enjoyment. Many of the ideas we have about sexual behaviours and relationships are heavily influenced by media, especially the Internet, in both positive and negative ways.

DEBATE QUESTION

What might be some of the pros and cons of exposing youth to sexual content in media (TV, Internet, magazines, etc.)?

REVIEW QUESTIONS

1. How do varying definitions of "having sex" reflect traditional sexual scripts? How do they reflect more recent changes in attitudes toward sex?

2. Is sexual compliance always a bad thing?

3. What are some different things that partners can incorporate into their sexual repertoire to enhance pleasure and sexual satisfaction?

4. Why might many of the gender differences in sexual behaviours and attitudes appear to be shrinking? Why might some differences (e.g., differences in masturbation frequency, or pornography use) remain significant?

5. What are some of the benefits and drawbacks of participating in a non-monogamous sexual relationship? What are some of the benefits and drawbacks of monogamy?

6. How can mass media influence individuals' sexual scripts? How might this influence be positive? How might it be negative?

SUGGESTIONS FOR FURTHER READING AND VIEWING

Recommended Websites

National Survey of Sexual Health and Behaviour: www.nationalsexstudy.indiana.edu
Sex Educator and Therapist Betty Dodson with Carlin Ross: www.dodsonandross
   .com
SexualityandU.ca: www.sexualityandu.ca
Teen Sexual Behaviour Calculator: www.healthcalculators.org/calculators/teen_
   sexual_behavior.asp
Vibrators FAQ: www.vibrators-faq.com

Recommended Readings

Barbach, L. (1984). *For each other: Sharing sexual intimacy*. New York, NY: Signet.

Herbenick, D. (2009). *Because it feels good: A woman's guide to sexual pleasure and satisfaction*. Emmaus, PA: Rodale Books.

Mah, K., & Binik, Y.M. (2001). The nature of human orgasm: A critical review of major trends. *Clinical Psychology Review, 21*, 823–56. doi:10.1016/S0272-7358(00)00069-6

McCarthy, B.W., & McCarthy, E. (2009). *Discovering your couple sexual style: Sharing desire, pleasure, and satisfaction*. New York, NY: Taylor & Francis Group.

Petersen, J.L., & Hyde, J.S. (2010). A meta-analytic review of research on gender differences in sexuality, 1993–2007. *Psychological Bulletin, 136*, 21–38. doi:10.1037/a0017504

Zilbergeld, B. (1999). *The new male sexuality* (Rev. ed.). New York, NY: Bantam.

Recommended Viewing

Grupper, J. (Director). (2005). *Anatomy of sex* [Documentary]. USA: Tiger Tigress Productions.

National Geographic. (2008). *Taboo: Mating* [Documentary series episode]. In *Taboo*. USA: National Geographic Channel.

15 CHAPTER

Variations in Sexual Behaviour

KATHERINE S. SUTTON
AND CAROLINE F. PUKALL

LEARNING OBJECTIVES

In this chapter, you will

- find out about sexual behaviours that are commonly considered to be "atypical" or "paraphilic";
- discover that non-harmful expressions of certain paraphilic behaviours can be part of a healthy and fulfilling sex life;
- encounter various theories that attempt to explain the development and maintenance of paraphilias; and
- learn about various approaches to treating paraphilias in cases where the behaviours they entail cause harm in the person with the paraphilia and/or others.

Morpheous Speaks, and You'd Better Listen!

Morpheous is a Toronto-based kink author, sex educator, and photographer. He would like to set the record straight for some people who have the wrong idea about kink/BDSM:

The world has changed radically for the kink and BDSM community over the past 20 years. The terms *kink* and *BDSM* can be both inclusive and exclusive of one another. The working definition of *kink* refers to a wide range of sexualistic practices that are both playful and intense and all degrees in between. BDSM is an overlapping term that encompasses bondage and discipline, dominance and submission, and sadomasochism. Both kink or "kinky" and BDSM terms and practices can overlap in someone's interests and participation. Kink might include fetishism, consensual objectification, or the use of conventional and non-conventional sexual toys, while BDSM regularly incorporates role-playing and other mental aspects that reflect the participants' kinky interests. Information and knowledge grows, and the Internet has helped sexuality that was mostly marginalized to gain a greater acceptance. For good or bad, the Internet has changed it forever.

Let me explain.

The Internet pulled kink and BDSM from the shadows of clubs and a "secret" underworld and laid it out in the light of day. Of course there are those die-hards who started in the older clubs where you needed to know someone before you were ever invited to a BDSM or kink party and who felt that the Internet was cheapening their own growth and experience by suddenly casting all their "secrets" to the general public. I disagree. I started going to fetish parties in 1991. I was there at the time when you had to know someone to get in. What I observed was that, perhaps because the BDSM community was thought by many to be a sort of "secret underground club," much knowledge and education was also "underground," and a lot of people were misinformed, especially about safer-sex kinky practices. We know better now. By making knowledge and education available to the general public, not only does it potentially reduce the chance of harm (depending on the practitioners), but it gives people a firmer foundation to discuss their desires in an arena that is larger than ever previously imagined. Social networking has given many like-minded people a voice to express their desires and to find other people who are supportive of their desires (although sometimes people then forget their manners when interacting face-to-face!).

In my writing, lectures, and travels, my ultimate goal is to bring people together and to show that the more we are different, the more we remain the same around the world. Kinky and BDSM practitioners all want love and acceptance from those close to them—after all, who doesn't? Love and acceptance doesn't look any different for a classic nuclear family enjoying a picnic down by the park gazebo than it does for a six-way poly-gay leather family at a collaring ceremony. Being connected to others is what brings about the best of our humanity. Compassion comes from supporting your loved ones and learning to love others that may have desires that differ from your own. Regardless of the activities we enjoy, or where we enjoy them, the heart of kinky sex for me is connecting with others. I always tell those first starting out in an exploration of their sexuality that their Internet life is like a flashlight—it helps you find what you are looking for but it is just a tool to get there, it isn't the end goal. I want to reassure them that their desires aren't so different from others and that acceptance of their desires through consensual activities can be a lot of fun and can also be emotionally fulfilling. There should be joy in playtime and taking creative licence to give away your agency in making choices. There is a certain psychological freedom in your chosen role (dominant, submissive) for a few hours, days, or even a lifetime, and this choice is always an active one; it is never passive, even when you are the submissive partner.

It is essential to have the ability to share joy and laughter in a classroom and in a relationship. We call it "playtime" for a reason. As a formally trained educator, it is my personal belief that the use of play in learning to absorb and retain information is second to none. Children learn best this way, why is it adults forget this simple lesson as they get older? The new people I see in the lifestyle who start coming out to events are just as shy and nervous as the veterans were when they were in the same position long ago. I believe that being shy and nervous is an evolution of oneself, rather than a personal trait. I encourage new people to volunteer, help out, and become involved with the kink and BDSM communities.

Explore all the subtle nuances in your sex life in a healthy, positive way, and remember that there is joy in the lifestyle; in addition, remember that there are people who have been where you are now and who can help encourage and support you in your journey of sexual and self-exploration.

Craig Henshaw (B.Ed.), a.k.a. Morpheous

QUESTIONS FOR CRITICAL THOUGHT AND REFLECTION

1. What are your initial thoughts and feelings after reading this personal account of the BDSM community? Why do you think you feel this way?
2. How could someone approach her or his sexual partner with a "kinky" idea?

Introduction: What Is "Normal" Sexual Behaviour?

Normal is a difficult term to define. *Oxford Dictionaries Online* defines the adjective as "conforming to a standard; usual, typical, or expected," and also "(of a person) free from physical or mental disorders." Given the great amount of diversity in today's world, and the high prevalence of mental and physical illnesses, it would be surprising if many people met the definition for *normal*.

So how do we define what is "normal" sexual behaviour? We could first examine the issue from a statistical point of view. How many people need to engage in a particular sexual behaviour before it becomes normative? Before we can answer this question, however, we must consider how we might determine the prevalence of sexual behaviours, and how reliable our methods might be. Surveys, such as those used by Kinsey or the *Durex Sexual Wellbeing Global Survey* (2005), may shed some light on what goes on behind closed doors, but sex is a difficult topic for many people to discuss, and not everyone is open to participating in a survey on sexual behaviour. Plus, people may refrain from reporting their involvement in certain behaviours that they deem to be "abnormal" or that are illegal, for fear that they will face serious social or legal repercussions.

We could also take a socio-cultural approach to defining normalcy. All societies throughout history and around the world have established sexual "norms" in an attempt to control the sexuality of their members. When we think about "normal" sexual behaviour in the Western world, what comes to mind is typically filtered through a Judeo-Christian lens. Historically, this has meant that "normal" sexual behaviour is what occurs between one man and one woman who engage in sexual intercourse, likely in the missionary position, for the sole purpose of procreation (recall the supposedly popular Victorian wedding night advice to British brides to "lie back and think of England"). Within this socio-cultural context, such sexual intimacy was preceded by a period of courtship, perhaps arranged and supervised by family members, and sex was permitted only following the exchange of wedding vows. Of course, not many Westerners today follow this "norm," and it is not customary in other cultures. Thus, a socio-cultural approach can identify what is considered to be normal behaviour only in a certain time and place. That being said, there are some standard global taboos that cut across most cultural boundaries, such as **incest**, and non-consensual sex is rarely looked upon favourably.

A third approach defines behaviours that do not cause harm to any person as normal. By extension, this approach may also define behaviours that are consensual as normal, by the reasoning that that a person may be harmed by being involved in an activity to which she or he has not consented. As you might expect, definitions that are based on the concepts of *harm* and *consent* are also affected by socio-cultural influences. What we think of as harmful or as signifying consent changes over time and

incest Sexual activity between persons of a close enough genetic relationship that they are not legally permitted to marry.

from society to society, and our definitions of such concepts are often based on societal values and morals, not scientific fact. For example, in times when engaging in sexual behaviours for pleasure was not looked upon favourably, masturbation was thought to cause a variety of illnesses, and engaging in oral and/or anal sex was thought to be a sign of mental illness. Despite the potential limitations of this approach, however, it is thought to be relatively neutral and is thus used by many sex researchers.

How Are Atypical Sexual Behaviours Defined?

Atypical sexual behaviours are referred to as *paraphilias*, a word derived from the Greek *para* ("deviation") and *philia* ("love" or "attraction"). Typically, researchers, mental health practitioners, and others involved in the study of atypical sexual behaviours define paraphilias according to the guidelines set out in the *Diagnostic and Statistical Manual of Mental Disorders* (*DSM*). The most recent edition of the *DSM* (*DSM-5*) characterizes paraphilias as intense and persistent sexual interests other than sexual interest in genital stimulation or preparatory fondling with phenotypically normal, physically mature, consenting human partners. The *DSM-5* defines a **paraphilic disorder** as a paraphilia that is currently causing distress or impairment to the individual, or a paraphilia that causes personal harm, or risk of harm, to others when acted upon (APA, 2013).

The paraphilias exist on a continuum that ranges from "normal" to abnormal. Indeed, many people are aroused by or engage in some degree of the paraphilias described below from time to time, and occasional paraphilic interests are not considered abnormal or deviant, so you can breathe a sigh of relief! Paraphilic interests can be exclusive, meaning that the paraphilic object is the only thing that turns the person on sexually, or they can be non-exclusive, meaning that the person is aroused by more culturally typical sexual interactions as well as the paraphilic object. This distinction between exclusive and non-exclusive paraphilias may be an important one to make for providing appropriate treatments (see the section on treatment of paraphilic disorders later in this chapter).

Diagnosing Paraphilic Disorders

The *DSM* offers a comprehensive description of the signs and symptoms that are necessary to identify paraphilias and diagnose someone with a particular paraphilic disorder. Criterion A specifies the qualitative nature of the paraphilia (e.g., exposing one's genitals to strangers), and Criterion B specifies the negative consequences of the paraphilia (i.e., distress, impairment, or harm to others). Note that a paraphilia is a necessary but not sufficient condition for having a paraphilic disorder, and a paraphilia does not necessarily justify or require clinical intervention. In keeping with the distinction between paraphilias and paraphilic disorders, the term *diagnosis* is reserved for those individuals who meet both Criterion A and Criterion B (i.e., those who have a paraphilic disorder). If an individual meets Criterion A but not Criterion B (e.g., a case of transvestic fetishism in which a person cross-dresses but is not distressed by his or her behaviour), then that person is said to have a paraphilia, but not a paraphilic disorder. This characterization allows researchers and clinicians to differentiate between non-distressing paraphilic behaviours (e.g., sadomasochism) and diagnosable levels of paraphilic behaviours (e.g., sadistic disorder). In addition, for a diagnosis, the paraphilic disorder must have been present for at least six months. While it is argued that the six-month duration may be arbitrary, many believe that this is an adequate amount of time to establish that the paraphilic interest is not simply a transient reaction to a stressor or a passing interest.

paraphilia Any intense and persistent sexual interest other than sexual interest in genital stimulation or preparatory fondling with phenotypically normal, physically mature, consenting human partners.

paraphilic disorder A paraphilia that causes distress or impairment to the individual, or that may harm others when acted upon.

What Are the Commonly Identified Atypical Sexual Behaviours?

For the purposes of this chapter, paraphilias have been categorized into two major sections: paraphilias/paraphilic disorders that involve consenting partners, and paraphilic disorders that involve non-consenting people; the latter type are also those that are against the law in North America. Pedophilia will be considered in depth, and several other paraphilias/paraphilic disorders will be discussed in brief. Much of the information we have about paraphilic disorders comes from assessment and treatment of those who are criminally convicted of an offence and from individual case studies. We also have some information on paraphilias from those who are willing to participate in anonymous sex surveys, the first of which was conducted by Alfred Kinsey (see Chapter 1). Keep in mind that it is difficult to research characteristics of people who engage in atypical sexual behaviours because these behaviours are generally expressed in private, what happens behind closed bedroom doors is still considered by many to be a taboo topic, and atypical sexual behaviours and thoughts are often discouraged by society. For these reasons, many people are reluctant to participate in studies of atypical sexual behaviours, even in anonymous research, particularly if the behaviour is illegal or would have severe social repercussions (e.g., because they live in a small town, or because their partner is unaware of their atypical interests or behaviours).

Paraphilias and Paraphilic Disorders that Involve Consenting Partners

FETISHISTIC DISORDER

The term *fetish* was originally used to describe urges, fantasies, and behaviours in which non-living objects or specific body parts (known as partialism) are eroticized. Currently, fetishistic disorder involves the persistent and repetitive use of or dependence on non-living objects or a highly specific focus on a (typically non-genital) body part as a primary element associated with sexual arousal; this focus must cause significant personal distress or psychosocial role impairment. If a person has a leather fetish (Figure 15.1), for example, but does not report any clinical impairment in association with it, then this person would simply have a fetish, and not a fetishistic disorder. The *DSM-5* includes a caveat that the fetish cannot be limited to articles of female clothing exclusively used in cross-dressing or to devices specifically used for tactile genital stimulation, such as vibrators.

In the more extreme cases of fetishism/fetishistic disorder, the individual is unable to orgasm or even to become aroused unless the fetish object is present. Many people have milder fetishes in which they are aroused by objects such as lingerie; in these cases, the object does not play a central role in the individual's sexual experience, but rather acts to enhance it. Most fetishes are directly related to the human body or objects that are in close association with the body. Fetish objects also tend to be female gender–specific, such as women's shoes or lingerie (Cantor et al., 2009). A recent

FIGURE 15.1 This is an example of an outfit that might be arousing for an individual with a leather fetish.

online study of people with fetishes found that 33 per cent of individuals with object fetishes described their fetish object as something worn on the legs or buttocks, 32 per cent listed footwear, and 12 per cent listed underwear (Scorolli, Ghirlanda, Enquist, Zattoni, & Jannini, 2007). The same study found that feet and/or toes are the most commonly fetishized body parts, with 47 per cent of partialists reporting a foot/toe fetish. In addition, fetishes for bodily fluids and specific body sizes (e.g., large body size) were each reported by 9 per cent of the sample. Many individuals have more than one fetish (Scorolli et al., 2007), and fetishism can overlap with other paraphilias, such as sadism and masochism (Kafka, 2010).

Fetishes typically develop in early childhood or adolescence, and they appear almost exclusively in males. There is also some evidence suggesting that fetishes are a conditioned behaviour in which sexual arousal or orgasm is paired with a particular object. For example, one experiment showed that males in a laboratory setting could be conditioned to become sexually aroused to pictures of shoes (Rachman, 1966).

TRANSVESTIC DISORDER

The diagnosis of transvestic disorder applies to individuals whose cross-dressing or thoughts of cross-dressing are always or often accompanied by sexual excitement and who are emotionally distressed by this pattern, or who feel that it impairs social or interpersonal functioning. The *DSM-5* provides two specifiers for this diagnosis in men. (1) If an individual also reports sexual arousal to the fabrics, materials, or garments he is wearing, he is diagnosed with transvestic disorder with fetishism. (2) If the individual is sexually aroused by thoughts of himself as a female, he is diagnosed with transvestic disorder with autogynephilia (i.e., a male's paraphilic tendency to be sexually aroused by the thought or image of himself as a woman). The transvestic disorder diagnosis does not apply to all individuals who cross-dress, even if their cross-dressing is a habitual behaviour; as with the other paraphilias, distress must be present for diagnosis (Figure 15.2).

Most individuals with transvestic fetishism (or transvestic disorder) begin cross-dressing in childhood and masturbating while cross-dressing during adolescence (Dzelme & Jones, 2001). The median age at which men with transvestic fetishism (or transvestic disorder) first cross-dress is approximately 8.5 years (Bullough & Bullough, 1997). This fetish is usually harmless, and treatment is often sought only when a romantic/sexual partner is distressed by the behaviour. Men with this fetish are typically married and college educated (Docter & Prince, 1997). One study found that most wives of men with transvestic fetishism (or transvestic disorder) knew about their husband's cross-dressing from early on in the relationship (Bullough & Weinberg, 1988).

Transvestic disorder differs from transgenderism, which involves a person dressing as the other sex due to gender dysphoria (see Chapter 10); however, they can overlap. The *DSM-5* notes that the presence of the specifier of autogynephilia increases the likelihood of gender dysphoria in men with transvestic disorder (APA, 2013). There has been much

FIGURE 15.2 Male cross-dressers may be best known by the general public as "drag queens" or "female impersonators," who dress in women's clothing to entertain or to provide commentary on the portrayal of gender; however, there are many men who regularly cross-dress in the privacy of their own homes or in public because they find it sexually arousing. It is only the men in this latter category who are said to have transvestic fetishism.

debate in the academic and public spheres around this condition. Much of the debate surrounds the question of whether autogynephilia has been inappropriately applied as a label for some individuals with gender dysphoria (see Chapter 10). Autogynephilia is conceptualized as an erotic target location error (Freund & Blanchard, 1993) or an autoerotic paraphilia (a paraphilia relating to sexual arousal brought about by transformed images of oneself rather than of someone in the environment); it is considered to represent a misdirected male heterosexuality (Blanchard, 1991). Rather than an attraction to an external female, men with autogynephilia experience attraction to the

Ethical Debate

Voluntary Amputation

In 1997, a Scottish surgeon was approached by a man with an unusual request: to have his lower left leg amputated on the grounds that this part of his body felt alien to him. It was otherwise a healthy leg. Dr Smith consulted with psychiatrists and, after much deliberation, performed the amputation. A follow-up appointment two and a half years later indicated that the patient was satisfied with the results of the surgery; he reported that his life was much better since the amputation. Dr Smith was scheduled to conduct similarly motivated amputations of healthy limbs on other patients when the story hit the media and resulted in a public outcry. Smith was instructed to stop these procedures, and as far as we know, no hospital today performs amputations on healthy limbs. "Would-be amputees," or "wannabes," may number in the thousands, and some have their own websites meant to promote awareness for their condition (see www.reddit.com/r/IAmA/comments/9f8vg/i_need_to_be_an_amputee _yes_i_am_a_genuine for one example). Some individuals would even like to have parts of their genitals removed, as in the case of voluntary eunuchs (Johnson, Brett, Roberts, & Wassersug, 2007; see the chapter-opening case study in Chapter 4). Why would someone want a healthy part of their body amputated?

The answer is, of course, controversial and incomplete. Some believe that wannabes suffer from a form of body dysmorphic disorder in which they feel that their body is not "whole" if it is in fact whole; they have an overwhelming desire to take away a part of their body to feel as if they fit well in their bodies. For example, Smith's first patient indicated that his left leg was simply not a part of him. Others state that they will not feel "whole" with legs

(or arms, or some other body part). These wannabes want the amputation performed in order to feel complete in their bodies, perhaps similar to those with gender identity disorder who feel complete only when their external body matches with their felt gender. Other individuals, however, are sexually turned on by thoughts of being an amputee (termed *apotemnophilia*), or they are sexually attracted to amputees (termed *acrotomophilia*), or both. Indeed, there are likely several subgroups of wannabes.

With a lack of access to medical assistance, wannabes who desperately desire amputations may feel they are forced to take drastic measures on their own. Reports in the press have documented cases in which people have attempted to amputate parts of their bodies with such tools as shotguns and homemade guillotines, or with amateur freezing methods. There is no question that these individuals can suffer serious medical consequences, or even die, from these attempts. In some cases, individuals may become so frustrated by their condition that they contemplate or even attempt suicide.

When doctors are faced with the fact that the harm of amputation can actually be *less* than the harm of living with a whole body, how does the motto of "do no harm" fit in these cases? How ethical would it be to perform these surgeries? How liable would a surgeon be if she or he performed the procedure and the patient later regretted the decision? Is regret ever felt in these cases? Would a surgeon treat a wannabe who does not exhibit sexual arousal to the thought of being an amputee differently from a wannabe who has a form of body dysmorphic disorder? How is amputation of healthy limbs in these cases different from other forms of cosmetic surgery?

woman internal to themselves (Cantor et al., 2009). Other erotic target location error paraphilias include infantilism (an autoerotic form of pedophilia) and apotemnophilia (an autoerotic form of acrotomophilia, which is sexual arousal for amputees; see the "Ethical Debate" box). In the *DSM-5*, these paraphilic disorders are generally labelled as "other specified paraphilic disorders" (see Table 15.1, on p. 380).

SEXUAL SADISM AND MASOCHISM, AND THEIR ASSOCIATED DISORDERS

Sexual sadism and masochism are often discussed together because the roles are complementary. Their combination may be referred to as *sadomasochism*. Note that engaging in sadism and/or masochism with a fully informed, willing, and consenting partner is considered part of the "kink" or BDSM lifestyle, and many argue that this behaviour should not be pathologized (see Moser & Kleinplatz, 2005, and the "Culture and Diversity" box in Chapter 16). Some people, however, derive pleasure from sadistic and masochistic behaviours with the intent to cause serious harm or death to others or themselves. Indeed, such cases are pathological.

BDSM

BDSM, known more generally as "kink," is often confused with the *DSM* definitions of sadism and masochism. Part of BDSM encompasses sadism and masochism, but it also involves bondage and discipline, and domination and submission. Each of these areas

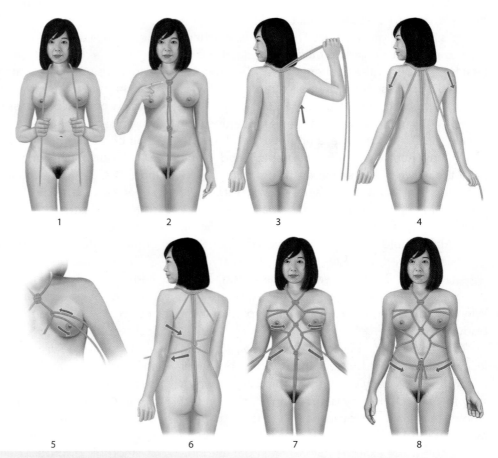

FIGURE 15.3 Japanese rope bondage, known in Japan as *kinbaku*, has recently become popular in North American BDSM communities. The practice consists of consensual bondage of an individual using decorative knots following specific aesthetic rules.

most often consists of consensual sexual behaviours, although there are some sexual sadists who engage in non-consensual sexual activities; however, these non-consensual practices are not related to the subculture of BDSM. Charles Moser observed more than two hundred BDSM parties over 25 years and published an article outlining the rules of etiquette and safety, as well as the norms. He concluded that overt genital play is not common, and that strict rules and safety precautions for BDSM activity are put in place before any activity occurs (Moser, 1998).

To get all the definitions right, here is an outline:

*   *bondage* and *discipline* (BD): Bondage is the use of restraints, from simple use of handcuffs or ribbons, to elaborate rituals and art forms such as Japanese rope bondage (Figure 15.3). Discipline may include painful whipping, biting, and the application of hot wax or other painful stimuli. It may also include sensory deprivation and humiliating behaviours such as boot-licking or behaving like a dog, or the use of feces or urine (Figure 15.4).
*   *dominance* and *submission* (DS): DS is about elaborate "play" scripts that can be specific to sexual interactions, or that can permeate into all areas of an individual's life through the formation of a DS romantic relationship. The dominant partner is often referred to as the "master" or the "top," and the submissive partner is often referred to as the "slave" or "bottom." There are also people called "switch" who change roles. People who engage in these exchanges are very meticulous and cautious in setting up the script and establishing consent and boundaries prior to beginning the scenario or relationship, to avoid any lasting physical (or psychological) damage. Negotiation is a key component, and "safe words" are determined beforehand for the submissive partner to use if she or he wants to stop the role play.
*   *sadomasochism* (SM): SM involves rituals and scripts surrounding the infliction of pain (sadism) or the receiving of pain (masochism) in a sexual context. Pain outside of a set sexual script (e.g., stubbing a toe or cutting a finger) is not arousing for individuals who engage in BDSM.

The sexual practices involved in BDSM rarely result in clinically significant psychological impairment; when they do, it tends to be because of the stigma expressed by mainstream society. Increased awareness in the media and popular books like *Fifty Shades of Grey*, however, may help with making the BDSM lifestyle more widely understood and accepted. Although the book *Fifty Shades of Grey* focusses on a character who is experiencing psychological problems, there is no evidence that psychological impairment or distress is any more prevalent in those who practise BDSM as compared with the general population (Richters, Visser, Grulich, & Rissel, 2008).

A wide variety of people engage in BDSM activities to varying degrees. According to the *Durex Sexual Wellbeing Global Survey* (2005) conducted in over 40 countries, 5 per cent of respondents identified with a BDSM community, and approximately 20 per cent of respondents had engaged in some form of bondage or light spanking during sex on

FIGURE 15.4 BDSM often involves scenes in which one partner consensually humiliates the other partner. Scenes are arranged in advance, and rules and limitations are determined prior to the start of the scene.

at least one occasion. Kinsey found, in his sexuality surveys, that approximately one half of males and females had experienced an erotic response as a result of being bitten while engaging in sexual activity, and that 12 per cent of females and 24 per cent of males reported an erotic response to a story about sadomasochism (Kinsey, Pomeroy, Martin, & Gebhard, 1953). Although the prevalence rate of BDSM activity is higher among men than among women, women are well represented in the BDSM community. (*The Story of O*, a novel published in 1954 that was made into a film in 1975, provides an interesting take on BDSM from a female perspective.)

Sexual Sadism Disorder

A sexual sadist is someone who derives sexual pleasure from inflicting physical pain or psychological suffering on another person, often to gain power or to humiliate the other person. The term *sadism* comes from the period of the French Revolution and is derived from the name of Donatien Alphonse François, Marquis de Sade. He wrote about his sadistic experiences, starting with the libertine novel *Justine*, also known as *Les Malheurs de la Vertu* (1791; Figure 15.5). His writings and behaviour landed him in mental asylums and prison on numerous occasions throughout his life. (The film *Quills* [2000] provides an overview of his life.)

Sexual sadism disorder involves recurrent and intense sexual arousal from the physical or psychological suffering of another person, as manifested by fantasies, urges, or behaviours; note that for the diagnosis to be applied, one must have acted upon these urges with a non-consenting person, or the sexual urges or fantasies must cause significant distress or impairment (APA, 2013).

FIGURE 15.5 This nineteenth-century illustration depicts a scene from the Marquis de Sade's famous novel *Justine*. The Marquis de Sade is often referred to as a "libertine," which is defined as an individual who lacks moral restraint. The philosophical movement of libertinism, which focusses on freedom and physical pleasure, was popular in the seventeenth and eighteenth centuries.

Sexual Masochism and Its Associated Disorder

A masochist is a person who derives sexual pleasure by experiencing pain, humiliation, or suffering. The term *masochism* was created in 1886 by Richard von Krafft-Ebing; it derives from the name of Leopold von Sacher-Masoch (1836–1895), who wrote novels about his masochistic fantasies. Sexual masochism disorder involves recurrent and intense sexual arousal from the act of being humiliated, beaten, bound, or otherwise made to suffer, as manifested by fantasies, urges, or behaviours; recall that for the diagnosis to be applied, the sexual urges, fantasies, or behaviours must cause significant distress or impairment (APA, 2013).

Theories of Development of Sexual Sadism and Masochism

Some theorists have proposed that sadomasochism, as with fetishes (see above), develops based on certain childhood or adolescent experiences. For example, being punished after being caught masturbating as a child may lead one to associate pain (if spanked) or humiliation with sexual arousal; however, Moser (1979) found that the majority of sadomasochists did not recall any erotic enjoyment from punishment as children. Masochism may also be explained by a desire to escape from self-awareness and remove pressures and responsibilities of everyday life. Perhaps the more burdens and pressures there are in one's life, the more desire one has to engage in masochism and give up all control and relinquish oneself to another (Baumeister, 1988). For the sadistic partner, the treatment of the submissive as a vehicle for his or her own sexual pleasure, rather than as an equal partner, may diminish some of the anxiety associated with sex (Baumeister, 1988).

HYPERSEXUALITY

The recent media craze over Tiger Woods's supposed "sex addiction" has brought a great deal of attention to the area of hypersexuality, an excessive, insatiable sex drive that leads a person to continually pursue sexual encounters, despite negative consequences. Historically, such behaviours were referred to as *nymphomania* in females and *satyriasis* in males. In one study, hypersexual behaviour in males and females was found to be associated with other risk-taking behaviours such as smoking, heavy drinking, and drug use. This study defined hypersexuality by preference for casual sex, extra-partnered sex, and group sex; a high frequency of masturbation and pornography use; and a high number of sexual partners (Långström & Hanson, 2006). Other studies have found high rates of comorbidity (co-occurrence) with substance-use disorders, depression, anxiety, and personality disorders (e.g., Raymond, Coleman, & Miner, 2003).

According to some researchers, hypersexuality is characterized by dysregulation in impulse control, resulting in excessive frequency and intensity of maladaptive sexual behaviours (e.g., Schwartz & Abramowitz, 2005). Other models proposed to explain hypersexuality have been based on the principles of addiction (e.g., Carnes, 1983; Potenza, 2006) and compulsivity (e.g., Coleman, 1987). Some researchers suggest that there is substantial overlap among these models (Hollander & Rosen, 2000). For example, the addiction model contains elements of impulsivity and compulsivity and may be referred to by any of these terms, and each model implicates difficulties with motivation and emotional regulation. The relative contribution of these constructs may vary over the course of the disorder, with early behaviours presenting as impulsivity problems and later behaviours having more in common with compulsions (Koob, 2006). These models are proposed to co-occur within individuals (Grant & Potenza, 2006).

Hypersexuality is estimated to affect between 3 and 6 per cent of the general population; however, there is currently no official *DSM-5* psychiatric diagnosis for people with a "sex addiction." Although eventually rejected, "hypersexual disorder" was proposed for inclusion in the appendix of the *DSM-5*. Diagnosis of hypersexuality can be covered through the *International Classification of Diseases* (*ICD-10*) of the World Health Organization, with the diagnostic code F52.7 (excessive sexual drive). The *ICD-10* also includes a diagnosis for excessive masturbation, classified under F98.8 (other specified behavioural and emotional disorders with onset usually occurring in childhood and adolescence).

In order to identify hypersexuality, even if we are unable to diagnose it using the *DSM*, we must consider the question, "What is an excessive frequency of sexual behaviour?" We may cite studies indicating that male undergraduate students masturbate an average of 12 times per month, and female undergraduates, 4.7 times per month (Pinkerton, Bogart, Cecil, & Abramson, 2002), and that the average number of times individuals aged 20 to 29 have sex per year is 117 (Durex, 2005). Keep in mind, though, that preference for frequency of sexual activity, including masturbation, is simply that—a personal preference; as a result, the meaning of "excessive frequency" will be different for every person. In addition, few individuals can be expected to exhibit statistically average tendencies, as statistical averages merely represent a calculated central value of a wide range of data points. Thus, hypersexual disorder does not simply entail engaging in sexual behaviour more frequently than what is deemed to be average; individuals who meet the proposed criteria for hypersexual disorder have significant impairment in their relationships, work, and education because they spend so much time thinking about or pursing sexual activities.

persistent genital arousal disorder (PGAD) Spontaneous, persistent, uncontrollable genital arousal that is not associated with sexual desire.

priapism A persistent, often painful erection.

Hypersexuality should not be confused with **persistent genital arousal disorder (PGAD)** in women or **priapism** in men, which are conditions that are not associated with persistent psychological sexual arousal, but rather with uncontrollable genital arousal.

Paraphilic Disorders that Involve Non-consenting People: The Courtship Disorders

A courtship disorder is a disturbance in one or more phases of the common Western notion of partnered sexual activity, which include (1) looking for and finding a partner; (2) approaching that partner with conversation; (3) non-genital physical touching; and (4) sexual intercourse (Freund & Blanchard, 1986). It is hypothesized that individuals with courtship disorders experience one or more of these phases in a distorted manner. Distortions of each phase will be discussed below: (1) voyeuristic disorder; (2) exhibitionistic disorder (and telephone scatologia); and (3) frotteuristic disorder. Biastophilia will also be discussed, although it is not currently a *DSM-5* diagnosis. Placing each of these disorders under the umbrella term of *courtship disorders* makes sense because they are highly comorbid (Freund & Blanchard, 1986); indeed, men with one of these disorders show elevated penile responses to stimuli depicting images associated with the other disorders (reported in Cantor et al., 2009). In addition, these paraphilic disorders are similar to one another in that they all often involve non-consenting victims. It is hypothesized that these disorders may develop because the individuals lack the proper social skills to approach partnered activity in a consenting manner.

VOYEURISTIC DISORDER

Voyeuristic disorder is diagnosed when an individual has recurrent and intense sexual arousal from observing an unsuspecting person who is naked, in the process of disrobing, and/or engaging in sexual activity, as manifested by fantasies, urges, or behaviours; in addition, the person has either acted upon these urges with a non-consenting person, or the urges and fantasies have caused distress or impairment (APA, 2013). Many studies around the world have found high prevalence rates of voyeuristic behaviours in both clinical (i.e., patient) and general populations (Långström, 2010). Although voyeurs may derive some satisfaction from "peep shows" or live-feed Internet pornography, the *unsuspecting* piece of the definition is a key component of their sexual arousal. Indeed, most voyeurs do not get a kick out of seeing naked people on a nude beach! In this scenario, naked people would not be an uncommon sight; plus, the fear of getting caught—which adds to the arousal of a voyeur—is absent, as the nudity is socially acceptable. Webcam broadcasts showing unsuspecting people in partial or full undress (e.g., in fitting rooms or washrooms) now exist and may provide an outlet for voyeurs; however, the excitement of potentially being caught in this act is diminished.

Many individuals show an interest in watching nude people, but this does not mean that they meet the criteria for a diagnosis of voyeuristic disorder. One study found that among university students, 84 per cent of males and 74 per cent of females would secretly watch an attractive person undress or two attractive people have sex if they were guaranteed not to be caught (Rye & Meaney, 2007). And you are not a voyeur if you like watching porn on the Internet or going to strip clubs from time to time. Voyeuristic behaviour becomes abnormal when it becomes preferred to partnered sex, when it interferes with a person's daily activities, or when it involves crimes such as breaking and entering. Although some women enjoy viewing pornography, going to strip clubs, or looking at sexually explicit magazines such as *Playgirl*, there are very few women who would meet the criteria for voyeuristic disorder. Indeed, the terms *voyeurism* and *voyeuristic disorder* are usually applied to heterosexual males.

A study of 62 treatment-seeking voyeurs found that approximately one-third of them had their first arousing voyeuristic experience before puberty and about half of them knew they had an interest in voyeurism before age 15. Voyeurism is often comorbid with many other paraphilias, including sadism, masochism, and exhibitionism (Abel, Becker, Cunningham-Rathner, Mittelman, & Rouleau, 1988). Voyeurism rarely leads to more intrusive sexual activities, such as rape, but this progression cannot be ruled out (Holmes, 1991). There is a positive association between voyeuristic behaviour and having more psychological and substance use problems, lower life satisfaction, and greater sexual interest (Långström & Seto, 2006).

EXHIBITIONISTIC DISORDER

Exhibitionistic disorder involves recurrent and intense sexual arousal from the exposure of one's genitals to an unsuspecting person; to be diagnosed with this disorder, the individual must have acted upon these urges with a non-consenting person or experienced distress or impairment from the urges or fantasies (APA, 2013; Figure 15.6). It is the victim's reaction that creates the sexual excitement for the exhibitionist. Acts of exhibitionism (often referred to as "indecent exposure") are among the most common of the law-breaking sexual behaviours (Långström & Seto, 2006). Such behaviours usually begin in adolescence, and their frequency decreases with age (Seligman & Hardenburg, 2000). The majority of exhibitionists masturbate to ejaculation while they expose themselves (Freund, Watson, & Rienzo, 1988). They may also masturbate to thoughts about the exposure at later times. Most exhibitionists are not looking to scare their victims. Rather, they hope that their victims might want to have sexual intercourse with them, or they hope for positive or neutral reaction from their victims (Freund et al., 1988).

As is the case with most paraphilias, exhibitionism is far more common in men than it is in women. Anecdotal evidence suggests that one possible explanation for this difference can be that men have fewer socially acceptable outlets for exposing themselves than women do—for example, at strip clubs, topless beaches, or events such as Mardi Gras. Or, it may simply be that this and other paraphilias, as we understand them at this time, generally apply more to males than to females.

TELEPHONE SCATOLOGIA

Telephone scatologia is diagnosed under the category of "other specified paraphilic disorder"; however, it will be discussed in this section due to its shared features with exhibitionistic disorder. Telephone scatologia is a form of verbal exhibitionism in which a person becomes aroused by making sexually explicit telephone calls, based on the reaction of the victim. The caller may masturbate during the call or while thinking about the call afterward. Some callers speak in obscene terms, indicating to the victim what they would like to do, and even threatening to come to the victim's home. Other callers may pose as police or survey representatives, including sex researchers, in order to ask personal questions or coerce the individual into performing various sexual acts while on the phone. Charges for making such calls can include sexual harassment and stalking.

FIGURE 15.6 Most acts of exhibitionism involve men exposing their genitals to women or children in relatively isolated settings, such as parks.

FROTTEURISTIC DISORDER

Frotter is a French verb meaning "rubbing" or "friction." Frotteuristic disorder is characterized by the act of fantasizing about, or actually engaging in, rubbing against or touching a non-consenting person for sexual gratification; to be diagnosed with this disorder, an individual must have either acted on these urges with a non-consenting person or experienced distress or impairment from the urges or fantasies (APA, 2013). Sometimes the touching, rather than rubbing, of others is referred to as **toucherism**. These behaviours usually occur in public, crowded areas where, if caught, the perpetrator can claim that the rubbing or touching was an accident. The frotteur is usually male, and victims are typically female. There have not been any large-scale non-clinical surveys to date to estimate the prevalence of frotteurism. In clinical samples, frotteurism was found to be highly comorbid with exhibitionism and voyeurism (Freund, Seto, & Kuban, 1997).

toucherism The act of fantasizing about touching, or actually touching, a non-consenting person for sexual gratification.

BIASTOPHILIA

Biastophilia is the erotic interest in committing rape (for a full discussion on rape, see Chapter 17). This paraphilia is not included in the *DSM-5*, though it was proposed to be included under the title of paraphilic coercive disorder. Not all rapists have biastophilia, and some individuals may suffer from this disorder without having committed rape. Those with biastophilia prefer rape to sexual interaction with consenting partners. Some non-paraphilic, non-criminal men and women report experiencing some rape fantasies (Arndt, Foehl, & Good, 1985); however, this paraphilia is far more common in men than in women.

Pedophilic Disorder

Age of consent, meaning the age at which an individual is recognized to be able to consent to sexual activity, varies by country and has evolved throughout history. Biologically, humans are ready to have sex when they are capable of reproduction; for girls, this occurs with first ovulation (shortly before menarche), and for boys it occurs with first ejaculation, around puberty. Culturally, though, the appropriate age for sexual activity is an entirely different standard. Although early marriages have been common throughout history, intercourse is typically not condoned or permitted until at least puberty. Sexual interest in children who are not of reproductive maturity by biological standards—that is, those who are prepubescent or pubescent—is considered paraphilic. This biological definition of age of sexual maturity is often, but not always, consistent with the legal age of consent in any given criminal code.

According to the *DSM-5*, the diagnosis of pedophilic disorder is specifically for individuals who have recurrent, intense, sexually arousing fantasies or urges involving sexual activity with a prepubescent child or children, generally aged 13 or younger, and who have acted upon these urges, or in whom the urges or fantasies cause marked distress or interpersonal difficulty (APA, 2013). **Pedophiles** typically report attraction to children of specific age ranges, and there is growing evidence that they may possess different characteristics based upon the age they are attracted to. Pedophilic disorder can involve exclusive pedophilia (i.e., the attraction is to children only) or non-exclusive pedophilia (i.e., the attraction is to adults as well as children).

pedophile An individual with an exclusive or non-exclusive sexual preference for children.

There have been many criticisms regarding *DSM* definitions of pedophilia, and many clinicians and researchers report that the criteria have limited utility (Marshall, 2007). A specific criticism of the current *DSM* definition is the exclusion of specifiers that would increase accuracy of diagnosis, namely by specifying whether the individual is sexually attracted to prepubescent children (Tanner stage 1), pubescent children (Tanner stages 2 and 3), or both. These specifiers would have been termed *classic type*, *hebephilic type*, and *pedohebephilic type*, respectively (Blanchard, 2013). Various criticisms that were made about the *DSM-IV-TR* also do not appear to have been resolved in the current *DSM*. First, Criterion B seems to be redundant, as anyone with sexual fantasies, urges, or behaviours toward children in our society is going to be socially impaired in some way because of our societal norms and laws against such attraction (O'Donohue, Regev, & Hagstrom, 2000). In addition, the definition seems to allow for the disorder to be diagnosed on a history of sexual acts alone, thereby blurring the line between the mental disorder of pedophilia and criminal sexual acts against children (First & Frances, 2008). It is important to note that while there is overlap between people who sexually offend against children and people who are diagnosed pedophiles, one is not the same as the other. The prevalence of pedophilia ranges from 40 to 50 per cent among males who sexually offend against children (Blanchard, Klassen, Dickey, Kuban, & Blak, 2001; Seto & Lalumière, 2001). Yet not all pedophiles actually offend against children (Federoff, Smolewska, Selhi, Ng, & Bradford, 2001), and we have no good studies to cite how common pedophilia is in the general population. Seto, Cantor, and Blanchard (2006) found that men who watch child pornography are "strongly" aroused by it, but these pedophilic interests do not necessarily result in contact offences.

Clearly, with the rise of the Internet there has been an increase in the accessibility of sexually explicit material, child pornography included. The Internet allows people to access pornography in the privacy of their own homes, giving people access to things they may not have sought out in more public spheres. So what consequence does this have on sexual offending? A meta-analysis found that only 12 per cent of sex offenders who are charged with online (child pornography) offences have a criminal history of one or more contact sexual offences; however, 55 per cent of men with a child pornography charge admitted to having had a contact offence for which they were not caught (Seto, Hanson, & Babchishin, 2011). Another meta-analysis of studies with a follow-up of 1.5 to 6 years post offence found that 2 per cent of online offenders committed a contact sexual offence and 3.4 per cent committed a new child pornography offence (Seto et al., 2011). Interestingly, it was found that online offenders with a history of contact offences had higher **recidivism** rates than contact-only sex offenders (Harris & Hanson, 2004), but those with no history of contact offences almost never committed any future contact offences (Babchishin, Hanson, & Hermann, 2011). Although the harm caused by contact offences is often more visible, it is important not to minimize the negative impact of online offences. The more demand there is for child pornography, the more children are harmed in the creation of the pornography to meet that demand.

recidivism Committing another crime.

In contrast to media depictions, most pedophiles do not prey on strangers, and most are not violent. Rather, they work hard to groom and coerce a specific child they are close to, such as a biological relative, a step-child, or a neighbour. Incest offenders have significantly lower rates of recidivism compared to non-incest offenders; offenders with only female child victims and older offenders also have significantly lower recidivism rates. The best predictor of recidivism that we have to date is arousal to children as measured by **penile plethysmography (PPG)** (Hanson & Bussière, 1998). Younger unrelated male victims, and more of them, correlate with higher sexual arousal levels to children (Seto & Lalumière, 2001). In self-report studies, findings suggest that pedophiles have greater preference for boys (e.g., Wilson & Cox, 1983); however, girls are preferred among men in forensic (i.e., criminal) samples (Blanchard et al., 2001). Participation and progress in treatment predicts lower rates of recidivism (Barbaree, Langton, & Peacock, 2006).

penile plethysmography (PPG) The direct measurement of changes in penile blood volume in response to external sexual stimuli.

Some pedophiles have put forth several arguments in support of what they feel is their "right" to have sex with children. Their most persistent argument is that contemporary societal values are too restrictive, and that general attitudes toward sexual matters change over time, as they have in the cases of masturbation and same-sex sexual behaviours; of course, this argument largely ignores the issue of consent. They also note that other paraphilias (e.g., "homosexuality") have been removed from the *DSM* and that sex with children has existed throughout history. While it is true that sex with pubescent children has existed throughout history, one is hard pressed to find any example of widely condoned sex with a prepubescent child. One organization that promotes the interests of pedophiles is the North American Man–Boy Love Association (NAMBLA). This group argues that sex with younger boys in the context of a loving relationship is not harmful and that this is a very different situation from that of individuals who prey on young boys exclusively for their own sexual gratification. Another attempt to justify pedophilic behaviour comes from men who have gone to countries such as Cambodia or Thailand and provided housing or school tuition for children in exchange for sex; these men often argue that the children's lives are better because of their "generosity" (see the "Culture and Diversity" box). Naturally, there is little support for any of these arguments among members of the larger society. But it's not all bad news! Dan Savage, of the syndicated sex-advice column *Savage Love*, has reported on what he calls: "Gold Star Pedophiles." These individuals have pedophilic interests, but they have not acted on these interests. Unfortunately, there is little in the way of research (or treatment), since these individuals are fearful of coming forward. Germany has an innovative project for such individuals: Prevention Project Dunkelfeld. This project aims to provide confidential and free support and counselling to individuals who are interested in children, and want help to manage those interests, but they are unknown to legal authorities. Their website is captioned "Do you like children in ways you shouldn't?" and can be found at www.dont-offend.org.

Other Specified Paraphilic Disorders

The category of "other specified paraphilic disorders" is reserved for paraphilic disorders that do not fit into the other categories of paraphilic disorders identified in the *DSM*. Necrophilia, apotemnophilia, and telephone scatologia are examples of other specified paraphilic disorders; Table 15.1 contains some additional examples. Many paraphilic disorders in this category may overlap with other paraphilic disorders.

TABLE 15.1 Examples of paraphilias in the "other specified paraphilic disorders" category.

Paraphilic Disorder	Description
Bestiality/Zoophilia	Erotic interest in non-human animals. The attraction is to particular species, breeds, and biological sex.
Asphyxiophilia	Erotic interest in using techniques such as strangulation or suffocation by oneself or a partner to create an oxygen deficiency in the brain, which enhances sexual excitement and orgasm. The wish to die from lack of oxygen is not a part of this sexual practice; however, it is probably the unintended consequence more often that we think.
Coprophilia	Erotic interest in contact with feces. This may overlap with sadomasochism.
Urophilia	Erotic interest in contact with urine. This may overlap with sadomasochism.
Necrophilia	Erotic interest in sexual contact with a dead person. This may include mutilation of the corpse following sexual activity.
Hyphephilia	Arousal to the feeling of a particular texture (e.g., leather, hair, fur).
Klismaphilia	Arousal to enemas, the injection of liquid into the rectum through the anus, usually for cleansing or for stimulating evacuation of the bowels.
Stigmatophilia	Arousal to partners who are pierced or tattooed.

Culture & Diversity

The Child Sex Trade in Southeast Asia

Child sex tourists are people who travel to various countries around the world in order to engage in sex with children without legal consequences (or at least with less chance of being arrested). Historically, this travel has been primarily to Southeast Asian countries such as Thailand and Cambodia; however, more recent tourist sites for child sex trade include Mexico, Central American countries, and Caribbean countries such as the Dominican Republic.

It is estimated that more than a million children are forced into the sex trade each year (US Department of Justice, n.d.). Poverty is a driving force of the child sex trade, and clients often attempt to justify their actions by claiming that the money they provide in exchange for having sex with children improves the lives of the children, their families, and others in the community. Governments of countries in which **sex tourism** operates do not openly condone the sex trade, but they may turn a blind eye because of the profit the tourism generates for their countries. Other ways perpetrators justify their behaviour is by thinking that children outside of Western countries are less inhibited sexually, and that because there is a child sex trade in these countries, having sex with children must be less of a social taboo there, so they are not harming the children in the same way as they would be in the Western world. There may also be a racialized view of "us" (the tourists) and "other" (the local children), with the sex tourists viewing the "others" as less human than themselves.

An article in *The Globe and Mail* (Stackhouse, 1997) offers some insight into the mentality of child sex tourists. It discusses the arrest of a Canadian man, Manfred Gast, who retired to Cambodia in 1993 and was formally charged with "debauchery" by Cambodian police. Gast justified his "relationship" with one young boy in particular by saying that he found him as a street orphan and provided him with "shelter, food, games, and about $1 a day in pocket money." He stated, "Did I fondle him? Yes. But you must understand the boy never had a home and no one ever cared for him." He further stated that this boy was too young to ejaculate and, therefore, the relationship was not sexual. He saved oral sex and penetrative activities for the older boys he abused.

The US and Canada have both begun to prosecute people for crimes committed against children while out of their home country. Since 1997, Canada has had a sex tourism law that allows for the prosecution of Canadian citizens and permanent residents who commit sexual crimes outside of Canada; however, it is costly and difficult to investigate and prove such offences (for more on human trafficking, see Chapter 17). Donald Bakker was the first Canadian to be convicted of this offence, in 2005. There is criticism that Canada has convicted only this one individual since the enactment of this law, suggesting that officials are not following through with a tough enough stance on child rights.

> **sex tourism** Travel for the purposes of engaging in uninhibited sex.

What Factors Play a Role in the Development and Maintenance of Paraphilias/Paraphilic Disorders?

There is not one scientifically accepted theory to explain the development and maintenance of paraphilias/paraphilic disorders. In fact, we are still not sure exactly what factors or combination of factors play a role, but it is likely that the contributing factors differ from individual to individual. Explanations also differ depending upon the specific type of paraphilia that is exhibited; however, given the great extent of comorbidity among the paraphilias/paraphilic disorders, they likely have many shared etiological factors. Some proposed theories are outlined below, from some of the classic theories based on psychoanalysis to theories based on modern scientific studies using brain-imaging techniques.

Psychoanalytic Theory

According to psychoanalytic theory, paraphilias are thought to result from castration anxiety and the Oedipus complex (see Chapter 2), explaining why they are more common in males than in females. In this explanation, the fetish object is an unconscious replacement for the mother's missing penis and therefore reduces the male's castration anxiety evoked by the missing penis of his female partner (Steele, 1996). The fetish object is hypothesized to be the object last seen by the boy prior to his realization that his mother does not have a penis, and this is why it is typically something feminine (Wiederman, 2003). According to psychoanalytic theories, all paraphilias are hypothesized to involve issues about masculinity or femininity. For example, exposing one's penis is an assertion of masculinity (Kaplan, 1991). Object-relations theorists propose that sexual abuse or trauma in early childhood results in an inability to maintain healthy sexual and romantic adult relationships. Proponents of this theory believe that this hypothesis may explain courtship disorders, sexual satisfaction through objects/fetishes, and relationships based on a disproportionate use of power, including pedophilia. Several studies have demonstrated that child sex offenders (not necessarily pedophiles) report less secure childhood and adult attachments than non-sex offenders do (Smallbone, 2006).

Behavioural Theory

Freud thought of children as "polymorphous perverse," meaning that they could become aroused to anything. Although Freud's theories follow a very different psychological model, in this case his idea fits with the theories about how paraphilias develop later put forth by social learning and behavioural theorists. These theories propose that the development of paraphilias occurs through classical conditioning, in which the paraphilic object or action comes to be paired with sexual arousal over one or more trials in which sexual arousal is accidentally associated with it. According to John Money (1984), if normal sexual curiosity is punished or discouraged, a child may redirect her or his sexual energy toward a permitted object, resulting in the development of a paraphilia. In males, this association may also occur accidentally through the experience of an unanticipated erection being associated with whatever activity the male is involved in at the time. The media may play a role in this as well by sexualizing items such as shoes, cigarettes, and cars in advertising and elsewhere. Along this line, feminists argue that if society encourages the objectification of women, it would be natural to associate feminine objects with sexual arousal, thus explaining many fetishes. Objectification of women may also explain paraphilias that involve violence toward women.

Neurological Findings

More recent studies have begun to explore the role of altered brain functioning and structure in paraphilias. So far, these studies have mainly focussed on identifying factors that may relate to pedophilia. **Neuro-cognitive testing** has demonstrated, for example, that pedophiles have lower IQs than non-pedophile offenders, and surveys reveal that they are more likely to have repeated school grades or received special education (Cantor et al., 2004; Cantor et al., 2006). These findings do not appear to extend to other paraphilias/paraphilic disorders, though more research is needed (Cantor et al., 2009). Brain-imaging studies show that, in comparison to non-pedophiles, pedophiles show deficits in brain activation associated with sexuality when they are viewing sexual pictures of adults (Walter et al., 2007) and significantly more activation in an emotional processing area of the brain (the amygdala) when looking at pictures of children wearing swimsuits (Sartorius et al., 2008). A recent imaging study found that brain response patterns to sexual stimuli are able to identify a group of averaged brains of pedophiles

neuro-cognitive testing The administration of tests that contain tasks designed to measure the functioning associated with a particular brain area in order to diagnose deficits and strengths in the manner in which a person perceives and navigates the world.

from non-pedophiles (Ponseti et al., 2012) though the technology is certainly not such that one could be identified as having pedophliic interests simply from undergoing a brain scan! Studies also demonstrate structural differences in the brains of pedophiles versus non-pedophiles. Pedophiles have decreased gray matter volume in the orbito-frontal cortex, the cerebellum, and the ventral striatum (Schiffer et al., 2007; Figure 15.7), as well as in the right amygdala (Schiltz et al., 2007). When pedophiles were compared with men with a history of committing non-sexual crimes, no decrease in grey matter was found between the groups; however, a decrease in white matter volume of the temporal and parietal lobes was noted, as well as a number of deficits in the cortical regions known to be associated with the recognition of sexual stimuli (Cantor et al., 2008). Such studies suggest that people with certain brain characteristics may have a susceptibility to pedophilia, though further research is needed.

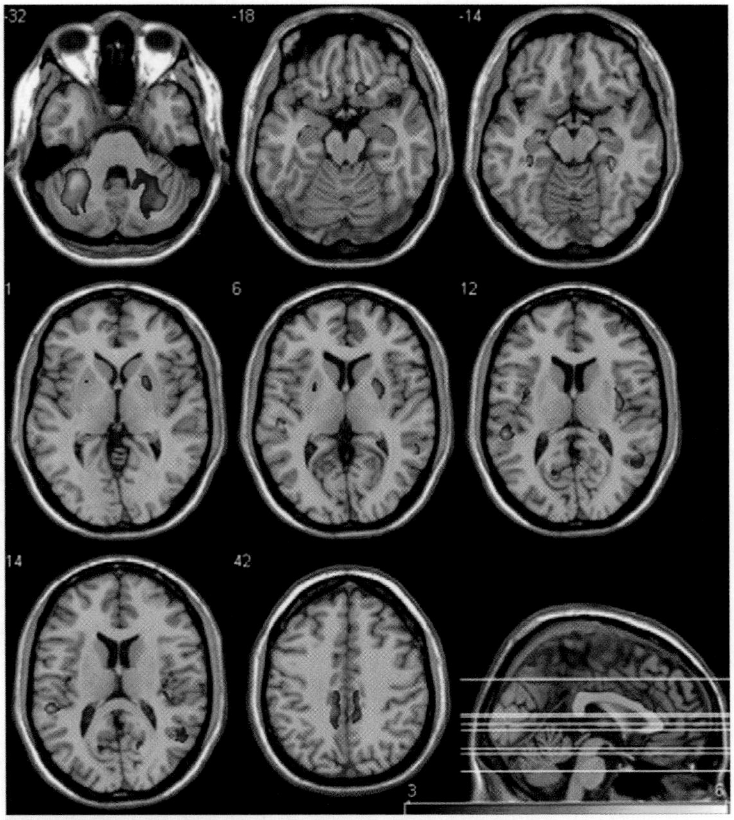

Theories of Development and Maintenance of Pedophilic Disorder

Far more research has been done on pedophilic disorder than on other paraphilic disorders because of the high prevalence of men who are arrested for child sexual offences. As suggested in

FIGURE 15.7 Did you know that we are in the early stages of examining paraphilias using brain imaging? Schiffer et al. (2007) have found that brain scans of pedophiles show decreased gray matter volume in the orbitofrontal cortex, the cerebellum, and the ventral striatum as compared with males who do not have paraphilic or pedophilic interests.

the previous section, one theory about the development of paraphilic disorder is that it may relate to certain functional and structural developments in the brain. Another theory is that, in certain cases, it may stem from sexual abuse suffered as a child. Although not all victims of child sexual abuse develop pedophilic disorder or sexually offend against children, there are a high number of child sex offenders who were abused as children; one study estimated 35 per cent (Bradford, 2001). Choice of age and gender of the victims may also be reflective of child abusers' own abuse (Pollock & Hashmall, 1991).

Other theories have suggested that individuals with certain behavioural characteristics may be more likely to develop pedophilic disorder and/or commit sexual offences against children. For those who sexually abuse children, three main risk factors are currently proposed: (1) sexual deviance, for example pedophilic disorder; (2) antisocial traits (i.e., traits associated with antisocial personality disorder); and (3) intimacy deficits, including poor social skills and identification with children (Seto et al., 2011). These factors are also used in assessment of risk of recidivism.

Another widely held theory, which is not mutually exclusive to the above noted theories, is that pedophiles who sexually abuse children likely suffer from thinking errors, or **cognitive distortions**. Indeed, the model of cognitive distortion is the predominant model that is currently used to understand sexual offending. Cognitive distortions are often statements that individuals make to themselves that act as excuses to allow them to rationalize, justify, minimize, or deny that they are behaving in an

cognitive distortions
Thinking errors or irrational thoughts.

inappropriate manner. Common examples of cognitive distortions in sex offenders who abuse children include "the child seduced me," "it's better he/she learn about sex from me than from some stranger," "he/she is too young to remember," and "I am doing nothing wrong, people have been having sex with children for centuries, it is our uptight Judeo-Christian societal values that are harming the child, not me."

Sex Differences in Paraphilias

As mentioned previously, paraphilias are more common in males than in females. Various explanations have been proposed to account for this difference. One explanation, for example, is that there may be more males than females with paraphilias because of the evolutionary sex differences based on males being able to inseminate multiple female partners for biological fitness. From this point of view, it would be beneficial for males to become aroused to a variety of stimuli that do not contain emotional content, such as fetish objects (Wilson, 1987). Another explanation is based on the observation that it may be the combination of sexually explicit stimuli and widespread prohibitions about sexual behaviour that drives some paraphilias (Steele, 1996). This explanation might partially explain the male–female difference in paraphilias because most of the sexual stimuli in Western culture are aimed at a male audience (Wiederman, 2003).

Assessment of Paraphilic Disorders

In order to develop a treatment plan for an individual diagnosed with a paraphilic disorder, one must first understand the nature of the paraphilia and the impact that it is having on the person's life. Assessment consists of an interview, including a general background of the client (e.g., family and educational history); a mental and physical health history; and an extensive sexual and relationship history. **Malingering** and downplaying of symptoms should also be assessed, especially in forensic populations; however, clinicians need to maintain awareness that, even when the person is not intentionally trying to deceive them, the person may not have the insight or be able to articulate his or her history in a way that they can take what the person says at face value. Assessment may also include **psychometrics**. For example, intelligence tests, personality inventories, and measures of mental health may be used to enhance a clinician's understanding of her or his client. It is essential that assessment of forensic populations also includes risk assessment measures for rates of recidivism.

For research purposes and in criminal cases, particularly those involving offences against children, penile plethysmography (PPG) may be used to assess paraphilic interests. PPG is the direct measurement of changes in penile blood volume, which is an indicator of level of sexual arousal; increased penile blood flow in response to external stimuli is indicative of sexual preference for that stimuli. PPG can be used to assess age and gender preference and preference for coercive versus consenting sexual interactions by having the man listen to auditory stimuli (e.g., audio recordings) and/or look at visual stimuli (e.g., slides or videos) depicting sexual scenarios or individuals that vary by age, gender, and degree of consent. There are presently two methods for collecting data on PPG: circumferential and volumetric (Figure 15.8). The circumferential method measures blood flow through a penile strain gauge placed approximately two-thirds of the way down the man's penis. For the volumetric method, the man's penis is placed in a condom and then into an airtight glass tube; as he gets an erection, air is displaced and changes in volume are measured to assess level of erection. The volumetric method is more sensitive than the circumferential method in detecting

malingering Intentionally faking or exaggerating symptoms for personal gain.

psychometrics Measurement, development, or administration of psychological tests.

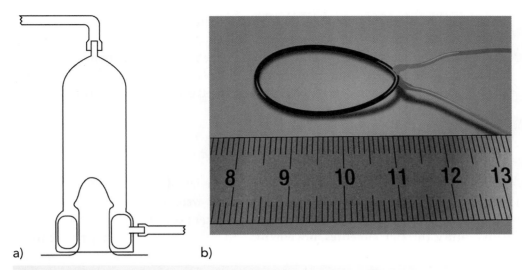

a) b)

FIGURE 15.8 a) The first volumetric penile plethysmograph was developed in the 1950s by Kurt Freund. It was originally used to detect men attempting to get out of military service with false claims of being gay, although Freund also used this technology in his research for detecting courtship disorders and pedophilia. b) A more common method, due to its ease of use, is the circumferential method, which relies on, for example, a mercury-in-rubber strain gauge. This device is placed around the shaft of the penis and measures minute changes in circumference.

small changes in penile blood volume, although the circumferential method is used more often because it is simpler and less invasive, with the man being able to place the strain gauge on himself (Kuban, Barbaree, & Blanchard, 1999).

Criticisms for PPG include the lack of standardized guidelines for using these methods, including lack of a standardized cut-off rate for how much of an increase in circumference or volume reliably indicates sexual preference for a particular item. These tests may also be subject to manipulation on the part of clients, by trying to suppress or enhance their arousal as they deem appropriate; we cannot ever fully assess the degree to which clients are paying attention to the presented stimuli. That being said, studies using phallometric testing have found that men with prior offences against children who self-report not being attracted to children still show greater arousal to depictions of children than they do to depictions of adults, and they show greater arousal to children than do sex offenders with sex offences only against adults (e.g., Blanchard et al., 2001). Interestingly, heterosexual male volunteers without sexual interest in children display some arousal to prepubescent girls on phallometric testing that exceeds their arousal to male stimuli; however, the response is less than that to stimuli depicting adult females (Freund, McKnight, Langevin, & Cibiri, 1972).

Although we have similar means to measure sexual arousal in women, physiological testing measures are not used in cases of female sex offenders. Researchers have demonstrated that in contrast to men, who demonstrate physical arousal that is consistent with their self-reported turn-ons (e.g., straight men respond to female stimuli and not male stimuli), women become genitally aroused to a variety of sexual stimuli, including stimuli that they do not rate as mentally arousing, such as sex scenes that are inconsistent with their sexual orientation or even scenes of bonobo monkeys copulating. This finding makes it difficult to assess sexual preferences as a means of assessing risk for recidivism in women (Chivers, Rieger, Latty, & Bailey, 2004).

In the US, polygraph tests (a.k.a. lie detectors) may also be used in the assessment and risk management of sex offenders. Those who use the test believe that it provides the clinician with highly accurate information, when used appropriately (Grubin, 2008); however, there are many criticisms of this method as well (Meijet, Verschuere, Merckelbach, & Crombez, 2008). One suggested benefit to the use of polygraph tests is that it might increase the number of truthful disclosures because of the "bogus pipe-line" paradigm in which people reveal more just based on the belief that the device can detect their lies (see Chapter 10).

Treatment of Paraphilic Disorders

eugenics movement A social movement in which society is thought to be improved by controlling the passing on of heredi-tary information through controlling which members of society are allowed to procreate.

Treatment of paraphilic disorders dates back to the late nineteenth century and the medicalization of sexual deviance. Almost all cases were identified in men, and the initial treatment was surgical castration. This treatment continued well into the twen-tieth century, through **eugenics movements** and attempts to reduce the risk of recid-ivism. There is no good evidence to suggest that paraphilic interests can be changed. However, treatment can focus on the management of the interest, and when consen-sual, the integration of the paraphilic interest in a way that is healthier and more accept-able for the individual can be achieved. The role of psychotherapy in the treatment of individuals with paraphilic disorders began with behaviour therapy and aversion treat-ments in the 1960s, and the current trend is to use **cognitive-behavioural therapy (CBT)** treatment (Gordon, 2008). Psychotherapeutic treatments can be individual or group based. Group treatments are useful because they can help to reduce isolation and shame, and they often encourage clients to challenge one another as peers. In the past and today, treatment efforts have focussed on individuals with paraphilic disor-ders who have also engaged in illegal behaviours related to their paraphilias, and it is these sort of treatment efforts that are focussed on below.

cognitive-behavioural therapy (CBT) Therapy based on the view that internal mental processes reciprocally interact with behaviours and emotional responses.

CBT and Relapse-Prevention Techniques

Most sex offender treatment follows the CBT model (Kaplan & Kreuger, 2012), usually paired with relapse-prevention (RP). Much of the work is typically done in group set-tings. Treatment intensity (frequency and duration of meetings) depends on recidivism risk. A variety of treatment approaches are in use today, but it is generally agreed upon that group treatment using CBT/relapse prevention with a social-skills component is the gold standard. As with much psychotherapy, therapist characteristics that maxi-mize treatment outcome include empathy, warmth, directiveness, and rewardingness (Beech & Hamilton-Giachritsis, 2005). This model focusses on challenging an offend-er's cognitive distortions about sexual offending; encouraging the offender to empa-thize with others; getting the offender to take responsibility for offending, including a disclosure of the offence to the group; identifying personal risks for offending, includ-ing paraphilic sexual preferences; and developing personalized safety plans to address those risks (Marshall, Marshall, Serran, & Fernandez, 2006).

Self-Esteem and Social-Skills Training

Self-esteem and social-skills training is typically done in a group setting, in conjunc-tion with the CBT/relapse-prevention model. This therapy is intended to target the risk factor of loneliness and to help build social skills for engagement with age-appropri-ate colleagues and future partners. Assertiveness, anger, impulsivity, mood manage-ment, and healthy relationships are all topics that may be covered in this training. Development of social skills and reintegration into society are important factors in reducing recidivism; however, society often does not take rehabilitation into account, focussing instead on punishment (see the "Research vs Real Life" box).

Research VS Real Life

Sex Offender Registries

Megan's Law is an American law that was passed on a federal level in 1996. This law was developed in response to the murder of seven-year-old Megan Kanka, who was lured into her neighbour's home and raped, strangled, and suffocated. Little did the neighbourhood know that her neighbour was a sex offender with two prior convictions. Megan's Law mandates that communities have access to information about the presence of convicted sex offenders in their neighbourhoods. This information includes the offenders' names, addresses, photographs, and crimes. The amount of information made available to the public and the amount of time a convicted sex offender is registered for is dependent upon the state. Megan's Law has led to the development of several mobile applications ("apps") that allow individuals in the US to track sex offenders. These apps provide the addresses of and other information about registered sex offenders in a given region. One of the first such apps, Offender Locator, quickly became one of the top-10 paid iPhone apps shortly after its release in 2009 (Siegler, 2009). Another app, Sex Offender Tracker, has also become popular, particularly after it was endorsed by Antoine Dodson, whose *Bed Intruder Song* went viral in 2010. These apps have remained popular despite objections that charging for them constitutes the selling of personal information, making them illegal in some states. Canada also has a National Sex Offender Registry, which was established by the Sex Offender Information Registration Act, passed in 2004. The difference between the Canadian registry and the US registry is that the public does not have access to the registry in Canada. Its purpose is to provide useful information to police services in the tracking and investigation of sexual crimes.

How many of the sex offenders identified on sex offender registries are actually a risk to the community? Findings depend upon how we define recidivism—whether it is a new charge, a new conviction, a self-report of a new offence, or simply a suspicion that a new offence has occurred. An amalgamation of a series of studies on recidivism, as measured by charges and/or convictions, has revealed that the risk of recidivism for offenders having committed contact sexual offences was approximately 13 per cent after 5 to 6 years (Hanson & Bussière, 1998), and approximately 33 per cent after 20 to 30 years (Hanson, Steffy, & Gauthier, 1993). Other studies have shown that the longer a person abstains from reoffending, the lower their risk becomes, such that, for example, risk in the first year of release is higher than risk in the tenth year. Unfortunately, many sexual offences are also never reported, causing a perpetual underestimation of the actual risk of recidivism, and of course offenders whose crimes are not reported will never be found in a sex offender registry.

Much of the criticism of sex offender registries is based upon the US model in which there is public access. One criticism is that public access to tools such as sex offender apps may give people a false sense of security because they believe that they know where all the sex offenders are located and may not consider the many sex offenders in existence who have never been convicted or individuals who have yet to commit their first offence. Another criticism is that public access to sex offender registries may lead to social isolation of individuals listed in these registries, and loneliness is a big risk factor for recidivism. Thus, public awareness of a sex offender's identity may actually increase his or her risk of reoffending.

Another thing to consider is who is on the registry. Convictions are not standardized; for example, a conviction of sexual assault can mean anything from something the public might think of as harassment (e.g., slapping someone on the buttocks) to violent rape. In addition, there are certain cases in which individuals might be convicted of a criminal sexual offence for actions that are of little harm to the general public. A relatively recent example concerns **sexting** among adolescents. Some teens in the US have recently been arrested with child pornography charges

> **sexting** The sending of sexually explicit photographs or messages via mobile phone.

after sharing naked pictures of themselves via their mobile phones with their boyfriends or girlfriends. One particular case in Pennsylvania involved three teenage girls sending nude photos of themselves to three male classmates. The girls were charged with manufacturing and disseminating child pornography. The boys were accused of possessing child pornography. Should these teens be on the sex offender registry? In many states they will be required to!

Satiation Therapy

Satiation therapy requires the client to masturbate to an appropriate fantasy and then masturbate again immediately following orgasm to an undesired fantasy. The idea behind this treatment is that the decreased sex drive on the second masturbation attempt will make the experience less exciting, and eventually the pairing between the undesired fantasy and sexual arousal will diminish.

Orgasmic Reconditioning

Orgasmic reconditioning requires the client to masturbate to the paraphilic fantasy until the point of orgasm, at which time the fantasy is switched to a more socially acceptable one. The goal is for the client to come to associate orgasm with a more appropriate stimulus.

Aversion Therapy

In aversion therapy, fantasies of the paraphilic behaviour are linked with an unpleasant stimulus, such as an unpleasant smell or an electric shock. This form of therapy is meant to condition the client to associate the unpleasant stimulus with the paraphilic behaviour, so that he or she no longer associates the paraphilic behaviour with pleasure.

Community-Based Support Programs

Community-based support programs for hypersexuality are often modelled on the 12-step program of Alcoholics Anonymous, and they are often used to treat "sexual addictions." Examples include Sexaholics Anonymous (SA) and Sex and Love Addicts Anonymous (SLAA). Community-based support programs are also offered for sexual offenders. These include, Circles of Support and Accountability (COSA) and programs run through the John Howard Society, both of which provide community support for convicted sex offenders once they are released.

Medical Treatments

Paraphilic disorders, often those that have resulted in legal repercussions, or those that have not responded well to other treatments may warrant pharmacological treatment, starting with a course of anti-depressants. If these are not effective within four to six weeks, a small dose of an anti-androgen may be added to reduce sex drive (Bradford, 2001). Anti-androgens can be delivered orally, often with the patient self-administering the drugs, or through intramuscular injections by a physician. Injections are the preferred method for ensuring treatment adherence and monitoring for cases that involve criminal activity.

Chemical castration is not always an effective treatment option, for a variety of reasons. For instance, compliance with chemical castration is often a problem due to the variety of side effects, such as feminization of the body in terms of fat distribution, reduced body hair, and loss of muscle mass. In addition, the reduction in sex drive is not limited to sexual arousal related to the paraphilia, so chemical castration is likely to interfere with other treatments designed to encourage appropriate partnered sexual activity in order to reduce the risk of recidivism. Further, patients may decide to take sexual enhancement/erectile functioning drugs to overturn the effects of the anti-androgen. Finally, this treatment may not be useful for particularly violent offenders or those for whom the ability to achieve an erection is not part of the offence. In fact, even following surgical castration, serious reoffences, including murder, have been reported (Raboch, Cerna, & Zemek, 1987).

CHAPTER SUMMARY

The issue of defining "normal" versus "abnormal" sexual behaviour can be approached from a variety of view points, including statistical, socio-cultural, and whether it causes harm. Readers are encouraged to think about their own views of "normal" sexuality and take their personal and socio-cultural contexts into account. The *DSM* captures a number of "abnormal" sexual activities under the diagnostic label of *paraphilic disorder*. There are a number of concerns about this classification of sexuality, and scientists and clinicians alike agree that criminal sexual behaviours need not be thought of as paraphilias to be illegal, and that normalizing particular paraphilias does not mean that we are condoning illegal activities. There are many paraphilic activities that do not meet the *DSM'S* Criterion B for causing distress, and research indicates that individuals with paraphilias do not differ from people with "normal" sexuality on a variety of psychological and social-functioning measures. The paraphilic disorders identified in the *DSM-5* are summarized in the chapter, along with relevant information about characteristics of those who meet criteria for them. One paraphilic disorder in particular that draws a great deal of attention is pedophilic disorder, as some people who suffer from this disorder also engage in the criminal activity of sexually abusing children. Although we do not know exactly what causes pedophilia/pedophilic disorder or other paraphilias/paraphilic disorders, several theories have been proposed. Treatment for diagnosed paraphilic disorders requires assessment of the impact the disorder has on the individual's life, and it generally involves individual or group psychotherapeutic treatments.

DEBATE QUESTIONS

What are the pros and cons to having an application that lists information about sex offenders in your area? Would it be wise to place your peace of mind regarding the safety of your children on this information, especially since many children are victimized by someone well known to them, such as a male relative?

REVIEW QUESTIONS

1. What are three ways in which "normal" sexuality can be defined?
2. What is Criterion B in the *DSM*, and why is it important to consider when discussing the paraphilic disorders?
3. What are the courtship disorders, and why are they defined as such?
4. What might be the ethical implications of using brain imaging to identify pedophiles?
5. What are the three main risk factors used in the assessment of recidivism of sex offenders who target children?
6. How are sex offenders different from pedophiles? How are they different from sadists?

SUGGESTIONS FOR FURTHER READING AND VIEWING

Recommended Websites

DSM-5: www.dsm5.org
Association for the Treatment of Sexual Abusers (ATSA): www.atsa.com
Sex Education Links, on paraphilias: www.bigeye.com/sexeducation/paraphilias.html

Recommended Reading

Blaney, P.H., & Milton, T. (Eds). (2009). *Oxford textbook of psychopathology* (2nd ed.). New York, NY: Oxford University Press.

Browne, R.B. (1982). *Objects of special devotion: Fetishes and fetishism in popular culture*. New York, NY: Bowling Green University Popular Press.

Hirschfeld, M., Lombardi-Nash, M.A., & Bullogh, V.L. (1991). *Transvestites: The erotic drive to cross dress*. Buffalo, NY: Prometheus Books.

Marshall, W.L., Marshall, L.E., Serran, G.A., & Fernandez, Y.M. (2006). *Treating sexual offenders: An integrated approach*. New York, NY: Routledge.

Morpheous. (2008). *How to be kinky: A beginner's guide to BDSM*. San Francisco, CA: Green Candy Press.

Ost, S. (2009). *Child pornography and sexual grooming: Legal and societal responses*. New York, NY: Cambridge University Press.

Young, K.S. (2001). *Cybersex: Uncovering the secret world of Internet sex*. London, UK: Carleton Publishing Group.

Recommended Viewing

Broomfield, N. (Director). (1996). *Fetishes* [Documentary]. United States: Lafayette Films.

Gilbert, M. (Director). (2003). *Whole* [Documentary]. United States: Frozen Feet Films.

Jaeckin, J. (Director). (1975). *The Story of O* [Motion picture]. United States: A.D. Creation.

Kaufman, P. (Director). (2000). *Quills* [Motion picture]. United States: Fox Searchlight.

16 CHAPTER

Sexual Dysfunctions

PEGGY J. KLEINPLATZ

LEARNING OBJECTIVES

In this chapter, you will

- discover some common causes of sexual difficulties;
- learn about the major sexual problems that men and women may face;
- consider some of the underlying factors that can contribute to sexual difficulties; and
- become familiar with the kinds of help that are available for people who seek treatment for sexual concerns.

A New Baby

Imagine that you are a therapist. A woman, 25 years of age, comes to see you complaining of lack of interest in sex. She looks tired and pale, and her clothes and hair are dishevelled. You ask her when the problem began. She says that it started six months ago. You ask if any changes occurred in her life at that time. She answers that yes, that is when her baby was born. In fact, that is her baby you hear crying in your waiting room, in the arms of this woman's husband, who has asked her to seek treatment. She says she hasn't wanted to have sex since the baby came along.

We will return to this woman as we try to make sense of what constitutes a sexual problem, what the causes might be, what kinds of treatment are available, and how to seek help for them.

QUESTIONS FOR CRITICAL THOUGHT AND REFLECTION

1. What additional questions might you ask this woman and her husband to assess for possible sexual difficulties?
2. How do we even know whether there is a difficulty here? If there is one, whose difficulty is it?
3. What might be causing this couple's sexual concern? Is there likely one root cause, or might there be a number of factors that contribute to the problem?

Introduction

People can experience a wide array of sexual difficulties. Some of these difficulties are formally recognized in the "Bible" of psychiatric diagnoses, the *Diagnostic and Statistical Manual of Mental Disorders* (*DSM*), currently in its fifth edition (*DSM-5*; APA, 2013). In the *DSM*, sexual problems are referred to as "sexual dysfunctions" or "sexual disorders." All diagnoses listed in the *DSM*—including ones related to sexual expressions and behaviours—are considered as **psychopathology** (i.e., mental illness). Other sexual problems, many of which are exceedingly common, are not recognized as mental disorders but still cause much distress. Dysfunctions identified in the *DSM* and some other common sexual problems will be covered below.

psychopathology Mental illness.

Causes of Sexual Problems

The causes of sexual problems are generally divided into four categories: intrapsychic, interpersonal/relational, cultural/psychosocial, and organic. Many sexual problems tend to be multi-causal and multi-determined, meaning that different causes jointly create them. For example, having been sexually assaulted, being in a relationship where she or he cannot talk about the trauma, and being on anti-anxiety medication with sexual side-effects may combine to create sexual arousal difficulties for a 20-year-old university student. Although sex therapists and researchers often speak as if the causes of sexual problems exist in separate categories and are unrelated to one another, these distinctions tend to be artificial. For example, when we speak about the role of sex guilt in inhibiting sexual expression, this guilt resides not only within the individual but also within a cultural and relational context; it may be more common in certain cultures. Similarly, fear of getting pregnant may hold a young couple back from expressing their sexual feelings to each other, but the resulting inability to "let go" during sex may also be the consequence of living in a small Northern Ontario town with little access to confidentiality for teens seeking contraception.

Intrapsychic Factors in the Development of Sexual Problems

Psychological factors that play a role in the origins of sexual problems begin to develop in early childhood, based on interactions with and observations of family members. Indeed, much of what we learn about our bodies and sexuality is conveyed at home long before we reach formal school-based sex education. For example, the way parents diaper and bathe their child, whether they touch their child in general, and their child's genitals in particular, with affection or revulsion, leaves an impact on the child's feelings about his or her body, body image, and broader sense of self. The parents' emotional and sexual relationship with each other also transmits a great deal about whether intimacy is safe and to be sought after or something fraught with danger and to be approached warily. Ultimately, both the parents' relationship with each other and their relationships with their children help to lay the foundations for warm and loving attachments or difficulties with being close in adulthood.

Most people will say that their parents never taught them about sex but neglect to notice how much they learned from their parents' silence surrounding sexuality. It is the sense of taboo around sexuality that is acquired early and wordlessly that may often make it difficult to communicate freely in adulthood about one's sexual desires. Lack of discussion or, commonly, mislabelling may lead to the absence of an accurate vocabulary relating to sexual matters, which can create awkwardness in expressing one's desires later in life. Thus, even a "normal" Canadian childhood can lead to discomfort with sexuality. This discomfort may be intensified if one is sexually abused in childhood or sexually assaulted thereafter. In such cases, doubts about who can be trusted and feelings of being unsafe in one's own body, of shame and guilt about sexuality—notwithstanding being the victim—emerge as causes of intrapsychic and relational contributors to sexual difficulties (Finkelhor, 2008; Maltz, 2001, 2012).

In adolescence and adulthood, another slew of factors can predispose an individual to the development of sexual difficulties. Low self-esteem, fear of being inadequate, or fear of pregnancy and sexually transmitted infections (STIs) can make it harder to anticipate and enjoy sexual experiences. In addition, cultural expectations that everyone should be sexually active and skillful and find sex easy and effortless create the foundations for **performance anxiety**.

performance anxiety
Worries about one's ability to "perform" sexually (e.g., getting and keeping erections, having an orgasm at the "right" time) that can interfere with experiencing pleasure during sex or even while thinking about having sex.

Interpersonal/Relational Factors in the Development of Sexual Problems

Sometimes the appearance of sexual problems in an individual may actually be a symptom of underlying difficulties in a relationship. For example, inadequate communication between partners can lead to sexual difficulties. Indeed, one of the most common problems that couples report in therapy is the inability to communicate (Figure 16.1).

Lack of communication in day-to-day discussions and interactions, however, is not usually an issue. The problem comes with conflict resolution. As is the case with most interpersonal skills, conflict-resolution skills are generally learned in childhood. Children who observe their parents working through conflicts in a productive manner

"No, there's nothing on my mind, but if there was I don't want to talk about it."

FIGURE 16.1 Poor communication can lead to frustration, anxiety, and less intimacy between members of a couple.

FIGURE 16.2 Does this couple look satisfied? The inability to express anger constructively in relationships is a major relational contributor to sexual problems.

will learn how to manage conflict constructively in their own adult relationships. In contrast, children who observe their parents engaging in unproductive conflict-resolution habits—for example, feigning contentment while ignoring obvious problems, or hurling insults at each other without addressing the real issue—will not know how to argue constructively. Individuals who do not learn good conflict-resolution skills will be unable to express the normal anger that surfaces in every relationship, and many end up suppressing their feelings, often out of a fear that expressing their anger will hurt their partners or damage the relationships. When two people in an intimate, sexual relationship are unable to express their anger safely and effectively, they will eventually be unable to express or even experience passion (Figure 16.2). The suppression of anger then becomes a major relational contributor to sexual problems.

The inability to resolve fights effectively can also contribute to and exacerbate other relational causes of sexual problems. It can lead, for example, to various kinds of power struggles or pursuit and withdrawal dynamics, which may then get played out in bed (Betchen, 2005). Picture a couple who argues about how to, or how often to, or who should initiate sex. Sometimes the argument really is about sex; at other times, it is merely a stand-in for the expression of feelings about other fights that never got resolved.

Other interpersonal sources of sexual difficulties include affairs, jealousy, and distrust. Being disappointed in sex within a particular relationship or in all relationships to date is also a major factor in sexual problems (McCarthy & McCarthy, 2003). Similarly, fear of being disappointed and hurt again after a betrayal has occurred can make it difficult to be sufficiently emotionally engaged for sexual intimacy to occur.

Cultural/Psychosocial Factors in the Development of Sexual Problems

There are many cultural mechanisms for formally and informally teaching children about a given society's sexual values. These include religious teachings, family-based teachings, and formal school-based sex education as well as the learning that comes from the lack thereof, and the imagery that comes through our media. In North America, the cultural factors that influence our ideas about sexuality are very diverse; as a result, there is no absolute consensus on what is "normal" and what is "pathological" in relation to sexuality. (See the "Culture and Diversity" box.)

RELIGIOUS TEACHINGS

Most religious traditions promote certain sexual values and advise their followers on what sexual behaviours are and are not permissible. Historically, beginning with European colonization, the major religious tradition in Canada was Christianity. For many years, the majority of people in Quebec identified as Roman Catholic, and the majority of people in the rest of Canada identified as Protestant. In recent decades, however, the influence of Christian churches has declined, with fewer adult Canadians self-defining as practising Christians. In addition, a variety of non-Christian religions

Culture & Diversity

BDSM and the DSM

How are we to know what is normal and what is pathological? Since 1980, the APA has required that the diagnostic criteria in the *DSM* be based on empirical evidence rather than social biases or theoretical orientation. That leaves the APA struggling with how to handle sexual behaviours that are considered socially unacceptable but where there is no evidence of psychopathology per se. Are sexual minorities to be diagnosed as pathological?

A good example of the complexity involved in making such a determination involves BDSM (see Chapter 15 for more on BDSM). Historically, BDSM has been equated with the paraphilias sexual sadism and sexual masochism, which are described in the *DSM*. The criteria for these paraphilias listed in the *DSM* include distress and dysfunction. The problem here is that although "vanilla folk" (i.e., people not interested in BDSM) may find "kinky" sex repulsive, there is no evidence that BDSM causes distress or dysfunction in its practitioners. That may be because the BDSM community promotes the behavioural code of "safe, sane, and consensual," thus self-regulating BDSM practices

by encouraging participants to be well-informed and to insist on mutual consent in advance. Even those few who report distress are generally responding to stigma directed against them—and the consequences of this stigma, including loss of jobs, security clearances, and custody of children—rather than their own personal feelings (Moser & Kleinplatz, 2005).

In 2009, Richard Krueger, a member of the Sexual and Gender Identity Disorders Workgroup of the *DSM-5*, reported that in 25,150,180 office visits to psychiatrists and 333,873,400 visits to primary-care physicians in the United States, not a single case of sexual sadism or sexual masochism was recorded. The Workgroup recommended that the paraphilias, including sexual sadism and sexual masochism, be acknowledged in the DSM-5 as a variation in sexual interest that is not automatically deemed pathological; rather, sadism and masochism should be diagnosed as pathological only when they are accompanied by distress and dysfunction. These recommendations were accepted by the APA and are reflected in the *DSM-5*.

have become established in Canada, and the Canadian population has become increasingly heterogeneous in terms of its religious practices. As a result, there can be no assumption of uniformity in sexual values rooted in religious beliefs across Canada or even within regions.

FAMILY-BASED TEACHINGS

Family-based teachings generally involve explicit as well as implicit lessons. In terms of what most people learn from their families implicitly, there is little open nudity in most Canadian households past early childhood, if that, suggesting that nudity should be avoided or hidden away. Explicit lessons tend to be aimed at teaching children what *not* to do, without any positive messages about how to express one's sexuality in a healthy way. For example, parents are often concerned about how to get their children to quit "touching themselves," and they generally find euphemistic terms for the areas to be avoided (*down there, your privates, wee wee, ding dong*, and so on). The use of such language and the admonishments about touching one's own genitals—let alone exploring others' in the course of ordinary childhood sex play—tend to leave a strong impression on children that their genitals are forbidden zones. Thus, it is no wonder that many children come to believe, "Sex is dirty. Save it for someone you love." Other lessons may be incomplete or imprecise, leaving children more confused than informed about sexual issues. The minimum that parents teach their children about where babies come from tends to explain the rudiments of pregnancy and reproduction but little about sex.

SCHOOL-BASED SEX EDUCATION

Formal sex education in Canada (see Chapter 19) is provincially rather than federally regulated. As a result, the content, amount, and timing of sex education all vary from province to province (Weaver, Byers, Sears, Cohen, & Randall, 2002). Within each province, there is hardly uniformity, with much decision-making as to implementation of sex education programs left in the hands of individual school boards. Overall, sex education in Canada seems to convey the basics of reproductive biology and how to avoid STIs, with little to no mention of sexual feelings, desire, or pleasure. The silence surrounding these topics suggests to students that their feelings connected to sex and their desires for sexual pleasure are taboo. The consequence of this approach to sex education is that students are far less prepared to deal with the complexities of adult sexuality than are students raised in countries that offer more comprehensive sex education (Kirby, Laris, & Rolleri, 2005; SIECCAN, 2009).

SOURCES OF MISINFORMATION

In the vacuum created by inadequate sex education, myths about sexuality flourish, and many of these myths have a direct bearing on the development of sexual dysfunctions (Figure 16.3). Unfortunately, these myths are frequently reinforced in popular media, especially on the Internet, where many young Canadians go to learn about sex. Sexually explicit videos can be a particularly misleading source of misinformation, as they reinforce unattainable body-image ideals and unrealistic performance expectations, making viewers feel defective by comparison. What many viewers do not realize is that these videos are not even remotely accurate or educational; rather, they are fictional portrayals of sex.

Organic Factors in the Development of Sexual Problems

Anything that can affect the body (positively or negatively) can affect sexuality. The effects of disease, disability, and drugs on the vascular, neurological, and endocrine systems in particular can have serious implications for sexual function. For example, cardiovascular disease—along with treatments for it, such as antihypertensive and diuretic medications prescribed for high blood pressure—can affect sexual arousal and response adversely. Indeed, anything that can restrict blood flow to the heart can also impair blood flow to the genitals. As such, erectile dysfunction is increasingly coming to be seen as the "canary in the coalmine" for cardiovascular disease in men, and men with erectile difficulties are encouraged to see their physicians. Although physicians tend not to warn women of the potential sexual effects of cardiovascular disease or the treatments for this disease, both processes can similarly interfere with the physiological aspects of sexual arousal in women (e.g., lubrication).

Myths about Sexuality

- "Real" sex equals intercourse.
- Sexual satisfaction equals orgasm.
- Bigger is better (when it comes to breasts and penises).
- A man always wants and is always ready to have sex.
- Women's sexuality is more complicated than men's.
- Sex should be natural and spontaneous.
- Talking ruins the mood.
- You shouldn't start anything you can't finish.
- Sex goes downhill after marriage; it gets even worse after you have children.

FIGURE 16.3 Examples of myths about sexuality that have a direct bearing on the development of sexual dysfunctions.

THE ROLE OF HORMONES

Many people are under the impression that sexual desire is driven by hormones. That is certainly the impression left by daytime talk shows and popular men's and women's magazines. Particularly ubiquitous is the notion that low libido is caused by low testosterone, notwithstanding the lack of evidence in support of this belief (Davis, Davison, Donath, & Bell, 2005; Wierman et al., 2006). In reality, the causes of sexual desire problems tend to be quite complex. However, there are a number of organic factors that do commonly contribute to low desire. These include hypothyroidism (a condition characterized by low thyroid hormone levels) and anemia (a decrease in red blood cells commonly caused by iron deficiency or other disease processes), both of which should be ruled out when an individual reports high levels of fatigue in association with low desire.

Physical factors may be particularly significant causes of low sexual desire in women who have recently given birth. Consider the example of the 25-year-old woman reporting low desire that appears at the beginning of this chapter. In this woman's case, her family physician might want to inquire as to whether her childbirth experience six months prior had involved unusual or prolonged bleeding and to see if her hemoglobin levels have rebounded from even the normal blood loss of childbirth. If they have not, the physician could prescribe an iron supplement until her iron is back in the normal range. In addition, if she is breastfeeding, her elevated prolactin (a pituitary hormone related to the breastfeeding reflex) levels could be increasing vaginal dryness, thus creating pain on penetration, which can then secondarily lead to reduction of desire. If she feels subjectively aroused but has vaginal dryness, she can use a lubricant for the duration of breastfeeding. Furthermore, most six-month-old babies are not yet sleeping through the night, and she—and her husband—may be too exhausted for sex. As you can see, even though there is no medical disorder here, there are a number of organic factors that may be contributing to this woman's "normal" and certainly common reduction in sexual desire.

NEUROLOGICAL DISORDERS AND CENTRAL NERVOUS SYSTEM INJURIES

Disorders, diseases, and injuries that cause damage to the central nervous system (e.g., multiple sclerosis, spinal cord injuries) can affect sensation and/or movement and thus have an adverse impact on sexual functioning or response. An insightful and informative discussion of issues related to impaired neurological functioning and sex can be found in the highly acclaimed, Canadian-authored book *The Ultimate Guide to Sex and Disability*, which is recommended to those with disabilities and chronic diseases and their partners (Kaufman, Silverberg, & Odette, 2007).

Diabetes makes for an interesting example of a disease that affects sexuality both as an endocrine (i.e., hormonal) disorder and, in its latter stages, as a disorder that affects the nervous system. Diabetes can lead to **peripheral neuropathy**, which can affect sexual functioning by reducing blood flow to the genitals and eventually causing deterioration in nerve function. Although it is now routine for endocrinologists to warn men about the possibility of erectile dysfunction with diabetes, women are not generally told about the corresponding difficulties in lubrication and sensation. If this pattern is beginning to sound familiar, it is because there is, indeed, a pattern: To the extent that we as a society define "sex" as intercourse, we tend to pay considerable attention to whatever organic (or other) factors might interfere with sexual function so as to impede penetration. From that vantage point, having a hard penis tops the list of requirements. Factors that reduce pleasure but do not automatically prevent penetration (such as reduced female sexual arousal) often do not receive the same level of attention from health care providers.

peripheral neuropathy
Damage to the nerves outside of the brain or spinal cord, which can cause pain, weakness, or numbness.

psychogenic Stemming from psychological causes.

iatrogenic Originating from medical, pharmacological, or surgical treatment.

aphrodisiac A substance alleged to induce sexual desire.

DRUG-RELATED CAUSES OF SEXUAL DIFFICULTIES

Perhaps the most common organic causes of sexual difficulties at present are drug-related. Interestingly, in 1970, Masters and Johnson wrote that 90 per cent of the causes of sexual dysfunction were **psychogenic** and only 10 per cent were organic. By the mid-1980s, even before the more recent explosion of medications on the market, Masters and Johnson (1986) had revised their original estimate to 20 per cent organic; they accounted for this doubling of organic etiology to prescription drug–related **iatrogenic** disorders. More recently, since the advent of Viagra in the late 1990s, many people associated with the pharmaceutical industry have argued that erectile disorder (ED) is 90 per cent organic and 10 per cent psychogenic. Overall, the prevailing discourse about ED remains dualistic—mind *versus* body—rather than holistic, or focussing on mind–body integration.

All manner of drugs can affect sexual functioning, response, and desire. This includes prescription drugs, over-the-counter medications, and recreational drugs. Among the most common medications that have an adverse impact on sexuality are those used to treat cardiovascular diseases, arthritis, high cholesterol, and cancer, as well as most psychiatric drugs. The drugs used for treatment of depression (and often anxiety), that is, the selective serotonin reuptake inhibitors (SSRIs) and the selective norepinephrine reuptake inhibitors (SNRIs), often have devastating effects on sexuality. Some are more likely to affect arousal (e.g., Prozac), some inhibit orgasm (e.g., Paxil), and some have a negative impact on desire (e.g., Effexor), though most seem to have non-specific effects that can affect all aspects of sexuality and that may affect different individuals in different ways (e.g., Celexa, Pristiq). Some recreational drugs, including those that depress the central nervous system (e.g., alcohol, narcotics) and those that act as stimulants (e.g., cocaine, methamphetamine), are used for their alleged **aphrodisiac** properties or because they are believed to have disinhibiting effects on desire. Unfortunately, true aphrodisiacs do not exist (although placebo effects are quite common with drugs and alcohol). In actuality, use of drugs and alcohol can have a negative impact on one's sexual abilities and interactions. Consider, for example, that as the popularity of binge drinking on college campuses has grown, so have transitory episodes of ED among university students, often referred to colloquially as "whiskey dick." In addition, the use of alcohol impairs judgment and has also been correlated with sexual assault and with failure to practise safer sex. Long-term use of any recreational drugs can have chronic, adverse effects on sexual functioning and desire.

Hormonal Contraceptives

One additional category of medications of special relevance to young adults in connection with sexual difficulties is hormonal contraceptives. In Canada, the use of hormonal contraceptives is so heavily promoted that young people often use the term *birth control* as if it were synonymous with oral contraceptives (OCs) or with Depo-Provera ("the shot") while forgoing other contraceptive options (e.g., the diaphragm, IUDs, and condoms, except for STI prevention). However, some hormonal contraceptives are known to have adverse effects on arousal and desire. Depo-Provera in particular has been linked with low desire. This drug is popular in general in Canada, and it is often prescribed for new mothers as it does not interfere with breastfeeding. If we return again to our 25-year-old new mother with low desire, the use of Depo-Provera may be an important factor in her low desire. Another drug that has such a powerful impact on the entire endocrine system that it interferes with ovulation in women and can cause a reduction in sexual desire contains cyproterone acetate, and it is sold in Canada under the brand name *Diane* and the generic name *Ginette*. Although never approved by Health Canada for anything except treatment of the most severe cases of cystic acne, Diane has been prescribed "off-label" (meaning without Health Canada's approval for this purpose) as a contraceptive. The inhibitory impact of both Depo-Provera and cyproterone acetate (the active ingredient in Diane) on sexual desire is well known—indeed, both drugs were originally designed and are still used for chemical castration, to cut off all sexual desire, in convicted serial rapists—yet most women are not warned about this effect when they are given a prescription for these drugs. The possibility that all OCs can have an adverse impact on desire has been suggested in the scientific literature only recently (Panzer et al., 2006), and there remains no clear literature on which dosages of which OCs might be harmful, what exactly the effects might be, what characteristics might make a woman more susceptible to negative effects, or how long the effects might last.

Sexual Difficulties in Men and Women

Sexual Difficulties in Men

ERECTILE DYSFUNCTION

The best known of the male sexual difficulties is ED, even though it is not the most common. ED tends to involve difficulty with maintaining erections more than diffi-culty with actually becoming erect. Like all sexual problems, it can occur across all circumstances, in which case it is called "generalized," or it can occur only in particular situations (e.g., with a partner but not in self-stimulation). In the years since the 1999 release of Viagra in Canada, *public* discussion of erectile problems has become ubi-quitous (Figure 16.4). Unfortunately, the discourse has not necessarily made private couples' communication any easier, nor has it expanded our understanding of either male sexuality or its problems.

Possible Causes

Anything that might interfere with blood flow to the penis or enjoyment of tactile stimu-lation can impede erection. Thus, the organic causes of ED include cardiovascular disease, diabetes, and the side effects of many medications, including psychotropic and anti-hypertensive drugs. Other causes run the gamut from interpersonal conflict, communi-cation problems, and work stress, to a history of sexual abuse. Sexual myths, including the idea that real men are always ready, willing, and able to have intercourse, contribute to the pressure men feel to get and keep erections hard enough for penetration. Of course, not being able to get an erection is a normal response when a man is with a partner he does not find arousing, or when the stimulation he receives does not turn him on.

> **phosphodiesterase type-5 inhibitors (PDE-5 inhibitors)** Erectogenic drugs that work by helping to dilate the arteries of the penis.

Options

The erectogenic drugs Viagra, Levitra, and Cialis, known collectively as the **phosphodiesterase type-5 inhibitors** (or simply the PDE-5 inhibitors), work by helping the arter-ies of the corpora cavernosa to dilate more readily and stay that way, but only if the man is sexually stimulated. These drugs are neither aphrodisiacs nor "automatic" erection pills, and they do not create erections in men who are not subjectively aroused. Thus, a man who takes these drugs

FIGURE 16.4 Erection problems? Dealing with erectile problems has become increasingly public since the 1999 release of Viagra in Canada.

will still need to communicate with his partner about getting the kind(s) of stimulation he likes for the PDE-5 inhibitors to be effective. This factor was a surprise to the many men who assumed that Viagra would be a quick fix no matter how they felt, an assumption that may contribute to unexpectedly low compliance rates in use of the PDE-5 inhibitors. Indeed, most men who receive a prescription for Viagra do not fill it, and of those who do, only about 50 per cent refill it. Men with a family history of vision or hearing loss or who are using nitrates (e.g., nitroglycerine spray) for cardiovascular disease must discuss these possible contraindications before receiving a prescription for any of these drugs. In addition, there has been greater success in treatment of ED with sex therapy, or with the combination of sex therapy and the PDE-5 inhibitors than with the PDE-5 inhibitors alone (Althof, 2001; Perelman, 2000).

RAPID EJACULATION

Each semester, I play a little thought experiment with my sex therapy students: Suppose you are a sex therapist and a patient comes to you complaining that "sex has barely begun" by the time it is over. "A few thrusts is all it takes before I reach orgasm, and then it's game over. . . . I'm done. I wish I could last longer." What do you do? My students quickly begin to discuss the advantages and disadvantages of various treatment strategies for men who ejaculate too soon, when I stop them to point out that they have taken it for granted that the patient is male. The prevailing assumption, although we might deny it, is that there is a correct timing for orgasm, that men should "last" as long as possible, and that women should reach orgasm very quickly. Thus, my students assume that the patient is male because they believe that no woman would complain about reaching "premature" orgasm. Unfortunately, the social values and beliefs behind such assumptions have made their way into the realm of scientific sexology as if they were objective diagnostic indicators of sexual dysfunction and criteria for effective treatment outcome. In considering what constitutes "normal" sexual functioning, therefore, we must be very aware of how our assumptions about sex and sexuality influence our perceptions.

Rapid ejaculation is the most common of the male sexual dysfunctions (and it is also commonly known as *premature ejaculation*). Both the terminology and the definition for this problem illustrate the challenges in conceptualizing it. Masters and Johnson (1970) first defined what was then called "premature ejaculation" as a man's inability to maintain his erection without ejaculating long enough to bring his partner to orgasm during intercourse at least 50 per cent of the time. This definition came with a few problems. First, it assumes that heterosexual intercourse is essential to everyone's idea of "having sex," thus excluding gay men entirely as well as heterosexual men who prefer to spend more time on non-coital activities. Second, Masters and Johnson's reasoning at the time was based on the idea that all women should attain orgasm via intercourse alone, given sufficient time. However, a number of studies have demonstrated that this assumption is erroneous; in theory, then, according to Masters and Johnson's definition, a man could be capable of thrusting for hours at a time and still be diagnosed as a premature ejaculator if his partner did not have an orgasm. Third, this definition begs the questions, "premature" for what, and as compared to what exactly? Is there a "correct" time to ejaculate? (And who is holding the stopwatch?) Later definitions focussed on number of thrusts or time to ejaculation, although these definitions also came with the problem of determining how fast is too fast. More recent definitions have focussed on distress over lack of sufficient pleasure for the man or his partner (male or female), and whether ejaculation occurs during intercourse or other sexual activities (cf., Metz & McCarthy, 2003; Zilbergeld, 1999). The *DSM-5* calls this condition *premature (early) ejaculation* and defines it in terms of **intra-vaginal ejaculatory latency (IELT)**. The new criteria would have men diagnosed as premature (early) ejaculators if they ejaculate within 60 seconds of penetration 75 per cent of the time for a period of six months or longer (Segraves, 2010), if it causes distress for the individual experiencing the symptoms.

intra-vaginal ejaculatory latency (IELT) The duration from the moment of vaginal penetration until a man ejaculates in the vagina.

Possible Causes

There has been little agreement on the possible causes of rapid ejaculation. Some have suggested that this difficulty results from anxiety, lack of control, genetic factors, or penile hypersensitivity. Others have hypothesized that the problem was created by the adolescent hurrying through solo or partnered sex to avoid being caught by his parents. There have been minimal data supporting any of these hypotheses. In cases where a man has "diagnosed" himself as having rapid ejaculation, the cause of the "problem" may be his own unrealistic expectations.

Options

The assessment of and treatment for rapid ejaculation reveal a great deal about conventional thinking surrounding sexuality itself. When men seek out sex therapy for treatment of rapid ejaculation, it is often with the assumption that remaining harder for longer is what it takes to satisfy a woman sexually. Quite typically, men undertake therapy alone, without consulting their partners about their aspirations—let alone whether these do, in fact, correspond to their partners' wishes. As such, it can be quite revealing when patients describe their previous "home remedy" efforts to "cure" themselves.

Many men mention "double-bagging" (i.e., wearing two condoms simultaneously, one inside the other) in order to reduce sensation and "last" longer. This strategy can actually backfire in that wearing two condoms at the same time makes it more likely that both will fall off and leave the couple unprotected against pregnancy and STIs. A second common approach is to order products over the Internet with names like "Stay-Hard Cream." These items contain topical anaesthetics such as lidocaine (the same kind of drug use by dentists to freeze a patient's mouth), again to reduce sensation. These products cause numbness to the penis—as well as numbness and often burning to the vagina or anus of the man's partner. In addition to attempting to decrease physical sensation, many men try to think distracting thoughts (e.g., recalling an especially grisly episode of *CSI*) to prevent orgasm. When women hear of these efforts, they are typically surprised to learn that their partners believe that numbing themselves either physically or emotionally is a solution to the "problem," especially because many of these women may not have perceived that there was a problem at all.

In therapy, men often report being so distressed by failing their partners that they are overcome with shame and guilt. They are usually relieved to discover that many people prefer manual or oral stimulation over intercourse as a route to orgasm. Thus, psychoeducational counselling tends to provide instant relief from performance anxiety and feelings of inadequacy. This results in a shift in orientation from wanting to "last longer" to exploring the question, "How can we give each other more pleasure?" Further, as Zilbergeld (1999) points out, helping the man to increase his threshold for pleasure rather than trying to reduce sensation (as is the focus of most home remedies) makes for more satisfying sexual experiences.

Nonetheless, some physicians prescribe, off-label, medications that reduce sexual pleasure and sensation to treat rapid ejaculation. In the 1990s, once the side effect of SSRIs on sexual response had been observed, physicians began prescribing these drugs to men with rapid ejaculation, knowing that it would slow them down markedly (cf.,

Assalian, 1994). What is unquestionably an unwanted side effect of SSRI treatment for most people has been considered a boon to some men with rapid ejaculation.

DELAYED EJACULATION

While rapid ejaculation is among the most commonly reported of sexual dysfunctions, delayed ejaculation (DE) is the most under reported of male sexual difficulties (Apfelbaum, 2000). The notion that a man can never thrust for too long is so entrenched in our fantasy images of male sexuality that the idea that a man should complain of thrusting endlessly without ejaculating seems hard to fathom. This is why Apfelbaum (2000) refers to men with DE as the "workhorses" of the sex world. Neither heterosexual men nor their partners generally note DE as a problem (unless, for example, the woman cannot get pregnant) because the man who can thrust endlessly is seen as a sexual superstar in a culture more focussed on performance than pleasure. It is also important to remember that when a woman complains of pain on intercourse that goes on all night, it can sometimes be her "symptom" of his DE.

In the past, DE was known, rather insensitively, as *ejaculatory incompetence*, and later as *retarded ejaculation*. Today, it is increasingly referred to as *delayed ejaculation* or as *male anorgasmia* or *male coital anorgasmia*, as it involves difficulty with orgasm. Some men with DE report never having been able to experience orgasm; however, such cases are rare and tend to have an organic basis. More commonly, men who are diagnosed with DE are able to ejaculate alone but have difficulty with a partner, particularly during vaginal or anal intercourse. Whereas all of these situations were once reported relatively infrequently, an increased incidence has been noted in the literature since the late 1990s (e.g., Waldinger, 2010).

anorgasmia Persistent inability to have an orgasm.

Possible Causes

A major cause of secondary (i.e., recent onset) DE is the use of psychotropic drugs, especially anti-depressants (e.g., SSRIs and SNRIs) and anti-psychotics (e.g., Zyprexa, Abilify). In cases in which the man has never been able to have an orgasm, even while sleeping, the cause tends to be organic. In other cases, the basis for delayed ejaculation has been challenging to identify. Some have suggested that men who can ejaculate alone but not with a partner may have developed an idiosyncratic masturbatory style (e.g., Perelman, 2010). Others have posited that the issue is with the widespread notion that the mere presence of an erection must signify that a man *wants* to engage in intercourse. This assumption can lead couples to engage in sex based on minimal cues of arousal (i.e., an erection) rather than waiting for higher levels of excitement to occur. At merely threshold levels, much can go awry; when couples wait for arousal to become quite intense, it is much less likely that sexual dysfunctions will arise (Schnarch, 1997).

The notion that performance and arousal/pleasure may be conflated in men with DE is supported by the recent literature (Beckman, Waern, Gustafson, & Skoog, 2008; Kleinplatz, 2008). Further, the use of erectogenic drugs may also reinforce the conflation of performance and arousal/pleasure. Indeed, since 1998, when the PDE-5 inhibitors were first released in the US, it has been easier for a man to engage in penetrative sex even if he is not especially excited. As the use of erectogenic drugs has spread, so have reports of DE.

Options

We need to pay more attention to how men actually feel *during* sex. Men and their partners should be aware that an erection does not always signal that a man *wants* to engage in intercourse, and men should be enabled to admit to their partners when they do not. Men may be aroused just enough to have an erection but not enough to ejaculate;

their thrusting on and on may be a clue that they need more stimulation rather than a sign that they are "good to go" for hours. For some men, the solution may be to pay more attention to their pleasure, to increase their arousal to a level that will allow them to experience orgasm. For others, it may be to broaden their repertoire of stimulation techniques. Some clinicians point out that men with difficulties experiencing orgasm with a partner may be best understood as clinically equivalent to women with anorgasmia—that is, they are sufficiently aroused to respond physiologically (i.e., with an erection) but not enough to experience orgasm and have difficulty saying so (Apfelbaum, 2000; see the discussion on anorgasmia in women later in this chapter). For those who experience secondary DE as a side effect of psychotropic drugs, a physician-supervised withdrawal from medication may improve the situation.

DYSPAREUNIA

Pain during intercourse—or, more broadly, pain related to sex—is known as dyspareunia. Most of the literature on dyspareunia focusses on women; such pain in men has generally been overlooked. Many men do not report sex-related pain until it has become severe enough to compel medical attention.

Possible Causes

A multitude of diseases can cause pain at erection or during and after ejaculation. These include STIs, benign or cancerous diseases of the prostate and testes, and Peyronie's disease (i.e., plaques forming within the penis that cause painful curvature of the penis), among many others.

Options

Treatment options for dyspareunia in men generally focus on treating the underlying disease(s). The treatment is usually conducted by urologists.

Sexual Difficulties in Women

Many often speak as if the sexual dysfunctions that women can experience are unrelated to one another, each existing separately. A more helpful way of thinking of these difficulties is that each may have an impact on the other, as discussed below.

FEMALE SEXUAL AROUSAL DISORDER

Female sexual arousal disorder (FSAD) is usually conceived of as a difficulty with vaginal lubrication. Although this notion is partially correct, lack of lubrication may not signify a sexual dysfunction at all. If a woman is not sexually aroused, it is normal that she would not lubricate. Although this seems like common sense, it is surprising how often couples seek treatment for lack of lubrication when a female partner's lack of arousal signifies an appropriate (lack of) response to an unappealing encounter—not a disorder. Rather frequently, gynaecologists refer women to sex therapy for pain on intercourse after first suggesting that they try applying a lubricant to ease penetration. Yet such "solutions" ignore the fact that the woman was not subjectively sexually excited; they attempt merely to circumvent the symptom without looking too closely at her sex life. Such treatment methods illuminate how some clinicians define not only the nature of the problem but the nature of "sex" itself. For these clinicians, the goal of treatment is to enable the woman to engage in "sex" despite her lack of pleasure. This approach illuminates the belief that sexual dysfunctions are conceived as impediments to intercourse rather than as obstacles to pleasure.

Until recently, the DSM treated female sexual arousal difficulties as a distinct disorder, akin to erectile dysfunction in men. In the DSM-5, this distinction has been retained for men but not for women. (Please see below, in the section on desire disorders, for more on the collapsing of arousal and desire categories in women only.)

Possible Causes

There are a variety of factors that can prevent a woman from feeling aroused during sex. These include a lack of attraction to her partner, a recent argument that has yet to be resolved, a history of sexual assault, ongoing fatigue and stress, and fear of pregnancy or STIs. Sometimes, a woman will not become aroused because the nature or quality of the sexual contact itself is not particularly stimulating or erotic for her. Cultural values that discourage open expression of sexual wishes can prevent a woman from asking for what she wants. In addition, as mentioned previously in the section on drug-related causes of sexual difficulties, certain drugs can interfere with sexual desire and arousal in men and women.

If, on the other hand, a woman is feeling subjectively aroused but is not lubricating, other factors may be at play. For example, when a woman is breastfeeding or postmenopausal, the reduction in estrogen may result in reduced lubrication, even when she feels very aroused. In some cases, drug side-effects can create vaginal dryness. One especially common example in young adults is the use of anti-histamines and decongestants for allergies; the same drugs that dry out weepy eyes and runny noses will also dry out the mucous membranes of the vagina. Some oral contraceptives will also reduce lubrication, as will diuretics taken for hypertension (i.e., high blood pressure) and chemotherapy and radiation for cancer, even when the treatment is not directed toward the genitals.

Options

In cases where a woman is not lubricating even though she feels aroused, application of a commercial lubricant may be helpful. Yet it is important to recognize that a lubricant cannot act as a magical cure in cases where the problem is with lack of arousal. Rather, women in this situation should be encouraged to take a close look at their sex lives to identify factors contributing to their lack of arousal. As noted above, treatments for lack of lubrication too often focus on enabling a woman to engage in intercourse despite her lack of pleasure in doing so.

It is important for women to select a lubricant carefully. Although extreme vaginal dryness (e.g., in women undergoing chemotherapy or radiation for cancer treatment) may benefit from application of an oil-based (ideally plant-based but not petroleum-based) lubricant, such as almond oil, these lubricants can destroy latex condoms. Thus, women who choose to use oil-based lubricants are advised to use an alternative to latex condoms, such as polyurethane or nitrile condoms. If a woman is using latex condoms for partnered intercourse, she and her partner should ensure that they are using water- or silicone-based lubricants, which will not compromise the integrity of the latex.

ANORGASMIA

As noted previously, anorgasmia is generally defined as a persistent inability to achieve orgasm. As with all sexual dysfunctions, it can be primary, meaning lifelong, or secondary, that is, of recent onset. Primary anorgasmia is often related to a woman's lack of knowledge of her own body and sexual response, in particular her lack of understanding of what leads to orgasm. In fact, Barbach (2000) has suggested that the term *anorgasmia* be replaced with *preorgasmia* in relation to women with the primary form of this condition to indicate that it is not that these women cannot have an orgasm, but merely that they have not experienced one, *yet*. Secondary anorgasmia—that is, difficulty with orgasm in a woman who had previously been orgasmic—is generally more complex in origin and in treatment.

Possible Causes

As suggested above, the most frequent cause of primary anorgasmia is a woman's lack of knowledge about her own body and sexuality. In particular, many women are not aware of the importance of clitoral stimulation. The clitoris is the only organ in the human body whose sole function is pleasure (by comparison, the penis also functions for reproduction and urination); it is densely loaded with nerve endings, far more so than the vagina (see Chapter 4). The silence surrounding female sexual development often inhibits girls from exploring their bodies sexually as early in life as their male peers typically do (Tolman, 2002); in North America, women do not typically begin self-stimulation until late adolescence or thereafter. In addition, some women never engage in sexual self-discovery. Therefore, many women come to partnered sexual activities with considerably less awareness of what might give them pleasure than do men. Lacking knowledge from within and in the absence of comprehensive sex education, they are prey to myths about female sexuality that are ubiquitous in the media (Barbach, 2000). These myths are especially prevalent in sexually explicit images and films on the Internet, which often depict women as able to have multiple orgasms in response to vaginal or, increasingly, anal penetration alone. Such inaccurate displays of sexual response convince many viewers that this is how women *should* reach orgasm. It is a surprise to many women and their partners that most women require clitoral stimulation for orgasm to occur. Indeed, women who seek help for primary anorgasmia typically present as believing that "real" women need only intercourse to have an orgasm.

Secondary anorgasmia is typically caused by pharmacological side effects. In particular, the SSRIs and anti-psychotics are well known to disrupt orgasm in women and in men. It may also be linked to psychological or interpersonal difficulties affecting the woman in her relationship.

Options

Much of the treatment for cases of primary anorgasmia involves psychoeducational counselling and, to that end, **bibliotherapy**. This type of therapy involves offering information on female anatomy—and focussing on the crucial role of clitoral stimulation—and practical exercises and instruction. Two of the more popular books used in bibliotherapy (i.e., Barbach, 2000; Heiman & LoPiccolo, 1988) outline programs that use cognitive-behavioural exercises focussed on genital exploration and clitoral stimulation to help women experience their first orgasms (Figure 16.5). Many women are reassured to hear that it requires more than a few moments of self-stimulation for a woman to have an initial orgasm. After working through such programs and engaging in sexual self-exploration, it is essential that a woman teach her partner what she has learned about her body rather than relying on the partner to somehow figure out how to give her pleasure (Dodson, 2002). Curiously, some couples regard the suggestion that a woman's partner might stimulate her clitoris during "sex" as "cheating." Such a response highlights how cultural definitions of "sex" as only intercourse generate sexual problems.

bibliotherapy The use of readings and written assignments in psychotherapy.

FIGURE 16.5 Can masturbation make your sex life better? Self-stimulation is a key component of becoming orgasmic.

Women dealing with secondary anorgasmia will need to work carefully with a skilled clinician to assess the iatrogenic or other cause(s) of their difficulties in order to proceed with the best course of action.

DYSPAREUNIA

Women's genital or pelvic pain during or after sexual activity, especially intercourse, is referred to as dyspareunia. Women can experience dyspareunia in a variety of ways. Some women describe itching or burning of the vulva or the vagina, while others report sharp or persistent pain deep within the pelvis. Pain may occur during or after sexual activity, and some women with dyspareunia also experience genital pain from just walking or crossing their legs.

Most women will experience transitory pain on intercourse at some point in their lives, and such experiences are not always cause for concern. Continuing pain is another matter and requires medical attention. Unfortunately, both the patient's and the physician's discomfort with sexual matters can impede thorough and efficient assessment as to the origin of the woman's pain. Most physicians are not trained to ask about sexual concerns, and most patients will not feel free to raise the subject (Maurice, 1999). Women who do seek treatment for dyspareunia will often report to their sex therapists that their physicians noticed no abnormalities on their annual physicals. However, unless a woman specifically tells her physician about pain associated with sex, the physician will not know to look for it; he or she will not perform a focussed genital/pelvic examination (Moser, 1999, 2005).

Possible Causes

The possible kinds and causes of genital/pelvic pain are almost innumerable (Goldstein, Pukall, & Goldstein, 2009); this section lists only some of the most commonly observed. Sharp pain at one side of the pelvis may correspond to ovulation. Deep pelvic pain, especially with penetration, may be caused by endometriosis. Pain of the vulva may result from a wide variety of dermatological conditions, or it may be related to herpes blisters, genital warts, or consequences of other STIs. Pain that presents as itching may be caused by a yeast infection. Burning pain, particularly when it is experienced around the vaginal opening, may occur if a woman engages in intercourse without being sexually aroused. Perineal pain can be caused by STIs or by irritation from vaginal infections or from incisions or tears at childbirth that have not healed properly. Vaginal pain can be caused by persistent thrusting combined with vaginal dryness, and deep vaginal pain may be caused by banging of the cervix, pelvic inflammatory disease, or even ovarian cancer. Vaginal pain resulting from vaginal dryness may have deeper underlying causes such as lack of arousal due to psychological, relationship, or situational issues, or the dryness may be a side effect of certain medications.

As the above discussion indicates, the linkages among the various sexual difficulties begin to become obvious in discussing the causes of dyspareunia. It is not as though the difficulties listed thus far each exist in a vacuum. Being subjectively turned off corresponds with lack of lubrication. Proceeding with sexual intercourse while lacking in even minimal arousal surely will not lead to orgasm but may result in dyspareunia. Further, if pain on intercourse occurs often enough to make a woman cringe at the thought of next having sex, this may lead to vaginismus and/or lack of sexual desire in the future (see below).

Options

Much of the terminology that has gone in and out of fashion over the last 15 years or so—including vulvodynia (pain in the vulva), vulvar vestibulitis (pain at the vaginal opening), and provoked vestibulodynia (pain at the vaginal opening when stimulated)—has added to the confusion surrounding diagnosis and treatment. Many patients walk into their physicians' offices explaining that they have genital/pelvic pain and seem relieved to walk out with one of the "diagnoses" listed here. Unfortunately, these diagnoses offer patients only a description (the words are borrowed from Greek and describe pain in the genitals, with *dynia* being Greek for "pain") and provide no explanatory information. These terms do not specify the cause of the pain, but merely its location (which the woman already knew and articulated when she made the appointment). This adds to the patient's eventual frustration that the prescribed treatment does not actually address the cause of her pain but only provides false comfort in dealing with her symptom. It is crucial that the physician actually take the time to reproduce the pain during the examination in order to determine its origin and ascertain the diagnosis and treatment correctly.

Often, women will be told that the physician could not find the cause of her pain. Such patients are often left with the impression that the problem is all in their heads. This situation highlights the importance of finding a skilled clinician and maintaining a good working relationship between patient and physician (Goldstein et al., 2009). Effective treatment of dyspareunia focusses on treating the underlying cause(s) of the pain.

The whole idea of treating dyspareunia on its own, as an isolated condition, and listing it as a sexual dysfunction in the *DSM* has long been controversial. Binik and his colleagues (e.g., Binik, 2009a) have written a series of influential articles that have taken issue with the concept of "sexual pain," questioning why pain in the genitals or pelvis ought to be understood differently from back pain or headaches. What, they ask, distinguishes this pain as "sexual," except for its location? Binik reminds clinicians that many cases of alleged dyspareunia actually involve a myriad of organic disorders or pain syndromes that may not even be localized to the genitals or pelvis and that may cause pain unrelated to intercourse. Binik's (2009a) recommendation that dyspareunia and vaginismus (see below) be combined in the *DSM-5* as *genito-pelvic pain/penetration disorder* was accepted. His rationale for this amalgamation was that the emphasis of the definition should be on assessing and treating *pain* without the implicit focus on "sex." Furthermore, the ideal clinical team should include all the relevant health care professionals, from sex therapists to gynecologists to pelvic floor physiotherapists, to help the patient with hands-on pain relief.

VAGINISMUS

Vaginismus involves a fear of penetration or a fear of pain on penetration combined with an involuntary spasm at the opening of the vagina, which makes penetration difficult or impossible. This sexual problem is often associated with a history of pain on intercourse or on prior attempts at penetration. For some women, the difficulty occurs with attempts at all types of penetration, including insertion of tampons or fingers, and during pelvic examinations. For other women, the problem is associated exclusively with intercourse. Men whose partners are diagnosed with vaginismus inevitably describe feeling as if they have hit a "brick wall" about an inch or so into the vagina. Some note that attempts at penetration are rather painful for the penile glans. These sorts of descriptions can be very helpful to a clinician trying to make a diagnosis, as she or he may be unable to examine the patient directly due to the patient's pain and trepidation.

Both the existence of vaginismus as a distinct clinical entity and the causes of it are in dispute. Binik and his colleagues have long questioned whether vaginismus can be identified reliably across patients and physicians. Recently, as noted above, the *DSM-5* has combined the diagnosis of vaginismus with that of dyspareunia under the category of genito-pelvic pain/penetration disorder. Certainly, the origins of both seem to be related.

Possible Causes

Vaginismus is best understood in terms of cause as well as meaning or purpose. To view it merely as a disorder to be overcome rather than as a symptom of underlying fear or reluctance fails to illuminate vaginismus in all its complexity. Vaginismus may be best understood as an adaptive response to fear or reluctance to engage in intercourse rather than as merely a dysfunction to be eliminated (Kleinplatz, 1998). To the extent that conventional models of sexuality tend to focus on obstacles to functioning, vaginismus is indeed the ultimate in dysfunctions, literally obstructing intercourse.

Many factors can contribute to women's underlying fear or reluctance. Some women who cannot endure penetration have a history of exposure to sex-negative messages alongside a current reluctance to become pregnant. Such a combination has been found more frequently in societies known for their negative messages about sex and severe consequences for unwanted pregnancies. In addition, many women who are diagnosed with vaginismus have a history of poor sex education with little accurate information about their own anatomy (Kleinplatz, 1998). Indeed, the norm is that women with vaginismus tend to have received "information" that instilled or reinforced certain myths about sexuality itself. These myths include the ideas that "losing one's virginity" will be extremely painful with lots of bleeding, that men are "after just one thing," and that girls will have to "take it," no matter how unpleasant, if they want to "keep" their guys. Certainly, the normal physiological response to fear and anxiety is the constriction of one's musculature; thus, fear of pain on penetration becomes a self-fulfilling prophecy. It is also fairly common for women diagnosed with vaginismus to have a history of sexual abuse or assault. Indeed, the sudden appearance of secondary vaginismus after a lifelong history of easy penetration may suggest a recent genital trauma. However, it is the combination of sex-negative messages and sexual abuse or assault that seems especially to engender the symptoms of vaginismus (Kleinplatz, 1998).

Medical textbooks have long noted that a visual inspection of the vaginal opening of a woman experiencing vaginismus reveals that the patient's musculature seems to be poised as a woman's lips saying "no." Indeed, "no" to what? To pain? To intercourse itself? To this particular way of having sex? To this particular partner? To having sex with men entirely? When a physician is diagnosing vaginismus in a patient, she or he should investigate these questions before proceeding to eliminate the symptom of what may well be an adaptive response to the patient's inability to articulate her reluctance with words.

Options

Treatment of vaginismus has traditionally involved the use of graduated plastic dilators inserted into the vagina in combination with relaxation training and pelvic floor exercises (e.g., Binik, Bergeron, & Khalifé, 2007). The goal of this sort of treatment has been to permit vaginal containment of penis-sized objects, and this objective has been attained successfully from the beginnings of sex therapy. Masters and Johnson (1970) and Kaplan (1974) reported virtually 100 per cent success rates. In fact, Hawton and Catalan (1990) went so far as to suggest that "vaginismus is an excellent sexual dysfunction for trainee therapists to treat because the approach is reasonably straightforward and success is likely to result" (p. 47). However, there has been some criticism of the methods and goals of such treatments (Kleinplatz, 1996, 1998, 2001a; Shaw, 1994). It is precisely in the reports of the success of these treatments that the underlying assumptions of sex therapy become illuminated. The fact that this treatment aims for normative functioning rather than sexual pleasure becomes especially apparent when the goal is to enable intercourse regardless of how the participants really feel about their sex lives (see the "Research vs Real Life" box).

Sexual Desire Disorders in Men and Women

Two desire disorders were listed in the *DSM-IV-TR*, both of which were said to affect men as well as women: hypoactive sexual desire disorder (HSDD) and sexual aversion disorder (APA, 2000). HSDD is commonly thought of as low desire or low libido. Sexual aversion is not a general reluctance to have sex so much as it is characterized by an intensely negative or fearful response to a *specific* aspect of sexual interaction. For example, an individual with sexual aversion disorder might look forward to and enjoy having sex until coming into contact with her partner's moustache or feeling his partner's bodily fluids, at which time the person might freeze, shut down, or experience panic. This reaction is often found among survivors of sexual trauma. Sexual aversion disorder has been removed from the *DSM-5*. This may hamper therapists who are attempting to distinguish low desire from aversive reactions.

Desire disorders have a revealing history in the *DSM*. In the first two editions of the *DSM*, published in 1952 (*DSM-I*) and 1968 (*DSM-II*), there was no diagnosis for low

Research VS Real Life

Botox Injections for Vaginismus

A new treatment for vaginismus has recently been introduced by American cosmetic surgeon Peter Pacik (2010), and its popularity is spreading across Canada. Unlike low desire, which is generally believed to have notoriously poor treatment outcomes, the existing treatments for vaginismus are generally thought to be highly effective. Because the new treatment involves a novel procedure rather than a new drug, it does not require Health Canada's approval. The treatment is intended for women who have vaginismus, many of whom report being under severe pressure to fulfill their husbands' and families' expectation—and the social expectation—that they be "complete" wives and mothers.

The treatment begins with the woman being put under general anaesthesia, at which point her husband enters the room. As the husband observes, the physician injects Botox into three areas surrounding the woman's vaginal opening, to paralyze her pelvic floor muscles, and then introduces a series of dilators into her vagina. When the woman wakes up, she experiences the sensation of penetration, often for the first time, as a result of a dilator protruding one inch from her vagina. Increasingly large dilators continue to be inserted over the next two days and must remain in the woman's vagina overnight while waiting for the Botox to take effect. The treatment takes three days, during which time the patient remains in the clinic, and the effects of the Botox generally last three to four months.

Some question the clinical wisdom and the ethics involved in using such an invasive procedure, with the potential for serious adverse medical and psychological effects, when safer, less invasive treatment options are readily available. Others question the fundamental goal of the treatment paradigm and whether these methods and goals are in the patient's best interests. When a woman is so fearful of penetration that her muscles clamp shut, who is to decide that overriding her fear while she is unconscious is a good idea? The procedure will "work" to open up her vagina, but what of the woman attached? Will it "work" for her? Who gets to determine what is in the patient's best interests? How might the patient's interests differ from those of the physicians and clinicians involved in performing this procedure? How might their goals differ?

desire. Too much desire was pathologized as nymphomania in women and satyriasis or Don Juanism in men, although in practice it was mainly women who were treated as nymphomaniacs; men who had extremely active sex lives were deemed . . . lucky. Much changed with the advent of the *DSM*-III in 1980. The idea of gender bias in the *DSM* became unacceptable. Furthermore, in the period just after the so-called "sexual revolution," suddenly one could not have too much sex. As a result, too low desire was introduced into the *DSM* as inhibited sexual desire (ISD), a diagnosis that could be applied to men and women, and was soon renamed hypoactive sexual desire disorder.

High desire is not currently listed as a disorder in the *DSM*, although a variety of celebrity sex scandals have led to speculation as to whether out-of-control sexual behaviour is actually "sexual addiction." Although the term *sex addiction* has captured the popular imagination, the notion of sex as something that one can be addicted to—in the same way that one can be addicted to heroin or cocaine, for example—does not fit with the thinking of most specialists in sex therapy or addiction treatment. Kafka (2010) had proposed that hypersexual disorder be introduced into the *DSM-5* but suggested that most "patients" would be male and noted that there was little research on hypersexuality in women. This proposal was rejected by the APA, and there is no category for high desire in the *DSM-5*.

SEXUAL DESIRE DISCREPANCY

The most common problem among couples who seek sex therapy is sexual desire discrepancy. This difficulty arises when one partner's desire for sex is noticeably greater than the other's. One partner may claim that the other has no libido, while the other may state that the partner with the greater desire is a "sex addict." In such cases, it is sometimes hard to distinguish which partner—if either—even has a problem. All that is clear is that when two people with such divergent levels of sexual interest are partnered, they share a problem.

A close look at sexual desire reveals how various intrapsychic, interpersonal/relational, cultural/psychosocial, and organic factors can contribute to sexual difficulties. The links—indeed, the domino effect played by one sexual problem leading to another—become illuminated when looking at sexual desire problems. To get a sense of how complex the factors that contribute to issues with sexual desire may be, let's return once more to the 25-year-old woman who complains of lack of interest in sex six months after having had a baby. This woman is seeking treatment because her husband reports that her lack of desire is a problem. But is there a problem? If there is, what might the nature of the problem be?

As noted previously in this chapter, a major factor contributing to this woman's lack of desire is likely exhaustion. The woman is probably not getting much sleep, and sleep deprivation is a common cause of low desire. That is, the underlying problem is lack of sleep; one of its many manifestations is low desire. If caring for the child is causing her to lose more sleep than her husband is losing, the result may be a disparity in their levels of sexual desire. This disparity may be alleviated if the father assumes responsibility for a larger share of the housework and child care, especially at night.

Another problem may be that this couple have little support from their families or the general community, and they may be feeling overwhelmed by their situation. In North America, the cultural expectation is often that new parents should be able to handle all their parental responsibilities on their own. In addition, young couples tend to be mobile and not live in close proximity to their families. Thus, there may be few options for new parents to get away and recharge their batteries, particularly if they have little extra money for babysitters.

Is her desire truly decreased or have complications from a routine, Canadian childbirth in combination with her elevated prolactin while breastfeeding led to vaginal dryness and pain on intercourse? As discussed above, vaginal dryness is normal in breastfeeding women, but if she and her husband are not aware of this, they may perceive her reduced lubrication as lack of arousal. This perception may cause both partners to turn away from each other. In addition, attempts at intercourse may be painful due to the woman's lack of lubrication, and with time the woman may come to associate pain with intercourse; this association will likely further reduce her sexual desire. If this woman had been told by her obstetrician to use a lubricant while breastfeeding, these outcomes could have been avoided. If she had given birth in a country where an episiotomy is the exception rather than the norm, her pain from a poorly healed incision scar could have been avoided, too.

Differing approaches to communication in general and conflict resolution in particular may also lead to problems of sexual desire. Picture the wife as having come from a family where the parents never argued in front of the children; when conflict was unresolved, the parents simply withdrew emotionally. In addition, picture the husband as having come from a family that engaged in open and intense disagreement, some of which became quite heated, but that quickly overlooked, if not forgot, whatever was said in anger. Their role models for how to deal with conflict are widely divergent. They do not know how to manage conflict in ways that feel mutually respectful and affirming. These two young parents are navigating what it means to be a family while sleep deprived and prone to bickering. Thus, disagreements may result in the husband yelling, while the wife retreats. If he then pursues her in bed, she may refuse his advances, feeling offended by his wanting to have sex so shortly after yelling at her. If this happens often enough, they may come to view her as having a problem of low desire.

Once the couple have decided that the woman has a problem of low desire, they may focus on trying to overcome or work around this problem, rather than confronting the root issue of poor conflict-resolution skills. For example, the wife may begin to agree to her husband's sexual initiations out of commitment to their relationship, and to avoid further conflict over lack of sex, even though it is without *sexual* desire. They may also have read that women's desire tends to be receptive rather than coming from within (Basson, 2007). As a result, she may attempt to "just do it" (see Weiner-Davis, 2003) in the hope that desire will follow, which may lead to her participating in sex while not aroused and eventually hurrying through intercourse to "get it over with." Over time, the couple may become less sexually engaged during sexual relations, the quality of sex may decrease, with less and less "foreplay," and the "goal" of sex may become "just doing it," rather than enjoyment. The woman can say she has "done it" while both of them silently remember a time when they anticipated leisurely encounters rather than dreading these hurried, laboured events (see Kleinplatz, 2010a, 2011). Indeed, sex may come to feel more like work than pleasure.

After six months of this pattern becoming entrenched, the woman may be referred to a sex therapist for treatment of HSDD. The role of the clinician here is to carefully assess the biomedical (organic), psychosocial, intrapsychic, and relational factors that combine to look like one (or each) of them has a disorder. If the therapist mistakenly attempts to fix only the symptom of lack of interest in sex, the outcome of therapy is likely to be dismal. Indeed, it is common wisdom that sexual desire problems are the most difficult of all sexual disorders to treat, with the poorest outcome (Leiblum, 2010). However, when the therapist untangles and addresses the numerous and interconnected underlying problems, the "disorder" may dissipate (Kleinplatz, 2010b).

Is there such a thing as a "pure" desire disorder—that is, one in which the root or essence of the problem is lack of sexual desire? Yes, but instances of such disorders seem to be rare, representing only a small fraction of desire discrepancy problems experienced by couples. More often, as the above example illustrates, the matter is much more complex. In the face of this complexity, Brotto (2010) proposed that the sections on sexual arousal disorders in men (i.e., erectile dysfunction) and HSDD remain separate in the *DSM*, but that FSAD and HSDD in women be collapsed into one category to be known as *sexual interest/arousal disorder* or *sexual arousability disorder*. Brotto's recommendation was accepted and appears in the *DSM-5*.

Therapy for Sexual Difficulties

The modern history of treatment for sexual dysfunctions begins with William Masters and Virginia Johnson (1970) of St Louis, Missouri. Prior to the development of their treatment paradigm, sexual problems were the province of clergymen, general psychotherapists, or marriage counsellors (the latter two of whom were using psychodynamic/insight-oriented models at the time). Approaches taken by such professionals were intended to embrace the whole person/couple but were time-consuming and none too effective. When Masters and Johnson released their classic book *Human Sexual Inadequacy* in 1970, they created the new field of sex therapy.

Masters and Johnson decided to tackle the presenting symptom itself in the briefest, most direct manner they could devise. Masters, a gynecologist, believed that sexual functioning needed to be brought out of the domain of philosophy, religion, and depth psychotherapy and should be the subject of scientific inquiry. Human sexual functioning, he decreed, was no different from urination, defecation, and respiration (Masters & Johnson, 1986). The study of each involved the scientific investigation of a bodily function, albeit one that could be impeded in its natural expression by psychosocial obstacles (just as might occur with constipation). This sentiment paved the way for the development of the treatment of sexual difficulties as a scientific endeavour. Simultaneously, this stance reified the belief that sex was *best* understood as a primarily physical phenomenon. The consequences of this position and the accompanying assumptions remain embedded in sexology over forty years later.

The treatment model developed by Masters and Johnson consisted of brief, intensive, behaviourally oriented sex therapy. The goal of treatment was to eliminate obstacles to sexual functioning (as defined in their human sexual response cycle; see Chapter 4) so that "normal" sexual response could be restored. Masters and Johnson observed that couples with sexual problems are often leery of "starting anything" with the implications of it potentially leading to sex, so they avoid touch entirely. Furthermore, when such couples do have sex, the tone is pressured, with a focus on measuring up and staying hard (in men with ED) or on reaching the set goal of having a well-timed orgasm (in men and women). The associated fears are known as performance anxiety. Masters and Johnson referred to the focus on monitoring one's functioning as **spectatoring**.

Masters and Johnson's major therapy innovation, which remains a mainstay in the treatment of sexual dysfunctions at present, was the use of **sensate focus exercises**. This technique both restores affection between partners and simultaneously prevents the fear and demand characteristics associated with sex from arising. In the initial stage, the sex therapist asks the couple to spend time each day touching each other, for approximately 20 minutes each, with no breast, genital, or anal contact permitted. This phase allows couples to reconnect physically without having the expectation that sex will follow. Thus, performance anxiety is circumvented and the individuals are

spectatoring Monitoring one's own sexual performance (as if one were watching from the bleachers) rather than simply enjoying giving and receiving sexual pleasure.

sensate focus exercises Sex therapy exercises developed by Masters and Johnson that involve couples focussing on the sensation of touching and being touched by each other.

able to attend to the sheer sensations of touching and being touched without having to wonder if their genitals will function adequately. In the second phase, couples are instructed to touch one another from head to toe, including the genitalia, without focussing on any particular area and with no particular aim, other than enjoying the pleasure of touch. The third phase consists of a variety of different exercises specific to a given difficulty, but in most cases the couple is instructed to engage in **non-demand genital pleasuring**. The objective at this point is to allow the couple to experience heightened sexual pleasure as well as to target the sexual symptom for elimination without triggering the anxiety and spectatoring engendered by the expectation of intercourse. For example, a man with ED is encouraged to let his partner stimulate him to the point of erection and then pause the stimulation repeatedly, allowing his erection to subside; eventually, his fear of losing his erection dissipates, thus enabling him to enjoy giving and receiving pleasure regardless of how hard his penis might—or might not—be. Ironically, the therapy is deemed to be successful when the man regains his capacity to achieve and maintain an erection rigid enough for penetration. This measure suggests that although Masters and Johnson were allegedly aiming to reduce the prevailing performance orientation to sex (which persists today), their actual goals may have been to enable sexual performance, particularly intercourse as illuminated by their criteria for effective treatment outcome (Kleinplatz, 2004, 2012a).

> **non-demand genital pleasuring** An element of Masters and Johnson's sensate focus exercises in which the couple focusses on stimulating each other's genitals without engaging in intercourse.

An important precept in Masters and Johnson's paradigm is that the couple rather than only the individual with the symptom/problem should always be the unit targeted in therapy. Even when the problem is clearly and distinctly located in the man or woman (e.g., his rapid ejaculation or her inability to have an orgasm), given that the problem occurs within their relationship, both partners must be involved in solving the problem.

In the forty or so years since the development of this treatment paradigm, successive trends for the treatment of sexual difficulties have come and gone. In the 1970s, Masters and Johnson's model was adopted widely and rapidly across disciplinary lines. Sex therapy emerged as a distinct subfield within the broad array of mental health and medical professionals. In 1974, Helen Singer Kaplan, a psychiatrist with a psychoanalytic background, encouraged therapists to add remote influences (i.e., early life experiences) to the assessment of sexual problems, rather than focussing only on recent or immediate contributors. Nonetheless, even Kaplan said that there was little need to go beyond treating the immediate symptom unless the sexual difficulty proved unusually recalcitrant to remediation.

Sex Therapy in the New Millennium

The focus on eliminating sexual symptoms as obstacles to normative sexual functioning has remained a feature of the predominant treatment models. To the extent that sex therapy has been effective at ameliorating symptoms of sexual difficulties, it has been easy to overlook the conflating of symptoms with underlying problems (Kleinplatz, 2001b, 2004, 2012a). The confusion and the paradigm that has been built upon it have been strengthened by the success of the PDE-5 inhibitors in ameliorating the functioning of men with ED. As discussed above, PDE-5 inhibitors have been promoted as the "solution" to ED, even though they do not solve all of the underlying issues associated with ED (e.g., lack of arousal resulting from lack of appropriately arousing stimulation). In the years leading up to the release of Viagra, the notion was promoted widely that not only would erectogenic drugs facilitate blood flow to the penis but that the problem was, in essence, a matter of hydraulics (e.g., Goldstein in Burns & Braun, 1998, and in Leland, 1997). This sort of reasoning—that if the symptom can be relieved by agent A, the problem is the lack of agent A—is interesting. It is equivalent to saying that if Aspirin works on headaches, the cause of headaches is lack of Aspirin. (This type of logical fallacy is known as *post hoc ergo propter hoc*.) This approach has infused many current clinical and research initiatives directed at the treatment of sexual difficulties (see the "Ethical Debate" box).

In recent years, the field of sex therapy has grown increasingly fragmented. Much of the treatment of sexual difficulties is now provided by individuals with minimal training in sexuality or in individual and couples therapy. Since the mid-1990s, the increasing medicalization of the field has meant less emphasis on the complexity of sexual difficulties, to an extent that Masters and Johnson could not have envisioned. Unfortunately, over the course of these same years, the reduction in hours devoted to medical school training in sexual matters has left physicians poorly equipped to deal with sexual difficulties (Kleinplatz, 2012a). This makes it all the more important that an individual or couple with sexual difficulties seek out a clinician with expertise in both human sexuality and psychotherapy. The rationale for certification in sex

Ethical Debate

Pink Viagra for Women?

In the past ten years, at least five drugs have been touted as "pink Viagra for women," promising effective treatment of low sexual desire in women. None of these drugs have been approved by either the Food and Drug Administration (FDA) or Health Canada, and those that have undergone the approval process have been found to be ineffective, unsafe, or both. However, in the years leading up to the manufacturers' hoped-for release of their new blockbuster drug, the potential value of such "treatments" tends to receive much attention in the media. One of the more conspicuous arguments in recent years has been that women are entitled to pharmaceutical treatment for their sexual disorders just as men are entitled to the PDE-5 inhibitors. Sue Goldstein, an administrator who oversaw clinical trials sponsored by Boehringer Ingelheim for their drug Flibanserin (which was rejected by both the FDA and Health Canada in 2010), has strongly supported such arguments:

> Would anyone deny a man the right to an erection? Would anyone deny a woman the right to have her breast cancer or heart disease treated? . . . When is it really my turn? (S.W. Goldstein, 2009, p. 302)

On the other side are a variety of women's health advocates and public policy experts who question (1) whether low desire is necessarily problematic,

and if so, whether it is necessarily pathological; (2) whether low desire is to be understood as a biochemical disorder or something more complex; (3) whether low desire is a disease (e.g., like breast cancer); (4) whether low desire can be understood at all—and therefore treated effectively—outside its intrapsychic, interpersonal, or psychosocial contexts, and (5) whether low desire necessarily requires treatment (cf., Moynihan & Mintzes, 2010). Moynihan and Mintzes (2010) regard the pharmaceutical companies' attempts to drum up a market for a "problem" that is neither clearly a disease nor one for which there is actually an effective treatment as a classic example of "disease mongering." They point out that pharmaceutical firms often exaggerate the magnitude of the "problem" and the benefits of the "solution" while minimizing the potential harm associated with unproven treatments.

Who do you think should get to decide how serious the complaint is and what the nature of the problem might be? Who should determine how problems are to be defined? How is low desire similar to or different from breast cancer or erectile dysfunction? Should the media promote (and should Health Canada approve) drugs without data as to safety and effectiveness so that women can feel that their problems, too, "count"? Who gets to determine which treatments should be available when the data are not clear?

therapy is consumer protection—protection of the public from medical and mental health professionals who have inadequate knowledge of and training in human sexuality (Kleinplatz, 2009, 2012b). The requirements for certification in sex therapy presuppose that one has already been trained in and demonstrated competence in individual and couples therapy. For more information on training and certification in sex therapy, see the websites of the American Association of Sexuality Educators, Counsellors, and Therapists (www.aasect.org) and the Board of Examiners in Sex Therapy and Counselling in Ontario (http://bestco.info).

CHAPTER SUMMARY

Sexual difficulties are complex and difficult to conceptualize, understand, assess, diagnose, and treat. They stem from a wide array of intrapsychic, interpersonal, psychosocial, and organic causes. Although, historically, some researchers and clinicians have divided sexual dysfunctions into those of psychological origin versus those of physical origin, it is always the whole person or relationship that needs help—never merely the parts. In addition, although the temptation on the part of the individual, the couple, the clinician, and society is to focus on the physical symptoms of a sexual disorder, the more important and potentially more useful approach is to attend to the underlying problem(s) rather than only its manifestations.

DEBATE QUESTIONS

Suppose a drug were created (or a substance were discovered) that could cause instant desire. What would be the arguments for and against prescribing it to the 25-year-old woman whose case was given at the opening of this chapter? Would giving this drug to her be doing her a favour or causing her harm?

REVIEW QUESTIONS

1. What are the four major categories of factors causing sexual difficulties? What are some examples of causal factors within each of these broad categories?

2. Which common drugs (prescription and recreational) have an adverse impact on sexual functioning or desire?

3. How can one sexual problem lead to the development of other sexual dysfunctions?

4. In making treatment decisions, what are the criteria for deciding what constitutes a beneficial treatment? What are the criteria for effective treatment? Are these the same thing?

SUGGESTIONS FOR FURTHER READING AND VIEWING

Recommended Websites

American Association of Sexuality Educators, Counsellors, and Therapists: www.aasect.org

Annual Guelph Sexuality Conference: www.open.uoguelph.ca/sexconf

Board of Examiners in Sex Therapy and Counselling in Ontario: www.bestco.info

International Society for Sexual Medicine: www.issm.info

International Society for the Study of Women's Sexual Health: www.isswsh.org

Sex Information and Education Council of Canada (SIECCAN): www.sieccan.org
Society for Sex Therapy and Research: www.sstarnet.org
Society for the Scientific Study of Sexuality (SSSS): www.sexscience.org
World Professional Association for Transgender Health: www.wpath.org

Recommended Readings

Balon, R. (2008). *Sexual dysfunction: The brain-body connection.* Basel, Germany: Karger.

Barbach, L. (2000). *For yourself: The fulfillment of female sexuality.* New York, NY: Signet Books.

Dodson, B. (2002). *Orgasms for two.* New York, NY: Harmony.

Finkelhor, D. (2008). *Childhood victimization.* New York, NY: Oxford University Press.

Goldstein, A.T., Pukall, C., & Goldstein, I. (2009). *Female sexual pain disorders: Evaluation and management.* Hoboken, NJ: Wiley-Blackwell.

Goldstein, A.T., Pukall, C., & Goldstein, I. (2011). *When sex hurts: A woman's guide to banishing sexual pain.* Cambridge, MA: DaCapoPress.

Kaufman, M., Silverberg, C., & Odette, F. (2007). *The ultimate guide to sex and disability.* San Francisco, CA: Cleis Press.

Kleinplatz, P. (2012). *New directions in sex therapy: Innovations and alternatives.* New York, NY: Routledge.

Kleinplatz, P.J., Ménard, A.D., Paquet, M.-P., Paradis, N., Campbell, M., Zuccarini, D., & Mehak, L. (2009). The components of optimal sexuality: A portrait of "great sex." *Canadian Journal of Human Sexuality, 18,* 1–13.

Leiblum, S.R. (Ed). (2010). *Treating sexual desire disorders: A clinical casebook.* New York, NY: Guilford.

McAnulty, R.D., & Burnette, M.M. (Eds). (2006). *Sex and sexuality: Sexual function and dysfunction* (Vol. 2). Westport, CT: Praeger.

McCarthy, B., & McCarthy, E. (2003). *Rekindling desire: A step-by-step program to help low-sex and no-sex marriages.* New York, NY: Brunner-Routledge.

Nathan, S. (2010). When do we say a woman's sexuality is dysfunctional? In S. Levine, C. Reisen, & S. Althof (Eds), *Handbook of clinical sexuality for mental health professionals* (2nd ed.) (pp. 143–58). New York, NY: Brunner-Routledge.

Working Group for a New View of Women's Sexual Problems. (2001). A new view of women's sexual problems. *Women & Therapy, 24,* 1–8.

Zilbergeld, B. (1999). *The new male sexuality.* New York, NY: Bantam Books.

Recommended Viewing

Canner, E. (Director). (2009). *Orgasm Inc.* [Documentary]. USA: Astrea Media.

17 CHAPTER

The Dark Side of Sex: Assault and Harassment

SCOTT T. RONIS

LEARNING OBJECTIVES

In this chapter, you will

- learn what constitutes sexual assault and sexual harassment;
- consider various explanations for why sexual assault and sexual harassment occur; and
- encounter useful advice on what to do if you or someone you know has been sexually assaulted or harassed.

Trying to Move On: A Rape Survivor's Story

I was 15. When I got home from school that day, I found my older sister's boyfriend sitting on the couch, just sitting there all by himself. There was no one else at home—I guess that goes to show me that we should lock the door. My sister had already left for her night course, and my mom was working until 9:00.

I asked him what he was doing there, since my sister was out, and he said, "just hangin'." He moved over, and I sat down beside him because I didn't want to be rude. We started shooting the shit about some stuff, when he decided to tell me that he broke up with my sister. Then he started getting weird. He said the breakup was all *my* fault, and that I *owed* him. The way he said it really creeped me out, so I started to get up to leave.

All of a sudden, he grabbed my arm really hard. I think I cried out, because then he pulled me toward him and covered my mouth with his other hand. I tried to get away, but he was so much bigger than me. I was like 115 lbs and 5'3, and he was built like a football player. At one point I managed to knee him near the balls, but he only held me tighter.

He started groping my breasts and licking my neck with his disgusting tongue. He kept grabbing my hand and trying to get me to touch his dick. After a while he stood up and pulled me to my feet. I started twisting to get away, but he picked me up and started carrying me to my bedroom at the back of the house. I tried grabbing at the furniture, the walls, anything I could get my hands on, but nothing worked.

When we got to my room he hurled me onto the bed and threw himself on top of me. He kissed me all over my face and tried to make me kiss him back. When he reached down and started unbuttoning my pants, I felt like I was gonna puke. I was dizzy. Before I knew what was happening he was inside me. I tried with everything I had to push him off but he was too heavy. Eventually I gave up and waited for it to be over.

The whole time he kept mumbling things that didn't make sense. He said that I made this happen because I'd done something stupid. That I needed to learn my lesson. That he knew I wanted it. All I could think was that I had no idea what he meant. After he came, he looked me over and and said I was "a decent lay." When he saw that I was crying, he said I should feel lucky to have been with such a hot guy like him. Then he pulled his pants up and left the house.

My first thought was that I needed to get what remained of him off of me. I ran to the shower and made the water run as hot as I could stand it. I scrubbed at my skin until it was bright red. When I was finished I went back to my bedroom, changed the sheets on my bed, and cried in silence. I didn't tell anyone what had happened because I was afraid of what they would think of me. I felt ashamed and disgusted.

For the next two years or so, I had sex with any guy who seemed even remotely interested. I figured giving it up willingly was better than being forced to take it. It got to the point that it was the only way I could relate to guys. I also started drinking a lot and taking whatever drugs I could find, to dull the pain and forget.

After I finished high school I tried to clean myself up and even started having a real relationship with a nice guy. But I couldn't have sex with him without crying and feeling dirty. I dated him for a few months but it didn't work out. One of our biggest issues, and one of my biggest issues in general when it comes to guys, was trust. I just can't bring myself to trust men. I don't feel safe around them, and I'm worried that they'll take advantage if I let my guard down. I'm in therapy now, and the sessions are helping me sort things out. I feel stronger than I have in a long time, and my strength is what, I believe, will ultimately help me put this trauma behind me and move on.

—Based on a rape survivor's account

QUESTIONS FOR CRITICAL THOUGHT AND REFLECTION

1. Do you feel the above case represents a common type of sexual assault? If so, how? If not, why not?
2. What sociocultural factors contribute to girls being sexually assaulted?
3. What programs do you think should be implemented to (a) prevent people from being sexually assaulted in the first place, and (b) decrease the potentially negative effects that victims may have following a sexual assault?
4. What should non-offending parents do to maintain open communication so that their child will talk to them about the incident if she or he is sexually assaulted?

Introduction: Why Is It Important to Understand the Dark Side of Sex?

Although sexual activity is generally considered to be positive and a sign of emotional affection between consenting partners, it can also involve coercion or physical assault. It is important to consider the *dark side of sex* to understand the full range of sexual behaviours and desires and to be able to respond to unwanted sexual advances. In addition, because relevant public policies and practices are based in part on an understanding of unwanted sexual behaviours, knowledge of this area has implications for decreasing the prevalence of such behaviours. Thus, this chapter will cover the topics of **sexual assault** and **rape**, **sexual harassment**, and **stalking** by considering the current conceptual and legal definitions, typical contexts in which each occurs, and the subsequent effects of these acts. There has been substantial focus on these areas during the last thirty years, in both scientific research and the legal system.

Sexual Assault and Rape

Our understanding of sexual assault and rape and of the possible consequences of these acts hinges on how these acts are defined, and how we conceptualize the individuals who commit these acts. Various authoritative resources and world-recognized bodies—such as the *Diagnostic and Statistical Manual of Mental Disorders*, fifth edition (*DSM-5*; American Psychiatric Association, 2013), the Criminal Code of Canada, and the World Health Organization (WHO; Krug, Dahlberg, Mercy, Zwi, & Lozano, 2002)— have defined or classified rape and sexual assault in different ways. Surprisingly, sexual assault and rape are not specifically defined or classified in the *DSM-5*. Instead, they are considered to be possible elements or consequences of certain paraphilic disorders. As you learned in Chapter 15, the *DSM-5* describes paraphilia as "intense and persistent sexual interest other than sexual interest in genital stimulation or preparatory fondling with phenotypically normal, physically mature, consenting human partners" and paraphilic disorder as "a paraphilia that is currently causing distress or impairment to the individual or a paraphilia whose satisfaction has entailed personal harm, or risk of harm, to others." Therefore, a paraphilia is necessary but not sufficient for a diagnosis of a paraphilic disorder. Two primary paraphilic disorders that may be diagnosed in some individuals who commit sexual assault include frotteuristic disorder and sexual sadism disorder. In particular, rape has typically been cited under the clinical criteria for sexual sadism disorder, which is defined by recurrent and intense sexual arousal from the pain or humiliation of a person and is manifested by fantasies, urges, or behaviours; however, this description applies to only a small minority of instances of rape or sexual assault (Craissati, 2005). Indeed, researchers have argued that individuals who commit rape or sexual assault are often unlikely to meet these criteria (see Gannon & Ward, 2008). As a result, professionals involved in diagnosing individuals who have histories of sexually assaulting others are often recommended to consider using the *DSM* category of "paraphilia not otherwise specified" (i.e., "unspecified paraphilic disorder" in *DSM-5*) because of its broader criteria (Marshall, 2007).

The *International Classification of Diseases*, tenth edition (*ICD-10*; WHO, 1992), which is used internationally to classify medical diseases and other health problems, similarly does not have an explicit diagnosis for those who commit rape or sexual assault. Instead, it lists several "disorders of sexual preference," which include fetishism, exhibitionism, pedophilia, sadomasochism, and an unspecified disorder of sexual preference. Långström and colleagues (Långström, Sjöstedt, & Grann, 2004) examined previous *ICD* psychiatric diagnoses of 1215 adult males who had been convicted of serious sexual

---

sexual assault A range of non-consensual sexual experiences, including unwanted touching; oral, anal, and vaginal intercourse; and sexual violence.

rape The act of initiating sexual intercourse with a person without his or her consent; it may involve physical force, verbal coercion, abuse of authority, or an incapacity to provide valid consent.

sexual harassment Any unwanted sex-related behaviours that are considered by the recipient to be offensive, threatening, or demeaning.

stalking Harassing behaviour such as repeatedly following, intimidating, or tracking another person against his or her will.

crimes (i.e., rape, child molestation) and released from Swedish prisons between 1993 and 1997. The researchers were surprised to find that the most prevalent diagnoses for the sexual offenders were alcohol abuse or alcohol dependence (7.8 per cent), drug abuse (2.8 per cent), personality disorder (1.8 per cent), and psychosis (1.4 per cent), while only 0.2 per cent had a sexual preference disorder diagnosis. This seems absolutely astonishing for a group of people whose principal conviction was for deviant sexual behaviour! Overall, it seems that the diagnostic classifications for individuals with histories of committing sexual assault do not specifically capture the patterns exhibited by these individuals, or they are too general. Thus, based on the diagnoses in the major classification systems, it is unclear how sexual assault is defined, how many people engage in such behaviour, and what should be done in terms of treatment or other interventions.

The legal definition of rape and sexual assault in Canada has shifted in the last three decades from one focussed specifically on the *sexual* nature of the offence to one focussed more generally on the *violent* nature of the crime. Prior to 1983, the law defined rape exclusively as forced heterosexual intercourse enacted by a man on a woman (i.e., sexual penetration of a woman's vagina by a man's penis), outside of marriage. The rape law was criticized for being limited to sexual penetration, defining only males as perpetrators and females as victims, and excluding husbands from being charged with rape. In addition, a victim's prior sexual activities could be considered as evidence of her consent, which called into question her credibility as a victim. Under this law, many cases of rape did not proceed to trial or were dismissed in the courts simply because the woman had engaged in prior consensual sex with the alleged perpetrator or had engaged in sexual intercourse with a number of other partners prior to her involvement with the alleged perpetrator.

In 1983, the Criminal Code of Canada was amended, with an expanded definition of sexual assault under the general heading of "Assault," to make it easier for victims to report sexual assaults to police (Kong, Johnson, Beattie, & Cardillo, 2003; see Figure 17.1). The Parliament of Canada removed *rape* and *indecent assault* as specific offences and replaced them with three levels of seriousness of *sexual assault*: (1) sexual assault; (2) sexual assault with a weapon, threats to a third party, or causing bodily harm; and (3) aggravated sexual assault (Criminal Code, sections 271–3). The level of seriousness of the assault was determined by the amount of force used and the degree of injury sustained by the victim. In essence, these amendments made it possible for a spouse of either sex to be charged with sexual assault. Furthermore, the primary aims of the changes were to de-emphasize the sexual nature of the offence and to improve the conditions for the victims of sexual assault, so they no longer needed to defend their reputation in court.

Although many people today still use the term *rape* to refer to forced sexual intercourse, the Canadian Criminal Code exclusively uses the term *sexual assault* to refer to a range of non-consensual sexual experiences, including unwanted touching; oral, anal, and vaginal intercourse; and sexual violence. Consent is not obtained simply because of marital or cohabitational status or because of previous consensual relations. In addition, neither a silent or ambiguous response to sexual initiation nor tacit approval given while under the influence of alcohol or drugs (Figure 17.2) or while unconscious is a satisfactory indicator of sexual consent. Finally, the partner, with few exceptions, must be 16 years of age or older to legally consent to sexual intercourse. There are "close-in-age" exceptions (see Table 17.1), which state that 14- and 15-year olds can have consensual sex with someone who is less than five years older, and 12- or 13-year olds can have consensual sex with someone who is less than two years older. Note,

Assault

(1) A person commits an assault when

  (a) without the consent of another person, he applies force intentionally to that other person, directly or indirectly;

  (b) he attempts or threatens, by an act or a gesture, to apply force to another person, if he has, or causes that other person to believe on reasonable grounds that he has, present ability to effect his purpose; or

  (c) while openly wearing or carrying a weapon or an imitation thereof, he accosts or impedes another person or begs.

(2) This section applies to all forms of assault, including sexual assault, sexual assault with a weapon, threats to a third party or causing bodily harm and aggravated sexual assault.

(3) For the purposes of this section, no consent is obtained where the complainant submits or does not resist by reason of

  (a) the application of force to the complainant or to a person other than the complainant;

  (b) threats or fear of the application of force to the complainant or to a person other than the complainant;

  (c) fraud; or

  (d) the exercise of authority.

(4) Where the accused alleges that he believed that the complainant consented to the conduct that is the subject matter of the charge, a judge, if satisfied that there is sufficient evidence and that, if believed by the jury, the evidence would constitute a defence, shall instruct the jury, when reviewing all the evidence relating to the determination of the honesty of the accused's belief, to consider the presence or absence of reasonable grounds for that belief.

FIGURE 17.1 The offence of sexual assault is defined in Section 265 of the Criminal Code of Canada. (Note that the use of male pronouns is not meant to indicate that it is only males who commit sexual assault. Although many offences in the Canadian Criminal Code are phrased in gender-neutral language, this one is not.)

however, that these exceptions do not apply when one of the individuals is in a position of trust or has authority over the other, when one of the individuals is dependent on the other, or when one partner is somehow exploiting the other. Furthermore, the law provides protections for people with mental or physical disabilities, regardless of age.

Take a moment to think about the situation in which a teenager who is 16 years old, perhaps in Grade 11, is dating someone who is 13 years old, perhaps in Grade 9. By law, if they are having sex, the 16-year-old is committing sexual assault against the 13-year-old. As such, the older person could receive a lengthy jail sentence. Do you think this is warranted? Now, think about a person who is 15 years old having sex with someone who is 13 years old. If the 15-year-old turns 16 before the younger person turns 14, the consensual sex they are having would then become illegal. Providing further complication is the fact that according to Canadian federal criminal statutes, the age of consent for vaginal sex is 16 (with close-in-age exceptions for youth aged 12 years or older), whereas the age of consent for anal sex is 18 (with no close-in-age exceptions). Although cases have not been prosecuted differently based on the type of intercourse, the distinct laws remain. Clearly, these laws symbolize the reach of traditional social values and seem to be biased against people who have anal sex.

Prevalence and Incidence of Sexual Assault

Researchers have used multiple methods to estimate the scope of sexual assault (Gannon & Ward, 2008). For example, some researchers have used surveys to obtain **prevalence estimates**, by identifying the percentage of surveyed individuals who report having been sexually assaulted or having sexually assaulted someone else at least once. Others have used official reports to obtain **incidence estimates**, by examining the number of sexual assaults that are officially reported. Both types of estimates are biased and are assumed to undercount incidents of sexual assault.

Prevalence estimates of sexual assault vary substantially, depending on the definitions, measures, and samples used. In 1993, Statistics Canada conducted the first nationally representative survey dedicated to studying violence against women, which was called the Violence Against Women Survey (VAWS). The VAWS was a special one-time survey funded by the federal government that established a baseline and an understanding of physical and sexual violence among Canadian women; its methodology has since been replicated in other countries. The survey found that 51 per cent of all Canadian women had been sexually or physically abused by a man at least once, and that approximately 60 per cent of these women had survived more than one incident of violence. However, researchers have since pointed out that design flaws in the study may have led to an elevated perception of the problem of violence against women.

Since 1993, a number of smaller surveys investigating sexual assault have been conducted in Canada, both in the general population and on university campuses, and the findings are sobering. For instance, according to Statistics Canada's 2004 General Social

prevalence estimates
Estimates based on the percentage of surveyed individuals who report having participated in or experienced a certain condition in a given period of time.

incidence estimates
Estimates based on the documented instances of a certain condition in a given period of time.

TABLE 17.1 This table illustrates whether a sexual relationship between two people of different ages is legally consensual in Canada. Red indicates that consent cannot be given, orange indicates that consent can be given in some cases, and yellow indicates that consent can be given in all cases.

The youth is . . .	Under 12	12	13	14	15	16	17	18	19	20
And the other person is . . .										
Under 12	No*	No	No	No	No	No	No	No	No	No
Same age	No	Yes	Yes	Yes	Yes	Yes	Yes	Yes	Yes	Yes
Less than one year older	No	Yes	Yes	Yes	Yes	Yes	Yes	Yes	Yes	Yes
Less than two years older	No	Yes	Yes	Yes	Yes	Yes	Yes	Yes	Yes	Yes
Less than three years older	No	No	No	Yes	Yes	Yes	Yes	Yes	Yes	Yes
Less than four years older	No	No	No	Yes	Yes	Yes	Yes	Yes	Yes	Yes
Less than five years older	No	No	No	Yes	Yes	Yes	Yes	Yes	Yes	Yes
More than five years older	No	No	No	No	No	Yes	Yes	Yes	Yes	Yes

*Children under the age of 12 cannot legally consent to any sexual activity. However, it is not an offence if two children under the age of 12 engage in sexual activities with each other.

Note: Even close-in-age exceptions are not considered consensual when one of the individuals is in a position of trust or authority with the other, one is in a relationship of dependency with the other, or if the relationship between them is found to be exploitative. Furthermore, there are protections for people mental or physical disabilities, regardless of age.

Survey (GSS), which was conducted with a nationally representative sample of respondents, there were approximately 1977 incidents of sexual assault per 100,000 people aged 15 years or older. The rates of sexual victimization were nearly five times higher for females than for males. Interestingly, of the three types of violent crimes recorded by the GSS, sexual assault was the least likely to be reported to the authorities, with less than 10 per cent of incidents being reported compared to 47 per cent of robberies and 40 per cent of general physical assaults. It seems clear that, despite widespread education against blaming victims, women are still hesitant to report sexual assaults. University women are at particularly high risk for sexual assault, with between 20 and 25 per cent reporting having experienced an attempted or completed rape up to the time when they were surveyed (Belknap, 2010). Furthermore, one study found that 7 out of 10 women at university reported experiencing "emotional manipulation" by a male partner who was trying to get them to engage in sex-

FIGURE 17.2 So-called "date rape drugs" include alcohol and drugs such as flunitrazepam (roofies, e.g., Rohypnol), GHB (liquid ecstasy), and ketamine (special K). Many of these drugs are easily administered (e.g., in a drink) and odourless and tasteless, and they can cause confusion, drowsiness, disorientation, and decreased inhibitions, as well as more serious side effects.

ual activity (Struckman-Johnson, Struckman-Johnson, & Anderson, 2003). Prevalence rates among children and teens are somewhat lower than rates among adults, but they remain alarmingly high. Indeed, in a random sample of 2000 children aged 10 to 16 years, Boney-McCoy and Finkelhor (1995) found that 7.6 per cent had been sexually victimized during the previous year. This finding is especially alarming given that children who experience unwanted sexual intercourse and other types of unwanted sexual activities have been shown to be two to four times more likely to be sexually assaulted after age 16 (Coid et al., 2001).

Surveys of university men have found that 25 to 57 per cent acknowledged having committed sexual assault, including using verbal manipulation, emotional manipulation, deceit, or extreme verbal pressure to obtain sex with a non-consensual partner (Byers & Eno, 1991; Struckman-Johnson et al., 2003). Although one may explain these high rates as a consequence of the high frequency of intimate interactions that typically take place on university campuses, similar rates have been found among men in the general community (Senn, Desmarais, Verberg, & Wood, 2000). Thus, there seems to be substantial evidence that many men engage in coercive tactics to get their partners to have sex with them.

It is nearly impossible to understand the actual number of victims and perpetrators of sexual crimes based on the people who are taken into custody (see Figure 17.3). Because so many sexual crimes go unreported to authorities (Belknap, 2010; Suarez & Gadalla, 2010), incidence estimates, which are based on official records, likely underestimate the number of sexual assaults and the percentage of the population who experience unwanted sexual contact. According to data from the Uniform Crime Reporting Survey published in 2012, there were approximately 22,000 arrests for sexual assault in Canada in the past year.

Human Sex Trafficking

Human sex trafficking, a modern term for a form of sexual slavery, involves the buying, selling, and smuggling of human beings for the purposes of forcing them to perform sexual acts. Sex trafficking is an international concern. Because of social, political,

human sex trafficking
A form of slavery in which individuals are forced to engage in sexual acts for others' profit.

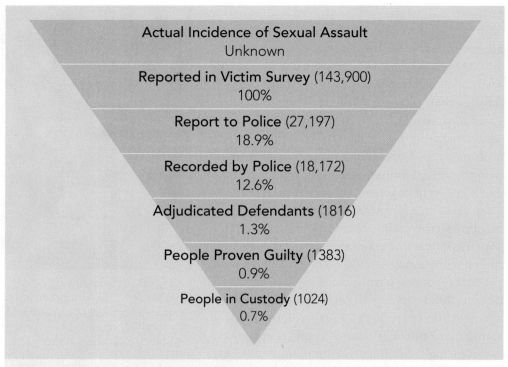

FIGURE 17.3 The results of a study of recidivism of sexual offenders in Australia indicated that few cases of sexual assault proceed to the point where the accused is sentenced to incarceration (Gelb, 2007). Only a small fraction of sexual assaults are actually reported to the police in the first place, and there are several points in the justice system where the cases are filtered out and do not proceed further.

and economic strife throughout the world, and because of widespread disparity among social and/or economic groups, certain individuals may become susceptible to being trafficked or endure exploitative conditions.

While many of us do not think about humans being trafficked into Canada, this unfortunately happens. In this country, the victims of human trafficking are primarily found in some avenue of the sex trade, including forced prostitution or the adult service industry (e.g., exotic dance clubs, massage parlours, escort agencies). Although some immigrants choose to work for legitimate adult service businesses, there is great risk for foreign workers to be sexually exploited. The Royal Canadian Mounted Police (2010) reported that 800 to 1200 people are trafficked in and through Canada each year. Individuals caught for trafficking another human being can receive a prison term of up to 14 years, although most perpetrators spend less than three years in custody. Many traffickers are finding Canada a relatively easy target, compared to countries with high minimum sentences for human trafficking, in which to have a sex trafficking business.

Effects of Sexual Assault

A large number of studies have investigated the short- and long-term psychological, social, and physical health reactions of females following sexual assault. Overall findings indicate that sexual assault is one of the most severe of all traumas, potentially impacting a woman's adjustment for a year or more! Studies have shown that women experience persistent negative effects following assaults committed by strangers as well as by acquaintances or someone that they know well. Furthermore, sexual assaults involving verbal coercion or physical incapacitation (e.g., drug-facilitated sexual assault) can have similarly persistent effects compared to those involving violence or other forms of physical aggression (Brown, Testa, & Messman-Moore, 2009).

To help explain victims' typical response patterns to sexual assault, Burgess and Holmstrom (1974) coined the term ***rape trauma syndrome (RTS)***, which describes a two-phase response pattern consisting of an acute, or disruptive, phase and a reorganization phase. During the *acute phase*, which begins immediately following a sexual assault, it is common for victims to experience a range of emotional reactions such as anxiety, intense fear, anger, depression, disbelief, and vulnerability. In particular, a woman may blame herself for what happened, possibly reflecting broader sociocultural attitudes that assign blame to women for their own victimization and, by default, excuse the perpetrator (Glenn & Byers, 2009). Indeed, she may think to herself, "I should have known better than to go out at night by myself," or she may wonder, "did I lead him on and give him the wrong messages?" or "why did I trust that guy?" Other victims may report feeling numb and disorganized or may even deny that they were sexually assaulted as an avoidance response against potentially overwhelming feelings of confusion and shock (particularly if they were assaulted by a partner or someone in whom they trusted). The emotional reactions in this phase often escalate and persist for one to two months but then slowly begin to decrease, although the sexual assault is never forgotten (Rothbaum, Foa, Riggs, Murdock, & Walsh, 1992). In the *reorganization phase*, which can last from months to years, victims attempt to restore order in their lives and re-establish a sense of control. Many victims report that making some lifestyle changes, such as changing where they live or what they do for work, helps them to regain control and can even lead to positive growth (Frazier, Mortensen, & Steward, 2005).

Although research has demonstrated that the majority of victims recover from the trauma of sexual assault within five years, nearly one third of victims have substantial difficulty that persists years beyond the acute aftermath of the incident (Rothbaum et al., 1992). A significant number of sexual assault survivors develop **post-traumatic stress disorder (PTSD)**, an official *DSM* diagnosis that describes the persistent psychological symptoms (e.g., insomnia, depression, flashbacks, nightmares, avoidance behaviour patterns) that a person may have following a traumatic event. There is some evidence that susceptibility to PTSD in response to a traumatic event is hereditary. Thus, it might be written into some peoples' genes that a traumatic event triggers PTSD, whereas the same event for other people does not trigger the same response. According to the cognitive-behavioural perspective, which asserts that internal mental processes reciprocally interact with behaviours and emotional responses, PTSD becomes persistent when survivors develop a memory schema about the trauma and their responses to it (Ehlers & Clark, 2000). This memory schema is continually activated by individual or interpersonal cues, which leads to a sense of serious current threat and maladaptive interpretations of new events. Once activated, the perception of current threat is also accompanied by intrusions (e.g., flashbacks) and other symptoms, such as hyperarousal or anxiety.

Although we automatically assume that a person who is sexually assaulted will experience short- and/or long-term negative effects, some researchers have actually suggested that some people experience **post-traumatic growth** as a result of their sexual assault. Qualitative studies have found respondents who say, for example, that they spend more time with people who are important to them or that have transformed what they consider to be important in their lives following a sexual assault. Of course, it is hard to know whether these reported changes are significant relative to any negative impacts. Furthermore, we should consider that people can experience alternating periods of distress and positive growth for a long time after the assault. It is also possible that perceived growth can be actual change or primarily a defensive illusion that

rape trauma syndrome (RTS)
A two-phase stress response pattern that typically follows a sexual assault.

post-traumatic stress disorder (PTSD) An anxiety disorder that can develop after exposure to a life-threatening or serious anxiety-producing event and can cause persistent and chronic psychological symptoms, such as flashbacks, nightmares, avoidance of stimuli associated with the trauma, hyperarousal, and anxiety.

post-traumatic growth
Positive psychological change following a major negative event.

one has been transformed positively as a way to cope with or make sense of the trauma (Park, 2010). Overall, the notion of post-traumatic growth is complex.

The effects of sexual assault usually extend beyond the victim. When a family member or intimate partner is sexually assaulted, it is normal to feel anger, frustration, and intense feelings of revenge. In addition, while a person typically wants to support his or her family member or partner, he or she may experience guilt, self-blame, or a sense of loss or emotional withdrawal from the survivor. For example, a non-offending parent may feel guilty for not picking up on previous signals that would have indicated her child was being sexually abused. Overall, it is important that negative feelings be acknowledged and for family members and partners to obtain emotional support, as this will likely serve as a foundation to provide critical care to the survivor.

Recovery is affected by multiple factors related to the sexual assault, social support and professional help received following the assault, and the degree to which a victim blames himself or herself. Some victims report that the actual sexual assault was second to the response received from others in terms of its impact on their well-being. Support from family members, significant others, and colleagues or acquaintances can lead to decreased self-blame and other negative feelings and better likelihood for recovery. Alternatively, a lack of support can lead to revictimization and longer-lasting negative consequences. As such, police officers, medical physicians, and other first responders are often trained on how to work with individuals who allege that sexual assault has occurred, because the response of these professionals can substantially impact the emotional effects of sexual assault on victims.

Victims of sexual assault often find an easier road to recovery by obtaining professional help (Figure 17.4). The most widely studied treatment for sexual assault victims is cognitive-behavioural therapy, which includes stress inoculation training (SIT), prolonged exposure (PE), and cognitive processing therapy (CPT) (Vickerman & Margolin, 2009). Briefly, SIT involves psychoeducation to normalize fear and avoidance behaviours, establishing and assigning hierarchical exposure assignments to target assault-related phobias (e.g., darkness, strange places, unknown men), and training in various coping strategies (e.g., muscle relaxation exercises, guided self-dialogue, role playing). PE focusses on decreasing anxiety with sexual assault memories and helps victims to establish more organized trauma stories by teaching them coping exercises and by imaginably re-exposing them to the assault while they repeatedly retell the details of their assault. CPT helps victims to integrate their trauma into pre-existing cognitive schemas, thus decreasing avoidance and intrusive thoughts. Similar to SIT and PE, CPT involves psychoeducation, exposure, and cognitive techniques. Patients are asked to write personal accounts of their trauma and to explore the personal meanings of the trauma in journals and then review and question what they have written during and between sessions. Another exposure-based treatment, **eye movement desensitization and reprocessing (EMDR)**, has been shown to be effective in some small studies, although it is unclear which components of the treatment are necessary for improvement. EMDR is a psychotherapy approach that integrates psychodynamic, cognitive-behavioural, interpersonal, experiential, and body-centred therapies. However,

eye movement desensitization and reprocessing (EMDR) A form of psychotherapy to alleviate trauma-related symptoms and associated distressing memories through exposure to stimuli of traumatic events while simultaneously focussing on dual attention stimulus (e.g., hand-tapping, electronic- or therapist-directed lateral eye movement).

FIGURE 17.4 Although the effects of sexual assault are different for everyone, many people find that professional psychotherapy can help in dealing with trauma and consequences of the assault.

what distinguishes EMDR from other therapies is its emphasis on the element of bilateral stimulation through eye movements, tones, or finger tapping during imaginal exposure exercises. Supportive counselling (e.g., talk therapy) and pharmacotherapy (e.g., antidepressant medication) have also been shown to be effective for some individuals and for addressing some symptoms.

Reasons for Sexual Assault

In determining the reasons for sexual assault, it is important to separate fact from myth and situational characteristics from personal characteristics. Criminologists have attempted to explain individuals' risk of sexual assault victimization by the convergence of several factors: risky situations, suitable targets, motivated perpetrators, and an absence of capable guardians (Ullman, 2007). Indeed, there are a variety of contextual factors that can contribute to the occurrence of a sexual assault (Figure 17.5). Furthermore, researchers who study the people who commit sexual assaults have distinguished between trait characteristics (i.e., characteristics that do not change easily) and state/dynamic characteristics (i.e., personal characteristics that change according to personal or situational factors). Knowledge of state/dynamic characteristics can most directly help individuals decrease their likelihood of being sexually assaulted, whereas trait characteristics are most often addressed through broad policy reform and intervention strategies in society. This section will cover **rape myths** as well as certain correlates of sexual assaults.

rape myths Inaccurate beliefs about sexual assault.

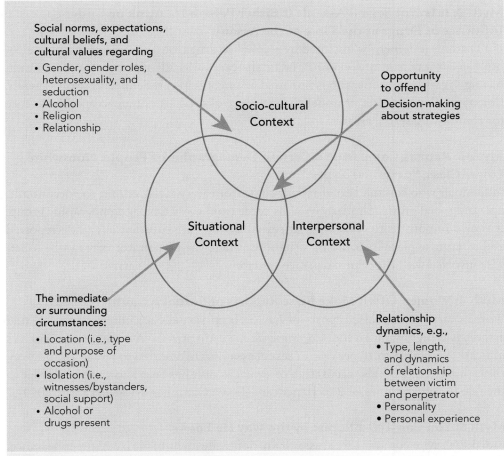

FIGURE 17.5 Several overlapping contextual factors can lead to the occurrence of a sexual assault.

RAPE MYTHS

Rape myths are widely held by both men and women, young and old, rich and poor. They have tremendous impacts on how victims of sexual assault view themselves and are viewed by others, and they offer assailants false information to draw on as they attempt to rationalize their crimes (Suarez & Gadalla, 2010). Furthermore, these myths legitimize sexual assault or even cause society to deny that it occurs. In effect, they can help perpetuate sexual assault.

While many rape myths are outright false, some contain kernels of truth, in that they have developed out of observations that are true in some cases. For example, while the myth that sexual assault usually occurs outside is not true, some sexual assaults do occur outdoors. Thus, it is important to understand particular rape myths and critically analyze the reasons these myths exist. Below are brief discussions of 10 of the most prominent and persistent myths about when and why sexual assaults occur.

Myth 1: Women Cause Men to Sexually Assault by the Way They Look or Dress.

This myth is simply not true. Studies have shown that women are sexually assaulted while wearing different types of clothes, and women of all ages and physical body types have been sexually assaulted. One study that interviewed individuals who were arrested for sexual assaults found that the thing they most often look for is a victim who seems to be vulnerable, not one who is particularly attractive or dressed in a certain way (Stevens, 1994).

Myth 2: It Is Not Sexual Assault If Either Person Is Drunk or Under the Influence of Drugs at the Time of the Assault.

If a person's judgment is impaired by alcohol or drugs, or if the use of drugs or alcohol has left a person unconscious, he or she cannot legally give consent. As a result, having sex with someone who is impaired or unconscious is defined as sexual assault. Conversely, being drunk or under the influence of drugs is not an acceptable defence for committing sexual assault.

Myth 3: Rapists Come from a Certain Demographic of People: Non-white, Lower Class, "Criminal Types."

Individuals who commit sexual assault come from every racial, ethnic, socioeconomic, age, and social group. Similarly, victims come from every type of demographic group. It is also important to consider that sexual assaults are substantially underreported and often take place in domestic situations, where the perpetrator may not be otherwise involved with the criminal justice system.

Myth 4: Women Often Make False Reports of Sexual Assault.

Women rarely make false reports of having been sexually assaulted. In fact, sexual assault is a highly underreported crime. Some estimates from victimization surveys indicate that only 5 to 10 per cent of sexual assaults are reported to police. In addition, the estimated rate of false accusation of sexual assault has been shown to be similar to the rate for other crimes, at 2 to 10 per cent (Lisak, Gardinier, Nicksa, & Cote, 2010).

Myth 5: You Can Tell a Rapist by the Way He Looks.

Individuals who commit sexual assault are not easily identifiable based on appearance. Some may appear friendly, normal, and non-threatening. Many are young, married, and have children.

Myth 6: Sexual Assault Usually Occurs Outside and at Night.

This myth is only partly true. While 43 per cent of sexual assaults were found to occur between 6 p.m. and midnight and 24 per cent were found to occur between midnight and 6 a.m., these assaults were not typically occurring out in public (Greenfeld, 1997). Indeed, most assaults (60 per cent) occur in a private home, with the largest percentage (38 per cent) occurring in the victim's own home.

Myth 7: Sexual Assault Usually Occurs between Strangers.

Despite the fear that dangerous men are lurking in bushes or dark alleys waiting for their potential victims, most sexual assaults are committed by someone known to the victim. This is especially true among university students (see Figure 17.6).

Myth 8: Sexual Assault Is an Impulsive Act of Sexual Gratification.

Sexual assault is primarily an act of violence and is used as a way to obtain power over another person. Although a person may *want* to have sex, he or she has the ability to not act on such desires or motivations. A person's suggestion to the contrary should be seen as more of a threat than an indication of desire or physical necessity (e.g., a man's statement that he will be in great physical pain without having sex is as an invalid, coercive tactic).

Myth 9: If a Victim Didn't Physically Fight Back, She or He Wasn't Really Sexually Assaulted.

Different people respond to traumatic, life-threatening events in different ways. Some people may fight their assailant with all of their strength, whereas others may respond in a non-aggressive, seemingly passive manner. Whatever a person does to survive an assault should not reflect on the nature of the crime committed against him or her.

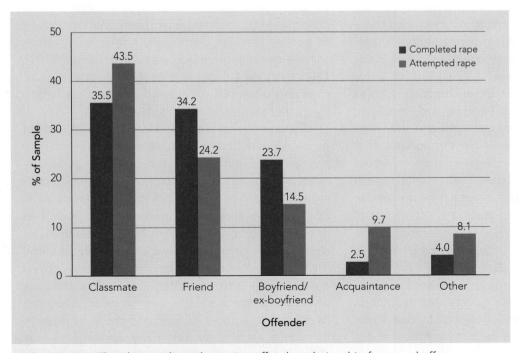

FIGURE 17.6 This chart outlines the victim–offender relationship for sexual offences committed by single offenders against female undergraduate students. As noted in this chart, an undergraduate woman is much more likely to be sexually assaulted by a classmate, friend, boyfriend, or acquaintance than by individuals outside these categories.

Myth 10: A Person Cannot Be Sexually Assaulted by Her or His Intimate Partner.

Within an intimate relationship, each partner must give consent each time sexual relations occur, and each may choose to say "no" for any reason. If one partner forces the other to have sex against her or his will, the act constitutes sexual assault. In addition, if a person changes her or his mind about having sex after first consenting, that person's partner should stop. Continuing with the sexual activity despite a partner's protests, or using verbal or physical coercion to obtain sex, is non-consensual and is legally considered to be sexual assault.

marital rape Within a spousal relationship, any unwanted intercourse or penetration (oral, vaginal, or anal) obtained by force, by threat of force, or when a spouse is unable to consent.

Most countries offer their citizens the legal right to say "no" to sex with anyone, including a spouse or a partner. Indeed, as noted previously in this chapter, sexual assault within a marriage has been illegal in Canada since 1983 (but see the "Culture and Diversity" box for differing views on **marital rape**). Yet marital rape does occur even where it is illegal, and an estimated 7 to 25 per cent of wives are raped at least once during their marriage (Russell, 1990).

SITUATIONAL CHARACTERISTICS

The characteristics of situations can play a role in sexual assault. For example, sexual assaults are more likely to occur in secluded places, such as a house; at parties at which

Culture & Diversity

Marital Rape Lost in Translation

Marital rape (or "spousal rape" or "intimate partner sexual aggression") is a form of domestic, or intimate partner, violence that is criminalized in various countries throughout the world. However, it remains legal or at least tolerated in many countries. As of 2006, marital rape was considered a prosecutable crime in at least 104 countries. In other countries, such as Afghanistan, Sudan, Egypt, Nigeria, and Honduras, sexual intercourse is a conjugal right and thus rape is not considered possible within the spousal relationship. Regardless of the legal differences across countries, the trauma associated with marital rape is similar to the effects of sexual assault by a stranger. Furthermore, because marital rape is often part of a broader pattern of an abusive relationship and is often not a one-time event, there may be cumulative negative effects (Cattaneo, DeLoveh, & Zweig, 2008).

Nevertheless, marital rape is not viewed as negatively in some cultures as it generally is in Canada and in much of the Western world. In one study comparing perspectives in various countries, about 10 to 20 per cent of the women surveyed in 5 out of 10 countries believed that a woman does not have a right to refuse sex to her husband under any

circumstances (García-Moreno, Jansen, Ellsberg, Heise, & Watts, 2005). In other studies, men in some countries (e.g., Pakistan, Egypt) are commonly found to beat their wives, particularly if their wives refuse to have sex with them (Ali, Israr, Ali, & Janjua, 2009). Overall, studies suggest that marital rape is common and often not considered abnormal or wrong by men or women in some cultures.

Cultures and laws collide in countries like Canada or the United States because of the ever-growing population of immigrants who come from other cultures and countries where women's rights and conjugal relationships are viewed in very different ways. For example, an immigrant woman who has been or continues to be sexually assaulted in her relationship with her partner may not consider this a crime if it was condoned in her country or culture of origin. She may also not report her partner because of language barriers or for fear of being deported or abused by authorities from whom she might seek help. Furthermore, as with many women, she may depend completely on the perpetrating spouse for financial support, which makes it difficult for her to report her spouse.

people are under the influence of alcohol or other drugs; or in situations where the victim is known to the perpetrator (e.g., romantic or non-romantic acquaintance relationships). In particular, alcohol use has been shown to play a significant role in sexually coercive behaviour in both university and criminal samples. In one study (Abbey, 2002), at least half of the sexual assaults among university students involved alcohol consumption by either the perpetrator or the victim, or both. Among sexual offenders at risk for recidivism, access to potential victims, limited social supports, and substance misuse are key situational factors that increase the likelihood of reoffending (Hanson & Harris, 2000).

PERSONAL CHARACTERISTICS

Identifying personal characteristics associated with sexual offending is important for risk assessment and treatment as well as in helping to solve criminal investigations (Beauregard, 2010). Studies have typically examined characteristics related to demographics, individual adjustment (e.g., cognitions, emotional and behavioural patterns), victimization histories, and interpersonal relations of individuals who have been arrested for sexual crimes. Although the research is limited in terms of appropriate comparisons (e.g., nonsexual offenders), studies have found some differences in personal characteristics between sexual offenders and people in the general population. For example, and perhaps most obvious, males are disproportionately the perpetrators of sexual assaults. According to 2007 police-reported data (Brennan & Taylor-Butts, 2008), 97 per cent of individuals accused of sexual offences in Canada were male; this percentage was significantly higher than the percentage of individuals accused of all other types of violent crimes who were male (78 per cent). In addition, although individuals who commit sexual assault come from all socioeconomic levels, a disproportionately high number come from the lower strata.

A number of researchers have attempted to identify the individual risk factors for sexual offending that may be targeted in treatment interventions (for a discussion, see Gannon & Ward, 2008). For example, Craissati (2005) emphasized five core dynamic risk factors (i.e., factors that can be modified or that change over time): intimacy deficits, offence-supportive social influences, offence-supportive attitudes, limited sexual self-regulation, and limited general self-regulation. Typical intimacy deficits may develop from beliefs that women are devious, an inability to understand women's facial affective cues, or a lack of empathy. In terms of social influences, individuals who commit sexual offences often associate with people who are supportive of their behaviour in various ways—for example, these people may demonstrate antisocial attitudes, reinforce negative beliefs about women, or commit sexual offences with the offender. In regard to the offence-supportive attitudes, sexual offenders are likely to hold strong attitudes of entitlement, which include blaming the victim, failing to take responsibility for their actions, and minimizing the negative impact of their actions on the victim. Finally, limited sexual and general self-regulation refers to sexual offenders' limited ability to inhibit strong behavioural urges.

Martin Lalumière and colleagues (Lalumière, Harris, Quinsey, & Rice, 2005) have provided a comprehensive discussion of the etiology, or causes, of sexually assaultive behaviour. Based on a synthesis of the forensic psychological literature on individual differences, they described three main routes to sexual offending: (1) **young male syndrome**, (2) **competitive disadvantage**, and (3) **psychopathy**. Young male syndrome refers to a route in which some individuals, usually young men, are willing to engage in risky, violent, and competitive behaviour in order to demonstrate their dominance and willingness to incur risks to attain goals. The incidence of their behaviour,

young male syndrome A theorized route to delinquent and/or criminal acts in which individuals engage in risky, violent, and competitive behaviour, especially during adolescence and early adulthood, to demonstrate their dominance and willingness to incur risks to attain goals.

competitive disadvantage A theorized developmental pattern in which the witnessing and expression of aggressive behaviours as well as a disadvantaged environment lead to chronic patterns of deviant behaviour in adulthood.

psychopathy A theorized developmental pattern in which an individual's antisocial behaviour is life persistent, has no known environmental causes, and involves manipulation and exploitation of others for personal gain.

including sexual assault and other crimes, peaks in late adolescence and early adulthood and then desists when important life events (e.g., employment, marriage) occur in adulthood. Competitive disadvantage and psychopathy both represent life-course-persistent routes to delinquency (including sexual assault), whereby antisocial and aggressive behaviours are expressed in childhood and continue at chronic levels late into adulthood. The distinction between the two is that competitive disadvantage describes a route in which some children begin life with neurodevelopmental insults (i.e., brain damage due to acute or chronic trauma) and are raised in disadvantaged environments (e.g., single-parent, poor, chaotic, and/or abusive households), whereas psychopaths show no signs of early neurodevelopmental perturbations. Also, certain neurodevelopmental incidents in the competitive disadvantaged pattern may result in deviant sexual preferences (e.g., sexual interest in children), whereas psychopaths are more likely to have more extensive and versatile criminal histories, are more likely to act for premeditated rather than reactive reasons, and show no remorse or guilt for their misbehaviours.

Some researchers and theorists have proposed that certain personal characteristics may make certain individuals more vulnerable to sexual assault. This view is expressed in **victim precipitation theory**, which has been faulted for shifting at least part of the responsibility for an assault from the perpetrator to the victim. Nevertheless, several studies have examined demographic factors and psychosocial histories of victims of sexual assault to determine personal factors that might be related to victimization. Although such studies have found that most demographic variables are not significantly associated with sexual assault, some correlates of victimization have been reported. As noted earlier, victim substance use is associated with sexual victimization (Abbey, 2002). In addition, previous sexual victimization, poor psychological adjustment, and insecurity about relationships with men are predictive of revictimization (Daigle, Fisher, & Cullen, 2008).

Some researchers have summarized what helps (and does not help) in preventing sexual victimization among women. Self-defence training and assertiveness training (see Figure 17.7) have been shown to decrease the likelihood of sexual assault and increase self-protective behaviours, assertive sexual communication, and self-efficacy in thwarting potential perpetrators. Specifically, effective strategies that are often demonstrated in these training programs include verbal and/or physical resistance (e.g., screaming, yelling, biting, scratching, hitting) and non-forceful physical resistance (e.g., fleeing, guarding one's body with one's arms, struggling). Programs that focus on increasing knowledge about sexual assault and changing attitudes that are believed to contribute to sexual assault have not effectively decreased the likelihood of sexual assault or changed peoples' attitudes. Moreover, non-forceful verbal resistance strategies (e.g., pleading, crying, reasoning with an attacker) are typically ineffective and are related to greater odds of sexual assault completion. The efficacy of newly developed technologies such as electrified anti-rape underwear and the Rape aXe system (see Figure 17.8) in preventing sexual victimization has yet to be determined through scientific investigation.

victim precipitation theory
A theory that suggests that victims are in part responsible for their assaults due to their own particular behaviours or characteristics.

FIGURE 17.7 Many experts have indicated that learning effective self-defence techniques can help women protect themselves against sexual assault.

Practical Advice Following a Sexual Assault

Sexual assaults—regardless of whether they involve violence or verbal coercion, or whether they are perpetrated by a stranger, an acquaintance, or an intimate partner—are almost always traumatic events. What happens immediately following such events can have a tremendous impact on the psychological outcome for the victim as well as on any legal consequences for the perpetrator(s). If you or someone you know is sexually assaulted, the first thing to keep in mind is that sexual assault is definitively against the law and that a victim should not feel blame for what happened. Although a victim is not responsible for the sexual assault, he or she may be able to take control over what happens after the event. If any medical care is needed, this should be obtained immediately. A victim should be encouraged to report the assault to the police. If someone you know has recently been sexually assaulted, you should provide support and encouragement as well as available options, but do not pressure the person to take a particular action.

Forensic examinations can be useful for providing key evidence that can be used in the identification and prosecution of a perpetrator. Internal forensic samples can be collected within 72 hours of an assault, and other evidence such as hair or stains on clothes or bedding can be obtained up to a week after the assault. However, the recovery of DNA diminishes dramatically with time, so it is important for the victim to be examined as soon as possible following the assault. Ideally, to help maintain any evidence, victims should not go to the toilet, eat or drink, bathe or shower, change their clothes, or disturb any evidence at the scene of the incident. This can be difficult to do, as was noted in the personal account at the beginning of the chapter.

Other steps can be taken following a sexual assault to ensure the physical and mental health of the victim. The victim can take medication within 72 hours of the assault to help prevent HIV/AIDS as well as other sexually transmitted infections. In addition, although the risk of becoming pregnant as a result of a sexual assault is low for a woman who is already using a continuous form of birth control, the victim may choose to take certain drugs to prevent a pregnancy. Further, many victims find it helpful to talk to a mental health professional or to get support from someone they trust, especially if they fear future assaults or retaliation for pressing charges. Going through the legal process can be unnerving for many, and most police jurisdictions have programs in place to help victims learn about and acclimate to the process so that they avoid further trauma.

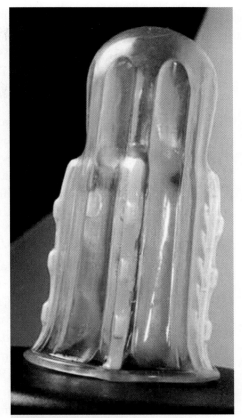

FIGURE 17.8 As a way of dealing with high rates of sexual assault among women in South Africa, Sonnet Ehlers designed the Rape aXe system for women to wear in their vaginas. The device resembles a latex female condom but contains razor-sharp barbs, which attach themselves to the penis when the device is penetrated by an attacker. The device must be surgically removed from the attacker's body, which could potentially result in the positive identification of the attacker.

Legal Sanctions for Sexual Assault

In Canada, the legal sanctions for sexual assault vary depending on whether the perpetrator is convicted of (1) sexual assault; (2) sexual assault with a weapon; or (3) aggravated sexual assault. If a person is found guilty of the first of these offences, the maximum sentence can range from 18 months (and/or a $5,000 fine) to 10 years in prison, depending on whether the crown prosecutor proceeds with a summary conviction or an indictment. In sentencing, judges often consider a number of factors, including the assailant's previous criminal record, the personal circumstances of the offender, the circumstances of the case, and the severity and physical harm of the crime. If the sexual assault involved the use of a weapon, the maximum penalty is 14 years. If the offence was listed as an aggravated sexual assault (i.e., an assault in which the perpetrator wounds, maims, disfigures, or endangers the life of the victim), the maximum penalty is life in prison. See the "Ethical Debate" box for a discussion about some of Canada's current sanctioning practices.

According to Statistics Canada, the median sentence for sexual assault and for other sexual offences is 360 days. In comparison, the median sentence for robbery is 540 days. Given that sexual assault involves a violation of one's personal body whereas robbery involves violation of one's property, the relative weight of these sentences seems to be flawed (Renner, Alksnis, & Park, 1997). On the other hand, the recidivism rate (i.e., the rate of people who will commit crimes upon release) is lower for sexual offenders than for offenders in general.

Sexual Victimization of Men

One myth about sexual assault that has not yet been addressed in the chapter is that only women are victims of sexual assault. While the majority of sexual assault victims are women, it has been estimated that 4 to 20 per cent of men in the general population have a history of being sexually victimized (Weiss, 2010). However, the true prevalence of male sexual victimization is not known because sexual assault among men, even in comparison to sexual assault among women, may be seriously underreported (King & Woollett, 1997). The underreporting by men is perhaps due to the social beliefs about vulnerability and masculinity or questions about the nature of unwanted intercourse among men, especially in cases where the perpetrator is female (Mezey & King, 1989). As a result of low reported prevalence, there is limited research on males who are sexually victimized. Most of the research that has been conducted has focussed on sexual victimization of men who have sex with other men, homeless male youth, or men in sexually segregated institutions such as prison.

It is possible for a man to be sexually victimized by a woman; it is also quite likely for a man to respond with a physical erection despite being victimized (Mezey & King,

Ethical Debate

Ethical Issues in Rounding Up the Usual "Sex-spects"

Sexual assault in all forms is wrong, and the law is very clear about punishments that should be given to people who commit various types of crimes. In addition to serving sentences of incarceration, paying fines, and/or performing mandated acts of civil retribution, individuals who are convicted of sexual crimes in Canada must register their names and their residential addresses with local authorities. For the offenders considered to be most at risk for future sexual crimes, local law enforcement agencies may notify the community in which the formerly incarcerated individual resides through the media, flyers, newspapers, or telephone. You might ask yourself, "How are these sentences determined, and why do sexual offenders receive differential punishments compared to others who commit murder, other violent crimes, burglary, and so on?" Registries and community notification laws are maintained under the guise of promoting public safety. The notion is that if the police know where sexual offenders live (at least the ones who have been caught), they will be able to secure the neighbourhoods with greater concentrations of registered sexual offenders; further, this information may prove useful when investigating new sexual crimes. While this may seem like a good practice on the surface, does it do more harm than good? Is it ethical?

1989). Research in New Brunswick has found that it is fairly common for men to report being forced or pressured into experiencing unwanted sexual activity (O'Sullivan, Byers, & Finkelman, 1998). The results showed that 19 per cent of men had experienced unwilling sexual activity in the previous year, and 9 per cent of women reported having used sexual coercion.

A recent study (Smith & Ford, 2010) focussed on data from a representative sample of 1400 male youth aged 18 to 24 years in the United States, taken from the National Survey of Family Growth. In this sample, 23 males (1.6 per cent) reported being sexually victimized by a male perpetrator, with the majority of the last incidents happening before age 15. Furthermore, 94 young men (6.7 per cent) reported that they had been forced by a woman to have vaginal sex. In contrast to youth sexually victimized by male perpetrators, the majority of youth sexually victimized by females reported being last victimized between the ages of 18 and 22. Youth who had been victimized by males and youth who had been victimized by females were similarly likely to report being physically hurt (14.6 and 11.1 per cent, respectively), pressured verbally (57.1 and 56.1 per cent), and given alcohol or drugs (46.2 and 46.6 per cent) in relation to their assault. However, more youth who had been victimized by males reported being physically held down (39.6 vs 30.8 per cent), physically threatened (41.5 vs 13.3 per cent), and victimized by a perpetrator who was older or bigger (59.2 vs 25.7 per cent).

It has been suggested that the effects of sexual assault among males tend to be largely the same as for females (Abdullah-Khan, 2008). Indeed, research has found that adult male victims of sexual assault, similar to female victims, are likely to report a number of physical and mental health problems (Choudhary, Coben, & Bossarte, 2008). Specifically, men who have been sexually assaulted often experience depression, anxiety, PTSD, anger, and emotional withdrawal. They have also been found to be at risk for attempting suicide (Mezey & King, 1989). Moreover, men who experience sexual assault victimization are more likely to report poor physical health, low life satisfaction, activity limitations, and infrequent emotional or social support (Choudhary, Coben, & Bossarte, 2010). In her study of people who called the United Kingdom's Survivors UK helpline from 1994 to 2001, Abdullah-Khan (2008) found that 39 of the callers were male survivors of sexual assault. One survivor, Patrick, aged 27, detailed the effects of his sexual assault experience in the following way:

> I still get flashbacks and memories and find it very hard to trust people. I get a lot of times when I withdraw and find it difficult to carry on at times. I still have times when I feel like ending my life. I still have difficulties sexually. I broke off with my previous boyfriend because I couldn't cope with a committed relationship. Sex brought flashbacks. When I'm on my own I find it very tough. I also had a breakdown. (Abdullah-Khan, 2008, p. 199)

Childhood Sexual Abuse

In addition to the Canadian laws on sexual assault, there are currently several statutes in the Criminal Code of Canada that specifically address the sexual abuse of children. The crimes of sexual interference, invitation to sexual touching, and sexual exploitation involve sexual contact between a child and an adult, either directly or indirectly. There is also a law against incest, which prohibits someone from knowingly having sexual intercourse with his or her parent, child, sibling (including half-sibling), grandparent, or grandchild. The overall prevalence rates for child sexual abuse in Canada are 4.8 per cent for men and 15.2 per cent for women (based on studies that included retrospective reports of adults on their experiences prior to 18 years of age; Pereda,

FIGURE 17.9 First Nations communities continue to feel the profound and long-lasting effects of the high rates of sexual victimization of Aboriginal boys and girls who were forced into government-run residential schools in the nineteenth and twentieth centuries. Prime Minister Stephen Harper delivered an official apology to former residential school students on 11 June 2008, and an independent assessment process was set up to address compensations in sexual abuse cases. Aboriginal leaders have strongly criticized the Canadian government's response as inadequate.

Guilera, Forns, & Gómez-Benito, 2009). Historically, the prevalence rates have been higher among children from First Nations communities (see Figure 17.9).

Nico Trocmé and his colleagues at McGill University have conducted the ongoing Canadian Incidence Study on the incidence of child abuse and neglect, including sexual abuse, based on reports from child welfare agencies and child protection services around the country. In general, they have found a drop in reported and substantiated sexual abuse cases from 1998 to 2008, although it is unclear whether this drop reflects a lower rate of sexual abuse perpetrated against children or merely a decrease in the disclosure of such abuse.

Child sexual abuse has been linked to a number of problems not only immediately following an experience but also years later. For example, it is associated with a higher incidence of depression, anxiety, PTSD, sexual dysfunctions, and interpersonal problems in adulthood (Sachs-Ericsson et al., 2010). Similarly, several studies examining the consequences of incest in general have demonstrated that individuals who have been victims of incest have difficulties in maintaining appropriate relations with others (e.g., Brand & Alexander, 2003). However, other studies examining childhood sexual abuse and incest have provided evidence that the negative effects of these experiences may be overstated in many studies and can be accounted for by negative family functioning or variability across individuals (e.g., McClure, Chavez, Agars, Peacock, & Matosian, 2008). Although children are fairly resilient to negative experiences, including sexual abuse, it seems clear that children who are sexually abused should get help to handle these experiences and the relationships with their family members. It is also important to keep in mind that some youth who are sexually abused also engage in coercive sexual acts with others, thus making it difficult to distinguish victims from perpetrators. A discussion about how we should treat youth who commit sexual crimes features in the "Research vs Real Life" box.

Sexual Harassment

Currently, there are four definitions of sexual harassment, each based on a unique perspective: (1) legal; (2) psychological, or subjective; (3) behavioural; and (4) sex-based (O'Leary-Kelly, Bowes-Sperry, Bates, & Lean, 2009). Under Canadian federal and provincial laws, sexual harassment is considered to be any unwanted conduct, comment, gesture, or contact of a sexual nature; it is a form of sexual discrimination and is therefore illegal. Included in the legal definition are two types of sexual harassment: *quid pro quo*, which entails coercing a person to comply with sexual advances in exchange for something of benefit to her or him (e.g., a job or a promotion, higher grades), and *hostile work environment*, which involves unwanted sexual advances that might cause offence or humiliation. According to the psychological definition, sexual harassment is any unwanted sex-related behaviours that are considered by the recipient to be offensive or threatening. From the behavioural perspective, specific sex-related behaviours (e.g., making a sexual advance at an inappropriate time or in an inappropriate place, telling a sexual joke) are considered to be sexual harassment regardless of whether a

Research **VS** Real Life

Should We Treat Juvenile Sexual Offenders Like Adult Sexual Offenders?

The juvenile justice and mental health treatments for juvenile sexual offenders are typically patterned on the treatments for adult sexual offenders, which are based on the available research on risks and correlates of sexual offending in adults. Although there are some similarities between adult sexual offenders and juvenile sexual offenders in terms of their histories, it is important for researchers, policy makers, and treatment providers to account for the developmental needs of adolescents. Recent research on the characteristics of juvenile sexual offenders has suggested that, to be effective, treatments should address multiple contextual factors associated with juvenile sexual offending, including behaviour problems, family relations, peer relations, and academic performance (Ronis & Borduin, 2007). Unfortunately, most mental health treatment approaches for juvenile sexual offenders do not take such factors into consideration, instead focussing only on helping these youths to overcome deviant thoughts and behaviours. Why do you think there is a disconnection between research findings and treatment with juvenile sexual offenders? Are there political or public pressures to maintain a system in which juvenile sexual offenders are collectively treated in ways that contradict the research evidence?

particular recipient is uncomfortable with such advances. Finally, sex-based harassment is behaviour that "derogates, demeans, or humiliates an individual based on that individual's sex" (Berdahl, 2007, p. 641) and can include seemingly neutral acts, such as giving someone the silent treatment or excluding someone from group events.

Sexual Harassment as an Employee

Sexual harassment in the workplace can interfere with a person's ability to do his or her job and may have negative effects on careers (those of the victim or the perpetrator) and/or on the overall workplace environment (see Figure 17.10). Surveys indicate that sexual harassment at work is actually very common (O'Leary-Kelly et al., 2009). The people most vulnerable to sexual harassment are those in lower-paying or less secure jobs; those who are of a non-dominant race, religion, or gender; people with a disability; those who are younger or older relative to most co-workers; and LGBTTIQQ individuals.

Both the Canadian Human Rights Act and the Canada Labour Code protect employees from sexual harassment. In fact, employers are required by the Canada Labour Code to develop public anti-harassment policies and to make every reasonable effort to ensure that no employee is subjected to sexual harassment. In Canada, many employers, and most certainly federally regulated ones, follow the guidelines set out by the Canadian Human Rights Commission (2006). With these protections in place, what should you do if you feel you are not being treated fairly and respectfully in the workplace? In most cases, because people who engage in sexually harassing

FIGURE 17.10 Sexual harassment in the workplace can have detrimental effects for the individuals directly involved as well as the organization as a whole. Most workplaces have policies in place to prevent and handle these types of situations.

behaviour may not be consciously aware that they are doing so, letting the person or people know how you feel about their behaviour will often lead to an elimination of such behaviour and may also improve the overall work environment. If you do not feel you can speak directly to these people or if they continue to engage in the behaviour after you have spoken with them, you should speak with a manager or an anti-harassment counsellor. From this point, the employer has the responsibility to investigate the complaint and to work toward resolving any issues. Although it is difficult to completely eliminate sexual harassment in some workplaces, no person should be required to confront and deal with discrimination on his or her own.

Sexual Harassment as a Student

You may have heard of friends or classmates who have been involved in a situation in which an instructor has suggested that their grade could be altered in exchange for engaging in some type of sexual conduct, or you may have been involved in such a situation yourself. Perhaps you have witnessed an instructor make sexual comments, make a sexual joke via the Internet, or present visually offensive sexual material that interfered with your ability to focus on your school work. These examples of sexual harassment in school may seem shocking, but sexual harassment is common among university students. Indeed, it has been estimated that 25 to 30 per cent of university students have experienced sexual harassment (Ménard, Hall, Phung, Ghebrial, & Martin, 2003). Importantly, many students do not disclose being victims of sexual harassment, so the actual numbers of victims on university campuses is likely much higher.

There are several reasons students may decide not to disclose their experiences of sexual harassment. First, students may blame themselves and perceive that they were responsible for negative interactions with the perpetrator. Second, they may perceive that the authorities to whom they might report the incident would not take their side or not be willing to discipline the perpetrator. Thus, if a university does not present as being an advocate for students, it is less likely that students will feel free to disclose harassment. Third, they may not perceive the event as serious, or they may rationalize away their concerns when thinking about the event in retrospect. In essence, victims may feel that the event does not fit their individual script for what the crime might entail. Finally, they may feel reluctant to disclose based on their relationship to the offender. For example, a student may feel more reluctant to report a tenured professor than she or he would a staff member (e.g., an executive assistant, a janitor) due to fear of potential retaliation from the professor or from school officials.

Effects of Sexual Harassment

The effects of harassment on victims can be traumatic and often cause long-term difficulties in both their professional and personal lives. Severe or chronic sexual harassment can lead to psychological, physical health, and interpersonal problems similar to those experienced following sexual assault. Specifically, sexual harassment often causes or at least maintains such problems as low self-esteem, irritability, withdrawal, depression, anxiety, inability to focus on work, and lack of interest in academic or occupational tasks. A person who is sexually harassed may have somatic symptoms, such as panic attacks, nausea, or sleeplessness. In terms of interpersonal problems, sexual harassment can lead to resentment and mistrust of others and a related change in life patterns (e.g., not going out with friends or co-workers). In the most severe cases of sexual harassment, many of these problems can contribute to suicide.

Studies show that an organizational environment may be affected as a result of sexual harassment and other events and situations related to the sexual harassment. Chelsea

Willness and her colleagues (Willness, Steel, & Lee, 2007) at the University of Calgary conducted a meta-analysis on the consequences of workplace sexual harassment. In this study, they found that not only were victims susceptible to decreased productivity but their co-workers also showed decreased productivity as well as increased conflict among each other. This was seen as contributing to increased absenteeism, loss of staff through resignations or firings, and overall decreased job satisfaction. Similarly, sexual harassment in schools can lead to students, not only previous victims, leaving school to avoid future harassment. Organizations can work to avoid such consequences by adopting clear anti-harassment policies and by acting quickly to resolve any complaints through a fair and thorough process. This will prevent future incidents of sexual harassment as well as stop a snowball effect of negative organizational consequences. As a co-worker or as a student colleague, you should work to avoid exacerbating a problem—offer support to anyone who reports having experienced sexual harassment, but avoid participating in idle gossip or spreading rumours related to the incident.

Reasons for Sexual Harassment

Why does sexual harassment occur in this day and age, when policies and regulations unequivocally prohibit such discriminatory practices? Although there is no clear answer to this question, it is likely that sexual harassment occurs due to a complex combination of sociocultural, organizational, and individual factors. To date, there have been five widely accepted theories of sexual harassment that have attempted to succinctly explain why sexual harassment occurs: sociocultural theory; organizational theory; sex-role spillover theory; natural/biological, or evolutionary, theory; and four-factor theory. This section will briefly cover each of the theories.

SOCIOCULTURAL THEORY

Sociocultural theories, based largely on feminist perspectives, suggest that gender inequality and sexism in society leads to sexual harassment. That is, sexual harassment occurs in various forms because of society's stereotypical view that males are dominant and superior to women. In turn, sexual harassment then contributes to maintaining gender stratifications by highlighting sex-role expectations. These gender stratifications occur at individual (e.g., among employees) and organizational levels. According to this theory, men and women are socialized to expect specific ways of interaction, with men as aggressive and dominant and women as passive and accepting.

ORGANIZATIONAL THEORY

According to organizational theory, sexual harassment occurs because of a wide range of organizational issues such as power and status inequalities. Similar to the sociocultural theory, the organizational theory suggests that power differentials within an organization affect the likelihood that sexual harassment will take place. However, the difference is that the focus of power differentials is not gender specific. Sexual harassment, which can be perpetrated by males or females, is often seen as an attempt to gain power within an organization. In addition to power differentials, organizational theory encompasses other contributing factors of sexual harassment, including permissiveness of the organizational climate, gendered occupations, and organizational ethics and norms.

A relatively recent and widely reported case that illustrates some of the key tenets of the organizational theory of sexual harassment is that of successful business executive and one-time Republican front-runner for US president Herman Cain. In late 2011, there were reports that Cain had sexually harassed several female employees during his tenure as CEO at the National Restaurant Association. In at least two of the cases, the women had previously settled civil suits with the association in exchange for their agreement to not discuss the allegations further. One of the women who publicly came forward reported that Cain had sexually assaulted her when she approached him for assistance in getting her job back at the association or finding a new job; when she questioned him about what he was doing, he replied, "You want a job, right?" Based on the allegations, this presents an apparent example of *quid pro quo* sexual harassment, in which an individual in a position of great authority attempted to use his power over this woman to gain sexual favours.

SEX-ROLE SPILLOVER THEORY

Although the organizational theory helps to explain contextual factors of sexual harassment, it does not focus on the influence of individual differences in attitudes and beliefs. In contrast, the sex-role spillover theory attempts to integrate contextual characteristics and individual gender-based beliefs. The foundation of this theory is that men and women have pre-existing beliefs and gender-based expectations for how to behave in various settings (e.g., workplace, school), regardless of whether these beliefs and expectations are applicable to a particular setting. For example, a harasser may have the belief that a woman should not be in a position of managing others despite the organizational perspective that workers should be able to advance and be in leadership positions without regard to gender. As a result of this gap between the individual belief and the organizational perspective, conflict is likely to arise in which the harasser's sex-role stereotypes are different from actual gender roles. Further, this would explain why some women in positions not traditionally held by women (e.g., high-ranking female military officers, female CEOs of large corporations) experience sexual harassment.

NATURAL/BIOLOGICAL THEORY

The natural/biological theory posits that sexual harassment signifies an expression of sexual attraction. According to this theory, because men have a stronger innate drive to be sexually aggressive and find a mate than do women, men who sexually harass women are simply using their power to try to maximize their chances of gaining sexual access and procreating. Thus, sexually aggressive behaviour may occur at work or in other inappropriate situations to increase these chances. Although this theory has a significant strength in acknowledging the impact of innate human instincts, there are several weaknesses. For example, sexual harassment in particular and sexual coercion in general are treated in very simplistic ways, with a lack of consideration of other individual and interpersonal factors. Also, proving the validity of this theory is difficult given that studies cannot be easily designed to test it.

FOUR-FACTOR THEORY

The four-factor theory incorporates key components of the previously mentioned theories. According to this theory, there need to be four conditions present for sexual harassment to occur: (1) the person needs to be motivated to harass by any number of factors (e.g., power, sexual attraction), (2) the person must overcome cognitive inhibitions to *not harass*, (3) the person must overcome societal and cultural inhibitions to *not harass* (e.g., an organization's anti-harassment policies), and (4) the person must overcome any resistance by the victim. Relative to the single-factor theories, the four-factor theory has been better supported by empirical research findings. Therefore, it seems likely that a combination of individual, sociocultural, and organizational factors lead to sexual harassment.

Legal Sanctions for Sexual Harassment

The punishment for sexual harassment, unlike the punishment for most other sexual crimes, does not include incarceration. However, according to the Canadian Human Rights Act, a person who is found guilty of sexual harassment can be liable for a fine of up to $50,000. Furthermore, the penalty for sexual harassment often goes beyond legal sanctions. Depending on the severity of the complaint(s), an employee can be subject to written reprimands (that are placed in the employee's file), fines, suspension with or without pay, demotion, transfer, or outright dismissal from a position. In addition, if an employee remains in the workplace, he or she will often be required to complete anti-harassment training sessions. Employers often have no tolerance for sexual harassment in the workplace.

Because sexual harassment typically occurs in situations where there is a large power differential, victims are often hesitant to file complaints. Knowing this, the Canadian Human Rights Commission has outlined suggestions for handling unsubstantiated complaints made in good faith, confidentiality, and retaliation in the workplace. If a person files in good faith a complaint that is not supported during an investigation and the complaint is ultimately dismissed, it is suggested that there be no penalty for the accused person or for the person who made the complaint. Regarding confidentiality, the Commission suggests that employers not disclose the names of any of the involved parties or the circumstances related to a complaint, except to investigate or as required by law. Finally, retaliation against someone who has filed a complaint is a serious disciplinary breach. Thus, anyone, such as another co-worker, who is found to retaliate against a person who has complained of harassment can be considered guilty of harassment and penalized accordingly.

Stalking

Stalking, known as criminal harassment in the Canadian Criminal Code, can be defined as harassing behaviour such as repeatedly following, intimidating, or tracking another person against his or her will. This also includes watching the places that the person lives or frequents and engaging in threatening conduct directed at a person related to the targeted individual. Often, the purpose of stalking behaviour is to attempt to control someone or to force a relationship with someone who is unwilling or otherwise unavailable. While the definition of stalking may seem simple, it is actually very complex. Although criminal harassment (i.e., stalking) is against the law, the behaviours that contribute to it (e.g., calling someone on the phone, instant messaging a person, inquiring about someone's whereabouts) are typically not. Complicating the definition of stalking even further is the fact that stalking behaviour is often defined based on the victim's perceptions of being harassed or threatened rather than on the perpetrator's intentions and actual behaviours.

You might wonder how typical it is for a person to be stalked (see Figure 17.11) or whether there are particular characteristics associated with being stalked. Studies in representative samples have generally found that approximately 12 to 16 per cent of women and 4 to 7 per cent of men report having been stalked at least once in their lifetime (Kropp, Hart, & Lyon, 2002). Although stalking affects a variety of people, young and old, rich and poor, single and partnered, certain personal characteristics have been found to be associated with victims of stalking. Research findings demonstrate that women are victimized more frequently than are men, with a ratio of about 3 to 1 (Spitzberg, 2002). In addition, the largest group of victims consists of individuals who are between 18 and 30 years old, at the higher end of the socioeconomic continuum, single, and living alone. Furthermore, high-risk groups include people with highly visible jobs (e.g., actors, politicians, public servants) or jobs that require engaging with young, single people (e.g., teacher, counsellor); gay men; and those with a history of sexual assault or physical abuse.

Effects of Stalking

Although one might not consider being stalked to be as traumatic as being sexual assaulted, it is important to consider that stalking is usually more chronic than sexual assault. In fact, several studies examining the duration periods of stalking have found that victims report an average range of 13 to 58 months (e.g., Blaauw, Winkel, Arensman, Sheridan, & Freeve, 2002). Perhaps as a result of this duration, stalking can have severe psychological, economical, and social impacts on victims. In general, victims are likely to exhibit depression, confusion, fear, distrust of others, anger or aggression, sleep disturbances, appetite problems, and psychosomatic symptoms (e.g., headaches, nausea). In addition, victims often report suffering financially due to decreasing the hours they work or attend school, an action they may take because they fear being followed by their perpetrator or because they are dealing with psychological issues. Moreover, victims may spend more money on security at home or in other places to try to protect themselves from actual and potential stalkers. Finally, in terms of social impacts, victims may avoid going out with friends or doing outside activities, which, in turn, may lead to increased isolation and other related difficulties due to lack of social support.

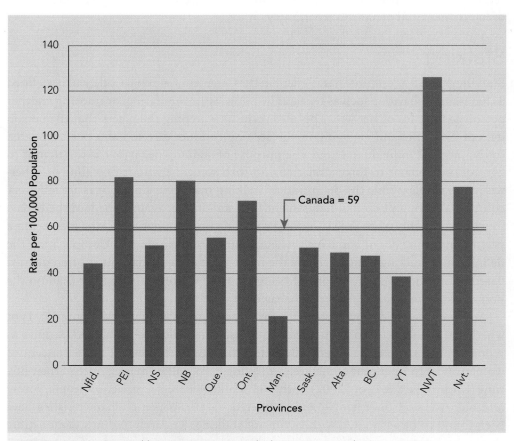

FIGURE 17.11 Criminal harassment in Canada, by province and territory, 2009.

Characteristics of Stalkers

Just as victims of stalking do not all share the same characteristics, not all stalkers are of the same type. However, there are some general or common characteristics that many stalkers display. As one might expect based on the typical gender of victims, about three-fourths of stalkers are male (Spitzberg, 2002). Stalkers tend to be older than other criminals, with the typical age being between 35 and 40 (Mullen, Pathé, Purcell, & Stuart, 1999). Not surprisingly, many stalkers have various psychological problems. Mullen and colleagues (1999) reported that 42 per cent of their sample of stalkers had a *DSM*-identified disorder, with the primary diagnoses being delusional disorder, personality disorder, substance-related disorder, or psychotic disorder. A criminal history is not uncommon for stalkers, as demonstrated by studies with criminal and victim samples (Blaauw et al., 1999; Mullen et al., 1999).

Reasons for Stalking

To understand and describe possible motivations for stalking, researchers have often attempted to develop classification systems. These classification systems are typically based on characteristics of the victim or the perpetrator, the relationship between these individuals, or the nature of the stalking behaviours. Overall, experts have noted that stalkers typically fit into two broad categories: (1) stalkers obsessed with a stranger, and (2) stalkers obsessed with someone they know. Stalkers obsessed with a stranger (e.g., a celebrity) often think that they will be able to gain the attention and favour of their victim. Alternatively, they may believe that their victim is already in love with them but unable to reciprocate their feelings because of external influences (e.g., being married to someone else, pressure from the media). Stalkers who are fixated on someone they know (e.g., an ex-partner, a spouse, a co-worker) presumably want to control this person because they disapprove of her or his current circumstances or behaviour, or because they believe that they love this person. In Canada, about 12 per cent of victims of criminal harassment are harassed by a stranger, while the rest know the person who is stalking them (Department of Justice Canada, 2003).

Legal Sanctions for Stalking

The punishment for committing criminal harassment in Canada is an imprisonment for a term not exceeding 10 years. However, there are also other sanctions that can be imposed on the perpetrator if he or she has committed a related crime. Importantly, if you or someone you know is feeling threatened, it is possible to achieve legal protection and perhaps a higher level of safety by obtaining a **peace bond**, which may be granted by a judge, a justice of the peace, or a magistrate for a period of 12 months and can be renewed on a yearly basis if necessary. Violation of a peace bond can lead to a person's arrest, and a judge can impose a sentence of a fine of up to $2000 and/or a jail term of up to 6 months. You may also consider obtaining a civil court order, such as a **restraining order** or a **protection order**. A restraining order is typically taken out against a spouse or a partner; it serves basically the same function as a peace bond, but it does not carry with it the same penalties if the person disobeys it. A protection order is a better option in cases of family violence; it may, for example, give temporary custody of children and the home to the victim, and it may order no contact between the victim and the partner. Although a peace bond or civil court order cannot protect a victim from someone who chooses to ignore it, obtaining such an order can be a useful proactive step in many cases.

peace bond A court order requiring a person to keep a certain distance from you, your workplace, your home, or any member of your family.

restraining order A family court order that forbids a spouse, a partner, or another family member from harassing the victim and sets limits on the conditions under which the person can contact the victim.

protection order A civil court order available in some provinces that provides various emergency and long-term orders to protect victims of family violence.

CHAPTER SUMMARY

Sexual assault is defined in the Criminal Code of Canada as a range of non-consensual sexual experiences, with three levels of seriousness, depending on the amount of physical force used. The Code defines consent as the explicit approval by a willing partner who is over 16 years of age, conscious, and not under the influence of alcohol or other drugs. The prevalence of sexual assault in Canada is not known, as many instances go underreported, and relatively few of the cases that are reported result in a conviction. Victims of sexual assault can experience both short- and long-term psychological, social, and physical consequences, some of which may be moderated through professional treatment. Although several static and dynamic factors have been linked to sexual offending behaviour, there are no clear predictors of who will engage in such behaviour. Self-defence and assertiveness training are the most effective tools for reducing one's risk of becoming the victim of a sexual assault.

Sexual harassment involves unwelcome sexual advances involving coercion or humiliation, generally in workplace or educational settings. Sexual harassment can have negative effects for the individuals directly involved as well as for the general workplace or educational environment. There are five major theoretical views of sexual harassment: sociocultural, organizational, sex-role spillover, natural/biological (or evolutionary), and four-factor. Stalking, or criminal harassment, involves repeated harassing behaviour such as tracking a person, watching places that a person frequents, and engaging in threatening conduct. Stalking can have severe negative effects on the victim, perhaps due to the typical lengthy duration of the offending experiences.

DEBATE QUESTIONS

What are the reasons for and against making people who have been arrested for sexual crimes register as sexual offenders? Is there evidence to support or refute the arguments for and against these policies?

REVIEW QUESTIONS

1. How is legal consent defined in terms of sexual assault, and how has this definition changed over the years in Canada? What are the close-in-age exceptions, and how is consent for having vaginal sex characterized differently from consent for having anal sex?

2. Who can be the victim of sexual assault? What types of people commit sexual assault? What situational and personal characteristics have been identified as correlates of sexual assault?

3. What are the five theories of sexual harassment discussed in this chapter? How are they similar to and/or different from one another?

4. How can sexual harassment affect a person's mental health and occupational well-being?

5. What are some strategies for dealing with or preventing sexual harassment?

6. What are the effects of stalking, or criminal harassment, on victims, and what might explain why the effects can often be as negative as those for sexual assault?

SUGGESTIONS FOR FURTHER READING AND VIEWING

Recommended Websites

Canadian Association of Sexual Assault Centres: www.casac.ca

Canadian Human Rights Commission: www.chrc-ccdp.ca

Centre for Research and Education on Violence against Women and Children: www
.crvawc.ca

Male Survivor: www.malesurvivor.org

Men Can Stop Rape: www.mencanstoprape.org

Minnesota Center against Violence and Abuse: www.mincava.umn.edu

Rape Is: www.rapeis.org

Slutwalk Toronto: www.slutwalktoronto.com

Stop Rape Now, UN Action Against Sexual Violence in Conflict: www.stoprapenow.org

Recommended Reading

Alcott, L.M. (1995). *A long fatal love chase*. New York, NY: Random House.

Easteal, P., & McOrmond-Plummer, L. (2006). *Real rape, real pain: Help for women sexually assaulted by male partners*. Melbourne, Australia: Hybrid Publishers.

Saguy, A.C. (2003). *What is sexual harassment? From Capitol Hill to the Sorbonne*. Berkeley, CA: University of California Press.

Sebold, A. (2002). *Lucky: A memoir*. Boston, MA: Back Bay Books.

Swift, C.F. (Ed). (1995). *Sexual assault and abuse: Sociocultural context of prevention*. Binghamton, NY: Haworth Press.

UFCW Canada National Council Women's Advisory Committee. (2010). *Workplace sexual harassment: Reference and rights guide*. Retrieved from http://www.ufcw.ca/templates/ufcwcanada/images/women/publicatios/harassment_brosh_jan2011_en.pdf

Recommended Viewing

Bienstock, R.E., Golubev, F., & Jacobovici, S. (Producers), & Bienstock, R.E. (Director). (2006). *Sex slaves* [Documentary]. Canada: Canadian Broadcasting Corporation.

Daniels, L. (Producer), & Kassell, N. (Director). (2004). *The woodsman* [Motion picture]. United States: Dash Films.

Daniels, L., Siegel-Magness, S., & Magness, G. (Producers), & Daniels, L. (Director). (2009). *Precious* [Motion picture]. United States: Lionsgate.

Jaffe, S.R., & Lansing, S. (Producers), & Kaplan, J. (Director). (1988). *The accused* [Motion picture]. United States: Paramount Pictures.

Simmons, A.S. (Producer), & Simmons, A.S. (Director). (2007). *Unveiling the Silence: No! The Rape Documentary* [Documentary]. United States: AfroLez Productions.

18 CHAPTER

Selling and Buying Sex

KEVIN ALDERSON

LEARNING OBJECTIVES

In this chapter, you will

- learn about why people buy and sell sexual experiences and sexually explicit materials;
- begin to think about the impact the sex industry has on the physical and psychological health of those who work in it; and
- consider social and legal issues related to the selling and buying of sex.

What Do You Do with Tracy?

Imagine that you are a child counsellor. Graham and Ronnie, a married couple with highly conservative Christian beliefs, come to you with their 13-year-old daughter, Tracy, for counselling. Tracy was caught by police giving oral sex to a young man in a city park. Graham was shocked to find out she was doing it for money! Graham tells you that Tracy has been given everything a girl could want; although they are not rich, both he and Ronnie have high middle-class incomes. Ronnie remains silent during the meeting, speaking only to answer questions. It appears to you that she feels like a failure as a mom and that she is also very embarrassed by the situation.

Tracy appears sullen, and when you try to engage her, she talks back sarcastically and says that there is nothing wrong with what she is doing. She tells you that lots of other girls are doing the same thing and insists that it is no big deal.

QUESTIONS FOR CRITICAL THOUGHT AND REFLECTION

1. What actions would you suggest Graham and Ronnie take to reduce the likelihood that Tracy will continue this behaviour?
2. How would you go about finding out if in fact other girls that Tracy knows are involved in **sex trade work (STW)**?
3. What impact would it have in working with this family if you discovered that a pimp was involved?
4. How would you go about trying to get through to Tracy so that she might stop engaging in STW?
5. What do you believe is an appropriate punishment for men who hire individuals whom they know to be underage for sexual purposes?

Introduction

Few subjects bring up more emotionally charged controversy than human sexuality. Most societies around the world and throughout history have regulated sexual behaviour, creating and enforcing a continuum between sex-related behaviours considered absolutely acceptable and those considered absolutely heinous or despicable. Such a continuum exists in relation to what aspects of sexuality can be bought and sold. Sexually suggestive content has become pervasive and widely acceptable in many areas of commerce—sex is used to sell everything from cars to cosmetics, and sexually suggestive performances are commonplace in the popular culture (Figure 18.1). Sexually explicit materials such as hard-core magazines and Internet pornography are not approved of by all, yet they remain widely available and commonly consumed. Still less acceptable are activities that directly relate to the selling and buying of sex itself. Indeed, while the selling and buying of sex is not technically illegal in Canada, it is illegal for anyone to publicly offer or seek out sex in exchange for money, and it is illegal for anyone to operate or visit an establishment in which sex trade work (STW) takes place; these restrictions make it nearly impossible for STW to occur in this country in a purely legal context. While many people have made legitimate points both for and against permitting STW among consenting

> **sex trade work (STW)** Work that involves a transaction between a seller and a buyer of sexual services.

FIGURE 18.1 The music recording industry knows that sex sells. Here Lady Gaga is strutting her stuff during a performance.

adults, most would agree that non-consensual STW—such as that related to human trafficking, or that involving children—is morally wrong and rightly prohibited by law. This chapter will explore these and other avenues for the buying and selling of sex, focussing mainly on STW, exotic dancing, and sexually explicit material.

Growth of the Sex Industry

sex industry The commercial enterprises that deal with the buying and selling of sex-related services.

escort agency A company that sends out sex trade workers to off-site locations, such as homes, hotels, and motels.

pornification The process of making or becoming more visibly or explicitly sexual.

With few exceptions, the various factions of the **sex industry** are growing rapidly. In the US, for example, the percentage of men reporting paying women for sex doubled from 2.0 per cent in 1990 to 4.2 per cent in 2000, despite the fact that STW is currently illegal in 49 states (Spice, 2007). Huge growth has also been witnessed in **escort agencies**, exotic dance clubs, and sex tours. The growth has been particularly high in sex services that are being bought and sold over the Internet (Sanders, 2010; Figure 18.2). Sociologist Brian McNair coined the term *pornification* to describe how sex is becoming increasingly visible and more explicit in our society.

This growth may not be surprising given that sex trade work (STW) is a mega-dollar industry. The value of the strip club industry alone is currently estimated to be worth $75 billion globally (Figure 18.3). Revenues from STW provide some Asian countries with nearly 14 per cent of their gross national product. Much of this revenue comes from sex tourism, a growing practice whereby vacationers travel to countries with few legal sanctions against any type of STW to enjoy uninhibited sex (see Chapter 15). Human sex trafficking, which often involves the selling of girls and women across international borders to provide sexual services (see Chapter 17), is also on the rise and brings in great profit for the criminals who run human trafficking operations; it has become so widespread that it has been referred to as the "new slave trade."

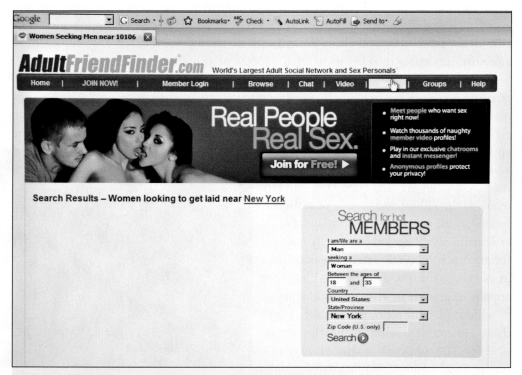

FIGURE 18.2 The Internet is increasingly being used to promote and facilitate all types of sexual services.

Selling and Buying Sex

Over the years, the selling and buying of sex has been interpreted and defined in various ways. For example, in 1988, the World Health Organization (WHO) defined *prostitution* as a "process that involves a transaction between a seller and buyer of a sexual service." More recently, the WHO (2011) suggested that the term *sex work* is more appropriate to describe the act of exchanging sex for materials as a survival strategy (WHO, 2011, para. 3). However, neither term seems appropriate for our purposes, for different reasons. If the process is called *prostitution*, the one providing the service is consequently called a *prostitute*, a demeaning term that suggests an immorality of the person that goes beyond what they do. On the other hand, *sex worker* sounds like an occupation that would be fun and without negative consequences; unfortunately, this is rarely the case. In light of these concerns, a third option—***sex trade workers (STWs)***—may be preferable, as it emphasizes involvement in the *sex trade* and is neither demoralizing nor glamorizing of those who engage in this work. Thus, the term *sex trade workers* will be used in this chapter, in an attempt to be morally neutral and non-derogatory, while at the same time not diminishing the psychological harm and physical risk this work poses to many in this industry.

FIGURE 18.3 Strippers, or exotic dancers, are part of a growing multi-billion dollar industry.

sex trade workers (STWs) People practising sex trade work.

Whatever terminology is used, we must recognize that many different types of people exchange sex for materials for many different reasons. While some people engage in STW as a survival strategy to pay for basic human necessities, others are forced into the sex trade, and still others choose this sort of work because they think it might be fun or thrilling, because they are looking for a new experience, or because they are seeking financial prosperity. In addition, we should keep in mind that there are many subtleties to what is defined as "sex for materials," and many interactions that could be described in this way are not typically understood to be sex trade work. For example, a person might engage in sexual activity with someone she or he met at a bar who has been buying drinks for her or him all night, or with an employer or manager who has promised a promotion in exchange for sex. Another, more problematic example is that of teenage girls who give blow jobs in exchange for pretty clothes or the means to buy pretty clothes. Sharlene Azam, a Canadian journalist and filmmaker, received a lot of press for her book and documentary called *Oral Sex Is the New Goodnight Kiss* (Azam, 2009). While her findings were not based on systematic research, Azam found that some teenage girls (as young as 13!) are being recruited into having sex with up to seven men a night, several times a week. Surprisingly, these girls, like Tracy, come from affluent Canadian suburbs.

Situations in which sex is exchanged for money or goods often elicit strong moral responses. Sometimes the matter is very clear and most people would make similar moral judgments of the situation. For example, most Canadians would agree that it is morally wrong for an adult to pay a child for sex. Indeed, Canadian laws reflect this moral stance, and any adult caught in such a situation can be charged and convicted of a criminal offence. Yet opinions are less uniform when it comes to paying a consenting adult for sex. Indeed, opinion polls suggest that Canadians are divided in their views regarding this sort of STW. Young (2008) reported that 68 per cent believed the sex trade was immoral, while 65 per cent reported that it should be legal but regulated.

Sex Trade Work

Despite moral objections, STW occurs frequently in North America and across the globe, particularly in densely populated cities. STW generates a great amount of revenue, and many women and men make their living by engaging in STW. Given the widespread disapproval of STW and the illegality of many activities related to this work, it is difficult to obtain solid estimates of how many people work in the sex trade. One US study (Potterat, Woodhouse, Muth, & Muth, 1990) found that the prevalence of STWs in one large urban centre was 23 full-time STWs for every 100,000 individuals, but no reliable nation-wide estimates are available for either the US or Canada.

A Snapshot of the History of STW in Canada

The first prohibition against STW in Canada occurred in 1759 with the passing of the Nova Scotia Act, which made street-based STW a criminal offence (Hallgrimsdottir, Phillips, Benoit, & Walby, 2008). Interestingly, while the laws were made more stringent in the second half of the nineteenth century, they were not strongly enforced in this period. STW was instead regulated mostly through vagrancy statutes targeted at women found on the street. During this time, STW in Canada happened mostly in brothels (Shaver, 2011). In fact, in Victoria, British Columbia, brothels outnumbered churches by a ratio of 6 to 1, and in the 1870s there were nine brothels in Victoria's Chinatown district alone (Hallgrimsdottir et al., 2008)! In 1892, laws relating to street-based STW and the operation of brothels were incorporated into the Criminal Code of Canada. STW flourished during World War I, a time when women could not work, and decreased during World War II, perhaps because more women were entering the workforce due to the labour shortage (Shaver, 2011).

In the following years, more women than men were charged with STW–related offences under the Criminal Code. In the 1970s and 1980s, in response to public concern regarding street-based STW, the laws were refined to cover public communication regarding the buying or selling of sex, to extend liability to the clients who paid for sex, to apply the laws equally to men and women, and to strengthen prohibitions related to the prostitution of underage individuals. More recently, advocacy groups have rallied to support the rights of STWs, often arguing for the decriminalization of sex work as a means of making the work safer for all involved. The legality of STW–related activities continues to be a subject of much debate across the country (Shaver, 2011).

Legal Aspects of STW

While STW itself has never been illegal in Canada, current laws prohibit four activities related to it: (1) living off the avails of prostitution; (2) owning, operating, or occupying a bawdy house (i.e., a brothel); (3) communicating for the purpose of prostitution; and (4) knowingly transporting a person to a bawdy house. This approach is consistent with most Canadians' view that the sex trade is a problem that needs to be dealt with through the criminal justice system (Benoit & Millar, 2001).

In general, there are four legal options for dealing with STW: **criminalization**, **legalization** (regulation), **abolition**, and **decriminalization**. Most who advocate criminalization today focus their concerns on street-based and underage STWs. Those who support legalizing and regulating STW note that regulations relating to the licensing of STWs, compulsory medical examinations, zoning, and/or registration of brothels would likely have a positive impact on STWs and society in general. Abolitionism has a clear benefit in that it focusses on punishing those who exploit, coerce, or otherwise harm STWs. No country has fully adopted abolitionism. Finally, decriminalization is

criminalization of STW A legal option for dealing with sex trade work by making it and/or activities related to it illegal.

legalization of STW A legal option for dealing with sex trade work by making it legal but subject to regulations.

abolition of STW A legal option for dealing with sex trade work by allowing it and punishing those who exploit or coerce sex trade workers.

decriminalization of STW A legal option for dealing with sex trade work by repealing all laws governing it.

preferred by those who see the buying and selling of sex as a personal choice between consenting adults. The intent is to affirm STWs and provide them a legitimate place in society. In 2003, New Zealand became the first country to decriminalize STW (see the "Culture and Diversity" box).

Types of STW

When most people think of STWs, their minds usually go to those who work "on the street," or outdoors (Figure 18.4). Yet it is estimated that less than 20 per cent of STW occurs outdoors (Benoit & Millar, 2001). Indeed, the vast majority of STWs are solicited while remaining indoors (e.g., those working for escort agencies or who advertise over the Internet). In Vancouver alone, there are hundreds of escort agencies, dating services, and massage parlours that operate as legitimate businesses but that also act as commercial sex outlets (Figure 18.5). Windsor, Ontario, has licensed escorts as a means of providing legitimacy to both the agencies and

FIGURE 18.4 Street-based STW remains popular in most countries throughout the world.

Culture & Diversity

The Decriminalization of STW in New Zealand and Australia

In 2003, the Prostitution Reform Act decriminalized STW in New Zealand. This act removed legal prohibitions against all aspects of STW, including street-based work, brothels, and pimping. This legislation did not pass without great controversy, however. In fact, the parliamentary vote was only 60 votes in favour, with 59 votes opposed and one abstention! Moralists have used this narrow margin to argue that the law should be repealed, and they have argued that the number of STWs has increased since the Act was passed. Empirical research, however, has suggested that an increase in the number of STWs has *not* occurred in New Zealand (Abel, Fitzgerald, & Brunton, 2009).

Astier (2009) interviewed several STWs in New Zealand, and most spoke very highly about the changes that have occurred since STW was decriminalized. "Lucy," age 23, was quoted as follows: "I make twice what I was earning in retail. I am appreciated by customers and my boss. I can work whenever I want to—it's by far the most gratifying work I've ever had." "Anna" also had good things to say about STW: "I had sex, money, and men! . . . We get so pissed off when politicians portray us as victims." Nonetheless, Astier concluded that the society still

views this work negatively. For example, the city of Christchurch attempted to impose a zoning law that would have kept STWs out of most areas. If STWs had not fought against it, this law may well have passed.

STW has also been decriminalized in various parts of Australia. Recently, Seib, Dunne, Fischer, and Najman (2010) compared sexual practices of STWs before and after decriminalization occurred. Their findings indicated a reduction in oral sex without condoms and a slight decrease in STWs providing vaginal sex, but there was no decrease in the frequency of anal sex. Interestingly, a significant increase was found in the provision of "exotic" sexual practices, including activities related to bondage, submission, and fantasy/fetish. Thus, it appears that when STW is decriminalized, customers may become increasingly likely to request "fringe" sexual practices. It is not clear why this is the case, but it may mean that as some sexual services become more mainstream, customers search for other services that remain taboo. In addition, there may be an element of some men's psyche that wants to make sex for pay bad in some respect. What do you think? What might be the appeal of engaging in sexual practices that appear forbidden in some regard?

FIGURE 18.5 All we know from the outside of this business is that it offers customers a massage and access to a sauna. Registered massage therapists in Canada operate according to an ethical code that forbids them from offering sexual services in addition to a massage, but a number of massage businesses employ unregistered individuals to provide sexual services.

the STWs who work for them. Many men travel from the US to Windsor to seek out sexual services without facing the risk of arrest.

There is no defined career path or ladder within STW, although different levels of status are generally attached to different types of STW. Street-based STWs are generally viewed as having the lowest status; they tend to earn the least and face the greatest risk of violence and ostracism. STWs who work for escort agencies, on the other hand, have the highest status, earn the most, and work under the most secure conditions. Some STWs work in more than one venue at the same time (e.g., outdoors, in a massage parlour, in an exotic dance club).

Who Works in the Sex Trade, and Why?

STWs are a heterogeneous group of people. Nevertheless, studies have suggested that there are some characteristics common among many of these individuals. Benoit and Millar (2001), for example, concluded that most STWs are female, and the majority of those they interviewed had not graduated from high school. Regarding street-based STWs, Shaver (2011) has suggested that most are "young, single, female, addicted, undereducated, from backgrounds with a history of poverty and abuse, and controlled by pimps" (Shaver, 2011, para. 19). Casey and Philips (2008), in their study of mostly female escorts in Victoria, British Columbia, found that over half had not completed high school. In terms of age, Benoit and Millar (2001) found that the average age of their respondents was 32, with the average age for entering the sex trade being 18. Shaver (2011) found a much lower average age range of 22 to 25 for street-based STWs.

In some cases, unstable family situations may contribute to individuals entering into STW. Indeed, a repeated finding in the literature is the high prevalence of STWs who were sexually and/or physically abused as children (Benoit & Millar, 2001; Farley, Lynne, & Cotton, 2005). Benoit and Millar (2001) indicated that 55 per cent of their sample of 201 female STWs reported a history of childhood sexual abuse. Aboriginal women are disproportionately found in STW and also report high rates of childhood abuse. In one sample, 82 per cent reported childhood sexual abuse and 72 per cent reported childhood physical abuse (Farley et al., 2005).

Researchers have found several other factors that may lead an individual to engage in STW. Benoit and Millar (2002) found that "economic duress and enticement were the two most common reasons for initial entry" (p. 7). Likewise, Shaver (2011) found that most street-based STWs enter the trade for financial reasons. Other reasons vary. Some people may enter the trade for a specific reason—for example, to earn money to pay off a debt, or to cover the costs of postsecondary education—and for a specific period of time. Others may choose a career in STW because they perceive certain benefits or advantages to the work compared to other options. Still others feel pulled into it, either by sex traffickers or in order to feed a drug addiction (Benoit & Millar, 2002). Of the female STWs interviewed by Dalla (2000), none imagined that they would one day work in the sex trade, and none saw it as a long-term career goal.

Individuals also have various reasons for remaining in STW. For some, the reason is simply that they cannot find a way to get out. Indeed, Benoit and Millar (2001) found that many of their respondents had tried to leave the sex trade, some many times, but most returned due to economic necessity. For others, it is a matter of preference. Many STWs report enjoying various aspects of their work—according to one study, 57 per cent of participants reported that they were happy with their work (Casey & Philips, 2008).

If You Sell Sex, Do You Enjoy Sex?

One might assume that most STWs are in the "business" because they enjoy sex. However, this is not always the case. One study found that, compared with male and transgender STWs, female STWs were the least likely to experience orgasm in their work and the most likely to report that they never enjoyed "giving clients hand jobs, having their breasts fondled, and providing oral sex" (Weinberg, Shaver, & Williams, 1999, p. 515). Individuals in the transgender sample were most likely to report enjoying breast fondling and receptive anal intercourse. In addition, it was apparent that female STWs attempt to work with their clients expeditiously and without regard to their own sexual enjoyment. The "recreational element" is less likely to be a part of women's overall experience of STW compared to men's (Weinberg et al., 1999). But not all female STWs report that their work lacks pleasure: some female STWs working in licensed brothels in Victoria, Australia, reported enjoying this work more than other jobs available to them (Bilardi et al., 2011). Working in a licensed establishment, however, is different from most STWs' experiences in Canada and the US.

Underage STWs

There are approximately two million known underage (i.e., under 18) STWs in the world. Unfortunately, in most countries, minors are the group most vulnerable to becoming victims of sex trafficking, and the trend for young males and females to enter STW appears to be growing. A recent study from Quebec found that in a sample of 815 high school students, 3 per cent reported having bought sex and 4 per cent reported having sold sex in their lifetime (Lavoie, Thibodeau, Gagné, & Hébert, 2010). Selling sex was associated with a history of sexual abuse and stressful life events. Buying sex was related to having favourable attitudes toward the sex trade and to having become engaged in sexually risqué activities, such as attending wet t-shirt contests or stripteases.

Homeless youth are most at risk of entering street-based STW, particularly if they lack employment in legitimate jobs. Many young people leave home without a source of income, and government support is negligible. Homelessness leads many youth to enter the sex trade to obtain what is necessary for their survival (i.e., food, shelter) as well as what they view as necessary for their survival (e.g., drugs).

Child STW is a common problem in Central America, South America, and Asia. Indeed, about half of all known child STWs live in Asia. Of the Asian nations, Thailand is the country in which the problem is most pronounced. Thailand has long been known for its sex trade, and it has a long history of child STW; according to STWs, sex work has become normalized there. Most child STWs in Thailand are females who remain financially reliant on others.

LGBTTIQQ-identified youth are at significantly greater risk of finding themselves involved in "survival" sex work, possibly because they are also at a greater risk of being rejected by their families and thus forced to support themselves. Marshall, Shannon, Kerr, Zhang, and Wood (2010) found that LGBTTIQQ youth in the sex trade were more likely to report inconsistent condom use with clients compared to non-LGBTTIQQ youth, thereby placing them at increased risk of HIV infection.

The Impact of STW on Physical and Psychological Health

As noted above, many STWs have a history of being sexually and/or physically abused as children. Unfortunately, many STWs, especially females, continue to suffer abuse in adulthood. Most female STWs report that they have been raped and physically assaulted since commencing STW. Studies based on data from several countries have found that 70 per cent of female STWs have been raped, 65 per cent have been physically assaulted by customers, and 66 per cent have been assault by pimps (Pines, as cited in Farley et al., 2005). Simply put, STW is dangerous. A Canadian commission reported that the death rate among female STWs is 40 times higher than that for the general population (Special Committee on Pornography and Prostitution, as cited in Farley et al., 2005). While male STWs generally feel relatively safe due to their physical size, transgender STWs tend to feel less safe compared to other STWs due to their greater experiences of harassment by police and physical assault from members of the general public.

Besides the ongoing threat of violence, STWs are also at an elevated risk of contracting HIV and other STIs. Researchers have found conflicting reports regarding the prevalence of condom use among STWs. While one study of STWs in Victoria, British Columbia, found that virtually all respondents reported practising safer sex while working (Benoit & Millar, 2001), a study of female STWs in a city in Eastern Canada found that most respondents did not use condoms at all or used them only sometimes in their private lives (Jackson, Sowinski, Bennett, & Ryan, 2005). Most studies in both North America and Australia have found that the majority of STWs wear condoms with their clients when having anal or vaginal sex but are less consistent when practising oral sex (Jackson et al., 2005). As noted in Chapter 8, unprotected oral sex entails risk of STI transmission. A study of injection drug users in Vancouver found elevated HIV infection rates among users involved in STW compared to those not involved in the sex trade (Wood et al., 2007). Members of the transgender community appear to be at the greatest risk of HIV infection when they enter STW. Studies consistently show that male-to-female STWs have high levels of HIV infection (Operario, Soma, & Underhill, 2008). It is possible that the vaginal tissue created during sex reassignment surgery may leave male-to-female transgendered individuals more susceptible to HIV infection.

Along with the physical health consequences associated with STW, emotional and psychological harm is also apparent. Many women involved in STW feel stigmatized, ashamed, and degraded. Many also feel vulnerable, helpless, fearful, and disempowered. Such feelings affect these women's sense of self-worth. In a sample of 193 female STWs interviewed in Zurich, Germany, high rates of mental disorders was found, and it was concluded that the majority of the observed disorders was related to experiences of violence and the perceived burden of doing sex work (Rossler et al., 2010). In a study of 278 street-based STWs in the US city of Miami, over one-third reported experiencing moderate to severe anxiety symptoms and over half reported experiencing moderate to severe depression (Surratt, Kurtz, Weaver, & Inciardi, 2005). Indeed, many female STWs live with the fear and despair of being assaulted (Farley et al., 2005). Weinberg et al. (1999) emphasize that the emotional damage that may result from STW is mostly a consequence of negative social attitudes, lack of control over the work situation, or harassment from both clients and the police—not from the sex itself.

Due in large part to the negative stigma surrounding the sex industry, many STWs keep their work secret from their family and friends. As a result, they may have few people they feel they can turn to for social support. STWs may also feel a great deal of negative stress as a result of low income and lack of job security. One Canadian study found that among STWs the median annual income from sex activities was $18,000, with male STWs being financially worse off than female STWs (Benoit & Millar, 2001). In addition, few STWs can provide evidence of employment that can be used to verify income for loan applications. Further, STWs are not protected by labour codes, they are not entitled to parental leave, they do not receive compensation for workplace injuries, and they do not pay into or receive government pensions.

Male STWs

This section will highlight some of the ways in which male STWs' experiences of the sex trade differ from those of their female counterparts. The main difference is that while female STWs often experience violence against them and live in fear for their safety, violence against male STWs has not been documented as a significant problem. This might be the case for several reasons. First, customers are more likely to perceive male STWs as better able to defend themselves compared to female STWs. Second, customers who seek out male STWs—most of whom are gay or bisexual men, but also women and men who do not define as gay or bisexual—may be less likely to engage in violent behaviour. In particular, most gay men are less physically aggressive than are most heterosexual men; perhaps this is the case because when men become comfortable sexualizing other men, as most gay men have, it becomes incompatible for them to aggress against other men. Another reason may have to do with gender politics and the lower status of women compared to men. From a feminist perspective, so long as there is a power imbalance between the genders, women will be subjugated to varying extents by men. This power imbalance exists across society, but it is amplified in the sex trade, as disenfranchised female STWs are often viewed as having a lesser status than that of women who are not involved in the sex trade. Finally, because male STWs are generally not stigmatized or marginalized to the degree that female STWs are, and because they are particularly not stigmatized within the gay community, they may be less likely to be targeted for victimization.

Many male STWs' approaches toward and perceptions of the sex trade also differ from those of most female STWs. Men are increasingly entering STW with professional, positive attitudes toward it, and many are using relatively new technologies such as the Internet to facilitate their business. Those who advertise on the Internet are motivated by three main factors: (1) monetary benefits, (2) positive effects on the self, and (3) sexual pleasure (Uy, Parsons, Bimbi, Koken, & Halkitis, 2004). Uy et al. (2004) emphasize

street hustler A male sex trade worker who looks for customers on the street.

bar hustler A male sex trade worker who looks for customers in a bar.

call boy A male sex trade worker who either works for an escort agency or is self-employed as an escort.

kept boy A young male who is financially dependent on an older man, usually with the expectation that the younger individual will provide sexual services to the older man.

that Internet-based male STWs differ from those who work on the street in that they can be more selective about their clients and charge higher fees, and they experience greater control over their work schedule. Buyers looking for a male escort online can select one based on various attributes, such as age, height, penis size, and circumcision status. Many male escorts also mention health concerns in their online ads, for example by noting that they practise only "safer" sex.

HIERARCHY AND MOTIVATIONS AMONG MALE STWS

There is a hierarchy of male STWs, similar to that mentioned earlier in relation to indoor vs outdoor work. **Street hustlers** are considered to have the lowest status and receive the lowest pay (Figure 18.6). Next are **bar hustlers**, **call boys** (i.e., escorts), and finally **kept boys**. A kept boy is the male equivalent of a kept woman, and the man looking after him is commonly referred to as a *sugar daddy*. Another interesting finding that speaks of hierarchy is that escorts who advertise that they present as masculine charge higher prices for their work than do those who advertise that they present as feminine, with the difference in price being about 17 per cent (Logan, 2010). This is not surprising, given that many gay men prefer other men who are masculine for both sexual activity and for dating.

Most street hustlers and many other male STWs self-define as heterosexual, viewing their work in the sex trade mostly as a means of obtaining financial rewards. Nonetheless, while the majority of male STWs in a study by Weisburg (1985) suggested monetary reasons as their main motivation, sex (27 per cent) and adventure (19 per cent) were also strong motivators. Two other reasons include wanting to be involved in a delinquent lifestyle and making STW an occupational choice.

AGE AND MALE STWS

In general, clients who engage male STWs tend to prefer younger STWs. This is particularly true in countries that have become known as major destinations for sex tourists. Most male tourists in Prague and other places look for younger STWs, and consequently, male STWs often have a short career. Despite their short career, however, their reputation as a former STW can persist for a long time. As is the case with women who have worked in the sex trade, it can be difficult for these men to find other sources of income, given their limited experience with other types of work.

FIGURE 18.6 Many street hustlers, such as this male transvestite STW in New York City, dress provocatively in order to entice potential clients.

Exotic Dancing

Exotic dancing, commonly referred to as "stripping," has its roots in burlesque theatre. It generally involves one or more costumed performers dancing and removing their clothes on a stage, in front of audience members who sit by the stage or at tables where they can be served alcohol and sometimes food. In Canada and the US, it is illegal for live sex acts to occur on stage, although these sorts of performances are permitted in some other countries, such as Thailand. In a national sex survey conducted in the US by

Laumann, Gagnon, Michael, and Michaels (1994), 16 per cent of men and 4 per cent of women disclosed that they had ever attended a strip club.

Strip clubs are places where patrons (the buyers) can explore sexuality by interacting with women or men who are attractive and accessible. Kaufman (2009) reported that most men who visit strip clubs are looking for a sexual encounter, either in or out of the club itself. In accordance with local statutes, strip clubs establish rules that prohibit patrons from touching dancers in any way. Such rules allow dancers to maintain control over their interactions with customers. In some cases, physical contact can be negotiated in exchange for money, particularly in clubs that offer private dancing (also referred to as "table dancing" or "lap dancing"; see Figure 18.7). The popularity of private dancing has grown rapidly over the past decade. In some establishments, a private dance involves a patron and a dancer going go to a private area in the strip club where they are, for the most part, alone. These private areas are generally not completely private, however, thereby ensuring the safety of the dancer and some degree of restraint. Some dancers will also negotiate STW off premises for a price. Interestingly, the more that physical contact is disallowed in a club, the more the dancer can earn by offering it to a patron.

In order to do well financially, dancers must not only show off their physical attributes but also add a spark or an element of originality to their performance (Figure 18.8), and they must make connections with members of their audience. Dancers use several strategies to make customers feel sexually desirable and special, while at the same time making themselves seem emotionally and/or sexually available. The dancer's work is about impression management, creating a façade that will appeal to customers. Customers also create impressions, such as by implying an emotional attachment to a dancer, presenting as lonely, and/or boasting of financial resources or physical endowment.

exotic dancing Dancing that involves the removal of most or all of one's clothing with the intent of creating erotic arousal in the viewer.

FIGURE 18.7 This male exotic dancer is demonstrating lap dancing. Both male and female exotic dancers may offer lap dances within certain strip clubs that are known for this pay-as-you-go service.

FIGURE 18.8 This female exotic dancer is demonstrating her skills on a pole. Interestingly, "pole dancing" has also become a popular form of aerobic exercise, and various gyms and dance studios offer classes for fun!

New dancers are usually recruited through personal contact networks and then socialized into the occupation by experienced dancers. Dancers new to their work talk about the positive aspects, such as the money, flexible hours, and general enjoyment. Some dancers describe their time on stage as spiritual, and Barton and Hardesty (2010) interpret this as a time when dancers are in "flow," a term used to describe something akin to a peak experience. After a few years, however, many dancers begin to focus on the costs of their work, such as the effects of substance use and abuse, strain on the body, and the aggressiveness of some abusive patrons (Barton, 2007). Some dancers also report that their work interferes with their private lives. Indeed, many young dancers who hide their occupation from family and friends report feeling the strain of leading a "double life" (Trautner & Collett, 2010).

Exotic dancing certainly takes its toll on many performers. Barton (2007) describes how dancers manage the stress related to their work: by setting personal rules, by distancing themselves by believing they are not like the others, and by creating a "dancer persona." The persona is a stage identity—essentially, a character—with a name and a personality that differ from those of the performer. Maintaining this persona can cause additional mental stress, however, particularly for those dancers whose off-stage desires are not consistent with the demands of their job (e.g., a male dancer who defines as heterosexual but performs lap dances for gay men). Several of Barton's informants even described feeling fatigued and nauseous when thinking about and preparing to go to work. (See the "Ethical Debate" box for additional consideration of issues related to exotic dancing.)

Ethical Debate

What Approach Should We Take to Exotic Dancing in Canada?

There are several reasons that women and men strip for a living. In some cases, it is because they need to earn a decent income, and they do not have other employable skills that would provide them a similar standard of living. Some have argued, however, that this work should not be permitted because it sexualizes people's bodies in a way that creates the impression that some women and men ought to be subjugated. What do you think? Is it ethically okay to allow men and women to buy and/or sell exotic dancing? Should Canada strengthen its regulations on exotic dancing? Or, should it relax these regulations? To what extent should a society protect its members from experiences that may have harmful effects in the long run? What might be done to increase the status of exotic dancers so that they might feel better about themselves and the work they do?

Pornography, Erotica, and Sexually Explicit Material

Definitions of *sexually explicit material* (SEM) vary, depending on an individual's or group's views on sex and sexuality. Some feminists distinguish between erotic SEM and SEM that is violent and/or degrading to women (Garos, Beggan, Kluck, & Easton, 2004). In this section, this distinction will be maintained by the use of the word ***erotica*** to refer to sexual material that shows equal enjoyment of sexuality in both men and women, and the use of the word ***pornography*** to refer to sexual material that presents sexuality in a manner that is unequal, unbalanced, violent, or degrading toward men or women. Most sexually explicit videos today would fall more into the category of erotica rather than pornography (Garos et al., 2004). The term *sexually explicit material* will be used more generally, when erotica is not or has not been distinguished from pornography.

Access to sexually explicit material (SEM) has grown exponentially in recent decades. Carroll et al. (2008) note that the rapid proliferation of SEM is linked to the extensive availability of personal computers beginning in the early 1980s, widespread access to the Internet beginning in the mid-1990s, and the emergence of pay-per-view home movies beginning in the early 1990s. Today, despite reports that 54 to 58 per cent of Canadians believe that SEM is morally wrong (Young, 2008), many Canadians support the SEM industry by using and/or purchasing its products (Figure 18.9). Globally, the industry related to SEM generates over $55 billion in revenues annually, making it the third most profitable industry, following the trade of weapons and the trade of illicit drugs (Bullough & McAnulty, 2006). What influences the ongoing demand for SEM may be a desire for variety and novelty.

Watching SEM is far more common in men than in women (Garos et al., 2004; Petersen & Hyde, 2010). What do men focus on when they view SEM? Not surprisingly, research has shown that men tend to pay the most attention to members of the sex to which they are typically attracted. For example, one study that compared how men and women view SEM found that heterosexual men spend more time looking at women than at men in erotic photographs, whereas heterosexual women tend to pay equal attention to men and women in such photographs (Lykins, Meana, & Strauss, 2008). At the same time, some have argued that such findings may not accurately reflect what men do in more natural settings (e.g., at home), as men who are being tested in a laboratory—where they may have an increased concern for being "caught"—may focus on what they think would be socially appropriate. Regardless, empirical research does support differences between the types of visual stimuli that men and women find arousing. Men are generally more responsive to the sex of the actors (to the sex they are attracted to, whether female or male) than women are, and they prefer scenes where the actors can be objectified (i.e., scenes that depict people as merely visual objects, without regard for their psychosocial circumstances or other aspects that would evoke feelings of familiarity). Women, on the other hand, are more responsive to scenes into which they feel they can project themselves (Rupp & Wallen, 2008).

erotica Textual, visual, and audial material that promotes or creates sexual arousal and shows enjoyment of sexuality in an equal and balanced manner toward people of either sex.

pornography Textual, visual, and audial material that promotes or creates sexual arousal and presents sexuality in an unequal, unbalanced, violent, or degrading manner toward people of either sex.

FIGURE 18.9 Use of sexually explicit material by men is common, particularly among adolescents and younger men. For those consumers who enjoy sexually explicit magazines, there are many publications from which to choose.

Effects of Consuming SEM

Over the last thirty years, concerns regarding sexually explicit material have migrated from focussing on its moral impact to focussing on the social and psychological harm it may cause, particularly in terms of how it might affect the ways men treat women. Researchers have investigated such issues, questioning whether SEM generally has a harmful, neutral, or positive effect on people who are exposed to it. The following discussion provides a summary of some of their findings.

REPORTED EFFECTS OF SEM CONSUMPTION ON ADULTS

Many people assume that exposure to SEM is "all bad," and some studies do report negative effects. For example, the authors of one study concluded that exposure to pornography was associated with an increased risk of developing sexually deviant tendencies, committing sexual offences, developing problems in one's intimate relationships, and accepting rape myths (e.g., the myth that women really want sex even when they say "no"; see Chapter 17) (Oddone-Paolucci, Genuis, & Violato, 2000). In addition, Manning (2006) concluded that Internet SEM has several negative impacts on individuals (e.g., distorted perceptions of sexuality, devaluation of marriage and monogamy, increased aggression) and on marital relationships (e.g., threats to relationship stability, decreased sexual satisfaction, perception that viewing SEM betrays fidelity).

Other studies assert that SEM may provide positive educational benefits. In a study of gay men's use of SEM, Kendall (2004) concluded that gay men today are obsessed with hyper-masculinity, and that SEM promotes these images. He also surmised that SEM undermines safer sex practices and respectful practices, noting that gay men need to commit to more realistic and responsible practices built on respect and mutual caring. Indeed, it is important for all viewers of SEM to understand that the sexually explicit images they see are not "real," despite the claims of the provider. SEM offers only a fictional portrayal of sexual activity between actors and should not be used as a model for real-life sexual experiences with real people.

While such findings suggest that exposure to SEM is generally harmful, it is important to keep in mind that not all reported effects are negative, and not all findings are consistent. Indeed, Diamond (2009) notes that no empirical studies have statistically demonstrated that consumption of SEM causes social or moral harm to women. Even when looking at the consumption of violent pornography—which is actually relatively rare—a review found inconsistent negative effects (Ferguson & Hartley, 2009).

An important consideration is that individual reactions to SEM often differ. For example, while one person may view a sexually explicit work as promoting immorality and oppression, another person may view the same work as a creative, artistic expression of sexuality. Thus, it may not be SEM itself but rather individuals' interpretations of SEM—based on their pre-existing beliefs—that determine whether the effect will be positive, negative, or neutral. This view is supported in Seto, Maric, and Barbaree's (2001) critical review of the research examining the relationship between pornography and sexual aggression. These researchers found that individuals who are already predisposed toward sexual assault are the most likely to show a negative effect from watching pornography, while men who are not predisposed are unlikely to show any effect. Another study found that male undergraduate students who used SEM generally demonstrated permissive, but not aggressive, sexual attitudes (Taylor, 2006).

In addition, the effect might depend on the type of SEM viewed. For example, exposure to pornography, and violent pornography in particular, may be associated with negative effects, while exposure to erotica may be associated with positive effects. Indeed, the majority of studies that find negative effects focus on pornography. Studies that focus on erotica, on the other hand, typically report positive effects. In two studies conducted by Garos et al. (2004), for example, higher usage levels of erotica were correlated with less sexist attitudes. Heavier users of erotica may have politically tolerant views, leaving them receptive to both feminist thinking and the use of erotica. Viewing erotica may also have a positive impact on women's sexuality. Goodson, McCormick, and Evans (2001) suggested that SEM is valued by college women as a safe venue for exploring their sexuality. In another study, Senn and Desmarais (2004) found that women who viewed erotica reported an improvement in mood, while those who viewed pornography maintained a negative mood while watching this material. These researchers also found that women responded more favourably to SEM when they viewed this material with a same-sex friend or a male partner instead of by themselves.

Finally, there is evidence that use of SEM may have a positive impact in reducing instances of sex crimes. A literature review concluded that in places around the world where SEM has become more available, sex crimes have either decreased or remained the same (Diamond, 2009). Interestingly, a study of 97 sex offenders in Alberta and Ontario revealed that those who commit offences against children use child SEM infrequently and, compared to a control group, were actually less likely to have *ever* used it (Langevin et al., 1988). Based on these results, it might be time to discard the idea that watching pornography leads to sexual assault. (For food for thought related to sex and violence in the visual media, see the "Research vs Real Life" box.)

EFFECTS OF SEM EXPOSURE ON YOUTH

In the past, being exposed to SEM at a young age was likely limited to sneaking peeks at a parent's collection of *Playboy* or *Playgirl* magazines; today, however, SEM can be easily accessed on the Internet and through other visual media. It appears as though viewing SEM is developmentally appropriate at about age 14, and concerns that large numbers of children younger than 14 are viewing SEM seem to be unfounded. Data from 1501 children and adolescents (aged 10 to 17) indicated that 87 per cent of the sample who reported looking at SEM online and in magazines were 14 years of age or older (Ybarra & Mitchell, 2005). Approximately twice as many youth between the ages of 14 and 17 (20 per cent) watched SEM intentionally compared to youth between ages 10 and 13 (8 per cent).

Children and youth exposed to pornography before they are mentally and emotionally ready to understand what they see may experience several troubling consequences. Younger children may be disturbed and upset by the material. Flood (2009) maintained that consuming pornography at a young age encourages sexist and unhealthy notions of sex and relationships, and that it increases the likelihood of perpetrating assault. Supporting these conclusions is a research study conducted by Ybarra, Mitchell, Hamburger, Diener-West, and Leaf (2011). These researchers investigated longitudinal linkages between intentional use of violent pornography and aggressive behaviour in 10- to 15-year-olds surveyed nationally across the US over three different time periods. They found that there was a sixfold increase in the odds of self-reported sexually aggressive behaviour by those who intentionally consumed violent pornographic material.

Exposure to SEM may affect young boys differently than it affects young girls. A study of 471 Dutch adolescents aged 13 to 18 found that exposure to SEM was related to having more recreational attitudes toward sex, and also that the effects were mediated by gender and the extent to which the adolescents perceived the material as realistic (Peter & Valkenburg, 2006). The researchers found that male adolescents had more recreational attitudes toward sex and also perceived the SEM as more realistic

Research VS Real Life

How about Erotica Instead of Violence on Television?

Television today is filled with graphic images of violence. For example, series such as *Criminal Minds* and *CSI* expose us to nightly scenes of murder and torture. And it isn't only through fictional programming that we are exposed to violence. Throughout the day, televised news shows fill our minds with descriptions of how nasty, cruel, demented, or corrupt certain people have been, often showing video clips of these individuals in action. After being bombarded with such violent images throughout the day, we are expected to sleep well, dreaming no doubt of loving people doing loving things to one another.

Now think about it: doesn't erotica depict just that? Erotica is about presenting scenes and situations that are sensual, consensual, and sexual. It shows us what we hope to attain in our sex lives. Erotica is stimulating because we can imagine ourselves in the hot moments of steamy passion that it depicts. At least we can live vicariously through such depictions if our own sex lives are currently rather mundane or non-existent. The screen brings it all to life! How often do you feel horror or fear when you view erotica? Contrast that with how you feel when you view stories about the latest child who has been abducted, or the rapist or serial killer ravaging *your* neighbourhood or *your* city. How about when you watch the latest documentary showing heinous acts against the victims of war?

Let's consider, for a moment, what has been revealed in the scientific literature. While no studies have conclusively proven the effects of exposure to either violence or sex on television, many have suggested certain correlations. In relation to exposure to violence on television, several studies have suggested that such exposure may lead to violent behaviour or at least desensitization toward violence, especially when this exposure occurs in childhood. In relation to exposure to erotica—or, more generally, exposure to SEM—the most consistent finding is a correlation between viewing such material and developing more permissive attitudes toward sex. Given such findings, which type of content, violence or erotica, has the potential to have the greater negative effect?

It seems we have it backwards. It is time we censure the graphic violence on television—it affects not only adults who choose to watch programs that contain violence, but also children who find ways to catch glimpses of this stuff when their parents are not diligently watching every move they make! No parent wants his or her child to become a violent individual with little to no conscience, and few people want to look at others that way, either—it is unhealthy to say the least. Put on some soothing erotica, then, and if children catch a glimpse, at least they will be getting some positive sex education. Really, don't we want *all* people to learn to become loving individuals, whatever their age?

Freud was right, you know: we have two primary instincts, or drives—sex ("libido," or life energy) and aggression ("thanatos," or death instinct). Which one do you want to spend the most time engaging? Given that people tend to be fascinated by both sex and violence, would we not do better to place greater restrictions on the amount and degree of violence permitted in visual media and become more permissive about the amount and degree of erotica permitted in visual media?

(i.e., accurately reflecting how men and women in actual relationships would conduct themselves sexually) than did the female participants.

There is some evidence that early exposure to SEM may contribute to earlier experience with partnered sexual activities. In a study of 437 participants ($M = 29.46$ years), males who watched Internet SEM between the ages of 12 and 17 reported having first oral sex at younger ages than those without Internet access. Both males and females with Internet access reported younger ages at first sexual intercourse (Kraus & Russell, 2008). Although some might be tempted to conclude that Internet access leads to earlier sexual experiences, keep in mind that other factors may also be responsible for this association, such as greater exposure to sexuality in the visual media in general and greater openness to discussing sexual issues.

Internet SEM

Many forms of SEM are widely available and easy to access on the Internet. Young (2008) reported that there are at least 4.2 million websites related to SEM on the Internet, and 25 per cent of all search engine requests are related to SEM. The Internet is a popular place for adolescents to find SEM. Indeed, in their study of 563 college students, Sabina, Wolak, and Finkelhor (2008) found that 93 per cent of the men and 62 per cent of the women they surveyed reported that they had been exposed to Internet SEM during adolescence, although exposure before age 13 was relatively uncommon. The researchers concluded that exposure to Internet SEM has become a normative experience.

Research efforts to investigate the impact of viewing online SEM have grown steadily along with the rise of the Internet. Most research has focussed on the possible negative effects of Internet SEM, with little attention paid to its potential benefits. One study of 1052 Dutch adolescents aged 13 to 20 concluded that exposure to Internet SEM resulted in reduced sexual satisfaction, particularly for those with little to no sexual experience. This effect occurred for both male and female participants (Peter & Valkenburg, 2009). In a study of 15,246 respondents in the US, 75 per cent of the men and 41 per cent of the women reported that they had intentionally downloaded SEM from the Internet (Albright, 2008). Gay men, heterosexual men, and lesbian women were the most likely groups to access SEM. Women reported more negative consequences from viewing this material, such as lowered body image, increased pressure to perform acts depicted in the films, and less actual (i.e., real life) sex. Men reported being more critical of their partner's bodies and less interested in actual sex.

Addiction to SEM

While most people who use SEM are able to do so without suffering any harm, for some it becomes an unhealthy habit that is hard to break. This problem may be brought on or exacerbated by the ease with which SEM can be found on the Internet at any time of day or night. Indeed, Mitchell, Becker-Blease, and Finkelhor (2005) have noted a marked increase in the number of clients seeking treatment for addiction related to Internet SEM.

What constitutes an addiction to SEM? Goodman (1990) has provided a definition of addiction that could be applied to excessive SEM use. According to Goodman, an addiction includes (a) an inability to resist urges; (b) recurring stress related to the problem; (c) feelings of loss of control; (d) derivation of short-term pleasure; (e) sense of relief while engaged in the problem; and (f) tolerance, resulting in an increase in the intensity and frequency of the problem. When assessing addiction, it is important to consider whether the behaviour in question has a negative impact on the individual's well-being; if it does not, there may be no problem. In addition, as Levine (2010) has suggested in his work on sexual addiction, only men with "psychological deterioration" resulting from their problematic sexual behaviour can reasonably be viewed as "sex addicts"; this same criterion should be applied to those who feel they have a problem with addiction to SEM.

Being a "Porn Star"

Besides examining the consumers of SEM, research has also focussed on the actors who perform in sexually explicit videos. One finding from a Canadian study by Polk and Cowan (1996) is that female porn stars are viewed more negatively than movie stars and women in general, but more positively than female STWs. Other studies and general reports have noted that STIs are common among porn actors, despite the fact that monthly STI screening is a requirement in the porn industry.

But what is it like to actually *be* in a pornographic film? Benjamin Scuglia (2004), a writer in the gay adult video industry who has interviewed and interacted with many porn actors, has provided a fascinating report from an insider's perspective. He notes that being on a porn set is boring, as the usual sexual practices are re-enacted repeatedly over many hours of filming. Like flipping hamburgers in a full-time job, repeating the same sex act again and again can quickly become boring. There is also a typical "formula" that is followed: "kiss-kiss-suck-suck-rim-fuck-change positions-fuck-cum-cum" (Scuglia, 2004, p. 186). Waiting for the essential "cum shot" can delay the shoot: some men have been known to take hours! Most porn stars do not find their work intrinsically pleasurable: after all, work *is* work. Sometimes the actors in the scene don't even like each other. Evidently this work is not as glamorous as many viewers may believe.

CHAPTER SUMMARY

Most aspects of the global sex industry have witnessed rapid expansion over the past decade, thanks in large part to rapid and affordable travel and to the convenience, accessibility, and anonymity of the Internet. While STW is available everywhere, studies continue to highlight the psychological and physical harm it does to STWs, particularly to the women who often find themselves in it for economic survival. Exotic dancing is another aspect of the sex industry that involves in-person contact between workers and clients. While most people would not consider exotic dancing to be high-status work, it is generally regarded as more legitimate than STW, and the dancers have a greater degree of control over their work than do most STWs. Many exotic dancers enter this work primarily for money and may at first enjoy it, but most begin to experience negative physical, emotional, and psychological effects after a few years. SEM offers consumers a less direct sexual experience, but it has the benefit of being easy to obtain without even leaving one's home. The effects of SEM continue to be researched, and most findings suggest it has a minimal effect on either the people who consume it or the greater society in which it is consumed. While parents often fear that their children will be exposed to SEM at too young of an age, research suggests that most children first encounter SEM around age 13, when most are developmentally ready to process what they see. Ultimately, despite moral and ethical objections from many, SEM and the sex industry are firmly rooted in the Canadian landscape, and they are unlikely to decrease in popularity any time soon.

DEBATE QUESTIONS

A question that rarely seems to get asked in the literature is, "What type of society do we want to create?" If by waving a magic wand you could change the way STW, exotic dancing, and SEM are accessed, provided, and regulated in Canada, what would characterize the new sex industry? What objections might some people have to the changes you would make?

REVIEW QUESTIONS

1. What are the four possible legal approaches to dealing with the sex trade?
2. What factors might influence a person to engage in STW?
3. What psychological and physical effects often result from STW?

4. How do exotic dancers titillate their audiences? What strategies do they use to cope with stress?

5. What does the bulk of research tell us about the impact of viewing SEM?

SUGGESTIONS FOR FURTHER READING AND VIEWING

Recommended Websites

Exotic Dancers: Resources and Advocacy: www.bayswan.org/EDAindex.html

Peers Victoria Resource Society: www.peers.bc.ca

Prostitution Resources: http://arapaho.nsuok.edu/~dreveskr/prolinks.html-ssi

Prostitution Resources: www.rapeis.org/activism/prostitution/prostitution.html

Bay Area Sex Worker Advocacy Network: www.bayswan.org

Prostitution Research and Education (FAQ): www.prostitutionresearch.com/c-prostitution-facts.html

Internet Censorship FAQ: www.spectacle.org/freespch/faq.html

Sex Professionals of Canada: www.spoc.ca

First Advocates: www.firstadvocates.org

Recommended Reading

Bornstein, C. (2011). *Battling pornography: The American feminist anti-pornography movement, 1976–1986*. New York, NY: Cambridge University Press.

Cooper, S.W., Estes, R.J., Giardino, A.P., Kellogg, N.D., & Vieth, V.I. (2005). *Medical, legal, & social science aspects of child sexual exploitation: A comprehensive review of pornography, prostitution, and Internet crimes, Vol. 1*. St Louis, MO: GW Medical.

Frances, R. (2007). *Selling sex: A hidden history of prostitution*. Sydney, Australia: University of New South Wales Press.

Levy, A. (2005). *Female chauvinist pigs: Woman and the rise of raunch culture*. New York, NY: Free Press.

National Network on Environments and Women's Health. (n.d.). *Towards healthy work environments for exotic dancers in Canada*. Retrieved from www.nnewh.org/images/upload/attach/7098star-policy-brief.pdf

Osanka, F.M., & Johann, S.L. (1990). *Sourcebook on pornography*. Lexington, MA: Lexington.

Recommended Viewing

Angle, J. (Director). (2012). *A fine line: A documentary on exotic dancers* [Documentary]. USA: Whistle Time Productions.

Goldberg, B. (Director). (2003). *Hot and bothered: Feminist pornography* [Documentary]. USA: National Film Network.

Lauterbach, K.R. (Director). (2012). *Flesh the movie: A documentary about sex trafficking in the US* [Documentary]. USA.

For a collection of free, short documentaries on prostitution and sex trafficking, see www.youtube.com/playlist?list=PLA45CD98C7592C348

For additional recommendations of films about sex work, see www.alternet.org/movies/127421/the_best_movies_about_sex_work

19 CHAPTER

Sex Education in Canada

STÉPHANIE C. BOYER
AND SHANNON M. COYLE

LEARNING OBJECTIVES

In this chapter, you will

- learn about the goals, theoretical background, and effectiveness of sex education in Canada;
- become familiar with formal and informal sources of information about sexual health; and
- explore barriers to accessing sex education in Canada.

Abracadabra: VAGINA!

Imagine that you are a sex therapist. Your first clients of the day are a couple that were referred to you by their family physician for sexual difficulties.

Janet and Brett have been married for just over three months, and they dated for two years prior to getting married. They met in high school and went to the same university, where Janet studied advertising and Brett completed a degree in law. They engaged in some sexual activity before marriage, but both wanted to wait until their wedding night to "officially" consummate their relationship. But on their wedding night they were unable to have intercourse. Brett recalls feeling as if there was a wall stopping his penis from entering Janet's vagina, and Janet explains that she felt discomfort with his attempts to penetrate. Chalking it up to the excitement of the day, they tried again the following night. No luck. They tried the next night, and the night after that. . . . After a few weeks of frustrating attempts, they went back to their previous sexual routine, feeling discouraged and not knowing what to do.

As a sex therapist, you can think of a number of possible differential diagnoses. Based on their description of the problem, you wonder if Janet may have a genital pain condition, perhaps due to an imperforate hymen or to vaginismus. You also wonder whether Brett's erections are hard enough for penetration. You recommend that they each see their family physician to examine the matter further in order to help you determine the source of the problem and the best course of treatment.

Janet and Brett return two weeks later with clean bills of health. Neither exam showed any sign of something that could be responsible for their inability to have intercourse. At this point, you start to think that you must be missing an important piece of the puzzle. Taking out a diagram of a vulva, you ask them to tell you more about what happened during their attempts to have sex. As they take you through their story one more time, you ask Brett to show you on the diagram exactly where it felt like he was hitting a "wall." He explains that he tried everywhere, but the entrance to the vagina was not visible. Upon further questioning, you realize that Brett and Janet did not know that the entrance to the vagina is found beneath the folds of the labia; they believed it would just "appear" once he gently pressed his penis in the right "spot." You spend the remainder of the session educating them about the male and female sexual response—and providing some much-needed information about anatomy! At their next and final session, they happily tell you the news that the problem is solved, while at the same time expressing serious frustration about not having learned about how intercourse "actually happens" in school. After five years of sex education, each knew about different methods of contraception and the signs and symptoms of sexually transmitted infections (STIs), and yet they weren't given enough information to be able to actually figure out how to have sex!

QUESTIONS FOR CRITICAL THOUGHT AND REFLECTION

1. Do you think that the mechanics of sex should be taught in school?
2. What other settings might be appropriate for teaching this information?
3. At what age might it be appropriate for young people to learn about the mechanics of sex?

Introduction

What comes to mind when you think of sex education? For some, it is a reminder of an awkward conversation with their parents or a memory of their first sexual experience, while others may recall learning about sex in a classroom. A person's view of her or his **sexual health** is influenced by many factors such as cultural beliefs and values, and personal experiences. Theorists, researchers, and policy-makers alike have been unable to create a universal definition of "sexual health" that fully captures its complexity (Sandfort & Ehrhardt, 2004). Working definitions have, however, been created to guide education programs and support human rights. For example, one widely used definition is that provided by the World Health Organization (WHO):

sexual health A state of sexual well-being that varies from person to person and is influenced by various socio-cultural factors and historical contexts.

Sexual health is a state of physical, emotional, mental and social well-being in relation to sexuality; it is not merely the absence of disease, dysfunction or infirmity. Sexual health requires a positive and respectful approach to sexuality and sexual relationships, as well as the possibility of having pleasurable and safe sexual experiences, free of coercion, discrimination and violence. For sexual health to be attained and maintained, the sexual rights of all persons must be respected, protected and fulfilled (WHO, 2002, p. 5).

Sexual health education is one such right to which all Canadians are entitled (Public Health Agency of Canada [PHAC], 2008). Nevertheless, as you will discover in this chapter, this topic remains hotly debated in Canada with regard to who teaches it, what topics to include, and when and where it is taught. Despite such debate, however, and regardless of whether sex education is obtained from parents, peers, or in school, teaching youth about sex in a personalized manner that relates to their own questions and concerns is the best way to ensure that they will understand and explore their sexuality in a healthy and independent way.

Sex Education in Canada

Goals and Principles

The ***Canadian Guidelines for Sexual Health Education*** (the *Canadian Guidelines*), first released in 1994 and most recently updated in 2008, was created to serve as a framework for developing, implementing, and evaluating sex education programs, as well as related services and policies, across Canada. This document defines sex education as "equipping individuals, couples, families, and communities with the information, motivation, and behavioural skills needed to enhance sexual health and avoid negative sexual health outcomes" (PHAC, 2008, p. 5). It also outlines two main goals in educating Canadians about sexuality: promoting **positive sexual health outcomes**, such as rewarding sexual relationships and informed reproductive decisions, and avoiding **negative sexual health outcomes**, such as STIs, unintended pregnancy, and sexual coercion (PHAC, 2008).

Reducing negative outcomes is typically emphasized in government policy related to sexual health. Giami (2002) analyzed sexual health policies in the US and England and found that the documents outlining these policies limited their discussion of sexual health to the negative consequences of sexual behaviour. The emphasis on preventing negative outcomes is likely to impact sex education curricula, and consequently, it is surprising to many that sex education is not just about avoiding STIs but also about promoting sexual pleasure! For example, a recent survey of Toronto youth found that respondents were most likely to report having learned about STIs, pregnancy, and contraception (65 to 78 per cent of respondents), and least likely to have learned about sexual satisfaction and pleasure (42 per cent of respondents) in formal sex education settings (Causarano, Pole, Flicker, & the Toronto Teen Survey Team, 2010). Nevertheless, promoting self-esteem, healthy relationships, and the development of one's sexual identity are equally important goals in sex education (PHAC, 2008).

Five key principles are identified in the *Canadian Guidelines* (PHAC, 2008) as contributing to effective sex education programs:

1. *Accessibility*. This principle states that sex education should be available to all Canadians. Programs should also address the diverse needs of our society in a nonjudgmental environment. This means not discriminating against individuals based on their socio-demographic characteristics (e.g., socio-economic status, religion,

sexual health education
A universal sexual right to access comprehensive sexual health information and other resources necessary to promote healthy sexuality and avoid negative outcomes.

Canadian Guidelines for Sexual Health Education
A comprehensive document that outlines best practices for teaching sexual health in Canada, based on research and clinical expertise from such fields as education, health promotion, medicine, nursing, psychology, and social work. (PHAC, 2008)

positive sexual health outcomes Positive outcomes relating to sexual satisfaction, exploring one's sexual identity, making informed sexual decisions, and maintaining a healthy mental and physical state free from STIs, sexual violence, sexual discrimination, and sexual abuse.

negative sexual health outcomes Negative consequences relating to sexual health behaviours, including STIs, unintended pregnancy, sexual violence, sexual discrimination, sexual abuse, and sexual coercion.

culture, race, gender identity, sexual orientation, and/or physical/cognitive ability). Discrimination could be direct—for instance, making negative comments about same-sex relationships in a classroom—or indirect, as is the case when individuals in rural areas do not have access to sexual health information and services, such as STI testing.

2. *Comprehensiveness.* Program content should cover all relevant areas, with age-appropriate topics presented beginning at the start of elementary school up to the end of high school. For instance, labelling body parts is suitable for the developmental level of Grade 1 students, but talking about contraception options at this age would not be! Beyond the content, the context or setting in which one learns about sex is also important. Sex education does not end once one leaves the classroom—counselling and health care services, caregivers, and the media all play a part in teaching us about sex. To ensure communication among these different sources of information, federal, provincial, and municipal governments should work together to coordinate sex education programs and related community services, and to support informal sexual health learning opportunities.

3. *Effective approaches.* Sex education should go beyond simply providing participants with information about sex; indeed, it should encourage personal insight and motivation to act on this information, and it should incorporate skill-building activities. For example, while information about the effectiveness of condoms is important to know, it may also be useful to have students discuss how comfortable they would feel about asking a partner to wear a condom, and to have them learn how to properly put on a condom. Further, the classic sex education exercise of putting a condom on a banana might be more entertaining than just focussing on numbers and descriptions.

4. *Training and support.* It would not be very useful to have people who are not knowledgeable about sexuality teach a sex education class. People providing sex education should know their stuff! School employees and others involved in formal teaching should undergo mandatory training. People who teach sex education on a more informal basis—such as parents—should also be given learning opportunities, to ensure they know enough about sex to provide others with reliable information. Formal program educators should also receive support from their organization, such as enough class time to cover sexual health topics, and continuing education opportunities.

5. *Program planning, evaluation, and revision.* Sex education programs should be developed to address the needs of the targeted audience and the community at large. Imagine the goals of a sex education program for college students: would the same goals apply to a program for preteens in a low socio-economic status area? There would be some overlap, but it is certain that the groups would differ in their previous knowledge, skills, and experiences. Once implemented, a program should be systematically evaluated to examine (i) its effect on the targeted sexual health behaviours (e.g., did more students use contraception during sex after attending the class?) and (ii) participants' satisfaction with the program (e.g., did students find the class useful? what could be improved?). Based on the results of such evaluations and new findings from sexual health research, program content and structure should be regularly updated.

Theory

How we understand why people decide to engage in certain sexual behaviours impacts how and what we teach about sex. A number of theoretical frameworks have been applied to sex education, including the information–motivation–behavioural skills (IMB) model developed by Jeffrey Fisher and William Fisher (see J.D. Fisher & Fisher,

1992, and W.A. Fisher & Fisher, 1993, as well as chapters 7 and 8, for more on this model). The IMB model was chosen as the focus of Canadian sex education policy because there is evidence showing that it can effectively be applied to sexual health issues of concern to Canadians (Figure 19.1), as programs based on this theory that target a variety of sexual health behaviours have been successful (see J.D. Fisher & Fisher, 2000, for a review). In addition to providing a useful theoretical framework, the IMB model also outlines steps for effective program development and evaluation: (1) determine the sexual health needs of the target population through research; (2) design a program to meet these needs; and (3) evaluate the program (J.D. Fisher & Fisher, 1992).

The IMB model specifies that sexual health behaviours are initiated and maintained by three factors:

1. *Information or knowledge about the behaviour,* which should be easily translated into action to reduce sexual health risks and promote healthy sexuality (W.A. Fisher & Fisher, 1993). For example, education about contraceptive methods should not just stop at a definition. Imagine you were first learning about what a condom is for, and all you were given was a short description and a picture; would that be enough for you to successfully use one? Probably not: how would you know where to find a condom, which side to use, or when to put it on? It is important to include practical information, such as where condoms can be found in one's local community, and how to discuss using condoms with a partner (PHAC, 2008).

2. *Motivation to apply knowledge in order to maintain sexual health,* which results from the combined effect of emotional, personal, and social motivations (W.A. Fisher & Fisher, 1998; PHAC, 2008) (see Figure 19.1 for examples of these three types of

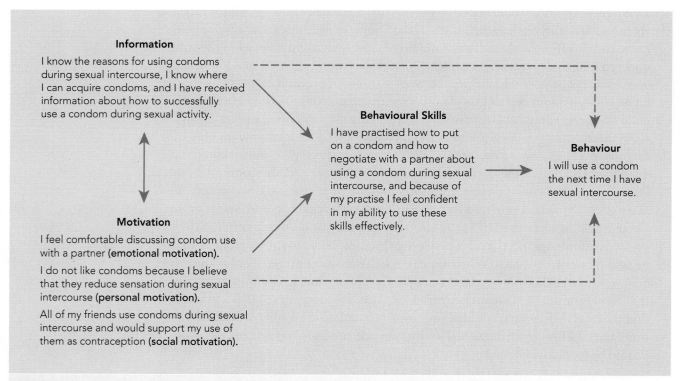

FIGURE 19.1 This application of the information–motivation–behavioural skills model to the topic of condom use highlights just a few of the many factors that can impact our sexual decisions and behaviour. Which part(s) of the model do you think impact your choices the most?

Source: Adapted from J.D. Fisher & Fisher (1992) and W.A. Fisher & Fisher (1993).

motivation). Emotional motivation is the level of comfort a person has with sexuality and specific sexual health behaviours. This level of comfort will influence whether someone will avoid or seek out information about sex. Personal motivation, on the other hand, refers to the beliefs and values a person has about practising specific sexual health behaviours. For example, if someone is not concerned about getting an STI during oral sex, he or she is less likely to use a condom in this situation. Social motivation relates to perceptions of social norms: in other words, what your friends think about engaging in a sexual health behaviour, like unsafe sex, and how much support you think you'll get from them if you engage in that behaviour.

3. *Behavioural skills enabling someone to engage in sexual health behaviour*, which includes objective skills (e.g., being able to negotiate condom use with a partner) as well as the feeling of being capable of performing a behaviour, termed *self-efficacy* (Bandura, 1989; W.A. Fisher & Fisher, 1993). So it is not just about whether you know what to do but whether you think you can do it and do it well! As seen in Figure 19.1, the IMB model assumes that information and motivation drive the development and application of related behavioural skills. These skills not only initiate sexual health behaviours, they also maintain them in order to aid in the reduction of risky sexual behaviours. Although both information and motivation are thought to influence whether behavioural skills are applied to reduce negative sexual behaviours, they are thought to be unrelated to one another. For example, although someone may know about the risks of contracting STIs from unprotected sex, that person may not necessarily engage in appropriate sexual health behaviours if she or he feels uncomfortable discussing condom use with a partner or believes no one in her or his peer group uses condoms.

If behavioural skills are not a crucial factor in whether or not a person engages in a behaviour, information and motivation can directly affect whether that person engages in the behaviour (rather than indirectly via the behavioural skills component of the model, as indicated by the broken lines in Figure 19.1). Taking an example provided by W.A. Fisher and Fisher (1998), imagine a young heterosexual woman who has been using oral contraceptive pills for several years, knows that taking these pills reduces the likelihood that she will experience an unintended pregnancy, and is motivated to continue taking these pills. She will likely not have to apply new or complicated skills to use these pills effectively to prevent pregnancy. On the other hand, if we look at the same young woman's use of condoms, she may have to use negotiation skills with a partner to ensure they use condoms consistently. In the first example, information and motivation would directly lead to use of the pills, while in the second example, the same woman would have to use her communication skills to use a condom, which would be driven by her knowledge and motivation to use condoms (W.A. Fisher & Fisher, 1998).

Curriculum and Delivery

Broadly speaking, there are two main types of sex education programs in North America: **comprehensive programs** and **abstinence-only programs**. Comprehensive sex education programs promote both abstaining from sexual activity and employing strategies to protect oneself from STIs and unintended pregnancy. This second goal is based on the understanding that many teenagers engage in sexual behaviour before marriage. Abstinence-only programs, on the other hand, typically solely promote postponing intercourse until marriage (or simply until later in life). Although many programs

comprehensive sexual health education Sexual health education programs that include information about contraception and avoidance of STIs as well as abstinence.

abstinence-only sexual health education Sexual health education programs focussed on teaching abstinence from sexual activity until marriage and/or a later time; information about contraception tends to be excluded from such programs.

can be easily identified as being comprehensive or abstinence-only, it is best to think about sex education programs along a continuum. There are all kinds of abstinence-only programs; not all of them are at the extreme we typically picture (Kirby, 2001). For example, some may discuss condoms but focus on the message that condoms are not 100 per cent effective in preventing negative outcomes (Kirby, 2001). Abstinence-only programs are more common in the US than in Canada, with 18 states requiring that curricula include information on the importance of sexual activity occurring only within marriage (Guttmacher Institute, 2011), and a large amount of US government funding is used to implement and promote abstinence-only programs (Kirby, 2008).

McKay and Bissell (2009) state that school-based sex education in Canada should not be based within an abstinence-only framework for two main reasons. First, abstinence-only programs can be viewed as unethical because they withhold some of the information people need to make informed decisions about their sexual health. Santelli et al. (2006) agree and further note that such programs are particularly inadequate for sexually experienced youth and LGBTQ youth. Indeed, Orton (1994) remarks that abstinence-only programs stigmatize youth "in whom abstinence is impossible, unrealistic, or not desirable" (p. 215). Many LGBTQ youth suffer because the heterosexist nature of abstinence-only curriculum ignores sexual diversity and may leave LGBTQ students feeling marginalized and uninformed; even worse, LGBTQ identities may be negatively and explicitly denounced in such programs (C.M. Fisher, 2009; Santelli et al., 2006). Second, the long-term effectiveness of abstinence-only programs on reducing sexual behaviour among teens has not been demonstrated in the majority of studies. For example, Kohler, Manhart, and Lafferty (2008) compared sexual behaviour among US teenagers 15 to 19 years of age who had received (1) no sex education, (2) abstinence-only education, or (3) comprehensive sex education. The results indicated that, similar to a complete lack of sex education, abstinence-only education programming did not decrease the likelihood of reporting a history of sexual intercourse, pregnancy, or STIs. On the other hand, comprehensive programs were associated with a decreased likelihood of pregnancy and of initiating sexual intercourse. Based on a review of abstinence-only versus comprehensive sex education programs, Kirby (2008) concluded that there was little evidence to support the widespread application of abstinence-only curricula.

So, what makes a sex education program effective? Based on a review of 73 studies investigating youth sex education programs conducted in Canada and the US, Kirby (2001) identified 10 characteristics that effective programs all had in common (Table 19.1). Overall, the programs that are the most effective provide clear, accurate information on a variety of sexual health topics relevant to students, involve practical examples and exercises, and are run by trained individuals who believe in the value of the program.

The *Canadian Guidelines* (PHAC, 2008) outlines recommendations for sex education, but as the title states, this document is a set of guidelines and not regulations. The breadth and depth—including the specific content—of school-based sex education programs is determined at the provincial level, by each provincial government. Content will therefore vary across Canada based on provincial curriculum guidelines for elementary and high school students. In addition, provincial curriculum objectives for sex education are broad, so individual school boards, schools, and even classrooms will differ in terms of how much class time is dedicated to sexual health and which topics are covered. As discussed in the Barriers to Sex Education section later in this chapter, a number of political and socio-demographic factors impact what is included in school-based sex education, which remains an issue of debate.

TABLE 19.1 Ten characteristics of effective sexual health education programs.

Characteristic	Description	Example/Further Details
Specific behaviour target(s)	The program specifically focusses on decreasing one or more behaviours linked to negative sexual health outcomes.	Example: A major behaviour change goal of a program to reduce unprotected sexual activity could be increasing use of condoms.
Theoretical foundation	The program is rooted in a theory that has been shown to be effective when applied to the reduction of other negative health-related behaviours.	Example: The program could be based on the IMB model.
Clear message	The program explicitly states and reinforces a specific message about safer sexual activity and contraception use.	Example: If the program message is that teens should use condoms every time they have sex, it should not only explore the pros and cons of engaging in unprotected sexual activity but unambiguously emphasize that unprotected sex is a negative and risky choice.
Basic information	The program gives basic, up-to-date information on the risks associated with sexual activity, and either (i) ways of abstaining from sexual intercourse or (ii) using condoms and other contraceptives to prevent unintended pregnancy and STIs.	Example: Rather than describing all of the possible methods of contraception, the program emphasizes the reasoning for protecting oneself during sexual activity and focusses on key method(s) of contraception, such as condoms.
Activities related to social environment	The program includes skill-building activities that help students deal with how social barriers, pressures, and norms can affect sexual behaviour.	Example: Activities could address the social barrier of feeling embarrassed about buying condoms, the social pressure from a partner to engage in sexual activity, and the social norm that "unprotected sex is not such a big deal."
Activities related to sexual communication	The program includes skill-building activities that help students learn sexual activity communication, negation, and refusal.	Example: Students could role-play to rehearse how to say "no" to unprotected sex.
Activities related to active application of knowledge	The program uses experiential exercises versus only didactic teaching methods so that participants will actively apply the program information to their own lives.	Example: Students could engage in small group discussions or exercises outside of class, such as locating sexual health services in their community.
Appropriate content	The program's behavioural goals, teaching methods, and materials are geared to its audience.	The goals are specific to the age, culture, and sexual experience of the program participants.
Appropriate program length	The program lasts long enough for activities to be effective.	The program length is of at least 14 hours.[a]
Knowledgeable and motivated educators	The program leaders are carefully selected, participate in training, and believe in the curriculum they are teaching.	Educators receive at least 6 hours of training.

[a]Kirby's study found that certain shorter programs were also effective, but in these cases the participants tended to be volunteers and the program activities were run in smaller groups.

Source: Adapted from Kirby (2001).

School-based programs are certainly not the only mode of delivery of sex education, but they are a crucial component of educating Canadians about sexual health. Unlike any other organization or agency, the school system has the potential to initiate contact with all of Canada's youth (Orton, 1994). A number of Canadian studies have shown that both parents and teens strongly support sex education occurring in school (e.g., Byers et al., 2003; Weaver, Byers, Sears, Cohen, & Randall, 2002). Starting sex education programs in elementary school may help to influence the decisions people make regarding sexual behaviours later in life (Boyce et al., 2006). For example, if someone learns about the importance of contraception only after engaging in unprotected sex for several years, it may be more difficult for that person to apply this new knowledge and change her or his behaviour, compared to someone who is armed with this information *before* she or he begins having sex. One could speculate that if sex education is provided only after someone becomes sexually active, it may have less of an impact on what she or he does. Of course, sex education may start in school, but it should not and does not end there. Knowing where to find sexual health information and services is crucial to leading a sexually healthy life.

Effectiveness of Sex Education: How Is Canada Doing?

As outlined in the *Canadian Guidelines* (PHAC, 2008) and the IMB model (J.D. Fisher & Fisher, 1992, W.A. Fisher & Fisher, 1993), sex education programs must be regularly evaluated and updated in order to be effective. One direct way to evaluate a program is to measure its impact on those who took part in it. Results from two comprehensive school-based sex education programs recently conducted in Ontario will be reviewed in this section:

1. The Girl Time program (Rye et al., 2008) for female Grade 7 students who were followed over a year after the program ended and attended a booster session in Grade 8.
2. A mandatory sex education program for Grade 9 students investigated by Smylie and colleagues (Smylie, Maticka-Tyndale, Boyd, & the Adolescent Sexual Health Planning Committee, 2008).

This section will also examine broad Canadian trends in knowledge, motivation (such as attitudes and subjective norms), and behaviour to assess how Canada as a whole is doing at educating and supporting Canadians regarding sexual health. Looking at these three areas in teens is an important starting point given the importance of school-based programs in Canada's sex education infrastructure, as well as the high rates of STIs in Canadian youth compared to adults (PHAC, 2009; Sellors et al., 2003). The following discussion will also draw on findings from two large national studies that have been conducted within the past decade to examine sexuality in Canadian youth: the Canadian Community Health Survey (CCHS) (Rotermann, 2005, 2008) and the Canadian Youth, Sexual Health, and HIV/AIDS Study (CYSHHAS) (Boyce, Doherty, Fortin, & MacKinnon, 2003; Boyce et al., 2006). Two major strengths of these studies are that (1) they were designed to correspond to a nationally representative sample of Canadian youth, and (2) they compared their findings to the results of earlier versions of the same surveys (conducted in 1995/1996 and 1989, respectively).

Knowledge

Sex education programs provide important information about the health risks associated with unprotected sexual activity and how to avoid these risks. The results of the Girl Time program indicated that sexual health knowledge did not differ between the program group and the control group before the program, but Girl Time participants had significantly more knowledge than the control group after the program (Rye et al., 2008). Additionally, although both groups gained sexual health knowledge in the 14 months following the program (which makes sense because we learn more as we grow up), the sexual health knowledge of Girl Time participants was still greater than that of the control group at this later time. Smylie and colleagues (2008) found that one month after the end of their program, participants had significantly more knowledge compared to students who had not participated in the program.

There is great emphasis on providing information about STIs, especially HIV, to Canadian youth. The CYSHHAS looked at knowledge about transmission, diagnosis, and treatment of STIs in grade 7, 9, and 11 students in schools across Canada (Boyce et al., 2003). Overall, the results were worrisome and disappointing: in 2002, students appeared to be less knowledgeable about STIs compared to students who did the survey in 1989. For example, fewer students in 2002 knew that HIV/AIDS cannot be cured if treated early. In addition, only 36 per cent of Grade 9 students knew that there is no vaccine available to prevent HIV/AIDS. Further, less than half of Grade 9 students knew that many people with STIs may not have symptoms, and only slightly more than half of Grade 11 students answered this question correctly.

When overall knowledge scores were calculated, the results were more encouraging: 60 and 87 per cent of Grade 9 and Grade 11 students, respectively, answered half or more of the questions correctly (Boyce et al., 2003). Were knowledge scores related to formal sex education in the survey? Overall, students who reported that school was their main source of information about HIV/AIDS were slightly more likely to have high versus low scores, although when individual grades were examined by gender this relationship was not consistently seen (Boyce et al., 2003). Similarly, students in grades 9 and 11 who reported spending more hours learning about HIV/AIDS were more likely to have higher knowledge scores. On the other hand, students who rated media as their main source of information about HIV/AIDS tended to have low scores. (See the Alternative Forms of Sex Education section that appears later in this chapter for more about the impact of media on learning about sex.)

Motivation

The CYSHHAS asked students not only about their knowledge of STIs but also about their perceived vulnerability to disease (Boyce et al., 2003). Approximately half of the students reported being worried about catching an STI. Students in grades 9 and 11 were also asked about their personal attitudes about sexual topics. Between 64 and 70 per cent of male and female students in each grade agreed that premarital sexual activity is acceptable if two people are in love. The acceptability of casual sex and masturbation varied by gender, with only a third of female students agreeing that masturbation is acceptable (Figure 19.2). It seems that both male and female students generally viewed masturbation, a healthy component of sexual expression that has been linked to a number of positive sexual outcomes (Coleman, 2003), as equally acceptable to engaging in casual sex, a behaviour associated with sexual risk-taking.

In general, findings about the impact of specific sex education programs on attitudes toward sexuality have been mixed. Despite encouraging increases in sexual

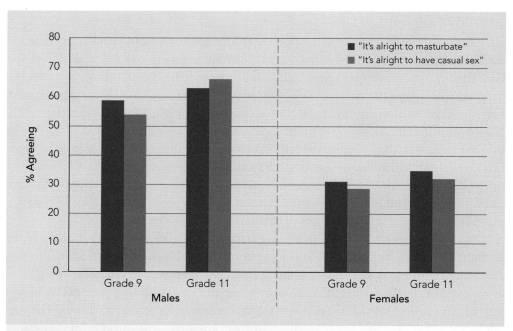

FIGURE 19.2 When male and female students participating in the CYSHHAS were asked whether they agree with the statements "it's alright to masturbate" and "it's alright to have casual sex," their responses revealed an interesting pattern. These results could suggest that different attitudes are conveyed to each gender about masturbation and casual sex. Does this surprise you?

Source: Adapted from Boyce et al. (2003).

health knowledge, the Girl Time program did not have a high impact on motivation; specifically, it had little effect on changing sexual attitudes and behavioural intentions (Rye et al., 2008); similar results were reported by Smylie et al. (2008). The authors of both studies indicated that because scores on certain motivation outcome measures were already high before the intervention (for example, participants already had strong intent to use contraception during sexual activity), there may have been a **ceiling effect**: there was little room for improvement from before to after the program because attitudes were already so positive at the start. So it seems that although teens have knowledge to gain in sex education classes, they may already be highly motivated to engage in healthy sexual behaviours before the program starts.

ceiling effect A levelling off of an effect when something reaches its maximum impact on something else.

Behaviour

To assess behavioural skills, the Girl Time study asked participants in the intervention and control groups about how hard it would be for them to engage in different sexual health behaviours and how effective they would be at engaging in these behaviours (Rye et al., 2008). The groups differed in their perceived self-efficacy: Girl Time participants had a significantly higher level of self-efficacy after the program and for the following year compared to the control group.

The findings presented above are encouraging, as knowledge, motivation, and behavioural skills are important areas theorized to impact sexual behaviour according to the IMB model. But what we really want to know is whether sex education interventions actually have a positive effect on adolescent sexual behaviour. To find out, and to determine how at risk Canadian youth are for negative sexual outcomes, we can examine several factors: participation in sexual activity, sexual frequency, number of sexual partners, condom use, and STI and pregnancy rates.

Participation in sexual activity. Despite some discouraging findings about the sexual health knowledge of high school students surveyed in the CYSHHAS, data from this study suggested that, overall, the number of students engaging in different sexual behaviours in 2002 was similar to what it was in 1989 (see Figure 19.3 for the specific percentage of students reporting that they had engaged in different sexual behaviours in 2002). These results suggest that Canadian youth were not more sexually active in 2002 than in 1989 (Boyce et al., 2003). In relation to sexual intercourse in particular, data from the CCHS suggested that fewer adolescents had engaged in sexual intercourse, and those who had were first initiating sex at a later age (Rotermann, 2008). From 1996/1997 to 2005, there was a drop in the number of 15- to 19-year-olds who reported having had sexual intercourse (47 to 43 per cent) and in the number of teens who reported having engaged in sexual intercourse before they turned 15 (12 to 8 per cent).

Sexual frequency. Of students who reported in the CYSHHAS that they had had sexual intercourse at least once, there was a relatively even split in sexual frequency: approximately one third reported having had intercourse only once, one third reported having had intercourse a few times, and one third reported having had intercourse often (Boyce et al., 2006). Compared to the 1989 responses, it appears that students in 2002 who reported being sexually active engaged in intercourse more frequently (Boyce et al., 2003).

Number of sexual partners. In the CYSHHAS, approximately half of the students in grades 9 and 11 who reported having had sexual intercourse had had only one sexual partner (Boyce et al., 2006). Compared to the results from 1989, these findings suggest that fewer teens have had multiple sexual partners. In the CCHS, teens were asked about their number of sexual partners within the past year: 33 per cent reported having had more than one partner, and this response was significantly more common in individuals 18 to 19 years of age (Rotermann, 2008).

Condom use. In the CCHS, 75 per cent of teens reported having used a condom the last time they had sexual intercourse. Condom use was more common in adolescents 15 to 17 years of age versus older adolescents (Rotermann, 2008). Similarly, in the CYSHHAS,

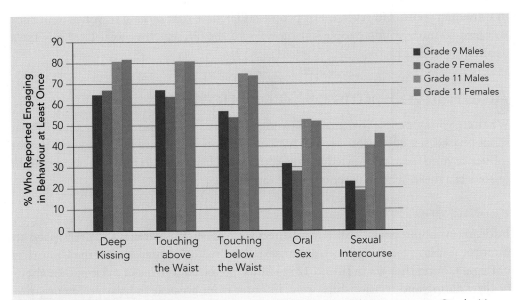

FIGURE 19.3 Not surprisingly, the CYSHHAS found higher sexual experience in Grade 11 versus Grade 9 students. This study also indicated that there are not large gender differences in the sexual experiences of Canadian students.

Source: Adapted from Boyce et al. (2003).

64 to 80 per cent of male and female students in grades 9 and 11 had used a condom during last intercourse (Boyce et al., 2003). One of the most commonly endorsed reasons for not having used a condom during last intercourse was not expecting to engage in sexual activity (Boyce et al., 2003).

STI rates. A recent report by PHAC (2009) found an increase in the reported incidence of chlamydia, gonorrhea, and syphilis infections from 1998 to 2007. The highest rates of chlamydia were in females 15 to 24 years of age, and the highest rates of gonorrhea were in females 15 to 24 years of age and males 20 to 24 years of age. In contrast, the highest rates of syphilis were in those 30 years of age and older. Similar increases in STI rates have been seen in other developed countries, particularly in younger populations in the US, Australia, and the UK (PHAC, 2009).

Pregnancy rates. How many Canadian teens are becoming pregnant? Statistics Canada has shown a consistent decrease in teen pregnancy rates since the 1990s (Statistics Canada, 2008). For example, from 1996 to 2005, the number of reported pregnancies in women under 20 years of age dropped from 38.7 to 24.6 out of 1000 women (Statistics Canada, 2008). This decrease in pregnancy rates has occurred despite similar rates of sexual activity (Boyce et al., 2006), suggesting that Canadian teens are using effective contraception methods to prevent pregnancy (McKay, 2004a).

In summary, Canada is doing relatively well when we compare youth sexual behaviour today to that in the past: adolescents appear to be delaying sexual intercourse, and Canadian teen pregnancy rates have been steadily decreasing. Nevertheless, rates of STIs continue to increase among young Canadians, which could be related to factors such as a decrease in knowledge about this topic in Canadian youth over time, as suggested in the CYSHHAS (Boyce et al., 2003). Additionally, although it is helpful to assess Canada as a whole, the rates of STIs and unintended pregnancies vary considerably from one end of Canada to the other (PHAC, 2009; Statistics Canada, 2008). Provinces and territories with the most elevated rates may benefit the most from increased support for education programs and other initiatives that promote sexual health. Continued development, application, and revision of programs such as those reviewed in this section will be an important step forward in improving sexual health in Canadian youth. However, many people still believe that talking to youth about sex will lead to more young people having sex—see the "Research vs Real Life" box for a debunking of this myth.

Alternative Forms of Sex Education

What are young people in Canada learning about sex from sources other than formal school-based sex education programs? This section will examine three sources that influence youth sexual knowledge, motivation, and behaviour as much as or more than lessons taught in school: parents, peers, and media.

Parents and Peers

Information about sexual health from direct sources, such as parents and peers, plays an important role in teaching youth about sexuality. In 2005, researchers at the University of Regina found that grade 10 and 12 students' preferred sources of information about healthy dating and relationships were, in order from greatest to least preference, personal experience, friends, and parents. Preferred sources of information on pregnancy and STI prevention were school, followed by parents, and friends (Hampton, Fahlman, Goertzen, & Jeffery, 2005). Similarly, the CYSHHAS found that school was the main source of information about sexuality, puberty, birth control, and HIV/AIDS in Grade 9

Research VS Real Life

Does Talking about Sex Lead to Sex?

Have you ever heard someone say that teaching about sex leads to sex? An enduring myth about sex education is that it will lead to earlier and more frequent sexual behaviour in youth. This criticism has been aimed predominantly at comprehensive sex education programs. It is one of the most common misconceptions the Canadian public has about school-based sex education (McKay, 2004b; McKay & Bissell, 2009), and it has been cited in the media as one of the most common parental objections to school-based sex education (Goldman, 2008).

So what does the research say about the impact of sex education on sexual behaviour? A recent literature review examined 83 studies of youth sex education programs (six of which were abstinence-only programs) carried out in school, health, and community settings around the world (Kirby, Laris, & Rolleri, 2006, 2007). All of these studies compared individuals participating in a sex education program to a non-intervention control group to determine whether sexual behaviour and other outcomes differed between program participants and non-participants. The authors of the review concluded that, overall, sex education programs did not speed up initiation of sexual intercourse: all but one of the studies found either a delay in initiation of intercourse among program participants or no difference between the groups in terms of age at first intercourse. Most studies also found that participation in sex education programs either reduced or did not change individuals' frequency of engaging in sexual intercourse. These findings were echoed in a meta-analysis of 174 studies that examined sex education programs focussing on HIV risk reduction (Smoak, Scott-Sheldon, Johnson, Carey, & the SHARP Research Team, 2006). The investigators found that program participants were less likely than control participants to engage in penetrative intercourse.

Based on these results, it seems safe to say that teaching young Canadians about sexual health—including how to protect themselves from STIs and unintended pregnancy—will not lead them to start engaging in sexual behaviour sooner or more frequently than Canadians who are not taught about sexual health. In fact, sex education may delay sexual activity. So the results are in: teaching people about sex does not lead them to rush out and have sex!

students (Boyce et al., 2003). Although parents were not cited as a primary source of information in this study, they may nevertheless have a direct or indirect effect on their child's sex education—for example, through discussions at home about sexuality or by moderating what their child watches on television.

PARENTS

The CYSHHAS also asked students to indicate the ease with which they could talk to their parents about sex. Participants' responses to this question suggest that the majority of Canadian youth do not feel comfortable discussing sexuality with their parents (Figure 19.4). This discomfort is not surprising given that most teens cringe at the idea of their parents knowing *anything* about sex, and that many parents feel equally uncomfortable about discussing sexuality with their child (check out the cartoon in Figure 19.5). The teen's reported lack of comfort with talking to their parents about sex may also explain why parents were not rated as a preferred source of information about sex in this study.

Despite the discomfort that may arise at the thought of speaking with one's parents about sex, research has shown that such discussions may have a positive effect. For example, adolescents whose parents discuss sexuality with them are more likely to delay engaging in sexual activity (Miller, Forehand, & Kotchick, 1999). The positive impact

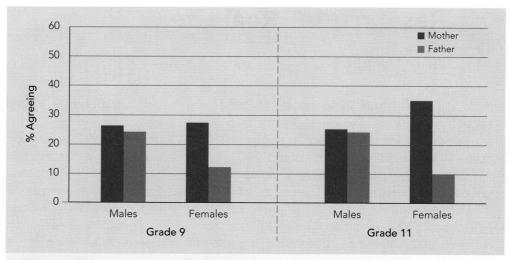

FIGURE 19.4 This graph shows the percentage of students who reported in the CYSHHAS that they agreed or strongly agreed that they could speak openly with each parent about sex. Notice that although rates are similar in male students for both parents, female students reported less comfort speaking with their father versus their mother about sex.

Source: Adapted from Boyce et al. (2003).

of parent involvement on sex education and behaviour has, however, been shown to be dependent on having a warm and connected relationship with one's parent(s) (Miller, Benson, & Galbraith, 2001) and other socio-demographic variables (Roche et al., 2005). Specifically, Roche et al. (2005) found that greater parental involvement was related to a lower likelihood of early initiation of sexual intercourse, but only when the family lived in a neighbourhood that was socio-economically advantaged.

PEERS

Peers play an important role in influencing youth sexual behaviour, as perceived norms for sexual activity are closely tied to one's social environment (Hampton et al., 2005). Hampton et al. (2005) have pointed out that young people tend to look to their peers for advice and for approval of their actions. In fact, they found that students' perceptions of whether their peers were engaging in sexual intercourse predicted initiation of intercourse. In other words, students who thought their peers were having sex were more likely to have done so themselves. Social norms about sexual behaviour are an important factor in a number of theories relating to sexual behaviour, including the IMB model (J.D. Fisher & Fisher, 1992; W.A. Fisher & Fisher, 1993).

Peer influence on sexuality is not necessarily negative. The *Canadian Guidelines* (PHAC, 2008)—recognizing that youth seek approval from their peers—recommends the use of peer-based teaching approaches. In fact, peer-to-peer sex education models have resulted in positive outcomes in certain Canadian communities (Adamcheck, 2006). Such approaches are likely successful because many youth feel more comfortable receiving information from peers, and they often consider information from a peer who has recently dealt with a sexual issue under consideration as more credible than similar information delivered by adults (Smylie et al., 2008).

Media

Beyond the more direct sources of sex education discussed thus far, Canadian youth receive influential information about sexuality from popular media sources like the

Internet, TV, movies, magazines, books, and songs. The average Canadian youth watches television for nearly 22 hours per week (Statistics Canada, 2006)—yes, almost an entire day every week in front of the TV! A number of studies have investigated sexual content in media consumed by North American youth. One such study found that 70 per cent of the top teen programs include sexual references (Kunkel, Eyal, Finnerty, Biely, & Donnerstein, 2005). Another found that 25 per cent of teen movie characters are shown engaging in sexual intercourse (Stern, 2005). Yet another found that 37 per cent of popular songs refer to sexual activity (Primack, Gold, Schwarz, & Dalton, 2008).

Typically, movies and television shows do not depict sexual behaviour openly; instead they refer to sexual acts through discussions and visual representations of actions occurring before and after what viewers assume to be sexual acts. Unfortunately, mainstream North American visual media tends to not provide educational messages alongside its references to sexuality. More specifically, the sexual encounters represented in visual media involve very little negotiation surrounding safe sex practices (see Figure 19.6). Rarely do you hear characters about to have sex ask questions such as "How many sexual partners have you had?" "Have you been tested for STIs?" and "What method of contraception should we use?" Research has shown that sex-related media content mostly involves talking about sex rather than depicting responsible sexual behaviours (L.D. Taylor, 2005), such as buying and using condoms.

There is no standard script in place that sets out how sexual content might be portrayed in media sources to provide useful information and reinforce positive sexual behaviours in viewers. In fact, the current sexual scripts depicted in mainstream North American media may be misleading, as they tend to be sensationalized and unrealistic. For example, the television show *Gossip Girl* frequently depicts poorly supervised high school students staying out late socializing, drinking, and engaging in various sexual behaviours without any negotiations of safe sex. Such sexual messages in television and movies may negatively affect youth sexual behaviour. Research has shown an association between watching media with sexual content and skewed beliefs about what is "normal" sexual behaviour (Ward, 2002) and expectations about how sexual relationships progress (L.D. Taylor, 2005). Consuming such media has also been shown to predict earlier initiation and faster progression of sexual behaviours (Collins et al., 2004). But not all exposure to sexual content on television is negative, as illustrated by a study about the impact of an episode of the popular sitcom *Friends*. This study, which was conducted by Collins, Elliott, Berry, Kanouse, and Hunter (2003), found that 65 per cent of adolescent viewers who had seen an episode of the show in which the character Rachel becomes pregnant recalled that the pregnancy had resulted from a condom failure.

Another media source that may have a strong influence on young people's expectations about sex is Internet pornography. With the existence of 4.2 billion pornography websites, which represent 12 per cent of all Internet websites (Ropelato, n.d.), it seems almost inevitable that youth using the Internet will be exposed to pornography, either on purpose or accidentally. Indeed, approximately 60 per cent of Canadians

FIGURE 19.5 Have your parents ever tried talking to you about sex? Was it awkward, or uncomfortable? Did you feel as though your parents were not communicating directly, or that they lacked accurate, up-to-date information about sexual issues? Did you just want to run out of the room and tell them that you already learned everything you need to know from friends or school? Many teenagers perceive communicating with their parents about sex as unbearable; as a result, they are more likely to turn to their peers, media sources, or school to help inform them about sex and sexuality.

FIGURE 19.6 Super-condom to the rescue! Wouldn't negotiating with a partner about safe sex practices be easier if a "super-condom" hero would just appear and have the conversation for you? Popular media tend to omit any dialogue about safe sex practices, but there may be room in the visual media landscape for a character such as "super-condom" to help teens understand the importance of discussing safe sex practices with a new partner prior to engaging in sexual activity.

aged 15 to 24 have encountered pornography online (Rotermann, 2001), and the average age of first exposure to Internet pornography is 11 (Ropelato, n.d.). Donnerstein and Smith (2001) have argued that Internet pornography may be more influential on the development of youth sexuality than is any other type of media. Due to ethical constraints that prevent exposing youth under the age of 18 to pornography for research, there are no available statistics on the impact of pornography on youth sexual behaviour and expectations (Malamuth & Huppin, 2005). We can speculate, however, that Internet pornography is misleading to youth because most of the images it presents do not embody the realities of most people's sex lives. In adults, exposure to pornography has been shown to negatively affect men's perceptions of women and women's perceptions of themselves (Paul, 2005). Extrapolating from such findings in adults, we may reasonably conclude that Internet pornography likely has a negative impact on children and teens who are exposed to it, especially in terms of how they perceive themselves and others.

With regard to LGBTTIQQ representation, mainstream visual media in North America has begun to include more LGBTTIQQ characters and discussions of issues related to sexual and gender diversity in the last several years. One criticism, however, is that bisexual, intersex, transgender, and asexual individuals are not often represented alongside gay and lesbian characters, restricting the focus of sexual and gender diversity in visual media to same-sex sexuality. On a positive note, research on gay and lesbian youth has shown that the Internet is a valuable media source for experimentation and self-definition (Brown, Keller, & Stern, 2009). LGBTTIQQ youth use the Internet to discuss sexual identities and queer politics, navigate the coming-out process, and discuss sexual practices, including educational information on sexual health and activity specific to same-sex relations (Bond, Hefner, & Drogos, 2008).

In conclusion, young Canadians who have access to visual media and the Internet will likely be exposed to sexual content. Whether purposefully or, more often, passively, the media is educating young people about sex, and it is not always in a positive, informative, and unbiased way. What can teens and those who care for them do to lessen the negative impact of sex-related messages from the media? One of the easiest and most effective solutions is to ensure that young people are media literate, meaning that they know how to critically assess what they see and read in the media, particularly on the Internet. Indeed, the *Canadian Guidelines* (PHAC, 2008) encourages educators to discuss media literacy with youth, and concerned organizations such as Media Smarts (http://mediasmarts.ca) provide aids to help educators teach students how to evaluate media sources. In the future, with the rise of mobile Internet devices and other communications technologies that offer constant access to media content, media literacy will undoubtedly become even more important as more and more young people find themselves bombarded with more and more media messages about sexuality.

Barriers to Sex Education

A variety of factors contribute to sex education's accessibility. Individuals who have difficulty accessing sex education and resources may be at a higher risk for negative sexual outcomes, as they may not receive the information and services required to make informed decisions (Orton, 1994). The *Canadian Guidelines* (PHAC, 2008) emphasizes the importance of creating environments conducive to sex education. Due to environmental factors, barriers may exist for certain populations to access sexual health information at the institutional or personal level.

Institutional Barriers

Each level of government in Canada has a direct impact on sex education (see Orton, 1994, for a discussion). Policies, budgets, and resources provided by higher levels of government (federal and provincial) to lower levels of government (provincial and municipal) impact the accessibility and comprehensiveness of sex education programs. The hierarchical system of the Canadian government means that top-level political decisions regarding sexual health programs and policies will inevitably trickle down and impact individual programs. Unfortunately, the politicians making these decisions often rely more on public opinion than on research findings about what types of programs might best meet the sexual health needs of Canadian youth.

Overall, Canada is regarded as a fairly accepting and progressive country when it comes to recognizing sexual and gender diversity among its citizens; the country's first legal same-sex marriages took place in Ontario in 2001, and in 2005 Canada became the fourth country to legalize same-sex marriage nationwide (CBC News, 2007; see Chapter 1). However, sex education remains predominately heterosexist: it is mainly focussed on addressing STIs and pregnancy prevention in a manner that assumes youth are engaging in heterosexual sexual activity. Delivering sex education based on this assumption ignores sexual and gender diversity, which means that LGBTTIQQ youth are not receiving adequate education specific to their identity and orientation. A recent study of Toronto teens found that only 51 per cent had received any formal education relating to sexual orientation (Causarano et al., 2010). Exclusion of these topics can be considered a violation of sexual rights for access to relevant and comprehensive sex education. More diversified programming is needed in school-based curricula to better represent all Canadian youth. Education is an important tool to aid in destabilizing the stigmatization surrounding LGBTTIQQ youth.

A recent example of how these issues may play out at the provincial level comes from efforts to change the sex education curriculum in Ontario. In April of 2010, a curriculum change was proposed that would have incorporated information about same-sex sexuality and gender diversity into the sexual health education curriculum, which had not been updated in over a *decade* (Ontario Ministry of Education and Training, 2010)! Two key reasons for the suggested changes were (1) to recognize the legal rights of LGBTTIQQ persons in Canada, and (2) to address technological advances that have introduced youth to visual media that regularly include images of sexual behaviour (see Ferguson, Benzie, & Rushowy, 2010). According to an article in the current affairs magazine *Maclean's* ("Religious Groups Fight Changes," 2010), due to mounting pressure from religious groups—with many Christian and Muslim parents planning to withdraw their children from school in protest—Ontario swiftly retracted its plan to introduce the new curriculum less than two days after proposing the changes. Father Alphonse de Valk (2010), a prominent activist for the Catholic Church, went so far as to say that the introduction of sexual orientation in the revised curriculum was a "poison pill" (p. 15). In spite of this example from Ontario, there have also been efforts by the federal government to formally recognize the importance of education about sexual and gender diversity (PHAC, 2010a, 2010b), and there is hope that this topic will one day be as integral a part of school-based educational programs as is the prevention of STIs and unintended pregnancy.

At the regional level, lack of support from the school board or staff can negatively impact school-based programs, illustrating why such support is a major principle in the *Canadian Guidelines* (PHAC, 2008). A qualitative study of female high school students in Nova Scotia found that these students perceived a number of obstacles to their sex education, including school staff and teachers seeing the class as a low priority and communicating negative attitudes about the class to students (Langille, MacKinnon, Marshall, & Graham, 2001). Lack of support for efforts to evaluate and improve youth sexual health may also be displayed more passively. For example, some researchers investigating adolescent sexual health have been denied access to survey specific schools. In the case of the CYSHHAS, certain school boards in Alberta and British Columbia denied access to their students for direct reasons, such as disapproval of the study's topic, and for indirect reasons, such as the survey being considered a low priority compared to other ongoing surveys (Boyce et al., 2003). Additionally, Catholic school boards uniformly refused to distribute a recent survey conducted by LGBT human rights organization Egale and the University of Winnipeg (C. Taylor et al., 2008; the findings of this survey will be discussed in the next section). As a result, the researchers could not examine the prevalence of homophobia and **transphobia** in the majority of Catholic schools. Such institutional decisions may result in a lack of awareness about issues of concern for sex education program participants, including their attitudes and level of knowledge about different issues. As outlined in the IMB model, assessment of needs is the first important step in designing effective interventions to stimulate behaviour change (J.D. Fisher & Fisher, 1992).

Religious values embedded within curricula may also impact access to sex education. Under the Constitution Act (1867), Protestants or Roman Catholics (whichever are the religious minority in the province in question) have the right to a separate publicly funded school board. Denominational school rights are currently applicable only in Ontario, Alberta, and Saskatchewan (Alberta Act, 1905; Constitution Act, 1982; Saskatchewan Act, 1905). As a result of the separation between separate and public school boards in these provinces, there may be differential emphasis on aspects of the provincial curriculum, and sexual topics may be discussed in separate schools in a manner that is consistent with religious values regarding sexuality (Meaney, Rye, Wood, & Solovieva, 2009). So you can see how various institutional decisions and policies can have a dramatic impact on one's experience of sex education. It is easy for these factors to fade into the background, which is all the more reason to keep their potential impact in mind.

transphobia The fear, dislike, and/or intolerance of transgender or gender non-conforming individuals.

Socio-demographic Factors

Socio-demographic factors such as culture, race, religion, sexual orientation, and socio-economic status have been examined to determine whether they are related to sexual health in youth. The Toronto Teen Survey, for example, sampled over 1000 people involved in a variety of community-based programs to investigate the relationship between sexual behaviour and socio-demographic characteristics. The results showed that respondents born outside of Canada and respondents who identified as Muslim were less likely to have engaged in sexual intercourse compared to the rest of the sample (Pole, Flicker, & the Toronto Teen Survey Team, 2010). Other variables, such as race and gender, were not found to be related to sexual behaviour. The survey also found that ethnicity and length of time spent living in Canada impacted the likelihood of teens having received sex education (Figure 19.7). Thus, it seems that some socio-demographic factors may be associated with positive sexual outcomes, such as being less likely to engage in intercourse during adolescence, while others may have no effect, and still others may be associated with negative outcomes, such as limited access to education that could help teens make informed sexual health decisions.

Most strikingly, individuals who identified as LBG2PQ (lesbian, bisexual, gay, two-spirited, pansexual, or queer) in the Toronto Teen Survey were more than twice as likely as youth identifying as heterosexual to have engaged in intercourse (Pole et al., 2010). This statistic may be unsurprising given the heterosexist approach taken by many educators, which can alienate LGBTTIQQ youth and leave them without the information they need to explore their own sexuality in a healthy way. As discussed previously, education about sexual orientation and gender diversity in school-based sexual health education programs is an important tool that may help to decrease negative outcomes experienced by LGBTTIQQ youth. A survey of almost 3700 high school students across Canada found that bullying, homophobia, and transphobia remain pervasive in schools: 74 per cent of trans students and 55 per cent of "sexual minority" (lesbian, gay, bisexual, queer, or questioning) students reported having been verbally harassed about their gender expression, about 10 per cent of LGBTQ students reported having heard homophobic comments daily or weekly from teachers, and 21 per cent of LGBTQ students reported being physically harassed or assaulted because of their sexual orientation. Not surprisingly, in light of these findings, 64 per cent of LGBTQ students also reported feeling unsafe at school (C. Taylor et al., 2011). Compared to their heterosexual peers, LGBTQ youth have a higher risk of suicide, school related-problems, homelessness/street involvement, physical violence, and substance use (Birkett, Espelage, & Koenig, 2009). LGBTQ youth also report higher rates of sexual abuse and unprotected sexual activity (Saewyc et al., 2006).

Individuals from cultural backgrounds that are very different from the dominant Canadian culture may also experience difficulty in accessing sexual health information that is relevant to them. In Canada, specific groups affected by cultural barriers to sex education include recent immigrants and Aboriginal peoples (see the "Culture and Diversity" box). Canadian approaches to teaching and monitoring sexual health in youth may directly oppose certain cultural beliefs and therefore be perceived as threatening to certain cultures. For example, a qualitative study found that adult Iranian immigrants perceived the refusal of schools and health care providers to release information about their children as showing a lack of understanding and respect for their values, rather than an effort to uphold individual rights and well-being (Shirpak, Maticka-Tyndale, & Chinichian, 2007). Acculturation of immigrant youth to Canadian culture may also create intergenerational issues among families (Pole et al., 2010). Exposure to and acceptance of Canadian sex education curricula may create tension between children and their parents as the children strive to manage competing aspects of their family's cultural beliefs and practices with those of their peers. Language may also be a barrier when providing sex education to newly immigrated families. To combat these and other issues commonly faced by immigrants, culturally sensitive initiatives have been established in Ontario and other regions of the country; these initiatives provide language interpreters if needed during communication with health care professionals, and they involve diverse cultural groups in the development of sexual health curricula (Shirpak et al., 2007). Indeed, the *Canadian Guidelines* (PHAC, 2008) and analysis

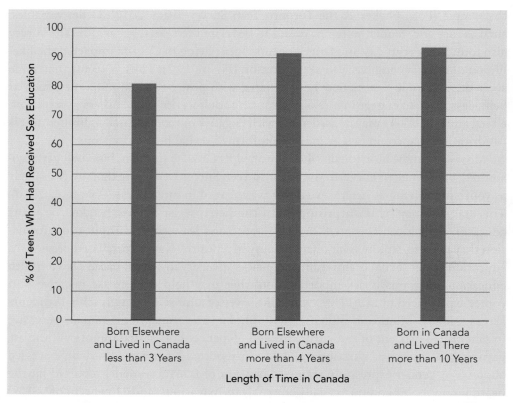

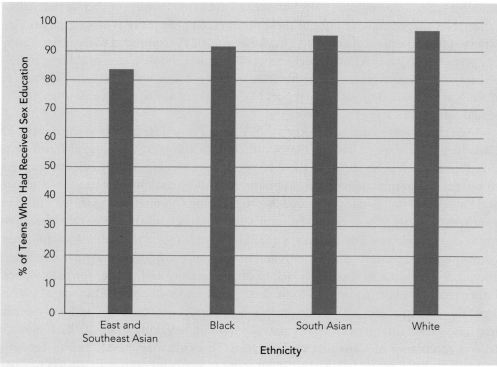

FIGURE 19.7 The Toronto Teen Survey found that regardless of age, gender, religion, socio-economic status, and sexual experience, youth who had lived in Canada less than three years were significantly less likely to have received any sex education compared to youth who had been born in Canada, as shown in the top graph. Additionally, East and Southeast Asian youth were significantly less likely to report having been provided with sex education compared to black, South Asian, and white youth, as shown in the bottom graph.

Source: Adapted from Salehi, Flicker, & the Toronto Teen Survey Team (2010).

of the Toronto Teen Survey results (Pole et al., 2010) emphasize the importance of maintaining cultural sensitivity—awareness and acceptance of cultural differences and similarities—in program initiatives. With regard to reproductive sexual health, it has been suggested that self-collected vaginal samples for cervical cancer screening may be more acceptable and respectful of cultures in which screening via a gynecological examination may be in direct opposition to cultural values (Brotto, Chou, Singh, & Woo, 2008). At the same time, Maticka-Tyndale (2008) has emphasized that although Canada has begun responding to issues arising due to clashing cultural values, the method of response has tended to be to allow parental restriction and denial of access to sex education, which reinforces group differences.

Another population to which specific attention is drawn in the *Canadian Guidelines* (PHAC, 2008) is Canadian street youth. A survey carried out in multiple centres by the

Culture & Diversity

Sex Education in Canadian Aboriginal Populations

Many barriers exist for Aboriginal peoples in gaining access to and making use of sexual health information in Canada. For example, language can be a barrier, as the majority of sex education materials are in Canada's national languages of French and English, which limits their utility and ease of applicability in Aboriginal communities (Hill, 2003). Additionally, many Aboriginal communities are in rural areas with limited or no access to technologies like computers or to certain forms of visual media, and this isolation can limit access to sexual health information that is more readily available in urban areas.

Some research has indicated that Aboriginal persons in Canada are at a greater risk for poor health than non-Aboriginal Canadians (Health Canada, 2009). For example, in the period from 2002 to 2005, the rate of HIV infection in Aboriginal persons was about 2.8 times higher than it was in non-Aboriginal persons in Canada (Health Canada, 2009).

LaRoque (1993) notes that one of the biggest problems in Aboriginal homes and communities is a lack of informative sex education. She states that parents and other adults are not providing such sex education to their youth, and Aboriginal youth are desperately in need of this education, as illustrated by this population's elevated risk of STIs. However, a step in the right direction has been made with the release of the first comprehensive Canadian resource on sexual and reproductive health within an Aboriginal cultural context, entitled *Finding Our*

Way: A Sexual and Reproductive Health Sourcebook for Aboriginal Communities (see the resource section at the end of the chapter for the website link).

Looking forward, Jessica Yee (2009), the founder of the Native Youth Sexual Health Network and a self-described "multiracial Indigenous hip-hop feminist reproductive justice freedom fighter," believes that

Examining cultural competency and sex education means using what we [Aboriginal people] already have in our culture to empower our youth to lead healthy, strong lives. . . . Rather than continuing to allow people outside our communities to dictate to us how to be "healthy". . . I decided to go directly to the source itself. . . . I asked youth of colour about their experiences with sex education and if colonization, in its many forms, affects how they view sexuality. (pp. 4–5)

What Yee found was that youth wanted to take more initiative and control of their sexual health by speaking with other youth and educating themselves beyond what they had access to in school. Thus, it seems that more attention must be paid not only to developing sex education that takes into account the cultural diversity represented in Canada, but also to finding ways to give youth of colour the right to self-determination when talking and learning about sexuality.

Canadian government from 1999 to 2003 (the Enhanced Surveillance of Canadian Street Youth) found that members of this often forgotten subset of the population are engaging in a number of high-risk sexual behaviours and practices (PHAC, 2006). This survey found that the average age of first intercourse among participants was 14, and the average number of sexual partners reported was over 17. Approximately half of the youth sampled in 2001 and 2003 reported not having used a condom the last time they engaged in sexual activity, with 19 to 25 per cent of street youth in the sex trade reporting that they had not used a condom with their last client; a whopping 21 per cent of all participants reported having been involved in sex trade work at some point in their lives (see Chapter 18 for more information about sex trade workers). Further, rates of STIs were found to be significantly greater in street youth compared to the rest of Canadian youth (PHAC, 2009): street youth are 10 to 30 times more likely to have chlamydia or gonorrhea (PHAC, 2006). These statistics reiterate that street youth are an important target population in Canada to provide with accessible sexual health information. Indeed, street youth are less likely than other youth to receive school-based sex education, and they may have more difficulty gaining access to sexual health services and resources. Initiatives and policies to provide support and reach out to street youth, such as government-funded drop-in centres and clinics where sexual health information and services are readily available, are crucial (PHAC, 2008).

Overall, it seems that the best way for Canada to support and inform populations that lack access to important and personally relevant sex education is to establish comprehensive sexual health programs based on cultural awareness, inclusivity, and acceptance of diverse attitudes toward sexuality. Indeed, the *Canadian Guidelines* (PHAC, 2008) encourages striving toward programming that is culturally sensitive, inclusive, non-judgmental, and respectful of individual sexual diversity. In addition, researchers must begin to more closely examine education opportunities and sexual health indicators in specific populations. They must also consider how personal risk factors may overlap in certain individuals. Imagine the issues that may arise for someone living in a rural area, identifying as queer, and attending a school that offers only abstinence-only sex education. Determining the additive effects of barriers and which barriers are most detrimental is another important step for future research and policies to address.

Sex Education for Older Adults

Sexuality in older adults has been a relatively neglected area of study, likely due to assumptions and taboos about sexual behaviour in this population, including the belief that older adults are not sexually active. Although there tends to be a decline in partnered sexual activity across the lifespan (e.g., Herbenick et al., 2010), recent research has demonstrated that a large proportion of older adults remain sexually active (see Chapter 9). In a nationally representative survey in the US, Lindau and colleagues (2007) found that 67 per cent of males and 40 per cent of females 65 to 74 years of age had engaged in sexual activity within the past 12 months. In individuals between 75 and 85 years of age, 39 per cent of males and 17 per cent of females reported having engaged in sexual activity in the same period. Of those who reported having engaged in sexual activity within the past year, more than half were sexually active at least two to three times per month.

Sex education is clearly relevant to older adults, and there are a number of reasons that such education may be particularly needed in this population. Older adults are less likely to have had access to the types of sex education programs and initiatives currently available when they were growing up. There also tend to be fewer sexual health resources specifically aimed at older adults. For example, a study of the HIV/ AIDS materials produced by all 50 US Public Health departments reported that the majority were aimed at young adults, with only 30 per cent primarily targeting an older adult audience (Orel, Wright, & Wagner, 2004). Additionally, some of the negative sexual outcomes that are of greatest concern for today's population, such as HIV/AIDS, did not pose as great a health risk when older adults were acquiring knowledge and developing attitudes and beliefs about sexual health. Although rates of chlamydia and gonorrhea remain relatively low in older adults compared to other Canadians, there was a substantial increase in STI rates from 1998 to 2007 in men over 60 years of age (PHAC, 2009). These increased rates may be linked to engaging in unprotected sexual activity and low rates of STI testing. A recent US survey of individuals over 50 found that only 20 per cent of men and 24 per cent of women had used a condom the last time they engaged in sexual activity, despite not being in a committed relationship in most instances (Schick et al., 2010). In addition, over 60 per cent had not received any STI testing within the past year, despite the fact that 5 per cent of the entire sample knew that the last partner they engaged in sexual intercourse with had an STI at the time!

Increased age is also associated with a number of sexual problems in men and women, likely due to the physiological changes that occur during the aging process (see Chapter 4) and poorer physical health. A nationally representative survey of adults in the US found that 44 per cent of women 65 to 85 years of age reported experiencing trouble with vaginal lubrication for at least several months over the past 12 months (Lindau et al., 2007). Lack of interest in sexual activity and inability to achieve orgasm were also reported by more than a third of the sample. In men 65 to 85 years of age, over 40 per cent reported having trouble achieving and/or maintaining an erection during sexual activity; overall, men in this age group were almost twice as likely as 57- to 64-year-olds to report erectile difficulties. In addition, one third of 75- to 85-year-old men reported being unable to achieve orgasm, and men in this age group were therefore more than twice as likely to experience this type of sexual problem in comparison to those 57 to 64 years of age. An additional issue for older adults who live in long-term care facilities is lack of privacy, which can make it difficult for them to develop sexual relationships (PHAC, 2008).

These findings indicate that physicians and other health care professionals need to take a role in inquiring about, as well as initiating proper assessment and treatment of, sexual problems in older adults. In addition, more research needs to be conducted on the sexual health and sexuality of older Canadian adults; few Canadian studies have been conducted in this population. Such research will aid in program and policy development, and it will help to adequately inform physicians about the types of sexual behaviours in which their older patients are engaging (Hinchliff & Gott, 2011). Encouragingly, some initiatives are being developed to educate older adults about the risks of unprotected sex. For example, a group of Miami senior citizens created a video about the importance of safe sex in older adults, told by clay figures, entitled "Sex and the Seniors" (Dellagloria, 2009).

Sex Education for Individuals with Disabilities

Individuals with disabilities have a variety of sexual health needs, which is something that has only recently begun to be acknowledged and addressed (Di Giulio, 2003). With regard to individuals with physical disabilities, it has been posited that societal views of people with physical disabilities as asexual stem from the assumption that their disability will interfere with their ability to engage in sexual activity, and that these

Ethical Debate

Sexuality in Individuals with Intellectual Disabilities

The criteria for a diagnosis of an intellectual disability are significant limitations in day-to-day skills (termed *adaptive function*) and significant limitations in intellectual ability, present before 18 years of age (Schalock et al., 2010). During the eugenics movement of the early twentieth century, many individuals with intellectual disabilities underwent involuntary sterilization to prevent them from having children (Kempton & Kahn, 1991). Although this practice is no longer common in Canada, sexuality in people with intellectual disabilities is still largely ignored, and many are discouraged from engaging in sexual activity. The sexual health and education of individuals with intellectual disabilities is an issue of great moral and ethical debate.

Although increasing attention has been brought to the sexual rights and sex education of individuals with intellectual disabilities in recent decades, societal stereotypes and negative attitudes still persevere with regard to the sexuality of these individuals (Watson, Venema, Molloy, & Reich, 2002). With respect to sexual behaviour, individuals with an intellectual disability tend to be viewed at extremes: asexual and childlike, or out of control (Szollos & McCabe, 1995). Despite any discrepancy between chronological and mental age, individuals with intellectual disabilities are sexual beings, sharing with all other human beings not only similar biological drives but also the desire for intimate relationships (McCabe, 1999).

Unfortunately, individuals with intellectual disabilities may come to internalize negative societal attitudes about their sexuality (Di Giulio, 2003), which may result in lack of sexual expression (Richards et al., 2008). A number of studies have reported that individuals with an intellectual disability have more conservative and negative attitudes about sexual behaviours compared to individuals without an intellectual disability (McCabe, 1999; McCabe & Cummins, 1996). Hingsburger and Tough (2002) described cases of patients seen at the York Behaviour Management Services Sexuality Clinic in Ontario in which caregiver communication of negative attitudes about sexuality were believed to have hindered the patients' ability to engage in healthy sexual behaviour and resulted in feelings of anxiety, fear, and shame surrounding sexual expression.

Acceptance (or lack thereof) of individuals with intellectual disabilities as sexual beings has a profound impact on their access to sex education. McCabe (1999) found that only 52 per cent of a sample of individuals with mild intellectual disability had received any type of formal or informal sex education, versus 90 per cent of a sample recruited from the general population. Many studies have found that individuals with intellectual disabilities have poorer knowledge than comparison groups about topics such as STIs, contraception, and healthy relationships (McCabe, 1999; McGillivray, 1999; Szollos & McCabe, 1995). These findings are troublesome because this lack of knowledge may put individuals with intellectual disabilities at higher risk for negative sexual outcomes. Indeed, there is a high incidence of sexual abuse in children and adults with intellectual disabilities, and lack of sexual knowledge has been associated with an increased risk of abuse (Sobsey & Varnhagen, 1991). In addition, McCabe and Cummins (1996) found that the only domains in which a group of individuals with mild intellectual disability did not report less sexual experience compared to undergraduate students were pregnancy and disease: the individuals in the intellectual disability group were significantly more likely to have been pregnant and to have had an STI.

Withholding comprehensive sex education from individuals with intellectual disabilities violates human rights relating to sexuality and well-being. It hampers their ability to avoid negative sexual outcomes (e.g., sexual abuse, STIs) and to achieve positive outcomes (e.g., sexual self-esteem, healthy interpersonal relationships). These outcomes are under the umbrella of sexual rights stipulated by the WHO, alongside access to sex education (WHO, 2002). As stated by Watson and colleagues (2002): "To deny a person's sexuality is to deny part of his or her personhood. To deny that an individual who has a developmental disability is a sexual being is thus to treat him or her as less than a full person. This is clearly an ethical issue" (p. 19).

individuals therefore do not have sexual needs or that sexual needs should therefore be suppressed within these individuals (Milligan & Neufeldt, 2001). On the contrary, research has shown that compared to a control sample, individuals with a physical disability report a higher level of sexual needs (McCabe, Cummins, & Deeks, 2000), suggesting that they have a strong desire to date and engage in intimate sexual relationships (McCabe, 1999). Individuals with a physical disability have also been shown to have significantly less knowledge about sex, less sexual experience, and more negative attitudes toward sexuality in comparison to people without disabilities; individuals with an intellectual disability were found to have the lowest knowledge and experience, and the most negative attitudes (McCabe, 1999; McCabe et al., 2000). (See the "Ethical Debate" box for a detailed discussion of the sexuality and sexual health of individuals with intellectual disabilities.)

Less sexual knowledge may put individuals with disabilities at increased risk for negative sexual outcomes, including sexual abuse, which is highly reported in individuals with disabilities (e.g., Sobsey & Varnhagen, 1991). There are a number of systemic barriers to sexual health that may impact individuals with disabilities, including (1) lower access to sex education and sexual health care, (2) lack of privacy, and (3) decreased opportunities for social interaction and intimate relationships (Di Giulio, 2003; Richards et al., 2008). Providing access to sex education from both formal and informal sources is an important first step toward promoting sexual health for people with disabilities. In youth with an intellectual disability, providing access goes beyond simply making programs and information available; it also requires presenting information at the person's individual level of understanding and using strategies that maximize her or his learning (Di Giulio, 2003). For example, using concrete examples that are relevant to the person's life and presenting the information in multiple ways may be helpful. In youth with physical disabilities, the comprehensiveness of sex education should be a focus (PHAC, 2008; Di Giulio, 2003), and attention should be paid to providing information about how someone's specific disability and medications may affect different aspects of her or his sexual function.

CHAPTER SUMMARY

This chapter has covered current policies relating to sex education in Canada and the theoretical underpinnings of this education, as well as barriers to accessing comprehensive sex education. Canadian research efforts in this domain continue to inform policy-makers, researchers, educators, parents, and youth about some of the sexual health areas Canada is doing well in and areas in need of improvement. Focussing on positive as well as negative outcomes in sexual health is an important goal that has not yet been widely translated into curricula and policy. Continued attention to diversity and efforts to meet the specific needs of populations that differ in age, ability, sexuality, gender, race, class, and religion will contribute to more inclusive sex education in Canada.

DEBATE QUESTIONS

Although sex education is included in the majority of school curricula, parents typically have the right to withdraw their children from these classes if they choose, such as under Bill 44 in Alberta. What would be the pros and cons of making sexual health curriculum mandatory for all students? How do ethical principles fit into each side of this debate?

REVIEW QUESTIONS

1. In what ways might school-based sex education exclude LGBTTIQQ individuals?

2. What forms of sex education, other than school-based lessons, are (a) the most informative and (b) the most influential?

3. What institutional and socio-demographic barriers prevent individuals from gaining access to sex education?

4. What improvements might be made to the ways in which sex education is taught in this country, in order meet the needs of the most young people? How might it be helpful to draw on informal sources of information to enhance classroom lessons?

5. How might the *Canadian Guidelines*' principles of accessibility, comprehensiveness, and effective approaches apply to teaching individuals with physical disabilities and intellectual disabilities about sexual health? What special concerns might educators and policy-makers need to address when designing and implementing sex education programs directed at each of these groups?

SUGGESTIONS FOR FURTHER READING AND VIEWING

Recommended Websites

Aboriginal Health Initiative (administered by the Society of Obstetricians and Gynaecologists of Canada): www.aboriginalsexualhealth.ca

Advocates for Youth (information for parents and teens): www.advocatesforyouth.org

Canadian Federation for Sexual Health (CFSH): www.cfsh.ca

Communities and Schools Promoting Health (sexual health lesson plans and activities): www.safehealthyschools.org/sexualityeducation/gateway.htm

Egale (Canadian LGBT human rights organization): www.egale.ca

Finding Our Way: A Sexual and Reproductive Health Sourcebook for Aboriginal Communities: www.anac.on.ca/sourcebook/toc.htm

Media Smarts: http://mediasmarts.ca

Native Youth Sexual Health Network: www.nativeyouthsexualhealth.com

Public Health Agency of Canada: www.phac-aspc.gc.ca

Sex Information and Education Council of Canada (SIECCAN): www.sieccan.org

Sexpressions (sex education and consulting services): http://sexpressions.ca

SexualityandU.ca (advice for teachers): www.sexualityandu.ca/teachers

TeachingSexualHealth.ca (Alberta-based sexual health education resource): www.teachingsexualhealth.ca

Teen Health Source (funded by Planned Parenthood Toronto): http://teenhealthsource.com

Recommended Readings

Bruess, C., & Greenberg, J. (2008). *Sexuality education: Theory and practice.* Mississauga, ON: Jones & Bartlett.

Irvine, J.M. (2004). *Talk about sex: The battles over sex education in the United States.* Berkeley: University of California Press.

Jensen, R.E. (2010). *Dirty words: The rhetoric of public sex education, 1870–1924.* Champaign: University of Illinois Press.

Johnson, M. (2012). *I heard it 'round the Internet: Sexual health education and authenticating online information.* Media Smarts. Retrieved from http://mediasmarts.ca/sites/default/files/pdfs/lesson-plan/Lesson_Sexual_Health_Education.pdf

Public Health Agency of Canada. (2008). *Canadian guidelines for sexual health education.* Ottawa, ON: Author. Available at www.phac-aspc.gc.ca/publicat/cgshe-ldnemss

Roman, L.G., & Erye, L. (1997). *Dangerous territories: Struggles for differences and equality in education.* New York, NY: Routledge.

Recommended Viewing

A2ZCDS.com (Directors). (2006). *Sex education: Pesky puberty* [DVD]. United States: Tapeworm.

Lipschutz, M., & Rosenblatt, R. (Directors). (2005). *The education of Shelby Knox: Sex, lies, and education.* United States: Incite Pictures.

For additional recommendations, see the Center for Sexual Pleasure and Health's list of top-10 sex education films: http://thecsph.org/our-resources/education/top-10-sex-education-films.

Glossary

abolition of STW A legal option for dealing with sex trade work by allowing it and punishing those who exploit or coerce sex trade workers.

abstinence Refraining from some or all aspects of sexual activity.

abstinence-only sexual health education Sexual health education programs focussed on teaching abstinence from sexual activity until marriage and/or a later time; information about contraception tends to be excluded from such programs.

accessory olfactory system A secondary system of smell, present in many mammals, that detects and processes pheromones.

adherence The degree to which an individual takes medication or complies with other instructions of a health care provider.

adipose tissue Body fat. It consists of a loose connective tissue composed of adipocytes, cells whose main role is to store energy.

adrenal glands Endocrine glands that make and secrete sex hormones such as estrogens and androgens, stress hormones such as cortisol, and catecholamines. Best known for mediating the "flight or fight" stress response.

adultery Sexual intercourse between a married individual and someone who is not his or her spouse.

affectional orientation The interaction between affect and cognition such that it produces attraction, erotic desire, and ultimately feelings of love for members of the other sex, the same sex, or both.

affiliation Attachment or connection with others of the same species, often to care for young, reduce stress, and/or confer a survival benefit on the group.

ageism Discrimination against people because of their age.

agenda-setting theory A theory that proposes that media influence our thoughts and behaviour by highlighting what we should pay attention to.

amenorrhea Suppression or absence of menstruation.

amniotic sac A sac, filled with amniotic fluid, that helps protect the embryo from outside damage and harmful temperature changes.

anal stage Psychosexual stage from ages two to four, during which a child's energy and needs are focussed on mastering elimination (i.e., toilet training).

anilingus Oral stimulation of the anus, perineum, and surrounding area.

anogenital Relating to the region of the anus and/or the genitals.

anorgasmia Persistent inability to have an orgasm.

anterior pituitary The gland within the pituitary that synthesizes and secretes hormones such as growth hormone (GH), thyroid-stimulating hormone (TSH), prolactin (PRL), luteinizing hormone (LH), and follicle-stimulating hormone (FSH).

anthropomorphizing Perceiving human qualities or characteristics in non-human entities.

anti-choice movement See **pro-choice movement**.

aphrodisiac A substance alleged to induce sexual desire (e.g., powdered rhinoceros horn, the use of which led to the term *horny*).

apocrine glands Glands that open at the surface of the skin and whose cells bleb off a portion of themselves in the release of their secretions. In humans, they are located only in certain areas, which include the axillae (armpits), the pubic area, and the breasts.

appetitive behaviours In male animals, behavioural patterns that orient a male toward a female.

archival data-mining Sorting through pre-existing data or records to uncover new insights into past phenomena.

areola The round, coloured area around the nipple.

aromatase An enzyme that converts androgens to estrogens.

arranged marriage A marriage in which family members, typically parents, choose a partner for a person to marry.

asexual identity An identity label acknowledging that a person perceives little or no interest in engaging sexually with others.

assortative mating The tendency to choose a partner who is similar to oneself on one or more characteristics.

asymptomatic Showing no symptoms or signs of a disease.

attractivity A female's visual, auditory, and/or chemical cues that provoke approach behaviours in males.

autogynephilia A sexual variation in which a man is sexually attracted to the thought of himself as a woman.

axon A thin fiber that projects from a nerve cell.

balls See **beads**.

bar hustler A male sex trade worker who looks for customers in a bar.

basal body temperature The lowest waking temperature.

BDSM A type of role play or lifestyle choice between two or more individuals that involves a wide range of activities involving safe and consensual manipulations of erotic power. The term stands for "bondage and discipline, dominance and submission, sadism and masochism."

beads A sex toy that consists of a series of balls connected by a string, and that can be inserted into the rectum or vagina and removed at varying speeds. Also known as *balls*.

behavioural confirmation A process whereby someone's expectations about an upcoming event influence his or her behaviour and thus cause the event to unfold in a way that is consistent with his or her expectations.

behavioural neuroscience The study of how parts of the peripheral nervous system (the nerves and nerve cells outside the central nervous system) and the central nervous system (the spinal cord and the brain), as well as hormones and other chemicals that affect these systems, influence animal behaviour.

behaviourism A theoretical approach that assumes that observable behaviours are the only measurable and therefore knowable indications of psychological processes. It views behaviours as resulting from conditioning.

bibliotherapy The use of readings and written assignments in psychotherapy.

biological sex The biological condition of being male and/or female, as determined by genes, chromosomes, hormones, and physical traits.

biphobia The fear, dislike, and/or intolerance of bisexual individuals.

bisexual identity An identity status denoting individuals who have come to identify themselves as having both other-sex and same-sex oriented cognition, affect, and/or behaviour, and who have adopted the construct of "bisexual" as having personal significance to them.

bisexual orientation An affectional orientation where affect and cognition are directed at members of both sexes, to one extent or another.

blind coders Coders who are not familiar with the specific hypotheses of the study.

block designs Research designs, used in brain imaging research, that consist of the alternating presence or absence of the stimuli of interest.

body humours The four humours of Hippocratic medicine believed to directly influence an individual's temperament and health: black bile, yellow bile, phlegm, and blood.

bonding Joining together for social and physical support, as through affiliation.

bottom A gay man who assumes the penetratee role in anal sex.

call boy A male sex trade worker who either works for an escort agency or is self-employed as an escort.

Canadian Guidelines for Sexual Health Education A comprehensive document that outlines best practices for teaching sexual health in Canada, based on research and clinical expertise from such fields of education, health promotion, medicine, nursing, psychology, and social work. (PHAC, 2008)

capacitation Removal of the plasma membrane overlying the sperm to allow for greater binding between the sperm and the egg.

case study An in-depth study of an individual or a group.

castration anxiety Anxiety due to fear of loss of or injury to one's genitals.

ceiling effect A levelling off of an effect when something reaches its maximum impact on something else.

cervical dysplasia Growth of abnormal cells on the surface of the cervix.

Charter of Rights and Freedoms The Canadian bill of rights entrenched in the Constitution of Canada, which sets out the rights of all Canadians.

chemical castration Administration of medication that suppresses androgens and, as a result, reduces a male's sex drive.

chorionic villi Finger-like projections that emerge from the sac that surrounds the developing fetus.

chromosomal sex Sex determined by the combination of sex chromosomes.

chronic pelvic pain (CPP) Chronic or recurrent pelvic pain that apparently has a gynecological origin but for which no definitive cause can be found.

classical conditioning A process through which an individual is repeatedly exposed to a neutral stimulus and an unconditioned stimulus at the same time, until the neutral stimulus comes to elicit a response initially brought forth by the unconditioned stimulus.

cloacal exstrophy A rare developmental variation in which the abdominal organs are exposed and the genitals develop abnormally.

cognitive distortions Thinking errors or irrational thoughts.

cognitive theories Theories that attempt to understand human behaviour by focussing on thought processes.

cognitive-behavioural therapy (CBT) Therapy based on the view that internal mental processes reciprocally interact with behaviours and emotional responses.

cohabitation People involved in a romantic and/or sexual relationship living together without being married. These partnerships are legally referred to as "common-law" relationships, and they are afforded under the law rights and benefits similar to those afforded to marriages.

Cohen's d effect size A measure of the strength of the relationship between two variables in a population.

coinfection Infection with two or more STIs at one time.

coitus Intercourse in which a man inserts his penis into a woman's vagina.

colostrum High protein, antibody-rich fluid that flows from the breast before the full onset of lactation.

commitment In the short term, the decision that one person loves another. In the long term, the decision to maintain the love that one has for another person.

common-law relationship A legally recognized relationship in which two people involved in a romantic relationship and who are not married have lived together for at least 12 months.

companionate love Affection and tenderness felt for someone with whom one's life is deeply connected.

competitive disadvantage A theorized developmental pattern in which the witnessing and expression of aggressive behaviours as well as a disadvantaged environment lead to chronic patterns of deviant behaviour in adulthood.

comprehensive sexual health education Sexual health education programs that include information about contraception and avoidance of STIs as well as abstinence.

conception Fertilization of the egg by the sperm.

concordance rate The probability that two individuals will have the same trait, given that one individual has the trait.

confounding variables Psychological, behavioural, and/or biological variables that change along with the manipulated experimental variable, thereby affecting a researcher's ability to discern a true cause-and-effect relationship between two variables.

consummatory behaviours In male animals, mounting, intromissions (penile-vaginal insertions), and ejaculation.

contempt A negative communication behaviour that entails putting down and/or expressing disrespect toward one's partner.

content analysis A method of data analysis by which a researcher identifies patterns or themes of meaning in a transcript or across observations, and often relates these patterns or themes to predetermined theories.

contraception The deliberate use of natural techniques, an artificially created barrier, or hormonal methods to prevent pregnancy as a result of sexual intercourse.

conversion therapy Therapy directed at changing a same-sex or bisexual orientation into a heterosexual orientation.

corpus luteum A temporary, functional cyst that develops out of the Graafian follicle after the follicle has released its egg; its major function is to produce progesterone and estradiol to support a pregnancy. If conception occurs, the placenta will eventually take over the role temporarily played by the corpus luteum. If conception does not occur, the corpus luteum stops functioning and menstruation follows.

correlational research designs Research designs that allow researchers to study how two or more variables covary, or change, in relation to one another.

couples' communication An ongoing exchange between two partners that unfolds over time and consists of verbal, behavioural, and affective exchanges.

criminalization of STW A legal option for dealing with sex trade work by making it and/or activities related to it illegal.

criticism A negative communication behaviour that entails attacking a partner's character or personality rather than focussing specifically on the behaviour that is upsetting.

cultivation theory A theory that proposes that media portrayals create a shared set of values and expectations about reality among media consumers.

cunnilingus Oral stimulation of a woman's genitals by a partner.

cybersex Sexual activity that takes place via the Internet.

decriminalization of STW A legal option for dealing with sex trade work by repealing all laws governing it.

defensiveness A negative communication behaviour in which someone protects himself or herself from a perceived verbal assault by denying responsibility, making excuses, or counter-complaining.

delayed control-group designs A research design that includes groups receiving the same treatment, tested at different points in time to better understand the time course of the treatment effects.

demand characteristics Experimental cues that indicate the type of behaviour or responding that the researcher expects.

demand-withdraw A communication pattern in which one partner puts pressure on the other (e.g., by nagging or criticizing), and the other partner does not engage or is defensive.

dependent variables The variables that are being measured in an experiment.

descriptive research designs Research designs that allow researchers to summarize patterns of sexual phenomena through observation and self-report.

Diagnostic and Statistical Manual of Mental Disorders (DSM) A handbook published by the American Psychiatric Association (APA) that describes and offers standard criteria for diagnosing mental disorders.

dildo A penetrative device, often shaped like a penis, that can be used to stimulate various parts of the body.

direct observation Observing and recording patterns in behaviour, either in a natural setting or in a laboratory.

disorders of sexual development (DSDs) A group of conditions in which the reproductive organs and/or genitals develop differently than expected.

Doppler ultrasonography A physiological method used to measure female and male sexual arousal by detecting properties of blood flow in genital tissue.

douche To flush out the inside of the vagina with a liquid. Also, a product designed for this purpose.

DSM See ***Diagnostic and Statistical Manual of Mental Disorders***.

dual control model of sexuality A theory that suggests that an individual's sexual responses are influenced by the balance between neurobiological, environmental, and cultural processes that activate or suppress sexual response.

dyspareunia Genital and/or pelvic pain during or after sexual activity.

eclampsia A life-threatening complication of pregnancy that is characterized by the presence of seizures.

ecological validity The extent to which the behaviours that are observed in a research setting are representative of what actually happens in the real world.

ectopic pregnancy A pregnancy in which the fertilized egg implants outside of the uterus.

effacement The thinning and shortening of the cervix late in pregnancy or during labour.

ego Within psychodynamic theory, the portion of an individual's personality that mediates between the realities of the outside world, the individual's urges and desires, and the individual's conscience.

elective abortion An abortion performed for reasons other than maternal or fetal health.

Electra complex In girls, an attachment to the mother followed by a shift in attachment to the father as a way to resolve penis envy.

empirical Methods that rely on direct observation and experiments, rather than theory alone, to confirm a phenomenon.

endemic Common or of chronic prevalence in a certain area.

endocrine organs Glands whose products (hormones) are secreted into the blood to affect tissues distant from the site of the gland.

endometriosis A condition in which the type of cells that normally line the uterus grow outside of the uterus, causing pain.

engagement The beginning of the descent of the fetus through the pelvic canal.

epididymitis Inflammation of the epididymis.

epidural Injection of local anesthetic into the epidural space of the spinal canal to produce numbness in the lower body.

episiotomy Incision of the perineum to help with passage of the baby.

erectile dysfunction The inability to develop or maintain an erection of sufficient rigidity to engage in intercourse.

erogenous zone An area of the body with heightened sensitivity. When such areas are stimulated, the result may be sexual arousal.

erotica Textual, visual, and audial material that promotes or creates sexual arousal and shows enjoyment of sexuality in an equal and balanced manner toward people of either sex.

escort agency A company that sends out sex trade workers to off-site locations, such as homes, hotels, and motels.

estrus cycle The physical processes that occur in the female reproductive tract caused by hormones in sexually mature mammals.

ethnocentrism The tendency to believe that one's ethnic or cultural group is the norm, and to view other ethnicities or cultures as abnormal or different.

eugenics movement A social movement in which society is thought to be improved by controlling the passing on of hereditary information through controlling which members of society are allowed to procreate.

eunuch A castrated human male.

event-related designs Research designs, used in brain imaging research, that incorporate different types of intermixed stimuli.

evolutionary biology The application of evolutionary theories to understand how species have adapted and changed over time.

evolutionary psychology The application of evolutionary theories to understand emotional and psychological processes, mainly in human beings.

exclusive breastfeeding Feeding an infant only breast milk.

exotic dancing Dancing that involves the removal of most or all of one's clothing with the intent of creating erotic arousal in the viewer. Commonly referred to as "stripping."

experimental research designs Research designs that use standardized procedures and randomization to evaluate the causal relationship between two variables.

extradyadic sex Sex that occurs outside the context of the primary relationship.

extramarital sex Sex that occurs outside the context of a marriage.

eye movement desensitization and reprocessing (EMDR) A form of psychotherapy to alleviate trauma-related symptoms and associated distressing memories through exposure to stimuli of traumatic events while simultaneously focussing on dual attention stimulus (e.g., hand-tapping, electronic- or therapist-directed lateral eye movement).

falsifiable Able to be proven false by research.

family planning Individual/partnered choice over the spacing and number of children a woman/couple will have.

feedback signal The part of a control system that provides a measure of the level of a certain substance.

fellatio Oral stimulation of a man's genitals by a partner.

feminist theory A theory based on the idea that society has been shaped around the desires of white heterosexual males, and that it thus fosters gender inequality.

feticide A deliberate act that causes the death of a fetus.

fixation A condition that occurs when needs are not met in childhood, resulting in blocked libidinal energy and unsuccessful resolution of the psychosexual stages of development.

flaccid Non-erect.

focus group A small group of demographically diverse individuals who participate in a guided discussion to help the researcher better understand a certain belief, behaviour, or phenomenon.

follicular phase The first phase of the menstrual cycle, during which the ovarian follicles mature and estrogen stimulates the growth of the endometrium. In this phase, estrogen levels are higher than progesterone levels.

forceps A tong-like instrument with cup-shaped ends that grasp the baby's head so the baby can be pulled from its mother's body through the birth canal.

frottage The sexual practice in which partners (clothed or not) rub or thrust their genitals against any part of the other person's body.

gamete A cell with half the number of chromosomes necessary for reproduction that fuses with another such cell during conception in order to make an embryo. In humans, females produce the larger gamete, ovum (or egg), and males produce the smaller gamete, the sperm.

gay identity An identity status denoting those individuals who have come to identify themselves as having primarily same-sex oriented cognition, affect, and/or behaviour, and who have adopted the construct of "gay" as having personal significance to them.

gender The psychological experience of femaleness and/or maleness.

gender dysphoria Distress resulting from the discrepancy between one's felt gender identity and one's biological sex and/or the gender one was assigned at birth.

gender identity The way in which one identifies with a gender category (e.g., man, woman, neither).

gender role The set of social and behavioural norms that are considered to be socially appropriate for individuals of a specific sex in the context of a specific culture.

gender schemas Mental frameworks based on understandings of how men and women typically behave.

gender socialization The learning of behaviour and attitudes considered appropriate for a given gender role.

gender stereotypes Widely held beliefs about the typical characteristics and behaviours of men and women.

genderqueer A person whose gender identification and self-presentation does not conform to gender categories.

generalizability The extent to which the conclusions drawn from particular findings in a sample population can be extended to principles that are present in the population at large.

genetic theory A theory that examines the role of genes in influencing behaviour.

genital stage Final psychosexual stage, which occurs during puberty; during this stage, an individual's sexual needs and feelings are directed toward others for sexual gratification.

genotype The genetic constitution of an organism, determined by genetic components inherited from the organism's parents.

gestation In mammals, the period of time in which a fetus/embryo develops in the uterus, beginning with fertilization and ending at birth.

girl-zines Self-published print or online magazines written by young women to express their thoughts and feelings about sexuality in a non-judgmental outlet. Also known as "grrrl-zines."

gonadal sex Sex determined by the presence of female gonads (ovaries) and/or male gonads (testicles).

gonadotropic hormones Hormones that stimulate the gonads.

gonads Glands in which gametes are produced; in humans, the ovaries and the testes.

Graafian follicle A mature ovarian follicle. It is a small sac, embedded in the ovary, that contains an egg. At puberty, each ovary has a large number of immature follicles (primordial follicles), each of which contains an undeveloped egg cell; many of these immature follicles will mature into a Graafian follicle. The egg is released from the follicle every month, at which time the shell of the follicle is primed to become the corpus luteum.

habituation A decrease in behavioural response to a repeated stimulus. Sexual habituation occurs when increased accessibility to a partner and predictability in sexual interactions leads to reduced sexual interest.

hard-core Explicitly depicting genitals and/or sexual penetration.

heritable Capable of being inherited, hereditary.

heterosexism Prejudice and discrimination against individuals of other sexual orientations and genders, based on the implicit assumption that heterosexuality is the norm.

heterosexual orientation An affectional orientation where affect and cognition are exclusively directed at members of the other sex.

homonegativity Explicitly negative attitudes toward gay and lesbian people.

homophily The principle that we are more likely to have contact and affiliate with, and therefore develop positive feelings toward. people who are similar to us.

homophobia The fear, dislike, and/or intolerance of gay and/or lesbian individuals.

hooking up Casual sex interactions with no strings attached.

hormonal sex Sex determined by levels of estrogens and androgens.

hormone A chemical released by a cell or group of cells (gland) in one part of an organism that affects cells in other parts of the organism via the circulatory system. Only a small amount of hormone is required to alter cellular metabolism.

human chorionic gonadotropin (HCG) A hormone produced by the chorionic villi of the placenta.

human sex trafficking A form of slavery in which individuals are forced to engage in sexual acts for others' profit.

humoural substances Any substance that forms part of the body fluids.

hymenoplasty A cosmetic surgery to reposition the remnants of the broken hymen or a small flap of vaginal skin to approximate the hymen.

hypogonadism A condition in which the gonads produce little or no hormones.

hypothalamus A portion of the brain, located below the thalamus, that contains numerous small groupings of neurons, all of which play a role in visceral functions such as sex, nursing, eating, biorhythms, and hormone production. Substances released by many of these neurons connect the nervous system to the endocrine system via the pituitary.

hypothesis A prediction, based on theory, about the expected outcomes of a research study.

hysteria A controversial mental illness/disease that was seen as being specific to women and characterized by the conversion of psychological stresses (specifically, sexual frustration) into physical symptom (e.g., gastrointestinal and nervous system problems), as well as volatile emotions and attention-seeking behaviours.

iatrogenic Originating from medical, pharmacological, or surgical treatment.

id Within psychodynamic theory, the portion of an individual's personality that represents unconscious and/or instinctual urges and desires.

identity disclosure The process of telling another person or other people your sexual identity label.

impression management A form of socially desirable responding in which someone deliberately responds in a way that makes him or her look good to others.

incest Sexual activity between persons of a close enough genetic relationship that they are not legally permitted to marry.

incidence The frequency of occurrence of new cases of an infection or a disease (or other condition) in a defined population.

incidence estimates Estimates based on the documented instances of a certain condition in a given period of time.

independent variables The variables that are being manipulated in an experiment.

infanticide The act of killing a child within a year of its birth.

infertility The inability to achieve pregnancy without the assistance of reproductive technologies.

infidelity Engaging in sexual and/or emotional relations with someone who is not one's primary partner when in a monogamous relationship.

information–motivation–behavioural skills (IMB) model A social psychology model that identifies three major components (information, motivation, and behavioural skills) that may directly or indirectly impact sexual health behaviours. The model also specifies a sequence of steps to successfully develop, implement, and update programs aiming to change sexual health behaviours.

interfemoral intercourse The sexual practice in which a man moves his penis between his partner's thighs without intromission.

internalized homophobia The fear, dislike, and/or intolerance that gay and lesbian individuals feel toward themselves and/or others with a same-sex orientation.

interpretation bias A bias that results from the fact that different people interpret behaviours and situations in different ways, based on their personal experiences, opinions, beliefs, and so on.

interrater reliability The extent to which two independent observers obtain the same results when using the same coding system.

intersex individuals Individuals whose reproductive and/or sexual anatomy develops differently from what is considered to be typical in either a female or a male.

intersexual selection Preferentially picking one mate over others.

interviews Self-report research tools designed to collect data about an individual's experiences and/or perceptions.

intimacy Feelings of closeness and connection that one feels with another.

intra-crural intercourse Rubbing the penis between the partner's thighs.

intrasexual competition Competition between members of the same sex for access to breeding with members of the other sex.

intra-vaginal ejaculatory latency (IELT) The duration from the moment of vaginal penetration until a man ejaculates in the vagina.

involuntary muscle A muscle that contracts without conscious control, usually found in the walls of internal organs.

jealousy A negative emotional response to potential or actual rejection from a partner or to loss of a relationship due to a rival.

kept boy A young male who is financially dependent on an older man, usually with the expectation that the younger individual will provide sexual services to the older man.

labial thermistor A physiological method used to measure female sexual arousal by recording the surface temperature of labia skin.

labiaplasty A form of cosmetic surgery to change the appearance of the labia minora.

lactational anovulation A lack of ovulation due to breast milk production.

latency stage Psychosexual stage from age six to puberty, during which all libidinal energy lies dormant.

legalization of STW A legal option for dealing with sex trade work by making it legal but subject to regulations. This option is also referred to as *regulation of STW*.

lesbian identity An identity status denoting those female-gendered individuals who have adopted the construct of "lesbian" as having personal significance to them.

lesions Abnormal changes to a body tissue.

LGBTTIQQ Lesbian, gay, bisexual, transgender, two-spirited, intersex, queer, questioning.

LGBTTIQQ affirmative therapy Therapy directed at helping LGBTTIQQ individuals view their sexual/affectional orientation, sexual identity, and/or gender identity in a positive light.

libertinism A philosophy, lifestyle, or pattern of behaviour characterized by self-indulgence and lack of restraint, especially one involving sexual promiscuity.

libidinal energy Psychic energy associated with mental desires and drives.

libido Sex drive; desire for sexual activity.

longitudinal studies Studies that examine psychological and/or behavioural information in a single individual or group over a long period of time (usually months to years).

love See **passionate love** and **companionate love**.

love stories Stories that express different beliefs and ideas about what love is like.

luteal phase The third phase of the menstrual cycle, which begins with the formation of the corpus luteum and ends in either pregnancy or involution of the corpus luteum. The main hormone associated with this stage is progesterone, which is highest during this phase of the cycle.

major histocompatibility complex (MHC) A group of genes that code for proteins found on the surfaces of cells that help the immune system recognize foreign substances.

malingering Intentionally faking or exaggerating symptoms for personal gain.

marital rape Within a spousal relationship, any unwanted intercourse or penetration (oral, vaginal, or anal) obtained by force, by threat of force, or when a spouse is unable to consent.

masochism The practice of deriving pleasure or sexual gratification from the experience of suffering physical pain or humiliation.

mass media All media technologies—including the Internet, television, newspapers, film, and radio—that are used for communicating with the public, and the organizations that distribute these technologies.

masturbation Manual stimulation of one's own genitals for sexual pleasure, commonly resulting in orgasm.

meconium The first stools passed by a newborn.

memory bias A bias that results from cognitive processes that interfere with the way in which a person remembers an event.

menarche The first incidence of menstruation.

menopause The stage of life at which a woman ceases to menstruate, usually between the ages of 45 and 55.

menses Menstrual flow.

menstruation The shedding of the uterine lining that has built up in anticipation of a fertilized egg.

mere-repeated-exposure effect The tendency for repeated exposure to a stimulus (e.g., another person) to increase our preference for that stimulus.

meta-analytic review A report that combines the effects found across multiple research studies.

milk let-down response A series of neural events that leads to milk ejection from the mammary glands (breasts). These include production and release of oxytocin from the hypothalamus, which causes cells around the breast alveoli to contract and eject milk down the milk ducts. This passing of the milk down the ducts is called the "let-down" (milk ejection) reflex.

misattribution of arousal When physiological arousal stemming from one state (e.g., fear) is misinterpreted as stemming from another state (e.g., love).

missionary position A position for sexual intercourse in which the heterosexual couple lies face to face with the woman underneath the man.

model organisms Animals that share important physiological and biological characteristics with humans, to the degree that they can be studied to reveal broad biological and behavioural patterns that are also present in humans.

monogamy The practice or state of being married to or in an intimate relationship with one person at a time.

monotheistic religions Religions that believe in only one deity, as opposed to those that believe in multiple deities.

mucosa The lining of the mouth, vagina, anus, and several other bodily orifices.

multiple orgasms More than one orgasm experienced within a short period of time.

myotonia The increased muscle tension in genital and non-genital areas of the body during sexual arousal.

natural selection The evolutionary process in which organisms best adapted to their environment are most likely to survive and reproduce.

negative reciprocity A communication pattern in which each partner tends to respond to the other with negative comments or behaviours, thereby escalating the conflict.

negative sexual health outcomes Negative consequences relating to sexual health behaviours, including STIs, unintended pregnancy, sexual violence, sexual discrimination, sexual abuse, and sexual coercion.

netiquette Rules outlining acceptable and unacceptable Internet activities.

neuro-cognitive testing The administration of tests that contain tasks designed to measure the functioning associated with a particular brain area in order to diagnose deficits and strengths in the manner in which a person perceives and navigates the world.

neurotransmitters Biochemicals made by the nervous system that transmit signals from one neuron to another.

nocturnal emission An involuntary ejaculation of semen during sleep (commonly known as "wet dream").

non-demand genital pleasuring An element of Masters and Johnson's sensate focus exercises in which the couple focusses on stimulating each other's genitals without engaging in intercourse.

non-random samples Study participants who have not been selected at random and therefore do not accurately represent the population of interest in terms of gender, racial, socioeconomic, behavioural, and/or other characteristics.

non-verbal communication All communication behaviours that are not words, including but not limited to body posture, voice qualities, facial expressions, and gestures.

nulliparous Never having given birth.

objectùm sexuality Emotional and physical attraction to and love for an object or objects.

Oedipus complex In boys, a desire for the mother's love coupled with fears of retaliation from the father.

online sexual activity (OSA) Activity that takes place via the Internet for any range of sexual purposes.

operant A behaviour.

operant conditioning A process through which an individual's behaviour is modified by the consequences or reinforcements that he or she receives.

operant conditioning chamber Originally, a small box that contains a lever or other device that an animal can use to receive reinforcement (e.g., food) or to avoid punishment (e.g., a shock); also known as "Skinner's box."

operationalize To clearly define a concept so that different people will understand it in the same way.

optimal sexuality Having sexual experiences that are (subjectively) extraordinary.

oral stage Psychosexual stage from birth to age two, during which an infant's energy and needs are focussed on the mouth.

orgasmic disorder Significant difficulty or inability to experience orgasm.

ovulation The second phase of the menstrual cycle, during which a mature egg is released from the ovaries; in the ovarian cycle, the stage just after the LH surge.

Pap test A test in which a sample of cells is taken from a woman's cervix with a small brush or spatula to detect precancerous changes, which may be due to HPV infection.

paraphilia Any intense and persistent sexual interest other than sexual interest in genital stimulation or preparatory fondling with phenotypically normal, physically mature, consenting human partners.

paraphilic disorder A paraphilia that causes distress or impairment to the individual, or that may harm others when acted upon.

parental investment theory A theory proposed by Robert Trivers (1972) that predicts that the sex making the larger investment in offspring will be more discriminating in mating.

parous Having given birth at least once.

parturition Childbirth; the process of delivering a baby and placenta from the uterus to the world outside of the mother's womb.

passionate love A state of intense longing for union with another.

pathogens Bacteria, parasites, or viruses that cause infection or disease.

pathologize The act of identifying a condition as abnormal or indicative of disease.

PDE-5 inhibitors See **phosphodiesterase type-5 inhibitors**.

peace bond A court order requiring a person to keep a certain distance from you, your workplace, your home, or any member of your family.

pedophile An individual with an exclusive or non-exclusive sexual preference for children. Pedophiles may or may not act on their sexual preferences. Individuals who engage in sexual activity with children are called child molesters; they may or may not be pedophiles.

pelvic inflammatory disease (PID) A bacterial infection of the female reproductive organs that causes lower abdominal pain. It can cause damage resulting in infertility, ectopic pregnancy, and chronic pelvic pain. PID is often caused by bacterial STIs.

penile agenesis A rare developmental variation in which a male child is born without a penis.

penile plethysmography (PPG) The direct measurement of changes in penile blood volume in response to external sexual stimuli.

penile strain gauge A physiological method used to assess male sexual arousal by measuring increases in penile circumference.

penis extender A device that attaches to the penis to make the penis seem longer and/or wider.

penis pump A device that draws blood into the penis, designed to assist men with erection difficulties.

penis ring A ring placed at the base of the penis to prolong erection by keeping the blood inside the penis.

perceptual confirmation A process whereby someone interprets an event in a way that is consistent with his or her expectations.

perfect use Ideal situation in which the birth control method is followed 100 per cent accurately.

performance anxiety Worries about one's ability to "perform" sexually (e.g., getting and keeping erections, achieving orgasm at the "right" time) that can interfere with experiencing pleasure during sex or even while thinking about having sex.

perimenopause The years prior to menopause when hormonal levels are fluctuating and declining and a woman is transitioning from having regular periods to not having any.

perineum The area between the pubic symphysis and the coccyx (tail bone).

peripheral neuropathy Damage to the nerves outside of the brain or spinal cord, which can cause pain, weakness, or numbness.

persistent genital arousal disorder (PGAD) Spontaneous, persistent, uncontrollable genital arousal that is not associated with sexual desire.

phallic stage Psychosexual stage from ages four to six, during which a child's energy and needs are focussed on the genitals.

phenotype The outward appearance or expression of a set of physical and behavioural traits, determined by genotype and environment.

pheromones Olfactory signals that trigger a social response in members of the same species.

phone sex Sexual activity that takes place via telephones, either through live conversations or by listening to sexually explicit pre-recorded messages.

phosphodiesterase type-5 inhibitors (PDE-5 inhibitors) Erectogenic drugs that work by helping to dilate the arteries of the penis.

physiological Relating to the physical functioning of living organisms.

pick-up line A verbal statement made by someone in order to initiate a romantic encounter.

placenta An organ that connects the fetus to the uterine wall for gas and nutrient exchange.

polyamory The practice of having multiple sexual and conjugal partners; being romantically and sexually involved with more than one person at the same time. Literally, the term *polyamory* means "the love of many" (*poly* = many, *amory* = love).

polyandry Polygamy in which a woman has more than one husband.

polygamy The practice or custom of having more than one wife or husband at the same time.

polygyny Polygamy in which a man has more than one wife.

pornification The process of making or becoming more visibly or explicitly sexual.

pornography Textual, visual, and audial material that promotes or creates sexual arousal and presents sexuality in an unequal, unbalanced, violent, or degrading manner toward people of either sex.

positive sexual health outcomes Positive outcomes relating to sexual satisfaction, exploring one's sexual identity, making informed sexual decisions, and maintaining a healthy mental and physical state free from STIs, sexual violence, sexual discrimination, and sexual abuse.

positivism The philosophy underlying scientific inquiry that requires that knowledge is based on reproducible experimental verification of natural phenomena, rather than on personal experience.

posterior pituitary A collection of axons projecting from the hypothalamus that terminates behind the anterior pituitary gland.

postpartum blues Mild depression, tearfulness, anxiety, and/or irritability occurring in the first few days after delivery.

postpartum depression (PPD) Severe depression occurring within the first year after giving birth.

postpartum psychosis (PPP) Psychosis occurring within the first three months postpartum.

post-traumatic growth Positive psychological change following a major negative event.

post-traumatic stress disorder (PTSD) An anxiety disorder that can develop after exposure to a life-threatening or serious anxiety-producing event and can cause persistent and chronic psychological symptoms, such as flashbacks, nightmares, avoidance of stimuli associated with the trauma, hyperarousal, and anxiety.

pre-copulatory behaviours In male animals, behaviours that reflect motivation toward a specific sexual target, which is influenced by concurrent sexual arousal.

precursor In biochemistry, a compound, cell, or cellular component from which another substance, cell, or cellular component is formed.

pre-ejaculate A clear fluid released from the tip of the penis when a man is sexually aroused.

premenstrual dysphoric disorder (PMDD) A mood disorder associated primarily with the luteal phase of the menstrual cycle and characterized by feelings of anxiety, anger, and depression.

premenstrual syndrome (PMS) A wide range of physical and/or emotional symptoms typically occurring 5 to 11 days prior to menstruation.

prevalence The current extent of an infection or disease (or other condition) in a defined population.

prevalence estimates Estimates based on the percentage of surveyed individuals who report having participated in or experienced a certain condition in a given period of time.

priapism A persistent, often painful erection.

primary reinforcer A powerful reward that is intrinsically satisfying.

primary sex characteristics The main sex organs that are necessary for reproduction.

primiparous Pregnant for the first time. Also, a woman who has been pregnant and given birth only once.

proceptivity A female's approach behaviour in response to contact with a male.

pro-choice movement A movement whose followers believe that a woman has the option to choose whether or not to terminate her pregnancy.

pro-life movement A movement whose followers believe that abortion is murder and should not be conducted under any circumstances (or under limited circumstances involving the physical health of the mother).

prostatectomy The surgical removal of all or part of the prostate gland, usually performed to remove cancer.

protection order A civil court order available in some provinces that provides various emergency and long-term orders to protect victims of family violence.

psychoanalysis Within psychodynamic theory, therapy conducted between a therapist (psychoanalyst) and a client, with the goal of examining, correcting, and balancing any disruptions in the client's personality.

psychoanalytic Relating to or incorporating the methods and theories of psychiatric treatment originated by Sigmund Freud.

psychodynamic theory A theory that attempts to explain the conscious and unconscious psychological forces that underlie human personality, motivation, and behaviour.

psychogenic Stemming from psychological causes.

psychometrics Measurement, development, or administration of psychological tests.

psychopathology Mental illness.

psychopathy A theorized developmental pattern in which an individual's antisocial behaviour is life persistent, has no known environmental causes, and involves manipulation and exploitation of others for personal gain.

puberty A stage of life, initiated by hormonal signals from the brain to the gonads, in which an adolescent reaches sexual maturity and becomes capable of reproduction. In response to the signals from the brain, the gonads produce hormones that stimulate libido as well as growth, function, and transformation of brain, bone, muscle, blood, skin, hair, breasts, and genitalia.

qualitative research methods Research methods that explore variation in the individual, interpersonal, and/or group understanding of phenomena by using flexible, open-ended questions.

quantitative research methods Research methods that measure and organize naturally occurring variation, often with the aim of identifying causal relationships.

quantitative sensory testing A standardized assessment of how an individual perceives distinct sensations caused by the placement of various stimuli (e.g., pressure, temperaure) onto the skin's surface.

quasi-experimental research designs Research designs that use standardized experiment-like procedures but that do not use random assignment and provide researchers with only a limited ability to manipulate independent variables.

queer identity An identity status that is intended to not label one's sexuality.

queerphobia The fear, dislike, and/or intolerance of members of the LGBTTIQQ community.

questionnaire A set of multiple-choice or short-answer questions that is designed to obtain specific information.

R rating Restricted rating from the Motion Picture Association of America, requiring individuals under the age of 17 to be accompanied by a parent or adult guardian.

rainbow parties Oral sex parties at which girls wear different colours of lipstick and leave rings of colour around the penises of the boys on whom they perform oral sex.

random assignment The process of dividing research participants into different treatment or experimental groups, so that each participant has an equal chance of being placed in any group.

random samples Study participants who have been selected at random to accurately represent the population of interest in terms of gender, racial, socioeconomic, behavioural, and/or other characteristics.

rape The act of initiating sexual intercourse with a person without his or her consent; it may involve physical force, verbal coercion, abuse of authority, or an incapacity to provide valid consent.

rape myths Inaccurate beliefs about sexual assault.

rape trauma syndrome (RTS) A two-phase stress response pattern that typically follows a sexual assault.

receptivity A female's capacity to engage in copulation.

receptor A molecule, most often found on the surface of a cell, that receives chemical signals originating external to the cell. When they bind to a receptor, these signals direct a cell to do something—for example, make proteins, grow, or establish an electrical signal to contact other cells.

recidivism Committing another crime.

refractory period In males, the period of time following orgasm in which another orgasm cannot occur regardless of stimulation received.

reinforcement Something that encourages a specific behaviour.

reproduction The process by which new organisms (offspring) are produced from progenitor organisms (parents). All individual organisms exist as the result of reproduction, either sexual or asexual.

reproductive fitness The ability to successfully pass on genes to the next generation.

research design A researcher's plan for how she or he will collect and analyze data.

responder bias The tendency for a participant to answer questions in a way she or he believes the researcher expects.

restraining order A family court order that forbids a spouse, a partner, or another family member from harassing the victim and sets limits on the conditions under which the person can contact the victim.

rhythm method A calendar-based method of family planning that estimates the start and end of the fertile time based on past cycle lengths and involves abstaining from intercourse during the fertile time.

sadism The practice of deriving pleasure or sexual gratification from inflicting pain, humiliation, or suffering on other people.

same-sex orientation An affectional orientation where affect and cognition are exclusively directed at members of the same sex.

scientific theory A set of thoroughly tested, generally agreed upon conclusions about, or explanations of, certain phenomena.

scissoring The sexual practice where two women wrap their legs around each other and rub their vulvas together.

secondary sex characteristics Features not directly related to reproduction that develop at puberty.

secretory cells Cells that secrete.

Section 15 of the Canadian Charter of Rights and Freedoms The section of the Charter that deals with equality rights, such as the right to equal treatment before and under the law as well as equal protection and benefit of the law.

self-deceptive enhancement A form of socially desirable responding in which someone inadvertently responds in a way that makes him or her look good to others, because he or she truly perceives himself or herself more positively than is accurate.

self-efficacy A person's belief that she or he can competently perform a specific behaviour.

self-identification The process of coming to accept for oneself a particular sexual identity label.

semenarche The first incidence of ejaculation.

sensate focus exercises Sex therapy exercises developed by Masters and Johnson that involve couples focussing on the sensation of touching and being touched by each other.

serial monogamy A pattern of consecutive, single-partnered intimate relationships.

sex See **biological sex**.

sex industry The commercial enterprises that deal with the buying and selling of sex-related services.

sex tourism Travel for the purposes of engaging in uninhibited sex.

sex trade work (STW) Work that involves a transaction between a seller and a buyer of sexual services.

sex trade workers (STWs) People practising sex trade work.

sex trafficking See **human sex trafficking**.

sexology The scientific study of human sexuality.

sexting The sending of sexually explicit photographs or messages via mobile phone.

sexual assault A range of non-consensual sexual experiences, including unwanted touching; oral, anal, and vaginal intercourse; and sexual violence.

sexual brain The part of the brain that mediates sexual behaviour.

sexual communication The processes by which intimate partners share their sexual likes and dislikes with each other and negotiate sexuality in their relationship.

sexual compliance An individual's willing consent to engage in sexual behaviour when she or he does not desire sexual activity.

sexual concordance Agreement between self-reported sexual arousal and genital arousal.

sexual consent An individual's agreement to engage in sexual behaviour.

sexual double standard A set of culturally maintained standards for sexual behaviour reflecting more permissive and less restricted sexual expression by men than by women; this double standard has been declining in North America in recent years.

sexual fantasies Sexual thoughts or images that stimulate a person physiologically and/or emotionally.

sexual harassment Any unwanted sex-related behaviours that are considered by the recipient to be offensive, threatening, or demeaning. It is a form of sexual discrimination. The legal definition includes two types (1) *quid pro quo*, which entail coercing a person to comply with sexual advances in exchange for employment or educational status or opportunity, and (2) *hostile work environment*, which involve unwanted sexual advances that might cause offence or humiliation.

sexual health A state of sexual well-being that varies from person to person and is influenced by various sociocultural factors and historical contexts.

sexual health education A universal sexual right to access comprehensive sexual health information and other resources necessary to promote healthy sexuality and avoid negative outcomes.

sexual identity label The general label one chooses to use to describe one's sexual attractions (typically gay, lesbian, bisexual, questioning, or queer).

sexual psychophysiology The study of physiological sexual processes that underlie psychological sexual responses.

sexual response cycle The four-stage model of physiological responses during sexual stimulation proposed/discovered by Masters and Johnson's research. The phases are excitement, plateau, orgasmic, and resolution.

sexual script A series of learned and predictable actions that lead up to sexual encounters.

sexual selection The evolutionary process of mate selection, which can be either intrasexual or intersexual.

sexual strategies theory A theory based on the idea that human mating strategies have evolved to overcome mating problems faced by our ancestors.

sexualization Making someone or something sexual.

sexually explicit material (SEM) Textual, visual, and/or audial material that promotes or creates sexual arousal.

sexually transmitted infection (STI) An illness, disease, or infection transmitted from one person to another by means of sexual behaviour, including sexual intercourse (both vaginal and anal), oral sex, and the use of shared sex toys.

smegma Secretions made up of dead skin cells, oils, and moisture, which can form in the genital folds of males and females.

smooth muscle Involuntary non-striated muscle.

social exchange theory A theory based on the idea that interpersonal relationships operate on a system of costs (or losses) and rewards (or gains), within which individuals try to maximize rewards and minimize costs, or at least find balance between the two.

social learning theory A theory based on the idea that learning occurs through modelling of observed behaviour. In some cases, individuals will model their attitudes and behaviours after fictional characters in the media.

social script theory A theory based on the idea that our social interactions tend to follow, or are at least heavily influenced by, predefined, culturally recognizable sequences of behaviours.

socially desirable responding The tendency to modify one's responses to a questionnaire or interview in order to make oneself appear in a favourable light.

sociobiological theory A theory based on the idea that the way we behave in social situations is influenced by our biological makeup, which has evolved over the history of our species.

sociological theory A theory that attempts to investigate and explain social phenomena by examining patterns and influences in various social contexts.

sociosexuality Individual difference in the willingness to engage in casual sexual activity.

soft-core Erotically suggestive without showing genitals or sexual penetration.

sonographic examination Diagnostic imaging using ultrasound to visualize the developing fetus.

specificity of sexual arousal Agreement between self-reported sexual attractions and sexual arousal patterns.

spectatoring Monitoring one's own sexual performance (as if one were watching from the bleachers) rather than simply enjoying giving and receiving sexual pleasure.

speculum A plastic or metal device shaped like a duck's bill, used to open a body cavity in a medical examination.

spermatogenesis Sperm production. In this process, primary sperm cells undergo meiosis and produce a number of cells, termed *spermatogonia*. Each primary spermatocyte divides into two secondary spermatocytes, and each secondary spermatocyte divides into two spermatids, or young spermatozoa. This takes place in the testes.

spermatozoa The mature male gametes in many sexually reproducing organisms.

spermicide A contraceptive substance that kills sperm to prevent impregnation.

spinal block Injection of local anesthetic into the spinal fluid to produce numbness in the lower body.

spousal rape See **marital rape**.

stalking Harassing behaviour such as repeatedly following, intimidating, or tracking another person against his or her will.

standardized questionnaire A research tool consisting of a fixed set of questions and corresponding response options.

stonewalling A negative communication behaviour that entails refusing to respond and resisting influence by not engaging in the discussion at hand.

street hustler A male sex trade worker who looks for customers on the street.

superego Within psychodynamic theory, the portion of an individual's personality that represents that person's internalized standards, which are based on social and parental learning.

survey method A research method in which participants are asked to respond to questionnaires.

theoretical bias A bias that can result from an individual's strict adherence to a specific theoretical approach.

therapeutic abortion An abortion performed when the mother's life is at risk, the pregnancy is likely to cause severe physical or mental health consequences in the mother, or the fetus has a congenital disorder associated with a significant risk of morbidity.

thermography In sex research, a physiological method used to measure female and male sexual arousal by using a heat-sensing camera to record the temperature of genital skin.

top A gay man who assumes the penetrator role in anal sex.

toucherism The act of fantasizing about touching, or actually touching, a non-consenting person for sexual gratification.

toxic shock syndrome (TSS) A serious but uncommon bacterial infection, originally associated with tampon use but now known to have an association with some contraceptive barrier methods.

trace A very small amount that is detectable by extremely sensitive instrumentation but not quantifiable.

transition related surgeries (TRSs) Surgical procedures to alter physical characteristics to resemble those typically associated with ones felt gender.

translational model A simplified representation of a more complex human condition or situation that generalizes an experimental finding to the clinical setting (and vice versa).

transman A biological female who identifies and presents as a man.

transphobia The fear, dislike, and/or intolerance of transgender individuals.

transwoman A biological male who identifies and presents as a woman.

tribadism The sexual practice where a woman rubs her vulva against any part of her partner's body.

typical use Realistic situation in which some people will inevitably make mistakes in use, perhaps because they are misinformed, intoxicated, tired, or forgetful.

ulcers Open sores.

unstandardized questionnaire A research tool consisting of a fixed set of questions, with room for individualized responses.

urethritis Inflammation of the urethra.

vacuum extractor A cup-shaped suction device that attaches to the baby's head to extract the baby from its mother's body through the birth canal.

vaginal photoplethysmography A physiological method used to indirectly measure vaginal blood flow associated with female sexual arousal.

vaginal pulse amplitude (VPA) A measure of short-term changes in vaginal blood flow, generally with each heartbeat.

vaginismus A condition in which vaginal penetration is difficult or impossible due to marked fear and/or tightening of the pelvic floor muscles.

vaginitis An inflammation of the vagina, usually due to infection, that can result in discharge, irritation, and pain of the vagina and vulva.

vasocongestion The increased vascular blood flow in the genitals (as well as certain non-genital regions) during sexual arousal, which results in swelling of the vagina and vulva in women and erection in men.

versatile A gay man who is willing to assume either the top or bottom role in anal sex.

vibrator A vibrating device used to stimulate various parts of the body.

victim precipitation theory A theory that suggests that victims are in part responsible for their assaults due to their own particular behaviours or characteristics.

viral load A measure of the amount of a virus that an infected person per millimetre of blood.

virilization The biological development of sex differences, specifically changes that make a male body different from a female body.

withdrawal A method of controlling fertility in which the man withdraws his penis from the woman's vagina before ejaculating, with the plan of preventing sperm from entering the cervix.

young male syndrome A theorized route to delinquent and/or criminal acts in which individuals engage in risky, violent, and competitive behaviour, especially during adolescence and early adulthood, to demonstrate their dominance and willingness to incur risks to attain goals.

References

CHAPTER 1

Ali, K. (2006). *Sexual ethics in Islam: Feminist reflections on Qur'an, hadith, and jurisprudence*. Oxford, England: Oneworld.

Andaló, P. (2003). Love, tears, betrayal . . . and health messages. *Perspectives in Health Magazine, 8*, 8–13.

Beck, V., Pollard, W., & Greenberg, B. (2000, November). *Tune in for health: Working with television entertainment shows and partners to deliver health information for at-risk audiences*. Paper presented at the annual meeting of the American Public Health Association, Boston.

Bishop, C. (1996). *Sex and spirit: Ecstasy, ritual, and taboo*. London, England: Duncan Baird.

Blair, K.L., & Holmberg, D. (2008). Perceived social network support and well-being in same-sex versus mixed-sex relationships. *Journal of Social and Personal Relationships, 25*, 769–91. doi:10.1177/0265407508096695

Catholics for a Free Choice. (1998). A matter of conscience: Catholics on contraception. Retrieved from www.catholicsforchoice.org/topics/prevention/documents/1998amatterofconsciece.pdf

CBC News. (2011, November 23). *Canada's polygamy legislation. B.C. Supreme court upholds polygamy laws*. Retrieved from www.cbc.ca/news/canada/story/2009/01/21/f-polygamy.html

CBC News Archive. (2012). *Sex education in the schools*. Retrieved from www.cbc.ca/archives/discover/programs/t/take-30/sex-education-in-the-schools.html

CBSC. (2004). *Canadian Broadcast Standards Council 2003/2004 annual report*. Retrieved from www.cbsc.ca/english/documents/annreports/annreport-2003-2004.pdf

Courtney, S. (2005). *Hollywood fantasies of miscegenation: Spectacular narratives of gender and race: 1903–1967*. New Jersey, NY: Princeton University Press.

Custer, L., Holmberg, D., Blair, K., & Orbuch, T. (2008). So how did you two meet? Narratives of relationship initiation. In S. Sprecher, A. Wenzel, & J. Harvey (Eds), *Handbook of relationship initiations* (pp. 453–69). New York, NY: Taylor & Francis.

DeLamater, J. (1987). Theories of human sexuality: A sociological approach. In J.H. Geer & W.T. O'Donohue (Eds), *Theories of human sexuality* (pp. 237–56). New York, NY: Plenum.

Diab, K. (2006, December 2). Under the veil of sexuality. *The Globe and Mail*. Retrieved from www.theglobeandmail.com

Dines, G., & Humez, J.M. (Eds). (2003). *Gender, race, and class in media: A text-reader* (2nd ed.). Thousand Oaks, CA: Sage.

Fischtein, D.S., Herold, E.S., & Desmarais, S. (2005). Canadian attitudes toward female topless behaviour: A national survey. *The Canadian Journal of Human Sexuality, 14*(3–4), 63–76. Retrieved from www.sieccan.org/cjhs.html

French, M. (2002). *From Eve to dawn: A history of women in the world* (Vol. 1). Toronto, ON: McArthur.

Galloway, K. (1997). *Dreaming of Eden: Reflections on Christianity and sexuality*. Glasgow, Scotland: Wild Goose.

Gallup and Robinson Research. (2012). Sex in advertising: A G & R essay. Retrieved from http://gallup-robinson.com/tableofcontents.html

Gauntlett, D. (1999). Gender and sexuality in Japanese anime. Retrieved from www.theory.org.uk/ctr-rol4.htm

Goodyear, S. (2011, September 26). A quarter of Canadians venturing into online dating. *Canoe*. Retrieved from http://lifewise.canoe.ca

Gregor, T. (1985). *Anxious pleasures: The sexual lives of an Amazonian people*. University of Chicago Press.

Guttmacher Institute. (2011). Facts on induced abortion in the United States. Retrieved from www.guttmacher.org/pubs/fb_induced_abortion.html

Heckel, N.M. (n.d.) Sex, society, and medieval women. Retrieved from www.lib.rochester.edu/camelot/medsex/text.htm

Herbenick, D., Reece, M., Sanders, S.A., Dodge, B., Ghassemi, A., & Fortenberry, J.D. (2009). Prevalence and characteristics of vibrator use by women in the United States: Results from a nationally representative study. *Journal of Sexual Medicine, 6*, 1857–66. doi:10.1111/j.1743-6109.2009.01318.x

Hite, S. (1976). *The Hite report: A national study of female sexuality*. New York, NY: Dell.

Hoskin, R.A. (2012, May). *Western conversion and the transmogrification of Sailor Moon*. Paper presented at the meeting of the Popular Culture Association of Canada, Niagara Falls, ON.

Houseman, J. (2011). *The psychosocial impact of television on queer women* (Doctoral dissertation, Alliant International University). Retrieved from http://gradworks.umi.com/34/17/3417162.html

Jelq, J. (2009). Our hero: Dr. Jocelyn Elders. Or, "firing the surgeon general." Retrieved from www.jackinworld.com/resources/general-articles/our-hero-dr-joycelyn-elders

Jones J. (1993). The construction of black sexuality: Towards normalizing the Black cinematic experience. In M. Diawara (Ed.), *Black American cinema* (pp. 247–56). New York, NY: Routledge.

Kellner, D. (2003). Cultural studies, multiculturalism and media culture. In G. Dines & J.M. Humez (Eds), *Gender, race and class in media: A critical reader* (pp. 9–20). Thousand Oaks, CA: Sage.

Kennedy, M.G., O'Leary, A., Beck, V., Pollard, K., & Simpson, P. (2004). Increases in calls to the CDC national STD and AIDS Hotline following AIDS-related episodes in a soap opera. *Journal of Communication, 54*, 287–301. doi:10.1093/joc/54.2.287

Knapp-Whittier, D., Kennedy, M.G., St Lawrence, J.S., Seeley, S., Beck, V. (2005). Embedding health messages into entertainment television: Effect on gay men's response to a syphilis outbreak. *Journal of Health Communication, 10*, 251–59. doi:10.1080/10810730590934271

Kohler, P.K., Manhart, L.E., & Lafferty, W.E. (2008). Abstinence-only and comprehensive sex education and the initiation of sexual activity and teen pregnancy. *Journal of Adolescent Health, 42*, 344–51. doi:10.1016/j.jadohealth.2007.08.026

Kugle, S. (2010). *Homosexuality in Islam: Critical reflection on gay, lesbian, and transgender Muslims*. Oxford, England: Oneworld.

Kung, H. (2005). *Women in Christianity*. New York, NY: Bowden.

Kunkel, D., Biely, E., Eyal, K., Cope-Farrar, K., Donnerstein, E., & Fandrich, R. (2003). *Sex on TV 3: A biennial report to the Kaiser Family Foundation*. Menlo Park, CA: Kaiser Family Foundation.

Kunkel, D., Eyal, K., Finnerty, K., Biely, E., & Donnerstein, E. (2005). *Sex on TV 4: A Kaiser Family Foundation report*. Retrieved from www.kff.org/entmedia/upload/sex-on-tv-4-full-report.pdf

Lane, F.S. (2000). *Obscene profits: The entrepreneurs of pornography in the cyber age*. New York, NY: Routledge.

Laumann, E.O., Gagnon, J.H., Michael, R.T., & Michaels, S. (1994). *The social organization of sexuality*. University of Chicago Press.

McKay, A., & Barrett, M. (2010). Trends in teen pregnancy rates from 1996–2006: A comparison of Canada, Sweden, USA, and England/Wales. *The Canadian Journal of Human Sexuality, 19,* 43–52. Retrieved from www.sieccan.org

Maines, R.P. (1999). *The technology of orgasm: Hysteria, the vibrator, and women's sexual satisfaction.* Baltimore, MD: Johns Hopkins University Press.

Marsh, J. (2011). *Sex and sexuality in the nineteenth century.* Retrieved from www.vam.ac.uk/content/articles/s/sex-and-sexuality-19th-century

Masters, W., & Johnson, V. (1966). *Human sexual response.* New York, NY: Lippincott Williams & Wilkins.

Parsons, S.F. (1996). *Feminism and Christian ethics.* Cambridge, MA: Cambridge University Press.

Reeder, E.D. (1995). *Pandora's box: Women in classical Greece.* Baltimore, MD: Princeton University Press.

Rich, T.R. (1999). Judaism 101: Kosher sex. Retrieved from www.jewfaq.org/sex.htm

Riddle, J. (1992). *Contraception and abortion from the ancient world to the renaissance.* Cambridge, MA: Harvard University Press.

Roberts, D.F., Henriksen, L., & Foehr, U.G. (2009). Adolescence, adolescents, and media. In R.M. Lerner & L. Steinberg (Eds), *Handbook of adolescent psychology* (Vol. 2, pp. 314–44). Hoboken, NJ: John Wiley & Sons.

Robinson, M.L. (1999, January 1). Film, TV, and real people. Retrieved from http://newenglandfilm.com/news/archives/99january/womeninfilm.htm

Rosenbloom, S. (2011, November 12). Love, lies and what they learned. *The New York Times.* Retrieved from www.nytimes.com/2011/11/13/fashion/online-dating-as-scientific-research.html?pagewanted=all&_r=0

Severn, J., Belch, G.E., & Belch, M.A. (1990). The effects of sexual and non-sexual advertising appeals and information level on cognitive processing and communication effectiveness. *Journal of Advertising, 19*(1), 14–22. Retrieved from http://journalofadvertising.org/ja/index.htm

Shaikh, S. (2003). Family planning, contraception and abortion in Islam: Undertaking Khilafah. In D.C. Maguire (Ed.), *Sacred rights: The case for contraception and abortion in world religions* (pp. 105–28). New York, NY: Oxford University Press.

Shaver, F.M. (2011). Prostitution. *The Canadian Encyclopedia.* Retrieved from www.thecanadianencyclopedia.com/articles/prostitution

Statistics Canada. (2011). *Gay pride . . . by the numbers.* Retrieved from www42.statcan.gc.ca/smr08/2011/smr08_158_2011-eng.htm

Turner, J.S. (2011). Sex and the spectacle of music videos: An examination of the portrayal of race and sexuality in music videos. *Sex Roles, 64,* 173–91. doi:10.1007/s11199-010-0766-6

Tyree, R. (1998). *Pandora.* Retrieved from www.arthistory.sbc.edu/imageswomen/papers/tyreepandora/pandora.html

Weitzer, J. (1999). *Sex for sale: Prostitution, pornography and the sex industry.* New York, NY: Routledge.

Wiesner-Hanks, M.E. (2000). *Christianity and sexuality in the early modern world: Regulating desire, reforming practice.* London, England: Routledge.

Witcombe, C.L.C.E. (2000). *Eve and the identity of women.* Retrieved from http://witcombe.sbc.edu/eve-women/1evewomen.html

Yelaja, P. (2011, July 20). Women's topless court victory 20 years later. *CBC News.* Retrieved from www.cbc.ca/news/canada/toronto/story/2011/07/19/gwen-jacobs.html

CHAPTER 2

Bailey, J.M., Dunne, M.P., & Martin, N.G. (2000). Genetic and environmental influences on sexual orientation and its correlates in an Australian twin sample. *Journal of Personality and Social Psychology, 78,* 524–36. doi:10.1037/0022-3514.78.3.524

Bailey, J.M., & Pillard, R.C. (1991). A genetic study of male sexual orientation. *Archives of General Psychiatry, 48,* 1089–96. doi:10.1001/archpsyc.1991.01810360053008

Bailey, J.M., Pillard, R.C., Neale, M.C., & Agyei, Y. (1993). Heritable factors influence sexual orientation in women. *Archives of General Psychiatry, 50,* 217–23. doi:10.1001/archpsyc.1993.01820150067007

Bancroft, J. (2009). *Human sexuality and its problems* (3rd ed.). Philadelphia, PA: Churchill Livingstone.

Bancroft, J., & Janssen, E. (2000). The dual control model of male sexual response: A theoretical approach to centrally mediated erectile dysfunction. *Neuroscience & Biobehavioral Reviews, 24,* 571–79. doi:10.1016/S0149-7634(00)0024-5

Bandura, A. (1977). Self-efficacy: Toward a unifying theory of behavioral change. *Psychological Review, 84,* 191–215. doi:10.1037/0033-295X.84.2.19

Barash, D.P. (1977). Sociobiology of rape in mallards (*Anas platyrhynchos*): Responses of the mated male. *Science, 197,* 788–89. doi:10.1126/science.197.4305.788

Bélanger, C. (2000a). *The Roman Catholic Church and Québec.* Retrieved from http://faculty.marianopolis.edu/c.belanger/quebechistory/readings/church.htm

Bélanger, C. (2000b). *The quiet revolution.* Retrieved from http://faculty.marianopolis.edu/c.belanger/quebechistory/events/quiet.htm

Bem, D.J. (1996). Exotic becomes erotic: A developmental theory of sexual orientation. *Psychological Review, 103,* 320–35. doi:10.1037//0033-295X.103.2.320

Bergeron, S., Binik, Y.M., Khalifé, S., Pagidas, K., Glazer, H.I., Meana, M., & Amsel, R. (2001). A randomized comparison of group cognitive-behavioral therapy, surface electromyographic biofeedback, and vestibulectomy in the treatment of dyspareunia resulting from vulvar vestibulitis. *Pain, 91,* 297–306. doi:10.1016/S0304-3959(00)00449-8

Bisson, M.A., & Levine, T.R. (2009). Negotiating a friends with benefits relationship. *Archives of Sexual Behavior, 38,* 66–73. doi:10.1007/s10508-007-9211-2

Breedlove, S., Rosenzweig, M., & Watson, N. (2007). *Biological psychology: An introduction to behavioural, cognitive and clinical neuroscience.* New York, NY: Pearson Education.

Brown, C.M., Traverso, G., & Fedoroff, J.P. (1996). Masturbation prohibition in sex offenders: A cross-over study. *Archives of Sexual Behaviour, 25,* 397–408. doi:10.1007/BF02437582

Buss, D.M., & Schmitt, D.P. (1993). Sexual strategies theory: An evolutionary perspective on human mating. *Psychological Review, 2,* 204–32. doi:10.1037//0033-295X.100.2.204

Byers, E.S., & Wang, A. (2004). Understanding sexuality in close relationships from the social exchange perspective. In J.H. Harvey, A. Wenzel, & S. Sprecher (Eds), *The handbook of sexuality in close relationships* (pp. 203–34). Mayway, NJ; Lawrence Erlbaum.

Carnes, P. (1983). *Out of the shadows: Understanding sexual addiction.* Minneapolis, MN: CompCare.

Dobson, K.S. (2002). *Handbook of cognitive-behavioral therapies.* New York, NY: Guilford Press.

Gagnon, J.H., & Simon, W. (1973). *Sexual conduct.* Chicago, IL: Aldine.

Graham, C.A., Sanders, S.A., & Milhausen, R.R. (2006). The sexual excitation and sexual inhibition inventory for women: Psychometric properties. *Archives of Sexual Behavior, 35,* 397–410. doi:10.1007/s10508-006-9041-7

Herdt, G.H. (1984). *Ritualized homosexuality in Melanesia.* Berkeley, CA: University of California Press.

Kafka, M.P. (2007). Paraphilia-related disorders: The evaluation and treatment of nonparaphilic hypersexuality. In S.R. Leiblum (Ed.), *Principles and practice of sex therapy* (4th ed., pp. 442–76). New York, NY: Guilford Press.

Kaschak, E., & Tiefer, L. (Eds). (2001). *A new view of women's sexual problems.* New York, NY: Routledge.

Knight, K. (n.d.). *"I'm just not that into him": A qualitative study of friends with benefits relationships among college students.* Manuscript submitted for publication.

Leiblum, S.R. (2007). *Principles and practice of sex therapy.* New York, NY: Guilford Press.

Liao, L.M., & Creighton, S.M. (2007). Requests for cosmetic genitoplasty: How should health care providers respond? *BMJ, 334,* 1090–92. doi:10.1136/bmj.39206.422269.BE

Pedlow, C.T., & Carey, M.P. (2000). Developmentally appropriate sexual risk reduction interventions for adolescents: Rationale, review of interventions, and recommendations for research and practice. *Annals of Behavioral Medicine, 27,* 172–84. doi:10.1207/s15324796abm2703_5

Prentky, R., Dowdell, E., Fedoroff, P., Burgess, A., Malamuth, N., & Schuler, A. (2010). *A multi-prong approach to strengthening internet child safety.* Washington, DC: United States Office of Juvenile Justice and Delinquency Prevention.

Reissing, E.D., Andruff, H.L., & Wentland, J.J. (2010). Looking back: The experience of first sexual intercourse and current sexual adjustment in young heterosexual adults. *Journal of Sex Research, 48,* 1–9. doi:10.1080/00224499.2010.538951

Reissing, E.D., Laliberté, G.M., & Davis, H.J. (2005). Young women's sexual adjustment: The role of sexual self-schema, sexual self-efficacy, sexual aversion and body attitudes. *Canadian Journal of Human Sexuality, 14*(3/4), 77–86. Retrieved from www.sieccan.org/cjhs.html

Statistics Canada. (2007). *Census snapshot of Canada—Families* (Catalogue no. 11-008). Ottawa, ON: Author.

Trivers, R.L. (1972). Parental investment and sexual selection. In B. Campbell (Ed.), *Sexual selection and the descent of man, 1871–1971* (pp. 136–79). Chicago, IL: Aldine.

Vasey, P.L., & VanderLaan, D.P. (2010). Avuncular tendencies and the evolution of male androphilia in Samoan *fa'afafine. Archives of Sexual Behavior, 39,* 821–30. doi:10.1007/s10508-008-9404-3

Wentland, J.J. & Reissing, E.D. (2011). Taking casual sex not too casually: Arriving at consensus definitions for different types of casual sexual relationships. *Canadian Journal of Human Sexuality, 20,* 75–91. Retrieved from www.sieccan.org/cjhs.html

Wilson, E.O. (1975). *Sociobiology: The new synthesis.* Cambridge, MA: Harvard University Press.

CHAPTER 3

American Psychiatric Association (2000). *Diagnostic and statistical manual of mental disorders* (4th Rev. ed.). Washington, DC: Author.

Amoroso, D.M., Brown, M., Pruesse, M., Ware, E.E., & Pilkey, D.W. (1970). An investigation of behavioral, psychological, and physiological reactions to pornographic stimuli. In *Technical reports of the Commission on Obscenity and Pornography* (Vol. 8). Washington, DC: US Government Printing Office.

Arthurs, O.J., & Boniface, S. (2002). How well do we understand the neural origins of the fMRI BOLD signal? *Trends in Neuroscience, 25,* 27–31. doi:10.1016/S0166-2236(00)01995-0

Bancroft, J., Graham, C.A., Janssen, E., & Sanders, S.A. (2009). The dual control model: Current status and future directions. *Journal of Sex Research, 46,* 121–42. doi:10.1080/00224490902747222

Basson, R. (2000). The female sexual response: A different model. *Journal of Sex & Marital Therapy, 26,* 51–65. doi:10.1080/009262300278641

Beach, F.A. (1976). Sexual attractivity, proceptivity, and receptivity in female mammals. *Hormones & Behavior, 7,* 105–38. doi:10.1016/0018-506X(76)90008-8

Brecher, E.M. (1969). *The sex researchers.* Boston, MA: Little, Brown.

Breuer, J., & Freud, S. (2005). *Studies on hysteria* (N. Luckhurst, Trans.). New York, NY: Penguin Books. (Original work published 1895)

Buisson, O., Foldes, P., Jannini, E., & Mimoun, S. (2010). Coitus as revealed by ultrasound in one volunteer couple. *Journal of Sexual Medicine, 7,* 2750–4. doi:10.1111/j.1743-6109.2010.01892.x

Burton, R.F. (Trans.). (1964). *The perfumed garden of the Shaykh Nefzawi.* New York, NY: Putnam. (Original work published 1886)

Carrère, S., & Gottman, J.M. (1999). Predicting divorce among newlyweds from the first three minutes of a marital conflict discussion. *Family Process, 38,* 293–301. doi:10.1111/j.1545-5300.1999.00293.x

Chivers, M.L., Seto, M.C., Lalumière, M.L., Laan, E., & Grimbos, T. (2010). Agreement of self-reported and genital measures of sexual arousal in men and women: A meta-analysis. *Archives of Sexual Behavior, 39,* 5–56. doi:10.1007/s10508-009-9556-9

Daniélou, A. (1993). *The complete Kama Sutra: The first unabridged modern translation of the classic Indian text.* Rochester, VT: Inner Traditions.

Davis, S.N.P., Maykut, C.A., Binik, Y.M., Amsel, R., & Carrier, S. (2011). Tenderness as measured by pressure pain thresholds extends beyond the pelvis in Chronic Pelvic Pain Syndrome in men. *Journal of Sexual Medicine, 8,* 232–39. doi:10.1111/j.1743-6109.2010.02041.x

Farmer, M.A., & Binik, Y.M. (2005). Psychology is from Mars, sexology is from Venus: Can they meet on Earth? *Canadian Psychology, 46,* 46–51. doi:10.1037/h0085824

Farmer, M.A., Taylor, A.M., Bailey, A.L., MacIntyre, L.C., Milagrosa, Z.E., Crissman, H., . . . Mogil, J.S. (2011). Repeated vulvovaginal fungal infections cause persistent pain in a mouse model of vulvodynia. *Science Translational Medicine, 3,*(101). doi:10.1126/scitranslmed.3002613

Gaither, G.A., Rosenkranz, R.R., Amato-Henderson, S., Plaud, J.J., & Bigwood, S.J. (1996). The effect of condoms in sexually explicit narratives on male sexual arousal. *Journal of Sex & Marital Therapy, 22,* 103–09. doi:10.1080/00926239608404914

Giuliano, F., Pfaus, J., Balasubramanian, S., Hedlund, P., Hisasue, S., Marson, L., & Wallen, K. (2010). Experimental models for the study of female and male sexual function. *Journal of Sexual Medicine, 7,* 2970–95. doi:10.1111/j.1743-6109.2010.01960.x

Graham, C.A., Sanders, S., Milhausen, R.R., McBride, K.R. (2004). Turning on and turning off: A focus group study of the factors that affect women's sexual arousal. *Archives of Sexual Behavior, 33*, 527–38. doi:10.1023/B:ASEB.0000044737.62561.fd

Hadley, M.E. (2005). Discovery that a melanocortin regulates sexual functions in male and female humans. *Peptides, 26*, 1687–9.

Hayes, R.D., Bennett, C.M., Dennerstein, L., Taffe, J.R., & Fairley, C.K. (2008). Are aspects of study design associated with the reported prevalence of female sexual difficulties? *Fertility and Sterility, 90*, 497–505. doi:10.1016/j.fertnstert.2007.07.1297

Kagerer, S., Klucken, T., Wehrum, S., Zimmermann, M., Schienle A., Walter, B., Vaitl, D., & Stark, R. (2011). Neural activation toward erotic stimuli in homosexual and heterosexual males. *The Journal of Sexual Medicine, 8*(11), 2132-3143.

Kinsey, A.C., Pomeroy, W.B., & Martin, C.E. (1948). *Sexual behaviour in the human male*. Philadelphia, PA: W.B. Saunders.

Kinsey, A.C., Pomeroy, W.B., Martin, C.E., & Gebhard, P.H. (1953). *Sexual behaviour in the human female*. Philadelphia, PA: W.B. Saunders.

Komisaruk, B.R., Whipple, B., Crawford, A., Liu, W.C., Kalnin, A., & Mosier, K. (2004). Brain activation during vaginocervical self-stimulation and orgasm in women with complete spinal cord injury: fMRI evidence of mediation by the vagus nerves. *Brain Research, 1024*, 77–88. doi:10.1016/j.brainres.2004.07.029

Krafft-Ebing, R. (1965). *Psychopathia sexualis: A medico-forensic study*. New York, NY: Stein and Day. (Original work published 1886)

Kukkonen, T.M., Paterson, L., Binik, Y.M., Amsel, R., Bouvier, F., & Khalifé, S. (2006). Convergent and discriminant validity of clitoral color Doppler ultrasonography as a measure of female sexual arousal. *Journal of Sex & Marital Therapy, 32*, 281–7. doi:10.1080/00926230600666220

Laumann, E.O., Paik, A., & Rosen, R.C. (1999). Sexual dysfunction in the United States: Prevalence and predictors. *Journal of the American Medical Association, 281*, 537–44. doi:10.1001/jama.281.6.537

Mah, K., & Binik, Y.M. (2002). Do all orgasms feel alike? Evaluating a two-dimensional model of the orgasm experience across gender and sexual context. *Journal of Sex Research, 39*, 104–13. doi:10.1080/00224490209552129

Masters, W. H., & Johnson, V. E. (1966). *Human sexual response*. Boston, MA: Little, Brown.

Masters, W. H., & Johnson, V. E. (1970). *Human sexual inadequacy*. New York, NY: Bantam Books.

Melody, M.E., & Peterson, L.M. (1999). *Teaching America about sex: Marriage guides and sex manuals from the late Victorians to Dr. Ruth*. New York University Press.

Meston, C.M., Heiman, J.R., Trapnell, P.D., & Paulhus, D.L. (1998). Socially desirable responding and sexuality self-reports. *Journal of Sex Research, 35*, 148–57. doi:10.1080/00224499809551928

Moynihan, R. (2003). The making of a disease: Female sexual dysfunction. *British Medical Journal, 326*, 45–7. doi:10.1136/bmj.326.7379.45

Ortigue, S., Bianchi-Demicheli, F., Patel, N., Frum, C., & Lewis, J.W. (2010). Neuroimaging of love: fMRI meta-analysis evidence toward new perspectives in sexual medicine. *Journal of Sexual Medicine, 7*, 3541–52. doi:10.1111/j.1743-6109.2010.01999.x

Paulhus, D.L. (2002). Socially desirable responding: The evolution of a construct. In H.I. Braun, D.N. Jackson, & D.E. Wiley (Eds), *The role of constructs in psychological and educational measurement* (pp. 46–69). Mahwah, NJ: Lawrence Erlbaum.

Payne, K.A., Binik, Y.M., Pukall, C.F., Thaler, L., Amsel, R., & Khalifé, S. (2007). Effects of sexual arousal on genital and non-genital sensation: A comparison of women with vulvar vestibulitis syndrome and healthy controls. *Archives of Sexual Behavior, 36*, 289–300. doi:10.1007/s10508-006-9089-4

Payne, K.A., Thaler, L., Kukkonen, T.M., Carrier, S., & Binik, Y.M. (2007). Sensation and sexual arousal in circumcised and uncircumcised men. *Journal of Sexual Medicine, 4*, 667–74. doi:10.1111/j.1743-6109.2007.00471.x

Pfaus, J.G., Kippin, T.E., & Coria-Avila, G. (2003). What can animal models tell us about human sexual response? *Annual Review of Sex Research, 14*, 1–63. Retrieved from www.tandfonline.com/toc/hjsr20/current

Pfaus, J.G., Shadiack, A., Van Soest, T., Tse, M., & Molinoff, P. (2004). Selective facilitation of sexual solicitation in the female rat by a melanocortin receptor agonist. *PNAS, 101*, 10201–204. doi:10.1073/pnas.0400491101

Pfaus, J.G., Smith, W.J., & Coopersmith, C.B. (1999). Appetitive and consummatory sexual behaviors of female rats in bilevel chambers. I. A correlational and factor analysis and the effects of ovarian hormones. *Hormones and Behavior, 35*, 224–40. doi:10.1006/hbeh.1999.1516

Pukall, C.F., Binik, Y.M., Khalifé, S., Amsel, R., & Abbott, F.V. (2002). Vestibular tactile and pain thresholds in women with vulvar vestibulitis syndrome. *Pain, 96*, 163–75. doi:10.1016/S0304-3959(01)00442-0

Pukall, C.F., Strigo, I.A., Binik, Y.M., Amsel, R., Khalifé, S., & Bushnell, M.C. (2005). Neural correlates of painful genital touch in women with vulvar vestibulitis syndrome. *Pain, 115*, 118–27. doi:10.1016/j.pain.2005.02.020

Robinson, P. (1976). *The modernization of sex*. New York: Harper Colophon Books.

Rotermann, M. (2008). Trends in teen sexual behavior and condom use. *Health Reports, 19*(3), 53–7.

Tiefer, L. (2001). A new view of women's sexual problems: Why new? Why now? *Journal of Sex Research, 38*, 89–96. doi:10.1080/00224490109552075

van Netten, J.J., Georgiadis, J.R., Nieuwenburg, A., & Kortekaas, R. (2008). 8–13 Hz fluctuations in rectal pressure are an objective marker of clitorally-induced orgasm in women. *Archives of Sexual Behavior, 37*, 279–85. doi:10.1007/s10508-006-9112-9

Woo, J.S., Brotto, L.A., & Gorzalka, B.B. (2011). The relationship between sex guilt and sexual desire in a community sample of Chinese and Euro-Canadian women. *Journal of Sex Research, 49*, 290–98. doi:10.1080/00224499.2010.551792

Woodard, T.L., & Diamond, M.P. (2009). Physiologic measures of sexual function in women: A review. *Fertility and Sterility, 92*, 19–34. doi:10.1016/j.fertnstert.2008.04.041

Yule, M., Woo, J.S., & Brotto, L.A. (2010). Sexual arousal in East Asian and Euro-Canadian women: A psychophysiological study. *Journal of Sexual Medicine, 7*, 3066–79. doi:10.1111/j.1743-6109.2010.01916.x

CHAPTER 4

American College of Obstetricians and Gynecologists. (2007). Vaginal "rejuvenation" and cosmetic vaginal procedures (ACOG Committee Opinion No. 378). *Obstetrics & Gynecology, 110*, 737–38. doi:10.1097/01.AOG.0000263927.82639.9b

Basson, R. (2002). A model of women's sexual arousal. *Journal of Sex & Marital Therapy, 28*, 1–10. doi:10.1080/009262302317250963

Bramwell, R., Morland, C., & Garden, A.S. (2007). Expectations and experience of labial reduction: A qualitative study. *Obstetrical & Gynecological Survey, 63*, 145–46. doi:10.1097/OGX.0b013e318165afcc

Buisson, O., Foldes, P., Jannini, E., & Mimoun, S. (2010). Coitus as revealed by ultrasound in one volunteer couple. *Journal of Sexual Medicine, 7*, 2750–54. doi:10.1111/j.1743-6109.2010.01892.x

Canadian Cancer Society. (2008). *Cervical cancer: How to reduce your risk* [Brochure]. Author.

Canadian Cancer Society. (2012). *Canadian Cancer Statistics 2012.* Toronto, Ontario: Canadian Cancer Society.

Chalmers, B., & Omer-Hashi, K. (2003). *Female genital mutilation and obstetric care.* Vancouver, British Columbia: Trafford.

Cook, R.J., & Dickens, B.M. (2009). Hymen reconstruction: Ethical and legal issues. *International Journal of Gynecology and Obstetrics, 107*, 266–69. doi:10.1016/j.ijgo.2009.07.032

Darling, C.A., Davidson, J.K., & Conway-Welch, C. (1990). Female ejaculation: Perceived origins, the Grafenberg spot/area, and sexual responsiveness. *Archives of Sexual Behavior, 19*, 29–47. doi:10.1007/BF01541824

Dickerman, J.D. (2007). Circumcision in the time of HIV: When is there enough evidence to revise the American Academy of Pediatrics' policy on circumcision? *Pediatrics, 119*, 1006–1007. doi:10.1542/peds.2007-0739

Dixson, B.J., Dixson, A.F., Bishop, P.J., & Parish, A. (2010). Human physique and sexual attractiveness in men and women: A New Zealand–US comparative study. *Archives of Sexual Behavior, 39*, 798–806. doi:10.1007/s10508-008-9441-y

Dixson, B.J., Dixson, A.F., Morgan, B., & Anderson, M.J. (2007). Human physique and sexual attractiveness: Sexual preferences of men and women in Bakossiland, Cameroon. *Archives of Sexual Behavior, 36*, 369–75. doi:10.1007/s10508-006-9093-8

Dunn, M.E., & Trost, J.E. (1989). Male multiple orgasms: A descriptive study. *Archives of Sexual Behavior, 18*, 377–87. doi:10.1007/BF01541970

Federman, D.D. (2006). The biology of human sex differences. *The New England Journal of Medicine, 354*, 1507–14. doi:10.1056/NEJMra052529

Fetus and Newborn Committee, Canadian Paediatric Society. (1996). Neonatal circumcision revisited. *Canadian Medical Association Journal, 154*, 769–80. Retrieved from www.cps.ca/en/documents/position/circumcision

Freud, S. (2000). *Three essays on the theory of sexuality* (J. Strachey, Ed. & Trans.). New York, NY: Basic Books (Original work published 1905).

Friedman, D.M. (2001). *A mind of its own: A cultural history of the penis.* New York, NY: Penguin Books.

Goodman, M.P., Bachmann, G., Johnson, C., Fourcroy, J.L., Goldstein, A., Goldstein, G., & Sklar, S. (2007). Is elective vulvar plastic surgery ever warranted, and what screening should be conducted preoperatively? *Journal of Sexual Medicine, 4*, 269–76. doi:10.1111/j.1743-6109.2007.00431.x

Goodman, M.P., Placik, O.J., Benson III, R.H., Miklos, J.R., Moore, R.D., Jason, R.A., . . . Gonzalez, F. (2010). A large multicenter outcome study of female genital plastic surgery. *Journal of Sexual Medicine, 7*, 1565–77. doi:10.1111/j.1743-6109.2009.01573.x

Grafenberg, E. (1950). The role of the urethra in female orgasm. *International Journal of Sexology, 3*, 145–48.

Herbenick, D., Schick, V., Reece, M., Sanders, S., & Fortenberry, J.D. (2010). Pubic hair removal among women in the United States: Prevalence, methods, and characteristics. *Journal of Sexual Medicine, 7*, 3322–30. doi:10.1111/j.1743-6109.2010.01935.x

Humphries, A.K., & Cioe, J. (2009). Reconsidering the refractory period: An exploratory study of women's post-orgasmic experiences. *The Canadian Journal of Human Sexuality, 18*, 127–34. Retrieved from www.sieccan.org/cjhs.html

Kaplan, H.S. (1974). *The new sex therapy: Active treatment of sexual dysfunctions.* New York, NY: Brunner/Mazel.

Kilmer, M. (1982). Genital phobia and depilation. *Journal of Hellenic Studies, 102*, 104–12. Retrieved from http://journals.cambridge.org/action/displayJournal?jid=JHS

Kinsey, A., Pomeroy, W.B., & Martin, C. (1948). *Sexual behavior in the human male.* Philadelphia, PA: Saunders.

Kinsey, A., Pomeroy, W.B., Martin, C., & Gebhard, P. (1953). *Sexual behavior in the human female.* Philadelphia, PA: Saunders.

Koch, P.B., Mansfield, P.K., Thurau, D., & Carey, M. (2005). "Feeling frumpy": The relationships between body image and sexual response changes in midlife women. *Journal of Sex Research, 42*, 215–23. doi:10.1080/00224490509552276

Koff, E., & Benavage, A. (1998). Breast size perception and satisfaction, body image, and psychological functioning in Caucasian and Asian American college women. *Sex Roles, 38*, 655–73. Retrieved from www.springer.com/psychology/personality+%26+social+psychology/journal/11199

Lundberg, P.O., Ertekin, C., Ghezzi, A., Swash, M., & Vodusek, D. (2001). Neurosexology: Guidelines for neurologists [Supplemental material]. *European Journal of Neurology, 8*, 2–24. doi:10.1046/j.1468-1331.2001.0080s3002.x

Mah, K., & Binik, Y.M. (2002). Do all orgasms feel alike? Evaluating a two-dimensional model of orgasm experience across gender and sexual context. *Journal of Sex Research, 39*, 104–13. doi:10.1080/00224490209552129

Masters, W.H., & Johnson, V.E. (1966). *Human sexual response.* New York, NY: Bantam Books.

Masters, W.H., Johnson, V. E., & Kolodny, R.C. (1988). *Human sexuality* (3rd ed.). Glenview, IL: Scott Foresman.

Morales, A., Heaton, J.P.W., & Carson, C.C., III (2000). Andropause: A misnomer for a true clinical entity. *Journal of Urology, 163*, 705–12. doi:10.1016/S0022-5347(05)67788-9

Narjani, A. (1924). Considérations sur les causes anatomiques de la frigidité chez la femme [Notes on the anatomical causes of frigidity in women]. *Bruxelles Médical, 27*, 768–78.

Nelson, H.D. (2008). Menopause. *Lancet, 371*, 760–70. doi:10.1016/S0140-6736(08)60346-3

Noone, R.B. (2010). An evidence-based approach to reduction mammoplasty. *Plastic and Reconstructive Surgery, 126*, 2171–76. doi:10.1097/PRS.0b013e3181f830d7

Nugteren, H.M., Balkema, G.T., Pascal, A.L., Weijmar Shultz, W.M.C., Nijman, J.M., & Van Driel, M.F. (2010). Penile enlargement: From medication to surgery. *Journal of Sex & Marital Therapy, 36*, 118–23. doi:10.1080/00926230903554453

Oderda, M., & Gontero, P. (2010). Non-invasive methods of penile lengthening: Fact or fiction? *British Journal of Urology International, 107*, 1278–82. doi:10.1111/j.1464-410X.2010.09647.x

Pagel, M., & Bodmer, W. (2003). A naked ape would have fewer parasites [Supplemental material]. *Proceedings of the Royal Society of London, 270*(117), 9–S119. doi:10.1098/rsbl.2003.0041

Payne, K., Thaler, L., Kukkonen, T., Carrier, S., & Binik, Y. (2007). Sensation and sexual arousal in circumcised and uncircumcised men. *Journal of Sexual Medicine, 4,* 667–74. doi:10.1111/j.1743-6109.2007.00471.x

Perry, J.D., & Whipple, B. (1981). Pelvic muscle strength of female ejaculators: Evidence in support of a new theory of orgasm. *The Journal of Sex Research, 17,* 22–39. doi:10.1080/00224498109551095

Public Health Agency of Canada. (2009). *What mothers say: The Canadian maternity experiences survey.* Ottawa, ON: Author. Retrieved from www.phac-aspc.gc.ca/rhs-ssg/pdf/survey-eng.pdf

Ramsey, A., Sweeney, C., Fraser, M., & Oades, G. (2009). Pubic hair and sexuality: A review. *Journal of Sexual Medicine, 6,* 2102–10. doi:10.1111/j.1743-6109.2009.01307.x

Riddell, L., Varto, H., & Hodgson, Z.G. (2010). Smooth talking: The phenomenon of pubic hair removal in women. *The Canadian Journal of Human Sexuality, 19,* 121–30. Retrieved from www.sieccan.org/cjhs.html

Rouzier, R., Louis-Sylvestre, C., Paniel, B.J., & Haddad, B. (2000). Hypertrophy of labia minora: Experience with 163 reductions. *American Journal of Obstetrics and Gynecology, 182,* 35–40. doi:10.1016/S0002-9378(00)70488-1

Sand, M., & Fisher, W. (2007). Women's endorsement of models of female sexual response: The nurses' sexuality study. *Journal of Sexual Medicine, 4,* 708–19. doi:10.1111/j.1743-6109.2007.00496.x

Sorrells, M.L., Snyder, J.L., Reiss, M.D., Eden, C., Milos, M.F., Wilcox, N., & Van Howe, R.S. (2007). Fine-touch pressure thresholds in the adult penis. *British Journal of Urology International, 99,* 846–69. doi:10.1111/j.1464-410X.2006.06685.x

Taddio, A., Katz, J., Hersich, A.L., & Koren, G. (1997). Effect of neonatal circumcision on pain response during subsequent routine vaccination. *Lancet, 349,* 599–603. doi:10.1016/S0140-6736(96)10316-0

Thorne, C.H. (2010). An evidence-based approach to augmentation mammoplasty. *Plastic and Reconstructive Surgery, 126,* 2184–88. doi:10.1097/PRS.0b013e3181f8302

Trager, J.D. (2006). Pubic hair removal—Pearls and pitfalls. *Journal of Pediatric and Adolescent Gynecology, 19,* 117–23. doi:10.1016/j.jpag.2006.01.051

van Netten, J.J., Georgiadis, J.R., Nieuwenburg, A., & Kortekaas, R. (2008). 8–13 Hz fluctuations in rectal pressure are an objective marker of clitorally-induced orgasm in women. *Archives of Sexual Behavior, 37,* 279–85. doi:10.1007/s10508-006-9112-9

Vardi, Y., Harshai, Y., Gil, T., & Gruenwald, I. (2008). A critical analysis of penile enhancement procedures for patients with normal penile size: Surgical techniques, success, and complications. *European Urology, 54,* 1042–50. doi:10.1016/j.eururo.2008.07.080

Wallen, K., & Lloyd, E.A. (2011). Female sexual arousal: Genital anatomy and orgasm in intercourse. *Hormones and Behavior, 59,* 780–92. doi:10.1016/j.yhbeh.2010.12.004

Warkentin, K.M., Gray, R.E., & Wassersug, R.J. (2006). Restoration of satisfying sex for a castrated cancer patient with complete impotence: A case study. *Journal of Sex and Marital Therapy, 32,* 389–99. doi:10.1080/00926230600835346

Weiss, H., Polonsky, J., Bailey, R., Hankins, C., Halperin, D., & Schmid, G. (2007). *Male circumcision: Global trends and determinants of prevalence, safety and acceptability.* Retrieved from http://whqlibdoc.who.int/publications/2007/9789241596169_eng.pdf

Wimpissinger, F., Stifter, K., Wolfgang, F., & Stackl, W. (2007). The female prostate: Perineal ultrasound and biochemical studies of female ejaculate. *Journal of Sexual Medicine, 4,* 1388–93. doi:10.1111/j.1743-6109.2007.00542.x

World Health Organization. (1997). *Female genital mutilation: A joint* WHO/UNICEF/UNFPA *statement.* Retrieved from http://whqlibdoc.who.int/publications/1997/9241561866.pdf

World Health Organization. (2001). *Female genital mutilation and harmful tradition practices* (Progress Report). Geneva, Switzerland: Author.

Wunsch, L., & Schober, J.M. (2007). Imaging and examination strategies of normal male and female sex development and anatomy. *Best Practice & Research Clinical Endocrinology & Metabolism, 21,* 367–79. doi:10.1016/J.BEEM.2007.06.002

Wylie, K.R., & Eardley, I. (2007). Penile size and the "small penis syndrome." *British Journal of Urology International, 99,* 1449–55. doi:10.1111/j.1464-410X.2007.06806.x

Zaviačič, M., Jakubovská, V., Belošovič, M., & Breza, J. (2000). Ultrastructure of the normal adult human female prostate gland (Skene's gland). *Anatomy and Embryology, 201,* 51–61. Retreived from www.springer.com/biomed/neuroscience/journal/429

CHAPTER 5

American Psychiatric Association. (1994). *Diagnostic and statistical manual of mental disorders* (4th ed.). Washington, DC: Author.

Bachmann, G., Bancroft, J., Braunstein, G., Burger, H., Davis, S., Dennerstein, L., . . . Traish, A. (2002). Female androgen insufficiency: The Princeton consensus statement on definition, classification, and assessment. *Fertility and Sterility, 77,* 660–65. doi:10.1016/S0015-0282(02)02969-2

Bartz, J.A., Zaki, J., Bolger, N., & Ochsner, K. (2011). Social effects of oxytocin in humans: Context and person matter. *Trends in Cognitive Sciences, 15,* 301–09. doi:10.1016/j.tics.2011.05.002

Basson, R., Brotto, L.A., Laan, E., Redmond, G., & Utian, W.H. (2005). Assessment and management of women's sexual dysfunctions: Problematic desire and arousal. *Journal of Sexual Medicine, 2,* 291–300. doi:10.1111/j.1743-6109.2005.20346.x

Bhutta, M. (2007). Sex and the nose: Human pheromonal responses. *Journal of the Royal Society of Medicine, 100,* 268–74. doi:10.1258/jrsm.100.6.268

Campbell, A. (2010). Oxytocin and human social behavior. *Personality and Social Psychology Review, 14,* 281–95. doi:10.1177/1088868310363594

Carmichael, M.S., Warburton, V.L., Dixen, J., & Davidson, J.M. (1994). Relationships among cardiovascular, muscular, and oxytocin responses during human sexual activity. *Archives of Sexual Behavior, 23,* 59–79. doi:10.1007/BF01541618

Corter, C.M., & Fleming, A.S. (2002). Psychobiology of maternal behavior in human beings. In M.H. Bornstein (Ed.), *Handbook of parenting: Biology and ecology of parenting* (Vol. 2, pp. 141–82). Mahwah, NJ: Lawrence Erlbaum.

Dabbs, J.M., Jr, & Mohammed, S. (1992). Male and female salivary testosterone concentrations before and after sexual activity. *Physiology and Behaviour, 52,* 195–97. doi:10.1016/0031-9384(92)90453-9

Dennerstein, L., Randolph, J., Taffe, J., Dudley, E., & Burger, H. (2002). Hormones, mood, sexuality, and the menopausal transition. *Fertility and Sterility*, *77*, 42–8. doi:10.1016/S0015-0282(02)03001-7

Einstein, G. (2007). *Sex and the brain: A reader*. Cambridge, MA: MIT Press.

Einstein, G. (2012). Measuring biological sex. In J.L. Oliffe & L. Greaves (Eds), *Design and conducting gender, sex, and health research* (pp. 85–102). Thousand Oaks, CA: Sage.

Einstein, G., & Flanagan, O.J. (2003). Sexual identities and narratives of self. In G.D. Fireman, T.E. McVay, Jr, & O.J. Flanagan (Eds), *Narrative and consciousness: Literature, psychology, and the brain* (pp. 209–31). New York, NY: Oxford University Press.

Exton, M.S., Kruger, T.H., Bursch, N., Haake, P., Knapp, W., Schedlowski, M., & Hartmann, U. (2001). Endocrine response to masturbation-induced orgasm in healthy men following a 3-week sexual abstinence. *World Journal of Urology*, *19*, 377–82. doi:10.1007/s003450100222

Goldey, K.L., & van Anders, S.M. (2011). Sexy thoughts: Effects of sexual cognitions on testosterone, cortisol, and arousal in women. *Hormones and Behavior*, *59*, 754–64. doi:10.1016/j.yhbeh.2010.12.005

Hummer, T.A., & McClintock, M.K. (2009). Putative human pheromone androstadienone attunes the mind specifically to emotional information. *Hormones and Behaviour*, *55*, 548–59. doi:10.1016/j.yhbeh.2009.01.002

Insel, T.R., & Young, L.J. (2001). The neurobiology of attachment. *Nature Reviews Neuroscience*, *2*, 129–36. doi:10.1038/35053579

Jacob, S., McClintock, M.K., Zelano, B., & Ober, C. (2002). Paternally inherited HLA alleles are associated with women's choice of male odor. *Nature Genetics*, *30*, 175–79. doi:10.1038/ng830

Kippin, T.E., & Pfaus, J.G. (2001a). The nature of the conditioned response mediating olfactory conditioned ejaculatory preference in the male rat. *Behavioural Brain Research*, *122*, 11–24. doi:10.1016/S0166-4328(01)00162-0

Kippin, T.E., & Pfaus, J.G. (2001b). The development of olfactory conditioned ejaculatory preferences in the male rat. I. Nature of the unconditioned stimulus. *Physiology & Behaviour*, *73*, 457–69. doi:10.1016/S0031-9384(01)00485-1

Mazur, A., & Michalek, J. (1998). Marriage, divorce, and male testosterone. *Social Forces*, *77*, 315–30. doi:10.2307/3006019

McClintock, M.K. (1971). Menstrual synchrony and suppression. *Nature*, *229*, 244–45. doi:10.1038/229244a0

Ortigue, S., Bianchi-Demicheli, F., Patel, N., Frum, C., & Lewis, J.W. (2010). Neuroimaging of love: fMRI meta-analysis evidence toward new perspectives in sexual medicine. *Journal of Sexual Medicine*, *7*, 3541–52.

Practice Committee of the ASRM. (2008). Androgen deficiency in the aging male. *Fertility and Sterility*, *90*, s83–7. Retrieved from www.fertstert.org

Raisman, G. (1997). An urge to explain the incomprehensible: Geoffrey Harris and the discovery of the neural control of the pituitary gland. *Annual Review of Neuroscience*, *20*, 533–66. doi:10.1146/annurev.neuro.20.1.533

Raisman, G., & Field, P.M. (1973). Sexual dimorphism in the neuropil of the preoptic area of the rat and its dependence on neonatal androgen. *Brain Research*, *54*, 1–29. doi:10.1016/0006-8993(73)90030-9

Roenneberg, T., & Aschoff, J. (1990). Annual rhythm of human reproduction: I. Biology, sociology, or both? *Journal of Biological Rhythms*, *5*, 95–216.

Rubinow D.R., & Schmidt, P.J. (2006). Gonadal steroid regulation of mood: The lessons of premenstrual syndrome? *Frontiers in Neuroendocrinology*, *27*, 210–16. doi:10.1016/j.yfrne.2006.02.003

Savic, I, Berglund, H., & Lindström, P. (2005). Brain response to putative pheromones in homosexual men. *Proceedings of the National Academy of Sciences*, *102*, 7356–61. doi:10.1073/pnas.0407998102

Schwartz, D., Romans, S., Meiyappan, S., DeSouza, M.J., & Einstein, G. (2012). The role of ovarian steroids in mood. *Hormones and Behavior*. doi:10.1016/j.yhbeh.2012.08.001

Shahrokh, D.K., Zhang, T.Y., Diorio, J., Gratton, A., & Meaney, M.J. (2010). Oxytocin-dopamine interactions mediate variations in maternal behavior in the rat. *Endocrinology*, *151*, 2276–86. doi:10.1210/en.2009-1271

Sherwin, B. (2002). Randomized clinical trials of combined estrogen-androgen preparations: Effects on sexual functioning. *Fertility and Sterility*, *77*(Suppl. 4), 49–54. doi:10.1016/S0015-0282(02)03002-9

Shifren, J.L., Braunstein, G.D., Simon, J.A., Casson, P.R., Buster, J.E., Redmond, G.P., . . . Mazer, N.A. (2000). Transdermal testosterone treatment in women with impaired sexual function after oophorectomy. *New England Journal of Medicine 343*(10): 682–8.

Smith, E.P., Boyd, J., Frank, G.R., Hioyuki, T., Cohen, R.M., Specker, B., . . . Korach, K.S. (1994). Estrogen resistance caused by a mutation in the estrogen-receptor gene in a man. *New England Journal of Medicine*, *331*, 1056–61. doi:10.1056/NEJM199410203311604

Spencer, J.B., Klein, M., Kumar, A., & Azziz, R. (2007). The age-associated decline of androgens in reproductive age and menopausal Black and White women. *Journal of Clinical Endocrinology & Metabolism*, *92*, 4730–33. doi:10.1210/jc.2006-2365

Theodoridou, A., Rowe, A.C., Penton-Voak, I.S., & Rogers, P. (2009). Oxytocin and social perception: Oxytocin increases perceived facial trustworthiness and attractiveness. *Hormones and Behaviour*, *56*, 128–32. doi:10.1016/j.yhbeh.2009.03.019

Toran-Allerand, C.D., Tinnikov, A.A., Singh, R.J., & Nethrapalli, I.S. (2005). 17alpha-estradiol: A brain-active estrogen? *Endocrinology*, *146*, 3843–50. doi:10.1210/en.2004-1616

Traish, A.M., Botchevar, E., & Kim, N.N. (2010). Biochemical factors modulating female genital sexual arousal physiology. *Journal of Sexual Medicine*, *7*, 2925–46. doi:10.1111/j.1743-6109.2010.01903.x

Tuiten, A., Van Honk, J., Koppeschaar, H., Bernaards, C., Thijssen, J., & Verbaten, R. (2000). Time course of effects of testosterone administration on sexual arousal in women. *Archives of General Psychiatry*, *57*, 149–53.

van Anders, S.M., Brotto, L., Farrell, J., & Yule, M. (2009). Associations among physiological and subjective sexual response, sexual desire, and salivary steroid hormones in healthy premenopausal women. *Journal of Sexual Medicine*, *6*, 739–51. doi:10.1111/j.1743-6109.2008.01123.x

van Anders, S.M., & Dunn, E.J. (2009). Are gonadal steroids linked with orgasm perceptions and sexual assertiveness in women and men? *Hormones and Behavior*, *56*, 206–13. doi:10.1016/j.yhbeh.2009.04.007

van Anders, S.M., Hamilton, L.D., Schmidt, N., & Watson, N.V. (2007). Associations between testosterone secretion and sexual activity in women. *Hormones and Behavior, 51,* 477–82. doi:10.1016/j.yhbeh.2007.01.003

van Anders, S.M., & Watson, N.V. (2006). Relationship status and testosterone in North American heterosexual and non-heterosexual men and women: Cross-sectional and longitudinal data. *Psychoneuroendocrinology, 31,* 715–23. doi:10.1016/j.psyneuen.2006.01.008

van Anders, S.M., & Watson, N.V. (2007). Testosterone levels in women and men who are single, in long-distance relationships, or same-city relationships. *Hormones and Behavior, 51,* 286–91. doi:10.1016/j.yhbeh.2006.11.005

Villemure, C., & Bushnell, M.C. (2007). The effects of the steroid androstadienone and pleasant odorants on the mood and pain perception of men and women. *European Journal of Pain, 11,* 181–91. doi:10.1016/j.ejpain.2006.02.005

Wedekind , C., Seebeck, T., Bettens, F., & Paepke , A.J. (1995). MHC-dependent mate preferences in humans. *Proceedings of the Royal Society B: Biological Sciences, 260,* 245–49. doi:10.1098/rspb.1995.0087

Wyart, C., Webster, W.W., Chen, J.H., Wilson, S.R., McClary, A., Khan, R.M., & Sobel, N. (2007). Smelling a single component of male sweat alters levels of cortisol in women. *Journal of Neuroscience, 27,* 1261–65. doi:10.1523/JNEUROSCI.4430-06.2007

Young, K.A., Gobrogge, K.L., Liu, Y., & Wang, Z. (2011). The neurobiology of pair bonding: Insights from a socially monogamous rodent. *Frontiers in Neuroendocrinology, 32,* 53–69. doi:10.1016/j.yfrne.2010.07.006

Zukov, I., Ptacek, R., Raboch, J., Domluvilova, D., Kuzelova, H. Fischer, S., & Kozelek, P. (2010). Premenstrual dysphoric disorder—Review of actual findings about mental disorders related to menstrual cycle and possibilities of their therapy. *Prague Medical Report, 111,* 12–24. Retrieved from http://pmr.cuni.cz/

CHAPTER 6

Adler, E., & Bancroft, J. (1998). The relationship between feeding persistence, sexuality and mood in postpartum women. *Psychological Medicine, 18,* 389–96. doi:10.1017/S0033291700007935

Amso, N.N., & O'Leary, A. (2008). Investigation and treatment of the infertile couple. In M. Scanlon & A. Rees (Eds), *Specialist training in endocrinology.* Philadelphia, PA: Elsevier.

Anderson, G.M. (2004). Making sense of rising caesarean section rates: Time to change our goals. *British Medical Journal, 329,* 696–97. doi:10.1136/bmj.329.7468.696

Andrews, F., & Halman, L.J. (1992). Infertility and subjective well-being: The mediating roles of self-esteem, interpersonal control, and interpersonal conflict. *Journal of Marriage and the Family, 54,* 408–17. doi:10.2307/353072

Assisted Human Reproduction Act of 2004, SC, c. 2. Retrieved from http://laws.justice.gc.ca/eng/acts/A-13.4

Assisted Human Reproduction Canada. (2011). Risks Associated with AHR. Retrieved from www.ahrc-pac.gc.ca/v2/patients/risks-risques-eng.php

Barrett, G., Pendry, E., Peacock, J., Victor, C., Thakar, R., & Manyonda, I. (2000). Women's sexual health after childbirth. *BJOG, 107*(2), 186–95.

Bastian, L.A., Nanda, K., Hasselblad, V., & Simel, D.L. (1998). Diagnostic efficiency of home pregnancy test kits: A meta-analysis. *Archives of Family Medicine, 7,* 465–69. doi:10.1001/archfami.7.5.465

Beck, C.T., & Gable, R.K. (2000). Postpartum depression screening scale: Development and psychometric testing. *Nursing Research, 49,* 272–82. doi:10.1097/00006199-200009000-00006

Beemsterboer, S.N., Homburg, R., Gorter, N.A., Schats, R., Hompes, P.G., & Lambalk, C.B. (2006). The paradox of declining fertility but increasing twinning rates with advancing maternal age. *Human Reproduction, 21,* 1531–32. doi:10.1093/humrep/del009

Blickstein, I., Goldman, R.D., & Mazkereth, R. (2000). Risk for one or two very low birth weight twins: A population study. *Obstetrics Gynecology, 96,* 400–02. doi:10.1016/S0029-7844(00)00942-X

Bloch, M., Rotenberg, N., Koren, D., & Klein, E. (2005). Risk factors associated with the development of postpartum mood disorders. *Journal of Affective Disorders, 88,* 9–18. doi:10.1016/j.jad.2005.04.007

Blondel, B., Kogan, M.D., Alexander, G.R., Dattani, N., Kramer, M.S., Macfarlane, A., . . . Wen, S.W. (2002). The impact of the increasing number of multiple births on the rates of preterm birth and low birthweight: An international study. *American Journal of Public Health, 92*(8),1323–30. doi:10.2105/AJPH.92.8.1323

Brinsden, P.R. (2003). Controlling the high order multiple birth rate: The European perspective. *Reproductive Biomedicine Online, 6*(3), 339–44. doi:10.1016/S1472-6483(10)61854-8

Cacciatore, J. (2010). The unique experiences of women and their families after the death of a baby. *Social Work in Health Care, 49,* 134–48. doi:10.1080/00981380903158078

Canadian Paediatric Society, Dietitians of Canada, Health Canada. (1998). *Nutrition for healthy term infants.* Ottawa, ON: Minister of Public Works and Government Services Canada.

Chaliha, C., Kalia, V., Stanton, S.L., Monga, A., & Sultan, A.H. (1999). Antenatal prediction of postpartum urinary and fecal incontinence. *Obstetrics & Gynecology, 94,* 689–94. Retrieved from http://journals.lww.com/greenjournal/pages/default.aspx

Chalmers, B. (1990). *Pregnancy and parenthood: Heaven or hell.* Sandton, South Africa: Berev.

Chalmers, B., Dzakpasu, S., Heaman, M., & Kaczorowski, J. (2008). The Canadian maternity experiences survey: An overview of findings. *Journal of Obstetrics and Gynaecology of Canada, 30,* 217–28. Retrieved from www.sogc.org/jogc/index_e.asp

Chalmers, B., Mangiaterra, V., & Porter, R. (2001). WHO principles of perinatal care: The essential antenatal, perinatal and postpartum care course. *Birth, 28*(3), 202–07. doi:10.1046/j.1523-536x.2001.00202.x

Chalmers, B., & Royle, C. (2009). Birth experience and satisfaction with care. In Public Health Agency of Canada, *What mothers say: The maternity experiences survey of the Canadian Perinatal Surveillance System* (pp.162–66). Retrieved from www.phac-aspc.gc.ca/rhs-ssg/survey-eng.php

Chalmers, B.E., & Chalmers, B.M. (1986). Post-partum depression: A revised perspective. *Journal of Psychosomatic Obstetrics and Gynecology, 5,* 93–105. doi:10.3109/01674828609016746

Choudhry, U.K. (1997). Traditional practices of women from India: Pregnancy, childbirth, and newborn care. *Journal of Obstetric, Gynecologic, and Neonatal Nursing, 26,* 533–39. doi:10.1111/j.1552-6909.1997.tb02156.x

Clements, K.M., Barfield, W.D., Ayadi, M.F., & Wilber, N. (2007). Preterm birth-associated cost of early intervention services:

An analysis by gestational age. *Pediatrics, 119*(4), e866–74. doi:10.1542/peds.2006-1729

Cohen-Dayag, A., Tur-Kaspa, I., Dor, J., Mashiach, S., & Eisenbach, M. (1995). Sperm capacitation in humans is transient and correlates with chemotactic responsiveness to follicular factors. *Proceedings of the National Academy of Sciences of the United States of America, 92*, 11039–43. doi:10.1073/pnas.92.24.11039

Conde-Agudelo, A., & Belizan, J.A. (2000). Risk factors for preeclampsia in a large cohort of Latin American and Caribbean women. *BJOG: An International Journal of Obstetrics & Gynaecology, 107*, 75–83. doi:10.1111/j.1471-0528.2000.tb11582.x

Connolly, A., Thorp, J., & Pahel, L. (2005). Effects of pregnancy and childbirth on postpartum sexual function: A longitudinal prospective study. *International Urogynecology Journal, 16*, 263–67. doi:10.1007/s00192-005-1293-6

Cook, J.L., Collins, J., Buckett, W., Racowsky, C., Hughes, E., & Jarvi, K. (2011). Assisted reproductive technology-related multiple births: Canada in an international context. *Journal of Obstetrics and Gynaecology Canada, 33*, 159–67. Retrieved from www.sogc.org/jogc/index_e.asp

Cousineau, T.M., & Domar, A.D. (2007). Psychological impact of infertility. *Best Practice & Research Clinical Obstetrics & Gynecology, 21*, 293–308. doi:10.1016/j.bpobgyn.2006.12.003

Cunningham, F.G., Leveno, K.J., Bloom, S.L., Hauth, J.C., Rouse, D.J., & Spong, C.Y. (2010). *Williams obstetrics* (23rd ed.). New York, NY: McGraw-Hill.

Davidson, M.R., London, M.L., & Ladewig, P.A.W. (2008). *Olds' maternal-newborn nursing and women's health across the lifespan* (8th ed.). Upper Saddle River, NJ: Pearson Prentice Hall.

De Judicibus, M.A., & McCabe, M.P. (2002). Psychological factors and the sexuality of pregnant and postpartum women. *Journal of Sex Research, 39*, 94–103. doi:10.1080/00224490209552128

Dennis, C.L. (2004). Can we identify mothers at risk for postpartum depression in the immediate postpartum period using the Edinburgh postnatal depression scale? *Journal of Affective Disorders, 78*, 163–69. doi:10.1016/S0165-0327(02)00299-9

Domar, A.D., Zuttermeister, P.C., & Friedman, R. (1993). The psychological impact of infertility: A comparison with patients with other medical conditions. *Journal of Psychosomatic Obstetrics & Gynaecology, 14*, 45–52. Retrieved from www.ispog.org/jpog

Enkin, M., Keirse, M.J.N.C., Neilson, J., Crowther, C., Duley, L., Hodnett, E., & Hofmeyr, G.J. (2001). Effective care in pregnancy and childbirth: A synopsis. *Birth, 28*, 41–51. doi:10.1046/j.1523-536x.2001.00041.x

Evans, M., Ciorica, D., Britt, D., & Fletscher, J. (2005). Update on selective reduction. *Prenatal Diagnosis, 25*, 807–13. doi:10.1002/pd.1261

Flaxman, S.M., & Sherman, P.W. (2000). Morning sickness: A mechanism for protecting mother and embryo. *The Quarterly Review of Biology, 5*, 113–48. doi:10.1086/393377

Gibbs, R.S., Karlan, B.Y., Haney, A.F., & Nygaard, I. (2008). *Danforth's obstetrics and gynecology* (10th ed.). Philadelphia, PA: Lippincott, Williams, & Wilkin.

Goodman, J.H. (2004). Paternal postpartum depression, its relationship to maternal postpartum depression, and implications for family health. *Journal of Advanced Nursing, 45*, 26–35. doi:10.1046/j.1365-2648.2003.02857.x

Greil, A.L. (1997). Infertility and psychological distress: A critical review of the literature. *Social Science and Medicine, 45*, 1679–1704. doi:10.1016/S0277-9536(97)00102-0

Guzick, D.S., Carson, S.A., Coutifaris, C., Overstreet, J., Factor-Litvak, P., Steinkampf, M.P., . . . Canfield, R.E. (1999). Efficacy of superovulation and intrauterine insemination treatment of infertility. *New England Journal of Medicine, 340*, 177–83. doi:10.1056/NEJM199901213400302

Hack, M., & Fanaroff, A.A. (1999). Outcomes of children of extremely low birthweight and gestational age in the 1990's. *Early Human Development, 53*(3), 193–218. doi:10.1016/S0378-3782(98)00052-8

Hartmann, K., Viswanathan, M., Palnieri, R., Gartlehner, G., Thorp, J., Lohr, K. (2005). Outcomes of routine episiotomy: A systematic review. *Journal of the American Medical Association, 293*(17), 2141–48. doi:10.1001/jama.293.17.2141

Health Canada. (2000). *Family-centred maternity and newborn care: National guidelines* (Catalogue No. H39-527/2000E). Ottawa, ON: Minister of Public Works and Government Services Canada. Retrieved from www.phac-aspc.gc.ca/dca-dea/prenatal/fcmc1-eng.php

Health Canada. (2008). *Assisted human reproduction at Health Canada.* Retrieved from www.hc-sc.gc.ca/hl-vs/reprod/hc-sc/index-eng.php

Health Canada. (2010). *Canadian gestational weight gain recommendations.* Retrieved from www.hc-sc.gc.ca/fn-an/nutrition/prenatal/qa-gest-gros-qr-eng.php

Hughes, P.M., Turton, P., & Evans, C.D.H. (1999). Stillbirth as a risk factor for depression and anxiety in the subsequent pregnancy: Cohort study. *British Medical Journal, 318*, 1721–24. doi:10.1136/bmj.318.7200.1721

IVF Canada. (2013). *Fees and charges.* Retrieved from www.ivfcanada.com/services/fees/general_fee_schedule.cfm

Jesudason, V., & Shirur, R. (1980). Selected socio-cultural aspects of food during pregnancy in the Telangana region of Andhra Pradesh. *Journal of Family Welfare, 27*, 3–15. Retrieved from http://medind.nic.in/jah/jahm.shtml

Joó, J.G., Beke, A., Berkes, E., Papp, Z., Rigó, J., Jr, & Papp, C. (2009). Fetal pathology in second-trimester miscarriages. *Fetal Diagnosis and Therapy, 25*, 186–91. doi:10.1159/000210832

Jordan, C., & Revenson, T.A. (1999). Gender differences in coping with infertility: A meta-analysis. *Journal of Behavior Medicine, 22*, 341–58. doi:10.1023/A:1018774019232

Joseph, K.S., Demissie, K., & Kramer, M.S. (2002). Obstetric intervention, stillbirth, and preterm birth. *Seminars in Perinatology, 26*, 250–59. doi:10.1053/sper.2002.34769

Joseph, K.S., Kramer, M.S., Marcoux, S., Ohlsson, A., Wen, S.W., Allen, A., & Platt, R. (1998). Determinants of preterm birth rates in Canada from 1981 through 1983 and from 1992 through 1994. *New England Journal of Medicine, 339*, 1434–39. doi:10.1056/NEJM199811123392004

Kakarla, N., & Bradshaw, K.D. (2003). Evaluation and management of infertile couples. In J.J. Sciarri (Ed.), *Gynecology and obstetrics* (Vol. 5). Hagerstown, MD: Harper & Row.

Klein, M.C., Kaczorowski, J., Hall, W.A., Fraswe, W., Liston, R.M., Eftekhary, S., . . . Chamberlaine, A. (2009). The attitudes of Canadian maternity care practitioners towards labour and birth: Many differences but important similarities. *Journal of Obstetrics and Gynaecology Canada, 31*, 827–40. Retrieved from www.jogc.com

Klock, S.C. (2004). Psychological issues related to infertility. In J.J. Sciarri (Ed.), *Gynecology and obstetrics* (Vol. 5). Hagerstown, MD: Harper & Row.

Kmietowicz, Z. (2004). NICE advises against Caesarean section on demand. *British Medical Journal, 328,* 1031. doi:10.11.1136/bmj.382.7447.1031

Kramer, M.S., Aboud, F., Mironova, E., Vanilovich, I., Platt, R.W., Matush, L., . . . Shapiro, S. (2008). Breastfeeding and child cognitive development: New evidence from a large randomized trial. *Archives of General Psychiatry, 65,* 578-84. doi:10.1001/archpsyc.65.5.578

Kramer, M.S., Chalmers, B., Hodnett, E.D., Sevkovskaya, Z., Dzikovich, I., Shapiro, S, . . . Helsing, E. (2001). Promotion of breastfeeding intervention trial (PROBIT): A randomized trial in the Republic of Belarus. *Journal of the American Medical Association, 285,* 413-20. doi:10.1001/jama.285.4.413

Kramer, M.S., Demissie, K., Hong, Y., Platt, R.W., Sauve, R., & Liston, R. (2000). The contribution of mild and moderate preterm birth to infant mortality. *Journal of the American Medical Association.* 284,843-49. doi:10.1001/jama.284.7.843

Kramer, M.S., & Kakuma, R. (2004). The optimal duration of exclusive breastfeeding: A systematic review. *Advances in Experimental Medical Biology, 554,* 63-77. Retrieved from www.springer.com/series/5584

LaMarre, A.K., Paterson, L.Q., & Gorzalka, B.B. (2003). Breastfeeding and postpartum maternal sexual functioning: A review. *Canadian Journal of Human Sexuality, 12,* 151-68. Retrieved from www.sieccan.org/cjhs.html

Leary, W. (1990, September 13). New focus on sperm brings fertility success. *The New York Times,* p. B11.

Lewis, P.R., Brown, J.B., Renfree, M.B., & Short, R.V. (1991). The resumption of ovulation and menstruation in a well-nourished population of women breastfeeding for an extended period of time. *Fertility and Sterility, 55,* 529-36. Retrieved from www.sciencedirect.com/science/journal/00150282

Little, C.M. (2010a). Nursing considerations in the case of multifetal pregnancy reduction. *MCN: The American Journal of Maternal/Child Nursing, 35,* 166-71. doi:10.1097/NMC.0b013e3181d765bc

Little, C.M. (2010b). One consequence of infertility treatment: Multifetal pregnancy. *MCN: The American Journal of Maternal/Child Nursing, 35,* 150-55. doi:10.1097/NMC.0b013e3181d765a8

Liu, S., Liston, R.M., Joseph, K.S., Heaman, M., Sauve R., & Kramer, M.S. (2007). Maternal mortality and severe morbidity associated with low-risk planned cesarean delivery versus planned vaginal delivery at term. *Canadian Medical Association Journal, 176,* 475-6. doi:10.1503/cmaj.060870

Lok, I.H., & Neugebauer, R. (2007). Psychological morbidity following miscarriage. *Best Practice & Research Clinical Obstetrics & Gynaecology, 21,* 229-47. doi:10.1016/j.bpobgyn.2006.11.007

Lucas, A., Morley, R., Cole, T.J., Lister, G., & Leeson-Payne, C. (1992). Breastmilk and subsequent intelligence quotient in children born preterm. *Lancet, 339,* 261-4. doi:10.1016/0140-6736(92)91329-7

Markman, H. & Kadushin, F. (1986). Preventive effects of Lamaze training for first-time parents: A short-term longitudinal study. *Journal of Consulting & Clinical Psychology, 54,* 872-74. doi:10.1037/0022-006X.54.6.872

Martin, J.A., & Park, M.M. (1999). *Trends in twin and triplet births: 1980–1997* (National Vital Statistics Report), *47*(24), 1-16. Retrieved from the Center for Disease Control and Prevention website: www.cdc.gov/nchs/data/nvsr/nvsr47/nvs47_24.pdf

Masters, W.H., & Johnson, V.E. (1966). *Human sexual response.* Boston, MA: Little-Brown.

McClure, R., & Brewer, R.T. (1980). Attitudes of new parents towards child and spouse with Lamaze or non-Lamaze methods of childbirth. *Journal of Human Behavior, 17,* 45-8. Retrieved from www.eric.ed.gov/

Medical Research Council Vitamin Study Research Group (1991). Prevention of neural tube defects: Results of the Medical Research Council Vitamin Study Group. *Lancet, 338,* 131-37. doi:10.1016/0140-6736(91)90133-A

Nag, M. (1994). Beliefs and practices about food during pregnancy: Implication for maternal nutrition. *Economic and Political Weekly, 29,* 2427-28. Retrieved from www.epw.in/

O'Brien, B. Young, D., & Chalmers, B. (2009). Pain management. In Public Health Agency of Canada, *What mothers say: The Canadian maternity experiences survey* (pp. 146-51). Retrieved from www.phac-aspc.gc.ca/rhs-ssg/pdf/survey-eng.pdf

Pook, M., Roehrle, B., & Krause, W. (1999). Individual prognosis for changes in sperm quality on the basis of perceived stress. *Psychotherapy and Psychosomatics, 68,* 95-101. doi:10.1159/000012319

Primakoff, P., & Myles, D.G. (2002). Penetration, adhesion, and fusion in mammalian sperm–egg interaction. *Science, 296,* 2183-85. doi:10.1126/science.1072029

Public Health Agency of Canada. (2008). *Canadian perinatal health report.* Ottawa, ON: Author.

Public Health Agency of Canada. (2009). *What mothers say: The Canadian maternity experiences survey.* Ottawa, Ontario: Author. Retrieved from www.phac-aspc.gc.ca/rhs-ssg/pdf/survey-eng.pdf

Raman, A.V. (1988). Traditional practices and nutritional taboos: Effects on mothers and perinatal outcome. *Nursing Journal of India, 79,* 143-66. Retrieved from www.tnaionline.org/thenursing.htm

Rea, M. (2004). Benefits of breastfeeding and women's health. *Jornal de Pediatria (Rio J), 80* (Suppl. 5), S142-46. doi:10.2223/JPED.1247

Riordan, J. (2005). *Breastfeeding and human lactation.* Sudbury, MA: Jones & Bartlett.

Rousseau, S., Lord, J., Lepage, Y., & Van Campenhout, J. (1983). The expectancy of pregnancy for "normal" infertile couple. *Fertility & Sterility, 40,* 768-72. Retrieved from www.fertstert.org/

Rowland, M., Foxcroft, L., Hopman, W.M., & Patel, R. (2005). Breastfeeding and sexuality immediately postpartum. *Canadian Family Physician, 51,* 1367-73. Retrieved from www.cfp.ca/

Saisto, T., Salmela-Aro, K., Nurmi, J.E., Kononen, T., & Halmesmaki, E. (2001). A randomized controlled trial of intervention in fear of childbirth. *Obstetrics and Gynecology, 98,* 820-26. doi:10.1016/S0029-7844(01)01552-6

Samuels, M., & Samuels, M. (1986). *The well pregnancy book.* New York, NY: Simon & Schuster.

Sibai, B.M., Ewell, M., Levine, R.J., Klebanoff, M.A., Esterlitz, J., Catalano, P.M., Goldenberg, R.L., & Joffe, G. (1997). Risk factors associated with preeclampsia in healthy nulliparous women. *American Journal of Obstetrics & Gynecology, 177,* 1003-10. doi:10.1016/S0002-9378(97)70004-8

Signorello, L.B., Harlow, B.L., Chekos, A.K., & Repke, J.T. (2001). Postpartum sexual functioning and its relationship to perineal trauma: A retrospective cohort study of primiparous women. *American Journal of Obstetrics & Gynecology, 184,* 881–90. doi:10.1067/mob.2001.113855

Slade, P., Escott, D., Spiby, H., Henderson, B., & Fraser, R.B. (2000). Antenatal predictors and use of coping strategies in labour. *Psychology & Health, 15,* 555–69. doi:10.1080/08870440008402013

Society of Obstetricians and Gynecologists of Canada. (2004, March 10). SOGC's position on elective C-sections [Press release]. Retrieved from www.SOGC.org.

Spehr, M., Gisselmann, G., Poplawski, A., Riffell, J., Wetzel, C., Zimmer, R., & Hatt, H. (2003). Identification of a testicular odorant receptor mediating human sperm chemotaxis. *Science, 299,* 2054–57. doi:10.1126/science.1080376

Stanton, C., Lawn, J.E., Rahman, H., Wilczynska-Ketende, K., & Hill, K. (2006). Stillbirth rates: Delivering estimates in 190 countries. *Lancet, 367,* 1487–94. doi:10.1016/S0140-6736(06)68586-3

Stewart, D. (2006). Life stage: Perinatal. In N. Diaz-Granados, D. Stewart, & University Health Network Women's Health program 2006 (Eds), A *literature review on depression among women: Focussing on Ontario* (pp.47–54). Retrieved from www.ontla.on.ca/library/repository/mon/24010/304938.pdf

Sunderam, S., Chang, J., Flowers, L., Kulkarni, A., Sentelle, G., Jeng, G., & Macaluso, M. (2006). Assisted reproductive technology surveillance—United States, 2006. *Surveillance Summaries, 58*(SS05), 1–25. Retrieved from www.cdc.gov/mmwr/preview/mmwrhtml/ss5805a1.htm

Turton, P., Evans, C., & Hughes, P. (2009). Long-term psychosocial sequelae of stillbirth: Phase II of a nested case-control cohort study. *Archives of Women's Mental Health, 12,* 35–41. doi:10.1007/s00737-008-0040-7

Turton, P. Hughes, P., Evans, C.D.H, & Fainman, D. (2001). The incidence and significance of post-traumatic stress disorder in the pregnancy after stillbirth. *British Journal of Psychiatry, 178,* 556–60. doi:10.1192/bjp.178.6.556

von Sydow, K. (1999). Sexuality during pregnancy and after childbirth: A metacontent analysis of 59 studies. *Journal of Psychosomatic Research, 47,* 27–49. doi:10.1016/S0022-3999(98)00106-8

Wass, D.M., Brown, G.A., Warren, P.S., & Saville, T.A. (1991). Completed follow-up of 1,000 consecutive transcervical chorionic villus samplings performed by a single operator. *Australian and New Zealand Journal of Obstetrics and Gynecology, 31,* 240–45. doi:10.1111/j.1479-828X.1991.tb02790.x

Weigel, R.M., & Weigel, M.M. (1989). Nausea and vomiting of early pregnancy and pregnancy outcome. A meta-analytical review. BJOG: *An International Journal of Obstetrics & Gynaecology, 96,* 1312–18. doi:10.1111/j.1471-0528.1989.tb03229.x

Wilcox, A.J., Baird, D.D., & Weinberg, C.R. (1999). Time of implantation of the conceptus and loss of pregnancy. *New England Journal of Medicine, 340,* 1796–99. doi:10.1056/NEJM199906103402304

Wilmut, I., Schnieke, A.E., McWhir, J., Kind, A.K., & Campbell, K.H. (1997). Viable offspring derived from fetal and adult mammalian cells. *Cloning and Stem Cells, 9*(1), 3–7. doi:10.1089/clo.2006.0002

Winston, R. (1997). The promise of cloning for human medicine: Not a moral threat but an exciting challenge. *British Journal of Medicine, 314,* 913. doi:10.1136/bmj.314.7085.913

World Health Organization (1996, May 25). *Infant and young child nutrition* (World Health Assembly Resolution 49.15). Retrieved from www.who.int/nutrition/topics/WHA49.15_iycn_en.pdf

World Health Organization & UNICEF. (2003). *Global strategy for infant and young child feeding.* Geneva, Switzerland: Author.

Wortham, J. (2009, January 2). Facebook won't budge on breastfeeding photos. *The New York Times.* Retrieved from http://bits.blogs.nytimes.com/2009/01/02/breastfeeding-facebook-photos

Worthington, E., Martin, G., Shumate, M., & Carpenter, J. (1983). The effect of brief Lamaze training and social encouragement on pain endurance in a cold pressor tank. *Journal of Applied Social Psychology, 13,* 223–33. doi:10.1111/j.1559-1816.1983.tb01736.x

Zax, M., Sameroff, A.J., & Farum, J.E. (1975). Childbirth education, maternal attitudes, and delivery. *American Journal of Obstetrics & Gynecology, 123,* 185–90. Retrieved from www.ajog.org

CHAPTER 7

Adler, N.E., David, H.P., Major, B.N., Roth, S.H., Russo, N.F., & Wyatt, G.E. (1992). Psychological factors in abortion: A review. *American Psychologist, 47,* 1194–1204. doi:10.1037/0003-066X.47.10.1194

American Psychological Association. (1989, January 18). APA research review finds no evidence of "post-abortion syndrome" but research studies on psychological effects of abortion inconclusive [Press release].

Appleby, B.M. (1999). *Responsible parenthood: Decriminalizing contraception in Canada.* Toronto, ON: University of Toronto Press. Retrieved from www.jstor.org/stable/3712293

Arévalo, M., Jennings, V., & Sinai, I. (2002). Efficacy of a new method of family planning: The standard days method. *Contraception, 65,* 333–38. doi:10.1016/S0010-7824(02)00288-3

Ashok, P.W., Penney, G.C., Flett, G.M., & Templeton, A. (1998). An effective regimen for early medical abortion: A report of 2000 consecutive cases. *Human Reproduction, 13,* 2962–65. doi:10.1093/humrep/13.10.2962

Baochang, G., Wang, F., Zhigang, G., Zhang, E. (2007). China's local and national fertility policies at the end of the twentieth century. *Population and Development Review, 33,* 129–47. doi:10.1111/j.1728-4457.2007.00161.x

Barot, S. (2008). Making the case for a "contraceptive convenience" agenda. *Guttmacher Policy Review, 11.* Retrieved from www.guttmacher.org/pubs/gpr/11/4/gpr110411.html

Billy, J.O.G., Grady, W.R., & Sill, M.E. (2009). Sexual risk-taking among adult dating couples in the United States. *Perspectives on Sexual and Reproductive Health, 41,* 74–83. doi:10.1363/4107409

Bishop, M.F. (2011). Birth control. In J.H. Marsh (Ed.), *The Canadian Encyclopedia.* Retrieved from www.thecanadianencyclopedia.com/index.cfm?PgNm=TCE&Params=a1AR TA0000779

Black, A., Francoeur, D., & Rowe, T. (2004a). Canadian contraception consensus (Part 1). *Journal of Obstetrics and Gynaecology Canada, 26,* 143–56. Retrieved from www.sogc.org/guidelines/public/143E-CPG1-February2004.pdf

Black, A., Francoeur, D., & Rowe, T. (2004b). Canadian contraception consensus (Part 2). *Journal of Obstetrics and Gynaecology Canada, 26,* 219–54. Retrieved from www.sogc.org/jogc/index_e.asp

Black, A., Francoeur, D., & Rowe, T. (2004c). Canadian contraception consensus (Part 3). *Journal of Obstetrics and Gynaecology*

Canada, 26, 347–87. Retrieved from www.sogc.org/jogc/index_e.asp

Byrne, D., & Fisher, W.A. (1983). *Adolescents, sex, and contraception.* Hillsdale, NJ: Lawrence Erlbaum.

Canada Adopts. (2001). *Adopting in Canada: FAQs.* Retrieved from http://canadaadopts.com/canada/faqs.shtml

Canadian Federation for Sexual Health. (2009, August 28). *Diaphragm.* Retrieved from www.cfsh.ca/Your_Sexual_Health/Contraception-and-Safer-Sex/Contraception-and-Birth-Control/Diaphragm.aspx

Canadian Institute for Health Information. (2009). *Induced abortions reported in Canada in 2009.* Retrieved from www.cihi.ca/CIHI-ext-portal/pdf/internet/TA_09_ALLDATATABLES20111028_EN

Carter, J.A., McNair, L.D., Corbin, W.R., & Williams, M. (1999). Gender differences related to heterosexual condom use: The influence of negotiation styles. *Journal of Sex & Marital Therapy, 25,* 217–25. doi:10.1080/00926239908403996

Chalmers, B. (1990). *African birth: Childbirth in cultural transition.* Sandton, South Africa: Berev.

Chalmers, B., Sand, M., Muggah, H., Oblivanova, L., Almazova, N., & Tkatchenko, E. (1998). Contraceptive knowledge, attitudes and use among women attending health clinics in St. Petersburg, Russian Federation. *The Canadian Journal of Human Sexuality, 7,* 129–37. Retrieved from www.sieccan.org/cjhs.html

Clifton, D., Kaneda, T., & Ashford, L. (2008). *Family planning worldwide: 2008 data sheet.* Washington, DC: Population Reference Bureau. Retrieved from www.prb.org/pdf08/fpds08.pdf

Cohen, S. (2009). Facts and consequences: Legality, incidence, and safety of abortion worldwide. *Guttmacher Policy Review, 12.* Retrieved from www.guttmacher.org/pubs/gpr/12/4/gpr120402.html

Collier, A. (2007). *The humble little condom: A history.* Amherst, NY: Prometheus Books.

Connell, E.B. (1999). Contraception in the prepill era. *Contraception, 59*(Suppl. 1), 7S–10S. doi:10.1016/S0010-7824(98)00130-9

Cooper, M.L. (2010). Toward a person × situation model of sexual risk-taking behaviors: Illuminating the conditional effects of traits across sexual situations and relationship contexts. *Journal of Personality and Social Psychology, 98,* 319–41. doi:10.1037/a0017785

Cunningham, G.R., Silverman, V.E., Thornby, J., Kohler, P.O. (1979). The potential for an androgen male contraceptive. *Journal of Clinical Endocrinology and Metabolism, 49,* 520–26.

Delaney, J., Lupton, M.J. & Toth, E. (1988). *The curse. A cultural history of menstruation.* Champaign, IL: First University of Illinois Press.

Delbanco, T.L., & Daley, J. (1996). Through the patient's eyes: Strategies toward more successful contraception. *Obstetrics and Gynaecology, 88*(Suppl. 3), 41S–7S. doi:10.1016/0029-7844(96)00243-8

Dixon-Mueller, R. (1993). *Population policy & women's rights: Transforming reproductive choice.* Santa Barbara, CA: ABC-CLIO.

Dryburgh, H. (2007). *Teenage pregnancy.* Statistics Canada Health Reports (No. 82-003). Ottawa, ON: Statistics Canada. Retrieved from www.statcan.gc.ca/kits-trousses/preg-gross/preg-gross-eng.htm

EKOS. (2010). *Canadians decisively pro-choice on abortion.* Ottawa: Author. Retrieved from www.ekospolitics.com/wp-content/uploads/full_report_april_11.pdf

Elam-Evans, L.D., Strauss, L.T., Herndon, J., Parker, W.Y., Whitehead, S., & Berg, C.J. (2002). Abortion surveillance—United States, 1999. *Morbidity Mortality Weekly Report, 51*(SS09), 1–28. Retrieved from Centers for Disease Control and Prevention website: www.cdc.gov/mmwr/preview/mmwrhtml/ss5109a1.htm

Finer, L.B., Frohwirth, L.F., Dauphinee, L.A., Singh, S., & Moore, A.M. (2005). Reasons US women have abortions: Quantitative and qualitative perspectives. *Perspectives on Sexual and Reproductive Health, 37,* 110–18. doi:10.1363/3711005

Fisher, W.A., Boroditsky, R., & Morris, B. (2004). The 2002 Canadian contraception study. *Journal of Obstetrics and Gynaecology Canada, 26,* 580–90. Part 1 retrieved from http://sexualityandu.ca/uploads/files/2002ContraceptionStudy_JOGC.pdf; Part 2 retrieved from www.sogc.org/jogc/index_e.asp

Fisher, W.A., & Fisher, J.D. (2003). The information-motivation-behavioural skills model as a general model of health behaviour change: Theoretical approaches to individual-level change. In J. Suls & K. Wallston (Eds), *Social psychological foundations of health.* Cambridge, MA: Blackwell.

Fisher, W.A., Grenier, G., Watters, W.W., Lamont, J., Cohen, M., & Askwith, J. (1988). Students' sexual knowledge, attitudes towards sex, and willingness to treat sexual concerns. *Journal of Medical Education, 63,* 379–96. Retrieved from www.jmededu.com/

Freedman, L.P., & Issacs, S.L. (1993). Human rights and reproductive choice. *Studies in Family Planning, 24,* 18–30. doi:10.2307/j100383

Glasier, A., Fairhurst, K., Wyke, S., Ziebland, S., Seaman, P., Walker, J., & Lakha, F. (2004). Advanced provision of emergency contraception does not reduce abortion rates. *Contraception, 69,* 361–66. doi:10.1016/j.contraception.2004.01.002

Gu, Y., Liang, X., Wu, W., Liu, M., Song, S., Cheng, L., . . . Yao, K. (2009). Multicenter contraceptive efficacy trial of injectable testosterone undecanoate in Chinese men. *Journal of Clinical Endocrinology & Metabolism, 94,* 1910–15. doi:10.1210/jc.2008-1846

Guttmacher Institute. (2012). *Facts on Induced Abortion Worldwide.* New York, NY: Author & WHO. Retrieved from www.who.int/reproductivehealth/publications/unsafe_abortion/induced_abortion_2012.pdf

Harris, M. (1977). *Cannibals and kings: The origins of cultures.* New York, NY: Random House.

Hatcher, R.A., Trussell, J., & Nelson, A.L. (Eds). (2007). *Contraceptive technology* (19th ed.). New York, NY: Ardent Media.

Heinemann, K., Saad, F., Wiesemes, M., White, S., & Heinemann, L. (2005). Attitudes toward male fertility control: Results of a multinational survey on four continents. *Human Reproduction, 20,* 549–56. doi:10.1093/humrep/deh574

Holt, V.L., Cushing-Haugen, K.L., & Daling, J.R. (2002). Body weight and risk of oral contraceptive failure. *Obstetrics & Gynecology, 99,* 820–27. doi:10.1016/S0029-7844(02)01939-7

Huang, Y., & Yang, D.L. (2006). China's unbalanced sex ratios: Politics and policy response. *The Chinese Historical Review, 13,* 1–15. Retrieved from www.chss.iup.edu/chr

Hynie, M., MacDonald, T.K., Marques, S. (2006). Self-conscious emotions and self-regulation in the promotion of condom use. *Personality and Social Psychology Bulletin*, 32, 1072–84. doi:10.1177/0146167206288060

Information Office of the State Council of the People's Republic of China. (1995). *Family planning in China: Social undertaking that benefits the people* [White paper]. Retrieved from www.china.org.cn/e-white/familypanning/13-3.htm

Johnston, W.R. (2005, August 13). *Worldwide abortion legislation.* Retrieved from www.johnstonsarchive.net/policy/abortion/wrjp335al.html

Jones, A. (2009). *Gendercide watch.* Retrieved from www.gendercide.org

Jones, R.K., Darroch, J.E., & Henshaw S.K. (2002). Contraceptive use among US women having abortions in 2000–2001. *Perspectives on Sexual and Reproductive Health*, 34, 294–303.

Kalmuss, D.S., & Namerow, P.B. (1994). Subsequent childbearing among teenage mothers: The determinants of closely spaced second birth. *Family Planning Perspectives*, 26(4), 149–53. doi:10.2307/2136238

Lei, M.L.S., Robson, S.C., & May, C.R. (2008). Experiences of abortion: A narrative review of qualitative studies. *BMC Health Services Research*, 8, 150–9. doi:10.1186/1472-6963-8-150

Lim, L. (2007, April 23). Cases of forced abortions surface in China. *NPR News.* Retrieved from www.npr.org

Lopez, A. (2011, June 6). North Carolina state senate approves bill requiring women to view ultrasound before abortion. *The Washington Independent.* Retrieved from http://washingtonindependent.com

MacDonald, N.E., Wells, G.A., Fisher, W.A., Warren, W.K., King, M.A., Doherty, J.A., & Bowie, W.R. (1990). High-risk STD/HIV behavior among college students. *The Journal of the American Medical Association*, 263, 3155–9. doi:10.1001/jama.1990.03440230051031

Major, B., Appelbaum, M., Beckman, L., Dutton, M., Russo, N.F., & West C. (2009). Abortion and mental health: Evaluating the evidence. *American Psychologist*, 64, 863–90. doi:10.1037/a0017497

Mitchinson, W. (1991). *The nature of their bodies: Women and their doctors in Victorian Canada.* Toronto, ON: University of Toronto Press.

Mrozek, A. (2011, March 10). *Making a mess of abortion statistics.* E-Review, 11(5). Retrieved from www.imfcanada.org/article_files/eReview_March_10_11.pdf

National Institutes of Health, US National Library of Medicine. (2011). *Tubal ligation.* Retrieved from www.nlm.nih.gov/medlineplus/ency/article/002913.htm

National Population and Family Planning Commission of China. (2010, March 29). *Most people want two children, survey says.* Retrieved from www.npfpc.gov.cn/international/pnews/201202/t20120220_381664.html

Nieschlag, E. (2010). Clinical trials in male hormonal contraception. *Contraception*, 82, 457–70. doi:10.1016/j.contraception.2010.03.020

Oudshoorn, N. (1999). On masculinities, technologies, and pain: The testing of male contraceptives in the clinic and the media. *Science, Technology, & Human Values*, 24, 265–89. doi:10.1177/016224399902400204

Population Reference Bureau. (2008). *Family planning worldwide: 2008 data sheet.* Retrieved from www.prb.org/pdf08/fpds08.pdf

Redmond, G., Godwin, A.J., Olson, W., Lippman, J.S. (1999). Use of placebo controls in an oral contraceptive trial: Methodological issues and adverse event incidence. *Contraception*, 60, 81–5. doi.org/10.1016/S0010-7824(99)00069-4

Roumen, F.J., Apter, D., Mulders, T.M., & Dieben, T.O. (2001). Efficacy, tolerability, and acceptability of a novel contraceptive vaginal ring releasing etonogestrel and ethinyl oestradiol. *Human Reproduction*, 16(3), 469–75.

Royal College of Obstetricians and Gynaecologists. (2004). *Male and female sterilisation: Evidence-based clinical guideline number 4.* London, UK: RCOG Press. Retrieved from www.rcog.org.uk/files/rcog-corp/uploaded-files/NEBSterilisationFull060607.pdf

Sedgh, G., Henshaw, S.K., Singh, S., Bankole, A., & Drescher, J. (2007). Legal abortion worldwide: Incidence and recent trends. *International Family Planning Perspectives*, 33, 106–16. doi:10.1363/3310607

Singh, S. (2006). Hospital admissions resulting from unsafe abortion: Estimates from 13 developing countries. *Lancet*, 368, 1887–92. doi:10.1016/S0140-6736(06)69778-X

Singh, S., Darroch, J.E., Vlassoff, M., & Nadeau, J. (2004). *Adding it up: The Benefits of Investing in Sexual and Reproductive Health Care.* New York: UNFPA/Alan Guttmacher Institute. Retrieved from http://siteresources.worldbank.org/INTPRH/Resources/376374-1261312056980/RHAP_Pub_8-23-10web.pdf

Singh, S., Wulf, D., Hussain, R., Bankole, A., & Sedgh, G. (2009). *Abortion worldwide: A decade of uneven progress.* Retrieved from Guttmacher Institute website: www.guttmacher.org/pubs/Abortion-Worldwide.pdf

Statistics Canada. (1999). *National population health survey data file: Custom tabulations* (Catalogue No. 82C0013). Ottawa, ON: Statistics Canada.

Task Force on Postovulatory Methods of Fertility Regulation. (1998). Randomized controlled trial of levonorgestrel versus the Yuzpe regimen of combined oral contraceptives for emergency contraception. *Lancet*, 352, 424–33. doi:10.1016/S0140-6736(98)05145-9

Taylor, J. (2005, February 8). *China—One child policy* [Transcript]. Sydney, Australia: Australian Broadcasting Company. Retrieved from www.abc.net.au/

Thomas, J.W., & Grindle, M.S. (1990, February). *National priorities and individual responses: The political economy of police reform.* Paper presented at the conference on the Politics of Induced Fertility Change in Developing Countries, Bellagio, Italy.

Tone, A. (2001). *Devices and desires: A history of contraceptives in America.* New York, NY: Hill and Wang.

Townsend, J.W., Sitruk-Ware, R., Williams, K., Askew, I., & Brill, K. (2011). New strategies for providing hormonal contraception in developing countries. *Contraception*, 83, 405–9. doi:10.1016/j.contraception.2010.08.015

Trussell, J. (2007a). Contraceptive efficacy. In R.A. Hatcher, J. Trussell, & A.L. Nelson (Eds), *Contraceptive technology* (19th ed., pp. 747–56). New York, NY: Ardent Media.

Trussell, J. (2007b). Choosing a contraceptive: Efficacy, safety, and personal considerations. In R.A. Hatcher, J. Trussell, A.L. Nelson, W. Cates, Jr, F.H. Stewart, & D. Kowal. *Contraceptive technology* (19th rev. ed., pp. 19–48). New York, NY: Ardent Media.

United Nations, Department of Economic and Social Affairs, Population Division. (2006). *World contraceptive use 2005* (UN Publication No. ST/ESA/SER.A/235). Retrieved from www

.un.org/esa/population/publications/contraceptive2005/2005_World_Contraceptive_files/WallChart_WCU2005.pdf

United Nations, Millennium Development Goals Indicators. (2010). *Condom use to overall contraceptive use among currently married women 15–49 years old, percentage* [Data file]. Retrieved from http://unstats.un.org/unsd/mdg/SeriesDetail.aspx?srid=733

Vignetta, C.E., Polis, C.B., Sridhara, S.K., & Blum, R.W. (2008). Abortion and long-term mental health outcomes: A systematic review of the evidence. *Contraception, 78,* 436–50. doi:10.1016/j.contraception.2008.07.005

Vlassoff, M., Walker, D., Shearer, J., Newlands, D., & Singh, S. (2009). Estimates of health care system costs of unsafe abortion in Africa and Latin America. *International Perspectives on Sexual and Reproductive Health, 35*(3), 114–22. doi:10.1363/3511409

Weller, S.C., Davis-Beaty, K. (2002). Condom effectiveness in reducing heterosexual HIV transmission. *Cochrane Database of Systematic Reviews, 1,* 1–22. doi:10.1002/14651858.CD003255

Wilcox, A.J., Dunson, D., & Baird, D.D. (2000). The timing of the "fertility window" in the menstrual cycle: Day specific estimates from a prospective study. *British Medical Journal, 321,* 1259. doi:10.1136/bmj.321.7271.1259

World Health Organization. (2001). *Improving access to quality care in family planning: Medical eligibility for contraceptive use* (2nd ed.). Geneva, Switzerland: Author.

Wu, F., & Arthur, J. (2010). *A survey of anti-choice protesting activity at Canadian abortion clinics.* Retrieved from Abortion Rights Coalition of Canada website: www.arcc-cdac.ca/presentations/ARCC-survey-protest-activity.pdf

Youssef, H. (1993). The history of the condom. *Journal of the Royal Society of Medicine, 86,* 226–8.

Zietsch, B.P., Verweij, K.J.H., Bailey, J.M., Wright, M.J., Martin, N.G. (2010). Genetic and environmental influences on risky sexual behavior and its relationship with personality. *Behavior Genetics, 40,* 12–21. doi:10.1007/s10519-009-9300-1

CHAPTER 8

Abdool Karim, Q., Abdool Karim, S.S., Frohlich, J.A., Grobler, A.C., Baxter, C., Mansoor, L.E., . . . Taylor, D. (2010). Effectiveness and safety of Tenofovir gel, an antiretroviral microbicide, for the prevention of HIV infection in women. *Science, 329,* 1168–74. doi:10.1126/science/1193748

ACT UP (AIDS Coalition to Unleash Power). (2011). [Website]. Retrieved from www.actupny.org

Bailey, R.C., Moses, S., Parker, C.B., Agot, K., Maclean, I., Krieger, J.N., . . . Ndinya-Achola, J.O. (2007). Male circumcision for HIV prevention in young men in Kisumu, Kenya: A randomised controlled trial. *Lancet, 369*(9562), 643–56. doi:10.1016/S0140-6736(07)60312-2

Bangsberg, D.R., & Deeks S.G. (2002). Is average adherence to HIV antiretroviral therapy enough? *Journal of General Internal Medicine, 17,* 812–13. doi:10.1046/j.1525-1497.2002.20812.x

Bayer, R., & Oppenheim, G.M. (2000). *AIDS doctors: Voices from the epidemic.* Oxford, England: Oxford University Press.

Burchell, A.N., Tellier, P.P., Hanley, J., Coutlee, F., & Franco, E.L. (2010). Human papillomavirus infections among couples in new sexual relationships. *Epidemiology, 21*(1), 31–7. doi:10.1097/EDE.0b103e3181c1e70b

Canadian AIDS Society. (2011a). *How do you get HIV (or not get HIV?).* Retrieved from www.cdnaids.ca/howdoyougethivornotgethiv

Canadian AIDS Society. (2011b). *How can I have sex more safely?* Retrieved from www.cdnaids.ca/howcanihavesexmoresafely

Canadian Cancer Society. (2011, September 14). *Treatment for cervical cancer.* Retrieved from www.cancer.ca/Canada-wide/About%20cancer/Types%20of%20cancer/Treatment%20for%20cervical%20cancer.aspx?sc_lang=en

Centers for Disease Control and Prevention. (2001). *AIDS cases and deaths, by year and age group, through December 2001.* Retrieved from www.cdc.gov/hiv/topics/surveillance/resources/reports/2001report/table21

Centers for Disease Control and Prevention. (2004). *Syringe disinfection for injection drug users.* Retrieved from www.cdc.gov/idu/facts/disinfection.pdf

Centers for Disease Control and Prevention. (2005). *Antiretroviral postexposure prophylaxis after sexual, injection-drug use, or other nonoccupational exposure to HIV in the United States.* Retrieved from www.cdc.gov/mmwr/preview/mmwrhtml/rr5402a1.htm

Centers for Disease Control and Prevention. (2010). [General letter]. Retrieved from www.cdc.gov/hiv/ehap/resources/direct/112310/hcp.htm

Centers for Disease Control and Prevention. (2011a). *Male latex condoms and sexually transmitted diseases.* Retrieved from www.cdc.gov/condomeffectiveness/latex.htm

Centers for Disease Control and Prevention. (2011b). *Viral hepatitis.* Retrieved from www.cdc.gov/hepatitis

Centers for Disease Control and Prevention. (2011c). *Bacterial vaginosis—CDC fact sheet.* Retrieved from www.cdc.gov/std/bv/stdfact-bacterial-vaginosis.htm

Chen, L.F., Hoy, J., & Lewin, S.R. (2007). Ten years of highly active antiretroviral therapy for HIV infection. *Medical Journal of Australia, 186*(3), 146–51.

Chin, J. (2007). *The AIDS pandemic: The collision of epidemiology with political correctness.* Oxford, England: Radcliffe.

Conway, B. (2007). The role of adherence to antiretroviral therapy in the management of HIV infection. *Journal of Acquired Immune Deficiency Syndromes, 45*(Suppl. 1), 14–8. doi:10.1097/QAI.0b13e80600766

Cornman, D.H., Kiene, S.C., Christie, S., Fisher, W.A., Shuper, P.A., Pillay, S., . . . & Fisher, J.D. (2008). Clinic-based intervention reduces unprotected sexual behavior among HIV-infected patients in Kwazulu-Natal, South Africa: Results of a Pilot Study. *Journal of Acquired Immune Deficiency Syndromes, 48*(5), 553–60. doi:10.1097/QAI.0b013e31817bebd7

Darrow W.W. (1998 [1977]). A few minutes with Venus, a lifetime with Mercury. In G.G. Brannigan, E.R. Allgeier, & A.R. Allgeier (Eds), *The sex scientists* (pp. 156–70). New York, NY: Addison, Wesley, Longman.

Darrow, W.W., Montanea, J.E., Fernandez, P.B., Zucker, U.F., Stephens, D.P., & Gladwin, H. (2004). Eliminating disparities in HIV disease: Community mobilization to prevent HIV transmission among Black & Hispanic young adults in Broward County, Florida. *Ethnicity & Disease, 14,* 108–16.

Dempsey, A.F., Gebremariam, A, Koutsky, L.A., & Manhart, L. (2008). Using risk factors to predict human papillomavirus infection: Implications for targeted vaccination strategies in young adult women. *Vaccine, 26*(8), 1111–17. doi:10.1016/j.vaccine.2007.11.088

Drolet, M., Brisson, M., Maunsell, E., Franco, E.L., Coutlée, F., Ferenczy, A. . . . Mansi, J.A. (2011). The impact of anogenital warts on health-related quality of life: A 6-month prospective study. *Sexually Transmitted Diseases, 38*(10), 949–56. doi:10.1097/OLQ.0b013e3182215512

D'Souza, G., Kreimer, A.R., Viscidi, R., Pawlita, M., Fakhry, C., Koch, W.M., . . . Gillison, M.L. (2010). Case-control study of human papillomavirus and oropharyngeal cancer. *New England Journal of Medicine, 356*, 1944–56.

Eurosurveillance Editorial Team. (2008). Swiss study suggests condom use not necessary for some HIV-positive patients. *Eurosurveillance, 13*(6). Retrieved from www.eurosurveillance.org/ViewArticle.aspx?ArticleId=8035

Fallopio, G. (1564). *De morbo Gallico liber absolutusmus*. Pavia, Italy.

Fischl, M.A., Dickinson, G.M., Scott, G.B., Kimas, N., Fletcher, M.A., & Parks, W. (1987). Evaluation of heterosexual partners, children, and household contacts of adults with AIDS. *Journal of the American Medical Association, 257*, 640–44. doi:10.1001/jama.1987.033900500266020

Fisher, J.D., Cornman, D.H., Norton, W.E., & Fisher, W.A. (2006). Involving behavioral scientists, health care providers, and HIV-infected patients as collaborators in theory-based HIV prevention and antiretroviral adherence interventions. *Journal of Acquired Immune Deficiency Syndrome, 43*(1), 10–17. doi:10.1097/01.qai.0000248335.90190.f9

Fisher, J.D., Cornman, D.H., Shuper, P.A., Christie, S., Pillay, S., MacDonald, S., . . . Fisher, W.A. (2012, July). *HIV prevention counseling intervention delivered during routine clinical care reduces HIV transmission risk behavior in HIV-infected South Africans receiving antiretroviral therapy: The Izindlela Zokuphila/Options for Health randomized trial*. International AIDS Conference, Washington, DC.

Fisher, J.D., Fisher, W.A., Cornman, D.H., Amico, K.R., Bryan, A., & Friedland, G.H. (2006). Clinician-delivered intervention during routine clinical care reduces unprotected sexual behavior among HIV-infected patients. *Journal of Acquired Immune Deficiency Syndrome, 41*(1), 44–52. doi:10.1097/01.qai.0000192000.15777.5c

Fisher, J.D., Fisher, W.A., & Shuper, P.A. (2009). The information motivation behavioral skills model of HIV preventive behavior. In R. DiClemente, R. Crosby, & M. Kegler (Eds), *Emerging theories in health promotion practice and research model of HIV preventive behavior* (2nd ed., pp. 22–63). San Francisco, CA: Jossey Bass.

Fisher, W.A. (1997). Do no harm: On the ethics of testosterone replacement therapy for persons carrying a lethal sexually transmitted disease. *Journal of Sex Research, 34*(1), 35–8. doi:10.1080/00224499709551862

Fisher, W.A., & Boroditsky, R. (2000). Sexual activity, contraceptive choice, and reproductive health risk among single Canadian women aged 15–19: Additional findings from the Canadian contraceptive study. *Canadian Journal of Human Sexuality, 9*(2), 79–93.

Fisher, W.A., Kohut, T., & Fisher, J.D. (2009). AIDS exceptionalism: On the social psychology of HIV prevention research. *Social Issues and Policy Review, 3*(1), 45–77. doi:10.1111/j.1751-2409.2009.01010.x

Fumaz, C.R., Munoz-Moreno, J., Molto, J., Ferrer, M.J., Lopez-Blazquez, R., Negredo, E., . . . Clotet, B. (2008). Sustained antiretroviral treatment adherence in survivors of the pre-HAART era: Attitudes and beliefs. *AIDS Care, 20*, 796–805. doi:10.1080/09540120701694022

Gay Men's Health Crisis. (2011). [Website]. Retrieved from www.gmhc.org

Gillison, M., Ang, K.K., Harris, J., Wheeler, R., Weber, R., Rosenthal, D.I., . . . Gillison, M.L. (2010). Human papillomavirus and survival of patients with oropharyngeal cancer. *New England Journal of Medicine, 363*(1), 24–35. doi:10.1056/NEJMoa0912217

Grant, R.M., Lama, J.R., Anderson, P.L., McMahan, V., Liu, A.Y., Vargas, L., . . . Glidden, D.V. (2010). Preexposure chemoprophylaxis for HIV prevention in men who have sex with men. *New England Journal of Medicine, 363*, 2587–99. doi:10.1056/NEJMoa1011205

Gulli, C. (2007, August 27). Our girls are not guinea pigs. *Macleans.ca*. Retrieved from www.macleans.ca/science/health/article.jsp?content=20070827_108312_108312

Hahn, B.H., Shaw, G.M., De Cock, K.M., & Sharp, P.M. (2000). AIDS as a zoonosis: Scientific and public health implications. *Science, 287*, 607–14. doi : 10.1126/science.287.5453.607

Thomas, E., and Maddin, S. (2011). *Herpes guide: How do I know if I have herpes?* Retrieved from www.herpesguide.ca

Karon, J.M., Fleming, P.L., Steketee, R.W., & De Cock, K.M. (2001). HIV in the United States at the turn of the century: An epidemic in transition. *American Journal of Public Health, 91*, 1060–68.

Kleeberger, C.A., Buechner, J., Palella, F., Detels, R., Riddler, S., Godfrey, R., & Jacobsen L.P. (2004). Changes in adherence to highly active antiretroviral therapy medications in the Multicenter AIDS Cohort Study. *AIDS, 18*, 683–8. doi:10.1097/00002030-200403050-00013

Korber, B., Muldoon, M., Theiler, J., Gao, F., Gupta, R., Lapedes, A., . . . Bhattacharya, T. (2000). Timing the ancestor of the HIV-1 pandemic strains. *Science, 288*, 1789–96. doi:10.1126/science.288.5472.1789

Lazo, M., Gange, S.J., Wilson, T.E., Anastos, K., Ostrow, D.G., Witt, M.D., Jacobson, L.P. (2007). Patterns and predictors of changes in adherence to highly active antiretroviral therapy: Longitudinal study of men and women. *Clinical Infectious Diseases, 45*, 1377–85. doi:10.1086/522762

Lippman, A., Melnychuk, R. Shimmin, C., & Boscoe, M. (2007). Human papillomavirus, vaccines and women's health: Questions and cautions. *Canadian Medical Association Journal, 177*(5), 484–7. doi:10.1503/cmaj.070944

MacDonald, N.E., Wells, G.A., Fisher, W.A., Warren, W.K., King, M.A., Doherty, J.A., & Bowie, W.R. (1990). High risk STD/HIV behaviour among college students. *Journal of the American Medical Association, 263*, 3155–9. doi:10.1001/jama.1990.03440230051031

Manhart, L.E., & Koutsky, L.A. (2002). Do condoms prevent genital HPV infection, external genital warts, or cervical neoplasia? A meta-analysis. *Sexually Transmitted Diseases, 29*(11), 725–35. doi:10.1097/00007435-200211000-00018

Nahmias, A.J., Weiss, J., Yao, X., Lee, F., Kodsi, R., Schanfield, M., Mathews, T., . . . Essex, M. (1986). Evidence for human infection with an HTLV III/LAV-like virus in Central Africa, 1959. *Lancet, 31*, 1279–80. doi:10.1016/S0140-6736(86)91422-4

Nasman, A., Attner, P., Hammarstedt, L., Du, J., Eriksson, M., Giraud, G., . . . Dalianis, T. (2009). Incidence of human papillomavirus (HPV) positive tonsillar carcinoma in Stockholm, Sweden: An epidemic of viral-induced carcinoma? *International Journal of Cancer, 125*(2), 362–6.

National Institutes of Health. (2011). *AIDS info: Guidelines for the use of antiretroviral agents in HIV-1-infected adults and adolescents*. Retrieved from http://aidsinfo.nih.gov/contentfiles/AdultandAdolescentGL.pdf

Paterson, D.L., Swindells, S., Mohr, J., Brester, M., Vergis, E.N., Squier, C., . . . Singh, N. (2000). Adherence to protease inhibitor therapy and outcomes in patients with HIV infection. *Annals of Internal Medicine, 133*, 21–30

Pirotta, M.V., Ung, L., Stein, A.N., Conway, L., Fairley, C.K., & Garland, S.M. (2009). Patterns of treatment of external genital warts in Australian sexual health clinics. *Sexually Transmitted Diseases, 36*(6), 375–9. doi:10.1136/sti.2009.037028

Pubic Health Agency of Canada. (2010). *Canadian guidelines on sexually transmitted infections.* Retrieved from www.phac-aspc.gc.ca/std-mts/sti-its/index-eng.php

Public Health Agency of Canada (2011a). *Reported cases and rates of chlamydia by age group and sex, 1991 to 2009.* Retrieved from www.phac-aspc.gc.ca/std-mts/sti-its_tab/chlamydia-eng.php

Public Health Agency of Canada. (2011b). *Surveillance Report to December 31, 2009.* Retrieved from www.phac-aspc.gc.ca/aids-sida/publication/survreport/2009/dec/8-eng.php

Pubic Health Agency of Canada. (2011c). Summary: Estimates of HIV prevalence and incidence in Canada, 2011. Retrieved from www.phac-aspc.gc.ca/aids-sida/publication/survreport/estimat2011-eng.php

Public Health Agency of Canada. (2011d). *Report on sexually transmitted infections in Canada: 2008.* Retrieved from www.phac-aspc.gc.ca/std-mts/report/sti-its2008/PDF/10-047-STI_report_eng-r1.pdf

Public Health Agency of Canada. (2011e). *Sexually transmitted infections: risk rater.* Retrieved from www.phac-aspc.gc.ca/publicat/std-mts/risk-eng.php#b

Public Health Agency of Canada. (2011f). *Sexually transmitted infections: Chlamydia.* Retrieved from www.phac-aspc.gc.ca/publicat/std-mts/chlam-eng.php

Public Health Agency of Canada. (2011g). *Sexually transmitted infections: Gonorrhea.* Retrieved from www.phac-aspc.gc.ca/publicat/std-mts/gonor-eng.php

Public Health Agency of Canada. (2011h). *Sexually transmitted infections: Syphilis.* Retrieved from www.phac-aspc.gc.ca/publicat/std-mts/syphilis-eng.php

Public Health Agency of Canada. (2011i). *Sexually transmitted infections: Herpes.* Retrieved from www.phac-aspc.gc.ca/publicat/std-mts/herpes-eng.php

Public Health Agency of Canada. (2011j). *Sexually transmitted infections: HPV.* Retrieved from www.phac-aspc.gc.ca/publicat/std-mts/hpv-eng.php

Public Health Agency of Canada. (2011k). *Statement on human papillomavirus vaccine.* Retrieved from www.phac-aspc.gc.ca/publicat/ccdr-rmtc/07vol33/acs-02

Public Health Agency of Canada. (2011l). *HIV/AIDS epi updates—July 2010: Chapter 1.* Retrieved from www.phac-aspc.gc.ca/aids-sida/publication/epi/2010/1-eng.php

Public Health Agency of Canada. (2011m). *Hepatitis.* Retrieved from www.phac-aspc.gc.ca/hep/index-eng.php#1

Public Health Agency of Canada. (2011n). *Trichomonas vaginalis.* Retrieved from www.phac-aspc.gc.ca/lab-bio/res/psds-ftss/trichomonas-eng.php

Public Health Agency of Canada. (2011o). *Sexually transmitted infections: Pubic Lice & Scabies.* Retrieved from www.phac-aspc.gc.ca/publicat/std-mts/pubic-eng.php

Public Health Agency of Canada. (2012). *Update on human papillomavirus (HPV) vaccines.* Retrieved from www.phac-aspc.gc.ca/publicat/ccdr-rmtc/12vol38/acs-dcc-1/index-eng.php#a5

Richardson, H., Kelsall, G., Tellier, P., Voyer, H., Abrahamowicz, M., Ferenczy, A., Coutlee, F., & Franco, E.L. (2003). The natural history of type-specific human papillomavirus infections in female university students. *Cancer Epidemiology, Biomarkers, and Prevention, 12*, 485–90.

Sepkowitz, K.A. (2001). AIDS—the first 20 years. *New England Journal of Medicine, 344*, 1764–72. doi:10.1056/NEJM200106073442306

Sexually transmitted disease (STD). (2013). In *Encyclopaedia Britannica.* Retrieved from www.britannica.com/EBchecked/topic/537217/sexually-transmitted-disease-STD

Shilts, R. (1987). *And the band played on: People, politics, and the AIDS epidemic.* New York, NY: St Martin's Press.

Society of Obstetricians and Gynaecologists of Canada. (2007, August 14). SOGC position statement on CMAJ commentary, "Human papillomavirus, vaccines and women's health: questions and cautions." Retrieved from www.sogc.org/media/guidelines-hpv-commentary_e.asp

Stall, R., & Mills, T.C. (2006). A quarter century of AIDS [Editorial]. *American Journal of Public Health, 96*, 959–61. doi:10.2105/AJPH.2006.089086

Steben, M., & Duarte-Franco, E. (2007). Human papillomavirus infection: Epidemiology and pathophysiology. *Gynecological Oncology, 107*, S2–S5. doi:10.1016/j.ygyno.2007.07.067

UNAIDS. (2012). *Global report: UNAIDS report on the global AIDS epidemic 2012.* Retrieved from www.unaids.org/en/media/unaids/contentassets/documents/epidemiology/2012/gr2012/20121120_UNAIDS_Global_Report_2012_en.pdf

University of California San Francisco Medical Center. (2011). *Viral hepatitis treatment.* Retrieved from www.ucsfhealth.org/conditions/viral_hepatitis/treatment.html

Wagner, G., Rabkin, J., & Rabkin, R. (1997a). Effects of testosterone replacement therapy on sexual interest, function, and behavior in HIV+ Men. *The Journal of Sex Research, 34*, 27–33. doi:10.1080/00224499709551861

Wagner, G., Rabkin, J., & Rabkin, R. (1997b). Response to commentaries. *Journal of Sex Research, 34*(1), 37. doi:10.1080/00224499709551864

Williams, S., Kimble, D., Covell, N., Weiss, L., Newton, K., Fisher, J., & Fisher, W.A. (1992). College students use implicit personality theory instead of safer sex. *Journal of Applied Social Psychology, 22*, 921–33. doi:10.1111/j.1559-1816.1992.tb00934.x

Winer, R.L., Hughes, J.P., Feng, Q., O'Reilly, S., Kiviat, N.B., Holmes, K.K., & Koutsky, L.A. (2006). Condom use and the risk of genital human papillomavirus infection in young women. *New England Journal of Medicine, 354*, 2645–54. doi:10.1056/NEJMoa053284

World Health Organization. (2007). *Female condom technical review committee summary report on FC2.* Retrieved from http://whqlibdoc.who.int/hq/2007/WHO_RHR_07.19_eng.pdf

CHAPTER 9

Ainsworth, M.D.S. (1973). The development of infant–mother attachment. In B. Caldwell & H. Ricciuti (Eds), *Review of child development research* (vol. 3, pp. 1–94). Chicago, IL: University of Chicago Press.

Allen, E.S., Atkins, D.C., Baucom, D.H., Snyder, D.K., Gordon, K.C., & Glass, S.P. (2005). Intrapersonal, interpersonal, and contextual factors in engaging in and responding to extramarital involvement. *Clinical Psychology: Science and Practice, 12,* 101–30. doi:10.1093/clipsy.bpi014

American Congress of Obstetricians and Gynecologists. (2010). *Midlife transitions: Perimenopause to menopause.* Retrieved from www.acog.org/publications/patient_education/ab013.cfm

Azam, S. (2009). *Oral sex is the new goodnight kiss.* Vancouver, BC: Reluctant Hero.

Bacon, C.G., Mittleman, M.A., Kawachi, I., Giovannucci, E., Glasser, D.B., & Rimm, E.B. (2003). Sexual function in men older than 50 years of age: Results from the health professionals follow-up study. *Annals of Internal Medicine, 139*(3), 161–8. Retrieved from http://annals.org/journal.aspx

Bancroft, J. (2009). *Human sexuality and its problems* (3rd ed.). Philadelphia, PA: Churchill Livingstone.

Biro, F.M., Galvez, M.P., Greenspan, L.C., Succop, P.A., Vangeepuram, N., Pinney, S.M., . . . Wolff, M.S. (2010). Pubertal assessment method and baseline characteristics in a mixed longitudinal study of girls. *Pediatrics, 126,* e583–90. doi:10.1542/peds.2009-3079

Bissell, M. (2000). Socio-economic outcomes of teen pregnancy and parenthood: A review of the literature. *Canadian Journal of Human Sexuality, 9,* 191–204. Retrieved from www.sieccan.org/cjhs.html

Boyce, W., Doherty-Poirier, M., MacKinnon, D., Fortin, C., Saab, H., King, M., & Gallupe, O. (2006). Sexual health of Canadian youth: Findings from the Canadian youth, sexual health and HIV/AIDS study. *The Canadian Journal of Human Sexuality, 15,* 59–68. Retrieved from www.sieccan.org/cjhs.html

Buss, D.M., Larsen, R.J., Westen, D., & Semmelroth, J. (1992). Sex differences in jealousy: Evolution, physiology, and psychology. *Psychological Science, 3,* 251–5. doi:10.1111/j.1467-9280.1992.tb00038.x

Call, V., Sprecher, S., & Schwartz, P. (1995). The incidence and frequency of marital sex in a national sample. *Journal of Marriage and the Family, 57,* 639–52. doi:10.2307/353919

Carpenter, L.M. (2002). Gender and the meaning and experience of virginity loss in the contemporary United States. *Gender and Society, 16,* 345–65. doi:10.1177/0891243202016003005

Chen, X.K., Wen, S.W., Fleming, N., Demissie, K., Rhoads, G.G., & Walker, M. (2007). Teenage pregnancy and adverse birth outcomes: A large population based retrospective cohort study. *International Journal of Epidemiology, 36,* 368–73. doi:10.1093/ije/dyl284

Clark, W., & Crompton, S. (2006). Till death do us part? The risk of first and second marriage dissolution. *Canadian Social Trends* (Statistics Canada, Catalogue no. 11-008E). Retrieved from www.statcan.gc.ca/pub/11-008-x/2006001/pdf/9198-eng.pdf

Dainton, M., & Aylor, B. (2001). A relational uncertainty analysis of jealousy, trust and maintenance in long-distance versus geographically close relationships. *Communication Quarterly, 49* 172–89. doi:10.1080/01463370109385624

Darroch, J.E., Singh, S., Frost, J.J., & Study Team. (2001). Differences in teenage pregnancy rates among five developed countries: The roles of sexual activity and contraceptive use. *Family Planning Perspectives, 33*(6), 244–50, 281. doi:10.2307/3030191

D'Augelli, A.R., & Hershberger, S.L. (1993). Lesbian, gay, and bisexual youth in community settings: Personal challenges and mental health problems. *American Journal of Community Psychology, 21,* 421–48. doi:10.1007/BF00942151

De Gaston, J.F., & Weed, S. (1996). Understanding gender difference in adolescent sexuality. *Adolescence, 31*(121), 217–29. Retrieved from www.eric.ed.gov

De Lamater, J., & Friedrich, W.N. (2002). Human sexual development. *The Journal of Sex Research, 39,* 10–14. doi:10.1080/00224490209552113

Dellmann-Jenkins, M., Bernard-Paolucci, T.A.S., & Rushing, B. (1994). Does distance make the heart grow fonder? A comparison of college students in long-distance and geographically close dating relationships. *College Student Journal, 28,* 212–19.

Dennerstein, L., Alexander, J.L., & Kotz, K. (2003). The menopause and sexual functioning: A review of the population-based studies. *Annual Review of Sex Research, 14,* 64–82. Retrieved from www.tandfonline.com/loi/hjsr20

Donnelly, D.A. (1993). Sexually inactive marriages. *The Journal of Sex Research, 30,* 171–9. doi:10.1080/00224499309551698

Fang, L., Oliver, A., Jayaraman, G.C., & Wong, T. (2010). Trends in age disparities between younger and middle-age adults among reported rates of chlamydia, gonorrhea, and infectious syphilis infections in Canada: Findings from 1997 to 2007. *Sexually Transmitted Diseases, 37,* 18–25. doi:10.1097/OLQ.0b013e3181b617dc

Friedrich, W.N., Grambsch, P., Broughton, D., Kuiper, J., & Beilke, R.L. (1991). Normative sexual behavior in children. *Pediatrics, 88*(3), 456–64. Retrieved from http://pediatrics.aappublications.org

Gottman, J.M., & Silver, N. (1999). *The seven principles for making marriage work.* New York, NY: Three Rivers Press.

Graham, C.A., Sanders, S.A., & Milhausen, R.R. (2006). The sexual excitation and sexual inhibition inventory for women: Psychometric properties. *Archives of Sexual Behavior, 35,* 397–410. doi:10.1007/s10508-006-9041-7

Guldner, G.T. & Swensen, C.H. (1995). Time spent together and relationship quality: Long-distance relationships as a test case. *Journal of Social and Personal Relationships, 12,* 313–20. doi:10.1177/0265407595122010

Haffner, D.W. (2008). *From diapers to dating: A parent's guide to raising sexually healthy children* (2nd rev. ed.). New York, NY: Newmarket Press.

Halpern-Felsher, B.L., Cornell, J.L., Kropp, R.Y., & Tschann, J.M. (2005). Oral versus vaginal sex among adolescents: Perceptions, attitudes and behavior. *Pediatrics, 115,* 845–51. doi:10.1542/peds.2004-2108

Herbenick, D., Reece, M., Schick, V., Sanders, S.A., Dodge, B., & Fortenberry, J.D. (2010). Sexual behaviors, relationships, and perceived health status among adult women in the United States: Results from a national probability sample. *Journal of Sexual Medicine, 7* (suppl. 5), 277–90. doi:10.1111/j.1743-6109.2010.02010.x

Herdt, G., & McClintock, M. (2000). The magical age of 10. *Archives of Sexual Behavior, 29,* 587–606. doi:10.1023/A:1002006521067

Holt, P.A.. & Stone, L.S. (1988). Needs, coping strategies, and coping outcomes associated with long-distance relationships. *Journal of College Student Development, 29,* 136–41.

Jacoby, S. (2005, July/August). Sex in America. *AARP Magazine.*

Kato, I., Toniolo, P., Akhmedkhanov, A., Koenig, K.L., Shore, R., & Zeleniuch-Jacquotte, A. (1998). Prospective study of factors influencing the onset of natural menopause. *Journal of Clinical Epidemiology, 51,* 1271–6. doi:10.1016/S0895-4356(98)00119-X

Kinsey, A.C., Pomeroy, W.B., & Martin, C.E. (1948). *Sexual behaviour in the human male*. Philadelphia, PA: W.B. Saunders Company.

Kinsey, A.C., Pomeroy, W.B., Martin, C.E., & Gebhard, P.H. (1953). *Sexual behaviour in the human female*. Philadelphia, PA: W.B. Saunders Company.

Laumann, E.O., Nicolosi, A., Glasser, D.B., Paik, A., Gingell, C., Moreira, E., & Wang, T. (2005). Sexual problems among women and men aged 40–80 y: Prevalence and correlates identified in the global study of sexual attitudes and behaviors. *International Journal of Impotence Research, 17*, 39–57. doi:10.1038/sj.ijir.3901250

Lawrance, K.-A., & Byers, E.S. (1995). Sexual satisfaction in long-term heterosexual relationships: The interpersonal exchange model of sexual satisfaction. *Personal Relationships, 2*, 267–85. doi:10.1111/j.1475-6811.1995.tb00092.x

Le Bourdais, C., & Lapierre-Adamcyk, E. (2004). Changes in conjugal life in Canada: Is cohabitation progressively replacing marriage? *Journal of Marriage and Family, 66*, 929–42. doi:10.1111/j.0022-2445.2004.00063.x

Leung, A.K., & Robson, W.L. (1993). Childhood masturbation. *Clinical Pediatrics, 32*, 238–41. doi:10.1177/000992289303200410

Lindau, S.T., Schumm, L.P., Laumann, E.O., Levinson, W., O'Muircheartaigh, C.A., & Waite, L.J. (2007). A study of sexuality and health among older adults in the United States. *The New England Journal of Medicine, 357*, 762–4. doi:10.1056/NEJMoa067423

Lindberg, L.D., Jones, R., & Santelli, J.S. (2008). Noncoital sexual activities among adolescents. *Journal of Adolescent Health, 43*, 231–8. doi:10.1016/j.jadohealth.2007.12.010

MacIntosh, H., Reissing, E.D., & Andruff, H. (2010). Same-sex marriage in Canada: The impact of legal marriage on the first cohort of gay and lesbian Canadians to wed. *The Canadian Journal of Human Sexuality, 19*(3), 79–90. Retrieved from www.sieccan.org/cjhs.html

McKay, A., & Barrett, M. (2010). Trends in teen pregnancy rates from 1996–2006: A comparison of Canada, Sweden, USA, and England/Wales. *The Canadian Journal of Human Sexuality, 19*, 43–52. Retrieved from www.sieccan.org/index.html

Maguire, K.C. (2007). "Will it ever end?": A (re)examination of uncertainty in college student long-distance dating relationships. *Communication Quarterly, 55*, 415–312. doi:10.1080/01463370701658002

Martinson, F.M. (1994). *The sexual life of children*. Westport, CT: Bergin and Garvey.

Masters, W.H., & Johnson, V.E. (1970). *Human sexual response*. Boston, MA: Little, Brown, and Company.

Meijer, B., & Bakker, H.H. (2003). Management of priapism in the newborn. *Urology, 61*, 224xvi–xviii. doi:10.1016/S0090-4295(02)02101-5

Milan, A. (2003). Would you live common law? (Catalogue no. 11-008). *Canadian Social Trends. 71*, 2–6. Ottawa, ON: Statistics Canada.

Mishna, F., Newman, P.A., Daley, A., & Solomon, S. (2009). Bullying of lesbian and gay youth: A qualitative investigation. *The British Journal of Social Work, 39*, 1598–614. doi:10.1093/bjsw/bcm148

Molla, M., Berhane, Y., & Lindtjorn, B. (2008). Traditional values of virginity and sexual behaviour in rural Ethiopian youth: Results from a cross-sectional study. *BMC Public Health, 8*(9), 1–10. doi:10.1186/1471-2458-8-9

Muise, A., Christofides, E., & Desmarais, S. (2009). More information than you ever wanted: Does Facebook bring out the green-eyed monster of jealousy? *CyberPsychology & Behavior, 12*, 441–4. doi:10.1089/cpb.2008.0263

Narchi, H. (2003). Infantile masturbation mimicking paroxysmal disorders. *Journal of Pediatric Neurology, 1*(1), 43–5. Retrieved from http://childscience.org/html/jpn/instructions.html

Okami, P., Olmstead, R., & Abramson, P.R. (1997). Sexual experiences in early childhood: 18-year longitudinal data from the UCLA Family Lifestyles Project. *The Journal of Sex Research, 34*, 339–47. doi:10.1080/00224499709551902

Ontario Federation for Cerebral Palsy. (2009). *Sexuality and cerebral palsy* [Booklet]. Toronto, ON: Author. Retrieved from www.ofcp.ca/pdf/book/sexuality_book.pdf

Pistole, M.C., Roberts, A., & Chapman, M.L. (2010). Attachment, relationship maintenance, and stress in long distance and geographically close romantic relationships. *Journal of Social and Personal Relationships, 27*, 535–52. doi:10.1177/0265407510363427

Randall, H.E., & Byers, E.S. (2003). What is sex? Students' definitions of having sex, sexual partner, and unfaithful sexual behaviour. *The Canadian Journal of Human Sexuality, 12*, 87–96. Retrieved from www.sieccan.org/cjhs.html

Reece, M., Herbenick, D., Schick, V., Sanders, S.A., Dodge, B., & Fortenberry, J.D. (2010). Sexual behaviors, relationships, and perceived health among adult men in the United States: Results from a national probability sample. *Journal of Sexual Medicine, 7*(Suppl. 5), 291–304. doi:10.1111/j.1743-6109.2010.02009.x

Reissing, E.D., Andruff, H.L., & Wentland, J.J. (2010). Looking back: The experience of first sexual intercourse and current sexual adjustment in young heterosexual adults. *Journal of Sex Research, 48*, 1–9. doi:10.1080/00224499.2010.538951

Rheaume, C., & Mitty, E. (2008). Sexuality and intimacy in older adults. *Geriatric Nursing, 29*, 342–9. doi:10.1016/j.gerinurse.2008.08.004

Saewyc, E., Poon, C., Wang, N., Homma, Y., Smith, A., & the McCreary Centre Society. (2007). *Not yet equal: The health of lesbian, gay, & bisexual youth in BC*. Vancouver, BC: McCreary Centre Society.

Sandnabba, K.N., Santtila, P., Wannäs, M., & Krook, K. (2003). Age and gender specific sexual behaviors in children. *Child Abuse & Neglect, 27*, 579–605. doi:10.1016/S0145-2134(03)00102-9

Santhya, K.G., Acharya, R., Jejeebhoy, S.J., & Ram, U. (2011). Timing of first sex before marriage and its correlates: Evidence from India. *Culture, Health & Sexuality, 13*, 327–41. doi:10.1080/13691058.2010.534819

Schuhrke, B. (2001). Young children's curiosity about other people's genitals. In T.G.M. Sandfort & J. Rademakers (Eds), *Childhood sexuality: Normal sexual beahvior and development* (pp. 27–48). New York, NY: Routledge.

Schwartz, I.M. (1999). Sexual activity prior to coital initiation: A comparison between males and females. *Archives of Sexual Behavior, 28*, 63–9. doi:10.1023/A:1018793622284

Shirozu, H., Koyanagi, T., Takashima, T., Horimoto, N., Akazawa, K., & Nakano, H. (1995). Penile tumescence in the human fetus at term: A preliminary report. *Early Human Development, 41*, 159–66. doi:10.1016/0378-3782(95)01618-D

SIECCAN. (2004). Adolescent sexual and reproductive health in Canada: A report card in 2004. *The Canadian Journal of Human Sexuality, 13*, 67–81. Retrieved from www.sieccan.org/cjhs.html

Skelton, D.A., & Dinan-Young, A.M. (2008). Ageing and older people. In J. Buckley (Ed.), *Exercise physiology in special populations* (pp.161–224). Philadelphia, PA: Churchill Livingston Elsevier.

Slater, A., & Tiggemann, M. (2002). A test of objectification theory in adolescent girls. *Sex Roles, 46,* 343–9. doi:10.1023/A:1020232714705

Smith, A., Lyons, A., Ferris, J., Richters, J., Pitts, M., Shelley, J., & Simpson, J.M. (2011). Sexual and relationship satisfaction among heterosexual men and women: The importance of desired frequency of sex. *Journal of Sex & Marital Therapy, 37,* 104–15. doi:10.1080/0092623X.2011.560531

Smock, P.J. (2000). Cohabitation in the United States: An appraisal of research themes, findings, and implications. *Annual Review of Sociology, 26,* 1–20. doi:10.1146/annurev.soc.26.1.1

Spanier, G.B. (1976). Measuring dyadic adjustment: New scales for assessing the quality of marriage and similar dyads. *Journal of Marriage and Family, 38,* 15–28. doi:10.2307/350547

Spitz, R.A. (1945). Hospitalism: An inquiry into the genesis of psychiatric conditions in early childhood. *The Psychoanalytic Study of the Child, 1,* 53–74.

Spitz, R.A. (1946). Hospitalism: A follow-up report. *The Psychoanalytic Study of the Child, 2,* 53–74.

Sprecher, S. (1999). "I love you more than yesterday": Romantic partners' perceptions of changes in love and related affect over time. *Journal of Personality and Social Psychology, 76,* 46–53. doi:10.1037//0022-3514.76.1.46

Stafford, L., & Reske, J.R. (1990). Idealization and communication in long-distance premarital relationships. *Family Relations, 39,* 274–9. Retrieved from www.jstor.org/stable/584871

Statistics Canada. (2007). *Legal marital status, common-law status, age groups, and sex for the population 15 years and over of Canada, provinces, territories, census divisions and census subdivisions, 2006 census* (Catalogue no. 97-552-XCB2006009). Ottawa, ON: Author.

Statistics Canada. (2009). *Nuptiality and divorce* (Catalogue no. 91-209-X). Ottawa, ON: Author.

Statistics Canada. (2013). *Family life—Marriage.* Retrieved from www4.hrsdc.gc.ca/.3ndic.1t.4r@-eng.jsp?iid=78

Stephen, T.D. (1986). Communication and interdependence in geographically separated relationships. *Human Communication Research, 13,* 191–210. doi:10.1111/j.1468-2958.1986.tb00102.x

van Horn, K.R., Arnone, A., Nesbitt, K., Desilets, L., Sears, T., Giffin, M., & Brudi, R. (1997). Physical distance and interpersonal characteristics in college students' romantic relationships. *Personal Relationships, 4,* 25–34. doi:10.1111/j.1475-6811.1997.tb00128.x

Vogel, L. (2010). Canadian baby boomers shirk safe sex. *Canadian Medical Association Journal, 18,* E827–8. doi:10.1503/cmaj.109-3729

Waite, L.J., Laumann, E.O., Das, A., & Schumm, L.P. (2009). Sexuality: Measures of partnership, practices, attitudes, and problems in the national social life, health, and aging study. *Journal of Gerontology: Psychological Sciences, 64B*(Suppl. 1), i56–66. doi:10.1093/geronb/gbp038

Walker, B.L., & Harrington, D. (2002). Effects of staff training on staff knowledge and attitudes about sexuality. *Educational Gerontology, 28,* 639–564. doi:10.1080/03601270290081452

Wentland, J.J., Herold, E.S., Desmarais, S., & Milhausen, R.R. (2009). Differentiating highly sexual women from less sexual women. *The Canadian Journal of Human Sexuality, 18,* 169–82. Retrieved from www.sieccan.org/cjhs.html

Wentland, J.J., & Reissing, E.D. (2011). Taking casual sex not too casually: Arriving at consensus definitions for different types of casual sexual relationships. *Canadian Journal of Human Sexuality, 20,* 75–91. Retrieved from www.sieccan.org/cjhs.html

Woo, J.S.T., & Brotto, L.A. (2008). Age of first sexual intercourse and acculturation: Effects on adult sexual responding. *Journal of Sexual Medicine, 5,* 571–82. doi:10.1111/j.1743-6109.2007.00740.x

Young, M., Denny, G., Luquis, R., & Young, T. (1998). Correlates of sexual satisfaction in marriage. *The Canadian Journal of Human Sexuality, 7*(2), 115–27. Retrieved from www.sieccan.org/cjhs.html

Zurbriggen, E.L., Collins, R.L., Lamb, S., Roberts, T.A., Tolman, D.L., Ward, L.M., & Blake, J. (2007). *Report of the APA task force on the sexualization of girls.* Washington, DC: American Psychological Association.

CHAPTER 10

Alexander, G.M., & Hines, M. (2002). Sex differences in response to children's toys in nonhuman primates. *Evolution and Human Behaviour, 23*(6), 467–79. doi:10.1016/S1090-5138(02)00107-1

Alexander, M.G., & Fisher, T.D. (2003). Truth and consequences: Using the bogus pipeline to examine sex differences in self-reported sexuality. *The Journal of Sex Research, 40,* 27–35. doi:10.1080/00224490309552164

Archer, J. (2004). Sex differences in aggression in real-world setting: A meta-analytic review. *Review of General Psychology, 8,* 291–322. doi:10.1037/1089-2680.8.4.291

Bailey, J.M. (2003). *The man who would be queen: The science of gender-bending and transsexualism.* Washington, DC: Joseph Henry Press.

Bailey, J.M., Gaulin, S., Agyei, Y., & Gladue, B.A. (1994). Effects of gender and sexual orientation on evolutionarily relevant aspects of human mating psychology. *Journal of Personality and Social Psychology, 66*(6), 1081–93. doi:10.1037/0022-3514.66.6.1081

Bailey, J.M., & Zucker, K.J. (1995). Childhood sex-typed behavior and sexual orientation: A conceptual analysis and quantitative review. *Developmental Psychology, 31,* 43–55. doi:10.1037/0012-1649.31.1.43

Bandura, A. (1986). *Social foundations of thought and action: A social cognitive theory.* Englewood Cliffs, NJ: Prentice Hall.

Bastida, M.G., Rey, R.A., Bergadá, I., Bedecarrás, P., Andreone, L., del Rey, G., . . . Gottlieb, S. (2007). Establishment of testicular endocrine function impairment during childhood and puberty in boys with Klinefelter syndrome. *Clinical Endocrinology, 67,* 863–70. doi:10.1111/j.1365-2265.2007.02977.x

Baumeister, R.F. (2000). Gender differences in erotic plasticity: The female sex drive as socially flexible and responsive. *Psychological Bulletin, 126*(3), 347–74. doi:10.1037//0033-2909.126.3.347

Baumeister, R.F., Catanese, K.R., & Vohs, K.D. (2001). Is there a gender difference in strength of sex drive? Theoretical views, conceptual distinctions, and a review of relevant evidence. *Personality and Social Psychology Review, 5,* 242–73. doi:10.1207/S15327957PSPR0503_5

Bem, S.L. (1981). Gender schema theory: A cognitive account of sex typing. *Psychological Review, 88,* 354–64. doi:10.1037/0033-295X.88.4.354

Bem, S.L. (1989). Genital knowledge and gender constancy in preschool children. *Child development, 60,* 649–62.

Blakemore, J.E.O., Berenbaum, S.A., & Liben, L.S. (2008). *Gender development*. New York, NY: Taylor & Francis Group.

Blanchard, R. (1989). The concept of autogynephilia and the typology of male gender dysphoria. *Journal of Nervous and Mental Disease, 177*, 616–23. doi:10.1097/00005053-198910000-00004

Blanchard, R., Clemmensen, L.H., & Steiner, B. (1987). Heterosexual and homosexual gender dysphoria. *Archives of Sexual Behaviour, 16*, 139–52. doi:10.1007/BF01542067

Blanchard, R., Steiner, B.W., Clemmensen, L.H., & Dickey, R. (1989). Prediction of regrets in postoperative transsexuals. *The Canadian Journal of Psychiatry, 34*, 43–5.

Bojesen, A., & Gravholt, C.H. (2007). Klinefelter syndrome in clinical practice. *Nature Clinical Practice Urology, 4*, 192–03. doi:10.1038/ncpuro0775

Cejka, M.A., & Eagly, A.H. (1999). Gender-stereotypic images of occupations correspond to the sex segregation of employment. *Personality and Social Psychology Bulletin, 25*, 413–23. doi:10.1177/0146167299025004002

Chandra, A., Mosher, W.D., & Copen, C. (2010). Sexual behavior, sexual attraction, and sexual identity in the United States: Data from the 2006–2008 National Survey of Family Growth. *National Health Statistics Reports, 36*, 1–49.

Chivers, M.L. (2010). A brief update on the specificity of sexual arousal. *Sexual and Relationship Therapy, 25*, 407–14.

Chivers, M.L., & Bailey, J.M. (2000). Sexual orientation of female-to-male transsexuals: A comparison of homosexual and non-homosexual types. *Archives of Sexual Behavior, 29*, 259–78. doi:10.1023/A:1001915530479

Chivers, M.L., Haberl, M., & Timmers, A.D. (2011, August). *Sexual arousal patterns of bisexually attracted women: Specificity of sexual arousal increases with same-sex attractions*. Poster presentation at the International Academy of Sex Research, Los Angeles, CA.

Chivers, M.L., Seto, M.C., & Blanchard, R. (2007). Gender and sexual orientation differences in sexual response to sexual activities versus gender of actors in sexual films. *Journal of Personality and Social Psychology, 93*(6), 1108–21.

Chivers, M.L., Seto, M.C., Lalumière, M.L, Laan, E., & Grimbos, T. (2010). Agreement of self-reported and genital measures of sexual arousal in men and women: A meta-analysis. *Archives of Sexual Behavior, 39*, 5–56. doi:10.1007/s10508-009-9556-9

Chivers, M.L., & Timmers, A.D. (2012). The effects of gender and relationship context cues in audio narratives on heterosexual women's and men's genital and subjective sexual response. *Archives of Sexual Behavior, 41*, 185–97. doi:10.1007/s10508-012-9937-3

Cohen, J. (1988). *Statistical power analysis for the behavioral sciences* (2nd ed.). Hillsdale, NJ: Erlbaum.

Cohen, L.L., & Shotland, R.L. (1996). Timing of first sexual intercourse in a relationship: Expectations, experiences, and perceptions of others. *The Journal of Sex Research, 33*, 291–9. doi:10.1080/00224499609551846

Coleman, E., Bockting, W., Botzer, M., Cohen-Kettenis, P., DeCuypere, G., Feldman, J., . . . Zucker, K. (2012). Standards of care for the health of transsexual, transgender, and gender nonconforming people, version 7. *International Journal of Transgenderism, 13*, 1553–2739. doi:10.1080/15532739.2011.700873

Condry, J., & Condry, S. (1976). Sex differences: A study of the eye of the beholder. *Child Development, 47*, 812–19. doi:10.2307/1128199

Conway, L. (2006). *Transvestic fetishism, also called "autogynephilia" for a while by Blanchard, Bailey and Lawrence (BBL): Are these labels or stigmata?* http://ai.eecs.umich.edu/people/conway/TS/Labels%20or%20Stigmata.html.

de Vries, M.W. (1984). Temperament and infant mortality among the Masai of East Africa. *The American Journal of Psychiatry, 141*, 1189–94. Retrieved from http://ajp.psychiatryonline.org

Diamond, M., & Watson, L.A. (2004). Androgen insensitivity syndrome and Klinefelter's syndrome: Sex and gender considerations. *Child and Adolescent Psychiatric Clinics of North America, 13*, 623–40. doi:10.1016/j.chc.2004.02.015

Docter, R.F. (1988). *Transvestites and transsexuals: Toward a theory of cross-gender behavior*. New York, NY: Plenum.

Dresser, R., & Frader, J. (2009). Off-label prescribing: A call for heightened professional and government oversight. *Journal of Law, Medicine, and Ethics, 37*, 476–86. doi:10.1111/j.1748-720X.2009.00408.x

Eagly, A.H., & Wood, W. (1999). The origins of sex differences in human behavior: Evolved dispositions versus social roles. *American Psychologist, 54*, 408–23. doi:10.1037/0003-066X.54.6.408

Eagly, A.H., Wood, W., & Diekman, A.B. (2000). Social role theory of sex differences and similarities: A current appraisal. In T. Eckes & H.M. Trautner (Eds), *The developmental social psychology of gender* (pp. 123–74). Manwah, NJ: Erlbaum.

Fagot, B.I., & Leinbach, M.D. (1989). The young child's gender schema: Environmental input, internal organization. *Child Development, 60*, 663–72.

Fernandez-Balsells, M.M., Muthusamy, K., Smushkin, G., Lampropulos, J.F., Elamin, M.B., Abu Elnour, N.O., . . . Murad, M.H. (2010). Prenatal dexamethasone use for prevention of virilization in preganancies at risk for classical congenital adrenal hyperplasia because of 21-hydroxylase (CYP21A2) deficiency: a systematic review and meta-analysis. *Clinical Endocrinology, 73*, 436–44. doi:10.1111/j.1365-2265.2010.03826.x

Fisher, T.D. (2009). The impact of socially conveyed norms on the reporting of sexual behavior and attitudes by men and women. *Journal of Experimental Social Psychology, 45*, 567–72. doi:10.1016/j.jesp.2009.02.007

Frisén, L., Nordenström, A., Falhammar, H., Filipsson, H., Holmdahl, G., Janson, P.O., . . . Nordenskjöld, A. (2009). Gender role behavior, sexuality, and psychosocial adaptation in women with congenital adrenal hyperplasia due to CYP21A2 deficiency. *Journal of Clinical Endocrinology & Metabolism, 94*, 3432–9. doi:10.1210/jc.2009-0636

Gangestad, S.W., & Simpson, J.A. (2000). The evolution of human mating: Trade-offs and strategic pluralism. *Behavioural and Brain Sciences, 23*(4), 573–644. doi:10.1017/S0140525X0000337X

Gastaud, F., Bouvattier, C., Duranteau, L., Brauner, R., Thibaud, E., Kutten, F., & Bougnères, P. (2007). Impaired sexual and reproductive outcomes in women with classical forms of congenital adrenal hyperplasia. *The Journal of Clinical Endocrinology & Metabolism, 92*, 1391–6. doi:10.1210/jc.2006-1757

Gray, J. (1992). *Men are from Mars, women are from Venus: A practical guide for improving communication and getting what you want in your relationships*. New York, NY: HarperCollins.

Green, R. (1987). *The "sissy boy" syndrome and the development of homosexuality*. New Haven, CT: Yale University Press.

Halpern, D.F. (2000). *Sex differences in cognitive abilities*. Mahwah, NJ: Lawrence Erlbaum.

Hines, M. (2004). *Brain gender*. New York, NY: Oxford University Press.

Hjerrild, B.E., Mortensen, K.H., & Gravholt, C.H. (2008). Turner syndrome and clinical treatment. *British Medical Bulletin, 86*, 77–93. doi:10.1093/bmb/ldn015

Hyde, J.S. (2005). The gender similarities. *American Psychologist, 60*(6), 581–92. doi:10.1037/0003-066X.60.6.581

James, A. (2004). *"Autogynephilia": a disputed diagnosis.* Retrieved from www.tsroadmap.com/info/autogynephilia.html

Kinsey, A.C., Pomeroy, W.B., Martin, C.E., & Gebhard, P.H. (1953). *Sexual behavior in the human female.* Philadelphia, PA: Saunders.

Kohlberg, L. (1966). A cognitive-developmental analysis of children's sex- role concepts andattitudes. In E. E. Maccody (Ed.), *The development of sex difference* (pp. 82–172). Stanford, CA: Stanford University Press.

Lajic, S., Nordenström, A., & Hirvikoski, T. (2011). Long-term outcome of prenatal dexamethasone treatment of 21-hydroxylase deficiency. *Pediatric Adrenal Diseases, 20,* 96–105. doi:10.1159/000321228

Lawrence, A. (2003). Factors associated with satisfaction or regret following male-to-female sex reassignment surgery. *Archives of Sexual Behaviour, 32,* 299–315. doi:10.1023/A:1024086814364

Lawrence, A. (2005). Sexuality before and after male-to-female sex reassignment surgery. *Archives of Sexual Behavior, 34,* 147–66. doi:10.1007/s10508-005-1793-y

Lawrence, A. (2010). Sexual orientation versus age of onset as bases for typologies (subtypes) for gender identity disorder in adolescents and adults. *Archives of Sexual Behavior, 39,* 514–45. doi:10.1007/s10508-009-9594-3

Leinbach, M.D., & Fagot, B.I. (1993). Gender-role development in young children: From discrimination to labeling. *Developmental Review, 13,* 205–24. doi:10.1006/drev.1993.1009

Lippa, R.A. (2005). *Gender, Nature, and Nurture* (2nd ed.). Mahwah, NJ: Lawrence Erlbaum.

Lippa, R.A. (2006). Is high sex drive associated with increased sexual attraction to both sexes? *Psychological Science, 17*(1), 46–52. doi:10.1111/j.1467-9280.2005.01663.x

Lippa, R.A. (2009). Sex differences in sex drive, sociosexuality, and height across 53 nations: Testing evolutionary and social structural theories. *Archives of Sexual Behavior, 38,* 631–51. doi:10.1007/s10508-007-9242-8

McCall, K.M., & Meston, C.M. (2007). The effects of false positive and false negative physiological feedback on sexual arousal: A comparison of women with or without sexual arousal disorder. *Archives of Sexual Behavior, 36,* 518–30. doi:10.1007/s10508-006-9140-5

Maglaty, J. (2011). *When did girls start wearing pink? Every generation brings a new definition of masculinity and femininity that manifests itself in children's dress.* Retrieved from www.smithsonianmag.com/arts-culture/When-Did-Girls-Start-Wearing-Pink.html#

Mathews, G.A., Fane, B.A., Conway, G.S., Brook, C.G.D., & Hines, M. (2009). Personality and congenital adrenal hyperplasia: Possible effects of prenatal androgen exposure. *Hormones & Behavior, 55,* 285–91. doi:10.1016/j.yhbeh.2008.11.007

Mendonca, B.B., Inacio, M., Costa, E.M.F., Arnhold, I.J.P., Silva, F.A.Q., Nicolau, W., . . . Wilson, J.D. (1996). Male pseudohermaphroditism due to steroid 5 alpha-reductase 2 deficiency: Diagnosis, psychological evaluation, and management. *Medicine, 75,* 64–76. doi:10.1097/00005792-199603000-00003

Messner, M.A. (2000). Barbie girls versus sea monsters: Children constructing gender. *Gender & Society, 25,* 227–49. doi:10.1177/089124300014006004

Meston, C.M., & Buss, D.M. (2009). *Why women have sex: Understanding sexual motivations from adventure to revenge (and everything in between).* New York, NY: Henry Holt and Company.

Meyer-Bahlburg, H.F.L. (2005). Gender identity outcome in female-raised 46, XY persons with penile agenesis, cloacal exstrophy of the bladder, or penile ablation. *Archives of Sexual Behavior, 34,* 423–38.

Meyer-Bahlburg, H.F.L., Dolezal, C., Baker, S.W., & New, M.I. (2008). Sexual orientation in women with classical or non-classical congenital adrenal hyperplasia as a function of degree of prenatal androgen excess. *Archives of Sexual Behavior, 37,* 85–99. doi:10.1007/s10508-007-9265-1

Minto, C.L., Liao, L.M., Woodhouse, C.R., Ransley, P.G., & Creighton, S.M. (2003). The effect of clitoral surgery on sexual outcome in individuals who have intersex conditions with ambiguous genitalia: A cross-sectional study. *The Lancet, 361,* 1252–7. doi:10.1016/S0140-6736(03)12980-7

Mock, S.E., & Eibach, R.P. (2011). Stability and change in sexual orientation identity over a 10-year period in adulthood. *Archives of Sexual Behavior.* doi 10.1007/s10508-011-9761-1

Nanda, S. (1999). *Neither man nor woman: The hijras of India* (2nd ed.). Belmont, CA: Wadsworth.

Newfield, E., Hart, S., Dibble, S., & Kohler, L. (2006). Female-to-male transgender quality of life. *Quality of Life Research, 15,* 1447–57. doi:10.1007/s11136-006-0002-3

Nordenström, A., Servin, A., Bohlin, G., Larsson, A., & Wedell, A. (2002). Sex-typed toy play behavior correlates with the degree of prenatal androgen exposure assessed by CYP21 genotype in girls with congenital adrenal hyperplasia. *The Journal of Clinical Endocrinology & Metabolism, 87,* 5119–24. doi:10.1210/jc.2001-011531

Petersen, J.L., & Hyde, J.S. (2010). A meta-analytic review of research on gender differences in sexuality, 1993–2007. *Psychological Bulletin, 136,* 21–38. doi:10.1037/a0017504

Poisson, J. (2011, May 21). Parents keep child's gender secret. *Toronto Star.* Retrieved from www.thestar.com/life/parent/2011/05/21/parents_keep_childs_gender_secret.html

Reiner, W.G., & Gearhart, J.P. (2004). Discordant sexual identity in some genetic males with cloacal exstrophy assigned to female sex at birth. *The New England Journal of Medicine, 350,* 333–41. doi:10.1056/NEJMoa022236

Roughgarden, J. (2004). *Evolution's Rainbow: Diversity, Gender and Sexuality in Nature and People.* Los Angeles: University of California Press.

Smith, T. (1992). Discrepancies between men and women in reporting number of sexual partners. *Social Biology, 39,* 203–11. doi:10.1080/19485565.1992.9988817

Steensma, T.D., Biemond, R., Boer, F.D., & Cohen-Kettenis, P.T. (2011). Desisting and persisting gender dysphoria after childhood: A qualitative study. *Clinical Child Psychology and Psychiatry, 16,* 499–516. doi:10.1177/1359104510378303

Stoller, R.J. (1980). Gender identity disorders. In H.I. Kaplan, A.M. Freedman, & B.J. Sadock (Eds), *Comprehensive textbook of psychiatry* (3rd ed., Vol. 2, pp. 1400–8). Baltimore, MD: Williams & Wilkins.

Thomas, J.R., & French, K.E. (1985). Gender differences across age in motor performance: A meta-analysis. *Psychological Bulletin, 98,* 260–82. doi:10.1037/0033-2909.98.2.260

Trivers, R.L. (1972). Parental investment and sexual selection. In B. Campbell (Ed.), *Sexual selection and the descent of man, 1871–1971* (pp. 136–79). Chicago, IL: Aldine.

United Nations Development Programme. (1995). *Human development report 1995.* New York, NY: Oxford University Press.

Valerio, M.W. (2006). *The testosterone files: My hormonal and social transformation from female to male.* Emeryville, CA: Seal Press.

Vawter, M.P., Harvey, P.D., & DeLisi, L.E. (2007). Dysregulation of x-linked gene expression in Klinefelter's syndrome and association with verbal cognition. *American Journal of Medical Genetics, 144B*, 728–34. doi:10.1002/ajmg.b.30454

Wallen, K. (2001). Sex and context: Hormones and primate sexual motivation. *Hormones and Behavior, 40*, 330–57. doi:10.1006/hbeh.2001.1696

Wallien, M.S., & Cohen-Kettenis, P.T. (2008). Psychosexual outcome of gender-dysphoric children. *Journal of the American Academy of Child and Adolescent Psychiatry, 47*, 1413–23. doi:10.1097/CHI.0b013e31818956b9

Ward, L.M. (2002). Does television exposure affect emerging adults' attitudes and assumptions about sexual relationships? Correlational and experimental confirmation. *Journal of Youth and Adolescence, 31*, 1–15. doi:10.1023/A:1014068031532

Witchel, S.F., & Azziz, R. (2011). Congenital adrenal hyperplasia. *Journal of Pediatric Adolescent Gynecology, 24*, 116–26.

Zeger, M.P.D., Zinn, A.R., Lahlou, N., Ramos, P., Kowal, K., Samango-Sprouse, C., & Ross, J. L. (2008). Effect of ascertainment and genetic features on the phenotype of Klinefelter syndrome. *Journal of Pediatrics, 5*, 716–22. doi:10.1016/j.jpeds.2007.10.019

Zucker, K., Bradley, S., Oliver, G., Blake, J., Fleming, S., & Hood, J. (2004). Self-reported sexual arousability in women with congenital adrenal hyperplasia. *Journal of Sex & Marital Therapy, 30*, 343–55. doi:10.1080/00926230490465109

Zurbriggen, E.L., & Morgan, E.M. (2006). Who wants to marry a millionaire? Reality dating television programs, attitudes toward sex, and sexual behaviors. *Sex Roles, 54*, 1–17. doi:10.1007/s11199-005-8865-2

CHAPTER 11

Alden, H.L., & Parker, K.F. (2005). Gender role ideology, homophobia and hate crime: Linking attitudes to macro-level anti-gay and lesbian hate crimes. *Deviant Behavior, 26*(4), 321–43. doi:10.1080/016396290931614

Alderson, K.G. (2003). The ecological model of gay male identity. *Canadian Journal of Human Sexuality, 12*(2), 75–85.

Alderson, K.G. (2013). *Counseling LGBTI clients.* Thousand Oaks, CA: Sage.

Alderson, K.G., Orzeck, T.L., Davis, S., & Boyes, M. (2013). *Affectional orientation: Defining and measuring it.* Manuscript in preparation.

Alexander, J.E. (2000). Biological influences on homosexuality: Current findings and future directions. *Psychology, Evolution & Gender, 2*(3), 241–52. Retrieved from www.tandfonline.com/loi/rpeg19

Andersson, G.T., Noack, T., Seierstad, A., & Weedon-Fekjaer, H. (2006). The demographics of same-sex marriages in Norway and Sweden. *Demography, 43*(1), 79–98. doi:10.1353/dem.2006.0001

Bagley, C., & Tremblay, P. (1997). Suicidal behaviors in homosexual and bisexual males. *Crisis: The Journal of Crisis Intervention and Suicide Prevention, 18*(1), 24–34. doi:10.1027/0227-5910.18.1.24

Bailey, J.V., Farquhar, C., Owen, C., & Whittaker, D. (2003). Sexual behaviour of lesbians and bisexual women. *Sexually Transmitted Infections, 79*(2), 147–50. doi:10.1136/sti.79.2.147

Balsam, K.F., Beauchaine, T.P., Rothblum, E.D., & Solomon, S.E. (2008). Three-year follow-up of same-sex couples who had civil unions in Vermont, same-sex couples not in civil unions, and heterosexual married couples. *Developmental Psychology, 44*(1), 102–16. doi:10.1037/0012-1649.44.1.102

Beard, J., & Glickauf-Hughes, C. (1994). Gay identity and sense of self: Rethinking male homosexuality. *Journal of Gay & Lesbian Psychotherapy, 2*(2), 21–37. doi:10.1300/J236v02n02_02

Becker, J.M. (2012, April 25). Exclusive: Dr Robert Spitzer apologizes to gay community for infamous "ex-gay" study. *Truth Wins Out.* Retrieved from www.truthwinsout.org/news/2012/04/24542

Biblarz, T.J., & Stacey, J. (2010). How does the gender of parents matter? *Journal of Marriage and Family, 72*(1), 3–22. doi:10.1111/j.1741-3737.2009.00678.x

Blanchard, R. (2004). Quantitative and theoretical analyses of the relation between older brothers and homosexuality in men. *Journal of Theoretical Biology, 230*, 173–87.

Blanchard, R., Cantor, J.M., Bogaert, A.F., Breedlove, S.M., & Ellis, L. (2006). Interaction of fraternal birth order and handedness in the development of male homosexuality. *Hormones and Behavior, 49*(3), 405–14. doi:http://dx.doi.org/10.1016/j.yhbeh.2005.09.002

Blumstein, P., & Schwartz, P. (1983). *American couples: Money, work and sex.* New York, NY: Beacon Press.

Bogaert, A.F. (2004). Asexuality: Prevalence and associated factors in a national probability sample. *Journal of Sex Research, 41*(3), 279–87. doi:10.1080/00224490409552235

Bogaert, A.F. (2006). Toward a conceptual understanding of asexuality. *Review of General Psychology, 10*(3), 241–50. doi:10.1037/1089-2680.10.3.241

Brotto, L.A., Knudson, G., Inskip, J., Rhodes, K., & Erskine, Y. (2010). Asexuality: A mixed-methods approach. *Archives of Sexual Behavior, 39*(3), 599–618. doi:10.1007/s10508-008-9434-x

Brown, W.M., Finn, C.J., Cooke, B.M., & Breedlove, S.M. (2002). Differences in finger length ratios between self-identified "butch" and "femme" lesbians. *Archives of Sexual Behavior, 31*(1), 123–7.

Bullough, V.L., & Bullough, B. (1997). The history of the science of sexual orientation 1880–1980: An overview. *Journal of Psychology & Human Sexuality, 9*(2), 1–16.

Cass, V. (1979). Homosexual identity formation: A theoretical model. *Journal of Homosexuality, 4*(3), 219–35.

Cass, V. (1996). Sexual orientation identity formation: A western phenomenon. In R.P. Cabaj & T.S. Stein (Eds), *Textbook of homosexuality and mental health* (pp. 227–51). Washington, DC: American Psychiatric Press.

Chow, P.K.-Y., & Cheng, S.-T. (2010). Shame, internalized heterosexism, lesbian identity, and coming out to others: A comparative study of lesbians in mainland China and Hong Kong. *Journal of Counseling Psychology, 57*(1), 92–104. doi:10.1037/a0017930

Cole, S.W., Kemeny, M.E., Taylor, S.E., & Visscher, B.R. (1996). Elevated physical health risk among gay men who conceal their homosexual identity. *Health Psychology, 15*, 243–51. doi:10.1037/0278-6133.15.4.243

Coleman, E.M., Hoon, P.W., & Hoon, E.F. (1983). Arousability and sexual satisfaction in lesbian and heterosexual women. *Journal of Sex Research, 19*, 58–73. doi:10.1080/00224498309551169

Cramer, R.J., Golom, F.D., LoPresto, C.T., & Kirkley, S.M. (2008). Weighing the evidence: Empirical assessment and ethical implications of conversion therapy. *Ethics & Behavior, 18*(1), 93–114. doi:10.1080/10508420701713014

DeLameter, J.D., & Hyde, J.S. (1998). Essentialism vs social constructionism in the study of human sexuality. *Journal of Sex Research, 35*(1), 10–18.

Diamond, L.M. (2008). Female bisexuality from adolescence to adulthood: Results from a 10-year longitudinal study. *Developmental Psychology, 44*(1), 5–14. doi:10.1037/0012-1649.44.1.5

Drummond, K.D., Bradley, S.J., Peterson-Badali, M., & Zucker, K.J. (2008). A follow-up study of girls with gender identity disorder. *Developmental Psychology, 44*(1), 34–45. doi:10.1037/0012-1649.44.1.34

Dworkin, S.H. (2000). Individual therapy with lesbian, gay, and bisexual clients. In R.M. Perez, K.A. Debord, & K.J. Bieschke (Eds), *Handbook of counseling and psychotherapy with lesbian, gay, and bisexual clients* (pp. 157–82). Washington, DC: American Psychological Association.

Erikson, E.H. (1968). *Identity: Youth and crisis.* New York, NY: Norton.

Frankowski, B.L. (2004). Sexual orientation and adolescents. *Pediatrics, 113*, 1827–32. doi:10.1542/peds.113.6.1827

Freud, S. (1959). An autobiographical study. In J. Strachey (Ed. & Trans.), *The standard edition of the complete psychological works of Sigmund Freud* (Vol. 20, pp. 1–74). London, UK: Hogarth Press. (Original work published 1925)

Gartrell, N., & Bos, H. (2010). US national longitudinal lesbian family study: Psychological adjustment of 17-year-old adolescents. *Pediatrics, 126*, 28–36. doi:10.1542/peds.2009-3153

Gottman, J., & Levenson, R. (2010). *The 12 year study. Gay and lesbian couples research: A case of similarities of same-sex and cross-sex relationships, differences between gay and lesbian couples.* Manuscript submitted for publication. Retrieved from www.gottman.com/SubPage.aspx?spdt_id=2&sp_id=100842&spt_id=1

Gruszczynska, A. (2009). Sowing the seeds of solidarity in public space: Case study of the Poznan March of Equality. *Sexualities, 12*(3), 312–33. doi:10.1177/1363460709103893

Hansbury, G. (2004). Sexual TNT: A transman tells the truth about testosterone. *Journal of Gay & Lesbian Psychotherapy, 8*(1), 7–18. doi:10.1300/J236v08n01_02

Herdt, G. (1997). *Same sex, different cultures.* Boulder, CO: Westview Press.

Hetrick, E.S., & Martin, A.D. (1984). Ego-dystonic homosexuality: A developmental view. In E.S. Herrick & T.S. Stein (Eds), *Innovations in psychotherapy with homosexuals* (pp. 1–21). Washington, DC: American Psychiatric Press.

Hinds, A. (2011, June 28). Higher percentage of same-sex couples have kids in conservative states and suburbs, Census says. *Family Matters.* Retrieved from http://parentables.howstuffworks.com/family-matters/higher-percentage-same-sex-couples-have-kids-conservative-states-and-suburbs-census-says.html

Hunter, E. (2008). What's good for the gays is good for the gander: Making homeless youth housing safer for lesbian, gay, bisexual, and transgender youth. *Family Court Review, 46*(3), 543–57. doi:10.1111/j.1744-1617.2008.00220.x

Hurley, M.C. (2005). *Sexual orientation and legal rights: A chronological overview.* Ottawa, ON: Library of Parliament. Retrieved from www2.parl.gc.ca/Content/LOP/ResearchPublications/prb0413-e.htm

Jannini, E.A., Blanchard, R., Camperio-Ciani, A., & Bancroft, J. (2010). Male homosexuality: Nature or culture? *Journal of Sexual Medicine, 7*(10), 3245–53. doi:10.1111/j.1743-6109.2010.02024.x

Kaiser Family Foundation. (2001). *Inside-out: A report on the experiences of lesbians, gays and bisexuals in America and the public's views on issues and policies related to sexual orientation.* Retrieved from www.kff.org/kaiserpolls/3193-index.cfm

Kirk, K.M., Bailey, J.M., & Martin, N.G. (2000). Etiology of male sexual orientation in an Australian twin sample. *Psychology, Evolution & Gender, 2*(3), 301–11. doi:10.1080/14616660010024418

Kitzinger, C., & Wilkinson, S. (1995). Transitions from heterosexuality to lesbianism: The discursive production of lesbian identities. *Developmental Psychology, 31*, 95–104. doi:10.1037/0012-1649.31.1.95

Klein, F., Sepekoff, B., & Wolf, T.J. (1985). Sexual orientation: A multi-variable dynamic process. *Journal of Homosexuality, 11*(1–2), 35–49. doi:10.1300/J082v11n01_04

Kurdek, L.A. (1998). Relationship outcomes and their predictors: Longitudinal evidence from heterosexual married, gay cohabiting, and lesbian cohabiting couples. *Journal of Marriage and the Family, 60*(3), 553–68. doi:10.2307/353528

Kurdek, L.A. (2006). Differences between partners from heterosexual, gay, and lesbian cohabiting couples. *Journal of Marriage and Family, 68*(2), 509–28. doi:10.1111/j.1741-3737.2006.00268.x

Lalumière, M.L., Blanchard, R., & Zucker, K.J. (2000). Sexual orientation and handedness in men and women: A meta-analysis. *Psychological Bulletin, 126*(4), 575–92.

Laumann, E.O., Gagnon, J.H., Michael, R.T., & Michaels, S. (1994). *The social organization of sexuality: Sexual practices in the United States.* Chicago, IL: University of Chicago Press.

Levay, S. (1991). A difference in hypothalamic structure between heterosexual and homosexual men. *Science, 253*(5023), 1034–7.

Loulan, J. (1988). Research on the sex practices of 1566 lesbians and the clinical applications. *Women & Therapy, 7*(2–3), 221–34. doi:10.1300/J015v07n02_18

Matteson, D.R. (1996). Psychotherapy with bisexual individuals. In R.P. Cabaj & T.S. Stein (Eds), *Textbook of homosexuality and mental health* (pp. 433–50). Washington, DC: American Psychiatric Association.

Money, J. (1987). Sin, sickness, or status? Homosexual gender identity and psychoneuroendocrinology. *American Psychologist, 42*(4), 384–99. doi:10.1037/0003-066X.42.4.384

Nicolosi, J., Byrd, A.D., & Potts, R.W. (2000). Retrospective self-reports of changes in homosexual orientation: A consumer survey of conversion therapy clients. *Psychological Reports, 86*, 1071–88. doi:10.2466/PR0.86.3.1071–88

Noack, T., Seierstad, A., & Weedon-Fekjaer, H. (2005). A demographic analysis of registered partnerships (legal same-sex unions): The case of Norway. *European Journal of Population, 21*(1), 89–109. doi:10.1007/s10680-005-3626-z

Page, E.H. (2004). Mental health services experiences of bisexual women and bisexual men: An empirical study. *The Journal of Bisexuality, 3*(3–4), 137–60. doi:10.1300/J159v04n01_11

Patterson, C.J. (2009). Children of lesbian and gay parents: Psychology, law, and policy. *American Psychologist, 64*(8), 727–36. doi:10.1037/0003-066X.64.8.727

Patterson, C.J., & Hastings, P. (2007). Socialization in context of family diversity. In J. Grusee & P.D. Hastings (Eds), *Handbook of socialization* (pp. 328–52). New York, NY: Guilford Press.

Pedersen, P.B., Crethar, H.C., & Carlson, J. (2008). *Inclusive cultural empathy: Making relationships central in counseling and psychotherapy.* Washington, DC: American Psychological Association.

Peplau, L.A., & Fingerhut, A.W. (2007). The close relationships of lesbian and gay men. *Annual Review of Psychology, 58*, 405–24. doi:10.1146/annurev.psych.58.110405.085701

Percy, W.A., III. (1996). *Pederasty and pedagogy in archaic Greece.* Chicago, IL: University of Illinois Press.

Prause, N., & Graham, C.A. (2007). Asexuality: Classification and characterization. *Archives of Sexual Behavior, 36*(3), 341–56. doi:10.1007/s10508-006-9142-3

Ramirez, O.M., & Brown, J. (2010). Attachment style, rules regarding sex, and couple satisfaction: A study of gay male couples. *Australian and New Zealand Journal of Family Therapy, 31*(2), 202–13. doi:10.1375/anft.31.2.202

Reasons, C.E., Conley, D.J., & Debro, J. (2002). *Race, class, gender and justice in the United States.* Boston, MA: Allyn & Bacon.

Relf, M.V. (2001). Childhood sexual abuse in men who have sex with men: The current state of the science. *Journal of the Association of Nurses in AIDS Care, 12*(5), 20–9. doi:10.1016/S1055-3290(06)60260-4

Reuben, D. (1969). *Everything you always wanted to know about sex but were afraid to ask.* Toronto, ON: Bantam.

Rosario, M., Schrimshaw, E.W., & Hunter, J. (2011). Different patterns of sexual identity development over time: Implications for the psychological adjustment of lesbian, gay, and bisexual youths. *Journal of Sex Research, 48*(1), 3–15. doi:10.1080/00224490903331067

Ross, M.W., & Schonnesson, L.N. (2000). HIV/AIDS and sexuality. In L.T. Szuchman & F. Muscarella (Eds), *Psychological perspectives on human sexuality* (pp. 383–415). New York, NY: John Wiley & Sons.

Rothblum, E.D. (2009). An overview of same-sex couples in relationships: A research area still at sea. In D.A. Hope (Ed.), *Contemporary perspectives on lesbian, gay, and bisexual identities* (pp. 113–39). New York, NY: Springer Science + Business Media.

Rust, P.C. (2001). Two many and not enough: The meanings of bisexual identities. *Journal of Bisexuality, 1*(1), 31–68. doi:10.1300/J159v01n01_04

Savin-Williams, R.C. (2005). *The new gay teenager.* Cambridge, MA: Harvard University Press.

Sophie, J. (1985/1986). A critical examination of stage theories of lesbian identity development. *Journal of Homosexuality, 12,* 39–51.

Spitalnick, J.S., & McNair, L.D. (2005). Couples therapy with gay and lesbian clients: An analysis of important clinical issues. *Journal of Sex and Marital Therapy, 31*(1), 43–56. doi:http://dx.doi.org/10.1080/00926230590475260

Spitzer, R.L. (2003). Can some gay men and lesbians change their sexual orientation? 200 participants reporting a change from homosexual to heterosexual orientation. *Archives of Sexual Behavior, 32*(5), 403–17. doi:10.1023/A:1025647527010

Stein, T.S. (1997). Deconstructing sexual orientation: Understanding the phenomena of sexual orientation. *Journal of Homosexuality, 34*(1), 81–6.

Storms, M.D. (1981). A theory of erotic orientation development. *Psychological Review, 88,* 340–53. doi:10.1037/0033-295X.88.4.340

Suarez, T., & Kauth, M.R. (2001). Assessing basic HIV transmission risks and the contextual factors associated with HIV risk behavior in men who have sex with men. *In Session: Psychotherapy in Practice, 57,* 655–69. doi:10.1002/jclp.1035

Sullivan, R., & Harrington, M. (2009). The politics and ethics of same-sex adoption. *Journal of GLBT Family Studies, 5*(3), 235–46. doi:10.1080/15504280903035662

Tasker, F. (2005). Lesbian mothers, gay fathers, and their children: A review. *Journal of Developmental & Behavioral Pediatrics, 26*(3), 224–40. Retrieved from http://journals.lww.com/jrnldbp/pages/default.aspx

Townsend, J.M. (1998). *What women want—what men want: Why the sexes still see love and commitment so differently.* New York, NY: Oxford University Press.

Turner, C.F., Villarroel, M.A., Chromy, J.R., Eggleston, E., & Rogers, S.M. (2005). Trends: Same-gender sex among US adults: trends across the twentieth century and during the 1990s. *Public Opinion Quarterly, 69*(3), 439–62. doi:10.1093/poq/nfi025

Wienke, C., & Hill, G.J. (2009). Does the "marriage benefit" extend to partners in gay and lesbian relationships? Evidence from a random sample of sexually active adults. *Journal of Family Issues, 30*(2), 259–89. doi:10.1177/0192513X08324382

Witelson, S.F., Kigar, D.L., Scamvougeras, A., Kideckel, D.M., Buck, B., Stanchev, P. L., . . . Black, S. (2008). Corpus callosum anatomy in right-handed homosexual and heterosexual men. *Archives of Sexual Behavior, 37*(6), 857–63. doi:10.1007/s10508-007-9276-y

Wolf, T.J. (1985). Marriages of bisexual men. *Journal of Homosexuality, 11*(1-2), 135–48. doi:10.1300/J082v11n01_11

CHAPTER 12

Acevedo, B.P., & Aron, A. (2009). Does a long-term relationship kill romantic love? *Review of General Psychology, 13*(1), 59–65. doi:10.1037/a0014226

Acevedo, B.P., Aron, A., Fisher, H.E., & Brown, L.L. (2011, January 5). Neural correlates of long-term intense romantic love. *Social Cognitive and Affective Neuroscience.* doi:10.1093/scan/nsq092

Acker, M., & Davis, M.H. (1992). Intimacy, passion, and commitment in adult romantic relationships: A test of the triangular theory of love. *Journal of Social and Personal Relationships, 9,* 21–50. doi:10.1177/0265407592091002

Back, M.D., Schmukle, S.C., & Egloff, B. (2008). Becoming friends by chance. *Psychological Science, 19*(5), 439–40. doi:10.1111/j.1467-9280.2008.02106.x

Bartels, A., & Zeki, S. (2004). The neural correlates of maternal and romantic love. *Neuroimage, 21,* 1155–66. doi:10.1016/j.neuroimage.2003.11.003

Bartholomew, K. (1990). Avoidance of intimacy: An attachment perspective. *Journal of Social and Personal Relationships, 7*(2), 147–78. doi:10.1177/0265407590072001

Bartholomew, K., & Horowitz, L.M. (1991). Attachment styles among young adults: A test of a four-category model. *Journal of Personality and Social Psychology, 61*(2), 226–44. doi:10.1037/0022-3514.61.2.226

Baumeister, R.F., Wotman, S.R., & Stillwell, A.M. (1993). Unrequited love: On heartbreak, anger, guilt, scriptlessness, and humiliation. *Journal of Personality and Social Psychology, 64,* 377–94. doi:10.1037//0022-3514.64.3.377

Ben-Ari, A., & Lavee, Y. (2007). Dyadic closeness in marriage: From the inside story to a conceptual model. *Journal of Social and Personal Relationships, 24*(5), 627–44. doi:10.1177/0265407507081451

Berscheid, E., & Walster, E. (1974). A little about love: A minor essay on a major topic. In T. Huston (Ed.), *Foundations of interpersonal attraction* (pp. 355–81). New York, NY: Academic Press.

Blow, A.J., & Hartnett, K. (2005). Infidelity in committed relationships II: A substantive review. *Journal of Marital and Family Therapy, 31*(2), 217–33. doi:10.1111/j.1752-0606.2005.tb01556.x

Bogaert, A.F., & Sadava, S. (2002). Adult attachment and sexual behavior. *Personal Relationships, 9*(2), 191–204. doi:10.1111/1475-6811.00012

Boies, S.C. (2002). University students' uses of and reactions to online sexual information and entertainment: Links to online and offline sexual behaviour. *The Canadian Journal of Human Sexuality, 11*(2), 77–89. Retrieved from www.sieccan.org/cjhs.html

Buss, D.M., Larsen, R.J., Westen, D., & Semmelroth, J. (1992). Sex differences in jealousy: Evolution, physiology, and psychology. *Psychological Science, 3*, 251–5. doi:10.1111/j.1467-9280.1992.tb00038.x

Buss, D.M., Abbot, M., Angleitner, A., Asherian, A., Biaggio, A., Blanco-Villasenor, A., . . . Yang, K.-S. (1990). International preferences in selecting mates: A study of 37 cultures. *Journal of Cross-Cultural Psychology, 21*(1), 5–47. doi:10.1177/0022022190211001

Byrne, D. & Nelson, D. (1965). Attraction as a linear function of proportion of positive reinforcements. *Journal of Personality and Social Psychology, 1*(6), 659–63. doi:10.1037/h0022073

Cunningham, M.R. (1989). Reactions to heterosexual opening gambits: Female selectivity and male responsiveness. *Personality and Social Psychology Bulletin, 15*(1), 27–41. doi:10.1177/0146167289151003

Desteno, D., Valdesolo, P., & Bartlett, M.Y. (2006). Jealousy and the threatened self: Getting to the heart of the green-eyed monster. *Journal of Personality and Social Psychology, 91*(4), 626–41. doi:10.1037/0022-3514.91.4.626

Diamond, L.M. (2004). Emerging perspectives on distinctions between romantic love and sexual desire. *Current Directions in Psychological Science, 13*(3), 116–19. doi:10.1111/j.0963-7214.2004.00287.x

Dion, K.L., & Dion, K.K. (1993). Gender and ethnocultural comparisons in styles of love. *Psychology of Women Quarterly, 17*(4), 463–73. doi:10.1111/j.1471-6402.1993.tb00656.x

Dutton, D.G., & Aron, A.P. (1974). Some evidence for heightened sexual attraction under conditions of high anxiety. *Journal of Personality and Social Psychology, 30*(4), 510–17. Retrieved from www.apa.org/pubs/journals/psp/index.aspx

Elphinston, R.A., & Noller, P. (2011). Time to face it! Facebook intrusion and the implications for romantic jealousy and relationship satisfaction. *Cyberpsychology, Behavior, and Social Networking, 14*(11), 631–5. doi:10.1089/cyber.2010.0318

Facebook. (2013). *Key facts.* Retrieved from http://newsroom.fb.com/Key-Facts

Fehr, B. (1988). Prototype analysis of the concepts of love and commitment. *Journal of Personality and Social Psychology, 55*(4), 557–79. doi:10.1037/0022-3514.55.4.557

Fisher, H. (2006). The drive to love: The neural mechanism for mate selection. In R.J. Sternberg & K. Weis (Eds), *The new psychology of love* (pp. 87–115). New Haven, CT: Yale.

Fisher, H., Aron, A., & Brown, L.L. (2005). Romantic love: An fMRI study of a neural mechanism for mate choice. *The Journal of Comparative Neurology, 493*(1), 58–62. doi:10.1002/cne.20772

Fisher, H.E., Brown, L.L., Aron, A., Strong, G., & Mashek, D. (2010). Reward, addiction, and emotion regulation systems associated with rejection in love. *Journal of Neurophysiology, 104*(1), 51–60. doi:10.1152/jn.00784.2009

Fraley, R.C., & Shaver, P.R. (2000). Adult romantic attachment: Theoretical developments, emerging controversies, and unanswered questions. *Review of General Psychology, 4*(2), 132–54. doi:10.1037/1089-2680.4.2.132

Fricker, J., & Moore, S. (2002). Relationship satisfaction: The role of love styles and attachment styles. *Current Research in Social Psychology, 7*(11), 182–204. Retrieved from www.uiowa.edu/~grpproc/crisp/crisp.html

Gangestad, S.W., & Scheyd, G.J. (2005). The evolution of human physical attractiveness. *Annual Review of Anthropology, 34*, 523–48. doi:10.1146/annurev.anthro.33.070203.143733

Garver-Apgar, C.E., Gangestad, S.W., Thornhill, R., Miller, R.D., & Olp, J.J. (2006). Major histocompatibility complex alleles, sexual responsivity, and unfaithfulness in romantic couples. *Psychological Science, 17*(10), 830–5. doi:10.1111/j.1467-9280.2006.01789.x

Gilbert, R.L., Gonzalez, M.A., & Murphy, N.A. (2011). Sexuality in the 3-D Internet and its relationship to real-life sexuality. *Psychology & Sexuality, 2*(2), 107–22. doi:10.1080/19419899.2010.536987

Gilbert, R.L., Murphy, N.A., & Ávalos, M.C. (2011). Realism, idealization, and potential negative impact of 3-D virtual relationships. *Computers in Human Behavior, 27*(5), 2039–204. doi:10.1016/j.chb.2011.05.011

Guerrero, L.K., Farinelli, L., & McEwan, B. (2009). Attachment and relational satisfaction: The mediating effect of emotional communication. *Communication Monographs, 76*(4), 487–514. doi:10.1080/03637750903300254

Hatfield, E., & Rapson, R.L. (1993). *Love, sex, and intimacy: Their psychology, biology, and history.* New York, NY: HarperCollins.

Hazan, C., & Shaver, P. (1987). Romantic love conceptualized as an attachment process. *Journal of Personality and Social Psychology, 52*(3), 511–24. doi:10.1037/0022-3514.52.3.511

Helsper, E.J., & Whitty, M.T. (2010). Netiquette within married couples: Agreement about acceptable online behavior and surveillance between partners. *Computers in Human Behavior, 26*(5), 916–26. doi:10.1016/j.chb.2010.02.006

Henderson, A.J.Z., Bartholomew, K., Trinke, S., & Kwong, M.J. (2005). When loving means hurting: An exploration of attachment and intimate abuse in a community sample. *Journal of Family Violence, 20*(4), 219–230. DOI: 10.1007/s10896-005-5985-y

Hendrick, C., & Hendrick, S. (1986). A theory and method of love. *Journal of Personality and Social Psychology, 50*(2), 392–402. doi:10.1037/0022-3514.50.2.392

Hendrick, S.S. (2004). Close relationship research: A resource for couple and family therapists. *Journal of Marital and Family Therapy, 30*(1), 13–27. doi:10.1111/j.1752-0606.2004.tb01219.x

Hendrick, S.S., & Hendrick, C. (1997). Love and satisfaction. In R.J. Sternberg, & M. Hojjat (Eds), *Satisfaction in close relationships* (pp. 56–78). New York, NY: Guildford.

Hendrick, S.S., & Hendrick, C. (2002). Linking romantic love with sex: Development of the perceptions of love and sex scale. *Journal of Social and Personal Relationships, 19*(3), 361–78. doi:10.1177/0265407502193004

Huber, J.D., & Herold, E.S. (2006). Sexually overt approaches in singles bars. *The Canadian Journal of Human Sexuality, 15*(3–4), 133–46. Retrieved from www.sieccan.org/cjhs.html

Kleinke, C.L., Meeker, F.B., & Staneski, R.A. (1986). Preference for opening lines: Comparing ratings by men and women. *Sex Roles, 15*(11–12), 585–600. doi:10.1007/BF00288216

Kleinplatz, P.J. (2010). Lessons from great lovers. In S.B. Levine, C.B. Risen, & S.E. Althof (Eds), *Handbook of clinical sexuality for mental health professionals* (pp. 57–72). New York, NY: Routledge.

Kleinplatz, P.J., & Ménard, A.D. (2007). Building blocks toward optimal sexuality: Constructing a conceptual model. *The Family Journal, 15*(1), 72–8. doi:10.1177/1066480706294126

Kleinplatz, P.J., Ménard, A.D., Paquet, M.-P., Paradis, N., Campbell, M., Zuccarino, D., & Mehak, L. (2009). The components of optimal sexuality: A portrait of "great sex". *The Canadian Journal of Human Sexuality, 18*(1–2), 1–13. Retrieved from www.sieccan.org/cjhs.html

Lacey, R.S., Reifman, A., Scott, J.P., Harris, S.M., & Fitzpatrick, J. (2004). Sexual-moral attitudes, love styles, and mate selection. *Journal of Sex Research, 41*(2), 121–8. doi:10.1080/00224490409552220

Langlois, J.H., Roggman, L.A., & Musselman, L. (1994). What is average and what is not average about attractive faces? *Psychological Science, 5*(4), 214–20. doi:10.1111/j.1467-9280.1994.tb00503.x

Lee, J.A. (1973). *Colours of love: An exploration of the ways of loving.* Toronto, ON: New Press.

Lemieux, R., & Hale, J.L. (2002). Cross-sectional analysis of intimacy, passion, and commitment: Testing the assumptions of the triangular theory of love. *Psychological Reports, 90,* 1009–14. doi:10.2466/PR0.90.3.1009-1014

Levine, R., Sato, S., Hashimoto, T., & Verma, J. (1995). Love and marriage in eleven cultures. *Journal of Cross-Cultural Psychology, 26*(5), 554–71. doi:10.1177/0022022195265007

Luo, S., & Zhang, G. (2009). What leads to romantic attraction: Similarity, reciprocity, security, or beauty? Evidence from a speed-dating study. *Journal of Personality, 77*(4), 933–63. doi:10.1111/j.1467-6494.2009.00570.x

MacIntosh, H., Reissing, E.D., & Andruff, H. (2010). Same-sex marriage in Canada: The impact of legal marriage on the first cohort of gay and lesbian Canadians to wed. *The Canadian Journal of Human Sexuality, 19*(3), 79–90. Retrieved from www.sieccan.org/cjhs.html

Mark, K.P., Janssen, E., Milhausen, R.R. (2011). Infidelity in heterosexual couples: Demographic, interpersonal, and personality-related predictors of extradyadic sex. *Archives of Sexual Behavior, 40*(5), 971–82. doi 10.1007/s10508-011-9771-z

Maticka-Tyndale, E., Herold, E.S., & Mewhinney, D. (1998). Casual sex on spring break: Intentions and behaviors of Canadian students. *Journal of Sex Research, 35*(3), 254–64. doi:10.1080/00224499809551941

Ménard, A.D., & Kleinplatz, P.J. (2008). Twenty-one moves guaranteed to make his thighs go up in flames: Depictions of "great sex" in popular magazines. *Sexuality & Culture, 12*(1), 1–20. doi:10.1007/s12119-007-9013-7

Meston, C.M., & Buss, D.M. (2007). Why humans have sex. *Archives of Sexual Behavior, 36,* 477–507. doi:10.1007/s10508-007-9175-2

Morahan-Martin, J., & Schumacher, P. (2003). Loneliness and social uses of the Internet. *Computers in Human Behavior, 19*(6), 659–71. doi:10.1016/S0747-5632(03)00040-2

Moreland, R.L., & Beach, S.R. (1992). Exposure effects in the classroom: The development of affinity among students. *Journal of Experimental Social Psychology, 28*(3), 255–76. doi:10.1016/0022-1031(92)90055-O

Moss, B.F., & Schwebel, A.I. (1993). Defining intimacy in romantic relationships. *Family Relations, 42*(1), 31–7. doi:10.2307/584918

Muise, A., Christofides, E., & Desmarais, S. (2009). More information than you ever wanted: Does Facebook bring out the green-eyed monster of jealousy? *Cyberpsychology & Behavior, 12*(4), 441–4. doi:10.1089/cpb.2008.0263

O'Leary, K.D., Acevedo, B.P., Aron, A., Huddy, L., & Mashek, D. (2012). Is long-term love more than a rare phenomenon? If so, what are its correlates? *Social Psychological and Personality Science, 3*(2). doi:10.1177/1948550611417015

Paul, E.L., & Hayes, K.A. (2002). The casualties of "casual sex": A qualitative exploration of the phenomenology of college students' hookups. *Journal of Social and Personal Relationships, 19*(5), 639–61. doi:10.1177/0265407502195006

Paul, E.L., McManus, B., & Hayes, A. (2000). "Hookups": Characteristics and correlates of college students' spontaneous and anonymous sexual experiences. *Journal of Sex Research, 37*(1), 76–88. doi:10.1080/00224490009552023

Penn, D.J., & Potts, W.K. (1999). The evolution of mating preferences and major histocompatibility complex genes. *The American Naturalist, 153*(2), 145–64. doi:10.1086/303166

Penn, R. (2011). Arranged marriages in Western Europe: Media representations and social reality. *Journal of Comparative Family Studies, 42*(5), 637–50. Retrieved from http://soci.ucalgary.ca/jcfs

Poyner-Del Vento, P.W., & Cobb, R. J. (2011). Chronic stress as a moderator of the association between depressive symptoms and marital satisfaction. *Journal of Social and Clinical Psychology, 30*(9), 905–36. doi:10.1521/jscp.2011.30.9.905

Previti, D., & Amato, P.R. (2004). Is infidelity a cause or a consequence of poor marital quality? *Journal of Social and Personal Relationships, 21*(2), 217–30. doi:10.1177/0265407504041384

Provost, M.P., Troje, N.F., & Quinsey, V.L. (2008). Short-term mating strategies and attraction to masculinity in point-light walkers. *Evolution and Human Behavior, 29*(1), 65–9. doi:10.1016/j.evolhumbehav.2007.07.007

Regan, P.C., Kocan, E.R., & Whitlock, T. (1998). Ain't love grand! A prototype analysis of the concept of romantic love. *Journal of Social and Personal Relationships, 15*(3), 411–20. doi:10.1177/0265407598153006

Rhodes, G., Sumich, A., & Byatt, G. (1999). Are average facial configurations attractive only because of their symmetry? *Psychological Science, 10*(52), doi:10.1111/1467-9280.00106

Roberts, S.C., Havlicek, J., Flegr, J., Hruskova, M., Little, A.C., Jones, B.C., . . . Petrie, M. (2004). Female facial attractiveness increases during the fertile phase of the menstrual cycle. *Proceedings of the Royal Society B: Biological Sciences, 271*(Suppl. 5), S270–2. doi 10.1098/rsbl.2004.0174

Sagarin, B.J., Becker, D.V., Guadagno, R.E., Nicastle, L.D., & Millevoi, A. (2003). Sex differences (and similarities) in jealousy: The moderating influence of infidelity experience and sexual orientation of the infidelity. *Evolution and Human Behavior, 24*(1), 17–23. doi:10.1016/S1090-5138(02)00106-X

Schaefer, M.T., & Olson, D.H. (1981). Assessing intimacy: The pair inventory. *Journal of Marital and Family Therapy, 7*(1), 47–60. doi:10.1111/j.1752-0606.1981.tb01351.x

Schneider, J.P. (2000). Effects of cybersex addiction on the family: Results of a survey. *Sexual Addiction & Compulsivity, 7*(1–2), 31–58. doi:10.1080/10720160008400206

Sims, K.E., & Meana, M. (2010). Why did passion wane? A qualitative study of married women's attributions for declines in sexual desire. *Journal of Sex and Marital Therapy, 36*(4), 360–80. doi:10.1080/0092623X.2010.498727

Singh, D., & Bronstad, P.M. (2001). Female body odour is a potential cue to ovulation. *Proceedings of the Royal Society B: Biological Sciences, 268*(1469), 797–801. doi:10.1098/rspb.2001.1589

Statistics Canada. (2009). *Canadian Internet use survey*. Retrieved from www.statcan.gc.ca/daily-quotidien/100510/dq100510a-eng.htm

Sternberg, R.J. (1986). A triangular theory of love. *Psychological Review, 93*(2), 119–35. doi:10.1037/0033-295X.93.2.119

Sternberg, R.J. (2006). A duplex theory of love. In R.J. Sternberg & K. Weis (Eds), *The new psychology of love* (pp. 184–99). New Haven, CT: Yale.

Sternberg, R.J., Hojjat, M., & Barnes, M.L. (2001). Empirical tests of aspects of a theory of love as a story. *European Journal of Personality, 15*(3), 199–218. doi:10.1002/per.405

Stinson, R.D. (2010). Hooking up in young adulthood: A review of factors influencing the sexual behavior of college students. *Journal of College Student Psychotherapy, 24*(2), 98–115. doi:10.1080/87568220903558596

Strachman, A., & Impett, E.A. (2009). Attachment orientations and daily condom use in dating relationships. *Journal of Sex Research, 46*(4), 319–29. doi:10.1080/00224490802691801

Swami, V., & Furnham, A. (2008). Is love really so blind? *Psychologist, 21*(2), 108–11.

Terry, J. (2010). Loving objects. *Trans-Humanities, 2*(1), 33–75.

Weber, K., Goodboy, A.K., & Cayanus, J.L. (2010). Flirting competence: An experimental study on appropriate and effective opening lines. *Communication Research Reports, 27*(2), 184–91. doi:10.1080/08824091003738149

Wedekind, C., Seebeck, T., Bettens, F., & Paepke, A.J. (1995). MHC-dependent mate preferences in humans. *Proceedings: Biological Sciences, 260*, 245–9. doi:10.1098/rspb.1995.0087

Whitchurch, E.R., Wilson, T.D., & Gilbert, D.T. (2011). "He loves me, he loves me not . . .": Uncertainty can increase romantic attraction. *Psychological Science, 22*(2), 172–5. doi:10.1177/0956797610393745

White, G.L., & Mullen, P.E. (1989). *Jealousy: Theory, research, and clinical strategies*. New York, NY: Guildford.

Widmer, E.D., Treas, J., & Newcomb, R. (1998). Attitudes toward nonmarital sex in 24 countries. *Journal of Sex Research, 35*(4), 349–58. doi:10.1080/00224499809551953

Wiederman, M.W. (1997). Extramarital sex: Prevalence and correlates in a national survey. *Journal of Sex Research, 34*(2), 167–74. doi:10.1080/00224499709551881

Worth, H., Reid, A., & McMillan, K. (2002). Somewhere over the rainbow: Love, trust, and monogamy in gay relationships. *Journal of Sociology, 38*(3), 237–53. doi:10.1177/1440783302128756642

Zeki, S., & Romaya, J.P. (2010). The brain reaction to viewing faces of opposite- and same-sex romantic partners. *PLoS ONE 5(12)*, e15802. doi:10.1371/journal.pone.0015802

CHAPTER 13

Artuso, A. (2010, April 20). Sex education program sparks outcry. *Toronto Sun*. Retrieved from www.torontosun.com/news/canada/2010/04/20/13658066.html

Ball, J., Cowan, P., & Cowan, C. (1995). Who's got the power? Gender differences in partners' perceptions of influence during marital problem-solving discussions. *Family Process, 34*, 303–21. doi:10.1111/j.1545-5300.1995.00303.x

Bradbury, T.N. (1994). Unintended effects of marital research on marital relationships. *Journal of Family Psychology, 8*(2), 187–201. doi:10.1037//0893-3200.8.2.187

CBC News. (2010, April 22). Sex-ed change needs "rethink": Ont. premier. Retrieved from www.cbc.ca/news/canada/toronto/story/2010/04/22/sex-ed.html

Christensen, A. (1987). Detection of conflict patterns in couples. In K. Hahlweg & M.J. Goldstein (Eds), *Understanding major mental disorders: The contribution of family interaction research*, (pp. 250–65). New York, NY: Family Process Press.

Christensen, A., & Heavey, C.L. (1990). Gender and social structure in demand/withdraw pattern of marital conflict. *Journal of Personality and Social Psychology, 59*, 73–81. doi:10.1037//0022-3514.59.1.73

Coan, J.A., & Gottman, J.M. (2007). The Specific Affect (SPAFF) coding system. In J.A. Coan & J.J.B. Allen (Eds), *Handbook of emotion elicitation and assessment* (pp.106–23). New York, NY: Oxford University Press.

Cohen, J.N., Byers, E.S., Sears, H.A., & Weaver, A.D. (2004). Sexual health education: Attitudes, knowledge, and comfort of teachers in New Brunswick schools. *The Canadian Journal of Human Sexuality, 13*(1), 1–15. Retrieved from www.sieccan.org/cjhs.html

Cupach, W., & Canary, D. (1995). Managing conflict and anger: Investigating the sex stereotype hypothesis. In P. Kalbfleisch & M. Cody (Eds), *Gender, power, and communication in human relationships* (pp. 233–52). Hillsdale, NJ: Lawrence Erlbaum

Cupach, W.R. & Metts, S. (1991). Sexuality and communication in close relationships. In K. McKinney & S. Sprecher (Eds), *Sexuality in close relationships* (pp. 93–110). Hillsdale, NJ: Lawrence Erlbaum.

Dawson, J., Fallis, E., & Rehman, U.S. (2010, October). *Why is this so difficult? Challenges of discussing sexual issues in committed relationship*. Paper presented at the Canadian Sex Research Forum, Toronto, ON.

Downey, G., Freitas, A.L., Michaelis, B., & Khouri, H. (1998). The self-fulfilling prophecy in close relationships: Rejection sensitivity and rejection by romantic partners. *Journal of Personality and Social Psychology, 75*, 545–60. doi:10.1037//0022-3514.75.2.545

Gilligan, C. (1982). *In a different voice: Psychological theory and women's development*. Cambridge, MA: Harvard University Press.

Gottman, J.M. (1979). *Marital interaction: Experimental investigations*. New York, NY: Academic Press.

Gottman, J.M. (1999). *The marriage clinic: A scientifically based marital therapy*. New York, NY: Norton Publications.

Gottman, J.M., & Carrère, S. (1994). Why can't men and women get along? Developmental roots and marital inequities. In D.J. Canary & L. Stafford (Eds), *Communication and relational maintenance* (pp. 203–29). San Diego, CA: Academic Press.

Gottman, J.M., & Levenson, R.W. (1988). The social psychophysiology of marriage. In P. Noller & M.A. Fitzpatrick (Eds), *Perspectives on marital interaction* (pp. 182–200). Clevedon, England: Multilingual Matters.

Gray, J. (1992). *Men are from Mars, women are from Venus*. New York, NY: Harper Collins.

Greenberg, L.S., & Goldman, R.N. (2008). Anger in couples therapy. In L.S. Greenberg & R.N. Goldman (Eds), *Emotion-focused couples therapy: The dynamics of emotion, love, and power* (pp. 227–57). Washington, DC: American Psychological Association. doi:10.1037/11750-010

Guerrero, L.K., & Floyd, K. (2006). *Nonverbal communication in close relationships*. Mahwah, NJ: Lawrence Erlbaum.

Halford, W.K., Hahlweg, K., & Dunne, M. (1990). The cross-cultural consistency of marital communication associated with marital distress. *Journal of Marriage and the Family, 52(2)*, 487–500. doi:10.2307/353042

Heavey, C.L., Layne, C., & Christensen, A. (1993). Gender and conflict structure in marital interaction: A replication and extension. *Journal of Consulting and Clinical Psychology, 61*, 16–27. doi:10.1037//0022-006X.61.1.16

Heyman, R.E. (2001). Observation of couple conflicts: Clinical assessment applications, stubborn truths, and shaky foundations. *Psychological Assessment, 13*(1), 5–35. doi:10.1037//1040-3590.13.1.5

Holmberg, D., & Blair, K.L. (2009). Sexual desire, communication, satisfaction, and preferences of men and women in same-sex versus mixed-sex relationships. *Journal of Sex Research, 46*(1), 57–66. doi:10.1080/00224490802645294

Holtzworth-Munroe, A., Smutzler, N., & Stuart, G.L. (1998). Demand and withdraw communication among couples experiencing husband violence. *Journal of Consulting and Clinical Psychology, 66*, 731–43. doi:10.1037//0022-006X.66.5.731

Jacobson, N.S. (1983). Beyond empiricism: The politics of marital therapy. *American Journal of Family Therapy, 11*(2), 11–24. doi:10.1080/01926188308250118

Kelly, M.P., Strassberg, D.S., & Turner, D.S. (2006). Behavioural assessment of couples' communication in female orgasmic disorder. *Journal of Sex & Marital Therapy, 32*, 81–95. doi:10.1080/00926230500442243

Levenson, R.W., & Gottman, J.M. (1983). Marital interaction: Physiological linkage and affective exchange. *Journal of Personality and Social Psychology, 45*, 587–97. doi:10.1037//0022-3514.45.3.587

Lloyd, S. (1987). Conflict in premarital relationships: Differential perceptions of males and females. *Family Relations, 36*, 290–94. doi:10.2307/583542

McKay, A. & Barrett, M. (1999). Pre-service sexual health education training of elementary, secondary, and physical health educators in Canadian faculties of education. *The Canadian Journal of Human Sexuality, 8*(2), 91–101. doi:1999-15699-002

McKay, A., Pietrusiak, M., & Holowaty, P. (1998). Parents' opinions and attitudes toward sexuality education in the schools. *Canadian Journal of Human Sexuality, 7*(2), 139–45. Retrieved from www.sieccan.org/cjhs.html

MacNeil, S., & Byers, E.S. (1997). The relationships between sexual problems, communication, and sexual satisfaction. *Canadian Journal of Human Sexuality, 6*, 277–83. Retrieved from www.sieccan.org/cjhs.html

MacNeil, S., & Byers, E.S. (2005). Dyadic assessment of sexual self-disclosure and sexual satisfaction in heterosexual dating couples. *Journal of Social and Personal Relationships, 22*, 169–81. doi:10.1177/0265407505050942

MacNeil, S., & Byers, E.S. (2009). Role of sexual self-disclosure in the sexual satisfaction of long-term heterosexual couples. *Journal of Sex Research, 46*, 3–14. doi:10.1080/00224490802398399

McNulty, J.K., & Karney, B.R. (2002). Expectancy confirmation in appraisals of marital interaction. *Personality and Social Psychology Bulletin, 28*, 764–75. doi:10.1177/0146167202289006

Margolin, G., & Wampold, B.E. (1981). Sequential analysis of conflict and accord in distressed and nondistressed marital partners. *Journal of Consulting and Clinical Psychology, 49*, 554–67. doi:10.1037//0022-006X.49.4.554

Margolin, G., John, R.S., & Gleberman, L. (1988). Affective responses to conflictual discussions in violent and nonviolent couples. *Journal of Consulting and Clinical Psychology, 56*, 24–33. doi:10.1037//0022-006X.56.1.24

Meaney, G.J., Rye, B.J., Wood, E., & Solovieva, E. (2009). Satisfaction with school-based sexual health education in a sample of university students recently graduated from Ontario high schools. *Canadian Journal of Human Sexuality, 18*, 107–25. Retrieved from www.sieccan.org/cjhs.html

Meston, C.M., Heiman, J.R., Trapnell, P.D., & Paulhus, D.L. (1998). Socially desirable responding and sexuality self-reports. *The Journal of Sex Research, 35*, 148–57. doi:10.1080/00224499809551928

Metts, S., & Cupach, R.W. (1989). The role of communication in sexuality. In K. McKinney & S. Sprecher (Eds), *Human sexuality: The societal and interpersonal context* (pp. 139–61). Norwood, NJ: Ablex.

Miller, D.T., & Turnbull, W. (1986). Expectancies and interpersonal processes. *Annual Review of Psychology, 37*, 233–56. doi:10.1146/annurev.ps.37.020186.001313

Paulhus, D.L. & Reid, D.B. (1991). Enhancement and denial in socially desirable responding. *Journal of Personality and Social Psychology, 60*, 307–17. doi:10.1037//0022-3514.60.2.307

Regulated Health Professions Act, 1991, S.O., 199, c.18. Retrieved from www.e-laws.gov.on.ca/html/statutes/english/elaws_statutes_91r18_e.htm

Rehman, U.S. & Holtzworth-Munroe, A. (2006). Gender differences in demand-withdraw: A cross-cultural analysis. *Journal of Consulting and Clinical Psychology, 74*, 755–66. www.apa.org/pubs/journals/ccp/index.aspx

Rehman, U.S. & Holtzworth-Munroe, A. (2007). A cross-cultural examination of the relation of marital communication behaviour to marital satisfaction. *Journal of Family Psychology, 21*, 759–63. doi:10.1037/0893-3200.21.4.759

Rehman, U., Janssen, E., Hahn, S., Heiman, J., Holtzworth-Munroe, A., Fallis, E., & Rafaeli, E. (2011). Marital satisfaction and communication behaviors during sexual and nonsexual conflict discussions in newlywed couples: A pilot study. *Journal of Sex and Marital Therapy, 37*, 94–103. doi:10.1080/0092623X.2011.547352

Rosenthal, R., & Jacobson, L. (1968). *Pygmalion in the classroom: Teacher expectation and pupils' intellectual development*. New York, NY: Holt, Rinehart & Winston.

Rubin, L.B. (1983). *Intimate strangers: Men and women together*. New York, NY: Harper & Row.

Sanford, K. (2003). Problem-solving conversations in marriage: Does it matter what topics couples discuss? *Personal Relationships, 10*, 97–112. doi:10.1111/1475-6811.00038

Vincent, J.P., Friedman, L.C., Nugent, J., & Messerly, L. (1979). Demand characteristics in observations of marital interaction. *Journal of Consulting and Clinical Psychology, 47*, 557–66. doi:10.1037//0022-006X.47.3.557

Weaver, A.D., Byers, E.S., Sears, H.A., Cohen, J.N., & Randall, H.E.S. (2002). Sexual health education at school and at home: Attitudes and experiences of New Brunswick parents. *Canadian Journal of Human Sexuality, 11*, 19–31. Retrieved from www.sieccan.org/cjhs.html

Winkler, I., & Doherty, W.J. (1983). Communication styles and marital satisfaction in Israeli and American couples. *Family Process, 22*, 229–37. doi:10.1111/j.1545-5300.1983.00221.x

Yarrow, C.J.S., & Osborne, P.J. (2004). The regulation of psychology in Ontario. In D.R. Evans (Ed.), *The law, standards, and ethics in the practice of psychology* (2nd ed., pp. 55-86). Toronto, ON: Emond Montgomery Publications.

CHAPTER 14

Ambert, A. (2005). *Same-sex couples and same-sex parent families: Relationships, parenting, and issues of marriage* (Rev. ed.). Ottawa, ON: Vanier Institute of the Family.

Ambert, A. (2009). *Divorce: Facts, causes, and consequences* (3rd ed.). Ottawa, ON: Vanier Institute of the Family.

Bala, N. (2009). Why Canada's prohibition of polygamy is constitutionally valid and sound social policy. *Canadian Journal of Family Law, 25*, 165-21. Retrieved from http://faculty.law.ubc .ca/cdnjfl/index.html

Barker, M., & Langdridge, D. (2010). Whatever happened to non-monogamies? *Critical Reflections on Recent Research and Theory, 13*, 748-72. doi:10.1177/1363460710384645

Barrett, A. (2004). Oral sex and teenagers: A sexual health educator's perspective. *The Canadian Journal of Human Sexuality, 13*, 197-200. Retrieved from www.sieccan.org/index.html

Barrett, M., King, A., Levy, J., Meticka-Tyndale, E., McKay, A., & Fraser, J. (2004). Canada. In R.T. Francoeur & R.J. Noonan (Eds), *The continuum complete international encyclopedia of sexuality*. New York, NY: Continuum. Retrieved from www .kinseyinstitute.org/ccies

Beres, M.A., Herold, E., & Maitland, S.B. (2004). Sexual consent behaviors in same-sex relationships. *Archives of Sexual Behavior, 33*, 475-86. doi:10.1023/B:ASEB.0000037428.41757.10

Bibby, R.W. (1995). *The Bibby report: Social trends Canadian style*. Toronto, ON: Stoddart.

Bibby, R.W. (2004). *Future families project: A survey of Canadian hopes and dreams*. Ottawa, ON: Vanier Institute of the Family. Retrieved from www.vanierinstitute.ca/include/get .php?nodeid=42

Bisson, M.A., & Levine, T.R. (2009). Negotiating a friends with benefits relationship. *Archives of Sexual Behavior, 38*, 66-73. doi:10.1007/s10508-007-9211-2

Boies, S.C. (2002). University students' uses of and reactions to online sexual information and entertainment: Links to online and offline sexual behaviour. *Canadian Journal of Human Sexuality, 11*(2), 77-89.

Brotto, L.A., Woo, J.S.T., & Ryder, A.G. (2007). Acculturation and sexual function in Canadian East Asian men. *Journal of Sexual Medicine, 4*, 72-82. doi:10.1111/j.1743-6109.2006.00388.x

Brown, J.D. (2002). Mass media influences on sexuality. *Journal of Sex Research, 39*, 42-5. doi:10.1080/00224490209552118

Brown, J.D., L'Engle, K.L., Pardun, C.J., Guo, G., Kenneavy, K., & Jackson, C. (2006). Sexy media matter: Exposure to sexual content in music, movies, television, and magazines predicts black and white adolescents' sexual behavior. *Pediatrics, 117*, 1018-27. doi:10.1542/peds.2005-1406

Bruce, A.S., & Severance, T.A. (2003). Swinging revisited. In C. Hensley & R. Tewksbury (Eds), *Sexual deviance: A reader* (pp. 245-60). Boulder, CO: Lynne Rienner.

Byers, E.S., Henderson, J., & Hobson, K.M. (2009). University students' definitions of sexual abstinence and having sex. *Archives of Sexual Behavior, 38*, 665-74. doi:10.1007/s10508-007-9289-6

Byers, E.S., & MacNeil, S. (2006). Further validation of the interpersonal exchange model of sexual satisfaction. *Journal of Sex and Marital Therapy, 32*, 53-69. doi:10.1080/ 00926230500232917

Chadwick Martin Bailey. (2010). Match.com and Chadwick Martin Bailey 2009-2010 studies: Recent trends: Online dating [Press release]. Retrieved from http://cp.match.com/ cppp/media/CMB_Study.pdf

Christopher, F.S., & Sprecher, S. (2000). Sexuality in dating, marriage, and other relationships: A decade review. *Journal of Marriage and the Family, 62*, 999-1017. doi:10.1111/ j.1741-3737.2000.00999.x

Clark, W. (2007). Delayed transitions of young adults. *Canadian Social Trends* (Catalogue No. 11.008). Ottawa, ON: Statistics Canada. Retrieved from www.statcan.gc.ca/pub/11-008-x/ 2007004/pdf/10311-eng.pdf

Cohen, J.N., Byers, E.S., & Walsh, L.P. (2008). Factors influencing the sexual relationships of lesbians and gay men. *International Journal of Sexual Health, 20*, 162-76. doi:10.1080/ 19317610802240105

Collins, R.L., Elliott, M.N., Berry, S.H., Kanouse, D.E., & Hunter, S.B. (2003). Entertainment television as a healthy sex educator: The impact of condom-efficacy information in an episode of Friends. *Pediatrics, 112*, 1115-21. doi:10.1542/peds.112.5 .1115

Cook, R.J., & Dickens, B.M. (2009). Hymen reconstruction: Ethical and legal issues. *International Journal of Gynecology and Obstetrics, 107*, 266-9. doi:10.1016/ijgo.2009.07.032

Cooper, M.L., Shapiro, C.M., & Powers, A.M. (1998). Motivations for sex and sexually risky behavior among adolescents and young adults: A functional perspective. *The Journal of Personality and Social Psychology, 75*, 1528-58. doi:10.1037/0022-3514.75.6.1528

Curtis, D. (2004). Commodities and sexual subjectivities: Desires. *Cultural Anthropology, 19*, 95-121. doi:10.1525/can.2004.19.1.95

Daneback, K., Mansson, S.A., & Ross, M.W. (2007). Using the Internet to find offline sex partners. *Cyberpsychology & Behavior, 10*, 100-7. doi:10.1089/cpb.2006.9986

Demaris, A. (2009). Distal and proximal influences on the risk of extramarital sex: A prospective study of longer duration marriages. *Journal of Sex Research, 46*, 597-607. doi:10.1080/00224490902915993

Donnelly, D., Burgess, E., Anderson, S., Davis, R., & Dillard, J. (2001). Involuntary celibates: A life course analysis. *Journal of Sex Research, 38*, 159-69. doi:10.1080/00224490109552083

Elbedour, S., Onwuegbuzie, A.J., Caridine, C., & Abu-Saad, E. (2002). The effect of polygamous marital structure on behavioral, emotional, and academic adjustment in children: A comprehensive review of the literature. *Clinical Child and Family Psychology Review, 5*, 255-71. doi:10.1023/A:1020925123016

Foxman, B., Aral, S.O., & Holmes, K.K. (2006). Common use in the general population of sexual enrichment AIDS and drugs to enhance sexual experience. *Sexually Transmitted Diseases, 33*, 156-62. doi:10.1097/01.olq.0000187210.53010.10

Furman, W., & Shaffer, L. (2010). Romantic partners, friends, friends with benefits, and casual acquaintances as sexual partners. *Journal of Sex Research, 47*, 1-11. doi:10.1080/00224499 .2010.535623

Gagnon, J.H. (1998). Sexual conduct revisited. In J.H. Gagnon (Ed.), *An interpretation of desire: Essays in the study of sexuality* (pp. 271-86). Chicago, IL: University of Chicago Press.

Goodson, P., McCormick, D., & Evans, A. (2000). Sex and the Internet: A survey instrument to assess college students' behavior and attitudes. *Cyber Psychology & Behavior, 3,* 129–49. doi:10.1089/109493100315987

Griffith, M. (2001). Sex on the Internet: Observations and implications for Internet sex addiction. *Journal of Sex Research, 38,* 333–42. doi:10.1080/00224490109552104

Grov, C., Gillespie, B.J., Royce, T., & Lever, J. (2010). Perceived consequences of casual online sexual activities on heterosexual relationships: A US online survey. *Archives of Sexual Behavior, 40,* 429–39. doi:10.1007/s10508-010-9598-z

Halpern, C.T., Waller, M.W., Spriggs, A., & Hallfors, D.D. (2006). Adolescent predictors of emerging adult sexual patterns. *Journal of Adolescent Health, 39,* e1–e10. doi:10.1016/j.jadohealth.2006.08.005

Halpern-Felsher, B.L., Cornell, J.L., Kropp, R.Y., & Tschann J.M. (2005). Oral versus vaginal sex among adolescents: Perceptions, attitudes, and behaviour. *Pediatrics, 115,* 845–51. doi:10.1542/peds.2004-2108

Herbenick, D., Reece, M., Sanders, S.A., Dodge, B., Ghassemi, A., & Fortenberry, J.D. (2010). Women's vibrator use in sexual partnerships: Results from a nationally representative survey in the United States. *Journal of Sex & Marital Therapy, 36,* 49–65. doi:10.1080/00926230903375677

Herbenick, D., Reece, M., Schick, V., Sanders, S.A., Dodge, B., & Fortenberry, J.D. (2010a). Sexual behavior in the United States: Results from a national probability sample of men and women ages 14–94. *Journal of Sexual Medicine, 7,* 255–65. doi:10.1111/j.1743-6109.2010.02012.x

Herbenick, D., Reece, M., Schick, V., Sanders, S.A., Dodge, B., & Fortenberry, J.D. (2010b). An event-level analysis of the sexual characteristics and composition among adults ages 18 to 59: Results from a national probability sample in the United States. *Journal of Sexual Medicine, 7*(5), 346–61. doi:10.1111/j.1743-6109.2010.02012.x

Hershberger, S.L., Pilkington, N.W., & D'Augelli, A.R. (1997). Predictors of suicide attempts among gay, lesbian, and bisexual youth. *Journal of Adolescent Research, 12,* 477–97. doi:10.1177/0743554897124004

Hickman, S.E., & Muehlenhard, C.L. (1999). By the semi-mystical appearance of a condom: How young women and men communicate sexual consent in heterosexual situations. *Journal of Sex Research, 36,* 258–72. doi:10.1080/00224499909551996

Holmberg, D., & Blair, K.L. (2009). Sexual desire, communication, satisfaction, and preferences of men and women in same-sex versus mixed-sex relationships. *Journal of Sex Research, 46,* 57–66. doi:10.1080/00224490802645294

Impett, E.A., Peplau, L.A., & Gable, S.L. (2005). Approach and avoidance sexual motives: Implications for personal and interpersonal well-being. *Personal Relationships, 12,* 465–82. doi:10.1111/j.1475-6811.2005.00126.x

Kandela, P. (1996). Egypt's trade in hymen repair. *Lancet, 347,* 1615. doi:10.1016/S0140-6736(96)91096-X

Kunkel, D., Eyal, K., Biely, E., Cope-Farrar, K., Donnerstein, E., & Fandrich, R. (2003). *Sex on TV 3: A biennial report to the Kaiser Family Foundation.* Menlo Park, CA: Kaiser Family Foundation.

Laflin, M.T., Wang, J., & Barry, M. (2008). A longitudinal study of adolescent transition from virgin to nonvirgin status. *Journal of Adolescent Health, 42,* 228–36. doi:10.1016/j.jadohealth.2007.08.014

Lawrance, K., & Byers, E.S. (1995). Sexual satisfaction in long-term heterosexual relationships: The interpersonal exchange model of sexual satisfaction. *Personal Relationships, 2,* 267–85. doi:10.1111/j.1475-6811.1995.tb00092.x

Lehmiller, J.J., Vanderdrift, L.E., & Kelly, J.R. (2010). Sex differences in approaching friends with benefits relationships. *Journal of Sex Research, 48,* 1–10. doi:10.1080/00224491003721694

Lindell, R. (2012, May 17). A racy sex exhibit leaves Ottawa hot under the collar. *Global News.* Retrieved from www.globalnews.ca/canada/sex+scandal/6442643504/story.html

Lim, G.Y, & Roloff, M.E. (1999). Attributing sexual consent. *Journal of Applied Communication Research, 27,* 1–23. doi:10.1080/00909889909365521

Logmans, A., Verhoeff, A., Raap, R.B., Creighton, F., & van Lent, M. (1998). Should doctors reconstruct the vaginal introitus of adolescent girls to mimic the virginal state? Who wants the procedure and why. *British Medical Journal, 316,* 459–60. doi:10.1136/bmj.316.7129.459

McKenna, K.Y.A., Green, A.S., & Gleason, M.E.J. (2002). Relationship formation on the internet: What's the big attraction? *Journal of Social Issues, 58,* 9–31. doi:10.1080/01494920903224350

MacNeil, S., & Byers, E.S. (2005). Dyadic assessment of sexual self-disclosure and sexual satisfaction in heterosexual dating couples. *Journal of Social and Personal Relationships, 22,* 169–81. doi:10.1177/0265407505050942

MacNeil, S., & Byers, E.S. (2009). Role of sexual self-disclosure in the sexual satisfaction of long-term heterosexual couples. *Journal of Sex Research, 46,* 3–14. doi:10.1080/00224490802398399

Mah, K., & Binik, Y.M. (2002). Do all orgasms feel alike? Evaluating a two-dimensional model of the orgasm experience across gender and sexual context. *Journal of Sex Research, 39,* 104–13. doi:10.1080?00224490209552129

Markman, H.J., Stanley, S.M., & Blumberg, S.L. (2010). *Fighting for your marriage* (3rd ed.). San Francisco, CA: Josey-Bass.

Maticka-Tyndale, E. (2001). Sexual health and Canadian youth: How do we measure up? *The Canadian Journal of Human Sexuality, 10,* 1–17. Retrieved from www.sieccan.org/cjhs.html

Miller, A.S., & Byers, E.S. (2004). Actual and desired duration of foreplay and intercourse: Discordance and misperceptions within heterosexual couples. *Journal of Sex Research, 41,* 301–9. doi:10.1080/00224490409552237

Morrison, T.G., Ellis, S.R., Morrison, M.A., Bearden, A., & Harriman, R.L. (2006). Exposure to sexually explicit material and variations in body esteem, genital attitudes, and sexual esteem among a sample of Canadian men. *The Journal of Men's Studies, 14,* 209–22. doi:10.3149/jms.1402.209

Petersen, J.L., & Hyde, J.S. (2010). A meta-analytic review of research on gender differences in sexuality, 1993–2007. *Psychological Bulletin, 136,* 21–38. doi:10.1037/a0017504

Price, J.H., Allensworth, D.D., & Hillman, K.S. (1985). Comparison of sexual fantasies of homosexuals and of heterosexuals. *Psychological Reports, 57,* 871–7. doi:10.2466/pr0.1985.57.3.871

Purnine, D.M., & Carey, M.P. (1997). Interpersonal communication and sexual adjustment: The roles of understanding and agreement. *Journal of Consulting and Clinical Psychology, 65,* 1017–25. doi:10.1037/0022-006X.65.6.1017

Randall, H.E., & Byers, E.S. (2003). What is sex? Students' definitions of having sex, sexual partner, and unfaithful sexual behaviour. *Canadian Journal of Human Sexuality, 12,* 87–96. Retrieved from www.sieccan.org/cjhs.html

Reece, M., Rosenberger, J.G., Schick, V., Herbenick, D., Dodge, B., & Novak, D.S. (2010). Characteristics of vibrator use by gay and bisexually identified men in the United States. *The Journal of Sexual Medicine, 7*, 3467-76. doi:10.1111/j.1743-6109.2010.01873.x

Renaud, C.A., & Byers, E.S. (1999). Exploring the frequency, diversity and content of university students' positive and negative sexual cognitions. *Canadian Journal of Human Sexuality, 8*, 17-30. Retrieved from www.sieccan.org/cjhs.html

Renaud, C.A., & Byers, E.S. (2001). Positive and negative sexual cognitions: Subjective experience and relationships to sexual adjustment. *Journal of Sex Research, 38*, 252-62. doi:10.1080/00224490109552094

Rosario, M., Meyer-Bahlberg, H.F.L., Hunter, J., Exner, T.M., Gwadz, M., & Keller, A.M. (1996). The psychosexual development of urban lesbian, gay, and bisexual youth. *Journal of Sex Research, 33*, 113-26. doi:10.1080/00224499609551823

Rosen, R., Brown, C., Heiman, J., Leiblum, S., Meston, C., Shabsigh, R. . . . D'Agostino, R. (2000). The female sexual function index (FSFI): A multidimensional self-report instrument for the assessment of female sexual function. *Journal of Sex and Marital Therapy, 26*, 191-208. doi:10.1016/j.fertnstert.2009.07.1173

Schick, V., Herbenick, D., Rosenberger, J.G., & Reece, M. (2011). Prevalence and characteristics of vibrator use among women who have sex with women. *Journal of Sexual Medicine, 8*, 3306-15.

Shaughnessy, K., Byers, E.S., & Walsh, L. (2010). Online sexual activity experience of heterosexual students: Gender similarities and differences. *Archives of Sexual Behavior, 40*, 419-27. doi:10.1007/s10508-010-9629-9

Sprecher, S. (2002). Sexual satisfaction in premarital relationships: Associations with satisfaction, love, commitment, and stability. *Journal of Sex Research, 39*, 190-6. doi:10.1080/00224490209552141

Sprecher, S. (2009). Relationship initiation and formation on the internet. *Marriage and Family Review, 45*, 761-82. doi:10.1080/01494920903224350

Sprecher, S., Barbee, A., & Schwartz, P. (1995). "Was it good for you, too?" Gender differences in first sexual intercourse experiences. *Journal of Sex Research, 32*, 3-15. doi:10.1080/00224499509551769

Statistics Canada. (2011). *General social survey 2010: Overview of the time use of Canadians* (Catalogue No. 89-647-XWE). Ottawa, ON: Author.

Traeen, B., Nilsen, T.S., & Stigum, H. (2006). Use of pornography in traditional media and on the Internet in Norway. *Journal of Sex Research, 43*, 245-54. doi:10.1080/00224490609552323

Tsui, L., & Nicoladis, E. (2004). Losing it: Similarities and differences in virginity loss experiences of men and women. *Canadian Journal of Human Sexuality, 13*, 95-106. doi:10.1080/00224499809551915

Vance, E.B., & Wagner, N.N. (1974). Written descriptions of orgasm: A study of sex differences. *Archives of Sexual Behavior, 5*, 87-98. doi:10.1007/BF01542242

Vannier, S.A., & O'Sullivan, L.F. (2010). Sex without desire: Characteristics of occasions of sexual compliance in young adults' committed relationships. *Journal of Sex Research, 47*, 429-39. doi:10.1080/00224490903132051

Ward, L.M., Day, K.M., & Epstein, M. (2006). Uncommonly good: Exploring how mass media may be a positive influence on young women's sexual health and development. *New Directions for Child and Adolescent Development, 112*, 57-70. doi:10.1002/cd.162

Weaver, A.D., MacKeigan, K.L., & MacDonald, H.A. (2011). Experiences and perceptions of young adults in friends with benefits relationships: A qualitative study. *Canadian Journal of Human Sexuality, 20*, 41-53. Retrieved from www.sieccan.org/cjhs.html

Zietsch, B.P., Miller, G.F., Bailey, J.M., & Martin, N.G. (2011). Female orgasm rates are largely independent of other traits: Implications for "female orgasmic disorder" and evolutionary theories of orgasm. *Journal of Sexual Medicine, 8*, 2305-16. doi:10.1111/j.1743-6109.2011.02300.x

CHAPTER 15

Abel, G.G., Becker, J.V., Cunningham-Rathner, J., Mittelman, M., & Rouleau, J.L. (1988). Multiple paraphilic diagnoses among sex offenders. *Bulletin of the American Academy of Psychiatry and Law, 16*, 153-68. Retrieved from www.aapl.org/journal.htm

American Psychiatric Association. (2013). *Diagnostic and statistical manual of mental disorders* (5th ed.). Washington, DC: Author.

Arndt, W.B., Foehl, J.C., & Good, F.E. (1985). Specific sexual fantasy themes: A multidimensional study. *Journal of Personality and Social Psychology, 48*(2), 472-80. doi:10.1037/0022-3514.48.2.472

Babchishin, K.M., Hanson, R.K., & Hermann, C.A. (2011). The characteristics of online sex offenders: A meta-analysis. *Sexual Abuse: A Journal of Research and Treatment, 23*, 92-123. doi:10.1177/1079063210370708

Barbaree, H.E., Langton, C.M., & Peacock, E.J. (2006). The factor structure of static actuarial items: Its relation to prediction. *Sexual Abuse: A Journal of Research and Treatment, 18*, 207-26. doi:10.1177/107906320601800207

Baumeister, R.F. (1988). Gender differences in masochistic scripts. *Journal of Sex Research, 25*, 478-9. doi:10.1080/00224498809551477

Beech, A.R., & Hamilton-Giachritsis, C.E. (2005). Relationship between therapeutic climate and treatment outcome in group-based sexual offender treatment programs. *Sexual Abuse: A Journal of Research and Treatment, 17*, 127-40. doi:10.1007/s11194-005-4600-3

Blanchard, R. (1989). The classification and labeling of non-homosexual gender dysphorias. *Archives of Sexual Behaviour, 18*, 315-34. doi:10.1007/BF01541951

Blanchard, R. (1991). Clinical observations and systematic studies of autogynephilia. *Journal of Sex and Marital Therapy, 17*, 235-51. doi:10.1080/00926239108404348

Blanchard, R. (In press). Dissenting opinion on DSM-5 pedophilic disorder. *Archives of Sexual Behaviour.* doi: 10.1007/s10508-013-0117-x

Blanchard, R., Klassen, P., Dickey, R., Kuban, M.E., & Blak, T. (2001). Sensitivity specificity of the phallometric test for pedophilia in nonadmitting sex offenders. *Psychological Assessment, 13*, 118-26. doi:10.1037/1040-3590.13.1.118

Bradford, J.M. (2001). The neurobiology, neuropharmacology, and pharmacological treatment of the paraphilias and compulsive sexual behaviour. *Canadian Journal of Psychiatry, 46*, 26-33. Retrieved from http://publications.cpa-apc.org/browse/sections/0

Bullough, B., & Bullough, V. (1997). Are transvestites necessarily heterosexual? *Archives of Sexual Behaviour, 26*, 1-12. doi:10.1023/A:1024589618410

Bullough, V., & Weinberg, T. (1988). Alienation, self-image, and the importance of support groups for the wives of transvestites. *Journal of Sex Research, 24*, 262–8. doi:10.1080/00224498809551422

Cantor, J.M., Blanchard, R., & Barbaree, H. (2009). Sexual disorders. In P.H. Blaney & T. Milton (Eds), *Oxford Textbook of Psychopathology* (pp. 527–48). New York, NY: Oxford University Press.

Cantor, J.M., Blanchard, R., Christensen, B.K., Dickey, R., Klassen, P.E., Beckstead, A.L. . . . Kuban, M.E. (2004). Intelligence, memory, and handedness in pedophilia. *Neuropsychology, 18*, 3–14. doi:10.1037/0894-4105.18.1.3

Cantor, J.M., Kabani, N., Christensen, B.K., Zipursky, R.B., Barbaree, H.E., Dickey, R. . . . Blanchard, R. (2008). Cerebral white matter deficiencies in pedophilic men. *Journal of Psychiatric Research, 42*, 167–83. doi:10.1016/j.jpsychires.2007.10.013

Cantor, J.M., Kuban, M.E., Blak, T., Klassen, P.E., Dickey, R., & Blanchard, R. (2006). Grade failure and special education placement in sexual offenders' educational histories. *Archives of Sexual Behaviour, 35*, 743–51. doi:10.1007/s10508-006-9018-6

Carnes, P. (1983). *The Sexual Addiction*. Hazelden, MN: CompCare.

Chivers, M.L., Rieger, G., Latty, E., & Bailey, J.M. (2004). A sex difference in the specificity of sexual arousal: 1. *Psychological Science, 15*, 736–44. doi:10.1111/j.0956-7976.2004.00750.x

Coleman, E. (1987). Sexual compulsivity: Definition, etiology, and treatment considerations. *Journal of Chemical Dependency Treatment, 1*, 189–204. doi:10.1300/J034v01n01_11

Docter, R.F., & Prince, V. (1997). Transvestism: A survey of 1032 cross-dressers. *Archives of Sexual Behaviour, 26*, 589–606. doi:10.1023/A:1024572209266

Durex. (2005). *Durex Sexual Wellbeing Global Survey*. Retrieved from www.durex.com/en-CA/SexualWellbeingSurvey/pages/default.aspx

Dzelme, K., & Jones, R.A. (2001). Male cross-dressers in therapy: A solution focused perspective for marriage and family therapists. *American Journal of Family Therapy, 29*, 293–305. doi:10.1080/01926180152588716

Federoff, J.P., Smolewska, K., Selhi. Z., Ng, E., & Bradford, J.M. (2001) Victimless pedophiles. Poster presented at the Annual Meeting of the International Academy of Sex Research, Montreal, Quebec.

First, M.B., & Frances, A. (2008). Issues for *DSM-V*: Unintended consequences of small changes: The case of paraphilias. *The American Journal of Psychiatry, 165*, 1240–1. doi:10.1176/appi.ajp.2008.08030361

Freund, K., & Blanchard, R. (1986). The concept of courtship disorder. *Journal of Sex and Marital Therapy, 12*, 79–92. doi:10.1080/00926238608415397

Freund, K., & Blanchard, R. (1993). Erotic target location errors in male gender dysphorics, pedophiles, and fetishists. *British Journal of Psychiatry, 162*, 558–63. doi:10.1192/bjp.162.4.558

Freund, K., McKnight, C.K., Langevin, R., & Cibiri, S. (1972). The female child as a surrogate object. *Archives of Sexual Behavior, 2*, 119–33. doi:10.1007/BF01541862

Freund, K., Seto, M.C., & Kuban, M. (1997). Frotteurism and the theory of courtship disorder. In D.R. Laws & W.T. O'Donohue (Eds), *Sexual deviance: Theory, assessment, and treatment* (pp. 111–30). New York, NY: Guilford Press.

Freund, K., Watson, R., & Rienzo, D. (1988). The value of self-reports in the study of voyeurism and exhibitionism. *Annals of Sex Research, 1*, 243–62. doi:10.1007/BF00852800

Gordon, H. (2008). The treatment of paraphilias: An historical perspective [Editorial]. *Criminal Behaviour and Mental Health, 18*, 79. doi:10.1002/cbm.687

Grant, J., & Potenza, M. (2006). Compulsive aspects of impulse-control disorders. *Psychiatric clinics of North America, 29*, 539–51. doi:10.1016/j.psc.2006.02.002

Grubin, D. (2008). The case for polygraph testing of sex offenders. *Legal and Criminological Psychology, 13*, 177–89. doi:10.1348/135532508X295165

Hanson, R.K., & Bussière, M.T. (1998). Predicting relapse: A meta-analysis of sexual offender recidivism studies. *Journal of Consulting and Clinical Psychology, 66*, 348–62. doi:10.1037/0022-006X.66.2.348

Hanson, R.K., Steffy, R.A., & Gauthier, R. (1993). Long-term recidivism of child molesters. *Journal of Consulting and Clinical Psychology, 61*, 646–52. doi:10.1037/0022-006X.61.4.646

Harris, A.J.R., & Hanson, R.K. (2004). *Sex offender recidivism: A simple question* (Corrections Users Report No. 2004-03). Retrieved from www.publicsafety.gc.ca/res/cor/rep/_fl/2004-03-se-off-eng.pdf

Hollander, E., & Rosen, J. (2000). Impulsivity. *Journal of Psychoparmacology, 14*(2, suppl. 1), 539–44.

Holmes, R. (1991). *Sex crimes*. Newbury Park, CA: Sage.

Johnson, T.W., Brett, M.A., Roberts L.F., & Wassersug, R.J. (2007). Eunuchs in contemporary society: Characterizing men who are voluntarily castrated (part I). *Journal of Sexual Medicine, 4*, 930–45. doi:10.1111/j.1743-6109.2007.00521.x

Kafka, M.P. (2010). Hypersexual disorder: A proposed diagnosis for *DSM-V*. *Archives of Sexual Behaviour, 39*, 377–400. doi:10.I007/s10508-009-9574-7

Kaplan, L.J. (1991). Women masquerading as women. In G.I. Fogel & W.A. Meyers (Eds), *Perversions and near-perversions in clinical practice: New psychoanalytic perspectives* (pp. 127–52). New Haven, CT: Yale University Press.

Kaplan, M.S., & Krueger, R.B. (2012). Cognitive-behavioral treatment of the paraphilias. *Israel Journal of Psychiatry & Related Sciences, 49*(4), 291–6.

Kinsey, A.C., Pomeroy, W.B., Martin, C.E., & Gebhard, P.H. (1953). *Sexual behaviour in the human female*. Philadelphia, PA: Saunders.

Koob, G. (2006). The neurobiology of addiction: A neuroadaptational view relevant for diagnosis. *Addiction, 101* (suppl. 1), 23–30. doi:10.1111/j.1360-0443.2006.01586.x

Kuban, M., Barbaree, H.E., & Blanchard, R. (1999). A comparison of volume and circumference phallometry: Response magnitude and method agreement. *Archives of Sexual Behaviour, 28*, 345–59. doi:10.1023/A:1018700813140

Långström, N. (2010). The *DSM* diagnostic criteria for exhibitionism, voyeurism, and frotteurism. *Archives of Sexual Behaviour, 39*, 317–24. doi:10.1007/s10508-009-9577-4.

Långström, N., & Hanson, R.K. (2006). High rates of sexual behavior in the general population: Correlates and predictors. *Archives of Sexual Behavior, 35*, 37–52. doi:10.1007/s10508-006-8993-y

Långström, N., & Seto, M.C. (2006). Exhibitionistic and voyeuristic behavior in a Swedish national population survey. *Archives of Sexual Behavior, 35*, 427–35. doi:10.1007/s10508-006-9042-6

Marshall, W.L. (2007). Diagnostic issues, multiple paraphilias, and comorbid disorders in sexual offenders: Their incidence and treatment. *Aggression and Violent Behavior, 12*, 16–35. doi:10.1016/j.avb.2006.03.001

Marshall, W.L., Marshall, L.E., Serran, G.A., & Fernandez, Y.M. (2006). *Treating sexual offenders: An integrated approach*. New York, NY: Routledge.

Meijet, E.H., Verschuere, B., Merckelbach, H.L.G.J., & Crombez, G. (2008). Sex offender management and using the polygraph: A critical review. *International Journal of Law and Psychiatry, 31*, 423–9. doi:10.1016/j.ijlp.2008.08.007

Money, J. (1984). Paraphilias: Phenomenology and classification. *American Journal of Psychotherapy, 38*, 164–79. Retrieved from www.ajp.org

Moser, C. (1979). *An exploratory descriptive study of self defined S/M (sadomasochistic) sample* (Unpublished doctoral dissertation). Institute for Advanced Study of Human Sexuality, San Francisco, CA.

Moser, C. (1998). S/M (sadomasochistic) interactions in semi-public settings. *Journal of Homosexuality, 36*, 19–29. doi:10.1300/J082v36n02_02

Moser, C., & Kleinplatz, P.J. (2005). *DSM-IV-TR* and the paraphilias: An argument for removal. *Journal of Psychology and Human Sexuality, 17*(3/4), 91–109. Retrieved from www.tandfonline.com/loi/wzph20

O'Donohue, W., Regev, L.G., & Hagstrom, A. (2000). Problems with the *DSM-IV* diagnosis of pedophilia. *Sexual Abuse: A Journal of Research and Treatment, 12*, 95–105. doi:10.1177/107906320001200202

Pinkerton, S.D., Bogart, L.M., Cecil, H., & Abramson, P.R. (2002). Factors associated with masturbation in a collegiate sample. *Journal of Psychology and Human Sexuality, 14*(2/3), 103–21. doi:10.1300/J056v14n02_07

Pollock, N.L., & Hashmall, J.M. (1991). The excuses of child molesters. *Behavioural Sciences and the Law, 9*, 53–9. doi:10.1002/bsl.2370090107

Ponseti, J., Granert, O., Jansen, O., Wolff, S., Beier, K., Neutze, J. . . . Bosinski, H. (2012). Assessment of pedophilia using hemodynamic brain response to sexual stimuli. *Archives of General Psychiatry, 69*, 187–94. doi:10.1001/archgenpsychiatry.2011.130

Potenza, M.N. (2006). Should addictive disorders include non-substance-related conditions? *Addiction, 101* (suppl. 1), 142–51. doi:10.1111/j.1360-0443.2006.01591.x

Raboch, J., Cerna, H., & Zemek, P. (1987). Sexual aggressivity and androgens. *British Journal of Psychiatry, 151*, 398–400. doi:10.1192/bjp.151.3.398

Rachman, S. (1966). Sexual fetishism: An experimental analogue. *Psychological Record, 16*, 293–6. Retrieved from http://thepsychologicalrecord.siuc.edu

Raymond, N.C., Coleman, E., & Miner, M.H. (2003). Psychiatric comorbidity and compulsive/impulsive traits in compulsive sexual behaviour. *Comprehensive Psychiatry, 44*, 370–80. doi:10.1016/S0010-440X(03)00110-X

Richters, J., Visser, R., Grulich, A., & Rissel, C. (2008). Selected abstracts of presentations during the world congress of sexology, 2007: Demographic and psychosocial features of participants in BDSM sex: Data from a national survey. *Journal of Sex Research, 45*, 90–117. Retrieved from www.tandfonline.com/toc/hjsr20/current

Rye, B.J., & Meaney, G.J. (2007). Voyeurism: It is good as long as we do not get caught. *International Journal of Sexual Health, 19*, 47–56. doi:10.1300/J514v19n01_06

Sartorius, A., Ruf, M., Kief, C., Demirakca, T., Bailer, J., Ende, G. . . . Dressing, H. (2008). Abnormal amygdala activation profile in pedophilia. *European Archives of Psychiatry and Clinical Neuroscience, 258*, 271–7. Doi:10.1007/s00406-008-0782-2.

Schiffer, B., Peschel, T., Paul, T., Gizewski, E., Forsting, M., Leygraf, N. . . . Krueger, T.H.C. (2007). Structural brain abnormalities in the frontostriatal system and cerebellum in pedophilia. *Journal of Psychiatric Research, 41*, 753–62. doi:10.1016/j.jpsychires.2006.06.003

Schiltz, K., Witzel, J., Northoff, G., Zierhut, K., Gubka, U., Fellmann, H. . . . Bogerts, B. (2007). Brain pathology in pedophilic offenders. *Archives of General Psychiatry, 64*, 737–46. doi:10.1001/archgenpsychiatry.2011.130

Schwartz, S.A., & Abramowitz, J.S. (2005). Contrasting non-paraphilic sexual addictions and OCD. In M.M. Antony (Series Ed.), *Series in Anxiety and Related Disorders: Concepts and Controversies in Obsessive-Compulsive Disorder* (pp. 177–84). doi:10.1007/0-387-23370-9_9

Scorolli, C., Ghirlanda, S., Enquist, M., Zattoni, S., & Jannini, E.A. (2007). Relative prevalence of different fetishes. *International Journal of Impotence Research, 19*, 432–7. doi:10.1038/sj.ijir.3901547

Seligman, L., & Hardenburg, S.A. (2000). Assessment and treatment of paraphilias. *Journal of Counselling and Development, 78*, 107–13. doi:10.1002/j.1556-6676.2000.tb02567.x

Seto, M.C., Cantor, J.M., & Blanchard, R. (2006). Child pornography offenses are a valid diagnostic indicator of pedophilia. *Journal of Abnormal Psychology, 115*, 610–15. doi:10.1037/0021-843X.115.3.610

Seto, M.C., Hanson, R.K., & Babchishin, K.M. (2011). Contact sexual offending by men with online sexual offenses. *Sexual Abuse: A Journal of Research and Treatment, 23*, 124–45. doi:10.1177/1079063210369013

Seto, M.C., & Lalumière, M.L. (2001). A brief scale to identify pedophilic interests among child molesters. *Sexual Abuse: A Journal of Research and Treatment, 13*, 15–25. doi:10.1023/A:1009510328588

Siegler, M.G. (2009, 25 July). The iPhone's latest hit app: A sex offender locator. Retrieved from http://techcrunch.com/2009/07/25/the-iphones-latest-hit-app-a-sex-offender-locator

Smallbone, S.W. (2006). An attachment-theoretical revision of Marshall and Barbaree's integrated theory of the etiology of sexual offending. In W.L. Marshall, Y.M. Fernandez, L.E. Marshall, & G.A. Serran (Eds), *Sex offender treatment: Controversial issues* (pp. 93–107). West Sussex, UK: John Wiley & Son.

Stackhouse, J. (1997, March 15). Canadian denies guilt in sex case. *The Globe and Mail.*

Steele, V. (1996). *Fetish: Fashion, sex, & power*. New York, NY: Oxford University Press.

US Department of Justice. (n.d.) *Trafficking and sex tourism*. Retrieved from www.justice.gov/criminal/ceos/index.html

Walter, M., Witzel, J., Wiebking, C., Gubka, U., Rotte, M., Schiltz, K. . . . Northoff, G. (2007). Pedophilia is linked to reduced activation in hypothalamus and lateral prefrontal cortex during erotic stimulation. *Biological Psychiatry, 62*, 698–701. doi:10.1016/j.biopsych.2006.10.018

Wiederman, M.W. (2003). Paraphilia and fetishism. *The Family Journal, 11*, 315–21. doi:10.1177/1066480703252663

Wilson, G.D. (1987). An ethological approach to sexual deviation. In G.D. Wilson (Ed.), *Variant sexuality: Research and theory*. Baltimore, MD: John Hopkins University Press.

Wilson, G., & Cox, D. (1983). Personality of paedophile club members. *Personality and Individual Differences, 4*, 323–9. doi:10.1016/0191-8869(83)90154-X

CHAPTER 16

Althof, S.E. (2001). My personal distress over the inclusion of personal distress. *Journal of Sex & Marital Therapy, 27*, 123–5. doi:10.1080/00926230152051761

American Psychiatric Association. (1980). *Diagnostic and statistical manual of mental disorders* (3rd ed.). Washington, DC: Author.

American Psychiatric Association. (2000). *Diagnostic and statistical manual of mental disorders* (4th ed., text rev.). Washington, DC: Author.

American Psychiatric Association. (2013). *Diagnostic and statistical manual of mental disorders* (5th ed.). Washington, DC: Author.

Apfelbaum, B. (2000). Retarded ejaculation: A much-misunderstood syndrome. In S.R. Leiblum & R.C. Rosen (Eds), *Principles and practice of sex therapy* (3rd ed., pp. 205–41). New York, NY: Guilford.

Assalian, P. (1994). Premature ejaculation: Is it really psychogenic? *Journal of Sex Education and Therapy, 20*, 1–4.

Barbach, L. (2000). *For yourself: The fulfilment of female sexuality.* New York, NY: Signet Books.

Basson, R. (2007). Sexual desire/arousal disorders in women. In S.R. Leiblum (Ed.), *Principles and practice of sex therapy* (4th ed., pp. 25–53). New York, NY: Guilford.

Beckman, N., Waern, M., Gustafson, D., & Skoog, I. (2008). Secular trends in self-reported sexual activity and satisfaction in Swedish 70 year olds: Cross-sectional survey of four populations, 1971–2001. *British Medical Journal, 337*(7662), 151–4. doi:10.1136/bmj.a279

Betchen, S.J. (2005). *Intrusive partners, elusive mates: The pursuer–distancer dynamic in couples.* New York, NY: Routledge.

Binik, Y.M. (2009a). The DSM diagnostic criteria for dyspareunia. *Archives of Sexual Behavior, 39*, 292–303. doi:10.1007/s10508-009-9563-x

Binik, Y.M. (2009b). The DSM diagnostic criteria for vaginismus. *Archives of Sexual Behavior, 39*, 278–91. doi:10.1007/s10508-009-9560-0

Binik, Y.M., Bergeron, S., & Khalifé, S. (2007). Dyspareunia and vaginismus: So-called sexual pain. In S.R. Leiblum (Ed.), *Principles and practice of sex therapy* (4th ed., pp. 124–56). New York, NY: Guilford.

Brotto. L.A. (2010). The DSM diagnostic criteria for hypoactive sexual desire disorder in women. *Archives of Sexual Behavior, 39*, 221–39. doi:10.1007/s10508-009-9543-1

Burns, B., & Braun, S. (Writers). (1998). The truth about impotence [Television series episode]. In B. Burns & B. Wheatley (Producers), *Nova*. Boston, MA: WGBH.

Davis, S.R., Davison, S.L., Donath, S., & Bell, R.J. (2005). Circulating androgen levels and self-reported sexual function in women. *Journal of the American Medical Association, 294*(1), 91–6. doi:10.1001/jama.294.1.91

Dodson, B. (2002). *Orgasms for two.* New York, NY: Harmony.

Finkelhor, D. (2008). *Childhood victimization.* New York, NY: Oxford University Press.

Goldstein, A.T., Pukall, C.F., & Goldstein, I. (Eds). (2009). *Female sexual pain disorders: Evaluation and management.* Hoboken, NJ: Wiley-Blackwell.

Goldstein, S.W. (2009). My turn . . . finally. *Journal of Sexual Medicine, 6*, 301–2. doi:10.1111/j.1743-6109.2008.01147.x

Hawton, K., & Catalan, J. (1990). Sex therapy for vaginismus: Characteristics of couples and treatment outcome. *Sexual and Marital Therapy, 5*, 39–48. doi:10.1080/02674659008407995

Heiman, J., & LoPiccolo, J. (1988). *Becoming orgasmic: A sexual and personal growth program for women.* New York, NY: Prentice Hall.

Kafka, M.P. (2010). Hypersexual disorder: A proposed diagnosis for DSM-V. *Archives of Sexual Behavior, 39*, 377–400. doi:10.1007/s10508-009-9574-7

Kaplan, H.S. (1974). *The new sex therapy.* New York, NY: Brunner/Mazel.

Kaufman, M., Silverberg, C., & Odette, F. (2007). *The ultimate guide to sex and disability.* San Francisco, CA: Cleis Press.

Kirby, D., Laris, B.A., & Rolleri, L. (2005). *Impact of sex and HIV education programs on sexual behaviors of youth in developing and developed countries.* Research Triangle Park, NC: Family Health International.

Kleinplatz, P.J. (1996). The erotic encounter. *Journal of Humanistic Psychology, 36*(3), 105–23. doi:10.1177/00221678960363008

Kleinplatz, P.J. (1998). Sex therapy for vaginismus: A review, critique and humanistic alternative. *Journal of Humanistic Psychology, 38*(2), 51–81. doi:10.1177/00221678980382004

Kleinplatz, P.J. (2001a). A critical evaluation of sex therapy: Room for improvement. In P.J. Kleinplatz (Ed.), *New directions in sex therapy: Innovations and alternatives* (pp. xi–xxxiii). Philadelphia, PA: Brunner-Routledge.

Kleinplatz, P.J. (2001b). A critique of the goals of sex therapy or the hazards of safer sex. In P.J. Kleinplatz (Ed.), *New directions in sex therapy: Innovations and alternatives* (pp. 109–32). Philadelphia, PA: Brunner-Routledge.

Kleinplatz, P.J. (2004). Beyond sexual mechanics and hydraulics: Humanizing the discourse surrounding erectile dysfunction. *Journal of Humanistic Psychology, 44*, 215–42. doi:10.1177/0022167804263130

Kleinplatz, P.J. (2008). Sexuality and older people: Doctors should ask patients, regardless of age, about sexuality. *British Medical Journal, 337*, a239. doi:10.1136/bmj.a239

Kleinplatz, P.J. (2009). Consumer protection is the major purpose of sex therapy certification. *Archives of Sexual Behavior, 38*, 1031–2. doi:10.1007/s10508-009-9473-y

Kleinplatz, P.J. (2010a). Lessons from great lovers. In S. Levine, S. Althof, & C. Risen (Eds), *Handbook of adult sexuality for mental health professionals* (2nd ed., pp. 57–72). New York, NY: Brunner-Routledge.

Kleinplatz, P.J. (2010b). "Desire disorders" or opportunities for optimal erotic intimacy. In S.R. Leiblum (Ed.), *Treating sexual desire disorders: A clinical casebook* (pp. 92–113). New York, NY: Guilford.

Kleinplatz, P.J. (2011). Arousal and desire problems: Conceptual, research and clinical considerations or the more things change the more they stay the same. *Sex and Relationship Therapy, 26*, 3–15. doi:10.1080/14681994.2010.521493

Kleinplatz, P.J. (2012a). Is that all there is? A new critique of the goals of sex therapy. In P.J. Kleinplatz (Ed.), *New directions in sex therapy: Innovations and alternatives* (2nd ed., pp.101–18). New York, NY: Routledge.

Kleinplatz, P.J. (2012b). Advancing sex therapy or is that the best you can do? In P.J. Kleinplatz (Ed.), *New directions in sex therapy: Innovations and alternatives* (2nd ed., pp. xix–xxxvi). New York, NY: Routledge.

Krueger, R.B. (2009). The DSM diagnostic criteria for sexual sadism. *Archives of Sexual Behaviour, 39*, 346–56. doi:10.1007/s10508-009-9586-3

Leiblum, S.R. (2010). Introduction and overview: Clinical perspectives on and treatment for sexual desire disorders. In

S. R. Leiblum (Ed.), *Treating sexual desire disorders: A clinical casebook* (pp. 1–22). New York, NY: Guilford.

Leland, J. (1997, November 17). A pill for impotence? *Newsweek*, pp. 62–9.

McCarthy, B., & McCarthy, E. (2003). *Rekindling desire: A step-by-step program to help low-sex and no-sex marriages*. New York, NY: Brunner-Routledge.

Maltz, W. (2001). *The sexual healing journey: A guide for survivors of sexual abuse*. New York, NY: Harper Paperbacks.

Maltz, W. (2012). Sex therapy with survivors of sexual abuse. In P.J. Kleinplatz (Ed), *New directions in sex therapy: Innovations and alternatives* (2nd ed., pp. 267–84). New York, NY: Routledge.

Masters, W.H., & Johnson, V.E. (1970). *Human sexual inadequacy*. New York, NY: Bantam Books.

Masters, W.H., & Johnson, V.E. (1986). *Sex therapy on its twenty-fifth anniversary: Why it survives*. St Louis, MO: Masters and Johnson Institute.

Maurice, W.L. (1999). *Sexual medicine in primary care*. St Louis, MO: Mosby.

Metz, E.M., & McCarthy, B.W. (2003). *Coping with premature ejaculation: How to overcome PE, please your partner and have great sex*. Oakland, CA: New Harbinger.

Moser, C. (1999). *Health care without shame: A handbook for the sexually diverse and their caregivers*. San Francisco, CA: Greenery Press.

Moser, C. (2005). How to ask sex questions during a medical interview. *San Francisco Medicine, 78*(2), 22–4. Retrieved from www.sfms.org/NewsPublication/SanFranciscoMedicine.aspx

Moser, C., & Kleinplatz, P.J. (2005). DSM-IV-TR and the paraphilias: An argument for removal. *Journal of Psychology and Human Sexuality, 17*(3–4), 91–109. doi:10.1300/J056v17n03_05

Moynihan, R., & Mintzes, B. (2010). *Sex, lies and pharmaceuticals: How drug companies plan to profit from female sexual dysfunction*. Vancouver, BC: Greystone Books.

Pacik, P.T. (2010). *When sex seems impossible: Stories of vaginismus and how you can achieve intimacy*. Manchester, NH: Odyne Publishing.

Panzer, C., Wise, S., Fantini, G., Kang, D., Munarriz, R., Guay, A., & Goldstein, I. (2006). Impact of oral contraceptives on sex hormone-binding globulin and androgen levels: A retrospective study in women with sexual dysfunction. *The Journal of Sexual Medicine, 3*, 104–11. doi:10.1111/j.1743-6109.2005.00198.x

Perelman, M.A. (2000). Integrating sildenafil: Its impact on sex therapy. *Sexual Dysfunction in Medicine, 1*, 98–104.

Perelman, M.A. (2010). Comments on "Considerations for a better definition of male orgasmic disorder in DSM-V." *Journal of Sexual Medicine, 7*, 697–9. doi:10.1111/j.1743-6109.2009.01683_1.x

Schnarch, D. (1997). *Passionate marriage: Love, sex, and intimacy in emotionally committed relationships*. New York, NY: Wiley.

Segraves, R.T. (2010). Considerations for an evidence-based definition of premature ejaculation in the DSM-V. *Journal of Sexual Medicine, 7*, 679–89. doi:10.1111/j.1743-6109.2009.01682.x

Shaw, J. (1994). Treatment of primary vaginismus: A new perspective. *Journal of Sex & Marital Therapy, 20*(1), 46–55. doi:10.1080/00926239408403416

SIECCAN. (2009). Sexual health education in the schools: Questions & answers (3rd ed.). *Canadian Journal of Human Sexuality, 18*(1–2), 47–60. Retrieved from www.sieccan.org/cjhs.html

Tolman, D.L. (2002). *Dilemmas of desire: Teenage girls talk about sexuality*. Cambridge, MA: Harvard University Press.

Waldinger, M.D. (2010). Premature ejaculation and delayed ejaculation. In S.B. Levine, C.B. Risen, & S.E. Althof (Eds), *Handbook of clinical sexuality for mental health professionals* (2nd ed., pp. 267–92). New York, NY: Routledge/Taylor & Francis.

Weaver, A.D., Byers, E.S., Sears, H.A., Cohen J.N., & Randall, H. (2002). Sexual health education at school and at home: Attitudes and experiences of New Brunswick parents. *Canadian Journal of Human Sexuality, 11*, 19–31.

Weiner-Davis, M. (2003). *The sex-starved marriage*. New York, NY: Simon & Schuster.

Wierman, M.E., Basson, R., Davis, S.R., Khosla, S., Miller, K.K., Rosner, W., & Santoro, N. (2006). Androgen therapy in women: An Endocrine Society clinical practice guideline. *Journal of Clinical Endocrinology & Metabolism, 91*, 3697–710. doi:10.1210/jc.2006-1121

Zilbergeld, B. (1999). *The new male sexuality*. New York, NY: Bantam Books.

CHAPTER 17

Abbey, A. (2002). Alcohol-related sexual assault: A common problem among college students. *Journal of Studies on Alcohol, Suppl. 14*, 118–28. Retrieved from http://jsad.com

Abdullah-Khan, N. (2008). *Male rape: The emergence of a social and legal issue*. New York, NY: Palgrave Macmillan.

Ali, F.A., Israr, S.M., Ali, B.S., & Janjua, N.Z. (2009). Association of various reproductive rights, domestic violence and marital rape with depression among Pakistani women. *BMC Psychiatry, 9*(1), 1–13. doi:10.1186/1471-244X-9-77

American Psychiatric Association. (2013). *Diagnostic and statistical manual of mental disorders* (5th ed.). Washington, DC: Author.

Beauregard, E. (2010). Rape and sexual assault in investigative psychology: The contribution of sex offenders' research to offender profiling. *Journal of Investigative Psychology and Offender Profiling, 7*(1), 1–13. doi:10.1002/jip.114

Belknap, J. (2010). Rape: Too hard to report and too easy to discredit victims. *Violence Against Women, 16*, 1335–44. doi:10.1177/1077801210387749

Berdahl, J.L. (2007). Harassment based on sex: Protecting social status in the context of gender hierarchy. *The Academy of Management Review, 32*, 641–58. doi:10.5465/AMR.2007.24351879

Blaauw, E., Winkel, F.W., Arensman, E., Sheridan, L., & Freeve, A. (2002). The toll of stalking: The relationship between features of stalking and psychopathology of victims. *Journal of Interpersonal Violence, 17*, 50–63. doi:10.1177/0886260502017001004

Boney-McCoy, S., & Finkelhor, D. (1995). Psychosocial sequelae of violent victimization in a national youth sample. *Journal of Consulting and Clinical Psychology, 63*, 726–36. doi:10.1037/0022-006X.63.5.726

Brand, B.L., & Alexander, P.C. (2003). Coping with incest: The relationship between recollections of childhood coping and adult functioning in female survivors of incest. *Journal of Traumatic Stress, 16*, 285–93. doi:10.1023/A:1023704309605

Brennan, S., & Taylor-Butts. A. (2008). *Sexual assault in Canada, 2004 and 2007* (No. 85F0033M). Ottawa, ON: Minister of Industry, Canadian Centre for Justice Statistics. Retrieved from www.statcan.gc.ca/pub/85f0033m/85f0033m2008019-eng.pdf

Brown, A.L., Testa, M., & Messman-Moore, T.L. (2009). Psychological consequences of sexual victimization resulting from force, incapacitation, or verbal coercion. *Violence Against Women, 15*, 898–919. doi:10.1177/1077801209335491

Burgess, A.W., & Holmstrom, L.L. (1974). Rape trauma syndrome. *The American Journal of Psychiatry, 131*, 981–6. doi:10.1176/appi.ajp.131.9.981

Byers, E.S., & Eno, R.J. (1991). Predicting men's sexual coercion and aggression from attitudes, dating history, and sexual response. *Journal of Psychology and Human Sexuality, 4*, 55–70. doi:10.1300/J056v04n03_04

Canadian Human Rights Commission. (2006). *Anti-harassment policies for the workplace: An employer's guide.* Ottawa, ON: Minister of Public Works and Government Services. Retrieved from www.chrc-ccdp.ca/pdf/ahpoliciesworkplace_en.pdf.

Cattaneo, L.B., DeLoveh, H.L.M., & Zweig, J.M. (2008). Sexual assault within intimate partner violence: Impact on helpseeking in a national sample. *Journal of Prevention and Intervention in the Community, 36*, 137–53. doi:10.1080/10852350802022415

Choudhary, E., Coben, J.H., & Bossarte, R.M. (2008). Gender and time differences in the associations between sexual violence victimization, health outcomes, and risk behaviors. *American Journal of Men's Health, 2*, 254–9. doi:10.1177/1557988307313819

Choudhary, E., Coben, J.H., & Bossarte, R.M. (2010). Adverse health outcomes, perpetrator characteristics, and sexual violence victimization among US adult males. *Journal of Interpersonal Violence, 25*, 1523–41. doi:10.1177/0886260509346063

Coid, J., Petruckevitch, A., Feder, G., Chung, W.-S., Richardson, J., & Moorey, S. (2001). Relation between childhood sexual and physical abuse and risk of revictimisation in women: A cross-sectional survey. *Lancet, 358*, 450–4. doi:10.1016/S0140-6736(01)05622-7

Craissati, J. (2005). Sexual violence against women: A psychological approach to the assessment and management of rapists in the community. *Probation Journal: The Journal of Community and Criminal Justice, 52*, 401–22. doi:10.1177/0264550505058950

Criminal Code, R.S.C. 1985, c. C-46. Retrieved from http://laws-lois.justice.gc.ca/PDF/C-46.pdf

Daigle, L.E., Fisher, B.S., & Cullen, F.T. (2008). The violent and sexual victimization of college women: Is repeat victimization a problem? *Journal of Interpersonal Violence, 23*, 1296–313. doi:10.1177/0886260508314293

Department of Justice Canada. (2003). *Stalking is a crime called criminal harassment.* Ottawa, ON: Minister of Justice and Attorney General of Canada. Retrieved from www.justice.gc.ca/eng/pi/fv-vf/pub/har/har_e-har_a.pdf

Ehlers, A., & Clark, D.M. (2000). A cognitive model of post-traumatic stress disorder. *Behaviour Research and Therapy, 38*, 319–45. doi:10.1016/S0005-7967(99)00123-0

Frazier, P.A., Mortensen, H., & Steward, J. (2005). Coping strategies as mediators of the relations among perceived control and distress in sexual assault survivors. *Journal of Counseling Psychology, 52*, 267–78. doi:10.1037/0022-0167.52.3.267

Gannon, T.A., & Ward, T. (2008). Rape: Psychopathology and theory. In D.R. Laws & W.T. O'Donohue (Eds), *Sexual deviance: Theory, assessment, and treatment* (2nd ed., pp. 336–55). New York, NY: Guilford.

García-Moreno, C., Jansen, H.A.F.M., Ellsberg, M., Heise, L., & Watts, C. (2005). *WHO multi-country study on women's health and domestic violence against women: Initial results on prevalence, health outcomes, and women's responses.* Geneva, Switzerland: World Health Organization. Retrieved from www.who.int/gender/violence/who_multicountry_study/en

Gelb, K. (2007). *Recidivism of sex offenders research paper.* Melbourne, Australia: Sentencing Advisory Council. Retrieved from www.sentencingcouncil.vic.gov.au/sites/sentencingcouncil.vic.gov.au/files/recidivism_of_sex_offenders_research_paper.pdf

Glenn, S.A., & Byers, E.S. (2009). The roles of situational factors, attributions, and guilt in the well-being of women who have experienced sexual coercion. *Canadian Journal of Human Sexuality, 18*(4), 201–19. Retrieved from www.sieccan.org/cjhs.html

Hanson, R.K., & Harris, A.J.R. (2000). Where should we intervene? Dynamic predictors of sex offense recidivism. *Criminal Justice and Behavior, 27*, 6–35. doi:10.1177/0093854800027001002

King, M., & Woollett, E. (1997). Sexually assaulted males: 115 men consulting a counseling service. *Archives of Sexual Behavior, 26*, 579–88. doi:10.1023/A:1024520225196

Kong, R., Johnson, H., Beattie, S., & Cardillo, A. (2003). Sexual offences in Canada. *Juristat, 23*(6), No. 85-002-XIE. Ottawa, ON: Statistics Canada.

Kropp, P.R., Hart, S.D., & Lyon, D.R. (2002). Risk assessment of stalkers: Some problems and possible solutions. *Criminal Justice and Behavior, 29*, 590–616. doi:10.1177/009385402236734

Krug, E.G., Dahlberg, L.L., Mercy, J.A., Zwi, A.B., & Lozano, R. (Eds). (2002). *World report on violence and health.* Geneva, Switzerland: World Health Organization.

Lalumière, M.L., Harris, G.T., Quinsey, V.L., & Rice, M.E. (2005). *The causes of rape: Understanding individual differences in male propensity for sexual aggression.* Washington, DC: American Psychological Association.

Långström, N., Sjöstedt, G., & Grann, M. (2004). Psychiatric disorders and recidivism in sexual offenders. *Sexual Abuse: A Journal of Research and Treatment, 16*, 139–50. doi:10.1177/107906320401600204

Lisak, D., Gardinier, L., Nicksa, S.C., & Cote, A.M. (2010). False allegations of sexual assault: An analysis of ten years of reported cases. *Violence Against Women, 16*, 1318–34. doi:10.1177/1077801210387747

McClure, F.H., Chavez, D.V., Agars, M.D., Peacock, M.J., & Matosian, A. (2008). Resilience in sexually abused women: Risk and protective factors. *Journal of Family Violence, 23*, 81–8. doi:10.1007/s10896-007-9129-4

Marshall, W.L. (2007). Diagnostic issues, multiple paraphilias, and comorbid disorders in sexual offenders: Their incidence and treatment. *Aggression and Violent Behavior, 12*, 16–35. doi:10.1016/j.avb.2006.03.001

Ménard, K.S., Hall, G.C.N., Phung, A.H., Ghebrial, M.F.E., & Martin, L. (2003). Gender differences in sexual harassment and coercion in college students: Developmental, individual, and situational determinants. *Journal of Interpersonal Violence, 18*, 1222–39. doi:10.1177/0886260503256654

Mezey, G., & King, M. (1989). The effects of sexual assault on men: A survey of 22 victims. *Psychological Medicine, 19*, 205–9. doi:10.1017/S0033291700011168

Mullen, P.E., Pathé, M., Purcell, R., & Stuart, W. (1999). Study of stalkers. *The American Journal of Psychiatry, 156*, 1244–9. Retrieved from http://ajp.psychiatryonline.org/journal.aspx?journalid=13

O'Leary-Kelly, A.M., Bowes-Sperry, L., Bates, C.A., & Lean, E.R. (2009). Sexual harassment at work: A decade (plus) of progress. *Journal of Management, 35*, 503–36. doi:10.1177/0149206308330555

O'Sullivan, L.F., Byers, E.S., & Finkelman, L. (1998). A comparison of male and female college students' experiences of sexual coercion. *Psychology of Women Quarterly, 22,* 177–95. doi:10.1111/j.1471-6402.1998.tb00149.x

Park, C.L. (2010). Making sense of the meaning literature: An integrative review of meaning making and its effects on adjustment to stressful life events. *Psychological Bulletin, 136,* 257–301. doi:10.1037/a0018301

Pereda, N., Guilera, G., Forns, M., & Gómez-Benito, J. (2009). The prevalence of child sexual abuse in community and student samples: A meta-analysis. *Clinical Psychology Review, 29,* 328–38. doi:10.1016/j.cpr.2009.02.007

Renner, K.E., Alksnis, C., & Park, L. (1997). The standard of social justice as a research process. *Canadian Psychology, 38,* 91–102. doi:10.1037/0708-5591.38.2.91

Ronis, S.T., & Borduin, C.M. (2007). Individual, family, peer, and academic characteristics of male juvenile sexual offenders. *Journal of Abnormal Child Psychology, 35,* 153–63. doi:10.1007/s10802-006-9058-3

Rothbaum, B.O., Foa, E.B., Riggs, D.S., Murdock, T., & Walsh, W. (1992). A prospective examination of post-traumatic stress disorder in rape victims. *Journal of Traumatic Stress, 5,* 455–72. doi:10.1002/jts.2490050309

Royal Canadian Mounted Police. (2010). *Human trafficking in Canada.* Ottawa, ON: Her Majesty the Queen in Right of Canada.

Russell, D.E.H. (1990). *Rape in marriage.* New York, NY: Macmillan Press.

Sachs-Ericsson, N., Gayman, M.D., Kendall-Tackett, K., Lloyd, D.A., Medley, A., Collins, N., . . . Sawyer, K. (2010). The long-term impact of childhood abuse on internalizing disorders among older adults: The moderating role of self-esteem. *Aging and Mental Health, 14,* 489–501. doi:10.1080/13607860903191382

Senn, C., Desmarais, S., Verberg, N., & Wood, E. (2000). Predicting coercive sexual behavior across the lifespan in a random sample of Canadian men. *Journal of Social and Personal Relationships, 17,* 95–113. doi:10.1177/0265407500171005

Smith, L.H., & Ford, J. (2010). History of forced sex and recent sexual risk indicators among young adult males. *Perspectives on Sexual and Reproductive Health, 42,* 87–92. doi:10.1363/4208710

Spitzberg, B.H. (2002). The tactical topography of stalking victimization and management. *Trauma, Violence, and Abuse, 3,* 261–88. doi:10.1177/1524838002237330

Stevens, D.J. (1994). Predatory rapists and victim selection techniques. *The Social Science Journal, 31,* 421–33. doi:10.1016/0362-3319(94)90033-7

Struckman-Johnson, C., Struckman-Johnson, D., & Anderson, P.B. (2003). Tactics of sexual coercion: When men and women won't take no for an answer. *Journal of Sex Research, 40,* 76–86. doi:10.1080/00224490309552168

Suarez, E., & Gadalla, T.M. (2010). Stop blaming the victim: A meta-analysis on rape myths. *Journal of Interpersonal Violence, 25,* 2010–35. doi:10.1177/0886260509354503

Ullman, S.E. (2007). Relationship to perpetrator, disclosure, social reactions, and PTSD symptoms in child sexual abuse survivors. *Journal of Child Sexual Abuse, 16,* 19–36. doi:10.1300/J070v16n01_02

Greenfeld, L.A. (1997). *Sex offenses and offenders: An analysis of data on rape and sexual assault.* Washington, DC: US Department of Justice. Retrieved from http://bjs.gov/content/pub/pdf/SOO.PDF

Vickerman, K.A., & Margolin, G. (2009). Rape treatment outcome research: Empirical findings and state of the literature. *Clinical Psychology Review, 29,* 431–48. doi:10.1016/j.cpr.2009.04.004

Weiss, K.G. (2010). Male sexual victimization: Examining men's experiences of rape and sexual assault. *Men and Masculinities, 12,* 275–98. doi:10.1177/1097184X08322632

Willness, C.R., Steel, P., & Lee, K. (2007). A meta-analysis of the antecedents and consequences of workplace sexual harassment. *Personnel Psychology, 60,* 127–62. doi:10.1111/j.1744-6570.2007.00067.x

World Health Organization. (1992). *The ICD-10 classification of mental and behavioural disorders: Clinical descriptions and diagnostic guidelines* (10th rev.). Geneva, Switzerland: Author.

CHAPTER 18

Abel, G.M., Fitzgerald, L.J., & Brunton, C. (2009). The impact of decriminalisation on the number of sex workers in New Zealand. *Journal of Social Policy, 38*(3), 515–31. doi:10.1017/S0047279409003080

Albright, J.M. (2008). Sex in America online: An exploration of sex, marital status, and sexual identity in internet sex seeking and its impacts. *Journal of Sex Research, 45*(2), 175–86. doi:10.1080/00224490801987481

Astier, H. (2009, March 17). Selling sex legally in New Zealand. *BBC News.* Retrieved from http://news.bbc.co.uk/2/hi/7927461.stm

Azam, S. (2009). *Oral sex is the new goodnight kiss: The sexual bullying of girls* [Book and documentary]. Available from www.thenewgoodnightkiss.com

Barton, B. (2007). Managing the toll of stripping: Boundary setting among exotic dancers. *Journal of Contemporary Ethnography, 36*(5), 571–96. doi:10.1177/0891241607301971

Barton, B., & Hardesty, C.L. (2010). Spirituality and stripping: Exotic dancers narrate the body ekstasis. *Symbolic Interaction, 33*(2), 280–96. doi:10.1525/si.2010.33.2.280

Benoit, C., & Millar, A. (2001). *Short report: Dispelling myths and understanding realities: Working conditions, health status and exiting experiences of sex workers.* Retrieved from www.peers.bc.ca/images/DispMythsshort.pdf

Bilardi, J.E., Miller, A., Hocking, J.S., Keogh, L., Cummings, R., Chen, M.Y., . . . Fairley, C.K. (2011). The job satisfaction of female sex workers working in licensed brothels in Victoria, Australia. *Journal of Sexual Medicine, 8*(1), 116–22. doi:10.1111/j.1743-6109.2010.01967.x

Bullough, V.L., & McAnulty, R.D. (2006). The sex trade: Exotic dancing and prostitution. In R.D. McAnulty & M.M. Burnette (Eds), *Sex and sexuality, Vol 1: Sexuality today: Trends and controversies* (pp. 299–320). Westport, CT: Praeger/Greenwood.

Carroll, J.S., Padilla-Walker, L.M., Nelson, L.J., Olson, C.D., Barry, C.M., & Madsen, S.D. (2008). Generation XXX: Pornography acceptance and use among emerging adults. *Journal of Adolescent Research, 23*(1), 6–30. doi:10.1177/0743558407306348

Casey, L., & Philips, R. (2008). *Behind closed doors: Summary of findings, November 2008.* Retrieved from www.peers.bc.ca/images/BehindClosedDoors.pdf

Dalla, R.L. (2000). Exposing the "Pretty Woman" myth: A qualitative examination of the lives of female streetwalking prostitutes. *Journal of Sex Research, 37*(4), 344–53. doi:10.1080/00224490009552057

Diamond, M. (2009). Pornography, public acceptance and sex related crime: A review. *International Journal of Law and Psychiatry, 32*(5), 304–14. doi:10.1016/j.ijlp.2009.06.004

Farley, M., Lynne, J., & Cotton, A.J. (2005). Prostitution in Vancouver: Violence and the colonization of First Nations women. *Transcultural Psychiatry, 42*(2), 242–71. doi:10.1177/1363461505052667

Ferguson, C.J., & Hartley, R.D. (2009). The pleasure is momentary . . . the expense damnable? The influence of pornography on rape and sexual assault. *Aggression and Violent Behavior, 14*(5), 323–9. doi:10.1016/j.avb.2009.04.008

Flood, M. (2009). The harms of pornography exposure among children and young people. *Child Abuse Review, 18*(6), 384–400. doi:10.1002/car.1092

Garos, S., Beggan, J.K., Kluck, A., & Easton, A. (2004). Sexism and pornography use: Toward explaining past (null) results. *Journal of Psychology & Human Sexuality, 16*(1), 69–96. doi:10.1300/J056v16n01_05

Goodman, A. (1990). Addiction: Definition and implications. *British Journal of Addictions, 85*(11), 1403–8. doi:10.1111/j.1360-0443.1990.tb01620.x

Goodson, P., McCormick, D., & Evans, A. (2001). Searching for sexually explicit material on the Internet: An exploratory study of college students' behavior and attitudes. *Archives of Sexual Behavior, 30*, 101–17. doi:10.1023/A:1002724116437

Hallgrimsdottir, H.K., Phillips, R., Benoit, C., & Walby, K. (2008). Sporting girls, streetwalkers, and inmates of houses of ill repute: Media narratives and the historical mutability of prostitution stigmas. *Sociological Perspectives, 51*(1), 119–38. doi:10.1525/sop.2008.51.1.119

Jackson, L.A., Sowinski, B., Bennett, C., & Ryan, D. (2005). Female sex trade workers, condoms, and the public-private divide. *Journal of Psychology & Human Sexuality, 17*(1–2), 83–105. doi:10.1300/J056v17n01_06

Kaufman, M.R. (2009). "It's just a fantasy for a couple of hours": Ethnography of a nude male show bar. *Deviant Behavior, 30*(5), 407–33. doi:10.1080/01639620802296220

Kendall, C.N. (2004). Educating gay male youth: Since when is pornography a path towards self-respect? *Journal of Homosexuality, 47*(3–4), 83–128. doi:10.1300/J082v47n03_06

Kraus, S.W., & Russell, B. (2008). Early sexual experiences: The role of Internet access and sexually explicit material. *CyberPsychology & Behavior, 11*(2), 162–8. doi:10.1089/cpb.2007.0054

Langevin, R., Lang, R., Wright, P., Handy, L., Frenzel, R., & Black, E. (1988). Pornography and sexual offenses. *Annals of Sex Research, 1*(3), 335–62. doi:10.1007/BF00878103

Laumann, E.O., Gagnon, J.H., Michael, R.T., & Michaels, S. (1994). *The social organization of sexuality: Sexual practices in the United States.* Chicago, IL: University of Chicago Press.

Lavoie, F., Thibodeau, C., Gagné, M.-H., & Hébert, M. (2010). Buying and selling sex in Québec adolescents: A study of risk and protective factors. *Archives of Sexual Behavior, 39*(5), 1147–60. doi:10.1007/s10508-010-9605-4

Levine, S.B. (2010). What is sexual addiction? *Journal of Sex & Marital Therapy, 36*(3), 261–75. doi:10.1080/00926231003719681

Logan, T.D. (2010). Personal characteristics, sexual behaviors, and male sex work: A quantitative approach. *American Sociological Review, 75*(5), 679–704. doi:10.1177/0003122410379581

Lykins, A.D., Meana, M., & Strauss, G.P. (2008). Sex differences in visual attention to erotic and non-erotic stimuli. *Archives of Sexual Behavior, 37*(2), 219–28. doi:10.1007/s10508-007-9208-x

Manning, J.C. (2006). The impact of Internet pornography on marriage and the family: A review of the research. *Sexual Addiction & Compulsivity, 13*(2–3), 131–65. doi:10.1080/10720160600870711

Marshall, B.D.L., Shannon, K., Kerr, T., Zhang, R. & Wood, E. (2010). Survival sex work and increased HIV risk among sexual minority street-involved youth. *JAIDS, 53*(5), 661–4. doi:10.1097/QAI.0b013e3181c300d7

Mitchell, K.J., Becker-Blease, K.A., & Finkelhor, D. (2005). Inventory of problematic Internet experiences encountered in clinical practice. *Professional Psychology: Research and Practice, 36*(5), 498–509. doi:10.1037/0735-7028.36.5.498

Oddone-Paolucci, E., Genuis, M., & Violato, C. (2000). A meta-analysis of the published research on the effects of pornography. In C. Violato, E. Oddone-Paolucci, & M. Genuis (Eds), *The changing family and child development* (pp. 48–59). Aldershot, UK: Ashgate.

Operario, D., Soma, T., & Underhill, K. (2008). Sex work and HIV status among transgender women: Systematic review and meta-analysis. *JAIDS, 48*(1), 97–103. doi:10.1097/QAI.0b013e31816e3971

Peter, J., & Valkenburg, P.M. (2006). Adolescents' exposure to sexually explicit online material and recreational attitudes toward sex. *Journal of Communication, 56*(4), 639–60. doi:10.1111/j.1460-2466.2006.00313.x

Peter, J., & Valkenburg, P.M. (2009). Adolescents' exposure to sexually explicit Internet material and sexual satisfaction: A longitudinal study. *Human Communication Research, 35*(2), 171–94. doi:10.1111/j.1468-2958.2009.01343.x

Petersen, J.L., & Hyde, J.S. (2010). A meta-analytic review of research on gender differences in sexuality, 1993–2007. *Psychological Bulletin, 136*(1), 21–38. doi:10.1037/a0017504

Polk, R.K., & Cowan, G. (1996). Perceptions of female pornography stars. *Canadian Journal of Human Sexuality, 5*(3), 221–9. Retrieved from www.sieccan.org/cjhs.html

Potterat, J.J., Woodhouse, D.E., Muth, J.B., & Muth, S.Q. (1990). Estimating the prevalence and career longevity of prostitute women. *The Journal of Sex Research, 27*, 233–43. doi:10.1080/00224499009551554

ProCon.org. (2011, December 22). One hundred countries and their prostitution policies. *Procon.org.* Retrieved from http://prostitution.procon.org/view.resource.php?resourceID=000772

Rossler, W., Koch, U., Lauber, C., Hass, A.-K., Altwegg, M., Ajdacic-Gross, V., & Landolt, K. (2010). The mental health of female sex workers. *Acta Psychiatrica Scandinavica, 122*(2), 143–52. doi:10.1111/j.1600-0447.2009.01533.x

Rupp, H.A., & Wallen, K. (2008). Sex differences in response to visual sexual stimuli: A review. *Archives of Sexual Behavior, 37*(2), 206–18. doi:10.1007/s10508-007-9217-9

Sabina, C., Wolak, J., & Finkelhor, D. (2008). The nature and dynamics of Internet pornography exposure for youth. *CyberPsychology & Behavior, 11*(6), 691–3. doi:10.1089/cpb.2007.0179

Sanders, T. (2010). The sex industry, regulation and the Internet. In Y. Jewkes & M. Yar (Eds), *Handbook of Internet crime* (pp. 302–19). Devon, UK: Willan.

Scuglia, B. (2004). Sex pigs: Why porn is like sausage, or the truth is that—behind the scenes—porn is not very sexy. *Journal of Homosexuality, 47*(3–4), 185–8. doi:10.1300/J082v47n03_10

Seib, C., Dunne, M.P., Fischer, J., & Najman, J.M. (2010). Commercial sexual practices before and after legalization in Australia. *Archives of Sexual Behavior, 39*(4), 979–89. doi:10 .1007/s10508-008-9458-2

Senn, C.Y., & Desmarais, S. (2004). Impact of interaction with a partner or friend on the exposure effects of pornography and erotica. *Violence and Victims, 19*(6), 645–58. doi:10.1891/ vivi.19.6.645.66347

Seto, M.C., Maric, A., & Barbaree, H.E. (2001). The role of pornography in the etiology of sexual aggression. *Aggression and Violent Behavior, 6*(1), 35–53. doi:10.1016/S1359-1789(99)00007-5

Shaver, F.M. (2011). Prostitution. In *The Canadian Encyclopedia.* Retrieved from www.thecanadianencyclopedia.com/index .cfm?PgNm=TCE&Params=A1ARTA0006521

Spice, W. (2007). Management of sex workers and other high-risk groups. *Occupational Medicine, 57*(5), 322–8. doi:10.1093/ occmed/kqm045

Surratt, H.L., Kurtz, S.P., Weaver, J.C., & Inciardi, J A. (2005). The connections of mental health problems, violent life experiences, and the social milieu of the "stroll" with the HIV risk behaviors of female street sex workers. *Journal of Psychology & Human Sexuality, 17*(1–2), 23–44. doi:10.1300/ J056v17n01_03

Taylor, L.D. (2006). College men, their magazines, and sex. *Sex Roles, 55*(9–10), 693–702. doi:10.1007/s11199-006-9124-x

Trautner, M.N., & Collett, J.L. (2010). Students who strip: The benefits of alternate identities for managing stigma. *Symbolic Interaction, 33*(2), 257–79. doi:10.1525/si.2010.33.2.257

Uy, J.M., Parsons, J.T., Bimbi, D.S., Koken, J.A., & Halkitis, P.N. (2004). Gay and bisexual male escorts who advertise on the Internet: Understanding reasons for and effects of involvement in commercial sex. *International Journal of Men's Health, 3*(1), 11–26. doi:10.3149/jmh.0301.11

Weinberg, M.S., Shaver, F.M., & Williams, C.J. (1999). Gendered sex work in the San Francisco Tenderloin. *Archives of Sexual Behavior, 28*(6), 503–21. doi:10.1023/A:1018765132704

Weisburg, K.D. (1985). *Children of the night: A study of adolescent prostitution.* Lexington, MA: Lexington.

Wood, E., Schachar, J., Li, K., Stoltz, J.-A., Shannon, K., Miller, C., … Kerr, T. (2007). Sex trade involvement is associated with elevated HIV incidence among injection drug users in Vancouver. *Addiction Research & Theory, 15*(3), 321–5. doi:10.1080/ 16066350701254258

World Health Organization. (1988). *STD control in prostitution: Guidelines for policy. WHO consultation on prevention and control of sexually transmitted diseases in population groups at risk.* Geneva, Switzerland: Author.

World Health Organization. (2011). *HIV/AIDS: Sex workers.* Retrieved from www.euro.who.int/en/what-we-do/health -topics/communicable-diseases/hivaids/policy/sex-workers

Ybarra, M.L., & Mitchell, K.J. (2005). Exposure to Internet pornography among children and adolescents: A national survey. *CyberPsychology & Behavior, 8*(5), 473–86. doi:10.1089/ cpb.2005.8.473

Ybarra, M.L., Mitchell, K.J., Hamburger, M., Diener-West, M., & Leaf, P.J. (2011). X-rated material and perpetration of sexually aggressive behavior among children and adolescents: Is there a link? *Aggressive Behavior, 37*(1), 1–18. doi:10.1002/ ab.20367

Young, A. (2008). The state is still in the bedrooms of the nation: The control and regulation of sexuality in Canadian criminal law. *Canadian Journal of Human Sexuality, 17*(4), 203–20. Retrieved from www.sieccan.org/cjhs.html

CHAPTER 19

Adamcheck, S.E. (2006). *Youth peer education in reproductive health and HIV/AIDS: Progress, process, and programming for the future. Youth Issues paper 7.* Washington, DC: Family Health International. Retrieved from www.fhi.org/NR/rdonlyres/ em7o6gq65ntn3p5cdtq2g3pqut5rxhs7afrnu64vmmva36a ydt65naap6vaxyezz42bvaeuoohof6a/YI7.pdf

Alberta Act, 4-5 Edward VII, c. 3 § 17 (1905).

Bandura, A. (1989). Perceived self-efficacy in the exercise of control over AIDS infection. In V. M. Mays, G.W. Alhee, & S.M. Schneider (Eds), *Primary prevention of AIDS* (pp. 128–41). Newbury Park, CA: Sage.

Birkett, M., Espelage, D.L., & Koenig, B. (2009). LGB and questioning students in schools: The moderating effects of homophobic bullying and school climate on negative outcomes. *Journal of Youth and Adolescence, 38*, 989–1000. doi:10.1007/ s10964-008-9389-1

Bond, B., Hefner, V., & Drogos, K. (2008). Information-seeking practices during the sexual development of lesbian, gay, and bisexual individuals: The influence and effects of coming out in a mediated environment. *Sexuality & Culture, 13*, 32–51. doi:10.1007/s12119-008-9041-y

Boyce, W., Doherty, M., Fortin, C., & MacKinnon, D. (2003). *Canadian youth, sexual health, and HIV/AIDS study: Factors influencing knowledge, attitudes, and behaviours.* Toronto, ON: Council of Ministers of Education, Canada. Retrieved from www .cmec.ca

Boyce, W., Doherty-Poirier, M., MacKinnon, D., Fortin, C., Saab, H., King, M., & Gallupe, O. (2006). Sexual health of Canadian youth: Findings from the Canadian youth, sexual health, and HIV/AIDS study. *Canadian Journal of Human Sexuality, 15*, 59–68. Retrieved from www.sieccan.org/cjhs.html

Brotto, L.A., Chou, A.Y., Singh, T., & Woo, J.S.T. (2008). Reproductive health practices among Indian, Indo-Canadian, Canadian East Asian, and Euro-Canadian women: The role of acculturation. *Journal of Obstetrics and Gynaecology Canada, 30*, 229–38. Retrieved from www.sogc.org/jogc

Brown, J.D., Keller, S., & Stern, S. (2009). Sex, sexuality, sexting, and sexed: Adolescents and the media. *The Prevention Researcher, 16*(4), 12–16. Retrieved from www.tpronline.org/ index.cfm

Byers, E.S., Sears, H.A., Voyer, S.D., Thurlow, J.L., Cohen, J.N., & Weaver, A.D. (2003). An adolescent perspective on sexual health education at school and at home: I. High school students. *Canadian Journal of Human Sexuality, 12*, 1–17. Retrieved from www.sieccan.org/cjhs.html

Causarano, N., Pole, J.D., Flicker, S., & the Toronto Teen Survey Team. (2010). Exposure to and desire for sexual health education among, urban youth: Associations with religion and other factors. *The Canadian Journal of Human Sexuality, 19*, 169–84. Retrieved from www.sieccan.org/cjhs.html

CBC News. (2007, March 1). Same-sex rights: Canada timeline. *CBC News.* Retrieved from www.cbc.ca/news/background/ samesexrights/timeline_canada.html

Coleman, E. (2003). Masturbation as a means of achieving sexual health. *Journal of Psychology & Human Sexuality, 14*, 5–16. doi:10.1300/J056v14n02_02

Collins, R.L., Elliott, M.N., Berry, S.H., Kanouse, D.E., & Hunter, S.B. (2003). Entertainment television as a healthy sex educator: The impact of condom-efficacy information in an episode of *Friends. Pediatrics, 112*, 1115–21. doi:10.1542/peds.112.5.1115

Collins, R.L., Elliott, M.N., Berry, S.H., Kanouse, D.E., Kunkel, D., Hunter, S.B., & Miu, A. (2004). Watching sex on television predicts adolescent initiation of sexual behaviour. *Pediatrics, 114*, e280–9. doi:10.1542/peds.2003-1065-L

Constitution Act, 30-31 Victoria, c. 3§ 93 (1867, 1982).

Dellagloria, R. (2009, February 11). Seniors learn ins and outs of safe sex. *Miami Herald*. Retrieved from www.globalaging.org/health/us/2009/safesex.htm

de Valk, A. (2010, September). McGuinty's poison pill for Ontario schools. *Catholic Insight*. Retrieved from http://catholicinsight.com/online/features/article_1025.shtml

Di Giulio, G. (2003). Sexuality and people living with physical or developmental disabilities: A review of key issues. *The Canadian Journal of Human Sexuality, 12*, 53–68. Retrieved from www.sieccan.org/cjhs.html

Donnerstein, E., & Smith, S. (2001). Sex in the media: Theory, influences, and solutions. In D.G. Singer & J.L. Singer (Eds), *Handbook of children and the media* (pp. 289–307). Thousand Oaks, CA: Sage Publications.

Ferguson, R., Benzie, R., & Rushowy, K. (2010, April 22). McGuinty backs down on sex ed changes. *Toronto Star*. Retrieved from www.thestar.com/breakingnews/article/799313--mcguinty-postpones-sex-ed-changes?bn=1

Fisher, C.M. (2009). Queer youth experiences with abstinence-only-until-marriage sexuality education: "I can't get married so where does that leave me?". *Journal of LGBT Youth, 6*, 61–79. doi:10.1080/19361650802396775

Fisher, J.D., & Fisher, W.A. (1992). Changing AIDS-risk behavior. *Psychological Bulletin, 111*, 455–74. doi:10.1037/0033-2909.111.3.455

Fisher, J.D., & Fisher, W.A. (2000). Theoretical approaches to individual-level change in HIV risk behavior. In J.L. Peterson & R.J. DiClemente (Eds), *Handbook of HIV prevention, AIDS prevention and mental health* (pp. 3–55). Dordrecht, Netherlands: Kluwer Academic.

Fisher, W.A., & Fisher, J.D. (1993). A general social psychological model for changing AIDS risk behavior. In J. Pryor & G. Reeder (Eds), *The social psychology of HIV infection* (pp. 127–53). Hillsdale, NJ: Psychology Press.

Fisher, W.A., & Fisher, J.D. (1998). Understanding and promoting sexual and reproductive health behavior: Theory and method. *Annual Review of Sex Research, 9*, 39–76. Retrieved from www.tandf.co.uk/journals/spissue/hjsr-si.asp

Giami, A. (2002). Sexual health: The emergence, development, and diversity of a concept. *Annual Review of Sex Research, 13*, 1–35. Retrieved from www.tandf.co.uk/journals/spissue/hjsr-si.asp

Goldman, J.D.G. (2008). Responding to parental objections to school sexuality education: A selection of 12 objections. *Sex Education, 8*, 415–38. doi:10.1080/14681810802433952

Guttmacher Institute. (2011). *State policies in brief: Sex and HIV education*. New York, NY: Author.

Hampton, M.R., Fahlman, S.A., Goertzen, J.R., & Jeffery, B.L. (2005). A process evaluation of the youth educating about health (YEAH) program: A peer-designed and peer-led sexual health education program. *Canadian Journal of Human Sexuality, 14*, 129–41. Retrieved from www.sieccan.org/cjhs.html

Health Canada. (2009). *A statistical profile on the health of First Nations in Canada: Self-rated health and selected conditions, 2002 to 2005* (Catalogue No. H34-193/2-2008E-PDF). Ottawa, ON: Author. Retrieved from www.hc-sc.gc.ca/fniah-spnia/pubs/aborig-autoch/2009-stats-profil-vol3/index-eng.php#a536

Herbenick, D., Reece, M., Schick, V., Sanders, A., Dodge, B., & Fortenberry, J.D. (2010). Sexual behavior in the United States: Results from a national probability sample of men and women ages 14-94. *Journal of Sexual Medicine, 7*, 255–265. doi:10.1111/j.1743-6109.2010.02012.x

Hill, D.M. (2003). HIV/AIDS among Canada's First Nations people: A look at disproportionate risk factors as compared to the rest of Canada. *Canadian Journal of Native Studies, 23*, 349–59. Retrieved from www2.brandonu.ca/library/cjns

Hinchliff, S., & Gott, M. (2011). Seeking medical help for sexual concerns in mid- and later life: A review of the literature. *Journal of Sex Research, 48*, 106–17. doi:10.1080/00224499.2010.548610

Hingsburger, D., & Tough, S. (2002). Healthy sexuality: Attitudes, systems, and policies. *Research & Practice for Persons with Severe Disabilities, 27*, 8–17. doi:10.2511/rpsd.27.1.8

Johnson, M. (2012). *I heard it 'round the Internet: Sexual health education and authenticating online information*. Media Smarts. Retrieved from http://mediasmarts.ca/sites/default/files/pdfs/lesson-plan/Lesson_Sexual_Health_Education.pdf

Kempton, W., & Kahn, E. (1991). Sexuality and people with intellectual disabilities: A historical perspective. *Sexuality and Disability, 9*, 93–111. doi:10.1007/BF01101735

Kirby, D. (2001). *Emerging answers: Research findings on programs to reduce teen pregnancy*. Washington, DC: National Campaign to Prevent Teen Pregnancy.

Kirby, D. (2008). The impact of abstinence and comprehensive sex and STD/HIV education programs on adolescent sexual behavior. *Sexuality Research & Social Policy, 5*, 18–27. doi:10.1525/srsp.2008.5.3.18

Kirby, D., Laris, B., & Rolleri, L. (2006). *The impact of sex and HIV education programs in schools and communities on sexual behaviors among young adults*. Research Triangle Park, NC: Family Health International.

Kirby, D., Laris, B., & Rolleri, L. (2007). Sex and HIV education programs: Their impact on sexual behaviors of young people throughout the world. *Journal of Adolescent Health, 40*, 206–217. doi:10.1016/j.jadohealth.2006.11.143

Kohler, P.K., Manhart, L.E., & Lafferty, W.E. (2008). Abstinence-only and comprehensive sex education and the initiation of sexual activity and teen pregnancy. *Journal of Adolescent Health, 42*, 344–51. doi:10.1016/j.jadohealth.2007.08.026

Kunkel, D., Eyal, K., Finnerty, K., Biely, E., & Donnerstein, E. (2005). *Sex on TV4: A biennial report to the Kaiser Family Foundation*. Menlo Park, CA: The Henry J. Kaiser Foundation. Retrieved from www.kff.org/entmedia/7398.cfm

Langille, D., MacKinnon, D., Marshall, E., & Graham, J. (2001). So many bricks in the wall: Young women in Nova Scotia speak about barriers to school-based sexual health education. *Sex Education, 1*, 245–57. doi:10.1080/14681810120080640

LaRoque, E.D. (1993). Violence in Aboriginal communities. In L.T. Montour (Ed), *The path to healing: Report of the national round table on Aboriginal health and social issues* (pp. 72–89). Ottawa, ON: Canadian Government Publishing. Retrieved from http://dsp-psd.pwgsc.gc.ca/Collection/H72-21-100-1994E.pdf

Lindau, S.T., Schumm, L.P., Laumann, E.O., Levinson, W., O'Muircheartaigh, C.A., & Waite, L.J. (2007). A study of sexuality and health among older adults in the United States.

New England Journal of Medicine, 357, 762–74. doi:10.1056/NEJMoa067423.

Lindberg, L.D., Santelli, J.S., & Singh, S. (2006). Changes in formal sex education: 1995–2002. *Perspectives on Sexual & Reproductive Health, 38*, 182–9. doi:10.1363/3818206

McCabe, M.P. (1999). Sexual knowledge, experience, and feelings among people with disability. *Sexuality and Disability, 17*, 157–70. doi:10.1023/A:1021476418440

McCabe, M.P., & Cummins, R.A. (1996). The sexual knowledge, experience, feelings, and needs of people with mild intellectual disabilities. *Education and Training in Mental Retardation and Developmental Disabilities, 31*, 13–21.

McCabe, M.P., Cummins, R., & Deeks, A. (2000). Sexuality and quality of life among people with physical disability. *Sexuality and Disability, 18*, 123–31. doi:10.1023/A:1005562813603

McGillivray, J.A. (1999). Levels of knowledge and risk of contracting HIV/AIDS amongst young adults with mild/moderate intellectual disability. *Journal of Applied Research in Intellectual Disabilities, 12*, 113–26. doi:10.1111/j.1468-3148.1999.tb00070.x

McKay, A. (2004a). Adolescent sexual and reproductive health in Canada: A report card in 2004. *Canadian Journal of Human Sexuality, 13*, 67–81. Retrieved from www.sieccan.org/cjhs.html

McKay, A. (2004b). Sexual health education in the schools: Questions & answers. *Canadian Journal of Human Sexuality, 13*, 129–41. Retrieved from www.sieccan.org/cjhs.html

McKay, A., & Bissell, M. (2009). Sexual health education in the schools: Questions & answers (3rd ed.). *Canadian Journal of Human Sexuality, 18*, 47–60. Retrieved from www.sieccan.org/cjhs.html

Malamuth, N., & Huppin, M. (2005). Pornography and teenagers: The importance of individual differences. *Adolescent Medicine Clinics, 16*, 315–326. doi:10.1016/j.admecli.2005.02.004

Maticka-Tyndale, E. (2008). Sexuality and sexual health of Canadian adolescents: Yesterday, today, and tomorrow. *Canadian Journal of Human Sexuality, 17*, 85–95. Retrieved from www.sieccan.org/cjhs.html

Meaney, G.J., Rye, B.J., Wood, E., & Solovieva, E. (2009). Satisfaction with school-based sexual health education in a sample of university students recently graduated from Ontario high schools. *Canadian Journal of Human Sexuality, 18*, 107–25. Retrieved from www.sieccan.org/cjhs.html

Miller, B.C., Benson, B., & Galbraith, K.A. (2001). Family relationships and adolescent pregnancy risk: A research synthesis. *Developmental Review, 21*, 1–38. doi:10.1006/drev.2000.0513

Miller, K.S., Forehand, R., & Kotchick, B.A. (1999). Adolescent sexual behavior in two ethnic minority samples: The role of family variables. *Journal of Marriage and the Family, 61*, 85–98. doi:10.2307/353885

Milligan, M.S., & Neufeldt, A.H. (2001). The myth of asexuality: A survey of social and empirical evidence. *Sexuality and Disability, 19*, 91–109. doi:10.1023/A:1010621705591

Ontario Ministry of Education and Training. (2010). *The Ontario curriculum grades 1 to 8. Health and physical education: Interim edition*. Toronto, ON: Author. Retrieved from www.edu.gov.on.ca/eng/curriculum/elementary/health.html

Orel, N.A., Wright, J.M., & Wagner, J. (2004). Scarcity of HIV/AIDS risk-reducing materials targeting the needs of older adults among state departments of public health. *The Gerontologist, 44*, 693–6. doi:10.1093/geront/44.5.693

Orton, M.J. (1994). Institutional barriers to sexual health: Issues at the federal, provincial, and local programs levels—Ontario as a case study. *Canadian Journal of Human Sexuality, 3*, 209–25. Retrieved from www.sieccan.org/cjhs.html

Paul, P. (2005). *Pornified: How pornography is transforming our lives, our relationships, and our families*. New York, NY: Time Books.

Pole, J.D., Flicker, S., & the Toronto Teen Survey Team. (2010). Sexual behaviour profile of a diverse group of urban youth: An analysis of the Toronto Teen Survey. *Canadian Journal of Human Sexuality, 19*, 145–56. Retrieved from www.sieccan.org/cjhs.html

Primack, B., Gold, M.A., Schwarz, F.B., & Dalton, M.A. (2008). Degrading and non-degrading sex in popular music: A content analysis. *Public Health Reports, 123*, 593–600. Retrieved from www.publichealthreports.org/archives/issueopen.cfm?articleID=2095

Public Health Agency of Canada. (2006). *Sexually transmitted infections in Canadian street youth: Findings from enhanced surveillance of Canadian street youth, 1999–2003*. Ottawa, ON: Author. Retrieved from www.phac-aspc.gc.ca/std-mts/reports_06/sti-youth-eng.php

Public Health Agency of Canada. (2008). *Canadian guidelines for sexual health education*. Ottawa, ON: Author. Retrieved from www.phac-aspc.gc.ca/publicat/cgshe-ldnemss/index-eng.php

Public Health Agency of Canada. (2009). *Brief report on sexually transmitted infections in Canada: 2007*. Ottawa, ON: Author. Retrieved from www.phac-aspc.gc.ca/publicat/2009/sti-its/index-eng.php

Public Health Agency of Canada. (2010a). *Questions and answers: Gender identity in schools*. Ottawa, ON: Author. Retrieved from www.phac-aspc.gc.ca/publicat/qagis-qrise/pdf/qagis-qrise-eng.pdf

Public Health Agency of Canada. (2010b). *Questions and answers: Sexual orientation in schools*. Ottawa, ON: Author. Retrieved from www.phac-aspc.gc.ca/publicat/qasos-qose/pdf/qasos-qose-eng.pdf

Religious groups fight changes to Ontario sex ed curriculum. (2010, April 22). *Macleans.ca*. Retrieved from www2.macleans.ca/2010/04/22/religious-groups-fight-changes-to-ontario-sex-ed-curriculum

Richards, D., Miodrag, N., Watson, S.L., Feldman, M., Aunos, M., Cox-Lindenbaum, D., & Griffiths, D. (2008). Sexual and human rights of persons with intellectual disabilities. In F. Owen & D. Griffiths (Eds), *Challenges to the human rights of people with intellectual disabilities* (pp. 184–218). London, UK: Jessica Kingsley Publisher.

Roche, K.M., Mekos, D., Alexander, C.S., Astone, N.M., Bandeen-Roche, K., & Ensminger, M.E. (2005). Parenting influences on early sex initiation among adolescents: How neighborhood matters. *Journal of Family Issues, 26*, 32–54. doi:10.1177/0192513X04265943

Ropelato, J. (n.d.). *Internet pornography statistics*. Retrieved from http://internet-filter-review.toptenreviews.com/internet-pornography-statistics.html

Rotermann, M. (2001). Wired young Canadians. *Canadian Social Trends, 63*, 4–8. Retrieved from www.statcan.gc.ca/studies-etudes/11-008/feature-caracteristique/5022699-eng.pdf

Rotermann, M. (2005). Sex, condoms and STDs among young people. *Health Reports, 16*, 39–45. Retrieved from www.statcan.gc.ca/ads-annonces/82-003-x/index-eng.htm

Rotermann, M. (2008). Trends in sexual behaviour and condom use. *Health Reports, 19*, 53–7. Retrieved from www.statcan.gc.ca/ads-annonces/82-003-x/index-eng.htm

Rye, B.J., Yessis, J., Brunk, T., McKay, A., Morris, S., & Meaney, G.J. (2008). Outcome evaluation of Girl Time: Grade 7/8 health sexuality program. *Canadian Journal of Human Sexuality, 17,* 15–36. Retrieved from www.sieccan.org/cjhs.html

Saewyc, E., Skay, C., Richens, K., Reis, E., Poon, C., & Murphy, A. (2006). Sexual orientation, sexual abuse, and HIV-risk behaviors among adolescents in the Pacific Northwest. *American Journal of Public Health, 96,* 1104–10. doi:10.2105/AJPH.2005.065870

Salehi, R., Flicker, S., & the Toronto Teen Survey Team. (2010). Predictors to sexual health education among teens who are newcomers to Canada. *Canadian Journal of Human Sexuality, 19,* 157–67. Retrieved from www.sieccan.org/cjhs.html

Sandfort, T.G.M., & Ehrhardt, A.A. (2004). Sexual health: A useful public health paradigm or a moral imperative? *Archives of Sexual Behavior, 33,* 181–7. doi:10.1023/B:ASEB .0000026618.16408.e0

Santelli, J., Ott, M.A., Lyon, M., Rogers, J., Summers, D., & Schleifer, R. (2006). Abstinence and abstinence-only education: A review of US policies and programs. *Journal of Adolescent Health, 38,* 72–81. doi:10.1016/j.jadohealth.2005.10.006.

Saskatchewan Act, 4-5 Edward VII, c. 42 § 17 (1905).

Schalock, R.L., Borthwick-Duffy, S.A., Bradley, V.J., Buntinx, W.H.E., Coulter, D.L., Craig, E.M., . . . Yeager, M.H. (2010). *Intellectual disability: Definition, classification, and systems of supports* (11th ed.). Washington, DC: American Association on Intellectual and Developmental Disabilities.

Schick, V., Herbenick, D., Reece, M., Sanders, S.A., Dodge, B., Middlestadt, S.E.,& Fortenberry, J.D. (2010). Sexual behaviors, condom use, and sexual health of Americans over 50: Implications for sexual health promotion for older adults. *Journal of Sexual Medicine, 7,* 315–29. doi:10.1111/ j.1743-6109.2010.02013.x

Sellors, J.W., Karwalajtys, T.L., Kaczorowski, J.B., Mahony, J.B., Lytwyn, A., Chong, S., . . . Lorincz, A. (2003). Incidence, clearance, and predictors of human papillomavirus infection in women. *Canadian Medical Association Journal, 168,* 421–5. Retrieved from www.cmaj.ca

Shirpak, K.R., Maticka-Tyndale, E., & Chinichian, M. (2007). Iranian immigrants' perceptions of sexuality in Canada: A symbolic interactionist approach. *Canadian Journal of Human Sexuality, 16,* 113–28. Retrieved from www.sieccan.org/cjhs .html

Smoak, N.D., Scott-Sheldon, L.A.J., Johnson, B.T., Carey, M.P., & the SHARP Research Team. (2006). Sexual risk reduction interventions do not inadvertently increase overall frequency of sexual behavior: A meta-analysis of 174 studies with 116, 735 participants. *Acquired Immune Deficiency Syndrome, 41,* 374–84. doi:10.1097/01.qai.0000185575.36591.fc.

Smylie, L., Maticka-Tyndale, E., Boyd, D., & the Adolescent Sexual Health Planning Committee. (2008). Evaluation of a school-based sex education programme delivered to grade nine students in Canada. *Sex Education, 8,* 25–46. doi:10.1080/14681810701811795

Sobsey, D., & Varnhagen, C.K. (1991). Sexual abuse and exploitation of disabled individuals. In C.R. Bagley & R.J. Thomlison (Eds), *Child sexual abuse: Critical perspectives on prevention, intervention, and treatment* (pp. 203–16). Toronto, ON: Wall Emerson.

Statistics Canada. (2006, March 31). Television viewing. *The Daily.* Retrieved from www.statcan.gc.ca/daily-quotidien/060331/ dq060331b-eng.htm

Statistics Canada. (2008). *Pregnancy outcomes 2005* (Catalogue No. 82-224-X). Ottawa, ON: Author. Retrieved from http:// dsp-psd.pwgsc.gc.ca/collection_2008/statcan/82-224-X/82 -224-XIE2005000.pdf

Stern, S. (2005). Self-absorbed, dangerous, and disengaged: What popular films tell us about teenagers. *Mass Communication & Society, 8,* 23–38. doi:10.1207/s15327825mcs0801_3

Szollos, A.A., & McCabe, M.P. (1995). The sexuality of people with mild intellectual disability: Perceptions of clients and caregivers. *Australia & New Zealand Journal of Developmental Disabilities, 20,* 205–22. doi:10.1080/07263869500035561

Taylor, L.D. (2005). Effects of visual and verbal sexual television content and perceived realism on attitudes and beliefs. *Journal of Sex Research, 42,* 130–7. doi:10.1080/00224490509552266

Taylor, C., Peter, T., McMinn, T.L., Elliott, T., Beldom, S., Ferry, A., . . . Schachter, K. (2011). *Every class in every school: The first national climate survey on homophobia, biphobia, and transphobia in Canadian schools. Final report.* Toronto, ON: Egale Canada Human Rights Trust.

Taylor, C., Peter, T., Schachter, K., Paquin, S., Beldom, S., Gross, Z., & McMinn, T.L. (2008). *Youth speak up about homophobia and transphobia: The first national climate survey on homophobia in Canadian schools. Phase one report.* Toronto, ON: Egale Canada Human Rights Trust.

Ward, L.M. (2002). Does television exposure affect emerging adults' attitudes and assumptions about sexual relationships? Correlational and experimental confirmation. *Journal of Youth & Adolescence, 31,* 1–15. doi:10.1023/A:1014068031532

Watson, S.L., Venema, T., Molloy, W., & Reich, M. (2002). Sexual rights and individuals who have a developmental disability. In D. Griffiths, D. Richards, P. Fedoroff, & S.L. Watson (Eds), *Ethical dilemmas: Sexuality and developmental disabilities* (pp. 9–51). Kingston, NY: NADD.

Weaver, A.D., Byers, S.E., Sears, H.A., Cohen, J.N., & Randall, H.E.S. (2002). Sexual health education at school and at home: Attitudes and experiences of New Brunswick parents. *Canadian Journal of Human Sexuality, 11,* 19–31. Retrieved from www.sieccan.org/cjhs.html

World Health Organization. (2002). *Defining sexual health. Report of a technical consultation on sexual health.* Geneva, Switzerland: Author. Retrieved from www.who.int

Yee, J. (2009, February). Introduction. *Our Schools/Our Selves, 18*(2), 1–6. Retrieved from www.policyalternatives.ca/sites/ default/files/uploads/publications/Our_Schools_Ourselves/ OSOS_94_Sex_Ed_and_Youth.pdf

Photo Credits

Chapter 1 opener: Edward Kinsman/Photo Researchers/Getty Images; **Fig. 1.1:** Alex Noriega; **Fig. 1.2:** © Retro Atelier/iStock; **Fig. 1.3:** © Moviestore collection Ltd/Alamy; **Fig. 1.4:** Photo by James Devaney/WireImage; **Fig. 1.5:** New Vision Technologies Inc/Photo Disc/Getty Images; **Fig. 1.6**: © Robert Harding Picture Library Ltd/Alamy; **Fig. 1.7:** National Museum of Spain; **Fig. 1.8:** Image courtesy of The Advertising Archives; **Fig. 1.9:** www.CartoonStock.com/Roy Delgado; **Fig. 1.10:** The Canadian Press/Jonathan Hayward

Chapter 2 opener: Daniel Day/Stone/Getty Images; **Fig. 2.1:** Photo by Erik Hill/Anchorage Daily News/MCT via Getty Images; **Fig. 2.3:** National Library of Medicine/Science Photo Library; **Fig. 2.5:** Mark Anderson, Andertoons.com; **Fig. 2.6:** © digitalskillet/iStock; **Fig. 2.7:** © cosmin4000; **Fig. 2.8 (left and right):** John Devries/Science Photo Library

Chapter 3 opener: © Pencho Tihov/Alamy; **Fig. 3.1:** Courtesy of The Kinsey Institute for Research in Sex, Gender and Reproduction. Photo by William Dellenback; **Fig. 3.2:** Photo by NBC/NBCU Photo Bank via Getty Images; **Fig. 3.4:** © Aurora Photos/Alamy; **Fig. 3.5:** © Steve Debenport/iStock.com; **Fig. 3.7:** Melissa Farmer

Chapter 4 opener: okeyphotos/E+/Getty Images; **Fig. 4.3:** Panel One of Ten from the Great Wall of Vagina by Jamie McCartney; **Fig. 4.9 (left and right):** http://adultcirc20.blogspot.ca; **Fig. 4.15:** © Alllex/iStock; **Fig. 4.16:** W.W. Schultz/British Medical Journal/Science Photo Library

Chapter 5 opener: Michael W Davidson/Photo Researchers/Getty; **Fig. 5.5:** Peter Gardiner/Science Photo Library; **Fig. 5.7:** © tiburonstudios/iStock.com; **Fig. 5.8:** Courtesy of Todd H. Ahern

Chapter 6 opener: Aneyeforit/Dreamstime.com/GetStock.com; **Fig. 6.1:** © David Marchal/iStock.com; **Fig. 6.2:** Dr G. Moscoso/Science Photo Library; **Fig. 6.3:** Steve Allen/Science Photo Library; **Fig. 6.4:** © mevans/iStockphoto.com; **Fig. 6.5:** Eddie Lawrence/Science Photo Library; **Fig. 6.6:** © builttospill1/iStock.com; **Fig. 6.7:** Joti/Science Photo Library; **Fig. 6.8:** Josh Sher/Science Photo Library; **Fig. 6.9:** Ron Sutherland/Science Photo Library

Chapter 7 opener: Paul Edmondson/Getty; **Fig. 7.1:** IISH/Stefan R. Landsberger Collections; **Fig. 7.2:** The Canadian Press; **Table 7.2 (a):** © claylib/iStock.com; **Table 7.2 (b):** Redbaron/Dreamstime.com; **Table 7.2 (c):** © vario images GmbH & Co.KG/Alamy; **Table 7.2 (d):** © winterling/iStock.com; **Table 7.2 (e):** Scott Camazine/Science Photo Library; **Table 7.2 (f):** Saturn Stills/Science Photo Library; **Table 7.2 (g):** © EduardoLuzzatti/iStock.com; **Table 7.2 (h):** Gary Parker/Science Photo Library; **Table 7.2 (j):** Gary Parker/Science Photo Library; **Table 7.2 (k):** © jenjen42/iStock.com; **Table 7.2 (l):** Gary Parker/Science Photo Library; **Table 7.2 (m):** nito/Shutterstock; **Table 7.2 (n):** © malerapaso/iStock.com; **Fig. 7.4:** Fertility UK; **Fig. 7.5:** kyoshino/Thinkstock; **Fig. 7.6:** © Justin Horrocks/iStock.com; **Fig. 7.7:** © Joel Gordon Photography; **Fig. 7.8:** © Mathieu Belanger/Reuters/Corbis

Chapter 8 opener: © Jagadeesh Nv/epa/Corbis; **Fig. 8.1:** Global Protection Corp; **Fig. 8.3:** © Corbis; **Fig. 8.4:** Reprinted with the permission of the AIDS Committee of Toronto (ACT); **Fig. 8.5:** Reprinted with permission of The Gazette; **Figs 8.8 to 8.13 and 8.16 to 8.18:** © Mark Steban. Reproduced by permission and subject to the copyright laws of Canada

Chapter 9 opener: © Roy McMahon/Corbis; **Fig. 9.1:** Alexander Tsiaras/Science Photo Library; **Fig. 9.2:** © mbogacz/iStock.com; **Fig. 9.3:** Andrew Mayovskyy/123RF; **Fig. 9.4:** wavebreakmedia/Shutterstock; **Fig. 9.5:** © 1MoreCreative/iStockphpto.com; **Fig. 9.6:** criben/Shutterstock.com; **Fig. 9.7:** © tom carter/Alamy; **Fig. 9.8:** © Janine Wiedel Photolibrary/Alamy; **Fig. 9.9:** © ozgurdonmaz/iStock.com; **Fig. 9.10 (left):** © Mlenny/Indian Teenagers; **Fig. 9.10 (right):** © Grant Rooney Premium/Alamy; **Fig. 9.11:** © Hope Milam/iStock.com; **Fig. 9.12:** © peepo/iStock.com; **Fig. 9.13:** feverpitched/123RF

Chapter 10 opener: Coco Layne; **Fig. 10.1:** Courtesy of the Kinsey Institute for Research in Sex, Gender and Reproduction. Photographer unknown; **Fig. 10.2:** CP Photo/Winnipeg Free Press/Files; **Fig. 10.3:** Courtesy Dr Milton Diamond; **Fig. 10.5:** Photo courtesy of Daniel Fay, MD, Daniel Hawley, MD, Doug Storm, MD, and MedPix®; **Fig. 10.6:** Photo courtesy Katie Baratz Dalke; **Fig. 10.7:** The Canadian PressToronto Star-Steve Russell; **Fig. 10.8:** © TongRo Images/Corbis; **Fig. 10.9:** © RIA Novosti/Alamy; **Fig. 10.10:** Ethan Daniel

Chapter 11 opener: Reuters/Antonio Bronic; **Fig. 11.3:** © dmbaker/iStock.com; **Fig. 11.4:** © David Hathcox; **Fig. 11.6:** smithore/Can Stock Photo; **Fig. 11.7:** © srki72/Demotix/Demotix/Corbis; **Fig. 11.8:** Lisa F. Young/Shutterstock; **Fig. 11.9:** © tiburonstudios/iStock.com

Chapter 12 opener: © Ocean/Corbis; **Fig. 12.1:** Kate Jacobs/Science Photo Library; **Fig. 12.2:** Courtesy Professor Gillian Rhodes; **Fig. 12.3:** Lisa DeBruine and Ben Jones (University of Glasgow); **Fig. 12.4:** © Izabela Habur/iStock.com; **Fig. 12.5:** © 2010 Sardonic Salad; **Fig. 12.7:** Mark Anderson, Andertoons.com; **Fig. 12.10:** Jim Lo Scalzo/US News and World Report/Aurora Photos/GetStock.com; **Fig. 12.11:** Stockbyte/Getty Images

Chapter 13 opener: © Tobbe/Corbis; **Fig. 13.1:** © monkeybusinessimages; **Fig. 13.2:** © Jennifer_Sharp/iStock.com; **Fig. 13.3:** © Jean Sorenson; **Fig. 13.4:** Randy Glasbergen; **Fig. 13.6:** © Julie Smith/maXximages.com; **Fig. 13.8:** The Canadian Press/Mark Spowart

Chapter 14 opener: © mother image/Bedford/Corbis; **Fig. 14.9:** © EdStock/iStock.com; **Fig. 14.11:** © EdStock/iStock.com

Chapter 15 opener: Reuters/Hannibal Hanschke/(Germany); **Fig. 15.1:** DoctorKan/Can Stock Photo; **Fig. 15.2:** Katstudio/Shutterstock; **Fig. 15.4:** Anatoly Tiplyashin/Shutterstock; **Fig. 15.5:** © Pictorial Press Ltd/Alamy; **Fig. 15.6:** © whiteboxmedia limited/Alamy; **Fig. 15.7:** Schiffer, B., Pesche, T., Paul, T., Gizewski, E., Forsting, M., Leygraf, N., et al. 2007, Structural brain abnormalities in the frontostriatal system and cerebellum in pedophilia.

Journal of Psychiatric Research, 41, 753-762. doi:10.1016/j
.jpsychires.2006.06.003.

Chapter 16 opener: Reuters/Luke MacGregor (Britain Society);
Fig. 16.1: www.CartoonStock.com/Chapman; **Fig. 16.2:**
© Justin Horrocks/iStock.com; **Fig. 16.4:** © RapidEye/iStock
.com; **Fig. 16.5:** © JochenSchoenfeld/iStock.com

Chapter 17 opener: © Radius Images/Corbis; **Fig. 17.2:**
© Chris Rout/Alamy; **Fig. 17.2:** © PaulaConnelly/iStock.com;
Fig. 17.7: © YouraPechkin/iStock.com; **Fig. 17.9:** The Canadian
Press/Fred Chartrand; **Fig. 17.10:** © Alina Vincent Photography,
LLC/iStock.com

Chapter 18 opener: Colin Young/Thinkstock;
Fig. 18.1: © Pictorial Press Ltd/Alamy; **Fig. 18.2:** © Joel
Gordon Photography; **Fig. 18.3:** areacan/Can Stock Photo;
Fig. 18.4: © RapidEye/iStock.com; **Fig. 18.5:** © Jeffrey
Blackler/Alamy; **Fig. 18.6:** © Joel Gordon Photography;
Fig. 18.7: Randy Miramontez/Shutterstock.co;
Fig. 18.8: hurricanehank/Can Stock Photo; **Fig. 18.9:** © Joel
Gordon Photography

Chapter 19 opener: © Mode Images/Alamy; **Fig. 19.5:** www
.CartoonStock.com /Guy&Rodd; **Fig. 19.6:** www.CartoonStock
.com/Paul Kinsella

Index